105297
C000278750

Official 1985
National Footb
Record
& Fact Book

A National Football League Book.

Workman Publishing Co., New York.

National Football League, 1985

410 Park Avenue, New York, N.Y. 10022   (212) 758-1500

Commissioner: Pete Rozelle
Executive Vice President & League Counsel: Jay Moyer
Treasurer: John Schoemer
Executive Director: Don Weiss
Director of Administration: Joe Rhein
Director of Communications: Joe Browne
Director of Operations: Jan Van Duser
Director of Broadcasting: Val Pinchbeck, Jr.
Director of Public Relations: Jim Heffernan
Director of Security: Warren Welsh
Assistant Director of Security: Charles R. Jackson
Director of Player Personnel: Joel Bussert
Supervisor of Officials: Art McNally
Assistant Supervisor of Officials: Jack Reader
Assistant Supervisor of Officials: Nick Skorich
Director of Special Events: Jim Steeg
Assistant Director of Special Events: Susan McCann
Assistant Counsel: Jim Noel
Controller: Tom Sullivan
Director of Player Relations: Mel Blount

American Football Conference
President: Lamar Hunt, Kansas City Chiefs
Assistant to President: Al Ward
Director of Information: Pete Abitante

National Football Conference
President: Wellington Mara, New York Giants
Assistant to President: Bill Granholm
Director of Information: Dick Maxwell

Cover Photograph by Paul Jasienski.

Copyright 1985 by the National Football League.
All rights reserved. The information in this publication
has been compiled for use by the news media to aid
in reporting of the games and teams of the National
Football League. No part of this book may be repro-
duced or transmitted in any form or by any means,
electronic or mechanical, including photocopying,
recording, or by any information storage and re-
trieval system, without permission in writing from the
National Football League.

Printed in the United States of America.

A National Football League Book.
Compiled by the NFL Public Relations Department
   and Seymour Siwoff.
Edited by Pete Abitante, NFL Public Relations and
   Chuck Garrity, Jr., NFLP Creative Services.
Statistics by Elias Sports Bureau.
Produced by NFL Properties, Inc., Creative Services
   Division.

Workman Publishing Co.
1 West 39th Street, New York, N.Y. 10018
Manufactured in the United States of America.
First printing, July 1985.

10 9 8 7 6 5 4 3 2 1

Contents

1985 NFL Schedule 4
Important Dates. 11
Waivers, Active List, Reserve List, Trades,
   Annual Player Limits. 12
Tie-Breaking Procedures. 13
Figuring the 1986 NFL Schedule 14
Look For in 1985 16
Active Coaches Career Records 17
Coaches With 100 Career Victories 17
AFC Active Statistical Leaders. 18
NFC Active Statistical Leaders. 19
Draft List for 1985 20
American Football Conference
   Buffalo Bills 24
   Cincinnati Bengals 28
   Cleveland Browns. 32
   Denver Broncos 36
   Houston Oilers. 40
   Indianapolis Colts 44
   Kansas City Chiefs 48
   Los Angeles Raiders 52
   Miami Dolphins 56
   New England Patriots. 60
   New York Jets 64
   Pittsburgh Steelers 68
   San Diego Chargers. 72
   Seattle Seahawks. 76
National Football Conference
   Atlanta Falcons 82
   Chicago Bears. 86
   Dallas Cowboys 90
   Detroit Lions. 94
   Green Bay Packers. 98
   Los Angeles Rams 102
   Minnesota Vikings. 106
   New Orleans Saints 110
   New York Giants 114
   Philadelphia Eagles 118
   St. Louis Cardinals 122
   San Francisco 49ers. 126
   Tampa Bay Buccaneers. 130
   Washington Redskins. 134
Trades. 140
1984 Preseason Standings and Results 141
1984 Regular Season Standings and Results 142
1984 Week by Week. 144
1984 Professional Football Awards 165
1984 All-Pro Teams. 166
1984 Paid Attendance Breakdown. 168
NFL Paid Attendance. 169
NFL's 10 Biggest Weekends 169
NFL's 10 Highest Scoring Weekends 169
Top 10 Televised Sports Events 169
1984 Ten Best Rushing Performances 170
1984 Ten Best Passing Performances. 171
1984 Ten Best Receiving Performances 172
1984 Statistics
   American Football Conference Team Offense . . . 174
   American Football Conference Team Defense. 175
   National Football Conference Team Offense 176
   National Football Conference Team Defense. 177
   AFC, NFC, and NFL Team Summary. 178
   Club Leaders 179
   Club Rankings by Yards. 179
   Takeaways and Giveaways. 179
   Individual Scoring 180
   Individual Field Goals. 183
   Individual Rushing 184
   Individual Passing. 187
   Individual Pass Receiving 189
   Individual Interceptions 192
   Individual Punting 194
   Individual Punt Returns 195
   Individual Kickoff Returns 196
   Individual Fumbles 198
   Individual Sacks 202
Pro Football Hall of Fame 206
A Chronology of Professional Football. 209
Past Standings 215
All-Time Team vs. Team Results. 222
Super Bowl Game Summaries 244
Playoff Game Summaries
   AFC Championship Games. 249
   NFC Championship Games 250
   AFC Divisional Playoff Games 252
   NFC Divisional Playoff Games 253
   AFC First-Round Playoff Games 253
   NFC First-Round Playoff Games 253
AFC-NFC Pro Bowl Game Summaries. 254
AFC vs. NFC, 1970-1984 257
Monday Night Results 258
Overtime Games. 260
Number-One Draft Choices. 263
All-Time Records. 266
Outstanding Performers 285
Yearly Statistical Leaders 289
Super Bowl Records. 295
Postseason Game Records 302
AFC-NFC Pro Bowl Records. 310
1985 Roster of Officials 316
Official Signals. 318
Digest of Rules 322

All times P.M. local daylight.
Nationally televised games in parentheses. CBS and NBC television
doubleheader games in the regular season to be announced.

Preseason/First Week

Saturday, August 3	Houston ___ vs. New York Giants ___ at Canton, Ohio	(ABC) 2:30
Friday, August 9	Buffalo ___ at Detroit ___	8:00
	Chicago ___ at St. Louis ___	7:30
Saturday, August 10	Cleveland ___ at San Diego ___	6:00
	Green Bay ___ at Dallas ___	8:00
	Houston ___ at Los Angeles Rams ___	7:00
	Kansas City ___ at Cincinnati ___	7:00
	Minnesota ___ at Miami ___	8:00
	New Orleans ___ at New England ___	3:30
	New York Giants ___ at Denver ___	7:00
	Philadelphia ___ at New York Jets ___	8:30
	Pittsburgh ___ at Tampa Bay ___	8:00
	San Francisco ___ at Los Angeles Raiders ___	6:00
	Seattle ___ at Indianapolis ___	7:30
	Washington ___ at Atlanta ___	8:00

Preseason/Second Week

Thursday, August 15	St. Louis ___ at Los Angeles Rams ___	7:00
Friday, August 16	Detroit ___ at Seattle ___	7:30
Saturday, August 17	Atlanta ___ at Tampa Bay ___	8:00
	Buffalo ___ at Miami ___	8:00
	Dallas ___ at San Diego ___	(CBS) 6:00
	Green Bay ___ at New York Giants ___	8:00
	Houston ___ at New Orleans ___	7:00
	Indianapolis ___ at Chicago ___	6:00
	New England ___ at Kansas City ___	7:30
	New York Jets ___ at Cincinnati ___	7:00
	Philadelphia ___ at Cleveland ___	7:30
	Pittsburgh ___ at Minnesota ___	7:00
Sunday, August 18	Washington ___ at Los Angeles Raiders ___	(NBC) 1:00
Monday, August 19	Denver ___ at San Francisco ___	(ABC) 6:00

Preseason/Third Week

Friday, August 23	Cincinnati ___ at Detroit ___	8:00
	Los Angeles Rams ___ vs. Philadelphia ___ at Columbus, Ohio	7:30
	New England ___ at Washington ___	8:00
	Pittsburgh ___ at St. Louis ___	7:30
Saturday, August 24	Atlanta ___ vs. Green Bay ___ at Milwaukee	7:00
	Cleveland ___ at Buffalo ___	6:00
	Indianapolis ___ at Denver ___	7:00
	Kansas City ___ at Houston ___	8:00
	Miami ___ at Los Angeles Raiders ___	(NBC) 6:00
	New York Jets ___ at New York Giants ___	8:00
	San Diego ___ at San Francisco ___	(CBS) 12:00
	Seattle ___ at Minnesota ___	7:00
	Tampa Bay ___ at New Orleans ___	7:00
Monday, August 26	Chicago ___ at Dallas ___	(ABC) 7:00

Preseason/Fourth Week

Thursday, August 29	Detroit ____ at Philadelphia ____	7:30
Friday, August 30	Cincinnati ____ at Indianapolis ____	7:30
	Los Angeles Raiders ____ at Cleveland ____	7:30
	Miami ____ at Atlanta ____	8:00
	Minnesota ____ at Denver ____	7:00
	New Orleans ____ at San Diego ____	7:00
	New York Giants ____ at Pittsburgh ____	7:30
	San Francisco ____ at Seattle ____	(NBC) 6:00
	Washington ____ at Tampa Bay ____	8:00
Saturday, August 31	Buffalo ____ at Chicago ____	6:00
	Houston ____ at Dallas ____	(CBS) 8:00
	New England ____ at Los Angeles Rams ____	7:00
	New York Jets ____ at Green Bay ____	7:00
	St. Louis ____ at Kansas City ____	7:30

First Week

Sunday, September 8 **(NBC-TV doubleheader)**	Denver ____ at Los Angeles Rams ____	1:00
	Detroit ____ at Atlanta ____	1:00
	Green Bay ____ at New England ____	1:00
	Indianapolis ____ at Pittsburgh ____	1:00
	Kansas City ____ at New Orleans ____	12:00
	Miami ____ at Houston ____	12:00
	New York Jets ____ at Los Angeles Raiders ____	1:00
	Philadelphia ____ at New York Giants ____	1:00
	St. Louis ____ at Cleveland ____	1:00
	San Diego ____ at Buffalo ____	4:00
	San Francisco ____ at Minnesota ____	12:00
	Seattle ____ at Cincinnati ____	1:00
	Tampa Bay ____ at Chicago ____	12:00
Monday, September 9	Washington ____ at Dallas ____	(ABC) 8:00

Second Week

Thursday, September 12	Los Angeles Raiders ____ at Kansas City ____	(ABC) 7:00
Sunday, September 15 **(CBS-TV doubleheader)**	Atlanta ____ at San Francisco ____	1:00
	Buffalo ____ at New York Jets ____	1:00
	Cincinnati ____ at St. Louis ____	12:00
	Dallas ____ at Detroit ____	1:00
	Houston ____ at Washington ____	1:00
	Indianapolis ____ at Miami ____	1:00
	Los Angeles Rams ____ at Philadelphia ____	1:00
	Minnesota ____ at Tampa Bay ____	4:00
	New England ____ at Chicago ____	12:00
	New Orleans ____ at Denver ____	2:00
	New York Giants ____ at Green Bay ____	3:00
	Seattle ____ at San Diego ____	1:00
Monday, September 16	Pittsburgh ____ at Cleveland ____	(ABC) 9:00

Third Week

Thursday, September 19	Chicago ____ at Minnesota ____	(ABC) 7:00
Sunday, September 22 **(CBS-TV doubleheader)**	Cleveland ____ at Dallas ____	12:00
	Denver ____ at Atlanta ____	1:00
	Detroit ____ at Indianapolis ____	12:00
	Houston ____ at Pittsburgh ____	1:00
	Kansas City ____ at Miami ____	4:00
	New England ____ at Buffalo ____	1:00
	New York Jets ____ vs. Green Bay ____ at Milwaukee	3:00
	Philadelphia ____ at Washington ____	1:00
	St. Louis ____ at New York Giants ____	1:00
	San Diego ____ at Cincinnati ____	1:00
	San Francisco ____ at Los Angeles Raiders ____	1:00
	Tampa Bay ____ at New Orleans ____	12:00
Monday, September 23	Los Angeles Rams ____ at Seattle ____	(ABC) 6:00

Fourth Week

Sunday, September 29	Atlanta ___ at Los Angeles Rams ___	1:00
(NBC-TV doubleheader)	Cleveland ___ at San Diego ___	1:00
	Dallas ___ at Houston ___	12:00
	Green Bay ___ at St. Louis ___	12:00
	Indianapolis ___ at New York Jets ___	4:00
	Los Angeles Raiders ___ at New England ___	1:00
	Miami ___ at Denver ___	2:00
	Minnesota ___ at Buffalo ___	1:00
	New Orleans ___ at San Francisco ___	1:00
	New York Giants ___ at Philadelphia ___	1:00
	Seattle ___ at Kansas City ___	12:00
	Tampa Bay ___ at Detroit ___	1:00
	Washington ___ at Chicago ___	12:00
Monday, September 30	Cincinnati ___ at Pittsburgh ___	(ABC) 9:00

Fifth Week

Sunday, October 6	Buffalo ___ at Indianapolis ___	12:00
(NBC-TV doubleheader)	Chicago ___ at Tampa Bay ___	1:00
	Dallas ___ at New York Giants ___	(ABC) 9:00
	Detroit ___ at Green Bay ___	12:00
	Houston ___ at Denver ___	2:00
	Kansas City ___ at Los Angeles Raiders ___	1:00
	Minnesota ___ at Los Angeles Rams ___	1:00
	New England ___ at Cleveland ___	1:00
	New York Jets ___ at Cincinnati ___	4:00
	Philadelphia ___ at New Orleans ___	12:00
	Pittsburgh ___ at Miami ___	1:00
	San Diego ___ at Seattle ___	1:00
	San Francisco ___ at Atlanta ___	1:00
Monday, October 7	St. Louis ___ at Washington ___	(ABC) 9:00

Sixth Week

Sunday, October 13	Atlanta ___ at Seattle ___	1:00
(CBS-TV doubleheader)	Buffalo ___ at New England ___	1:00
	Chicago ___ at San Francisco ___	1:00
	Cleveland ___ at Houston ___	12:00
	Denver ___ at Indianapolis ___	12:00
	Detroit ___ at Washington ___	1:00
	Kansas City ___ at San Diego ___	1:00
	Los Angeles Rams ___ at Tampa Bay ___	1:00
	Minnesota ___ vs. Green Bay ___ at Milwaukee	12:00
	New Orleans ___ at Los Angeles Raiders ___	1:00
	New York Giants ___ at Cincinnati ___	1:00
	Philadelphia ___ at St. Louis ___	12:00
	Pittsburgh ___ at Dallas ___	12:00
Monday, October 14	Miami ___ at New York Jets ___	(ABC) 9:00

Seventh Week

Sunday, October 20	Cincinnati ___ at Houston ___	12:00
(NBC-TV doubleheader)	Dallas ___ at Philadelphia ___	1:00
	Indianapolis ___ at Buffalo ___	1:00
	Los Angeles Raiders ___ at Cleveland ___	1:00
	Los Angeles Rams ___ at Kansas City ___	12:00
	New Orleans ___ at Atlanta ___	1:00
	New York Jets ___ at New England ___	4:00
	St. Louis ___ at Pittsburgh ___	1:00
	San Diego ___ at Minnesota ___	12:00
	San Francisco ___ at Detroit ___	1:00
	Seattle ___ at Denver ___	2:00
	Tampa Bay ___ at Miami ___	4:00
	Washington ___ at New York Giants ___	1:00
Monday, October 21	Green Bay ___ at Chicago ___	(ABC) 8:00

Eighth Week

Sunday, October 27 **(CBS-TV doubleheader)**	Atlanta ____ at Dallas ____	12:00
	Buffalo ____ at Philadelphia ____	1:00
	Denver ____ at Kansas City ____	12:00
	Green Bay ____ at Indianapolis ____	1:00
	Houston ____ at St. Louis ____	12:00
	Miami ____ at Detroit ____	1:00
	Minnesota ____ at Chicago ____	12:00
	New England ____ at Tampa Bay ____	1:00
	New York Giants ____ at New Orleans ____	3:00
	Pittsburgh ____ at Cincinnati ____	4:00
	San Francisco ____ at Los Angeles Rams ____	1:00
	Seattle ____ at New York Jets ____	1:00
	Washington ____ at Cleveland ____	1:00
Monday, October 28	San Diego ____ at Los Angeles Raiders ____	(ABC) 6:00

Ninth Week

Sunday, November 3 **(NBC-TV doubleheader)**	Chicago ____ at Green Bay ____	12:00
	Cincinnati ____ at Buffalo ____	1:00
	Cleveland ____ at Pittsburgh ____	1:00
	Denver ____ at San Diego ____	1:00
	Detroit ____ at Minnesota ____	12:00
	Kansas City ____ at Houston ____	12:00
	Los Angeles Raiders ____ at Seattle ____	1:00
	Miami ____ at New England ____	1:00
	New Orleans ____ at Los Angeles Rams ____	1:00
	New York Jets ____ at Indianapolis ____	4:00
	Philadelphia ____ at San Francisco ____	1:00
	Tampa Bay ____ at New York Giants ____	1:00
	Washington ____ at Atlanta ____	1:00
Monday, November 4	Dallas ____ at St. Louis ____	(ABC) 8:00

Tenth Week

Sunday, November 10 **(CBS-TV doubleheader)**	Atlanta ____ at Philadelphia ____	1:00
	Cleveland ____ at Cincinnati ____	1:00
	Dallas ____ at Washington ____	4:00
	Detroit ____ at Chicago ____	12:00
	Green Bay ____ at Minnesota ____	12:00
	Houston ____ at Buffalo ____	1:00
	Indianapolis ____ at New England ____	1:00
	Los Angeles Raiders ____ at San Diego ____	1:00
	Los Angeles Rams ____ at New York Giants ____	1:00
	New York Jets ____ at Miami ____	4:00
	Pittsburgh ____ at Kansas City ____	12:00
	St. Louis ____ at Tampa Bay ____	1:00
	Seattle ____ at New Orleans ____	12:00
Monday, November 11	San Francisco ____ at Denver ____	(ABC) 7:00

Eleventh Week

Sunday, November 17 **(NBC-TV doubleheader)**	Buffalo ____ at Cleveland ____	1:00
	Chicago ____ at Dallas ____	12:00
	Cincinnati ____ at Los Angeles Raiders ____	1:00
	Kansas City ____ at San Francisco ____	1:00
	Los Angeles Rams ____ at Atlanta ____	1:00
	Miami ____ at Indianapolis ____	1:00
	Minnesota ____ at Detroit ____	4:00
	New England ____ at Seattle ____	1:00
	New Orleans ____ vs. Green Bay ____ at Milwaukee	12:00
	Pittsburgh ____ at Houston ____	12:00
	St. Louis ____ at Philadelphia ____	1:00
	San Diego ____ at Denver ____	2:00
	Tampa Bay ____ at New York Jets ____	1:00
Monday, November 18	New York Giants ____ at Washington ____	(ABC) 9:00

Twelfth Week

Sunday, November 24
(CBS-TV doubleheader)

Atlanta ___ at Chicago ___	12:00
Cincinnati ___ at Cleveland ___	1:00
Denver ___ at Los Angeles Raiders ___	1:00
Detroit ___ at Tampa Bay ___	1:00
Green Bay ___ at Los Angeles Rams ___	1:00
Indianapolis ___ at Kansas City ___	3:00
Miami ___ at Buffalo ___	1:00
New England ___ at New York Jets ___	1:00
New Orleans ___ at Minnesota ___	12:00
New York Giants ___ at St. Louis ___	3:00
Philadelphia ___ at Dallas ___	3:00
San Diego ___ at Houston ___	12:00
Washington ___ at Pittsburgh ___	1:00

Monday, November 25

Seattle ___ at San Francisco ___	(ABC) 6:00

Thirteenth Week

Thursday, November 28
(Thanksgiving Day)

New York Jets ___ at Detroit ___	(NBC) 12:30
St. Louis ___ at Dallas ___	(ABC) 3:00

Sunday, December 1
(CBS-TV doubleheader)

Buffalo ___ at San Diego ___	1:00
Cleveland ___ at New York Giants ___	1:00
Denver ___ at Pittsburgh ___	1:00
Houston ___ at Cincinnati ___	1:00
Kansas City ___ at Seattle ___	1:00
Los Angeles Raiders ___ at Atlanta ___	4:00
Los Angeles Rams ___ at New Orleans ___	12:00
Minnesota ___ at Philadelphia ___	1:00
New England ___ at Indianapolis ___	1:00
San Francisco ___ at Washington ___	4:00
Tampa Bay ___ at Green Bay ___	12:00

Monday, December 2

Chicago ___ at Miami ___	(ABC) 9:00

Fourteenth Week

Sunday, December 8
(NBC-TV doubleheader)

Atlanta ___ at Kansas City ___	12:00
Cleveland ___ at Seattle ___	1:00
Dallas ___ at Cincinnati ___	1:00
Detroit ___ at New England ___	1:00
Indianapolis ___ at Chicago ___	12:00
Los Angeles Raiders ___ at Denver ___	2:00
Miami ___ at Green Bay ___	12:00
New Orleans ___ at St. Louis ___	12:00
New York Giants ___ at Houston ___	3:00
New York Jets ___ at Buffalo ___	1:00
Pittsburgh ___ at San Diego ___	(ABC) 6:00
Tampa Bay ___ at Minnesota ___	3:00
Washington ___ at Philadelphia ___	1:00

Monday, December 9

Los Angeles Rams ___ at San Francisco ___	(ABC) 6:00

Fifteenth Week

Saturday, December 14

Chicago ___ at New York Jets ___	(CBS) 12:30
Kansas City ___ at Denver ___	(NBC) 2:00

Sunday, December 15
(NBC-TV doubleheader)

Buffalo ___ at Pittsburgh ___	1:00
Cincinnati ___ at Washington ___	1:00
Green Bay ___ at Detroit ___	1:00
Houston ___ at Cleveland ___	1:00
Indianapolis ___ at Tampa Bay ___	1:00
Minnesota ___ at Atlanta ___	1:00
New York Giants ___ at Dallas ___	12:00
Philadelphia ___ at San Diego ___	1:00
St. Louis ___ at Los Angeles Rams ___	1:00
San Francisco ___ at New Orleans ___	12:00
Seattle ___ at Los Angeles Raiders ___	1:00

Monday, December 16

New England ___ at Miami ___	(ABC) 9:00

Sixteenth Week

Friday, December 20	Denver ___ at Seattle ___	(ABC) 5:00
Saturday, December 21	Pittsburgh ___ at New York Giants ___	(NBC) 12:30
	Washington ___ at St. Louis ___	(CBS) 3:00
Sunday, December 22	Atlanta ___ at New Orleans ___	12:00
(CBS-TV doubleheader)	Buffalo ___ at Miami ___	1:00
	Chicago ___ at Detroit ___	1:00
	Cincinnati ___ at New England ___	1:00
	Cleveland ___ at New York Jets ___	1:00
	Dallas ___ at San Francisco ___	1:00
	Green Bay ___ at Tampa Bay ___	1:00
	Houston ___ at Indianapolis ___	4:00
	Philadelphia ___ at Minnesota ___	12:00
	San Diego ___ at Kansas City ___	12:00
Monday, December 23	L.A. Raiders ___ at L.A. Rams ___	(ABC) 6:00

First-Round Playoff Games

Site Priorities

Two wild card teams (fourth- and fifth-best records) from each conference will enter the first round of the playoffs. The wild cards from the same conference will play each other. Home clubs will be the clubs with the best won-lost-tied percentage in the regular season. If tied in record, the tie will be broken by the tie-breaking procedure already in effect.

Sunday, December 29, 1985 American Football Conference

_____ at _____ (NBC)

National Football Conference

_____ at _____ (CBS)

Divisional Playoff Games

Site Priorities

In each conference, the two division winners with the highest won-lost-tied percentage during the regular season will be the home teams. The division winner with the best percentage will be host to the wild card winner from the first-round playoff, and the division winner with the second-best percentage will be host to the third division winner, unless the wild card team is from the same division as the winner with the highest percentage. In that case, the division winner with the best percentage will be host to the third division winner and the second highest division winner will be host to the wild card.

Saturday, January 4, 1986 American Football Conference

_____ at _____ (NBC)

National Football Conference

_____ at _____ (CBS)

Sunday, January 5, 1986 American Football Conference

_____ at _____ (NBC)

National Football Conference

_____ at _____ (CBS)

Conference Championship Games, Super Bowl XX, and AFC-NFC Pro Bowl

Site Priorities for Championship Games

The home teams will be the surviving divisional playoff winners with the best won-lost-tied percentage during the regular season. The wild card team will never be the home team, in either the divisional playoffs or the championship games. Any ties in won-lost-tied percentage will be broken by the tie-breaking procedures already in effect.

Sunday, January 12, 1986 American Football Conference Championship Game

_____ at _____ (NBC)

National Football Conference Championship Game

_____ at _____ (CBS)

Sunday, January 26, 1986 Super Bowl XX at Louisiana Superdome, New Orleans, Louisiana

_____ vs. _____ (NBC)

Sunday, February 2, 1986 AFC-NFC Pro Bowl at Honolulu, Hawaii

AFC _____ vs. NFC _____ (ABC)

Postseason Games

Sunday, December 29	AFC and NFC First-Round Playoffs (NBC and CBS)
Saturday, January 4	AFC and NFC Divisional Playoffs (NBC and CBS)
Sunday, January 5	AFC and NFC Divisional Playoffs (NBC and CBS)
Sunday, January 12	AFC and NFC Championship Games (NBC and CBS)
Sunday, January 26	Super Bowl XX at Louisiana Superdome, New Orleans (NBC)
Sunday, February 2	AFC-NFC Pro Bowl, Honolulu, Hawaii (ABC)

Nationally Televised Games

(All games carried on NBC Network Radio.)

Regular Season

Monday, September 9	Washington at Dallas (night, ABC)
Thursday, September 12	Los Angeles Raiders at Kansas City (night, ABC)
Monday, September 16	Pittsburgh at Cleveland (night, ABC)
Thursday, September 19	Chicago at Minnesota (night, ABC)
Monday, September 23	Los Angeles Rams at Seattle (night, ABC)
Monday, September 30	Cincinnati at Pittsburgh (night, ABC)
Sunday, October 6	Dallas at New York Giants (night, ABC)
Monday, October 7	St. Louis at Washington (night, ABC)
Monday, October 14	Miami at New York Jets (night, ABC)
Monday, October 21	Green Bay at Chicago (night, ABC)
Monday, October 28	San Diego at Los Angeles Raiders (night, ABC)
Monday, November 4	Dallas at St. Louis (night, ABC)
Monday, November 11	San Francisco at Denver (night, ABC)
Monday, November 18	New York Giants at Washington (night, ABC)
Monday, November 25	Seattle at San Francisco (night, ABC)
Thursday, November 28	(Thanksgiving) New York Jets at Detroit (day, NBC)
	St. Louis at Dallas (day, CBS)
Monday, December 2	Chicago at Miami (night, ABC)
Sunday, December 8	Pittsburgh at San Diego (night, ABC)
Monday, December 9	Los Angeles Rams at San Francisco (night, ABC)
Saturday, December 14	Chicago at New York Jets (day, CBS)
	Kansas City at Denver (day, NBC)
Monday, December 16	New England at Miami (night, ABC)
Friday, December 20	Denver at Seattle (night, ABC)
Saturday, December 21	Pittsburgh at New York Giants (day, NBC)
	Washington at St. Louis (day, CBS)
Monday, December 23	Los Angeles Raiders at Los Angeles Rams (night, ABC)

AFC-NFC Interconference Games

(Sunday unless noted; all times local.)

September 8	Denver at Los Angeles Rams	1:00
	Green Bay at New England	1:00
	Kansas City at New Orleans	12:00
	St. Louis at Cleveland	1:00
September 15	Cincinnati at St. Louis	12:00
	Houston at Washington	1:00
	New England at Chicago	12:00
	New Orleans at Denver	2:00
September 22	Cleveland at Dallas	12:00
	Denver at Atlanta	1:00
	Detroit at Indianapolis	12:00
	New York Jets vs. Green Bay at Milwaukee	3:00
	San Francisco at Los Angeles Raiders	1:00
September 23	Los Angeles Rams at Seattle (Monday night)	6:00
September 29	Dallas at Houston	12:00
	Minnesota at Buffalo	1:00
October 13	Atlanta at Seattle	1:00
	New Orleans at Los Angeles Raiders	1:00
	New York Giants at Cincinnati	1:00
	Pittsburgh at Dallas	12:00
October 20	Los Angeles Rams at Kansas City	12:00
	St. Louis at Pittsburgh	1:00
	San Diego at Minnesota	12:00
	Tampa Bay at Miami	4:00
October 27	Buffalo at Philadelphia	1:00
	Green Bay at Indianapolis	1:00
	Houston at St. Louis	12:00
	Miami at Detroit	1:00
	New England at Tampa Bay	1:00
	Washington at Cleveland	1:00
November 10	Seattle at New Orleans	12:00
November 11	San Francisco at Denver (Monday night)	7:00

November 17	Kansas City at San Francisco	1:00
	Tampa Bay at New York Jets	1:00
November 24	Washington at Pittsburgh	1:00
November 25	Seattle at San Francisco (Monday night)	6:00
November 28	New York Jets at Detroit (Thanksgiving)	12:30
December 1	Cleveland at New York Giants	1:00
	Los Angeles Raiders at Atlanta	4:00
December 2	Chicago at Miami (Monday night)	9:00
December 8	Atlanta at Kansas City	12:00
	Detroit at New England	1:00
	Dallas at Cincinnati	1:00
	Indianapolis at Chicago	12:00
	Miami at Green Bay	12:00
	New York Giants at Houston	3:00
December 14	Chicago at New York Jets (Saturday)	12:30
December 15	Cincinnati at Washington	1:00
	Indianapolis at Tampa Bay	1:00
	Philadelphia at San Diego	1:00
December 21	Pittsburgh at New York Giants (Saturday)	12:30
December 23	Los Angeles Raiders at Los Angeles Rams (Monday night)	6:00

Monday Night Games at a Glance

(All times local; televised by ABC and broadcast by NBC Network Radio.)

September 9	Washington at Dallas	8:00
September 16	Pittsburgh at Cleveland	9:00
September 23	Los Angeles Rams at Seattle	6:00
September 30	Cincinnati at Pittsburgh	9:00
October 7	St. Louis at Washington	9:00
October 14	Miami at New York Jets	9:00
October 21	Green Bay at Chicago	8:00
October 28	San Diego at Los Angeles Raiders	6:00
November 4	Dallas at St. Louis	8:00
November 11	San Francisco at Denver	7:00
November 18	New York Giants at Washington	9:00
November 25	Seattle at San Francisco	6:00
December 2	Chicago at Miami	9:00
December 9	Los Angeles Rams at San Francisco	6:00
December 16	New England at Miami	9:00
December 23	Los Angeles Raiders at Los Angeles Rams	6:00

Sunday, Thursday, & Friday Prime Time Night Games at a Glance

(All times local; televised by ABC and broadcast by NBC Network Radio.)

Thursday, September 12	Los Angeles Raiders at Kansas City	7:00
Thursday, September 19	Chicago at Minnesota	7:00
Sunday, October 6	Dallas at New York Giants	9:00
Sunday, December 8	Pittsburgh at San Diego	6:00
Friday, December 20	Denver at Seattle	5:00

Important Dates

For the 1985 Season

July 5	Claiming period of 24 hours begins in waiver system. All waivers for the rest of the year are no-recall and no-withdrawal.
Mid-July	Preseason training camps open.
August 3	Hall of Fame Game, Canton, Ohio: Houston vs. New York Giants.
August 8-11	First preseason weekend.
August 15-19	Second preseason weekend.
August 20	Roster cutdown to maximum of 60 players.
August 23-26	Third preseason weekend.
August 27	Roster cutdown to maximum of 50 players.
August 29-31	Fourth preseason weekend.
September 2	Roster cutdown to maximum of 45 players.
September 8-9	Regular season opens.
September 24	Priority on multiple waiver claims in the same conference now based on the current season's standings.
October 15	Trading of player contracts/rights ends at 4:00 p.m. E.S.T.
December 16-17	Balloting for AFC-NFC Pro Bowl.
December 20	Deadline for waiver requests in 1985.
December 22-23	Regular season closes.
December 25	Deadline for postseason participant to sign free agents for playoffs.
December 29	AFC and NFC First-Round Playoff Games.
January 4-5	AFC and NFC Divisional Playoff Games.
January 12	AFC and NFC Conference Championship Games.
January 26	Super Bowl XX at Louisiana Superdome, New Orleans, Louisiana.
February 2	AFC-NFC Pro Bowl at Aloha Stadium, Honolulu, Hawaii.
February 3	Trading period begins.
March 10-14	NFL Annual Meeting at Rancho Mirage, California.

For the 1986 Season

August 2	Hall of Fame Game, Canton Ohio: Kansas City vs. Los Angeles Rams.
August 8-10	First preseason weekend.
September 7-8	Regular season opens.
December 21-22	Regular season closes.
December 28	AFC and NFC First-Round Playoff Games.
January 3-4	AFC and NFC Divisional Playoff Games.
January 11	AFC and NFC Conference Championship Games.
January 25	Super Bowl XXI at Rose Bowl, Pasadena, California.
February 1	AFC-NFC Pro Bowl at Aloha Stadium, Honolulu, Hawaii.
March 16-20	NFL Annual Meeting at Maui, Hawaii.

For the 1987 Season

August 8	Hall of Fame Game, Canton, Ohio: New England vs. St. Louis.
August 14-16	First preseason weekend.
September 13-14	Regular season opens.
December 27-28	Regular season closes.
January 3	AFC and NFC First-Round Playoff Games.
January 9-10	AFC and NFC Divisional Playoff Games.
January 17	AFC and NFC Conference Championship Games.
January 31	Super Bowl XXII at San Diego Jack Murphy Stadium, San Diego, California.
February 7	AFC-NFC Pro Bowl.
March 18-22	NFL Annual Meeting at Phoenix, Arizona.

For the 1988 Season

January 22, 1989	Super Bowl XXIII at Dolphins Stadium, Miami, Florida.
January 29	AFC-NFC Pro Bowl.
March 20-24	NFL Annual Meeting at Palm Springs, California.

For the 1989 Season

January 28, 1990	Super Bowl XXIV at Louisiana Superdome, New Orleans, Louisiana.
February 4	AFC-NFC Pro Bowl.
March 25-30	NFL Annual Meeting at Maui, Hawaii.

Waivers

The waiver system is a procedure by which player contracts or NFL rights to players are made available by a club to other clubs in the League. During the procedure the 27 other clubs either file claims to obtain the players or waive the opportunity to do so—thus the term "waiver." Claiming clubs are assigned players on a priority based on the inverse of won-and-lost standing. The claiming period normally is 10 days during the offseason and 24 hours from early July through December. In some circumstances another 24 hours is added on to allow the original club to rescind its action (known as a recall of a waiver request) and/or the claiming club to do the same (known as withdrawal of a claim). If a player passes through waivers unclaimed and is not recalled by the original club, he becomes a free agent. All waivers from July through December are no-recall and no withdrawal. Under the Collective Bargaining Agreement, from February 1 through October 15, any veteran who has acquired four years of pension credit may, if about to be assigned to another club through the waiver system, reject such assignment and become a free agent.

Active List

The Active List is the principal status for players participating for a club. It consists of all players under contract, including option, who are eligible for preseason, regular season, and postseason games. Clubs are allowed to open training camp with an unlimited number of players but thereafter must meet a series of mandatory roster reductions prior to the season opener. Teams will be permitted to dress up to 45 players for each regular season and postseason game during the 1985 season. The Active List maximums and dates for 1985 are:

August 20 . . . . 60 players
August 27 . . . . 50 players
September 2 . . . . 45 players

Reserve List

The Reserve List is a status for players who, for reasons of injury, retirement, military service, or other circumstances, are not immediately available for participation with a club. Those players in the category of Reserve/Injured who were physically unable to play football for a minimum of four weeks from the date of going onto Reserve may be re-activated by their clubs upon clearing procedural recall waivers; in addition, each club will have five free re-activations for players meeting the four-week requirement, but only one of the free re-activations can be used for a player placed on Reserve/Injured prior to or concurrent with the final cutdown on September 2. Clubs participating in postseason competition will be granted an additional free re-activation. Players not meeting the four-week requirement may not return in the same season to the Active List of the club which originally placed them on Reserve, but may be assigned through the waiver system to other clubs. Players in the category of Reserve/Retired may not be reinstated during the period from 30 days before the end of the regular season on through the postseason.

Trades

Unrestricted trading between the AFC and NFC is allowed in 1985 through October 15, after which trading of player contracts/rights will end until February 3, 1986.

Annual Player Limits

NFL

Year(s)	Limit
1985	45
1983-84	49
1982	45†–49
1978–81	45
1975–77	43
1974	47
1964–73	40
1963	37
1961–62	36
1960	38
1959	36
1957–58	35
1951–56	33
1949–50	32
1948	35
1947	35*–34
1945–46	33
1943–44	28
1940–42	33
1938–39	30
1936–37	25
1935	24
1930–34	20
1926–29	18
1925	16

†45 for first two games
*35 for first three games

AFL

Year(s)	Limit
1966–69	40
1965	38
1964	34
1962–63	33
1960–61	35

Tie-Breaking Procedures

The following procedures will be used to break standings ties for postseason playoffs and to determine regular season schedules.

To Break a Tie Within a Division

If, at the end of the regular season, two or more clubs in the same division finish with identical won-lost-tied percentages, the following steps will be taken until a champion is determined.

Two Clubs

1. Head-to-head (best won-lost-tied percentage in games between the clubs).
2. Best won-lost-tied percentage in games played within the division.
3. Best won-lost-tied percentage in games played within the conference.
4. Best won-lost-tied percentage in common games, if applicable.
5. Best net points in division games.
6. Best net points in all games.
7. Strength of schedule.
8. Best net touchdowns in all games.
9. Coin toss.

Three or More Clubs

(Note: If two clubs remain tied after a third club is eliminated during any step, tie-breaker reverts to step 1 of two-club format.)

1. Head-to-head (best won-lost-tied percentage in games among the clubs).
2. Best won-lost-tied percentage in games played within the division.
3. Best won-lost-tied percentage in games played within the conference.
4. Best won-lost-tied percentage in common games.
5. Best net points in division games.
6. Best net points in all games.
7. Strength of schedule.
8. Best net touchdowns in all games.
9. Coin toss.

To Break a Tie for the Wild Card Team

If it is necessary to break ties to determine the two Wild Card clubs from each conference, the following steps will be taken.

1. If the tied clubs are from the same division, apply division tie-breaker.
2. If the tied clubs are from different divisions, apply the following steps.

Two Clubs

1. Head-to-head, if applicable.
2. Best won-lost-tied percentage in games played within the conference.
3. Best won-lost-tied percentage in common games, minimum of four.
4. Best average net points in conference games.
5. Best net points in all games.
6. Strength of schedule.
7. Best net touchdowns in all games.
8. Coin toss.

Three or More Clubs

(Note: If two clubs remain tied after other clubs are eliminated, tie-breaker reverts to step 1 of applicable two-club format.)

1. Head-to-head sweep. (Applicable only if one club has defeated each of the others, or if one club has lost to each of the others.)
2. Best won-lost-tied percentage in games played within the conference.
3. Best won-lost-tied percentage in common games, minimum of four.
4. Best average net points in conference games.
5. Best net points in all games.
6. Strength of schedule.
7. Best net touchdowns in all games.
8. Coin toss.

Tie-Breaking Procedure for Selection Meeting

If two or more clubs are tied for selection order, the conventional strength of schedule tie-breaker will be applied, subject to the following exceptions for playoff teams.

1. The Super Bowl winner will be last and the Super Bowl loser will be next-to-last.
2. Any non-Super Bowl playoff team involved in a tie moves down in drafting priority as follows:
   A. Participation by a club in the playoffs without a victory adds one-half victory to the club's regular season won-lost-tied record.
   B. For each victory in the playoffs, one full victory will be added to the club's regular season won-lost-tied record.
3. Clubs with the best won-lost-tied records after these steps are applied will drop to their appropriate spots at the bottom of the tied segment. In no case will the above process move a club lower than the segment in which it was initially tied.

Figuring the 1986 NFL Schedule

As soon as the final game of the 1985 NFL regular season (Los Angeles Raiders at Los Angeles Rams, December 23) has been completed, it will be possible to determine the 1986 opponents of the 28 teams.

Each 1986 team schedule is based on a formula initiated for the 1978 season that uses the team's won-lost-tied percentage from the current season as the primary guide.

For years the NFL had been seeking an easily understood, balanced schedule that would provide for both competitive equality and a variety of opponents. It was easy to segregate groups of teams into tight divisions, have them play the majority of their games within those divisions, and let the division winners emerge into a structured playoff system. But the result was that many attractive teams with star players never appeared in other cities unless those clubs happened to be matched in the playoffs.

The new approach to scheduling gives the fans the best of both systems, a neat competitive format and variety at the same time. It also reduces inequalities in the strength of schedules that popped up too often in the past under the system of rotating opponents over a period of years.

Under the present format, schedules of any NFL team are figured according to one of the following three formulas. (The reference point for the figuring is the final standing. Ties for position in any of the divisions are broken according to the tie-breaking procedures outlined on page 13. The chart on the following page is included for use as you go through each step.)

A. First- through fourth-place teams in a five-team division (AFC East, AFC West, NFC East, NFC Central).

1. Home-and-home round-robin within the division (8 games).
2. One game each with the first- through fourth-place teams in a division of the other conference. In 1986, AFC East will play NFC West, AFC West will play NFC East, and AFC Central will play NFC Central (4 games).
3. The first-place team plays the first- and fourth-place teams in the other divisions within the conference. The second-place team plays the second- and third-place teams in the other division within the conference. The third-place team plays the third- and second-place teams in the other divisions within the conference. The fourth-place team plays the fourth- and first-place teams in the other divisions within the conference (4 games).

This completes the 16-game schedule.

B. First- through fourth-place teams in a four-team division (AFC Central, NFC West).

1. Home-and-home round-robin within the division (6 games).
2. One game with each of the fifth-place teams in the conference (2 games).
3. The same procedure that is listed in step A2 (4 games).
4. The same procedure that is listed in step A3 (4 games).

This completes the 16-game schedule.

C. The fifth-place teams in a division (AFC East, AFC West, NFC East, NFC Central).

1. Home-and-home round-robin within the division (8 games).
2. One game with each team in the four-team division of the conference (4 games).
3. A home-and-home with the other fifth-place team in the conference (2 games).
4. One game each with the fifth-place teams in the other conference (2 games).

This completes the 16-game schedule.

The 1986 Opponent Breakdown chart on the following page does not include the round-robin games within the division. Those are automatically on a home-and-away basis.

1985 NFL Standings

AFC

EAST AE

1 _____
2 _____
3 _____
4 _____
5 _____

CENTRAL AC

1 _____
2 _____
3 _____
4 _____

WEST AW

1 _____
2 _____
3 _____
4 _____
5 _____

NFC

EAST NE

1 _____
2 _____
3 _____
4 _____
5 _____

WEST NW

1 _____
2 _____
3 _____
4 _____

CENTRAL NC

1 _____
2 _____
3 _____
4 _____
5 _____

A Team's 1986 Schedule

Team Name _____

_____
_____
_____
_____
_____
_____
_____
_____
_____
_____
_____
_____
_____
_____
_____
_____
_____

1986 Opponent Breakdown

AE AFC EAST	HOME	AWAY	AC AFC CENTRAL	HOME	AWAY	AW AFC WEST	HOME	AWAY	NE NFC EAST	HOME	AWAY	NC NFC CENTRAL	HOME	AWAY	NW NFC WEST	HOME	AWAY
AE-1	AC-4	AC-1	**AC-1**	AE-1	AE-4	**AW-1**	AE-4	AE-1	**NE-1**	NW-4	NW-4	**NC-1**	NE-4	NE-1	**NW-1**	NE-1	NE-4
	AW-1	AW-4		AW-4	AW-1		AC-1	AC-4		NC-1	NC-1		NW-1	NW-4		NC-4	NC-1
	NW-2	NW-1		AW-5	AE-5		NE-2	NE-1		AW-1	AW-2		AC-1	AC-2		NC-5	NE-5
	NW-4	NW-3		NC-2	NC-1		NE-4	NE-3		AW-3	AW-4		AC-3	AC-4		AE-1	AE-2
				NC-4	NC-3											AE-3	AE-4
AE-2	AC-3	AC-2	**AC-2**	AE-2	AE-3	**AW-2**	AE-3	AE-2	**NE-2**	NW-3	NW-2	**NC-2**	NE-3	NE-2	**NW-2**	NE-2	NE-3
	AW-2	AW-3		AW-3	AW-2		AC-2	AC-3		NC-2	NC-3		NW-2	NW-3		NC-3	NC-2
	NW-1	NW-2		AE-5	AW-5		NE-1	NE-2		AW-2	AW-1		AC-2	AC-1		NE-5	NC-5
	NW-3	NW-4		NC-1	NC-2		NE-3	NE-4		AW-4	AW-3		AC-4	AC-3		AE-2	AE-1
				NC-3	NC-4											AE-4	AE-3
AE-3	AC-2	AC-3	**AC-3**	AE-3	AE-2	**AW-3**	AE-2	AE-3	**NE-3**	NW-2	NW-3	**NC-3**	NE-2	NE-3	**NW-3**	NE-3	NE-2
	AW-3	AW-2		AW-2	AW-3		AC-3	AC-2		NC-3	NC-2		NW-3	NW-2		NC-2	NC-3
	NW-2	NW-1		AW-5	AE-5		NE-2	NE-1		AW-1	AW-2		AC-1	AC-2		NC-5	NE-5
	NW-4	NW-3		NC-2	NC-1		NE-4	NE-3		AW-3	AW-4		AC-3	AC-4		AE-1	AE-2
				NC-4	NC-3											AE-3	AE-4
AE-4	AC-1	AC-4	**AC-4**	AE-4	AE-1	**AW-4**	AE-1	AE-4	**NE-4**	NW-1	NW-4	**NC-4**	NE-1	NE-4	**NW-4**	NE-4	NE-1
	AW-4	AW-1		AW-1	AW-4		AC-4	AC-1		NC-4	NC-1		NW-4	NW-1		NC-1	NC-4
	NW-1	NW-2		AE-5	AW-5		NE-1	NE-2		AW-2	AW-1		AC-2	AC-1		NE-5	NC-5
	NW-3	NW-4		NC-1	NC-2		NE-3	NE-4		AW-4	AW-3		AC-4	AC-3		AE-2	AE-1
				NC-3	NC-4											AE-4	AE-3
AE-5	AC-1	AC-2				**AW-5**	AC-2	AC-1	**NE-5**	NW-1	NW-2	**NC-5**	NW-2	NW-1			
	AC-3	AC-4					AC-4	AC-3		NW-3	NW-4		NW-4	NW-3			
	AW-5	AW-5					AE-5	AE-5		NC-5	NC-5		NE-5	NE-5			
	NE-5	NC-5					NC-5	NE-5		AW-5	AE-5		AE-5	AW-5			

Look for in 1985

Things that could happen in 1985:

• Eric Dickerson, Los Angeles Rams, could become only the third player in NFL history to lead the league in rushing in each of his first three seasons. The others: Jim Brown (who led in each of his first five years) and Earl Campbell.

• John Riggins, Washington, needs 562 rushing yards to move past O. J. Simpson into fourth place in NFL history in career rushing yardage. Riggins enters the season with 10,675 yards; Simpson finished with 11,236.

• Riggins needs 10 rushing touchdowns to tie Jim Brown's NFL record of 106. Riggins also enters the season with 108 total touchdowns (including 12 on pass receptions), to rank third behind Brown (126) and Lenny Moore (113).

• Tony Dorsett, Dallas, needs 475 yards rushing to become the sixth NFL player to accumulate 10,000 total yards.

• Ottis Anderson, St. Louis, needs 718 yards rushing to crack the NFL's all-time top 10 in that category. Anderson starts the season in eleventh place with 7,364 yards; Larry Csonka is tenth at 8,081.

• Walter Payton, Chicago, needs just two touchdowns to join Jim Brown, Lenny Moore, John Riggins, Don Hutson, and Franco Harris in the group of NFL players to have scored 100 career touchdowns.

• If Payton rushes for 1,000 yards this year, it would be his ninth such season, which would break the mark of eight that he currently shares with Franco Harris.

• Ken Anderson, Cincinnati, needs 204 completions to pass Johnny Unitas into second place in NFL history. Anderson starts the season with 2,627 in 181 NFL games, while Unitas had 2,830 in 211 games. The all-time leader is Fran Tarkenton, who had 3,686 in 246 games. Dan Fouts, San Diego, also could challenge Unitas; Fouts enters the season in fifth place with 2,585 completions.

• Fouts also only needs 812 yards passing to move past Jim Hart into third place in NFL history. Fouts starts the season with 33,854 yards in 144 games; Hart passed for 34,665 yards in 201 games.

• Steve Largent, Seattle, needs 55 receptions to become the fifth NFL player to accumulate 600 career receptions. If Largent catches 50 or more passes this season, it will be his eighth such year, breaking the NFL record of seven, which Largent currently shares with four other players.

• Ozzie Newsome, Cleveland, needs 60 receptions to become the fourteenth NFL player to catch 500 passes in his career.

• Dave Jennings, New York Giants, is 69 punts short of joining John James and Jerrel Wilson as the only NFL players to punt 1,000 times.

• Billy Johnson, Atlanta, needs 55 yards on punt returns to surpass the NFL record of 3,008 career yards, held by Rick Upchurch. Johnson also has 240 career punt returns, 18 short of the league record held by Emlen Tunnell.

• Jan Stenerud, Minnesota, needs to play in nine games to pass Earl Morrall into third place in NFL history. Stenerud begins the season with 247 games; Morrall had 255.

Active Coaches' Career Records

Start of 1985 Season

Coach	Team(s)	Regular Season					Postseason				Career			
		Yrs.	Won	Lost	Tied	Pct.	Won	Lost	Tied	Pct.	Won	Lost	Tied	Pct.
Joe Gibbs	Washington Redskins	4	41	16	0	.719	6	2	0	.750	47	18	0	.723
Don Shula	Baltimore Colts, Miami Dolphins	22	227	82	6	.730	15	12	0	.555	242	94	6	.716
Tom Flores	Los Angeles Raiders	6	58	31	0	.651	8	2	0	.800	66	33	0	.666
Tom Landry	Dallas Cowboys	25	223	126	6	.637	20	15	0	.571	243	141	6	.631
Chuck Knox	Los Angeles Rams, Buffalo Bills, Seattle Seahawks	12	112	62	1	.643	7	9	0	.438	119	71	1	.626
Chuck Noll	Pittsburgh Steelers	16	142	88	1	.617	15	7	0	.682	157	95	1	.623
Bud Grant	Minnesota Vikings	17	151	87	5	.633	10	12	0	.455	161	99	5	.617
Don Coryell	St. Louis Cardinals, San Diego Chargers	12	102	68	1	.599	3	6	0	.333	105	74	1	.586
Bill Walsh	San Francisco 49ers	6	49	40	0	.551	7	1	0	.875	56	41	0	.577
Dan Reeves	Denver Broncos	4	34	23	0	.596	0	2	0	.000	34	25	0	.576
John Robinson	Los Angeles Rams	2	19	13	0	.594	1	2	0	.333	20	15	0	.571
O.A. (Bum) Phillips	Houston Oilers, New Orleans Saints	10	78	69	0	.531	4	3	0	.571	82	72	0	.532
Leeman Bennett	Atlanta Falcons, Tampa Bay Buccaneers	7	46	41	0	.529	1	3	0	.250	47	44	0	.516
Mike Ditka	Chicago Bears	3	21	20	0	.512	1	1	0	.500	22	21	0	.512
Forrest Gregg	Cleveland Browns, Cincinnati Bengals, Green Bay Packers	8	58	56	0	.509	2	2	0	.500	60	58	0	.508
Sam Wyche	Cincinnati Bengals	1	8	8	0	.500	0	0	0	.000	8	8	0	.500
Raymond Berry	New England Patriots	1	4	4	0	.500	0	0	0	.000	4	4	0	.500
Marty Schottenheimer	Cleveland Browns	1	4	4	0	.500	0	0	0	.000	4	4	0	.500
Jim Hanifan	St. Louis Cardinals	5	34	38	1	.473	0	1	0	.000	34	39	1	.466
John Mackovic	Kansas City Chiefs	2	14	18	0	.438	0	0	0	.000	14	18	0	.438
Joe Walton	New York Jets	2	14	18	0	.438	0	0	0	.000	14	18	0	.438
Bill Parcells	New York Giants	2	12	19	1	.391	1	1	0	.500	13	20	1	.397
Dan Henning	Atlanta Falcons	2	11	21	0	.344	0	0	0	.000	11	21	0	.344
Kay Stephenson	Buffalo Bills	2	10	22	0	.313	0	0	0	.000	10	22	0	.313
Marion Campbell	Atlanta Falcons, Philadelphia Eagles	4	17	39	1	.307	0	0	0	.000	17	39	1	.307
Hugh Campbell	Houston Oilers	1	3	13	0	.188	0	0	0	.000	3	13	0	.188
Rod Dowhower	Indianapolis Colts	0	0	0	0	.000	0	0	0	.000	0	0	0	.000
Darryl Rogers	Detroit Lions	0	0	0	0	.000	0	0	0	.000	0	0	0	.000

Coaches With 100 Career Victories

Start of 1985 Season

Coach	Team(s)	Regular Season					Postseason				Career			
		Yrs.	Won	Lost	Tied	Pct.	Won	Lost	Tied	Pct.	Won	Lost	Tied	Pct.
George Halas	Chicago Bears	40	319	148	31	.672	6	3	0	.667	325	151	31	.672
Tom Landry	Dallas Cowboys	25	223	126	6	.637	20	15	0	.571	243	141	6	.631
Don Shula	Baltimore Colts, Miami Dolphins	22	227	82	6	.730	15	12	0	.555	242	94	6	.716
Earl (Curly) Lambeau	Green Bay Packers, Chicago Cardinals, Washington Redskins	33	231	133	23	.627	3	2	0	.600	234	135	23	.626
Paul Brown	Cleveland Browns, Cincinnati Bengals	21	166	100	6	.621	4	8	0	.333	170	108	6	.609
Bud Grant	Minnesota Vikings	17	151	87	5	.633	10	12	0	.455	161	99	5	.617
Chuck Noll	Pittsburgh Steelers	16	142	88	1	.617	15	7	0	.682	157	95	1	.623
Steve Owen	New York Giants	23	151	100	17	.595	3	8	0	.273	154	108	17	.582
Hank Stram	Kansas City Chiefs, New Orleans Saints	17	131	97	10	.571	5	3	0	.625	136	100	10	.573
Weeb Ewbank	Baltimore Colts, New York Jets	20	130	129	7	.502	4	1	0	.800	134	130	7	.507
Sid Gillman	Los Angeles Rams, San Diego Chargers, Houston Oilers	18	122	99	7	.550	1	5	0	.167	123	104	7	.541
Chuck Knox	Los Angeles Rams, Buffalo Bills, Seattle Seahawks	12	112	62	1	.643	7	9	0	.438	119	71	1	.626
George Allen	Los Angeles Rams, Washington Redskins	12	116	47	5	.705	2	7	0	.222	118	54	5	.681
John Madden	Oakland Raiders	10	103	32	7	.750	9	7	0	.563	112	39	7	.731
Ray (Buddy) Parker	Chicago Cardinals, Detroit Lions, Pittsburgh Steelers	15	104	75	9	.577	3	1	0	.750	107	76	9	.581
Vince Lombardi	Green Bay Packers, Washington Redskins	10	96	34	6	.728	9	1	0	.900	105	35	6	.740
Don Coryell	St. Louis Cardinals, San Diego Chargers	12	102	68	1	.599	3	6	0	.333	105	74	1	.586

AFC ACTIVE STATISTICAL LEADERS

LEADING ACTIVE PASSERS, AMERICAN FOOTBALL CONFERENCE
1,000 or more attempts

	Yrs.	Att.	Comp.	Pct. Comp.	Yards	Avg. Gain	TD	Pct. TD	Had Int.	Pct. Int.	Rate Pts.
Ken Anderson, Cin.	14	4420	2627	59.4	32497	7.35	194	4.4	158	3.6	82.0
Dan Fouts, S.D.	12	4380	2585	59.0	33854	7.73	201	4.6	185	4.2	81.2
Bill Kenney, K.C.	5	1397	776	55.5	10163	7.27	60	4.3	52	3.7	77.5
Gary Danielson, Clev.	8	1684	952	56.5	11885	7.06	69	4.1	71	4.2	74.7
Steve Grogan, N.E.	10	2681	1389	51.8	20270	7.56	139	5.2	162	6.0	68.9
Jim Zorn, Sea.	9	2990	1593	53.3	20122	6.73	107	3.6	133	4.4	67.9
David Woodley, Pitt.	5	1117	593	53.1	7201	6.45	42	3.8	49	4.4	67.4
Jim Plunkett, Raiders	13	3346	1739	52.0	23093	6.90	147	4.4	186	5.6	65.6
Bob Avellini, N.Y.J.	9	1110	560	50.5	7111	6.41	33	3.0	69	6.2	54.8

TOP 10 ACTIVE RUSHERS, AFC
2,000 or more yards

	Yrs.	Att.	Yards	TD
1. Mike Pruitt, Clev.	9	1593	6540	47
2. Greg Pruitt, Raiders	12	1196	5672	27
3. Pete Johnson, Mia.	8	1489	5626	76
4. Curtis Dickey, Ind.	5	791	3456	26
5. Wayne Morris, S.D.	9	899	3387	38
6. Cullen Bryant, Sea.	12	848	3262	20
7. Freeman McNeil, N.Y.J.	4	677	3133	14
8. Anthony Collins, N.E.	4	725	3104	23
9. Marcus Allen, Raiders	3	701	2879	33
10. Tony Nathan, Mia.	6	558	2653	11

Other Leading Rushers

Charles Alexander, Cin.	6	704	2489	11
Kenny King, Raiders	6	563	2410	7
Randy McMillan, Ind.	4	611	2409	14
Frank Pollard, Pitt.	5	537	2283	14
Andra Franklin, Mia.	4	622	2232	22
Ken Anderson, Cin.	14	396	2220	20
Sammy Winder, Den.	3	559	2169	8
Steve Grogan, N.E.	10	377	2061	29
Theotis Brown, K.C.	6	549	2046	30

TOP 10 ACTIVE PASS RECEIVERS, AFC
200 or more receptions

	Yrs.	No.	Yards	TD
1. Charlie Joiner, S.D.	16	657	10774	56
2. Steve Largent, Sea.	9	545	8772	72
3. Cliff Branch, Raiders	13	501	8685	67
4. Ozzie Newsome, Clev.	7	440	5570	34
5. Nat Moore, Mia.	11	421	6414	60
6. Isaac Curtis, Cin.	12	416	7101	53
7. Kellen Winslow, S.D.	6	399	5176	37
8. Wes Chandler, S.D.	7	393	6243	40
9. Charle Young, Sea.	12	390	4755	25
10. John Stallworth, Pitt.	11	387	6799	55

Other Leading Pass Receivers

Dave Casper, Raiders	11	378	5216	52
Henry Marshall, K.C.	9	343	5321	32
Greg Pruitt, Raiders	12	328	3069	18
Stanley Morgan, N.E.	8	312	6441	42
Wesley Walker, N.Y.J.	8	312	5735	46
Mike Pruitt, Clev.	9	255	1761	5
Tony Nathan, Mia.	6	253	2407	13
Cris Collinsworth, Cin.	4	246	3828	20
Steve Watson, Den.	6	236	4331	27
Jerry Butler, Buff.	5	222	3229	25
Todd Christensen, Raiders	6	222	2879	25
Bruce Harper, N.Y.J.	8	220	2409	12
Preston Dennard, Buff.	7	219	3483	28
Dan Doornink, Sea.	7	201	1854	11

TOP 10 ACTIVE SCORERS, AFC
250 or more points

	Yrs.	TD	FG	PAT	TP
1. Pat Leahy, N.Y.J.	11	0	158	306	780
2. Chris Bahr, Raiders	9	0	146	321	759
3. Rolf Benirschke, S.D.	8	0	130	287	677
4. Uwe von Schamann, Mia.	6	0	101	237	540
5. Tony Franklin, N.E.	6	0	102	214	520
6. Matt Bahr, Clev.	6	0	104	203	515
7. Nick Lowery, K.C.	6	0	112	177	513
8. Pete Johnson, Mia.	8	82	0	0	492
9. Jim Breech, Cin.	6	0	96	202	490
10. Benny Ricardo, S.D.	7	0	92	171	447

Other Leading Scorers

Steve Largent, Sea.	9	73	0	0	438
Cliff Branch, Raiders	13	67	0	0	402
Nat Moore, Mia.	11	61	0	0	366
Charlie Joiner, S.D.	16	56	0	0	336
John Stallworth, Pitt.	11	56	0	0	336
Dave Casper, Raiders	11	53	0	0	318
Isaac Curtis, Cin.	12	53	0	0	318
Mike Pruitt, Clev.	9	52	0	0	312
Gary Anderson, Pitt.	3	0	61	105	288
Greg Pruitt, Raiders	12	47	0	0	282
Wesley Walker, N.Y.J.	8	46	0	0	276
Marcus Allen, Raiders	3	44	0	0	264
Stanley Morgan, N.E.	8	43	0	0	258
Wayne Morris, S.D.	9	43	0	0	258
Norm Johnson, Sea.	3	0	48	112	256

TOP 10 ACTIVE INTERCEPTORS, AFC
20 or more interceptions

	Yrs.	No.	Yards	TD
1. Donnie Shell, Pitt.	11	43	371	1
2. Steve Foley, Den.	9	39	536	1
Dave Brown, Sea.	10	39	527	3
4. Mike Haynes, Raiders	9	35	613	2
5. John Harris, Sea.	7	34	405	2
6. Lyle Blackwood, Mia.	12	33	575	2
Lester Hayes, Raiders	8	33	538	3
8. Terry Jackson, Sea.	7	28	360	3
Jack Lambert, Pitt.	11	28	243	0
10. Kenny Easley, Sea.	4	24	435	3
Tim Fox, S.D.	9	24	368	0

Other Leading Interceptors

Louis Breeden, Cin.	7	22	413	1
Steve Freeman, Buff.	10	22	329	3
Darrol Ray, N.Y.J.	5	21	581	3
Gregg Bingham, Hou.	12	21	279	0
Ray Clayborn, N.E.	8	20	382	0
Tom Jackson, Den.	12	20	340	3

TOP 10 ACTIVE PUNT RETURNERS, AFC
40 or more punt returns

	Yrs.	No.	Yards	Avg.	TD
1. Mike Martin, Cin.	2	47	603	12.8	0
2. Louis Lipps, Pitt.	1	53	656	12.4	1
3. Tommy Vigorito, Mia.	3	57	633	11.1	2
4. James Brooks, Cin.	5	52	565	10.9	0
5. J. T. Smith, K.C.	7	220	2322	10.6	4
6. Kirk Springs, N.Y.J.	4	51	534	10.5	1
7. Mike Haynes, Raiders	9	111	1159	10.4	2
Stanley Morgan, N.E.	8	92	960	10.4	1
9. Greg Pruitt, Raiders	12	194	2007	10.3	1
10. Cullen Bryant, Sea.	12	71	707	10.0	0

Other Leading Punt Returners

Bruce Harper, N.Y.J.	8	183	1784	9.7	1
Roland James, N.E.	5	40	387	9.7	1
Mark Clayton, Mia.	2	49	471	9.6	1
Tony Nathan, Mia.	6	51	484	9.5	1
Butch Johnson, Den.	9	146	1313	9.0	0
Cle Montgomery, Raiders	5	62	538	8.7	1
Paul Skansi, Sea.	2	59	508	8.6	0
Nesby Glasgow, Ind.	6	79	651	8.2	1
Larry Anderson, Ind.	7	75	582	7.8	0
John Simmons, Cin.	4	42	295	7.0	0
Wes Chandler, S.D.	7	58	387	6.7	0
Robb Riddick, Buff.	3	46	289	6.3	0
Lyle Blackwood, Mia.	12	68	319	4.7	0

TOP 10 ACTIVE KICKOFF RETURNERS, AFC
40 or more kickoff returns

	Yrs.	No.	Yards	Avg.	TD
1. Ray Clayborn, N.E.	8	57	1538	27.0	3
2. Cullen Bryant, Sea.	12	69	1813	26.3	3
3. Fulton Walker, Mia.	4	123	2944	23.9	1
4. Greg Pruitt, Raiders	12	106	2514	23.7	1
5. Carlos Carson, K.C.	5	52	1208	23.2	0
Butch Johnson, Den.	9	79	1832	23.2	0
7. Nesby Glasgow, Ind.	6	84	1904	22.7	0
8. Larry Anderson, Ind.	7	189	4217	22.3	1
Lionel James, S.D.	1	43	959	22.3	0
Bruce Harper, N.Y.J.	8	243	5407	22.3	0

Other Leading Kickoff Returners

Dwight Walker, Clev.	3	42	922	22.0	0
James Brooks, Cin.	5	112	2449	21.9	0
Wes Chandler, S.D.	7	47	1021	21.7	0
David Verser, Cin.	4	61	1310	21.5	0
Van Williams, Buff.	2	64	1370	21.4	0
Tony Nathan, Mia.	6	53	1133	21.4	0
Zachary Dixon, Sea.	6	128	2634	20.6	1
Anthony Collins, N.E.	4	64	1317	20.6	0
Cle Montgomery, Raiders	5	125	2556	20.4	0
Kurt Sohn, N.Y.J.	3	41	827	20.2	0
Anthony Hancock, K.C.	3	58	1156	19.9	0
Robb Riddick, Buff.	3	42	825	19.6	0
Steve Wilson, Den.	6	58	1107	19.1	0

TOP 10 ACTIVE PUNTERS, AFC
50 or more punts

	Yrs.	No.	Avg.	LG
1. Rohn Stark, Ind.	3	235	44.9	72
2. Reggie Roby, Mia.	2	125	43.8	69
3. Rich Camarillo, N.E.	4	225	43.3	76
4. Ray Guy, Raiders	12	870	42.8	74
5. Maury Buford, S.D.	3	150	42.7	71
6. Jim Arnold, K.C.	2	191	42.4	64
7. John Kidd, Buff.	1	88	42.0	63
Steve Cox, Clev.	4	190	42.0	69
9. Luke Prestridge, Sea.	6	421	41.9	89
10. Pat McInally, Cin.	9	643	41.8	67

Other Leading Punters

Craig Colquitt, Pitt.	6	429	41.3	74
Jeff Gossett, Clev.	3	132	40.6	60
Chris Norman, Den.	1	96	40.1	83
Jeff West, Sea.	9	610	38.1	62

NFC ACTIVE STATISTICAL LEADERS

LEADING ACTIVE PASSERS, NATIONAL FOOTBALL CONFERENCE
1,000 or more attempts

	Yrs.	Att.	Comp.	Pct. Comp.	Yards	Avg. Gain	TD	Pct. TD	Had Int.	Pct. Int.	Rate Pts.
Joe Montana, S.F.	6	2077	1324	63.7	15609	7.52	106	5.1	54	2.6	92.7
Neil Lomax, St.L.	4	1355	782	57.7	10192	7.52	61	4.5	43	3.2	83.3
Danny White, Dall.	9	1943	1155	59.4	14754	7.59	109	5.6	90	4.6	82.7
Joe Theismann, Wash.	11	3301	1877	56.9	23432	7.10	152	4.6	122	3.7	79.0
Steve Bartkowski, Atl.	10	3219	1802	56.0	22732	7.06	149	4.6	140	4.3	75.5
Vince Ferragamo, Rams	7	1288	730	56.7	9376	7.28	70	5.4	71	5.5	74.8
Ron Jaworski, Phil.	11	3313	1759	53.1	22827	6.89	151	4.6	133	4.0	73.5
Tommy Kramer, Minn.	8	2380	1326	55.7	15631	6.57	100	4.2	102	4.3	72.0
Lynn Dickey, G.B.	12	2811	1575	56.0	21116	7.51	126	4.5	162	5.8	71.0
Phil Simms, N.Y.G.	5	1529	792	51.8	10269	6.72	61	4.0	61	4.0	69.9
Steve DeBerg, T.B.	7	2256	1292	57.3	14593	6.47	78	3.5	102	4.5	69.4
Joe Ferguson, Det.	12	4166	2188	52.5	27590	6.62	181	4.3	190	4.6	68.9
Richard Todd, N.O.	9	2935	1594	54.3	20419	6.96	121	4.1	157	5.3	67.8
Archie Manning, Minn.	13	3642	2011	55.2	23911	6.57	125	3.4	173	4.8	67.1

TOP 10 ACTIVE RUSHERS, NFC
2,000 or more yards

	Yrs.	Att.	Yards	TD
1. Walter Payton, Chi.	10	3047	13309	89
2. John Riggins, Wash.	13	2740	10675	96
3. Tony Dorsett, Dall.	8	2136	9525	59
4. Earl Campbell, N.O.	7	2029	8764	73
5. Ottis Anderson, St.L.	6	1690	7364	40
6. Wilbert Montgomery, Phil.	8	1465	6538	45
7. William Andrews, Atl.	5	1263	5772	29
8. Wendell Tyler, S.F.	8	1142	5384	44
9. Billy Sims, Det.	5	1131	5106	42
10. Joe Washington, Atl.	8	1143	4629	11

Other Leading Rushers

George Rogers, Wash.	4	995	4267	23
Rob Carpenter, N.Y.G.	8	1110	4159	29
Ted Brown, Minn.	6	961	3959	29
Eric Dickerson, Rams	2	769	3913	32
Tony Galbreath, N.Y.G.	9	976	3750	34
Scott Dierking, T.B.	8	734	2915	18
Gerry Ellis, G.B.	5	648	2910	18
James Wilder, T.B.	4	758	2878	24
Eddie Lee Ivery, G.B.	6	531	2272	21
Lynn Cain, Atl.	6	604	2263	19
Gerald Riggs, Atl.	3	531	2222	26
Archie Manning, Minn.	13	384	2197	18
Ron Springs, Dall.	6	604	2180	28

TOP 10 ACTIVE PASS RECEIVERS, NFC
200 or more receptions

	Yrs.	No.	Yards	TD
1. Pat Tilley, St.L.	9	416	6228	31
2. Tony Galbreath, N.Y.G.	9	401	3223	8
3. James Lofton, G.B.	7	397	7663	41
4. Sammy White, Minn.	9	385	6324	50
5. Walter Payton, Chi.	10	373	3456	9
6. Dwight Clark, S.F.	6	367	4961	31
7. Joe Washington, Atl.	8	358	3085	17
8. Tony Hill, Dall.	8	356	6105	41
9. John Jefferson, G.B.	7	348	5684	47
10. Freddie Solomon, S.F.	10	346	5587	47

Other Leading Pass Receivers

David Hill, Rams	9	304	3634	26
Art Monk, Wash.	5	302	4256	22
Duriel Harris, Dall.	9	299	5031	20
Ted Brown, Minn.	6	294	2427	10
Tony Dorsett, Dall.	8	292	2539	8
Russ Francis, S.F.	9	275	3916	36
Paul Coffman, G.B.	7	273	3557	33
William Andrews, Atl.	5	272	2612	11
Wilbert Montgomery, Phil.	8	266	2447	12
Ottis Anderson, St.L.	6	266	2179	5
Billy Johnson, Atl.	10	261	3240	20
John Riggins, Wash.	13	244	2072	12
Earnest Gray, N.Y.G.	6	243	3768	27
James Wilder, T.B.	4	243	2038	4
Jimmie Giles, T.B.	8	235	3596	25
Kevin House, T.B.	5	231	3919	26
Roy Green, St.L.	6	222	3958	33
Ron Springs, Dall.	6	222	2028	10
Mike Barber, Rams	9	220	2751	17
Gerry Ellis, G.B.	5	219	2050	10
Earl Cooper, S.F.	5	209	1863	12
Leonard Thompson, Det.	10	201	3626	25

TOP 10 ACTIVE SCORERS, NFC
250 or more points

	Yrs.	TD	FG	PAT	TP
1. Jan Stenerud, Minn.	18	0	358	539	1613
2. Mark Moseley, Wash.	14	0	266	426	1224
3. Ray Wersching, S.F.	12	0	171	319	832
4. Rafael Septien, Dall.	8	0	146	335	773
5. John Riggins, Wash.	13	108	0	0	648
6. Bob Thomas, Chi.	10	0	133	248	647
7. Walter Payton, Chi.	10	98	0	0	588
8. Neil O'Donoghue, St.L.	8	0	102	221	527
9. Ed Murray, Det.	5	0	108	166	490
10. Earl Campbell, N.O.	7	73	0	0	438

Other Leading Scorers

Tony Dorsett, Dall.	8	68	0	0	408
Mick Luckhurst, Atl.	4	0	68	146	350
Wilbert Montgomery, Phil.	8	58	0	0	348
Wendell Tyler, S.F.	8	58	0	0	348
Freddie Solomon, S.F.	10	56	0	0	336
Sammy White, Minn.	9	50	0	0	300
John Jefferson, G.B.	7	47	0	0	282
Billy Sims, Det.	5	47	0	0	282
Ottis Anderson, St.L.	6	45	0	0	270
Tony Galbreath, N.Y.G.	9	42	2	1	259
James Lofton, G.B.	7	42	0	0	252

TOP 10 ACTIVE INTERCEPTORS, NFC
20 or more interceptions

	Yrs.	No.	Yards	TD
1. Dennis Thurman, Dall.	7	31	541	3
2. Gary Fencik, Chi.	9	30	408	1
Herman Edwards, Phil.	8	30	90	0
4. Cedric Brown, T.B.	9	29	593	2
5. Nolan Cromwell, Rams	8	28	537	3
6. Gary Green, Rams	8	27	418	1
Mark Murphy, Wash.	8	27	282	0
8. Dwight Hicks, S.F.	6	26	518	3
Mario Clark, S.F.	9	26	438	0
10. Everson Walls, Dall.	4	25	276	0

Other Leading Interceptors

Gerald Small, Atl.	7	24	380	1
Eric Harris, Rams	5	21	329	1

TOP 10 ACTIVE PUNT RETURNERS, NFC
40 or more punt returns

	Yrs.	No.	Yards	Avg.	TD
1. Henry Ellard, Rams	2	46	620	13.5	3
2. Billy Johnson, Atl.	10	240	2954	12.3	6
3. Dana McLemore, S.F.	3	83	1008	12.1	3
4. LeRoy Irvin, Rams	5	144	1448	10.1	4
5. Ricky Smith, Wash.	3	54	537	9.9	0
6. Robbie Martin, Det.	4	118	1118	9.5	2
Gary Allen, Dall.	3	63	599	9.5	1
8. Jeff Fisher, Chi.	4	120	1125	9.4	1
9. Mike Nelms, Wash.	5	212	1948	9.2	2
10. Freddie Solomon, S.F.	10	177	1614	9.1	4
Zack Thomas, T.B.	2	54	493	9.1	1

Other Leading Punt Returners

Stump Mitchell, St.L.	4	145	1280	8.8	1
Jeff Groth, N.O.	6	104	887	8.5	0
James Jones, Dall.	4	87	736	8.5	0
Rich Mauti, Wash.	7	76	612	8.1	0
Theo Bell, T.B.	8	189	1511	8.0	0
Leon Bright, T.B.	4	129	1025	7.9	0
Phillip Epps, G.B.	3	85	673	7.9	0
Dwight Hicks, S.F.	6	54	403	7.5	0
Willard Harrell, St.L.	10	123	854	6.9	2
Ron Fellows, Dall.	4	46	308	6.7	0
Phil McConkey, N.Y.G.	1	46	306	6.7	0
Evan Cooper, Phil.	1	40	250	6.3	0

TOP 10 ACTIVE KICKOFF RETURNERS, NFC
40 or more kickoff returns

	Yrs.	No.	Yards	Avg.	TD
1. Duriel Harris, Dall.	9	56	1416	25.3	0
2. Billy Johnson, Atl.	10	123	2941	23.9	2
3. Mike Nelms, Wash.	5	175	4128	23.6	0
Brian Baschnagel, Chi.	9	89	2102	23.6	1
5. Darrin Nelson, Minn.	3	63	1468	23.3	0
6. Roy Green, St.L.	6	83	1917	23.1	1
7. Wayne Wilson, N.O.	6	68	1565	23.0	0
8. Rich Mauti, Wash.	7	124	2838	22.9	0
9. Stump Mitchell, St.L.	4	142	3238	22.8	1
10. Ricky Smith, Wash.	3	67	1505	22.5	1

Other Leading Kickoff Returners

James Owens, T.B.	6	127	2801	22.1	2
Alvin Hall, Det.	4	83	1828	22.0	1
Mike McCoy, G.B.	8	54	1187	22.0	0
Jimmy Rogers, N.O.	5	77	1678	21.8	0
Barry Redden, Rams	3	64	1390	21.7	0
Del Rodgers, G.B.	2	59	1279	21.7	1
Ken Jenkins, Det.	2	40	855	21.4	0
Mike Morton, T.B.	3	89	1885	21.2	0
James Jones, Dall.	4	61	1283	21.0	0
Kenny Duckett, N.O.	3	64	1338	20.9	0
Dana McLemore, S.F.	3	49	1009	20.6	0
Gary Allen, Dall.	3	56	1136	20.3	0
Ron Fellows, Dall.	4	73	1478	20.2	0
Leon Bright, T.B.	4	66	1331	20.2	0
Drew Hill, Rams	5	171	3438	20.1	1
Zack Thomas, T.B.	2	46	924	20.1	0
Willard Harrell, St.L.	10	97	1921	19.8	0
Jeff Moore, Wash.	6	40	784	19.6	0
Beasley Reece, T.B.	9	40	775	19.4	0
Mark Lee, G.B.	5	45	859	19.1	0
Harlan Huckleby, G.B.	5	70	1300	18.6	0
Robbie Martin, Det.	4	59	1061	18.0	0

TOP 10 ACTIVE PUNTERS, NFC
50 or more punts

	Yrs.	No.	Avg.	LG
1. Brian Hansen, N.O.	1	69	43.8	66
2. Mike Horan, Phil.	1	92	42.2	69
3. Frank Garcia, T.B.	3	165	42.0	64
Bucky Scribner, G.B.	2	154	42.0	70
5. Dave Jennings, N.Y.G.	11	931	41.7	73
6. Carl Birdsong, St.L.	4	275	41.3	75
Mike Black, Det.	2	147	41.3	63
8. Ralph Giacomarro, Atl.	2	138	41.1	58
9. Greg Coleman, Minn.	8	602	40.5	73
Max Runager, S.F.	6	371	40.5	64

Other Leading Punters

John Misko, Rams	3	201	40.4	67
Danny White, Dall.	9	609	40.2	73
Dave Finzer, Chi.	1	83	40.1	87
John Warren, Dall.	2	60	39.2	54
Jeff Hayes, Wash.	3	195	38.8	59

50th Annual NFL Draft, April 30–May 1, 1985

Atlanta Falcons

1. Fralic, Bill—2, T, Pittsburgh, from Houston through Minnesota
Choice to Minnesota
2. Choice to Washington
Gann, Mike, 45, DE, Notre Dame, from St. Louis
3. Choice to Minnesota
4. Harry, Emile, 89, WR, Stanford
5. Choice to St. Louis
6. Choice to Miami
Pleasant, Reggie—152, DB, Clemson, from New Orleans
7. Choice to Cincinnati
8. Lee, Ashley—201, DB, Virginia Tech
Washington, Ronnie—215, LB, Northeast Louisiana, from New England
9. Moon, Micah—228, LB, North Carolina
10. Martin, Brent—257, C, Stanford
11. Ayres, John—284, DB, Illinois
12. Whisenhunt, Ken—313, TE, Georgia Tech

Buffalo Bills

1. Smith, Bruce—1, DE, Virginia Tech
Burroughs, Derrick—14, DB, Memphis State, from Green Bay
2. Traynowicz, Mark—29, T, Nebraska
Burkett, Chris—42, WR, Jackson State, from Green Bay
3. Reich, Frank—57, QB, Maryland
Garner, Hal—63, LB, Utah State, from Cleveland
4. Reed, Andre—86, WR, Kutztown State
Hellestrae, Dale—112, T, Southern Methodist, from San Francisco
5. Choice to Los Angeles Rams
Teal, Jimmy—130, WR, Texas A&M, from Dallas
6. Hamby, Mike—141, DT, Utah State
7. Pitts, Ron—169, DB, UCLA
8. Robinson, Jacque—197, RB, Washington
9. Jones, Glenn—225, DB, Norfolk State
10. Babyar, Chris—253, G, Illinois
11. Seawright, James—282, LB, South Carolina
12. Choice to Washington
Woodside, Paul—333, K, West Virginia, from Seattle

Chicago Bears

1. Perry, William—22, DT, Clemson
2. Phillips, Reggie—49, DB, Southern Methodist
3. Maness, James—78, WR, Texas Christian
4. Butler, Kevin—105, K, Georgia
5. Choice to New York Jets
6. Choice to Los Angeles Rams
7. Bennett, Charles—190, DE, Southwestern Louisiana
8. Buxton, Steve—217, T, Indiana State
9. Sanders, Thomas—250, RB, Texas A&M
10. Coryatt, Pat—273, DT, Baylor
11. Morrissey, James—302, LB, Michigan State
12. Choice to San Diego

Cincinnati Bengals

1. Brown, Eddie—13, WR, Miami
King, Emanuel—25, LB, Alabama, from Seattle
2. Zander, Carl—43, LB, Tennessee
3. Thomas, Sean—70, DB, Texas Christian
4. Tuggle, Anthony—97, DB, Nicholls State
5. Degrate, Tony—127, DT, Texas
Davis, Lee—129, DB, Mississippi, from New England
6. Stokes, Eric—148, T, Northeastern, from Tampa Bay
7. Locklin, Kim—172, RB, New Mexico State, from Atlanta
Walter, Joe—181, T, Texas Tech
8. Strobel, Dave—211, LB, Iowa
9. Cruise, Mark—238, DE, Northwestern
10. King, Bernard—265, LB, Syracuse
11. Stanfield, Harold—296, TE, Mississippi College
12. Garza, Louis—322, T, New Mexico State
6. Lester, Keith—154, TE, Murray State

Cleveland Browns

1. Choice to Green Bay through Buffalo
2. Allen, Greg—35, RB, Florida State
3. Choice to Buffalo
4. Choice to Miami
5. Choice to Dallas through Buffalo
6. Krerowicz, Mark—147, G, Ohio State
7. Langhorne, Reginald—175, WR, Elizabeth City State
8. Banks, Fred—203, WR, Liberty Baptist
9. Choice to Philadelphia
10. Williams, Larry—259, G, Notre Dame
11. Tucker, Travis—287, TE, Southern Connecticut
12. Swanson, Shane—315, WR, Nebraska

Dallas Cowboys

1. Brooks, Kevin—17, DE, Michigan
2. Penn, Jesse—44, LB, Virginia Tech
3. Ker, Crawford—76, G, Florida
4. Lavette, Robert—103, RB, Georgia Tech
5. Walker, Herschel—114, RB, Georgia, from Houston
Darwin, Matt—119, C, Texas A&M, from Cleveland through Buffalo
Choice to Buffalo
6. Ploeger, Kurt—144, DE, Gustavus Adolphus, from Indianapolis
Moran, Matt—157, G, Stanford
7. Powe, Karl—178, WR, Alabama State, from New York Jets through Kansas City
Herrmann, Jim—184, DE, Brigham Young
8. Gonzales, Leon—216, WR, Bethune-Cookman
9. Strasburger, Scott—243, LB, Nebraska
10. Jones, Joe—270, TE, Virginia Tech
11. Dellocono, Neal—297, LB, UCLA
12. Jordan, Karl—324, LB, Vanderbilt

Denver Broncos

1. Sewell, Steve—26, RB, Oklahoma
2. Johnson, Vance—31, WR, Arizona, from Houston
Fletcher, Simon—54, DE, Houston
3. Choice to Houston
4. McGregor, Keli—110, TE, Colorado State
5. Choice to Houston
Hinson, Billy—139, G, Florida, from Miami
6. Choice to New York Jets
7. Cameron, Dallas—194, NT, Miami
8. Riley, Eric—222, DB, Florida State
9. Smith, Daryl—249, DB, North Alabama
10. Funck, Buddy—269, QB, New Mexico, from New England
Anderson, Ron—278, LB, Southern Methodist
11. Rolle, Gary—306, WR, Florida
12. Lynch, Dan—334, G, Washington State

Detroit Lions

1. Brown, Lomas—6, T, Florida
2. Glover, Kevin—34, C, Maryland
3. Johnson, James—62, LB, San Diego State
4. Hancock, Kevin—90, LB, Baylor
5. McIntosh, Joe—118, RB, North Carolina State
6. Short, Stan—146, G, Penn State
7. Staten, Tony—174, DB, Angelo State
8. Caldwell, Scotty—202, RB, Texas-Arlington
9. James, June—230, LB, Texas
10. Beauford, Clayton—258, WR, Auburn
11. Harris, Kevin—286, DB, Georgia
12. Weaver, Mike—314, G, Georgia

Green Bay Packers

1. Ruettgers, Ken—7, T, Southern California, from Cleveland through Buffalo
Choice to Buffalo
2. Choice to Buffalo
3. Moran, Rich—71, G, San Diego State
4. Stanley, Walter—98, WR, Mesa, Colo.
5. Noble, Brian—125, LB, Arizona State
6. Lewis, Mark—155, TE, Texas A&M
7. Wilson, Eric—171, LB, Maryland, from Minnesota
Ellerson, Gary—182, RB, Wisconsin
8. Stills, Ken—209, DB, Wisconsin
9. Johnson, Morris—239, G, Alabama A&M
10. Burgess, Ronnie—266, DB, Wake Forest
11. Shield, Joe—294, QB, Trinity, Conn.
12. Meyer, Jim—323, P, Arizona State

Houston Oilers

1. Choice to Atlanta through Minnesota
Childress, Ray—3, DE, Texas A&M, from Minnesota
Johnson, Richard—11, DB, Wisconsin, from New Orleans
2. Choice to Denver
Byrd, Richard—36, DE, Southern Mississippi, from Tampa Bay through Denver
3. Choice to New York Giants
Kelley, Mike—82, C, Notre Dame, from Denver
4. Briehl, Tom—87, LB, Stanford
5. Choice to Dallas
Bush, Frank—133, LB, North Carolina State, from Los Angeles Rams through Kansas City
Johnson, Lee—138, K, Brigham Young, from Denver
6. Choice to Los Angeles Raiders
Krakoski, Joe—153, LB, Washington, from Kansas City
7. Akiu, Mike—170, WR, Hawaii
8. Thomas, Chuck—199, C, Oklahoma
9. Tasker, Steve—226, RB, Northwestern
10. Golic, Mike—255, DE, Notre Dame
11. Drewrey, Willie—281, KR, West Virginia
12. Vonder Haar, Mark—311, DT, Minnesota

Indianapolis Colts

1. Bickett, Duane—5, LB, Southern California
2. Anderson, Don—32, DB, Purdue
3. Young, Anthony—61, DB, Temple
4. Broughton, Willie—88, DE, Miami
5. Caron, Roger—117, T, Harvard
6. Choice to Dallas
7. Harbour, James—173, WR, Mississippi
8. Nichols, Ricky—200, WR, East Carolina
9. Boyer, Mark—229, TE, Southern California
10. Pinesett, Andre—256, DT, Cal State-Fullerton
11. Choice to Los Angeles Rams
12. Burnette, Dave—312, T, Central Arkansas

Kansas City Chiefs

1. Horton, Ethan—15, RB, North Carolina
2. Hayes, Jonathan—41, TE, Iowa
3. Choice to San Diego
4. Olderman, Bob—99, G, Virginia
5. King, Bruce—126, RB, Purdue
6. Bostic, Jonathan—149, DB, Bethune-Cookman, from Philadelphia
Choice to Houston
7. Thomson, Vince—180, DE, Missouri
Western, from San Diego
Heffernan, Dave—183, G, Miami
8. Hillary, Ira—210, WR, South Carolina
9. Armentrout, Mike—237, DB, Southwest Missouri
10. Smith, Jeff—267, RB, Nebraska
11. Jackson, Chris—293, C, Southern Methodist
12. Le Bel, Harper—321, C, Colorado State

Los Angeles Raiders

1. Hester, Jessie—23, WR, Florida State
2. Choice to New England
3. Moffett, Tim—79, WR, Mississippi
Adams, Stefon—80, DB, East Carolina, from Washington through Houston
4. Kimmel, Jamie—107, LB, Syracuse, from Washington
Choice to New England
5. Reeder, Dan—135, RB, Delaware
6. Hilger, Rusty—143, QB, Oklahoma State, from Houston
Choice to Minnesota
7. Belcher, Kevin—186, T, Wisconsin, from New York Giants
Pattison, Mark—188, WR, Washington, from New England
Clark, Bret—191, DB, Nebraska
Haden, Nick—192, C, Penn State, from Washington through New England
8. Wingate, Leonard—220, DT, South Carolina State
9. Sydnor, Chris—246, DB, Penn State
10. McKenzie, Reggie—275, LB, Tennessee, from Washington
Myres, Albert—276, DB, Tulsa
11. Strachan, Steve—303, RB, Boston College
12. Polk, Raymond—332, DB, Oklahoma State

Los Angeles Rams

1. Gray, Jerry—21, DB, Texas
2. Scott, Chuck—50, WR, Vanderbilt
3. Hatcher, Dale—77, P, Clemson
4. Choice to Minnesota
5. Greene, Kevin—113, LB, Auburn, from Buffalo
Choice to Houston through Kansas City
6. Young, Mike—161, WR, UCLA, from Chicago
Johnson, Damone—162, TE, Cal Poly-SLO
7. Bradley, Danny—189, RB, Oklahoma
8. McIntyre, Marlon—218, RB, Pittsburgh
9. Swanson, Gary—245, LB, Cal Poly-SLO
10. Love, Duval—274, G, UCLA
11. Flutie, Doug—285, QB, Boston College, from Indianapolis
Brown, Kevin—301, DB, Northwestern
12. Choice to Tampa Bay

Miami Dolphins

1. Hampton, Lorenzo—27, RB, Florida
2. Choice to San Diego
3. Little, George—65, DT, Iowa, from Philadelphia
   Moyer, Alex—83, LB, Northwestern
4. Smith, Mike—91, DB, Texas-El Paso, from Cleveland
   Dellenbach, Jeff—111, T, Wisconsin
5. Choice to Denver
6. Shorthose, George—145, WR, Missouri, from Atlanta
   Davenport, Ron—167, RB, Louisville
7. Reveiz, Fuad—195, K, Tennessee
8. Sharp, Dan—223, TE, Texas Christian
9. Hinds, Adam—251, DB, Oklahoma State
10. Pendleton, Mike—279, DB, Indiana
11. Jones, Mike—307, RB, Tulane
12. Noble, Ray—335, DB, California

Minnesota Vikings

1. Choice to Houston
   Doleman, Chris—4, LB, Pittsburgh, from Atlanta
2. Holt, Issiac—30, DB, Alcorn State
3. Lowdermilk, Kirk—59, C, Ohio State
   Meamber, Tim—60, LB, Washington, from Atlanta
   Long, Tim—66, T, Memphis State, from San Diego
4. Rhymes, Buster—85, WR, Oklahoma
   Morrell, Kyle—106, DB, Brigham Young, from Los Angeles Rams
5. MacDonald, Mark—115, G, Boston College
   Bono, Steve—142, QB, UCLA
   Newton, Tim—164, NT, Florida, from Los Angeles Raiders
7. Choice to Green Bay
8. Blair, Nikita—198, LB, Texas-El Paso
9. Covington, Jaime—227, RB, Syracuse
10. Johnson, Juan—254, WR, Langston
11. Williams, Tim—283, DB, North Carolina A&T
12. Jones, Byron—310, NT, Tulsa

New England Patriots

1. Choice to San Francisco
   Matich, Trevor—28, C, Brigham Young, from San Francisco
2. Veris, Garin—48, DE, Stanford
   Bowman, Jim—52, DB, Central Michigan, from Los Angeles Raiders
   Thomas, Ben—56, DE, Auburn, from San Francisco
3. Choice to San Francisco
   McMillian, Audrey—84, DB, Houston, from San Francisco
4. Toth, Tom—102, T, Western Michigan
   Phelan, Gerard—108, WR, Boston College, from Los Angeles Raiders
5. Choice to Cincinnati
6. Choice to Philadelphia
7. Choice to Los Angeles Raiders
8. Choice to Atlanta
   Hodge, Milford—224, DT, Washington State, from San Francisco
9. Choice to Pittsburgh
10. Choice to Denver
11. Lewis, Paul—295, RB, Boston U.
12. Mumford, Tony—328, RB, Penn State

New Orleans Saints

1. Choice to Houston
   Toles, Alvin—24, LB, Tennessee, from Washington
2. Gilbert, Daren—38, T, Cal State-Fullerton
3. Del Rio, Jack—68, LB, Southern California
4. Allen, Billy—95, DB, Florida State
5. Choice to Washington
6. Choice to Atlanta
7. Martin, Eric—179, WR, Louisiana State
8. Kohlbrand, Joe—206, DE, Miami
9. Johnson, Earl—236, DB, South Carolina
10. Choice to Washington
11. Choice to Washington
12. Songy, Treg—320, DB, Tulane

New York Giants

1. Adams, George—19, RB, Kentucky
2. Robinson, Stacy—46, WR, North Dakota State
3. Davis, Tyrone—58, DB, Clemson, from Houston
   Johnston, Brian—73, C, North Carolina
4. Bavaro, Mark—100, TE, Notre Dame
5. Henderson, Tracy—132, WR, Iowa State
6. Oliver, Jack—159, G, Memphis State
   Pembrook, Mark—165, DB, Cal State-Fullerton, from Seattle
7. Choice to Los Angeles Raiders
8. Rouson, Lee—213, RB, Colorado
9. Wright, Frank—240, NT, South Carolina
10. Dubroc, Gregg—272, LB, Louisiana State
11. Young, Allen—299, DB, Virginia Tech
12. Welch, Herb—326, DB, UCLA

New York Jets

1. Toon, Al—10, WR, Wisconsin
2. Lyles, Lester—40, DB, Virginia
3. Elder, Donnie—67, DB, Memphis State
4. Allen, Doug—94, WR, Arizona State
5. Benson, Troy—120, LB, Pittsburgh, from Tampa Bay
   Luft, Brian—124, DT, Southern California
   Smith, Tony—134, WR, San Jose State, from Chicago
6. Deaton, Jeff—151, G, Stanford
   Miano, Rich—166, DB, Hawaii, from Denver
7. Choice to Dallas through Kansas City
8. Monger, Matt—208, LB, Oklahoma State
9. Waters, Mike—235, RB, San Diego State
10. Glenn, Kerry—262, DB, Minnesota
11. White, Brad—292, DE, Texas Tech
12. Wallace, Bill—319, WR, Pittsburgh

Philadelphia Eagles

1. Allen, Kevin—9, T, Indiana
2. Cunningham, Randall—37, QB-P, Nevada-Las Vegas
3. Choice to Miami
4. Naron, Greg—93, G, North Carolina
5. Jiles, Dwayne—121, LB, Texas Tech
6. Choice to Kansas City
   Reeves, Ken—156, T, Texas A&M, from New England
7. Choice to Washington
8. Polley, Tom—205, LB, Nevada-Las Vegas
9. Toub, Dave—231, C, Texas-El Paso, from Cleveland
   Drake, Joe—233, DT, Arizona
10. Kelso, Mark—261, DB, William & Mary
11. Hunter, Herman—289, RB, Tennessee State
12. Russell, Todd—317, DB, Boston College

Pittsburgh Steelers

1. Sims, Darryl—20, DE, Wisconsin
2. Behning, Mark—47, T, Nebraska
3. Hobley, Liffort—74, DB, Louisiana State
4. Turk, Dan—101, C, Wisconsin
5. Choice to Seattle
   Jacobs, Cam—136, LB, Kentucky, from Washington
6. Carr, Gregg—160, LB, Auburn
7. Andrews, Alan—187, TE, Rutgers
8. Newsome, Harry—214, P, Wake Forest
9. Small, Fred—241, LB, Washington
   Harris, Andre—242, DB, Minnesota, from New England
10. White, Oliver—268, TE, Kentucky
11. Matichak, Terry—300, DB, Missouri
12. Sanchez, Jeff—327, DB, Georgia

St. Louis Cardinals

1. Nunn, Freddie—18, LB, Mississippi
2. Choice to Atlanta
   Bergold, Scott—51, T, Wisconsin, from Washington through Atlanta
3. Smith, Lance—72, T, Louisiana State
4. Wolfley, Ron—104, RB, West Virginia
5. Dunn, K.D.—116, TE, Clemson, from Atlanta
   Wong, Louis—131, G, Brigham Young
6. Novacek, Jay—158, WR, Wyoming
7. Choice to Washington through Kansas City
8. Monaco, Rob—212, G, Vanderbilt
9. Williams, Scott—244, TE, Georgia
10. Williams, Dennis—271, RB, Furman
11. Anderson, Ricky—298, K, Vanderbilt
12. Young, Lonnie—325, DB, Michigan State

San Diego Chargers

1. Lachey, Jim—12, G, Ohio State
2. Davis, Wayne—39, DB, Indiana State
   Dale, Jeffery—55, DB, Louisiana State, from Miami
3. Choice to Minnesota
   Hendy, John—69, DB, Long Beach State, from Kansas City
4. Mojsiejenko, Ralf—96, K, Michigan State
5. Choice to Seattle
6. Lewis, Terry—150, DB, Michigan State
7. Choice to Kansas City
   Fellows, Mark—196, LB, Montana State, from San Francisco
8. Adams, Curtis—207, RB, Central Michigan
9. Berner, Paul—234, QB, Pacific
   Remsberg, Dan—252, T, Abilene Christian, from San Francisco
10. King, David—264, DB, Auburn
11. Smith, Jeff—291, NT, Kentucky
12. Simmons, Tony—318, DE, Tennessee
    Pearson, Bret—329, TE, Wisconsin, from Chicago

San Francisco 49ers

1. Rice, Jerry—16, WR, Mississippi Valley State, from New England
   Choice to New England
2. Choice to New England
3. Moore, Ricky—75, RB, Alabama, from New England
   Choice to New England
4. Choice to Buffalo
5. Collie, Bruce—140, T, Texas-Arlington
6. Barry, Scott—168, QB, Cal-Davis
7. Choice to San Diego
8. Choice to New England
9. Choice to San Diego
10. Choice to Seattle
11. Wood, David—308, DE, Arizona
12. Chumley, Donald—336, DT, Georgia

Seattle Seahawks

1. Choice to Cincinnati
2. Gill, Owen—53, RB, Iowa
3. Greene, Danny—81, WR, Washington
4. Davis, Tony—109, TE, Missouri
5. Napolitan, Mark—123, C, Michigan State, from San Diego
   Brown, Arnold—128, DB, North Carolina Central, from Pittsburgh
   Jones, Johnnie—137, RB, Tennessee
6. Choice to New York Giants
7. Mattes, Ron—193, T, Virginia
8. Lewis, Judious—221, WR, Arkansas State
9. Otto, Bob—248, DE, Idaho State
10. Conner, John—277, QB, Arizona
    Bowers, James—280, DB, Memphis State, from San Francisco
11. Cooper, Louis—305, LB, Western Carolina
12. Choice to Buffalo

Tampa Bay Buccaneers

1. Holmes, Ron—8, DE, Washington
2. Choice to Houston through Denver
3. Randle, Ervin—64, LB, Baylor
4. Heaven, Mike—92, DB, Illinois
5. Choice to New York Jets
6. Choice to Cincinnati
7. Prior, Mike—176, DB, Illinois State
8. Freeman, Phil—204, WR, Arizona
9. Calabria, Steve—232, QB, Colgate
10. Igwebuike, Donald—260, K, Clemson
11. Williams, James—288, RB, Memphis State
12. Rockford, Jim—316, DB, Oklahoma
    Melka, Jim—330, LB, Wisconsin, from Los Angeles Rams

Washington Redskins

1. Choice to New Orleans
2. Nixon, Tory—33, DB, San Diego State, from Atlanta
   Choice to St. Louis through Atlanta
3. Choice to Los Angeles Raiders through Houston
4. Choice to Los Angeles Raiders
5. Cherry, Raphel—122, RB, Hawaii, from New England
   Choice to Pittsburgh
6. Lee, Danzell—163, TE, Lamar
7. Harris, Jamie—177, KR, Oklahoma State, from Philadelphia
   Vital, Lionel—185, RB, Nicholls State, from St. Louis through Kansas City
   Choice to Los Angeles Raiders through New England
8. Wilburn, Barry—219, DB, Mississippi
9. Geier, Mitch—247, G, Troy State
10. Orr, Terry—263, RB, Texas, from New Orleans
    Choice to Los Angeles Raiders
11. McKenzie, Raleigh—290, G, Tennessee, from New Orleans
    Kimble, Garry—304, DB, Sam Houston State
12. Hamel, Dean—309, DT, Tulsa, from Buffalo
    Winn, Bryant—331, LB, Houston

THE AFC

Buffalo Bills
Cincinnati Bengals
Cleveland Browns
Denver Broncos
Houston Oilers
Indianapolis Colts
Kansas City Chiefs
Los Angeles Raiders
Miami Dolphins
New England Patriots
New York Jets
Pittsburgh Steelers
San Diego Chargers
Seattle Seahawks

BUFFALO BILLS

American Football Conference
Eastern Division

Team Colors: Royal Blue, Scarlet Red, and White

One Bills Drive
Orchard Park, New York 14127
Telephone: (716) 648-1800

Club Officials

President: Ralph C. Wilson, Jr.
Executive-Vice President: Patrick J. McGroder, Jr.
Vice President-Administration and General
  Manager: Terry Bledsoe
Treasurer: David N. Olsen
Vice President-Head Coach: Kay Stephenson
Vice President-Player Personnel: Norm Pollom
Vice President-Public Relations: L. Budd Thalman
Ticket Director: Jim Cipriano
Assistant Ticket Director: Adam Ziccardi
Assistant Public Relations Director: Dave Senko
Assistant Director of Player Personnel:
  Bob Ferguson
Pro Personnel: Bill Polian
Director of Purchasing and Marketing:
  Bill Munson
Trainers: Ed Abramoski, Bud Carpenter
Equipment Manager: Dave Hojnowski
Strength and Conditioning Coordinator:
  Rusty Jones

Stadium: Rich Stadium • **Capacity:** 80,290
  One Bills Drive
  Orchard Park, New York 14127

Playing Surface: AstroTurf

Training Camp: Fredonia State University
  Fredonia, New York 14063

1985 SCHEDULE

Preseason
Aug. 10	at Detroit	8:00
Aug. 17	at Miami	8:00
Aug. 24	**Cleveland**	6:00
Aug. 31	at Chicago	6:00

Regular Season
Sept. 8	**San Diego**	4:00
Sept. 15	at New York Jets	1:00
Sept. 22	**New England**	1:00
Sept. 29	**Minnesota**	1:00
Oct. 6	at Indianapolis	12:00
Oct. 13	at New England	1:00
Oct. 20	**Indianapolis**	1:00
Oct. 27	at Philadelphia	1:00
Nov. 3	**Cincinnati**	1:00
Nov. 10	**Houston**	1:00
Nov. 17	at Cleveland	1:00
Nov. 24	**Miami**	1:00
Dec. 1	at San Diego	1:00
Dec. 8	**New York Jets**	1:00
Dec. 15	at Pittsburgh	1:00
Dec. 22	at Miami	1:00

BILLS COACHING HISTORY

(154-202-8)
1960-61	Buster Ramsey	11-16-1
1962-65	Lou Saban	38-19-3
1966-68	Joe Collier*	13-17-1
1968	Harvey Johnson	1-10-1
1969-70	John Rauch	7-20-1
1971	Harvey Johnson	1-13-0
1972-76	Lou Saban**	32-28-1
1976-77	Jim Ringo	3-20-0
1978-82	Chuck Knox	38-38-0
1983-84	Kay Stephenson	10-22-0

*Released after two games in 1968
**Resigned after five games in 1976

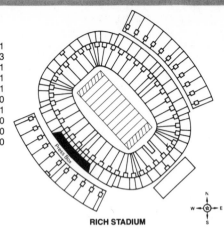

RICH STADIUM

RECORD HOLDERS

Individual Records — Career
Category	Name	Performance
Rushing (Yds.)	O.J. Simpson, 1969-1977	10,183
Passing (Yds.)	Joe Ferguson, 1973-1984	27,590
Passing (TDs)	Joe Ferguson, 1973-1984	181
Receiving (No.)	Elbert Dubenion, 1960-67	296
Receiving (Yds.)	Elbert Dubenion, 1960-67	5,304
Interceptions	George (Butch) Byrd, 1964-1970	40
Punting (Avg.)	Paul Maguire, 1964-1970	42.1
Punt Return (Avg.)	Keith Moody, 1976-79	10.5
Kickoff Return (Avg.)	Wallace Francis, 1973-74	27.2
Field Goals	John Leypoldt, 1971-76	74
Touchdowns (Tot.)	O.J. Simpson, 1969-1977	70
Points	O.J. Simpson, 1969-1977	420

Individual Records — Single Season
Category	Name	Performance
Rushing (Yds.)	O.J. Simpson, 1973	2,003
Passing (Yds.)	Joe Ferguson, 1981	3,652
Passing (TDs)	Joe Ferguson, 1983	26
Receiving (No.)	Frank Lewis, 1981	70
Receiving (Yds.)	Frank Lewis, 1981	1,244
Interceptions	Billy Atkins, 1961	10
	Tom Janik, 1967	10
Punting (Avg.)	Billy Atkins, 1961	44.5
Punt Return (Avg.)	Keith Moody, 1977	13.1
Kickoff Return (Avg.)	Ed Rutkowski, 1963	30.2
Field Goals	Pete Gogolak, 1965	28
Touchdowns (Tot.)	O.J. Simpson, 1975	23
Points	O.J. Simpson, 1975	138

Individual Records — Single Game
Category	Name	Performance
Rushing (Yds.)	O.J. Simpson, 11-25-76	273
Passing (Yds.)	Joe Ferguson, 10-9-83	419
Passing (TDs)	Joe Ferguson, 9-23-79	5
	Joe Ferguson, 10-9-83	5
Receiving (No.)	Glenn Bass, 12-3-61	12
	Bill Miller, 10-5-63	12
Receiving (Yds.)	Jerry Butler, 9-23-79	255
Interceptions	Many times	3
	Last time by Jeff Nixon, 9-7-80	
Field Goals	Pete Gogolak, 12-5-65	5
Touchdowns (Tot.)	Cookie Gilchrist, 12-8-63	5
Points	Cookie Gilchrist, 12-8-63	30

1984 TEAM STATISTICS

	Buffalo	Opp.
Total First Downs	263	345
Rushing	98	134
Passing	149	186
Penalty	16	25
Third Down: Made/Att.	86/243	87/203
Fourth Down: Made/Att.	11/26	7/10
Total Net Yards	4341	5582
Avg. Per Game	271.3	348.9
Total Plays	1046	1052
Avg. Per Play	4.2	5.3
Net Yards Rushing	1643	2106
Avg. Per Game	102.7	131.6
Total Rushes	398	531
Net Yards Passing	2698	3476
Avg. Per Game	168.6	217.3
Tackled/Yards Lost	60/554	26/191
Gross Yards	3252	3667
Att./Completions	588/298	495/300
Completion Pct.	50.7	60.6
Had Intercepted	30	16
Punts/Avg.	90/41.1	72/39.1
Net Punting Avg.	32.7	32.2
Penalties/Yards Lost	121/997	87/734
Fumbles/Ball Lost	31/14	36/21
Touchdowns	31	56
Rushing	9	19
Passing	18	32
Returns	4	5
Avg. Time of Possession	28:43	31:17

1984 TEAM RECORD
Preseason (1-3)

Date	Buffalo		Opponents
8/4	3	Seattle	7
8/11	23	*New England	13
8/18	12	*Detroit	17
8/26	7	Chicago	38
	45		75

Regular Season (2-14)

Date	Buffalo		Opp.	Att.
9/2	17	*New England	21	48,528
9/9	7	St. Louis	37	35,785
9/17	17	*Miami	21	65,455
9/23	26	*New York Jets	28	48,330
9/30	17	Indianapolis	31	60,032
10/7	17	*Philadelphia	27	37,555
10/14	28	Seattle	31	59,034
10/21	7	*Denver	37	31,204
10/28	7	Miami	38	58,824
11/4	10	*Cleveland	13	33,343
11/11	10	New England	38	43,313
11/18	14	*Dallas	3	74,391
11/25	14	Washington	41	51,513
12/2	21	*Indianapolis	15	20,693
12/8	17	New York Jets	21	45,378
12/16	21	Cincinnati	52	55,771
	250		454	769,149

*Home Game

Score by Periods

Buffalo	66	57	64	63	—	250
Opponents	113	148	72	121	—	454

Attendance
Home 359,499   Away 409,650   Total 769,149
Single game home record, 79,933 (10-3-83)
Single season home record, 601,712 (1981)

1984 INDIVIDUAL STATISTICS

Rushing

	Att.	Yds.	Avg.	LG	TD
Bell	262	1100	4.2	85	7
Neal	49	175	3.6	10	1
Ferguson	19	102	5.4	20	0
Moore	24	84	3.5	21	0
Kofler	10	80	8.0	19	0
V. Williams	18	51	2.8	7	0
Brookins	2	27	13.5	16	0
Dufek	9	22	2.4	13	1
Hunter	1	6	6.0	6	0
Riddick	3	3	1.0	6	0
Franklin	1	−7	−7.0	−7	0
Buffalo	398	1643	4.1	85	9
Opponents	531	2106	4.0	31t	19

Passing

	Att.	Comp.	Pct.	Yds.	TD	Int.	Tkld.	Rate
Ferguson	344	191	55.5	1991	12	17	35/357	63.5
Dufek	150	74	49.3	829	4	8	10/86	52.9
Kofler	93	33	35.5	432	2	5	15/111	35.8
Mosley	1	0	0.0	0	0	0	0/0	39.6
Buffalo	588	298	50.7	3252	18	30	60/554	56.3
Opponents	495	300	60.6	3667	32	16	26/191	91.5

Receiving

	No.	Yds.	Avg.	LG	TD
Franklin	69	862	12.5	64t	4
Bell	34	277	8.1	37	1
Hunter	33	331	10.0	30	2
Moore	33	172	5.2	14	0
Dennard	30	417	13.9	68t	7
Riddick	23	276	12.0	38	0
Dawkins	21	295	14.0	37t	2
Brookins	18	318	17.7	70t	1
Neal	9	76	8.4	18	0
Barnett	8	67	8.4	18	0
Brammer	7	49	7.0	12	0
V. Williams	5	46	9.2	32	1
Mosley	4	38	9.5	17	0
White	4	28	7.0	11	0
Buffalo	298	3252	10.9	70t	18
Opponents	300	3667	12.2	65t	32

Interceptions

	No.	Yds.	Avg.	LG	TD
Romes	5	130	26.0	55	0
Freeman	3	45	15.0	45	0
Carpenter	3	11	3.7	11	0
Smerlas	1	25	25.0	25	0
Kush	1	15	15.0	15	0
L. Smith	1	7	7.0	7	0
Bellinger	1	0	0.0	0	0
L. Johnson, Clev.-Buff.	1	0	0.0	0	0
Talley	1	0	0.0	0	0
Buffalo	16	233	14.6	55	0
Opponents	30	416	13.9	59t	4

Punting

	No.	Yds.	Avg.	In 20	LG
Kidd	88	3696	42.0	16	63
Buffalo	90	3696	41.1	16	63
Opponents	72	2812	39.1	22	69

Punt Returns

	No.	FC	Yds.	Avg.	LG	TD
Wilson	33	8	297	9.0	65t	1
Buffalo	33	8	297	9.0	65t	1
Opponents	52	10	597	11.5	39	0

Kickoff Returns

	No.	Yds.	Avg.	LG	TD
V. Williams	39	820	21.0	65	0
Wilson	34	576	16.9	36	0
Bell	1	15	15.0	15	0
David	1	6	6.0	6	0
White	1	5	5.0	5	0
Buffalo	76	1422	18.7	65	0
Opponents	44	958	21.8	59	0

Scoring

	TD R	TD P	TD Rt	PAT	FG	Saf	TP
Bell	7	1	0	0/0	0/0	0	48
Dennard	0	7	0	0/0	0/0	0	42
Danelo	0	0	0	17/17	8/16	0	41
Franklin	0	4	0	0/0	0/0	0	24
Nelson	0	0	0	14/14	3/5	0	23
Dawkins	0	2	0	0/0	0/0	0	12
Hunter	0	2	0	0/0	0/0	0	12
Brookins	0	1	0	0/0	0/0	0	6
David	0	0	1	0/0	0/0	0	6
Dufek	1	0	0	0/0	0/0	0	6
Keating	0	0	1	0/0	0/0	0	6
Neal	1	0	0	0/0	0/0	0	6
Sanford	0	0	1	0/0	0/0	0	6
V. Williams	0	1	0	0/0	0/0	0	6
Wilson	0	0	1	0/0	0/0	0	6
Buffalo	9	18	4	31/31	11/21	0	250
Opponents	19	32	5	56/56	20/28	1	454

FIRST-ROUND SELECTIONS

(If Club had no first-round selection, first player drafted is listed with round in parentheses.)

Year	Player, College, Position
1960	Richie Lucas, Penn State, QB
1961	Ken Rice, Auburn, T
1962	Ernie Davis, Syracuse, RB
1963	Dave Behrman, Michigan State, C
1964	Carl Eller, Minnesota, DE
1965	Jim Davidson, Ohio State, T
1966	Mike Dennis, Mississippi, RB
1967	John Pitts, Arizona State, S
1968	Haven Moses, San Diego State, WR
1969	O.J. Simpson, Southern California, RB
1970	Al Cowlings, Southern California, DE
1971	J. D. Hill, Arizona State, WR
1972	Walt Patulski, Notre Dame, DE
1973	Paul Seymour, Michigan, TE
	Joe DeLamielleure, Michigan State, G
1974	Reuben Gant, Oklahoma State, TE
1975	Tom Ruud, Nebraska, LB
1976	Mario Clark, Oregon, DB
1977	Phil Dokes, Oklahoma State, DT
1978	Terry Miller, Oklahoma State, RB
1979	Tom Cousineau, Ohio State, LB
	Jerry Butler, Clemson, WR
1980	Jim Ritcher, North Carolina State, C
1981	Booker Moore, Penn State, RB
1982	Perry Tuttle, Clemson, WR
1983	Tony Hunter, Notre Dame, TE
	Jim Kelly, Miami, QB
1984	Greg Bell, Notre Dame, RB
1985	Bruce Smith, Virginia Tech, DE
	Derrick Burroughs, Memphis State, DB

BUFFALO BILLS 1985 VETERAN ROSTER

No.	Name	Pos.	Ht.	Wt.	Birth-date	NFL Exp.	College	Birthplace	Residence	'84 Games/Starts
75	†Acker, Bill	NT	6-3	255	11/7/56	6	Texas	Freer, Tex.	Freer, Tex.	15/0
50	Azelby, Joe	LB	6-1	225	3/5/62	2	Harvard	New York, N.Y.	Dumont, N.J.	14/0
84	Barnett, Buster	TE	6-5	235	11/24/58	5	Jackson State	Brooksville, Miss.	Jackson, Miss.	16/7
43	Bayless, Martin	S	6-2	195	10/11/62	2	Bowling Green	Dayton, Ohio	Dayton, Ohio	16/1*
28	Bell, Greg	RB	5-10	210	8/1/62	2	Notre Dame	Columbus, Ohio	East Aurora, N.Y.	16/15
36	Bellinger, Rodney	CB	5-8	181	6/4/62	2	Miami	Miami, Fla.	Coral Gables, Fla.	10/2
86	Brammer, Mark	TE	6-3	235	5/3/58	6	Michigan State	Traverse City, Mich.	Orchard Park, N.Y.	12/1
81	Brookins, Mitchell	WR	5-11	196	12/10/60	2	Illinois	Chicago, Ill.	Chicago, Ill.	16/0
80	Butler, Jerry	WR	6-0	178	10/12/57	6	Clemson	Greenwood, S.C.	East Amherst, N.Y.	0*
30	Carpenter, Brian	CB	5-10	170	11/27/60	4	Michigan	Flint, Mich.	Flint, Mich.	16/10*
63	Cross, Justin	T	6-6	265	4/29/59	4	Western State, Colo.	Montreal, Canada	Hampton Beach, N.H.	7/0
59	David, Stan	LB	6-3	210	2/17/62	2	Texas Tech	North Platte, Neb.	Tucumcari, N.M.	16/3
89	†Dawkins, Julius	WR	6-1	196	1/4/61	3	Pittsburgh	Monessen, Pa.	Pittsburgh, Pa.	16/3
83	Dennard, Preston	WR	6-1	183	11/28/55	8	New Mexico	Cordele, Ga.	West Seneca, N.Y.	16/13
70	Devlin, Joe	T	6-5	250	2/23/54	9	Iowa	Phoenixville, Pa.	Eden, N.Y.	16/16
19	†Dufek, Joe	QB	6-4	215	8/23/61	2	Yale	Kent, Ohio	West Seneca, N.Y.	5/5
85	Franklin, Byron	WR	6-1	185	9/4/58	4	Auburn	Florence, Ala.	East Aurora, N.Y.	16/16
22	†Freeman, Steve	S	5-11	185	5/8/53	11	Mississippi State	Lamesa, Tex.	Memphis, Tenn.	15/15
53	Grant, Will	C	6-3	255	3/7/54	8	Kentucky	Milton, Mass.	Boston, N.Y.	16/16
55	†Haslett, Jim	LB	6-3	232	12/9/56	7	Indiana, Pa.	Pittsburgh, Pa.	Orchard Park, N.Y.	15/15
25	Hill, Rod	CB	6-0	188	3/14/59	3	Kentucky State	Detroit, Mich.	Amherst, N.Y.	2/0
87	Hunter, Tony	TE	6-4	237	5/22/60	3	Notre Dame	Cincinnati, Ohio	Cincinnati, Ohio	11/9
91	Johnson, Ken	DE	6-5	253	3/25/55	7	Knoxville College	Nashville, Tenn.	Nashville, Tenn.	16/16
48	Johnson, Lawrence	CB	5-11	204	9/11/57	6	Wisconsin	Gary, Ind.	Solon, Ohio	16/3*
72	Jones, Ken	T	6-5	260	12/1/52	10	Arkansas State	St. Louis, Mo.	Niagara Falls, N.Y.	16/16
52	†Keating, Chris	LB	6-2	233	10/12/57	7	Maine	Boston, Mass.	Boston, Mass.	16/6
4	Kidd, John	P	6-3	201	8/22/61	2	Northwestern	Findlay, Ohio	Findlay, Ohio	16/0
10	†Kofler, Matt	QB	6-3	192	8/30/59	4	San Diego State	Kelso, Wash.	El Cajon, Calif.	16/0
42	†Kush, Rod	S	6-0	188	1/31/53	6	Nebraska-Omaha	Omaha, Neb.	Gretna, Neb.	16/5
61	Lynch, Tom	G	6-5	250	5/24/55	9	Boston College	Chicago, Ill.	Salem, N.H.	16/0
54	Marve, Eugene	LB	6-2	230	8/14/60	4	Saginaw Valley State	Flint, Mich.	East Amherst, N.Y.	16/16
95	McNanie, Sean	DE	6-5	252	9/9/61	2	San Diego State	Mundelein, Ill.	El Cajon, Calif.	15/1
34	Moore, Booker	FB	5-11	224	6/23/59	4	Penn State	Flint, Mich.	East Aurora, N.Y.	15/15
88	Mosley, Mike	WR	6-1	186	6/30/58	4	Texas A&M	Hillsboro, Tex.	Humble, Tex.	4/0
41	Neal, Speedy	FB	6-2	254	8/26/62	2	Miami	Key West, Fla.	Key West, Fla.	12/1
13	Nelson, Chuck	K	5-11	175	2/23/60	3	Washington	Seattle, Wash.	Seattle, Wash.	7/0
38	Nixon, Jeff	S	6-3	190	10/13/56	5	Richmond	Fursten Feldbruck, Ger.	Blasdell, N.Y.	0*
49	Norris, Ulysses	TE	6-4	232	1/15/57	7	Georgia	Monticello, Ga.	Rochester, Mich.	14/0
58	Potter, Steve	LB	6-3	235	11/6/57	5	Virginia	Bradford, Pa.	Palm Beach, Fla.	10/0
79	†Prater, Dean	DE	6-4	245	9/28/58	4	Oklahoma State	Altus, Okla.	Vernon, Tex.	13/0
40	†Riddick, Robb	RB	6-0	195	4/26/57	4	Millersville State	Quakertown, Pa.	West Seneca, N.Y.	16/0
51	Ritcher, Jim	G	6-3	251	5/21/58	6	North Carolina State	Berea, Ohio	Raleigh, N.C.	14/14
26	Romes, Charles	CB	6-1	190	12/16/54	9	North Carolina Central	Durham, N.C.	Buffalo, N.Y.	16/16
57	Sanford, Lucius	LB	6-2	216	2/14/56	8	Georgia Tech	Atlanta, Ga.	Buffalo, N.Y.	8/8
76	Smerlas, Fred	NT	6-3	270	4/8/57	7	Boston College	Waltham, Mass.	Waltham, Mass.	16/16
56	Talley, Darryl	LB	6-4	235	7/10/60	3	West Virginia	East Cleveland, Ohio	Orchard Park, N.Y.	16/16
	†Taylor, Roger	T	6-6	275	1/5/58	2	Oklahoma State	Shawnee, Okla.	Blue Springs, Mo.	0*
65	†Vogler, Tim	C	6-3	245	10/2/56	7	Ohio State	Covington, Ohio	Hamburg, N.Y.	16/2
60	Wenglikowski, Al	LB	6-1	220	8/3/60	2	Pittsburgh	Franklin, Ohio	Franklin, Ohio	5/0
27	White, Craig	WR	6-1	194	10/8/61	2	Missouri	Fillmore, Mo.	Lawrence, Kan.	14/0
77	Williams, Ben	DE	6-3	260	9/1/54	10	Mississippi	Yazoo City, Miss.	Jackson, Miss.	15/15
23	†Williams, Van	RB	6-0	208	3/15/59	3	Carson-Newman	Johnson City, Tenn.	Johnson City, Tenn.	16/0
21	Wilson, Donald	S	6-2	190	7/21/61	2	North Carolina State	Washington, D.C.	Washington, D.C.	16/11

* Bayless played 3 games with St. Louis, 13 with Buffalo in '84; Butler, Nixon, and Taylor missed '84 season due to injuries; Carpenter played 3 games with Washington, 13 with Buffalo; L. Johnson played 6 games with Cleveland, 10 with Buffalo.

†Option playout; subject to developments.

Traded—Guard Jon Borchardt to Seattle; Quarterback Joe Ferguson to Detroit.

Also played with Bills in '84—LB Trey Junkin (2 games), LB Mark Merrill (2), WR John Mistler (1), CB Lucious Smith (4), DE Scott Virkus (2).

COACHING STAFF

Head Coach,
Kay Stephenson

Pro Career: Starts third season as Bills head coach. Promoted to Buffalo head job on February 1, 1983. Served as Bills' quarterback coach from 1978-82. Signed as a free agent with the San Diego Chargers in 1967 before being traded to Bills in 1968. Injured in 1968-69 and was with Oakland and Atlanta briefly before retiring in 1970. Played one year with the Jacksonville Sharks of the WFL in 1974. Joined Jacksonville coaching staff as offensive coordinator and director of player personnel in 1975. Quarterback coach with the Los Angeles Rams in 1977 before joining the Bills in 1978. Career record: 10-22.

Background: Attended Pensacola, Fla., High School and the University of Florida where he was backup quarterback to Steve Spurrier 1963-66. Assistant football coach at Rice University in 1971. Head coach and Athletic Director at Baker County, Fla., High School in 1973.

Personal: Born December 17, 1944, DeFuniak Springs, Fla. Kay and wife, Mary Jac, live in Orchard Park, N.Y. Has a daughter, Sheryl, 21.

Assistant Coaches

Art Asselta, tight ends; born March 2, 1946, Utica, N.Y., lives in Orchard Park, N.Y. Quarterback-receiver Ithaca College 1965-67. No pro playing experience. College coach: Northern Colorado 1973-74, San Francisco State 1975-77, University of the Pacific 1978-79. Pro coach: Montreal Alouettes (CFL) 1980, Hamilton Tiger-Cats (CFL) 1981, Montreal Concordes (CFL) 1982, Winnipeg Blue Bombers (CFL) 1983-84. First year with Bills.

Hank Bullough, assistant head coach-defensive coordinator; born January 24, 1934, Scranton, Pa., lives in Orchard Park, N.Y. Lineman Michigan State 1951-54. Pro lineman Green Bay Packers 1955, 1958. College coach: Michigan State 1959-69. Pro coach: Baltimore Colts 1970-72, New England Patriots 1973-79, Cincinnati Bengals 1980-83, Pittsburgh (USFL) 1984 (head coach), first year with Bills.

Kay Dalton, quarterbacks; born May 4, 1932, Moab, Utah, lives in Orchard Park, N.Y. Tight end Colorado State 1950-54. No pro playing experience. College coach: Trinidad State 1958-60, Western State 1961-65, Colorado 1971-72. Pro coach: Montreal Alouettes (CFL) 1966-69 (head coach), British Columbia Lions (CFL) 1970, Denver Broncos 1973-76, Buffalo Bills 1977, Kansas City Chiefs 1978-82, Houston Oilers 1983-84, rejoined Bills in 1985.

Monte Kiffin, linebackers; born February 29, 1940, Lexington, Neb., lives in Orchard Park, N.Y. Defensive end Nebraska 1961-63. Pro defensive end Winnipeg Blue Bombers (CFL) 1965-66. College coach: Nebraska 1966-76, Arkansas 1977-79, North Carolina State 1980-82 (head coach). Pro coach: Green Bay Packers 1983, joined Bills in 1984.

Bob Leahy, receivers; born September 5, 1946, Passaic, N.J., lives in Orchard Park, N.Y. Quarterback Emporia State 1967-69. Pro quarterback Pittsburgh Steelers 1970-71. College coach: Pittsburgh 1973-75, 1977, Washington State 1976, California 1978, Oklahoma State 1979-82. Pro coach: Michigan Panthers (USFL) 1983-84, Minnesota Vikings 1984, first year with Bills.

Dick Moseley, defensive backs; born August 1, 1933, Detroit, Mich., lives in Orchard Park, N.Y. Offensive-defensive back Eastern Michigan 1951-54. No pro playing experience. College coach: Eastern Michigan 1968-70, Wichita State 1971, Minnesota 1972-78, Colorado 1979-82. Pro coach: New Jersey Generals (USFL) 1983, Pittsburgh Maulers (USFL) 1984, first year with Bills.

BUFFALO BILLS 1985 FIRST-YEAR ROSTER

Name	Pos.	Ht.	Wt.	Birth-date	College	Birthplace	Residence	How Acq.
Albright, Ira	FB	5-11	253	1/2/59	Northeastern State	Dallas, Tex.	Dallas, Tex.	FA
Alexander, Larry (1)	DE	6-3	255	11/21/59	San Jose State	Los Angeles, Calif.	San Jose, Calif.	FA
Babyar, Chris	G	6-4	264	6/1/62	Illinois	Bloomingdale, Ill.	Bloomingdale, Ill.	D10
Bateson, Robert	LB	6-1	230	5/14/61	Cortland State	Philadelphia, Pa.	Eden, N.Y.	FA
Burkett, Chris	WR	6-4	202	8/23/62	Jackson State	Laurel, Miss.	Collins, Miss.	D2a
Burroughs, Derrick	CB	6-1	176	5/18/62	Memphis State	Mobile, Ala.	Mobile, Ala.	D1a
Christy, Greg	T	6-4	285	4/29/62	Pittsburgh	Natrona Hts., Pa.	Freeport, Pa.	FA
Curry, Robert	NT	6-2	265	5/27/62	Missouri	Pensacola, Fla.	Arlington, Tex.	FA
Davis, Russell (1)	TE	6-5	230	6/16/60	Maryland	Harrisburg, Pa.	Steelton, Pa.	FA
DeVane, William (1)	NT	6-2	275	5/28/62	Clemson	Jacksonville, N.C.	Jacksonville, N.C.	FA
Emerson, Darryl (1)	WR	6-0	190	12/15/60	Maryland	Buffalo, N.Y.	Buffalo, N.Y.	FA
Everett, Emil	K	6-1	185	3/2/62	Wittenberg	Buffalo, N.Y.	Amherst, N.Y.	FA
Gallery, Jim (1)	K	6-1	193	9/15/61	Minnesota	Redwood Falls, Minn.	Mochow, Minn.	FA
Garner, Hal	LB	6-4	219	1/18/62	Utah State	New Iberia, La.	Logan, Utah	D3a
Gipson, Reggie (1)	RB	6-2	205	7/27/60	Alabama A&M	Birmingham, Ala.	Brighton, Ala.	FA
Gulley, Anthony	WR	6-1	200	1/3/63	Texas Christian	Camden, Ark.	Dallas, Tex.	FA
Hamby, Mike	NT	6-4	253	11/2/62	Utah State	Salt Lake City, Utah	Lehi, Utah	D6
Harbison, Charles (1)	S	6-1	195	10/27/59	Gardner-Webb	Gaston Co., N.C.	Lincolnton, N.C.	FA
Hellestrae, Dale	T	6-5	261	7/11/62	Southern Methodist	Phoenix, Ariz.	Scottsdale, Ariz.	D4a
Howell, Leroy (1)	DE	6-4	260	11/4/62	Appalachian State	Columbia, S.C.	Columbia, S.C.	D9('84)
Johnson, Randy	RB	5-11	210	4/11/62	Texas-Arlington	Dallas, Tex.	Dallas, Tex.	FA
Jones, Glenn	CB	5-10	170	12/4/60	Norfolk State	Norfolk, Va.	Norfolk, Va.	D9
Johnston, Michael	K	5-11	185	9/20/61	Notre Dame	Rochester, N.Y.	Rochester, N.Y.	FA
Norwood, Scott (1)	K	6-0	207	7/17/60	James Madison	Alexandria, Va.	Annandale, Va.	FA
Payne, Jimmy (1)	DE	6-4	265	2/9/60	Georgia	Athens, Ga.	Athens, Ga.	D4('83)
Perryman, James	S	6-0	180	12/23/60	Millikin	Oakland, Calif.	Bethel Park, Pa.	FA
Pitts, Ron	CB	5-10	175	10/14/62	UCLA	Detroit, Mich.	Orchard Park, N.Y.	D7
Reed, Andre	WR	6-0	180	1/29/64	Kutztown State	Allentown, Pa.	Allentown, Pa.	D4
Reich, Frank	QB	6-3	208	12/4/61	Maryland	Freeport, N.Y.	Lebanon, Pa.	D3
Richardson, Eric (1)	WR	6-1	183	4/11/62	San Jose State	San Francisco, Calif.	San Jose, Calif.	D2('84)
Robinson, Jacque	RB	5-11	215	3/5/63	Washington	Oakland, Calif.	San Jose, Calif.	D8
Sanchez, Emilio	K	5-11	220	11/8/59	Cal State-Fullerton	Mexico City, Mexico	Valinda, Calif.	FA
Seawright, James	LB	6-2	219	3/30/62	South Carolina	Greenville, S.C.	Simpsonville, S.C.	D11
Smith, Bruce	DE	6-4	285	6/18/63	Virginia Tech	Norfolk, Va.	Norfolk, Va.	D1
Tate, Golden (1)	WR	6-3	197	7/5/60	Tennessee State	Greenville, Miss.	San Jose, Calif.	FA
Teal, Jimmy	WR	5-10	170	8/18/62	Texas A&M	Lufkin, Tex.	Diboll, Tex.	D5
Thompson, Emmuel (1)	CB	5-11	175	11/15/59	Texas A&I	Houston, Tex.	Houston, Tex.	FA
Tolliver, Mike	WR	5-11	180	12/23/60	Stanford	Tacoma, Wash.	Redwood City, Calif.	FA
Traynowicz, Mark	T-G	6-5	267	11/20/62	Nebraska	Omaha, Neb.	Bellevue, Neb.	D2
Woodside, Paul	K	5-11	170	9/2/63	West Virginia	Fairfax, Va.	Falls Church, Va.	D12

Players who report to an NFL team for the first time are designated on rosters as rookies (R). If a player reported to an NFL training camp in a previous year but was not on the active squad for three or more regular season or postseason games, he is listed on the first-year roster and designated by a (1). Thereafter, a player who is on the active squad for three or more regular season or postseason games is credited with an additional year of playing experience.

NOTES

_____

_____

_____

_____

_____

_____

_____

_____

_____

Elijah Pitts, running backs; born February 3, 1938, Mayflower, Ark., lives in Orchard Park, N.Y. Running back Philander Smith 1957-60. Pro running back Green Bay Packers 1961-69, 1971, Los Angeles Rams 1970, Chicago Bears 1970, New Orleans Saints 1970. Pro coach: Los Angeles Rams 1974-77, Buffalo Bills 1978-80, Houston Oilers 1981-83, Hamilton Tiger-Cats (CFL) 1984, rejoined Bills in 1985.

Jim Ringo, offensive coordinator-offensive line; born November 21, 1932, Orange, N.J., lives in Orchard Park, N.Y. Center Syracuse 1950-52. Pro center Green Bay Packers 1953-63, Philadelphia Eagles 1964-66. Pro coach: Chicago Bears 1969-71, Buffalo Bills 1972-77 (1976-77 head coach), New England Patriots 1978-81, Los Angeles Rams 1982, New York Jets 1983-84, rejoined Bills in 1985. Member Pro Football Hall of Fame.

Ardell Wiegandt, defensive line; born June 28, 1940, in Lakota, N.D., lives in Orchard Park, N.Y. Guard-linebacker North Dakota State 1963-65. No pro playing experience. College coach: North Dakota State 1969-74, Wyoming 1983-84. Pro coach: Birmingham Americans (WFL) 1975, Calgary Stampeders (CFL) 1977-81 (head coach 1980-81), Montreal Concordes (CFL) 1982. first year with Bills.

CINCINNATI BENGALS

**American Football Conference
Central Division**

Team Colors: Black, Orange, and White

**200 Riverfront Stadium
Cincinnati, Ohio 45202
Telephone: (513) 621-3550**

Club Officials

President: John Sawyer
General Manager: Paul E. Brown
Assistant General Manager: Michael Brown
Business Manager: Bill Connelly
Consultant: John Murdough
Director of Public Relations: Allan Heim
Director of Player Personnel: Pete Brown
Ticket Manager: Paul Kelly
Trainer: Marv Pollins
Equipment Managers: Tom Gray, Al Davis

Stadium: Riverfront Stadium • **Capacity:** 59,754
200 Riverfront Stadium
Cincinnati, Ohio 45202

Playing Surface: AstroTurf

Training Camp: Wilmington College
Wilmington, Ohio 45177

1985 SCHEDULE

Preseason
Aug. 10	**Kansas City**	7:00
Aug. 17	**New York Jets**	7:00
Aug. 23	at Detroit	8:00
Aug. 30	at Indianapolis	7:30

Regular Season
Sept. 8	**Seattle**	1:00
Sept. 15	at St. Louis	12:00
Sept. 22	**San Diego**	1:00
Sept. 30	at Pittsburgh (Monday)	9:00
Oct. 6	**New York Jets**	4:00
Oct. 13	**New York Giants**	1:00
Oct. 20	at Houston	12:00
Oct. 27	**Pittsburgh**	4:00
Nov. 3	at Buffalo	1:00
Nov. 10	**Cleveland**	1:00
Nov. 17	at Los Angeles Raiders	1:00
Nov. 24	at Cleveland	1:00
Dec. 1	**Houston**	1:00
Dec. 8	**Dallas**	1:00
Dec. 15	at Washington	1:00
Dec. 22	at New England	1:00

BENGALS COACHING HISTORY

(123-128-1)

1968-75	Paul Brown	55-59-1
1976-78	Bill Johnson*	18-15-0
1978-79	Homer Rice	8-19-0
1980-83	Forrest Gregg	34-27-0
1984	Sam Wyche	8-8-0

*Resigned after five games in 1978

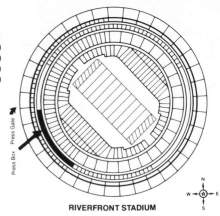

RIVERFRONT STADIUM

RECORD HOLDERS
Individual Records—Career

Category	Name	Performance
Rushing (Yds.)	Pete Johnson, 1977-1983	5,421
Passing (Yds.)	Ken Anderson, 1973-1984	32,497
Passing (TDs)	Ken Anderson, 1973-1984	194
Receiving (No.)	Isaac Curtis, 1973-1984	420
Receiving (Yds.)	Isaac Curtis, 1973-1984	7,106
Interceptions (No.)	Ken Riley, 1969-1983	63
Punting (Avg.)	Dave Lewis, 1970-73	43.9
Punt Return (Avg.)	Mike Martin, 1983-84	12.8
Kickoff Return (Avg.)	Lemar Parrish, 1970-78	24.7
Field Goals	Horst Muhlmann, 1969-1974	120
Touchdowns (Tot.)	Pete Johnson, 1977-1983	70
Points	Horst Muhlmann, 1969-1974	549

Individual Records—Single Season

Category	Name	Performance
Rushing (Yds.)	Pete Johnson, 1981	1,077
Passing (Yds.)	Ken Anderson, 1981	3,754
Passing (TDs)	Ken Anderson, 1981	29
Receiving (No.)	Dan Ross, 1981	71
Receiving (Yds.)	Cris Collinsworth, 1983	1,130
Interceptions	Ken Riley, 1976	9
Punting (Avg.)	Dave Lewis, 1970	46.2
Punt Return (Avg.)	Mike Martin, 1984	15.7
Kickoff Return (Avg.)	Lemar Parrish, 1980	30.2
Field Goals	Horst Muhlmann, 1972	27
Touchdowns (Tot.)	Pete Johnson, 1981	16
Points	Jim Breech, 1981	115

Individual Records—Single Game

Category	Name	Performance
Rushing (Yds.)	Pete Johnson, 12-17-78	160
Passing (Yds.)	Ken Anderson, 11-17-75	447
Passing (TDs)	Many times	4
	Last time by Ken Anderson, 11-29-81	
Receiving (No.)	Many times	10
	Last time by Cris Collinsworth, 9-27-81	
Receiving (Yds.)	Cris Collinsworth, 10-2-83	216
Interceptions	Many times	3
	Last time by Ken Riley, 11-28-83	
Field Goals	Horst Muhlmann, 11-8-70, 9-24-72	5
Touchdowns (Tot.)	Larry Kinnebrew, 10-28-84	4
Points	Horst Muhlmann, 11-8-70	19
	Horst Muhlmann, 12-17-72	19

1984 TEAM STATISTICS

	Cincinnati	Opp.
Total First Downs	339	322
Rushing	135	115
Passing	179	191
Penalty	25	16
Third Down: Made/Att.	93/211	82/202
Fourth Down: Made/Att.	10/14	5/11
Total Net Yards	5480	5259
Avg. Per Game	342.5	328.7
Total Plays	1081	1034
Avg. Per Play	5.1	5.1
Net Yards Rushing	2179	1868
Avg. Per Game	136.2	116.8
Total Rushes	540	477
Net Yards Passing	3301	3391
Avg. Per Game	206.3	211.9
Tackled/Yards Lost	45/358	40/298
Gross Yards	3659	3689
Att./Completions	496/306	517/302
Completion Pct.	61.7	58.4
Had Intercepted	22	25
Punts/Avg.	67/42.3	67/41.4
Net Punting Avg.	35.3	31.6
Penalties/Yards Lost	85/693	90/743
Fumbles/Ball Lost	32/17	27/15
Touchdowns	39	39
Rushing	18	21
Passing	17	15
Returns	4	3
Avg. Time of Possession	30:50	29:10

1984 TEAM RECORD
Preseason (3-1)

Date	Cincinnati		Opponents
8/4	21	New York Jets	15
8/11	13	Tampa Bay	21
8/18	25	Chicago	17
8/24	35	*Detroit	14
	94		67

Regular Season (8-8)

Date	Cincinnati		Opp.	Att.
9/2	17	Denver	20	74,178
9/9	22	*Kansas City	27	47,111
9/16	23	New York Jets	43	64,193
9/23	14	*Los Angeles Rams	24	45,406
10/1	17	Pittsburgh	38	57,098
10/7	13	*Houston	3	43,647
10/14	14	New England	20	48,154
10/21	12	*Cleveland	9	50,667
10/28	31	Houston	13	34,010
11/4	17	San Francisco	23	58,324
11/11	22	Pittsburgh	20	52,497
11/18	6	*Seattle	26	50,280
11/25	35	*Atlanta	14	44,678
12/2	20	Cleveland (OT)	17	51,774
12/9	24	New Orleans	21	40,855
12/16	52	*Buffalo	21	55,771
	339		339	818,633

*Home Game   (OT) Overtime

Score by Periods

Cincinnati	53	105	77	101	3	—	339
Opponents	40	98	78	123	0	—	339

Attendance

Home 390,047   Away 428,586   Total 818,633
Single game home record, 60,284 (10-17-71)
Single season home record, 422,430 (1981)

1984 INDIVIDUAL STATISTICS

Rushing

	Att.	Yds.	Avg.	LG	TD
Kinnebrew	154	623	4.0	23	9
Alexander	132	479	3.6	22	2
Brooks	103	396	3.8	33	2
Jennings	79	379	4.8	20t	2
Schonert	13	77	5.9	17	1
S. Wilson	17	74	4.4	9	0
Anderson	11	64	5.8	14	0
Esiason	19	63	3.3	9	2
Farley	7	11	1.6	5	0
Collinsworth	1	7	7.0	7	0
Verser	2	5	2.5	3	0
Martin	1	3	3.0	3	0
Harris	1	-2	-2.0	-2	0
Cincinnati	540	2179	4.0	33	18
Opponents	477	1868	3.9	36t	21

Passing

	Att.	Comp.	Pct.	Yds.	TD	Int.	Tkld.	Rate
Anderson	275	175	63.6	2107	10	12	24/191	81.0
Schonert	117	78	66.7	945	4	7	16/115	77.8
Esiason	102	51	50.0	530	3	3	5/52	62.9
McInally	2	2	100.0	77	0	0	0/0	118.8
Cincinnati	496	306	61.7	3659	17	22	45/358	77.2
Opponents	517	302	58.4	3689	15	25	40/298	70.0

Receiving

	No.	Yds.	Avg.	LG	TD
Collinsworth	64	989	15.5	57t	6
Harris	48	759	15.8	80t	2
Jennings	35	346	9.9	43	3
Brooks	34	268	7.9	27t	2
Alexander	29	203	7.0	22	0
Holman	21	239	11.4	27	1
Kreider	20	243	12.2	27	1
Kinnebrew	19	159	8.4	22	1
Curtis	12	135	11.3	22	0
Martin	11	164	14.9	42	0
Verser	6	113	18.8	28	0
S. Wilson	2	15	7.5	11	0
Kern	2	14	7.0	9	0
Farley	2	11	5.5	10	0
Muñoz	1	1	1.0	1t	0
Cincinnati	306	3659	12.0	80t	17
Opponents	302	3689	12.2	76	15

Interceptions

	No.	Yds.	Avg.	LG	TD
Breeden	4	96	24.0	70	0
Jackson	4	32	8.0	28t	1
Kemp	4	27	6.8	14	0
Horton	3	48	16.0	48t	1
Simmons	2	43	21.5	43t	1
R. Williams	2	33	16.5	33	0
R. Griffin	2	13	6.5	13	0
J. Griffin	1	57	57.0	57t	1
Cameron	1	15	15.0	15	0
Turner	1	4	4.0	4	0
Schuh	1	0	0.0	0	0
Cincinnati	25	368	14.7	70	4
Opponents	22	364	16.5	52t	2

Punting

	No.	Yds.	Avg.	In 20	LG
McInally	67	2832	42.3	19	61
Cincinnati	67	2832	42.3	19	61
Opponents	67	2771	41.4	12	62

Punt Returns

	No.	FC	Yds.	Avg.	LG	TD
Martin	24	5	376	15.7	55	0
Simmons	12	6	98	8.2	30	0
Horton	2	0	-1	-0.5	1	0
Cincinnati	38	11	473	12.4	55	0
Opponents	38	3	310	8.2	19	0

Kickoff Returns

	No.	Yds.	Avg.	LG	TD
Jennings	22	452	20.5	46	0
Martin	19	386	20.3	44	0
Brooks	7	144	20.6	37	0
Farley	6	93	15.5	32	0
Verser	3	46	15.3	23	0
Simmons	1	15	15.0	15	0
Harris	1	12	12.0	12	0
Kinnebrew	1	7	7.0	7	0
G. Williams	1	0	0.0	0	0
Cincinnati	61	1155	18.9	46	0
Opponents	69	1446	21.0	73	1

Scoring

	TD R	TD P	TD Rt	PAT	FG	Saf	TP
Breech	0	0	0	37/37	22/31	0	103
Kinnebrew	9	1	0	0/0	0/0	0	60
Collinsworth	0	6	0	0/0	0/0	0	36
Jennings	2	3	0	0/0	0/0	0	30
Brooks	2	2	0	0/0	0/0	0	24
Alexander	2	0	0	0/0	0/0	0	12
Esiason	2	0	0	0/0	0/0	0	12
Harris	0	2	0	0/0	0/0	0	12
J. Griffin	0	0	1	0/0	0/0	0	6
Holman	0	1	0	0/0	0/0	0	6
Horton	0	0	1	0/0	0/0	0	6
Jackson	0	0	1	0/0	0/0	0	6
Kreider	0	1	0	0/0	0/0	0	6
Muñoz	0	1	0	0/0	0/0	0	6
Schonert	1	0	0	0/0	0/0	0	6
Simmons	0	0	1	0/0	0/0	0	6
Cincinnati	18	17	4	37/39	22/31	1	339
Opponents	21	15	3	37/39	22/27	1	339

FIRST-ROUND SELECTIONS

(If Club had no first-round selection, first player drafted is listed with round in parentheses.)

Year	Player, College, Position
1968	Bob Johnson, Tennessee, C
1969	Greg Cook, Cincinnati, QB
1970	Mike Reid, Penn State, DT
1971	Vernon Holland, Tennessee State, T
1972	Sherman White, California, DE
1973	Isaac Curtis, San Diego State, WR
1974	Bill Kollar, Montana State, DT
1975	Glenn Cameron, Florida, LB
1976	Billy Brooks, Oklahoma, WR
	Archie Griffin, Ohio State, RB
1977	Eddie Edwards, Miami, DT
	Wilson Whitley, Houston, DT
	Mike Cobb, Michigan State, TE
1978	Ross Browner, Notre Dame, DT
	Blair Bush, Washington, C
1979	Jack Thompson, Washington State, QB
	Charles Alexander, Louisiana State, RB
1980	Anthony Muñoz, Southern California, T
1981	David Verser, Kansas, WR
1982	Glen Collins, Mississippi State, DE
1983	Dave Rimington, Nebraska, C
1984	Ricky Hunley, Arizona, LB
	Pete Koch, Maryland, DE
	Brian Blados, North Carolina, T
1985	Eddie Brown, Miami, WR
	Emanuel King, Alabama, LB

CINCINNATI BENGALS 1985 VETERAN ROSTER

No.	Name	Pos.	Ht.	Wt.	Birth-date	NFL Exp.	College	Birthplace	Residence	'84 Games/Starts
40	Alexander, Charles	RB	6-1	226	7/28/57	7	Louisiana State	Galveston, Tex.	Baton Rouge, La.	16/12
14	Anderson, Ken	QB	6-3	212	2/15/49	15	Augustana, Ill.	Batavia, Ill.	Ft. Mitchell, Ky.	11/9
53	Barker, Leo	LB	6-1	221	11/7/59	2	New Mexico State	Panama	Las Cruces, N.M.	16/0
74	Blados, Brian	T	6-4	295	1/11/62	2	North Carolina	Arlington, Va.	Arlington, Va.	16/14
	Bird, Steve	WR	5-11	176	10/20/60	3	Western Kentucky	Indianapolis, Ind.	Corbin, Ky.	9/0*
61	Boyarsky, Jerry	NT	6-3	290	5/15/59	5	Pittsburgh	Scranton, Pa.	Olyphant, Pa.	15/0
3	Breech, Jim	K	5-6	161	4/11/56	7	California	Sacramento, Calif.	Cincinnati, Ohio	16/0
34	Breeden, Louis	CB	5-11	185	10/26/53	8	North Carolina Central	Hamlet, N.C.	Cincinnati, Ohio	16/15
21	Brooks, James	RB	5-10	182	12/28/58	5	Auburn	Warner Robins, Ga.	Warner Robins, Ga.	15/11
50	Cameron, Glenn	LB	6-2	228	2/21/53	11	Florida	Coral Gables, Fla.	Gainesville, Fla.	16/14
76	Collins, Glen	DE	6-6	265	7/10/59	4	Mississippi State	Jackson, Miss.	Jackson, Miss.	16/0
80	Collinsworth, Cris	WR	6-5	192	1/27/59	5	Florida	Dayton, Ohio	Tampa, Fla.	15/14
85	Curtis, Isaac	WR	6-1	192	10/20/50	13	San Diego State	Santa Ana, Calif.	Cincinnati, Ohio	16/13
73	Edwards, Eddie	DE	6-5	256	4/25/54	9	Miami	Sumter, S.C.	Marietta, Ga.	16/16
7	Esiason, Boomer	QB	6-4	220	4/17/61	2	Maryland	East Islip, N.Y.	Cincinnati, Ohio	10/4
33	Farley, John	RB	5-10	202	8/11/61	2	Cal State-Sacramento	Stockton, Calif.	Stockton, Calif.	13/0
58	Frazier, Guy	LB	6-2	221	7/20/59	5	Wyoming	Detroit, Mich.	Cincinnati, Ohio	16/5
22	Griffin, James	S	6-2	197	9/7/61	3	Middle Tennessee State	Camilla, Ga.	Pelham, Ga.	16/0
83	Harris, M.L.	TE	6-5	238	1/16/54	6	Kansas State	Columbus, Ohio	Cincinnati, Ohio	16/16
27	Hicks, Bryan	S	6-0	192	1/24/57	4	McNeese State	Lake Charles, La.	Florence, Ky.	0*
82	Holman, Rodney	TE	6-3	232	4/20/60	4	Tulane	Ypsilanti, Mich.	Slidell, La.	16/2
20	Horton, Ray	CB	5-11	190	4/12/60	3	Washington	Tacoma, Wash.	Seattle, Wash.	15/13
37	Jackson, Robert	S	5-10	186	10/10/58	4	Central Michigan	Grand Rapids, Mich.	Hamilton, Ohio	16/16
36	Jennings, Stanford	RB	6-1	205	3/12/62	2	Furman	Summerville, S.C.	Summerville, S.C.	15/4
26	Kemp, Bobby	S	6-0	191	5/29/59	5	Cal State-Fullerton	Oakland, Calif.	Cincinnati, Ohio	10/8
89	Kern, Don	TE	6-4	225	8/25/62	2	Arizona State	Los Gatos, Calif.	Los Gatos, Calif.	16/0
28	Kinnebrew, Larry	RB	6-1	252	6/11/59	3	Tennessee State	Rome, Ga.	Rome, Ga.	16/4
71	Koch, Pete	NT	6-6	265	1/23/62	2	Maryland	Nassau County, N.Y.	New Hyde Park, N.Y.	16/0
64	Kozerski, Bruce	C	6-4	275	4/2/62	2	Holy Cross	Plains, Pa.	Haverhill, Mass.	16/1
86	Kreider, Steve	WR	6-3	192	5/12/58	7	Lehigh	Reading, Pa.	Cincinnati, Ohio	16/3
69	Krumrie, Tim	NT	6-2	262	5/20/60	3	Wisconsin	Eau Claire, Wis.	Eau Claire, Wis.	16/16
55	Maidlow, Steve	LB	6-2	234	6/6/60	3	Michigan State	Lansing, Mich.	Cincinnati, Ohio	16/2
88	Martin, Mike	WR	5-10	186	11/18/60	3	Illinois	Washington, D.C.	Champaign, Ill.	15/0
87	McInally, Pat	P	6-6	212	5/7/53	10	Harvard	Villa Park, Calif.	Villa Park, Calif.	16/0
65	Montoya, Max	G	6-5	275	5/12/56	7	UCLA	Alexander, Ala.	Villa Hills, Ky.	16/15
78	Muñoz, Anthony	T	6-6	278	8/19/58	6	Southern California	Ontario, Calif.	Cincinnati, Ohio	16/16
68	Obrovac, Mike	G	6-6	275	10/11/55	4	Bowling Green	Canton, Ohio	Cincinnati, Ohio	0*
42	Pickering, Clay	WR	6-5	215	6/2/61	2	Maine	Jacksonville, Fla.	Cincinnati, Ohio	3/0
75	Reimers, Bruce	T	6-7	280	9/18/60	2	Iowa State	Algona, Iowa	Humboldt, Iowa	15/0
52	Rimington, Dave	C	6-3	288	8/13/62	3	Nebraska	Omaha, Neb.	Crestview Hills, Ky.	16/16
15	Schonert, Turk	QB	6-1	190	1/15/57	6	Stanford	Placentia, Calif.	Park Hills, Ky.	8/3
59	Schuh, Jeff	LB	6-2	229	5/22/58	5	Minnesota	Crystal, Minn.	Brooklyn Park, Minn.	16/11
25	Simmons, John	CB	5-11	192	12/1/58	5	Southern Methodist	Little Rock, Ark.	Cincinnati, Ohio	16/2
56	Simpkins, Ron	LB	6-1	235	4/2/58	5	Michigan	Detroit, Mich.	Hamilton, Ohio	16/11
62	Smith, Gary	G	6-2	265	1/27/60	2	Virginia Tech	Bitburg AFB, Germany	Blacksburg, Va.	8/2
35	Turner, Jimmy	CB	6-0	187	6/15/59	3	UCLA	Sherman, Tex.	Sherman, Tex.	16/8
81	Verser, David	WR	6-1	202	3/1/58	5	Kansas	Kansas City, Kan.	Cincinnati, Ohio	11/0
84	†Williams, Gary	WR	6-2	215	9/4/59	2	Ohio State	Wilmington, Ohio	Cincinnati, Ohio	8/1
57	Williams, Reggie	LB	6-0	228	9/19/54	10	Dartmouth	Flint, Mich.	Cincinnati, Ohio	16/16
77	Wilson, Mike	T	6-5	271	5/28/55	8	Georgia	Norfolk, Va.	Gainesville, Ga.	16/16

* Bird played 8 games with St. Louis, 1 with San Diego in '84; Hicks and Obrovac missed '84 season due to injury.

†Option playout; subject to developments.

Traded—Quarterback Bryan Clark to Miami.

Also played with Bengals in '84—S Ralph Battle (3 games), DE Ross Browner (16), CB Ray Griffin (12), LB Brian Pillman (6), LB Rick Razzano (10), RB Stanley Wilson (1).

COACHING STAFF

Head Coach, Sam Wyche

Pro Career: Became the fifth head coach in Cincinnati history when he was named to lead the Bengals on December 28, 1983. Played quarterback with Bengals 1968-70, Washington Redskins 1971-73, Detroit Lions 1974-75, St. Louis 1976, and Buffalo 1977. Quarterback coach with the San Francisco 49ers 1979-82. Career record: 8-8.

Background: Attended North Fulton High School in Atlanta and Furman University where he was the quarterback from 1962-66. Assistant coach at South Carolina in 1967. Head coach at Indiana University in 1983.

Personal: Born January 5, 1945, in Atlanta, Ga. Sam and his wife, Jane, have two children—Zak and Kerry. They live in Cincinnati.

Assistant Coaches

Jim Anderson, running backs; born March 27, 1948, Harrisburg, Pa., lives in Cincinnati. Linebacker-defensive end Cal Western (U.S. International) 1969-70. No pro playing experience. College coach: Cal Western 1970-71, Scottsdale Community College 1973, Nevada-Las Vegas 1974-75, Southern Methodist 1977-80, Stanford 1981-83. Pro coach: Joined Bengals in 1984.

Bruce Coslet, wide receivers-passing game; born August 5, 1946, Oakdale, Calif., lives in Cincinnati. Tight end University of the Pacific 1967-69. Pro tight end Cincinnati Bengals 1969-76. Pro coach: San Francisco 49ers 1980, joined Bengals in 1981.

Bill Johnson, tight ends; born July 14, 1926, Tyler, Tex., lives in Cincinnati. Center Texas A&M 1944-46. Pro center San Francisco 49ers 1948-55. Pro coach: San Francisco 49ers 1956-67, Cincinnati Bengals 1968-78 (head coach 1976-78), Tampa Bay Buccaneers 1979-82, Detroit Lions 1983-84, rejoined Bengals in 1985.

Dick LeBeau, defensive coordinator-defensive backs; born September 9, 1937, London, Ohio, lives in Cincinnati. Halfback Ohio State 1957-59. Pro defensive back Detroit Lions 1959-72. Pro coach: Philadelphia Eagles 1973-75, Green Bay Packers 1976-79, joined Bengals in 1980.

Jim McNally, offensive line-running game; born December 13, 1943, Buffalo, New York, lives in Cincinnati. Guard University of Buffalo 1961-65. No pro playing experience. College coach: Buffalo 1966-69, Marshall 1973-75, Boston College 1976-78, Wake Forest 1979. Pro coach: Joined Bengals in 1980.

Dick Selcer, linebackers; born August 22, 1937, Cincinnati, Ohio, lives in Cincinnati. Running back Notre Dame 1955-58. No pro playing experience. College coach: Xavier, Ohio 1962-64, 1970-71 (head coach), Cincinnati 1965-66, Brown 1967-69, Wisconsin 1972-74, Kansas State 1975-77, Southwestern Louisiana 1978-80. Pro coach: Houston Oilers 1981-83, joined Bengals in 1984.

Bill Urbanik, defensive line; born December 27, 1946, Donora, Pa., lives in Cincinnati. Lineman Ohio State 1965-68. No pro playing experience. College coach: Marshall 1971-73, 1975, Northern Illinois 1976-78, Wake Forest 1978-83. Pro coach: Joined Bengals in 1984.

Kim Wood, strength; born July 12, 1945, Barrington, Ill., lives in Cincinnati. Running back Wisconsin 1965-68. No pro playing experience. Pro coach: Joined Bengals in 1975.

CINCINNATI BENGALS 1985 FIRST-YEAR ROSTER

Name	Pos.	Ht.	Wt.	Birth-date	College	Birthplace	Residence	How Acq.
Brown, Eddie	WR	6-0	185	12/17/62	Miami	Miami, Fla.	Miami, Fla.	D1
Collins, Larry	RB	6-1	219	10/30/63	Rice	Houston, Tex.	Houston, Tex.	FA
Cruise, Keith	DE	6-3	260	1/17/63	Northwestern	St. Louis, Mo.	Evanston, Ill.	D9
Davis, Lee	CB	6-1	198	12/18/62	Mississippi	Okalona, Miss.	University, Miss.	D5a
Degrate, Anthony	NT	6-3	287	4/25/62	Texas	Snyder, Tex.	Snyder, Tex.	D5
Garza, Louis	T	6-3	300	11/17/62	New Mexico State	San Antonio, Tex.	San Antonio, Tex.	D12
King, Bernard	LB	6-1	228	7/5/62	Syracuse	Forsyth, Ga.	Forsyth, Ga.	D10
King, Emanuel	LB	6-4	245	8/15/63	Alabama	Leroy, Ala.	Leroy, Ala.	D1a
Kinlaw, Rodney	NT	6-3	280	7/31/62	Central State, Ohio	Paris, France	Columbus, Ohio	FA
Lester, Keith	TE	6-5	244	5/28/62	Murray State	Bartow, Fla.	Clearwater, Fla.	D6a
Lewis, Mike	WR	6-3	185	2/2/61	Maryland	Rocky Mount, N.C.	Beltsville, Md.	FA
Locklin, Kim	RB	6-0	200	11/21/63	New Mexico State	Rockdale, Tex.	Las Cruces, N.M.	D7
Peace, Wayne	QB	6-2	215	11/3/61	Florida	Gainesville, Fla.	Lakeland, Fla.	SD('84)
Rogers, Rick	RB	6-1	210	3/26/63	Michigan	Baton Rouge, La.	Inkster, Mich.	FA
Singleton, John	DE	6-6	260	12/22/56	Texas-El Paso	Houston, Tex.	Houston, Tex.	FA
Smith, Darrell	WR	6-2	195	11/5/61	Central State, Ohio	Youngstown, Ohio	Wilberforce, Ohio	FA
Smith, Terry	WR	6-1	183	5/27/62	Indiana	Fairfield, Ohio	Fairfield, Ohio	FA
Stanfield, Harold	TE	6-3	244	1/1/63	Mississippi College	Houston, Miss.	Houston, Miss.	D11
Stokes, Eric	T	6-3	285	1/13/62	Northeastern Iowa	Derby, Conn.	Boston, Mass.	D6
Strobel, Dave	LB	6-3	230	4/3/62	Iowa	St. Paul, Minn.	Iowa City, Iowa	D8
Thomas, Sean	CB	6-0	190	4/12/62	Texas Christian	Oakland, Calif.	Sacramento, Calif.	D3
Tuggle, Anthony	CB	6-1	211	9/16/63	Nicholls State	Baton Rouge, La.	Baton Rouge, La.	D4
Walter, Joe	T	6-6	290	6/18/63	Texas Tech	Dallas, Tex.	Lubbock, Tex.	D7a
Zander, Carl	LB	6-2	235	3/23/63	Tennessee	Mendham, N.J.	Knoxville, Tenn.	D2

Players who report to an NFL team for the first time are designated on rosters as rookies (R). If a player reported to an NFL training camp in a previous year but was not on the active squad for three or more regular season or postseason games, he is listed on the first-year roster and designated by a (1). Thereafter, a player who is on the active squad for three or more regular season or postseason games is credited with an additional year of playing experience.

NOTES

_____
_____
_____
_____
_____
_____
_____
_____
_____
_____
_____
_____
_____
_____
_____
_____
_____
_____
_____
_____
_____
_____
_____
_____

CLEVELAND BROWNS

BROWNS COACHING HISTORY

(293-193-9)

1950-62	Paul Brown	115-49-5
1963-70	Blanton Collier	79-38-2
1971-74	Nick Skorich	30-26-2
1975-77	Forrest Gregg*	18-23-0
1977	Dick Modzelewski	0-1-0
1978-84	Sam Rutigliano**	47-52-0
1984	Marty Schottenheimer	4-4-0

*Released after 13 games in 1977
**Released after eight games in 1984

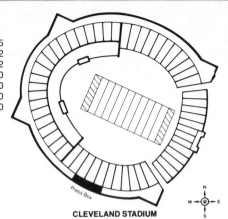

CLEVELAND STADIUM

**American Football Conference
Central Division**

Team Colors: Seal Brown, Orange, and White

**Tower B
Cleveland Stadium
Cleveland, Ohio 44114
Telephone: (216) 696-5555**

Club Officials

President: Arthur B. Modell
Executive Vice President/Legal and
  Administrative: Jim Bailey
Executive Vice President/Football
  Operations: Ernie Accorsi
Vice President/Finance: Mike Poplar
Vice President/Player Personnel: Bill Davis
Vice President/Public Relations: Kevin Byrne
Director of Player Relations: Paul Warfield
Director of Operations: Denny Lynch
Director of Advertising: John Minco
Director of Pro Personnel: Chip Falivene
Director of Security: Ted Chappelle
Area Scouts: Dom Anile, Dave Beckman,
  Tom Heckert, Tom Miner, Mike Santiago
Film Coordinator: Ed Ulinski
Ticket Director: Bill Breit
Head Trainer: Bill Tessendorf
Equipment Manager: Charley Cusick

Stadium: Cleveland Stadium • **Capacity:** 80,098
  West 3rd Street
  Cleveland, Ohio 44114

Playing Surface: Grass

Training Camp: Lakeland Community College
  Mentor, Ohio 44094

1985 SCHEDULE

Preseason

Aug. 10	at San Diego	6:00
Aug. 17	**Philadelphia**	7:30
Aug. 24	at Buffalo	6:00
Aug. 31	**Los Angeles Raiders**	7:30

Regular Season

Sept. 8	**St. Louis**	1:00
Sept. 16	**Pittsburgh** (Monday)	9:00
Sept. 22	at Dallas	12:00
Sept. 29	at San Diego	1:00
Oct. 6	**New England**	1:00
Oct. 13	at Houston	12:00
Oct. 20	**Los Angeles Raiders**	1:00
Oct. 27	**Washington**	1:00
Nov. 3	at Pittsburgh	1:00
Nov. 10	at Cincinnati	1:00
Nov. 17	**Buffalo**	1:00
Nov. 24	**Cincinnati**	1:00
Dec. 1	at New York Giants	1:00
Dec. 8	at Seattle	1:00
Dec. 15	**Houston**	1:00
Dec. 22	at New York Jets	1:00

RECORD HOLDERS

Individual Records—Career

Category	Name	Performance
Rushing (Yds.)	Jim Brown, 1957-1965	12,312
Passing (Yds.)	Brian Sipe, 1974-1983	23,713
Passing (TDs)	Brian Sipe, 1974-1983	154
Receiving (No.)	Ozzie Newsome, 1978-1984	440
Receiving (Yds.)	Ozzie Newsome, 1978-1984	5,570
Interceptions	Thom Darden, 1972-74, 1976-1981	45
Punting (Avg.)	Horace Gillom, 1950-56	43.8
Punt Return (Avg.)	Greg Pruitt, 1973-1981	11.8
Kickoff Return (Avg.)	Greg Pruitt, 1973-1981	26.3
Field Goals	Lou Groza, 1950-59, 1961-67	234
Touchdowns (Tot.)	Jim Brown, 1957-1965	126
Points	Lou Groza, 1950-59, 1961-67	1,349

Individual Records—Single Season

Category	Name	Performance
Rushing (Yds.)	Jim Brown, 1963	1,863
Passing (Yds.)	Brian Sipe, 1980	4,132
Passing (TDs)	Brian Sipe, 1980	30
Receiving (No.)	Ozzie Newsome, 1983, 1984	89
Receiving (Yds.)	Paul Warfield, 1968	1,067
Interceptions	Thom Darden, 1978	10
Punting (Avg.)	Gary Collins, 1965	46.7
Punt Return (Avg.)	Leroy Kelly, 1965	15.6
Kickoff Return (Avg.)	Bo Scott, 1969	28.9
Field Goals	Matt Bahr, 1984	24
Touchdowns (Tot.)	Jim Brown, 1965	21
Points	Jim Brown, 1965	126

Individual Records—Single Game

Category	Name	Performance
Rushing (Yds.)	Jim Brown, 11-24-57	237
	Jim Brown, 11-19-61	237
Passing (Yds.)	Brian Sipe, 10-25-81	444
Passing (TDs)	Frank Ryan, 12-12-64	5
	Bill Nelsen, 11-2-69	5
	Brian Sipe, 10-7-79	5
Receiving (No.)	Ozzie Newsome, 10-14-84	14
Receiving (Yds.)	Ozzie Newsome, 10-14-84	191
Interceptions	Many times	3
	Last time by Hanford Dixon, 12-19-82	
Field Goals	Don Cockroft, 10-19-75	5
Touchdowns (Tot.)	Dub Jones, 11-25-51	6
Points	Dub Jones, 11-25-51	36

1984 TEAM STATISTICS

	Cleveland	Opp.
Total First Downs	295	270
Rushing	89	103
Passing	180	145
Penalty	26	22
Third Down: Made/Att.	89/228	86/217
Fourth Down: Made/Att.	6/13	4/13
Total Net Yards	4828	4641
Avg. Per Game	301.8	290.1
Total Plays	1039	995
Avg. Per Play	4.6	4.7
Net Yards Rushing	1696	1945
Avg. Per Game	106.0	121.6
Total Rushes	489	494
Net Yards Passing	3132	2696
Avg. Per Game	195.8	168.5
Tackled/Yards Lost	55/358	43/353
Gross Yards	3490	3049
Att./Completions	495/273	458/261
Completion Pct.	55.2	57.0
Had Intercepted	23	20
Punts/Avg.	76/42.3	77/40.6
Net Punting Avg.	33.7	34.6
Penalties/Yards Lost	111/928	108/765
Fumbles/Ball Lost	31/16	34/15
Touchdowns	25	30
Rushing	10	10
Passing	14	15
Returns	1	5
Avg. Time of Possession	30:53	29:07

1984 TEAM RECORD
Preseason (1-3)

Date	Cleveland		Opponents	
8/4	14	*Pittsburgh	31	
8/13	21	Los Angeles Rams	10	
8/18	13	Kansas City	31	
8/23	19	Philadelphia	20	
	67		92	

Regular Season (5-11)

Date	Cleveland		Opp.	Att.
9/3	0	Seattle	33	59,540
9/9	17	Los Angeles Rams	20	43,043
9/16	14	*Denver	24	61,980
9/23	20	*Pittsburgh	10	77,312
9/30	6	Kansas City	10	39,225
10/7	16	*New England	17	53,036
10/14	20	*New York Jets	24	55,673
10/21	9	Cincinnati	12	50,667
10/28	14	*New Orleans	16	52,489
11/4	13	Buffalo	10	33,343
11/11	7	*San Francisco	41	60,092
11/18	23	Atlanta	7	28,280
11/25	27	*Houston	10	46,077
12/2	17	*Cincinnati	20	51,774
12/9	20	Pittsburgh (OT)	23	55,825
12/16	27	Houston	20	33,676
	250		297	802,032

*Home Game   (OT) Overtime

Score by Periods

Cleveland	54	81	44	71	0	—	250
Opponents	61	97	53	83	3	—	297

Attendance

Home 458,433   Away 343,599   Total 802,032
Single game home record, 85,703 (9-21-70)
Single season home record, 620,496 (1980)

1984 INDIVIDUAL STATISTICS

Rushing

	Att.	Yds.	Avg.	LG	TD
Green	202	673	3.3	29	0
Pruitt	163	506	3.1	14	6
Byner	72	426	5.9	54	2
White	24	62	2.6	8	0
J. Davis	3	15	5.0	8	1
Holt	1	12	12.0	12	0
B. Davis	1	6	6.0	6	0
McDonald	22	4	0.2	10	1
Walker	1	−8	−8.0	−8	0
Cleveland	489	1696	3.5	54	10
Opponents	494	1945	3.9	64	10

Passing

	Att.	Comp.	Pct.	Yds.	TD	Int.	Tkld.	Rate
McDonald	493	271	55.0	3472	14	23	53/345	67.3
Cox	1	1	100.0	16	0	0	0/0	118.8
Flick	1	1	100.0	2	0	0	2/13	79.2
Cleveland	495	273	55.2	3490	14	23	55/358	67.5
Opponents	458	261	57.0	3049	15	20	43/353	70.0

Receiving

	No.	Yds.	Avg.	LG	TD
Newsome	89	1001	11.2	52	5
Brennan	35	455	13.0	52	3
Harris	32	512	16.0	43	2
Feacher	22	382	17.4	64	1
Adams	21	261	12.4	24	0
Holt	20	261	13.1	36	0
Green	12	124	10.3	44t	1
Byner	11	118	10.7	26	0
Walker	10	122	12.2	25	0
B. Davis	7	119	17.0	43t	2
Pruitt	5	29	5.8	9	0
White	5	29	5.8	17	0
Young	1	47	47.0	47	0
Bolden	1	19	19.0	19	0
Stracka	1	15	15.0	15	0
McDonald	1	−4	−4.0	−4	0
Cleveland	273	3490	12.8	64	14
Opponents	261	3049	11.7	61t	15

Interceptions

	No.	Yds.	Avg.	LG	TD
Gross	5	103	20.6	47	0
Dixon	5	31	6.2	18	0
Cousineau	2	9	4.5	9	0
E. Johnson	2	3	1.5	3	0
Rogers	1	39	39.0	39	0
Minnifield	1	26	26.0	26	0
Perry	1	17	17.0	17	0
Banks	1	8	8.0	8	0
L. Johnson	1	0	0.0	0	0
Rockins	1	0	0.0	0	0
Cleveland	20	236	11.8	47	0
Opponents	23	518	22.5	85	3

Punting

	No.	Yds.	Avg.	In 20	LG
Cox	74	3213	43.4	16	69
Cleveland	76	3213	42.3	16	69
Opponents	77	3123	40.6	21	61

Punt Returns

	No.	FC	Yds.	Avg.	LG	TD
Brennan	25	10	199	8.0	19	0
Harris	9	0	73	8.1	13	0
Walker	6	3	50	8.3	13	0
Cleveland	40	13	322	8.1	19	0
Opponents	43	7	489	11.4	42	0

Kickoff Returns

	No.	Yds.	Avg.	LG	TD
Byner	22	415	18.9	28	0
B. Davis	18	369	20.5	40	0
P. Brown	8	136	17.0	27	0
White	5	80	16.0	23	0
Young	5	134	26.8	36	0
Nicolas	1	12	12.0	12	0
Contz	1	10	10.0	10	0
Holt	1	1	1.0	1	0
Cleveland	61	1157	19.0	40	0
Opponents	52	1159	22.3	46	0

Scoring

	TD R	TD P	TD Rt	PAT	FG	Saf	TP
Bahr	0	0	0	25/25	24/32	0	97
Pruitt	6	0	0	0/0	0/0	0	36
Newsome	0	5	0	0/0	0/0	0	30
Brennan	0	3	0	0/0	0/0	0	18
Byner	2	0	1	0/0	0/0	0	18
B. Davis	0	2	0	0/0	0/0	0	12
Harris	0	2	0	0/0	0/0	0	12
J. Davis	1	0	0	0/0	0/0	0	6
Feacher	0	1	0	0/0	0/0	0	6
Green	0	1	0	0/0	0/0	0	6
McDonald	1	0	0	0/0	0/0	0	6
Cox	0	0	0	0/0	1/3	0	3
Cleveland	10	14	1	25/25	25/35	0	250
Opponents	10	15	5	30/30	29/33	0	297

FIRST-ROUND SELECTIONS

(If Club had no first-round selection, first player drafted is listed with round in parentheses.)

Year	Player, College, Position
1950	Ken Carpenter, Oregon State, B
1951	Ken Konz, Louisiana State, B
1952	Bert Rechichar, Tennessee, DB
	Harry Agganis, Boston U., QB
1953	Doug Atkins, Tennessee, DE
1954	Bobby Garrett, Stanford, QB
	John Bauer, Illinois, G
1955	Kurt Burris, Oklahoma, C
1956	Preston Carpenter, Arkansas, B
1957	Jim Brown, Syracuse, B
1958	Jim Shofner, Texas Christian, DB
1959	Rich Kreitling, Illinois, DE
1960	Jim Houston, Ohio State, DE
1961	Bobby Crespino, Mississippi, TE
1962	Gary Collins, Maryland, WR
	Leroy Jackson, Western Illinois, RB
1963	Tom Hutchinson, Kentucky, WR
1964	Paul Warfield, Ohio State, WR
1965	James Garcia, Purdue, T (2)
1966	Milt Morin, Massachusetts, TE
1967	Bob Matheson, Duke, LB
1968	Marvin Upshaw, Trinity, Texas, DT-DE
1969	Ron Johnson, Michigan, RB
1970	Mike Phipps, Purdue, QB
	Bob McKay, Texas, T
1971	Clarence Scott, Kansas State, CB
1972	Thom Darden, Michigan, DB
1973	Steve Holden, Arizona State, WR
	Pete Adams, Southern California, T
1974	Billy Corbett, Johnson C. Smith, T (2)
1975	Mack Mitchell, Houston, DE
1976	Mike Pruitt, Purdue, RB
1977	Robert Jackson, Texas A&M, LB
1978	Clay Matthews, Southern California, LB
	Ozzie Newsome, Alabama, TE
1979	Willis Adams, Houston, WR
1980	Charles White, Southern California, RB
1981	Hanford Dixon, Southern Mississippi, DB
1982	Chip Banks, Southern California, LB
1983	Ron Brown, Arizona State, WR (2)
1984	Don Rogers, UCLA, DB
1985	Greg Allen, Florida State, RB (2)

CLEVELAND BROWNS 1985 VETERAN ROSTER

No.	Name	Pos.	Ht.	Wt.	Birth-date	NFL Exp.	College	Birthplace	Residence	'84 Games/ Starts
80	Adams, Willis	TE-WR	6-2	200	8/22/56	6	Houston	Weimar, Tex.	Houston, Tex.	16/1
52	Ambrose, Dick	LB	6-0	228	1/17/53	10	Virginia	New Rochelle, N.Y.	Fairview Park, Ohio	0*
53	†Anderson, Stuart	LB	6-1	225	12/25/59	4	Virginia	Mathews, Va.	Fairfax, Va.	6/0*
61	Baab, Mike	C	6-4	270	12/6/59	4	Texas	Ft. Worth, Tex.	Lakewood, Ohio	16/16
9	Bahr, Matt	K	5-10	175	7/6/56	7	Penn State	Philadelphia, Pa.	Pittsburgh, Pa.	16/0
99	Baldwin, Keith	DE	6-4	270	10/13/60	4	Texas A&M	Houston, Tex.	Lakewood, Ohio	16/16
56	Banks, Chip	LB	6-4	233	9/18/59	4	Southern California	Ft. Lawton, Okla.	Augusta, Ga.	16/16
24	Best, Greg	S	5-10	185	1/14/60	3	Kansas State	New Brighton, Pa.	Berea, Ohio	5/0
77	Bolden, Rickey	T	6-6	250	9/8/61	2	Southern Methodist	Dallas, Tex.	Westlake, Ohio	12/9
47	†Braziel, Larry	CB	6-0	184	9/25/54	7	Southern California	Ft. Worth, Tex.	Randallstown, Md.	13/1
86	Brennan, Brian	WR	5-9	178	2/15/62	2	Boston College	Bloomfield, Mich.	Rocky River, Ohio	15/4
49	Burrell, Clinton	S	6-1	192	9/4/56	6	Louisiana State	Franklin, La.	Middleburg Heights, Ohio	13/0
44	Byner, Earnest	RB	5-10	215	9/15/62	2	East Carolina	Milledgeville, Ga.	Westlake, Ohio	16/3
96	Camp, Reggie	DE	6-4	270	2/28/61	3	California	San Francisco, Calif.	Bratenahl, Ohio	16/16
75	Contz, Bill	T	6-5	260	5/12/61	3	Penn State	Belle Vernon, Pa.	North Royalton, Ohio	15/9
50	Cousineau, Tom	LB	6-3	225	5/6/57	4	Ohio State	Bloomington, Ind.	Rocky River, Ohio	16/16
15	Cox, Steve	P-K	6-4	195	5/11/58	5	Arkansas	Shreveport, La.	Jonesboro, Ark.	16/0
18	t-Danielson, Gary	QB	6-2	196	9/10/51	9	Purdue	Detroit, Mich.	Troy, Mich.	15/14
85	Davis, Bruce	WR	5-8	160	2/25/63	2	Baylor	Dallas, Tex.	Beachwood, Ohio	14/1
38	Davis, Johnny	FB	6-1	235	7/17/56	8	Alabama	Montgomery, Ala.	Richmond Heights, Ohio	16/4
64	DeLamielleure, Joe	G	6-3	260	3/16/51	13	Michigan State	Detroit, Mich.	Charlotte, N.C.	16/16
29	Dixon, Hanford	CB	5-11	182	12/25/58	5	Southern Mississippi	Mobile, Ala.	Lakewood, Ohio	16/16
74	Farren, Paul	T	6-5	260	12/24/60	3	Boston University	Cohasset, Mass.	Parma, Ohio	15/6
83	Feacher, Ricky	WR	5-10	180	2/11/54	10	Mississippi Valley State	Crystal River, Fla.	Warrensville Hts., Ohio	16/3
10	Flick, Tom	QB	6-3	190	8/30/58	4	Washington	Patuxent River, Md.	Rocky River, Ohio	1/0
94	Franks, Elvis	DE	6-4	265	7/9/57	6	Morgan State	Doucette, Tex.	South Euclid, Ohio	16/0
79	Golic, Bob	NT	6-2	260	10/26/57	6	Notre Dame	Cleveland, Ohio	Mentor, Ohio	15/15
30	Green, Boyce	RB	5-11	215	6/24/60	3	Carson-Newman	Port Royal, S.C.	Parma, Ohio	16/10
27	Gross, Al	S	6-3	186	1/4/61	3	Arizona	Stockton, Calif.	Parma, Ohio	16/16
78	Hairston, Carl	DE	6-4	260	12/15/52	10	Maryland-East. Shore	Martinsville, Va.	Virginia Beach, Va.	16/0
81	Holt, Harry	TE	6-4	230	12/29/57	3	Arizona	Harlingen, Tex.	Mentor, Ohio	12/8
68	Jackson, Robert	G	6-5	260	4/1/53	11	Duke	Charlotte, N.C.	Bay Village, Ohio	16/16
51	Johnson, Eddie	LB	6-1	215	2/3/59	5	Louisville	Albany, Ga.	Brookpark, Ohio	16/16
1	Johnson, Nate	WR-KR	6-0	195	5/12/57	2	Hillsdale	St. Petersburg, Fla.	Berea, Ohio	0*
90	Jones, Willie	DE	6-4	257	11/22/57	4	Florida State	Dublin, Ga.	Berea, Ohio	0*
88	Lewis, Darryl	TE	6-6	226	4/16/61	2	Texas-Arlington	Mt. Pleasant, Tex.	Berea, Ohio	2/0
62	Lilja, George	T	6-4	262	3/3/58	4	Michigan	Evergreen Park, Ill.	Berea, Ohio	7/1*
59	Marshall, David	LB	6-3	220	1/3/61	2	Eastern Michigan	Cleveland, Ohio	Cleveland, Ohio	16/0
57	Matthews, Clay	LB	6-2	235	3/15/56	8	Southern California	Palo Alto, Calif.	Los Angeles, Calif.	16/16
16	McDonald, Paul	QB	6-2	185	2/23/58	6	Southern California	Montebello, Calif.	Rocky River, Ohio	16/16
31	Minnifield, Frank	CB	5-9	180	1/1/60	2	Louisville	Lexington, Ky.	Lexington, Ky.	15/12
82	Newsome, Ozzie	TE	6-2	232	3/16/56	8	Alabama	Muscle Shoals, Ala.	Bratenahl, Ohio	16/15
58	Nicolas, Scott	LB	6-3	226	8/7/60	4	Miami	Wichita Falls, Tex.	Olmsted Falls, Ohio	16/0
7	Nugent, Terry	QB	6-4	218	12/5/61	2	Colorado State	Merced, Calif.	Lakewood, Ohio	0*
	t-Oatis, Victor	WR	6-0	184	1/6/59	2	N.W. Louisiana	Monroe, La.	Natchitoches, La.	0*
43	Pruitt, Mike	FB	6-0	225	4/3/54	10	Purdue	Chicago, Ill.	Westlake, Ohio	10/7
72	Puzzuoli, Dave	NT	6-3	260	1/12/61	3	Pittsburgh	Stamford, Conn.	Berea, Ohio	16/1
63	Risien, Cody	T	6-7	280	3/22/57	6	Texas A&M	Bryan, Tex.	Olmsted Falls, Ohio	0*
37	Rockins, Chris	S	6-0	195	5/18/62	2	Oklahoma State	Sherman, Tex.	Lakewood, Ohio	16/2
20	Rogers, Don	S	6-1	206	9/17/62	2	UCLA	Texarkana, Ark.	Sacramento, Calif.	15/14
87	Stracka, Tim	TE	6-3	225	9/27/59	3	Wisconsin	Madison, Wis.	Cleveland, Ohio	6/1
12	Taylor, Jim Bob	QB	6-2	200	9/9/59	2	Georgia Tech	San Antonio, Tex.	Berea, Ohio	0*
89	Walker, Dwight	WR	5-10	185	1/10/59	4	Nicholls State	Metairie, La.	Parma, Ohio	11/1
55	Weathers, Curtis	LB	6-5	230	9/16/56	7	Mississippi	Memphis, Tenn.	Berea, Ohio	16/1
25	White, Charles	RB	5-10	190	1/22/58	5	Southern California	Los Angeles, Calif.	Strongsville, Ohio	10/1
21	Whitwell, Mike	S	6-0	175	11/14/58	3	Texas A&M	Kenedy, Tex.	Middleburg Heights, Ohio	0*
84	Young, Glen	WR-KR	6-2	205	10/11/60	3	Mississippi State	Greenwood, Miss.	Berea, Ohio	2/1

* Ambrose was physically unable to perform in '84; Anderson played 2 games with Washington, 4 with Cleveland in '84; Nate Johnson last active with N.Y. Giants in '80; Jones last active with Oakland in '81; Lilja played 3 games with N.Y. Jets, 4 with Cleveland in '84; Nugent active for 16 games, but did not play; Oatis, Risien, and Whitwell missed '84 season due to injury; Taylor last active with Baltimore in '83.

†Option playout; subject to developments.

t-Browns traded for Danielson (Detroit), Oatis (Indianapolis).

Retired—Tom DeLeone, 13-year center, 15 games in '84; Doug Dieken, 14-year tackle, 16 games in '84; 15 games in '84; Rod Perry, 10-year cornerback, 8 games in '84.

Also played with Browns in '84—RB James Black (2 games), KR Preston Brown (2), LB Jim Dumont (12), WR Duriel Harris (11), CB Lawrence Johnson (6), T Ted Petersen (4).

COACHING STAFF

Head Coach,
Marty Schottenheimer

Pro Career: Became the sixth head coach in Cleveland history on October 22, 1984, when he was promoted from defensive coordinator. Replaced Sam Rutigliano at midseason and guided Browns to a 4-4 finish. Joined the Cleveland staff in 1980 as defensive coordinator. Served as an assistant coach with Portland Storm (WFL) in 1974, was linebacker coach and defensive coordinator with New York Giants 1975-77, and linebacker coach with Detroit Lions 1978-79. Drafted in the seventh round of the 1965 draft by the Buffalo Bills. Played linebacker for Bills 1965-68 and for Boston Patriots 1969-70. Career record: 4-4.

Background: All-America linebacker at University of Pittsburgh 1962-65. Following retirement from pro football, worked as a real estate developer in both Miami and Denver from 1971-74.

Personal: Born September 23, 1943, Canonsburg, Pa. Marty and his wife, Patricia, live in Strongsville, Ohio, and have two children—Kristen and Brian.

Assistant Coaches

Tom Bettis, defensive coordinator; born March 17, 1933, Chicago, Ill. lives in Strongsville, Ohio. Guard Purdue 1951-54. Pro linebacker Green Bay Packers 1955-61, Pittsburgh Steelers 1962, Chicago Bears 1963. Pro Coach: Kansas City Chiefs 1966-77 (head coach for final seven games of 1977), St. Louis Cardinals 1978-84, first year with Browns.

Bill Cowher, special teams; born May 8, 1957, Pittsburgh, Pa., lives in Strongsville, Ohio. Linebacker North Carolina State 1975-78. Pro linebacker Cleveland Browns 1980-82, Philadelphia Eagles 1983-84. Pro coach: First year with Browns.

Steve Crosby, assistant to head coach and running backs; born July 3, 1950, Pawnee Rock, Kan., lives in Cleveland, Ohio. Running back Fort Hayes (Kan.) College 1971-73. Pro running back New York Giants 1974-76. Pro coach: Miami Dolphins 1977-82, Atlanta Falcons 1983-84, first year with Browns.

Greg Landry, quarterbacks; born December 18, 1946, Nashua, N.H., lives in Strongsville, Ohio. Quarterback Massachusetts 1964-67. Quarterback Detroit Lions 1968-78, Baltimore Colts 1979-81, Chicago Blitz (USFL) 1983, Arizona Wranglers (USFL) 1984, Chicago Bears 1984. Pro coach: First year with Browns.

Richard Mann, receivers; born April 20, 1947, Aliquippa, Pa., lives in Strongsville, Ohio. Wide receiver Arizona State 1966-68. No pro playing experience. College coach: Arizona State 1974-79, Louisville 1980-81. Pro coach: Indianapolis Colts 1982-84, first year with Browns.

Howard Mudd, offensive line; born February 10, 1942, Midland, Mich., lives in Medina, Ohio. Guard Hillsdale 1961-63. Pro guard San Francisco 49ers 1964-69, Chicago Bears 1970-71. College coach: California 1972-73. Pro coach: San Diego Chargers 1974-76, San Francisco 49ers 1977, Seattle Seahawks 1978-82, joined Browns in 1983.

Tom Olivadotti, linebackers; born September 22, 1945, Long Branch, N.J., lives in Strongsville, Ohio. Defensive end-wide receiver Upsala 1963-66. No pro playing experience. College coach: Princeton 1975-77, Boston College 1978-79, Miami 1980-83. Pro coach: First year with Browns.

Joe Pendry, offensive coordinator, born August 5, 1947, Matheny, W.Va., lives in Strongsville, Ohio. Tight end West Virginia 1966-67. No pro playing experience. College coach: West Virginia 1967-74, 1976-77, Kansas State 1975, Pittsburgh 1978-79, Michigan State 1980-81. Pro coach: Philadelphia Stars (USFL) 1983, Pittsburgh Maulers (head coach) (USFL) 1984, first year with Browns.

Tom Pratt, defensive line, born June 21, 1935, Edgerton, Wis., lives in Medina, Ohio. Linebacker Miami 1954-56. No pro playing experience. College coach: Miami 1957-59, Southern Mississippi 1960-62. Pro coach: Kansas City Chiefs 1963-77, New Orleans Saints 1978-80, joined Browns in 1981.

CLEVELAND BROWNS 1985 FIRST-YEAR ROSTER

Name	Pos.	Ht.	Wt.	Birth-date	College	Birthplace	Residence	How Acq.
Addison, Chuck	WR-KR	6-3	200	8/31/60	Delaware State	Biloxi, Miss.	Winton, Calif.	FA
Allen, Greg	RB	6-0	200	6/4/63	Florida State	Milton, Fla.	Tallahassee, Fla.	D2
Banks, Fred	WR	5-10	177	5/26/62	Liberty Baptist	Columbus, Ga.	Lynchburg, Va.	D8
Black, James (1)	RB	5-11	198	4/3/62	Akron	Lima, Ohio	Berea, Ohio	FA
Blair, Anthony	WR	5-11	170	9/9/57	Tennessee	Alliance, Ohio	Knoxville, Tenn.	FA
Bolzan, Scott	T	6-3	270	7/25/62	Northern Illinois	Chicago, Ill.	Tinley Park, Ill.	FA
Bond, John (1)	TE	6-4	210	3/19/61	Mississippi State	Starkville, Miss.	Schlater, Miss.	SD('84)
Boone, Jamie	CB-S	6-0	205	3/6/59	Miami	Louisville, Ky.	Berea, Ohio	FA
Brown, Greg (1)	LB	6-2	225	12/27/61	Miami	Monterey, Calif.	Berea, Ohio	FA
Brunot, Rick (1)	T	6-4	250	11/6/61	Youngstown State	Meadville, Pa.	Conneaut, Ohio	FA
Carpenter, Dean (1)	K	5-10	175	10/6/59	Chicago	Chicago, Ill.	Malibu, Calif.	FA
Collier, Steve	DE	6-6	304	4/19/63	Bethune-Cookman	Chicago, Ill.	Chicago, Ill.	FA
Colson, Eddie	FB	5-10	228	9/8/63	North Carolina	Oahu, Hawaii	Carrboro, N.C.	FA
Craver, Jon (1)	LB	6-3	240	3/24/61	James Madison	York, Pa.	Middleburg Hts., Ohio	FA
Daly, Ray	CB-S	5-11	195	12/9/62	Virginia	Washington, D.C.	Charlottesville, Va.	FA
Daum, Mark	LB	6-4	237	2/26/62	Nebraska	Kadoka, S.D.	Lincoln, Neb.	FA
Fontenot, Herman	WR	6-0	206	9/12/63	Louisiana State	Beaumont, Tex.	Baton Rouge, La.	FA
Gambrell, Michael (1)	C-G	6-3	262	7/24/62	Louisiana State	Lake Charles, La.	Berea, Ohio	FA
Goedecker, Mike (1)	TE	6-1	225	8/25/59	Miami	Rochester, Pa.	Monaca, Pa.	FA
Hamilton, Waymon (1)	FB	6-0	227	5/31/61	Brigham Young	Brawley, Calif.	Pleasant Grove, Utah	FA
Harrison, Marck	RB	5-7	186	4/20/61	Wisconsin	Columbus, Ohio	Columbus, Ohio	FA
Hayes, Nat	LB	6-0	225	2/17/62	Wichita State	St. Louis, Mo.	Wichita, Kan.	FA
Hicks, Randy	DE	6-3	235	12/10/61	Kent State	Rochester, Minn.	Kent, Ohio	FA
Hill, Troy	CB-S	5-11	174	2/18/62	Pittsburgh	New Brunswick, N.J.	Pittsburgh, Pa.	FA
Hoggard, D.D. (1)	CB	6-0	188	5/20/61	North Carolina State	Ahoskie, N.C.	Burke, Va.	FA
Hunter, Keith	CB-S	5-11	199	5/16/61	Iowa	New York, N.Y.	Newark, N.J.	FA
Jefferson, Pernell	CB-S	5-9	190	6/4/63	Guilford	Stuart, Fla.	Benson, N.C.	FA
Kenebrew, Len	WR	6-3	188	7/11/62	Indiana	Chicago, Ill.	Lauderhill, Ill.	FA
Krerowicz, Mark	G	6-4	285	3/1/63	Ohio State	Toledo, Ohio	Columbus, Ohio	D6
Langhorne, Reginald	WR	6-1	203	4/7/63	Elizabeth City State	Suffolk, Va.	Carrollton, Va.	D7
Lee, Tony	K	6-1	180	10/7/61	Toledo	Fostoria, Ohio	Fostoria, Ohio	FA
Lewis, Fred	LB	6-3	228	7/25/62	Louisiana State	Lake Charles, La.	Baton Rouge, La.	FA
Mack, Kevin	RB	6-0	212	8/9/62	Clemson	Kings Mountain, N.C.	Berea, Ohio	SD('84)
McCormack, Glenn (1)	C-G	6-5	257	1/28/60	Arizona	San Diego, Calif.	Tucson, Ariz.	FA
Minor, Terry	CB-S	6-2	202	5/28/62	Knoxville College	Knoxville, Tenn.	Knoxville, Tenn.	FA
Moore, Robert	RB	5-11	203	3/20/61	Syracuse	Deptford, N.J.	Westville Grove, N.J.	FA
Morrill, David	NT	6-2	260	4/27/63	Ohio State	Dayton, Ohio	Dayton, Ohio	FA
Otte, Richard (1)	WR	5-11	185	8/6/61	N.E. Missouri State	Perryville, Mo.	St. Louis, Mo.	FA
Polenz, Mark (1)	C-G	6-5	270	6/3/61	Central Michigan	Lansing, Mich.	Berea, Ohio	FA
Siegrist, Ernest	TE	6-2	220	9/5/62	E. Stroudsburg State	Plainfield, N.J.	Watchung, N.J.	FA
Sikora, Robert (1)	T	6-8	285	6/14/62	Indiana	Youngstown, Ohio	Avon, Ohio	FA
Simecka, Bennie	C	6-4	282	2/28/62	Kansas	Topeka, Kan.	Lawrence, Kan.	FA
St. Louis, Todd (1)	RB-KR	5-10	195	7/18/62	Augustana, S.D.	Milwaukee, Wis.	Holiday, Fla.	FA
Swanson, Shane	WR-KR	5-9	195	10/4/62	Nebraska	Tracy, Calif.	Lincoln, Neb.	D12
Taylor, Henry	LB	5-10	225	9/24/63	Florida State	Milledgeville, Ga.	Tallahassee, Fla.	FA
Tolle, Stewart	NT	6-3	265	2/7/62	Bowling Green	Columbus, Ohio	Alliance, Ohio	FA
Tripoli, Paul	CB-S	6-0	197	12/14/61	Alabama	Utica, N.Y.	Tuscaloosa, Ala.	FA
Tucker, Travis	TE	6-3	227	9/19/63	So. Connecticut	Brooklyn, N.Y.	Brooklyn, N.Y.	D11
Vernasco, John (1)	QB	6-2	200	2/8/61	Evansville	Mishawaka, Ind.	Berea, Ohio	FA
White, James	T	6-3	245	7/5/62	Louisiana State	Rayville, La.	Baton Rouge, La.	FA
Williams, Larry	G	6-5	269	7/3/63	Notre Dame	Orange, Calif.	Notre Dame, Ind.	D10
Wright, Felix (1)	S	6-2	190	6/22/59	Drake	Carthage, Mo.	Strongsville, Ohio	FA

Players who report to an NFL team for the first time are designated on rosters as rookies (R). If a player reported to an NFL training camp in a previous year but was not on the active squad for three or more regular season or postseason games, he is listed on the first-year roster and designated by a (1). Thereafter, a player who is on the active squad for three or more regular season or postseason games is credited with an additional year of playing experience.

NOTES

_____
_____
_____
_____
_____
_____

Dave Redding, strength and conditioning; born June 14, 1952, North Platte, Neb., lives in Medina, Ohio. Defensive end Nebraska 1972-75. No pro playing experience. College coach: Nebraska 1976, Washington State 1977, Missouri 1978-81. Pro coach: Joined Browns in 1982.

Darvin Wallis, special assistant-defense; born February 14, 1949, Ft. Branch, Ind., lives in Middleburg Heights, Ohio. No college or pro playing experience. College coach: Adams State 1976-77, Tulane 1978-79, Mississippi 1980-81. Pro coach: Joined Browns in 1982.

DENVER BRONCOS

**American Football Conference
Western Division**

Team Colors: Orange, Royal Blue,
and White

**5700 Logan Street
Denver, Colorado 80216
Telephone: (303) 296-1982**

Club Officials

President, Chief Executive Officer:
Patrick D. Bowlen
Vice President-Head Coach: Dan Reeves
General Manager: John Beake
Treasurer: Robert M. Hurley
Director of Administration: Sandy Waters
Coordinator of College Scouting: Reed Johnson
Coordinator of Combine Scouting: Carroll Hardy
Director of Media Relations: Jim Saccomano
Ticket Manager: Gail Stuckey
Director of Player and Community
Relations: Charlie Lee
Equipment Manager: Bill Harpole
Trainer: Steve Antonopulos

Stadium: Denver Mile High Stadium •
Capacity: 75,100
1900 West Eliot
Denver, Colorado 80204

Playing Surface: Grass (PAT)

Training Camp: University of Northern Colorado
Greeley, Colorado 80639

1985 SCHEDULE

Preseason

Aug. 10	**New York Giants**	7:00
Aug. 19	at San Francisco	6:00
Aug. 24	**Indianapolis**	7:00
Aug. 30	**Minnesota**	7:00

Regular Season

Sept. 8	at Los Angeles Rams	1:00
Sept. 15	**New Orleans**	2:00
Sept. 22	at Atlanta	1:00
Sept. 29	**Miami**	2:00
Oct. 6	**Houston**	2:00
Oct. 13	at Indianapolis	12:00
Oct. 20	**Seattle**	2:00
Oct. 27	at Kansas City	12:00
Nov. 3	at San Diego	1:00
Nov. 11	**San Francisco** (Monday)	7:00
Nov. 17	**San Diego**	2:00
Nov. 24	at Los Angeles Raiders	1:00
Dec. 1	at Pittsburgh	1:00
Dec. 8	**Los Angeles Raiders**	2:00
Dec. 14	**Kansas City** (Saturday)	2:00
Dec. 20	at Seattle (Friday)	5:00

BRONCOS COACHING HISTORY

(158-197-9)

1960-61	Frank Filchock	7-20-1
1962-64	Jack Faulkner*	9-22-1
1964-66	Mac Speedie**	6-19-1
1966	Ray Malavasi	4-8-0
1967-71	Lou Saban***	20-42-3
1971	Jerry Smith	2-3-0
1972-76	John Ralston	34-33-3
1977-80	Robert (Red) Miller	42-25-0
1981-84	Dan Reeves	34-25-0

*Released after four games in 1964
**Resigned after two games in 1966
***Resigned after nine games in 1971

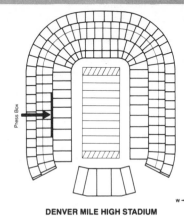

DENVER MILE HIGH STADIUM

RECORD HOLDERS
Individual Records—Career

Category	Name	Performance
Rushing (Yds.)	Floyd Little, 1967-1975	6,323
Passing (Yds.)	Craig Morton, 1977-1982	11,895
Passing (TDs)	Craig Morton, 1977-1982	74
Receiving (No.)	Lionel Taylor, 1960-66	543
Receiving (Yds.)	Lionel Taylor, 1960-66	6,872
Interceptions	Goose Gonsoulin, 1960-66	43
Punting (Avg.)	Jim Fraser, 1962-64	45.2
Punt Return (Avg.)	Rick Upchurch, 1975-1983	12.1
Kickoff Return (Avg.)	Abner Haynes, 1965-66	26.3
Field Goals	Jim Turner, 1971-79	151
Touchdowns (Tot.)	Floyd Little, 1967-1975	54
Points	Jim Turner, 1971-79	742

Individual Records—Single Season

Category	Name	Performance
Rushing (Yds.)	Otis Armstrong, 1974	1,407
Passing (Yds.)	Craig Morton, 1981	3,195
Passing (TDs)	Frank Tripucka, 1960	24
Receiving (No.)	Lionel Taylor, 1961	100
Receiving (Yds.)	Steve Watson, 1981	1,244
Interceptions	Goose Gonsoulin, 1960	11
Punting (Avg.)	Jim Fraser, 1963	46.1
Punt Return (Avg.)	Floyd Little, 1967	16.9
Kickoff Return (Avg.)	Bill Thompson, 1969	28.5
Field Goals	Gene Mingo, 1962	27
Touchdowns (Tot.)	Floyd Little, 1972, 1973	13
	Steve Watson, 1981	13
Points	Gene Mingo, 1962	137

Individual Records—Single Game

Category	Name	Performance
Rushing (Yds.)	Otis Armstrong, 12-8-74	183
Passing (Yds.)	Frank Tripucka, 9-15-62	447
Passing (TDs)	Frank Tripucka, 10-28-62	5
	John Elway, 11-18-84	5
Receiving (No.)	Lionel Taylor, 11-29-64	13
	Bobby Anderson, 9-30-73	13
Receiving (Yds.)	Lionel Taylor, 11-27-60	199
Interceptions	Goose Gonsoulin, 9-18-60	4
	Willie Brown, 11-15-64	4
Field Goals	Gene Mingo, 10-6-63	5
	Rich Karlis, 11-20-83	5
Touchdowns (Tot.)	Many times	3
	Last time by Steve Watson, 9-20-81	
Points	Gene Mingo, 12-10-60	21

1984 TEAM STATISTICS

	Denver	Opp.
Total First Downs	299	311
Rushing	121	90
Passing	152	206
Penalty	26	15
Third Down: Made/Att.	67/206	85/240
Fourth Down: Made/Att.	6/7	8/23
Total Net Yards	4935	5687
Avg. Per Game	308.4	355.4
Total Plays	1018	1123
Avg. Per Play	4.8	5.1
Net Yards Rushing	2076	1664
Avg. Per Game	129.8	104.0
Total Rushes	508	435
Net Yards Passing	2859	4023
Avg. Per Game	178.7	251.4
Tackled/Yards Lost	35/257	57/430
Gross Yards	3116	4453
Att./Completions	475/263	631/346
Completion Pct.	55.4	54.8
Had Intercepted	17	31
Punts/Avg.	96/40.1	81/41.5
Net Punting Avg.	35.4	35.1
Penalties/Yards Lost	78/636	104/891
Fumbles/Ball Lost	36/17	44/24
Touchdowns	42	26
Rushing	12	10
Passing	22	16
Returns	8	—
Avg. Time of Possession	28:56	31:04

1984 TEAM RECORD
Preseason (3-1)

Date	Denver		Opponents
8/4	13	*Washington	16
8/11	21	*San Francisco	20
8/18	31	*Indianapolis	0
8/24	24	Atlanta	13
	89		49

Regular Season (13-3)

Date	Denver		Opp.	Att.
9/2	20	*Cincinnati	17	74,178
9/9	0	Chicago	27	54,335
9/16	24	Cleveland	14	61,980
9/23	21	*Kansas City	0	74,263
9/30	16	*Los Angeles Raiders	13	74,833
10/7	28	Detroit	7	55,836
10/15	17	*Green Bay	14	62,546
10/21	37	Buffalo	7	31,204
10/28	22	L.A. Raiders (OT)	19	91,020
11/4	26	*New England	19	74,908
11/11	16	San Diego	13	53,181
11/18	42	*Minnesota	21	74,716
11/25	24	*Seattle	27	74,922
12/2	13	Kansas City	16	35,537
12/9	16	*San Diego	13	74,867
12/15	31	Seattle	14	64,411
	353		241	1,032,737

*Home Game   (OT) Overtime

Score by Periods

Denver	75	125	68	82	3	—	353
Opponents	49	74	45	73	0	—	241

Attendance
Home 585,233   Away 447,504   Total 1,032,737
Single game home record, 75,008 (10-16-78)
Single season home record, 598,402 (1981)

1984 INDIVIDUAL STATISTICS

Rushing

	Att.	Yds.	Avg.	LG	TD
Winder	296	1153	3.9	24	4
Willhite	77	371	4.8	52	2
Elway	56	237	4.2	21	1
Parros	46	208	4.5	25	2
Lang	8	42	5.3	15	2
Brewer	10	28	2.8	8	0
Kubiak	9	27	3.0	17	1
Myles	5	7	1.4	2	0
Johnson	1	3	3.0	3	0
Denver	508	2076	4.1	52	12
Opponents	435	1664	3.8	72t	10

Passing

	Att.	Comp.	Pct.	Yds.	TD	Int.	Tkld.	Rate
Elway	380	214	56.3	2598	18	15	24/158	76.8
Kubiak	75	44	58.7	440	4	1	10/86	87.6
Stankavage	18	4	22.2	58	0	1	1/13	17.4
Willhite	2	1	50.0	20	0	0	0/0	85.4
Denver	475	263	55.4	3116	22	17	35/257	76.1
Opponents	631	346	54.8	4453	16	31	57/430	65.2

Receiving

	No.	Yds.	Avg.	LG	TD
Watson	69	1170	17.0	73	7
Winder	44	288	6.5	21	2
Johnson	42	587	14.0	49	6
Willhite	27	298	11.0	63	0
Sawyer	17	122	7.2	25	0
Kay	16	136	8.5	21	3
J. Wright	11	118	10.7	21	1
Sampson	9	123	13.7	25	1
Alexander	8	132	16.5	41	1
Parros	6	25	4.2	9	0
Lang	4	24	6.0	9t	1
Summers	3	32	10.7	16	0
Myles	2	22	11.0	12	0
Brewer	2	20	10.0	16	0
Kubiak	1	20	20.0	20	0
Logan	1	3	3.0	3	0
Studdard	1	−4	−4.0	−4	0
Denver	263	3116	11.8	73	22
Opponents	346	4453	12.9	80t	16

Interceptions

	No.	Yds.	Avg.	LG	TD
Foley	6	97	16.2	40t	1
Harden	6	79	13.2	45t	1
Wilson	4	59	14.8	22	0
D. Smith	3	13	4.3	10	0
Mecklenburg	2	105	52.5	63	0
Robbins	2	62	31.0	62t	1
Busick	2	21	10.5	16	0
Woodard	1	27	27.0	27t	1
R. Jackson	1	23	23.0	23	0
Ryan	1	13	13.0	13	0
Comeaux	1	5	5.0	5	0
Lilly	1	5	5.0	5	0
L. Wright	1	1	1.0	1	0
Denver	31	510	16.5	63	4
Opponents	17	189	11.1	35	0

Punting

	No.	Yds.	Avg.	In 20	LG
Norman	96	3850	40.1	16	83
Denver	96	3850	40.1	16	83
Opponents	81	3361	41.5	22	62

Punt Returns

	No.	FC	Yds.	Avg.	LG	TD
Willhite	20	9	200	10.0	35	0
Thomas	20	3	118	5.9	15	0
Wilson	1	0	0	0.0	0	0
Denver	41	12	318	7.8	35	0
Opponents	44	25	335	7.6	24	0

Kickoff Returns

	No.	Yds.	Avg.	LG	TD
Lang	19	404	21.3	38	0
Thomas	18	351	19.5	33	0
Willhite	4	109	27.3	40	0
Dennison	2	27	13.5	16	0
Harden	1	4	4.0	4	0
A. Smith	1	2	2.0	2	0
Denver	45	897	19.9	40	0
Opponents	55	1181	21.5	62	0

Scoring

	TD R	TD P	TD Rt	PAT	FG	Saf	TP
Karlis	0	0	0	38/41	21/28	0	101
Watson	0	7	0	0/0	0/0	0	42
Johnson	0	6	0	0/0	0/0	0	36
Winder	4	2	0	0/0	0/0	0	36
Kay	0	3	0	0/0	0/0	0	18
Lang	2	1	0	0/0	0/0	0	18
Foley	0	0	2	0/0	0/0	0	12
Parros	2	0	0	0/0	0/0	0	12
Willhite	2	0	0	0/0	0/0	0	12
Alexander	0	1	0	0/0	0/0	0	6
Elway	1	0	0	0/0	0/0	0	6
Harden	0	0	1	0/0	0/0	0	6
R. Jones	0	0	1	0/0	0/0	0	6
Kubiak	1	0	0	0/0	0/0	0	6
Robbins	0	0	1	0/0	0/0	0	6
D. Smith	0	0	1	0/0	0/0	0	6
Sampson	0	1	0	0/0	0/0	0	6
J. Wright	0	1	0	0/0	0/0	0	6
L. Wright	0	0	1	0/0	0/0	0	6
Woodard	0	0	1	0/0	0/0	0	6
Denver	12	22	8	38/42	21/28	0	353
Opponents	10	16	0	26/26	19/33	1	241

FIRST-ROUND SELECTIONS

(If Club had no first-round selection, first player drafted is listed with round in parentheses.)

Year	Player, College, Position
1960	Roger LeClerc, Trinity, Connecticut, C
1961	Bob Gaiters, New Mexico State, RB
1962	Merlin Olsen, Utah State, DT
1963	Kermit Alexander, UCLA, CB
1964	Bob Brown, Nebraska, T
1965	Dick Butkus, Illinois, LB (2)
1966	Jerry Shay, Purdue, DT
1967	Floyd Little, Syracuse, RB
1968	Curley Culp, Arizona State, DE (2)
1969	Grady Cavness, Texas-El Paso, DB (2)
1970	Bob Anderson, Colorado, RB
1971	Marv Montgomery, Southern California, T
1972	Riley Odoms, Houston, TE
1973	Otis Armstrong, Purdue, RB
1974	Randy Gradishar, Ohio State, LB
1975	Louis Wright, San Jose State, DB
1976	Tom Glassic, Virginia, G
1977	Steve Schindler, Boston College, G
1978	Don Latimer, Miami, DT
1979	Kelvin Clark, Nebraska, T
1980	Rulon Jones, Utah State, DE (2)
1981	Dennis Smith, Southern California, DB
1982	Gerald Willhite, San Jose State, RB
1983	Chris Hinton, Northwestern, G
1984	Andre Townsend, Mississippi, DE (2)
1985	Steve Sewell, Oklahoma, RB

DENVER BRONCOS 1985 VETERAN ROSTER

No.	Name	Pos.	Ht.	Wt.	Birth-date	NFL Exp.	College	Birthplace	Residence	'84 Games/Starts
80	Alexander, Ray	WR	6-3	180	1/8/62	2	Florida A&M	Miami, Fla.	Aurora, Colo.	8/0
54	†Bishop, Keith	G-C	6-3	265	3/10/57	5	Baylor	San Diego, Calif.	Englewood, Colo.	16/14
65	Bowyer, Walt	DE	6-4	252	9/8/60	3	Arizona State	Pittsburgh, Pa.	Aurora, Colo.	16/1
26	Brewer, Chris	RB	6-1	193	1/23/62	2	Arizona	Denver, Colo.	Aurora, Colo.	13/0
64	Bryan, Billy	C	6-2	255	9/21/55	8	Duke	Burlington, N.C.	Englewood, Colo.	16/16
58	Busick, Steve	LB	6-4	227	12/10/58	5	Southern California	Los Angeles, Calif.	Aurora, Colo.	16/16
68	†Carter, Rubin	NT	6-0	256	12/12/52	11	Miami	Pompano Beach, Fla.	Aurora, Colo.	15/15
79	Chavous, Barney	DE	6-3	258	3/22/51	13	South Carolina State	Aiken, S.C.	Aurora, Colo.	15/15
59	Comeaux, Darren	LB	6-1	227	4/15/60	4	Arizona State	San Diego, Calif.	San Diego, Calif.	16/0
63	Cooper, Mark	G	6-5	267	2/14/60	3	Miami	Miami, Fla.	Miami, Fla.	15/4
55	Dennison, Rick	LB	6-3	220	6/22/58	4	Colorado State	Kalispel, Mont.	Louisville, Colo.	16/15
7	Elway, John	QB	6-3	202	6/28/60	3	Stanford	Port Angeles, Wash.	Aurora, Colo.	15/14
43	Foley, Steve	S	6-2	190	11/11/53	9	Tulane	New Orleans, La.	New Orleans, La.	16/16
62	Freeman, Mike	G	6-3	256	10/13/61	2	Arizona	Mt. Holly, N.J.	Aurora, Colo.	9/0
66	Garnett, Scott	NT	6-2	271	12/3/62	2	Washington	Pasadena, Calif.	Pasadena, Calif.	16/1
72	Graves, Marsharne	T	6-3	272	7/8/62	2	Arizona	Memphis, Tenn.	San Francisco, Calif.	1/0
31	Harden, Mike	CB	6-1	192	2/16/58	6	Michigan	Memphis, Tenn.	Aurora, Colo.	16/16
74	Hood, Winford	G	6-3	262	3/29/62	2	Georgia	Atlanta, Ga.	Atlanta, Ga.	16/2
60	Howard, Paul	G	6-3	260	9/12/50	12	Brigham Young	San Jose, Calif.	Golden, Colo.	16/14
98	Hunley, Ricky	LB	6-2	238	11/11/61	2	Arizona	Petersburg, Va.	Aurora, Colo.	8/0
66	Hyde, Glenn	G-C	6-3	255	3/14/51	9	Pittsburgh	Boston, Mass.	Denver, Colo.	0*
28	Jackson, Roger	S	6-0	186	2/28/59	4	Bethune-Cookman	Macon, Ga.	Macon, Ga.	16/0
57	Jackson, Tom	LB	5-11	220	4/4/51	13	Louisville	Cleveland, Ohio	Morrison, Colo.	16/16
86	Johnson, Butch	WR	6-1	187	5/28/54	10	Cal-Riverside	Los Angeles, Calif.	Castle Rock, Colo.	16/9
75	Jones, Rulon	DE	6-6	260	3/25/58	6	Utah State	Salt Lake City, Utah	Brighton, Colo.	16/16
3	Karlis, Rich	K	6-0	180	5/23/59	4	Cincinnati	Salem, Ohio	Aurora, Colo.	16/0
88	Kay, Clarence	TE	6-2	237	7/30/61	2	Georgia	Seneca, S.C.	Seneca, S.C.	16/13
8	Kubiak, Gary	QB	6-0	192	8/15/61	3	Texas A&M	Houston, Tex.	Plantersville, Tex.	7/2
33	Lang, Gene	RB	5-10	196	3/15/62	2	Louisiana State	Pass Christian, Miss.	Pass Christian, Miss.	16/0
76	Lanier, Ken	T	6-3	269	7/8/59	5	Florida State	Columbus, Ohio	Aurora, Colo.	16/15
22	Lilly, Tony	S	6-0	199	2/16/62	2	Florida	Alexandria, Va.	Aurora, Colo.	13/0
42	Manning, Wade	CB	5-11	190	7/25/55	4	Ohio State	Meadville, Pa.	Denver, Colo.	0*
69	Manor, Brison	DE	6-4	248	8/10/52	9	Arkansas	Bridgeton, N.J.	North Little Rock, Ark.	10/0*
77	Mecklenburg, Karl	DE-LB	6-3	250	9/1/60	3	Minnesota	Edina, Minn.	Westminster, Colo.	16/1
29	Myers, Wilbur	S	5-11	195	8/17/61	2	Delta State	Bassfield, Miss.	Bassfield, Miss.	0*
39	Myles, Jesse	RB	5-10	210	9/28/60	3	Louisiana State	New Orleans, La.	Aurora, Colo.	7/0
1	Norman, Chris	P	6-2	198	5/25/62	2	South Carolina	Albany, Ga.	Putney, Ga.	16/0
24	Parros, Rick	RB	5-11	200	6/14/58	5	Utah State	Brooklyn, N.Y.	Aurora, Colo.	15/2
48	Robbins, Randy	CB	6-2	189	9/14/62	2	Arizona	Casa Grande, Ariz.	Casa Grande, Ariz.	16/1
50	Ryan, Jim	LB	6-1	215	5/18/57	7	William & Mary	Bellmawr, N.J.	Englewood, Colo.	16/14
84	Sampson, Clint	WR	5-11	183	1/4/61	3	San Diego State	Los Angeles, Calif.	Los Angeles, Calif.	12/3
83	Sawyer, John	TE	6-2	230	7/26/53	10	Southern Mississippi	Baker, La.	Ethel, La.	10/8
91	Shaffer, Craig	LB	6-1	227	3/31/59	4	Indiana State	Terre Haute, Ind.	Terre Haute, Ind.	4/0*
56	Smith, Aaron	LB	6-2	225	8/10/62	2	Utah State	Los Angeles, Calif.	Aurora, Colo.	10/0
49	Smith, Dennis	S	6-3	200	2/3/59	5	Southern California	Santa Monica, Calif.	Aurora, Colo.	15/15
70	Studdard, Dave	T	6-4	260	11/22/55	7	Texas	San Antonio, Tex.	Littleton, Colo.	16/16
85	Summers, Don	TE	6-4	226	2/2/61	2	Boise State	Grants Pass, Ore.	Boise, Idaho	16/2
61	Townsend, Andre	DE-NT	6-3	265	10/8/62	2	Mississippi	Chicago, Ill.	University, Miss.	16/0
81	Watson, Steve	WR	6-4	195	5/28/57	7	Temple	Baltimore, Md.	Aurora, Colo.	16/16
47	Willhite, Gerald	RB	5-10	200	5/30/59	4	San Jose State	Sacramento, Calif.	Rancho Cordova, Calif.	16/1
45	Wilson, Steve	CB	5-10	195	8/25/57	7	Howard	Los Angeles, Calif.	Richardson, Tex.	15/1
23	Winder, Sammy	RB	5-11	203	7/15/59	4	Southern Mississippi	Madison, Miss.	Aurora, Colo.	16/15
52	†Woodard, Ken	LB	6-1	218	1/22/60	4	Tuskegee Institute	Detroit, Mich.	Westminster, Colo.	16/2
87	Wright, Jim	TE	6-3	240	9/1/56	6	Texas Christian	Fort Hood, Tex.	Houston, Tex.	16/10
20	Wright, Louis	CB	6-2	200	1/31/53	11	San Jose State	Gilmer, Tex.	Aurora, Colo.	16/15

* Hyde last active with Baltimore in '82; Manning last active with Denver in '82; Manor played 6 games with Tampa Bay, 4 with Denver in '84; Myers missed '84 season due to injury; Shaffer played 4 games with St. Louis in '84.

†Option playout; subject to developments.

Traded—Quarterback Scott Brunner to Green Bay.

Retired—Bob Swenson, 8-year linebacker, injured reserve in '84.

Also played with Broncos in '84—WR Dave Logan (4 games), WR Zack Thomas (12), QB Scott Stankavage (1).

COACHING STAFF

Head Coach,
Dan Reeves

Pro Career: Became ninth head coach in Broncos history on February 28, 1981, after spending entire pro career as both player and coach with Dallas Cowboys. Guided Broncos to AFC West championship with a 13-3 record in 1984, and a 9-7 mark and playoff berth in 1983. His teams were 10-6 in 1981 and 2-7 in 1982. He joined the Cowboys as a free agent running back in 1965 and became a member of the coaching staff in 1970 when he undertook the dual role of player-coach for two seasons. Was Cowboys offensive backfield coach from 1972-76 and became offensive coordinator in 1977. Was an all-purpose running back during his eight seasons as a player, rushing for 1,990 yards and catching 129 passes for 1,693. Career record: 34-25.

Background: Quarterback at South Carolina from 1962-64 and was inducted into the school's Hall of Fame in 1978.

Personal: Born January 19, 1944, Rome, Ga. Dan and his wife, Pam, live in Denver and have three children—Dana, Laura, and Lee.

Assistant Coaches

Marvin Bass, special assistant; born August 28, 1919, Norfolk, Va., lives in Denver. Tackle William & Mary 1940-42. No pro playing experience. College coach: William & Mary 1944-46, North Carolina 1949, 1953-55, South Carolina 1956-59, 1961-65, Georgia Tech 1960, Richmond 1973. Pro coach: Washington Redskins 1952, Montreal Beavers (Continental League) 1966-67, Montreal Alouettes (CFL) 1968, Buffalo Bills 1969-71, Birmingham Americans (WFL) 1974-75, joined Broncos in 1982.

Joe Collier, assistant head coach, defense; born June 7, 1932, Rock Island, Ill., lives in Denver. End Northwestern 1950-53. No pro playing experience. College coach: Western Illinois 1957-59. Pro coach: Boston Patriots 1960-62, Buffalo Bills 1963-68 (head coach 1966-68), joined Broncos in 1969.

Chan Gailey, special teams, defensive assistant; born January 5, 1952, Americus, Ga., lives in Denver. Quarterback Florida 1971-74. No pro playing experience. College coach: Troy State 1976-77, 1983-84 (head coach), Air Force Academy 1978-82. Pro coach: First year with Broncos.

Alex Gibbs, head offensive line, running game; born February 11, 1941, Morganton, N.C., lives in Denver. Running back-defensive back Davidson 1959-63. No pro playing experience. College coach: Duke 1969-70, Kentucky 1971-72, West Virginia 1973-74, Ohio State 1975-78, Auburn 1979-81, Georgia 1982-83. Pro coach: Joined Broncos in 1984.

Stan Jones, defensive line; born November 24, 1931, Altoona, Pa., lives in Denver. Tackle Maryland 1950-53. Pro lineman Chicago Bears 1954-65, Washington Redskins 1966. Pro coach: Denver Broncos 1967-71, Buffalo Bills 1972-75, rejoined Broncos in 1976.

Al Miller, strength and conditioning; born August 29, 1947, El Dorado, Ark., lives in Denver. Wide receiver Northeast Louisiana 1966-69. No pro playing experience. College coach: Northwestern Louisiana 1974-78, Mississippi State 1980, Northeast Louisiana 1981, Alabama 1982-84. Pro coach: First year with Broncos.

Myrel Moore, linebackers; born March 9, 1934, Sebastopol, Calif., lives in Denver. Receiver California 1955-57. Pro defensive back Washington Redskins 1958. College coach: Santa Ana, Calif., J.C. 1959-62, California 1963-71. Pro coach: Denver Broncos 1972-77, Oakland Raiders 1978-79, rejoined Broncos in 1982.

Nick Nicolau, running backs, play-action passing game; born May 5, 1933, New York, N.Y., lives in Denver. Running back Southern Connecticut 1957-59. No pro playing experience. College coach: Southern Connecticut 1960, Springfield 1961, Bridgeport 1962-69 (head coach 1965-69), Massachusetts 1970, Connecticut 1971-72, Kentucky 1973-75, Kent State 1976. Pro coach: Hamilton Tiger-Cats (CFL) 1977, Montreal Alouettes (CFL) 1978-79, New Orleans Saints 1980, joined Broncos in 1981.

DENVER BRONCOS 1985 FIRST-YEAR ROSTER

Name	Pos.	Ht.	Wt.	Birth-date	College	Birthplace	Residence	How Acq.
Anderson, Ron	LB	6-2	215	9/16/62	Southern Methodist	Morton, Tex.	Levelland, Tex.	D10a
Baran, Dave	T-G	6-5	275	6/28/63	UCLA	Philadelphia, Pa.	Los Angeles, Calif.	FA
Bednarik, Mike	T-G	6-7	245	9/6/63	Moorhead State	Chicago, Ill.	Moorhead, Minn.	FA
Boadway, Steve	LB	6-3	230	6/20/63	Arizona	Bakersfield, Calif.	Tucson, Ariz.	FA
Booth, David	LB	6-3	220	12/20/62	Memphis State	Waycross, Ga.	Millwood, Ga.	FA
Brown, Michael	RB	5-11	200	2/19/61	Texas	Dallas, Tex.	Dallas, Tex.	FA
Brown, Rod	CB-S	6-0	180	10/6/62	Oklahoma State	Gainesville, Tex.	Gainesville, Tex.	FA
Cameron, Dallas	NT	6-2	245	11/6/62	Miami	Lake City, S.C.	Melbourne, Fla.	D7
Ceaser, Nat	CB-S	6-3	196	1/28/61	Auburn	Valdosta, Ga.	Valdosta, Ga.	FA
Dillingham, Dave	T-G	6-5	270	3/2/62	Oklahoma	Kansas City, Mo.	Tulsa, Okla.	FA
Fletcher, Simon	NT	6-5	240	2/18/62	Houston	Bay City, Tex.	Bay City, Tex.	D2a
Funck, Buddy	QB	6-2	195	3/22/65	New Mexico	Albuquerque, N.M.	Ft. Worth, Tex.	D10
Gallon, Russell	NT	6-8	285	7/14/62	Florida	Tampa, Fla.	Tampa, Fla.	FA
Greene, Ricky	CB-S	5-9	185	8/25/61	Nebraska	Amherst, Tex.	Lincoln, Neb.	FA
Groover, Richard	CB-S	5-11	185	8/21/62	Livingston	Winter Haven, Fla.	Winter Haven, Fla.	FA
Heine, John	LB	6-2	240	11/17/62	California	Honolulu, Hawaii	Berkeley, Calif.	FA
Hinson, Billy	T-G	6-1	278	1/8/63	Florida	Folkston, Ga.	Hilliard, Fla.	D5
Hornfeck, Ray	CB-S	5-10	180	12/30/62	New Mexico	Elizabeth, Pa.	Tucson, Ariz.	FA
Hunter, Daniel	CB	5-11	175	9/1/62	Henderson State	Arkadelphia, Ark.	Arkadelphia, Ark.	FA
Jarman, Murray (1)	WR	6-6	209	1/26/61	Clemson	Birmingham, Ala.	Boca Raton, Fla.	D12('84)
Johnson, Vance	WR	5-11	174	3/13/63	Arizona	Trenton, N.J.	Tucson, Ariz.	D2
Kelly, Clarence	CB-S	6-0	170	11/29/62	Akron	Cleveland, Ohio	Cleveland, Ohio	FA
Kilgo, John	T-G	6-3	275	10/8/61	Boise State	Oxfordshire, England	Boise, Idaho	FA
Kragen, Greg	NT	6-3	245	3/4/62	Utah State	Chicago, Ill.	Logan, Utah	FA
Lewis, Robert	RB	6-0	185	10/13/62	Texas Tech	Greenville, Tex.	Greenville, Tex.	FA
Linderholm, Rick	T-G	6-5	265	3/31/62	Montana	Golden Valley, Minn.	Missoula, Mont.	FA
Lynch, Dan	G	6-3	265	6/21/62	Washington State	Rochester, Minn.	Spokane, Wash.	D12
McGregor, Keli	TE	6-7	252	1/23/63	Colorado State	Primghar, Iowa	Lakewood, Colo.	D4
McRae, Scott	LB	6-3	235	9/1/62	Alabama	Albuquerque, N.M.	Huntsville, Ala.	FA
Naran, Randy	QB	6-1	198	1/20/62	Nebraska-Omaha	Omaha, Neb.	Omaha, Neb.	FA
Pack, David	WR	6-2	200	10/23/62	Southwestern	Nashville, Tenn.	Nashville, Tenn.	FA
Riley, Eric	CB	6-0	170	8/15/62	Florida State	Ft. Myers, Fla.	Ft. Myers, Fla.	D8
Roberts, Aaron	RB	6-0	190	12/26/62	Michigan State	Highland Park, Mich.	Detroit, Mich.	FA
Rolle, Gary	WR	5-11	169	2/16/62	Florida	Augsburg, Germany	Miami, Fla.	D11
Rutt, Thomas	T-G	6-5	275	11/23/62	Montana	Billings, Mont.	Missoula, Mont.	FA
Schulter, Joe	RB	6-2	222	1/20/61	Azusa Pacific	Austin, Tex.	San Dimas, Calif.	FA
Sewell, Steve	RB	6-3	210	4/2/63	Oklahoma	San Francisco, Calif.	San Francisco, Calif.	D1
Shupe, Mark	T-G	6-5	270	4/25/62	Arizona State	Lafayette, Ind.	Mesa, Ariz.	FA
Sims, Jack	T-G	6-2	250	4/21/62	Hawaii	San Mateo, Calif.	Vallejo, Calif.	FA
Smith, Daryl	CB	6-0	180	5/8/63	North Alabama	Opelika, Ala.	Opelika, Ala.	D9
Swing, Dale	T-G	6-2	248	11/23/62	Clemson	Lexington, N.C.	Lexington, N.C.	FA
Taylor, Derrick	RB	5-9	185	7/21/61	Southern Illinois	Chicago, Ill.	Chicago, Ill.	FA
Thurson, Tommy	LB	6-3	235	11/16/62	Georgia	Jay, Fla.	Jacksonville, Fla.	FA
Trahan, John	WR	5-9	165	4/19/61	Southern Colorado	Grand Forks, N.D.	Denver, Colo.	FA
Whitehead, Derrick	NT-DE	6-5	265	5/29/62	Eastern Michigan	Detroit, Mich.	Detroit, Mich.	FA
Wiley, Bryan	RB	6-1	205	12/5/62	UCLA	Los Angeles, Calif.	Harbor City, Calif.	FA
Woodson, Anthony	LB	6-2	220	7/12/62	Hawaii	San Francisco, Calif.	Vallejo, Calif.	FA
Wright, Will	LB	6-4	225	10/13/62	E. New Mexico	Perryton, Tex.	La Mesa, Tex.	FA
Willis, Larry	WR	5-10	170	7/13/63	Fresno State	Santa Monica, Calif.	Santa Monica, Calif.	FA
Young, Joe	T-G	6-2	270	4/9/61	Texas Christian	Frankfurt, Germany	Dallas, Tex.	FA
Younger, Robert	T-G	6-3	255	12/14/61	E. Tennessee St.	Newbern, Tenn.	Newbern, Tenn.	FA

Players who report to an NFL team for the first time are designated on rosters as rookies (R). If a player reported to an NFL training camp in a previous year but was not on the active squad for three or more regular season or postseason games, he is listed on the first-year roster and designated by a (1). Thereafter, a player who is on the active squad for three or more regular season or postseason games is credited with an additional year of playing experience.

NOTES

_____

_____

_____

_____

Mike Shanahan, offensive coordinator, wide receivers; born August 24, 1952, Oak Park, Ill., lives in Denver. Quarterback Eastern Illinois 1970-73. No pro playing experience. College coach: Oklahoma 1975-76, Northern Arizona 1977, Eastern Illinois 1978, Minnesota 1979, Florida 1980-83. Pro coach: Joined Broncos in 1984.

Doc Urich, tight ends, assistant offensive line; born September 10, 1928, Wapakoneta, Ohio, lives in Denver. End Miami (Ohio) 1948-50. No pro playing experience. College coach: Miami (Ohio) 1951-54, Northwestern 1955-63, Notre Dame 1964-65, Buffalo 1966-68 (head coach), Northern Illinois 1969-70 (head coach). Pro coach: Buffalo Bills 1971, Denver Broncos 1972-77, Washington Redskins 1978-80, Green Bay Packers 1981-83, rejoined Broncos in 1984.

Charlie West, defensive backs; born August 31, 1946, Big Spring, Tex., lives in Denver. Defensive back Texas El-Paso 1963-67. Pro defensive back Minnesota Vikings 1968-73, Detroit Lions 1974-78, Denver Broncos 1978-79. College coach: MacAlister 1981, California 1982. Pro coach: Joined Broncos in 1983.

HOUSTON OILERS

American Football Conference
Central Division

Team Colors: Columbia Blue, Scarlet, and White

Box 1516
Houston, Texas 77001
Telephone: (713) 797-9111

Club Officials
President: K. S. (Bud) Adams, Jr.
Executive Vice President-General Manager:
Ladd K. Herzeg
Vice President-Player Personnel: Mike Holovak
Director of Administration: Rick Nichols
Media Relations Director: Bob Hyde
Marketing/Media Relations: Gregg Stengel
Ticket Manager: David Fuqua
Head Trainer: Jerry Meins
Assistant Trainer: Joel Krekelberg
Equipment Manager: Gordon Batty

Stadium: Astrodome • **Capacity:** 50,496
Loop 610, Kirby and Fannin Streets
Houston, Texas 77054

Playing Surface: AstroTurf

Training Camp: Angelo State University
San Angelo, Texas 76901

1985 SCHEDULE

Preseason
Aug. 3	N.Y. Giants at Canton, Ohio	2:30
Aug. 10	at Los Angeles Rams	7:00
Aug. 17	at New Orleans	8:00
Aug. 24	**Kansas City**	8:00
Aug. 31	at Dallas	8:00

Regular Season
Sept. 8	**Miami**	12:00
Sept. 15	at Washington	1:00
Sept. 22	at Pittsburgh	1:00
Sept. 29	**Dallas**	12:00
Oct. 6	at Denver	2:00
Oct. 13	**Cleveland**	12:00
Oct. 20	**Cincinnati**	12:00
Oct. 27	at St. Louis	12:00
Nov. 3	**Kansas City**	12:00
Nov. 10	at Buffalo	1:00
Nov. 17	**Pittsburgh**	12:00
Nov. 24	**San Diego**	12:00
Dec. 1	at Cincinnati	1:00
Dec. 8	**New York Giants**	3:00
Dec. 15	at Cleveland	1:00
Dec. 22	at Indianapolis	4:00

OILERS COACHING HISTORY
(160-203-6)

1960-61	Lou Rymkus*	12-7-1
1961	Wally Lemm	10-2-0
1962-63	Frank (Pop) Ivy	17-12-0
1964	Sammy Baugh	4-10-0
1965	Hugh Taylor	4-10-0
1966-70	Wally Lemm	28-38-4
1971	Ed Hughes	4-9-1
1972-73	Bill Peterson**	1-18-0
1973-74	Sid Gillman	8-15-0
1975-80	O.A. (Bum) Phillips	59-38-0
1981-83	Ed Biles***	8-23-0
1983	Chuck Studley	2-8-0
1984	Hugh Campbell	3-13-0

*Released after five games in 1961
**Released after five games in 1973
***Released after six games in 1983

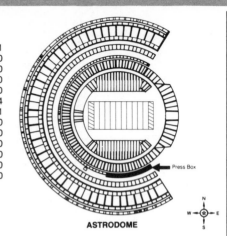

ASTRODOME

RECORD HOLDERS
Individual Records—Career

Category	Name	Performance
Rushing (Yds.)	Earl Campbell, 1978-1984	8,574
Passing (Yds.)	George Blanda, 1960-66	19,149
Passing (TDs)	George Blanda, 1960-66	165
Receiving (No.)	Charley Hennigan, 1960-66	410
Receiving (Yds.)	Ken Burrough, 1971-1982	6,907
Interceptions	Jim Norton, 1960-68	45
Punting (Avg.)	Jim Norton, 1960-68	42.3
Punt Return (Avg.)	Billy Johnson, 1974-1980	13.2
Kickoff Return (Avg.)	Bobby Jancik, 1962-67	26.4
Field Goals	George Blanda, 1960-66	91
Touchdowns (Tot.)	Earl Campbell, 1978-1984	73
Points	George Blanda, 1960-66	596

Individual Records—Single Season

Category	Name	Performance
Rushing (Yds.)	Earl Campbell, 1980	1,934
Passing (Yds.)	Warren Moon, 1984	3,338
Passing (TDs)	George Blanda, 1961	36
Receiving (No.)	Charley Hennigan, 1964	101
Receiving (Yds.)	Charley Hennigan, 1961	1,746
Interceptions	Fred Glick, 1963	12
	Mike Reinfeldt, 1979	12
Punting (Avg.)	Jim Norton, 1965	44.2
Punt Return (Avg.)	Billy Johnson, 1977	15.4
Kickoff Return (Avg.)	Ken Hall, 1960	31.2
Field Goals	Toni Fritsch, 1979	21
Touchdowns (Tot.)	Earl Campbell, 1979	19
Points	George Blanda, 1960	115

Individual Records—Single Game

Category	Name	Performance
Rushing (Yds.)	Billy Cannon, 12-10-61	216
Passing (Yds.)	George Blanda, 10-29-61	464
Passing (TDs)	George Blanda, 11-19-61	7
Receiving (No.)	Charley Hennigan, 10-13-61	13
Receiving (Yds.)	Charley Hennigan, 10-13-61	272
Interceptions	Many times	3
	Last time by Willie Alexander, 11-14-71	
Field Goals	Skip Butler, 10-12-75	6
Touchdowns (Tot.)	Billy Cannon, 12-10-61	5
Points	Billy Cannon, 12-10-61	30

1984 TEAM STATISTICS

	Houston	Opp.
Total First Downs	284	345
Rushing	95	158
Passing	164	168
Penalty	25	19
Third Down: Made/Att.	64/193	104/218
Fourth Down: Made/Att.	5/16	8/11
Total Net Yards	4884	5968
Avg. Per Game	305.3	373.0
Total Plays	969	1075
Avg. Per Play	5.0	5.6
Net Yards Rushing	1656	2789
Avg. Per Game	103.5	174.3
Total Rushes	433	596
Net Yards Passing	3228	3179
Avg. Per Game	201.8	198.7
Tackled/Yards Lost	49/382	32/267
Gross Yards	3610	3446
Att./Completions	487/282	447/271
Completion Pct.	57.9	60.6
Had Intercepted	15	13
Punts/Avg.	88/39.6	64/42.2
Net Punting Avg.	31.4	37.7
Penalties/Yards Lost	99/813	105/876
Fumbles/Ball Lost	36/16	24/11
Touchdowns	28	53
Rushing	13	27
Passing	14	23
Returns	1	3
Avg. Time of Possession	28:02	31:58

1984 TEAM RECORD
Preseason (1-3)

Date	Houston		Opponents
8/4	17	Tampa Bay	30
8/11	36	*New York Jets	17
8/18	19	*New Orleans	31
8/25	24	Dallas	31
	96		109

Regular Season (3-13)

Date	Houston		Opp.	Att.
9/2	14	*Los Angeles Raiders	24	49,092
9/9	21	*Indianapolis	35	43,820
9/16	14	San Diego	31	52,726
9/23	10	Atlanta	42	45,248
9/30	10	*New Orleans	27	43,108
10/7	3	Cincinnati	13	43,637
10/14	10	Miami	28	54,080
10/21	21	*San Francisco	34	39,900
10/28	13	*Cincinnati	31	34,010
11/4	7	Pittsburgh	35	48,892
11/11	17	Kansas City	16	39,472
11/18	31	*New York Jets	20	40,141
11/25	10	Cleveland	27	46,077
12/2	23	*Pittsburgh (OT)	20	39,782
12/9	16	Los Angeles Rams	27	49,092
12/16	20	*Cleveland	27	33,676
	240		437	702,953

*Home Game   (OT) Overtime

Score by Periods

Houston	27	82	50	78	3	—	240
Opponents	113	111	92	121	0	—	437

Attendance

Home 323,529   Away 379,224   Total 702,753
Single game home record, 55,293 (12-10-79)
Single season home record, 400,156 (1980)

1984 INDIVIDUAL STATISTICS

Rushing

	Att.	Yds.	Avg.	LG	TD
Moriarty	189	785	4.2	51t	6
Campbell	96	278	2.9	22	4
Edwards	60	267	4.5	20	1
Moon	58	211	3.6	31	1
Luck	10	75	7.5	18	1
Joyner	14	22	1.6	9	0
Walls	4	20	5.0	20	0
Mullins	1	0	0.0	0	0
Cooper	1	−2	−2.0	−2	0
Houston	433	1656	3.8	51t	13
Opponents	596	2789	4.7	54	27

Passing

	Att.	Comp.	Pct.	Yds.	TD	Int.	Tkld.	Rate
Moon	450	259	57.6	3338	12	14	47/371	76.9
Luck	36	22	61.1	256	2	1	2/11	89.6
Moriarty	1	1	100.0	16	0	0	0/0	118.8
Houston	487	282	57.9	3610	14	15	49/382	78.0
Opponents	447	271	60.6	3446	23	13	32/267	89.8

Receiving

	No.	Yds.	Avg.	LG	TD
Smith	69	1141	16.5	75t	4
J. Williams	41	545	13.3	32	3
Dressel	40	378	9.5	42	2
Moriarty	31	206	6.6	24	1
Holston	22	287	13.0	28	1
Edwards	20	151	7.6	20	0
Bryant	19	278	14.6	28	0
Walls	18	291	16.2	76	1
McCloskey	9	152	16.9	51	1
Mullins	6	85	14.2	25	1
Roaches	4	69	17.3	24	0
Campbell	3	27	9.0	15	0
Houston	282	3610	12.8	76	14
Opponents	271	3446	12.7	80t	23

Interceptions

	No.	Yds.	Avg.	LG	TD
Tullis	4	48	12.0	22	0
Hartwig	3	23	7.7	19	0
Brown	1	26	26.0	26	0
Eason	1	20	20.0	20	0
Lyday	1	12	12.0	12	0
Allen	1	2	2.0	2	0
Brazile	1	2	2.0	2	0
Abraham	1	1	1.0	1	0
Thompson	0	5	—	5	0
Houston	13	139	10.7	26	0
Opponents	15	214	14.3	47	2

Punting

	No.	Yds.	Avg.	In 20	LG
James	88	3482	39.6	20	55
Houston	88	3482	39.6	20	55
Opponents	64	2702	42.2	18	69

Punt Returns

	No.	FC	Yds.	Avg.	LG	TD
Roaches	26	8	152	5.8	18	0
Houston	26	8	152	5.8	18	0
Opponents	60	9	618	10.3	55	0

Kickoff Returns

	No.	Yds.	Avg.	LG	TD
Roaches	30	679	22.6	49	0
Walls	15	289	19.3	29	0
Allen	11	210	19.1	23	0
R. Williams	5	84	16.8	21	0
Brown	3	17	5.7	17	0
Joyner	3	57	19.0	24	0
Thompson	1	16	16.0	16	0
J. Williams	1	0	0.0	0	0
Houston	69	1352	19.6	49	0
Opponents	51	986	19.3	39	0

Scoring

	TD R	TD P	TD Rt	PAT	FG	Saf	TP
Cooper	0	0	0	13/13	11/13	0	46
Moriarty	6	1	0	0/0	0/0	0	42
Kempf	0	0	0	14/14	4/6	0	26
Campbell	4	0	0	0/0	0/0	0	24
Smith	0	4	0	0/0	0/0	0	24
J. Williams	0	3	0	0/0	0/0	0	18
Dressel	0	2	0	0/0	0/0	0	12
Bostic	0	0	1	0/0	0/0	0	6
Edwards	1	0	0	0/0	0/0	0	6
Holston	0	1	0	0/0	0/0	0	6
Luck	1	0	0	0/0	0/0	0	6
McCloskey	0	1	0	0/0	0/0	0	6
Moon	1	0	0	0/0	0/0	0	6
Mullins	0	1	0	0/0	0/0	0	6
Walls	0	1	0	0/0	0/0	0	6
Houston	13	14	1	27/28	15/19	0	240
Opponents	27	23	3	51/53	22/30	1	437

FIRST-ROUND SELECTIONS

(If Club had no first-round selection, first player drafted is listed with round in parentheses.)

Year	Player, College, Position
1960	Billy Cannon, Louisiana State, RB
1961	Mike Ditka, Pittsburgh, E
1962	Ray Jacobs, Howard Payne, DT
1963	Danny Brabham, Arkansas, LB
1964	Scott Appleton, Texas, DT
1965	Lawrence Elkins, Baylor, WR
1966	Tommy Nobis, Texas, LB
1967	George Webster, Michigan State, LB
	Tom Regner, Notre Dame, G
1968	Mac Haik, Mississippi, WR (2)
1969	Ron Pritchard, Arizona State, LB
1970	Doug Wilkerson, N. Carolina Central, G
1971	Dan Pastorini, Santa Clara, QB
1972	Greg Sampson, Stanford, DE
1973	John Matuszak, Tampa, DE
	George Amundson, Iowa State, RB
1974	Steve Manstedt, Nebraska, LB (4)
1975	Robert Brazile, Jackson State, LB
	Don Hardeman, Texas A&I, RB
1976	Mike Barber, Louisiana Tech, TE (2)
1977	Morris Towns, Missouri, T
1978	Earl Campbell, Texas, RB
1979	Mike Stensrud, Iowa State, DE (2)
1980	Angelo Fields, Michigan State, T (2)
1981	Michael Holston, Morgan State, WR (3)
1982	Mike Munchak, Penn State, G
1983	Bruce Matthews, Southern California, T
1984	Dean Steinkuhler, Nebraska, T
1985	Ray Childress, Texas A&M, DE
	Richard Johnson, Wisconsin, DB

HOUSTON OILERS 1985 VETERAN ROSTER

No.	Name	Pos.	Ht.	Wt.	Birth-date	NFL Exp.	College	Birthplace	Residence	'84 Games/Starts
56	†Abraham, Robert	LB	6-1	230	7/13/60	4	North Carolina State	Myrtle Beach, S.C.	Houston, Tex.	16/16
29	Allen, Patrick	CB	5-10	173	8/26/61	2	Utah State	Seattle, Wash.	Seattle, Wash.	16/0
75	†Baker, Jesse	DE	6-5	271	7/10/57	7	Jacksonville State	Conyers, Ga.	Stafford, Tex.	16/16
54	†Bingham, Gregg	LB	6-1	232	3/13/51	13	Purdue	Evanston, Ill.	Missouri City, Tex.	16/16
25	Bostic, Keith	S	6-1	210	1/17/61	2	Michigan	Ann Arbor, Mich.	Ann Arbor, Mich.	16/16
52	Brazile, Robert	LB	6-4	253	2/7/53	11	Jackson State	Mobile, Ala.	Houston, Tex.	16/16
24	Brown, Steve	CB	5-11	189	5/20/60	3	Oregon	Sacramento, Calif.	Houston, Tex.	16/16
81	Bryant, Steve	WR	6-2	197	10/10/59	4	Purdue	Los Angeles, Calif.	Houston, Tex.	14/3
8	Cooper, Joe	K	5-10	175	10/30/60	2	California	Fresno, Calif.	Fresno, Calif.	7/0
31	Donaldson, Jeff	S	6-0	193	4/19/62	2	Colorado	Ft. Collins, Colo.	Ft. Collins, Colo.	16/2
88	Dressel, Chris	TE	6-4	238	2/7/61	3	Stanford	Placentia, Calif.	Palo Alto, Calif.	16/16
21	Eason, Bo	S	6-2	200	3/10/61	2	Cal-Davis	Walnut Grove, Calif.	Walnut Grove, Calif.	10/1
32	Edwards, Stan	RB	6-0	210	5/20/60	4	Michigan	Detroit, Mich.	Detroit, Mich.	14/1
78	Foster, Jerome	DE	6-2	263	7/25/60	3	Ohio State	Detroit, Mich.	Southfield, Mich.	9/3
77	France, Doug	T	6-5	278	4/26/53	10	Ohio State	Dayton, Ohio	Fountain Valley, Calif.	0*
59	Grimsley, John	LB	6-2	232	2/25/62	2	Kentucky	Canton, Ohio	Houston, Tex.	16/0
39	Harris, Tim	RB	5-9	206	6/15/61	2	Washington State	Compton, Calif.	Compton, Calif.	0*
84	†Holston, Mike	WR	6-3	191	1/8/58	5	Morgan State	Washington, D.C.	Houston, Tex.	16/3
66	Howell, Pat	G	6-6	265	3/12/57	7	Southern California	Fresno, Calif.	Clovis, Calif.	11/5
97	Johnson, Mike	DE	6-5	253	4/24/62	2	Illinois	Chicago, Ill.	Chicago, Ill.	16/0
57	Joiner, Tim	LB	6-4	248	1/7/61	3	Louisiana State	Newport, Calif.	Baton Rouge, La.	11/0
38	Joyner, Willie	RB	5-10	200	4/2/62	2	Maryland	Brooklyn, N.Y.	Landover, Md.	10/0
4	†Kempf, Florian	K	5-9	170	5/25/56	4	Pennsylvania	Philadelphia, Pa.	Philadelphia, Pa.	9/0
27	Kennedy, Mike	S	6-0	195	2/26/59	3	Toledo	Toledo, Ohio	Toledo, Ohio	11/0
10	Luck, Oliver	QB	6-2	196	4/5/60	4	West Virginia	Cleveland, Ohio	Houston, Tex.	4/0
28	Lyday, Allen	CB-S	5-10	186	9/16/60	2	Nebraska	Wichita, Kan.	Lincoln, Neb.	4/0
93	Lyles, Robert	LB	6-1	223	3/21/61	2	Texas Christian	Los Angeles, Calif.	Houston, Tex.	6/0
74	Matthews, Bruce	T	6-4	280	8/8/61	3	Southern California	Arcadia, Calif.	Sierra Madre, Calif.	16/16
89	McCloskey, Mike	TE	6-5	246	2/2/61	3	Penn State	Philadelphia, Pa.	Philadelphia, Pa.	15/0
26	Meadows, Darryl	S	6-1	198	2/15/61	3	Toledo	Cincinnati, Ohio	Cincinnati, Ohio	14/0
91	Meads, Johnny	LB	6-2	225	6/25/61	2	Nicholls State	New Orleans, La.	Houston, Tex.	16/0
1	Moon, Warren	QB	6-3	208	11/18/56	2	Washington	Los Angeles, Calif.	Sugar Land, Tex.	16/16
76	Moran, Eric	T	6-5	282	6/10/60	2	Washington	Spokane, Wash.	Seattle, Wash.	8/1
30	Moriarty, Larry	RB	6-1	240	4/24/58	3	Notre Dame	Santa Barbara, Calif.	Santa Barbara, Calif.	14/9
80	Mullins, Eric	WR	5-11	181	7/30/62	2	Stanford	Houston, Tex.	Houston, Tex.	13/2
63	Munchak, Mike	G	6-3	286	3/5/60	4	Penn State	Scranton, Pa.	Sugar Land, Tex.	16/16
12	Ransom, Brian	QB	6-3	202	7/9/60	3	Tennessee State	Omaha, Neb.	Houston, Tex.	0*
53	Riley, Avon	LB	6-3	236	2/10/58	5	UCLA	Savannah, Ga.	Stafford, Tex.	16/16
55	Romano, Jim	C	6-3	255	9/7/59	4	Penn State	Glen Cove, N.Y.	Fulton, Calif.	14/9*
73	Salem, Harvey	T	6-6	285	1/15/61	3	California	Berkeley, Calif.	Berkeley, Calif.	16/15
62	†Schuhmacher, John	G	6-3	277	9/23/55	6	Southern California	Salem, Ore.	Sugar Land, Tex.	16/10
83	Smith, Tim	WR	6-2	206	3/20/57	6	Nebraska	Tucson, Ariz.	Stafford, Tex.	16/14
72	Sochia, Brian	NT	6-3	254	7/21/61	3	Northwest Oklahoma St.	Massena, N.Y.	Houston, Tex.	16/3
70	Steinkuhler, Dean	T	6-3	273	1/27/61	2	Nebraska	Syracuse, Neb.	Sugar Land, Tex.	10/10
67	Stensrud, Mike	NT	6-5	280	2/19/56	7	Iowa State	Lake Mills, Iowa	Missouri City, Tex.	14/14
98	Studaway, Mark	DE	6-3	269	9/20/60	2	Tennessee	Memphis, Tenn.	Memphis, Tenn.	6/0
51	†Thompson, Ted	LB	6-1	218	1/17/53	11	Southern Methodist	Atlanta, Tex.	Missouri City, Tex.	16/0
20	Tullis, Willie	CB	6-0	195	4/5/58	5	Troy State	Newville, Ala.	Houston, Tex.	16/15
82	Walls, Herkie	WR	5-8	160	7/18/61	3	Texas	Garland, Tex.	Carrollton, Tex.	14/10
87	Williams, Jamie	TE	6-4	232	2/25/60	3	Nebraska	Davenport, Iowa	Houston, Tex.	16/16
33	t-Woolfolk, Butch	RB	6-1	207	3/1/60	4	Michigan	Milwaukee, Wis.	Secaucus, N.J.	15/8

* France missed '84 season due to injury; Harris last active with Pittsburgh in '83; Ransom active for 16 games but did not play; Romano played 6 games with L.A. Raiders, 8 with Houston in '84.

†Option playout; subject to developments.

t-Oilers traded for Woolfolk (N.Y. Giants).

Traded—Defensive end Bob Hamm to Kansas City.

Also played with Oilers in '84—DE Bryan Caldwell (8 games), RB Earl Campbell (6), C David Carter (7), RB Donnie Craft (1), T Ellis Gardner (1), S Carter Hartwig (14), LB Daryl Hunt (5), P John James (16), KR-WR Carl Roaches (16).

COACHING STAFF

Head Coach, Hugh Campbell

Pro Career: Begins second season as Oilers head coach following 3-13 campaign in 1984. Became Oilers' thirteenth head coach on January 3, 1984, after spending 1983 season as head coach with the Los Angeles Express of USFL where he compiled an 8-10 record. From 1977-1982, Campbell was head coach of the Edmonton Eskimos of the Canadian Football League; was Western Division champion all six years in Edmonton and was five-time winner of Grey Cup from 1978-1982. Campbell's .773 winning percentage as head coach is best in CFL history. Pro player with Saskatchewan Roughriders of the CFL from 1963-1967, and again in 1969. Still holds numerous Roughriders and CFL receiving records. Originally a fourth-round draft pick of San Francisco 49ers as wide receiver. Career record: 3-13.

Background: Wide receiver at Washington State from 1959-62. Named to several bowl games after senior season. Assistant coach at Washington State from 1965-69. Head coach of Whitworth College in Spokane, Washington, from 1970-76.

Personal: Born May 21, 1941, San Jose, California. Hugh and wife, Louise, live in Missouri City, Tex., and have four children—Robin, Jill, Rick, and Molly.

Assistant Coaches

John Devlin, linebackers; born April 12, 1937, Norristown, Pa., lives in Houston, Tex. Tackle West Chester State 1956-58. No pro playing experience. College coach: Army 1963-65, Virginia Tech 1966-70, Florida State 1971-72, Maryland 1973-81, Kentucky 1982-83. Pro coach: Joined Oilers in 1984.

Joe Faragalli, offensive coordinator; born April 18, 1929, Philadelphia, Pa., lives in Missouri City, Tex. Tackle-defensive tackle Villanova 1950-53. No pro playing experience. College coach: Villanova 1962-66, Brown 1970-73, Marshall 1973. Pro coach: Winnipeg Blue Bombers (CFL) 1967-69, 1974-77, Edmonton Eskimos (CFL) 1977-80, Saskatchewan Roughriders (CFL) 1980-82 (head coach), Cincinnati Bengals 1984, first year with Oilers.

Gene Gaines, special teams; born June 26, 1938, Los Angeles, Calif., lives in Houston, Tex. Running back-defensive back UCLA 1958-60. Pro running back Ottawa Rough Riders (CFL) 1962-69, Montreal Alouettes (CFL) 1961, 1970-76. Pro coach: Montreal Alouettes (CFL) 1976-81, Edmonton Eskimos (CFL) 1982, Los Angeles Express (USFL) 1983, joined Oilers in 1984.

Jerry Glanville, defensive coordinator; born October 14, 1941, Detroit, Mich., lives in Houston, Tex. Guard-linebacker Northern Michigan 1961-63. No pro playing experience. College coach: Northern Michigan 1966, Western Kentucky 1967, Georgia Tech 1968-73. Pro coach: Detroit Lions 1974-76, Atlanta Falcons 1977-82, Buffalo Bills 1983, joined Oilers in 1984.

Kenny Houston, defensive backfield; born November 12, 1944, Lufkin, Tex., lives in Kingwood, Tex. Linebacker Prairie View A&M 1962-66. Pro defensive back Houston Oilers 1967-72, Washington Redskins 1973-1980. Pro coach: Joined Oilers in 1982.

Bruce Lemmerman, receivers; born October 4, 1945, Los Angeles, Calif., lives in Houston, Tex. Quarterback San Fernando Valley State 1965-67. Pro quarterback Atlanta Falcons 1968-70, Edmonton Eskimos (CFL) 1971-79, Hamilton Tiger-Cats (CFL) 1980. Pro coach: Edmonton Eskimos 1981-82, Los Angeles Express (USFL) 1983, joined Oilers in 1984.

Bob Padilla, defensive line; born February 11, 1936, Santa Ana, Calif., lives in Houston, Tex. Lineman Fresno State 1955-58. No pro playing experience. College coach: Fresno State 1968-72, 1978-79, San Jose State 1973-75, Michigan State 1976-78, Washington State 1980-81, Arizona State 1982-83. Pro coach: Joined Oilers in 1984.

Al Roberts, running backs; born January 6, 1944, Fresno, Calif., lives in Houston, Tex. Running back Puget Sound 1963-65. No pro playing experience. College coach: Washington 1977-82. Pro coach: Los Angeles Express (USFL) 1983, joined Oilers in 1984.

Bill Walsh, offensive line; born September 8, 1927, Phillipsburg, N.J., lives in Houston, Tex. Center Notre Dame 1945-48. Pro center Pittsburgh Steelers 1949-54. College coach: Notre Dame 1955-58, Kansas State 1959. Pro coach: Kansas City Chiefs 1960-74, Atlanta Falcons 1975-82, joined Oilers in 1983.

HOUSTON OILERS 1985 FIRST-YEAR ROSTER

Name	Pos.	Ht.	Wt.	Birth-date	College	Birthplace	Residence	How Acq.
Akiu, Mike	WR	5-9	185	2/12/62	Hawaii	Kailua, Hawaii	Kailua, Hawaii	D7
Briehl, Tom	LB	6-3	247	9/8/62	Stanford	Phoenix, Ariz.	Scottsdale, Ariz.	D4
Bush, Frank	LB	6-1	218	1/10/63	North Carolina St.	Athens, Ga.	Athens, Ga.	D5
Byrd, Richard	DE	6-3	255	3/20/62	So. Mississippi	Jackson, Miss.	Jackson, Miss.	D2
Campbell, Donnie	QB	6-5	218	12/18/61	Kansas State	Lyons, Kan.	Lyons, Kan.	FA
Childress, Ray	DE	6-6	267	10/20/62	Texas A&M	Dallas, Tex.	Dallas, Tex.	D1
Drewrey, Willie	WR-KR	5-7	158	4/28/63	West Virginia	Columbus, N.J.	McGuire AFB, N.J.	D11
Fuller, Ardell	WR	6-1	182	12/13/62	Vanderbilt	Gaffney, S.C.	Gaffney, S.C.	FA
Golic, Mike	NT-DE	6-5	265	12/12/62	Notre Dame	Willowick, Ohio	Willowick, Ohio	D10
Gordon, Scott (1)	G	6-4	265	9/23/60	Santa Clara	Palo Alto, Calif.	Houston, Tex.	FA
Hare, Frank	NT	6-2	244	2/13/63	Kentucky	Atlanta, Ga.	Lexington, Ky.	FA
Hall, Brian	CB	6-2	200	10/8/61	Oklahoma	Houston, Tex.	Houston, Tex.	FA
Harlien, Matt	T	6-4	270	9/16/60	Texas Tech	Corpus Christi, Tex.	Corpus Christi, Tex.	FA
Harraka, Greg	T-G	6-2	266	6/1/62	Maryland	Paterson, N.J.	Germantown, Md.	FA
Johnson, Lee	P-K	6-1	204	11/2/61	Brigham Young	Dallas, Tex.	Houston, Tex.	D5a
Johnson, Richard	CB	6-0	195	10/20/62	Wisconsin	Harvey, Ill.	Dixmoor, Ill.	D1a
Jordan, Kent (1)	TE	6-7	235	10/29/59	St. Mary's, Calif.	Berkeley, Calif.	Piedmont, Calif.	FA
Kelley, Mike	C-G	6-5	266	8/27/62	Notre Dame	Westfield, Mass.	Westfield, Mass.	D3
Kellermeyer, Doug (1)	T	6-2	265	6/1/61	Brigham Young	Bucyrus, Ohio	Scottsdale, Ariz.	FA
Krakoski, Joe	LB	6-1	224	11/11/62	Washington	Aurora, Ill.	Fremont, Calif.	D6
Schlecht, Mark (1)	P	6-2	200	6/17/59	Nebraska-Omaha	West Point, Neb.	West Point, Neb.	FA
Tasker, Steve	KR	5-9	185	4/10/62	Northwestern	Leoti, Kan.	Wichita, Kan.	D9
Thomas, Chuck	C	6-2	270	2/24/60	Oklahoma	Houston, Tex.	Houston, Tex.	D8
Turner, Greg	CB-S	5-11	192	6/12/62	Arizona	Toledo, Ohio	Tucson, Ariz.	FA
Vonder Haar, Mark	T	6-5	255	2/6/62	Minnesota	Hibbings, Minn.	Hibbings, Minn.	D12
Weil, Jack (1)	P	5-11	175	3/16/62	Wyoming	Denver, Colo.	Broomfield, Colo.	FA

Players who report to an NFL team for the first time are designated on rosters as rookies (R). If a player reported to an NFL training camp in a previous year but was not on the active squad for three or more regular season or postseason games, he is listed on the first-year roster and designated by a (1). Thereafter, a player who is on the active squad for three or more regular season or postseason games is credited with an additional year of playing experience.

NOTES

43

INDIANAPOLIS COLTS

**American Football Conference
Eastern Division**

Team Colors: Royal Blue, White, and Silver

**P.O. Box 54000
Indianapolis, Indiana 46254
Telephone: (317) 252-2658**

Club Officials

President-Treasurer: Robert Irsay
Vice President-General Manager: James Irsay
Vice President-General Counsel:
  Michael G. Chernoff
Assistant General Manager: Bob Terpening
Director of Player Personnel: Jack Bushofsky
Director of College Scouting: Clyde Powers
Controller: Kurt Humphrey
Director of Operations: Pete Ward
Director of Public Relations: Bob Eller
Assistant Director of Public Relations:
  Craig Kelley
Purchasing Administrator: David Filar
Equipment Manager: Jon Scott
Cinematographer: Marty Heckscher
Assistant Cinematographer: John Starliper
Cheerleader Director: Meg Irsay

Stadium: Hoosier Dome • **Capacity:** 60,127
  100 South Capitol Avenue
  Indianapolis, Indiana 46225

Playing Surface: AstroTurf

Training Camp: Anderson College
  Anderson, Indiana 46011

1985 SCHEDULE

Preseason

Aug. 10	**Seattle**	7:30
Aug. 17	at Chicago	6:00
Aug. 24	at Denver	7:00
Aug. 30	**Cincinnati**	7:30

Regular Season

Sept. 8	at Pittsburgh	1:00
Sept. 15	at Miami	1:00
Sept. 22	**Detroit**	12:00
Sept. 29	at New York Jets	4:00
Oct. 6	**Buffalo**	12:00
Oct. 13	**Denver**	12:00
Oct. 20	at Buffalo	1:00
Oct. 27	**Green Bay**	1:00
Nov. 3	**New York Jets**	4:00
Nov. 10	at New England	1:00
Nov. 17	**Miami**	1:00
Nov. 24	at Kansas City	3:00
Dec. 1	**New England**	1:00
Dec. 8	at Chicago	12:00
Dec. 15	at Tampa Bay	1:00
Dec. 22	**Houston**	4:00

COLTS COACHING HISTORY

(233-213-7)

1953	Keith Molesworth	3-9-0
1954-62	Weeb Ewbank	60-53-1
1963-69	Don Shula	73-25-4
1970-72	Don McCafferty*	26-11-1
1972	John Sandusky	4-5-0
1973-74	Howard Schnellenberger**	4-13-0
1974	Joe Thomas	2-9-0
1975-79	Ted Marchibroda	41-36-0
1980-81	Mike McCormack	9-23-0
1982-84	Frank Kush***	11-28-1
1984	Hal Hunter	0-1-0

  *Released after five games in 1972
 **Released after three games in 1974
***Resigned after 15 games in 1984

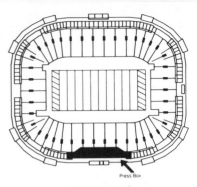

HOOSIER DOME

RECORD HOLDERS
Individual Records—Career

Category	Name	Performance
Rushing (Yds.)	Lydell Mitchell, 1972-77	5,487
Passing (Yds.)	Johnny Unitas, 1956-1972	39,768
Passing (TDs)	Johnny Unitas, 1956-1972	287
Receiving (No.)	Raymond Berry, 1955-1967	631
Receiving (Yds.)	Raymond Berry, 1955-1967	9,275
Interceptions	Bob Boyd, 1960-68	57
Punting (Avg.)	Rohn Stark, 1982-84	44.9
Punt Return (Avg.)	Wendell Harris, 1964	12.6
Kickoff Return (Avg.)	Jim Duncan, 1969-1971	32.5
Field Goals	Lou Michaels, 1964-69	107
Touchdowns (Tot.)	Lenny Moore, 1956-1967	113
Points	Lenny Moore, 1956-1967	678

Individual Records—Single Season

Category	Name	Performance
Rushing (Yds.)	Lydell Mitchell, 1976	1,200
Passing (Yds.)	Johnny Unitas, 1963	3,481
Passing (TDs)	Johnny Unitas, 1959	32
Receiving (No.)	Joe Washington, 1979	82
Receiving (Yds.)	Raymond Berry, 1960	1,298
Interceptions	Tom Keane, 1953	11
Punting (Avg.)	David Lee, 1966	45.6
Punt Return (Avg.)	Wendell Harris, 1964	12.6
Kickoff Return (Avg.)	Jim Duncan, 1970	35.4
Field Goals	Raul Allegre, 1983	30
Touchdowns (Tot.)	Lenny Moore, 1964	20
Points	Lenny Moore, 1964	120

Individual Records—Single Game

Category	Name	Performance
Rushing (Yds.)	Norm Bulaich, 9-19-71	198
Passing (Yds.)	Johnny Unitas, 9-17-67	401
Passing (TDs)	Gary Cuozzo, 11-14-65	5
Receiving (No.)	Lydell Mitchell, 12-15-74	13
	Joe Washington, 9-2-79	13
Receiving (Yds.)	Raymond Berry, 11-10-57	224
Interceptions	Many times	3
	Last time by Lyle Blackwood, 11-20-77	
Field Goals	Raul Allegre, 10-30-83	5
Touchdowns (Tot.)	Many times	4
	Last time by Lydell Mitchell, 10-12-75	
Points	Many times	24
	Last time by Lydell Mitchell, 10-12-75	

1984 TEAM STATISTICS

	Indianapolis	Opp.
Total First Downs	254	343
Rushing	114	124
Passing	117	194
Penalty	23	25
Third Down: Made/Att.	64/214	98/230
Fourth Down: Made/Att.	15/24	8/17
Total Net Yards	4132	5577
Avg. Per Game	258.3	348.6
Total Plays	979	1116
Avg. Per Play	4.2	5.0
Net Yards Rushing	2025	2007
Avg. Per Game	126.6	125.4
Total Rushes	510	559
Net Yards Passing	2107	3570
Avg. Per Game	131.7	223.1
Tackled/Yards Lost	58/436	42/320
Gross Yards	2543	3890
Att./Completions	411/206	515/298
Completion Pct.	50.1	57.9
Had Intercepted	22	18
Punts/Avg.	98/44.7	80/42.0
Net Punting Avg.	37.2	36.6
Penalties/Yards Lost	95/798	98/813
Fumbles/Ball Lost	35/16	29/13
Touchdowns	28	50
Rushing	13	16
Passing	13	31
Returns	2	3
Avg. Time of Possession	27:24	32:36

1984 TEAM RECORD
Preseason (1-3)

Date	Indianapolis		Opponents
8/4	3	Miami	24
8/11	26	*New York Giants	20
8/18	0	Denver	31
8/25	17	Green Bay	34
	46		109

Regular Season (4-12)

Date	Indianapolis		Opp.	Att.
9/2	14	*New York Jets	23	60,398
9/9	35	Houston	21	43,820
9/16	33	*St. Louis	34	60,274
9/23	7	Miami	44	55,415
9/30	31	*Buffalo	17	60,032
10/7	7	*Washington	35	60,012
10/14	7	Philadelphia	16	50,277
10/21	17	*Pittsburgh	16	60,026
10/28	3	Dallas	22	58,724
11/4	10	*San Diego	38	60,143
11/11	9	New York Jets	5	51,066
11/18	17	*New England	50	60,099
11/25	7	Los Angeles Raiders	21	40,289
12/2	15	Buffalo	21	20,693
12/9	17	*Miami	35	60,411
12/16	10	New England	16	22,383
	239		414	823,972

*Home Game

Score by Periods

Indianapolis	31	87	46	75	—	239
Opponents	92	143	74	105	—	414

Attendance

Home 481,305   Away 342,667   Total 823,972
Single game home record, 61,479 (11-11-83)
Single season home record, 481,305 (1984)

1984 INDIVIDUAL STATISTICS
Rushing

	Att.	Yds.	Avg.	LG	TD
McMillan	163	705	4.3	31t	5
Dickey	131	523	4.0	30	3
Middleton	92	275	3.0	20	1
Pagel	26	149	5.7	23	1
Schlichter	19	145	7.6	22	1
Moore	38	127	3.3	18	2
Wonsley	37	111	3.0	13	0
Stark	2	0	0.0	0	0
P. Smith	2	−10	−5.0	−3	0
Indianapolis	510	2025	4.0	31t	13
Opponents	559	2007	3.6	30	16

Passing

	Att.	Comp.	Pct.	Yds.	TD	Int.	Tkld.	Rate
Pagel	212	114	53.8	1426	8	8	28/201	71.8
Schlichter	140	62	44.3	702	3	7	23/170	46.2
Herrmann	56	29	51.8	352	1	6	7/65	37.8
Dickey	1	1	100.0	63	1	0	0/0	158.3
Moore	1	0	0.0	0	0	0	0/0	39.6
Stark	1	0	0.0	0	0	1	0/0	0.0
Indianapolis	411	206	50.1	2543	13	22	58/436	57.9
Opponents	515	298	57.9	3890	31	18	42/320	87.3

Receiving

	No.	Yds.	Avg.	LG	TD
Butler	43	664	15.4	74t	6
Porter	39	590	15.1	63t	2
Bouza	22	270	12.3	22	0
McMillan	19	201	10.6	44	0
Middleton	15	112	7.5	16	1
Young	14	164	11.7	28	2
Dickey	14	135	9.6	33	0
Sherwin	11	169	15.4	26	0
Henry	11	139	12.6	19t	2
Moore	9	52	5.8	12	0
Wonsley	9	47	5.2	17	0
Indianapolis	206	2543	12.3	74t	13
Opponents	298	3890	13.1	80t	31

Interceptions

	No.	Yds.	Avg.	LG	TD
Daniel	6	25	4.2	18	0
Randle	3	66	22.0	54	0
Krauss	3	20	6.7	18	0
Burroughs	3	9	3.0	6	0
Kafentzis	1	59	59.0	59t	1
Glasgow	1	8	8.0	8	0
Davis	1	3	3.0	3	0
Indianapolis	18	190	10.6	59t	1
Opponents	22	423	19.2	50	2

Punting

	No.	Yds.	Avg.	In 20	LG
Stark	98	4383	44.7	21	72
Indianapolis	98	4383	44.7	21	72
Opponents	80	3363	42.0	29	66

Punt Returns

	No.	FC	Yds.	Avg.	LG	TD
L. Anderson	27	7	182	6.7	19	0
Glasgow	7	2	79	11.3	35	0
Bouza	3	3	17	5.7	11	0
Padjen	1	0	0	0	0	0
Indianapolis	38	12	278	7.3	35	0
Opponents	62	15	600	9.7	38	0

Kickoff Returns

	No.	Yds.	Avg.	LG	TD
L. Anderson	22	525	23.9	69	0
P. Smith	32	651	20.3	96t	1
Kafentzis	5	69	13.8	22	0
Wonsley	4	52	13.0	20	0
Moore	2	19	9.5	10	0
Middleton	1	11	11.0	11	0
Hathaway	1	2	2.0	2	0
Sherwin	1	2	2.0	2	0
Radachowsky	1	0	0.0	0	0
Indianapolis	69	1331	19.3	96t	1
Opponents	42	849	20.2	45	0

Scoring

	TD R	TD P	TD Rt	PAT	FG	Saf	TP
Allegre	0	0	0	14/14	11/18	0	47
Butler	0	6	0	0/0	0/0	0	36
McMillan	5	0	0	0/0	0/0	0	30
Biasucci	0	0	0	13/14	3/5	0	22
Dickey	3	0	0	0/0	0/0	0	18
Henry	0	2	0	0/0	0/0	0	12
Middleton	1	1	0	0/0	0/0	0	12
Moore	2	0	0	0/0	0/0	0	12
Porter	0	2	0	0/0	0/0	0	12
Young	0	2	0	0/0	0/0	0	12
Kafentzis	0	0	1	0/0	0/0	0	6
Pagel	1	0	0	0/0	0/0	0	6
P. Smith	0	0	1	0/0	0/0	0	6
Schlichter	1	0	0	0/0	0/0	0	6
Humiston	0	0	0	0/0	0/0	1	2
Indianapolis	13	13	2	27/28	14/23	1	239
Opponents	16	31	3	47/50	21/23	2	414

FIRST-ROUND SELECTIONS

(If Club had no first-round selection, first player drafted is listed with round in parentheses.)

Year	Player, College, Position
1953	Billy Vessels, Oklahoma, B
1954	Cotton Davidson, Baylor, B
1955	George Shaw, Oregon, B
	Alan Ameche, Wisconsin, FB
1956	Lenny Moore, Penn State, B
1957	Jim Parker, Ohio State, G
1958	Lenny Lyles, Louisville, B
1959	Jackie Burkett, Auburn, C
1960	Ron Mix, Southern California, T
1961	Tom Matte, Ohio State, RB
1962	Wendell Harris, Louisiana State, S
1963	Bob Vogel, Ohio State, T
1964	Marv Woodson, Indiana, CB
1965	Mike Curtis, Duke, LB
1966	Sam Ball, Kentucky, T
1967	Bubba Smith, Michigan State, DT
	Jim Detwiler, Michigan, B
1968	John Williams, Minnesota, G
1969	Eddie Hinton, Oklahoma, WR
1970	Norman Bulaich, Texas Christian, RB
1971	Don McCauley, North Carolina, RB
	Leonard Dunlap, North Texas State, DB
1972	Tom Drougas, Oregon, T
1973	Bert Jones, Louisiana State, QB
	Joe Ehrmann, DT, Syracuse
1974	John Dutton, Nebraska, DE
	Roger Carr, Louisiana Tech, WR
1975	Ken Huff, North Carolina, G
1976	Ken Novak, Purdue, DT
1977	Randy Burke, Kentucky, WR
1978	Reese McCall, Auburn, TE
1979	Barry Krauss, Alabama, LB
1980	Curtis Dickey, Texas A&M, RB
	Derrick Hatchett, Texas, DB
1981	Randy McMillan, Pittsburgh, RB
	Donnell Thompson, North Carolina, DT
1982	Johnie Cooks, Mississippi State, LB
	Art Schlichter, Ohio State, QB
1983	John Elway, Stanford, QB
1984	Leonard Coleman, Vanderbilt, DB
	Ron Solt, Maryland, G
1985	Duane Bickett, Southern California, LB

INDIANAPOLIS COLTS 1985 VETERAN ROSTER

No.	Name	Pos.	Ht.	Wt.	Birth-date	NFL Exp.	College	Birthplace	Residence	'84 Games/Starts
2	Allegre, Raul	K	5-10	165	6/15/59	3	Texas	Torreon, Coaguila, Mexico	Austin, Tex.	12/0
30	†Anderson, Larry	S	5-11	194	9/25/56	8	Louisiana Tech	Monroe, La.	Shreveport, La.	12/0
61	Bailey, Don	C	6-4	257	3/24/61	2	Miami	Miami, Fla.	Miami, Fla.	10/0
	Baldischwiler, Karl	T	6-5	260	1/19/56	7	Oklahoma	Okmulgee, Okla.	Oklahoma City, Okla.	0*
97	Beach, Pat	TE	6-4	243	12/28/59	3	Washington State	Grant's Pass, Ore.	Indianapolis, Ind.	0*
48	†Bell, Mark	TE	6-5	246	8/30/57	6	Colorado State	Wichita, Kan.	Wichita, Kan.	16/0
5	Biasucci, Dean	K	6-0	188	7/25/62	2	Western Carolina	Niagra Falls, N.Y.	Miramar, Fla.	15/0
85	Bouza, Matt	WR	6-3	209	4/8/59	4	California	San Jose, Calif.	Walnut Creek, Calif.	16/4
52	Bracelin, Greg	LB	6-1	216	4/16/57	6	California	Lawrence, Kan.	Littleton, Colo.	16/7
45	†Burroughs, James	CB	6-1	187	1/21/58	4	Michigan State	Pahokee, Fla.	West Palm Beach, Fla.	6/5
80	Butler, Ray	WR	6-3	197	6/28/56	6	Southern California	Sweeney, Tex.	Lake Jackson, Tex.	16/15
72	Call, Kevin	T	6-7	289	11/13/61	2	Colorado State	Boulder, Colo.	Fort Collins, Colo.	15/0
98	Cooks, Johnie	LB	6-4	243	11/23/58	4	Mississippi State	Leland, Miss.	Leland, Miss.	16/13
38	Daniel, Eugene	CB	5-11	179	5/4/61	2	Louisiana State	Baton Rouge, La.	Baton Rouge, La.	15/14
27	Davis, Preston	CB	5-11	180	3/10/62	2	Baylor	Lubbock, Tex.	Waco, Tex.	12/8
33	Dickey, Curtis	RB	6-0	222	11/27/56	6	Texas A&M	Madisonville, Tex.	Houston, Tex.	10/9
53	Donaldson, Ray	C	6-4	273	5/17/58	6	Georgia	Rome, Ga.	Rome, Ga.	16/16
65	Gardner, Ellis	T-G	6-5	250	9/16/61	3	Georgia Tech	Chattanooga, Tenn.	Indianapolis, Ind.	9/0*
25	Glasgow, Nesby	S	5-10	180	4/15/57	7	Washington	Los Angeles, Calif.	Indianapolis, Ind.	16/16
58	Hathaway, Steve	LB	6-4	238	4/26/62	2	West Virginia	Jackson Heights, N.Y.	Beaver, Pa.	6/1
88	Henry, Bernard	WR	6-1	180	4/9/60	4	Arizona State	Los Angeles, Calif.	Los Angeles, Calif.	14/0
75	Hinton, Chris	G	6-4	283	7/31/61	3	Northwestern	Chicago, Ill.	Indianapolis, Ind.	6/6
57	†Humiston, Mike	LB	6-3	240	1/8/59	5	Weber State	Oceanside, Calif.	Chico, Calif.	16/1
51	†Jones, Ricky	LB	6-2	230	3/9/55	8	Tuskegee Institute	Birmingham, Ala.	Birmingham, Ala.	0*
29	†Kafentzis, Mark	S	5-10	200	6/30/58	4	Hawaii	Richland, Wash.	Indianapolis, Ind.	16/14
63	Kirchner, Mark	T	6-3	261	10/19/59	3	Baylor	Pasadena, Tex.	Houston, Tex.	11/1
55	Krauss, Barry	LB	6-3	249	3/17/57	7	Alabama	Pompano Beach, Fla.	Indianapolis, Ind.	16/16
56	Maxwell, Vernon	LB	6-2	238	10/25/61	3	Arizona State	Birmingham, Ala.	Carson, Calif.	16/15
32	McMillan, Randy	FB	6-0	212	12/17/58	5	Pittsburgh	Havre de Grace, Md.	Timonium, Md.	16/16
43	Middleton, Frank	RB	5-11	201	10/28/60	2	Florida A&M	Savannah, Ga.	Atlanta, Ga.	16/5
76	Mills, Jim	T	6-9	281	9/23/61	3	Hawaii	Vancouver, Canada	Richmond, Canada	14/13
23	Moore, Alvin	RB	6-0	198	5/30/59	3	Arizona State	Randolph, Ariz.	Tempe, Ariz.	13/2
93	Odom, Cliff	LB	6-2	235	9/15/58	5	Texas-Arlington	Beaumont, Tex.	Arlington, Tex.	16/15
90	Padjen, Gary	LB	6-2	241	7/2/58	4	Arizona State	Salt Lake City, Utah	Indianapolis, Ind.	16/0
18	Pagel, Mike	QB	6-2	205	9/13/60	4	Arizona State	Douglas, Ariz.	Chandler, Ariz.	11/9
78	Parker, Steve	DE	6-3	262	9/21/59	3	Eastern Illinois	Evanston, Ill.	Ontario, Canada	9/1
71	†Petersen, Ted	T	6-5	253	2/7/55	9	Eastern Illinois	Kankakee, Ill.	Pittsburgh, Pa.	9/4*
87	†Porter, Tracy	WR	6-2	202	6/1/59	5	Louisiana State	Baton Rouge, La.	Baton Rouge, La.	16/12
21	Radachowsky, George	CB-S	5-11	178	9/7/62	2	Boston College	Danbury, Conn.	Danbury, Conn.	16/0
35	Randle, Tate	CB	6-0	196	8/15/59	4	Texas Tech	Fredericksburg, Tex.	Odessa, Tex.	16/6
10	Schlichter, Art	QB	6-3	210	4/25/60	3	Ohio State	Fayette, Colo.	Bloomingberg, Ohio	9/5
95	Scott, Chris	DE	6-5	253	12/11/61	2	Purdue	Berea, Ohio	Indianapolis, Ind.	14/2
83	Sherwin, Tim	TE	6-6	245	5/4/58	4	Boston College	Watervliet, N.Y.	Indianapolis, Ind.	16/8
91	Smith, Byron	DE	6-5	264	12/21/62	2	California	Los Angeles, Calif.	Inglewood, Calif.	3/0
86	Smith, Phil	WR	6-3	188	4/28/61	3	San Diego State	Los Angeles, Calif.	Compton, Calif.	16/0
66	Solt, Ron	G	6-3	275	5/19/62	2	Maryland	Wilkes-Barre, Pa.	Wilkes-Barre, Pa.	16/16
3	Stark, Rohn	P	6-3	203	6/4/59	4	Florida State	Minneapolis, Minn.	Indianapolis, Ind.	16/0
99	Thompson, Donnell	DE	6-5	263	10/27/58	5	North Carolina	Lumberton, N.C.	Chapel Hill, N.C.	10/10
64	Utt, Ben	G	6-5	280	6/13/59	4	Georgia Tech	Richmond, Calif.	Indianapolis, Ind.	16/15
94	Virkus, Scott	DE	6-5	248	9/8/59	3	San Francisco C.C.	Palo Alto, Calif.	Rochester, N.Y.	6/0*
92	White, Brad	NT	6-2	260	8/18/58	5	Tennessee	Rexburg, Idaho	Knoxville, Tenn.	15/2
39	Williams, Newton	FB	5-10	219	5/19/59	3	Arizona State	Charlotte, N.C.	Charlotte, N.C.	0*
40	Williams, Vaughn	CB-S	6-2	193	12/14/61	2	Stanford	Greeley, Colo.	Auburn, Wash.	10/1
96	Winter, Blaise	DE	6-3	262	1/31/62	2	Syracuse	Blauvelt, N.Y.	Blauvelt, N.Y.	16/15
69	Wisniewski, Leo	NT	6-1	259	11/6/59	4	Penn State	Hancock, Mich.	Tampa, Fla.	14/14
34	Wonsley, George	RB	6-0	212	11/23/60	2	Mississippi State	Moss Point, Miss.	Moss Point, Miss.	14/0
81	Young, Dave	TE	6-5	243	2/9/59	4	Purdue	Akron, Ohio	Indianapolis, Ind.	13/9

* Baldischwiler, Beach, Jones, and N. Williams missed '84 season due to injury; Gardner active for 1 game with Houston but did not play, played 9 games with Indianapolis in '84; Petersen played 4 games with Cleveland, 5 with Indianapolis; Virkus played 5 games with New England, 1 with Indianapolis.

†Option playout; subject to developments.

Traded—Quarterback Mark Herrmann to San Diego, WR Victor Oatis to Cleveland.

Also played with Colts in '84—S Kim Anderson (1 game), C Grant Feasel (6), CB-S Bo Scott Metcalf (2), DE Henry Waechter (1), G Steve Wright (16).

COACHING STAFF

Head Coach, Rod Dowhower

Pro Career: Named the Colts' eleventh head coach on January 28, 1985. This is Dowhower's first head coaching position in the NFL. No pro playing experience.

Background: First started coaching as a graduate assistant at San Diego State under Don Coryell in 1966 as quarterback and receivers coach. He was elevated to offensive coordinator in 1968, and served in that capacity until 1972. Dowhower joined the St. Louis Cardinals with Coryell in 1973 as quarterbacks and receivers coach. He moved to UCLA from 1974-75 as offensive coordinator under Dick Vermeil. Following a season as offensive coordinator at Boise State in 1976, Dowhower joined Bill Walsh's staff at Stanford as quarterback coach. He landed his first head coaching job at Stanford in 1979, posting a 5-5-1 record. Dowhower moved back to the NFL from 1980-82 as the offensive coordinator with Denver. He moved to the St. Louis Cardinals, where he was offensive coordinator from 1983-84.

Personal: Born April 15, 1943, Ord, Nebraska. Rod and his wife, Nancy, have two sons, Brian and Deron. They live in Indianapolis.

Assistant Coaches

John Becker, quarterbacks; born February 16, 1943, Alexandria, Va., lives in Indianapolis. Cal State-Northridge 1965. No pro playing experience. College coach: UCLA 1970, New Mexico State 1971, New Mexico 1972-73, Los Angeles Valley College 1974-76 (head coach), Oregon 1977-79. Pro coach: Philadelphia Eagles 1980-83, Buffalo Bills 1984, first year with Colts.

George Catavolos, secondary; born May 8, 1945, Cleveland, Ohio, lives in Indianapolis. Defensive back Purdue 1965-67. No pro playing experience. College coach: Purdue 1968-69, 1971-76, Middle Tennessee State 1969, Louisville 1970, Kentucky 1977-81, Tennessee 1982-83. Pro coach: Joined Colts in 1984.

George Hill, defensive coordinator; born April 28, 1933, Bay Village, Ohio, lives in Indianapolis. Tackle-fullback Denison 1954-57. No pro playing experience. College coach: Findlay 1959, Denison 1960-64, Cornell 1965, Duke 1966-70, Ohio State 1971-78. Pro coach: Philadelphia Eagles 1979-84, first year with Colts.

Tom Lovat, offensive line-assistant head coach; born December 28, 1938, Bingham, Utah, lives in Indianapolis. Guard-linebacker Utah 1958-60. No pro playing experience. College coach: Utah 1967, 1972-76 (1974-76 head coach), Idaho State 1968-70, Stanford 1977-79. Pro coach: Saskatchewan Roughriders (CFL) 1971, 1977-79, Green Bay Packers 1980, St. Louis Cardinals 1981-84, first year with Colts.

Billie Matthews, offensive coordinator-running backs; born March 15, 1930, Houston, Tex., lives in Indianapolis. Quarterback Southern University 1948-51. No pro playing experience. College coach: Kansas 1970, UCLA 1971-78. Pro coach: San Francisco 49ers 1979-82, Philadelphia Eagles 1983-84, first year with Colts.

Chip Myers, receivers; born July 9, 1945, Panama City, Fla., lives in Indianapolis. Receiver Northwest Oklahoma 1964-66. Pro receiver San Francisco 49ers 1967, Cincinnati Bengals 1969-75. College coach: Illinois 1980-82. Pro coach: Tampa Bay Buccaneers 1983-84, first year with Colts.

Keith Rowen, special teams-assistant offensive line; born September 2, 1952, New York, N.Y., lives in Indianapolis. College coach: Stanford 1975-76, Long Beach State 1977-78, Arizona 1979-82. Pro coach: Boston/New Orleans Breakers (USFL) 1983-84, Cleveland Browns 1984, first year with Colts.

Steve Sidwell, defensive line; born August 30, 1944, Winfield, Kan., lives in Indianapolis. Center-linebacker Colorado 1963-66. No pro playing experience. College coach: Colorado 1968-73, Nevada-Las Vegas 1974, Southern Methodist 1976-81. Pro coach: New England Patriots 1982-84, first year with Colts.

Rick Venturi, linebackers; born February 23, 1946, Taylorville, Ill., lives in Indianapolis. Quarterback Northwestern 1965-67. No pro playing experience. College coach: Northwestern 1968-72, 1978-80 (head coach), Purdue 1973-76, Illinois 1977. Pro coach: Joined Colts in 1982.

Tom Zupancic, strength; born September 14, 1955, Indianapolis, Ind., lives in Indianapolis. Defensive-offensive tackle Indiana Central 1975-78. No pro playing experience. Pro coach: Joined Colts in 1984.

INDIANAPOLIS COLTS 1985 FIRST-YEAR ROSTER

Name	Pos.	Ht.	Wt.	Birth-date	College	Birthplace	Residence	How Acq.
Aikens, Carl	WR	6-1	187	6/5/62	Northern Illinois	Great Lakes, Ill.	Chicago, Ill.	FA
Anderson, Don	CB	5-10	185	7/8/63	Purdue	Detroit, Mich.	West Lafayette, Ind.	D2
Basso, Phil	QB	6-1	175	4/27/61	Liberty Baptist	Smithtown, N.Y.	Hialeah, Fla.	FA
Bickett, Duane	LB	6-5	232	12/1/62	Southern California	Los Angeles, Calif.	Los Angeles, Calif.	D1
Blackburn, Drew	G	6-4	265	3/31/62	Mississippi College	Mobile, Ala.	Decatur, Miss.	FA
Boyer, Mark	TE	6-4	232	9/16/62	Southern California	Huntington, Calif.	Los Angeles, Calif.	D9
Bromley, Phil	C	6-2	255	11/18/62	Florida	Jackson, Mich.	Pensacola, Fla.	FA
Brooks, Mark	FB	6-0	235	5/15/63	Notre Dame	Cincinnati, Ohio	Cincinnati, Ohio	FA
Broughton, Willie	DE	6-5	245	9/9/64	Miami	Fort Pierce, Fla.	Miami, Fla.	D4
Brown, Orlando	RB	5-10	200	12/31/62	Indiana	Memphis, Tenn.	Memphis, Tenn.	FA
Brown, Ray	DE	6-4	260	8/28/61	Clemson	Rome, Ga.	Rome, Ga.	FA
Burnette, David	T	6-6	278	3/24/61	Central Arkansas	Parkin, Ark.	Conway, Ark.	D12
Caron, Roger	T	6-5	270	6/3/62	Harvard	Norwell, Mass.	Boston, Mass.	D5
Crnkovich, Nick	TE	6-4	238	4/7/63	Wabash	East Chicago, Ind.	Highland, Ind.	FA
Dwenger, Rick	FB	5-10	217	5/12/61	Indiana State	Columbus, Ind.	Columbus, Ind.	FA
Gandy, Geff	LB	6-2	238	5/1/60	Baylor	Dallas, Tex.	Boerne, Tex.	FA
Grant, Randy	WR	5-11	175	6/2/63	Illinois	Hayward, Calif.	Livermore, Calif.	FA
Gross, James	LB	6-1	230	11/7/61	Maryland	Landover, Md.	College Park, Md.	FA
Harbour, James	WR	6-0	190	11/10/62	Mississippi	Meridian, Miss.	Oxford, Miss.	D7
Harris, Neil	CB-S	6-0	195	2/12/62	Nebraska	Kansas City, Kan.	Lincoln, Neb.	FA
Lowry, Orlando	LB	6-4	230	8/14/61	Ohio State	Cleveland, Ohio	Shaker Heights, Ohio	FA
Merritts, James	NT	6-2	264	3/22/61	West Virginia	Roaring Spr., W.Va.	Holidaysburg, Pa.	FA
Nichols, Ricky	WR	5-10	180	7/27/62	East Carolina	Norfolk, Va.	Chesapeake, Va.	D8
Peoples, Carlton	CB	6-0	181	11/9/60	Tennessee	Memphis, Tenn.	Memphis, Tenn.	FA
Pinesett, Andre	DE	6-2	245	7/25/61	Cal State-Fullerton	Los Angeles, Calif.	Los Angeles, Calif.	D10
Poles, Robert	DE	6-5	275	2/24/61	Boston College	Fort Bragg, N.C.	Rochester, N.Y.	FA
Richardson, Ed	LB	6-2	225	11/9/61	Clemson	Thomasville, N.C.	Thomasville, N.C.	FA
Sinclair, Ian	C	6-4	253	7/22/60	Miami	Toronto, Canada	Miami, Fla.	FA
Smith, Eric	S	5-10	186	12/22/59	Southern Methodist	Houston, Tex.	Houston, Tex.	FA
Smith, Mark	WR	6-0	180	4/4/62	North Carolina	Fayetteville, N.C.	Fayetteville, N.C.	FA
Taylor, Garfield	RB	6-1	198	2/3/61	Kansas	Miami, Fla.	Miami, Fla.	FA
Tootle, Jeff	LB	6-2	230	8/29/62	Mesa College	Salina, Kan.	Aurora, Colo.	FA
Underwood, Gene	CB	5-11	175	1/6/61	Cal Poly-SLO	Laurel, Miss.	Merced, Calif.	FA
Washington, Tim (1)	CB-S	5-11	187	11/7/59	Fresno State	Fresno, Calif.	Fresno, Calif.	FA
Williams, Oliver	WR	6-3	195	10/17/60	Illinois	Chicago, Ill.	Los Angeles, Calif.	FA
Wray, Steve	QB	6-2	215	1/24/60	Franklin, Ind.	Nuremburg, Germany	Plainfield, Ind.	FA
Young, Anthony	S	6-0	187	10/8/63	Temple	Pemberton, N.J.	Philadelphia, Pa.	D3
Ziolkowski, Ron	LB	6-1	230	4/5/62	James Madison	Pittsburgh, Pa.	Pittsburgh, Pa.	FA

Players who report to an NFL team for the first time are designated on rosters as rookies (R). If a player reported to an NFL training camp in a previous year but was not on the active squad for three or more regular season or postseason games, he is listed on the first-year roster and designated by a (1). Thereafter, a player who is on the active squad for three or more regular season or postseason games is credited with an additional year of playing experience.

NOTES

_____
_____
_____
_____
_____
_____
_____
_____
_____
_____
_____

KANSAS CITY CHIEFS

**American Football Conference
Western Division**

Team Colors: Red, Gold, and White

**One Arrowhead Drive
Kansas City, Missouri 64129
Telephone: (816) 924-9300**

Club Officials

Owner: Lamar Hunt
President: Jack Steadman
Vice President-General Manager: Jim Schaaf
Vice President-Administration: Don Steadman
Treasurer: Randy Cooper
Secretary: Jim Seigfried
Director of Player Personnel: Les Miller
Director of Public Relations and Community
  Relations: Bob Sprenger
Media Services Manager: Gary Heise
Community Relations Manager: Brenda Boatright
Director of Sales and Promotions: Mitch Wheeler
Director of Arrowhead Stadium: David Smith
Stadium Operations: Bob Wachter
Ticket Manager: Joe Mazza
Manager of Information Systems: Andy Sawyer
Trainer: Dave Kendall
Equipment Coordinator: John Phillips

Stadium: Arrowhead Stadium • **Capacity:** 78,067
  One Arrowhead Drive
  Kansas City, Missouri 64129

Playing Surface: AstroTurf-8

Training Camp: William Jewell College
  Liberty, Missouri 64068

1985 SCHEDULE

Preseason

Aug. 10	at Cincinnati	7:00
Aug. 17	**New England**	7:30
Aug. 24	at Houston	8:00
Aug. 31	**St. Louis**	7:30

Regular Season

Sept. 8	at New Orleans	12:00
Sept. 12	**L.A. Raiders** (Thursday)	7:00
Sept. 22	at Miami	4:00
Sept. 29	**Seattle**	12:00
Oct. 6	at Los Angeles Raiders	1:00
Oct. 13	at San Diego	1:00
Oct. 20	**Los Angeles Rams**	12:00
Oct. 27	**Denver**	12:00
Nov. 3	at Houston	12:00
Nov. 10	**Pittsburgh**	12:00
Nov. 17	at San Francisco	1:00
Nov. 24	**Indianapolis**	3:00
Dec. 1	at Seattle	1:00
Dec. 8	**Atlanta**	12:00
Dec. 14	at Denver (Saturday)	2:00
Dec. 22	**San Diego**	12:00

CHIEFS COACHING HISTORY

Dallas Texans 1960-62
(186-169-10)

1960-74	Hank Stram	129-79-10
1975-77	Paul Wiggin*	11-24-0
1977	Tom Bettis	1-6-0
1978-82	Marv Levy	31-42-0
1983-84	John Mackovic	14-18-0

*Released after seven games in 1977

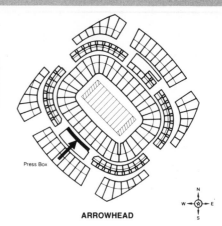

Press Box

ARROWHEAD

N
W—E
S

RECORD HOLDERS
Individual Records—Career

Category	Name	Performance
Rushing (Yds.)	Ed Podolak, 1969-1977	4,451
Passing (Yds.)	Len Dawson, 1962-1975	28,507
Passing (TDs)	Len Dawson, 1962-1975	237
Receiving (No.)	Otis Taylor, 1965-1975	410
Receiving (Yds.)	Otis Taylor, 1965-1975	7,306
Interceptions	Emmitt Thomas, 1966-1978	58
Punting (Avg.)	Jerrel Wilson, 1963-1977	43.5
Punt Return (Avg.)	J.T. Smith, 1979-1984	10.6
Kickoff Return (Avg.)	Noland Smith, 1967-69	26.8
Field Goals	Jan Stenerud, 1967-1979	279
Touchdowns (Tot.)	Otis Taylor, 1965-1975	60
Points	Jan Stenerud, 1967-1979	1,231

Individual Records—Single Season

Category	Name	Performance
Rushing (Yds.)	Joe Delaney, 1981	1,121
Passing (Yds.)	Bill Kenney, 1983	4,348
Passing (TDs)	Len Dawson, 1964	30
Receiving (No.)	Carlos Carson, 1983	80
Receiving (Yds.)	Carlos Carson, 1983	1,351
Interceptions	Emmitt Thomas, 1974	12
Punting (Avg.)	Jerrel Wilson, 1965	46.0
Punt Return (Avg.)	Abner Haynes, 1960	15.4
Kickoff Return (Avg.)	Dave Grayson, 1962	29.7
Field Goals	Jan Stenerud, 1968, 1970	30
Touchdowns (Tot.)	Abner Haynes, 1962	19
Points	Jan Stenerud, 1968	129

Individual Records—Single Game

Category	Name	Performance
Rushing (Yds.)	Joe Delaney, 11-15-81	193
Passing (Yds.)	Len Dawson, 11-1-64	435
Passing (TDs)	Len Dawson, 11-1-64	6
Receiving (No.)	Ed Podolak, 10-7-73	12
Receiving (Yds.)	Curtis McClinton, 12-19-65	213
Interceptions	Bobby Ply, 12-16-62	4
	Bobby Hunt, 12-4-64	4
Field Goals	Jan Stenerud, 11-2-69	5
	Jan Stenerud, 12-7-69	5
	Jan Stenerud, 12-19-71	5
Touchdowns (Tot.)	Abner Haynes, 11-26-61	5
Points	Abner Haynes, 11-26-61	30

1984 TEAM STATISTICS

	Kansas City	Opp.
Total First Downs	295	335
Rushing	88	121
Passing	178	192
Penalty	29	22
Third Down: Made/Att.	72/220	90/246
Fourth Down: Made/Att.	1/6	9/24
Total Net Yards	5095	5625
Avg. Per Game	318.4	351.6
Total Plays	1034	1159
Avg. Per Play	4.9	4.9
Net Yards Rushing	1527	1980
Avg. Per Game	95.4	123.8
Total Rushes	408	523
Net Yards Passing	3568	3645
Avg. Per Game	223.0	227.8
Tackled/Yards Lost	33/301	50/364
Gross Yards	3869	4009
Att./Completions	593/305	586/332
Completion Pct.	51.4	56.7
Had Intercepted	22	30
Punts/Avg.	98/44.9	91/40.0
Net Punting Avg.	37.5	33.8
Penalties/Yards Lost	98/801	108/951
Fumbles/Ball Lost	34/15	18/11
Touchdowns	35	38
Rushing	12	10
Passing	21	19
Returns	2	9
Avg. Time of Possession	27:25	32:35

1984 TEAM RECORD
Preseason (1-3)

Date	Kansas City		Opponents	
8/4	20	*New Orleans	34	
8/10	10	St. Louis	14	
8/18	31	*Cleveland	13	
8/24	7	New England	36	
	68		97	

Regular Season (8-8)

Date	Kansas City		Opp.	Att.
9/2	37	Pittsburgh	27	56,709
9/9	27	Cincinnati	22	47,111
9/16	20	*Los Angeles Raiders	22	75,111
9/23	0	Denver	21	74,263
9/30	10	*Cleveland	6	39,225
10/7	16	*New York Jets	17	48,895
10/14	31	*San Diego	13	62,233
10/21	7	New York Jets	28	66,782
10/28	24	*Tampa Bay	20	38,984
11/4	0	Seattle	45	61,396
11/11	16	*Houston	17	39,472
11/18	7	Los Angeles Raiders	17	48,575
11/25	27	New York Giants	28	74,383
12/2	16	*Denver	13	35,537
12/9	34	*Seattle	7	31,860
12/16	42	San Diego	21	40,221
	314		324	840,757

*Home Game

Score by Periods

Kansas City	57	105	61	91	—	314
Opponents	37	127	73	87	—	324

Attendance
Home 371,317   Away 469,440   Total 840,757
Single game home record, 82,094 (11-5-72)
Single season home record, 509,291 (1972)

1984 INDIVIDUAL STATISTICS

Rushing

	Att.	Yds.	Avg.	LG	TD
Heard	165	684	4.1	69t	4
Brown	97	337	3.5	25	4
B. Jackson	50	225	4.5	16	1
Lacy	46	165	3.6	24t	2
Blackledge	18	102	5.7	26	1
Paige	3	19	6.3	9	0
Gunter	15	12	0.8	4	0
Ricks	2	1	0.5	1	0
J. Arnold	1	0	0.0	0	0
Osiecki	1	−2	−2.0	−2	0
Carson	1	−8	−8.0	−8	0
Kenney	9	−8	−0.9	1	0
Kansas City	408	1527	3.7	69t	12
Opponents	523	1980	3.8	52	10

Passing

	Att.	Comp.	Pct.	Yds.	TD	Int.	Tkld.	Rate
Kenney	282	151	53.5	2098	15	10	18/163	80.7
Blackledge	294	147	50.0	1707	6	11	14/136	59.2
Osiecki	17	7	41.2	64	0	1	1/2	27.6
Kansas City	593	305	51.4	3869	21	22	33/301	68.5
Opponents	586	332	56.7	4009	19	30	50/364	67.3

Receiving

	No.	Yds.	Avg.	LG	TD
Marshall	62	912	14.7	37	4
Carson	57	1078	18.9	57	4
Brown	38	236	6.2	17	0
Paige	30	541	18.0	65t	4
Scott	28	253	9.0	27	3
Heard	25	223	8.9	17	0
B. Jackson	15	101	6.7	11	1
Lacy	13	87	6.7	20	2
W. Arnold	11	95	8.6	15	1
Hancock	10	217	21.7	46t	1
Smith	8	69	8.6	16	0
Beckman	7	44	6.3	9	1
Little	1	13	13.0	13	0
Kansas City	305	3869	12.7	65t	21
Opponents	332	4009	12.1	80t	19

Interceptions

	No.	Yds.	Avg.	LG	TD
Cherry	7	140	20.0	67	0
Ross	6	124	20.7	71t	1
Lewis	4	57	14.3	31	0
Radecic	2	54	27.0	35	1
McAlister	2	33	16.5	22	0
Burruss	2	16	8.0	16	0
Daniels	2	11	5.5	11	0
Hill	2	−1	−0.5	0	0
C. Jackson	1	16	16.0	16	0
Blanton	1	14	14.0	14	0
Kremer	1	1	1.0	1	0
Kansas City	30	465	15.5	71t	2
Opponents	22	683	31.0	99t	7

Punting

	No.	Yds.	Avg.	In 20	LG
J. Arnold	98	4397	44.9	22	63
Kansas City	98	4397	44.9	22	63
Opponents	91	3642	40.0	23	83

Punt Returns

	No.	FC	Yds.	Avg.	LG	TD
Smith	39	14	332	8.5	27	0
Hancock	3	1	14	4.7	7	0
Kansas City	42	15	346	8.2	27	0
Opponents	60	6	461	7.7	25	0

Kickoff Returns

	No.	Yds.	Avg.	LG	TD
Paige	27	544	20.1	45	0
Smith	19	391	20.6	39	0
Ricks	5	83	16.6	21	0
Hancock	2	32	16.0	17	0
Scott	1	9	9.0	9	0
Carson	1	2	2.0	2	0
Cherry	1	0	0.0	0	0
Kansas City	56	1061	18.9	45	0
Opponents	64	1354	21.2	47	0

Scoring

	TD R	TD P	TD Rt	PAT	FG	Saf	TP
Lowery	0	0	0	35/35	23/33	0	104
Brown	4	0	0	0/0	0/0	0	24
Carson	0	4	0	0/0	0/0	0	24
Heard	4	0	0	0/0	0/0	0	24
Lacy	2	2	0	0/0	0/0	0	24
Marshall	0	4	0	0/0	0/0	0	24
Paige	0	4	0	0/0	0/0	0	24
Scott	0	3	0	0/0	0/0	0	18
B. Jackson	1	1	0	0/0	0/0	0	12
W. Arnold	0	1	0	0/0	0/0	0	6
Beckman	0	1	0	0/0	0/0	0	6
Blackledge	1	0	0	0/0	0/0	0	6
Hancock	0	1	0	0/0	0/0	0	6
Radecic	0	0	1	0/0	0/0	0	6
Ross	0	0	1	0/0	0/0	0	6
Kansas City	12	21	2	35/35	23/33	0	314
Opponents	10	19	9	37/37	19/27	1	324

FIRST-ROUND SELECTIONS

(If Club had no first-round selection, first player drafted is listed with round in parentheses.)

Year	Player, College, Position
1960	Don Meredith, Southern Methodist, QB
1961	E.J. Holub, Texas Tech, C
1962	Ronnie Bull, Baylor, RB
1963	Buck Buchanan, Grambling, DT
	Ed Budde, Michigan State, G
1964	Pete Beathard, Southern California, QB
1965	Gale Sayers, Kansas, RB
1966	Aaron Brown, Minnesota, DE
1967	Gene Trosch, Miami, DE-DT
1968	Mo Moorman, Texas A&M, G
	George Daney, Texas-El Paso, G
1969	Jim Marsalis, Tennessee State, CB
1970	Sid Smith, Southern California, T
1971	Elmo Wright, Houston, WR
1972	Jeff Kinney, Nebraska, RB
1973	Gary Butler, Rice, TE (2)
1974	Woody Green, Arizona State, RB
1975	Elmore Stephens, Kentucky, TE (2)
1976	Rod Walters, Iowa, G
1977	Gary Green, Baylor, DB
1978	Art Still, Kentucky, DE
1979	Mike Bell, Colorado State, DE
	Steve Fuller, Clemson, QB
1980	Brad Budde, Southern California, G
1981	Willie Scott, South Carolina, TE
1982	Anthony Hancock, Tennessee, WR
1983	Todd Blackledge, Penn State, QB
1984	Bill Maas, Pittsburgh, DT
	John Alt, Iowa, T
1985	Ethan Horton, North Carolina, RB

KANSAS CITY CHIEFS 1985 VETERAN ROSTER

No.	Name	Pos.	Ht.	Wt.	Birth-date	NFL Exp.	College	Birthplace	Residence	'84 Games/ Starts
76	Alt, John	T	6-7	278	5/30/62	2	Iowa	Stuttgart, Germany	New Hope, Minn.	15/1
6	Arnold, Jim	P	6-2	212	1/31/61	3	Vanderbilt	Dalton, Ga.	Lee's Summit, Mo.	16/0
87	Arnold, Walt	TE	6-3	234	8/31/58	6	New Mexico	Galveston, Tex.	Albuquerque, N.M.	14/4*
68	Auer, Scott	G-T	6-4	255	10/4/61	2	Michigan State	Ft. Wayne, Ind.	Ft. Wayne, Ind.	16/0
77	Baldinger, Rich	T-G	6-4	285	12/31/59	4	Wake Forest	Camp Le Jeune, N.C.	Massapequa, N.Y.	14/0
99	Bell, Mike	DE	6-4	250	8/30/57	6	Colorado State	Wichita, Kan.	Overland Park, Kan.	15/14
14	Blackledge, Todd	QB	6-3	225	2/25/61	3	Penn State	Canton, Ohio	Lee's Summit, Mo.	11/8
57	Blanton, Jerry	LB	6-1	236	12/10/56	7	Kentucky	Toledo, Ohio	Lee's Summit, Mo.	10/9
27	Brown, Theotis	RB	6-2	225	4/20/57	7	UCLA	Chicago, Ill.	Kansas City, Mo.	14/7
66	Budde, Brad	G	6-4	260	5/9/58	6	Southern California	Detroit, Mich.	Overland Park, Kan.	16/16
34	Burruss, Lloyd	S	6-0	202	10/31/57	5	Maryland	Charlottesville, Va.	Charlottesville, Va.	16/16
88	Carson, Carlos	WR	5-11	180	12/28/58	6	Louisiana State	Lake Worth, Fla.	Grandview, Mo.	16/16
20	Cherry, Deron	S	5-11	190	9/12/59	5	Rutgers	Riverside, N.J.	Kansas City, Mo.	16/16
65	Condon, Tom	G	6-3	275	12/26/52	12	Boston College	Derby, Conn.	Kansas City, Mo.	16/16
50	Daniels, Calvin	LB	6-3	236	12/26/58	4	North Carolina	Morehead City, N.C.	Grandview, Mo.	16/16
73	†Dawson, Mike	NT	6-3	245	10/16/53	10	Arizona	Tucson, Ariz.	Tucson, Ariz.	9/0
38	Gunter, Michael	RB	5-11	205	1/18/61	2	Tulsa	Gladewater, Tex.	Blue Springs, Mo.	4/0
90	t-Hamm, Bob	DE	6-4	263	4/24/59	3	Nevada-Reno	Kansas City, Mo.	Reno, Nev.	12/12
82	Hancock, Anthony	WR-KR	6-0	200	6/10/60	4	Tennessee	Cleveland, Ohio	Independence, Mo.	14/0
44	Heard, Herman	RB	5-10	184	11/24/61	2	Southern Colorado	Denver, Colo.	Kansas City, Mo.	16/9
60	Herkenhoff, Matt	T	6-4	275	4/2/51	10	Minnesota	Melrose, Minn.	Overland Park, Kan.	15/15
23	Hill, Greg	CB	6-1	189	2/12/61	3	Oklahoma State	Orange, Tex.	Houston, Tex.	15/1
93	Holle, Eric	DE-NT	6-4	250	9/5/60	2	Texas	Austin, Tex.	Austin, Tex.	16/1
43	Jackson, Billy	RB	5-10	215	9/13/59	5	Alabama	Phenix City, Ala.	Phenix City, Ala.	16/9
52	Jolly, Ken	LB	6-2	220	2/28/62	2	Mid-America Nazarene	Dallas, Tex.	Kansas City, Mo.	16/0
9	Kenney, Bill	QB	6-4	211	1/20/55	7	Northern Colorado	San Francisco, Calif.	Lee's Summit, Mo.	9/8
91	Kremer, Ken	NT	6-4	260	7/16/57	7	Ball State	Hammond, Ind.	Merriam, Kan.	16/1
40	Lacy, Ken	RB	6-0	222	11/1/60	2	Tulsa	Dallas, Tex.	Dallas, Tex.	15/4
26	Lane, Skip	CB-S	6-1	208	1/30/60	2	Mississippi	Norwalk, Conn.	Westport, Conn.	4/0*
29	Lewis, Albert	CB	6-2	190	10/6/60	3	Grambling	Mansfield, La.	Lee's Summit, Mo.	15/15
71	†Lindstrom, Dave	DE	6-6	255	11/16/54	8	Boston University	Cambridge, Mass.	Overland Park, Kan.	16/2
62	Lingner, Adam	C-G	6-4	250	11/2/60	3	Illinois	Indianapolis, Ind.	Lee's Summit, Mo.	16/0
84	Little, Dave	TE	6-2	239	4/18/61	2	Middle Tennessee State	Selma, Calif.	Fresno, Calif.	10/1
8	Lowery, Nick	K	6-4	189	5/27/56	6	Dartmouth	Munich, Germany	Lee's Summit, Mo.	16/0
72	Lutz, David	T	6-5	285	12/30/59	3	Georgia Tech	Monroe, N.C.	Peachland, N.C.	7/6
63	Maas, Bill	NT	6-4	265	3/2/62	2	Pittsburgh	Newton Square, Pa.	Lee's Summit, Mo.	14/14
94	McAlister, Ken	LB	6-5	220	4/15/60	4	San Francisco	Oakland, Calif.	Kansas City, Mo.	15/9
89	Marshall, Henry	WR	6-2	220	8/9/54	10	Missouri	Broxton, Ga.	Kansas City, Mo.	16/16
11	Osiecki, Sandy	QB	6-5	202	5/18/60	2	Arizona State	Ansonia, Conn.	Lee's Summit, Mo.	4/0
83	Paige, Stephone	WR	6-1	180	10/15/61	3	Fresno State	Slidell, La.	Fresno, Calif.	16/1
95	Paine, Jeff	LB	6-2	224	8/19/61	2	Texas A&M	Garland, Tex.	Richardson, Tex.	14/3
21	Parker, Kerry	CB	6-1	200	10/3/55	2	Grambling	New Orleans, La.	New Orleans, La.	15/0
97	Radecic, Scott	LB	6-3	240	6/14/62	2	Penn State	Pittsburgh, Pa.	State College, Pa.	16/2
30	Robinson, Mark	S	5-10	206	9/13/62	2	Penn State	Silver Spring, Md.	Kansas City, Mo.	16/0
31	Ross, Kevin	CB	5-9	180	1/16/62	2	Temple	Paulsboro, N.J.	Camden, N.J.	16/16
70	†Rourke, Jim	T-G	6-5	263	2/10/57	6	Boston College	Weymouth, Mass.	North Abington, Mass.	13/10
53	Rush, Bob	C	6-5	264	2/27/55	8	Memphis State	Santa Monica, Calif.	Germantown, Tenn.	16/16
81	Scott, Willie	TE	6-4	245	2/13/59	5	South Carolina	Newberry, S.C.	Columbia, S.C.	15/12
86	Smith, J.T.	WR-KR	6-2	185	10/29/55	8	North Texas State	Leonard, Tex.	Big Spring, Tex.	15/0
59	Spani, Gary	LB	6-2	228	1/9/56	8	Kansas State	Satanta, Kan.	Lee's Summit, Mo.	14/14
67	Still, Art	DE	6-7	257	12/5/55	8	Kentucky	Camden, N.J.	Liberty, Mo.	16/16
35	Thomas, Ken	RB	5-9	211	2/11/60	2	San Jose State	Hanford, Calif.	Blue Springs, Mo.	0*
56	Zamberlin, John	LB	6-2	226	2/13/56	7	Pacific Lutheran	Tacoma, Wash.	Tacoma, Wash.	8/7

* W. Arnold played 4 games with Washington, 10 with Kansas City in '84; Lane played 3 games with N.Y. Jets, 1 with Kansas City; Thomas missed '84 season due to injury.

†Option playout; subject to developments.

t-Chiefs traded for Hamm (Houston).

Traded—Linebacker Charles Jackson to New York Jets.

Also played with Chiefs in '84—TE Ed Beckman (13 games), CB Van Jakes (8), RB Lawrence Ricks (5), QB David Whitehurst (active for 5 games but did not play).

COACHING STAFF

Head Coach,
John Mackovic

Pro Career: Begins third season as Chiefs head coach. Came to the Chiefs after serving as quarterback coach with Dallas Cowboys in 1981-82. No pro playing experience. Career record: 14-18.

Background: Played quarterback for Wake Forest 1961-64. Was freshman coach at Army in 1967-68 before joining San Jose State as offensive coordinator 1969-70. Returned to Army as an assistant 1971-72, then to Arizona 1973-76, and Purdue 1977. Became head coach at Wake Forest 1978-80 before going to the Cowboys.

Personal: Born October 1, 1943, Barberton, Ohio. John and his wife, Arlene, live in Kansas City, and have two children—Aimee and John III.

Assistant Coaches

David Brazil, defensive assistant; born March 25, 1936, Detroit, Mich., lives in Kansas City. No college or pro playing experience. College coach: Holy Cross 1968-69, Tulsa 1970-71, Eastern Michigan 1972-74, Boston College 1978-79. Pro coach: Detroit Wheels (WFL) 1975, Chicago Fire (WFL) 1976, joined Chiefs in 1984.

Walt Corey, defensive line; born May 9, 1938, Latrobe, Pa., lives in Kansas City. Defensive end Miami 1957-59. Pro linebacker Kansas City Chiefs 1960-66. College coach: Utah State 1967-69, Miami 1970-71. Pro coach: Kansas City Chiefs 1971-74, Cleveland Browns 1975-77, rejoined Chiefs in 1978.

Dan Daniel, inside linebackers; born April 10, 1933, Huron, S.D., lives in Kansas City. Quarterback-defensive back Huron College 1958-62. No pro playing experience. College coach: MacAlister College 1965, Colorado State 1966-69, Navy 1970, Wyoming 1971, Houston 1972-77. Pro coach: Edmonton Eskimos (CFL) 1978-81, Calgary Stampeders (CFL) 1982, joined Chiefs in 1983.

Marty Galbraith, offensive line; born February 3, 1950, Joplin, Mo., lives in Overland Park, Kan. Defensive back Missouri Southern State 1970-72. No pro playing experience. College Coach: Northwest Missouri State 1973, Purdue 1977, Wake Forest 1978-82. Pro Coach: Tampa Bay Bandits (USFL) 1983-84, first year with Chiefs.

Doug Graber, defensive backs and defensive quality control; born September 26, 1944, Detroit, Mich., lives in Kansas City. Defensive back Wayne State 1963-66. No pro playing experience. College coach: Michigan Tech 1969-71, Eastern Michigan 1972-75, Ball State 1976-77, Wisconsin 1978-81, Montana State 1982 (head coach). Pro coach: Joined Chiefs in 1983.

J. D. Helm, offensive assistant; born December 27, 1940, El Dorado Springs, Mo., lives in Overland Park, Kan. Running back Kansas 1959-60. No pro playing experience. College coach: Brigham Young 1969-75. Pro coach: Joined Chiefs in 1976.

C. T. Hewgley, offensive and defensive lines-coordinator of strength and conditioning program; born August 22, 1925, Nashville, Tenn., lives in Kansas City. Tackle Wyoming 1947-50. No pro playing experience. College coach: Miami 1968-70, Wyoming 1971-73, Nebraska-Omaha 1974 (head coach), Michigan State 1976-79, Arizona State 1980-82. Pro coach: Joined Chiefs in 1983.

Pete McCulley, quarterbacks; born November 29, 1931, Franklin, Miss., lives in Kansas City. Quarterback Louisiana Tech 1954-56. No pro playing experience. College coach: Stephen F. Austin 1959, Houston 1960-61, Baylor 1963-69, Navy 1970-72. Pro coach: Baltimore Colts 1973-75, Washington Redskins 1976-77, San Francisco 49ers 1978 (head coach nine games), New York Jets 1979-82, joined Chiefs in 1983.

Willie Peete, offensive backs; born September 14, 1937, Mesa, Ariz., lives in Kansas City. Wide receiver Arizona 1956-59. No pro playing experience. College coach: Arizona 1970-82. Pro coach: Joined Chiefs in 1983.

KANSAS CITY CHIEFS 1985 FIRST-YEAR ROSTER

Name	Pos.	Ht.	Wt.	Birth-date	College	Birthplace	Residence	How Acq.
Aldisert, Caesar	LB	6-3	220	12/13/62	Pittsburgh	Pittsburgh, Pa.	Pittsburgh, Pa.	FA
Armentrout, Mike	S	5-10	193	6/9/63	Southwest Missouri	Champaign, Ill.	Springfield, Mo.	D9
Bostic, John	CB	5-9	175	10/6/62	Bethune-Cookman	Titusville, Fla.	Jacksonville, Fla.	D6
Burse, William	LB	6-2	232	9/3/61	Kentucky State	Christams, Ky.	Hopkinsville, Ky.	FA
Byford, Bill	DE	6-3	247	12/9/62	N.W. Oklahoma	Stillwater, Okla.	Enid, Okla.	FA
Cocroft, Sherman (1)	S	6-1	193	8/29/61	San Jose State	Mobile, Ala.	Watsonville, Calif.	FA
Courtney, Matt	S	5-11	188	12/21/61	Idaho State	Greeley, Colo.	Littleton, Colo.	FA
Daniels, Bob	DE	6-2	255	3/10/63	Kansas State	Wichita, Kan.	Manhattan, Kan.	FA
Eisher, Doug	G	6-2	260	3/16/62	Nevada-Las Vegas	Pomona, Calif.	Chino, Calif.	FA
Fiala, Dan	LB	6-3	220	2/3/63	Colorado State	Omaha, Neb.	Denver, Colo.	FA
Fojtik, Brad	DE-NT	6-5	270	9/17/61	Florida State	Winter Haven, Fla.	Auburndale, Fla.	FA
Goodell, Terry	T	6-3	258	2/12/62	Central Michigan	Mt. Pleasant, Mich.	Mt. Pleasant, Mich.	FA
Green, Willie	LB	6-2	228	6/5/61	Arizona State	Youngstown, Ohio	Tempe, Ariz.	FA
Gwinn, Derek (1)	G	6-3	251	12/20/60	Georgia Tech	Winter Park, Fla.	Winter Park, Fla.	FA
Harrington, Scott	NT	6-1	260	4/2/63	Boston College	Norwood, Mass.	Norwood, Mass.	FA
Hayes, Jonathan	TE	6-5	233	8/11/62	Iowa	Pittsburgh, Pa.	Bridgefield, Pa.	D2
Heffernan, Dave	T-G-C	6-3	255	10/28/62	Miami	Boston, Mass.	Miami, Fla.	D7a
Hill, Andy	WR	5-8	169	1/26/62	Missouri	Kansas City, Mo.	Trenton, Mo.	FA
Hillary, Ira	WR	5-10	186	11/13/62	South Carolina	Edgefield, S.C.	Edgefield, S.C.	D8
Horton, Ethan	RB	6-2	229	12/19/62	North Carolina	Kannapolis, N.C.	Kannapolis, N.C.	D1
Jackson, Chris	C	6-3	265	8/21/61	Southern Methodist	Suffern, N.Y.	Suffern, N.Y.	D11
Jones, E.J. (1)	RB	5-11	219	2/1/62	Kansas	Chicago, Ill.	Chicago, Ill.	FA
King, Bruce	RB	6-1	219	1/7/63	Purdue	Dale, Ind.	Dale, Ind.	D5
Lane, Skip (1)	S	6-1	208	1/30/60	Mississippi	Norwalk, Conn.	Westport, Conn.	FA
Lang, Mark (1)	LB	6-2	235	6/27/61	Texas	Nonahans, Tex.	Kansas City, Mo.	D12('84)
LeBel, Harper	C	6-4	251	7/14/63	Colorado State	Granada Hills, Calif.	Sherman Oaks, Calif.	D12
McCashland, Mike	S	6-0	194	6/15/61	Nebraska	Lincoln, Neb.	Lincoln, Neb.	FA
Merritt, Charles	LB	6-1	229	1/13/63	Carson-Newman	Valdosta, Ga.	Valdosta, Ga.	FA
Nelson, Dirk	P	6-0	195	7/23/62	Kansas	Wichita, Kan.	Derby, Kan.	FA
O'Brien, Joe	NT	6-1	258	11/17/61	Montana State	Spencer, Iowa	Le Mats, Iowa	FA
Olderman, Robert	G	6-4	272	6/5/62	Virginia	Brookville, Pa.	Atlanta, Ga.	D4
Polk, Scott	LB	6-3	227	11/10/61	Texas A&M	Dallas, Tex.	Dallas, Tex.	FA
Pryor, David (1)	P	6-3	230	6/18/60	Southern California	Compton, Calif.	Marina Del Rey, Calif.	FA
Robinson, Charles	T	6-3	263	2/25/63	Bethune-Cookman	Orlando, Fla.	Orlando, Fla.	FA
Robinson, Eric	RB	5-8	183	12/12/60	Indiana State	Washington, D.C.	Gaithersburg, Md.	FA
Russell, Kevin	QB	6-0	180	6/12/62	California St., Pa.	East Lansing, Mich.	Pittsburgh, Pa.	FA
Schwartzburg, Dodge	K	5-7	166	5/6/62	Kansas	Elgin, Ill.	Lawrence, Kan.	FA
Smith, Chris	RB	6-0	222	6/1/63	Notre Dame	Cincinnati, Ohio	Cincinnati, Ohio	FA
Smith, Jeff	RB	5-9	201	3/22/62	Nebraska	Wichita, Kan.	Wichita, Kan.	D10
Stephenson, Larry	QB	6-2	194	4/23/61	Livingston	Montgomery, Ala.	Livingston, Ala.	FA
Stevens, Rufus (1)	WR	6-3	182	1/13/61	Grambling	Monroe, La.	Monroe, La.	D6('84)
Thompson, Bennie	S	6-0	197	2/10/63	Grambling	New Orleans, La.	New Orleans, La.	FA
Thomson, Vince	DE	6-4	265	9/4/63	Missouri Western	St. Louis, Mo.	St. Louis, Mo.	D7
Turner, Bill	C	6-5	272	3/24/63	Texas-El Paso	Alamogordo, N.M.	Tularosa, N.M.	FA
Voelker, Randy	G	6-4	263	5/17/63	Kansas State	Clay Center, Kan.	Manhattan, Kan.	FA
Walter, John	TE	6-2	227	12/15/62	Penn State	Camden, N.J.	Westmont, N.J.	FA
Williams, Jeff	WR	6-2	184	8/28/62	Hampton Institute	Pompano Beach, Fla.	Pompano Beach, Fla.	FA
Wood, David	WR	6-1	190	1/26/62	West Texas State	Stillwater, Okla.	Canyon, Tex.	FA
Young, Renard	CB	5-10	178	7/31/61	Nevada-Las Vegas	Los Angeles, Calif.	Los Angeles, Calif.	FA

Players who report to an NFL team for the first time are designated on rosters as rookies (R). If a player reported to an NFL training camp in a previous year but was not on the active squad for three or more regular season or postseason games, he is listed on the first-year roster and designated by a (1). Thereafter, a player who is on the active squad for three or more regular season or postseason games is credited with an additional year of <u>playing experience</u>.

NOTES

_____

_____

_____

_____

_____

_____

_____

Jim Vechiarella, outside linebackers-special teams; born February 20, 1937, Youngstown, Ohio, lives in Kansas City. Linebacker Youngstown State 1955-57. No pro playing experience. College coach: Youngstown State 1964-74, Southern Illinois 1976-77, Tulane 1978-80. Pro coach: Charlotte Hornets (WFL) 1975, Los Angeles Rams 1981-82, joined Chiefs in 1983.

Richard Williamson, receivers; born April 13, 1941, Fort Deposit, Ala., lives in Kansas City. Wide receiver Alabama 1959-60. No pro playing experience. College coach: Arkansas 1968-69, 1972-74, Alabama 1963-67, 1970-71, Memphis State 1975-80. Pro coach: Joined Chiefs in 1983.

LOS ANGELES RAIDERS

**American Football Conference
Western Division**

Team Colors: Silver and Black

332 Center Street
El Segundo, California 90245
Telephone: (213) 322-3451

Club Officials

Managing General Partner: Al Davis
Executive Assistant: Al LoCasale
Player Personnel: Ron Wolf
Business Manager: Ken LaRue
Senior Administrators: Tom Grimes, Irv Kaze,
 John Herrera
Marketing/Promotions: Mike Ornstein
Community Relations: Gil Hernandez,
 Calvin Peterson
Ticket Operations: Peter Eiges
Trainers: George Anderson, H. Rod Martin
Equipment Manager: Richard Romanski

Stadium: Los Angeles Memorial Coliseum •
 Capacity: 92,516
 3911 South Figueroa Street
 Los Angeles, California 90037

Playing Surface: Grass

Training Camp: Hilton Hotel
 Oxnard, California 93030

1985 SCHEDULE

Preseason

Aug. 10	**San Francisco**	6:00
Aug. 18	**Washington**	1:00
Aug. 24	**Miami**	6:00
Aug. 30	at Cleveland	7:30

Regular Season

Sept. 8	**New York Jets**	1:00
Sept. 12	at Kansas City (Thursday)	7:00
Sept. 22	**San Francisco**	1:00
Sept. 29	at New England	1:00
Oct. 6	**Kansas City**	1:00
Oct. 13	**New Orleans**	1:00
Oct. 20	at Cleveland	1:00
Oct. 28	**San Diego** (Monday)	6:00
Nov. 3	at Seattle	1:00
Nov. 10	at San Diego	1:00
Nov. 17	**Cincinnati**	1:00
Nov. 24	**Denver**	1:00
Dec. 1	at Atlanta	4:00
Dec. 8	at Denver	2:00
Dec. 15	**Seattle**	1:00
Dec. 23	at L.A. Rams (Monday)	6:00

RAIDERS COACHING HISTORY

Oakland 1960-81
(245-131-11)

1960-61	Eddie Erdelatz*	6-10-0
1961-62	Marty Feldman**	2-15-0
1962	Red Conkright	1-8-0
1963-65	Al Davis	23-16-3
1966-68	John Rauch	35-10-1
1969-78	John Madden	112-39-7
1979-84	Tom Flores	66-33-0

*Released after two games in 1961
**Released after five games in 1962

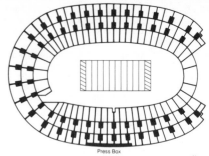

Press Box

MEMORIAL COLISEUM

RECORD HOLDERS
Individual Records — Career

Category	Name	Performance
Rushing (Yds.)	Mark van Eeghen, 1974-1981	5,907
Passing (Yds.)	Ken Stabler, 1970-79	19,078
Passing (TDs)	Ken Stabler, 1970-79	150
Receiving (No.)	Fred Biletnikoff, 1965-1978	589
Receiving (Yds.)	Fred Biletnikoff, 1965-1978	8,974
Interceptions	Willie Brown, 1967-1978	39
Punting (Avg.)	Ray Guy, 1973-1984	42.8
Punt Return (Avg.)	Claude Gibson, 1963-65	12.6
Kickoff Return (Avg.)	Jack Larscheid, 1960-61	28.4
Field Goals	George Blanda, 1967-1975	156
Touchdowns (Tot.)	Fred Biletnikoff, 1967-1978	77
Points	George Blanda, 1967-1975	863

Individual Records — Single Season

Category	Name	Performance
Rushing (Yds.)	Mark van Eeghen, 1977	1,273
Passing (Yds.)	Ken Stabler, 1979	3,615
Passing (TDs)	Daryle Lamonica, 1969	34
Receiving (No.)	Todd Christensen, 1983	92
Receiving (Yds.)	Art Powell, 1964	1,361
Interceptions	Lester Hayes, 1980	13
Punting (Avg.)	Ray Guy, 1973	45.3
Punt Return (Avg.)	Claude Gibson, 1963	14.4
Kickoff Return (Avg.)	Harold Hart, 1975	30.5
Field Goals	George Blanda, 1973	23
Touchdowns (Tot.)	Marcus Allen, 1984	18
Points	George Blanda, 1968	117

Individual Records — Single Game

Category	Name	Performance
Rushing (Yds.)	Clem Daniels, 10-20-63	200
Passing (Yds.)	Cotton Davidson, 10-25-64	427
Passing (TDs)	Tom Flores, 12-22-63	6
	Daryle Lamonica, 10-19-69	6
Receiving (No.)	Dave Casper, 10-3-76	12
Receiving (Yds.)	Art Powell, 12-22-63	247
Interceptions	Many times	3
	Last time by Charles Phillips, 12-8-75	
Field Goals	Many times	4
	Last time by Chris Bahr, 10-23-83	
Touchdowns (Tot.)	Art Powell, 12-22-63	4
	Marcus Allen, 9-24-84	4
Points	Art Powell, 12-22-63	24
	Marcus Allen, 9-24-84	24

1984 TEAM STATISTICS

	L.A. Raiders	Opp.
Total First Downs	301	297
Rushing	114	107
Passing	162	147
Penalty	25	43
Third Down: Made/Att.	80/223	72/239
Fourth Down: Made/Att.	6/9	5/11
Total Net Yards	5244	4644
Avg. Per Game	327.8	290.3
Total Plays	1061	1089
Avg. Per Play	4.9	4.3
Net Yards Rushing	1886	1892
Avg. Per Game	117.9	118.3
Total Rushes	516	517
Net Yards Passing	3358	2752
Avg. Per Game	209.9	172.0
Tackled/Yards Lost	54/360	64/516
Gross Yards	3718	3268
Att./Completions	491/266	508/254
Completion Pct.	54.2	50.0
Had Intercepted	28	20
Punts/Avg.	91/41.9	117/43.3
Net Punting Avg.	35.4	35.6
Penalties/Yards Lost	143/1209	121/1061
Fumbles/Ball Lost	42/20	28/14
Touchdowns	44	33
Rushing	19	12
Passing	21	19
Returns	4	2
Avg. Time of Possession	29:26	30:34

1984 TEAM RECORD
Preseason (1-3)

Date	Los Angeles Raiders		Opponents
8/4	10	San Francisco	13
8/10	21	Washington	20
8/19	23	*Miami	29
8/24	14	*New York Jets	20
	68		82

Regular Season (11-5)

Date	Los Angeles Raiders		Opp.	Att.
9/2	24	Houston	14	49,092
9/9	28	*Green Bay	7	46,269
9/16	22	Kansas City	20	75,111
9/24	33	*San Diego	30	76,131
9/30	13	Denver	16	74,833
10/7	28	*Seattle	14	77,904
10/14	23	*Minnesota	20	49,276
10/21	44	San Diego	37	57,442
10/28	19	*Denver (OT)	22	91,020
11/4	6	Chicago	17	59,858
11/12	14	Seattle	17	64,001
11/18	17	*Kansas City	7	48,575
11/25	21	*Indianapolis	7	40,289
12/2	45	Miami	34	71,222
12/10	24	Detroit	3	66,710
12/16	7	*Pittsburgh	13	83,056
	368		278	1,030,789

*Home Game   (OT) Overtime

Score by Periods

L.A. Raiders	57	85	79	147	0	—	368
Opponents	47	75	58	95	3	—	278

Attendance
Home 512,520   Away 518,269   Total 1,030,789
Single game home record, 90,334 (1-1-84)
Single season home record, 557,881 (1972;
Oakland Coliseum); 512,520 (1984; L.A. Coliseum).

1984 INDIVIDUAL STATISTICS

Rushing

	Att.	Yds.	Avg.	LG	TD
Allen	275	1168	4.2	52t	13
Hawkins	108	376	3.5	17	3
King	67	254	3.8	18	0
Wilson	30	56	1.9	14	1
Plunkett	16	14	0.9	9	1
Humm	2	7	3.5	9	0
Willis	5	4	0.8	2	0
McCall	1	3	3.0	3	0
Jensen	3	3	1.0	2	1
Montgomery	1	1	1.0	1	0
Pruitt	8	0	0.0	3	0
L.A. Raiders	516	1886	3.7	52t	19
Opponents	517	1892	3.7	32t	12

Passing

	Att.	Comp.	Pct.	Yds.	TD	Int.	Tkld.	Rate
Wilson	282	153	54.3	2151	15	17	37/228	71.7
Plunkett	198	108	54.5	1473	6	10	13/103	67.6
Humm	7	4	57.1	56	0	1	3/27	43.5
Allen	4	1	25.0	38	0	0	1/2	66.7
Raiders	491	266	54.2	3718	21	28	54/360	69.3
Opponents	508	254	50.0	3268	19	20	64/516	66.6

Receiving

	No.	Yds.	Avg.	LG	TD
Christensen	80	1007	12.6	38	7
Allen	64	758	11.8	92	5
Barnwell	45	851	18.9	51t	2
Branch	27	401	14.9	47	0
Williams	22	509	23.1	75t	4
King	14	99	7.1	15	0
Hawkins	7	51	7.3	15	0
Casper	4	29	7.3	13	2
Pruitt	2	12	6.0	8	0
Jensen	1	1	1.0	1t	1
L.A. Raiders	266	3718	14.0	92	21
Opponents	254	3268	12.9	70t	19

Interceptions

	No.	Yds.	Avg.	LG	TD
Haynes	6	220	36.7	97t	1
McElroy	4	42	10.5	31	0
Martin	2	31	15.5	17	1
M. Davis	2	11	5.5	11	0
Barnes	1	15	15.0	15	0
Van Pelt	1	9	9.0	9	0
J. Davis	1	8	8.0	8	0
Hayes	1	3	3.0	3	0
McKinney	1	0	0.0	0	0
Watts	1	0	0.0	0	0
L.A. Raiders	20	339	17.0	97t	2
Opponents	28	300	10.7	71t	2

Punting

	No.	Yds.	Avg.	In 20	LG
Guy	91	3809	41.9	25	63
L.A. Raiders	91	3809	41.9	25	63
Opponents	117	5071	43.3	23	65

Punt Returns

	No.	FC	Yds.	Avg.	LG	TD
Pruitt	53	16	473	8.9	38	0
Montgomery	14	1	194	13.9	69t	1
L.A. Raiders	67	17	667	10.0	69t	1
Opponents	34	14	345	10.1	35	0

Kickoff Returns

	No.	Yds.	Avg.	LG	TD
Williams	24	621	25.9	62	0
Montgomery	26	555	21.3	42	0
Pruitt	3	16	5.3	13	0
Jensen	1	11	11.0	11	0
Willis	1	13	13.0	13	0
McKinney	1	0	0.0	0	0
L.A. Raiders	56	1216	21.7	62	0
Opponents	61	1063	17.4	38	0

Scoring

	TD R	TD P	TD Rt	PAT	FG	Saf	TP
Allen	13	5	0	0/0	0/0	0	108
Bahr	0	0	0	40/42	20/27	0	100
Christensen	0	7	0	0/0	0/0	0	42
Williams	0	4	0	0/0	0/0	0	24
Hawkins	3	0	0	0/0	0/0	0	18
Martin	0	0	2	0/0	0/0	1	14
Barnwell	0	2	0	0/0	0/0	0	12
Casper	0	2	0	0/0	0/0	0	12
Jensen	1	1	0	0/0	0/0	0	12
Haynes	0	0	1	0/0	0/0	0	6
Montgomery	0	0	1	0/0	0/0	0	6
Plunkett	1	0	0	0/0	0/0	0	6
Wilson	1	0	0	0/0	0/0	0	6
L.A. Raiders	19	21	4	40/44	20/27	2	368
Opponents	12	19	2	29/33	17/21	0	278

FIRST-ROUND SELECTIONS

(If Club had no first-round selection, first player drafted is listed with round in parentheses.)

Year	Player, College, Position
1960	Dale Hackbart, Wisconsin, CB
1961	Joe Rutgens, Illinois, DT
1962	Roman Gabriel, North Carolina State, QB
1963	George Wilson, Alabama, RB (6)
1964	Tony Lorick, Arizona State, RB
1965	Harry Schuh, Memphis State, T
1966	Rodger Bird, Kentucky, S
1967	Gene Upshaw, Texas A&I, G
1968	Eldridge Dickey, Tennessee State, QB
1969	Art Thoms, Syracuse, DT
1970	Raymond Chester, Morgan State, TE
1971	Jack Tatum, Ohio State, S
1972	Mike Siani, Villanova, WR
1973	Ray Guy, Southern Mississippi, K-P
1974	Henry Lawrence, Florida A&M, T
1975	Neal Colzie, Ohio State, DB
1976	Charles Philyaw, Texas Southern, DT (2)
1977	Mike Davis, Colorado, DB (2)
1978	Dave Browning, Washington, DE (2)
1979	Willie Jones, Florida State, DE (2)
1980	Marc Wilson, Brigham Young, QB
1981	Ted Watts, Texas Tech, DB
	Curt Marsh, Washington, T
1982	Marcus Allen, Southern California, RB
1983	Don Mosebar, Southern California, T
1984	Sean Jones, Northeastern, DE (2)
1985	Jesse Hester, Florida State, WR

LOS ANGELES RAIDERS 1985 VETERAN ROSTER

No.	Name	Pos.	Ht.	Wt.	Birth-date	NFL Exp.	College	Birthplace	Residence	'84 Games/Starts
97	Ackerman, Rick	NT	6-4	250	6/16/59	4	Memphis State	LaGrange, Ill.	Chula Vista, Calif.	15/2*
59	Adams, Stanley	LB	6-2	215	5/22/60	2	Memphis State	Marion, Ark.	Crawfordsville, Ark.	4/3
32	Allen, Marcus	RB	6-2	205	3/22/60	4	Southern California	San Diego, Calif.	Brentwood, Calif.	16/16
77	Alzado, Lyle	DE	6-3	260	4/3/49	14	Yankton	Brooklyn, N.Y.	Manhattan Beach, Calif.	16/16
10	Bahr, Chris	K	5-10	170	2/3/53	10	Penn State	State College, Pa.	Rancho Palos Verdes, Calif.	16/0
56	Barnes, Jeff	LB	6-2	230	3/1/55	9	California	Philadelphia, Pa.	Hayward, Calif.	16/5
80	Barnwell, Malcolm	WR	5-11	185	6/28/58	5	Virginia Union	Charleston, S.C.	Midlothian, Va.	16/15
86	Belk, Rocky	WR	6-0	185	6/20/60	2	Miami	Alexandria, Va.	Alexandria, Va.	0*
21	Branch, Cliff	WR	5-11	170	8/1/48	14	Colorado	Houston, Tex.	Redondo Beach, Calif.	14/14
66	Bryant, Warren	T	6-7	285	11/11/55	9	Kentucky	Miami, Fla.	Roswell, Ga.	9/0*
54	Byrd, Darryl	LB	6-1	220	9/3/60	3	Illinois	San Diego, Calif.	Union City, Calif.	16/1
57	Caldwell, Tony	LB	6-1	225	4/1/61	3	Washington	Los Angeles, Calif.	Seattle, Wash.	16/0
87	Casper, Dave	TE	6-4	240	2/2/52	12	Notre Dame	Bemidji, Minn.	Waconia, Minn.	7/0
46	Christensen, Todd	TE	6-3	230	8/3/56	7	Brigham Young	Bellefonte, Pa.	El Segundo, Calif.	16/16
50	†Dalby, Dave	C	6-3	255	8/19/50	14	UCLA	Alexandria, Minn.	Pleasanton, Calif.	16/14
79	Davis, Bruce	T	6-6	280	6/21/56	7	UCLA	Rutherfordton, N.C.	Palos Verdes, Calif.	16/15
45	Davis, James	CB	6-0	190	6/12/57	4	Southern	Los Angeles, Calif.	Baton Rouge, La.	15/0
36	Davis, Mike	S	6-3	205	4/15/56	8	Colorado	Los Angeles, Calif.	Palos Verdes, Calif.	16/16
8	Guy, Ray	P	6-3	195	12/22/49	13	Southern Mississippi	Swainsboro, Ga.	Hattiesburg, Miss.	16/0
73	Hannah, Charley	G	6-5	260	7/26/55	9	Alabama	Canton, Ga.	Tampa, Fla.	15/9
27	Hawkins, Frank	RB	5-9	210	7/3/59	5	Nevada-Reno	Las Vegas, Nev.	Las Vegas, Nev.	16/0
37	Hayes, Lester	CB	6-0	200	1/22/55	9	Texas A&M	Houston, Tex.	Marina Del Rey, Calif.	16/16
22	Haynes, Mike	CB	6-2	190	7/1/53	10	Arizona State	Denison, Tex.	Hermosa Beach, Calif.	16/16
11	Humm, David	QB	6-2	190	4/2/52	11	Nebraska	Las Vegas, Nev.	Las Vegas, Nev.	3/0
31	Jensen, Derrick	TE-RB	6-1	215	4/27/56	7	Texas-Arlington	Waukegan, Ill.	Marina Del Rey, Calif.	16/0
99	Jones, Sean	DE	6-7	265	12/19/62	2	Northeastern	Kingston, Jamaica	Marina Del Rey, Calif.	16/0
74	Jordan, Shelby	T	6-7	280	1/23/52	10	Washington, Mo.	St. Louis, Mo.	Rancho Palos Verdes, Calif.	11/1
52	Junkin, Trey	LB	6-2	220	1/23/61	3	Louisiana Tech	Little Rock, Ark.	Winnfield, La.	14/0*
33	King, Kenny	RB	5-11	205	3/7/57	7	Oklahoma	Clarendon, Tex.	Marina Del Rey, Calif.	16/16
62	Kinlaw, Reggie	NT	6-2	245	1/9/57	6	Oklahoma	Miami, Fla.	Northridge, Calif.	13/13
	Krimm, John	S	6-1	190	5/30/60	2	Notre Dame	Philadelphia, Pa.	River Ridge, La.	0*
70	Lawrence, Henry	T	6-4	270	9/26/51	12	Florida A&M	Danville, Pa.	Palmetto, Fla.	16/16
75	Long, Howie	DE	6-5	270	1/6/60	5	Villanova	Sommerville, Mass.	Redondo Beach, Calif.	16/16
60	Marsh, Curt	G	6-5	270	8/25/59	4	Washington	Tacoma, Wash.	Snohomish, Wash.	16/7
53	Martin, Rod	LB	6-2	225	4/7/54	9	Southern California	Welch, W. Va.	Manhattan Beach, Calif.	16/16
65	Marvin, Mickey	G	6-4	265	10/5/55	9	Tennessee	Hendersonville, N.C.	Etowah, N.C.	9/6
43	McCall, Joe	RB	6-0	195	2/17/62	2	Pittsburgh	Miami, Fla.	Miami, Fla.	3/0
26	McElroy, Vann	S	6-2	190	1/13/60	4	Baylor	Birmingham, Ala.	Manhattan Beach, Calif.	16/16
23	McKinney, Odis	S	6-2	190	5/19/57	8	Colorado	Detroit, Mich.	Woodland Hills, Calif.	16/1
55	Millen, Matt	LB	6-2	250	3/12/58	6	Penn State	Hokendauqua, Pa.	Whitehall, Pa.	16/12
28	†Montgomery, Cle	WR	5-8	180	7/1/56	5	Abilene Christian	Greenville, Miss.	Los Angeles, Calif.	16/0
72	Mosebar, Don	G	6-6	260	9/11/61	3	Southern California	Yakima, Wash.	Manhattan Beach, Calif.	10/10
51	†Nelson, Bob	LB	6-4	235	6/30/53	9	Nebraska	Stillwater, Minn.	Wayzata, Minn.	12/11
81	Parker, Andy	TE	6-5	240	9/8/61	2	Utah	Redlands, Calif.	Laguna Hills, Calif.	9/0
71	Pickel, Bill	NT	6-5	260	11/5/59	3	Rutgers	Queens, N.Y.	Maspeth, N.Y.	16/3
16	Plunkett, Jim	QB	6-2	220	12/5/47	15	Stanford	San Jose, Calif.	Atherton, Calif.	8/6
34	Pruitt, Greg	RB	5-10	190	8/18/51	13	Oklahoma	Houston, Tex.	Shaker Heights, Ohio	15/0
88	Seale, Sam	WR	5-9	175	10/6/62	2	Western State, Colo.	Barbados, West Indies	East Orange, N.J.	12/0
58	Squirek, Jack	LB	6-4	230	2/16/59	4	Illinois	Cleveland, Ohio	Torrance, Calif.	12/7
30	Toran, Stacey	S	6-2	200	11/10/61	2	Notre Dame	Indianapolis, Ind.	Indianapolis, Ind.	16/0
93	Townsend, Greg	DE	6-3	240	11/3/61	3	Texas Christian	Los Angeles, Calif.	Culver City, Calif.	16/0
91	Van Pelt, Brad	LB	6-5	235	4/5/51	13	Michigan State	Owosso, Mich.	Manhattan Beach, Calif.	9/8
20	Watts, Ted	CB	6-0	190	5/29/59	5	Texas Tech	Tarpon Springs, Fla.	Los Angeles, Calif.	16/0
67	Wheeler, Dwight	C-T	6-3	275	1/3/55	7	Tennessee State	Memphis, Tenn.	Nashville, Tenn.	4/0
85	Williams, Dokie	WR	5-11	180	8/25/60	3	UCLA	Oceanside, Calif.	Los Angeles, Calif.	16/3
38	Willis, Chester	RB	5-11	200	5/2/58	5	Auburn	Elberton, Ga.	Gainesville, Ga.	16/0
6	Wilson, Marc	QB	6-6	205	2/15/57	6	Brigham Young	Bremerton, Wash.	Woodinville, Wash.	16/10

* Ackerman played 9 games with San Diego, 6 with Raiders in '84; Belk last played with Cleveland in '83; Bryant played 4 games with Atlanta, 5 with Raiders; Junkin played 2 games with Buffalo, 12 with Washington; Krimm last played with New Orleans in '82.

†Option playout; subject to developments.

Also played with Raiders in '84—NT Greg Boyd (5 games), QB Jerry Golsteyn (active for 1 game but did not play); LB Larry McCoy (4), LB Mark Merrill (3), T Ed Muransky (3), C Jim Romano (6), RB Jimmy Smith (7).

COACHING STAFF

Head Coach, Tom Flores

Pro Career: Begins seventh year as head coach. Guided Raiders to 38-9 victory over Redskins in Super Bowl XVIII and 27-10 win over Eagles in Super Bowl XV. Has been with Raiders' organization as either a player or coach for 20 years. Played six years at quarterback for Raiders 1960-61, 1963-66. After spending two years (1967-68) with the Buffalo Bills and two seasons (1969-70) with the Kansas City Chiefs, Flores returned to Oakland as receivers coach in February, 1972. Ranks as Raiders number-three all-time passer with 11,635 yards and 92 touchdowns. He also passed for a club-record six touchdowns in one game in 1963. Career record: 66-33.

Background: Quarterback at Fresno, Calif., J.C. 1954-55 and Pacific 1956-57. Coached at his alma mater in 1959 before joining Raiders as a quarterback in 1960.

Personal: Born March 21, 1937, in Fresno, Calif. Tom and his wife, Barbara, live in Manhattan Beach, Calif. They have twin sons, Mark and Scott, and a daughter, Kimberly.

Assistant Coaches

Sam Boghosian, offensive line; born December 22, 1931, Fresno, Calif., lives in El Segundo, Calif. Guard UCLA 1951-54. No pro playing experience. College coach: UCLA 1955-64, Oregon State 1965-73. Pro coach: Houston Oilers 1974-75, Seattle Seahawks 1976-77, joined Raiders in 1979.

Willie Brown, defensive backfield; born December 2, 1940, Yazoo City, Miss., lives in Rancho Palos Verdes, Calif. Defensive back Grambling 1959-62. Pro cornerback Denver Broncos 1963-66, Oakland Raiders 1967-78. Pro coach: Joined Raiders in 1979.

Chet Franklin, defensive backfield; born March 19, 1935, Ontario, Ore., lives in Los Angeles. Guard Utah 1954-56. No pro playing experience. College coach: Stanford 1959, Oklahoma 1960-62, Colorado 1963-70. Pro coach: San Francisco 49ers 1971-74, Kansas City Chiefs 1975-77, New Orleans Saints 1978-79, joined Raiders in 1980.

Larry Kennan, quarterbacks; born June 13, 1944, Pomona, Calif., lives in Rancho Palos Verdes, Calif. Quarterback LaVerne College 1962-65. College coach: Colorado 1969-72, Nevada-Las Vegas 1973-75, Southern Methodist 1976-78, Lamar 1979-81. Pro coach: Joined Raiders in 1982.

Earl Leggett, defensive line; born May 5, 1933, Jacksonville, Fla., lives in Fountain Valley, Calif. Tackle Hinds J.C. 1953-54, Louisiana State 1955-56. Pro defensive tackle Chicago Bears 1957-65, Los Angeles Rams 1966, New Orleans Saints 1967-68. College coach: Nicholls State 1971, Texas Christian 1972-73. Pro coach: Southern California Sun (WFL) 1974-75, Seattle Seahawks 1976-77, San Francisco 49ers 1978, joined Raiders in 1980.

Bob Mischak, tight ends, strength and conditioning; born October 25, 1932, Newark, N.J., lives in El Segundo, Calif. Guard Army 1951-53. Pro guard New York Giants 1958, New York Titans 1960-62, Oakland Raiders 1963-65. College coach: Army 1966-72. Pro coach: Joined Raiders in 1973.

Steve Ortmayer, football operations and special teams; born February 13, 1944, Painesville, Ohio, lives in Rancho Palos Verdes, Calif. LaVerne College 1966. No college or pro playing experience. College coach: Colorado 1967-73, Georgia Tech 1974. Pro coach: Kansas City Chiefs 1975-77, joined Raiders in 1978.

Art Shell, offensive line; born November 26, 1946, Charleston, S.C., lives in El Segundo, Calif. Tackle Maryland State 1965-67. Pro offensive tackle Oakland Raiders 1968-81, Los Angeles Raiders 1982. Pro coach: Joined Raiders in 1983.

Tom Walsh, receivers; born April 16, 1949, Vallejo, Calif., lives in Manhattan Beach, Calif. UC-Santa Barbara 1971. No college or pro playing experience. College coach: University of San Diego 1972-76, U.S. International 1979, Murray State 1980, Cincinnati 1981. Pro coach: Joined Raiders in 1982.

LOS ANGELES RAIDERS 1985 FIRST-YEAR ROSTER

Name	Pos.	Ht.	Wt.	Birth-date	College	Birthplace	Residence	How Acq.
Adams, Stefon	CB	5-10	190	8/11/63	East Carolina	High Point, N.C.	High Point, N.C.	D3a
Belcher, Kevin	T	6-5	310	11/9/61	Wisconsin	Bridgeport, Conn.	Bridgeport, Conn.	D7
Bias, Moe	LB	6-2	230	9/1/61	Illinois	Los Angeles, Calif.	Los Angeles, Calif.	FA
Carter, Archie	LB	6-3	220	9/15/60	Illinois	Shreveport, La.	Los Angeles, Calif.	FA
Coppens, John	QB	6-2	210	10/9/62	Illinois State	South Bend, Ind.	Mishawaka, Ind.	FA
Haden, Nick	C	6-2	270	11/7/62	Penn State	Pittsburgh, Pa.	McKees Rocks, Pa.	D7b
Hagood, Rickey (1)	NT	6-1	285	4/24/61	South Carolina	Easley, S.C.	Columbia, S.C.	FA
Hester, Jessie	WR	5-11	170	1/21/63	Florida State	Belle Glade, Fla.	Belle Glade, Fla.	D1
Hilger, Rusty	QB	6-4	200	5/9/62	Oklahoma State	Oklahoma City, Okla.	Oklahoma City, Okla.	D6
James, Ronnie (1)	RB	6-2	235	1/2/61	Grambling	Los Angeles, Calif.	Houston, Tex.	FA
Jensen, Russ (1)	QB	6-2	215	7/13/61	California Lutheran	Whittier, Calif.	La Mirada, Calif.	FA
Johnson, Bobby (1)	RB	6-1	185	9/30/62	San Jose State	Monterey, Calif.	Monterey, Calif.	FA
Kimmel, Jamie	LB	6-3	240	3/29/62	Syracuse	Johnson City, N.Y.	Kirkwood, N.Y.	D4
Lubischar, Steve (1)	LB	6-2	220	6/29/62	Boston College	Long Branch, N.J.	Oceanport, N.J.	FA
McCall, Jeff (1)	TE	6-2	220	7/4/60	Clemson	Fayetteville, N.C.	Marietta, Ga.	FA
McKenzie, Reggie	LB	6-1	235	2/8/63	Tennessee	Knoxville, Tenn.	Knoxville, Tenn.	D10
Moffett, Tim	WR	6-1	180	2/28/62	Mississippi	Laurel, Miss.	Taylorsville, Miss.	D3
Myres, Albert	S	6-0	195	5/5/63	Tulsa	Shreveport, La.	Houston, Tex.	D10a
Niualiku, George (1)	G	6-3	265	4/30/61	California	Nukuawfa, Tonga	San Francisco, Calif.	FA
Pattison, Mark	WR	6-2	190	12/13/61	Washington	Seattle, Wash.	Seattle, Wash.	D7a
Polk, Raymond	CB	5-9	190	6/10/62	Oklahoma State	Ft. Campbell, Ky.	Sherman, Tex.	D12
Reeder, Dan	RB	5-11	225	3/18/61	Delaware	Shamokin, Pa.	Newark, Del.	D5
Strachan, Steve	RB	6-1	215	3/22/63	Boston College	Winchester, Mass.	Burlington, Mass.	D11
Snydor, Chris	S	6-0	195	8/14/62	Penn State	Bryn Mawr, Pa.	Rosemont, Pa.	D9
Wahl, Steve (1)	G	6-6	250	8/10/60	Cal Poly-SLO	San Jose, Calif.	Santa Cruz, Calif.	FA
Williams, Quency (1)	DE	6-2	225	4/10/61	Auburn	Douglas, Ga.	Inglewood, Calif.	FA
Williams, Ricky (1)	CB	6-1	195	4/27/60	Langston	Santa Monica, Calif.	Santa Monica, Calif.	FA
Willis, Mitch (1)	NT	6-8	280	3/16/62	Southern Methodist	Dallas, Tex.	Arlington, Tex.	D7('84)
Wingate, Leonard	NT	6-3	265	11/3/61	South Carolina St.	Charleston, S.C.	Charleston, S.C.	D8

Players who report to an NFL team for the first time are designated on rosters as rookies (R). If a player reported to an NFL training camp in a previous year but was not on the active squad for three or more regular season or postseason games, he is listed on the first-year roster and designated by a (1). Thereafter, a player who is on the active squad for three or more regular season or postseason games is credited with an additional year of playing experience.

NOTES

_____
_____
_____
_____
_____
_____
_____
_____
_____
_____
_____
_____
_____

Ray Willsey, offensive backfield; born September 30, 1929, Regina, Saskatchewan, lives in Redondo Beach, Calif. Quarterback-defensive back California 1951-52. Pro back Edmonton Eskimos (CFL) 1953. College coach: California 1954-55, 1964-71 (head coach), Washington 1956, Texas 1957-59. Pro coach: St. Louis Cardinals 1960-61, 1973-77, Washington Redskins 1962-63, joined Raiders in 1978.

Bob Zeman, linebackers; born February 22, 1937, Wheaton, Ill., lives in Manhattan Beach, Calif. Fullback-halfback Wisconsin 1957-59. Pro defensive back Los Angeles-San Diego Chargers 1960-61, 1965-66, Denver Broncos 1962-63. College coach: Northwestern 1968-69, Wisconsin 1970. Pro coach: Oakland Raiders 1971-77, Denver Broncos 1978-82, Buffalo Bills 1983, rejoined Raiders in 1984.

American Football Conference
Eastern Division

Team Colors: Aqua, Coral, and White

4770 Biscayne Boulevard
Suite 1440
Miami, Florida 33137
Telephone: (305) 576-1000

Club Officials

President: Joseph Robbie
Vice President/General Manager:
  J. Michael Robbie
Vice President/Head Coach: Don Shula
Vice President/Public Affairs: Joe Abrell
Director of Pro Personnel: Charley Winner
Director of Player Personnel: Chuck Connor
Director of Publicity: Chip Namias
Ticket Director: Steve Dangerfield
Controller: Howard Rieman
Traveling Secretary: Brian J. Wiedmeier
Trainer: Bob Lundy
Equipment Manager: Bob Monica

Stadium: Orange Bowl • **Capacity:** 75,206
  1501 N.W. Third Street
  Miami, Florida 33125

Playing Surface: Grass

Training Camp: St. Thomas University
  16400-D N.W. 32nd Avenue
  Miami, Florida 33054

1985 SCHEDULE

Preseason

Aug. 10	**Minnesota**	8:00
Aug. 17	**Buffalo**	8:00
Aug. 24	at Los Angeles Raiders	6:00
Aug. 30	at Atlanta	8:00

Regular Season

Sept. 8	at Houston	12:00
Sept. 15	**Indianapolis**	1:00
Sept. 22	**Kansas City**	4:00
Sept. 29	at Denver	2:00
Oct. 6	**Pittsburgh**	1:00
Oct. 14	at New York Jets (Monday)	9:00
Oct. 20	**Tampa Bay**	4:00
Oct. 27	at Detroit	1:00
Nov. 3	at New England	1:00
Nov. 10	**New York Jets**	4:00
Nov. 17	at Indianapolis	1:00
Nov. 24	at Buffalo	1:00
Dec. 2	**Chicago** (Monday)	9:00
Dec. 8	at Green Bay	12:00
Dec. 16	**New England** (Monday)	9:00
Dec. 22	**Buffalo**	1:00

DOLPHINS COACHING HISTORY
(184-108-4)

1966-69	George Wilson	15-39-2
1970-84	Don Shula	169-69-2

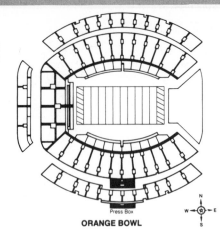

ORANGE BOWL

RECORD HOLDERS
Individual Records—Career

Category	Name	Performance
Rushing (Yds.)	Larry Csonka, 1968-1974, 1979	6,737
Passing (Yds.)	Bob Griese, 1967-1980	25,092
Passing (TDs)	Bob Griese, 1967-1980	192
Receiving (No.)	Nat Moore, 1974-1984	421
Receiving (Yds.)	Nat Moore, 1974-1984	6,415
Interceptions	Jake Scott, 1970-75	35
Punting (Avg.)	Reggie Roby, 1983-84	43.8
Punt Return (Avg.)	Freddie Solomon, 1975-77	11.4
Kickoff Return (Avg.)	Mercury Morris, 1969-1975	26.5
Field Goals	Garo Yepremian, 1970-78	165
Touchdowns (Tot.)	Nat Moore, 1974-1984	61
Points	Garo Yepremian, 1970-78	830

Individual Records—Single Season

Category	Name	Performance
Rushing (Yds.)	Delvin Williams, 1978	1,258
Passing (Yds.)	Dan Marino, 1984	5,084
Passing (TDs)	Dan Marino, 1984	48
Receiving (No.)	Mark Clayton, 1984	73
Receiving (Yds.)	Mark Clayton, 1984	1,389
Interceptions	Dick Westmoreland, 1967	10
Punting (Avg.)	Reggie Roby, 1984	44.7
Punt Return (Avg.)	Freddie Solomon, 1975	12.3
Kickoff Return (Avg.)	Duriel Harris, 1976	32.9
Field Goals	Garo Yepremian, 1971	28
Touchdowns (Tot.)	Mark Clayton, 1984	18
Points	Garo Yepremian, 1971	117

Individual Records—Single Game

Category	Name	Performance
Rushing (Yds.)	Mercury Morris, 9-30-73	197
Passing (Yds.)	Dan Marino, 12-2-84	470
Passing (TDs)	Bob Griese, 11-24-77	6
Receiving (No.)	Duriel Harris, 10-28-79	10
Receiving (Yds.)	Nat Moore, 10-4-81	210
Interceptions	Dick Anderson, 12-3-73	4
Field Goals	Garo Yepremian, 9-26-71	5
Touchdowns (Tot.)	Paul Warfield, 12-15-73	4
Points	Paul Warfield, 12-15-73	24

1984 TEAM STATISTICS

	Miami	Opp.
Total First Downs	387	314
Rushing	115	130
Passing	243	172
Penalty	29	12
Third Down: Made/Att.	103/200	90/219
Fourth Down: Made/Att.	6/11	17/21
Total Net Yards	6936	5420
Avg. Per Game	433.5	338.8
Total Plays	1070	1051
Avg. Per Play	6.5	5.2
Net Yards Rushing	1918	2155
Avg. Per Game	119.9	134.7
Total Rushes	484	458
Net Yards Passing	5018	3265
Avg. Per Game	313.6	204.1
Tackled/Yards Lost	14/128	42/339
Gross Yards	5146	3604
Att./Completions	572/367	551/310
Completion Pct.	64.2	56.3
Had Intercepted	18	24
Punts/Avg.	51/44.7	83/41.9
Net Punting Avg.	38.1	35.8
Penalties/Yards Lost	67/527	93/772
Fumbles/Ball Lost	26/10	23/12
Touchdowns	70	39
Rushing	18	16
Passing	49	22
Returns	3	1
Avg. Time of Possession	30:18	29:42

1984 TEAM RECORD
Preseason (3-1)

Date	Miami		Opponents
8/4	24	*Indianapolis	3
8/11	29	Minnesota	7
8/19	29	Los Angeles Raiders	23
8/24	13	Tampa Bay	14
	95		47

Regular Season (14-2)

Date	Miami		Opp.	Att.
9/2	35	Washington	17	52,683
9/9	28	*New England	7	66,083
9/17	21	Buffalo	17	65,455
9/23	44	*Indianapolis	7	55,415
9/30	36	St. Louis	28	46,991
10/7	31	Pittsburgh	7	59,103
10/14	28	*Houston	10	54,080
10/21	44	New England	24	60,711
10/28	38	*Buffalo	7	58,824
11/4	31	New York Jets	17	72,655
11/11	24	*Philadelphia	23	70,227
11/18	28	San Diego (OT)	34	53,041
11/26	28	*New York Jets	17	74,884
12/2	34	*Los Angeles Raiders	45	71,222
12/9	35	Indianapolis	17	60,411
12/17	28	*Dallas	21	74,139
	513		298	995,924

*Home Game   (OT) Overtime

Score by Periods

Miami	58	170	150	135	0	—	513
Opponents	52	81	55	104	6	—	298

Attendance
Home 524,874   Away 471,050   Total 995,924
Single game home record, 78,939 (1-2-72)
Single season home record, 532,005 (1972)

1984 INDIVIDUAL STATISTICS

Rushing

	Att.	Yds.	Avg.	LG	TD
Bennett	144	606	4.2	23	7
Nathan	118	558	4.7	22	1
Carter	100	495	5.0	35	1
P. Johnson, S.D.-Mia.	87	205	2.4	9	12
P. Johnson, Mia.	68	159	2.3	9	9
Franklin	20	74	3.7	12	0
Clayton	3	35	11.7	30	0
Moore	1	3	3.0	3	0
Strock	2	-5	-2.5	0	0
Marino	28	-7	-0.3	10	0
Miami	484	1918	4.0	35	18
Opponents	458	2155	4.7	52t	16

Passing

	Att.	Comp.	Pct.	Yds.	TD	Int.	Tkld.	Rate
Marino	564	362	64.2	5084	48	17	13/120	108.9
Strock	6	4	66.7	27	0	0	0/0	76.4
Jensen	1	1	100.0	35	1	0	1/8	158.3
Clayton	1	0	0.0	0	0	1	0/0	0.0
Miami	572	367	64.2	5146	49	18	14/128	108.5
Opponents	551	310	56.3	3604	22	24	42/339	71.4

Receiving

	No.	Yds.	Avg.	LG	TD
Clayton	73	1389	19.0	65t	18
Duper	71	1306	18.4	80t	8
Nathan	61	579	9.5	26	2
Moore	43	573	13.3	37t	6
D. Johnson	34	426	12.5	42	3
Hardy	28	257	9.2	19	5
Cefalo	18	185	10.3	25t	2
Jensen	13	139	10.7	20	2
Rose	12	195	16.3	34t	2
Carter	8	53	6.6	15	0
Bennett	6	44	7.3	20	1
P. Johnson, S.D.-Mia.	2	7	3.5	7	0
Miami	367	5146	14.0	80t	49
Opponents	310	3604	11.6	76t	22

Interceptions

	No.	Yds.	Avg.	LG	TD
G. Blackwood	6	169	28.2	50	0
Judson	4	121	30.3	60t	1
McNeal	3	41	13.7	30	1
L. Blackwood	3	29	9.7	15	0
Lankford	3	25	8.3	22	0
B. Brown	1	53	53.0	53	0
Kozlowski	1	26	26.0	26	0
Duhe	1	7	7.0	7	0
Sowell	1	7	7.0	7	0
Brudzinski	1	0	0.0	0	0
Miami	24	478	19.9	86t	2
Opponents	18	377	20.9	97t	1

Punting

	No.	Yds.	Avg.	In 20	LG
Roby	51	2281	44.7	15	69
Miami	51	2281	44.7	15	69
Opponents	83	3476	41.9	16	89

Punt Returns

	No.	FC	Yds.	Avg.	LG	TD
Walker	21	14	169	8.0	33	0
Clayton	8	2	79	9.9	22	0
Heflin	6	1	76	12.7	37	0
Kozlowski	4	4	41	10.3	20	0
G. Blackwood	0	4	0	—	0	0
L. Blackwood	0	2	0	—	0	0
Miami	39	27	365	9.4	37	0
Opponents	17	13	138	8.1	18	0

Kickoff Returns

	No.	Yds.	Avg.	LG	TD
Walker	29	617	21.3	41	0
Heflin	9	130	14.4	26	0
Clayton	2	15	7.5	14	0
Kozlowski	2	23	11.5	12	0
Hill	1	14	14.0	14	0
Duhe	1	0	0.0	0	0
Miami	44	799	18.2	41	0
Opponents	66	1368	20.7	42	0

Scoring

	TD R	TD P	TD Rt	PAT	FG	Saf	TP
Clayton	0	18	0	0/0	0/0	0	108
von Schamann	0	0	0	66/70	9/19	0	93
P. Johnson, S.D.-Mia.	12	0	0	0/0	0/0	0	72
P. Johnson, Miami	9	0	0	0/0	0/0	0	54
Bennett	7	1	0	0/0	0/0	0	48
Duper	0	8	0	0/0	0/0	0	48
Moore	0	6	0	0/0	0/0	0	36
Hardy	0	5	0	0/0	0/0	0	30
D. Johnson	0	3	0	0/0	0/0	0	18
Nathan	1	2	0	0/0	0/0	0	18
Cefalo	0	2	0	0/0	0/0	0	12
Jensen	0	2	0	0/0	0/0	0	12
Rose	0	2	0	0/0	0/0	0	12
Baumhower	0	0	1	0/0	0/0	0	6
Carter	1	0	0	0/0	0/0	0	6
Judson	0	0	1	0/0	0/0	0	6
McNeal	0	0	1	0/0	0/0	0	6
Miami	18	49	3	66/70	9/19	0	513
Opponents	16	22	1	37/38	9/17	0	298

FIRST-ROUND SELECTIONS

(If Club had no first-round selection, first player drafted is listed with round in parentheses.)

Year	Player, College, Position
1966	Jim Grabowski, Illinois, RB
	Rick Norton, Kentucky, QB
1967	Bob Griese, Purdue, QB
1968	Larry Csonka, Syracuse, RB
	Doug Crusan, Indiana, T
1969	Bill Stanfill, Georgia, DE
1970	Jim Mandich, Michigan, TE (2)
1971	Otto Stowe, Iowa State, WR (2)
1972	Mike Kadish, Notre Dame, DT
1973	Chuck Bradley, Oregon, C (2)
1974	Donald Reese, Jackson State, DE
1975	Darryl Carlton, Tampa, T
1976	Larry Gordon, Arizona State, LB
	Kim Bokamper, San Jose State, LB
1977	A.J. Duhe, Louisiana State, DT
1978	Guy Benjamin, Stanford, QB (2)
1979	Jon Giesler, Michigan, T
1980	Don McNeal, Alabama, DB
1981	David Overstreet, Oklahoma, RB
1982	Roy Foster, Southern California, G
1983	Dan Marino, Pittsburgh, QB
1984	Jackie Shipp, Oklahoma, LB
1985	Lorenzo Hampton, Florida, RB

MIAMI DOLPHINS 1985 VETERAN ROSTER

No.	Name	Pos.	Ht.	Wt.	Birth-date	NFL Exp.	College	Birthplace	Residence	'84 Games/ Starts
70	†Barnett, Bill	DE	6-4	260	5/10/56	6	Nebraska	St. Paul, Minn.	Lincoln, Neb.	16/1
73	Baumhower, Bob	NT	6-5	265	8/4/55	9	Alabama	Portsmouth, Va.	Ft. Lauderdale, Fla.	15/15
34	Bennett, Woody	FB	6-2	225	3/24/55	7	Miami	York, Pa.	York, Pa.	16/9
78	Benson, Charles	DE	6-3	267	11/21/60	3	Baylor	Houston, Tex.	Miami, Fla.	16/0
75	Betters, Doug	DE	6-7	265	6/11/56	8	Nevada-Reno	Lincoln, Neb.	Whitefish, Mont.	16/16
47	†Blackwood, Glenn	S	6-0	190	2/23/57	7	Texas	San Antonio, Tex.	Miami, Fla.	16/16
42	†Blackwood, Lyle	S	6-1	190	5/24/51	13	Texas Christian	San Antonio, Tex.	Austin, Tex.	16/16
58	Bokamper, Kim	DE	6-6	255	9/25/54	9	San Jose State	San Diego, Calif.	Ft. Lauderdale, Fla.	11/10
56	Bowser, Charles	LB	6-3	235	10/2/59	4	Duke	Plymouth, N.C.	Plymouth, N.C.	15/15
53	Brophy, Jay	LB	6-3	233	7/27/60	2	Miami	Akron, Ohio	Akron, Ohio	11/5
43	Brown, Bud	S	6-0	194	4/19/61	2	Southern Mississippi	DeKalb, Miss.	DeKalb, Miss.	16/0
51	Brown, Mark	LB	6-2	225	7/18/61	3	Purdue	Los Angeles, Calif.	Los Angeles, Calif.	16/9
59	†Brudzinski, Bob	LB	6-4	223	1/1/55	9	Ohio State	Fremont, Ohio	Orange, Calif.	16/16
23	Carter, Joe	RB	5-11	198	6/23/62	2	Alabama	Starkville, Miss.	Starkville, Miss.	13/2
71	Charles, Mike	NT	6-4	285	9/23/62	3	Syracuse	Newark, N.J.	North Miami, Fla.	10/6
	t-Clark, Bryan	QB	6-2	196	7/27/60	3	Michigan State	Redwood City, Calif.	San Mateo, Calif.	1/0*
76	Clark, Steve	G	6-4	255	8/2/60	4	Utah	Salt Lake City, Utah	Salt Lake City, Utah	12/0
83	Clayton, Mark	WR	5-9	175	4/8/61	3	Louisville	Indianapolis, Ind.	Indianapolis, Ind.	15/15
77	Duhe, A.J.	LB	6-4	235	6/11/56	9	Louisiana State	New Orleans, La.	Miami Shores, Fla.	12/8
85	Duper, Mark	WR	5-9	187	1/25/59	4	Northwestern State, La.	Pineville, La.	Miami, Fla.	16/16
61	Foster, Roy	G	6-4	275	5/24/60	4	Southern California	Los Angeles, Calif.	Los Angeles, Calif.	16/16
37	Franklin, Andra	FB	5-10	225	8/22/59	4	Nebraska	Anniston, Ala.	Miami, Fla.	2/2
79	Giesler, Jon	T	6-5	260	12/23/56	7	Michigan	Toledo, Ohio	Cooper City, Fla.	16/16
74	Green, Cleveland	T	6-3	262	9/11/57	7	Southern	Bolton, Miss.	Edwards, Miss.	16/12
84	Hardy, Bruce	TE	6-5	232	6/1/56	8	Arizona State	Murray, Utah	South Jordan, Utah	16/5
88	Heflin, Vince	WR	6-0	185	7/7/59	4	Central State, Ohio	Dayton, Ohio	Hialeah, Fla.	16/0
90	Hester, Ron	LB	6-2	222	5/26/59	2	Florida State	Atlanta, Ga.	Umatilla, Fla.	0*
31	†Hill, Eddie	RB	6-2	210	5/13/57	7	Memphis State	Nashville, Tenn.	Plantation, Fla.	16/0
11	†Jensen, Jim	WR	6-4	215	11/14/58	5	Boston University	Abington, Pa.	Pembroke Pines, Fla.	16/2
87	†Johnson, Dan	TE	6-3	240	5/17/60	3	Iowa State	Minneapolis, Minn.	Pembroke Pines, Fla.	16/16
46	Johnson, Pete	FB	6-0	250	3/22/54	9	Ohio State	Peach County, Ga.	Miramar, Fla.	16/0*
49	Judson, William	CB	6-1	190	3/26/59	4	South Carolina State	Detroit, Mich.	Miami, Fla.	16/16
40	Kozlowski, Mike	S	6-1	198	2/24/56	6	Colorado	Newark, N.J.	Plantation, Fla.	16/0
68	Laakso, Eric	T	6-4	260	11/29/56	8	Tulane	New York, N.Y.	Cooper City, Fla.	4/4
44	†Lankford, Paul	CB	6-2	184	6/15/58	4	Penn State	New York, N.Y.	Miami, Fla.	16/6
72	Lee, Ronnie	G	6-4	265	12/24/56	7	Baylor	Pine Bluff, Ark.	Miami, Fla.	16/0
13	Marino, Dan	QB	6-4	214	9/15/61	3	Pittsburgh	Pittsburgh, Pa.	Pittsburgh, Pa.	16/16
28	McNeal, Don	CB	5-11	192	5/6/58	5	Alabama	Atmore, Ala.	Miami, Fla.	11/10
89	†Moore, Nat	WR	5-9	188	9/19/51	12	Florida	Tallahassee, Fla.	Miami, Fla.	16/1
22	Nathan, Tony	RB	6-0	206	12/14/56	7	Alabama	Birmingham, Ala.	Miami Lakes, Fla.	16/12
64	Newman, Ed	G	6-2	255	6/4/51	13	Duke	Woodbury, N.Y.	Miami, Fla.	16/16
55	Rhone, Earnie	LB	6-2	224	8/20/53	10	Henderson, Ark.	Ogden, Ark.	Texarkana, Tex.	15/10
4	Roby, Reggie	P	6-2	243	7/30/61	3	Iowa	Waterloo, Iowa	Miami, Fla.	16/0
80	†Rose, Joe	TE	6-3	230	6/24/57	6	California	Marysville, Calif.	Ft. Lauderdale, Fla.	9/0
50	Shipp, Jackie	LB	6-2	236	3/19/62	2	Oklahoma	Stillwater, Okla.	Stillwater, Okla.	16/0
45	Sowell, Robert	CB	5-11	175	6/23/61	3	Howard	Columbus, Ohio	Columbus, Ohio	16/0
57	Stephenson, Dwight	C	6-2	255	11/20/57	6	Alabama	Murfreesboro, N.C.	Miami, Fla.	16/16
10	†Strock, Don	QB	6-5	220	11/27/50	12	Virginia Tech	Pottstown, Pa.	Miami Springs, Fla.	16/0
60	Toews, Jeff	G-C	6-3	255	11/4/57	7	Washington	San Jose, Calif.	Davie, Fla.	16/0
32	Vigorito, Tom	RB	5-10	190	10/23/59	3	Virginia	Passaic, N.J.	Pembroke Pines, Fla.	0*
5	von Schamann, Uwe	K	6-1	185	4/23/56	7	Oklahoma	West Berlin, Germany	Norman, Okla.	16/0
41	†Walker, Fulton	CB	5-11	196	4/30/58	5	West Virginia	Martinsburg, W. Va.	Martinsburg, W. Va.	12/0

* B. Clark active for 2 games with San Francisco but did not play, active for 2 games with Cincinnati and played in 1 in '84; Hester and Vigorito missed '84 season due to injury; P. Johnson played 3 games with San Diego, 13 with Miami.

†Option playout; subject to developments.

Retired—Jimmy Cefalo, 6-year wide receiver, 16 games in '84; Bob Kuechenberg, 14-year guard, injured reserve in '84.

t-Dolphins traded for B. Clark (Cincinnati).

Also played with Dolphins in '84—WR Fernanza Burgess (3 games), TE John Chesley (1), LB Ed Judie (2), LB Rodell Thomas (14).

COACHING STAFF

Head Coach, Don Shula

Pro Career: Beginning his twenty-third season as an NFL head coach, and sixteenth with the Dolphins. Miami has won or shared first place in the AFC East in 12 of his 15 years. Has highest winning percentage (.716) among active NFL coaches with 100 or more wins. Captured back-to-back NFL championships, defeating Washington 14-7 in Super Bowl VII and Minnesota 24-7 in Super Bowl VIII. Lost to Dallas 24-3 in Super Bowl VI, to Washington 27-17 in Super Bowl XVII, and to San Francisco 38-16 in Super Bowl XIX. His 1972 17-0 club is the only team in NFL history to go undefeated throughout the regular season and postseason. Started his pro playing career with Cleveland Browns as defensive back in 1951. After two seasons with Browns, spent 1953-56 with Baltimore Colts and 1957 with Washington Redskins. Joined Detroit Lions as defensive coach in 1960 and was named head coach of the Colts in 1963. Baltimore had a 13-1 record in 1968 and captured NFL championship before losing to New York Jets in Super Bowl III. Overall record: 242-94-6.

Background: Outstanding offensive player at John Carroll University in Cleveland before becoming defensive specialist as a pro. His alma mater gave him his doctorate in humanities, May 1973. Served as assistant coach at Virginia in 1958 and at Kentucky in 1959.

Personal: Born January 4, 1930, in Painesville, Ohio. Don and his wife, Dorothy, live in Miami Lakes and have five children—David, Donna, Sharon, Annie, and Mike.

Assistant Coaches

Tom Keane, special teams; born September 7, 1926, Bellaire, Ohio, lives in Miami. Back Ohio State 1944, West Virginia 1946-47. Pro back Los Angeles Rams 1948-51, Dallas Texans 1952, Baltimore Colts 1953-54, Chicago Cardinals 1955. Pro coach: Chicago Cardinals 1957, Calgary Stampeders (CFL) 1960, Wheeling (UFL) 1961-64, Pittsburgh Steelers 1965, joined Dolphins in 1966.

Bob Matheson, linebackers; born November 25, 1944, Boone, N.C., lives in Hollywood, Fla. Linebacker Duke 1964-66. Pro linebacker Cleveland Browns 1967-70, Miami Dolphins 1971-79. College coach: Duke 1981-82. Pro coach: Joined Dolphins in 1983.

Mel Phillips, defensive backfield; born January 6, 1942, Shelby, N.C., lives in North Miami. Defensive back-running back North Carolina A&T 1965-66. Pro defensive back San Francisco 49ers 1966-77. Pro coach: Detroit Lions 1980-84, first year with Dolphins.

John Sandusky, offense-offensive line; born December 28, 1925, Philadelphia, Pa., lives in Cooper City, Fla. Tackle Villanova 1946-49. Pro tackle Cleveland Browns 1950-55, Green Bay Packers 1956. College coach: Villanova 1957-58. Pro coach: Baltimore Colts 1959-72 (head coach 1972), Philadelphia Eagles 1973-75, joined Dolphins in 1976.

Mike Scarry, defensive line; born February 1, 1920, Duquesne, Pa., lives in Miami. Center Waynesburg 1939-41. Pro center Cleveland Rams 1944-45, Cleveland Browns (AAFC) 1946-47. College coach: Western Reserve 1948-49, Santa Clara 1950-52, Loras 1953, Washington State 1954-55, Cincinnati 1956-62, Waynesburg 1963-65 (head coach). Pro coach: Washington Redskins 1966-68, joined Dolphins in 1970.

David Shula, receivers-quarterbacks; born May 28, 1959, Lexington, Ky., lives in Miami Lakes. Wide receiver Dartmouth 1977-80. Pro receiver Baltimore Colts 1981. Pro coach: Joined Dolphins in 1982.

Chuck Studley, defense; born January 17, 1929, Maywood Ill., lives in Miami Lakes. Guard Illinois 1949-51. No pro playing experience. College coach: Illinois 1955-59, Massachusetts 1960 (head coach), Cincinnati 1961-68 (head coach). Pro coach: Cincinnati Bengals 1969-78, San Francisco 49ers 1979-82, Houston Oilers 1983 (interim head coach), joined Dolphins in 1984.

Carl Taseff, offensive backfield; born September 28, 1928, Cleveland, Ohio, lives in Pembroke Pines, Fla. Back John Carroll 1947-50. Pro defensive back Cleveland Browns 1951, Baltimore Colts 1953-61, Philadelphia Eagles 1961, Buffalo Bills 1962. Pro coach: Boston Patriots 1964, Detroit Lions 1965-66, joined Dolphins in 1970.

Junior Wade, strength-conditioning; born February 2, 1947, Bath, S.C., lives in Hialeah, Fla. South Carolina State 1969. No college or pro playing experience. Pro coach: Joined Dolphins in 1975, coach since 1983.

MIAMI DOLPHINS 1985 FIRST-YEAR ROSTER

Name	Pos.	Ht.	Wt.	Birthdate	College	Birthplace	Residence	How Acq.
Ballard, Quinton	NT	6-3	290	11/18/60	Elon College	Ahoski, N.C.	Gates, N.C.	FA
Carson, Malcolm	C-G	6-2	260	11/1/59	Tenn.-Chattanooga	Birmingham, Ala.	Chattanooga, Tenn.	FA
Carvalho, Bernard	G-T	6-4	262	9/29/61	Hawaii	Lihua Kauai, Hawaii	Kapaa Kauai, Hawaii	FA
Chesley, John	TE	6-5	235	7/2/62	Oklahoma State	Washington, D.C.	Washington, D.C.	FA
Curry, Ivory	S	5-11	180	2/6/61	Florida	Miami, Fla.	Miami, Fla.	FA
Davenport, Ron	FB	6-2	225	12/22/62	Louisville	Sum. Set, Bermuda	Louisville, Ky.	D6a
Dellenbach, Jeff	T	6-6	280	2/14/63	Wisconsin	Wausau, Wis.	Madison, Wis.	D4a
Flores, Sam	K	6-0	185	11/8/61	C.W. Post	Miami, Fla.	Hialeah, Fla.	FA
Hampton, Lorenzo	RB	6-0	212	3/12/62	Florida	Lake Wales, Fla.	Lake Wales, Fla.	D1
Hanks, Duan	WR	6-0	180	7/28/61	Stephen F. Austin	Detroit, Mich.	Detroit, Mich.	FA
Harris, Johnny	DE	6-4	266	8/3/60	Mississippi Valley	Demopolis, Ala.	Demopolis, Ala.	FA
Higgins, Robert	LB	6-1	220	11/19/59	Emporia State	Topeka, Kan.	Topeka, Kan.	FA
Hinds, Adam	S	6-3	201	7/21/61	Oklahoma State	St. Louis, Mo.	St. Louis, Mo.	D9
Jones, Mike	RB	5-11	187	8/2/63	Tulane	Ocilla, Ga.	Philadelphia, Ga.	D11
Lavin, Pete	S	6-1	195	4/17/61	Whittier College	Los Angeles, Calif.	Los Angeles, Calif.	FA
Little, George	NT	6-3	254	6/27/63	Iowa State	McKeesport, Pa.	Iowa City, Iowa	D3
Moyer, Alex	LB	6-2	223	10/25/63	Northwestern	Ecorse, Mich.	Evanston, Ill.	D3a
Nelson, David	RB	6-1	235	11/23/63	Heidelberg	Miami, Fla.	North Miami, Fla.	FA
Noble, Ray	CB	6-0	170	12/19/62	California	Seaside, Calif.	Berkeley, Calif.	D12
Pendleton, Mike	CB-S	6-2	185	4/11/61	Indiana	Evansville, Ind.	Evansville, Ind.	D10
Radle, Thomas	TE	6-5	240	5/27/61	VMI	Cleveland, Ohio	Winchester, Va.	FA
Reveiz, Fuad	K	6-0	228	2/4/63	Tennessee	Bogota, Columbia	Knoxville, Tenn.	D7
Sharp, Dan	TE	6-3	230	2/5/62	Texas Christian	Dallas, Tex.	Ft. Worth, Tex.	D8
Shorthose, George	WR	6-0	200	12/22/61	Missouri	Stanton, Calif.	Columbia, Mo.	D6
Smith, Mike	CB-S	6-0	174	10/24/62	Texas-El Paso	Houston, Tex.	El Paso, Tex.	D4
Smythe, Mark	DE	6-3	265	12/12/59	Indiana	Bloomington, Ind.	Bloomington, Ind.	FA
Thaxton, James	CB-S	5-11	175	3/16/62	Louisiana Tech	Monroe, La.	Monroe, La.	FA
Thurman, Tony	CB	6-0	194	3/15/62	Boston College	Jacksonville, Fla.	Lynn, Mass.	FA
Vanderwende, Kyle	QB	6-2	215	9/6/63	Miami	Palm Beach, Fla.	Coral Gables, Fla.	FA
Washington, Keith	WR	5-11	190	10/8/59	No college	Albany, N.Y.	Boynton Beach, Fla.	FA
White, Mike	G-C	6-3	241	10/21/61	Alabama	Decatur, Ga.	Tuscaloosa, Ala.	FA
Weir, Robert	DE	6-3	274	2/4/61	Southern Methodist	Birmingham, England	Dallas, Tex.	FA

Players who report to an NFL team for the first time are designated on rosters as rookies (R). If a player reported to an NFL training camp in a previous year but was not on the active squad for three or more regular season or postseason games, he is listed on the first-year roster and designated by a (1). Thereafter, a player who is on the active squad for three or more regular season or postseason games is credited with an additional year of playing experience.

NOTES

NEW ENGLAND PATRIOTS

**American Football Conference
Eastern Division**

Team Colors: Red, White, and Blue

Sullivan Stadium
Route 1
Foxboro, Massachusetts 02035
Telephone: (617) 543-7911, 262-1776

Club Officials

President: William H. Sullivan, Jr.
Executive Vice President: Charles W. Sullivan
Vice President: Francis J. (Bucko) Kilroy
General Manager: Patrick J. Sullivan
Director of Player Development: Dick Steinberg
Director of Pro Scouting: Bill McPeak
Director of College Scouting: Joe Mendes
Executive Director of Player Personnel:
  Darryl Stingley
Personnel Scouts: George Blackburn,
  Larry Cook, Charlie Garcia, Pat Naughton,
  Bob Teahan
Director of Public Relations: Dave Wintergrass
Director of Publicity: Jim Greenidge
Assistant Publicity Director: Mike Loftus
Box Office Manager: Ken Sternfeld
Trainer: Ron O'Neil
Equipment Manager: George Luongo
Film Manager: Ken Deininger

Stadium: Sullivan Stadium • **Capacity:** 60,890
  Route 1
  Foxboro, Massachusetts 02035

Playing Surface: Super Turf

Training Camp: Bryant College
  Smithfield, Rhode Island 02917

1985 SCHEDULE

Preseason
Aug. 10   **New Orleans** 3:30
Aug. 17   at Kansas City 7:30
Aug. 23   at Washington 8:00
Aug. 31   at Los Angeles Rams 7:00

Regular Season
Sept. 8   **Green Bay** 1:00
Sept. 15   at Chicago 12:00
Sept. 22   at Buffalo. 1:00
Sept. 29   **Los Angeles Raiders** 1:00
Oct. 6   at Cleveland 1:00
Oct. 13   **Buffalo** 1:00
Oct. 20   **New York Jets** 4:00
Oct. 27   at Tampa Bay. 1:00
Nov. 3   **Miami** 1:00
Nov. 10   **Indianapolis** 1:00
Nov. 17   at Seattle. 1:00
Nov. 24   at New York Jets 1:00
Dec. 1   at Indianapolis 1:00
Dec. 8   **Detroit**. 1:00
Dec. 16   at Miami (Monday). 9:00
Dec. 22   **Cincinnati** 1:00

PATRIOTS COACHING HISTORY

Boston 1960-70
(164-189-9)

1960-61	Lou Saban*	7-12-0
1961-68	Mike Holovak.	53-47-9
1969-70	Clive Rush**.	5-18-0
1970-72	John Mazur***	9-19-0
1972	Phil Bengtson.	1-4-0
1973-78	Chuck Fairbanks.	46-42-0
1979-81	Ron Erhardt	21-27-0
1982-84	Ron Meyer****	18-16-0
1984	Raymond Berry	4-4-0

  *Released after five games in 1961
  **Released after nine games in 1970
  ***Released after nine games in 1972
  ****Released after eight games in 1984

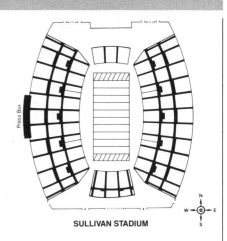

SULLIVAN STADIUM

RECORD HOLDERS
Individual Records—Career

Category	Name	Performance
Rushing (Yds.)	Sam Cunningham, 1973-79, 1981-82	5,453
Passing (Yds.).	Steve Grogan, 1975-1984.	20,270
Passing (TDs)	Steve Grogan, 1975-1984	139
Receiving (No.)	Stanley Morgan, 1977-1984	312
Receiving (Yds.)	Stanley Morgan, 1977-1984	6,441
Interceptions	Ron Hall, 1961-67.	29
Punting (Avg.)	Rich Camarillo, 1981-84	43.3
Punt Return (Avg.)	Mack Herron, 1973-75	12.0
Kickoff Return (Avg.)	Horace Ivory, 1977-1981	27.6
Field Goals	Gino Cappelletti, 1960-1970	176
Touchdowns (Tot.)	Sam Cunningham, 1973-79, 1981-82	49
Points	Gino Cappelletti, 1960-1970	1,130

Individual Records—Single Season

Category	Name	Performance
Rushing (Yds.)	Jim Nance, 1966	1,458
Passing (Yds.).	Vito (Babe) Parilli, 1964	3,465
Passing (TDs)	Vito (Babe) Parilli, 1964	31
Receiving (No.)	Derrick Ramsey, 1984	66
Receiving (Yds.)	Stanley Morgan, 1981	1,029
Interceptions	Ron Hall, 1964	11
Punting (Avg.)	Rich Camarillo, 1983	44.6
Punt Return (Avg.)	Mack Herron, 1974	14.8
Kickoff Return (Avg.)	Raymond Clayborn, 1977	31.0
Field Goals	John Smith, 1980	26
Touchdowns (Tot.)	Steve Grogan, 1976.	13
	Stanley Morgan, 1979	13
Points	Gino Cappelletti, 1964.	155

Individual Records—Single Game

Category	Name	Performance
Rushing (Yds.)	Tony Collins, 9-18-83.	212
Passing (Yds.).	Vito (Babe) Parilli, 10-16-64.	422
Passing (TDs)	Vito (Babe) Parilli, 11-15-64	5
	Vito (Babe) Parilli, 10-15-67	5
	Steve Grogan, 9-9-79	5
Receiving (No.)	Art Graham, 11-20-66	11
Receiving (Yds.)	Stanley Morgan, 11-8-81	182
Interceptions	Many times	3
	Last time by Roland James, 10-23-83	
Field Goals	Gino Cappelletti, 10-4-64	6
Touchdowns (Tot.)	Many times	3
	Last time by Derrick Ramsey, 11-18-84	
Points	Gino Cappelletti, 12-18-65	28

1984 TEAM STATISTICS

	New England	Opp.
Total First Downs	315	311
Rushing	104	109
Passing	186	182
Penalty	25	20
Third Down: Made/Att.	86/217	91/229
Fourth Down: Made/Att.	5/6	9/18
Total Net Yards	5263	5100
Avg. Per Game	328.9	318.8
Total Plays	1048	1066
Avg. Per Play	5.0	4.8
Net Yards Rushing	2032	1886
Avg. Per Game	127.0	117.9
Total Rushes	482	498
Net Yards Passing	3231	3214
Avg. Per Game	201.9	200.9
Tackled/Yards Lost	66/454	55/452
Gross Yards	3685	3666
Att./Completions	500/292	513/283
Completion Pct.	58.4	55.2
Had Intercepted	14	17
Punts/Avg.	92/42.4	83/40.3
Net Punting Avg.	35.0	33.5
Penalties/Yards Lost	86/674	87/773
Fumbles/Ball Lost	29/15	33/8
Touchdowns	42	42
Rushing	15	11
Passing	26	25
Returns	1	6
Avg. Time of Possession	29:51	30:09

1984 TEAM RECORD
Preseason (2-2)

Date	New England		Opponents
8/3	20	*New York Giants	48
8/11	13	Buffalo	23
8/17	31	Washington	27
8/24	36	*Kansas City	7
	100		105

Regular Season (9-7)

Date	New England		Opp.	Att.
9/2	21	Buffalo	17	48,528
9/9	7	Miami	28	66,083
9/16	38	*Seattle	23	43,140
9/23	10	*Washington	26	60,503
9/30	28	New York Jets	21	68,978
10/7	16	Cleveland	16	53,036
10/14	20	*Cincinnati	14	48,154
10/21	24	*Miami	44	60,711
10/28	30	*New York Jets	20	60,513
11/4	19	Denver	26	74,908
11/11	38	*Buffalo	10	43,313
11/18	50	Indianapolis	17	60,009
11/22	17	Dallas	20	55,341
12/2	10	*St. Louis	33	53,540
12/9	17	Philadelphia	27	41,581
12/16	16	*Indianapolis	10	22,383
	362		352	860,721

*Home Game

Score by Periods

New England	68	74	108	112	—	362
Opponents	78	115	84	75	—	352

Attendance
Home 392,257   Away 468,464   Total 860,721
Single game home record, 61,457 (12-5-71)
Single season home record, 475,081 (1978)

1984 INDIVIDUAL STATISTICS

Rushing

	Att.	Yds.	Avg.	LG	TD
C. James	160	790	4.9	73	1
Tatupu	133	553	4.2	20t	4
Collins	138	550	4.0	21	5
Eason	40	154	3.9	25t	5
Grogan	7	12	1.7	1	0
Fryar	2	−11	−5.5	1	0
Starring	2	−16	−8.0	0	0
New England	482	2032	4.2	73	15
Opponents	498	1886	3.8	53	11

Passing

	Att.	Comp.	Pct.	Yds.	TD	Int.	Tkld.	Rate
Eason	431	259	60.1	3228	23	8	59/409	93.4
Grogan	68	32	47.1	444	3	6	7/45	46.4
Kerrigan	1	1	100.0	13	0	0	0/0	118.8
New Eng.	500	292	58.4	3685	26	14	66/454	87.1
Opponents	513	283	55.2	3666	25	17	55/452	80.3

Receiving

	No.	Yds.	Avg.	LG	TD
D. Ramsey	66	792	12.0	34	7
Starring	46	657	14.3	65t	4
Dawson	39	427	10.9	27	4
Morgan	38	709	18.7	76t	5
C. James	22	159	7.2	16	0
Jones	19	244	12.8	22	2
Tatupu	16	159	9.9	24	0
Collins	16	100	6.3	19	0
Fryar	11	164	14.9	26	1
C. Weathers	8	115	14.4	29	2
Hawthorne	7	127	18.1	26	0
Robinson	4	32	8.0	17	1
New England	292	3685	12.6	76t	26
Opponents	283	3666	13.0	68t	25

Interceptions

	No.	Yds.	Avg.	LG	TD
Clayborn	3	102	34.0	85	0
Lippett	3	23	7.7	13	0
Marion	2	39	19.5	26	0
R. James	2	14	7.0	14	0
Gibson	2	4	2.0	4	0
Sanford	2	2	1.0	2	0
Dombroski	1	23	23.0	23	0
Blackmon	1	3	3.0	3	0
Nelson	1	0	0.0	0	0
New England	17	210	12.4	85	0
Opponents	14	237	16.9	86t	3

Punting

	No.	Yds.	Avg.	In 20	LG
Prestridge	44	1884	42.8	8	89
Camarillo	48	2020	42.1	12	61
New England	92	3904	42.4	20	89
Opponents	83	3347	40.3	17	64

Punt Returns

	No.	FC	Yds.	Avg.	LG	TD
Fryar	36	10	347	9.6	55	0
Starring	10	1	73	7.3	16	0
C. Weathers	1	0	7	7.0	7	0
Gibson	1	0	3	3.0	3	0
R. James	0	2	0	—	0	0
Sanford	0	2	0	—	0	0
New England	48	15	430	9.0	55	0
Opponents	45	12	442	9.8	47t	1

Kickoff Returns

	No.	Yds.	Avg.	LG	TD
Collins	25	544	21.8	46	0
J. Williams	23	461	20.0	29	0
Fryar	5	95	19.0	22	0
K. L. Lee	3	43	14.3	17	0
Robinson	3	38	12.7	14	0
Smith	1	22	22.0	22	0
Jones	1	20	20.0	20	0
Hawthorne	1	14	14.0	14	0
Tatupu	1	9	9.0	9	0
New England	63	1246	19.8	46	0
Opponents	73	1373	18.8	69	0

Scoring

	TD R	TD P	TD Rt	PAT	FG	Saf	TP
Franklin	0	0	0	42/42	22/28	0	108
D. Ramsey	0	7	0	0/0	0/0	0	42
Collins	5	0	0	0/0	0/0	0	30
Eason	5	0	0	0/0	0/0	0	30
Morgan	0	5	0	0/0	0/0	0	30
Dawson	0	4	0	0/0	0/0	0	24
Starring	0	4	0	0/0	0/0	0	24
Tatupu	4	0	0	0/0	0/0	0	24
Jones	0	2	1	0/0	0/0	0	18
C. Weathers	0	2	0	0/0	0/0	0	12
Fryar	0	1	0	0/0	0/0	0	6
C. James	1	0	0	0/0	0/0	0	6
Robinson	0	1	0	0/0	0/0	0	6
R. James	0	0	0	0/0	0/0	1	2
New England	15	26	1	42/42	22/28	1	362
Opponents	11	25	6	37/42	21/31	0	352

FIRST-ROUND SELECTIONS

(If Club had no first-round selection, first player drafted is listed with round in parentheses.)

Year	Player, College, Position
1960	Ron Burton, Northwestern, RB
1961	Tommy Mason, Tulane, RB
1962	Gary Collins, Maryland, WR
1963	Art Graham, Boston College, WR
1964	Jack Concannon, Boston College, QB
1965	Jerry Rush, Michigan State, DE
1966	Karl Singer, Purdue, T
1967	John Charles, Purdue, S
1968	Dennis Byrd, North Carolina State, DE
1969	Ron Sellers, Florida State, WR
1970	Phil Olsen, Utah State, DE
1971	Jim Plunkett, Stanford, QB
1972	Tom Reynolds, San Diego State, WR (2)
1973	John Hannah, Alabama, G
	Sam Cunningham, Southern California, RB
	Darryl Stingley, Purdue, WR
1974	Steve Corbett, Boston College, G (2)
1975	Russ Francis, Oregon, TE
1976	Mike Haynes, Arizona State, DB
	Pete Brock, Colorado, C
	Tim Fox, Ohio State, DB
1977	Raymond Clayborn, Texas, DB
	Stanley Morgan, Tennessee, WR
1978	Bob Cryder, Alabama, G
1979	Rick Sanford, South Carolina, DB
1980	Roland James, Tennessee, DB
	Vagas Ferguson, Notre Dame, RB
1981	Brian Holloway, Stanford, T
1982	Kenneth Sims, Texas, DT
	Lester Williams, Miami, DT
1983	Tony Eason, Illinois, QB
1984	Irving Fryar, Nebraska, WR
1985	Trevor Matich, Brigham Young, C

NEW ENGLAND PATRIOTS 1985 VETERAN ROSTER

No.	Name	Pos.	Ht.	Wt.	Birth-date	NFL Exp.	College	Birthplace	Residence	'84 Games/ Starts
85	Adams, Julius	DE	6-3	265	4/26/48	14	Texas Southern	Macon, Ga.	Roberta, Ga.	16/1
55	Blackmon, Don	LB	6-2	230	3/14/58	5	Tulsa	Pompano Beach, Fla.	Norfolk, Mass.	16/16
58	Brock, Pete	C	6-3	225	7/14/54	10	Colorado	Portland, Ore.	Norfolk, Mass.	12/12
3	Camarillo, Rich	P	5-11	191	11/29/59	5	Washington	Whittier, Calif.	Foxboro, Mass.	7/0
26	Clayborn, Ray	CB	6-0	186	1/2/55	9	Texas	Ft. Worth, Tex.	Austin, Tex.	16/16
33	Collins, Tony	RB-KR	5-11	212	5/27/50	5	East Carolina	Sanford, Fla.	North Easton, Mass.	16/5
87	Dawson, Lin	TE	6-3	240	6/24/59	5	North Carolina State	Norfolk, Va.	Kinston, N.C.	16/15
47	†Dombroski, Paul	S	6-0	185	8/8/56	6	Linfield College	Sumter, S.C.	Burlington, Mass.	14/0
11	Eason, Tony	QB	6-4	212	10/8/59	3	Illinois	Walnut Grove, Calif.	Walnut Grove, Calif.	16/13
56	Fairchild, Paul	G	6-2	235	8/14/61	2	Kansas	Carroll, Iowa	Glidden, Iowa	7/0
1	†Franklin, Tony	K	5-8	182	11/18/56	7	Texas A&M	Big Spring, Tex.	South Easton, Mass.	16/0
80	Fryar, Irving	WR-KR	6-0	200	9/28/62	2	Nebraska	Mount Holly, N.J.	Lincoln, Neb.	14/3
43	Gibson, Ernest	CB	5-10	185	10/3/61	2	Furman	Jacksonville, Fla.	Jacksonville, Fla.	15/8
59	†Golden, Tim	LB	6-1	220	11/15/59	4	Florida	Pahokee, Fla.	Gainesville, Fla.	15/0
14	Grogan, Steve	QB	6-4	210	7/24/53	11	Kansas State	San Antonio, Tex.	Foxboro, Mass.	3/3
68	Haley, Darryl	T	6-4	275	2/16/61	4	Utah	Gardena, Calif.	Salt Lake City, Utah	16/16
73	Hannah, John	G	6-3	265	4/4/51	13	Alabama	Canton, Ga.	Westwood, Mass.	15/15
40	Hawthorne, Greg	WR-RB	6-3	225	9/5/56	7	Baylor	Ft. Worth, Tex.	Ft. Worth, Tex.	14/1
70	†Henson, Luther	NT	6-0	275	3/25/59	4	Ohio State	Sandusky, Ohio	Sandusky, Ohio	9/0
76	Holloway, Brian	T	6-7	285	7/25/59	5	Stanford	Omaha, Neb.	Stephentown, N.Y.	16/16
51	Ingram, Brian	LB	6-4	235	10/31/59	4	Tennessee	Memphis, Tenn.	Stone Mountain, Ga.	12/0
32	James, Craig	RB	6-0	215	1/2/61	2	Southern Methodist	Jacksonville, Tex.	Dallas, Tex.	15/7
38	James, Roland	S	6-2	191	2/18/58	6	Tennessee	Jamestown, Ohio	Rehoboth, Mass.	15/15
83	Jones, Cedric	WR	6-0	184	6/1/60	4	Duke	Norfolk, Va.	Roanoke Rapids, N.C.	14/3
19	†Kerrigan, Mike	QB	6-3	205	4/27/60	3	Northwestern	Chicago, Ill.	Chicago, Ill.	1/0
22	†Lee, Keith	S	5-11	193	12/22/57	5	Colorado State	San Antonio, Tex.	North Attleboro, Mass.	15/0
42	Lippett, Ronnie	CB	5-11	180	12/10/60	3	Miami	Melbourne, Fla.	Sebring, Fla.	16/8
31	Marion, Fred	S	6-2	191	8/2/59	4	Miami	Gainesville, Fla.	Plainville, Mass.	16/10
50	McGrew, Larry	LB	6-5	233	7/23/57	5	Southern California	Berkeley, Calif.	Richmond, Calif.	16/15
23	McSwain, Rod	CB	6-1	198	1/28/62	2	Clemson	Caroleen, N.C.	Caroleen, N.C.	15/0
67	Moore, Steve	T	6-4	285	10/1/60	3	Tennessee State	Memphis, Tenn.	Walpole, Mass.	16/0
86	Morgan, Stanley	WR	5-11	181	2/17/55	9	Tennessee	Easley, N.C.	Germantown, Tenn.	13/12
75	†Morriss, Guy	C	6-4	270	5/13/51	13	Texas Christian	Colorado City, Tex.	Konawa, Okla.	16/5
57	Nelson, Steve	LB	6-2	230	4/26/51	12	North Dakota State	Farmington, Minn.	Norfolk, Mass.	16/16
98	Owens, Dennis	NT	6-1	258	2/24/60	4	North Carolina State	Clinton, N.C.	Huntsville, Ala.	16/16
88	Ramsey, Derrick	TE	6-5	235	12/23/56	8	Kentucky	Hastings, Fla.	Oakland, Calif.	16/13
52	Rembert, Johnny	LB	6-3	234	1/19/61	3	Clemson	Hollandale, Miss.	Arcadia, Fla.	7/0
95	Reynolds, Ed	LB	6-5	230	9/23/61	3	Virginia	Stuttgart, Germany	Ridgeway, Va.	16/0
41	Robinson, Bo	RB	6-2	235	5/27/56	7	West Texas State	Lamesa, Tex.	Duluth, Ga.	16/1
65	Rogers, Doug	DE	6-5	270	6/23/60	4	Stanford	Bakersfield, Calif.	Bakersfield, Calif.	12/0
25	Sanford, Rick	S	6-1	192	1/9/57	7	South Carolina	Rock Hill, S.C.	Foxboro, Mass.	16/7
77	Sims, Ken	DE	6-5	271	10/31/59	4	Texas	Kosse, Tex.	Austin, Tex.	16/16
81	Starring, Stephen	WR-KR	5-10	172	7/30/61	3	McNeese State	Baton Rouge, La.	Lake Charles, La.	16/16
30	Tatupu, Mosi	RB	6-0	227	4/26/55	8	Southern California	Pago Pago, Amer. Samoa	Plainville, Mass.	16/4
56	Tippett, Andre	LB	6-3	241	12/27/59	4	Iowa	Birmingham, Ala.	North Easton, Mass.	16/16
82	Weathers, Clarence	WR	5-9	170	1/10/62	3	Delaware State	Greens Pond, S.C.	Ft. Pierce, Fla.	9/0
24	Weathers, Robert	RB	6-2	222	9/13/60	4	Arizona State	Westfield, N.Y.	Stoughton, Mass.	2/0
53	Weishuhn, Clayton	LB	6-2	221	10/9/59	3	Angelo State	San Angelo, Tex.	San Angelo, Tex.	1/1
54	Williams, Ed	LB	6-4	244	8/9/61	2	Texas	Odessa, Tex.	Odessa, Tex.	14/0
44	Williams, Jon	RB-KR	5-9	205	6/1/61	2	Penn State	Somerville, N.J.	Somerville, N.J.	9/0
72	Williams, Lester	NT	6-3	272	1/19/59	4	Miami	Miami, Fla.	Ft. Lauderdale, Fla.	7/0
90	Williams, Toby	DE	6-3	265	11/19/59	3	Nebraska	Washington, D.C.	Mansfield, Mass.	16/15
61	Wooten, Ron	G	6-4	273	6/28/59	4	North Carolina	Bourne, Mass.	Norfolk, Mass.	16/16

†Option playout; subject to developments.

Also played with Patriots in '84—P Luke Prestridge (9 games), KR-CB-S Ricky Smith (1), DE Scott Virkus (5).

COACHING STAFF

Head Coach, Raymond Berry

Pro Career: Became ninth head coach in Patriots history when he was named to replace Ron Meyer on October 25, 1984, after eighth game of the season. Played receiver for the Baltimore Colts 1955-67. Made 631 catches for 9,275 yards and 68 touchdowns in his playing career. His number of career catches is presently fourth best in NFL history, while his receiving yardage is fifth best ever, and his career touchdown catches fourteenth. Helped Colts to two world championships (1958 and 1959) and to NFL Championship Game (1964). Named all-pro three times (1958-60) and played in five Pro Bowl games. Led NFL in receiving 1958-60. Holds NFL Championship Game records for yardage (178) and receptions (12), set in 1958 sudden-death title game vs. New York Giants. Was inducted into the Pro Football Hall of Fame on July 29, 1973, six years after his retirement. Was receivers coach with Dallas Cowboys in 1968-69, Detroit Lions 1973-75, Cleveland Browns 1976-77, and New England Patriots 1978-81. Career record: 4-4.

Background: Attended Paris (Texas) High School and Southern Methodist 1951-54, where played receiver. Coached receivers at University of Arkansas 1970-72.

Personal: Born February 27, 1933, in Corpus Christi, Texas. Raymond and his wife, Sally, reside in Medfield, Mass. with their children—Mark, Suzanne, and Ashley.

Assistant Coaches

Dean Brittenham, strength-conditioning; born June 25, 1931, Brady, Neb. lives in Foxboro, Mass. 1957 graduate of University of Nebraska, attending on basketball scholarship. No college or pro playing experience. College coach: University of Kansas 1962-64, Occidental 1965-67, Nebraska 1968-71. Pro coach: Kansas City Chiefs 1969-70, New Orleans Saints 1977-78, Denver Broncos 1982-83, Minnesota Vikings 1984, first year with Patriots.

Jim Carr, defensive backs; born March 25, 1933, Kayford, W.Va., lives in North Attleboro, Mass. Running back-defensive back-linebacker at Morris Harvey (now Univ. of Charleston, W.Va.) 1951-54. Pro running back, defensive back, linebacker Chicago Cardinals 1955-57, Montreal Alouettes (CFL) 1958, Philadelphia Eagles 1959-63, Washington Redskins 1964-65. Pro coach: Minnesota Vikings 1966-68, Chicago Bears 1969, 1973-74, Philadelphia Eagles 1970-72, Detroit Lions 1975-76, Buffalo Bills 1977, San Francisco 49ers 1978, Minnesota Vikings 1979-81, Denver Gold (USFL) 1983-84, first year with Patriots.

Bobby Grier, offensive backs; born November 10, 1942, Detroit, Mich., lives in Holliston, Mass. Running back Iowa 1961-64. No pro playing experience. College coach: Eastern Michigan 1974-77, Boston College 1978-80. Pro coach: Joined Patriots in 1981. Moved to team's scouting department 1982-84. Rejoined Patriots as coach in 1985.

Rod Humenuik, assistant head coach-offense, offensive line; born June 17, 1938, Detroit, Mich., lives in Foxboro, Mass. Guard Southern California 1956-58. Pro guard Winnipeg Blue Bombers (CFL) 1960-62. College coach: Fullerton, J.C. 1964-65, Southern California 1966-70, Cal State-Northridge 1971-72 (head coach). Pro coach: Toronto Argonauts (CFL) 1973-74, Cleveland Browns 1975-82, Kansas City Chiefs 1983-84, first year with Patriots.

Harold Jackson, assistant receivers coach; born January 6, 1946, Hattiesburg, Miss., lives in Foxboro, Mass. Receiver Jackson State 1964-67. Pro wide receiver Los Angeles Rams 1968, 1973-77, Philadelphia Eagles 1969-72, New England Patriots 1978-81, Seattle Seahawks 1983. Pro coach: First year with Patriots.

NEW ENGLAND PATRIOTS 1985 FIRST-YEAR ROSTER

Name	Pos.	Ht.	Wt.	Birth-date	College	Birthplace	Residence	How Acq.
Andreoli, John (1)	LB	6-2	230	3/30/60	Holy Cross	Jacksonville, N.C.	Worcester, Mass.	FA
Askew, Ricky (1)	TE	6-5	225	2/22/61	Rice	Altus, Okla.	Ealess, Tex.	FA
Baugh, Kevin (1)	WR	5-10	178	9/27/61	Penn State	Yonkers, N.Y.	Deer Park, N.Y.	FA
Bowman, Jim	S	6-2	210	10/26/63	Central Michigan	Cadillac, Mich.	Cadillac, Mich.	D2a
Creswell, Smiley (1)	DE	6-4	251	12/11/59	Michigan State	Everett, Wash.	Monroe, Wash.	D5('83)
Garron, Arnold	S	6-1	195	4/15/62	New Hampshire	Berwyn, Ill.	Framingham, Mass.	FA
Hodge, Milford	NT	6-3	278	3/11/61	Washington State	Hollywood, Calif.	San Bruno, Calif.	D8
Lewis, Paul	RB	5-8	197	9/12/62	Boston U.	Boston, Mass.	Boston, Mass.	D11
Matich, Trevor	C	6-4	270	10/9/61	Brigham Young	Sacramento, Calif.	Sacramento, Calif.	D1
McMillian, Audrey	CB-S	5-11	190	8/13/62	Houston	Carthage, Tex.	Carthage, Tex.	D3
Mocarski, Robert	T-G	6-4	265	5/9/63	Boston U.	Brooklyn, N.Y.	New Hyde Park, N.Y.	FA
Mumford, Tony	RB	6-0	215	6/14/63	Penn State	Yeadon, Pa.	Lindenwold, N.J.	D12
Pereira, Dave	CB-S	5-11	196	3/15/63	Boston College	Providence, R.I.	Providence, R.I.	FA
Phelan, Gerard	WR	6-0	190	1/20/63	Boston College	Willingboro, N.J.	Rosemont, Pa.	D4a
Ramsey, Tom (1)	QB	6-0	189	7/9/61	UCLA	Encino, Calif.	Palos Verdes, Ca.	D10('83)
Robinson, Melvin	WR	5-8	167	9/4/62	Houston	Garland, Tex.	Garland, Tex.	FA
Schubert, Eric	K	5-8	193	5/28/62	Pittsburgh	Abington, Pa.	Wanaque, N.J.	FA
Steevens, John	C-G	6-3	265	12/28/60	Fresno State	Pasadena, Calif.	Claremont, Calif.	FA
Thomas, Ben	DE	6-4	280	7/2/61	Auburn	Ashburn, Ga.	Ashburn, Ga.	D2b
Toth, Tom	T	6-5	275	5/23/62	Western Michigan	Blue Island, Ill.	Orland, Park, Ill.	D4
Veris, Garin	DE	6-4	255	2/27/63	Stanford	Chillicothe, Ohio	Chillicothe, Ohio	D2
Williams, Craig (1)	RB	6-1	225	4/4/62	Lafayette	Jamaica, N.Y.	Attleboro, Mass.	FA
Williams, Derwin (1)	WR	6-0	170	5/6/61	New Mexico	Brownwood, Tex.	Albuquerque, N.M.	FA
Windham, David (1)	LB	6-2	240	3/14/61	Jackson State	Mobile, Ala.	Providence, R.I.	D9('84)

Players who report to an NFL team for the first time are designated on rosters as rookies (R). If a player reported to an NFL training camp in a previous year but was not on the active squad for three or more regular season or postseason games, he is listed on the first-year roster and designated by a (1). Thereafter, a player who is on the active squad for three or more regular season or postseason games is credited with an additional year of playing experience.

NOTES

_____

_____

_____

_____

_____

_____

_____

_____

_____

_____

_____

Ed Khayat, defensive line; born September 14, 1935, Moss Point, Miss. lives in Foxboro, Mass. Offensive-defensive end Millsaps 1953, Perkinston J.C. 1954, Tulane 1955-56. Pro defensive end-defensive tackle Washington Redskins 1957, 1962-63, Philadelphia Eagles 1958-61, 1964-65, Boston Patriots 1966. Pro coach: New Orleans Saints 1967-70, Philadelphia Eagles 1971-72 (head coach), Detroit Lions 1973-74, Atlanta Falcons 1975-76, Baltimore Colts 1977-81, Detroit Lions 1982-84, first year with Patriots.

John Polonchek, special assistant to head coach; born January 1, 1928, in Granastrov, Czechoslokia, lives in Foxboro, Mass. Running back-defensive back Michigan State 1947-50. No pro playing experience. College coach: Michigan State 1950, 1955-57, Colorado 1959-60. Pro coach: Oakland Raiders 1967-71, Green Bay Packers 1972-74, New England Patriots 1975-81, New Jersey Generals (USFL) 1982-83, rejoined Patriots in 1985.

Rod Rust, defensive coordinator; born August 2, 1928, Webster City, Iowa, lives in Foxboro, Mass. Center-linebacker Iowa State 1947-49. No pro playing experience. College coach: New Mexico 1960-62, Stanford 1963-66, North Texas State 1967-72 (head coach). Pro coach: Montreal Alouettes (CFL) 1973-75, Philadelphia Eagles 1976-77, Kansas City Chiefs 1978-82, joined Patriots in 1983.

Dante Scarnecchia, special teams-tight ends; born February 15, 1948, Los Angeles, Calif., lives in Wrentham, Mass. Center Taft (Calif.), J.C. 1966-67, California Western 1968-70. No pro playing experience. College coach: California Western 1970-72, Iowa State 1973-74, Southern Methodist 1975-76, 1980-81, Pacific 1977-78, Northern Arizona 1979. Pro coach: Joined Patriots in 1982.

Don Shinnick, linebackers; born May 15, 1935, Kansas City, Mo. lives in Walpole, Mass. Guard-defensive back-running back-linebacker UCLA 1954-56. Pro linebacker Baltimore Colts 1957-69. College coach: Central Methodist College (Fayette, Missouri; head coach) 1979-81. Pro coach: Chicago Bears 1970-71, St. Louis Cardinals 1972, Oakland Raiders 1973-77, first year with Patriots.

Les Steckel, quarterbacks-receivers; born July 1, 1946, in Whitehall, Pa., lives in Foxboro, Mass. Running back, Kansas 1964-68. No pro playing experience. College coach: Colorado 1972-76, Navy 1977. Pro coach: San Francisco 49ers 1978, Minnesota Vikings 1979-84 (head coach, 1984), first year with Patriots.

NEW YORK JETS

American Football Conference
Eastern Division

Team Colors: Kelly Green and White

598 Madison Avenue
New York, New York 10022
Telephone: (212) 421-6600

Club Officials

Chairman of the Board: Leon Hess
President-Chief Operating Officer: Jim Kensil
Secretary and Administrative Manager:
   Steve Gutman
Director of Player Personnel: Mike Hickey
Pro Personnel Director: Jim Royer
Talent Scouts: Joe Collins, Don Grammer,
   Sid Hall, Marv Sunderland
Director of Public Relations: Frank Ramos
Assistant Director of Public Relations: Ron Cohen
Director of Operations: Tim Davey
Traveling Secretary: Mike Kensil
Ticket Manager: Bob Parente
Film Director: Jim Pons
Trainer: Bob Reese
Assistant Trainer: Pepper Burruss
Equipment Manager: Bill Hampton

Stadium: Giants Stadium • **Capacity:** 76,891
      East Rutherford, New Jersey 07073

Playing Surface: AstroTurf

Training Center: 1000 Fulton Avenue
      Hempstead, New York 11550
      (516) 538-6600

1985 SCHEDULE

Preseason

Aug. 10	**Philadelphia**	8:30
Aug. 17	at Cincinnati	7:00
Aug. 24	at New York Giants	8:00
Aug. 31	at Green Bay	7:00

Regular Season

Sept. 8	at Los Angeles Raiders	1:00
Sept. 15	**Buffalo**	1:00
Sept. 22	vs. Green Bay at Milwaukee	3:00
Sept. 29	**Indianapolis**	4:00
Oct. 6	at Cincinnati	4:00
Oct. 14	**Miami** (Monday)	9:00
Oct. 20	at New England	4:00
Oct. 27	**Seattle**	1:00
Nov. 3	at Indianapolis	4:00
Nov. 10	at Miami	4:00
Nov. 17	**Tampa Bay**	1:00
Nov. 24	**New England**	1:00
Nov. 28	at Detroit (Thanksgiving)	12:30
Dec. 8	at Buffalo	1:00
Dec. 14	**Chicago** (Saturday)	12:30
Dec. 22	**Cleveland**	1:00

JETS COACHING HISTORY

New York Titans 1960-62
(161-196-7)

1960-61	Sammy Baugh	14-14-0
1962	Clyde (Bulldog) Turner	5-9-0
1963-73	Weeb Ewbank	74-77-6
1974-75	Charley Winner*	9-14-0
1975	Ken Shipp	1-4-0
1976	Lou Holtz**	3-10-0
1976	Mike Holovak	0-1-0
1977-82	Walt Michaels	41-49-1
1983-84	Joe Walton	14-18-0

*Released after nine games in 1975
**Resigned after 13 games in 1976

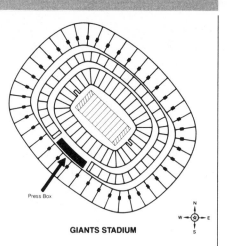

GIANTS STADIUM

RECORD HOLDERS

Individual Records—Career

Category	Name	Performance
Rushing (Yds.)	Emerson Boozer, 1966-1975	5,104
Passing (Yds.)	Joe Namath, 1965-1976	27,057
Passing (TDs)	Joe Namath, 1965-1976	170
Receiving (No.)	Don Maynard, 1960-1972	627
Receiving (Yds.)	Don Maynard, 1960-1972	11,732
Interceptions	Bill Baird, 1963-69	34
Punting (Avg.)	Curley Johnson, 1961-68	42.8
Punt Return (Avg.)	Dick Christy, 1961-63	16.2
Kickoff Return (Avg.)	Bobby Humphery, 1984	30.7
Field Goals	Pat Leahy, 1974-1984	158
Touchdowns (Tot.)	Don Maynard, 1960-1972	88
Points	Pat Leahy, 1974-1984	780

Individual Records—Single Season

Category	Name	Performance
Rushing (Yds.)	Freeman McNeil, 1984	1,070
Passing (Yds.)	Joe Namath, 1967	4,007
Passing (TDs)	Al Dorow, 1960	26
	Joe Namath, 1967	26
Receiving (No.)	George Sauer, 1967	75
Receiving (Yds.)	Don Maynard, 1967	1,434
Interceptions	Dainard Paulson, 1964	12
Punting (Avg.)	Curley Johnson, 1965	45.3
Punt Return (Avg.)	Dick Christy, 1961	21.3
Kickoff Return (Avg.)	Bobby Humphery, 1984	30.7
Field Goals	Jim Turner, 1968	34
Touchdowns (Tot.)	Art Powell, 1960	14
	Don Maynard, 1965	14
	Emerson Boozer, 1972	14
Points	Jim Turner, 1968	145

Individual Records—Single Game

Category	Name	Performance
Rushing (Yds.)	Matt Snell, 10-17-64	180
Passing (Yds.)	Joe Namath, 9-24-72	496
Passing (TDs)	Joe Namath, 9-24-72	6
Receiving (No.)	Clark Gaines, 9-21-80	17
Receiving (Yds.)	Don Maynard, 11-17-68	228
Interceptions	Dainard Paulson, 9-28-63	3
	Bill Baird, 10-31-64	3
	Rich Sowells, 9-23-73	3
Field Goals	Jim Turner, 11-3-68	6
	Bobby Howfield, 12-3-72	6
Touchdowns (Tot.)	Many times	3
	Last time by Wesley Walker, 9-23-84	
Points	Jim Turner, 11-3-68	19
	Pat Leahy, 9-16-84	19

1984 TEAM STATISTICS

	N.Y. Jets	Opp.
Total First Downs	310	341
Rushing	118	117
Passing	176	198
Penalty	16	26
Third Down: Made/Att.	90/217	85/214
Fourth Down: Made/Att.	8/19	5/14
Total Net Yards	5148	5566
Avg. Per Game	321.8	347.9
Total Plays	1044	1052
Avg. Per Play	4.9	5.3
Net Yards Rushing	2189	2064
Avg. Per Game	136.8	129.0
Total Rushes	504	497
Net Yards Passing	2959	3502
Avg. Per Game	184.9	218.9
Tackled/Yards Lost	52/382	44/360
Gross Yards	3341	3862
Att./Completions	488/272	511/312
Completion Pct.	55.7	61.1
Had Intercepted	21	15
Punts/Avg.	75/39.1	67/42.6
Net Punting Avg.	33.8	36.3
Penalties/Yards Lost	96/779	87/723
Fumbles/Ball Lost	26/13	34/18
Touchdowns	40	41
Rushing	17	16
Passing	20	24
Returns	3	1
Avg. Time of Possession	30:02	29:58

1984 TEAM RECORD
Preseason (1-3)

Date	New York Jets		Opponents
8/4	15	*Cincinnati	21
8/11	17	Houston	36
8/18	14	New York Giants	20
8/24	20	Los Angeles Raiders	14
	66		91

Regular Season (7-9)

Date	New York Jets			Opp.	Att.
9/2	23	Indianapolis		14	60,398
9/6	17	*Pittsburgh		23	70,564
9/16	43	*Cincinnati		23	64,193
9/23	28	Buffalo		26	48,330
9/30	21	*New England		28	68,978
10/7	17	Kansas City		16	48,895
10/14	24	Cleveland		20	55,673
10/21	28	*Kansas City		7	66,782
10/28	20	New England		30	60,513
11/4	17	*Miami		31	72,655
11/11	5	*Indianapolis		9	51,066
11/18	20	Houston		31	40,141
11/26	17	Miami		28	74,884
12/2	10	*New York Giants		20	74,975
12/8	21	*Buffalo		17	45,378
12/16	21	Tampa Bay		41	43,817
	332			364	947,242

*Home Game

Score by Periods

New York Jets	68	104	63	97	—	332
Opponents	73	90	95	106	—	364

Attendance

Home 514,591   Away 432,651   Total 947,242
Single game home record, 74,975 (12-2-84)
Single season home record, 514,591 (1984)

1984 INDIVIDUAL STATISTICS

Rushing

	Att.	Yds.	Avg.	LG	TD
McNeil	229	1070	4.7	53	5
Hector	124	531	4.3	64	1
Barber	31	148	4.8	18	2
Minter	34	136	4.0	14	1
Paige	35	130	3.7	24	7
Ryan	23	92	4.0	16	0
Harper	10	48	4.8	16	1
O'Brien	16	29	1.8	7	0
Dennison	1	4	4.0	4	0
Walker	1	1	1.0	1	0
Avellini, Chi.-Jets	3	−5	−1.7	0	0
N.Y. Jets	504	2189	4.3	64	17
Opponents	497	2064	4.2	51t	16

Passing

	Att.	Comp.	Pct.	Yds.	TD	Int.	Tkld.	Rate
Ryan	285	156	54.7	1939	14	14	30/214	72.0
O'Brien	203	116	57.1	1402	6	7	22/168	74.0
Avellini, Chi.-Jets	53	30	56.6	288	0	3	5/43	48.3
N.Y. Jets	488	272	55.7	3341	20	21	52/382	72.8
Opponents	511	312	61.1	3862	24	15	44/360	87.9

Receiving

	No.	Yds.	Avg.	LG	TD
Shuler	68	782	11.5	49	6
Walker	41	623	15.2	44t	7
Jones	32	470	14.7	37	1
McNeil	25	294	11.8	32	1
Hector	20	182	9.1	26	0
Gaffney	19	285	15.0	29	0
Dennison	16	141	8.8	20	1
Humphery	14	206	14.7	44t	1
Minter	10	109	10.9	39t	1
Barber	10	79	7.9	17	0
Paige	6	31	5.2	10	1
Harper	5	71	14.2	28	0
Klever	3	29	9.7	13	1
Sohn	2	28	14.0	16	0
Bruckner	1	11	11.0	11	0
N.Y. Jets	272	3341	12.3	49	20
Opponents	312	3862	12.4	80t	24

Interceptions

	No.	Yds.	Avg.	LG	TD
Carter	4	26	6.5	19	0
Ray	2	54	27.0	28	0
Lynn	2	16	8.0	16	0
Schroy	2	13	6.5	13	0
Buttle	2	5	2.5	5	0
Mullen	1	25	25.0	25	0
Springs	1	13	13.0	13	0
Clifton	1	0	0.0	0	0
N.Y. Jets	15	152	10.1	28	0
Opponents	21	207	9.9	30	0

Punting

	No.	Yds.	Avg.	In 20	LG
Ramsey	74	2935	39.7	19	64
N.Y. Jets	75	2935	39.1	19	64
Opponents	67	2854	42.6	18	82

Punt Returns

	No.	FC	Yds.	Avg.	LG	TD
Springs	28	10	247	8.8	33	0
Minter	4	2	44	11.0	18	0
Bruckner	2	0	25	12.5	20	0
Mullen	1	0	8	8.0	8	0
N.Y. Jets	35	12	324	9.3	33	0
Opponents	37	19	242	6.5	21	0

Kickoff Returns

	No.	Yds.	Avg.	LG	TD
Humphery	22	675	30.7	97t	1
Springs	23	521	22.7	73	0
Minter	10	224	22.4	52	0
Paige	3	7	2.3	7	0
Mullen	2	34	17.0	23	0
Bruckner	1	17	17.0	17	0
Davidson	1	9	9.0	9	0
Gaffney	1	6	6.0	6	0
Banker	1	5	5.0	5	0
Shuler	1	0	0.0	0	0
N.Y. Jets	65	1498	23.0	97t	1
Opponents	48	1030	21.5	54	0

Scoring

	TD R	TD P	TD Rt	PAT	FG	Saf	TP
Leahy	0	0	0	38/39	17/24	0	89
Paige	7	1	0	0/0	0/0	0	48
Walker	0	7	0	0/0	0/0	0	42
McNeil	5	1	0	0/0	0/0	0	36
Shuler	0	6	0	0/0	0/0	0	36
Barber	2	0	0	0/0	0/0	0	12
Humphery	0	1	1	0/0	0/0	0	12
Minter	1	1	0	0/0	0/0	0	12
Buttle	0	0	1	0/0	0/0	0	6
Dennison	0	1	0	0/0	0/0	0	6
Gastineau	0	0	1	0/0	0/0	0	6
Harper	1	0	0	0/0	0/0	0	6
Hector	1	0	0	0/0	0/0	0	6
Jones	0	1	0	0/0	0/0	0	6
Klever	0	1	0	0/0	0/0	0	6
Ryan	0	0	0	1/0	0/0	0	1
N.Y. Jets	17	20	3	39/39	17/24	1	332
Opponents	16	24	1	40/41	26/37	0	364

FIRST-ROUND SELECTIONS

(If Club had no first-round selection, first player drafted is listed with round in parentheses.)

Year	Player, College, Position
1960	George Izo, Notre Dame, QB
1961	Tom Brown, Minnesota, G
1962	Sandy Stephens, Minnesota, QB
1963	Jerry Stovall, Louisiana State, S
1964	Matt Snell, Ohio State, RB
1965	Joe Namath, Alabama, QB
	Tom Nowatzke, Indiana, RB
1966	Bill Yearby, Michigan, DT
1967	Paul Seiler, Notre Dame, T
1968	Lee White, Weber State, RB
1969	Dave Foley, Ohio State, T
1970	Steve Tannen, Florida, CB
1971	John Riggins, Kansas, RB
1972	Jerome Barkum, Jackson State, WR
	Mike Taylor, Michigan, LB
1973	Burgess Owens, Miami, DB
1974	Carl Barzilauskas, Indiana, DT
1975	Anthony Davis, Southern California, RB (2)
1976	Richard Todd, Alabama, QB
1977	Marvin Powell, Southern California, T
1978	Chris Ward, Ohio State, T
1979	Marty Lyons, Alabama, DE
1980	Johnny (Lam) Jones, Texas, WR
1981	Freeman McNeil, UCLA, RB
1982	Bob Crable, Notre Dame, LB
1983	Ken O'Brien, Cal-Davis, QB
1984	Russell Carter, Southern Methodist, DB
	Ron Faurot, Arkansas, DE
1985	Al Toon, Wisconsin, WR

NEW YORK JETS 1985 VETERAN ROSTER

No.	Name	Pos.	Ht.	Wt.	Birth-date	NFL Exp.	College	Birthplace	Residence	'84 Games/ Starts
60	Alexander, Dan	G	6-4	260	6/17/55	9	Louisiana State	Houston, Tex.	Houston, Tex.	16/16
35	Augustyniak, Mike	FB	5-11	226	7/17/56	4	Purdue	Fort Wayne, Ind.	Port Washington, N.Y.	0*
17	Avellini, Bob	QB	6-2	209	8/28/53	11	Maryland	Queens, N.Y.	Chicago, Ill.	4/1*
95	Baldwin, Tom	DT	6-4	270	5/13/61	2	Tulsa	Abergreen Park, Ill.	Tulsa, Okla.	16/2
63	Banker, Ted	G-C	6-2	255	2/17/61	2	Southeast Missouri	St. Louis, Mo.	Millstadt, Ill.	4/0
31	†Barber, Marion	FB	6-2	224	12/6/59	4	Minnesota	Ft. Lauderdale, Fla.	Plymouth, Minn.	14/5
58	Bell, Bobby	LB	6-3	217	2/7/62	2	Missouri	St. Paul, Minn.	Columbia, Mo.	15/2
78	Bennett, Barry	DT	6-4	260	12/10/55	8	Concordia	Long Prairie, Minn.	Buffalo, Minn.	15/13
64	Bingham, Guy	C-G-T	6-3	255	2/25/58	6	Montana	Koizumi Gumma Ken, Jap.	Missoula, Mont.	16/0
23	Bligen, Dennis	RB	5-11	215	3/3/62	2	St. John's	New York, N.Y.	Queens Village, N.Y.	1/0
83	Bruckner, Nick	WR	5-11	185	5/19/61	3	Syracuse	Astoria, N.Y.	Selden, N.Y.	16/0
51	Buttle, Greg	LB	6-3	232	6/20/54	10	Penn State	Atlantic City, N.J.	Jericho, N.Y.	14/13
27	Carter, Russell	CB-S	6-2	195	2/10/62	2	Southern Methodist	Ardmore, Pa.	Dallas, Tex.	11/8
59	Clifton, Kyle	LB	6-4	233	8/23/62	2	Texas Christian	Onley, Tex.	Fort Worth, Tex.	16/9
50	Crable, Bob	LB	6-3	234	9/22/59	4	Notre Dame	Cincinnati, Ohio	Loveland, Ohio	5/2
88	Davidson, Chy	WR	5-11	175	5/9/59	2	Rhode Island	Queens, N.Y.	Cambria Heights, N.Y.	3/0
22	†Dennis, Mike	S-CB	5-10	195	6/6/58	4	Wyoming	Los Angeles, Calif.	Pasadena, Calif.	6/2
86	Dennison, Glenn	TE	6-3	225	11/17/61	2	Miami	Beaver Falls, Pa.	Old Brookville, N.Y.	16/9
52	†Eliopulos, Jim	LB	6-2	229	4/18/59	3	Wyoming	Dearborn, Mich.	Cheyenne, Wyo.	11/0
74	Faurot, Ron	DE-LB	6-7	262	1/27/62	2	Arkansas	Wichita, Kan.	Hurst, Tex.	15/9
65	Fields, Joe	C	6-2	253	11/14/53	11	Widener	Woodbury, N.J.	Moorestown, N.J.	16/16
38	Floyd, George	S-CB	5-11	190	12/21/60	3	Eastern Kentucky	Tampa, Fla.	Florence, Ky.	8/2
81	Gaffney, Derrick	WR	6-1	182	5/24/55	8	Florida	Jacksonville, Fla.	Orange Park, Fla.	12/7
99	Gastineau, Mark	DE	6-5	265	11/20/56	7	East Central Oklahoma	Ardmore, Okla.	Halesite, N.Y.	16/16
94	Guilbeau, Rusty	LB	6-4	237	11/20/58	4	McNeese State	Sunset, La.	Sunset, La.	16/2
39	Hamilton, Harry	S	6-0	193	11/29/62	2	Penn State	Jamaica, N.Y.	Wilkes-Barre, Pa.	8/0
42	Harper, Bruce	RB-KR	5-8	179	6/20/55	9	Kutztown State	Englewood, N.J.	Norwood, N.J.	4/0
34	Hector, Johnny	RB	5-11	197	11/26/60	3	Texas A&M	Lafayette, La.	New Iberia, La.	13/2
84	Humphery, Bobby	WR-KR	5-10	170	8/23/61	2	New Mexico State	Lubbock, Tex.	Las Cruces, N.M.	16/4
40	Jackson, Bobby	CB	5-10	180	12/23/56	8	Florida State	Albany, Ga.	Westbury, N.Y.	3/2
55	t-Jackson, Charles	LB	6-2	222	3/22/55	8	Washington	Berkeley, Calif.	Fairway, Kan.	4/4
80	Jones, Johnny (Lam)	WR	5-11	180	4/4/58	6	Texas	Lawton, Okla.	Lampasas, Tex.	8/8
73	Klecko, Joe	DT-DE	6-3	263	10/15/53	9	Temple	Chester, Pa.	Malvern, Pa.	12/11
89	Klever, Rocky	TE	6-3	225	7/10/59	3	Montana	Portland, Ore.	Anchorage, Alaska	16/2
5	Leahy, Pat	K	6-0	193	3/19/51	12	St. Louis University	St. Louis, Mo.	St. Louis, Mo.	16/0
29	Lynn, Johnny	CB-S	6-0	198	12/19/56	6	UCLA	Los Angeles, Calif.	Pasadena, Calif.	14/14
93	Lyons, Marty	DE-DT	6-5	269	1/15/57	7	Alabama	Tokoma Park, Md.	Gallion, Ala.	13/10
68	†McElroy, Reggie	T	6-6	270	3/4/60	3	West Texas State	Beaumont, Tex.	Westbury, N.Y.	16/16
24	McNeil, Freeman	RB	5-11	212	4/22/59	5	UCLA	Jackson, Miss.	Huntington, N.Y.	12/12
56	Mehl, Lance	LB	6-3	233	2/14/58	6	Penn State	Bellaire, Ohio	Point Lookout, N.Y.	16/15
25	Minter, Cedric	RB-KR	5-10	200	11/13/58	2	Boise State	Charleston, S.C.	Boise, Idaho	8/2
20	Mullen, Davlin	CB-KR	6-1	177	2/17/60	3	Western Kentucky	McKeesport, Pa.	Houston, Tex.	15/6
7	O'Brien, Ken	QB	6-4	214	11/27/60	3	Cal-Davis	Brooklyn, N.Y.	Sacramento, Calif.	10/5
49	Paige, Tony	FB	5-10	230	10/14/62	2	Virginia Tech	Washington, D.C.	Blacksburg, Va.	16/3
79	Powell, Marvin	T	6-5	270	8/30/55	9	Southern California	Fort Bragg, N.C.	East Meadow, N.Y.	16/16
28	Ray, Darrol	S	6-1	198	6/25/58	6	Oklahoma	San Francisco, Calif.	Hempstead, N.Y.	15/12
10	Ryan, Pat	QB	6-3	210	9/16/55	8	Tennessee	Hutchinson, Kan.	Knoxville, Tenn.	16/11
48	Schroy, Ken	S	6-2	198	9/22/52	9	Maryland	Valley Forge, Pa.	Garden City, N.Y.	12/7
82	Shuler, Mickey	TE	6-3	231	8/21/56	8	Penn State	Harrisburg, Pa.	Marysville, Pa.	16/16
87	†Sohn, Kurt	WR	5-11	180	6/26/57	4	Fordham	Ithaca, N.Y.	Levittown, N.Y.	5/0
21	Springs, Kirk	S-KR	6-0	192	8/10/58	5	Miami, Ohio	Cincinnati, Ohio	Cincinnati, Ohio	16/11
53	Sweeney, Jim	G-C	6-4	260	8/8/62	2	Pittsburgh	Pittsburgh, Pa.	Pittsburgh, Pa.	10/2
70	Waldemore, Stan	G-T	6-4	269	2/20/55	8	Nebraska	Newark, N.J.	East Hanover, N.J.	14/14
85	Walker, Wesley	WR	6-0	182	5/26/55	9	California	San Bernardino, Calif.	Dix Hills, N.Y.	12/10
57	Woodring, John	LB	6-2	232	4/4/59	5	Brown	Philadelphia, Pa.	Port Washington, N.Y.	15/5

* Augustyniak missed '84 season due to injury; Avellini played 4 games with Chicago in '84.

†Option playout; subject to developments.

t-Jets traded for C. Jackson (Kansas City).

Also played with Jets in '84—S Fernanza Burgess (11 games), C George Lilja (3), CB-S Skip Lane (3), P Chuck Ramsey (16), DT-DE Ben Rudolph (16).

COACHING STAFF

Head Coach,
Joe Walton

Pro Career: Begins third year as head coach of the Jets. Entered pro coaching ranks as an assistant with the New York Giants in 1969-73. Joined the Washington Redskins' staff in 1974 and became the Redskins' offensive coordinator in 1978. Originally came to the Jets as the offensive coordinator in 1981. Career record: 14-18.

Background: Played tight end for the University of Pittsburgh 1953-56, before playing professionally for the Washington Redskins 1957-60 and the New York Giants 1961-63. Walton did some radio work before joining the Giants' staff as a scout in 1967-68.

Personal: Born December 15, 1935, Beaver Falls, Pa. Joe and his wife, Ginger, have three children— Jodi, Stacy, and Joseph, Jr. They live in Long Island.

Assistant Coaches

Bill Austin, offensive line; born October 18, 1928, San Pedro, Calif., lives in Long Island. Tackle Oregon State 1947-49. Pro guard New York Giants 1949-50, 1953-57. College coach: Wichita State 1958. Pro coach: Green Bay Packers 1959-64, Los Angeles Rams 1965, Pittsburgh Steelers (head coach) 1966-68, Washington Redskins 1969-70 (head coach 1970), 1973-77, Chicago Bears 1971, St. Louis Cardinals 1972, New York Giants 1979-82, New Jersey Generals (USFL) 1983-84, first year with Jets.

Zeke Bratkowski, quarterbacks; born October 20, 1931, Danville, Ill., lives in Long Island. Quarterback Georgia 1951-53. Pro quarterback Chicago Bears 1954, 1957-60, Los Angeles Rams 1961-63, Green Bay Packers 1963-68, 1971. Pro coach: Green Bay Packers 1969-70, 1975-81, Chicago Bears 1972-74, Indianapolis Colts 1982-84, first year with Jets.

Ray Callahan, defensive line; born April 28, 1933, Lebanon, Ky., lives in Long Island. Guard-linebacker Kentucky 1952-56. No pro playing experience. College coach: Kentucky 1963-67, Cincinnati 1968-72 (head coach 1969-72). Pro coach: Baltimore Colts 1973, Florida Blazers (WFL) 1974, Chicago Bears 1975-77, Houston Oilers 1981-82, joined Jets in 1983.

Bud Carson, defensive coordinator; born April 28, 1931, Brackenridge, Pa., lives in Long Island. Defensive back North Carolina 1948-52. No pro playing experience. College coach: North Carolina 1957-64, South Carolina 1965, Georgia Tech 1966-71 (head coach). Pro coach: Pittsburgh Steelers 1972-77, Los Angeles Rams 1978-81, Baltimore Colts 1982, Kansas City Chiefs 1983-84, first year with Jets.

Mike Faulkiner, special assistant to the head coach; born March 27, 1947, Cameron, W. Va., lives in Long Island. Quarterback-defensive back West Virginia Tech 1967-70. No pro playing experience. College coach: Eastern Illinois 1981. Pro coach: Toronto Argonauts (CFL) 1979, New York Giants 1980, Montreal Alouettes (CFL) 1982, joined Jets in 1983.

Bobby Hammond, running backs; born February 20, 1952, Orangeburg, S.C., lives in New York. Running back Morgan State 1973-75. Pro running back New York Giants 1976-79, Washington Redskins 1979-80. Pro coach: Joined Jets in 1983.

Rich Kotite, offensive coordinator-receivers; born October 13, 1942, Brooklyn, N.Y., lives in Long Island. End Wagner 1963-65. Pro tight end New York Giants 1967, 1969-72, Pittsburgh Steelers 1968. College coach: Tennessee-Chattanooga 1973-76. Pro coach: New Orleans Saints 1977, Cleveland Browns 1978-82, joined Jets in 1983.

Larry Pasquale, special teams; born April 21, 1941, New York, N.Y., lives in New York. Quarterback Bridgeport 1961-63. No pro playing experience. College coach: Slippery Rock State 1967, Boston University 1968, Navy 1969-70, Massachusetts 1971-75, Idaho State 1976. Pro coach: Montreal Alouettes (CFL) 1977-78, Detroit Lions 1979, joined Jets in 1980.

NEW YORK JETS 1985 FIRST-YEAR ROSTER

Name	Pos.	Ht.	Wt.	Birth-date	College	Birthplace	Residence	How Acq.
Allen, Doug	WR	5-10	180	4/22/63	Arizona State	Columbus, Ohio	Baldwin Park, Calif.	D4
Armstrong, Tron (1)	WR	6-2	200	8/18/61	Eastern Kentucky	St. Petersburg, Fla.	Richmond, Ky.	D5('84)
Barnes, Duane	T	6-5	268	8/1/60	West Virginia	Pittsburgh, Pa.	Pittsburgh, Pa.	FA
Benson, Troy	LB	6-2	235	7/30/63	Pittsburgh	Altoona, Pa.	Altoona, Pa.	D5
Biestek, Robert	FB	6-2	235	6/7/61	Boston College	Meriden, Conn.	Old Saybrook, Conn.	FA
Bradley, Ramiro (1)	T	6-5	285	9/17/58	Kansas State	Trenton, N.J.	Manhattan, Kan.	FA
Campbell, Todd	DT	6-1	265	1/28/61	West Virginia	New Kensington, Pa.	Coral Springs, Fla.	FA
Collins, Scott (1)	LB	6-1	235	11/10/60	Oregon Tech	San Diego, Calif.	Huntington Bch., Calif.	FA
Cone, Ronny (1)	FB	6-2	225	4/27/61	Georgia Tech	Bulloch County, Ga.	Statesboro, Ga.	D10('84)
Deaton, Jeff	G-T	6-3	280	4/26/62	Stanford	Mankato, Minn.	St. Cloud, Minn.	D6
Durden, Mike	CB-S	6-1	185	5/4/59	UCLA	Los Angeles, Calif.	Los Angeles, Calif.	FA
Elder, Donnie	CB	5-9	175	12/13/62	Memphis State	Chattanooga, Tenn.	Chattanooga, Tenn.	D3
Franklin, Derrick	CB	5-10	179	7/13/61	Fresno State	Fresno, Calif.	Fresno, Calif.	FA
Furnas, Mike (1)	RB	6-0	235	4/18/61	Tennessee	Miami, Okla.	Knoxville, Tenn.	FA
Gardner, Kenneth (1)	TE	6-4	220	1/25/60	Tennessee State	Springfield, Tenn.	Nashville, Tenn.	FA
Glenn, Kerry	CB	5-9	175	3/31/62	Minnesota	East St. Louis, Ill.	East St. Louis, Ill.	D10
Green, Darren	WR	5-9	168	3/19/62	Kansas	Lawrence, Kan.	Lawrence, Kan.	FA
Griggs, Billy (1)	TE	6-3	230	8/4/62	Virginia	Camden, N.J.	Pensauken, N.J.	D8('84)
Gunter, Gregory	C	6-3	265	5/16/62	C.W. Post	Glen Cove, N.Y.	Sea Cliff, N.Y.	FA
Harris, Willie (1)	CB-S	6-1	185	4/4/60	North Carolina	Wilson, N.C.	Wilson, N.C.	FA
Howard, Doug (1)	G	6-6	268	6/14/59	North Carolina State	Washington, D.C.	Berwyn, Pa.	FA
Hunter, Jimmy (1)	LB	6-2	225	4/10/60	Indiana	Birmingham, Ala.	Tampa, Fla.	FA
Kaifes, Eric (1)	P	6-4	215	7/16/60	Southern Methodist	Kansas City, Kan.	Kansas City, Kan.	FA
Luft, Brian	DT	6-6	270	9/5/63	Southern California	Fresno, Calif.	Fresno, Calif.	D5a
Lyles, Lester	S	6-3	215	12/27/62	Virginia	Washington, D.C.	Washington, D.C.	D2
McArthur, Kevin (1)	LB	6-1	223	5/11/62	Lamar	Cameron, La.	Beaumont, Tex.	FA
McCarthy, John	QB	6-4	208	1/31/61	Williams	New York, N.Y.	Oradell, N.J.	FA
Messemer, James	K	6-4	215	8/3/59	Texas Tech	Jersey City, N.J.	Englewood, Colo.	FA
Miano, Rich	S	6-0	200	9/3/62	Hawaii	Newton, Mass.	Honolulu, Hawaii	D6a
Monger, Matt	LB	6-1	235	11/15/61	Oklahoma State	Denver, Colo.	Miami, Okla.	D8
Newman, Donald	S	6-2	205	11/22/58	Idaho	New Orleans, La.	New Orleans, La	FA
Ogren, Mark (1)	LB	6-3	219	11/16/61	Minnesota-Duluth	Duluth, Minn.	Port Wing, Wis.	FA
Pendock, Bill	DT	6-2	269	3/7/61	Syracuse	Syracuse, N.Y.	Liverpool, N.Y.	FA
Phelps, Randy	WR	6-2	190	8/16/59	North Carolina State	Plymouth, N.C.	Cary, N.C.	FA
Reda, Louis (1)	S	6-0	192	10/10/61	Delaware	Bronx, N.Y.	Yonkers, N.Y.	FA
Schuchts, Wayne (1)	QB-P	6-2	205	3/25/61	Virginia	Pittsburgh, Pa.	Hollywood, Fla.	FA
Shumate, Mark	DT	6-5	265	3/30/60	Wisconsin	Madison, Wis.	Poynette, Wis.	FA
Smith, Tony	WR	5-11	170	6/28/62	San Jose State	San Diego, Calif.	San Diego, Calif.	D5b
Tate, Benjamin (1)	FB	6-0	230	8/29/61	N. Carolina Central	Philadelphia, Pa.	Berlin, Md.	FA
Toon, Al	WR	6-4	200	4/30/63	Wisconsin	Newport News, Va.	Newport News, Va.	D1
Viaene, Jim	DT	6-2	263	3/19/62	Wisconsin-Superior	Tacoma, Wash.	Appleton, Wis.	FA
Wallace, Bill	WR	6-2	190	2/14/62	Pittsburgh	Greensburg, Pa.	Flemington, N.J.	D12
Waters, Mike	FB	6-2	225	3/15/62	San Diego State	Chula Vista, Calif.	Ridgecrest, Calif.	D9
White, Brad	DE	6-6	245	9/26/61	Texas Tech	Lanesa, Tex.	Tahoka, Tex.	D11
Williams, James (1)	TE	6-1	223	4/18/61	Wyoming	Tuscaloosa, Ala.	Syracuse, N.Y.	FA
Woetzel, Keith (1)	LB	6-2	222	11/15/60	Rutgers	Waldwick, N.J.	Waldwick, N.J.	FA
Wright, Bret (1)	P	6-4	205	1/5/62	S.E. Louisiana	Ponchatoula, La.	Denham Sp., La.	D8a('84)

Players who report to an NFL team for the first time are designated on rosters as rookies (R). If a player reported to an NFL training camp in a previous year but was not on the active squad for three or more regular season or postseason games, he is listed on the first-year roster and designated by a (1). Thereafter, a player who is on the active squad for three or more regular season or postseason games is credited with an additional year of playing experience.

NOTES

_____
_____
_____
_____
_____
_____
_____
_____
_____

Dan Radakovich, linebackers ; born November 27, 1935, Duquesne, Pa., lives in Long Island. Center-linebacker Penn State 1954-56. No pro playing experience. College coach: Penn State 1960-69, Cincinnati 1970, Colorado 1972-73, North Carolina State 1982. Pro coach: Pittsburgh Steelers 1971, 1974-77, San Francisco 49ers 1978, Los Angeles Rams 1979-81, Denver Broncos 1983, Minnesota Vikings 1984, first year with Jets.

PITTSBURGH STEELERS

**American Football Conference
Central Division**

Team Colors: Black and Gold

**Three Rivers Stadium
300 Stadium Circle
Pittsburgh, Pennsylvania 15212
Telephone:** (412) 323-1200

Club Officials

Chairman of the Board: Arthur J. Rooney, Sr.
President: Daniel M. Rooney
Vice President: John R. McGinley
Vice President: Arthur J. Rooney, Jr.
Traveling Secretary: Jim Boston
Controller: Dennis P. Thimons
Assistant Controller: Dan Ferens
Publicity Director: Joe Gordon
Director of Player Personnel: Dick Haley
Assistant Director of Player Personnel:
   William Nunn, Jr.
Pro Talent Scout: Tom Modrak
Talent Scout-West Coast: Bob Schmitz
College Talent Scout: Joe Krupa
Director of Ticket Sales: Geraldine R. Glenn
Trainer: Ralph Berlin
Equipment Manager: Anthony Parisi

Stadium: Three Rivers Stadium •
   Capacity: 59,000
   300 Stadium Circle
   Pittsburgh, Pennsylvania 15212

Playing Surface: AstroTurf

Training Camp: St. Vincent College
   Latrobe, Pennsylvania 15650

1985 SCHEDULE

Preseason

Aug. 10	at Tampa Bay	8:00
Aug. 17	at Minnesota	7:00
Aug. 23	at St. Louis	7:30
Aug. 30	**New York Giants**	7:30

Regular Season

Sept. 8	**Indianapolis**	1:00
Sept. 16	at Cleveland (Monday)	9:00
Sept. 22	**Houston**	1:00
Sept. 30	**Cincinnati** (Monday)	9:00
Oct. 6	at Miami	1:00
Oct. 13	at Dallas	12:00
Oct. 20	**St. Louis**	1:00
Oct. 27	at Cincinnati	4:00
Nov. 3	**Cleveland**	1:00
Nov. 10	at Kansas City	12:00
Nov. 17	at Houston	12:00
Nov. 24	**Washington**	1:00
Dec. 1	**Denver**	1:00
Dec. 8	at San Diego	6:00
Dec. 15	**Buffalo**	1:00
Dec. 21	at N.Y. Giants (Saturday)	12:30

STEELERS COACHING HISTORY

(318-350-20)

1933	Forrest (Jap) Douds	3-6-2
1934	Luby DiMelio	2-10-0
1935-36	Joe Bach	10-14-0
1937-39	Johnny Blood (McNally)	6-19-0
1939-40	Walter Kiesling	3-13-3
1941	Bert Bell	0-2-0
	Aldo (Buff) Donelli	0-5-0
1941-44	Walter Kiesling*	13-20-2
1945	Jim Leonard	2-8-0
1946-47	Jock Sutherland	13-10-1
1948-51	Johnny Michelosen	20-26-2
1952-53	Joe Bach	11-13-0
1954-56	Walter Kiesling	14-22-0
1957-64	Raymond (Buddy) Parker	51-47-6
1965	Mike Nixon	2-12-0
1966-68	Bill Austin	11-28-3
1969-84	Chuck Noll	157-95-1

*Co-Coach with Earl (Greasy) Neale in Philadelphia-Pittsburgh merger in 1943 and with Phil Handler in Chicago Cardinals-Pittsburgh merger in 1944.

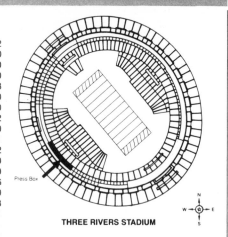

THREE RIVERS STADIUM

RECORD HOLDERS

Individual Records—Career

Category	Name	Performance
Rushing (Yds.)	Franco Harris, 1972-1983	11,950
Passing (Yds.)	Terry Bradshaw, 1970-1983	27,989
Passing (TDs)	Terry Bradshaw, 1970-1983	212
Receiving (No.)	John Stallworth, 1974-1984	387
Receiving (Yds.)	John Stallworth, 1974-1984	6,799
Interceptions	Mel Blount, 1971-1983	57
Punting (Avg.)	Bobby Joe Green, 1960-61	45.7
Punt Return (Avg.)	Bobby Gage, 1949-1950	14.9
Kickoff Return (Avg.)	Lynn Chandnois, 1950-56	29.6
Field Goals	Roy Gerela, 1971-78	146
Touchdowns (Tot.)	Franco Harris, 1972-1983	100
Points	Roy Gerela, 1971-78	731

Individual Records—Single Season

Category	Name	Performance
Rushing (Yds.)	Franco Harris, 1975	1,246
Passing (Yds.)	Terry Bradshaw, 1979	3,724
Passing (TDs)	Terry Bradshaw, 1978	28
Receiving (No.)	John Stallworth, 1984	80
Receiving (Yds.)	John Stallworth, 1984	1,395
Interceptions	Mel Blount, 1975	11
Punting (Avg.)	Bobby Joe Green, 1961	47.0
Punt Return (Avg.)	Bobby Gage, 1949	16.0
Kickoff Return (Avg.)	Lynn Chandnois, 1952	35.2
Field Goals	Roy Gerela, 1973	29
Touchdowns (Tot.)	Franco Harris, 1976	14
Points	Roy Gerela, 1973	123

Individual Records—Single Game

Category	Name	Performance
Rushing (Yds.)	John Fuqua, 12-20-70	218
Passing (Yds.)	Bobby Layne, 12-3-58	409
Passing (TDs)	Terry Bradshaw, 11-15-81	5
Receiving (No.)	J.R. Wilburn, 10-22-67	12
Receiving (Yds.)	Buddy Dial, 10-22-61	235
Interceptions	Jack Butler, 12-13-53	4
Field Goals	Many times	4
	Last time by Gary Anderson, 11-6-83	
Touchdowns (Tot.)	Ray Mathews, 10-17-54	4
	Roy Jefferson, 11-3-68	4
Points	Ray Mathews, 10-17-54	24
	Roy Jefferson, 11-3-68	24

1984 TEAM STATISTICS

	Pittsburgh	Opp.
Total First Downs	302	282
Rushing	117	87
Passing	167	167
Penalty	18	28
Third Down: Made/Att.	91/226	73/222
Fourth Down: Made/Att.	10/19	8/14
Total Net Yards	5420	4916
Avg. Per Game	338.8	307.3
Total Plays	1052	1016
Avg. Per Play	5.2	4.8
Net Yards Rushing	2179	1617
Avg. Per Game	136.2	101.1
Total Rushes	574	454
Net Yards Passing	3241	3299
Avg. Per Game	202.6	206.2
Tackled/Yards Lost	35/278	47/390
Gross Yards	3519	3689
Att./Completions	443/240	515/299
Completion Pct.	54.2	58.1
Had Intercepted	25	31
Punts/Avg.	70/41.2	90/42.4
Net Punting Avg.	34.7	32.5
Penalties/Yards Lost	112/948	107/945
Fumbles/Ball Lost	40/15	30/11
Touchdowns	45	35
Rushing	13	12
Passing	25	19
Returns	7	4
Avg. Time of Possession	30:33	29:27

1984 TEAM RECORD

Preseason (3-1)

Date	Pittsburgh		Opponents
8/4	31	Cleveland	14
8/11	20	*Philadelphia (OT)	17
8/16	20	Dallas	10
8/25	9	New York Giants	16
	80		57

Regular Season (9-7)

Date	Pittsburgh		Opp.	Att.
9/2	27	*Kansas City	37	56,709
9/6	23	New York Jets	17	70,564
9/16	24	*Los Angeles Rams	14	58,104
9/23	10	Cleveland	20	77,312
10/1	38	*Cincinnati	17	57,098
10/7	7	*Miami	31	59,103
10/14	20	San Francisco	17	59,110
10/21	16	Indianapolis	17	60,026
10/28	35	*Atlanta	10	55,971
11/4	35	*Houston	7	48,892
11/11	20	Cincinnati	22	52,497
11/19	24	New Orleans	27	66,005
11/25	52	*San Diego	24	55,856
12/2	20	Houston (OT)	23	39,782
12/9	23	*Cleveland	20	55,825
12/16	13	Los Angeles Raiders	7	83,056
	387		310	955,910

*Home Game   (OT) Overtime

Score by Periods

Pittsburgh	50	147	95	95	0	—	387
Opponents	26	105	69	107	3	—	310

Attendance

Home 447,558   Away 508,352   Total 955,910
Single game home record, 59,263 (10-16-83)
Single season home record, 462,567 (1983)

1984 INDIVIDUAL STATISTICS

Rushing

	Att.	Yds.	Avg.	LG	TD
Pollard	213	851	4.0	52	6
Abercrombie	145	610	4.2	31	1
Erenberg	115	405	3.5	31t	2
Corley	18	89	4.9	23	0
Veals	31	87	2.8	9	0
Lipps	3	71	23.7	36t	1
Malone	25	42	1.7	13t	3
Gillespie	7	18	2.6	9	0
Woodley	11	14	1.3	7	0
Colquitt	1	0	0.0	0	0
Spencer	1	0	0.0	0	0
Capers	1	−3	−3.0	−3	0
Campbell	3	−5	−1.7	0	0
Pittsburgh	574	2179	3.8	52	13
Opponents	454	1617	3.6	31	12

Passing

	Att.	Comp.	Pct.	Yds.	TD	Int.	Tkld.	Rate
Malone	272	147	54.0	2137	16	17	25/211	73.4
Woodley	156	85	54.5	1273	8	7	10/67	79.9
Campbell	15	8	53.3	109	1	1	0/0	71.3
Pittsburgh	443	240	54.2	3519	25	25	35/278	75.6
Opponents	515	299	58.1	3689	19	31	47/390	67.5

Receiving

	No.	Yds.	Avg.	LG	TD
Stallworth	80	1395	17.4	51	11
Lipps	45	860	19.1	80t	9
Erenberg	38	358	9.4	25	1
Pollard	21	186	8.9	18	0
Thompson	17	291	17.1	59	3
Abercrombie	16	135	8.4	59	0
Capers	7	81	11.6	19	0
Kolodziejski	5	59	11.8	22	0
Cunningham	4	64	16.0	29	1
D. Nelson	2	31	15.5	19	0
Sweeney	2	25	12.5	16	0
Garrity	2	22	11.0	12	0
Gillespie	1	12	12.0	12	0
Pittsburgh	240	3519	14.7	80t	25
Opponents	299	3689	12.3	68	19

Interceptions

	No.	Yds.	Avg.	LG	TD
Shell	7	61	8.7	52t	1
Washington	6	138	23.0	69t	2
Woodruff	5	56	11.2	42t	1
Hinkle	3	77	25.7	43	0
E. Williams	3	49	16.3	44	0
Merriweather	2	9	4.5	8	0
Woods	2	0	0.0	0	0
C. Brown	1	31	31.0	31	0
Cole	1	12	12.0	12	0
Clayton	1	0	0.0	0	0
Pittsburgh	31	433	14.0	69t	4
Opponents	25	371	14.8	70	1

Punting

	No.	Yds.	Avg.	In 20	LG
Colquitt	70	2883	41.2	21	62
Pittsburgh	70	2883	41.2	21	62
Opponents	90	3818	42.4	13	60

Punt Returns

	No.	FC	Yds.	Avg.	LG	TD
Lipps	53	2	656	12.4	76t	1
Woods	6	0	40	6.7	14	0
Clayton	1	0	0	0.0	0	0
Long	1	0	0	0.0	0	0
Pittsburgh	61	2	696	11.4	76t	1
Opponents	37	6	351	9.5	58t	1

Kickoff Returns

	No.	Yds.	Avg.	LG	TD
Erenberg	28	575	20.5	47	0
Spencer	18	373	20.7	40	0
Veals	4	40	10.0	18	0
Corley	1	15	15.0	15	0
Gillespie	1	12	12.0	12	0
C. Brown	1	11	11.0	11	0
Catano	1	0	0.0	0	0
Pittsburgh	54	1026	19.0	47	0
Opponents	61	1338	21.9	97t	1

Scoring

	TD R	TD P	TD Rt	PAT	FG	Saf	TP
Anderson	0	0	0	45/45	24/32	0	117
Lipps	1	9	1	0/0	0/0	0	66
Stallworth	0	11	0	0/0	0/0	0	66
Pollard	6	0	0	0/0	0/0	0	36
Erenberg	2	1	0	0/0	0/0	0	18
Malone	3	0	0	0/0	0/0	0	18
Thompson	0	3	0	0/0	0/0	0	18
Washington	0	0	2	0/0	0/0	0	12
Woodruff	0	0	2	0/0	0/0	0	12
Abercrombie	1	0	0	0/0	0/0	0	6
Cunningham	0	1	0	0/0	0/0	0	6
Hinkle	0	0	1	0/0	0/0	0	6
Shell	0	0	1	0/0	0/0	0	6
Pittsburgh	13	25	7	45/45	24/32	0	387
Opponents	12	19	4	34/35	22/28	0	310

FIRST-ROUND SELECTIONS

(If Club had no first-round selection, first player drafted is listed with round in parentheses.)

Year	Player, College, Position
1936	Bill Shakespeare, Notre Dame, B
1937	Mike Basrak, Duquesne, C
1938	Byron (Whizzer) White, Colorado, B
1939	Bill Patterson, Baylor, B (3)
1940	Kay Eakin, Arkansas, B
1941	Chet Gladchuk, Boston College, C (2)
1942	Bill Dudley, Virginia, B
1943	Bill Daley, Minnesota, B
1944	Johnny Podesto, St. Mary's, California, B
1945	Paul Duhart, Florida, B
1946	Felix (Doc) Blanchard, Army, B
1947	Hub Bechtol, Texas, E
1948	Dan Edwards, Georgia, E
1949	Bobby Gage, Clemson, B
1950	Lynn Chandnois, Michigan State, B
1951	Butch Avinger, Alabama, B
1952	Ed Modzelewski, Maryland, B
1953	Ted Marchibroda, St. Bonaventure, B
1954	Johnny Lattner, Notre Dame, B
1955	Frank Varrichione, Notre Dame, T
1956	Gary Glick, Colorado A&M, B
	Art Davis, Mississippi State, B
1957	Len Dawson, Purdue, B
1958	Larry Krutko, West Virginia, B (2)
1959	Tom Barnett, Purdue, B (8)
1960	Jack Spikes, Texas Christian, RB
1961	Myron Pottios, Notre Dame, LB (2)
1962	Bob Ferguson, Ohio State, RB
1963	Frank Atkinson, Stanford, T (8)
1964	Paul Martha, Pittsburgh, S
1965	Roy Jefferson, Utah, WR (2)
1966	Dick Leftridge, West Virginia, RB
1967	Don Shy, San Diego State, RB (2)
1968	Mike Taylor, Southern California, T
1969	Joe Greene, North Texas State, DT
1970	Terry Bradshaw, Louisiana Tech, QB
1971	Frank Lewis, Grambling, WR
1972	Franco Harris, Penn State, RB
1973	J.T. Thomas, Florida State, DB
1974	Lynn Swann, Southern California, WR
1975	Dave Brown, Michigan, DB
1976	Bennie Cunningham, Clemson, TE
1977	Robin Cole, New Mexico, LB
1978	Ron Johnson, Eastern Michigan, DB
1979	Greg Hawthorne, Baylor, RB
1980	Mark Malone, Arizona State, QB
1981	Keith Gary, Oklahoma, DE
1982	Walter Abercrombie, Baylor, RB
1983	Gabriel Rivera, Texas Tech, DT
1984	Louis Lipps, Southern Mississippi, WR
1985	Darryl Sims, Wisconsin, DE

PITTSBURGH STEELERS 1985 VETERAN ROSTER

No.	Name	Pos.	Ht.	Wt.	Birth-date	NFL Exp.	College	Birthplace	Residence	'84 Games/ Starts
34	Abercrombie, Walter	RB	6-0	210	9/26/59	4	Baylor	Waco, Tex.	Waco, Tex.	14/7
1	Anderson, Gary	K	5-11	170	7/16/59	4	Syracuse	Parys, South Africa	Pittsburgh, Pa.	16/0
77	August, Steve	T	6-5	258	9/4/54	9	Tulsa	Jeannette, Pa.	Seattle, Wash.	11/7*
54	Bingham, Craig	LB	6-2	220	9/29/59	4	Syracuse	Kingston, Jamaica	Pittsburgh, Pa.	11/1
71	Boures, Emil	G-T	6-1	261	1/29/60	4	Pittsburgh	Bridgeport, Pa.	Pittsburgh, Pa.	8/6
23	Brown, Chris	CB-S	6-0	195	4/11/62	2	Notre Dame	Owensboro, Ky.	Owensboro, Ky.	16/4
79	Brown, Larry	T	6-4	270	6/16/49	15	Kansas	Jacksonville, Fla.	Pittsburgh, Pa.	7/7
10	Campbell, Scott	QB	6-0	201	4/15/62	2	Purdue	Hershey, Pa.	Hershey, Pa.	5/0
80	Capers, Wayne	WR	6-2	193	5/17/61	3	Kansas	Miami, Fla.	Miami, Fla.	16/0
78	Catano, Mark	DE	6-3	265	1/26/62	2	Valdosta State	Yonkers, N.Y.	Peekskill, N.Y.	16/0
33	Clayton, Harvey	CB	5-9	180	4/4/61	3	Florida State	Kendall, Fla.	Florida City, Fla.	14/0
56	Cole, Robin	LB	6-2	225	9/11/55	9	New Mexico	Los Angeles, Calif.	Washington, Pa.	16/16
5	Colquitt, Craig	P	6-1	182	6/9/54	7	Tennessee	Knoxville, Tenn.	Knoxville, Tenn.	16/0
40	Corley, Anthony	RB	6-0	210	8/10/60	2	Nevada-Reno	Reno, Nev.	Reno, Nev.	14/0
89	Cunningham, Bennie	TE	6-5	255	12/23/54	10	Clemson	Laurens, S.C.	Piedmont, S.C.	7/4
67	Dunn, Gary	NT	6-3	265	8/24/53	9	Miami	Coral Gables, Fla.	Miami, Fla.	16/16
94	Echols, Terry	LB	6-0	220	1/10/62	2	Marshall	Mullens, W. Va.	Corrine, W. Va.	4/0
24	Erenberg, Rich	RB-KR	5-10	200	4/17/62	2	Colgate	Baltimore, Md.	Chappaqua, N.Y.	16/9
92	Gary, Keith	DE	6-3	260	9/14/59	3	Oklahoma	Bethesda, Md.	Pittsburgh, Pa.	16/11
26	Gillespie, Scoop	RB	5-10	185	2/26/62	2	William Jewell	St. Louis, Mo.	St. Louis, Mo.	14/0
95	Goodman, John	DE	6-6	255	11/12/58	5	Oklahoma	Oklahoma City, Okla.	Garland, Tex.	14/14
53	Hinkle, Bryan	LB	6-2	220	6/4/59	4	Oregon	Long Beach, Calif.	Pittsburgh, Pa.	15/15
62	Ilkin, Tunch	T	6-3	255	9/23/57	6	Indiana State	Istanbul, Turkey	Pittsburgh, Pa.	16/16
29	Johnson, Ron	S	5-11	195	6/8/56	8	Eastern Michigan	Detroit, Mich.	Pittsburgh, Pa.	15/0
90	Kohrs, Bob	LB	6-3	235	11/8/58	5	Arizona State	Phoenix, Ariz.	Pittsburgh, Pa.	10/0
84	Kolodziejski, Chris	TE	6-3	231	1/5/61	2	Wyoming	Augsburg, Germany	Pittsburgh, Pa.	7/3
58	Lambert, Jack	LB	6-4	220	7/8/52	12	Kent State	Mantua, Ohio	Pittsburgh, Pa.	8/3
83	Lipps, Louis	WR-KR	5-10	190	8/9/62	2	Southern Mississippi	New Orleans, La.	Reserve, La.	14/8
50	Little, David	LB	6-1	230	1/3/59	5	Florida	Miami, Fla.	Miami, Fla.	16/13
74	Long, Terry	G	5-11	272	7/21/59	2	East Carolina	Columbia, S.C.	Pittsburgh, Pa.	12/7
16	Malone, Mark	QB	6-4	218	11/22/58	6	Arizona State	El Cajon, Calif.	Pittsburgh, Pa.	13/9
57	Merriweather, Mike	LB	6-2	215	11/26/60	4	Pacific	Albans, N.Y.	Stockton, Calif.	16/16
81	Nelson, Darrell	TE	6-2	235	10/27/61	2	Memphis State	Memphis, Tenn.	Memphis, Tenn.	11/9
64	Nelson, Edmund	NT-DE	6-3	270	4/3/60	4	Auburn	Live Oak, Fla.	Tampa, Fla.	16/5
30	Pollard, Frank	RB	5-10	218	6/15/57	6	Baylor	Meridian, Tex.	Meridian, Tex.	15/15
60	Rasmussen, Randy	C-G	6-1	253	9/27/60	2	Minnesota	Minneapolis, Minn.	Hopkins, Minn.	16/0
88	Rodgers, John	TE	6-2	238	2/7/60	2	Louisiana Tech	Omaha, Tex.	Daingerfield, Tex.	6/0
63	Rostosky, Pete	T	6-4	255	7/29/61	2	Connecticut	Monongahela, Pa.	Monongahela, Pa.	8/2
59	Seabaugh, Todd	LB	6-4	225	3/16/61	2	San Diego State	Encino, Calif.	San Diego, Calif.	16/0
31	Shell, Donnie	S	5-11	190	8/26/51	12	South Carolina State	Whitmire, S.C.	Columbia, S.C.	16/16
72	†Snell, Ray	T	6-4	265	2/24/58	6	Wisconsin	Baltimore, Md.	Tampa, Fla.	13/6
36	Spencer, Todd	RB	6-0	200	7/26/62	2	Southern California	Portland, Ore.	Los Angeles, Calif.	7/0
82	Stallworth, John	WR	6-2	191	7/15/52	12	Alabama A&M	Tuscaloosa, Ala.	Huntsville, Ala.	16/16
85	Sweeney, Calvin	WR	6-2	190	1/12/55	6	Southern California	Riverside, Calif.	Santa Monica, Calif.	9/1
87	Thompson, Weegie	WR	6-6	210	3/21/61	2	Florida State	Pensacola, Fla.	Midlothian, Va.	16/7
38	Veals, Elton	RB	5-11	230	3/26/61	2	Tulane	Baton Rouge, La.	Baton Rouge, La.	15/1
41	Washington, Sam	CB	5-8	180	3/7/60	4	Mississippi Valley State	Tampa, Fla.	Tampa, Fla.	14/14
52	Webster, Mike	C	6-1	250	3/18/52	12	Wisconsin	Tomahawk, Wis.	Pittsburgh, Pa.	16/16
21	Williams, Eric	S	6-1	183	2/21/60	3	North Carolina State	Raleigh, N.C.	Garner, N.C.	16/12
28	Williams, Robert	S	5-11	202	9/26/62	2	Eastern Illinois	Chicago, Ill.	Chicago, Ill.	2/0
93	Willis, Keith	DE	6-1	260	7/29/59	3	Northeastern	Newark, N.J.	Pittsburgh, Pa.	12/2
61	Wingle, Blake	G	6-2	267	4/17/60	3	UCLA	Pottsville, Pa.	Canonsburg, Pa.	15/10
73	Wolfley, Craig	G	6-1	255	5/19/58	6	Syracuse	Buffalo, N.Y.	Pittsburgh, Pa.	9/9
19	Woodley, David	QB	6-2	204	10/25/58	6	Louisiana State	Shreveport, La.	Davie, Fla.	7/7
49	Woodruff, Dwayne	CB	6-0	198	2/18/57	7	Louisville	Bowling Green, Ky.	Pittsburgh, Pa.	16/14
22	Woods, Rick	S	6-0	191	11/16/59	4	Boise State	Boise, Idaho	Pittsburgh, Pa.	15/4

* August played 6 games for Seattle, 5 with Pittsburgh in '84.

†Option playout; subject to developments.

Also played with Steelers in '84—WR Gregg Garrity (6 games).

COACHING STAFF

Head Coach,
Chuck Noll

Pro Career: Became first NFL coach to win four Super Bowls when Steelers defeated Los Angeles Rams 31-19 in Super Bowl XIV. Has put together 13 consecutive non-losing seasons and has guided Steelers into postseason play 11 of last 13 years. Led Steelers to consecutive NFL championships twice (1974-75, 1978-79). With 157 career wins is third among active NFL coaches behind Tom Landry (243) and Don Shula (242). Has sixth-highest winning percentage (.623) among active coaches and ranks seventh among the NFL's all-time winningest coaches with a 157-95-1 career record. Noll is one of only five all-time NFL head coaches to lead a team for 17 consecutive seasons—Curly Lambeau (29), Landry (25), Steve Owen (23), and Bud Grant (17). Played pro ball as guard-linebacker for Cleveland Browns from 1953-59. At age 28, he started coaching career as defensive coach with Los Angeles (San Diego) Chargers in 1960. Left after 1965 season to become Don Shula's defensive backfield assistant in Baltimore. Remained with Colts until taking over Pittsburgh reins as head coach in 1969.

Background: Was an all-state star at Benedictine High in Cleveland. Captained the University of Dayton team, playing both tackle and linebacker. He was drafted by the Browns in 1953.

Personal: Born in Cleveland on January 5, 1932. He and wife, Marianne, live in Pittsburgh and have one son—Chris.

Assistant Coaches

Ron Blackledge, offensive line-tackles/tight ends; born April 15, 1938, Canton, Ohio, lives in Pittsburgh. Tight end-defensive end Bowling Green 1957-59. No pro playing experience. College coach: Ashland 1968-69, Cincinnati 1970-72, Kentucky 1973-75, Princeton 1976, Kent State 1977-81 (head coach 1979-81). Pro coach: Joined Steelers in 1982.

Tony Dungy, defensive coordinator; born October 6, 1955, Jackson, Mich., lives in Pittsburgh. Quarterback Minnesota 1973-76. Pro safety Pittsburgh Steelers 1977-78, San Francisco 49ers 1979. College coach: Minnesota 1980. Pro coach: Joined Steelers in 1981.

Walt Evans, assistant conditioning coach; born May 15, 1951, Pittsburgh, Pa., lives in Pittsburgh. Marietta College 1974. No college or pro playing experience. Pro coach: Joined Steelers in 1983.

Dennis Fitzgerald, inside linebackers; born March 13, 1936, Ann Arbor, Mich., lives in Pittsburgh. Running back Michigan 1958-60. No pro playing experience. College coach: Michigan 1961-68, Kentucky 1969-70, Kent State 1971-77 (head coach 1975-77), Syracuse 1978-80, Tulane 1981. Pro coach: Joined Steelers in 1982.

Dick Hoak, offensive backfield; born December 8, 1939, Jeannette, Pa., lives in Greenburg, Pa. Halfback-quarterback Penn State 1958-60. Pro running back Pittsburgh Steelers 1961-70. Pro coach: Joined Steelers in 1972.

Jed Hughes, outside linebackers; born November 14, 1947, New York, N.Y., lives in Pittsburgh. Tight end Gettysburg 1968-70. No pro playing experience. College coach: Stanford 1971-72, Michigan 1973-75, UCLA 1976-81. Pro coach: Minnesota Vikings 1982-83, joined Steelers in 1984.

Hal Hunter, offensive line-guards/centers; born June 3, 1934, Canonsburg, Pa., lives in Pittsburgh. Linebacker-guard Pittsburgh 1955-57. No pro playing experience. College coach: Richmond 1958-61, West Virginia 1962-63, Maryland 1964-65, Duke 1966-70, Kentucky 1971-72, Indiana 1973-76, California State (Pa.) 1977-80 (head coach). Pro coach: Hamilton Tiger-Cats (CFL) 1981, Indianapolis Colts 1982-84, first year with Steelers.

Jon Kolb, defensive line-conditioning; born August 30, 1947, Ponca City, Okla., lives in Pittsburgh. Center-linebacker Oklahoma State 1966-68. Pro tackle Pittsburgh Steelers 1969-81. Pro coach: Joined Steelers in 1982.

PITTSBURGH STEELERS 1985 FIRST-YEAR ROSTER

Name	Pos.	Ht.	Wt.	Birth-date	College	Birthplace	Residence	How Acq.
Andrews, Alan	TE	6-5	235	2/15/62	Rutgers	Columbus, Ga.	Succasunna, N.J.	D7
Behning, Mark	T	6-6	291	9/26/61	Nebraska	Alpena, Mich.	Denton, Tex.	D2
Bowens, Nate	DE	6-4	232	6/9/62	S.W. Oklahoma St.	Brooklyn, N.Y.	Mahwah, N.J.	FA
Carr, Gregg	LB	6-1	219	3/31/62	Auburn	Birmingham, Ala.	Birmingham, Ala.	D6
Clark, Randy (1)	S	6-0	197	2/18/62	Marshall	Marshall, Mich.	Venice, Fla.	FA
Cleveland, DeCarlos (1)	DE	6-3	268	7/9/61	Kent State	Pittsburgh, Pa.	Lebanon, Pa.	FA
Dickey, Charlie	G	6-2	268	12/31/62	Arizona	Ottumwa, Iowa	Scottsdale, Ariz.	FA
Dixon, Tom (1)	C-G	6-1	252	8/21/61	Michigan	Chicago, Ill.	Oak Park, Mich.	FA
Edwards, Dave	S	6-0	195	3/31/62	Illinois	Senoia, Ga.	Urbana, Ill.	FA
Gothard, Preston	TE	6-4	235	2/23/62	Alabama	Montgomery, Ala.	Montgomery, Ala.	FA
Gowdy, Cornell	CB	6-1	195	10/2/63	Morgan State	Washington, D.C.	Capitol Heights, Md.	FA
Graham, Russ (1)	T	6-4	265	5/5/61	Oklahoma State	Borger, Tex.	Borger, Tex.	FA
Harris, Andre	CB	5-11	194	6/30/62	Minnesota	Chicago, Ill.	Chicago, Ill.	D9a
Hobley, Liffort	S	6-0	207	10/12/62	Louisiana State	Shreveport, La.	Baton Rouge, La.	D3
Howe, Glen (1)	T	6-6	270	10/18/61	So. Mississippi	New Albany, Miss.	New Albany, Miss.	FA
Huff, Alan	NT	6-3	255	10/20/63	Marshall	East Liverpool, Ohio	Chester, W. Va.	FA
Jacobs, Cam	LB	6-1	218	3/10/62	Kentucky	Oklahoma City, Okla.	Coral Gables, Fla.	D5
Little, Steve	NT	6-3	260	10/27/61	Iowa State	Peoria, Ill.	Ames, Iowa	FA
Madison, L. E. (1)	LB	6-1	225	7/15/62	Kansas State	Topeka, Kan.	Pittsburgh, Pa.	FA
Matichak, Terry	S	6-1	197	4/6/62	Missouri	Joliet, Ill.	Joliet, Ill.	D11
McJunkin, Kirk (1)	G	6-3	250	3/15/61	Texas	Dallas, Tex.	Dallas, Tex.	D10('84)
Newsome, Harry	P	6-0	186	1/25/63	Wake Forest	Cheraw, S.C.	Cheraw, S.C.	D8
Sanchez, Jeff	S	5-11	180	5/11/62	Georgia	Ft. Oglethorpe, Ga.	Yorba Linda, Calif.	D12
Scarsella, Dave	NT	6-4	265	2/10/63	Mercyhurst	Mahoning Co., Ohio	Youngstown, Ohio	FA
Sims, Darryl	DE	6-3	265	7/23/61	Wisconsin	Winston-Salem, N.C.	Winston-Salem, N.C.	D1
Small, Fred	LB	5-11	231	7/15/63	Washington	Los Angeles, Calif.	Los Angeles, Calif.	D9
Sutton, Mike (1)	S	6-0	190	9/27/61	William & Mary	Cherry Point, N.C.	Darlington, Pa.	FA
Turk, Dan	C	6-4	259	6/25/62	Wis.-Milwaukee	Milwaukee, Wis.	Greenfield, Wis.	D4
White, Oliver	TE	6-1	237	5/28/63	Kentucky	Barbourville, Ky.	Barbourville, Ky.	D10

Players who report to an NFL team for the first time are designated on rosters as rookies (R). If a player reported to an NFL training camp in a previous year but was not on the active squad for three or more regular season or postseason games, he is listed on the first-year roster and designated by a (1). Thereafter, a player who is on the active squad for three or more regular season or postseason games is credited with an additional year of playing experience.

NOTES

_____

_____

_____

_____

_____

_____

_____

_____

_____

_____

_____

_____

_____

_____

_____

_____

Tom Moore, offensive coordinator; born November 7, 1938, Owatonna, Minn., lives in Pittsburgh. Quarterback Iowa 1957-60. No pro playing experience. College coach: Iowa 1961-62, Dayton 1965-68, Wake Forest 1969, Georgia Tech 1970-71, Minnesota 1972-73, 1975-76. Pro coach: New York Stars (WFL) 1974, joined Steelers in 1977.

SAN DIEGO CHARGERS

**American Football Conference
Western Division**

Team Colors: Blue, Gold, and White

San Diego Jack Murphy Stadium
P.O. Box 20666
San Diego, California 92120
Telephone: (619) 280-2111

Club Officials

Chairman of the Board/President: Alex G. Spanos
General Manager: John R. Sanders
Assistant General Manager: Paul (Tank) Younger
Assistant to the President: Jack Teele
Director of Scouting: Ron Nay
Director of Public Relations: Rick Smith
Business Manager: Pat Curran
Director of Marketing: Rich Israel
Director of Ticket Operations: Joe Scott
Assistant Director of Public Relations:
  Bill Johnston
Chief Financial Officer: Jerry Murphy
Trainer: Ric McDonald
Equipment Manager: Sid Brooks

Stadium: San Diego Jack Murphy Stadium •
   Capacity: 60,100
     9449 Friars Road
     San Diego, California 92108

Playing Surface: Grass

Training Camp: University of California-
        San Diego
        La Jolla, California 92037

1985 SCHEDULE

Preseason

Aug. 10	**Cleveland**	6:00
Aug. 17	**Dallas**	6:00
Aug. 24	at San Francisco	12:00
Aug. 30	**New Orleans**	7:00

Regular Season

Sept. 8	at Buffalo	4:00
Sept. 15	**Seattle**	1:00
Sept. 22	at Cincinnati	1:00
Sept. 29	**Cleveland**	1:00
Oct. 6	at Seattle	1:00
Oct. 13	**Kansas City**	1:00
Oct. 20	at Minnesota	12:00
Oct. 28	at L.A. Raiders (Monday)	6:00
Nov. 3	**Denver**	1:00
Nov. 10	**Los Angeles Raiders**	1:00
Nov. 17	at Denver	2:00
Nov. 24	at Houston	12:00
Dec. 1	**Buffalo**	1:00
Dec. 8	**Pittsburgh**	6:00
Dec. 15	**Philadelphia**	1:00
Dec. 22	at Kansas City	12:00

CHARGERS COACHING HISTORY

Los Angeles 1960
(188-170-11)

1960-69	Sid Gillman*	83-51-6
1969-70	Charlie Waller	9-7-3
1971	Sid Gillman**	4-6-0
1971-73	Harland Svare***	7-17-2
1973	Ron Waller	1-5-0
1974-78	Tommy Prothro****	21-39-0
1978-84	Don Coryell	63-45-0

  *Retired after nine games in 1969
  **Released after 10 games in 1971
  ***Resigned after eight games in 1973
  ****Resigned after four games in 1978

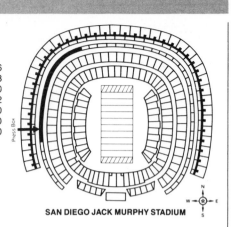

SAN DIEGO JACK MURPHY STADIUM

RECORD HOLDERS
Individual Records—Career

Category	Name	Performance
Rushing (Yds.)	Paul Lowe, 1960-67	4,963
Passing (Yds.)	Dan Fouts, 1973-1984	33,854
Passing (TDs)	John Hadl, 1962-1972	201
	Dan Fouts, 1973-1984	201
Receiving (No.)	Lance Alworth, 1962-1970	493
	Charlie Joiner, 1976-1984	493
Receiving (Yds.)	Lance Alworth, 1962-1970	9,585
Interceptions	Dick Harris, 1960-65	29
Punting (Avg.)	Dennis Partee, 1968-1975	41.2
Punt Return (Avg.)	Leslie (Speedy) Duncan, 1964-1970	12.3
Kickoff Return (Avg.)	Leslie (Speedy) Duncan, 1964-1970	25.2
Field Goals	Rolf Benirschke, 1977-1984	130
Touchdowns (Tot.)	Lance Alworth, 1962-1970	83
Points	Rolf Benirschke, 1977-1984	677

Individual Records—Single Season

Category	Name	Performance
Rushing (Yds.)	Earnest Jackson, 1984	1,179
Passing (Yds.)	Dan Fouts, 1981	4,802
Passing (TDs)	Dan Fouts, 1981	33
Receiving (No.)	Kellen Winslow, 1980	89
Receiving (Yds.)	Lance Alworth, 1965	1,602
Interceptions	Charlie McNeil, 1961	9
Punting (Avg.)	Dennis Partee, 1969	44.6
Punt Return (Avg.)	Leslie (Speedy) Duncan, 1965	15.5
Kickoff Return (Avg.)	Keith Lincoln, 1962	28.4
Field Goals	Rolf Benirschke, 1980	24
Touchdowns (Tot.)	Chuck Muncie, 1981	19
Points	Rolf Benirschke, 1980	118

Individual Records—Single Game

Category	Name	Performance
Rushing (Yds.)	Keith Lincoln, 1-5-64	206
Passing (Yds.)	Dan Fouts, 10-19-80	444
	Dan Fouts, 12-11-82	444
Passing (TDs)	Dan Fouts, 11-22-81	6
Receiving (No.)	Kellen Winslow, 10-7-84	15
Receiving (Yds.)	Wes Chandler, 12-20-82	260
Interceptions	Many times	3
	Last time by Pete Shaw, 11-2-80	
Field Goals	Many times	4
	Last time by Rolf Benirschke, 12-22-80	
Touchdowns (Tot.)	Kellen Winslow, 11-22-81	5
Points	Kellen Winslow, 11-22-81	30

1984 TEAM STATISTICS

	San Diego	Opp.
Total First Downs	374	322
Rushing	106	109
Passing	240	189
Penalty	28	24
Third Down: Made/Att.	115/244	83/197
Fourth Down: Made/Att.	9/21	9/10
Total Net Yards	6297	5936
Avg. Per Game	393.6	371.0
Total Plays	1154	1021
Avg. Per Play	5.5	5.8
Net Yards Rushing	1654	1851
Avg. Per Game	103.4	115.7
Total Rushes	456	457
Net Yards Passing	4643	4085
Avg. Per Game	290.2	255.3
Tackled/Yards Lost	36/285	33/218
Gross Yards	4928	4303
Att./Completions	662/401	531/323
Completion Pct.	60.6	60.8
Had Intercepted	21	19
Punts/Avg.	66/42.0	73/39.6
Net Punting Avg.	35.1	34.8
Penalties/Yards Lost	112/1023	108/905
Fumbles/Ball Lost	35/17	34/17
Touchdowns	48	51
Rushing	18	23
Passing	25	27
Returns	5	1
Avg. Time of Possession	31:43	28:17

1984 TEAM RECORD
Preseason (2-2)

Date	San Diego		Opponents
8/4	17	*Los Angeles Rams	10
8/11	13	*Dallas	24
8/18	35	*San Francisco	15
8/23	14	Los Angeles Rams	47
	79		96

Regular Season (7-9)

Date	San Diego		Opp.	Att.
9/2	42	Minnesota	13	57,276
9/9	17	Seattle	31	61,314
9/16	31	*Houston	14	52,726
9/24	30	Los Angeles Raiders	33	76,131
9/30	27	*Detroit	24	53,887
10/7	34	Green Bay	28	54,045
10/14	13	Kansas City	31	62,233
10/21	37	*Los Angeles Raiders	44	57,442
10/29	0	*Seattle	24	53,974
11/4	38	Indianapolis	10	60,143
11/11	13	*Denver	16	53,181
11/18	34	*Miami (OT)	28	53,041
11/25	24	Pittsburgh	52	55,856
12/3	20	*Chicago	7	45,470
12/9	13	Denver	16	74,867
12/16	21	*Kansas City	42	40,221
	394		413	911,807

*Home Game   (OT) Overtime

Score by Periods

San Diego	96	100	62	130	6	—	394
Opponents	60	127	135	91	0	—	413

Attendance

Home 409,942   Away 501,865   Total 911,807
Single game home record, 54,611 (12-31-72)
Single season home record, 411,661 (1981)

1984 INDIVIDUAL STATISTICS

Rushing

	Att.	Yds.	Avg.	LG	TD
Jackson	296	1179	4.0	32t	8
McGee	67	226	3.4	30	4
James	25	115	4.6	20	0
Muncie	14	51	3.6	11	0
P. Johnson	19	46	2.4	7	3
Thomas	14	43	3.1	9	2
Morris	5	12	2.4	5	1
Luther	4	11	2.8	7	0
Fouts	12	−29	−2.4	3	0
San Diego	456	1654	3.6	32t	18
Opponents	457	1851	4.1	81	23

Passing

	Att.	Comp.	Pct.	Yds.	TD	Int.	Tkld.	Rate
Fouts	507	317	62.5	3740	19	17	29/228	83.4
Luther	151	83	55.0	1163	5	3	7/57	82.7
Holohan	2	1	50.0	25	1	0	0/0	135.4
James	2	0	0.0	0	0	1	0/0	0.0
San Diego	662	401	60.6	4928	25	21	36/285	82.9
Opponents	531	323	60.8	4303	27	19	33/218	88.6

Receiving

	No.	Yds.	Avg.	LG	TD
Joiner	61	793	13.0	41	6
Holohan	56	734	13.1	51	1
Winslow	55	663	12.1	33	2
Chandler	52	708	13.6	63t	6
Sievers	41	438	10.7	32	3
Jackson	39	222	5.7	21	1
Duckworth	25	715	28.6	88t	4
James	23	206	9.0	31	0
Bendross	16	213	13.3	29	0
Egloff	11	92	8.4	17	0
McGee	9	76	8.4	43	2
Morris	5	20	4.0	9	0
Muncie	4	38	9.5	20	0
P. Johnson	2	7	3.5	7	0
Gissinger	1	3	3.0	3	0
Fouts	1	0	0.0	0	0
San Diego	401	4928	12.3	88t	25
Opponents	323	4303	13.3	75t	27

Interceptions

	No.	Yds.	Avg.	LG	TD
Byrd	4	157	39.3	99t	2
Lowe	3	61	20.3	32t	1
B. Smith	3	41	13.7	21	0
King	2	52	26.0	37	0
Turner	2	43	21.5	43	0
Young	2	31	15.5	31	0
L. Williams	1	66	66.0	66t	1
Fox	1	36	36.0	36	0
Gregor	1	12	12.0	12	0
L. Smith, Buff.-S.D.	1	7	7.0	7	0
San Diego	19	499	26.3	99t	4
Opponents	21	180	8.6	31	0

Punting

	No.	Yds.	Avg.	In 20	LG
Buford	66	2773	42.0	11	60
San Diego	66	2773	42.0	11	60
Opponents	73	2890	39.6	25	63

Punt Returns

	No.	FC	Yds.	Avg.	LG	TD
James	30	9	208	6.9	58t	1
Bird, St.L.-S.D.	6	0	60	10.0	17	0
Bird, S.D.	1	0	4	4.0	4	0
Henderson	1	2	0	0.0	0	0
L. Smith	1	0	0	0.0	0	0
Chandler	0	1	0	—	0	0
San Diego	33	12	212	6.4	58t	1
Opponents	43	5	399	9.3	27	0

Kickoff Returns

	No.	Yds.	Avg.	LG	TD
James	43	959	22.3	55	0
McGee	14	315	22.5	35	0
Bird, St.L.-S.D.	11	205	18.6	28	0
Egloff	2	20	10.0	11	0
Bird, S.D.	2	15	7.5	15	0
Jackson	1	10	10.0	10	0
Gofourth	1	0	0.0	0	0
San Diego	63	1319	20.9	55	0
Opponents	72	1437	20.0	44	0

Scoring

	TD R	TD P	TD Rt	PAT	FG	Saf	TP
Benirschke	0	0	0	41/41	17/26	0	92
Jackson	8	1	0	0/0	0/0	0	54
Chandler	0	6	0	0/0	0/0	0	36
Joiner	0	6	0	0/0	0/0	0	36
McGee	4	2	0	0/0	0/0	0	36
Duckworth	0	4	0	0/0	0/0	0	24
P. Johnson	3	0	0	0/0	0/0	0	18
Sievers	0	3	0	0/0	0/0	0	18
Ricardo	0	0	0	5/6	3/3	0	14
Byrd	0	0	2	0/0	0/0	0	12
Thomas	2	0	0	0/0	0/0	0	12
Winslow	0	2	0	0/0	0/0	0	12
Holohan	0	1	0	0/0	0/0	0	6
James	0	0	1	0/0	0/0	0	6
Lowe	0	0	1	0/0	0/0	0	6
Morris	1	0	0	0/0	0/0	0	6
L. Williams	0	0	1	0/0	0/0	0	6
San Diego	18	25	5	46/47	20/29	0	394
Opponents	23	27	1	50/51	19/25	0	413

FIRST-ROUND SELECTIONS

(If Club had no first-round selection, first player drafted is listed with round in parentheses.)

Year	Player, College, Position
1960	Monty Stickles, Notre Dame, E
1961	Earl Faison, Indiana, DE
1962	Bob Ferguson, Ohio State, RB
1963	Walt Sweeney, Syracuse, G
1964	Ted Davis, Georgia Tech, LB
1965	Steve DeLong, Tennessee, DE
1966	Don Davis, Cal State-Los Angeles, DT
1967	Ron Billingsley, Wyoming, DE
1968	Russ Washington, Missouri, DT
	Jimmy Hill, Texas A&I, DB
1969	Marty Domres, Columbia, QB
	Bob Babich, Miami, Ohio, LB
1970	Walker Gillette, Richmond, WR
1971	Leon Burns, Long Beach State, RB
1972	Pete Lazetich, Stanford, DE (2)
1973	Johnny Rodgers, Nebraska, WR
1974	Bo Matthews, Colorado, RB
	Don Goode, Kansas, LB
1975	Gary Johnson, Grambling, DT
	Mike Williams, Louisiana State, DB
1976	Joe Washington, Oklahoma, RB
1977	Bob Rush, Memphis State, C
1978	John Jefferson, Arizona State, WR
1979	Kellen Winslow, Missouri, TE
1980	Ed Luther, San Jose State, QB (4)
1981	James Brooks, Auburn, RB
1982	Hollis Hall, Clemson, DB (7)
1983	Billy Ray Smith, Arkansas, LB
	Gary Anderson, Arkansas, WR
	Gill Byrd, San Jose State, DB
1984	Mossy Cade, Texas, DB
1985	Jim Lachey, Ohio State, G

SAN DIEGO CHARGERS 1985 VETERAN ROSTER

No.	Name	Pos.	Ht.	Wt.	Birth-date	NFL Exp.	College	Birthplace	Residence	'84 Games/Starts
86	Bendross, Jesse	WR	6-0	197	5/19/61	2	Alabama	Donaldson, La.	Donaldson, La.	16/0
6	Benirschke, Rolf	K	6-1	184	2/7/55	9	Cal-Davis	Boston, Mass.	La Jolla, Calif.	14/0
50	Bradley, Carlos	LB	6-0	226	4/27/60	5	Wake Forest	Philadelphia, Pa.	Philadelphia, Pa.	8/1
7	Buford, Maury	P	6-1	191	2/18/60	4	Texas Tech	Mt. Pleasant, Tex.	Mt. Pleasant, Tex.	16/0
22	Byrd, Gill	CB	5-10	201	2/20/61	3	San Jose State	San Francisco, Calif.	San Diego, Calif.	13/13
89	Chandler, Wes	WR	6-0	182	8/22/56	8	Florida	New Smyrna Beach, Fla.	New Orleans, La.	15/15
91	Chickillo, Tony	NT	6-3	259	7/8/60	2	Miami	Miami, Fla.	Tampa, Fla.	1/0
77	Claphan, Sam	T	6-6	282	10/10/56	5	Oklahoma	Tahlequah, Okla.	Norman, Okla.	16/16
82	Duckworth, Bobby	WR	6-3	196	11/27/58	4	Arkansas	Crossett, Ark.	San Diego, Calif.	16/1
84	†Egloff, Ron	TE	6-5	227	10/2/55	9	Wisconsin	Plymouth, Mich.	Englewood, Colo.	12/4
78	Ehin, Chuck	DE	6-4	260	7/1/61	3	Brigham Young	Marysville, Calif.	San Diego, Calif.	16/15
68	Elko, Bill	NT	6-5	280	12/28/59	3	Louisiana State	New York, N.Y.	El Cajon, Calif.	15/12
76	Ferguson, Keith	DE	6-5	255	4/3/59	5	Ohio State	Miami, Fla.	San Diego, Calif.	16/16
14	Fouts, Dan	QB	6-3	203	6/10/51	13	Oregon	San Francisco, Calif.	Sisters, Ore.	13/13
48	†Fox, Tim	S	5-11	186	11/1/53	10	Ohio State	Canton, Ohio	Foxboro, Mass.	11/10
75	†Gissinger, Andrew	C-T	6-5	282	7/4/59	4	Syracuse	Barberton, Ohio	San Diego, Calif.	16/4
69	†Gofourth, Derrel	G-C	6-3	250	3/20/55	9	Oklahoma State	Little Parson, Kan.	Stillwater, Okla.	16/2
58	Green, Mike	LB	6-0	239	6/29/61	3	Oklahoma State	Port Arthur, Tex.	San Diego, Calif.	16/16
28	Greene, Ken	S	6-2	196	5/8/56	8	Washington State	Lewiston, Idaho	San Diego, Calif.	15/13
43	Gregor, Bob	S	6-2	191	2/10/57	5	Washington State	Riverside, Calif.	San Diego, Calif.	7/2
73	Guthrie, Keith	NT	6-3	267	8/17/62	2	Texas A&M	Tyler, Tex.	San Diego, Calif.	11/2
20	Henderson, Reuben	CB	6-0	196	10/3/58	5	San Diego State	Santa Monica, Calif.	San Diego, Calif.	12/0
	t-Herrmann, Mark	QB	6-5	199	1/8/59	5	Purdue	Cincinnati, Ohio	Englewood, Colo.	3/2
88	Holohan, Pete	TE	6-4	249	7/25/59	5	Notre Dame	Albany, N.Y.	San Diego, Calif.	15/4
41	Jackson, Earnest	RB	5-10	206	12/18/59	3	Texas A&M	Needville, Tex.	Dallas, Tex.	16/14
26	James, Lionel	KR-RB	5-6	172	5/25/62	2	Auburn	Albany, Ga.	Putney, Ga.	16/2
18	†Joiner, Charlie	WR	5-11	180	10/14/47	17	Grambling	Many, La.	Houston, Tex.	16/16
31	†Kay, Bill	CB	6-1	190	1/10/60	5	Purdue	Detroit, Mich.	Houston, Tex.	15/3*
57	†King, Linden	LB	6-4	250	6/28/55	8	Colorado State	Memphis, Tenn.	San Diego, Calif.	16/16
64	†Loewen, Chuck	G-T	6-4	268	1/23/57	5	South Dakota State	Mountain Lake, Minn.	San Diego, Calif.	13/0
51	Lowe, Woodrow	LB	6-0	219	6/9/54	10	Alabama	Columbus, Ga.	Seale, Ala.	15/15
62	Macek, Don	C	6-2	260	7/2/54	10	Boston College	Manchester, N.H.	San Diego, Calif.	13/13
12	Mathison, Bruce	QB	6-3	203	4/25/59	3	Nebraska	Superior, Wis.	San Diego, Calif.	2/0
21	McGee, Buford	RB	6-0	206	8/16/60	2	Mississippi	Durant, Miss.	Durant, Miss.	16/0
60	McKnight, Dennis	C-G	6-3	272	9/12/59	4	Drake	Dallas, Tex.	San Diego, Calif.	16/16
24	†McPherson, Miles	CB-S	5-11	191	3/30/60	4	New Haven University	Brooklyn, N.Y.	San Diego, Calif.	9/4
83	Micho, Bob	TE	6-3	227	3/7/62	2	Texas	Omaha, Neb.	San Diego, Calif.	6/0
25	†Morris, Wayne	RB	6-0	208	5/3/54	10	Southern Methodist	Dallas, Tex.	Dallas, Tex.	10/3
55	Nelson, Derrie	LB	6-1	238	2/8/58	3	Nebraska	York, Neb.	Fairmont, Neb.	6/0
93	Nelson, Shane	LB	6-1	232	5/25/55	8	Baylor	Mathis, Tex.	Lancaster, N.Y.	0*
52	†Preston, Ray	LB	6-0	221	1/25/54	10	Syracuse	Lawrence, Mass.	San Diego, Calif.	10/0
1	Ricardo, Benny	K	5-10	170	1/4/54	8	San Diego State	Asuncion, Paraguay	Costa Mesa, Calif.	2/0
90	Robinson, Fred	DE	6-4	240	10/22/61	2	Miami	Miami, Fla.	San Diego, Calif.	16/0
85	Sievers, Eric	TE	6-3	236	11/9/58	5	Maryland	Urbana, Ill.	San Diego, Calif.	14/13
54	Smith, Billy Ray	LB	6-3	231	8/10/61	3	Arkansas	Fayetteville, Ark.	San Diego, Calif.	16/16
45	Smith, Johnny Ray	CB	5-9	190	9/7/57	4	Lamar	Crockett, Tex.	Crockett, Tex.	1/0
33	Smith, Lucious	CB	5-10	190	1/17/57	6	Cal State-Fullerton	Columbus, Ga.	Anaheim, Calif.	13/6*
32	Thomas, Jewerl	RB	5-10	230	9/10/57	6	San Jose State	Hanford, Calif.	Carson, Calif.	7/0
59	Thrift, Cliff	LB	6-1	237	5/3/56	7	East Central Oklahoma	Dallas, Tex.	San Diego, Calif.	16/0
27	Turner, John	CB-S	6-0	193	2/22/56	8	Miami	Miami, Fla.	Miami, Fla.	15/6
23	Walters, Danny	CB	6-1	180	11/4/60	3	Arkansas	Prescott, Ark.	San Diego, Calif.	8/7
67	†White, Ed	T	6-2	284	4/4/47	17	California	San Diego, Calif.	Julian, Calif.	15/13
63	Wilkerson, Doug	G	6-3	253	3/27/47	16	North Carolina Central	Fayetteville, N.C.	Spring Valley, Calif.	16/16
92	†Williams, Eric	LB	6-2	235	6/17/55	9	Southern California	Sacramento, Calif.	St. Charles, La.	13/0
99	Williams, Lee	DE	6-6	270	10/15/62	2	Bethune-Cookman	Ft. Lauderdale, Fla.	Ft. Lauderdale, Fla.	8/0
80	Winslow, Kellen	TE	6-5	242	11/5/57	7	Missouri	St. Louis, Mo.	San Diego, Calif.	7/7
49	Young, Andre	S	6-0	190	11/22/60	4	Louisiana Tech	West Monroe, La.	West Monroe, La.	13/3

* Kay played 10 games with St. Louis, 5 with San Diego in '84; S. Nelson missed '84 season due to injury; L. Smith played 4 games with Buffalo, 9 with San Diego.

†Option playout; subject to developments.

t-Chargers traded for Herrmann (Indianapolis).

Also played with Chargers in '84—NT Rick Ackerman (9 games), WR Steve Bird (1), CB-S Scott Byers (6), CB-S Mike Dennis (2), TE Al Dixon (1), NT Rickey Hagood (2), NT Gary Johnson (4), RB Pete Johnson (3), QB Ed Luther (15), RB Chuck Muncie (1).

COACHING STAFF

Head Coach,
Don Coryell

Pro Career: Begins eighth year as San Diego's head coach. Became head coach of the Chargers after fourth game of 1978 season and led them to 8 wins in final 12 games. Before coming to Chargers was St. Louis Cardinals head coach for five seasons, compiling a 42-29-1 record and leading Cardinals to NFC East titles in 1974-75. Career record: 105-74-1.

Background: Played defensive back for University of Washington 1947-49. Assistant coach Punahou Academy, Honolulu, 1951. Head coach Farrington High School, Honolulu, 1952. Head coach University of British Columbia 1953-54. Head coach, Fort Ord, California, army team 1956. Head coach Whittier College 1957-59 (23-5-1). Offensive backfield coach at Southern California 1960. Head coach at San Diego State from 1961-72 where he compiled a 104-19-2 record.

Personal: Born October 17, 1924, in Seattle, Washington. Graduated from Lincoln High School, Seattle, in 1943. Served in United States Army 1943-46, released as first lieutenant. Don and his wife, Aliisa, live in El Cajon, Calif., and have two children—Mike and Mindy.

Assistant Coaches

Dave Adolph, assistant coach; born June 6, 1937, Akron, Ohio, lives in San Diego. Guard-linebacker Akron University 1955-58. No pro playing experience. College coach: Akron 1963-64, Connecticut 1956-68, Kentucky 1969-72, Illinois 1973-76, Ohio State 1977-78. Pro coach: Cleveland Browns 1979-84, first year with Chargers.

Tom Bass, defensive coordinator; born August 2, 1936, Riverside, Calif., lives in San Diego. Linebacker San Jose State 1955-57. No pro playing experience. College coach: San Jose State 1958-59, San Diego State 1960-62. Pro coach: San Diego Chargers 1964-67, Cincinnati Bengals 1968-69, Tampa Bay Buccaneers 1977-81, rejoined Chargers in 1982.

Hank Bauer, special offensive assistant; born July 15, 1954, Scottsbluff, Neb., lives in San Diego. Running back California Lutheran College 1972-75. Pro running back San Diego 1977-82. Pro coach: Joined Chargers 1983.

Marv Braden, special offensive assistant; born January 25, 1938, Kansas City, Mo., lives in San Diego. Linebacker Southwest Missouri State 1956-59. No pro playing experience. College coach: Northeast Missouri State 1967-68 (head coach), U.S. International 1969-72, Iowa State 1973, Southern Methodist 1974-75, Michigan State 1976. Pro coach: Denver Broncos 1977-80, joined Chargers in 1981.

Gunther Cunningham, defensive line; born June 19, 1946, Munich, Germany, lives in San Diego. Linebacker Oregon 1965-67. No pro playing experience. College coach: Oregon 1969-71, Arkansas 1972, Stanford 1973-76, California 1977-80. Pro coach: Hamilton Tiger-Cats (CFL) 1981, Indianapolis Colts 1982-84, first year with Chargers.

Earnel Durden, offensive backs; born January 24, 1937, Los Angeles, Calif., lives in La Mesa, Calif. Halfback Oregon State 1956-58. No pro playing experience. College coach: Compton, Calif., J.C. 1966-67, Long Beach State 1968, UCLA 1969-70. Pro coach: Los Angeles Rams 1971-72, Houston Oilers 1973, joined Chargers in 1974.

Dave Levy, offensive coordinator; born October 25, 1932, Carrollton, Mo., lives in Solana Beach, Calif. Guard UCLA 1953-54. No pro playing experience. College coach: UCLA 1954, Long Beach City College 1955, Southern California 1960-75. Pro coach: Joined Chargers in 1980.

Al Saunders, receivers; born February 1, 1947, London, England, lives in San Diego. Defensive back San Jose State 1966-68. No pro playing experience. College coach: Southern California 1970-71, Missouri 1972, Utah State 1973-75, California 1976-81, Tennessee 1982. Pro coach: Joined Chargers in 1983.

Name	Pos.	Ht.	Wt.	Birth-date	College	Birthplace	Residence	How Acq.
Adams, Curtis	RB	6-0	185	4/30/62	Central Michigan	Muskegon, Mich.	Muskegon, Mich.	D8
Barnes, Zach (1)	DE	6-5	267	11/9/60	Alabama State	Dothan, Ala.	San Diego, Calif.	D9('84)
Berner, Paul	QB	6-2	210	12/18/60	Pacific	San Diego, Calif.	San Diego, Calif.	D9
Casarino, Dario	P	6-7	240	9/30/57	Washington	St. Helena, Calif.	Hollister, Calif.	FA
Costello, Rocky	K	5-10	165	10/31/61	Fresno State	Long Beach, Calif.	La Mirada, Calif.	FA
Craighead, Bobby (1)	RB	6-1	201	6/7/61	Northeast Louisiana	McComb, Miss.	Monroe, La.	D8('84)
Crawford, Larry	S	6-0	187	12/18/59	Iowa State	Miami, Fla.	Vancouver, Canada	FA
Dale, Jeff	S	6-3	210	10/6/62	Louisiana State	Pineville, La.	Winnfield, La.	D2a
Davis, Jeff	S	6-1	190	4/20/61	South Dakota	Sanford, Fla.	Titusville, Fla.	FA
Davis, Wayne	CB	5-11	175	7/17/63	Indiana State	Cincinnati, Ohio	Cincinnati, Ohio	D2
Fellows, Mark	LB	6-0	220	2/26/63	Montana State	Billings, Mont.	Choteau, Mont.	D7
Forte, Dewey (1)	NT	6-5	290	8/31/61	Bethune-Cookman	Lakeland, Fla.	Lakeland, Fla.	SD('84)
Guendling, Mike (1)	LB	6-3	241	6/18/62	Northwestern	Elk Grove, Ill.	San Diego, Calif.	D2('84)
Hawn, Jim (1)	G	6-4	254	5/6/61	Arizona State	Des Moines, Iowa	San Diego, Calif.	FA
Hendy, John	CB	5-10	187	10/9/62	Long Beach State	Guatemala City, Guat.	Santa Clara, Calif.	D3
King, David	CB	5-9	175	5/19/63	Auburn	Mobile, Ala.	Fairhope, Ala.	D10
Knight, Steve (1)	G-T	6-4	277	3/13/62	Tennessee	Abingdon, Va.	Irving, Tex.	FA
Lachey, Jim	T	6-6	278	6/4/63	Ohio State	St. Henry, Ohio	Columbus, Ohio	D1
Lewis, Terry	CB	5-11	190	12/9/62	Michigan State	Detroit, Mich.	Highland Park, Mich.	D6
Mojsiejenko, Ralf	P-K	6-3	198	1/28/63	Michigan State	West Germany	Bridgman, Mich.	D4
O'Bard, Ronnie (1)	CB	5-10	185	6/11/58	Brigham Young	San Diego, Calif.	El Cajon, Calif.	FA
Olson, Ken	K	5-11	190	9/15/59	Salisbury State	Washington, D.C.	Tampa, Fla.	FA
Pearson, Bret	TE	6-4	230	3/31/62	Wisconsin	Menomone, Mich.	Menomone, Mich.	D12a
Pickett, Edgar	LB	6-1	235	1/30/62	Clemson	Lexington, N.C.	Lexington, N.C.	FA
Rackley, Dave	CB	5-9	170	2/2/61	Texas Southern	Miami, Fla.	Houston, Tex.	FA
Remsberg, Dan	T	6-4	275	4/7/62	Abilene Christian	Temple, Tex.	Temple, Tex.	D9a
Simmons, Tony	DE	6-4	256	12/18/62	Tennessee	Oakland, Tenn.	Knoxville, Tenn.	D12
Smith, Jeff	NT	6-2	265	1/19/63	Kentucky	Marion, Ky.	Springfield, Ky.	D11
Steels, Anthony	RB-KR	5-9	195	1/8/59	Nebraska	Sacramento, Calif.	Riverside, Calif.	FA
Stevenson, Mark	C-G	6-3	277	2/24/56	Western Illinois	Waukegan, Ill.	Tempe, Ariz.	FA
White, Bill (1)	RB	5-11	190	1/3/59	Missouri	St. Louis, Mo.	Montgomery, Ala.	FA
Wilson, Earl	DE	6-4	268	9/13/58	Kentucky	Long Branch, N.J.	Lexington, Ky.	FA
Wilson, Mark (1)	S	5-11	198	10/8/60	Abilene Christian	Tampa, Fla.	Throckmorton, Tex.	FA
Woodard, Ray (1)	DE	6-6	274	10/20/61	Texas	Lufkin, Tex.	Lufkin, Tex.	D8('84)
Yancy, Billy	S	5-10	175	6/16/58	Fresno State	Limestone, Maine	Los Angeles, Calif.	FA

Players who report to an NFL team for the first time are designated on rosters as rookies (R). If a player reported to an NFL training camp in a previous year but was not on the active squad for three or more regular season or postseason games, he is listed on the first-year roster and designated by a (1). Thereafter, a player who is on the active squad for three or more regular season or postseason games is credited with an additional year of playing experience.

NOTES

_____
_____
_____
_____
_____
_____
_____
_____
_____
_____

Jim Wagstaff, defensive backfield; born June 12, 1936, American Falls, Idaho, lives in San Diego. Back Idaho State 1954-58. Pro defensive back Chicago Cardinals 1959, Buffalo Bills 1960-61. College coach: Boise State 1969-72. Pro coach: Los Angeles Rams 1973-77, Buffalo Bills 1978-80, joined Chargers in 1981.

Chuck Weber, linebackers; born March 26, 1930, Philadelphia, Pa., lives in El Cajon, Calif. Linebacker West Chester State 1949-53. Pro linebacker Cleveland Browns 1955-56, Chicago Cardinals 1956-58, Philadelphia Eagles 1959-61. Pro coach: Boston Patriots 1964-67, San Diego Chargers 1968-69, Cincinnati Bengals 1970-75, St. Louis Cardinals 1976-77, Cleveland Browns 1978-79, Baltimore Colts 1980-81, rejoined Chargers in 1982.

Ernie Zampese, quarterbacks-passing game; born March 12, 1936, Santa Barbara, Calif., lives in San Diego. Halfback Southern California 1956-58. No pro playing experience. College coach: Hancock, Calif., J.C. 1962-65, Cal Poly-SLO 1966, San Diego State 1967-75. Pro coach: San Diego Chargers 1976, rejoined Chargers in 1978.

**American Football Conference
Western Division**

Team Colors: Blue, Green, and Silver

5305 Lake Washington Boulevard
Kirkland, Washington 98033
Telephone: (206) 827-9777

Club Officials

President-General Manager: Mike McCormack
Assistant General Manager: Chuck Allen
Director of Player Personnel: Mike Allman
Public Relations Director: Gary Wright
Assistant Public Relations Director: Dave Neubert
Business Manager: Mickey Loomis
Ticket Manager: James Nagaoka
Trainer: Jim Whitesel
Equipment Manager: Walt Loeffler

Stadium: Kingdome • **Capacity:** 64,984
201 South King Street
Seattle, Washington 98104

Playing Surface: AstroTurf

Training Camp: Eastern Washington University
Cheney, Washington 99004

1985 SCHEDULE

Preseason

Aug. 10	at Indianapolis	7:30
Aug. 16	**Detroit**	7:30
Aug. 24	at Minnesota	7:00
Aug. 30	**San Francisco**	6:00

Regular Season

Sept. 8	at Cincinnati	1:00
Sept. 15	at San Diego	1:00
Sept. 23	**L.A. Rams** (Monday)	6:00
Sept. 29	at Kansas City	12:00
Oct. 6	**San Diego**	1:00
Oct. 13	**Atlanta**	1:00
Oct. 20	at Denver	2:00
Oct. 27	at New York Jets	1:00
Nov. 3	**Los Angeles Raiders**	1:00
Nov. 10	at New Orleans	12:00
Nov. 17	**New England**	1:00
Nov. 25	at San Francisco (Monday)	6:00
Dec. 1	**Kansas City**	1:00
Dec. 8	**Cleveland**	1:00
Dec. 15	at Los Angeles Raiders	1:00
Dec. 20	**Denver** (Friday)	5:00

SEAHAWKS COACHING HISTORY

(63-75-0)

1976-82	Jack Patera*	35-59-0
1982	Mike McCormack	4-3-0
1983-84	Chuck Knox	24-13-0

*Released after two games in 1982

KINGDOME

RECORD HOLDERS

Individual Records—Career

Category	Name	Performance
Rushing (Yds.)	Sherman Smith, 1976-1982	3,429
Passing (Yds.)	Jim Zorn, 1976-1984	20,042
Passing (TDs)	Jim Zorn, 1976-1984	107
Receiving (No.)	Steve Largent, 1976-1984	545
Receiving (Yds.)	Steve Largent, 1976-1984	7,772
Interceptions	Dave Brown, 1976-1984	39
Punting (Avg.)	Herman Weaver, 1977-1980	40.0
Punt Return (Avg.)	Paul Johns, 1981-84	11.2
Kickoff Return (Avg.)	Zachary Dixon, 1983-84	23.4
Field Goals	Efren Herrera, 1978-1981	64
Touchdowns (Tot.)	Steve Largent, 1976-1984	73
Points	Steve Largent, 1976-1984	438

Individual Records—Single Season

Category	Name	Performance
Rushing (Yds.)	Curt Warner, 1983	1,449
Passing (Yds.)	Dave Krieg, 1984	3,671
Passing (TDs)	Dave Krieg, 1984	32
Receiving (No.)	Steve Largent, 1981	75
Receiving (Yds.)	Steve Largent, 1979	1,237
Interceptions	John Harris, 1981	10
Punting (Avg.)	Herman Weaver, 1980	41.8
Punt Return (Avg.)	Kenny Easley	12.1
Kickoff Return (Avg.)	Al Hunter, 1978	24.1
Field Goals	Efren Herrera, 1980	20
	Norm Johnson, 1984	20
Touchdowns (Tot.)	David Sims, 1978	15
	Sherman Smith, 1979	15
Points	Norm Johnson, 1984	110

Individual Records—Single Game

Category	Name	Performance
Rushing (Yds.)	Curt Warner, 11-27-83	207
Passing (Yds.)	Dave Krieg, 11-20-83	418
Passing (TDs)	Dave Krieg, 12-2-84	5
Receiving (No.)	David Hughes, 9-27-81	12
	Steve Largent, 11-25-84	12
Receiving (Yds.)	Steve Largent, 11-25-84	191
Interceptions	Kenny Easley, 9-3-84	3
Field Goals	Norm Johnson, 9-3-84	5
Touchdowns (Tot.)	Many times	3
	Last time by Steve Largent, 10-29-84	
Points	Many times	18
	Last time by Steve Largent, 10-29-84	

1984 TEAM STATISTICS

	Seattle	Opp.
Total First Downs	287	288
Rushing	94	99
Passing	171	160
Penalty	22	29
Third Down: Made/Att.	84/222	73/215
Fourth Down: Made/Att.	4/9	9/20
Total Net Yards	5068	4963
Avg. Per Game	316.8	310.2
Total Plays	1034	1051
Avg. Per Play	4.9	4.7
Net Yards Rushing	1645	1789
Avg. Per Game	102.8	111.8
Total Rushes	495	475
Net Yards Passing	3423	3174
Avg. Per Game	213.9	198.4
Tackled/Yards Lost	42/328	55/398
Gross Yards	3751	3572
Att./Completions	497/283	521/265
Completion Pct.	56.9	50.9
Had Intercepted	26	38
Punts/Avg.	95/37.5	83/40.3
Net Punting Avg.	33.3	33.0
Penalties/Yards Lost	128/1179	114/883
Fumbles/Ball Lost	24/13	47/25
Touchdowns	51	34
Rushing	10	11
Passing	32	18
Returns	9	5
Avg. Time of Possession	30:46	29:14

1984 TEAM RECORD
Preseason (4-1)

Date	Seattle		Opponents
7/28	38	Tampa Bay	0
8/4	7	*Buffalo	3
8/11	28	Detroit	24
8/17	17	*St. Louis	7
8/24	7	San Francisco	17
	97		51

Regular Season (12-4)

Date	Seattle		Opp.	Att.
9/3	33	*Cleveland	0	59,540
9/9	31	*San Diego	17	61,314
9/16	23	New England	38	43,140
9/23	38	*Chicago	9	61,520
9/30	20	Minnesota	12	57,171
10/7	14	Los Angeles Raiders	28	77,904
10/14	31	*Buffalo	28	59,034
10/21	30	Green Bay	24	52,286
10/29	24	San Diego	0	53,974
11/4	45	*Kansas City	0	61,396
11/12	17	*Los Angeles Raiders	14	64,001
11/18	26	Cincinnati	6	50,280
11/25	27	Denver	24	74,922
12/2	38	*Detroit	17	62,441
12/9	7	Kansas City	34	31,860
12/15	14	*Denver	31	64,411
	418		282	935,194

*Home Game

Score by Periods

Seattle	92	135	100	91	—	418
Opponents	60	86	62	74	—	282

Attendance
Home 493,657   Away 441,537   Total 935,194
Single game home record, 64,411 (12-15-84)
Single season home record, 493,657 (1984)

1984 INDIVIDUAL STATISTICS

Rushing

	Att.	Yds.	Avg.	LG	TD
Hughes	94	327	3.5	14	1
Lane	80	299	3.7	40t	4
Doornink	57	215	3.8	25	0
Morris	58	189	3.3	16	0
Krieg	46	186	4.0	37t	3
F. Harris	68	170	2.5	16	0
Dixon	52	149	2.9	17	2
C. Bryant	20	58	2.9	8	0
Warner	10	40	4.0	9	0
Largent	2	10	5.0	6	0
C. Young	1	5	5.0	5	0
Zorn	7	−3	−0.4	7	0
Seattle	495	1645	3.3	40t	10
Opponents	475	1789	3.8	25t	11

Passing

	Att.	Comp.	Pct.	Yds.	TD	Int.	Tkld.	Rate
Krieg	480	276	57.5	3671	32	24	40/314	83.3
Zorn	17	7	41.2	80	0	2	1/8	16.4
Morris	0	0	—	0	0	0	1/6	0.0
Seattle	497	283	56.9	3751	32	26	42/328	80.6
Opponents	521	265	50.9	3572	18	38	55/398	54.2

Receiving

	No.	Yds.	Avg.	LG	TD
Largent	74	1164	15.7	65	12
Turner	35	715	20.4	80t	10
C. Young	33	337	10.2	31	1
Doornink	31	365	11.8	32	2
Hughes	22	121	5.5	25	1
Johns	17	207	12.2	32	1
Walker	13	236	18.2	41	1
Lane	11	101	9.2	55t	1
Morris	9	61	6.8	18	0
Tice	8	90	11.3	30	3
Castor	8	89	11.1	21	0
Skansi	7	85	12.1	27	0
Metzelaars	5	80	16.0	25	0
C. Bryant	3	20	6.7	11	0
Scales	2	22	11.0	11	0
Dixon	2	6	3.0	6	0
Pratt	1	30	30.0	30	0
Warner	1	19	19.0	19	0
F. Harris	1	3	3.0	3	0
Seattle	283	3751	13.3	80t	32
Opponents	265	3572	13.5	92	18

Interceptions

	No.	Yds.	Avg.	LG	TD
Easley	10	126	12.6	58t	2
D. Brown	8	179	22.4	90t	2
J. Harris	6	79	13.2	29	0
Simpson	4	138	34.5	76t	2
T. Jackson	4	78	19.5	62t	1
Taylor	3	63	21.0	37	0
Gaines	1	18	18.0	18	0
Scholtz	1	15	15.0	15	0
J. Bryant	1	1	1.0	1	0
Seattle	38	697	18.3	90t	7
Opponents	26	333	12.8	42	3

Punting

	No.	Yds.	Avg.	In 20	LG
West	95	3567	37.5	24	60
Seattle	95	3567	37.5	24	60
Opponents	83	3345	40.3	14	63

Punt Returns

	No.	FC	Yds.	Avg.	LG	TD
Easley	16	5	194	12.1	42	0
Skansi	16	2	145	9.1	16	0
Johns	11	4	140	12.7	47t	1
Dixon	1	0	5	5.0	5	0
Seattle	44	11	484	11.0	47t	1
Opponents	32	39	205	6.4	65t	1

Kickoff Returns

	No.	Yds.	Avg.	LG	TD
Dixon	25	446	17.8	36	0
Hughes	17	348	20.5	38	0
Morris	8	153	19.1	34	0
C. Bryant	3	53	17.7	21	0
J. Harris	1	7	7.0	7	0
Seattle	54	1007	18.6	38	0
Opponents	67	1116	16.7	46	0

Scoring

	TD R	TD P	TD Rt	PAT	FG	Saf	TP
N. Johnson	0	0	0	50/51	20/24	0	110
Largent	0	12	0	0/0	0/0	0	72
Turner	0	10	0	0/0	0/0	0	60
Lane	4	1	0	0/0	0/0	0	30
Krieg	3	0	0	0/0	0/0	0	18
Tice	0	3	0	0/0	0/0	0	18
D. Brown	0	0	2	0/0	0/0	0	12
Dixon	2	0	0	0/0	0/0	0	12
Doornink	0	2	0	0/0	0/0	0	12
Easley	0	0	2	0/0	0/0	0	12
Hughes	1	1	0	0/0	0/0	0	12
Johns	0	1	1	0/0	0/0	0	12
Simpson	0	0	2	0/0	0/0	0	12
T. Jackson	0	0	1	0/0	0/0	0	6
Nash	0	0	1	0/0	0/0	0	6
Walker	0	1	0	0/0	0/0	0	6
C. Young	0	1	0	0/0	0/0	0	6
J. Bryant	0	0	0	0/0	0/0	1	2
Seattle	10	32	9	50/51	20/24	1	418
Opponents	11	18	5	34/34	14/22	1	282

FIRST-ROUND SELECTIONS

(If Club had no first-round selection, first player drafted is listed with round in parentheses.)

Year	Player, College, Position
1976	Steve Niehaus, Notre Dame, DT
1977	Steve August, Tulsa, G
1978	Keith Simpson, Memphis State, DB
1979	Manu Tuiasosopo, UCLA, DT
1980	Jacob Green, Texas A&M, DE
1981	Ken Easley, UCLA, DB
1982	Jeff Bryant, Clemson, DE
1983	Curt Warner, Penn State, RB
1984	Terry Taylor, Southern Illinois, DB
1985	Owen Gill, Iowa, RB (2)

SEATTLE SEAHAWKS 1985 VETERAN ROSTER

No.	Name	Pos.	Ht.	Wt.	Birth-date	NFL Exp.	College	Birthplace	Residence	'84 Games/ Starts
69	Abramowitz, Sid	T	6-6	280	5/21/60	3	Tulsa	Culver City, Calif.	Tulsa, Okla.	4/0
65	Bailey, Edwin	G	6-4	265	5/15/59	5	South Carolina State	Savannah, Ga.	Kirkland, Wash.	12/8
	t-Borchardt, Jon	G	6-5	255	8/13/57	7	Montana State	Minneapolis, Minn.	Tamarac, Fla.	16/16
22	†Brown, Dave	CB	6-2	190	1/16/53	11	Michigan	Akron, Ohio	Woodinville, Wash.	16/16
32	†Bryant, Cullen	FB	6-1	236	5/20/51	13	Colorado	Fort Sill, Okla.	Colorado Springs, Colo.	9/2
77	Bryant, Jeff	DE	6-5	270	5/22/60	4	Clemson	Atlanta, Ga.	Stone Mountain, Ga.	16/16
59	Bush, Blair	C	6-3	252	11/25/56	8	Washington	Fort Hood, Tex.	Edmonds, Wash.	16/16
96	Butler, Chuck	LB	6-0	220	12/18/61	2	Boise State	New Haven, Conn.	Bellevue, Wash.	8/0
53	†Butler, Keith	LB	6-4	238	5/16/56	8	Memphis State	Anniston, Ala.	Bothell, Wash.	16/16
83	Castor, Chris	WR	6-0	170	8/13/60	3	Duke	Burlington, N.C.	Redmond, Wash.	15/0
78	Cryder, Bob	T	6-4	282	9/7/56	8	Alabama	East St. Louis, Ill.	Kirkland, Wash.	16/10
31	†Dixon, Zachary	RB	6-1	204	3/5/57	7	Temple	Dorchester, Mass.	Redmond, Wash.	13/2
33	Doornink, Dan	FB	6-3	210	2/1/56	8	Washington State	Wapato, Wash.	Kirkland, Wash.	16/3
35	†Dufek, Don	S	6-0	195	4/28/54	9	Michigan	Ann Arbor, Mich.	Redmond, Wash.	9/0
45	Easley, Kenny	S	6-3	206	1/15/59	5	UCLA	Chesapeake, Va.	Bellevue, Wash.	16/16
68	Edwards, Randy	DE	6-4	255	3/9/61	2	Alabama	Marietta, Ga.	Tuscaloosa, Ala.	13/0
64	Essink, Ron	T	6-6	275	7/30/58	6	Grand Valley State	Zeeland, Mich.	Kirkland, Wash.	16/16
74	†Fanning, Mike	DE	6-6	255	2/2/53	11	Notre Dame	Mt. Clemens, Mich.	Inola, Okla.	16/0
56	Gaines, Greg	LB	6-3	220	10/16/58	4	Tennessee	Martinsville, Va.	Kirkland, Wash.	16/11
79	Green, Jacob	DE	6-3	255	1/21/57	6	Texas A&M	Pasadena, Tex.	Woodinville, Wash.	16/16
44	Harris, John	S	6-2	200	6/13/56	8	Arizona State	Fort Benning, Ga.	Woodinville, Wash.	16/16
63	Hicks, Mark	LB	6-2	225	11/7/60	2	Arizona State	Los Angeles, Calif.	Kirkland, Wash.	0*
46	†Hughes, David	FB	6-0	220	6/1/59	5	Boise State	Honolulu, Hawaii	Kirkland, Wash.	16/6
55	Jackson, Michael	LB	6-1	220	7/15/57	7	Washington	Pasco, Wash.	Bellevue, Wash.	8/5
24	Jackson, Terry	CB	5-11	197	12/9/55	8	San Diego State	Sherman, Tex.	Bellevue, Wash.	16/0
9	Johnson, Norm	K	6-2	193	5/31/60	4	UCLA	Inglewood, Calif.	Redmond, Wash.	16/0
60	Kaiser, John	LB	6-3	221	6/6/62	2	Arizona	Oconomowoc, Wis.	Tucson, Ariz.	16/0
62	†Kauahi, Kani	C	6-2	260	9/6/59	4	Hawaii	Kehaka, Hawaii	Kirkland, Wash.	16/0
17	Krieg, Dave	QB	6-1	185	10/20/58	6	Milton	Iola, Wis.	Kirkland, Wash.	16/16
37	Lane, Eric	RB	6-0	195	1/6/59	5	Brigham Young	Oakland, Calif.	Edmonds, Wash.	15/7
80	Largent, Steve	WR	5-11	184	9/28/54	10	Tulsa	Tulsa, Okla.	Tulsa, Okla.	16/16
73	Mangiero, Dino	NT	6-2	270	12/19/58	6	Rutgers	New York, N.Y.	West Orange, N.J.	15/0
67	†McKenzie, Reggie	G	6-5	255	7/27/50	14	Michigan	Detroit, Mich.	Kirkland, Wash.	10/8
51	Merriman, Sam	LB	6-3	225	5/5/61	3	Idaho	Tucson, Ariz.	Moscow, Idaho	16/0
88	Metzelaars, Pete	TE	6-7	240	5/24/60	4	Wabash	Three Rivers, Mich.	Woodinville, Wash.	9/4
71	Millard, Bryan	T	6-5	284	12/2/60	2	Texas	Sioux City, Tex.	Redmond, Wash.	14/0
43	Morris, Randall	RB	6-0	190	4/22/61	2	Tennessee	Anniston, Ala.	Bellevue, Wash.	10/2
21	Moyer, Paul	S	6-1	201	7/26/61	3	Arizona State	Anaheim, Calif.	Villa Park, Calif.	16/0
72	Nash, Joe	NT	6-2	250	10/11/60	4	Boston College	Boston, Mass.	West Roxbury, Mass.	16/16
61	Pratt, Robert	G	6-4	250	5/25/51	12	North Carolina	Richmond, Va.	Richmond, Va.	16/16
57	Robinson, Shelton	LB	6-2	233	9/14/60	4	North Carolina	Goldsboro, N.C.	Kirkland, Wash.	16/16
84	†Scales, Dwight	WR	6-2	182	5/30/53	9	Grambling	Little Rock, Ark.	Huntsville, Ala.	4/0
58	Scholtz, Bruce	LB	6-6	240	9/26/58	4	Texas	La Grange, Tex.	Bellevue, Wash.	16/16
75	Schreiber, Adam	G	6-4	284	2/20/62	2	Texas	Galveston, Tex.	Bellevue, Wash.	6/0
42	Simpson, Keith	CB	6-1	195	3/9/56	8	Memphis State	Memphis, Tenn.	Kirkland, Wash.	15/15
82	Skansi, Paul	WR	5-11	190	1/11/61	3	Washington	Tacoma, Wash.	Seattle, Wash.	7/0
20	Taylor, Terry	CB	5-10	175	7/18/61	2	Southern Illinois	Warren, Ohio	Bellevue, Wash.	16/1
86	†Tice, Mike	TE	6-7	250	2/2/59	5	Maryland	Bayshore, N.Y.	Woodinville, Wash.	16/8
81	Turner, Daryl	WR	6-3	198	12/15/61	2	Michigan State	Wadley, Ga.	Flint, Mich.	16/8
89	Walker, Byron	WR	6-4	190	7/28/60	4	Citadel	Scott Base, Ill.	Warner Robins, Ga.	16/0
28	Warner, Curt	RB	5-11	205	3/18/61	2	Penn State	Wyoming, W. Va.	Redmond, Wash.	1/1
8	†West, Jeff	P	6-2	205	4/6/53	10	Cincinnati	Ravenna, Ohio	Redmond, Wash.	16/0
54	Williams, Eugene	LB	6-1	220	6/15/60	3	Tulsa	Longview, Tex.	Bellevue, Wash.	0*
87	†Young, Charle	TE	6-4	234	2/5/51	13	Southern California	Fresno, Calif.	Woodinville, Wash.	15/13
50	Young, Fredd	LB	6-1	225	11/14/61	2	New Mexico State	Dallas, Tex.	Dallas, Tex.	16/0
10	Zorn, Jim	QB	6-2	200	5/10/53	10	Cal Poly-Pomona	Whittier, Calif.	Mercer Island, Wash.	16/0

* Hicks and Williams missed '84 season due to injury.

†Option playout; subject to developments.

t-Seahawks traded for Borchardt (Buffalo).

Retired—Joe Norman, 5-year linebacker, injured reserve in '84.

Also played with Seahawks in '84—T Steve August (6 games), FB Franco Harris (8), WR Paul Johns (4), S Ray Wilmer (3).

COACHING STAFF

Head Coach, Chuck Knox

Pro Career: Named head coach of Seahawks on January 26, 1983, after five seasons as head coach of Buffalo where he led Bills to AFC East title in 1980. Led Los Angeles Rams to five straight NFC West titles before taking over Bills in 1978. Pro assistant with New York Jets 1963-66, coaching offensive line, before moving to Detroit in 1967. Served Lions in same capacity until named head coach of Rams in 1973. No pro playing experience. Career record: 119-71-1.

Background: Played tackle for Juniata College in Huntingdon, Pa., 1950-53. Was assistant coach at his alma mater in 1954, then spent 1955 season as line coach at Ellwood City High School in Pennsylvania. Moved to Wake Forest as an assistant coach in 1959-60, then Kentucky in 1961-62.

Personal: Born April 27, 1932, Sewickley, Pa. Chuck and his wife, Shirley, live in Bellevue, Wash. and have four children—Chris, Kathy, Colleen, and Chuck.

Assistant Coaches

Tom Catlin, assistant head coach-defensive coordinator-linebackers; born September 8, 1931, Ponca City, Okla., lives in Kirkland, Wash. Center-linebacker Oklahoma 1950-52. Pro linebacker Cleveland Browns 1953-54, 1957-58, Philadelphia Eagles 1959. College coach: Army 1956. Pro coach: Dallas Texans-Kansas City Chiefs 1960-65, Los Angeles Rams 1966-77, Buffalo Bills 1978-82, joined Seahawks in 1983.

George Dyer, defensive line; born May 4, 1940, Alhambra, Calif., lives in Redmond, Wash. Center-linebacker U.C. Santa Barbara 1961-63. No pro playing experience. College coach: Humboldt State 1964-66, Coalinga, Calif., J.C. 1967 (head coach), Portland State 1968-71, Idaho 1972, San Jose State 1973, Michigan State 1977-79, Arizona State 1980-81. Pro coach: Winnipeg Blue Bombers (CFL) 1974-76 (head coach), Buffalo Bills 1982, joined Seahawks in 1983.

Chick Harris, offensive backfield; born September 21, 1945, Durham, N.C., lives in Redmond, Wash. Running back Northern Arizona 1966-69. No pro playing experience. College coach: Colorado State 1970-72, Long Beach State 1973-74, Washington 1975-80. Pro coach: Buffalo Bills 1981-82, joined Seahawks in 1983.

Ralph Hawkins, defensive backfield; born May 4, 1935, Washington, D.C., lives in Redmond, Wash. Quarterback-defensive back Maryland 1953-55. Pro defensive back New York Titans (AFL) 1960. College coach: Maryland 1959-60, 1967, Southern Methodist 1961, Kentucky 1962-65, Army 1966, Cincinnati 1968. Pro coach: Buffalo Bills 1969-71, 1981-82, Washington Redskins 1973-77, Baltimore Colts 1978, New York Giants 1979-80, joined Seahawks in 1983.

Ken Meyer, quarterbacks; born July 14, 1926, Erie, Pa., lives in Bellevue, Wash. Quarterback Denison 1947-50. No pro playing experience. College coach: Denison 1952-57, Wake Forest 1958-59, Florida State 1960-62, Alabama 1963-67, Tulane 1981-82. Pro coach: San Francisco 49ers 1968, 1977 (head coach), New York Jets 1969-72, Los Angeles Rams 1973-76, Chicago Bears 1978-80, joined Seahawks in 1983.

Steve Moore, receivers; born August 19, 1947, Los Angeles, Calif., lives in Bellevue, Wash. Running back U.C. Santa Barbara 1968-69. No pro playing experience. College coach: U.C. Santa Barbara 1970-71, Army 1975, Rice 1976-77. Pro coach: Buffalo Bills 1978-82, joined Seahawks in 1983.

Ray Prochaska, offensive coordinator; born August 9, 1919, Ulysses, Neb., lives in Redmond, Wash. End Nebraska 1939-40. Pro end Cleveland Rams 1941. College coach: Nebraska 1946-54. Pro coach: Edmonton (CFL) 1955-57, Chicago-St. Louis Cardinals 1958-65, Los Angeles Rams 1966-70, 1973-77, Cleveland Browns 1971-72, Buffalo Bills 1978-82, joined Seahawks in 1983.

SEATTLE SEAHAWKS 1985 FIRST-YEAR ROSTER

Name	Pos.	Ht.	Wt.	Birthdate	College	Birthplace	Residence	How Acq.
Babka, Beau	G	6-2	290	10/5/62	Hawaii	Los Angeles, Calif.	Los Angeles, Calif.	FA
Beverley, Anthony	LB	6-1	220	1/7/63	Southern Methodist	Denison, Tex.	San Antonio, Tex.	FA
Blazek, Pete	T	6-6	270	8/6/61	Georgia Tech	Waukesha, Wis.	Atlanta, Ga.	FA
Bowers, James	S	6-2	195	8/8/62	Memphis State	Memphis, Tenn.	Memphis, Tenn.	D10a
Brown, Arnold	CB	5-11	185	8/27/62	N. Carolina Central	Wilmington, N.C.	Wilmington, N.C.	D5a
Conner, John	QB	6-2	200	5/9/61	Arizona	Palo Alto, Calif.	Los Altos, Calif.	D10
Cooper, Louis	LB	6-2	235	8/5/63	Western Carolina	Marion, S.C.	Marion, S.C.	D11
Cortes, Julio	LB	6-1	217	8/13/62	Miami	New York, N.Y.	Miami, Fla.	FA
Davis, Tony	TE	6-5	248	2/11/62	Missouri	Santa Ana, Calif.	Boulder, Colo.	D4
Dorning, Dale	DE	6-5	237	2/7/62	Oregon	Burien, Wash.	Auburn, Wash.	FA
Gargus, James	P	6-3	226	2/13/61	Texas Christian	Dallas, Tex.	Kaufman, Tex.	FA
Gilbert, Gale	QB	6-3	215	12/20/61	California	Red Bluff, Calif.	Berkeley, Calif.	FA
Gill, Owen	FB	6-1	230	2/19/62	Iowa	London, England	Iowa City, Iowa	D2
Greene, Danny	WR	5-11	195	12/26/61	Washington	Compton, Calif.	Seattle, Wash.	D3
Grimminger, Harry	G	6-3	272	4/11/62	Nebraska	Boulder, Colo.	Grand Island, Neb.	FA
Haeusler, Greg	LB	6-1	223	8/12/62	Southern Mississippi	South Hampton, N.Y.	Destin, Fla.	FA
Haysbert, Adam	WR	6-0	182	2/16/62	Brigham Young	San Francisco, Calif.	San Mateo, Calif.	FA
Hines, Ernest	T	6-5	285	9/7/62	Norfolk State	Portsmouth, Va.	Portsmouth, Va.	FA
Hudetz, Bob	LB	6-1	238	6/13/62	Oregon	Warrenville, Ill.	Warrenville, Ill.	FA
Jones, Johnnie	RB	5-10	192	6/30/62	Tennessee	Covington, Tenn.	Millington, Tenn.	D5b
La Bomme, Don	RB	6-0	216	10/23/62	Washington State	Los Angeles, Calif.	Pacoima, Calif.	FA
Latham, Matt	S	6-0	175	1/6/62	Connecticut	Haward, Ill.	Pawcatuck, Conn.	FA
Lewis, Judious	WR	5-9	175	9/11/62	Arkansas State	Elkhart, Ind.	Marion, Ark.	D8
Manley, Bruce	S	6-1	180	2/12/61	Norfolk State	Virginia Beach, Va.	Norfolk, Va.	FA
Marshall, Kurt	TE	6-4	248	5/5/62	Murray State	Rockford, Ill.	Rockford, Ill.	FA
Mattes, Ron	T	6-6	285	8/8/63	Virginia	Shenandoah, Pa.	Ringtown, Pa.	D7
Mergenhagen, Paul	NT	6-4	260	7/20/62	Baylor	Abilene, Tex.	Abilene, Tex.	FA
Morgan, Steve	RB	5-10	200	7/27/61	Toledo	Springfield, Ohio	Springfield, Ohio	FA
Murray, T.J.	P	6-2	235	9/17/62	Catholic University	Springfield, Va.	Springfield, Va.	FA
Napolitan, Mark	C	6-3	265	2/4/62	Michigan State	Dearborn, Mich.	Trenton, Mich.	D5
Neville, Thomas	T	6-5	290	9/4/61	Fresno State	Great Falls, Mont.	Fresno, Calif.	FA
Otto, Bob	DE	6-6	250	12/16/62	Idaho State	Tucson, Ariz.	Sacramento, Calif.	D9
Robinson, Eugene	CB	6-0	180	5/28/63	Colgate	Hartford, Conn.	Hartford, Conn.	FA
Scott, Michael	WR	6-0	190	3/19/63	Pacific	Pass Christian, Miss.	Richmond, Calif.	FA
Staples, Lenson	LB	6-2	245	5/8/63	Missouri	St. Louis, Mo.	University City, Mo.	FA
Tushar, John	G	6-3	260	2/23/62	Cincinnati	St. Louis, Mo.	North Olmstead, Ohio	FA
Walker, Carlton	G	6-3	280	1/17/62	Utah	Tampa, Fla.	Tampa, Fla.	FA
Winfrey, Leon	WR	5-9	170	10/6/60	Morris Brown	Augusta, Ga.	Thomson, Ga.	FA
Wood, Barry	T	6-6	265	4/26/63	Connecticut	Altoona, Pa.	Altoona, Pa.	FA
Wood, Tony	K	5-9	195	3/20/63	Tulane	Lexington, Ky.	Cape Coral, Fla.	FA
Wrice, Tony	CB	5-11	179	7/8/63	Northwestern, Iowa	Philadelphia, Pa.	Atlantic, Iowa	FA
Wynter, Gino	WR	6-0	190	11/22/59	Vanderbilt	Panama	Miami, Fla.	FA

Players who report to an NFL team for the first time are designated on rosters as rookies (R). If a player reported to an NFL training camp in a previous year but was not on the active squad for three or more regular season or postseason games, he is listed on the first-year roster and designated by a (1). Thereafter, a player who is on the active squad for three or more regular season or postseason games is credited with an additional year of playing experience.

NOTES

_____
_____
_____
_____
_____
_____
_____
_____
_____
_____

Kent Stephenson, offensive line; born February 4, 1942, Anita, Iowa, lives in Kirkland, Wash. Guard-nose tackle Northern Iowa 1962-64. No pro playing experience. College coach: Wayne State 1965-68, North Dakota 1969-71, Southern Methodist 1972-73, Iowa 1974-76, Oklahoma State 1977-78, Kansas 1979-82. Pro coach: Michigan Panthers (USFL) 1983-84, first year with Seahawks.

Rusty Tillman, tight ends-special teams; born February 27, 1948, Beloit, Wis., lives in Kirkland, Wash. Linebacker Northern Arizona 1967-69. Pro linebacker Washington Redskins 1970-77. Pro coach: Joined Seahawks in 1979.

Joe Vitt, special assignments; born August 23, 1954, Camden, N.J., lives in Kirkland, Wash. Linebacker Towson State 1973-75. No pro playing experience. Pro coach: Baltimore Colts 1979-81, joined Seahawks in 1982.

THE NFC

Atlanta Falcons
Chicago Bears
Dallas Cowboys
Detroit Lions
Green Bay Packers
Los Angeles Rams
Minnesota Vikings
New Orleans Saints
New York Giants
Philadelphia Eagles
St. Louis Cardinals
San Francisco 49ers
Tampa Bay Buccaneers
Washington Redskins

ATLANTA FALCONS

**National Football Conference
Western Division**

Team Colors: Red, Black, White,
and Silver

Suwanee Road at I-85
Suwanee, Georgia 30174
Telephone: (404) 588-1111

Club Officials

Chairman of the Board: Rankin M. Smith, Sr.
President: Rankin Smith, Jr.
Executive Vice President: Eddie LeBaron
General Manager: Tom Braatz
Corporate Secretary: Taylor Smith
Chief Financial Officer: Jim Hay
Director of Pro Personnel: Bill Jobko
Scouts: Bob Cegelski, Bob Fry, John Jelacic,
    Bob Riggle, Bill Striegel
Ticket Manager: Ken Grantham
Assistant Ticket Manager: Jack Ragsdale
Director Public Relations/Promotions:
    Charlie Dayton
Assistant Director of Public Relations:
    Bob Dickinson
Assistant Director of Community Affairs:
    Carol Henderson
Head Trainer: Jerry Rhea
Assistant Trainer: Billy Brooks
Equipment Manager: Whitey Zimmerman
Assistant Equipment Manager: Horace Daniel

Stadium: Atlanta-Fulton County Stadium •
    Capacity: 60,748
    521 Capitol Avenue, S.W.
    Atlanta, Georgia 30312

Playing Surface: Grass

Training Camp: Suwanee Road at I-85
    Suwanee, Georgia 30174

1985 SCHEDULE

Preseason

Aug. 10	**Washington**	8:00
Aug. 17	at Tampa Bay	8:00
Aug. 24	Green Bay at Milwaukee	7:00
Aug. 30	**Miami**	8:00

Regular Season

Sept. 8	**Detroit**	1:00
Sept. 15	at San Francisco	1:00
Sept. 22	**Denver**	1:00
Sept. 29	at Los Angeles Rams	1:00
Oct. 6	**San Francisco**	1:00
Oct. 13	at Seattle	1:00
Oct. 20	**New Orleans**	1:00
Oct. 27	at Dallas	12:00
Nov. 3	**Washington**	1:00
Nov. 10	at Philadelphia	1:00
Nov. 17	**Los Angeles Rams**	1:00
Nov. 24	at Chicago	12:00
Dec. 1	**Los Angeles Raiders**	4:00
Dec. 8	at Kansas City	12:00
Dec. 15	**Minnesota**	1:00
Dec. 22	at New Orleans	12:00

FALCONS COACHING HISTORY

(108-165-4)

1966-68	Norb Hecker*	4-26-1
1968-74	Norm Van Brocklin**	37-49-3
1974-76	Marion Campbell***	6-19-0
1976	Pat Peppler	3-6-0
1977-82	Leeman Bennett	47-44-0
1983-84	Dan Henning	11-21-0

  *Released after three games in 1968
 **Released after eight games in 1974
***Released after five games in 1976

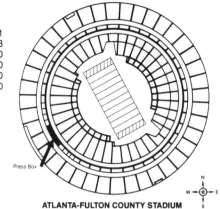

Press Box

ATLANTA-FULTON COUNTY STADIUM

RECORD HOLDERS
Individual Records—Career

Category	Name	Performance
Rushing (Yds.)	William Andrews, 1979-1983	5,772
Passing (Yds.)	Steve Bartkowski, 1975-1984	22,730
Passing (TDs)	Steve Bartkowski, 1975-1984	149
Receiving (No.)	Alfred Jenkins, 1975-1983	359
Receiving (Yds.)	Alfred Jenkins, 1975-1983	6,257
Interceptions	Rolland Lawrence, 1973-1981	39
Punting (Avg.)	Billy Lothridge, 1966-1971	41.3
Punt Return (Avg.)	Al Dodd, 1973-74	11.8
Kickoff Return (Avg.)	Ron Smith, 1966-67	24.3
Field Goals	Mick Luckhurst, 1981-84	68
Touchdowns (Tot.)	Alfred Jenkins, 1975-1983	40
	William Andrews, 1979-1983	40
Points	Mick Luckhurst, 1981-84	350

Individual Records—Single Season

Category	Name	Performance
Rushing (Yds.)	William Andrews, 1983	1,567
Passing (Yds.)	Steve Bartkowski, 1981	3,830
Passing (TDs)	Steve Bartkowski, 1980	31
Receiving (No.)	William Andrews, 1981	81
Receiving (Yds.)	Alfred Jenkins, 1981	1,358
Interceptions	Rolland Lawrence, 1975	9
Punting (Avg.)	Billy Lothridge, 1968	44.3
Punt Return (Avg.)	Gerald Tinker, 1974	13.9
Kickoff Return (Avg.)	Dennis Pearson, 1978	26.7
Field Goals	Nick Mike-Mayer, 1973	26
Touchdowns (Tot.)	Alfred Jenkins, 1981	13
	Gerald Riggs, 1984	13
Points	Mick Luckhurst, 1981	114

Individual Records—Single Game

Category	Name	Performance
Rushing (Yds.)	Gerald Riggs, 9-2-84	202
Passing (Yds.)	Steve Bartkowski, 11-15-81	416
Passing (TDs)	Randy Johnson, 11-16-69	4
	Steve Bartkowski, 10-19-80	4
	Steve Bartkowski, 10-18-81	4
Receiving (No.)	William Andrews, 11-15-81	15
Receiving (Yds.)	Alfred Jackson, 12-2-84	193
Interceptions	Many times	2
	Last time by Bobby Butler, 9-2-84	
Field Goals	Nick Mike-Mayer, 11-4-73	5
	Tim Mazzetti, 10-30-78	5
Touchdowns (Tot.)	Many times	3
	Last time by Lynn Cain, 10-22-84	
Points	Many times	18
	Last time by Lynn Cain, 10-22-84	

1984 TEAM STATISTICS

	Atlanta	Opp.
Total First Downs	292	317
Rushing	123	131
Passing	151	162
Penalty	18	24
Third Down: Made/Att.	77/218	94/212
Fourth Down: Made/Att.	17/30	8/15
Total Net Yards	5044	5279
Avg. Per Game	315.3	329.9
Total Plays	1034	1019
Avg. Per Play	4.9	5.2
Net Yards Rushing	1994	2153
Avg. Per Game	124.6	134.6
Total Rushes	489	538
Net Yards Passing	3050	3126
Avg. Per Game	190.6	195.4
Tackled/Yards Lost	67/496	38/287
Gross Yards	3546	3413
Att./Completions	478/294	443/262
Completion Pct.	61.5	59.1
Had Intercepted	20	12
Punts/Avg.	70/40.8	60/41.6
Net Punting Avg.	32.6	35.2
Penalties/Yards Lost	125/1011	93/820
Fumbles/Ball Lost	39/21	36/20
Touchdowns	31	48
Rushing	16	16
Passing	14	27
Returns	1	5
Avg. Time of Possession	30:14	29:46

1984 TEAM RECORD
Preseason (1-3)

Date	Atlanta		Opponents
8/4	6	Minnesota	37
8/11	21	New Orleans	31
8/18	52	*Tampa Bay	21
8/24	13	*Denver	24
	92		113

Regular Season (4-12)

Date	Atlanta		Opp.	Att.
9/2	36	New Orleans	28	66,652
9/9	24	*Detroit (OT)	27	49,878
9/16	20	Minnesota	27	53,955
9/23	42	*Houston	10	45,248
9/30	5	San Francisco	14	57,990
10/7	30	Los Angeles Rams	28	47,832
10/14	7	*New York Giants	19	50,268
10/22	10	*Los Angeles Rams	24	52,861
10/28	10	Pittsburgh	35	55,971
11/5	14	Washington	27	51,301
11/11	13	*New Orleans	17	40,590
11/18	7	*Cleveland	23	28,280
11/25	14	Cincinnati	35	44,678
12/2	17	*San Francisco	35	29,644
12/9	6	Tampa Bay	23	33,808
12/16	26	*Philadelphia	10	15,582
	281		382	724,538

*Home Game   (OT) Overtime

Score by Periods

Atlanta	45	83	87	66	0	—	281
Opponents	80	141	93	65	3	—	382

Attendance
Home 312,351   Away 412,187   Total 724,538
Single game home record, 59,257 (10-30-77)
Single season home record, 442,457 (1980)

1984 INDIVIDUAL STATISTICS

Rushing

	Att.	Yds.	Avg.	LG	TD
Riggs	353	1486	4.2	57	13
Cain	77	276	3.6	31t	3
Moroski	21	98	4.7	17	0
Archer	6	38	6.3	12	0
Bartkowski	15	34	2.3	8	0
Hodge	2	17	8.5	9	0
Stamps	3	15	5.0	8	0
C. Benson	3	8	2.7	6	0
B. Johnson	3	8	2.7	11	0
Austin	4	7	1.8	3	0
Pridemore	1	7	7.0	7	0
Giacomarro	1	0	0.0	0	0
Atlanta	489	1994	4.1	57	16
Opponents	538	2153	4.0	52	16

Passing

	Att.	Comp.	Pct.	Yds.	TD	Int.	Tkld.	Rate
Bartkowski	269	181	67.3	2158	11	10	40/300	89.7
Moroski	191	102	53.4	1207	2	9	20/151	56.8
Archer	18	11	61.1	181	1	1	7/45	90.3
Atlanta	478	294	61.5	3546	14	20	67/496	76.6
Opponents	443	262	59.1	3413	27	12	38/287	92.5

Receiving

	No.	Yds.	Avg.	LG	TD
Bailey	67	1138	17.0	61	6
A. Jackson	52	731	14.1	50t	2
Riggs	42	277	6.6	21	0
Cox	34	329	9.7	23t	3
C. Benson	26	244	9.4	30	0
B. Johnson	24	371	15.5	45t	3
Hodge	24	234	9.8	26	0
Cain	12	87	7.3	18	0
Seay, Wash.-Atl.	9	111	12.3	19	1
Landrum	6	66	11.0	30	0
Stamps	4	48	12.0	31	0
Curran	1	7	7.0	7	0
Matthews	1	7	7.0	7	0
Tuttle	1	7	7.0	7	0
Atlanta	294	3546	12.1	61	14
Opponents	262	3413	13.0	64t	27

Interceptions

	No.	Yds.	Avg.	LG	TD
K. Johnson	5	75	15.0	28	0
Butler	2	25	12.5	25	0
Pridemore	2	0	0.0	0	0
J. Jackson	1	35	35.0	35t	1
Britt	1	10	10.0	10	0
Small	1	2	2.0	2	0
Atlanta	12	147	12.3	35t	1
Opponents	20	304	15.2	54t	2

Punting

	No.	Yds.	Avg.	In 20	LG
Giacomarro	68	2855	42.0	12	58
Atlanta	70	2855	40.8	12	58
Opponents	60	2497	41.6	17	63

Punt Returns

	No.	FC	Yds.	Avg.	LG	TD
B. Johnson	15	1	152	10.1	37	0
K. Johnson	10	1	79	7.9	14	0
Curran	9	1	21	2.3	10	0
Seay, Wash.-Atl.	8	1	10	1.3	7	0
Seay, Atl.	7	1	12	1.7	7	0
Atlanta	41	4	264	6.4	37	0
Opponents	42	4	450	10.7	69t	1

Kickoff Returns

	No.	Yds.	Avg.	LG	TD
K. Johnson	19	359	18.9	27	0
Stamps	19	452	23.8	50	0
Curran	11	219	19.9	42	0
Tate	9	148	16.4	31	0
Seay, Wash.-Atl.	5	108	21.6	28	0
Seay, Atl.	2	55	27.5	28	0
Austin	4	77	19.3	23	0
B. Johnson	2	39	19.5	21	0
Gaison	1	15	15.0	15	0
Matthews	1	3	3.0	3	0
Malancon	1	0	0.0	0	0
Tyrrell	1	0	0.0	0	0
Atlanta	70	1367	19.5	50	0
Opponents	48	1053	21.9	50	0

Scoring

	TD R	TD P	TD Rt	PAT	FG	Saf	TP
Luckhurst	0	0	0	31/31	20/27	0	91
Riggs	13	0	0	0/0	0/0	0	78
Bailey	0	6	0	0/0	0/0	0	36
Cain	3	0	0	0/0	0/0	0	18
Cox	0	3	0	0/0	0/0	0	18
B. Johnson	0	3	0	0/0	0/0	0	18
A. Jackson	0	2	0	0/0	0/0	0	12
J. Jackson	0	0	1	0/0	0/0	0	6
Seay, Wash.-Atl.	0	1	0	0/0	0/0	0	6
Bryan	0	0	0	0/0	0/0	1	2
Case	0	0	0	0/0	0/0	1	2
Atlanta	16	14	1	31/31	20/27	2	281
Opponents	16	27	5	46/48	16/30	0	382

FIRST-ROUND SELECTIONS

(If Club had no first-round selection, first player drafted is listed with round in parentheses.)

Year	Player, College, Position
1966	Tommy Nobis, Texas, LB
	Randy Johnson, Texas A&I, QB
1967	Leo Carroll, San Diego State, DE (2)
1968	Claude Humphrey, Tennessee State, DE
1969	George Kunz, Notre Dame, T
1970	John Small, Citadel, LB
1971	Joe Profit, Northeast Louisiana, RB
1972	Clarence Ellis, Notre Dame, DB
1973	Greg Marx, Notre Dame, DT (2)
1974	Gerald Tinker, Kent State, WR (2)
1975	Steve Bartkowski, California, QB
1976	Bubba Bean, Texas A&M, RB
1977	Warren Bryant, Kentucky, T
	Wilson Faumuina, San Jose State, DT
1978	Mike Kenn, Michigan, T
1979	Don Smith, Miami, DE
1980	Junior Miller, Nebraska, TE
1981	Bobby Butler, Florida State, DB
1982	Gerald Riggs, Arizona State, RB
1983	Mike Pitts, Alabama, DE
1984	Rick Bryan, Oklahoma, DT
1985	Bill Fralic, Pittsburgh, T

ATLANTA FALCONS 1985 VETERAN ROSTER

No.	Name	Pos.	Ht.	Wt.	Birth-date	NFL Exp.	College	Birthplace	Residence	'84 Games/Starts
31	Andrews, Wiliam	RB	6-0	213	12/25/55	6	Auburn	Thomasville, Ga.	Duluth, Ga.	0*
16	Archer, Dave	QB	6-2	203	2/15/62	2	Iowa State	Fayetteville, N.C.	Ames, Iowa	2/0
39	Austin, Cliff	RB	6-0	190	3/2/60	3	Clemson	Atlanta, Ga.	Lithonia, Ga.	15/0
82	Bailey, Stacey	WR	6-0	157	2/10/60	4	San Jose State	San Rafael, Calif.	Duluth, Ga.	16/16
10	†Bartkowski, Steve	QB	6-4	218	11/12/52	11	California	Des Moines, Iowa	Duluth, Ga.	11/11
69	Benish, Dan	DT	6-5	265	11/21/61	3	Clemson	Youngstown, Ohio	Lawrenceville, Ga.	15/8
87	Benson, Cliff	TE	6-4	234	8/28/61	2	Purdue	Cook County, Ill.	Atlanta, Ga.	16/16
53	Benson, Thomas	LB	6-2	235	9/6/61	2	Oklahoma	Ardmore, Okla.	Norcross, Ga.	16/0
26	Britt, James	CB	6-0	185	9/12/60	3	Louisiana State	Minden, La.	Tucker, Ga.	16/16
77	Bryan, Rick	DE	6-4	260	3/20/62	2	Oklahoma	Tulsa, Okla.	Coweta, Okla.	16/16
73	Burley, Gary	DT	6-3	290	12/8/52	10	Pittsburgh	Columbus, Ohio	Cincinnati, Ohio	12/8
23	Butler, Bobby	CB	5-11	175	5/28/59	5	Florida State	Boynton Beach, Fla.	Norcross, Ga.	15/15
21	Cain, Lynn	RB	6-1	205	10/16/55	7	Southern California	Los Angeles, Calif.	Dunwoody, Ga.	15/2
25	Case, Scott	S	6-0	178	5/17/62	2	Oklahoma	Waynoka, Okla.	Buford, Ga.	16/0
70	Chapman, Mike	C-G	6-4	250	2/10/61	2	Texas	Laredo, Tex.	Austin, Tex.	4/0
88	Cox, Arthur	TE	6-2	255	2/5/61	3	Texas Southern	Plant City, Fla.	Norcross, Ga.	16/16
89	Curran, William	WR	5-11	175	12/30/59	4	UCLA	Inglewood, Calif.	Ventura, Calif.	14/0
50	Curry, Buddy	LB	6-4	228	6/4/58	6	North Carolina	Danville, Va.	Norcross, Ga.	16/16
71	†Dufour, Dan	T-C	6-5	280	10/18/60	3	UCLA	Lynn, Mass.	Pasadena, Calif.	6/3
58	Frye, David	LB	6-2	213	6/21/61	3	Purdue	Cincinnati, Ohio	Norcross, Ga.	16/11
34	†Gaison, Blane	S	6-1	188	5/13/58	5	Hawaii	Kanehoe, Hawaii	Kanehoe, Hawaii	15/0
1	Giacomarro, Ralph	P	6-1	194	1/17/61	3	Penn State	Passaic, N.J.	Alpharetta, Ga.	16/0
75	Harris, Roy	DT	6-2	266	3/26/61	2	Florida	Winter Garden, Fla.	Duluth, Ga.	15/0
30	Haworth, Steve	S	6-0	188	9/16/61	3	Oklahoma	Clark AFB, Philippines	Durant, Okla.	5/0
83	Hodge, Floyd	WR	6-0	195	7/18/59	4	Utah	Compton, Calif.	Duluth, Ga.	12/1
8	Holly, Bob	QB	6-2	205	6/1/60	4	Princeton	Belleville, N.J.	Greenwich, Conn.	0*
85	Jackson, Alfred	WR	6-0	190	8/3/55	8	Texas	Cameron, Tex.	Austin, Tex.	16/15
51	Jackson, Jeff	LB	6-1	228	10/9/61	2	Auburn	Shreveport, La.	Norcross, Ga.	16/0
81	Johnson, Billy	WR	5-9	177	1/27/52	10	Widener	Bouthwyn, Pa.	Duluth, Ga.	6/0
37	Johnson, Kenny	S	5-11	172	1/7/58	6	Mississippi State	Moss Point, Miss.	Moss Point, Miss.	16/16
78	Kenn, Mike	T	6-7	266	2/9/56	8	Michigan	Evanston, Ill.	Roswell, Ga.	14/14
54	†Kuykendall, Fulton	LB	6-4	228	6/10/53	11	UCLA	Coronado, Calif.	Roswell, Ga.	16/0
80	Landrum, Mike	TE	6-2	231	11/6/61	2	Southern Mississippi	Laurel, Miss.	Laurel, Miss.	15/0
55	Levenick, Dave	LB	6-3	220	5/29/59	3	Wisconsin	Milwaukee, Wis.	Cumming, Ga.	8/0
18	†Luckhurst, Mick	K	6-2	183	3/31/58	5	California	Redbourn, England	Buford, Ga.	16/0
52	Malancon, Rydell	LB	6-1	219	1/10/62	2	Louisiana State	Vacherie, La.	Vacherie, La.	7/0
49	Matthews, Allama	TE	6-2	230	8/24/61	3	Vanderbilt	Jacksonville, Fla.	Norcross, Ga.	6/0
62	Miller, Brett	T	6-7	285	10/2/58	3	Iowa	Lynwood, Calif.	Alpharetta, Ga.	15/13
15	†Moroski, Mike	QB	6-4	203	9/4/57	7	Cal-Davis	Novato, Calif.	Cumming, Ga.	16/5
64	†Pellegrini, Joe	G-C	6-4	258	4/8/57	5	Harvard	Boston, Mass.	Cedarhurst, N.Y.	15/3
74	Pitts, Mike	DT	6-5	270	9/25/60	3	Alabama	Pell City, Ala.	Norcross, Ga.	14/13
27	Pridemore, Tom	S	5-11	186	4/29/56	8	West Virginia	Ansted, W. Va.	Gainesville, Ga.	16/16
72	Provence, Andrew	DE	6-3	260	3/8/61	3	South Carolina	Savannah, Ga.	Duluth, Ga.	16/3
59	Rade, John	LB	6-1	225	8/31/60	3	Boise State	Ceres, Calif.	Doraville, Ga.	7/7
56	Richardson, Al	LB	6-3	222	9/23/57	6	Georgia Tech	Miami, Fla.	Stone Mountain, Ga.	16/14
42	Riggs, Gerald	RB	6-1	230	11/6/60	4	Arizona State	Tulluha, La.	Alpharetta, Ga.	15/14
67	†Sanders, Eric	T	6-7	280	10/22/58	5	Nevada-Reno	Reno, Nev.	Roswell, Ga.	10/2
61	Scully, John	G	6-6	255	8/2/58	5	Notre Dame	Long Island, N.Y.	Roswell, Ga.	16/16
41	†Seay, Virgil	WR	5-8	180	1/1/58	5	Troy State	Moultrie, Ga.	Fairfax, Va.	14/2*
48	Small, Gerald	CB	5-11	192	8/10/56	8	San Jose State	Washington, N.C.	Miami, Fla.	16/1
65	†Smith, Don	DE	6-5	270	5/9/57	7	Miami	Oakland, Calif.	Holiday, Fla.	16/16
84	Stamps, Sylvester	RB	5-7	166	2/24/61	2	Jackson State	Vicksburg, Miss.	Vicksburg, Miss.	10/0
68	†Thielemann, R.C.	G	6-4	262	8/12/55	9	Arkansas	Houston, Tex.	Norcross, Ga.	16/16
86	Tuttle, Perry	WR	6-0	180	8/2/59	4	Clemson	Lexington, N.C.	Norcross, Ga.	8/0*
32	Tyrrell, Tim	RB	6-1	201	2/19/61	2	Northern Illinois	Chicago, Ill.	Hoffman Estates, Ill.	11/0
57	Van Note, Jeff	C	6-2	250	2/7/46	17	Kentucky	South Orange, N.J.	Roswell, Ga.	16/13
24	t-Washington, Joe	RB	5-10	179	9/24/53	10	Oklahoma	Crockett, Tex.	Lutherville, Md.	7/0

* Andrews missed '84 season due to injury; Holly active for 4 games with Atlanta, 7 with Philadelphia in '84 but did not play; Seay played 11 games with Washington, 3 with Atlanta in '84; Tuttle played 3 games with Tampa Bay, 5 with Atlanta.

†Option playout; subject to developments.

t-Falcons traded for Washington (Washington).

Also played with Falcons in '84—T Warren Bryant (4 games), RB Rodney Tate (7), RB Richard Williams (1), DE Jeff Yeates (8).

COACHING STAFF

Head Coach, Dan Henning

Pro Career: Begins third season as Falcons head coach. Came from the Washington Redskins where he was assistant head coach under Joe Gibbs, helping the Redskins to a 20-9 record in 1981 and 1982 and a Super Bowl victory in 1983. Also was an assistant with Houston 1972, New York Jets 1976-78, and Miami Dolphins 1979-80. Played quarterback for the San Diego Chargers 1964-67. Career record: 11-21.

Background: Played quarterback for William & Mary 1960-63. Began college coaching career with Florida State 1968-70, 1974, Virginia Tech 1971, 1973.

Personal: Born June 21, 1942, Bronx, N.Y. Dan and his wife, Sandy, have five children—Mary K., Patty, Danny, Terry, and Mike. They live in Roswell, Ga.

Assistant Coaches

Larry Beightol, offensive line; born November 21, 1942, in Pittsburgh, Pa., lives in Atlanta. Guard-linebacker Catawba College 1965-67. No pro playing experience. College coach: William & Mary 1968-71, North Carolina State 1972-75, Auburn 1976, Arkansas 1977-78, Louisiana Tech 1979, Missouri 1980-84. Pro coach: First year with Falcons.

George Dostal, strength and conditioning; born October 25, 1934, Cleveland, Ohio, lives in Lawrenceville, Ga. Fullback-linebacker Kent State 1964-67. No pro playing experience. College coach: Clemson 1977-82. Pro coach: Joined Falcons in 1983.

Sam Elliott, running backs; born August 3, 1946, Huntington, W. Va., lives in Norcross, Ga. Quarterback-defensive back Ohio State 1965-67. No pro playing experience. College coach: Ohio State 1968, Florida State 1969-70, 1974, Kent State 1971-73. Pro coach: Joined Falcons in 1983.

Ted Fritsch, special teams; born August 26, 1950, Green Bay, Wis., lives in Marietta, Ga. Center St. Norbert 1969-71. Pro center Atlanta Falcons 1972-75, Washington Redskins 1976-79. Pro coach: Joined Falcons in 1983.

Bob Harrison, receivers; born September 9, 1941, Cleveland, Ohio, lives in Roswell, Ga. End Kent State 1961-64. No pro playing experience. College coach: Kent State 1969-70, Iowa 1971-73, Cornell 1974, North Carolina State 1975-76, Tennessee 1977-82. Pro coach: Joined Falcons in 1983.

Bobby Jackson, linebackers; born February 16, 1940, Forsyth, Ga., lives in Roswell, Ga. Linebacker-running back Samford 1959-62. No pro playing experience. College coach: Florida State 1965-69, Kansas State 1970-74, Louisville 1975-76, Tennessee 1977-82. Pro coach: Joined Falcons in 1983.

Joe Madden, defensive assistant-research and development; born March 5, 1935, Washington, D.C., lives in Atlanta. Back Maryland 1954-56. No pro playing experience. College coach: Mississippi State 1962, Morehead State 1963, Wake Forest 1964-67, Iowa State 1968-71, Kansas State 1972, Pittsburgh 1973-76, Tennessee 1977-79. Pro coach: Detroit Lions 1980-84, first year with Falcons.

John Marshall, defensive coordinator; born October 2, 1945, Arroyo Grande, Calif., lives in Roswell, Ga. Oregon 1968. No pro playing experience. College coach: Oregon 1970-76, Southern California 1977-79. Pro coach: Green Bay Packers 1980-82, joined Falcons in 1983.

Garry Puetz, assistant offensive line; born March 14, 1952, Chicago, Ill., lives in Lithonia, Ga. Offensive lineman Valparaiso 1969-72. Pro offensive lineman New York Jets 1973-78, Tampa Bay Buccaneers 1978, Philadelphia Eagles 1979, New England Patriots 1979-81, Washington Redskins 1982. Pro coach: Joined Falcons in 1983.

ATLANTA FALCONS 1985 FIRST-YEAR ROSTER

Name	Pos.	Ht.	Wt.	Birth-date	College	Birthplace	Residence	How Acq.
Ayres, John	CB	5-11	183	9/6/63	Illinois	Richmond, Calif.	Oakland, Calif.	D11
Bailey, Eric	TE	6-5	227	5/12/63	Kansas State	Ft. Worth, Tex.	Ft. Worth, Tex.	FA
Bennett, Ben (1)	QB	6-1	196	5/5/62	Duke	Sunnyvale, Calif.	Sunnyvale, Calif.	D6('84)
Best, Chuck	LB	6-1	240	11/22/61	New Mexico	Dallas, Tex.	Plano, Tex.	FA
Butler, Carl	RB	5-11	222	10/8/62	Michigan State	Eloy, Ariz.	Eloy, Ariz.	FA
Cason, Wendell	CB	5-11	183	1/22/63	Oregon	Carson, Calif.	Carson, Calif.	FA
Dean, Melvin	CB	5-10	175	9/9/63	Pittsburgh	Cordele, Ga.	Cordele, Ga.	FA
Fralic, Bill	T	6-5	285	10/31/62	Pittsburgh	Penn Hills, Pa.	Pittsburgh, Pa.	D1
Gann, Mike	DE	6-5	256	10/19/63	Notre Dame	Stillwater, Okla.	Orlando, Fla.	D2
Goff, Willard	DT	6-3	265	10/17/61	West Texas State	Springfield, Colo.	Springfield, Colo.	FA
Harry, Emile	WR	5-10	168	4/5/63	Stanford	Fountain Valley, Calif.	Fountain Valley, Calif.	D4
Heeres, Greg	QB	6-3	194	5/30/63	Hope	Grand Rapids, Mich.	Grand Rapids, Mich.	FA
Holmes, Don (1)	WR	5-10	180	4/1/63	Mesa	Miami, Fla.	Grand. Jct., Colo.	D12('84)
Jefferson, Don	CB	6-1	195	8/26/63	Florida A&M	Tallahassee, Fla.	Tallahassee, Fla.	FA
Jones, Cedric	RB	5-9	185	2/18/63	Florida State	Valdosta, Ga.	Valdosta, Ga.	FA
Jones, Michael	WR	5-11	170	6/13/62	Wisconsin	Chicago, Ill.	Chicago, Ill.	FA
Lee, Ashley	S	6-1	196	4/2/61	Virginia Tech	Franklin, Va.	Franklin, Va.	D8
Llewellyn, Nick	G	6-1	264	3/1/62	Missouri	St. Louis, Mo.	Columbia, Mo.	FA
Lowe, Marshall	WR	6-0	183	4/6/61	Alcorn State	Jackson, Miss.	Pickens, Miss.	FA
Mack, Tracey	LB	6-0	214	12/29/61	Missouri	Rock Hill, Mo.	Rock Hill, Mo.	FA
Martin, Brent	C	6-3	268	6/5/63	Stanford	Madera, Calif.	Madera, Calif.	D10
McDonald, Terry	LB	6-1	218	11/29/63	San Jose State	Oakland, Calif.	Oakland, Calif.	FA
Moon, Micah	LB	6-1	230	11/15/62	North Carolina	Altavista, Va.	Altavista, Va.	D9
Noirfalise, Harold	RB	6-2	215	12/26/61	Missouri Southern	Elberfeld, Ind.	Houston, Mo.	FA
Norman, Tommy (1)	WR	5-11	174	10/25/64	Jackson State	Greenville, Miss.	Greenville, Miss.	D11('84)
Pleasant, Reggie	CB	5-9	175	5/2/62	Clemson	Sumter, S.C.	Sumter, S.C.	D6
Price, Arthur	LB	6-2	220	5/17/62	Wisconsin	Newport News, Va.	Newport News, Va.	FA
Scoby, Joe	DE	6-4	278	1/29/62	Grambling	Monroe, La.	Monroe, La.	FA
Smoldt, Dave	TE	6-2	229	11/7/61	Iowa State	Cedar Rapids, Iowa	Cedar Rapids, Iowa	FA
Sullivan, Randy	RB	5-10	198	9/26/62	Morehead State	Stuart, Minn.	Stuart, Minn.	FA
Walker, Greg	T	6-4	254	1/19/63	Mississippi	Meridian, Miss.	Meridian, Miss.	FA
Wallace, Mike	WR	6-0	185	5/10/63	Kansas State	Ft. Worth, Tex.	Ft. Worth, Tex.	FA
Ward, Alvin	G	6-1	260	10/24/62	Miami	Chicago, Ill.	Chicago, Ill.	FA
Washington, Ronnie	LB	6-1	234	7/29/63	N.E. Louisiana State	Monroe, La.	Monroe, La.	D8a
Whisenhunt, Ken	TE	6-2	226	2/28/62	Georgia Tech	Augusta, Ga.	Augusta, Ga.	D12
Young, Almon	G	6-2	275	7/3/62	Bethune-Cookman	Eustis, Fla.	Umatilla, Fla.	FA

Players who report to an NFL team for the first time are designated on rosters as rookies (R). If a player reported to an NFL training camp in a previous year but was not on the active squad for three or more regular season or postseason games, he is listed on the first-year roster and designated by a (1). Thereafter, a player who is on the active squad for three or more regular season or postseason games is credited with an additional year of playing experience.

NOTES

Dan Sekanovich, assistant head coach-defensive line; born July 27, 1933, Hazleton, Pa., lives in Roswell, Ga. Defensive end Tennessee 1951-53. Pro defensive end Montreal Alouettes (CFL) 1955. College coach: Susquehanna 1961-63, Connecticut 1964-67, Pittsburgh 1968, Navy 1969-70, Kentucky 1971-72. Pro coach: Montreal Alouettes (CFL) 1973-76, New York Jets 1977-82, joined Falcons in 1983.

Jack Stanton, defensive backfield; born June 7, 1938, Bridgeville, Pa., lives in Atlanta. Halfback North Carolina State 1958-60. Defensive back Toronto Argonauts (CFL) 1961, Pittsburgh Steelers 1961. College coach: George Washington 1967, North Carolina State 1968-72, Florida State 1973, 1976-83, North Carolina 1974-75. Pro coach: Joined Falcons in 1984.

CHICAGO BEARS

**National Football Conference
Central Division**

Team Colors: Navy Blue, Orange,
and White

**Corporate Headquarters: Halas Hall
250 North Washington, Lake Forest,
Illinois 60045
Telephone: (312) 295-6600**

Club Officials

Chairman of the Board: Edward W. McCaskey
President and Chief Executive Officer: Michael B.
McCaskey
Vice President and General Manager, Treasurer:
Jerome R. Vainisi
Vice President: Charles A. Brizzolara
Secretary: Virginia H. McCaskey
Dir., Player Personnel: Bill Tobin
Dir., Community Involvement: Pat McCaskey
Dir., Marketing/Communications: Bill McGrane
Dir., Media Relations: Ken Valdiserri
Media Relations Assistant: Bryan Harlan
Ticket Manager: George Arneson
Trainer: Fred Caito
Assistant Trainer: Brian McCaskey
Strength Coordinator: Clyde Emrich
Equipment Manager: Ray Earley
Assistant Equipment Manager: Gary Haeger
Scouts: Jim Parmer, Rod Graves, Don King

Stadium: Soldier Field • **Capacity:** 65,790
425 McFetridge Place
Chicago, Illinois 60605

Playing Surface: AstroTurf

Training Camp: Wisconsin-Platteville
Platteville, Wisconsin 53818

1985 SCHEDULE

Preseason

Aug. 9	at St. Louis	7:30
Aug. 17	**Indianapolis**	6:00
Aug. 26	at Dallas	7:00
Aug. 31	**Buffalo**	6:00

Regular Season

Sept. 8	**Tampa Bay**	12:00
Sept. 15	**New England**	12:00
Sept. 19	at Minnesota (Thursday)	7:00
Sept. 29	**Washington**	12:00
Oct. 6	at Tampa Bay	1:00
Oct. 13	at San Francisco	1:00
Oct. 21	**Green Bay** (Monday)	8:00
Oct. 27	**Minnesota**	12:00
Nov. 3	at Green Bay	12:00
Nov. 10	**Detroit**	12:00
Nov. 17	at Dallas	12:00
Nov. 24	**Atlanta**	12:00
Dec. 2	at Miami (Monday)	9:00
Dec. 8	**Indianapolis**	12:00
Dec. 14	at N.Y. Jets (Saturday)	12:30
Dec. 22	at Detroit	1:00

BEARS COACHING HISTORY

**Chicago Staleys 1921
(490-328-42)**

1920-29	George Halas	85-31-19
1930-32	Ralph Jones	24-10-7
1933-42	George Halas*	88-25-4
1942-45	Hunk Anderson-
Luke Johnsos**	24-12-2
1946-55	George Halas	77-42-2
1956-57	John (Paddy) Driscoll	14-10-1
1958-67	George Halas	75-53-6
1968-71	Jim Dooley	20-36-0
1972-74	Abe Gibron	11-30-1
1975-77	Jack Pardee	20-23-0
1978-81	Neill Armstrong	30-35-0
1982-84	Mike Ditka	22-21-0

*Retired November 1 to re-enter Navy
**Co-coaches

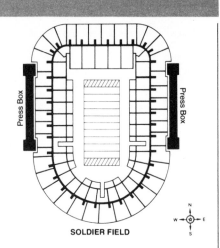

SOLDIER FIELD

RECORD HOLDERS
Individual Records—Career

Category	Name	Performance
Rushing (Yds.)	Walter Payton, 1975-1984	13,309
Passing (Yds.)	Sid Luckman, 1939-1950	14,686
Passing (TDs)	Sid Luckman, 1939-1950	137
Receiving (No.)	Walter Payton, 1975-1984	373
Receiving (Yds.)	Johnny Morris, 1958-1967	5,059
Interceptions	Richie Petitbon, 1959-1968	37
Punting (Avg.)	George Gulyanics, 1947-1952	44.5
Punt Return (Avg.)	Ray (Scooter) McLean, 1940-47	14.8
Kickoff Return (Avg.)	Gale Sayers, 1965-1971	30.6
Field Goals	Bob Thomas, 1975-1984	128
Touchdowns (Tot.)	Walter Payton, 1975-1984	98
Points	Bob Thomas, 1975-1984	629

Individual Records—Single Season

Category	Name	Performance
Rushing (Yds.)	Walter Payton, 1977	1,852
Passing (Yds.)	Bill Wade, 1962	3,172
Passing (TDs)	Sid Luckman, 1943	28
Receiving (No.)	Johnny Morris, 1964	93
Receiving (Yds.)	Johnny Morris, 1964	1,200
Interceptions	Roosevelt Taylor, 1963	9
Punting (Avg.)	Bobby Joe Green, 1963	46.4
Punt Return (Avg.)	Harry Clark, 1943	15.8
Kickoff Return (Avg.)	Gale Sayers, 1967	37.7
Field Goals	Mac Percival, 1968	25
Touchdowns (Tot.)	Gale Sayers, 1965	22
Points	Gale Sayers, 1965	132

Individual Records—Single Game

Category	Name	Performance
Rushing (Yds.)	Walter Payton, 11-20-77	275
Passing (Yds.)	Johnny Lujack, 12-11-49	468
Passing (TDs)	Sid Luckman, 11-14-43	7
Receiving (No.)	Jim Keane, 10-23-49	14
Receiving (Yds.)	Harlon Hill, 10-31-54	214
Interceptions	Many times	3
	Last time by Ross Brupbacher, 12-12-76	
Field Goals	Roger LeClerc, 12-3-61	5
	Mac Percival, 10-20-68	5
Touchdowns (Tot.)	Gale Sayers, 12-12-65	6
Points	Gale Sayers, 12-12-65	36

1984 TEAM STATISTICS

	Chicago	Opp.
Total First Downs	297	216
Rushing	164	72
Passing	115	122
Penalty	18	22
Third Down: Made/Att.	106/257	55/208
Fourth Down: Made/Att.	9/23	2/11
Total Net Yards	5437	3863
Avg. Per Game	339.8	241.4
Total Plays	1100	885
Avg. Per Play	4.9	4.4
Net Yards Rushing	2974	1377
Avg. Per Game	185.9	86.1
Total Rushes	674	378
Net Yards Passing	2463	2486
Avg. Per Game	153.9	155.4
Tackled/Yards Lost	36/232	72/583
Gross Yards	2695	3069
Att./Completions	390/226	435/198
Completion Pct.	57.9	45.5
Had Intercepted	15	21
Punts/Avg.	85/39.2	100/41.6
Net Punting Avg.	35.3	34.6
Penalties/Yards Lost	114/851	86/698
Fumbles/Ball Lost	31/16	33/13
Touchdowns	37	29
Rushing	22	10
Passing	14	14
Returns	1	5
Avg. Time of Possession	35:08	24:52

1984 TEAM RECORD
Preseason (1-3)

Date	Chicago		Opponents
8/4	10	*St. Louis	19
8/11	10	Green Bay	17
8/18	17	*Cincinnati	25
8/26	38	Buffalo	7
	75		68

Regular Season (10-6)

Date	Chicago		Opp.	Att.
9/2	34	*Tampa Bay	14	58,802
9/9	27	*Denver	0	54,335
9/16	9	Green Bay	7	55,942
9/23	9	Seattle	38	61,520
9/30	14	*Dallas	23	63,623
10/7	20	*New Orleans	7	53,752
10/14	21	St. Louis	38	49,554
10/21	44	Tampa Bay	9	60,003
10/28	16	*Minnesota	7	57,517
11/4	17	*Los Angeles Raiders	6	59,858
11/11	13	Los Angeles Rams	29	62,021
11/18	16	*Detroit	14	54,911
11/25	34	Minnesota	3	56,881
12/3	7	San Diego	20	45,470
12/9	14	*Green Bay	20	59,374
12/16	30	Detroit	13	53,252
	325		248	906,815

*Home Game

Score by Periods

Chicago	91	107	62	65	—	325
Opponents	33	73	53	89	—	248

Attendance
Home 462,172   Away 444,643   Total 906,815
Single game home record, 80,259 (11-24-66)
Single season home record, 511,541 (1981)

1984 INDIVIDUAL STATISTICS

Rushing

	Att.	Yds.	Avg.	LG	TD
Payton	381	1684	4.4	72t	11
Suhey	124	424	3.4	21	4
McMahon	39	276	7.1	30	2
C. Thomas	40	186	4.7	37	1
Lisch	18	121	6.7	31	0
Fuller	15	89	5.9	26	1
Gentry	21	79	3.8	28	1
Jordan	11	70	6.4	29	0
Hutchison	14	39	2.8	6	1
McKinnon	2	12	6.0	21	0
Landry	2	1	0.5	1t	1
Baschnagel	1	0	0.0	0	0
Finzer	2	0	0.0	5	0
Moorehead	1	−2	−2.0	−2	0
Avellini	3	−5	−1.7	0	0
Chicago	674	2974	4.4	72t	22
Opponents	378	1377	3.6	36	10

Passing

	Att.	Comp.	Pct.	Yds.	TD	Int.	Tkld.	Rate
McMahon	143	85	59.4	1146	8	2	10/48	97.8
Lisch	85	43	50.6	413	0	6	13/91	35.1
Fuller	78	53	67.9	595	3	0	7/41	103.3
Avellini	53	30	56.6	288	0	3	5/43	48.3
Landry	20	11	55.0	199	1	3	0/0	66.5
Payton	8	3	37.5	47	2	1	0/0	57.8
Baschnagel	2	1	50.0	7	0	0	0/0	58.3
Suhey	1	0	0.0	0	0	0	1/9	39.6
Chicago	390	226	57.9	2695	14	15	36/232	75.1
Opponents	435	198	45.5	3069	14	21	72/583	60.0

Receiving

	No.	Yds.	Avg.	LG	TD
Payton	45	368	8.2	31	0
Suhey	42	312	7.4	23	2
Gault	34	587	17.3	61t	6
Moorehead	29	497	17.1	50	1
McKinnon	29	431	14.9	32t	3
Dunsmore	9	106	11.8	25	1
Saldi	9	90	10.0	20	0
C. Thomas	9	39	4.3	9	0
Baschnagel	6	53	8.8	17	0
Gentry	4	29	7.3	13	0
Anderson	3	77	25.7	49t	1
Krenk	2	31	15.5	24	0
McMahon	1	42	42.0	42	0
Cameron	1	13	13.0	13	0
Cabral	1	7	7.0	7	0
Hutchison	1	7	7.0	7	0
Jordan	1	6	6.0	6	0
Chicago	226	2695	11.9	61t	14
Opponents	198	3069	15.5	88t	14

Interceptions

	No.	Yds.	Avg.	LG	TD
Fencik	5	102	20.4	61	0
Frazier	5	89	17.8	33	0
Bell	4	46	11.5	36t	1
Richardson	2	7	3.5	7	0
Harris	1	34	34.0	34	0
Duerson	1	9	9.0	9	0
Singletary	1	4	4.0	4	0
Schmidt	1	0	0.0	0	0
Gayle	1	−1	−1.0	−1	0
Chicago	21	290	13.8	61	1
Opponents	15	241	16.1	66t	3

Punting

	No.	Yds.	Avg.	In 20	LG
Finzer	83	3328	40.1	26	87
Chicago	85	3328	39.2	26	87
Opponents	100	4160	41.6	12	62

Punt Returns

	No.	FC	Yds.	Avg.	LG	TD
Fisher	57	11	492	8.6	28	0
McKinnon	5	0	62	12.4	18	0
Duerson	1	0	4	4.0	4	0
Chicago	63	11	558	8.9	28	0
Opponents	41	12	249	6.1	21	0

Kickoff Returns

	No.	Yds.	Avg.	LG	TD
Cameron	26	485	18.7	40	0
Gentry	11	209	19.0	33	0
Jordan	5	62	12.4	22	0
Duerson	4	95	23.8	26	0
Bell	2	33	16.5	17	0
Gault	1	12	12.0	12	0
Chicago	49	896	18.3	40	0
Opponents	68	1443	21.2	97t	1

Scoring

	TD R	TD P	TD Rt	PAT	FG	Saf	TP
B. Thomas	0	0	0	35/37	22/28	0	101
Payton	11	0	0	0/0	0/0	0	66
Gault	0	6	0	0/0	0/0	0	36
Suhey	4	2	0	0/0	0/0	0	36
McKinnon	0	3	0	0/0	0/0	0	18
McMahon	2	0	0	0/0	0/0	0	12
Anderson	0	1	0	0/0	0/0	0	6
Bell	0	0	1	0/0	0/0	0	6
Dunsmore	0	1	0	0/0	0/0	0	6
Fuller	1	0	0	0/0	0/0	0	6
Gentry	1	0	0	0/0	0/0	0	6
Hutchison	1	0	0	0/0	0/0	0	6
Landry	1	0	0	0/0	0/0	0	6
Moorehead	0	1	0	0/0	0/0	0	6
C. Thomas	1	0	0	0/0	0/0	0	6
Chicago	22	14	1	35/37	22/28	1	325
Opponents	10	14	5	26/29	16/22	0	248

FIRST-ROUND SELECTIONS
(If club had no first-round selection, first player drafted is listed with round in parentheses.)

Since 1948

Year	Player, College, Position
1948	Bobby Layne, Texas, B
	Max Baumgardner, Texas, E
1949	Dick Harris, Texas, C
1950	Chuck Hunsinger, Florida, B
	Fred Morrison, Ohio State, B
1951	Bob Williams, Notre Dame, B
	Billy Stone, Bradley, B
	Gene Schroeder, Virginia, E
1952	Jim Dooley, Miami, B
1953	Billy Anderson, Compton (Calif.) JC, B
1954	Stan Wallace, Illinois, B
1955	Ron Drzewiecki, Marquette, B
1956	Menan (Tex) Schriewer, Texas, E
1957	Earl Leggett, Louisiana State, T
1958	Chuck Howley, West Virginia, G
1959	Don Clark, Ohio State, B
1960	Roger Davis, Syracuse, G
1961	Mike Ditka, Pittsburgh, E
1962	Ronnie Bull, Baylor, RB
1963	Dave Behrman, Michigan State, C
1964	Dick Evey, Tennessee, DT
1965	Dick Butkus, Illinois, LB
	Gale Sayers, Kansas, RB
	Steve DeLong, Tennessee, T
1966	George Rice, Louisiana State, DT
1967	Loyd Phillips, Arkansas, DE
1968	Mike Hull, Southern California, RB
1969	Rufus Mayes, Ohio State, T
1970	George Farmer, UCLA, WR (3)
1971	Joe Moore, Missouri, RB
1972	Lionel Antoine, Southern Illinois, T
	Craig Clemons, Iowa, DB
1973	Wally Chambers, Eastern Kentucky, DE
1974	Waymond Bryant, Tennessee State, LB
	Dave Gallagher, Michigan, DT
1975	Walter Payton, Jackson State, RB
1976	Dennis Lick, Wisconsin, T
1977	Ted Albrecht, California, T
1978	Brad Shearer, Texas, DT (3)
1979	Dan Hampton, Arkansas, DT
	Al Harris, Arizona State, DE
1980	Otis Wilson, Louisville, LB
1981	Keith Van Horne, Southern California, T
1982	Jim McMahon, Brigham Young, QB
1983	Jimbo Covert, Pittsburgh, T
	Willie Gault, Tennessee, WR
1984	Wilber Marshall, Florida, LB
1985	William Perry, Clemson, DT

CHICAGO BEARS 1985 VETERAN ROSTER

No.	Name	Pos.	Ht.	Wt.	Birth-date	NFL Exp.	College	Birthplace	Residence	'84 Games/ Starts
86	Anderson, Brad	WR	6-2	196	1/21/61	2	Arizona	Glendale, Ariz.	Chicago, Ill.	13/3
60	Andrews, Tom	C	6-4	261	1/11/62	2	Louisville	Parma, Ohio	Louisville, Ky.	7/0
84	Baschnagel, Brian	WR	5-11	185	1/8/54	10	Ohio State	Kingston, N.Y.	Chicago, Ill.	16/1
79	Becker, Kurt	G	6-5	270	12/22/58	4	Michigan	Aurora, Ill.	Chicago, Ill.	16/16
25	†Bell, Todd	S	6-1	205	11/28/58	5	Ohio State	Middletown, Ohio	Middletown, Ohio	16/16
62	Bortz, Mark	G	6-6	271	2/12/61	3	Iowa	Pardeeville, Wis.	Vernon Hills, Ill.	15/15
54	†Cabral, Brian	LB	6-1	227	6/23/56	7	Colorado	Ft. Benning, Ga.	Libertyville, Ill.	16/0
30	Cameron, Jack	WR	6-0	182	11/5/61	2	Winston-Salem State	Durham, N.C.	Durham, N.C.	16/1
74	Covert, Jim	T	6-4	283	3/22/60	3	Pittsburgh	Conway, Pa.	Deerfield, Ill.	16/16
95	Dent, Richard	DE	6-5	253	12/13/60	3	Tennessee State	Atlanta, Ga.	Vernon Hills, Ill.	16/10
22	Duerson, Dave	S	6-1	205	11/28/60	3	Notre Dame	Muncie, Ind.	Mundelein, Ill.	16/0
88	Dunsmore, Pat	TE	6-3	237	10/2/59	3	Drake	Duluth, Minn.	Deerfield, Ill.	11/0
64	Fada, Rob	G	6-2	272	5/7/61	3	Pittsburgh	Fairborn, Ohio	Vernon Hills, Ill.	14/1
45	Fencik, Gary	S	6-1	197	6/11/54	10	Yale	Chicago, Ill.	Chicago, Ill.	16/16
15	Finzer, Dave	P	6-0	195	2/3/59	2	DePauw	Chicago, Ill.	Glenview, Ill.	16/0
24	Fisher, Jeff	CB	5-10	195	2/25/58	5	Southern California	Culver City, Calif.	Libertyville, Ill.	16/0
21	Frazier, Leslie	CB	6-0	189	4/3/59	5	Alcorn State	Columbus, Miss.	Vernon Hills, Ill.	11/11
71	Frederick, Andy	T	6-6	265	7/25/54	9	New Mexico	Oak Park, Ill.	Libertyville, Ill.	16/2
4	Fuller, Steve	QB	6-4	195	1/5/57	7	Clemson	Enid, Okla.	Spartanburg, S.C.	6/4
83	Gault, Willie	WR	6-0	178	9/5/60	3	Tennessee	Griffin, Ga.	Lake Forest, Ill.	16/15
23	Gayle, Shaun	CB	5-11	191	3/8/62	2	Ohio State	Hampton, Va.	Chicago, Ill.	15/6
29	Gentry, Dennis	RB	5-8	184	2/10/59	4	Baylor	Lubbock, Tex.	Temple, Tex.	16/0
99	Hampton, Dan	DT	6-5	266	9/19/57	7	Arkansas	Oklahoma City, Okla.	Cabot, Ark.	15/15
90	†Harris, Al	LB	6-5	253	12/31/56	7	Arizona State	Bangor, Me.	Wheeling, Ill.	16/16
73	Hartenstine, Mike	DE	6-3	258	7/27/53	11	Penn State	Allentown, Pa.	Lake Bluff, Ill.	16/14
63	Hilgenberg, Jay	C	6-3	255	3/21/59	5	Iowa	Iowa City, Iowa	Iowa City, Iowa	16/16
75	Humphries, Stefan	G	6-3	265	1/20/62	2	Michigan	Broward, Fla.	Chicago, Ill.	10/0
32	Hutchison, Anthony	RB	5-10	186	2/4/61	3	Texas Tech	Houston, Tex.	San Antonio, Tex.	12/0
49	Jordan, Donald	RB	6-0	210	2/9/62	2	Houston	Houston, Tex.	Houston, Tex.	13/0
98	†Keys, Tyrone	DE	6-7	267	10/24/59	3	Mississippi State	Brookhaven, Miss.	Los Angeles, Calif.	14/7
89	Krenk, Mitch	TE	6-2	225	11/19/59	2	Nebraska	Crete, Neb.	Dallas, Tex.	8/0
12	Lisch, Rusty	QB	6-4	215	12/21/56	6	Notre Dame	Bellevue, Ill.	Bellevue, Ill.	7/1
82	†Margerum, Ken	WR	6-0	180	10/5/58	4	Stanford	Fountain Valley, Calif.	Stanford, Calif.	0*
58	Marshall, Wilber	LB	6-1	225	4/18/62	2	Florida	Titusville, Fla.	Mims, Fla.	15/1
85	McKinnon, Dennis	WR	6-1	185	8/22/61	3	Florida	Quitman, Ga.	Gurnee, Ill.	12/12
9	McMahon, Jim	QB	6-1	185	8/21/59	4	Brigham Young	Jersey City, N.J.	Northbrook, Ill.	9/9
76	†McMichael, Steve	DT	6-2	263	10/17/57	6	Texas	Houston, Tex.	Lake Bluff, Ill.	16/16
87	†Moorehead, Emery	TE	6-2	225	3/22/54	9	Colorado	Evanston, Ill.	Broomfield, Colo.	16/9
34	Payton, Walter	RB	5-10	202	7/25/54	11	Jackson State	Columbia, Miss.	Barrington, Ill.	16/16
53	Rains, Dan	LB	6-1	222	4/26/56	3	Cincinnati	Rochester, Pa.	Aliquippa, Pa.	16/0
27	Richardson, Mike	CB	6-0	188	5/23/61	3	Arizona State	Compton, Calif.	Los Angeles, Calif.	15/15
59	Rivera, Ron	LB	6-3	244	1/7/62	2	California	Monterey, Calif.	Berkeley, Calif.	15/0
81	†Saldi, Jay	TE	6-3	227	10/8/54	10	South Carolina	White Plains, N.Y.	Grayslake, Ill.	15/7
50	Singletary, Mike	LB	6-0	228	10/9/58	5	Baylor	Houston, Tex.	Houston, Tex.	16/16
26	Suhey, Matt	RB	5-11	216	7/7/58	5	Penn State	State College, Pa.	Highland Park, Ill.	16/16
16	Thomas, Bob	K	5-10	177	8/7/52	10	Notre Dame	Rochester, N.Y.	Naperville, Ill.	16/0
33	Thomas, Calvin	RB	5-11	235	1/7/60	4	Illinois	St. Louis, Mo.	Forest Park, Ill.	16/0
78	†Van Horne, Keith	T	6-6	265	11/6/57	5	Southern California	Mt. Lebanon, Pa.	Deerfield, Ill.	14/14
70	Waechter, Henry	DT	6-5	270	2/13/59	4	Nebraska	Dubuque, Iowa	Lincoln, Neb.	3/2*
55	Wilson, Otis	LB	6-2	231	9/15/57	6	Louisville	New York, N.Y.	Libertyville, Ill.	15/15

* Margerum missed '84 season due to injury; Waechter played 1 game with Indianapolis, 2 with Chicago in '84.

†Option playout; subject to developments.

Retired—Jim Osborne, 13-year defensive tackle, 16 games in '84.

Also played with Bears in '84—QB Bob Avellini (5 games), QB Greg Landry (2), S Kevin Potter (1), CB Terry Schmidt (16).

COACHING STAFF

Head Coach, Mike Ditka

Pro Career: Became tenth head coach of Bears on January 20, 1982, after serving nine years as an offensive assistant with Dallas. Led Bears to first divisional title and first championship of any kind in 21 years following Bears 1985 NFC Championship Game appearance (lost to San Francisco 23-0). Bears 11-7 record included a divisional playoff win over Washington (23-19). The 45-year-old Ditka owns a 22-21 record since taking over the coaching reins and in the last two years has won 16 of his last 24 games, including 9 of his last 11 home games. Ditka is a 24-year veteran of the NFL as both a player and a coach. Had 12-year playing career as a tight end with Chicago (1961-66), Philadelphia (1967-68), and Dallas (1969-72). A first-round draft choice by Chicago in 1961, Ditka was NFL rookie of the year, all-NFL (1961-64), and played in five Pro Bowls (1962-66). He joined Cowboys coaching staff in 1973. In addition to working with Dallas special teams, he coached Cowboys' receivers. During his NFL career, he has been in league playoffs 14 seasons and been a member of teams that have been NFC champions five times and NFL champions three times. Career record: 22-21.

Background: Played at Pittsburgh from 1958-60 and was a unanimous All-America his senior year. A two-way performer, he played both tight end and linebacker. He also was one of the nation's leading punters with a 40-plus yard average over three years.

Personal: Born October 18, 1939, Carnegie, Pa. Mike and his wife, Diana, live in Grayslake, Ill., and have four chidren—Michael, Mark, Megan, and Matt.

Assistant Coaches

Jim Dooley, research and quality control; born February 8, 1930, Stoutsville, Mo., lives in Chicago. End Miami 1949-51. Pro receiver Chicago Bears 1952-61. Pro coach: Chicago Bears 1962-71 (head coach 1968-71), Buffalo Bills 1972, rejoined Bears in 1981.

Dale Haupt, defensive line; born April 12, 1929, Manitowic, Wis., lives in Libertyville, Ill. Guard Wyoming 1951-53. Pro guard Green Bay Packers 1954. College coach: Tennessee 1960-63, Iowa State 1964-65, Richmond 1966-71, North Carolina State 1972-76, Duke 1977. Pro coach: Joined Bears in 1978.

Ed Hughes, offensive coordinator; born October 23, 1927, Buffalo, N.Y., lives in Libertyville, Ill. Halfback Tulsa 1952-53. Pro defensive back Los Angeles Rams 1954-55, New York Giants 1956-58. Pro coach: Dallas Texans 1960-62, Denver Broncos 1963, Washington Redskins 1964-67, San Francisco 49ers 1968-70, Houston Oilers 1971 (head coach), St. Louis Cardinals 1972, Dallas Cowboys 1973-76, Detroit Lions 1977, New Orleans Saints 1978-80, Philadelphia Eagles 1981, joined Bears in 1982.

Steve Kazor, special teams; born February 24, 1948, New Kensington, Pa. lives in Vernon Hills, Ill. Nose tackle Westminister College 1967-70. No pro playing experience. College coach: Colorado State 1975, Wyoming 1976, Texas-El Paso 1979-80, Emporia State 1981 (head coach). Pro coach: Joined Bears in 1983.

Jim LaRue, defensive backfield; born August 11, 1925, Clinton, Okla., lives in Libertyville, Ill. Halfback Carson-Newman 1943, Duke 1944-45, Maryland 1947-49. No pro playing experience. College coach: Maryland 1950, Kansas State 1951-54, Houston 1955-56, Southern Methodist 1957-58, Arizona 1959-66 (head coach), Utah 1967-73, Wake Forest 1974-75. Pro coach: Buffalo Bills 1976-77, joined Bears in 1978.

Ted Plumb, receivers; born August 20, 1939, Reno, Nev., lives in Buffalo Grove, Ill. End Baylor 1959-61. No pro playing experience. College coach: Cerritos, Calif., J.C. 1966-67, Texas Christian 1968-70, Tulsa 1971, Kansas 1972-73. Pro coach: New York Giants 1974-76, Atlanta Falcons 1977-79, joined Bears in 1980.

CHICAGO BEARS 1985 FIRST-YEAR ROSTER

Name	Pos.	Ht.	Wt.	Birth-date	College	Birthplace	Residence	How Acq.
Bennett, Charles	DT	6-5	250	2/9/63	Southwest Louisiana	Alligator, Miss.	Alligator, Miss.	D7
Butkus, Mark (1)	DT	6-4	260	12/3/61	Illinois	Lansing, Ill.	Lansing, Ill.	D11('84)
Butler, Kevin	K	6-1	190	7/24/62	Georgia	Savannah, Ga.	Stone Mountain, Ga.	D4
Buxton, Steve	G-T	6-6	268	12/23/61	Indiana State	Sullivan, Ill.	Sullivan, Ill.	D8
Christopher, John	P	6-3	205	12/10/60	Moorhead State	Sandusky, Ohio	Norwalk, Ohio	FA
Coryatt, Pat	DT	6-2	287	6/18/61	Baylor	Trinidad	Baytown, Tex.	D10
Gray, Kevin	CB-S	6-0	188	9/11/57	Eastern Illinois	Chicago, Ill.	Chicago, Ill.	FA
Jackson, Jackie	RB	6-0	185	7/20/63	Southwestern	Tulsa, Okla.	Winfield, Kan.	FA
Johnson, Stan	WR	6-3	200	9/16/63	Wis.-LaCrosse	Milwaukee, Wis.	Pewaukee, Wis.	FA
Kallmeyer, Bruce (1)	K	5-10	180	2/8/62	Kansas	Kansas City, Mo.	Shawnee Mission, Kan.	FA
Long, Matt	C	6-3	265	3/16/61	San Diego State	Ventura, Calif.	Ventura, Calif.	FA
Maness, James	WR	6-1	174	5/1/63	Texas Christian	Decatur, Tex.	Decatur, Tex.	D3
Miller, Ken	CB-S	5-10	180	6/24/58	Eastern Michigan	Pine Bluff, Ark.	Ann Arbor, Mich.	FA
Morrissey, Jim	LB	6-2	207	12/24/62	Michigan State	Flint, Mich.	Flint, Mich.	D11
Newell, Shaun	DT-DE	6-3	257	2/26/62	Utah	Riverside, Calif.	Riverside, Calif.	FA
Norman, Tim	G	6-6	270	7/10/59	Illinois	Oak Park, Ill.	Winfield, Ill.	FA
Perry, William	DT	6-2	318	12/16/62	Clemson	Akin, S.C.	Clemson, S.C.	D1
Phillips, Eddie	RB	5-11	208	2/23/61	Iowa	Columbus, Miss.	Chicago, Ill.	FA
Phillips, Reggie	CB-S	5-10	168	12/12/60	Southern Methodist	Houston, Tex.	Houston, Tex.	D2
Pierce, Larry	DT	6-5	245	1/30/62	Nevada-Reno	San Jose, Calif.	San Jose, Calif.	FA
Potter, Kevin	CB-S	5-10	183	12/19/59	Missouri	St. Louis, Mo.	St. Louis, Mo.	FA
Price, Jeff	WR	6-0	195	4/18/63	Purdue	Newport News, Va.	Newport News, Va.	FA
Rammuno, Joe	T	6-3	265	2/1/62	Wyoming	Steamboat Spr., Colo.	Steamboat Spr., Colo.	FA
Riccio, Kevin	TE	6-5	240	5/26/61	Virginia	Babylon, N.Y.	West Islip, N.Y.	FA
Robinson, Roger	CB	6-3	185	8/6/62	Tennessee State	Stubenville, Ohio	Stubenville, Ohio	FA
Rowell, Eugene	T-DT	6-3	265	2/15/58	Dubuque	San Diego, Calif.	Chicago, Ill.	FA
Sanders, Thomas	RB	5-11	195	1/4/62	Texas A&M	Giddings, Tex.	Giddings, Tex.	D9
Satterfield, Glenn	CB-S	5-10	185	6/23/62	Angelo State	Georgetown, Tex.	Georgetown, Tex.	FA
Spivak, Joe	G	6-0	280	2/19/62	Illinois State	Chicago, Ill.	Normal, Ill.	FA
Stewart, Ricky	FB	5-10	219	3/1/62	McNeese State	Baton Rouge, La.	Baton Rouge, La.	FA
Stoopa, Mike	CB-S	6-2	182	12/13/61	Iowa	Youngstown, Ohio	Youngstown, Ohio	FA
Storey, Kenneth	WR	6-2	185	11/9/60	Cameron College	Plainview, Tex.	Plainview, Tex.	FA
Taylor, Ken	CB	6-1	185	9/2/63	Oregon State	San Jose, Calif.	San Jose, Calif.	FA
Thomas, Anthony	FB	5-10	195	11/15/62	Abilene Christian	Jasper, Tex.	Jasper, Tex.	FA
Tomczak, Mike	QB	6-1	192	10/23/62	Ohio State	Calumet City, Ill.	Calumet City, Ill.	FA
Vestman, Kurt (1)	TE	6-3	235	7/5/60	Idaho	Bainbridge, Wash.	Moscow, Idaho	D10('84)
Viracola, Mike	P	5-11	180	6/28/62	Notre Dame	Dallas, Tex.	Dallas, Tex.	FA
Ward, Rick	K	6-2	210	4/5/62	East Oregon State	Roseburg, Ore.	Roseburg, Ore.	FA
Wrightman, Tim (1)	TE	6-3	233	3/27/60	UCLA	Harbor City, Calif.	Chicago, Ill.	FA

Players who report to an NFL team for the first time are designated on rosters as rookies (R). If a player reported to an NFL training camp in a previous year but was not on the active squad for three or more regular season or postseason games, he is listed on the first-year roster and designated by a (1). Thereafter, a player who is on the active squad for three or more regular season or postseason games is credited with an additional year of playing experience.

NOTES

_____

_____

_____

_____

_____

_____

_____

_____

_____

_____

_____

Johnny Roland, offensive backs; born May 21, 1943, Corpus Christi, Tex., lives in Vernon Hills, Ill. Running back Missouri 1963-65. Pro running back St. Louis Cardinals 1966-72, New York Giants 1973. College coach: Notre Dame 1975. Pro coach: Green Bay Packers 1974, Philadelphia Eagles 1976-78, joined Bears in 1983.

Buddy Ryan, defensive coordinator; born February 16, 1934, Frederick, Okla., lives in Lincolnshire, Ill. Guard Oklahoma State 1952-55. No pro playing experience. College coach: Buffalo 1961-65, Vanderbilt 1966, University of Pacific 1967. Pro coach: New York Jets 1968-75, Minnesota Vikings 1976-77, joined Bears in 1978.

Dick Stanfel, offensive line; born July 20, 1927, San Francisco, Calif., lives in Libertyville, Ill. Guard San Francisco 1948-51. Pro guard Detroit Lions 1952-55, Washington Redskins 1956-58. College coach: Notre Dame 1959-62, California 1963. Pro coach: Philadelphia Eagles 1964-70, San Francisco 49ers 1971-75, New Orleans Saints 1976-80 (head coach, 4 games in 1980), joined Bears in 1981.

**National Football Conference
Eastern Division**

Team Colors: Royal Blue, Metallic Silver
Blue, and White

**One Cowboy Parkway
Irving, Texas 75063
Telephone: (214) 369-8000**

Club Officials

General Partner: H.R. Bright
President-General Manager: Texas E. Schramm
Vice President-Personnel Development:
  Gil Brandt
Vice President-Treasurer: Don Wilson
Vice President-Administration: Joe Bailey
Public Relations Director: Doug Todd
Business Manager: Dan Werner
Assistant Public Relations Director: Greg Aiello
Ticket Manager: Steve Orsini
Trainers: Don Cochren, Ken Locker
Equipment Manager: William T. (Buck) Buchanan
Cheerleaders Director: Suzanne Mitchell

Stadium: Texas Stadium • **Capacity:** 63,749
Irving, Texas 75062

Playing Surface: Texas Turf

Training Camp: California Lutheran College
  Thousand Oaks, California 91360

1985 SCHEDULE

Preseason

Aug. 10	**Green Bay**	8:00
Aug. 17	at San Diego	6:00
Aug. 26	**Chicago**	7:00
Aug. 31	**Houston**	8:00

Regular Season

Sept. 9	**Washington** (Monday)	8:00
Sept. 15	at Detroit	1:00
Sept. 22	**Cleveland**	12:00
Sept. 29	at Houston	12:00
Oct. 6	at New York Giants	9:00
Oct. 13	**Pittsburgh**	12:00
Oct. 20	at Philadelphia	1:00
Oct. 27	**Atlanta**	12:00
Nov. 4	at St. Louis (Monday)	8:00
Nov. 10	at Washington	4:00
Nov. 17	**Chicago**	12:00
Nov. 24	**Philadelphia**	3:00
Nov. 28	**St. Louis** (Thanksgiving)	3:00
Dec. 8	at Cincinnati	1:00
Dec. 15	**New York Giants**	12:00
Dec. 22	at San Francisco	1:00

COWBOYS COACHING HISTORY

(243-141-6)

1960-84 Tom Landry 243-141-6

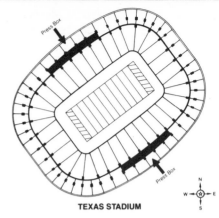

TEXAS STADIUM

RECORD HOLDERS
Individual Records — Career

Category	Name	Performance
Rushing (Yds.)	Tony Dorsett, 1977-1984	9,525
Passing (Yds.)	Roger Staubach, 1969-1979	22,700
Passing (TDs)	Roger Staubach, 1969-1979	153
Receiving (No.)	Drew Pearson, 1973-1983	489
Receiving (Yds.)	Drew Pearson, 1973-1983	7,822
Interceptions	Mel Renfro, 1964-1977	52
Punting (Avg.)	Sam Baker, 1962-63	45.1
Punt Return (Avg.)	Bob Hayes, 1965-1974	11.1
Kickoff Return (Avg.)	Mel Renfro, 1964-1977	26.4
Field Goals	Rafael Septien, 1978-1984	128
Touchdowns (Tot.)	Bob Hayes, 1965-1974	76
Points	Rafael Septien, 1978-1984	687

Individual Records — Single Season

Category	Name	Performance
Rushing (Yds.)	Tony Dorsett, 1981	1,646
Passing (Yds.)	Danny White, 1983	3,980
Passing (TDs)	Danny White, 1983	29
Receiving (No.)	Ron Springs, 1983	73
Receiving (Yds.)	Bob Hayes, 1966	1,232
Interceptions	Everson Walls, 1981	11
Punting (Avg.)	Sam Baker, 1962	45.4
Punt Return (Avg.)	Bob Hayes, 1968	20.8
Kickoff Return (Avg.)	Mel Renfro, 1965	30.0
Field Goals	Rafael Septien, 1981	27
Touchdowns (Tot.)	Dan Reeves, 1966	16
Points	Rafael Septien, 1983	123

Individual Records — Single Game

Category	Name	Performance
Rushing (Yds.)	Tony Dorsett, 12-4-77	206
Passing (Yds.)	Don Meredith, 11-10-63	460
Passing (TDs)	Many times	5
	Last time by Danny White, 10-30-83	
Receiving (No.)	Lance Rentzel, 11-19-67	13
Receiving (Yds.)	Bob Hayes, 11-13-66	246
Interceptions	Herb Adderley, 9-26-71	3
	Lee Roy Jordan, 11-4-73	3
	Dennis Thurman, 12-13-81	3
Field Goals	Many times	4
	Last time by Rafael Septien, 9-21-81	
Touchdowns (Tot.)	Many times	4
	Last time by Duane Thomas, 12-18-71	
Points	Many times	24
	Last time by Duane Thomas, 12-18-71	

1984 TEAM STATISTICS

	Dallas	Opp.
Total First Downs	323	283
Rushing	93	106
Passing	202	155
Penalty	28	22
Third Down: Made/Att.	83/238	83/247
Fourth Down: Made/Att.	3/7	5/16
Total Net Yards	5320	5036
Avg. Per Game	332.5	314.8
Total Plays	1121	1094
Avg. Per Play	4.7	4.6
Net Yards Rushing	1714	2226
Avg. Per Game	107.1	139.1
Total Rushes	469	510
Net Yards Passing	3606	2810
Avg. Per Game	225.4	175.6
Tackled/Yards Lost	48/389	57/390
Gross Yards	3995	3200
Att./Completions	604/322	527/250
Completion Pct.	53.3	47.4
Had Intercepted	26	28
Punts/Avg.	108/38.2	99/42.8
Net Punting Avg.	34.0	36.3
Penalties/Yards Lost	100/947	95/868
Fumbles/Ball Lost	35/17	35/16
Touchdowns	34	36
Rushing	12	8
Passing	19	23
Returns	3	5
Avg. Time of Possession	29:00	31:00

1984 TEAM RECORD

Preseason (3-1)

Date	Dallas		Opponents
8/4	31	*Green Bay	17
8/11	24	San Diego	13
8/16	10	*Pittsburgh	20
8/25	31	*Houston	24
	96		74

Regular Season (9-7)

Date	Dallas		Opp.	Att.
9/3	20	Los Angeles Rams	13	65,403
9/9	7	New York Giants	28	75,921
9/16	23	*Philadelphia	17	64,695
9/23	20	*Green Bay	6	64,425
9/30	23	Chicago	14	63,623
10/7	20	*St. Louis	31	61,678
10/14	14	Washington	34	55,431
10/21	30	*New Orleans (OT)	27	51,161
10/28	22	*Indianapolis	3	58,724
11/4	7	*New York Giants	19	60,235
11/11	24	St. Louis	17	48,721
11/18	3	Buffalo	14	74,391
11/22	20	*New England	17	55,341
12/2	26	Philadelphia	10	66,322
12/9	28	*Washington	30	64,286
12/17	21	Miami	28	74,139
	308		308	1,004,496

*Home Game   (OT) Overtime

Score by Periods

Dallas	65	89	56	95	3	—	308
Opponents	64	81	91	72	0	—	308

Attendance

Home 480,545   Away 523,951   Total 1,004,496
Single game home record, 80,259 (11-24-66)
Single season home record, 511,541 (1981)

1984 INDIVIDUAL STATISTICS

Rushing

	Att.	Yds.	Avg.	LG	TD
Dorsett	302	1189	3.9	31t	6
Newsome	66	268	4.1	30	5
Springs	68	197	2.9	16	1
D. White	6	21	3.5	8	0
Hogeboom	15	19	1.3	11	0
J. Jones	8	13	1.6	6	0
Hill	1	7	7.0	7	0
Donley	2	5	2.5	6	0
Smith	1	−5	−5.0	−5	0
Dallas	469	1714	3.7	31t	12
Opponents	510	2226	4.4	85t	8

Passing

	Att.	Comp.	Pct.	Yds.	TD	Int.	Tkld.	Rate
D. White	233	126	54.1	1580	11	11	22/178	71.5
Hogeboom	367	195	53.1	2366	7	14	26/211	63.7
Renfro	2	1	50.0	49	1	0	0/0	135.4
Dorsett	1	0	0.0	0	0	1	0/0	0.0
Springs	1	0	0.0	0	0	0	0/0	39.6
Dallas	604	322	53.3	3995	19	26	48/389	66.6
Opponents	527	250	47.4	3200	23	28	57/390	59.3

Receiving

	No.	Yds.	Avg.	LG	TD
Cosbie	60	789	13.2	36	4
Hill	58	864	14.9	66t	5
Dorsett	51	459	9.0	68t	1
Springs	46	454	9.9	57t	3
Renfro	35	583	16.7	60t	2
Harris, Clev.-Dall.	33	521	15.8	43	2
Harris, Dall.	1	9	9.0	9	0
Donley	32	473	14.8	49t	2
Newsome	26	263	10.1	29	0
J. Jones	7	57	8.1	19	1
Cornwell	2	23	11.5	13	1
Carmichael	1	7	7.0	7	0
Smith	1	7	7.0	7	0
Phillips	1	6	6.0	6	0
Pozderac	1	1	1.0	1	0
Dallas	322	3995	12.4	68t	19
Opponents	250	3200	12.8	80t	23

Interceptions

	No.	Yds.	Avg.	LG	TD
Downs	7	126	18.0	27t	1
Thurman	5	81	16.2	43	1
Clinkscale	3	32	10.7	23	0
Walls	3	12	4.0	12	0
Fellows	3	3	1.0	3	0
Hegman	3	3	1.0	3	0
Lockhart	1	32	32.0	32	0
V. Scott	1	5	5.0	5	0
Bates	1	3	3.0	3	0
Dickerson	1	0	0.0	0	0
Dallas	28	297	10.6	43	2
Opponents	26	372	14.3	49	4

Punting

	No.	Yds.	Avg.	In 20	LG
D. White	82	3151	38.4	21	54
Warren	21	799	38.0	3	48
Miller	5	173	34.6	1	41
Dallas	108	4123	38.2	25	54
Opponents	99	4236	42.8	23	59

Punt Returns

	No.	FC	Yds.	Avg.	LG	TD
Allen	54	15	446	8.3	18	0
Harris, Clev.-Dall.	9	0	73	8.1	13	0
Dallas	54	15	446	8.3	18	0
Opponents	55	19	230	4.2	19	0

Kickoff Returns

	No.	Yds.	Avg.	LG	TD
Allen	33	666	20.2	34	0
McSwain	20	403	20.2	32	0
Fellows	6	94	15.7	23	0
Salonen	2	30	15.0	22	0
Granger	2	6	3.0	5	0
Dallas	63	1199	19.0	34	0
Opponents	65	1310	20.2	64	0

Scoring

	TD R	TD P	TD Rt	PAT	FG	Saf	TP
Septien	0	0	0	33/34	23/29	0	102
Dorsett	6	1	0	0/0	0/0	0	42
Hill	0	5	0	0/0	0/0	0	30
Newsome	5	0	0	0/0	0/0	0	30
Cosbie	0	4	0	0/0	0/0	0	24
Springs	1	3	0	0/0	0/0	0	24
Donley	0	2	0	0/0	0/0	0	12
Harris, Clev.-Dall.	0	2	0	0/0	0/0	0	12
Renfro	0	2	0	0/0	0/0	0	12
Cornwell	0	1	0	0/0	0/0	0	6
Downs	0	0	1	0/0	0/0	0	6
Jeffcoat	0	0	1	0/0	0/0	0	6
J. Jones	0	1	0	0/0	0/0	0	6
Thurman	0	0	1	0/0	0/0	0	6
Dutton	0	0	0	0/0	0/0	1	2
Dallas	12	19	3	33/34	23/29	1	308
Opponents	8	23	5	35/36	19/28	0	308

FIRST-ROUND SELECTIONS

(If Club had no first-round selection, first player drafted is listed with round in parentheses.)

Year	Player, College, Position
1960	None
1961	Bob Lilly, Texas Christian, DT
1962	Sonny Gibbs, Texas Christian, QB (2)
1963	Lee Roy Jordan, Alabama, LB
1964	Scott Appleton, Texas, DT
1965	Craig Morton, California, QB
1966	John Niland, Iowa, G
1967	Phil Clark, Northwestern, DB (3)
1968	Dennis Homan, Alabama, WR
1969	Calvin Hill, Yale, RB
1970	Duane Thomas, West Texas State, RB
1971	Tody Smith, Southern California, DE
1972	Bill Thomas, Boston College, RB
1973	Billy Joe DuPree, Michigan State, TE
1974	Ed (Too Tall) Jones, Tennessee State, DE
	Charley Young, North Carolina State, RB
1975	Randy White, Maryland, LB
	Thomas Henderson, Langston, LB
1976	Aaron Kyle, Wyoming, DB
1977	Tony Dorsett, Pittsburgh, RB
1978	Larry Bethea, Michigan State, DE
1979	Robert Shaw, Tennessee, C
1980	Bill Roe, Colorado, LB (3)
1981	Howard Richards, Missouri, T
1982	Rod Hill, Kentucky State, DB
1983	Jim Jeffcoat, Arizona State, DE
1984	Billy Cannon, Jr., Texas A&M, LB
1985	Kevin Brooks, Michigan, DE

DALLAS COWBOYS 1985 VETERAN ROSTER

No.	Name	Pos.	Ht.	Wt.	Birth-date	NFL Exp.	College	Birthplace	Residence	'84 Games/Starts
36	Albritton, Vince	S	6-2	209	7/23/62	2	Washington	Oakland, Calif.	Oakland, Calif.	16/0
31	Allen, Gary	RB	5-10	179	4/23/60	4	Hawaii	Baldwin Park, Calif.	Baldwin Park, Calif.	16/0
76	Aughtman, Dowe	G	6-3	258	1/28/61	2	Auburn	Brewton, Ala.	Brewton, Ala.	7/0
62	Baldinger, Brian	G-T	6-4	258	1/7/59	4	Duke	Massapequa, N.Y.	Dallas, Tex.	16/4
40	Bates, Bill	S	6-1	201	6/6/61	3	Tennessee	Knoxville, Tenn.	Knoxville, Tenn.	12/2
47	Clinkscale, Dextor	S	5-11	189	4/13/58	5	South Carolina State	Greenville, S.C.	Dallas, Tex.	15/15
61	Cooper, Jim	T	6-5	267	9/28/55	9	Temple	Philadelphia, Pa.	Richardson, Tex.	7/7
85	Cornwell, Fred	TE	6-6	237	8/7/61	2	Southern California	Osborne, Kan.	Canyon Country, Calif.	14/1
84	Cosbie, Doug	TE	6-6	235	2/27/56	7	Santa Clara	Mountain View, Calif.	McKinney, Tex.	16/16
55	DeOssie, Steve	LB	6-2	248	11/22/62	2	Boston College	Tacoma, Wash.	Dallas, Tex.	16/0
51	†Dickerson, Anthony	LB	6-2	222	6/9/57	6	Southern Methodist	Texas City, Tex.	Garland, Tex.	16/15
33	Dorsett, Tony	RB	5-11	185	4/7/54	9	Pittsburgh	Aliquippa, Pa.	Dallas, Tex.	16/16
26	Downs, Michael	S	6-3	195	6/9/59	5	Rice	Dallas, Tex.	Dallas, Tex.	16/16
78	Dutton, John	DT	6-7	267	2/6/51	12	Nebraska	Evansville, Ind.	Dallas, Tex.	16/16
27	Fellows, Ron	CB	6-0	174	11/7/58	5	Missouri	South Bend, Ind.	Dallas, Tex.	16/16
28	Granger, Norm	RB	5-9	220	9/14/61	2	Iowa	Newark, N.J.	Newark, N.J.	15/0
86	Harris, Duriel	WR	5-11	176	11/27/54	10	New Mexico State	Port Arthur, Tex.	Dallas, Tex.	16/11*
58	Hegman, Mike	LB	6-1	231	1/17/53	10	Tennessee State	Memphis, Tenn.	Plano, Tex.	16/16
15	Hewko, Bob	QB	6-3	195	6/8/60	2	Florida	Abington, Pa.	Tampa, Fla.	0*
80	Hill, Tony	WR	6-2	198	6/23/56	9	Stanford	San Diego, Calif.	Dallas, Tex.	11/11
14	Hogeboom, Gary	QB	6-4	200	8/21/58	6	Central Michigan	Grand Rapids, Mich.	McKinney, Tex.	16/10
97	Hopkins, Thomas	T	6-6	260	1/13/60	2	Alabama A&M	Butler, Ala.	North Olmstead, Ohio	0*
21	Howard, Carl	CB	6-2	188	9/20/61	2	Rutgers	Newark, N.J.	Irvington, N.J.	10/0
79	Hunt, John	G	6-4	253	11/6/62	2	Florida	Orlando, Fla.	Orlando, Fla.	2/1
77	Jeffcoat, Jim	DE	6-5	257	4/1/61	3	Arizona State	Long Branch, N.J.	Dallas, Tex.	16/16
72	Jones, Ed	DE	6-9	287	2/23/51	11	Tennessee State	Jackson, Tenn.	Farmers Branch, Tex.	16/16
23	Jones, James	RB	5-10	189	12/6/58	5	Mississippi State	Vicksburg, Miss.	Dallas, Tex.	9/0
73	Kitson, Syd	G	6-4	262	9/27/58	5	Wake Forest	Orange, N.J.	New Providence, N.J.	9/3*
56	Lockhart, Eugene	LB	6-2	233	3/8/61	2	Houston	Crockett, Tex.	Dallas, Tex.	15/8
35	McSwain, Chuck	RB	6-0	190	2/21/61	3	Clemson	Rutherford, N.C.	Forest City, N.C.	15/0
30	Newsome, Timmy	RB	6-1	232	5/17/58	6	Winston-Salem State	Ahoskie, N.C.	Dallas, Tex.	15/4
16	Pelluer, Steve	QB	6-4	210	7/29/62	2	Washington	Bellevue, Wash.	Issaquah, Wash.	1/0
65	Petersen, Kurt	G	6-4	267	6/17/57	6	Missouri	St. Louis, Mo.	Carrollton, Tex.	13/13
81	Phillips, Kirk	WR	6-1	202	7/31/60	2	Tulsa	Poteau, Okla.	Dallas, Tex.	8/0
75	Pozderac, Phil	T	6-9	276	12/19/59	4	Notre Dame	Cleveland, Ohio	Carrollton, Tex.	15/14
64	Rafferty, Tom	C	6-3	254	8/2/54	10	Penn State	Syracuse, N.Y.	Dallas, Tex.	16/16
82	Renfro, Mike	WR	6-0	188	6/19/55	8	Texas Christian	Fort Worth, Tex.	Fort Worth, Tex.	16/11
70	Richards, Howard	T	6-6	260	8/7/59	5	Missouri	St. Louis, Mo.	Dallas, Tex.	11/4
50	Rohrer, Jeff	LB	6-3	225	12/25/58	4	Yale	Manhattan Beach, Calif.	Dallas, Tex.	16/0
89	Salonen, Brian	TE	6-2	227	7/29/61	2	Montana	Glasgow, Mont.	Great Falls, Mont.	16/0
66	Schultz, Chris	T	6-8	265	2/16/60	2	Arizona	Burlington, Ontario	Dallas, Tex.	0*
22	Scott, Victor	CB-S	5-11	196	6/1/62	2	Colorado	St. Louis, Mo.	East St. Louis, Ill.	16/0
1	Septien, Rafael	K	5-10	180	12/12/53	9	Southwest Louisiana	Mexico City, Mexico	Dallas, Tex.	16/0
60	Smerek, Don	DT	6-7	255	12/20/57	4	Nevada-Reno	Waterford, Mich.	Anna, Tex.	16/0
20	Springs, Ron	RB	6-1	224	11/1/56	7	Ohio State	Williamsburg, Va.	Dallas, Tex.	16/12
32	Thurman, Dennis	CB	5-11	175	4/13/56	8	Southern California	Los Angeles, Calif.	Farmers Branch, Tex.	16/0
63	Titensor, Glen	G	6-4	264	2/21/58	5	Brigham Young	Westminster, Calif.	Carrollton, Tex.	15/12
71	Tuinei, Mark	DT	6-5	274	3/31/60	3	Hawaii	Oceanside, Calif.	Honolulu, Hawaii	16/0
57	Turner, Jimmie	LB	6-2	220	2/16/62	2	Presbyterian	Vienna, Ga.	Byronville, Ga.	5/0
24	Walls, Everson	CB	6-1	190	12/28/59	5	Grambling	Dallas, Tex.	Dallas, Tex.	16/16
5	Warren, John	P	6-0	207	11/8/60	3	Tennessee	Jessup, Ga.	Knoxville, Tenn.	3/0
11	White, Danny	QB-P	6-2	197	2/9/52	10	Arizona State	Mesa, Ariz.	Wylie, Tex.	14/6
54	White, Randy	DT	6-4	260	1/15/53	11	Maryland	Wilmington, Del.	Dallas, Tex.	16/16

* Harris played 11 games with Cleveland, 5 with Dallas in '84; Hewko last active with Tampa Bay in '83; Hopkins last active with Cleveland in '84; Kitson played 8 games with Green Bay, 1 with Dallas in '84; Schultz missed '84 season due to injury.

†Option playout; subject to developments.

Retired—Bob Breunig, 10-year linebacker, 8 games in '84; Billy Cannon, rookie linebacker, 8 games in '84; Herb Scott, 10-year guard, 15 games in '84.

Also played with Cowboys in '84—WR Harold Carmichael (2 games), WR Doug Donley (15), P Jim Miller (1), WR Waddell Smith (2).

COACHING STAFF

Head Coach,
Tom Landry

Pro Career: Landry, the Cowboys' only head coach in their 25-year history, has compiled 19 winning seasons in succession and his overall record of 243-141-6 is winningest among active coaches. Cowboys became the fourth team in NFL to win a second Super Bowl. They defeated Denver 27-10 in Super Bowl XII on January 15, 1978, at Louisiana Superdome. Dallas has played in four other Super Bowls (V, VI, X, and XIII), winning Game VI 24-3 over Miami. Pro defensive back with New York Yanks (AAFC) 1949, New York Giants 1950-55. Player-coach with Giants 1954-55, named all-pro in 1954. Defensive assistant coach with Giants 1956-59 before moving to Dallas as head coach in 1960.

Background: Halfback, University of Texas 1947-48, and played in Longhorns' victories over Alabama in 1948 Sugar Bowl and Georgia in 1949 Orange Bowl.

Personal: Born September 11, 1924, Mission, Tex. A World War II bomber pilot. Tom and his wife, Alicia, live in Dallas and have three children—Tom Jr., Kitty, and Lisa.

Assistant Coaches

Neill Armstrong, research and development; born March 9, 1926, Tishomingo, Okla., lives in Dallas. End Oklahoma State 1943-46. Pro end-defensive back Philadelphia Eagles 1947-51, Winnipeg Blue Bombers (CFL) 1951, 1953-54. College coach: Oklahoma State 1955-61. Pro coach: Houston Oilers 1962-63, Edmonton Eskimos (CFL) 1964-69 (head coach), Minnesota Vikings 1970-77, Chicago Bears 1978-81 (head coach), joined Cowboys in 1982.

Al Lavan, running backs; born September 13, 1946, Pierce, Fla., lives in Dallas. Defensive back Colorado State 1965-67. Pro defensive back Philadelphia Eagles 1968, Atlanta Falcons 1969-70. College coach: Colorado State 1972, Louisville 1973, Iowa State 1974, Georgia Tech 1977-78, Stanford 1979. Pro coach: Atlanta Falcons 1975-76, joined Cowboys in 1980.

Alan Lowry, special teams; born November 21, 1950, Irving, Tex., lives in Dallas. Defensive back-quarterback Texas 1970-72. No pro playing experience. College coach: Virginia Tech 1974, Wyoming 1975, Texas 1976-81. Pro coach: Joined Cowboys in 1982.

Jim Myers, assistant head coach-offensive line; born November 12, 1921, Madison, W. Va., lives in Dallas. Guard Tennessee 1941-42, 1946, Duke 1943. No pro playing experience. College coach: Wofford 1947, Vanderbilt 1948, UCLA 1949-56, Iowa State 1957 (head coach), Texas A&M 1958-61 (head coach). Pro coach: Joined Cowboys in 1962.

Dick Nolan, receivers; born March 26, 1932, Pittsburgh, Pa., lives in Dallas. Offensive-defensive back Maryland 1951-53. Pro defensive back New York Giants 1954-57, 1959-61, St. Louis Cardinals 1958, Dallas player-coach 1962. Pro coach: Dallas Cowboys 1963-67, San Francisco 49ers 1968-75 (head coach), New Orleans Saints 1977-80 (head coach), Houston Oilers 1981, rejoined Cowboys in 1982.

Jim Shofner, quarterbacks; born December 18, 1935, Grapevine, Tex., lives in Dallas. Running back Texas Christian 1955-57. Pro defensive back Cleveland Browns 1958-63. College coach: Texas Christian 1964-66, 1974-76 (head coach). Pro coach: San Francisco 49ers 1967-73, 1977, Cleveland Browns 1978-80, Houston Oilers 1981-82, joined Cowboys in 1983.

Gene Stallings, defensive backs; born March 2, 1935, Paris, Tex., lives in Dallas. End Texas A&M 1954-57. No pro playing experience. College coach: Texas A&M 1957, 1965-71 (head coach), Alabama 1958-64. Pro coach: Joined Cowboys in 1972.

Ernie Stautner, defensive coordinator-defensive line; born April 2, 1925, Kham, Bavaria, lives in Dallas. Tackle Boston College 1946-49. Pro defensive tackle Pittsburgh Steelers 1950-63. Pro coach: Pittsburgh Steelers 1963-64, Washington Redskins 1965, joined Cowboys in 1966.

Jerry Tubbs, linebackers; born January 23, 1935, Breckenridge, Tex., lives in Dallas. Center-linebacker Oklahoma 1954-56. Pro linebacker Chicago Cardinals 1957, San Francisco 49ers 1958-59, Dallas Cowboys 1960-67. Pro coach: Joined Cowboys in 1966 (player-coach 1966-67).

Bob Ward, conditioning; born July 4, 1933, Huntington Park, Calif., lives in Dallas. Fullback-quarterback Whitworth College 1952-54. Doctorate in physical education, Indiana University. No pro playing experience. College coach: Fullerton, Calif., J.C. (track) 1965-75. Pro coach: Joined Cowboys in 1975.

DALLAS COWBOYS 1985 FIRST-YEAR ROSTER

Name	Pos.	Ht.	Wt.	Birth-date	College	Birthplace	Residence	How Acq.
Arendt, Chris (1)	DE	6-5	239	5/31/61	Duke	Abbottstown, Pa.	Abbottstown, Pa.	FA
Brooks, Kevin	DE	6-7	262	2/9/63	Michigan	Highland Park, Mich.	Detroit, Mich.	D1
Darwin, Matt	C-G	6-4	260	3/11/63	Texas A&M	Houston, Tex.	Houston, Tex.	D5a
Dellocono, Neal	LB	6-0	219	6/1/63	UCLA	Baton Rouge, La.	Baton Rouge, La.	D11
Fitzpatrick, John (1)	T-G	6-3	285	6/6/61	Purdue	Chicago, Ill.	Greencastle, Ill.	FA
Fowler, Todd (1)	RB	6-3	212	6/9/62	Stephen F. Austin	Van, Tex.	Van, Tex.	SD('84)
Gonzales, Leon	WR	5-10	158	9/21/63	Bethune-Cookman	Jacksonville, Fla.	Jacksonville, Fla.	D8
Herrmann, Jim	DE	6-5	255	10/20/62	Brigham Young	Hartland, Wis.	Milwaukee, Wis.	D7a
Jenkins, Ron (1)	WR	5-11	166	2/28/61	Colorado State	Denver, Colo.	Rohnert Park, Calif.	FA
Jones, Joe	TE	6-4	247	6/26/62	Virginia Tech	Windber, Pa.	Johnstown, Pa.	D10
Jordan, Karl	LB	6-1	244	1/12/63	Vanderbilt	Huntsville, Ala.	Huntsville, Ala.	D12
Ker, Crawford	G	6-4	293	5/5/62	Florida	Dunedin, Fla.	Dunedin, Fla.	D3
Lavette, Robert	RB	5-11	192	9/8/63	Georgia Tech	Cartersville, Ga.	Cartersville, Ga.	D4
Moore, Malcolm (1)	WR	6-3	199	6/24/61	Southern California	San Fernando, Calif.	Inglewood, Calif.	SD('84)
Moran, Matt	G	6-4	265	5/14/62	Stanford	Fullerton, Calif.	Washington, D.C.	D6a
Penn, Jesse	LB	6-2	222	9/6/62	Virginia Tech	Martinsville, Ga.	Martinsville, Ga.	D2
Ploeger, Kurt	DT	6-5	265	12/1/62	Gustavus Adolphus	Le Sueur, Minn.	Eldora, Iowa	D6
Ponder, David (1)	DT	6-3	248	6/27/62	Florida State	Dade City, Fla.	Cairo, Ga.	FA
Powe, Karl	WR	6-2	177	1/17/62	Alabama State	Mobile, Ala.	Mobile, Ala.	D7
Puzar, John (1)	C	6-6	255	6/27/62	Long Beach State	Los Angeles, Calif.	Long Beach, Calif.	FA
Revell, Mike (1)	RB	5-11	197	1/23/62	Bethune-Cookman	Brooksville, Fla.	Brooksville, Fla.	FA
Strasburger, Scott	LB	6-2	204	2/14/63	Nebraska	Stuttgart, W. Germany	Holdrege, Neb.	D9

Players who report to an NFL team for the first time are designated on rosters as rookies (R). If a player reported to an NFL training camp in a previous year but was not on the active squad for three or more regular season or postseason games, he is listed on the first-year roster and designated by a (1). Thereafter, a player who is on the active squad for three or more regular season or postseason games is credited with an additional year of playing experience.

NOTES

_____

_____

_____

_____

_____

_____

_____

_____

_____

_____

_____

_____

_____

_____

_____

_____

_____

_____

_____

_____

_____

DETROIT LIONS

National Football Conference
Central Division

Team Colors: Honolulu Blue and Silver

Pontiac Silverdome
1200 Featherstone Road — Box 4200
Pontiac, Michigan 48057
Telephone: (313) 335-4131

Club Officials

President-Owner: William Clay Ford
Executive Vice President-General Manager:
Russell Thomas
Director of Football Operations-Head Coach:
Darryl Rogers
Director of Player Personnel: Joe Bushofsky
Controller: Charles Schmidt
College Scouts: Dirk Dierking, Ron Hughes,
Jim Owen
Director of Public Relations: George Heddleston
Assistant Director of Public Relations:
Bill Keenist
Public and Community Relations: Tim Pendell
Ticket Manager: Fred Otto
Trainer: Kent Falb
Strength and Conditioning: Don Clemons
Equipment Manager: Dan Jaroshewich

Stadium: Pontiac Silverdome • **Capacity:** 80,638
1200 Featherstone Road
Pontiac, Michigan 48057

Playing Surface: AstroTurf

Training Camp: Oakland University
Rochester, Michigan 48063

1985 SCHEDULE

Preseason

Aug. 10	**Buffalo**	8:00
Aug. 16	at Seattle	7:30
Aug. 25	**Cincinnati**	8:00
Aug. 29	at Philadelphia	7:30

Regular Season

Sept. 8	at Atlanta	1:00
Sept. 15	**Dallas**	1:00
Sept. 22	at Indianapolis	12:00
Sept. 29	**Tampa Bay**	1:00
Oct. 6	at Green Bay	12:00
Oct. 13	at Washington	1:00
Oct. 20	**San Francisco**	1:00
Oct. 27	**Miami**	1:00
Nov. 3	at Minnesota	12:00
Nov. 10	at Chicago	12:00
Nov. 17	**Minnesota**	4:00
Nov. 24	at Tampa Bay	1:00
Nov. 28	**N.Y. Jets** (Thanksgiving)	12:30
Dec. 8	at New England	1:00
Dec. 15	**Green Bay**	1:00
Dec. 22	**Chicago**	1:00

LIONS COACHING HISTORY

Portsmouth Spartans 1930-33
(347-336-32)

1930-36	George (Potsy) Clark	53-26-9
1937-38	Earl (Dutch) Clark	14-8-0
1939	Gus Henderson	6-5-0
1940	George (Potsy) Clark	5-5-1
1941-42	Bill Edwards*	4-9-1
1942	John Karcis	0-8-0
1943-47	Charles (Gus) Dorais	20-31-2
1948-50	Alvin (Bo) McMillin	12-24-0
1951-56	Raymond (Buddy) Parker	50-24-2
1957-64	George Wilson	55-45-6
1965-66	Harry Gilmer	10-16-2
1967-72	Joe Schmidt	43-35-7
1973	Don McCafferty	6-7-1
1974-76	Rick Forzano**	15-17-0
1976-77	Tommy Hudspeth	11-13-0
1978-84	Monte Clark	43-63-1

*Resigned after three games in 1942
**Resigned after four games in 1976

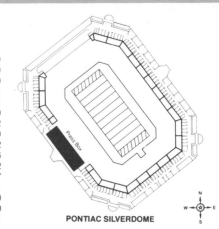

PONTIAC SILVERDOME

RECORD HOLDERS

Individual Records—Career

Category	Name	Performance
Rushing (Yds.)	Billy Sims, 1980-1984	5,106
Passing (Yds.)	Bobby Layne, 1950-58	15,710
Passing (TDs)	Bobby Layne, 1950-58	118
Receiving (No.)	Charlie Sanders, 1968-1977	336
Receiving (Yds.)	Gail Cogdill, 1960-68	5,220
Interceptions	Dick LeBeau, 1959-1972	62
Punting (Avg.)	Yale Lary, 1952-53, 1956-1964	44.3
Punt Return (Avg.)	Jack Christiansen, 1951-58	12.8
Kickoff Return (Avg.)	Pat Studstill, 1961-67	25.7
Field Goals	Errol Mann, 1969-1976	141
Touchdowns (Tot.)	Billy Sims, 1980-84	47
Points	Errol Mann, 1969-1976	636

Individual Records—Single Season

Category	Name	Performance
Rushing (Yds.)	Billy Sims, 1981	1,437
Passing (Yds.)	Gary Danielson, 1980	3,223
Passing (TDs)	Bobby Layne, 1951	26
Receiving (No.)	James Jones, 1984	77
Receiving (Yds.)	Pat Studstill, 1966	1,266
Interceptions	Don Doll, 1950	12
	Jack Christiansen, 1953	12
Punting (Avg.)	Yale Lary, 1963	48.9
Punt Return (Avg.)	Jack Christiansen, 1952	21.5
Kickoff Return (Avg.)	Tom Watkins, 1965	34.4
Field Goals	Ed Murray, 1980	27
Touchdowns (Tot.)	Billy Sims, 1980	16
Points	Doak Walker, 1950	128

Individual Records—Single Game

Category	Name	Performance
Rushing (Yds.)	Bob Hoernschemeyer, 11-23-50	198
Passing (Yds.)	Bobby Layne, 11-5-50	374
Passing (TDs)	Gary Danielson, 12-9-78	5
Receiving (No.)	Cloyce Box, 12-3-50	12
Receiving (Yds.)	Cloyce Box, 12-3-50	302
Interceptions	Don Doll, 10-23-49	4
Field Goals	Garo Yepremian, 11-13-66	6
Touchdowns (Tot.)	Cloyce Box, 12-3-50	4
Points	Cloyce Box, 12-3-50	24

1984 TEAM STATISTICS

	Detroit	Opp.
Total First Downs	306	328
Rushing	118	120
Passing	170	177
Penalty	18	31
Third Down: Made/Att.	84/215	98/216
Fourth Down: Made/Att.	9/19	4/9
Total Net Yards	5318	5319
Avg. Per Game	332.4	332.4
Total Plays	1038	1022
Avg. Per Play	5.1	5.2
Net Yards Rushing	2017	1808
Avg. Per Game	126.1	113.0
Total Rushes	446	519
Net Yards Passing	3301	3511
Avg. Per Game	206.3	219.4
Tackled/Yards Lost	61/486	37/271
Gross Yards	3787	3782
Att./Completions	531/298	466/288
Completion Pct.	56.1	61.8
Had Intercepted	22	14
Punts/Avg.	76/41.6	73/40.0
Net Punting Avg.	32.7	34.0
Penalties/Yards Lost	138/1165	107/978
Fumbles/Ball Lost	36/14	28/11
Touchdowns	32	48
Rushing	13	17
Passing	19	27
Returns	0	4
Avg. Time of Possession	29:43	30:17

1984 TEAM RECORD
Preseason (2-2)

Date	Detroit		Opponents
8/4	17	*Philadelphia	14
8/11	24	*Seattle	28
8/18	17	Buffalo	12
8/24	14	Cincinnati	35
	72		89

Regular Season (4-11-1)

Date	Detroit		Opp.	Att.
9/2	27	*San Francisco	30	56,782
9/9	27	Atlanta (OT)	24	49,878
9/16	17	Tampa Bay	21	44,560
9/23	28	*Minnesota	29	57,511
9/30	24	San Diego	27	53,887
10/7	7	*Denver	28	55,836
10/14	13	*Tampa Bay (OT)	7	44,308
10/21	16	Minnesota	14	57,953
10/28	9	Green Bay	41	54,289
11/4	23	*Philadelphia (OT)	23	59,141
11/11	14	Washington	28	50,212
11/18	14	Chicago	16	54,911
11/22	31	*Green Bay	28	63,698
12/2	17	Seattle	38	62,441
12/10	3	*Los Angeles Raiders	24	66,710
12/16	13	*Chicago	30	53,252
	283		408	885,369

*Home Game   (OT) Overtime

Score by Periods

Detroit	47	108	76	43	9	—	283
Opponents	108	133	57	110	0	—	408

Attendance
Home 457,238   Away 428,131   Total 885,369
Single game home record, 80,444 (12-20-81)
Single season home record, 622,593 (1980)

1984 INDIVIDUAL STATISTICS

Rushing

	Att.	Yds.	Avg.	LG	TD
Sims	130	687	5.3	81	5
J. Jones	137	532	3.9	34	3
Jenkins	78	358	4.6	25t	1
Danielson	41	218	5.3	40	3
Bussey	32	91	2.8	18	0
D'Addio	7	46	6.6	14	0
Witkowski	7	33	4.7	10	0
Nichols	3	27	9.0	13	0
Martin	1	14	14.0	14	0
Chadwick	1	12	12.0	12t	1
Machurek	1	9	9.0	9	0
Hipple	2	3	1.5	2	0
Black	3	−6	−2.0	4	0
L. Thompson	3	−7	−2.3	4	0
Detroit	446	2017	4.5	81	13
Opponents	519	1808	3.5	49	17

Passing

	Att.	Comp.	Pct.	Yds.	TD	Int.	Tkld.	Rate
Danielson	410	252	61.5	3076	17	15	41/335	83.1
Machurek	43	14	32.6	193	0	6	1/12	8.3
Hipple	38	16	42.1	246	1	1	7/62	62.0
Witkowski	34	13	38.2	210	0	0	11/74	59.7
J. Jones	5	3	60.0	62	1	0	1/3	143.3
Jenkins	1	0	0.0	0	0	0	0/0	39.6
Detroit	531	298	56.1	3787	19	22	61/486	73.2
Opponents	466	288	61.8	3782	27	14	37/271	94.2

Receiving

	No.	Yds.	Avg.	LG	TD
J. Jones	77	662	8.6	39	5
L. Thompson	50	773	15.5	66t	6
Chadwick	37	540	14.6	46	2
Nichols	34	744	21.9	77t	1
Sims	31	239	7.7	20	0
Jenkins	21	246	11.7	68	0
Lewis	16	236	14.8	58	3
Rubick	14	188	13.4	29	1
Bussey	9	63	7.0	19	0
Mandley	3	38	12.7	19	0
McCall	3	15	5.0	7	0
Danielson	1	22	22.0	22t	1
D'Addio	1	12	12.0	12	0
Martin	1	9	9.0	9	0
Detroit	298	3787	12.7	77t	19
Opponents	288	3782	13.1	73t	27

Interceptions

	No.	Yds.	Avg.	LG	TD
Watkins	6	0	0.0	0	0
Graham	3	22	7.3	15	0
Hall	2	64	32.0	36	0
McNorton	2	0	0.0	0	0
Fantetti	1	1	1.0	1	0
Detroit	14	87	6.2	36	0
Opponents	22	251	11.4	63	1

Punting

	No.	Yds.	Avg.	In 20	LG
Black	76	3164	41.6	13	63
Detroit	76	3164	41.6	13	63
Opponents	73	2921	40.0	13	60

Punt Returns

	No.	FC	Yds.	Avg.	LG	TD
Martin	25	8	210	8.4	23	0
Hall	7	1	30	4.3	11	0
Mandley	2	2	0	0.0	0	0
Jenkins	1	0	1	1.0	1	0
Johnson	1	0	0	0.0	0	0
Detroit	36	11	241	6.7	23	0
Opponents	49	2	516	10.5	69t	1

Kickoff Returns

	No.	Yds.	Avg.	LG	TD
Mandley	22	390	17.7	32	0
Hall	19	385	20.3	46	0
Jenkins	18	396	22.0	32	0
Martin	10	144	14.4	23	0
Meade	4	32	8.0	15	0
D'Addio	1	0	0.0	0	0
Detroit	74	1347	18.2	46	0
Opponents	60	1250	20.8	44	0

Scoring

	TD R	TD P	TD Rt	PAT	FG	Saf	TP
Murray	0	0	0	31/31	20/27	0	91
J. Jones	3	5	0	0/0	0/0	0	48
L. Thompson	0	6	0	0/0	0/0	0	36
Sims	5	0	0	0/0	0/0	0	30
Danielson	3	1	0	0/0	0/0	0	24
Chadwick	1	2	0	0/0	0/0	0	18
Lewis	0	3	0	0/0	0/0	0	18
Jenkins	1	0	0	0/0	0/0	0	6
Nichols	0	1	0	0/0	0/0	0	6
Rubick	0	1	0	0/0	0/0	0	6
Detroit	13	19	0	31/31	20/27	0	283
Opponents	17	27	4	48/48	24/29	0	408

FIRST-ROUND SELECTIONS

(If Club had no first-round selection, first player drafted is listed with round in parentheses.)

Year	Player, College, Position
1936	Sid Wagner, Michigan State, G
1937	Lloyd Cardwell, Nebraska, B
1938	Alex Wojciechowicz, Fordham, C
1939	John Pingel, Michigan State, B
1940	Doyle Nave, Southern California, B
1941	Jim Thomason, Texas A&M, B
1942	Bob Westfall, Michigan, B
1943	Frank Sinkwich, Georgia, B
1944	Otto Graham, Northwestern, B
1945	Frank Szymanski, Notre Dame, C
1946	Bill Dellastatious, Missouri, B
1947	Glenn Davis, Army, B
1948	Y. A. Tittle, Louisiana State, B
1949	John Rauch, Georgia, B
1950	Leon Hart, Notre Dame, E
	Joe Watson, Rice, C
1951	Dick Stanfel, San Francisco, G (2)
1952	Yale Lary, Texas A&M, B (3)
1953	Harley Sewell, Texas, G
1954	Dick Chapman, Rice, T
1955	Dave Middleton, Auburn, B
1956	Hopalong Cassady, Ohio State, B
1957	Bill Glass, Baylor, G
1958	Alex Karras, Iowa, T
1959	Nick Pietrosante, Notre Dame, B
1960	John Robinson, Louisiana State, S
1961	Danny LaRose, Missouri, T (2)
1962	John Hadl, Kansas, QB
1963	Daryl Sanders, Ohio State, T
1964	Pete Beathard, Southern California, QB
1965	Tom Nowatzke, Indiana, RB
1966	Nick Eddy, Notre Dame, RB (2)
1967	Mel Farr, UCLA, RB
1968	Greg Landry, Massachusetts, QB
	Earl McCullouch, Southern California, WR
1969	Altie Taylor, Utah State, RB (2)
1970	Steve Owens, Oklahoma, RB
1971	Bob Bell, Cincinnati, DT
1972	Herb Orvis, Colorado, DE
1973	Ernie Price, Texas A&I, DE
1974	Ed O'Neil, Penn State, LB
1975	Lynn Boden, South Dakota State, G
1976	James Hunter, Grambling, DB
	Lawrence Gaines, Wyoming, RB
1977	Walt Williams, New Mexico State, DB (2)
1978	Luther Bradley, Notre Dame, DB
1979	Keith Dorney, Penn State, T
1980	Billy Sims, Oklahoma, RB
1981	Mark Nichols, San Jose State, WR
1982	Jimmy Williams, Nebraska, LB
1983	James Jones, Florida, RB
1984	David Lewis, California, TE
1985	Lomas Brown, Florida, T

DETROIT LIONS 1985 VETERAN ROSTER

No.	Name	Pos.	Ht.	Wt.	Birth-date	NFL Exp.	College	Birthplace	Residence	'84 Games/ Starts
68	Baack, Steve	T	6-3	260	11/16/60	2	Oregon	Ames, Iowa	Eugene, Ore.	16/0
54	Barnes, Roosevelt	LB	6-2	228	8/3/58	4	Purdue	Ft. Wayne, Ind.	Ft. Wayne, Ind.	16/0
11	Black, Michael	P	6-1	197	1/18/61	3	Arizona State	Glendale, Calif.	Phoenix, Ariz.	16/0
80	Bland, Carl	WR	5-11	182	8/17/61	2	Virginia Union	Richmond, Va.	Richmond, Va.	3/0
89	Chadwick, Jeff	WR	6-3	190	12/16/60	3	Grand Valley State	Detroit, Mich.	Lake Orion, Mich.	16/3
53	†Cobb, Garry	LB	6-2	227	3/16/57	7	Southern California	Stamford, Conn.	West Bloomfield, Mich.	16/16
66	Cofer, Michael	DE	6-4	245	4/7/60	3	Tennessee	Knoxville, Tenn.	Knoxville, Tenn.	16/16
50	Curley, August	LB	6-2	226	1/24/60	3	Southern California	Little Rock, Ark.	Pontiac, Mich.	8/0
44	D'Addio, Dave	FB	6-1	229	7/13/61	2	Maryland	Newark, N.J.	Union, N.J.	16/2
72	Dieterich, Chris	G	6-3	260	7/27/58	6	North Carolina State	Freeport, N.Y.	Raleigh, N.C.	16/16
93	Dodge, Kirk	LB	6-1	231	6/4/62	2	Nevada-Las Vegas	Whittier, Calif.	La Habra, Calif.	11/0
58	†Doig, Steve	LB	6-2	245	3/28/60	4	New Hampshire	Melrose, Mass.	North Reading, Mass.	16/4
70	Dorney, Keith	T	6-5	265	12/3/57	7	Penn State	Macungie, Pa.	San Juan Capistrano, Ca.	16/16
61	Elias, Homer	G	6-2	255	5/1/55	8	Tennessee State	Ft. Benning, Ga.	Ft. Mitchell, Ala.	12/4
78	English, Doug	DT	6-5	258	8/25/53	10	Texas	Dallas, Tex.	Austin, Tex.	16/16
57	Fantetti, Ken	LB	6-1	232	4/7/57	7	Wyoming	Toledo, Ore.	Rochester, Mich.	14/13
12	t-Ferguson, Joe	QB	6-1	175	4/23/50	13	Arkansas	Alvin, Tex.	Shreveport, La.	12/11
65	†Fowler, Amos	C	6-2	253	2/11/56	7	Southern Mississippi	Pensacola, Fla.	Rochester, Mich.	15/7
26	Frizzell, William	CB	6-2	198	9/8/62	2	North Carolina Central	Greenville, N.C.	Greenville, N.C.	16/0
79	Gay, William	DE	6-4	257	5/28/55	8	Southern California	San Francisco, Calif.	Rochester, Mich.	16/16
33	Graham, William	S	5-11	191	9/27/59	4	Texas	Greenwood, Miss.	Austin, Tex.	14/13
67	Greco, Don	G	6-2	265	4/1/59	4	Western Illinois	St. Louis, Mo.	St. Charles, Mo.	16/16
62	Green, Curtis	DT	6-3	258	6/3/57	5	Alabama State	Quincy, Fla.	Quincy, Fla.	16/15
35	Hall, Alvin	S	5-10	184	8/12/58	5	Miami, Ohio	Dayton, Ohio	Rochester, Mich.	16/16
17	Hipple, Eric	QB	6-2	198	9/16/57	6	Utah State	Lubbock, Tex.	Bloomfield Hills, Mich.	8/1
31	Jenkins, Kenneth	RB	5-8	185	5/8/59	3	Bucknell	Washington, D.C.	Rochester, Mich.	14/3
21	Johnson, Demetrious	S	5-11	190	7/21/61	3	Missouri	St. Louis, Mo.	St. Louis, Mo.	16/3
51	Jones, David	C	6-2	257	10/25/61	2	Texas	Taipei, Taiwan	Austin, Tex.	10/0
30	Jones, James	FB	6-2	229	3/21/61	3	Florida	Pompano Beach, Fla.	Rochester, Mich.	16/16
92	†King, Angelo	LB	6-0	222	2/10/58	5	South Carolina State	Columbia, S.C.	Dallas, Tex.	16/0
73	Laster, Don	T	6-4	278	12/13/58	3	Tennessee State	Albany, N.Y.	Steubenville, Ohio	14/8
43	Latimer, Albert	S	5-11	181	10/14/57	3	Clemson	Winter Park, Fla.	West Bloomfield, Mich.	15/0
64	Lee, Larry	G	6-2	263	9/10/59	5	UCLA	Dayton, Ohio	Rochester, Mich.	15/6
87	Lewis, David	TE	6-3	235	6/8/61	2	California	Portland, Ore.	West Linn, Ore.	16/7
14	Machurek, Mike	QB	6-0	205	7/22/60	4	Idaho State	Las Vegas, Nev.	Rochester, Mich.	4/0
82	Mandley, Pete	WR	5-9	191	7/29/61	2	Northern Arizona	Mesa, Ariz.	Mesa, Ariz.	15/0
83	Martin, Robbie	WR	5-8	178	12/3/58	5	Cal Poly-SLO	Los Angeles, Calif.	San Luis Obispo, Calif.	14/0
81	McCall, Reese	TE	6-6	245	6/15/56	8	Auburn	Bessemer, Ala.	Rochester, Mich.	16/5
29	McNorton, Bruce	S-CB	5-10	175	2/28/59	4	Georgetown, Ky.	Daytona Beach, Fla.	Daytona Beach, Fla.	16/16
36	Meade, Mike	FB	5-10	227	2/12/60	4	Penn State	Dover, Del.	Newark, Del.	15/0
45	Morris, Tom	CB	5-10	165	4/2/60	3	Michigan State	Anniston, Ala.	Tampa, Fla.	0*
63	Moss, Martin	DE	6-3	255	12/16/58	4	UCLA	San Diego, Calif.	Van Nuys, Calif.	16/0
52	Mott, Steve	C	6-2	265	3/24/61	3	Alabama	New Orleans, La.	Birmingham, Mich.	6/6
3	Murray, Ed	K	5-9	175	8/29/56	6	Tulane	Halifax, Nova Scotia	Southfield, Mich.	16/0
86	Nichols, Mark	WR	6-1	208	10/29/59	5	San Jose State	Bakersfield, Calif.	Rochester, Mich.	15/9
84	Rubick, Rob	TE	6-2	234	9/27/60	4	Grand Valley State	Newberry, Mich.	Lake Orion, Mich.	16/9
20	Sims, Billy	RB	5-11	212	9/18/55	6	Oklahoma	St. Louis, Mo.	Hooks, Tex.	8/8
10	Stachowicz, Ray	P	6-0	192	3/6/59	3	Michigan State	Cleveland, Ohio	Broadview Heights, Ohio	0*
71	Strenger, Rich	T	6-7	276	3/10/60	2	Michigan	Port Washington, Wis.	Lake Orion, Mich.	1/1
39	Thompson, Leonard	WR	5-11	192	7/28/52	11	Oklahoma State	Tucson, Ariz.	Scottsdale, Ariz.	16/15
27	Watkins, Bobby	S-CB	5-10	184	5/31/60	4	Southwest Texas State	Cottonwood, Idaho	Dallas, Tex.	16/16
76	Williams, Eric	DT	6-4	260	2/24/62	2	Washington State	Stockton, Calif.	Stockton, Calif.	12/1
59	Williams, Jimmy	LB	6-2	230	11/15/60	4	Nebraska	Washington, D.C.	Rochester, Mich.	16/16
18	Witkowski, John	QB	6-1	205	6/18/62	2	Columbia	Flushing, N.Y.	Lindenhurst, N.J.	3/1

*Morris last active with Tampa Bay in '83; Stachowicz last active with Chicago in '83.

†Option playout; subject to developments.

t-Lions traded for Ferguson (Buffalo).

Traded—Quarterback Gary Danielson to Cleveland.

Retired—Dexter Bussey, 11-year running back, 16 games in '84.

Also played with Lions in '84—LB Terry Tautolo (4 games), CB-S Danny Wagoner (1), CB-S Gardner Williams (3).

COACHING STAFF

Head Coach,
Darryl Rogers

Pro Career: Became Lions' sixteenth head coach and director of football operations on February 6, 1985. No pro playing experience.

Background: Wide receiver who gained all-West Coast honors while playing at Fresno State. Served in U.S. Marine Corps and later earned his master's degree from Fresno State. Spent twenty years coaching in the collegiate ranks at Hayward State 1965, Fresno State 1966-72, San Jose State 1973-75 (head coach), Michigan State 1976-79 (head coach), Arizona State 1980-84 (head coach). Named national college coach of the year in 1978 while at Michigan State. Ranked as one of the winningest active coaches in the college ranks.

Personal: Born May 28, 1935, Los Angeles, Calif. Darryl and his wife, Marsha, live in Rochester, Mich., and have three daughters, Jamie, Keely, and Stacy.

Assistant Coaches

Bob Baker, offensive coordinator; born November 28, 1927, Lima, Ohio, lives in Rochester, Mich. Quarterback Ball State 1947-51. No pro playing experience. College coach: Indiana 1966-73, Michigan State 1977-79, Arizona State 1980-82. Pro coach: Calgary Stampeders (CFL) 1974-76 (head coach 1976), Los Angeles Rams 1983-84, first year with Lions.

Carl Battershell, special teams-tight ends; born November 5, 1948, Alliance, Ohio, lives in Rochester, Mich. Offensive tackle Bowling Green 1966-69. No pro playing experience. College coach: Bowling Green 1973-76, Syracuse 1977-79, West Virginia 1980-82, Arizona State 1983-84. Pro coach: First year with Lions.

Don Doll, special assignments; born August 29, 1926, Los Angeles, Calif., lives in Birmingham, Mich. Defensive back Southern California 1944, 1946-48. Pro defensive back Detroit Lions 1949-52, Washington Redskins 1953, Los Angeles Rams 1954. College coach: Washington 1955, Contra Costa, Calif., J.C. 1956, Southern California 1957-58, Notre Dame 1959-62. Pro coach: Detroit Lions 1963-64, Los Angeles Rams 1965, Washington Redskins 1966-70, Green Bay Packers 1971-73, Baltimore Colts 1974, Miami Dolphins, 1975-76, rejoined Lions in 1978.

Wayne Fontes, defensive coordinator; born February 17, 1940, New Bedford, Mass., lives in Auburn, Mich. Defensive back Michigan State 1959-62. Pro defensive back New York Titans (AFL) 1962. College coach: Dayton 1967-68, Iowa 1969-70, Southern California 1971-75. Pro coach: Tampa Bay Buccaneers 1976-84, first year with Lions.

Paul Lanham, receivers; born July 31, 1935, Ripley, W. Va., lives in Rochester, Mich. Linebacker Glenville State, W. Va. 1957-59. No pro playing experience. College coach: Dayton 1961, Colorado State 1962-69, Arkansas 1970-71. Pro coach: Washington Redskins 1973-77, Los Angeles Rams 1978-82, Chicago Blitz (USFL) 1983, Arizona Wranglers (USFL) 1984, first year with Lions.

Bill Muir, offensive line; born October 26, 1942, Pittsburgh, Pa., lives in Rochester, Mich. Tackle Susquehanna 1962-64. No pro playing experience. College coach: Susquehanna 1965, Delaware Valley 1966-67, Rhode Island 1970-71, Idaho State 1972-73, Southern Methodist 1976-77. Pro coach: Orlando (Continental Football League) 1968-69, Houston-Shreveport (WFL) 1975, New England Patriots 1982-84, first year with Lions.

Mike Murphy, linebackers; born September 25, 1944, New York, N.Y., lives in Auburn, Mich. Guard-linebacker Huron College, S.D. 1962-65. No pro playing experience. College coach: Vermont 1970-73, Idaho State 1974-76, Western Illinois 1977-78. Pro coach: Saskatchewan Roughriders (CFL) 1979-83, Chicago Blitz (USFL) 1984 first year with Lions.

Rex Norris, defensive line; born December 10, 1939, Tipton, Ind., lives in Auburn, Mich. Linebacker East Texas State 1964. No pro playing experience. College coach: Navarro, Tex., J.C. 1970-71, Texas A&M 1972, Oklahoma 1973-83, Arizona State 1984. Pro coach: First year with Lions.

Willie Shaw, defensive backs; born January 11, 1944, Glenmora, La., lives in Auburn, Mich. Defensive back New Mexico 1966-68. No pro playing experience. College coach: San Diego City College 1970-72, Stanford 1973-76, Long Beach State 1977-78, Oregon 1979, Arizona State 1980-84. Pro coach: First year with Lions.

Ivy Williams, offensive backs; born August 12, 1949, New York, N.Y., lives in Rochester, Mich. Running back Xavier (Ohio) 1968-72. No pro playing experience. College coach: Marshall 1974, Kansas State 1975-77, New Mexico State 1978, Kansas 1979-81, Arizona State 1982-84. Pro coach: First year with Lions.

DETROIT LIONS 1985 FIRST-YEAR ROSTER

Name	Pos.	Ht.	Wt.	Birth-date	College	Birthplace	Residence	How Acq.
Barrows, Scott	C	6-2	278	3/31/63	West Virginia	Marietta, Ohio	Marietta, Ohio	FA
Beauford, Clayton	WR	5-10	173	3/1/63	Auburn	Palatka, Fla.	Palatka, Fla.	D10
Brown, Lomas	T	6-4	282	3/30/63	Florida	Miami, Fla.	Miami, Fla.	D1
Caldwell, Scotty	RB	5-11	195	2/8/63	Texas-Arlington	Dallas, Tex.	Grand Prairie, Tex.	D8
Cross, Ron	S	6-2	196	1/3/63	Fresno State	Harbor City, Calif.	Los Angeles, Calif.	FA
Galloway, Duane (1)	CB	5-8	181	11/7/61	Arizona State	Los Angeles, Calif.	Los Angeles, Calif.	FA
Glover, Kevin	C-G	6-2	267	6/17/63	Maryland	Washington, D.C.	Upper Marlboro, Md.	D2
Graeber, Ken	NT	6-2	265	10/30/61	Nebraska	Tulsa, Okla.	Minneapolis, Minn.	FA
Hancock, Kevin	LB	6-2	223	1/6/62	Baylor	Longview, Tex.	Texas City, Tex.	D4
Harris, Kevin	S	6-0	196	9/27/63	Georgia	Arcadia, Fla.	Eustis, Fla.	D11
Keslar, Jack	T	6-4	294	6/5/62	West Virginia	Latrobe, Pa.	Ligonier, Pa.	FA
James, June	LB	6-1	218	12/2/62	Texas	Jennings, La.	Kansas City, Mo.	D9
Johnson, James	LB	6-2	236	6/21/62	San Diego State	Los Angeles, Calif.	Lake Elsinore, Calif.	D3
McIntosh, Joe	RB	5-10	189	12/9/63	North Carolina State	Lexington, N.C.	Lexington, N.C.	D5
Pierzynski, Jeff	LB	6-1	222	7/27/62	Eastern Michigan	Detroit, Mich.	Dearborn Hts., Mich.	FA
Royster, Mark	CB	6-0	195	12/28/61	Wichita State	Evansville, Ind.	Wichita, Kan.	FA
Short, Stan	C	6-4	270	9/20/63	Penn State	Ft. Riley, Kan.	Ft. Monmouth, N.J.	D6
Staten, Tony	CB	5-9	178	2/6/63	Angelo State	Washington, D.C.	San Antonio, Tex.	D7
Weaver, Mike	G	6-1	325	12/15/62	Georgia	Haines City, Fla.	Haines City, Fla.	D12

Players who report to an NFL team for the first time are designated on rosters as rookies (R). If a player reported to an NFL training camp in a previous year but was not on the active squad for three or more regular season or postseason games, he is listed on the first-year roster and designated by a (1). Thereafter, a player who is on the active squad for three or more regular season or postseason games is credited with an additional year of playing experience.

NOTES

**National Football Conference
Central Division**

Team Colors: Dark Green, Gold, and White

**1265 Lombardi Avenue
Green Bay, Wisconsin 54307-0628
Telephone:** (414) 494-2351

Club Officials

Chairman of the Board: Dominic Olejniczak
President, CEO: Robert Parins
Vice President: Tony Canadeo
Secretary: John Torinus
Treasurer: Phil Hendrickson
Assistant to the President: Bob Harlan
Assistant to the President: Tom Miller
Green Bay Ticket Director: Mark Wagner
Public Relations Director: Lee Remmel
Assistant Director of Public Relations:
　Scott Berchtold
Director of Player Personnel: Dick Corrick
Director of Player Procurement:
　Chuck Hutchison
Film Director: Al Treml
Trainer: Domenic Gentile
Equipment Manager: Bob Noel

Stadium: Lambeau Field • **Capacity:** 56,926
　　　P.O. Box 10628
　　　1265 Lombardi Avenue
　　　Green Bay, Wisconsin 54307-0628
　　　Milwaukee County Stadium •
　　　Capacity: 55,976
　　　Highway I-94
　　　Milwaukee, Wisconsin 53214

Playing Surfaces: Grass

Training Camp: St. Norbert College
　　　　　DePere, Wisconsin 54115

1985 SCHEDULE

Preseason

Aug. 10	at Dallas	8:00
Aug. 17	at New York Giants	8:00
Aug. 24	**Atlanta at Milwaukee**	3:00
Aug. 31	**New York Jets**	7:00

Regular Season

Sept. 8	at New England	1:00
Sept. 15	**New York Giants**	3:00
Sept. 22	**New York Jets** at Milw.	3:00
Sept. 29	at St. Louis	12:00
Oct. 6	**Detroit**	12:00
Oct. 13	**Minnesota** at Milwaukee	12:00
Oct. 21	at Chicago (Monday)	8:00
Oct. 27	at Indianapolis	1:00
Nov. 3	**Chicago**	12:00
Nov. 10	at Minnesota	12:00
Nov. 17	**New Orleans** at Milw.	12:00
Nov. 24	at Los Angeles Rams	1:00
Dec. 1	**Tampa Bay**	12:00
Dec. 8	**Miami**	12:00
Dec. 15	at Detroit	1:00
Dec. 22	at Tampa Bay	1:00

PACKERS COACHING HISTORY

(452-344-36)

1921-49	Earl (Curly) Lambeau	216-106-22
1950-53	Gene Ronzani	14-33-1
1954-57	Lisle Blackbourn	17-31-0
1958	Ray (Scooter) McLean	1-10-1
1959-67	Vince Lombardi	98-30-4
1968-70	Phil Bengtson	20-21-1
1971-74	Dan Devine	25-28-4
1975-83	Bart Starr	53-77-3
1984	Forrest Gregg	8-8-0

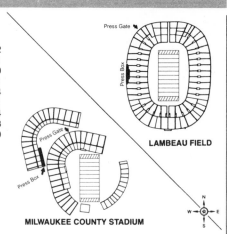

LAMBEAU FIELD

MILWAUKEE COUNTY STADIUM

RECORD HOLDERS

Individual Records—Career

Category	Name	Performance
Rushing (Yds.)	Jim Taylor, 1958-1966	8,207
Passing (Yds.)	Bart Starr, 1956-1971	23,718
Passing (TDs)	Bart Starr, 1956-1971	152
Receiving (No.)	Don Hutson, 1935-1945	488
Receiving (Yds.)	Don Hutson, 1935-1945	7,991
Interceptions	Bobby Dillon, 1952-59	52
Punt Return (Avg.)	Billy Grimes, 1950-52	13.2
Kickoff Return (Avg.)	Dave Hampton, 1970-71	28.9
Field Goals	Chester Marcol, 1972-1980	120
Touchdowns (Tot.)	Don Hutson, 1935-1945	105
Points	Don Hutson, 1935-1945	823

Individual Records—Single Season

Category	Name	Performance
Rushing (Yds.)	Jim Taylor, 1962	1,407
Passing (Yds.)	Lynn Dickey, 1983	4,458
Passing (TDs)	Lynn Dickey, 1983	32
Receiving (No.)	Don Hutson, 1942	74
Receiving (Yds.)	James Lofton, 1984	1,361
Interceptions	Irv Comp, 1943	10
Punting (Avg.)	Jerry Norton, 1963	44.7
Punt Return (Avg.)	Billy Grimes, 1950	19.1
Kickoff Return (Avg.)	Travis Williams, 1967	41.1
Field Goals	Chester Marcol, 1972	33
Touchdowns (Tot.)	Jim Taylor, 1962	19
Points	Paul Hornung, 1960	176

Individual Records—Single Game

Category	Name	Performance
Rushing (Yds.)	Jim Taylor, 12-3-61	186
Passing (Yds.)	Lynn Dickey, 10-12-80	418
Passing (TDs)	Many times	5
	Last time by Lynn Dickey, 9-4-83	
Receiving (No.)	Don Hutson, 11-22-42	14
Receiving (Yds.)	Bill Howton, 10-21-56	257
Interceptions	Bobby Dillon, 11-26-53	4
	Willie Buchanon, 9-24-78	4
Field Goals	Many times	4
	Last time by Jan Stenerud, 12-12-83	
Touchdowns (Tot.)	Paul Hornung, 12-12-65	5
Points	Paul Hornung, 10-8-61	33

1984 TEAM STATISTICS

	Green Bay	Opp.
Total First Downs	315	323
Rushing	120	136
Passing	168	166
Penalty	27	21
Third Down: Made/Att.	75/205	89/243
Fourth Down: Made/Att.	4/13	12/9
Total Net Yards	5449	5291
Avg. Per Game	340.6	330.7
Total Plays	1009	1140
Avg. Per Play	5.4	4.6
Net Yards Rushing	2019	2145
Avg. Per Game	126.2	134.1
Total Rushes	461	545
Net Yards Passing	3430	3146
Avg. Per Game	214.4	196.6
Tackled/Yards Lost	42/310	44/324
Gross Yards	3740	3470
Att./Completions	506/281	551/315
Completion Pct.	55.5	57.2
Had Intercepted	30	27
Punts/Avg.	85/42.3	89/40.9
Net Punting Avg.	35.2	36.1
Penalties/Yards Lost	110/915	145/1129
Fumbles/Ball Lost	17/7	33/15
Touchdowns	51	34
Rushing	18	14
Passing	30	16
Returns	3	4
Avg. Time of Possession	26:48	33:12

1984 TEAM RECORD
Preseason (2-2)

Date	Green Bay		Opponents
8/4	17	Dallas	31
8/11	17	*Chicago	10
8/18	24	Los Angeles Rams	27
8/25	34	*Indianapolis	17
	92		85

Regular Season (8-8)

Date	Green Bay		Opp.	Att.
9/2	24	*St. Louis	23	53,738
9/9	7	Los Angeles Raiders	28	46,269
9/16	7	*Chicago	9	55,942
9/23	6	Dallas	20	64,425
9/30	27	Tampa Bay (OT)	30	47,487
10/7	28	*San Diego	34	54,045
10/15	14	Denver	17	62,546
10/21	24	*Seattle	30	52,286
10/28	41	*Detroit	9	54,289
11/4	23	New Orleans	13	57,426
11/11	45	*Minnesota	17	52,931
11/18	31	*Los Angeles Rams	6	52,031
11/22	28	Detroit	31	63,698
12/2	27	*Tampa Bay	14	46,800
12/9	20	Chicago	14	59,374
12/16	38	Minnesota	14	51,197
	390		309	874,484

*Home Game (OT) Overtime

Score by Periods

Green Bay	79	121	108	82	0	—	390
Opponents	72	88	65	81	3	—	309

Attendance
Home 422,062   Away 452,422   Total 874,484
Single game home record, 56,267 (11-28-76; Lambeau Field) 56,258 (9-28-80; Milwaukee County Stadium)
Single season home record, 435,521 (1980)

1984 INDIVIDUAL STATISTICS

Rushing

	Att.	Yds.	Avg.	LG	TD
Ellis	123	581	4.7	50	4
Ivery	99	552	5.6	49	6
Clark	87	375	4.3	43t	4
Crouse	53	169	3.2	14	0
Huckleby	35	145	4.1	23	0
Rodgers	25	94	3.8	15	0
Lofton	10	82	8.2	26	0
Wright	8	11	1.4	5	0
Dickey	18	6	0.3	9	3
Campbell	2	2	1.0	5	0
West	1	2	2.0	2t	1
Green Bay	461	2019	4.4	50	18
Opponents	545	2145	3.9	39	14

Passing

	Att.	Comp.	Pct.	Yds.	TD	Int.	Tkld.	Rate
Dickey	401	237	59.1	3195	25	19	32/244	85.6
Wright	62	27	43.5	310	2	6	4/17	30.4
Campbell	38	16	42.1	218	3	5	5/46	47.8
Ellis	4	1	25.0	17	0	0	1/3	44.8
Scribner	1	0	0.0	0	0	0	0/0	39.6
Green Bay	506	281	55.5	3740	30	30	42/310	74.2
Opponents	551	315	57.2	3470	16	27	44/324	65.2

Receiving

	No.	Yds.	Avg.	LG	TD
Lofton	62	1361	22.0	79t	7
Coffman	43	562	13.1	44t	9
Ellis	36	312	8.7	22	2
Clark	29	234	8.1	20	2
Epps	26	435	16.7	56	3
Jefferson	26	339	13.0	33	0
Ivery	19	141	7.4	18	1
Crouse	9	93	10.3	25	1
Huckleby	8	65	8.1	13	0
West	6	54	9.0	29t	4
Rodgers	5	56	11.2	22	0
Childs	4	32	8.0	17	0
G. Lewis	4	29	7.3	15	0
Cassidy	2	16	8.0	10	0
Taylor	1	8	8.0	8	0
Moore	1	3	3.0	3t	1
Green Bay	281	3740	13.3	79t	30
Opponents	315	3470	11.0	50	16

Interceptions

	No.	Yds.	Avg.	LG	TD
Flynn	9	106	11.8	31	0
T. Lewis	7	151	21.6	99t	1
Lee	3	33	11.0	14	0
Anderson	3	24	8.0	22	0
Hood	1	8	8.0	8	0
Cumby	1	7	7.0	7	0
Brown	1	5	5.0	5t	1
Murphy	1	4	4.0	4	0
McLeod	1	0	0.0	0	0
Green Bay	27	338	12.5	99t	2
Opponents	30	317	10.6	53t	2

Punting

	No.	Yds.	Avg.	In 20	LG
Scribner	85	3596	42.3	18	61
Green Bay	85	3596	42.3	18	61
Opponents	89	3643	40.9	13	63

Punt Returns

	No.	FC	Yds.	Avg.	LG	TD
Epps	29	10	199	6.9	39	0
Flynn	15	4	128	8.5	20	0
Hayes	4	0	24	6.0	10	0
Murphy	0	2	0	—	0	0
Green Bay	48	16	351	7.3	39	0
Opponents	46	5	368	8.0	22	0

Kickoff Returns

	No.	Yds.	Avg.	LG	TD
Rodgers	39	843	21.6	97t	1
Huckleby	14	261	18.6	54	0
Epps	12	232	19.3	47	0
J. Smith, Wash-Raid-GB	2	38	19.0	22	0
D. Jones	1	19	19.0	19	0
Prather	1	7	7.0	7	0
Green Bay	67	1362	20.3	97t	1
Opponents	73	1171	16.0	51	0

Scoring

	TD R	TD P	TD Rt	PAT	FG	Saf	TP
Del Greco	0	0	0	34/34	9/12	0	61
Coffman	0	9	0	0/0	0/0	0	54
Ivery	6	1	0	0/0	0/0	0	42
Lofton	0	7	0	0/0	0/0	0	42
Clark	4	2	0	0/0	0/0	0	36
Ellis	4	2	0	0/0	0/0	0	36
West	1	4	0	0/0	0/0	0	30
Garcia	0	0	0	14/15	3/9	0	23
Dickey	3	0	0	0/0	0/0	0	18
Epps	0	3	0	0/0	0/0	0	18
Brown	0	0	1	0/0	0/0	0	6
Crouse	0	1	0	0/0	0/0	0	6
T. Lewis	0	0	1	0/0	0/0	0	6
Moore	0	1	0	0/0	0/0	0	6
Rodgers	0	0	1	0/0	0/0	0	6
Green Bay	18	30	3	48/51	12/21	0	390
Opponents	14	16	4	33/34	24/31	0	309

FIRST-ROUND SELECTIONS

(If Club had no first-round selection, first player drafted is listed with round in parentheses.)

Year	Player, College, Position
1936	Russ Letlow, San Francisco, G
1937	Ed Jankowski, Wisconsin, B
1938	Cecil Isbell, Purdue, B
1939	Larry Buhler, Minnesota, B
1940	Hal Van Every, Marquette, B
1941	George Paskvan, Wisconsin, B
1942	Urban Odson, Minnesota, T
1943	Dick Wildung, Minnesota, T
1944	Merv Pregulman, Michigan, G
1945	Walt Schlinkman, Texas Tech, G
1946	Johnny (Strike) Strzykalski, Marquette, B
1947	Ernie Case, UCLA, B
1948	Earl (Jug) Girard, Wisconsin, B
1949	Stan Heath, Nevada, B
1950	Clayton Tonnemaker, Minnesota, C
1951	Bob Gain, Kentucky, T
1952	Babe Parilli, Kentucky, QB
1953	Al Carmichael, Southern California, B
1954	Art Hunter, Notre Dame, T
	Veryl Switzer, Kansas State, B
1955	Tom Bettis, Purdue, G
1956	Jack Losch, Miami, B
1957	Paul Hornung, Notre Dame, B
	Ron Kramer, Michigan, E
1958	Dan Currie, Michigan State, C
1959	Randy Duncan, Iowa, B
1960	Tom Moore, Vanderbilt, RB
1961	Herb Adderley, Michigan State, CB
1962	Earl Gros, Louisiana State, RB
1963	Dave Robinson, Penn State, LB
1964	Lloyd Voss, Nebraska, DT
1965	Donny Anderson, Texas Tech, RB
	Larry Elkins, Baylor, E
1966	Jim Grabowski, Illinois, RB
	Gale Gillingham, Minnesota, T
1967	Bob Hyland, Boston College, C
	Don Horn, San Diego State, QB
1968	Fred Carr, Texas-El Paso, LB
	Bill Lueck, Arizona, G
1969	Rich Moore, Villanova, DT
1970	Mike McCoy, Notre Dame, DT
	Rich McGeorge, Elon, TE
1971	John Brockington, Ohio State, RB
1972	Willie Buchanon, San Diego State, DB
	Jerry Tagge, Nebraska, QB
1973	Barry Smith, Florida State, WR
1974	Barty Smith, Richmond, RB
1975	Bill Bain, Southern California, G (2)
1976	Mark Koncar, Colorado, T
1977	Mike Butler, Kansas, DE
	Ezra Johnson, Morris Brown, DE
1978	James Lofton, Stanford, WR
	John Anderson, Michigan, LB
1979	Eddie Lee Ivery, Georgia Tech, RB
1980	Bruce Clark, Penn State, DE
	George Cumby, Oklahoma, LB
1981	Rich Campbell, California, QB
1982	Ron Hallstrom, Iowa, G
1983	Tim Lewis, Pittsburgh, DB
1984	Alphonso Carreker, Florida State, DE
1985	Ken Ruettgers, Southern California, T

GREEN BAY PACKERS 1985 VETERAN ROSTER

No.	Name	Pos.	Ht.	Wt.	Birth-date	NFL Exp.	College	Birthplace	Residence	'84 Games/ Starts
59	Anderson, John	LB	6-3	229	2/14/56	8	Michigan	Waukesha, Wis.	Elm Grove, Wis.	16/16
93	†Brown, Robert	DE	6-2	250	5/21/60	4	Virginia Tech	Edenton, N.C.	Springville, Va.	16/0
18	t-Brunner, Scott	QB	6-5	200	3/24/57	5	Delaware	Sellersville, Pa.	Cranbury, N.J.	0*
58	Cannon, Mark	C	6-3	258	6/14/52	2	Texas-Arlington	Austin, Tex.	Green Bay, Wis.	16/0
76	Carreker, Alphonso	DE	6-6	260	5/25/62	2	Florida State	Columbus, Ohio	Tallahassee, Fla.	14/14
88	†Cassidy, Ron	WR	6-0	180	7/23/57	6	Utah State	Ventura, Calif.	Green Bay, Wis.	15/0
33	†Clark, Jessie	FB	6-0	233	1/3/60	3	Arkansas	Thebes, Ark.	Fayetteville, Ark.	11/10
82	Coffman, Paul	TE	6-3	225	3/29/56	7	Kansas State	St. Louis, Mo.	Lee's Summit, Mo.	14/13
21	Crouse, Ray	RB	5-11	214	3/16/59	2	Nevada-Las Vegas	Oakland, Calif.	Richmond, Calif.	16/0
52	Cumby, George	LB	6-0	224	7/5/56	6	Oklahoma	Gorman, Tex.	Green Bay, Wis.	16/16
10	Del Greco, Al	K	5-10	195	3/2/62	2	Auburn	Providence, R.I.	Auburn, Ala.	9/0
98	DeLuca, Tony	NT	6-4	250	11/16/60	2	Rhode Island	Greenwich, Conn.	Greenwich, Conn.	1/0
12	Dickey, Lynn	QB	6-4	203	10/19/49	15	Kansas State	Paola, Kan.	Lenexa, Kan.	15/15
99	Dorsey, John	LB	6-2	235	8/31/60	2	Connecticut	Leonardtown, Md.	Storrs, Conn.	16/0
53	Douglass, Mike	LB	6-0	214	3/15/55	8	San Diego State	St. Louis, Mo.	El Cajon, Calif.	16/16
61	Drechsler, Dave	G	6-3	264	7/18/60	3	North Carolina	Cleveland, N.C.	Green Bay, Wis.	16/3
31	Ellis, Gerry	FB	5-11	225	11/12/57	6	Missouri	Columbia, Mo.	Green Bay, Wis.	16/16
85	Epps, Phillip	WR	5-10	155	11/11/59	4	Texas Christian	Atlanta, Tex.	Ft. Worth, Tex.	16/4
41	Flynn, Tom	S	6-0	195	3/24/62	2	Pittsburgh	Verona, Pa.	Verona, Pa.	15/15
65	Hallstrom, Ron	T	6-6	283	6/11/59	4	Iowa	Holden, Mass.	Green Bay, Wis.	16/13
69	Harris, Leotis	G	6-1	265	6/28/55	7	Arkansas	Little Rock, Ark.	Little Rock, Ark.	0*
27	Hayes, Gary	CB	5-10	180	8/19/57	2	Fresno State	Tucson, Ariz.	Richmond, Calif.	16/0
78	Hoffman, Gary	T	6-7	282	9/28/61	2	Santa Clara	Sacramento, Calif.	Green Bay, Wis.	1/0
38	Hood, Estus	CB	5-11	189	11/14/55	8	Illinois	Hattiesburg, Miss.	Green Bay, Wis.	16/0
25	Huckleby, Harlan	RB	6-1	201	12/30/57	6	Michigan	Detroit, Mich.	Detroit, Mich.	16/0
74	Huffman, Tim	T	6-5	282	8/31/59	5	Notre Dame	Canton, Ohio	Green Bay, Wis.	16/15
79	Humphrey, Donnie	DE	6-3	275	4/20/61	2	Auburn	Madison City, Ala.	Huntsville, Ala.	16/16
40	Ivery, Eddie Lee	RB	6-0	214	7/30/57	6	Georgia Tech	McDuffie, Ga.	Thomson, Ga.	10/5
83	†Jefferson, John	WR	6-1	204	2/3/56	8	Arizona State	Dallas, Tex.	Dallas, Tex.	13/12
90	Johnson, Ezra	DE	6-4	259	10/2/55	9	Morris Brown	Shreveport, La.	Green Bay, Wis.	13/0
43	Jones, Daryll	S	6-0	190	3/23/62	2	Georgia	Columbus, Ga.	Jonesboro, Ga.	16/0
63	Jones, Terry	NT	6-2	253	11/8/56	8	Alabama	Sandersville, Ga.	Tuscaloosa, Ala.	16/16
68	Koch, Greg	T	6-4	276	6/14/55	9	Arkansas	Bethesda, Md.	Houston, Tex.	14/14
22	Lee, Mark	CB	5-11	188	3/20/58	6	Washington	Hanford, Calif.	Bellevue, Wash.	16/16
56	Lewis, Cliff	LB	6-1	224	11/9/59	5	Southern Mississippi	Brewton, Ala.	Ft. Walton Beach, Fla.	16/0
81	Lewis, Gary	TE	6-5	234	12/30/58	5	Texas-Arlington	Mt. Pleasant, Tex.	Arlington, Tex.	3/1
26	Lewis, Tim	CB	5-11	191	12/18/61	3	Pittsburgh	Perkasie, Pa.	Green Bay, Wis.	16/16
80	Lofton, James	WR	6-3	197	7/5/56	8	Stanford	Los Angeles, Calif.	Honolulu, Hawaii	16/16
94	Martin, Charles	DE	6-4	270	8/31/59	2	Livingston	Canton, Ga.	Birmingham, Ala.	16/2
54	McCarren, Larry	C	6-3	251	11/9/51	13	Illinois	Chicago, Ill.	Green Bay, Wis.	12/12
29	McCoy, Mike	S	5-11	190	8/16/53	9	Colorado	Memphis, Ark.	Green Bay, Wis.	0*
28	McLeod, Mike	S	6-0	180	5/4/58	2	Montana State	Bozeman, Mont.	Green Bay, Wis.	11/1
60	Moore, Blake	C-G	6-5	272	5/8/58	6	Wooster	Durham, N.C.	Cincinnati, Ohio	11/4
37	Murphy, Mark	S	6-2	201	4/22/58	5	West Liberty State	Canton, Ohio	North Canton, Ohio	16/16
51	†Prather, Guy	LB	6-2	229	3/28/58	5	Grambling	Olney, Md.	Reston, Va.	16/0
35	Rodgers, Del	RB	5-10	202	6/22/60	3	Utah	Tacoma, Wash.	Salinas, Calif.	14/0
55	Scott, Randy	LB	6-1	222	1/31/59	5	Alabama	Atlanta, Ga.	Atlanta, Ga.	16/16
13	†Scribner, Bucky	P	6-0	202	7/11/60	3	Kansas	Lawrence, Kan.	Overland Park, Kan.	16/0
67	Swanke, Karl	T	6-6	262	12/29/57	6	Boston College	Elmhurst, Ill.	Green Bay, Wis.	15/14
84	Taylor, Lenny	WR	5-10	179	2/15/61	2	Tennessee	Miami, Fla.	Miami, Fla.	2/0
70	Uecker, Keith	G-T	6-5	270	6/29/60	4	Auburn	Auburn, Ala.	Hollywood, Fla.	6/2
86	West, Ed	TE	6-1	242	8/2/61	2	Auburn	Colbert City, Ala.	Leighton, Ala.	16/0
50	Wingo, Rich	LB	6-1	227	7/16/56	6	Alabama	Elkhart, Ind.	Tuscaloosa, Ala.	16/0
16	Wright, Randy	QB	6-2	194	1/12/61	2	Wisconsin	St. Charles, Ill.	Green Bay, Wis.	8/1

* Brunner, Harris, and McCoy missed '84 season due to injury.

†Option playout; subject to developments.

t-Packers traded for Brunner (Denver).

Also played with Packers in '84—QB Rich Campbell (3 games), TE Henry Childs (3), K Eddie Garcia (7), T Boyd Jones (2), G Syd Kitson (8), NT Bill Neill (16), CB-S Dwayne O'Steen (4), RB Jimmy Smith (active for 1 game but did not play).

COACHING STAFF

Head Coach, Forrest Gregg

Pro Career: Registered 8-8 mark in first season at Green Bay helm, including 7-1 record over second half of season. Named Packers head coach on December 26, 1983, after compiling 34-27 record as Cincinnati's coach from 1980-83, including 1981 AFC Central title and Super Bowl XVI appearance. Was previously head coach of Cleveland Browns, where he compiled an 18-23 record from 1975-77, including 9-5 record in 1976. Also was head coach of Toronto Argonauts (CFL) in 1979 before signing to take over Bengals. Served as an NFL assistant coach from 1972-74. He was offensive line coach with San Diego Chargers in 1972-73 before joining Cleveland Browns in same capacity in 1974. Had outstanding 15-year playing career in NFL as a guard-tackle with Green Bay Packers 1956-70 (he played in the Packers' two Super Bowl wins) and as a player-coach with Dallas Cowboys in Super Bowl championship season of 1971. Inducted into the Pro Football Hall of Fame in 1977. Career record: 60-58.

Background: Tackle at Southern Methodist 1953-55. Twice named to the All-Southwest Conference team. Captain of the SMU team his senior year. Spent 1957 in military service.

Personal: Born October 18, 1933, in Birthright, Tex. Attended Sulphur Springs (Tex.) High School. He and his wife, Barbara, live in Green Bay and have two children—Forrest Jr. and Karen.

Assistant Coaches

Lew Carpenter, receivers; born January 12, 1932, Hayti, Mo., lives in Green Bay. Running back-end Arkansas 1950-52. Pro running back-defensive back-end Detroit Lions 1953-55, Cleveland Browns 1957-58, Green Bay Packers 1959-63. Pro coach: Minnesota Vikings 1964-66, Atlanta Falcons 1967-68, Washington Redskins 1969-70, St. Louis Cardinals 1971-72, Houston Oilers 1973-74, joined Packers in 1975.

Virgil Knight, strength-conditioning; born January 30, 1948, Clarksville, Ark., lives in Green Bay. Tight end Northeastern Oklahoma 1968-70. No pro playing experience. College coach: Arkansas Tech 1975-78, Florida 1979-80, Auburn 1981-83. Pro coach: First year with Packers.

Dick Modzelewski, defensive coordinator-defensive line; born January 16, 1931, West Natrona, Pa., lives in Green Bay. Tackle Maryland 1950-52. Pro defensive tackle Washington Redskins 1953-54, Pittsburgh Steelers 1955, New York Giants 1956-63, Cleveland Browns 1964-66. Pro coach: Cleveland Browns 1968-77, New York Giants 1978, Cincinnati Bengals 1979-83, joined Packers in 1984.

Herb Paterra, linebackers-special teams; born November 8, 1940, Grassport, Pa., lives in Green Bay. Offensive guard-linebacker Michigan State 1960-62. Pro linebacker Buffalo Bills 1963-64, Hamilton Tiger-Cats (CFL) 1965-68. College coach: Michigan State 1969-71, Wyoming 1972-74. Pro coach: Charlotte Hornets (WFL) 1975, Hamilton Tiger-Cats (CFL) 1978-79, Los Angeles Rams 1980-82, Edmonton Eskimos (CFL) 1983, joined Packers in 1984.

George Priefer, special teams-defensive assistant; born July 26, 1941, Lakewood, Ohio, lives in Green Bay. John Carroll University. No college or pro playing experience. College coach: Miami, Ohio 1977, North Carolina 1978-83. Pro coach: Joined Packers in 1984.

Ken Riley, secondary; born August 6, 1947, Bartow, Fla., lives in Green Bay. Defensive back Florida A&M 1966-68. Pro cornerback Cincinnati Bengals 1969-83. Pro coach: Joined Packers in 1984.

Bob Schnelker, offensive coordinator; born October 17, 1928, Galion, Ohio, lives in Green Bay. End Bowling Green 1946-50. Pro end Cleveland Browns 1953, New York Giants 1954-60, Minnesota Vikings 1961. Pro coach: Los Angeles Rams 1963-64, Green Bay Packers 1965-71, San Diego Chargers 1972-73, Miami Dolphins 1974, Kansas City Chiefs 1975-77, Detroit Lions 1978-81, rejoined Packers in 1982.

George Sefcik, offensive backfield; born December 27, 1939, Cleveland Ohio, lives in Green Bay. Halfback Notre Dame 1959-61. No pro playing experience. College coach: Notre Dame 1963-68, Kentucky 1969-72. Pro coach: Baltimore Colts 1973-74, Cleveland Browns 1975-77, Cincinnati Bengals 1978-83, joined Packers in 1984.

Jerry Wampfler, offensive line; born August 6, 1932, New Philadelphia, Ohio, lives in Green Bay. Tackle Miami, Ohio 1951-54. No pro playing experience. College coach: Presbyterian 1955, Miami, Ohio 1963-65, Notre Dame 1966-69, Colorado State 1970-72 (head coach). Pro coach: Philadelphia Eagles 1973-75, 1979-83, Buffalo Bills 1976-77, New York Giants 1978, joined Packers in 1984.

GREEN BAY PACKERS 1985 FIRST-YEAR ROSTER

Name	Pos.	Ht.	Wt.	Birth-date	College	Birthplace	Residence	How Acq.
Allen, Mark	CB-S	6-2	180	6/10/60	Brigham Young	Los Angeles, Calif.	Duarte, Calif.	FA
Bratel, Keith	WR	5-11	176	2/26/63	Carroll College	Milwaukee, Wis.	Waukesha, Wis.	FA
Cole, Curt	TE	6-4	230	1/2/61	Texas Tech	Austin, Tex.	Lubbock, Tex.	FA
Edwards, Keith	RB	6-0	210	4/4/62	Vanderbilt	Ocala, Fla.	Williston, Fla.	FA
Ellerson, Gary	RB	5-11	220	7/17/63	Wisconsin	Albany, Ga.	Albany, Ga.	D7a
Fowler, Delbert (1)	LB	6-3	220	5/4/58	West Virginia	Cleveland, Ohio	Cleveland, Ohio	FA
Harris, George W.	LB	6-3	228	12/2/60	Houston	Waco, Tex.	Waco, Tex.	FA
Johnson, Morris	T-G	6-2	317	6/25/62	Alabama A&M	Detroit, Mich	Detroit, Mich.	D9
Kapischke, Kurt	T-G	6-5	265	3/14/62	Augustana	Wiesbaden, Germany	Green Bay, Wis.	FA
Lewis, Mark	TE	6-2	218	5/20/61	Texas A&M	Houston, Tex.	College Station, Tex.	D6
Mayo, Blll	T-G	6-3	288	4/26/63	Tennessee	Chattanooga, Tenn.	Knoxville, Tenn.	FA
Meyer, Jim	P	6-4	204	1/3/62	Arizona State	Phoenix, Ariz.	Phoenix, Ariz.	D12
Moran, Rich	T-G	6-2	272	3/19/62	San Diego State	Boise, Idaho	San Diego, Calif.	D3
Mosley, Andre	CB	6-0	195	1/16/62	North Texas State	Lake Charles, La.	Denton, Tex.	FA
Noble, Brian	LB	6-3	237	9/6/62	Arizona State	Anaheim, Calif.	Anaheim, Calif.	D5
Quinlan, Peter	NT-DE	6-2	275	2/26/62	Holy Cross	Lowell, Mass.	Dracut, Mass.	FA
Ruettgers, Ken	T-G	6-5	267	8/20/62	Southern California	Bakersfield, Calif.	Bakersfield, Calif.	D1
Shield, Joe	QB	6-1	185	6/26/62	Trinity College	Brattleboro, Vt.	Hartford, Conn.	D11
Stanley, Walter	WR-KR	5-9	180	11/5/62	Mesa College	Chicago, Ill.	Grand Junction, Colo.	D4
Stills, Ken	CB-S	5-10	185	9/6/63	Wisconsin	Oceanside, Calif.	Madison, Wis.	D8
Walter, Ken	C-G	6-4	260	3/2/58	Texas Tech	Corsicana, Tex.	Richardson, Tex.	FA
White, Eddie	TE	6-3	240	12/9/60	Arkansas	Camden, Ark.	Fayetteville, Ark.	FA
Wilson, Eric	LB	6-1	247	10/17/62	Maryland	Charlottesville, Va.	Charlottesville, Va.	D7

Players who report to an NFL team for the first time are designated on rosters as rookies (R). If a player reported to an NFL training camp in a previous year but was not on the active squad for three or more regular season or postseason games, he is listed on the first-year roster and designated by a (1). Thereafter, a player who is on the active squad for three or more regular season or postseason games is credited with an additional year of playing experience.

NOTES

LOS ANGELES RAMS

National Football Conference
Western Division

Team Colors: Royal Blue, Gold, and White

Business Address:
2327 West Lincoln Avenue
Anaheim, California 92801

Ticket Office:
Anaheim Stadium
1900 State College Boulevard
Anaheim, California 92806
Telephone: (714) 535-7267
or (213) 585-5400

Club Officials

President: Georgia Frontiere
Vice President, Finance: John Shaw
Legal Counsel: Jay Zygmunt
Administrator, Football Operations: Jack Faulkner
Director of Operations: Dick Beam
Director of Player Personnel: John Math
Director of Public Relations: Pete Donovan
Assistant Director of Public Relations:
John Oswald
Director of Community Relations: Marshall Klein
Trainers: George Menefee, Jim Anderson,
Garrett Giemont
Equipment Manager: Don Hewitt
Assistant Equipment Manager: Todd Hewitt

Stadium: Anaheim Stadium • **Capacity:** 69,007
Anaheim, California 92806

Playing Surface: Grass

Training Camp: California State University
Fullerton, California 92634

1985 SCHEDULE

Preseason

Aug. 10	**Houston**	7:00
Aug. 15	**St. Louis**	7:00
Aug. 23	vs. Phil. at Columbus, Ohio	7:30
Aug. 31	**New England**	7:00

Regular Season

Sept. 8	**Denver**	1:00
Sept. 15	at Philadelphia	1:00
Sept. 23	at Seattle (Monday)	6:00
Sept. 29	**Atlanta**	1:00
Oct. 6	**Minnesota**	1:00
Oct. 13	at Tampa Bay	1:00
Oct. 20	at Kansas City	12:00
Oct. 27	**San Francisco**	1:00
Nov. 3	**New Orleans**	1:00
Nov. 10	at New York Giants	1:00
Nov. 17	at Atlanta	1:00
Nov. 24	**Green Bay**	1:00
Dec. 1	at New Orleans	12:00
Dec. 9	at San Francisco (Monday)	6:00
Dec. 15	**St. Louis**	1:00
Dec. 23	**L.A. Raiders** (Monday)	6:00

RAMS COACHING HISTORY

Cleveland 1937-45
(335-277-20)

1937-38	Hugo Bezdek*	1-13-0
1938	Art Lewis	4-4-0
1939-42	Earl (Dutch) Clark	16-26-2
1944	Aldo (Buff) Donelli	4-6-0
1945-46	Adam Walsh	15-5-1
1947	Bob Snyder	6-6-0
1948-49	Clark Shaughnessy	14-8-3
1950-52	Joe Stydahar**	18-9-0
1952-54	Hamp Pool	23-11-2
1955-59	Sid Gillman	28-32-1
1960-62	Bob Waterfield***	9-24-1
1962-65	Harland Svare	14-31-3
1966-70	George Allen	49-19-4
1971-72	Tommy Prothro	14-12-2
1973-77	Chuck Knox	57-20-1
1978-82	Ray Malavasi	43-36-0
1983-84	John Robinson	20-15-0

*Resigned after three games in 1938
**Resigned after one game in 1952
***Resigned after eight games in 1962

RECORD HOLDERS
Individual Records—Career

Category	Name	Performance
Rushing (Yds.)	Lawrence McCutcheon, 1973-79	6,186
Passing (Yds.)	Roman Gabriel, 1962-1972	22,223
Passing (TDs)	Roman Gabriel, 1962-1972	154
Receiving (No.)	Tom Fears, 1948-1956	400
Receiving (Yds.)	Elroy Hirsch, 1949-1957	6,289
Interceptions	Ed Meador, 1959-1970	46
Punting (Avg.)	Danny Villanueva, 1960-64	44.2
Punt Return (Avg.)	Henry Ellard, 1983-84	13.5
Kickoff Return (Avg.)	Jon Arnett, 1957-1963	24.9
Field Goals	Bruce Gossett, 1964-69	120
Touchdowns (Tot.)	Elroy Hirsch, 1949-1957	55
Points	Bob Waterfield, 1946-1952	573

Individual Records—Single Season

Category	Name	Performance
Rushing (Yds.)	Eric Dickerson, 1984	2,105
Passing (Yds.)	Vince Ferragamo, 1983	3,276
Passing (TDs)	Vince Ferragamo, 1980	30
Receiving (No.)	Tom Fears, 1950	84
Receiving (Yds.)	Elroy Hirsch, 1951	1,425
Interceptions	Dick (Night Train) Lane, 1952	14
Punting (Avg.)	Danny Villanueva, 1962	45.5
Punt Return (Avg.)	Woodley Lewis, 1952	18.5
Kickoff Return (Avg.)	Verda (Vitamin T) Smith, 1950	33.7
Field Goals	David Ray, 1973	30
Touchdowns (Tot.)	Eric Dickerson, 1983	20
Points	David Ray, 1973	130

Individual Records—Single Game

Category	Name	Performance
Rushing (Yds.)	Willie Ellison, 12-5-71	247
Passing (Yds.)	Norm Van Brocklin, 9-28-51	554
Passing (TDs)	Many times	5
	Last time by Vince Ferragamo, 10-23-83	
Receiving (No.)	Tom Fears, 12-3-50	18
Receiving (Yds.)	Jim Benton, 11-22-45	303
Interceptions	Many times	3
	Last time by Pat Thomas, 10-7-79	
Field Goals	Bob Waterfield, 12-9-51	5
Touchdowns (Tot.)	Bob Shaw, 12-11-49	4
	Elroy Hirsch, 9-28-51	4
	Harold Jackson, 10-14-73	4
Points	Bob Shaw, 12-11-49	24
	Elroy Hirsch, 9-28-51	24
	Harold Jackson, 10-14-73	24

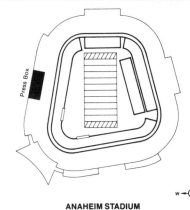

ANAHEIM STADIUM

1984 TEAM STATISTICS

	L.A. Rams	Opp.
Total First Downs	258	309
Rushing	140	108
Passing	100	179
Penalty	18	22
Third Down: Made/Att.	65/195	88/225
Fourth Down: Made/Att.	1/8	12/22
Total Net Yards	5006	5266
Avg. Per Game	312.9	329.1
Total Plays	931	1058
Avg. Per Play	5.4	5.0
Net Yards Rushing	2864	1600
Avg. Per Game	179.0	100.0
Total Rushes	541	449
Net Yards Passing	2142	3666
Avg. Per Game	133.9	229.1
Tackled/Yards Lost	32/240	43/298
Gross Yards	2382	3964
Att./Completions	358/176	566/346
Completion Pct.	49.2	61.1
Had Intercepted	17	17
Punts/Avg.	74/38.7	71/41.5
Net Punting Avg.	33.6	32.1
Penalties/Yards Lost	93/830	115/871
Fumbles/Ball Lost	31/18	42/22
Touchdowns	38	36
Rushing	16	15
Passing	16	18
Returns	6	3
Avg. Time of Possession	28:22	31:38

1984 TEAM RECORD
Preseason (2-2)

Date	Los Angeles Rams		Opponents
8/4	10	San Diego	17
8/13	10	*Cleveland	21
8/18	27	*Green Bay	24
8/23	47	*San Diego	14
	94		76

Regular Season (10-6)

Date	Los Angeles Rams		Opp.	Att.
9/3	13	*Dallas	20	65,403
9/9	20	*Cleveland	17	43,043
9/16	14	Pittsburgh	24	58,104
9/23	24	Cincinnati	14	45,406
9/30	33	*New York Giants	12	53,417
10/7	28	*Atlanta	30	47,832
10/14	28	New Orleans	10	63,161
10/22	24	Atlanta	10	52,861
10/28	0	*San Francisco	33	65,481
11/4	16	St. Louis	13	51,010
11/11	29	*Chicago	13	62,021
11/18	6	Green Bay	31	52,031
11/25	34	Tampa Bay	33	42,242
12/2	34	*New Orleans	21	49,348
12/9	27	*Houston	16	49,092
12/14	16	San Francisco	19	59,743
	346		316	860,195

*Home Game

Score by Periods

L.A. Rams	67	118	77	84	—	346
Opponents	55	110	57	94	—	316

Attendance
Home 435,637   Away 424,558   Total 860,195
Single game home record, 102,368 (11-10-57; L.A. Coliseum), 67,037 (12-23-84; Anaheim Stadium)
Single season home record, 519,175 (1973; L.A. Coliseum) 500,403 (1980; Anaheim Stadium)

1984 INDIVIDUAL STATISTICS

Rushing

	Att.	Yds.	Avg.	LG	TD
Dickerson	379	2105	5.6	66	14
Crutchfield	73	337	4.6	36	1
Redden	45	247	5.5	35	0
Kemp	34	153	4.5	23	1
Brown	2	25	12.5	16	0
Guman	1	2	2.0	2	0
Ferragamo	4	0	0.0	2	0
Ellard	3	−5	−1.7	5	0
L.A. Rams	541	2864	5.3	66	16
Opponents	449	1600	3.6	31t	15

Passing

	Att.	Comp.	Pct.	Yds.	TD	Int.	Tkld.	Rate
Kemp	284	143	50.4	2021	13	7	24/190	78.7
Ferragamo	66	29	43.9	317	2	8	7/42	29.2
Dills	7	4	57.1	44	1	1	1/8	75.9
Dickerson	1	0	0.0	0	0	1	0/0	0.0
L.A. Rams	358	176	49.2	2382	16	17	32/240	65.9
Opponents	566	346	61.1	3964	18	17	43/298	80.3

Receiving

	No.	Yds.	Avg.	LG	TD
Ellard	34	622	18.3	63t	6
Da. Hill	31	300	9.7	26	1
Brown	23	478	20.8	54	4
Dickerson	21	139	6.6	19	0
Guman	19	161	8.5	29	0
Dr. Hill	14	390	27.9	68	4
Grant	9	64	7.1	15	0
Farmer	7	75	10.7	23	0
Barber	7	42	6.0	11	0
J. McDonald	4	55	13.8	22	0
Redden	4	39	9.8	14	0
Crutchfield	2	11	5.5	7	1
Faulkner	1	6	6.0	6	0
L.A. Rams	176	2382	13.5	68	16
Opponents	346	3964	11.5	64t	18

Interceptions

	No.	Yds.	Avg.	LG	TD
Irvin	5	166	33.2	81t	2
Green	3	88	29.3	60	0
Cromwell	3	54	18.0	33t	1
Collins	2	43	21.5	40	0
Johnson	2	21	10.5	21	0
Newsome	1	31	31.0	31	0
Owens	1	−4	−4.0	−4	0
L.A. Rams	17	399	23.5	81t	3
Opponents	17	240	14.1	99t	2

Punting

	No.	Yds.	Avg.	In 20	LG
Misko	74	2866	38.7	21	58
L.A. Rams	74	2866	38.7	21	58
Opponents	71	2949	41.5	11	66

Punt Returns

	No.	FC	Yds.	Avg.	LG	TD
Ellard	30	3	403	13.4	83t	2
Irvin	9	0	83	9.2	22	0
Johnson	1	1	3	3.0	3	0
L.A. Rams	40	4	489	12.2	83t	2
Opponents	35	21	196	5.6	26	0

Kickoff Returns

	No.	Yds.	Avg.	LG	TD
Redden	23	530	23.0	40	0
Dr. Hill	26	543	20.9	40	0
Ellard	2	24	12.0	12	0
Irvin	2	33	16.5	22	0
Pleasant	2	48	24.0	29	0
Guman	1	43	43.0	43t	1
Crutchfield	1	20	20.0	20	0
Sully	1	3	3.0	3	0
L.A. Rams	58	1244	21.4	43t	1
Opponents	74	1288	17.4	43	0

Scoring

	TD R	TD P	TD Rt	PAT	FG	Saf	TP
Lansford	0	0	0	37/38	25/33	0	112
Dickerson	14	0	0	0/0	0/0	0	84
Ellard	0	6	2	0/0	0/0	0	48
Brown	0	4	0	0/0	0/0	0	24
Dr. Hill	0	4	0	0/0	0/0	0	24
Crutchfield	1	1	0	0/0	0/0	0	12
Irvin	0	0	2	0/0	0/0	0	12
Cromwell	0	0	1	0/0	0/0	0	6
Guman	0	0	1	0/0	0/0	0	6
Da. Hill	0	1	0	0/0	0/0	0	6
Kemp	1	0	0	0/0	0/0	0	6
Sully	0	0	0	0/0	0/0	1	2
Vann	0	0	0	0/0	0/0	1	2
L.A. Rams	16	16	6	37/38	25/33	3	346
Opponents	15	18	3	32/36	22/31	1	316

FIRST-ROUND SELECTIONS

(If Club had no first-round selection, first player drafted is listed with round in parentheses.)

Year	Player, College, Position
1937	Johnny Drake, Purdue, B
1938	Corbett Davis, Indiana, B
1939	Parker Hall, Mississippi, B
1940	Ollie Cordill, Rice, B
1941	Rudy Mucha, Washington, C
1942	Jack Wilson, Baylor, B
1943	Mike Holovak, Boston College, B
1944	Tony Butkovich, Illinois, B
1945	Elroy (Crazylegs) Hirsch, Wisconsin, B
1946	Emil Sitko, Notre Dame, B
1947	Herman Wedemeyer, St. Mary's, Cal., B
1948	Tom Keane, West Virginia, B (2)
1949	Bobby Thomason, Virginia Military, B
1950	Ralph Pasquariello, Villanova, B
	Stan West, Oklahoma, G
1951	Bud McFadin, Texas, G
1952	Bill Wade, Vanderbilt, QB
	Bob Carey, Michigan State, E
1953	Donn Moomaw, UCLA, C
	Ed Barker, Washington State, E
1954	Ed Beatty, Cincinnati, C
1955	Larry Morris, Georgia Tech, C
1956	Joe Marconi, West Virginia, B
	Charles Horton, Vanderbilt, B
1957	Jon Arnett, Southern California, B
	Del Shofner, Baylor, E
1958	Lou Michaels, Kentucky, T
	Jim Phillips, Auburn, E
1959	Dick Bass, Pacific, B
	Paul Dickson, Baylor, T
1960	Billy Cannon, Louisiana State, RB
1961	Marlin McKeever, Southern California, E-LB
1962	Roman Gabriel, North Carolina State, QB
	Merlin Olsen, Utah State, DT
1963	Terry Baker, Oregon State, QB
	Rufus Guthrie, Georgia Tech, G
1964	Bill Munson, Utah State, QB
1965	Clancy Williams, Washington State, CB
1966	Tom Mack, Michigan, G
1967	Willie Ellison, Texas Southern, RB (2)
1968	Gary Beban, UCLA, QB (2)
1969	Larry Smith, Florida, RB
	Jim Seymour, Notre Dame, WR
	Bob Klein, Southern California, TE
1970	Jack Reynolds, Tennessee, LB
1971	Isiah Robertson, Southern, LB
	Jack Youngblood, Florida, DE
1972	Jim Bertelsen, Texas, RB (2)
1973	Cullen Bryant, Colorado, DB (2)
1974	John Cappelletti, Penn State, RB
1975	Mike Fanning, Notre Dame, DT
	Dennis Harrah, Miami, T
	Doug France, Ohio State, T
1976	Kevin McLain, Colorado State, LB
1977	Bob Brudzinski, Ohio State, LB
1978	Elvis Peacock, Oklahoma, RB
1979	George Andrews, Nebraska, LB
	Kent Hill, Georgia Tech, T
1980	Johnnie Johnson, Texas, DB
1981	Mel Owens, Michigan, LB
1982	Barry Redden, Richmond, RB
1983	Eric Dickerson, Southern Methodist, RB
1984	Hal Stephens, East Carolina, DE (5)
1985	Jerry Gray, Texas, DB

LOS ANGELES RAMS 1985 VETERAN ROSTER

No.	Name	Pos.	Ht.	Wt.	Birth-date	NFL Exp.	College	Birthplace	Residence	'84 Games/ Starts
52	†Andrews, George	LB	6-3	225	11/28/55	7	Nebraska	Omaha, Neb.	Anaheim, Calif.	11/11
62	Bain, Bill	T	6-4	290	8/9/52	10	Southern California	Pico Rivera, Calif.	Dana Point, Calif.	16/16
86	Barber, Mike	TE	6-3	237	6/4/53	9	Louisiana Tech	White Oak, Tex.	Houston, Tex.	11/2
96	Barnett, Doug	LB	6-3	250	4/12/60	3	Azusa Pacific	Montebello, Calif.	Lake Arrowhead, Calif.	0*
73	†Bolinger, Russ	G	6-5	255	9/10/54	9	Long Beach State	Wichita, Kan.	Newport Beach, Calif.	16/0
90	Brady, Ed	LB	6-2	228	6/17/60	2	Illinois	Morris, Ill.	Costa Mesa, Calif.	16/0
89	Brown, Ron	WR	5-11	181	3/31/61	2	Arizona State	Los Angeles, Calif.	Inglewood, Calif.	16/0
50	Collins, Jim	LB	6-2	230	6/11/58	5	Syracuse	Orange, N.J.	Huntington Beach, Calif.	16/16
21	Cromwell, Nolan	S	6-1	200	1/30/55	9	Kansas	Smith Center, Kan.	Mission Viejo, Calif.	11/11
28	Croudip, David	CB	5-8	183	1/25/59	2	San Diego State	Indianapolis, Ind.	San Diego, Calif.	16/0
45	Crutchfield, Dwayne	RB	6-0	235	9/30/59	4	Iowa State	Cincinnati, Ohio	Cincinnati, Ohio	15/0
70	DeJurnett, Charles	NT	6-4	260	6/17/52	9	San Jose State	Picayune, Miss.	San Diego, Calif.	16/0
29	Dickerson, Eric	RB	6-3	220	9/2/60	3	Southern Methodist	Sealy, Tex.	Irvine, Calif.	16/16
8	Dils, Steve	QB	6-1	191	12/8/55	6	Stanford	Seattle, Wash.	Mission Viejo, Calif.	10/0*
71	Doss, Reggie	DE	6-4	263	12/7/56	8	Hampton Institute	Mobile, Ala.	Huntington Beach, Calif.	16/16
55	Ekern, Carl	LB	6-3	222	5/27/54	9	San Jose State	Richland, Wash.	Fountain Valley, Calif.	16/16
80	Ellard, Henry	WR	5-11	170	7/21/61	3	Fresno State	Fresno, Calif.	Fresno, Calif.	16/16
	Erxleben, Russell	P	6-4	221	1/13/57	5	Texas	Seguin, Tex.	Kenner, La.	0*
84	Farmer, George	WR	5-10	175	12/5/58	4	Southern	Los Angeles, Calif.	Los Angeles, Calif.	14/0
88	Faulkner, Chris	TE	6-4	260	4/13/60	2	Florida	Tipton, Ind.	Anaheim, Calif.	8/0
15	Ferragamo, Vince	QB	6-3	212	4/24/54	8	Nebraska	Torrance, Calif.	Orange, Calif.	3/3
82	Grant, Otis	WR	6-3	197	8/13/61	3	Michigan State	Atlanta, Ga.	Atlanta, Ga.	14/0
27	Green, Gary	CB	5-11	191	10/2/55	9	Baylor	San Antonio, Tex.	San Antonio, Tex.	16/16
44	Guman, Mike	RB	6-2	218	4/21/58	6	Penn State	Allentown, Pa.	Tustin, Calif.	16/13
60	Harrah, Dennis	G	6-5	265	3/9/53	11	Miami	Charleston, W. Va.	Long Beach, Calif.	16/16
26	Harris, Eric	CB	6-3	202	8/11/55	6	Memphis State	Memphis, Tenn.	Memphis, Tenn.	7/7
81	Hill, David	TE	6-2	228	1/1/54	10	Texas A&I	San Antonio, Tex.	Yorba Linda, Calif.	16/16
87	Hill, Drew	WR	5-9	170	10/5/56	7	Georgia Tech	Newnan, Ga.	Newnan, Ga.	16/16
72	Hill, Kent	G	6-5	260	3/7/57	7	Georgia Tech	Americus, Ga.	Americus, Ga.	16/16
47	Irvin, LeRoy	CB	5-11	184	9/15/57	6	Kansas	Fort Dix, N.J.	Fullerton, Calif.	16/16
59	Jerue, Mark	LB	6-3	229	1/15/60	3	Washington	Seattle, Wash.	Seattle, Wash.	16/0
77	Jeter, Gary	DE	6-4	260	3/24/55	9	Southern California	Weirton, W. Va.	Newport Beach, Calif.	5/0
20	Johnson, Johnnie	S	6-1	183	10/8/56	6	Texas	La Grange, Tex.	Huntington Beach, Calif.	9/7
24	†Jones, A.J.	RB	6-1	202	5/30/59	4	Texas	Youngstown, Ohio	Youngstown, Ohio	13/0
46	Kamana, John	RB	6-2	215	12/3/61	2	Southern California	Honolulu, Hawaii	Costa Mesa, Calif.	3/0
9	Kemp, Jeff	QB	6-0	201	7/11/59	5	Dartmouth	Santa Ana, Calif.	Orange, Calif.	14/13
76	Kowalski, Gary	T	6-5	275	7/2/60	2	Boston College	New Haven, Conn.	Anaheim, Calif.	0*
1	Lansford, Mike	K	6-0	183	7/20/58	4	Washington	Monterey Park, Calif.	Huntington Beach, Calif.	16/0
57	Laughlin, Jim	LB	6-1	222	7/5/58	6	Ohio State	Euclid, Ohio	Roswell, Ga.	3/0
83	McDonald, James	TE	6-5	230	3/29/61	3	Southern California	Long Beach, Calif.	Long Beach, Calif.	16/1
63	McDonald, Mike	LB	6-1	235	6/22/58	2	Southern California	Burbank, Calif.	Burbank, Calif.	16/0
69	†Meisner, Greg	NT	6-3	253	4/23/59	5	Pittsburgh	New Kensington, Pa.	Huntington Beach, Calif.	16/16
98	Miller, Shawn	NT	6-4	255	3/14/61	2	Utah State	Ogden, Utah	Ogden, Utah	8/0
6	Misko, John	P	6-5	207	10/1/54	4	Oregon State	Highland Park, Mich.	Strathmore, Calif.	16/0
22	Newsome, Vince	S	6-1	179	1/22/61	3	Washington	Braintree, England	Seattle, Wash.	16/7
58	†Owens, Mel	LB	6-2	224	12/7/58	5	Michigan	Detroit, Mich.	Balboa, Calif.	16/16
75	Pankey, Irv	T	6-4	267	12/15/58	5	Penn State	Aberdeen, Md.	Diamond Bar, Calif.	16/9
43	Pleasant, Mike	CB	6-1	195	8/16/58	2	Oklahoma	Muskogee, Okla.	San Diego, Calif.	5/0
30	Redden, Barry	RB	5-10	205	7/21/60	4	Richmond	Sarasota, Fla.	Anaheim, Calif.	14/0
93	Reed, Doug	DE	6-3	250	7/16/60	2	San Diego State	San Diego, Calif.	San Diego, Calif.	9/1
66	Reese, Booker	DE	6-6	260	9/20/59	4	Bethune-Cookman	Jacksonville, Fla.	Tampa, Fla.	10/0*
64	†Shearin, Joe	G	6-4	250	4/16/60	3	Texas	Dallas, Tex.	Austin, Tex.	15/0
78	Slater, Jackie	T	6-4	271	5/27/54	10	Jackson State	Jackson, Miss.	Anaheim, Calif.	7/7
61	Slaton, Tony	C	6-3	269	4/12/61	2	Southern California	Merced, Calif.	Merced, Calif.	0*
56	Smith, Doug	C	6-3	253	11/25/56	8	Bowling Green	Columbus, Ohio	Laguna Hills, Calif.	16/16
37	†Sully, Ivory	S	6-0	200	6/20/57	7	Delaware	Salisbury, Md.	Anaheim, Calif.	16/0
51	Vann, Norwood	LB	6-2	225	2/18/62	2	East Carolina	Philadelphia, Pa.	Magnolia, N.C.	16/0
54	Wilcher, Mike	LB	6-3	235	3/20/60	3	North Carolina	Washington, D.C.	Washington, D.C.	15/5
85	Youngblood, Jack	DE	6-4	242	1/26/50	15	Florida	Jacksonville, Fla.	Orange, Calif.	15/15

* Barnett and Kowalski missed '84 season due to injury; Dils played 3 games with Minnesota, 7 with Rams in '84; Erxleben last active with New Orleans in '83; Reese played 1 game with Tampa Bay, 9 with Rams; Slaton active for 3 games but did not play.

†Option playout; subject to developments.

Also played with Rams in '84—LB Jim Youngblood (5 games).

COACHING STAFF

Head Coach, John Robinson

Pro Career: Starts third season as Rams head coach. Guided Rams to 10-6 record and playoff berth for second straight year in 1984. Became seventeenth head coach in Rams history on February 14, 1983. Arrived with 23 years of coaching experience, including one on the professional level with the Raiders in 1975. No pro playing experience. Career record: 20-15.

Background: Played end at Oregon 1955-58. Began coaching career with his alma mater from 1960-71. Became an assistant at Southern California from 1972-74. Returned as head coach in 1976 before resigning after the 1982 season. Compiled seven-year .819 winning percentage at Southern California with 67 wins, 14 losses, and 2 ties.

Personal: Born July 25, 1935, in Chicago, Ill. John and his wife, Barbara, live in Fullerton and have four children—Teresa, Lynn, David, and Christopher.

Assistant Coaches

Lew Erber, wide receivers; born May 27, 1934, Clifton, N.J., lives in Corona del Mar, Calif. Wing back Montclair State, N.J. 1954-55. No pro playing experience. College coach: Iowa State 1967-69, California Western 1969-72, San Diego State 1973, California 1974. Pro coach: San Francisco 49ers 1975, Oakland Raiders 1976-81, New England Patriots 1982-84, first year with Rams.

Marv Goux, defensive line; born September 8, 1932, Santa Barbara, Calif., lives in Long Beach, Calif. Linebacker Southern California 1952, 1954-55. No pro playing experience. College coach: Southern California 1957-82. Pro coach: Joined Rams in 1983.

Gil Haskell, special teams; born September 24, 1943, San Francisco, Calif., lives in Diamond Bar, Calif. Defensive back San Francisco State 1961, 1963-65. No pro playing experience. College coach: Southern California 1978-82. Pro coach: Joined Rams in 1983.

Hudson Houck, offensive line; born January 7, 1943, Los Angeles, Calif., lives in Long Beach, Calif. Center Southern California 1962-64. No pro playing experience. College coach: Southern California 1970-72, 1976-82, Stanford 1973-75. Pro coach: Joined Rams in 1983.

Steve Shafer, defensive backs; born December 8, 1940, Glendale, Calif., lives in Anaheim, Calif. Quarterback-defensive back Utah State 1961-62. Pro defensive back British Columbia Lions (CFL) 1963-67. College coach: San Mateo, Calif., J.C. 1968-74 (head coach 1973-74), San Diego State 1975-82. Pro coach: Joined Rams in 1983.

Fritz Shurmur, defensive coordinator-inside linebackers; born July 15, 1932, Riverview, Mich., lives in Diamond Bar, Calif. Center Albion 1951-53. No pro playing experience. College coach: Albion 1956-61, Wyoming 1962-74 (head coach 1971-74). Pro coach: Detroit Lions 1975-77, New England Patriots 1978-81, joined Rams in 1982.

Bruce Snyder, running backs-running game coordinator; born March 14, 1940, Santa Monica, Calif., lives in Anaheim, Calif. Fullback Oregon 1960-62. No pro playing experience. College coach: Oregon 1966-72, Utah State 1973, Southern California 1974-75, Utah State 1976-82 (head coach). Pro coach: Joined Rams in 1983.

Norval Turner, tight ends-U-backs; born May 17, 1952, Martinez, Calif., lives in Long Beach, Calif. Quarterback Oregon 1972-74. College coach: Oregon 1975, Southern California 1976-84. Pro coach: First year with Rams.

Fred Whittingham, outside linebackers; born February 4, 1939, Boston, Mass., lives in Anaheim, Calif. Linebacker Cal Poly-SLO 1960-62. Pro linebacker Los Angeles Rams 1964, Philadelphia Eagles 1965-66, 1971, New Orleans Saints 1967-68, Dallas Cowboys 1969-70. College coach: Brigham Young 1973-81. Pro coach: Joined Rams in 1982.

LOS ANGELES RAMS 1985 FIRST-YEAR ROSTER

Name	Pos.	Ht.	Wt.	Birth-date	College	Birthplace	Residence	How Acq.
Bradley, Danny	RB	5-9	178	3/2/63	Oklahoma	Pine Bluff, Ark.	Pine Bluff, Ark.	D7
Brock, Dieter (1)	QB	6-0	195	2/12/51	Jacksonville State	Gadsden, Ala.	Anaheim, Calif.	FA
Brown, Kevin	S	6-0	189	5/10/63	Northwestern	Anchorage, Alaska	Middletown, Pa.	FA
Fisher, Roderick (1)	CB	5-10	190	11/23/61	Oklahoma State	Dallas, Tex.	Dallas, Tex.	D12('84)
Gibson, Steve	DE	6-3	260	5/5/62	Cal Poly-SLO	National City, Calif.	San Luis Obispo, Calif.	FA
Gray, Jerry	CB	6-0	190	12/2/62	Texas	Lubbock, Tex.	Lubbock, Tex.	D1
Greene, Kevin	LB	6-3	238	7/31/62	Auburn	New York, N.Y.	Granite City, Ill.	D5
Hatcher, Dale	P	6-2	195	4/5/63	Clemson	Cheraw, S.C.	Cheraw, S.C.	D3
Johnson, Damone	TE	6-4	230	3/2/62	Cal Poly-SLO	Santa Monica, Calif.	Santa Monica, Calif.	D6a
Love, Duval	G	6-3	263	6/24/63	UCLA	Los Angeles, Calif.	Fountain Valley, Calif.	D10
McIntyre, Marlon	RB	5-11	230	8/28/62	Pittsburgh	Belle Vernon, Pa.	Pricedale, Pa.	D8
McQuaid, Dan (1)	T	6-7	255	10/4/60	Nevada-Las Vegas	Cortland, Calif.	Cortland, Calif.	FA
Scott, Chuck	WR	6-2	202	5/24/63	Vanderbilt	Jacksonville, Fla.	Maitland, Fla.	D2
Shiner, Mike	T	6-8	285	1/27/61	Notre Dame	Palo Alto, Calif.	Sunnyvale, Calif.	FA
Stephens, Hal (1)	T	6-4	252	4/14/61	East Carolina	Whiteville, N.C.	Whiteville, N.C.	D5('84)
Swanson, Gary	LB	6-1	236	8/17/61	Cal Poly-SLO	Big Creek, Calif.	Big Creek, Calif.	D9
Tinsley, Scott (1)	QB	6-2	195	11/14/59	Southern California	Oklahoma City, Okla.	Oklahoma City, Okla.	FA
Wise, Francois	TE	6-5	240	5/15/58	Long Beach State	San Francisco, Calif.	Long Beach, Calif.	FA
Young, Michael	WR	6-1	185	2/2/62	UCLA	Hanford, Calif.	Visalia, Calif.	D6

Players who report to an NFL team for the first time are designated on rosters as rookies (R). If a player reported to an NFL training camp in a previous year but was not on the active squad for three or more regular season or postseason games, he is listed on the first-year roster and designated by a (1). Thereafter, a player who is on the active squad for three or more regular season or postseason games is credited with an additional year of playing experience.

NOTES

MINNESOTA VIKINGS

**National Football Conference
Central Division**

Team Colors: Purple, Gold, and White

**9520 Viking Drive
Eden Prairie, Minnesota 55344
Telephone:** (612) 828-6500

Club Officials

Board of Directors: Max Winter, Mike Lynn,
   John Skoglund, Jack Steele, Sheldon Kaplan
President: Max Winter
Executive Vice President-General Manager:
   Mike Lynn
Assistant to the General Manager/
   Director of Operations: Jeff Diamond
Director of Administration: Harley Peterson
Ticket Manager: Harry Randolph
Director of Football Operations: Jerry Reichow
Director of Player Personnel: Frank Gilliam
Head Scout: Ralph Kohl
Assistant Head Scout: Don Deisch
Scout: John Carson
Director of Public Relations: Merrill Swanson
Director of Communications and Community
   Relations: Kernal Buhler
Public Relations Assistant: Katie Hogan
Trainer: Fred Zamberletti
Equipment Manager: Dennis Ryan

Stadium: Hubert H. Humphrey Metrodome •
   Capacity: 62,212
   500 11th Avenue, So.
   Minneapolis, Minnesota 55415

Playing Surface: SuperTurf

Training Camp: Mankato State University
   Mankato, Minnesota 56001

1985 SCHEDULE

Preseason
Aug. 10	at Miami	8:00
Aug. 17	**Pittsburgh**	7:00
Aug. 24	**Seattle**	7:00
Aug. 30	at Denver	7:00

Regular Season
Sept. 8	**San Francisco**	12:00
Sept. 15	at Tampa Bay	4:00
Sept. 19	**Chicago** (Thursday)	7:00
Sept. 29	at Buffalo	1:00
Oct. 6	at Los Angeles Rams	1:00
Oct. 13	vs. Green Bay at Milw.	12:00
Oct. 20	**San Diego**	12:00
Oct. 27	at Chicago	12:00
Nov. 3	**Detroit**	12:00
Nov. 10	**Green Bay**	12:00
Nov. 17	at Detroit	4:00
Nov. 24	**New Orleans**	12:00
Dec. 1	at Philadelphia	1:00
Dec. 8	**Tampa Bay**	3:00
Dec. 15	at Atlanta	1:00
Dec. 22	**Philadelphia**	12:00

VIKINGS COACHING HISTORY
(193-163-9)

1961-66	Norm Van Brocklin	29-51-4
1967-83	Bud Grant	161-99-5
1984	Les Steckel	3-13-0

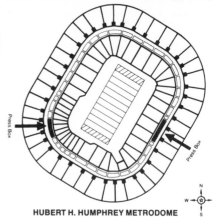

HUBERT H. HUMPHREY METRODOME

RECORD HOLDERS
Individual Records—Career
Category	Name	Performance
Rushing (Yds.)	Chuck Foreman, 1973-79	5,879
Passing (Yds.)	Fran Tarkenton, 1961-66, 1972-78	33,098
Passing (TDs)	Fran Tarkenton, 1961-66, 1972-78	239
Receiving (No.)	Ahmad Rashad, 1976-1982	400
Receiving (Yds.)	Sammy White, 1976-1984	5,925
Interceptions	Paul Krause, 1968-1979	53
Punting (Avg.)	Bobby Walden, 1964-67	42.9
Punt Return (Avg.)	Tommy Mason, 1961-66	10.5
Kickoff Return (Avg.)	Bob Reed, 1962-63	27.1
Field Goals	Fred Cox, 1963-1977	282
Touchdowns (Tot.)	Bill Brown, 1962-1974	76
Points	Fred Cox, 1963-1977	1,365

Individual Records—Single Season
Category	Name	Performance
Rushing (Yds.)	Chuck Foreman, 1976	1,155
Passing (Yds.)	Tommy Kramer, 1981	3,912
Passing (TDs)	Tommy Kramer, 1981	26
Receiving (No.)	Rickey Young, 1978	88
Receiving (Yds.)	Ahmad Rashad, 1979	1,156
Interceptions	Paul Krause, 1975	10
Punting (Avg.)	Bobby Walden, 1964	46.4
Punt Return (Avg.)	Billy Butler, 1963	10.5
Kickoff Return (Avg.)	John Gilliam, 1972	26.3
Field Goals	Fred Cox, 1970	30
Touchdowns (Tot.)	Chuck Foreman, 1975	22
Points	Chuck Foreman, 1975	132

Individual Records—Single Game
Category	Name	Performance
Rushing (Yds.)	Chuck Foreman, 10-24-76	200
Passing (Yds.)	Tommy Kramer, 12-14-80	456
Passing (TDs)	Joe Kapp, 9-28-69	7
Receiving (No.)	Rickey Young, 12-16-79	15
Receiving (Yds.)	Sammy White, 11-7-76	210
Interceptions	Many times	3
	Last time by Willie Teal, 11-28-82	
Field Goals	Fred Cox, 9-23-73	5
	Jan Stenerud, 9-23-84	5
Touchdowns (Tot.)	Chuck Foreman, 12-20-75	4
	Ahmad Rashad, 9-2-79	4
Points	Chuck Foreman, 12-20-75	24
	Ahmad Rashad, 9-2-79	24

1984 TEAM STATISTICS

	Minnesota	Opp.
Total First Downs	289	342
Rushing	111	144
Passing	150	182
Penalty	28	16
Third Down: Made/Att.	78/225	97/213
Fourth Down: Made/Att.	10/19	10/14
Total Net Yards	4716	6352
Avg. Per Game	294.8	397.0
Total Plays	1041	1062
Avg. Per Play	4.5	6.0
Net Yards Rushing	1844	2573
Avg. Per Game	115.3	160.8
Total Rushes	444	547
Net Yards Passing	2872	3779
Avg. Per Game	179.5	236.2
Tackled/Yards Lost	64/465	25/175
Gross Yards	3337	3954
Att./Completions	533/281	490/319
Completion Pct.	52.7	65.1
Had Intercepted	25	11
Punts/Avg.	82/42.4	68/40.8
Net Punting Avg.	36.6	35.6
Penalties/Yards Lost	90/762	113/1047
Fumbles/Ball Lost	39/16	35/18
Touchdowns	31	59
Rushing	10	20
Passing	18	35
Returns	3	4
Avg. Time of Possession	28:14	31:46

1984 TEAM RECORD
Preseason (1-3)

Date	Minnesota		Opponents
8/4	37	*Atlanta	6
8/11	7	*Miami	29
8/18	10	*Philadelphia	31
8/24	0	St. Louis	31
	54		97

Regular Season (3-13)

Date	Minnesota		Opp.	Att.
9/2	13	*San Diego	42	57,276
9/9	17	Philadelphia	19	55,942
9/16	27	*Atlanta	20	53,955
9/23	29	Detroit	28	57,511
9/30	12	*Seattle	20	57,171
10/7	31	Tampa Bay	35	47,405
10/14	20	Los Angeles Raiders	23	49,276
10/21	14	*Detroit	16	57,953
10/28	7	Chicago	16	57,517
11/4	27	*Tampa Bay	24	54,949
11/11	17	Green Bay	45	52,931
11/18	21	Denver	42	74,716
11/25	3	*Chicago	34	56,881
11/29	17	*Washington	31	55,017
12/8	7	San Francisco	51	56,670
12/16	14	*Green Bay	38	51,197
	276		484	896,367

*Home Game

Score by Periods

Minnesota	59	60	79	78	—	276
Opponents	137	146	109	92	—	484

Attendance
Home 444,399   Away 451,968   Total 896,367
Single game home record, 60,774 (10-2-83)
Single season home record, 464,902 (1983)

1984 INDIVIDUAL STATISTICS

Rushing

	Att.	Yds.	Avg.	LG	TD
Anderson	201	773	3.8	23	2
Brown	98	442	4.5	19	3
Dar. Nelson	80	406	5.1	39	3
Rice	14	58	4.1	16	1
Jones	4	45	11.3	36	0
Manning	11	42	3.8	16	0
Wilson	9	30	3.3	12	0
Waddy	3	24	8.0	11	0
Coleman	2	11	5.5	13	0
Lewis	2	11	5.5	6	0
Kramer	15	9	0.6	14	0
Jordan	1	4	4.0	4t	1
Dav. Nelson	1	3	3.0	3	0
Collins	3	-14	-4.7	1	0
Minnesota	444	1844	4.2	39	10
Opponents	547	2573	4.7	50	20

Passing

	Att.	Comp.	Pct.	Yds.	TD	Int.	Tkld.	Rate
Kramer	236	124	52.5	1678	9	10	24/145	70.6
Wilson	195	102	52.3	1019	5	11	20/159	52.5
Manning	94	52	55.3	545	2	3	18/153	66.1
Anderson	7	3	42.9	95	2	1	2/8	89.9
Coleman	1	0	0.0	0	0	0	0/0	39.6
Minnesota	533	281	52.7	3337	18	25	64/465	63.8
Opponents	490	319	65.1	3954	35	11	25/175	104.4

Receiving

	No.	Yds.	Avg.	LG	TD
Lewis	47	830	17.7	56	4
Brown	46	349	7.6	35	3
Jones	38	591	15.6	70t	1
Jordan	38	414	10.9	26	2
Dar. Nelson	27	162	6.0	17	1
White	21	399	19.0	47	1
Anderson	17	102	6.0	28t	1
Senser	15	110	7.3	26	0
Mularkey	14	134	9.6	26	2
Collins	11	143	13.0	43t	1
Rice	4	59	14.8	24	1
Kramer	1	20	20.0	20t	1
LeCount	1	14	14.0	14	0
Hasselbeck	1	10	10.0	10	0
Minnesota	281	3337	11.9	70t	18
Opponents	319	3954	12.4	68t	35

Interceptions

	No.	Yds.	Avg.	LG	TD
Bess	3	7	2.3	7	0
Swain	2	20	10.0	11	0
Teal	1	53	53.0	53t	1
Browner	1	20	20.0	20	0
Studwell	1	20	20.0	20	0
Hannon	1	0	0.0	0	0
Lee	1	0	0.0	0	0
McNeill	1	0	0.0	0	0
Minnesota	11	120	10.9	53t	1
Opponents	25	344	13.8	36t	2

Punting

	No.	Yds.	Avg.	In 20	LG
Coleman	82	3473	42.4	16	62
Minnesota	82	3473	42.4	16	62
Opponents	68	2777	40.8	17	61

Punt Returns

	No.	FC	Yds.	Avg.	LG	TD
Dar. Nelson	23	9	180	7.8	21	0
Lewis	4	1	31	7.8	13	0
Bess	2	0	9	4.5	7	0
Teal	1	0	0	0.0	0	0
Waddy	1	0	-3	-3.0	-3	0
Minnesota	31	10	217	7.0	21	0
Opponents	49	8	435	8.9	24	0

Kickoff Returns

	No.	Yds.	Avg.	LG	TD
Dar. Nelson	39	891	22.8	47	0
Anderson	30	639	21.3	41	0
Waddy	3	64	21.3	31	0
Bess	3	47	15.7	19	0
Rice	3	34	11.3	13	0
Smith	2	26	13.0	15	0
Rouse	2	22	11.0	15	0
Turner	2	21	10.5	14	0
Lewis	1	31	31.0	31	0
Dav. Nelson	1	0	0	0	0
Minnesota	86	1775	20.6	47	0
Opponents	59	1281	21.7	43	0

Scoring

	TD R	TD P	TD Rt	PAT	FG	Saf	TP
Stenerud	0	0	0	30/31	20/23	0	90
Brown	3	3	0	0/0	0/0	0	36
Lewis	0	4	0	0/0	0/0	0	24
Dar. Nelson	3	1	0	0/0	0/0	0	24
Anderson	2	1	0	0/0	0/0	0	18
Jordan	1	2	0	0/0	0/0	0	18
Mularkey	0	2	0	0/0	0/0	0	12
Rice	1	1	0	0/0	0/0	0	12
Browner	0	0	1	0/0	0/0	0	6
Collins	0	1	0	0/0	0/0	0	6
Jones	0	1	0	0/0	0/0	0	6
Kramer	0	1	0	0/0	0/0	0	6
C. Martin	0	0	1	0/0	0/0	0	6
Teal	0	0	1	0/0	0/0	0	6
White	0	1	0	0/0	0/0	0	6
Minnesota	10	18	3	30/31	20/23	0	276
Opponents	20	35	4	58/59	24/28	0	484

FIRST-ROUND SELECTIONS

(If Club had no first-round selection, first player drafted is listed with round in parentheses.)

Year	Player, College, Position
1961	Tommy Mason, Tulane, RB
1962	Bill Miller, Miami, WR (3)
1963	Jim Dunaway, Mississippi, T
1964	Carl Eller, Minnesota, DE
1965	Jack Snow, Notre Dame, WR
1966	Jerry Shay, Purdue, DT
1967	Clinton Jones, Michigan State, RB
	Gene Washington, Michigan State, WR
	Alan Page, Notre Dame, DT
1968	Ron Yary, Southern California, T
1969	Ed White, California, G (2)
1970	John Ward, Oklahoma State, DT
1971	Leo Hayden, Ohio State, RB
1972	Jeff Siemon, Stanford, LB
1973	Chuck Foreman, Miami, RB
1974	Fred McNeill, UCLA, LB
	Steve Riley, Southern California, T
1975	Mark Mullaney, Colorado State, DE
1976	James White, Oklahoma State, DT
1977	Tommy Kramer, Rice, QB
1978	Randy Holloway, Pittsburgh, DE
1979	Ted Brown, North Carolina State, RB
1980	Doug Martin, Washington, DT
1981	Mardye McDole, Mississippi State, WR (2)
1982	Darrin Nelson, Stanford, RB
1983	Joey Browner, Southern California, DB
1984	Keith Millard, Washington State, DE
1985	Chris Doleman, Pittsburgh, LB

MINNESOTA VIKINGS 1985 VETERAN ROSTER

No.	Name	Pos.	Ht.	Wt.	Birth-date	NFL Exp.	College	Birthplace	Residence	'84 Games/ Starts
46	Anderson, Alfred	RB	6-1	213	8/4/61	2	Baylor	Waco, Tex.	Waco, Tex.	16/14
69	Arbubakrr, Hasson	DE	6-4	250	12/9/60	3	Texas Tech	Newark, N.J.	Newark, N.J.	4/0
58	Ashley, Walker Lee	LB	6-0	240	7/28/60	3	Penn State	Bayonne, N.J.	Edina, Minn.	15/1
21	Bess, Rufus	CB	5-9	185	3/13/56	7	South Carolina State	Hartsville, S.C.	Hartsville, S.C.	16/13
59	Blair, Matt	LB	6-5	235	9/20/50	12	Iowa State	Honolulu, Hawaii	Prior Lake, Minn.	11/9
62	Boyd, Brent	G	6-3	275	3/23/57	5	UCLA	La Habra, Calif.	Leucadia, Calif.	0*
23	Brown, Ted	RB	5-10	210	2/2/57	7	North Carolina State	High Point, N.C.	Burnsville, Minn.	13/9
47	Browner, Joey	S	6-2	205	5/15/60	3	Southern California	Warren, Ohio	Burnsville, Minn.	16/8
82	Bruer, Bob	TE	6-5	240	5/22/54	6	Mankato State	Madison, Wis.	Edina, Minn.	0*
8	†Coleman, Greg	P	6-0	185	9/9/54	9	Florida A&M	Jacksonville, Fla.	Burnsville, Minn.	16/0
84	Collins, Dwight	WR	6-1	208	8/23/61	2	Pittsburgh	Rochester, N.Y.	Beaver Falls, Pa.	16/1
43	Colter, Jeff	CB	5-10	171	4/23/61	2	Kansas	Tucson, Ariz.	Tucson, Ariz.	16/0
73	†Elshire, Neil	DE	6-6	260	3/8/58	5	Oregon	Albany, Ore.	Lake Oswego, Ore.	12/10
64	Feasel, Grant	C-T	6-8	278	6/28/60	3	Abilene Christian	Barstow, Calif.	Rowlett, Tex.	15/3*
50	Fowlkes, Dennis	LB	6-2	230	3/11/61	3	West Virginia	Columbus, Ohio	Columbus, Ohio	14/0
25	Greene, Marcellus	CB	6-0	184	12/12/57	2	Arizona	Indianapolis, Ind.	Indianapolis, Ind.	14/0
90	Haines, John	NT	6-6	260	12/16/61	2	Texas	Fort Worth, Tex.	Fort Worth, Tex.	8/0
61	Hamilton, Wes	G	6-3	270	4/24/53	10	Tulsa	Texas City, Tex.	Burnsville, Minn.	4/1
45	Hannon, Tom	S	5-11	195	3/5/55	9	Michigan State	Massillon, Ohio	Eden Prairie, Minn.	16/16
60	Hernandez, Matt	T	6-6	262	10/16/61	3	Purdue	Detroit, Mich.	Wheaton, Ill.	13/0
51	Hough, Jim	G	6-2	275	8/4/56	8	Utah State	Lynwood, Calif.	Jordan, Minn.	9/3
76	Irwin, Tim	T	6-6	285	12/13/58	5	Tennessee	Memphis, Tenn.	Knoxville, Tenn.	16/16
65	Johnson, Charlie	NT	6-3	275	2/17/52	9	Colorado	West Columbia, Tex.	West Berlin, N.J.	16/15
52	Johnson, Dennis	LB	6-3	235	6/19/58	6	Southern California	Flint, Mich.	Torrance, Calif.	16/15
89	Jones, Mike	WR	5-11	176	4/14/60	3	Tennessee State	Chattanooga, Tenn.	Apple Valley, Minn.	16/14
83	Jordan, Steve	TE	6-3	230	1/10/61	4	Brown	Phoenix, Ariz.	Eagan, Minn.	14/14
9	Kramer, Tommy	QB	6-2	205	3/7/55	9	Rice	San Antonio, Tex.	Bloomington, Minn.	9/9
39	Lee, Carl	CB-S	5-11	185	4/6/61	3	Marshall	South Charleston, W. Va.	South Charleston, W. Va.	16/14
87	†Lewis, Leo	WR	5-8	170	9/17/56	5	Missouri	Columbia, Mo.	Knoxville, Tenn.	16/5
4	Manning, Archie	QB	6-3	211	5/9/49	15	Mississippi	Drew, Miss.	New Orleans, La.	6/2
56	†Martin, Chris	LB	6-2	230	12/19/60	3	Auburn	Huntsville, Ala.	New Orleans, La.	16/1
79	Martin, Doug	DE	6-3	255	5/22/57	6	Washington	Greenville, S.C.	Kirkland, Wash.	13/6
54	McNeill, Fred	LB	6-2	230	5/6/52	12	UCLA	Durham, Calif.	Edina, Minn.	13/13
86	Mularkey, Mike	TE	6-4	245	11/19/61	3	Florida	Miami, Fla.	Bloomington, Minn.	16/2
77	Mullaney, Mark	DE	6-6	245	4/30/53	11	Colorado State	Denver, Colo.	Denver, Colo.	7/6
20	†Nelson, Darrin	RB	5-9	180	1/2/59	4	Stanford	Sacramento, Calif.	Burnsville, Minn.	15/8
49	Nord, Keith	S	6-0	195	3/13/57	6	St. Cloud State	Minneapolis, Minn.	Minnetonka, Minn.	0*
36	Rice, Allen	RB-S	5-10	198	4/5/62	2	Baylor	Houston, Tex.	Houston, Tex.	14/0
78	†Riley, Steve	T	6-6	260	11/23/52	12	Southern California	Chula Vista, Calif.	Tustin, Calif.	16/16
68	†Rouse, Curtis	G	6-3	305	7/13/60	4	Tenn.-Chattanooga	Augusta, Ga.	Augusta, Ga.	16/15
67	†Sams, Ron	G	6-3	255	4/12/61	2	Pittsburgh	Bridgeville, Pa.	McDonald, Pa.	12/10
57	Sendlein, Robin	LB	6-3	225	12/1/58	5	Texas	Las Vegas, Nev.	Minnetonka, Minn.	15/8
81	†Senser, Joe	TE	6-4	235	8/18/56	6	West Chester State	Philadelphia, Pa.	Burnsville, Minn.	8/1
91	Smith, Gregory	NT	6-3	261	10/22/59	2	Kansas	Chicago, Ill.	Lena, Miss.	16/6
3	Stenerud, Jan	K	6-2	190	11/26/42	19	Montana State	Fetsund, Norway	Overland Park, Kan.	16/0
55	Studwell, Scott	LB	6-2	230	8/27/54	9	Illinois	Evansville, Ind.	Bloomington, Minn.	16/15
29	Swain, John	CB	6-1	195	9/4/59	5	Miami	Miami, Fla.	Burnsville, Minn.	15/10
66	Tausch, Terry	T	6-5	275	2/5/59	4	Texas	New Braunfels, Tex.	Plano, Tex.	16/16
37	Teal, Willie	CB	5-10	195	12/20/57	6	Louisiana State	Texarkana, Tex.	Baton Rouge, La.	11/4
24	Turner, Maurice	RB	5-11	199	9/10/60	2	Utah State	Salt Lake City, Utah	Layton, Utah	13/0
34	Wagoner, Dan	S	5-10	180	12/12/59	3	Kansas	High Point, N.C.	Lake Orion, Mich.	5/0*
85	White, Sammy	WR	5-11	195	3/16/54	10	Grambling	Winnsboro, La.	Monroe, La.	13/11
11	Wilson, Wade	QB	6-3	210	2/1/59	5	East Texas State	Greenville, Tex.	Dallas, Tex.	8/5

* Boyd, Bruer, and Nord missed '84 season due to injury; Feasel played 6 games with Indianapolis, 9 with Minnesota in '84; Wagoner played 1 game with Detroit, 4 with Minnesota in '84.

†Option playout; subject to developments.

Also played with Vikings in '84—G Malcolm Carson (1 game), DE Robert Cobb (2), QB Steve Dils (3), G Bill Dugan (1), TE Don Hasselbeck (16), DE Randy Holloway (8), WR Terry LeCount (2), RB David Nelson (2), LB Mark Stewart (4), NT Paul Sverchek (3), NT Rubin Vaughan (5), WR Billy Waddy (4).

COACHING STAFF

Head Coach, Bud Grant

Pro Career: Returns from one season as a consultant for eighteenth season as Vikings head coach. Has guided Minnesota to the playoffs 12 times and won 15 championships: 11 Central Division (1968-71, 1973-78, 1980), one NFL (1969), and three NFC (1973, 1974, and 1976). The Vikings, under Grant, played in four Super Bowls (IV, VIII, IX, XI). Head coach at Winnipeg of the Canadian Football League for 10 years before joining the Vikings in 1967. Grant's Winnipeg teams won six Western Conference championships and four Grey Cup championships. Played for the Philadelphia Eagles 1951-52 and ranked as the number-two receiver in NFL in 1952. Played 1953-56 with Winnipeg before being named head coach in 1957. NFL record: 161-99-5.

Background: Attended University of Minnesota and was two-time all-Big Ten end. Won four letters in football, two in basketball (forward), and three in baseball (pitcher-outfielder). Played football and basketball at Great Lakes in 1945, first year out of high school. Played 1950-51 with Minneapolis Lakers of the National Basketball Association. Canadian coach of the year in 1965; named Minnesota athlete of the half-century in 1951.

Personal: Born Harry P. Grant on May 20, 1927, Superior, Wis. Bud and his wife, Pat, live in Bloomington, Minn., and have six children—Kathleen, Laurie, Peter, Michael, Bruce, and Dan.

Assistant Coaches

Tom Batta, defensive assistant; born October 6, 1942, Youngstown, Ohio., lives in Bloomington, Minn. Offensive-defensive lineman Kent State 1961-63. No pro playing experience. College coach: Akron 1973, Colorado 1974-78, Kansas 1979-82, North Carolina State 1983. Pro coach: Joined Vikings in 1984.

Jerry Burns, assistant head coach-offensive coordinator; born January 24, 1927, Detroit, Mich., lives in Eden Prairie, Minn. Quarterback Michigan 1947-50. No pro playing experience. College coach: Hawaii 1951, Whittier 1952, Iowa 1954-65 (head coach 1961-65). Pro coach: Green Bay Packers 1966-67, joined Vikings in 1968.

Pete Carroll, defensive backs; born September 15, 1951, San Francisco, Calif., lives in Minneapolis, Minn. Defensive back Pacific 1969-72. No pro playing experience. College coach: Arkansas 1977, Iowa State 1978, Ohio State 1979, North Carolina State 1980-82, Pacific 1983. Pro coach: Buffalo Bills 1984, first year with Vikings.

Bob Hollway, defensive coordinator; born January 29, 1926, Ann Arbor, Mich., lives in Edina, Minn. End Michigan 1947-49. No pro playing experience. College coach: Maine 1951-52, Eastern Michigan 1953, Michigan 1954-66. Pro coach: Minnesota Vikings 1967-70, St. Louis Cardinals 1971-72 (head coach), Detroit Lions 1973-74, San Francisco 49ers 1975, Seattle Seahawks 1976-77, rejoined Vikings in 1978.

John Michels, offensive line; born February 15, 1931, Philadelphia, Pa., lives in Bloomington, Minn. Guard Tennessee 1949-52. Pro guard Philadelphia Eagles 1953, 1956, Winnipeg Blue Bombers (CFL) 1957. College coach: Texas A&M 1958. Pro coach: Winnipeg Blue Bombers (CFL) 1959-66, joined Vikings in 1967.

Floyd Reese, linebackers; born August 8, 1948, Springfield, Mo., lives in Bloomington, Minn. Defensive tackle UCLA 1967-69. No pro playing experience. College coach: UCLA 1970-73, Georgia Tech 1974. Pro coach: Detroit Lions 1975-77, San Francisco 49ers 1978, joined Vikings in 1979.

Dick Rehbein, kicking teams-tight ends; born November 22, 1955, Green Bay, Wis., lives in Edina, Minn. Center Ripon 1973-77. No pro playing experience. Pro coach: Green Bay Packers 1979-83, Los Angeles Express (USFL) 1984, joined Vikings in 1984.

MINNESOTA VIKINGS 1985 FIRST-YEAR ROSTER

Name	Pos.	Ht.	Wt.	Birth-date	College	Birthplace	Residence	How Acq.
Blair, Nikita	LB	6-2	224	11/19/62	Texas-El Paso	Dallas, Tex.	El Paso, Tex.	D8
Bono, Steve	QB	6-3	211	5/11/62	UCLA	Norristown, Pa.	Los Angeles, Calif.	D6
Borman, Dave	P	5-11	200	8/25/60	Northwest Missouri	Sioux Falls, Iowa	Algona, Iowa	FA
Brown, Melvin A. (1)	CB	5-11	187	10/25/58	Mississippi	Biloxi, Miss.	Biloxi, Miss.	D10('83)
Brown, Melvin L. (1)	WR	6-4	198	11/29/59	Alabama	Miami, Fla.	Florence, Ala.	FA
Covington, Jaime	RB	6-0	218	12/12/62	Syracuse	Flushing, N.Y.	Syracuse, N.Y.	D9
Doleman, Chris	LB	6-5	250	10/16/61	Pittsburgh	Indianapolis, Ind.	Pittsburgh, Pa.	D1
Gustafson, Jim (1)	WR	6-1	185	3/16/61	St. Thomas	Minneapolis, Minn.	St. Paul, Minn.	FA
Hechinger, Rick	G	6-5	255	6/19/62	Memphis State	Hampton, Va.	Minneapolis, Minn.	FA
Holt, Issiac	CB	6-1	197	10/4/62	Alcorn State	Birmingham, Ala.	Birmingham, Ala.	D2
Johnson, Juan	WR	5-11	185	2/21/62	Langston	Okmulgee, Okla.	Okmulgee, Okla.	D10
Jones, Byron	NT	6-3	276	7/5/62	Tulsa	Perth Amboy, N.J.	Altadena, Calif.	D12
Kidd, Keith (1)	WR	6-1	198	9/10/62	Arkansas	Crossette, Ark.	Fayetteville, Ark.	D9('84)
Lewis, David	RB	5-10	205	12/12/61	Northern Iowa	Minneapolis, Minn.	Minneapolis, Minn.	FA
Long, Tim	T	6-5	305	4/20/63	Memphis State	Cleveland, Tenn.	Memphis, Tenn.	D3b
Lowdermilk, Kirk	C	6-3	265	4/10/63	Ohio State	Canton, Ohio	Columbus, Ohio	D3
MacDonald, Mark	G	6-4	267	4/30/61	Boston College	West Roxbury, Mass.	West Roxbury, Mass.	D5
Meamber, Tim	LB	6-3	228	10/29/62	Washington	Yreka, Calif.	Redding, Calif.	D3a
Morrell, Kyle	S	6-1	189	10/9/63	Brigham Young	Scottsdale, Ariz.	Bountiful, Utah	D4a
Newton, Tim	NT	6-0	302	3/23/63	Florida	Orlando, Fla.	Gainesville, Fla.	D6a
Renn, Matt	C	6-1	267	4/30/63	Wis.-River Falls	Appleton, Wis.	Appleton, Wis.	FA
Rhymes, Buster	WR	6-1	212	1/27/62	Oklahoma	Miami, Fla.	Miami, Fla.	D4
Roanagle, Ted	CB-S	6-3	202	9/29/61	Portland State	Pasadena, Calif.	Aloha, Ore.	FA
Rush, Mark (1)	RB	6-2	230	3/31/59	Miami	Ft. Lauderdale, Fla.	Miami, Fla.	FA
Smith, Robert (1)	DE	6-5	245	12/3/62	Grambling	Bogalusa, La.	Bogalusa, La.	SD('84)
Spencer, James (1)	LB	6-2	236	11/22/61	Oklahoma State	Dallas, Tex.	Stillwater, Okla.	D10('84)
Williams, Tim	CB-S	6-1	200	2/21/63	North Carolina A&T	Greensboro, N.C.	Greensboro, N.C.	D11

Players who report to an NFL team for the first time are designated on rosters as rookies (R). If a player reported to an NFL training camp in a previous year but was not on the active squad for three or more regular season or postseason games, he is listed on the first-year roster and designated by a (1). Thereafter, a player who is on the active squad for three or more regular season or postseason games is credited with an additional year of playing experience.

NOTES

_____
_____
_____
_____
_____
_____
_____
_____
_____
_____
_____
_____
_____
_____
_____
_____
_____

Marc Trestman, running backs; born January 15, 1956, Minneapolis, Minn., lives in Minneapolis. Quarterback Minnesota 1976-78. No pro playing experience. College coach: Miami 1981-84. Pro coach: First year with Vikings.

Paul Wiggin, defensive line; born November 18, 1934, Modesto, Calif., lives in Eden Prairie, Minn. Offensive-defensive tackle Stanford 1953-57. Pro defensive end Cleveland Browns 1957-67. College coach: Stanford (head coach) 1980-83. Pro coach: San Francisco 49ers 1968-74, Kansas City Chiefs 1975-77 (head coach), New Orleans Saints 1978-80, first year with Vikings.

NEW ORLEANS SAINTS

**National Football Conference
Western Division**

Team Colors: Old Gold, Black, and White

**1500 Poydras Street
New Orleans, Louisiana 70112
Telephone: (504) 522-1500**

Club Officials

Managing General Partner: Tom Benson, Jr.
President: Eddie Jones
Head Coach-General Manager:
  O.A. (Bum) Phillips
Director of Football Operations: Pat Peppler
Director of Administration: Bruce Broussard
Director of Public Relations: Greg Suit
Assistant Director of Public Relations:
  Rusty Kasmiersky
Public Relations Assistant: Sylvia Alfortish
Ticket Manager: Sandy King
Marketing Director: Barra Birrcher
Administrative Assistant: Jack Cherry
Trainer: Dean Kleinschmidt
Equipment Manager: Dan Simmons

Stadium: Louisiana Superdome •
   Capacity: 71,647
   1500 Poydras Street
   New Orleans, Louisiana 70112

Playing Surface: AstroTurf

Training Camp: Louisiana Tech University
       Ruston, Louisiana 71272

1985 SCHEDULE

Preseason

Aug. 10	at New England	3:30
Aug. 17	**Houston**	7:00
Aug. 24	**Tampa Bay**	7:00
Aug. 30	at San Diego	7:00

Regular Season

Sept. 8	**Kansas City**	12:00
Sept. 15	at Denver	2:00
Sept. 22	**Tampa Bay**	12:00
Sept. 29	at San Francisco	1:00
Oct. 6	**Philadelphia**	12:00
Oct. 13	at Los Angeles Raiders	1:00
Oct. 20	at Atlanta	1:00
Oct. 27	**New York Giants**	3:00
Nov. 3	at Los Angeles Rams	1:00
Nov. 10	**Seattle**	12:00
Nov. 17	vs. Green Bay at Milw.	12:00
Nov. 24	at Minnesota	12:00
Dec. 1	**Los Angeles Rams**	12:00
Dec. 8	at St. Louis	12:00
Dec. 15	**San Francisco**	12:00
Dec. 22	**Atlanta**	12:00

SAINTS COACHING HISTORY

(78-176-5)

1967-70	Tom Fears*	13-34-2
1970-72	J.D. Roberts	7-25-3
1973-75	John North**	11-23-0
1975	Ernie Hefferle	1-7-0
1976-77	Hank Stram	7-21-0
1978-80	Dick Nolan***	15-29-0
1980	Dick Stanfel	1-3-0
1981-84	O.A. (Bum) Phillips	23-34-0

  *Released after seven games in 1970
  **Released after six games in 1975
  ***Released after 12 games in 1980

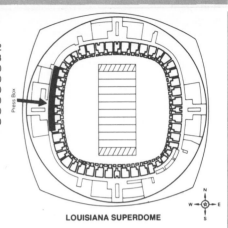

LOUISIANA SUPERDOME

RECORD HOLDERS

Individual Records—Career

Category	Name	Performance
Rushing (Yds.)	George Rogers, 1981-84	4,267
Passing (Yds.)	Archie Manning, 1971-1982	21,734
Passing (TDs)	Archie Manning, 1971-1982	115
Receiving (No.)	Dan Abramowicz, 1967-1973	309
Receiving (Yds.)	Dan Abramowicz, 1967-1973	4,875
Interceptions	Tommy Myers, 1972-1982	36
Punting (Avg.)	Tom McNeill, 1967-69	42.3
Punt Return (Avg.)	Gil Chapman, 1975	12.2
Kickoff Return (Avg.)	Walt Roberts, 1967	26.3
Field Goals	Charlie Durkee, 1967-68, 1971-72	52
Touchdowns (Tot.)	Dan Abramowicz, 1967-1973	37
Points	Charlie Durkee, 1967-68, 1971-72	243

Individual Records—Single Season

Category	Name	Performance
Rushing (Yds.)	George Rogers, 1981	1,674
Passing (Yds.)	Archie Manning, 1980	3,716
Passing (TDs)	Archie Manning, 1980	23
Receiving (No.)	Tony Galbreath, 1978	74
Receiving (Yds.)	Wes Chandler, 1979	1,069
Interceptions	Dave Whitsell, 1967	10
Punting (Avg.)	Brian Hansen, 1984	43.8
Punt Return (Avg.)	Gil Chapman, 1975	12.2
Kickoff Return (Avg.)	Don Shy, 1969	27.9
Field Goals	Tom Dempsey, 1969	22
Touchdowns (Tot.)	George Rogers, 1981	13
Points	Tom Dempsey, 1969	99

Individual Records—Single Game

Category	Name	Performance
Rushing (Yds.)	George Rogers, 9-4-83	206
Passing (Yds.)	Archie Manning, 12-7-80	377
Passing (TDs)	Billy Kilmer, 11-2-69	6
Receiving (No.)	Tony Galbreath, 9-10-78	14
Receiving (Yds.)	Wes Chandler, 9-2-79	205
Interceptions	Tommy Myers, 9-3-78	3
Field Goals	Garo Yepremian, 10-14-79	6
Touchdowns (Tot.)	Many times	3
	Last time by Wayne Wilson, 1-2-83	
Points	Many times	18
	Last time by Wayne Wilson, 1-2-83	

1984 TEAM STATISTICS

	New Orleans	Opp.
Total First Downs	298	298
Rushing	131	134
Passing	137	142
Penalty	30	22
Third Down: Made/Att.	89/224	83/220
Fourth Down: Made/Att.	8/22	8/11
Total Net Yards	5008	4914
Avg. Per Game	313.0	307.1
Total Plays	1044	1026
Avg. Per Play	4.8	4.8
Net Yards Rushing	2171	2461
Avg. Per Game	135.7	153.8
Total Rushes	523	549
Net Yards Passing	2837	2453
Avg. Per Game	177.3	153.3
Tackled/Yards Lost	45/361	55/420
Gross Yards	3198	2873
Att./Completions	476/246	422/239
Completion Pct.	51.7	56.6
Had Intercepted	28	13
Punts/Avg.	70/43.1	84/41.6
Net Punting Avg.	33.3	36.0
Penalties/Yards Lost	101/849	119/1025
Fumbles/Ball Lost	22/13	28/10
Touchdowns	34	41
Rushing	9	13
Passing	21	23
Returns	4	5
Avg. Time of Possession	30:13	29:47

1984 TEAM RECORD
Preseason (3-1)

Date	New Orleans		Opponents
8/4	34	Kansas City	20
8/11	31	*Atlanta	21
8/18	31	Houston	19
8/25	9	*Washington	14
	105		74

Regular Season (7-9)

Date	New Orleans		Opp.	Att.
9/2	28	*Atlanta	36	66,652
9/9	17	*Tampa Bay	13	54,686
9/16	20	San Francisco	30	57,611
9/23	34	*St. Louis	24	58,723
9/30	27	Houston	10	43,108
10/7	7	Chicago	20	53,752
10/14	10	*Los Angeles Rams	28	63,161
10/21	27	Dallas (OT)	30	51,161
10/28	16	Cleveland	14	52,489
11/4	13	*Green Bay	23	57,426
11/11	17	Atlanta	13	40,590
11/19	27	*Pittsburgh	24	66,005
11/25	3	*San Francisco	35	65,177
12/2	21	Los Angeles Rams	34	49,348
12/9	21	*Cincinnati	24	40,855
12/15	10	New York Giants	3	63,739
	298		361	884,483

*Home Game   (OT) Overtime

Score by Periods

New Orleans	61	101	37	99	0	—	298
Opponents	42	129	78	109	3	—	361

Attendance

Home 472,685   Away 411,798   Total 884,483
Single game home record, 76,490 (11-4-79)
Single season home record, 557,530 (1979)

1984 INDIVIDUAL STATISTICS

Rushing

	Att.	Yds.	Avg.	LG	TD
G. Rogers	239	914	3.8	28	2
Gajan	102	615	6.0	62t	5
Campbell, Hou.-N.O.	146	468	3.2	22	4
Campbell, N.O.	50	190	3.8	19	0
W. Wilson	74	261	3.5	36	1
Todd	28	111	4.0	15	0
Anthony	20	105	5.3	19	1
T. Wilson	2	8	4.0	5	0
Goodlow	1	5	5.0	5	0
Stabler	1	-1	-1.0	-1	0
Duckett	1	-3	-3.0	-3	0
D. Wilson	3	-7	-2.3	-2	0
Hansen	2	-27	-13.5	-12	0
New Orleans	523	2171	4.2	62t	9
Opponents	549	2461	4.5	66	13

Passing

	Att.	Comp.	Pct.	Yds.	TD	Int.	Tkld.	Rate
Todd	312	161	51.6	2178	11	19	33/267	60.6
D. Wilson	93	51	54.8	647	7	4	7/54	83.9
Stabler	70	33	47.1	339	2	5	5/40	41.3
Gajan	1	1	100.0	34	1	0	0/0	158.3
New Orleans	476	246	51.7	3198	21	28	45/361	63.3
Opponents	422	239	56.6	2873	23	13	55/420	83.0

Receiving

	No.	Yds.	Avg.	LG	TD
Gajan	35	288	8.2	51	2
Groth	33	487	14.8	31	0
W. Wilson	33	314	9.5	34t	3
Young	29	597	20.6	74	3
Brenner	28	554	19.8	57	6
Goodlow	22	281	12.8	23	3
Scott	21	278	13.2	37	1
Anthony	12	113	9.4	32	0
G. Rogers	12	76	6.3	15	0
Miller	8	81	10.1	22	1
Tice	6	55	9.2	17	1
Hardy	4	50	12.5	28t	1
Campbell, Hou-N.O.	3	27	9.0	15	0
Duckett	3	24	8.0	11	0
New Orleans	246	3198	13.0	74	21
Opponents	239	2873	12.0	50t	23

Interceptions

	No.	Yds.	Avg.	LG	TD
Waymer	4	9	2.3	9	0
Winston	2	90	45.0	47t	2
Wattelet	2	52	26.0	35t	1
Kovach	1	16	16.0	16	0
Poe	1	16	16.0	16	0
Jackson	1	14	14.0	14	0
B. Clark	1	9	9.0	9	0
Johnson	1	7	7.0	7	0
New Orleans	13	213	16.4	47t	3
Opponents	28	420	15.0	60	3

Punting

	No.	Yds.	Avg.	In 20	LG
Hansen	69	3020	43.8	9	66
New Orleans	70	3020	43.1	9	66
Opponents	84	3492	41.6	30	87

Punt Returns

	No.	FC	Yds.	Avg.	LG	TD
Fields	27	6	236	8.7	61	0
Groth	6	12	32	5.3	9	0
New Orleans	33	18	268	8.1	61	0
Opponents	47	5	550	11.7	76t	1

Kickoff Returns

	No.	Yds.	Avg.	LG	TD
Anthony	22	490	22.3	64	0
Duckett	29	580	20.0	39	0
Fields	19	356	18.7	31	0
W. Wilson	1	23	23.0	23	0
T. Wilson	1	16	16.0	16	0
New Orleans	72	1465	20.3	64	0
Opponents	45	916	20.4	35	0

Scoring

	TD R	TD P	TD Rt	PAT	FG	Saf	TP
Andersen	0	0	0	34/34	20/27	0	94
Gajan	5	2	0	0/0	0/0	0	42
Brenner	0	6	0	0/0	0/0	0	36
Campbell, Hou.-N.O.	4	0	0	0/0	0/0	0	24
W. Wilson	1	3	0	0/0	0/0	0	24
Goodlow	0	3	0	0/0	0/0	0	18
Young	0	3	0	0/0	0/0	0	18
G. Rogers	2	0	0	0/0	0/0	0	12
Wattelet	0	0	2	0/0	0/0	0	12
Winston	0	0	2	0/0	0/0	0	12
Anthony	1	0	0	0/0	0/0	0	6
Hardy	0	1	0	0/0	0/0	0	6
Miller	0	1	0	0/0	0/0	0	6
Scott	0	1	0	0/0	0/0	0	6
Tice	0	1	0	0/0	0/0	0	6
New Orleans	9	21	4	34/34	20/27	0	298
Opponents	13	23	5	41/41	24/33	1	361

FIRST-ROUND SELECTIONS

(If Club had no first-round selection, first player drafted is listed with round in parentheses.)

Year	Player, College, Position
1967	Les Kelley, Alabama, RB
1968	Kevin Hardy, Notre Dame, DE
1969	John Shinners, Xavier, G
1970	Ken Burrough, Texas Southern, WR
1971	Archie Manning, Mississippi, QB
1972	Royce Smith, Georgia, G
1973	Derland Moore, Oklahoma, DE (2)
1974	Rick Middleton, Ohio State, LB
1975	Larry Burton, Purdue, WR
	Kurt Schumacher, Ohio State, T
1976	Chuck Muncie, California, RB
1977	Joe Campbell, Maryland, DE
1978	Wes Chandler, Florida, WR
1979	Russell Erxleben, Texas, P-K
1980	Stan Brock, Colorado, T
1981	George Rogers, South Carolina, RB
1982	Lindsay Scott, Georgia, WR
1983	Steve Korte, Arkansas, G (2)
1984	James Geathers, Wichita State, DE
1985	Alvin Toles, Tennessee, LB

111

NEW ORLEANS SAINTS 1985 VETERAN ROSTER

No.	Name	Pos.	Ht.	Wt.	Birth-date	NFL Exp.	College	Birthplace	Residence	'84 Games/Starts
7	Andersen, Morten	K	6-2	205	8/19/60	4	Michigan State	Struer, Denmark	Harahan, La.	16/0
22	Anthony, Tyrone	RB	5-11	212	3/3/62	2	North Carolina	Winston-Salem, N.C.	Pfafftown, N.C.	15/0
85	Brenner, Hoby	TE	6-4	245	6/2/59	5	Southern California	Lynwood, Calif.	San Clemente, Calif.	16/16
67	†Brock, Stan	T	6-6	288	6/8/58	6	Colorado	Portland, Ore.	Mandeville, La.	14/14
35	Campbell, Earl	RB	5-11	233	3/29/55	8	Texas	Tyler, Tex.	Houston, Tex.	14/14*
65	†Carter, David	C	6-2	275	11/27/53	9	Western Kentucky	Vincennes, Ind.	Sugar Land, Tex.	14/0*
75	Clark, Bruce	DE	6-3	281	3/31/58	4	Penn State	New Castle, Pa.	Kenner, La.	15/15
68	Clark, Kelvin	G	6-3	273	1/30/56	7	Nebraska	Odessa, Tex.	Mandeville, La.	16/15
83	Duckett, Kenny	WR	6-0	179	10/1/59	4	Wake Forest	Winston-Salem, N.C.	Kenner, La.	11/0
63	Edelman, Brad	G	6-6	262	9/3/60	4	Missouri	Jacksonville, Fla.	Kenner, La.	11/11
99	Elliott, Tony	NT	6-2	280	4/23/59	4	North Texas State	New York, N.Y.	New Orleans, La.	4/3
26	Fields, Jitter	CB	5-8	188	8/16/62	2	Texas	Dallas, Tex.	Metairie, La.	13/0
46	Gajan, Hokie	FB	5-11	226	9/6/59	4	Louisiana State	Baton Rouge, La.	Mandeville, La.	14/14
20	Gary, Russell	S	5-11	196	7/31/59	5	Nebraska	Minneapolis, Minn.	New Orleans, La.	16/16
97	Geathers, James	DE	6-7	267	6/26/60	2	Wichita State	Georgetown, S.C.	Kenner, La.	16/0
88	Goodlow, Eugene	WR	6-2	181	12/19/58	3	Kansas State	St. Louis, Mo.	Miami, Fla.	10/6
86	Groth, Jeff	WR	5-10	181	7/2/57	7	Bowling Green	Mankato, Minn.	Destrehan, La.	16/13
10	Hansen, Brian	P	6-3	218	10/26/60	2	Sioux Falls	Hawarden, Iowa	Hawarden, Iowa	16/0
28	Harding, Greg	S	6-2	197	7/31/60	2	Nicholls State	New Orleans, La.	Houma, La.	3/0
87	†Hardy, Larry	TE	6-3	246	7/9/56	8	Jackson State	Mendenhall, Miss.	Jackson, Miss.	6/0
92	Haynes, James	LB	6-2	227	8/9/60	2	Mississippi Valley State	Tallulah, La.	Itta Bena, Miss.	10/0
61	Hilgenberg, Joel	C-G	6-3	253	7/10/62	2	Iowa	Iowa City, Iowa	Iowa City, Iowa	10/0
24	Hoage, Terry	S	6-3	199	4/11/62	2	Georgia	Ames, Iowa	Huntsville, Tex.	14/0
57	Jackson, Rickey	LB	6-2	239	3/20/58	5	Pittsburgh	Pahokee, Fla.	Kenner, La.	16/16
34	Johnson, Bobby	CB-S	6-0	187	9/1/60	3	Texas	La Grange, Tex.	Kenner, La.	16/0
60	Korte, Steve	C	6-2	271	1/15/60	3	Arkansas	Denver, Colo.	Mandeville, La.	15/15
52	Kovach, Jim	LB	6-2	239	5/1/56	7	Kentucky	Parma Heights, Ohio	Metairie, La.	15/15
64	Lafary, Dave	T	6-7	285	1/13/55	8	Purdue	Cincinnati, Ohio	Mandeville, La.	1/1
93	Lewis, Gary	NT	6-3	261	1/14/61	2	Oklahoma State	Oklahoma City, Okla.	Harahan, La.	0*
98	Lewis, Reggie	DE	6-2	251	1/20/54	4	San Diego State	New Orleans, La.	New Orleans, La.	13/0
29	†Lewis, Rodney	CB	5-11	186	4/2/59	3	Nebraska	Minneapolis, Minn.	Harahan, La.	16/0
19	†Merkens, Guido	QB-WR	6-1	197	8/14/55	8	Sam Houston State	San Antonio, Tex.	Kenner, La.	16/0
84	†Miller, Junior	TE	6-4	244	11/26/57	6	Nebraska	Midland, Tex.	Kenner, La.	15/0
74	Moore, Derland	NT	6-4	273	10/7/51	13	Oklahoma	Poplar Bluff, Mo.	Covington, La.	12/11
66	Oubre, Louis	G	6-4	272	5/15/58	4	Oklahoma	New Orleans, La.	Kenner, La.	12/5
51	Paul, Whitney	LB	6-3	218	10/8/55	10	Colorado	Galveston, Tex.	New Orleans, La.	16/16
53	Pelluer, Scott	LB	6-2	227	4/28/59	5	Washington State	Yakima, Wash.	Kenner, La.	16/0
25	†Poe, Johnnie	CB	6-1	194	8/29/59	5	Missouri	St. Louis, Mo.	Metairie, La.	16/16
58	†Redd, Glen	LB	6-1	231	6/17/58	4	Brigham Young	Ogden, Utah	Ogden, Utah	16/1
41	†Rogers, Jimmy	RB	5-10	195	6/29/55	6	Oklahoma	Earle, Ark.	Norman, Okla.	16/0
80	Scott, Lindsay	WR	6-1	200	12/6/60	4	Georgia	Jesup, Ga.	Kenner, La.	16/5
96	Thorp, Don	NT	6-4	260	7/10/62	2	Illinois	Chicago, Ill.	Champaign, Ill.	5/0
82	Tice, John	TE	6-5	243	6/22/60	3	Maryland	Bayshore, N.Y.	Kenner, La.	10/0
11	†Todd, Richard	QB	6-2	212	11/19/53	10	Alabama	Birmingham, Ala.	Sheffield, Ala.	15/14
72	Ward, Chris	T	6-3	269	12/16/55	8	Ohio State	Cleveland, Ohio	Kenner, La.	13/8
73	Warren, Frank	DE	6-4	278	9/14/59	5	Auburn	Birmingham, Ala.	Kenner, La.	16/3
49	†Wattelet, Frank	S	6-0	185	10/25/58	5	Kansas	Paola, Kan.	Kenner, La.	16/16
44	Waymer, Dave	CB	6-1	188	7/1/58	6	Notre Dame	Brooklyn, N.Y.	Los Angeles, Calif.	16/16
94	Wilks, Jim	DE	6-5	265	3/12/58	5	San Diego State	Los Angeles, Calif.	Altadena, Calif.	16/16
18	Wilson, Dave	QB	6-3	211	4/27/59	4	Illinois	Anaheim, Calif.	Anaheim, Calif.	5/2
45	†Wilson, Tim	FB	6-3	237	1/14/55	9	Maryland	New Castle, Del.	Richmond, Tex.	12/0
30	Wilson, Wayne	RB	6-3	220	9/4/57	7	Shepherd	Montgomery County, Md.	Columbia, Md.	14/2
56	Winston, Dennis	LB	6-0	244	10/25/55	9	Arkansas	Marianna, Ark.	Fayetteville, Ark.	16/16
89	†Young, Tyrone	WR	6-6	192	4/29/60	3	Florida	Ocala, Fla.	Kenner, La.	16/8

* Campbell played 6 games with Houston, 8 with New Orleans in '84; Carter played 7 games with Houston, 7 with New Orleans; G. Lewis last active with New Orleans in '83.

†Option playout; subject to developments.

Traded—Running back George Rogers to Washington.

Also played with Saints in '84—C John Hill (11 games), C Jim Pietrzak (10), QB Ken Stabler (3).

COACHING STAFF

Head Coach,
O. A. (Bum) Phillips

Pro Career: Starts eleventh season in the NFL and fifth with the Saints after signing with New Orleans as head coach on January 22, 1981. He had a career 59-38 record with the Oilers and twice played the AFC bridesmaid role with championship game losses to the Steelers in 1978 and 1979. Joined the Oilers on January 25, 1975, as head coach and general manager after serving as an assistant coach with the San Diego Chargers 1967-71 and as defensive coordinator with Oilers in 1974 prior to being named head coach. Career record: 82-72.

Background: Guard at Lamar Junior College 1941, 1946-47, Stephen F. Austin 1948-49. College assistant coach at Texas A&M 1957, Houston 1963-66, Southern Methodist 1971-72, and Oklahoma State 1973. Head coach at Texas-El Paso 1962.

Personal: Born September 29, 1923, in Orange, Tex. Bum and his wife, Helen, live in Destrehan, La., and have six children—Wade, Susan, Cicely, Dee Jean, Andrea, and Kim Ann.

Assistant Coaches

Andy Everest, tight ends; born October 27, 1924, Wichita Falls, Tex., lives in Destrehan, La. Guard Texas-El Paso 1947-50. No pro playing experience. College coach: Foot Hills College 1963-64, UC-Santa Barbara 1965-71, Southern Methodist 1972, North Texas State 1973-76. Pro coach: Joined Saints in 1981.

Mark Hatley, defensive backfield; born September 19, 1949, Bolger, Tex., lives in Destrehan, La. Linebacker Oklahoma State 1968-72. No pro playing experience. College coach: Oklahoma State 1973-76, Texas Christian 1977-82, Baylor 1983. Pro coach: First year with Saints (scout in '84).

King Hill, offensive coordinator; born November 8, 1936, Freeport, Tex., lives in Destrehan, La. Quarterback Rice 1954-58. Pro quarterback St. Louis Cardinals 1958-60, 1969, Philadelphia Eagles 1961-67, Minnesota Vikings 1968. Pro coach: Houston Oilers 1972-80, joined Saints in 1981.

John Levra, offensive backfield; born October 2, 1937, Arma, Kan., lives in Destrehan, La. Guard-linebacker Pittsburgh (Kan.) State 1963-65. No pro playing experience. College coach: Stephen F. Austin 1971-74, Kansas 1975-78, North Texas State 1979. Pro coach: British Columbia Lions (CFL) 1980, joined Saints in 1981.

Carl Mauck, offensive line; born July 7, 1947, McLeansboro, Ill., lives in New Orleans. Center Southern Illinois 1965-68. Pro center San Diego Chargers 1969-74, Houston Oilers 1975-80. Pro coach: Joined Saints in 1982.

Russell Paternostro, strength and conditioning; born July 21, 1940, New Orleans, lives in Jefferson, La. San Diego State. No college or pro playing experience. Pro coach: Joined Saints in 1981.

Wade Phillips, defensive coordinator; born June 21, 1947, Orange, Tex., lives in Destrehan, La. Linebacker Houston 1966-69. No pro playing experience. College coach: Oklahoma State 1973-75. Pro coach: Houston Oilers 1976-80, joined Saints in 1981.

Harold Richardson, receivers; born September 27, 1944, Houston, Tex., lives in Destrehan, La. Tight end Southern Methodist 1964-67. No pro playing experience. College coach: Southern Methodist 1971-72, Oklahoma State 1973-76, Texas Christian 1977-78, North Texas State 1979-80. Pro coach: Joined Saints in 1981.

Joe Spencer, quality control; born August 15, 1923, Cleveland County, Okla., lives in Destrehan, La. Tackle Oklahoma State 1942-47. Pro tackle Brooklyn Dodgers (AAFC) 1948, Cleveland Browns (AAFC) 1949, Green Bay Packers 1950-52. College coach: Austin, Tex., College 1952-60, Kansas 1972-73. Pro coach: Houston Oilers 1961-65, Edmonton Eskimos (CFL) 1966-67, New York Jets 1968-70, St. Louis Cardinals 1971, Chicago Fire (WFL) 1974, Kansas City Chiefs 1975-80, joined Saints in 1981.

John Paul Young, linebackers; born December 31, 1939, Dallas, Tex., lives in Destrehan, La. Linebacker Texas-El Paso 1959-61. No pro playing experience. College coach: Texas-El Paso 1962-63, Southern Methodist 1967-68, Oklahoma State 1969, Texas A&M 1970-77. Pro coach: Houston Oilers 1978-80, joined Saints in 1981.

Willie Zapalac, defensive line; born December 11, 1922, Sealy, Tex., lives in Destrehan, La. Fullback Texas A&M 1941-42, 1946. No pro playing experience. College coach: Texas A&M 1953-60, Texas Tech 1961-62, Oklahoma State 1963, Texas 1964-75. Pro coach: St. Louis Cardinals 1976-77, Buffalo Bills 1978-80, joined Saints in 1981.

NEW ORLEANS SAINTS 1985 FIRST-YEAR ROSTER

Name	Pos.	Ht.	Wt.	Birth-date	College	Birthplace	Residence	How Acq.
Allen, Billy	CB-S	5-11	210	9/25/58	Florida State	Cleveland, Ohio	Tallahassee, Fla.	D4
Dellocono, Michael	WR	5-9	176	6/25/61	Louisiana Tech	Baton Rouge, La.	Kenner, La.	FA
Del Rio, Jack	LB	6-4	235	4/4/63	Southern California	Castro Valley, Calif.	Castro Valley, Calif.	D3
Fowler, Bobby	TE	6-2	230	9/11/60	Louisiana Tech	Temple, Tex.	Angleton, Tex.	FA
Gilbert, Daren	T	6-6	285	10/3/63	Cal State-Fullerton	Compton, Calif.	Los Angeles, Calif.	D2
Johnson, Earl	CB	6-0	190	10/20/63	South Carolina	Daytona Beach, Fla.	Columbia, S.C.	D9
Kohlbrand, Joe	DE	6-4	242	3/18/63	Miami	Merritt Island, Fla.	Miami, Fla.	D8
Martin, Eric	WR	6-1	195	11/8/61	Louisiana State	Van Vleck, Tex.	Baton Rouge, La.	D7
Peters, Ken	TE	6-4	245	9/30/60	Houston	Dallas, Tex.	Houston, Tex.	FA
Songy, Treg	CB-S	6-1	195	6/15/63	Tulane	New Orleans, La.	New Orleans, La.	D12
Toles, Alvin	LB	6-1	211	3/23/63	Tennessee	Forsyth, Ga.	Knoxville, Tenn.	D1
Worsham, David	QB	6-3	207	4/15/59	Arkansas Tech	Corpus Christi, Tex.	San Antonio, Tex.	FA

Players who report to an NFL team for the first time are designated on rosters as rookies (R). If a player reported to an NFL training camp in a previous year but was not on the active squad for three or more regular season or postseason games, he is listed on the first-year roster and designated by a (1). Thereafter, a player who is on the active squad for three or more regular season or postseason games is credited with an additional year of playing experience.

NOTES

_____
_____
_____
_____
_____
_____
_____
_____
_____
_____
_____
_____
_____
_____
_____
_____
_____
_____
_____
_____
_____
_____

NEW YORK GIANTS

**National Football Conference
Eastern Division**

Team Colors: Blue, Red, and White

**Giants Stadium
East Rutherford, New Jersey 07073
Telephone:** (201) 935-8111

Club Officials

President: Wellington T. Mara
Vice President-Treasurer: Timothy J. Mara
Vice President-Secretary: Raymond J. Walsh
Vice President-General Manager: George Young
Assistant General Manager: Harry Hulmes
Controller: John Pasquali
Director of Player Personnel: Tom Boisture
Director of Pro Personnel: Tim Rooney
Director of Media Services: Ed Croke
Director of Promotions: Tom Power
Director of Special Projects: Victor Del Guercio
Box Office Treasurer: Jim Gleason
Trainer Emeritus: John Dziegiel
Head Trainer: Ronnie Barnes
Assistant Trainers: Dave Barringer, John Johnson
Equipment Manager: Ed Wagner, Jr.

Stadium: Giants Stadium • **Capacity:** 76,891
East Rutherford, N.J. 07073

Playing Surface: AstroTurf

Training Camp: Pace University
Pleasantville, New York 10570

1985 SCHEDULE

Preseason
Aug. 3	Houston at Canton, Ohio	2:30
Aug. 10	at Denver	7:00
Aug. 17	**Green Bay**	8:00
Aug. 24	**New York Jets**	8:00
Aug. 30	at Pittsburgh	7:30

Regular Season
Sept. 8	**Philadelphia**	1:00
Sept. 15	at Green Bay	3:00
Sept. 22	**St. Louis**	1:00
Sept. 29	at Philadelphia	1:00
Oct. 6	**Dallas**	9:00
Oct. 13	at Cincinnati	1:00
Oct. 20	**Washington**	1:00
Oct. 27	at New Orleans	3:00
Nov. 3	**Tampa Bay**	1:00
Nov. 10	**Los Angeles Rams**	1:00
Nov. 18	at Washington (Monday)	9:00
Nov. 24	at St. Louis	3:00
Dec. 1	**Cleveland**	1:00
Dec. 8	at Houston	3:00
Dec. 15	at Dallas	12:00
Dec. 21	**Pittsburgh** (Saturday)	12:30

GIANTS COACHING HISTORY
(409-358-32)
1925	Bob Folwell	8-4-0
1926	Joe Alexander	8-4-1
1927-28	Earl Potteiger	15-8-3
1929-30	LeRoy Andrews	26-5-1
1931-53	Steve Owen	154-108-17
1954-60	Jim Lee Howell	54-29-4
1961-68	Allie Sherman	57-54-4
1969-73	Alex Webster	29-40-1
1974-76	Bill Arnsparger*	7-28-0
1976-78	John McVay	14-23-0
1979-82	Ray Perkins	24-35-0
1983-84	Bill Parcells	13-20-1

*Released after seven games in 1976

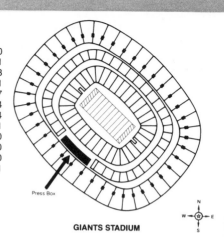

Press Box

GIANTS STADIUM

RECORD HOLDERS
Individual Records — Career
Category	Name	Performance
Rushing (Yds.)	Alex Webster, 1955-1964	4,638
Passing (Yds.)	Charlie Conerly, 1948-1961	19,488
Passing (TDs)	Charlie Conerly, 1948-1961	173
Receiving (No.)	Joe Morrison, 1959-1972	395
Receiving (Yds.)	Frank Gifford, 1952-1960, 1962-64	5,434
Interceptions	Emlen Tunnell, 1948-1958	74
Punting (Avg.)	Don Chandler, 1956-1964	43.8
Punt Return (Avg.)	Bob Hammond, 1976-78	9.1
Kickoff Return (Avg.)	Rocky Thompson, 1971-72	27.2
Field Goals	Pete Gogolak, 1966-1974	126
Touchdowns (Tot.)	Frank Gifford, 1952-1960, 1962-64	78
Points	Pete Gogolak, 1966-1974	646

Individual Records — Single Season
Category	Name	Performance
Rushing (Yds.)	Ron Johnson, 1972	1,182
Passing (Yds.)	Phil Simms, 1984	4,044
Passing (TDs)	Y.A. Tittle, 1963	36
Receiving (No.)	Earnest Gray, 1983	78
Receiving (Yds.)	Homer Jones, 1967	1,209
Interceptions	Otto Schnellbacher, 1951	11
	Jim Patton, 1958	11
Punting (Avg.)	Don Chandler, 1959	46.6
Punt Return (Avg.)	Merle Hapes, 1942	15.5
Kickoff Return (Avg.)	John Salscheider, 1949	31.6
Field Goals	Ali Haji-Sheikh, 1983	35
Touchdowns (Tot.)	Gene Roberts, 1949	17
Points	Ali Haji-Sheikh, 1983	127

Individual Records — Single Game
Category	Name	Performance
Rushing (Yds.)	Gene Roberts, 11-12-50	218
Passing (Yds.)	Y.A. Tittle, 10-28-62	505
Passing (TDs)	Y.A. Tittle, 10-28-62	7
Receiving (No.)	Many times	11
	Last time by Gary Shirk, 9-20-81	
Receiving (Yds.)	Del Shofner, 10-28-62	269
Interceptions	Many times	3
	Last time by Carl Lockhart, 12-4-66	
Field Goals	Joe Danelo, 10-18-81	6
Touchdowns (Tot.)	Ron Johnson, 10-2-72	4
	Earnest Gray, 9-7-80	4
Points	Ron Johnson, 10-2-72	24
	Earnest Gray, 9-7-80	24

1984 TEAM STATISTICS

	N.Y. Giants	Opp.
Total First Downs	310	296
Rushing	97	107
Passing	198	174
Penalty	15	15
Third Down: Made/Att.	85/232	84/224
Fourth Down: Made/Att.	3/11	4/9
Total Net Yards	5292	5193
Avg. Per Game	330.8	324.6
Total Plays	1083	1051
Avg. Per Play	4.9	4.9
Net Yards Rushing	1660	1818
Avg. Per Game	103.8	113.6
Total Rushes	493	474
Net Yards Passing	3632	3375
Avg. Per Game	227.0	210.9
Tackled/Yards Lost	55/434	48/361
Gross Yards	4066	3736
Att./Completions	535/288	529/288
Completion Pct.	53.8	54.4
Had Intercepted	18	19
Punts/Avg.	94/38.3	92/40.0
Net Punting Avg.	31.1	34.7
Penalties/Yards Lost	79/703	93/699
Fumbles/Ball Lost	17/9	24/16
Touchdowns	36	35
Rushing	12	10
Passing	22	20
Returns	2	5
Avg. Time of Possession	30:44	29:16

1984 TEAM RECORD
Preseason (3-1)

Date	New York Giants		Opponents
8/3	48	New England	20
8/11	20	Indianapolis	26
8/18	20	*New York Jets	14
8/25	16	*Pittsburgh	9
	104		69

Regular Season (9-7)

Date	New York Giants		Opp.	Att.
9/2	28	*Philadelphia	27	71,520
9/9	28	*Dallas	7	75,921
9/16	14	Washington	30	52,997
9/23	17	*Tampa Bay	14	72,650
9/30	12	Los Angeles Rams	33	53,417
10/8	10	*San Francisco	31	76,112
10/14	19	Atlanta	7	50,268
10/21	10	Philadelphia	24	64,677
10/28	37	*Washington	13	76,192
11/4	19	Dallas	7	60,235
11/11	17	Tampa Bay	20	46,534
11/18	16	*St. Louis	10	73,428
11/25	28	*Kansas City	27	74,383
12/2	20	New York Jets	10	74,975
12/9	21	St. Louis	31	49,973
12/15	3	*New Orleans	10	63,739
	299		301	1,037,021

*Home Game

Score by Periods

New York Giants	73	77	78	71	—	299
Opponents	45	90	71	95	—	301

Attendance
Home 583,945   Away 453,076   Total 1,037,021
Single game home record, 76,490 (11-4-79)
Single season home record, 583,945 (1984)

1984 INDIVIDUAL STATISTICS

Rushing

	Att.	Yds.	Avg.	LG	TD
Carpenter	250	795	3.2	22	7
Morris	133	510	3.8	28	4
Simms	42	162	3.9	21	0
Galbreath	22	97	4.4	11	0
Woolfolk	40	92	2.3	17	1
Cephous	3	2	0.7	2	0
Manuel	3	2	0.7	11	0
N.Y. Giants	493	1660	3.4	28	12
Opponents	474	1818	3.8	36	10

Passing

	Att.	Comp.	Pct.	Yds.	TD	Int.	Tkld.	Rate
Simms	533	286	53.7	4044	22	18	55/434	78.1
Galbreath	1	1	100.0	13	0	0	0/0	118.8
Rutledge	1	1	100.0	9	0	0	0/0	104.2
N.Y. Giants	535	288	53.8	4066	22	18	55/434	78.3
Opponents	529	288	54.4	3736	20	19	48/361	74.5

Receiving

	No.	Yds.	Avg.	LG	TD
Johnson	48	795	16.6	45	7
Mowatt	48	698	14.5	34	6
Gray	38	529	13.9	31	2
Galbreath	37	357	9.6	37	0
Manuel	33	619	18.8	53	4
Carpenter	26	209	8.0	19	1
B. Williams	24	471	19.6	65t	2
Morris	12	124	10.3	26	0
Woolfolk	9	53	5.9	13	0
McConkey	8	154	19.3	39	0
Mullady	2	35	17.5	22	0
Simms	1	13	13.0	13	0
Mistler	1	5	5.0	5	0
Belcher	1	4	4.0	4	0
N.Y. Giants	288	4066	14.1	65t	22
Opponents	288	3736	13.0	83t	20

Interceptions

	No.	Yds.	Avg.	LG	TD
Haynes	7	90	12.9	22	0
P. Williams	3	7	2.3	7	0
Kinard	2	29	14.5	29	0
Reasons	2	26	13.0	26	0
Hunt	1	14	14.0	14	0
Currier	1	7	7.0	7	0
Carson	1	6	6.0	6	0
Headen	1	4	4.0	4	0
Taylor	1	−1	−1.0	−1	0
N.Y. Giants	19	182	9.6	29	0
Opponents	18	222	12.3	36t	1

Punting

	No.	Yds.	Avg.	In 20	LG
Jennings	90	3598	40.0	22	54
Haji-Sheikh	0	0	—	0	0
N.Y. Giants	94	3598	38.3	22	54
Opponents	92	3677	40.0	22	69

Punt Returns

	No.	FC	Yds.	Avg.	LG	TD
McConkey	46	15	306	6.7	31	0
Manuel	8	3	62	7.8	22	0
Kinard	1	0	0	0.0	0	0
N.Y. Giants	55	18	368	6.7	31	0
Opponents	50	13	479	9.6	83t	2

Kickoff Returns

	No.	Yds.	Avg.	LG	TD
McConkey	28	541	19.3	33	0
Woolfolk	14	232	16.6	27	0
Cephous	9	178	19.8	30	0
Morris	6	69	11.5	14	0
McLaughlin	2	18	9.0	11	0
Daniel	1	52	52.0	52	0
Hill	1	27	27.0	27	0
N.Y. Giants	61	1117	18.3	52	0
Opponents	55	1088	19.8	56	0

Scoring

	TD R	TD P	TD Rt	PAT	FG	Saf	TP
Haji-Sheikh	0	0	0	32/35	17/33	0	83
Carpenter	7	1	0	0/0	0/0	0	48
Johnson	0	7	0	0/0	0/0	0	42
Mowatt	0	6	0	0/0	0/0	0	36
Manuel	0	4	0	0/0	0/0	0	24
Morris	4	0	0	0/0	0/0	0	24
Gray	0	2	0	0/0	0/0	0	12
B. Williams	0	2	0	0/0	0/0	0	12
Headen	0	0	1	0/0	0/0	0	6
McConkey	0	0	1	0/0	0/0	0	6
Woolfolk	1	0	0	0/0	0/0	0	6
N.Y. Giants	12	22	2	32/36	17/33	0	299
Opponents	10	20	5	34/35	17/26	3	301

FIRST-ROUND SELECTIONS

(If Club had no first-round selection, first player drafted is listed with round in parentheses.)

Year	Player, College, Position
1936	Art Lewis, Ohio U., T
1937	Ed Widseth, Minnesota, T
1938	George Karamatic, Gonzaga, B
1939	Walt Neilson, Arizona, B
1940	Grenville Lansdell, Southern California, B
1941	George Franck, Minnesota, B
1942	Merle Hapes, Mississippi, B
1943	Steve Filipowicz, Fordham, B
1944	Billy Hillenbrand, Indiana, B
1945	Elmer Barbour, Wake Forest, B
1946	George Connor, Notre Dame, T
1947	Vic Schwall, Northwestern, B
1948	Tony Minisi, Pennsylvania, B
1949	Paul Page, Southern Methodist, B
1950	Travis Tidwell, Auburn, B
1951	Kyle Rote, Southern Methodist, B
	Jim Spavital, Oklahoma A&M, B
1952	Frank Gifford, Southern California, B
1953	Bobby Marlow, Alabama, B
1954	Ken Buck, Pacific, C (2)
1955	Joe Heap, Notre Dame, B
1956	Henry Moore, Arkansas, B (2)
1957	Sam DeLuca, South Carolina, T (2)
1958	Phil King, Vanderbilt, B
1959	Lee Grosscup, Utah, B
1960	Lou Cordileone, Clemson, G
1961	Bruce Tarbox, Syracuse, G (2)
1962	Jerry Hillebrand, Colorado, LB
1963	Frank Lasky, Florida, T (2)
1964	Joe Don Looney, Oklahoma, RB
1965	Tucker Frederickson, Auburn, RB
1966	Francis Peay, Missouri, T
1967	Louis Thompson, Alabama, DT (4)
1968	Dick Buzin, Penn State, T (2)
1969	Fred Dryer, San Diego State, DE
1970	Jim Files, Oklahoma, LB
1971	Rocky Thompson, West Texas State, WR
1972	Eldridge Small, Texas A&I, DB
	Larry Jacobson, Nebraska, DE
1973	Brad Van Pelt, Michigan State, LB (2)
1974	John Hicks, Ohio State, G
1975	Al Simpson, Colorado State, T (2)
1976	Troy Archer, Colorado, DE
1977	Gary Jeter, Southern California, DT
1978	Gordon King, Stanford, T
1979	Phil Simms, Morehead State, QB
1980	Mark Haynes, Colorado, DB
1981	Lawrence Taylor, North Carolina, LB
1982	Butch Woolfolk, Michigan, RB
1983	Terry Kinard, Clemson, DB
1984	Carl Banks, Michigan State, LB
	Bill Roberts, Ohio State, T
1985	George Adams, Kentucky, RB

NEW YORK GIANTS 1985 VETERAN ROSTER

No.	Name	Pos.	Ht.	Wt.	Birth-date	NFL Exp.	College	Birthplace	Residence	'84 Games/Starts
67	Ard, Bill	G	6-3	270	3/12/59	5	Wake Forest	East Orange, N.J.	Westfield, N.J.	15/15
58	Banks, Carl	LB	6-4	235	8/29/62	2	Michigan State	Flint, Mich.	Flint, Mich.	16/4
73	Belcher, Kevin	G	6-3	276	2/23/61	3	Texas-El Paso	Detroit, Mich.	Montclair, N.J.	16/16
60	Benson, Brad	T	6-3	270	11/25/55	8	Penn State	Altoona, Pa.	Tuxedo, N.Y.	16/16
64	Burt, Jim	NT	6-1	260	6/7/59	5	Miami	Buffalo, N.Y.	Waldwick, N.J.	16/15
26	Carpenter, Rob	RB	6-1	226	4/20/55	9	Miami, Ohio	Lancaster, Ohio	Missouri City, Tex.	16/16
53	Carson, Harry	LB	6-2	240	11/26/53	10	South Carolina State	Florence, S.C.	Wash. Township, N.J.	16/16
31	Cephous, Frank	RB	5-10	205	7/4/61	2	UCLA	Philadelphia, Pa.	Newark, Del.	16/0
29	Currier, Bill	S	6-0	196	1/5/55	9	South Carolina	Richmond, Va.	Missouri City, Tex.	9/8
24	Daniel, Kenny	CB	5-10	180	6/1/60	2	San Jose State	Oakland, Calif.	Richmond, Calif.	15/1
37	Flowers, Larry	S	6-1	195	4/19/58	5	Texas Tech	Temple, Tex.	Temple, Tex.	16/0
30	Galbreath, Tony	RB	6-0	228	1/29/54	10	Missouri	Fulton, Mo.	Jefferson City, Mo.	16/0
61	Godfrey, Chris	G	6-3	265	5/17/58	3	Michigan	Detroit, Mich.	Berkeley Heights, N.J.	10/8
62	Goode, Conrad	T	6-6	285	1/19/62	2	Missouri	St. Louis, Mo.	St. Louis, Mo.	8/0
83	†Gray, Earnest	WR	6-3	191	3/2/57	7	Memphis State	Greenwood, Miss.	Memphis, Tenn.	12/11
6	Haji-Sheikh, Ali	K	6-0	170	1/11/61	3	Michigan	Ann Arbor, Mich.	Paramus, N.J.	16/0
79	Hardison, Dee	DE	6-4	274	5/2/56	8	North Carolina	Jacksonville, N.C.	Fayetteville, N.C.	15/5
	Hasselbeck, Don	TE	6-7	245	4/1/55	9	Colorado	Cincinnati, Ohio	Norfolk, Mass.	16/0*
36	†Haynes, Mark	CB	5-11	195	11/6/58	6	Colorado	Kansas City, Kan.	Woodridge, N.J.	15/15
54	Headen, Andy	LB	6-5	242	7/8/60	3	Clemson	Asheboro, N.C.	Liberty, N.C.	11/6
48	Hill, Kenny	S	6-0	195	7/25/58	5	Yale	Oak Grove, La.	Daly City, Calif.	12/7
15	Hostetler, Jeff	QB	6-3	212	4/22/61	2	West Virginia	Hollsopple, Pa.	Hollsopple, Pa.	0*
57	Hunt, Byron	LB	6-5	242	12/17/58	5	Southern Methodist	Longview, Tex.	Dallas, Tex.	13/6
13	Jennings, Dave	P	6-4	200	6/8/52	12	St. Lawrence	New York, N.Y.	Upper Saddle River, N.J.	16/0
88	Johnson, Bob	WR	5-11	171	12/14/61	2	Kansas	Shelbyville, Tenn.	Belleville, Ill.	16/16
51	Jones, Robbie	LB	6-2	230	12/25/59	2	Alabama	Demopolis, Ala.	Demopolis, Ala.	16/0
69	Jordan, David	G	6-6	276	7/14/62	2	Auburn	Birmingham, Ala.	Birmingham, Ala.	14/1
43	Kinard, Terry	S	6-1	200	11/24/59	3	Clemson	Bitburg, Germany	Sumter, S.C.	15/15
72	King, Gordon	T	6-6	275	2/3/56	7	Stanford	Madison, Wis.	Park Ridge, N.J.	0*
86	Manuel, Lionel	WR	5-11	175	4/13/62	2	Pacific	Cucamonga, Calif.	Cucamonga, Calif.	16/5
70	Marshall, Leonard	DE	6-3	285	10/22/61	3	Louisiana State	Franklin, La.	Jersey City, N.J.	16/11
75	Martin, George	DE	6-4	255	2/16/53	11	Oregon	Greenville, S.C.	Vacaville, Calif.	16/2
80	McConkey, Phil	WR	5-10	170	2/24/57	2	Navy	Buffalo, N.Y.	Pensacola Beach, Fla.	13/0
45	McDaniel, LeCharls	CB	5-9	169	10/15/58	5	Cal Poly-SLO	Ft. Bragg, N.C.	Lake Hiawatha, N.J.	0*
76	McGriff, Curtis	DE	6-5	276	5/17/58	6	Alabama	Donaldsville, Ga.	Gordon, Ala.	16/14
52	†McLaughlin, Joe	LB	6-1	235	7/1/57	7	Massachusetts	Springfield, Mass.	Stoneham, Mass.	16/5
71	Merrill, Casey	DE	6-4	260	7/16/57	7	Cal-Davis	Oakland, Calif.	Palm Desert, Calif.	16/0
20	Morris, Joe	RB	5-7	195	9/15/60	4	Syracuse	Ft. Bragg, N.C.	Wash. Township, N.J.	16/8
84	Mowatt, Zeke	TE	6-3	240	3/5/61	3	Florida State	Wauchula, Fla.	Tallahassee, Fla.	16/16
81	Mullady, Tom	TE	6-3	235	1/30/57	7	Rhodes College	Dayton, Ohio	Park Ridge, N.J.	16/0
63	Nelson, Karl	T	6-6	285	6/14/60	2	Iowa State	DeKalb, Ill.	DeKalb, Ill.	16/16
34	Patterson, Elvis	CB	5-11	188	10/21/60	2	Kansas	Bryan, Tex.	Houston, Tex.	15/0
55	Reasons, Gary	LB	6-4	234	2/18/62	2	N.W. Louisiana State	Crowley, Tex.	Crowley, Tex.	16/11
66	Roberts, Bill	T	6-5	280	8/5/62	2	Ohio State	Miami, Fla.	Miami, Fla.	11/8
17	Rutledge, Jeff	QB	6-1	195	1/22/57	7	Alabama	Birmingham, Ala.	Mission Viejo, Calif.	16/0
78	Sally, Jerome	NT	6-3	270	2/24/59	4	Missouri	Chicago, Ill.	Columbia, Mo.	16/1
11	†Simms, Phil	QB	6-3	214	11/3/56	7	Morehead State	Louisville, Ky.	Wyckoff, N.J.	16/16
56	Taylor, Lawrence	LB	6-3	243	2/4/59	5	North Carolina	Williamsburg, Va.	Upper Saddle River, N.J.	16/16
38	Tuggle, John	RB	6-1	210	1/31/61	2	California	Honolulu, Hawaii	San Jose, Calif.	0*
59	Umphrey, Rich	C	6-3	270	12/13/58	4	Colorado	Garden Grove, Calif.	Santa Ana, Calif.	15/0
87	Williams, Byron	WR	6-2	183	10/31/60	3	Texas-Arlington	Texarkana, Tex.	Duncanville, Tex.	16/0
23	Williams, Perry	CB	6-2	203	5/12/61	2	North Carolina State	Hamlet, N.C.	Hamlet, N.C.	16/16

* Hasselbeck played 16 games with Minnesota in '84; Hostetler active for 16 games but did not play; King and Tuggle missed '84 season due to injuries; McDaniel active for 2 games but did not play.

†Option playout; subject to developments.

Traded—Running back Butch Woolfolk to Houston.

Also played with Giants in '84—WR John Mistler (3 games), S Pete Shaw (16).

COACHING STAFF

Head Coach, Bill Parcells

Pro Career: Became twelfth head coach in New York Giants history on December 15, 1982. Parcells begins third campaign as head coach after spending two seasons as the Giants' defensive coordinator and linebacker coach. Started pro coaching career in 1980 as linebacker coach with New England. Career record: 13-20-1

Background: Linebacker at Wichita State 1961-63. College assistant Hastings (Neb.) 1964, Wichita State 1965, Army 1966-69, Florida State 1970-72, Vanderbilt 1973-74, Texas Tech 1975-77, Air Force 1978 (head coach).

Personal: Born August 22, 1941, Englewood, N.J. Bill and his wife, Judy, live in Upper Saddle River, N.J., and have three daughters—Suzy, Jill, and Dallas.

Assistant Coaches

Bill Belichick, defensive coordinator; born April 16, 1952, Nashville, Tenn., lives in East Rutherford, N.J. Center-tight end Wesleyan 1972-74. No pro playing experience. Pro coach: Baltimore Colts 1975, Detroit Lions 1976-77, Denver Broncos 1978, joined Giants in 1979.

Romeo Crennel, special teams; born June 18, 1947, Lynchburg, Va., lives in East Rutherford, N.J. Defensive lineman Western Kentucky 1966-69. No pro playing experience. College coach: Western Kentucky 1970-74, Texas Tech 1975-77, Mississippi 1978-79, Georgia Tech 1980. Pro coach: Joined Giants in 1981.

Ron Erhardt, offensive coordinator; born February 27, 1932, Mandan, N.D., lives in East Rutherford, N.J. Quarterback Jamestown (N.D.) College 1951-54. No pro playing experience. College coach: North Dakota State 1963-72 (head coach 1966-72). Pro coach: New England Patriots 1973-81 (head coach 1979-81), joined Giants in 1982.

Len Fontes, defensive backfield; born March 8, 1938, New Bedford, Mass., lives in East Rutherford, N.J. Defensive back Ohio State 1958-59. No pro playing experience. College coach: Eastern Michigan 1968, Dayton 1969-72, Navy 1973-76, Miami 1977-79. Pro coach: Cleveland Browns 1980-82, joined Giants in 1983.

Ray Handley, running backs; born October 8, 1944, Artesia, N.M., lives in East Rutherford, N.J. Running back Stanford 1963-65. No pro playing experience. College coach: Stanford 1967, 1971-74, 1979-83, Army 1968-69, Air Force 1975-78. Pro coach: Joined Giants in 1984.

Fred Hoaglin, offensive line; born January 28, 1944, Alliance, Ohio, lives in Sparta, N.J. Center Pittsburgh 1962-65. Pro center Cleveland Browns 1966-72, Baltimore Colts 1973, Houston Oilers 1974-75, Seattle Seahawks 1976. Pro coach: Detroit Lions 1978-84, first year with Giants.

Pat Hodgson, receivers; born January 30, 1944, Columbus, Ga., lives in East Rutherford, N.J. Tight end Georgia 1963-65. Pro tight end Washington Redskins 1966, Minnesota Vikings 1967. College coach: Georgia 1968-70, 1972-77, Florida State 1971, Texas Tech 1978. Pro coach: San Diego Chargers 1978, joined Giants in 1979.

Lamar Leachman, defensive line; born August 7, 1934, Cartersville, Ga., lives in East Rutherford, N.J. Center-linebacker Tennessee 1952-55. No pro playing experience. College coach: Richmond 1966-67, Georgia Tech 1968-71, Memphis State 1972, South Carolina 1973. Pro coach: New York Stars (WFL) 1974, Toronto Argonauts (CFL) 1975-77, Montreal Alouettes (CFL) 1978-79, joined Giants in 1980.

Johnny Parker, strength and conditioning; born February 1, 1947, Greenville, S.C., lives in East Rutherford, N.J. No pro playing experience. Graduate of Mississippi, M.A., Delta State University. College coach: South Carolina 1974-76, Indiana 1977-79, Louisiana State 1980, Mississippi 1981-83. Pro coach: Joined Giants in 1984.

NEW YORK GIANTS 1985 FIRST-YEAR ROSTER

Name	Pos.	Ht.	Wt.	Birth-date	College	Birthplace	Residence	How Acq.
Adams, George	RB	6-1	225	12/22/62	Kentucky	Lexington, Ky.	Lexington, Ky.	D1
Allen, Mark(1)	TE	6-4	225	4/29/60	Montclair State	Newark, N.J.	Livingston, N.J.	FA
Baker, Tony	RB	6-1	200	9/9/63	Cornell	Buffalo, N.Y.	Ithaca, N.Y.	FA
Battle, Ralph	CB-S	6-4	195	6/15/61	Jacksonville State	Huntsville, Ala.	Huntsville, Ala.	FA
Bavaro, Mark	TE	6-4	245	4/28/63	Notre Dame	East Boston, Mass.	Danvers, Mass.	D4
Belcher, Jack	C	6-4	278	4/17/61	Boston College	Boston, Mass.	Stoneham, Mass.	FA
Bell, Maurice	LB	6-2	222	3/14/62	Stephen F. Austin	Plainview, Tex.	Tyler, Tex.	FA
Bond, David(1)	NT	6-4	250	4/14/62	Virginia	Catskill, N.Y.	Fairfield, Conn.	FA
Bouier, Lorenzo(1)	RB	6-1	200	2/27/61	Maine	Hartford, Conn.	Hartford, Conn.	FA
Chambers, Lorenzo	RB	5-9	192	9/30/63	Dartmouth	Brooklyn, N.Y.	Brooklyn, N.Y.	FA
Chatman, Ricky	LB	6-2	230	1/4/62	Louisiana State	Jonesboro, Ark.	Winnfield, La.	FA
Colquitt, Jim	P	6-4	210	1/17/63	Tennessee	Knoxville, Tenn.	Knoxville, Tenn.	FA
Culpepper, Walt	LB	6-0	215	4/13/63	Georgia	Atlanta, Ga.	Atlanta, Ga.	FA
Davis, Tyrone	CB-S	6-1	190	11/17/61	Clemson	Athens, Ga.	Athens, Ga.	D3
Dubroc, Gregg	LB	6-3	230	1/15/62	Louisiana State	New Orleans, La.	New Orleans, La.	D10
Fourcade, John	QB	6-1	198	10/11/62	Mississippi	New Orleans, La.	Harvey, La.	FA
Gordon, Leon	CB-S	6-1	197	4/11/62	Virginia Tech	Charlottesville, Va.	Charlottesville, Va.	FA
Goodman, Don(1)	RB	5-11	200	4/23/59	Cincinnati	Los Angeles, Calif.	Los Angeles, Calif.	FA
Harmon, Mark	K	5-8	175	12/13/61	Stanford	Charleston, S.C.	Mountain View, Calif.	FA
Henderson, Tracy	WR	6-0	185	6/7/64	Iowa State	Melrose Park, Ill.	Haywood, Ill.	D5
Hooks, Mike	LB	6-3	235	5/21/62	Iowa	Omaha, Neb.	Iowa City, Iowa	FA
Johnson, Damian	T	6-5	290	12/18/62	Kansas State	Great Bend, Kan.	Great Bend, Kan.	FA
Johnston, Brian	C	6-3	275	11/26/62	North Carolina	Highland, Md.	Highland, Md.	D3a
Kowgios, Nick	RB	5-11	218	11/19/62	Lafayette	Yonkers, N.Y.	Yonkers, N.Y.	FA
Marvin, Al	NT	6-4	297	5/20/59	Alabama State	Andalusia, Ala.	Andalusia, Ala.	FA
Oliver, Jack	G	6-4	285	2/3/62	Memphis State	Washington, D.C.	Pensacola, Fla.	D6
Pembrook, Mark	CB-S	6-0	197	9/17/63	Cal State-Fullerton	Los Angeles, Calif.	Los Alamitos, Calif.	D6a
Rasheed, Eric	WR	5-7	158	4/29/63	Western Carolina	Atlanta, Ga.	Decatur, Ga.	FA
Robinson, Stacy	WR	5-11	186	2/19/62	North Dakota State	St. Paul, Minn.	St. Paul, Minn.	D2
Rouson, Lee	RB	6-1	210	10/18/62	Colorado	Elizabeth City, N.C.	Greensboro, N.C.	D8
Salter, Mark	G	6-4	240	10/16/63	Canisius	Lockport, N.Y.	Newfane, N.Y.	FA
Watson, Ron	CB-S	5-10	186	7/19/61	Clemson	Jackson, Miss.	Greenville, S.C.	FA
Welch, Herb	CB-S	5-11	180	1/12/61	UCLA	Los Angeles, Calif.	Downey, Calif.	D12
Winters, Larry	CB-S	6-1	210	2/14/60	St. Paul's	Marbury, Md.	Chapel Hill, N.C.	FA
Wright, Frank	NT	6-3	276	11/25/61	South Carolina	Greenwood, S.C.	Greenwood, S.C.	D9
Young, Al	CB-S	6-0	190	8/30/62	Virginia Tech	Hickory, N.C.	Hickory, N.C.	D11

Players who report to an NFL team for the first time are designated on rosters as rookies (R). If a player reported to an NFL training camp in a previous year but was not on the active squad for three or more regular season or postseason games, he is listed on the first-year roster and designated by a (1). Thereafter, a player who is on the active squad for three or more regular season or postseason games is credited with an additional year of playing experience.

NOTES

_____

_____

_____

_____

_____

_____

_____

_____

_____

_____

_____

Mike Pope, tight ends; born March 15, 1942, Monroe, N.C., lives in River Vale, N.J. Quarterback Lenoir Rhyne 1962-64. No pro playing experience. College coach: Florida State 1970-74, Texas Tech 1975-77, Mississippi 1978-82. Pro coach: Joined Giants in 1983.

Mike Sweatman, assistant special teams; born October 23, 1946, Kansas City, Mo., lives in Wayne, N.J. Linebacker Kansas 1964-67. No pro playing experience. College coach: Kansas 1973-74, 1979-82, Tulsa 1977-78, Tennessee 1983. Pro coach: Minnesota Vikings 1984, first year with Giants.

PHILADELPHIA EAGLES

**National Football Conference
Eastern Division**

Team Colors: Kelly Green, Silver,
and White

**Veterans Stadium
Broad Street and Pattison Avenue
Philadelphia, Pennsylvania 19148
Telephone: (215) 463-2500**

Club Officials

Owner: Norman Braman
Co-owner: Ed Leibowitz
Vice President-General Manager: Harry Gamble
Executive Director of Player Personnel:
    Lynn Stiles
Director of Communications: Ed Wisneski
Director of Public Relations: Jim Gallagher
Assistant Director of Public Relations:
    Ron Howard
Director of Sales and Marketing: Bob Caesar
Assistant Director of Sales and Marketing:
    Sherry Lewis
Director of Ticket Operations: Joyce Iman
Ticket Manager: Hugh Ortman
Business Manager: Mimi Box
Talent Scouts: Bill Baker, Lou Blumling
Trainer: Otho Davis
Assistant Trainer: Steve Watterson
Strength and Conditioning Coordinator:
    Tim Jorgensen
Equipment Manager: Rusty Sweeney
Film Director: Mike Dougherty

Stadium: Veterans Stadium •
    Capacity: 71,640
    Broad Street and Pattison Avenue
    Philadelphia, Pennsylvania 19148

Playing Surface: AstroTurf

Training Camp: West Chester University
    West Chester, Pennsylvania
    19380

1985 SCHEDULE

Preseason

Aug. 10	at New York Jets	8:30
Aug. 17	at Cleveland	7:30
Aug. 23	vs. L.A. Rams at Columbus, Ohio	7:30
Aug. 29	**Detroit**	7:30

Regular Season

Sept. 8	at New York Giants	1:00
Sept. 15	**Los Angeles Rams**	1:00
Sept. 22	at Washington	1:00
Sept. 29	**New York Giants**	1:00
Oct. 6	at New Orleans	12:00
Oct. 13	at St. Louis	12:00
Oct. 20	**Dallas**	1:00
Oct. 27	**Buffalo**	1:00
Nov. 3	at San Francisco	1:00
Nov. 10	**Atlanta**	1:00
Nov. 17	**St. Louis**	1:00
Nov. 24	at Dallas	3:00
Dec. 1	**Minnesota**	1:00
Dec. 8	**Washington**	1:00
Dec. 15	at San Diego	1:00
Dec. 22	at Minnesota	12:00

EAGLES COACHING HISTORY

(283-367-23)

1933-35	Lud Wray	9-21-1
1936-40	Bert Bell	10-44-2
1941-50	Earle (Greasy) Neale*	66-44-5
1951	Alvin (Bo) McMillin**	2-0-0
1951	Wayne Millner	2-8-0
1952-55	Jim Trimble	25-20-3
1956-57	Hugh Devore	7-16-1
1958-60	Lawrence (Buck) Shaw	20-16-1
1961-63	Nick Skorich	15-24-3
1964-68	Joe Kuharich	28-41-1
1969-71	Jerry Williams***	7-22-2
1971-72	Ed Khayat	8-15-2
1973-75	Mike McCormack	16-25-1
1976-82	Dick Vermeil	57-51-0
1983-84	Marion Campbell	11-20-1

*Co-coach with Walt Kiesling in Philadelphia-Pittsburgh
    merger in 1943
**Retired after two games in 1951
***Released after three games in 1971

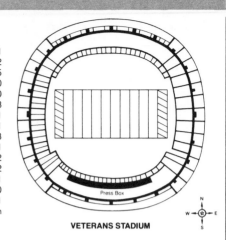

VETERANS STADIUM

Press Box

RECORD HOLDERS
Individual Records — Career

Category	Name	Performance
Rushing (Yds.)	Wilbert Montgomery, 1977-1984	6,538
Passing (Yds.)	Ron Jaworski, 1977-1984	22,108
Passing (TDs)	Ron Jaworski, 1977-1984	150
Receiving (No.)	Harold Carmichael, 1971-1983	589
Receiving (Yds.)	Harold Carmichael, 1971-1983	8,978
Interceptions	Bill Bradley, 1969-1976	34
Field Goals	Sam Baker, 1964-69	90
Touchdowns (Tot.)	Harold Carmichael, 1971-1983	79
Points	Bobby Walston, 1951-1962	881

Individual Records — Single Season

Category	Name	Performance
Rushing (Yds.)	Wilbert Montgomery, 1979	1,512
Passing (Yds.)	Sonny Jurgensen, 1961	3,723
Passing (TDs)	Sonny Jurgensen, 1961	32
Receiving (No.)	Mike Quick, 1983	69
Receiving (Yds.)	Mike Quick, 1983	1,409
Interceptions	Bill Bradley, 1971	11
Field Goals	Paul McFadden, 1984	30
Touchdowns (Tot.)	Steve Van Buren, 1945	18
Points	Paul McFadden, 1984	116

Individual Records — Single Game

Category	Name	Performance
Rushing (Yds.)	Steve Van Buren, 11-27-49	205
Passing (Yds.)	Bobby Thomason, 11-18-53	437
Passing (TDs)	Adrian Burk, 10-17-54	7
Receiving (No.)	Don Looney, 12-1-40	14
Receiving (Yds.)	Tommy McDonald, 12-10-60	237
Interceptions	Russ Craft, 9-24-50	4
Field Goals	Tom Dempsey, 11-12-72	6
Touchdowns (Tot.)	Many times	4
	Last time by Wilbert Montgomery, 10-7-79	
Points	Bobby Walston, 10-17-54	25

1984 TEAM STATISTICS

	Philadelphia	Opp.
Total First Downs	280	307
Rushing	83	123
Passing	176	171
Penalty	21	13
Third Down: Made/Att.	77/232	105/252
Fourth Down: Made/Att.	9/17	6/11
Total Net Yards	4698	5239
Avg. Per Game	293.6	327.4
Total Plays	1047	1108
Avg. Per Play	4.5	4.7
Net Yards Rushing	1338	2189
Avg. Per Game	83.6	136.8
Total Rushes	381	556
Net Yards Passing	3360	3050
Avg. Per Game	210.0	190.6
Tackled/Yards Lost	60/463	60/456
Gross Yards	3823	3506
Att./Completions	606/331	492/262
Completion Pct.	54.6	53.3
Had Intercepted	17	20
Punts/Avg.	92/42.2	89/39.3
Net Punting Avg.	35.6	33.6
Penalties/Yards Lost	77/632	96/904
Fumbles/Ball Lost	23/16	32/11
Touchdowns	27	36
Rushing	6	12
Passing	19	22
Returns	2	2
Avg. Time of Possession	29:30	30:30

1984 TEAM RECORD

Preseason (2-2)

Date	Philadelphia		Opponents
8/4	14	Detroit	17
8/11	17	Pittsburgh	20
8/18	31	Minnesota	10
8/23	20	*Cleveland	19
	82		66

Regular Season (6-9-1)

Date	Philadelphia		Opp.	Att.
9/2	27	New York Giants	28	71,520
9/9	19	*Minnesota	17	55,942
9/16	17	Dallas	23	64,695
9/23	9	*San Francisco	21	62,771
9/30	0	Washington	20	53,064
10/7	27	Buffalo	17	37,555
10/14	16	*Indianapolis	7	50,277
10/21	24	New York Giants	10	64,677
10/28	14	*St. Louis	34	54,310
11/4	23	Detroit (OT)	23	59,141
11/11	23	Miami	24	70,227
11/18	16	*Washington	10	63,117
11/25	16	St. Louis	17	39,858
12/2	10	*Dallas	26	66,322
12/9	27	*New England	17	41,581
12/16	10	Atlanta	26	15,582
	278		320	870,639

*Home Game (OT) Overtime

Score by Periods

Philadelphia	64	76	53	85	0	—	278
Opponents	61	102	74	83	0	—	320

Attendance

Home 458,997   Away 411,642   Total 870,639
Single game home record, 72,111 (11-1-81)
Single season home record, 557,325 (1980)

1984 INDIVIDUAL STATISTICS

Rushing

	Att.	Yds.	Avg.	LG	TD
Montgomery	201	789	3.9	27	2
Oliver	72	263	3.7	17	0
Haddix	48	130	2.7	21	1
M. Williams	33	83	2.5	8	0
Hardy	14	41	2.9	10	0
Pisarcik	7	19	2.7	16	2
Jaworski	5	18	3.6	10	1
Quick	1	−5	−5.0	−5	0
Philadelphia	381	1338	3.5	27	6
Opponents	556	2189	3.9	34	12

Passing

	Att.	Comp.	Pct.	Yds.	TD	Int.	Tkld.	Rate
Jaworski	427	234	54.8	2754	16	14	34/270	73.5
Pisarcik	176	96	54.5	1036	3	3	25/183	70.6
Montgomery	2	0	0.0	0	0	0	1/10	39.6
May	1	1	100.0	33	0	0	0/0	118.8
Philadelphia	606	331	54.6	3823	19	17	60/463	72.6
Opponents	492	262	53.3	3506	22	20	60/456	74.1

Receiving

	No.	Yds.	Avg.	LG	TD
Spagnola	65	701	10.8	34	1
Quick	61	1052	17.2	90t	9
Montgomery	60	501	8.4	28	0
Haddix	33	231	7.0	22	0
Oliver	32	142	4.4	21	0
Woodruff	30	484	16.1	38	3
Jackson	26	398	15.3	83t	1
Kab	9	102	11.3	26	3
M. Williams	7	47	6.7	15	0
Hoover	6	143	23.8	44	2
Garrity, Pitt.-Phil.	2	22	11.0	12	0
Hardy	2	22	11.0	13	0
Philadelphia	331	3823	11.5	90t	19
Opponents	262	3506	13.4	68	22

Interceptions

	No.	Yds.	Avg.	LG	TD
Ellis	7	119	17.0	31	0
Hopkins	5	107	21.4	33	0
Foules	4	27	6.8	20	0
Edwards	2	0	0.0	0	0
Wilson	1	28	28.0	28	0
Wilkes	1	6	6.0	6	0
Philadelphia	20	287	14.4	33	0
Opponents	17	211	12.4	43	1

Punting

	No.	Yds.	Avg.	In 20	LG
Horan	92	3880	42.2	21	69
Philadelphia	92	3880	42.2	21	69
Opponents	89	3497	39.3	19	64

Punt Returns

	No.	FC	Yds.	Avg.	LG	TD
Cooper	40	19	250	6.3	16	0
Philadelphia	40	19	250	6.3	16	0
Opponents	58	8	486	8.4	46	0

Kickoff Returns

	No.	Yds.	Avg.	LG	TD
Hayes	22	441	20.0	44	0
Cooper	17	299	17.6	48	0
Waters	13	319	24.5	89t	1
Everett	3	40	13.3	18	0
Ellis	2	25	12.5	15	0
Hardy	1	20	20.0	20	0
Strauthers	1	12	12.0	12	0
Philadelphia	59	1156	19.6	89t	1
Opponents	69	1298	18.8	51	0

Scoring

	TD R	TD P	TD Rt	PAT	FG	Saf	TP
McFadden	0	0	0	26/27	30/37	0	116
Quick	0	9	0	0/0	0/0	0	54
Kab	0	3	0	0/0	0/0	0	18
Woodruff	0	3	0	0/0	0/0	0	18
Hoover	0	2	0	0/0	0/0	0	12
Montgomery	2	0	0	0/0	0/0	0	12
Pisarcik	2	0	0	0/0	0/0	0	12
Haddix	1	0	0	0/0	0/0	0	6
Jackson	0	1	0	0/0	0/0	0	6
Jaworski	1	0	0	0/0	0/0	0	6
Kraynak	0	0	1	0/0	0/0	0	6
Spagnola	0	1	0	0/0	0/0	0	6
Waters	0	0	1	0/0	0/0	0	6
Philadelphia	6	19	2	26/27	30/37	0	278
Opponents	12	22	2	36/36	22/35	1	320

FIRST-ROUND SELECTIONS

(If Club had no first-round selection, first player drafted is listed with round in parentheses.)

Year	Player, College, Position
1936	Jay Berwanger, Chicago, B
1937	Sam Francis, Nebraska, B
1938	Jim McDonald, Ohio State, B
1939	Davey O'Brien, Texas Christian, B
1940	George McAfee, Duke, B
1941	Art Jones, Richmond, B (2)
1942	Pete Kmetovic, Stanford, B
1943	Joe Muha, Virginia Military, B
1944	Steve Van Buren, Louisiana State, B
1945	John Yonaker, Notre Dame, E
1946	Leo Riggs, Southern California, B
1947	Neill Armstrong, Oklahoma A&M, E
1948	Clyde (Smackover) Scott, Arkansas, B
1949	Chuck Bednarik, Pennsylvania, C
	Frank Tripucka, Notre Dame, B
1950	Harry (Bud) Grant, Minnesota, E
1951	Ebert Van Buren, Louisiana State, B
	Chet Mutryn, Xavier, B
1952	Johnny Bright, Drake, B
1953	Al Conway, Army, B (2)
1954	Neil Worden, Notre Dame, B
1955	Dick Bielski, Maryland, B
1956	Bob Pellegrini, Maryland, C
1957	Clarence Peaks, Michigan State, B
1958	Walt Kowalczyk, Michigan State, B
1959	J.D. Smith, Rice, T (2)
1960	Ron Burton, Northwestern, RB
1961	Art Baker, Syracuse, RB
1962	Pete Case, Georgia, G (2)
1963	Ed Budde, Michigan State, G
1964	Bob Brown, Nebraska, T
1965	Ray Rissmiller, Georgia, T (2)
1966	Randy Beisler, Indiana, DE
1967	Harry Jones, Arkansas, RB
1968	Tim Rossovich, Southern California, DE
1969	Leroy Keyes, Purdue, RB
1970	Steve Zabel, Oklahoma, TE
1971	Richard Harris, Grambling, DE
1972	John Reaves, Florida, QB
1973	Jerry Sisemore, Texas, T
	Charle Young, Southern California, TE
1974	Mitch Sutton, Kansas, DT (3)
1975	Bill Capraun, Miami, T (7)
1976	Mike Smith, Florida, DE (4)
1977	Skip Sharp, Kansas, DB (5)
1978	Reggie Wilkes, Georgia Tech, LB (3)
1979	Jerry Robinson, UCLA, LB
1980	Roynell Young, Alcorn State, DB
1981	Leonard Mitchell, Houston, DE
1982	Mike Quick, North Carolina State, WR
1983	Michael Haddix, Mississippi State, RB
1984	Kenny Jackson, Penn State, WR
1985	Kevin Allen, Indiana, T

PHILADELPHIA EAGLES 1985 VETERAN ROSTER

No.	Name	Pos.	Ht.	Wt.	Birth-date	NFL Exp.	College	Birthplace	Residence	'84 Games/ Starts
96	Armstrong, Harvey	NT	6-2	265	12/29/59	4	Southern Methodist	Houston, Tex.	Houston, Tex.	16/0
63	†Baker, Ron	G	6-4	270	11/19/54	8	Oklahoma State	Gary, Ind.	Stillwater, Okla.	16/16
98	Brown, Greg	DE	6-5	260	1/5/57	5	Kansas State	Washington, D.C.	Sicklerville, N.J.	16/16
11	Christensen, Jeff	QB	6-3	200	1/8/60	3	Eastern Illinois	Gibson City, Ill.	Saybrook, Ill.	0*
71	Clarke, Ken	NT	6-2	255	8/28/56	8	Syracuse	Savannah, Ga.	Savannah, Ga.	16/16
21	Cooper, Evan	CB-KR	5-11	180	6/28/62	2	Michigan	Miami, Fla.	Miami, Fla.	16/0
94	Darby, Byron	DE	6-4	260	6/4/60	3	Southern California	Los Angeles, Calif.	Sewell, N.J.	16/0
65	Dennard, Mark	C	6-1	252	11/2/55	7	Texas A&M	Bay City, Tex.	Bryan, Tex	16/16
46	†Edwards, Herman	CB	6-0	190	4/27/54	9	San Diego State	Fort Monmouth, N.J.	Seaside, Calif.	16/16
24	Ellis, Ray	S	6-1	192	4/27/59	5	Ohio State	Canton, Ohio	Philadelphia, Pa.	16/16
39	Everett, Major	FB	5-11	215	1/4/60	3	Mississippi College	Monticello, Miss.	New Hebron, Miss.	16/0
67	Feehery, Gerry	C	6-2	268	3/9/60	3	Syracuse	Philadelphia, Pa.	Springfield, Pa.	6/0
29	Foules, Elbert	CB	5-11	185	7/4/61	3	Alcorn State	Greenville, Miss.	Greenville, Miss.	16/12
86	Garrity, Gregg	WR	5-10	171	11/24/60	3	Penn State	Pittsburgh, Pa.	Bradford Woods, Pa.	10/0*
58	Griggs, Anthony	LB	6-3	230	2/12/60	4	Ohio State	Lawton, Okla.	Sicklerville, N.J.	16/16
26	Haddix, Michael	FB	6-2	225	12/27/61	3	Mississippi State	Tippah County, Miss.	Walnut, Miss.	14/14
47	Hardy, Andre	RB	6-1	233	11/28/61	2	St. Mary's, Calif.	San Diego, Calif.	San Diego, Calif.	6/0
68	Harrison, Dennis	DE	6-8	280	7/31/56	8	Vanderbilt	Cleveland, Ohio	Nashville, Tenn.	16/16
80	Hayes, Joe	WR-KR	5-9	185	9/15/60	2	Central State, Okla.	Dallas, Tex.	Dallas, Tex.	12/0
85	†Hoover, Melvin	WR	6-0	185	8/21/59	4	Arizona State	Charlotte, N.C.	Charlotte, N.C.	12/1
48	Hopkins, Wes	S	6-1	210	9/26/61	3	Southern Methodist	Birmingham, Ala.	Dallas, Tex.	16/15
2	Horan, Michael	P	5-11	190	2/1/59	2	Long Beach State	Orange, Calif.	Anaheim, Calif.	16/0
81	Jackson, Kenny	WR	6-0	180	2/15/62	2	Penn State	Neptune, N.J.	Cherry Hill, N.J.	11/9
7	Jaworski, Ron	QB	6-2	196	3/23/51	12	Youngstown State	Lackawanna, N.Y.	West Berlin, N.J.	13/13
84	Kab, Vyto	TE	6-5	240	12/23/59	4	Penn State	Albany, Ga.	Cherry Hill, N.J.	16/5
73	Kenney, Steve	G	6-4	270	12/26/55	6	Clemson	Wilmington, N.C.	Raleigh, N.C.	11/11
52	Kraynak, Rich	LB	6-1	225	1/20/60	3	Pittsburgh	Phoenixville, Pa.	Phoenixville, Pa.	14/0
5	May, Dean	QB	6-5	220	5/26/62	2	Louisville	Orlando, Fla.	Tampa, Fla.	2/0
8	McFadden, Paul	K	5-11	155	9/24/61	2	Youngstown State	Cleveland, Ohio	Euclid, Ohio	16/0
64	Miraldi, Dean	T	6-5	285	4/8/58	3	Utah	Culver City, Calif.	Balboa, Calif.	16/16
74	†Mitchell, Leonard	T	6-7	285	10/12/58	5	Houston	Houston, Tex.	Houston, Tex.	16/14
31	Montgomery, Wilbert	RB	5-10	194	9/16/54	9	Abilene Christian	Greenville, Miss.	West Berlin, N.J.	16/14
34	Oliver, Hubie	FB	5-10	212	11/12/57	4	Arizona	Elyria, Ohio	Elyria, Ohio	16/15
72	Pacella, Dave	G-C	6-3	266	2/7/60	2	Maryland	Sewickly, Pa.	College Park, Md.	16/0
62	†Perot, Petey	G	6-2	261	4/28/57	6	Northwestern Louisiana	Natchitoches, La.	Natchitoches, La.	12/5
9	Pisarcik, Joe	QB	6-4	217	7/2/52	9	New Mexico State	Wilkes-Barre, Pa.	Bradenton, Fla.	7/3
82	Quick, Mike	WR	6-2	190	5/14/59	4	North Carolina State	Hamlet, N.C.	Sicklerville, N.J.	14/14
55	Reichenbach, Mike	LB	6-2	235	9/14/61	2	East Stroudsburg State	Ford Meade, Md.	Bethlehem, Pa.	12/1
56	Robinson, Jerry	LB	6-2	225	12/18/56	7	UCLA	San Francisco, Calif.	West Chester, Pa.	15/15
79	Russell, Rusty	T	6-5	295	8/16/63	2	South Carolina	Orangeburg, S.C.	Orangeburg, S.C.	1/0
87	Sampleton, Lawrence	TE	6-5	233	9/25/59	4	Texas	Waelder, Tex.	Seguin, Tex.	16/0
53	Schulz, Jody	LB	6-4	235	8/17/60	3	East Carolina	Easton, Md.	Chester, Md.	15/2
88	Spagnola, John	TE	6-4	240	8/1/57	6	Yale	Bangor, Pa.	Cherry Hill, N.J.	16/16
93	†Strauthers, Thomas	DE	6-4	265	4/6/61	3	Jackson State	Wesson, Miss.	Sewell, N.J.	16/0
20	Waters, Andre	CB-KR	5-11	182	3/10/62	2	Cheyney State	Belle Glade, Fla.	Edgewater Park, N.J.	16/0
51	Wilkes, Reggie	LB	6-4	235	5/27/56	8	Georgia Tech	Pine Bluff, Ark.	Philadelphia, Pa.	14/14
59	†Williams, Joel	LB	6-1	225	12/13/56	7	Wisconsin-La Crosse	Miami, Fla.	Philadelphia, Pa.	16/16
32	Williams, Michael	RB	6-2	225	7/16/61	3	Mississippi College	Atmore, Ala.	Atmore, Ala.	16/1
22	Wilson, Brenard	S-CB	6-0	180	8/15/55	7	Vanderbilt	Daytona Beach, Fla.	Nashville, Tenn.	16/5
83	Woodruff, Tony	WR	6-0	185	11/12/58	4	Fresno State	Hazen, Ark.	Fresno, Calif.	16/5
43	Young, Roynell	CB	6-1	181	12/1/57	6	Alcorn State	New Orleans, La.	Houston, Tex.	7/0

* Christensen active for 3 games in '84, but did not play; Garrity played 6 games with Pittsburgh, 4 with Philadelphia.

†Option playout; subject to developments.

Retired—Bill Cowher, 4-year linebacker, 4 games in '84.

Also played with Eagles in '84—CB-S Lou Rash (4 games), T Jerry Sisemore (2).

COACHING STAFF

Head Coach, Marion Campbell

Pro Career: Campbell was named head coach of the Eagles on January 10, 1983, after six seasons as the club's defensive coordinator. Campbell's first association with the Eagles came in 1956 when, as a defensive lineman, he was traded to Philadelphia by San Francisco. He was the 49ers' fourth-round draft choice in 1951 but spent three years in the Army before he joined the 49ers. During his six-year playing career with the Eagles, Campbell played defensive tackle on the Eagles' 1960 NFL championship team and played in the 1960 and 1961 Pro Bowls. His pro coaching career began in 1962 as an assistant with the Boston Patriots. Two years later he moved into the NFL coaching ranks where he developed outstanding defensive lines at Minnesota (1964-66) and Los Angeles (1967-68). He joined Atlanta in 1969 and was the Falcons' head coach from November of 1974 to October of 1976. His head coaching record was 6-19, including a 4-10 mark in 1975, his only full season as a head coach. He was released by the Falcons after nine games in 1976 and joined the Eagles in 1977. Career record: 17-39-1.

Background: At the University of Georgia, where he played tackle, Campbell was an all-Southeastern Conference selection three times and the team's most valuable player his senior year.

Personal: Born May 25, 1929, in Chester, S.C. Marion and his wife, June, live in Medford, N.J., and have two children—Scott and Alicia.

Assistant Coaches

Tommy Brasher, defensive line; born December 30, 1940, El Dorado, Ark., lives in Moorestown, N.J. Linebacker Arkansas 1961-63. No pro playing experience. College coach: Arkansas 1970, Virginia Tech 1971-73, Northeast Louisiana 1974, 1976, Southern Methodist 1977-81. Pro coach: Shreveport (WFL) 1975, New England Patriots 1982-84, first year with Eagles.

Fred Bruney, assistant head coach-defensive backfield; born December 30, 1931, Martins Ferry, Ohio, lives in Medford, N.J. Back Ohio State 1949-52. Pro defensive back San Francisco 49ers 1953-56, Pittsburgh Steelers 1957, Washington Redskins 1958, Boston Patriots 1960-62. College coach: Ohio State 1959. Pro coach: Boston Patriots 1963, Philadelphia Eagles 1964-68, Atlanta Falcons 1969-76, rejoined Eagles in 1977.

Chuck Clausen, linebackers; born June 23, 1940, Anamosa, Iowa, lives in Mt. Laurel, N.J. Defensive lineman New Mexico 1961-63. No pro playing experience. College coach: William & Mary 1969-70, Ohio State 1971-75. Pro coach: Joined Eagles in 1976.

Tom Coughlin, wide receivers; born August 31, 1946, Waterloo, N.Y., lives in Medford, N.J. Wingback Syracuse 1965-67. No pro playing experience. College coach: Syracuse 1968, 1974-1980, Rochester Institute of Technology 1969-73 (head coach 1970-73), Boston College 1981-83. Pro coach: Joined Eagles in 1984.

Frank Gansz, tight ends-special teams; born November 22, 1938, Altoona, Pa., lives in Cherry Hill, N.J. Center Navy 1957-59. No pro playing experience. College coach: Air Force 1964-66, Colgate 1968, Navy 1969-72, Oklahoma State 1973, 1975, Army 1974, UCLA 1976-77. Pro coach: San Francisco 49ers 1978, Cincinnati Bengals 1979-80, Kansas City Chiefs 1981-82, joined Eagles in 1983.

Ken Iman, offensive line; born February 8, 1939, St. Louis, Mo., lives in Springfield, Pa. Center-linebacker Southeast Missouri State 1956-59. Pro center Green Bay Packers 1960-63, Los Angeles Rams 1964-74. Pro coach: Joined Eagles in 1976.

Milt Jackson, running backs; born October 16, 1943, Groesbeck, Tex., lives in Cherry Hill, N.J. Defensive back Tulsa 1966-67. Pro defensive back San Francisco 49ers 1967-68. College coach: Oregon State 1973, Rice 1974, California 1975-76, Oregon 1977-78, UCLA 1979. Pro coach: San Francisco 49ers 1980-82, Buffalo Bills 1983-84, first year with Eagles.

PHILADELPHIA EAGLES 1985 FIRST-YEAR ROSTER

Name	Pos.	Ht.	Wt.	Birth-date	College	Birthplace	Residence	How Acq.
Allen, Kevin	T	6-5	285	6/21/63	Indiana	Cincinnati, Ohio	Cincinnati, Ohio	D1
Brewster, Tim	TE	6-3	242	10/13/60	Illinois	Phillipsburg, N.J.	Washington, N.J.	FA
Caldwell, Bryan	DE	6-5	262	5/6/60	Arizona State	Oakland, Calif.	Mesa, Ariz.	FA
Chambers, Tim	CB-S-KR	5-10	185	12/5/62	Pennsylvania	Darby, Pa.	Newtown Square, Pa.	FA
Cunningham, Randall	QB-P	6-4	195	3/27/63	Nevada-Las Vegas	Santa Barbara, Calif.	Santa Barbara, Calif.	D2
Drake, Joe	NT	6-2	295	5/28/63	Arizona	San Francisco, Calif.	San Francisco, Calif.	D9a
Evans, Leon	DE	6-6	270	10/12/61	Miami	Washington, D.C.	Maple Shade, N.J.	FA
Harris, Michael	CB	5-11	180	3/30/63	Delaware	Wilmington, Del.	Wilmington, Del.	FA
Hunter, Herman	RB-KR	6-1	190	2/14/61	Tennessee State	Columbus, Ga.	Columbus, Ga.	D11
Irving, Mike	RB-KR	5-8	183	11/27/62	West Chester State	West Chester, Pa.	West Chester, Pa.	FA
Jelesky, Tom	T	6-6	290	10/4/60	Purdue	Gary, Ind.	Philadelphia, Pa.	FA
Jiles, Dwayne	LB	6-4	240	11/23/61	Texas Tech	Linden, Tex.	Douglassville, Tex.	D5
Kelso, Mark	S-KR	5-11	186	7/23/63	William & Mary	Pittsburgh, Pa.	Pittsburgh, Pa.	D10
Kimmel, Jon	LB	6-4	247	7/21/60	Colgate	Binghamton, N.Y.	Kirkwood, N.Y.	FA
Maune, Neil	G	6-4	281	11/4/60	Notre Dame	Washington, Mo.	Marthasville, Mo.	FA
Naron, Greg	G	6-4	270	10/21/63	North Carolina	Guilford County, N.C.	Climax, N.C.	D4
Polley, Tom	LB	6-3	235	2/17/62	Nevada-Las Vegas	Minneapolis, Minn.	St. Louis Park, Minn.	D8
Reeves, Ken	T-G	6-5	270	10/4/61	Texas A&M	Pittsburg, Tex.	Pittsburg, Tex.	D6
Russell, Todd	CB	6-1	190	9/5/61	Boston College	Birmingham, Ala.	Bedford, Mass.	D12
Slater, Sam	T	6-9	290	6/8/62	Weber State	Bronxville, N.Y.	Van Nuys, Calif.	FA
Tatum, Rowland	LB	6-2	240	11/20/62	Ohio State	Los Angeles, Calif.	Columbus, Ohio	FA
Toub, Dave	C	6-3	278	6/1/62	Texas-El Paso	Ossining, N.Y.	Mahopac, N.Y.	D9
Volpe, Pete	LB	5-11	220	5/3/62	Upsala	Red Bank, N.J.	Hazlet, N.J.	FA

Players who report to an NFL team for the first time are designated on rosters as rookies (R). If a player reported to an NFL training camp in a previous year but was not on the active squad for three or more regular season or postseason games, he is listed on the first-year roster and designated by a (1). Thereafter, a player who is on the active squad for three or more regular season or postseason games is credited with an additional year of playing experience.

NOTES

_____
_____
_____
_____
_____
_____
_____
_____
_____
_____
_____
_____
_____
_____
_____
_____
_____
_____
_____

Ted Marchibroda, offensive coordinator; born March 15, 1931, Franklin, Pa., lives in Mt. Laurel, N.J. Quarterback St. Bonaventure 1950-51, Detroit 1952. Pro quarterback Pittsburgh Steelers 1953, 1955-56, Chicago Cardinals 1957. Pro coach: Washington Redskins 1961-65, 1971-74, Los Angeles Rams 1966-70, Baltimore Colts 1975-79 (head coach), Chicago Bears 1981, Detroit Lions 1982-83, joined Eagles in 1984.

**National Football Conference
Eastern Division**

Team Colors: Cardinal Red, Black, and White

**Busch Stadium, Box 888
St. Louis, Missouri 63188
Telephone: (314) 421-0777**

Club Officials

Chairman: William V. Bidwill
President: Bing Devine
Vice President/Administration: Curt Mosher
Secretary and General Counsel: Thomas J. Guilfoil
Treasurer: Charley Schlegel
Director of Pro Personnel: Larry Wilson
Director of Player Personnel: George Boone
Public Relations Director: Michael Menchel
Media Coordinator: Greg Gladysiewski
Director of Community Relations: Adele Harris
Ticket Manager: Steve Walsh
Trainer: John Omohundro
Assistant Trainers: Jim Shearer, Ed Fleming
Equipment Manager: Bill Simmons
Assistant Equipment Managers: Mark Ahlemeier, Eric Youngstrom

Stadium: Busch Stadium •
Capacity: 51,392
200 Stadium Plaza
St. Louis, Missouri 63102

Playing Surface: AstroTurf

Training Camp: Eastern Illinois University
Charleston, Illinois 61920

1985 SCHEDULE

Preseason

Aug. 9	**Chicago**	7:30
Aug. 15	at Los Angeles Rams	7:00
Aug. 23	**Pittsburgh**	7:30
Aug. 31	at Kansas City	7:30

Regular Season

Sept. 8	at Cleveland	1:00
Sept. 15	**Cincinnati**	12:00
Sept. 22	at New York Giants	1:00
Sept. 29	**Green Bay**	12:00
Oct. 7	at Washington (Monday)	9:00
Oct. 13	**Philadelphia**	12:00
Oct. 20	at Pittsburgh	1:00
Oct. 27	**Houston**	12:00
Nov. 4	**Dallas** (Monday)	8:00
Nov. 10	at Tampa Bay	1:00
Nov. 17	at Philadelphia	1:00
Nov. 24	**New York Giants**	3:00
Nov. 28	at Dallas (Thanksgiving)	3:00
Dec. 8	**New Orleans**	12:00
Dec. 15	at Los Angeles Rams	1:00
Dec. 21	**Washington** (Saturday)	3:00

CARDINALS COACHING HISTORY

Chicago 1920-59
(336-434-38)

1920	Marshall Smith	5-2-1
1921-22	John (Paddy) Driscoll	12-6-3
1923-24	Arnold Horween	13-8-1
1925-26	Norman Barry	16-8-2
1927	Fred Gillies	3-7-1
1928	Guy Chamberlin	1-5-0
1929-30	Ernie Nevers	11-12-3
1931	LeRoy Andrews*	0-2-0
1931	Ernie Nevers	5-2-0
1932	Jack Chevigny	2-6-2
1933-34	Paul Schissler	6-15-1
1935-38	Milan Creighton	16-26-4
1939	Ernie Nevers	1-10-0
1940-42	Jimmy Conzelman	8-22-3
1943-45	Phil Handler**	1-29-0
1946-48	Jimmy Conzelman	27-10-0
1949	Phil Handler-Buddy Parker***	6-5-1
1950-51	Earl (Curly) Lambeau	8-16-0
1952	Joe Kuharich	4-8-0
1953-54	Joe Stydahar	3-20-1
1955-57	Ray Richards	14-21-1
1958-61	Frank (Pop) Ivy	17-31-2
1962-65	Wally Lemm	27-26-3
1966-70	Charley Winner	35-30-5
1971-72	Bob Hollway	8-18-2
1973-77	Don Coryell	42-29-1
1978-79	Bud Wilkinson****	9-20-0
1979	Larry Wilson	2-1-0
1980-84	Jim Hanifan	34-39-1

*Resigned after two games in 1931
**Co-coach with Walt Kiesling of 1944 Card-Pitt team
***Co-coaches
****Released after 13 games in 1979

RECORD HOLDERS

Individual Records—Career

Category	Name	Performance
Rushing (Yds.)	Ottis Anderson, 1979-1984	7,364
Passing (Yds.)	Jim Hart, 1966-1983	34,639
Passing (TDs)	Jim Hart, 1966-1983	209
Receiving (No.)	Jackie Smith, 1963-1977	480
Receiving (Yds.)	Jackie Smith, 1963-1977	7,918
Interceptions	Larry Wilson, 1960-1972	52
Punting (Avg.)	Jerry Norton, 1959-1961	44.9
Punt Return (Avg.)	Charley Trippi, 1947-1955	13.7
Kickoff Return (Avg.)	Ollie Matson, 1952, 1954-58	28.5
Field Goals	Jim Bakken, 1962-1978	282
Touchdowns (Tot.)	Sonny Randle, 1959-1966	60
Points	Jim Bakken, 1962-1978	1,380

Individual Records—Single Season

Category	Name	Performance
Rushing (Yds.)	Ottis Anderson, 1979	1,605
Passing (Yds.)	Neil Lomax, 1984	4,619
Passing (TDs)	Charley Johnson, 1963	28
	Neil Lomax, 1984	28
Receiving (No.)	Roy Green, 1983, 1984	78
Receiving (Yds.)	Roy Green, 1984	1,555
Interceptions	Bob Nussbaumer, 1949	12
Punting (Avg.)	Jerry Norton, 1960	45.6
Punt Return (Avg.)	John (Red) Cochran, 1949	20.9
Kickoff Return (Avg.)	Ollie Matson, 1958	35.5
Field Goals	Jim Bakken, 1967	27
Touchdowns (Tot.)	John David Crow, 1962	17
Points	Jim Bakken, 1967	117
	Neil O'Donoghue, 1984	117

Individual Records—Single Game

Category	Name	Performance
Rushing (Yds.)	John David Crow, 12-18-60	203
Passing (Yds.)	Neil Lomax, 12-16-84	468
Passing (TDs)	Jim Hardy, 10-2-50	6
	Charley Johnson, 9-26-65	6
	Charley Johnson, 11-2-69	6
Receiving (No.)	Sonny Randle, 11-4-62	16
Receiving (Yds.)	Sonny Randle, 11-4-62	256
Interceptions	Bob Nussbaumer, 11-13-49	4
	Jerry Norton, 11-20-60	4
Field Goals	Jim Bakken, 9-24-67	7
Touchdowns (Tot.)	Ernie Nevers, 11-28-29	6
Points	Ernie Nevers, 11-28-29	40

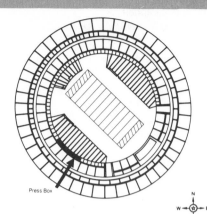

Press Box

BUSCH MEMORIAL STADIUM

1984 TEAM STATISTICS

	St. Louis	Opp.
Total First Downs	345	292
Rushing	129	108
Passing	200	157
Penalty	16	27
Third Down: Made/Att.	94/227	72/207
Fourth Down: Made/Att.	9/14	1/8
Total Net Yards	6345	5094
Avg. Per Game	396.6	318.4
Total Plays	1103	991
Avg. Per Play	5.8	5.1
Net Yards Rushing	2088	1923
Avg. Per Game	130.5	120.2
Total Rushes	488	442
Net Yards Passing	4257	3171
Avg. Per Game	266.1	198.2
Tackled/Yards Lost	49/377	55/403
Gross Yards	4634	3574
Att./Completions	566/347	494/251
Completion Pct.	61.3	50.8
Had Intercepted	16	21
Punts/Avg.	68/38.1	81/39.0
Net Punting Avg.	32.3	32.8
Penalties/Yards Lost	109/904	75/578
Fumbles/Ball Lost	32/20	20/12
Touchdowns	51	39
Rushing	21	11
Passing	28	26
Returns	2	2
Avg. Time of Possession	32:43	27:17

1984 TEAM RECORD
Preseason (3-1)

Date	St. Louis		Opponents
8/4	19	Chicago	10
8/10	14	*Kansas City	10
8/17	7	Seattle	17
8/24	31	*Minnesota	0
	71		37

Regular Season (9-7)

Date	St. Louis		Opp.	Att.
9/2	23	Green Bay	24	53,738
9/9	37	*Buffalo	7	35,785
9/16	34	Indianapolis	33	60,274
9/23	24	New Orleans	34	58,723
9/30	28	*Miami	36	46,991
10/7	31	Dallas	20	61,678
10/14	38	*Chicago	21	49,554
10/21	26	*Washington	24	50,262
10/28	34	Philadelphia	14	54,310
11/4	13	*Los Angeles Rams	16	51,010
11/11	17	*Dallas	24	48,721
11/18	10	New York Giants	16	73,428
11/25	17	*Philadelphia	16	39,858
12/2	33	New England	10	53,540
12/9	31	*New York Giants	21	49,973
12/16	27	Washington	29	54,299
	423		345	842,144

*Home Game

Score by Periods

St. Louis	72	134	102	115	—	423
Opponents	77	100	97	71	—	345

Attendance

Home 372,154   Away 469,990   Total 842,144
Single game home record, 51,010 (11-4-84)
Single season home record, 384,375 (1981)

1984 INDIVIDUAL STATISTICS

Rushing

	Att.	Yds.	Avg.	LG	TD
Anderson	289	1174	4.1	24	6
Mitchell	81	434	5.4	39	9
Ferrell	44	203	4.6	25	1
Lomax	35	184	5.3	20	3
Love	25	90	3.6	13	1
Harrell	6	7	1.2	4	1
Harrington	3	6	2.0	5	0
McIvor	3	5	1.7	6	0
Marsh	1	−5	−5.0	−5	0
Green	1	−10	−10.0	−10	0
St. Louis	488	2088	4.3	39	21
Opponents	442	1923	4.4	73	11

Passing

	Att.	Comp.	Pct.	Yds.	TD	Int.	Tkld.	Rate
Lomax	560	345	61.6	4614	28	16	49/377	92.5
McIvor	4	0	0.0	0	0	0	0/0	39.6
Mitchell	1	1	100.0	20	0	0	0/0	118.8
Perrin	1	1	100.0	0	0	0	0/0	79.2
St. Louis	566	347	61.3	4634	28	16	49/377	92.0
Opponents	494	251	50.8	3574	26	21	55/403	74.4

Receiving

	No.	Yds.	Avg.	LG	TD
Green	78	1555	19.9	83t	12
Anderson	70	611	8.7	57	2
Tilley	52	758	14.6	42	5
Marsh	39	608	15.6	47	5
Mitchell	26	318	12.2	44t	2
Ferrell	26	218	8.4	21	1
LaFleur	17	198	11.6	23	0
Harrell	14	106	7.6	15	0
Pittman	10	145	14.5	50	0
Love	7	33	4.7	16	1
Mack	5	61	12.2	22	0
Goode	3	23	7.7	10	0
St. Louis	347	4634	13.4	83t	28
Opponents	251	3574	14.2	90t	26

Interceptions

	No.	Yds.	Avg.	LG	TD
Washington	5	42	8.4	18	0
W. Smith	4	35	8.8	23	0
Perrin	4	22	5.5	22	0
L. Smith	2	31	15.5	25t	1
Griffin	2	0	0.0	0	0
Howard	2	−4	−2.0	1	0
Heflin	1	19	19.0	19	0
Junior	1	18	18.0	18	0
St. Louis	21	163	7.8	25t	1
Opponents	16	219	13.7	54	0

Punting

	No.	Yds.	Avg.	In 20	LG
Birdsong	67	2594	38.7	19	59
St. Louis	68	2594	38.1	19	59
Opponents	81	3157	39.0	11	59

Punt Returns

	No.	FC	Yds.	Avg.	LG	TD
Mitchell	38	3	333	8.8	39	0
Bird	5	0	56	11.2	17	0
Pittman	4	1	10	2.5	5	0
Green	0	1	0	—	0	0
St. Louis	47	5	399	8.5	39	0
Opponents	27	13	239	8.9	61	0

Kickoff Returns

	No.	Yds.	Avg.	LG	TD
Mitchell	35	804	23.0	56	0
Pittman	14	319	22.8	43	0
Harrell	13	231	17.8	28	0
Bird	9	190	21.1	28	0
Ferrell	1	0	0.0	0	0
Green	1	18	18.0	18	0
Love	1	1	1.0	1	0
St. Louis	74	1563	21.1	56	0
Opponents	85	1549	18.2	96t	1

Scoring

	TD R	TD P	TD Rt	PAT	FG	Saf	TP
O'Donoghue	0	0	0	48/51	23/35	0	117
Green	0	12	0	0/0	0/0	0	72
Mitchell	9	2	0	0/0	0/0	0	66
Anderson	6	2	0	0/0	0/0	0	48
Marsh	0	5	0	0/0	0/0	0	30
Tilley	0	5	0	0/0	0/0	0	30
Lomax	3	0	0	0/0	0/0	0	18
Ferrell	1	1	0	0/0	0/0	0	12
Love	1	1	0	0/0	0/0	0	12
Harrell	1	0	0	0/0	0/0	0	6
Howard	0	0	1	0/0	0/0	0	6
L. Smith	0	0	1	0/0	0/0	0	6
St. Louis	21	28	2	48/51	23/35	0	423
Opponents	11	26	2	36/39	25/38	0	345

FIRST-ROUND SELECTIONS

(If Club had no first-round selection, first player drafted is listed with round in parentheses.)

Year	Player, College, Position
1936	Jim Lawrence, Texas Christian, B
1937	Ray Buivid, Marquette, B
1938	Jack Robbins, Arkansas, B
1939	Charles (Ki) Aldrich, Texas Christian, C
1940	George Cafego, Tennessee, B
1941	John Kimbrough, Texas A&M, B
1942	Steve Lach, Duke, B
1943	Glenn Dobbs, Tulsa, B
1944	Pat Harder, Wisconsin, B
1945	Charley Trippi, Georgia, B
1946	Dub Jones, Louisiana State, B
1947	DeWitt (Tex) Coulter, Army, T
1948	Jim Spavital, Oklahoma A&M, B
1949	Bill Fischer, Notre Dame, G
1950	Jack Jennings, Ohio State, T (2)
1951	Jerry Groom, Notre Dame, C
1952	Ollie Matson, San Francisco, B
1953	Johnny Olszewski, California, B
1954	Lamar McHan, Arkansas, B
1955	Max Boydston, Oklahoma, E
1956	Joe Childress, Auburn, B
1957	Jerry Tubbs, Oklahoma, C
1958	King Hill, Rice, B
	John David Crow, Texas A&M, B
1959	Bill Stacy, Mississippi State, B
1960	George Izo, Notre Dame, QB
1961	Ken Rice, Auburn, T
1962	Fate Echols, Northwestern, DT
	Irv Goode, Kentucky, C
1963	Jerry Stovall, Louisiana State, S
	Don Brumm, Purdue, DE
1964	Ken Kortas, Louisville, DT
1965	Joe Namath, Alabama, QB
1966	Carl McAdams, Oklahoma, LB
1967	Dave Williams, Washington, WR
1968	MacArthur Lane, Utah State, RB
1969	Roger Wehrli, Missouri, DB
1970	Larry Stegent, Texas A&M, RB
1971	Norm Thompson, Utah, CB
1972	Bobby Moore, Oregon, RB-WR
1973	Dave Butz, Purdue, DT
1974	J.V. Cain, Colorado, TE
1975	Tim Gray, Texas A&M, DB
1976	Mike Dawson, Arizona, DT
1977	Steve Pisarkiewicz, Missouri, QB
1978	Steve Little, Arkansas, K
	Ken Greene, Washington State, DB
1979	Ottis Anderson, Miami, RB
1980	Curtis Greer, Michigan, DE
1981	E. J. Junior, Alabama, LB
1982	Luis Sharpe, UCLA, T
1983	Leonard Smith, McNeese State, DB
1984	Clyde Duncan, Tennessee, WR
1985	Freddie Joe Nunn, Mississippi, LB

ST. LOUIS CARDINALS 1985 VETERAN ROSTER

No.	Name	Pos.	Ht.	Wt.	Birth-date	NFL Exp.	College	Birthplace	Residence	'84 Games/ Starts
58	Ahrens, Dave	LB	6-3	230	12/5/58	5	Wisconsin	Cedar Falls, Iowa	Ballwin, Mo.	16/0
51	Allerman, Kurt	LB	6-2	232	8/30/50	9	Penn State	Glenridge, N.J.	Glencoe, Mo.	16/10
32	Anderson, Ottis	RB	6-2	220	1/19/57	7	Miami	West Palm Beach, Fla.	St. Louis, Mo.	15/15
60	Baker, Al	DE	6-6	270	12/9/56	8	Colorado State	Jacksonville, Fla.	Chesterfield, Mo.	15/15
52	Baker, Charlie	LB	6-2	234	9/26/57	6	New Mexico	Mt. Pleasant, Tex.	St. Louis, Mo.	9/6
18	Birdsong, Carl	P	6-0	192	1/1/59	5	S.W. Oklahoma State	Kaufman, Tex.	Amarillo, Tex.	16/0
71	Bostic, Joe	G	6-3	268	4/20/57	7	Clemson	Greensboro, N.C.	St. Louis, Mo.	16/16
64	Clark, Randy	C	6-3	254	7/27/57	6	Northern Illinois	Chicago, Ill.	Manchester, Mo.	16/16
62	Dardar, Ramsey	DT	6-2	264	10/3/59	2	Louisiana State	Lafayette, La.	St. Louis, Mo.	16/6
66	Dawson, Doug	G	6-3	267	12/27/61	2	Texas	Houston, Tex.	Houston, Tex.	15/1
73	Duda, Mark	DT	6-3	263	2/4/61	3	Maryland	Wilkes-Barre, Pa.	Plymouth, Pa.	8/6
86	Duncan, Clyde	WR	6-1	192	2/5/61	2	Tennessee	Oxon Hill, Md.	Temple Hills, Md.	8/0
31	Ferrell, Earl	RB	6-0	215	3/27/58	4	East Tennessee State	Halifax, Va.	South Boston, Va.	16/9
65	Galloway, David	DT	6-3	277	2/16/59	4	Florida	Tampa, Fla.	Creve Coeur, Mo.	14/14
84	Goode, John	TE	6-2	222	11/5/62	2	Youngstown State	Cleveland Heights, Ohio	Cleveland, Ohio	16/1
81	Green, Roy	WR	6-0	195	6/30/57	7	Henderson State	Magnolia, Ark.	St. Louis, Mo.	16/16
75	Greer, Curtis	DE	6-4	258	11/10/57	6	Michigan	Detroit, Mich.	St. Louis, Mo.	16/16
35	†Griffin, Jeff	CB	6-0	185	7/19/58	5	Utah	Carson, Calif.	Compton, Calif.	8/1
78	Grooms, Elois	DT	6-4	250	5/20/53	11	Tennessee Tech	Tomkinsville, Ky.	Mandeville, La.	11/6
39	Harrell, Willard	RB	5-9	190	9/16/52	11	Pacific	Stockton, Calif.	Maryland Heights, Mo.	16/0
36	Harrington, Perry	RB	5-11	210	3/13/58	6	Jackson State	Jackson, Miss.	Jackson, Miss.	6/0
50	Harris, Bob	LB	6-2	215	11/11/60	3	Auburn	Everett, Wash.	Lilburn, Ga.	16/3
46	Heflin, Victor	CB	6-0	184	7/7/60	3	Delaware State	Springfield, Mass.	Dayton, Ohio	16/0
59	Howard, Thomas	LB	6-2	220	8/18/54	9	Texas Tech	Lubbock, Tex.	Lubbock, Tex.	15/13
54	Junior, E.J.	LB	6-3	235	12/8/59	5	Alabama	Salisbury, N.C.	Florissant, Mo.	16/16
89	†LaFleur, Greg	TE	6-4	236	9/16/58	5	Louisiana State	Ville Platte, La.	Baton Rouge, La.	16/5
15	Lomax, Neil	QB	6-3	214	2/17/59	5	Portland State	Portland, Ore.	West Linn, Ore.	16/16
40	Love, Randy	RB	6-1	205	9/30/56	7	Houston	Wylie, Tex.	Garland, Tex.	16/1
82	Mack, Cedric	WR-CB	6-0	190	9/14/60	3	Baylor	Freeport, Tex.	Freeport, Tex.	12/0
12	Mackey, Kyle	QB	6-2	220	3/2/62	2	East Texas State	Fort Davis, Tex.	Arp, Tex.	0*
80	†Marsh, Doug	TE	6-3	238	6/18/58	6	Michigan	Akron, Ohio	Akron, Ohio	16/16
76	Mays, Stafford	DE	6-2	250	3/13/58	6	Washington	Lawrence, Kan.	Tacoma, Wash.	16/0
87	McGill, Eddie	TE	6-6	225	7/5/60	3	Western Carolina	Asheville, N.C.	Candler, N.C.	0*
14	McIvor, Rick	QB	6-4	210	9/26/60	2	Texas	Alpine, Tex.	Fort Davis, Tex.	4/0
30	Mitchell, Stump	RB	5-9	188	3/15/59	5	Citadel	St. Mary's, Ga.	St. Louis, Mo.	16/1
38	Nelson, Lee	S	5-10	185	1/30/54	10	Florida State	Kissimee, Fla.	Chesterfield, Mo.	16/6
57	Noga, Niko	LB	6-1	230	3/2/62	2	Hawaii	American Samoa	Waipahu, Hawaii	16/0
11	O'Donoghue, Neil	K	6-6	210	6/18/53	9	Auburn	Dublin, Ireland	Indian Rocks Beach, Fla.	16/0
23	Perrin, Benny	S	6-2	178	10/20/59	4	Alabama	Orange County, Calif.	Decatur, Ga.	16/16
85	†Pittman, Danny	WR	6-2	205	4/3/58	6	Wyoming	Memphis, Tenn.	Pasadena, Calif.	10/0
70	Plunkett, Art	T	6-7	270	3/8/59	5	Nevada-Las Vegas	Chicago, Ill.	Henderson, Nev.	16/0
72	Ralph, Dan	DT	6-4	260	3/9/61	2	Oregon	Northglenn, Colo.	Northglenn, Colo.	6/0
63	Robbins, Tootie	T	6-4	278	6/2/58	4	East Carolina	Windsor, N.C.	Florissant, Mo.	16/16
56	Scott, Carlos	C	6-4	300	7/2/60	3	Texas-El Paso	Hempstead, Tex.	Hempstead, Tex.	16/0
45	Smith, Leonard	S	5-11	190	9/2/60	3	McNeese State	New Orleans, La.	Chesterfield, Mo.	12/11
44	Smith, Wayne	CB	6-0	175	5/9/57	6	Purdue	Chicago, Ill.	Chicago, Ill.	16/15
68	Stieve, Terry	G	6-2	265	3/10/54	9	Wisconsin	Baraboo, Wis.	Ballwin, Mo.	14/14
83	†Tilley, Pat	WR	5-10	178	2/15/53	10	Louisiana Tech	Marshall, Tex.	Shreveport, La.	16/16
33	Walker, Quentin	WR	6-1	200	8/27/61	2	Virginia	Teaneck, N.J.	Teaneck, N.J.	3/0
48	Washington, Lionel	CB	6-0	184	10/21/60	3	Tulane	New Orleans, La.	Florissant, Mo.	15/15
42	Whitaker, Bill	S	6-0	182	11/18/59	5	Missouri	Kansas City, Mo.	Kansas City, Mo.	7/0

* Mackey active with St. Louis for 16 games but did not play; McGill missed '84 season due to injury.

†Option playout; subject to developments.

Also played with Cardinals in '84—G Dan Audick (7 games), S Martin Bayless (3), WR Steve Bird (8), LB Billy Davis (1), DE Randy Holloway (6), S Bill Kay (10), LB Craig Shaffer (4), T Luis Sharpe (16).

COACHING STAFF

Head Coach,
Jim Hanifan

Pro Career: Named head coach on January 30, 1980, and has improved Cardinals record in each of his five years. No stranger to city of St. Louis, where he began his pro coaching career in 1973 as offensive line coach. Served Cardinals in that capacity until 1979 when he left to become assistant head coach of San Diego Chargers. During his first tenure at St. Louis, his offensive lines allowed fewest quarterback sacks in NFL for three straight years (1974-76), including an NFL-record low of eight in 1975. Played end for the Toronto Argonauts (CFL) in 1955. Career record: 34-39-1.

Background: Played end for California 1952-54 and led the nation in receiving as a senior. Began coaching career at Charter Oak High School in Covina, Calif., in 1962. Was a college assistant for 14 years: Yuba, Calif., J.C. 1959-61, Glendale, Calif., J.C. 1964-65, Utah 1966-69, California 1970-71, San Diego State 1972.

Personal: Born September 21, 1933, in Compton, Calif. He and his wife, Mariana, live in St. Louis and have two children — Kathleen and James.

Assistant Coaches

Chuck Banker, offensive backs; born March 12, 1941, Prescott Ariz., lives in St. Louis. Linebacker-tight end Pasadena, Calif., City College 1959-60. No pro playing experience. College coach: Glendale, Calif., J.C. 1962-65, Utah 1966-67, 1974-75, Westminster 1968-70, Boise State 1976-79. Pro coach: Joined Cardinals in 1980. Served as special teams coach prior to 1985 season.

Rudy Feldman, linebackers; born May 18, 1932, San Francisco, Calif., lives in St. Louis. Guard UCLA 1950-53. No pro playing experience. College coach: Iowa State 1957, Oklahoma 1963-67, New Mexico 1968-73 (head coach). Pro coach: San Diego Chargers 1974-77, joined Cardinals in 1978.

Pete Hoener, strength and flexibility; born June 14, 1951, Peoria, Ill., lives in St. Louis. Defensive end Bradley 1969-70. No pro playing experience. College coach: Missouri 1975-76, Illinois State 1977, Indiana State 1978-84. Pro coach: First year with Cardinals.

Dick Jamieson, offensive coordinator; born November 13, 1937, Streator, Ill., lives in St. Louis. Quarterback Bradley 1955-58. Pro quarterback Baltimore Colts 1959, New York Titans 1960-61, Houston Oilers 1965. College coach: Bradley 1962-64, Missouri 1972-79. Pro coach: Joined Cardinals in 1980. Served as backfield coach prior to 1985 season.

Leon McLaughlin, special assistant; born May 30, 1925, San Diego, Calif., lives in St. Louis. Center-linebacker UCLA 1946-49. Pro center Los Angeles Rams 1951-55. College coach: Washington State 1956, Stanford 1959-65, San Fernando Valley State 1969-70 (head coach). Pro coach: Pittsburgh Steelers 1966-68, Los Angeles Rams 1971-72, Detroit Lions 1973-74, Green Bay Packers 1975-76, New England Patriots 1977, joined Cardinals in 1978.

Ernie McMillan, offensive line; born February 21, 1938, Chicago Heights, Ill., lives in St. Louis. End Illinois 1959-61. Pro offensive tackle St. Louis Cardinals 1961-74, Green Bay Packers 1975. Pro coach: Green Bay Packers 1977-83, joined Cardinals in 1984.

Floyd Peters, assistant head coach-defense; born May 21, 1936, Council Bluffs, Iowa, lives in St. Louis. Defensive tackle San Francisco State 1954-57. Pro defensive tackle Baltimore Colts 1958, Cleveland Browns 1959-62, Detroit Lions 1963, Philadelphia Eagles 1964-69, Washington Redskins 1970. Pro coach: Washington Redskins 1970, New York Giants 1974-75, San Francisco 49ers 1976-77, Detroit Lions 1978-81, joined Cardinals in 1982.

ST. LOUIS CARDINALS 1985 FIRST-YEAR ROSTER

Name	Pos.	Ht.	Wt.	Birth-date	College	Birthplace	Residence	How Acq.
Alston, Wilford	RB	5-10	205	2/28/60	Citadel	Beaufort, S.C.	Colorado Springs, Co.	FA
Anderson, Ricky	P-K	6-2	190	1/24/63	Vanderbilt	St. Petersburg, Fla.	St. Petersburg, Fla.	D11
Bergold, Scott	T	6-7	255	11/19/61	Wisconsin	Milwaukee, Wis.	Wauwatosa, Wis.	D2
Bowers, Alan (1)	RB	6-0	206	4/18/61	Illinois State	East St. Louis, Ill.	East St. Louis, Ill.	FA
Calhoun, Paul	CB-S	6-2	199	10/28/63	Kentucky	Louisville, Ky.	Louisville, Ky.	FA
Clark, Ralph	T	6-4	259	5/7/63	Northern Iowa	Minneapolis, Minn.	Minneapolis, Minn.	FA
Davis, Billy (1)	LB	6-4	200	12/6/61	Clemson	Alexandria, Va.	Alexandria, Va.	FA
Dunn, K.D.	TE	6-3	220	4/28/63	Clemson	Ft. Hood, Tex.	Decatur, Ga.	D5
Ferrell, David	LB	6-1	210	7/14/60	East Tennessee St.	South Boston, Va.	South Boston, Va.	FA
Holloway, Herman	RB	6-1	204	11/30/61	Arkansas-Pine Bluff	Birmingham, Ala.	Birmingham, Ala.	FA
Jones, Ed	DE	6-4	236	7/22/62	Virginia State	Hopewell, Va.	Hopewell, Va.	FA
Miller, Bob	C	6-2	248	3/2/62	Illinois	Elmhurst, Ill.	Schaumburg, Ill.	FA
Monaco, Rob	T	6-3	270	9/5/61	Vanderbilt	Hamden, Conn.	Hamden, Conn.	D8
Novacek, Jay	WR	6-4	211	10/24/62	Wyoming	Martin, S.D.	Gothenburg, Neb.	D6
Nunn, Freddie Joe	LB	6-4	233	4/9/62	Mississippi	Noxibee City, Wis.	Oxford, Miss.	D1
Patterson, Reno	DT	6-2	255	4/22/61	Bethune-Cookman	Chicago, Ill.	Chicago, Ill.	FA
Smith, Lance	G	6-2	273	1/1/63	Louisiana State	Kannapolis, N.C.	Baton Rouge, La.	D3
Thomas, Curtland (1)	WR	5-11	182	2/19/62	Missouri	St. Louis, Mo.	St. Louis, Mo.	FA
Walker, John (1)	RB	6-0	205	8/31/61	Texas	Killeen, Tex.	Killeen, Tex.	FA
West, James	LB	6-2	220	12/19/57	Texas Southern	Ft. Worth, Tex.	Houston, Tex.	FA
Williams, Dennis	RB	6-1	227	1/1/62	Furman	Anderson, S.C.	Greenville, S.C.	D10
Williams, Scott	TE	6-1	234	7/21/62	Georgia	Charlotte, N.C.	Charlotte, N.C.	D9
Wolfley, Craig	RB	6-0	222	10/14/62	West Virginia	Orchard Park, N.Y.	Orchard Park, N.Y.	D4
Wong, Louis	T	6-4	259	1/5/63	Brigham Young	Honolulu, Hawaii	Kaneohe, Hawaii	D5a
Young, Lonnie	CB-S	6-1	182	7/18/63	Michigan State	Flint, Mich.	Flint, Mich.	D12

Players who report to an NFL team for the first time are designated on rosters as rookies (R). If a player reported to an NFL training camp in a previous year but was not on the active squad for three or more regular season or postseason games, he is listed on the first-year roster and designated by a (1). Thereafter, a player who is on the active squad for three or more regular season or postseason games is credited with an additional year of playing experience.

NOTES

_____
_____
_____
_____
_____
_____
_____
_____
_____
_____
_____
_____
_____
_____
_____
_____
_____
_____

Jerry Smith, defensive line; born September 9, 1930, Dayton, Ohio, lives in St. Louis. Linebacker Wisconsin 1948-51. Pro linebacker San Francisco 49ers 1952-53, Green Bay Packers 1956. College coach: Dayton 1959. Pro coach: Boston Patriots 1960-61, Buffalo Bills 1962-68, New Orleans Saints 1969-70, Denver Broncos 1971, Houston Oilers 1972, Cleveland Browns 1973, Baltimore Colts 1974-76, San Diego Chargers 1977-83, first year with Cardinals.

Emmitt Thomas, receivers; born June 4, 1943, Angleton, Tex., lives in St. Louis. Quarterback-wide receiver Bishop College 1963-65. Pro defensive back Kansas City Chiefs 1966-78. College coach: Central Missouri State 1979-80. Pro coach: Joined Cardinals in 1981.

Lance Van Zandt, defensive backfield; born January 19, 1939, Amarillo, Tex., lives in St. Louis. Lamar 1961. No college or pro playing experience. College coach: New Mexico Highlands 1966-67, West Texas State 1968-69, Texas A&M 1970-71, Rice 1972, Oklahoma State, 1973-74, Kansas 1975-76, Nebraska 1977-80. Pro coach: New Orleans Saints 1981-84, first year with Cardinals.

SAN FRANCISCO 49ERS

**National Football Conference
Western Division**

Team Colors: Forty Niners Gold
and Scarlet

**711 Nevada Street
Redwood City, California 94061
Telephone (415) 365-3420**

Club Officials

Owner, Chairman of the Board: Edward J.
DeBartolo, Jr.
President, Head Coach: Bill Walsh
Vice President, General Manager: John McVay
Vice President of Marketing and Community
Affairs: Ken Flower
Director of Pro Scouting: Alan Webb
Director of College Scouting: Tony Razzano
Director of Public Relations: Jerry Walker
Publications Coordinator: Rodney Knox
Business Manager: Keith Simon
Ticket Manager: Ken Dargel
Trainer: Lindsy McLean
Assistant Trainer: John Miller
Equipment Manager: Bronco Hinek
Equipment Manager Emeritus: Chico Norton

Stadium: Candlestick Park • **Capacity:** 61,413
San Francisco, California 94124

Playing Surface: Grass

Training Camp: Sierra Community College
Rocklin, California 95677

1985 SCHEDULE

Preseason
Aug. 10	at Los Angeles Raiders	6:00
Aug. 19	**Denver**	6:00
Aug. 24	**San Diego**	12:00
Aug. 30	at Seattle	6:00

Regular Season
Sept. 8	at Minnesota	12:00
Sept. 15	**Atlanta**	1:00
Sept. 22	at Los Angeles Raiders	1:00
Sept. 29	**New Orleans**	1:00
Oct. 6	at Atlanta	1:00
Oct. 13	**Chicago**	1:00
Oct. 20	at Detroit	1:00
Oct. 27	at Los Angeles Rams	1:00
Nov. 3	**Philadelphia**	1:00
Nov. 11	at Denver (Monday)	7:00
Nov. 17	**Kansas City**	1:00
Nov. 25	**Seattle** (Monday)	6:00
Dec. 1	at Washington	4:00
Dec. 9	**L.A. Rams** (Monday)	6:00
Dec. 15	at New Orleans	12:00
Dec. 22	**Dallas**	1:00

49ERS COACHING HISTORY

(236-241-12)
1950-54	Lawrence (Buck) Shaw	33-25-2
1955	Norman (Red) Strader	4-8-0
1956-58	Frankie Albert	19-17-1
1959-63	Howard (Red) Hickey*	27-27-1
1963-67	Jack Christiansen	26-38-3
1968-75	Dick Nolan	56-56-5
1976	Monte Clark	8-6-0
1977	Ken Meyer	5-9-0
1978	Pete McCulley**	1-8-0
1978	Fred O'Connor	1-6-0
1979-84	Bill Walsh	56-41-0

*Resigned after three games in 1963
**Released after nine games in 1978

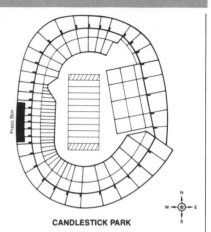

CANDLESTICK PARK

RECORD HOLDERS
Individual Records—Career
Category	Name	Performance
Rushing (Yds.)	Joe Perry, 1950-1960, 1963	7,344
Passing (Yds.)	John Brodie, 1957-1973	31,548
Passing (TDs)	John Brodie, 1957-1973	214
Receiving (No.)	Billy Wilson, 1951-1960	407
Receiving (Yds.)	Gene Washington, 1969-1977	6,664
Interceptions	Jimmy Johnson, 1961-1976	47
Punting (Avg.)	Tommy Davis, 1959-1969	44.7
Punt Return (Avg.)	Manfred Moore, 1974-75	14.7
Kickoff Return (Avg.)	Abe Woodson, 1958-1964	29.4
Field Goals	Ray Wersching, 1977-1984	139
Touchdowns (Tot.)	Ken Willard, 1965-1973	61
Points	Tommy Davis, 1959-1969	738

Individual Records—Single Season
Category	Name	Performance
Rushing (Yds.)	Wendell Tyler, 1984	1,262
Passing (Yds.)	Joe Montana, 1983	3,910
Passing (TDs)	John Brodie, 1965	30
Receiving (No.)	Dwight Clark, 1981	85
Receiving (Yds.)	Dave Parks, 1965	1,344
Interceptions	Dave Baker, 1960	10
Punting (Avg.)	Tommy Davis, 1965	45.8
Punt Return (Avg.)	Dana McLemore, 1982	22.3
Kickoff Return (Avg.)	Joe Arenas, 1953	34.4
Field Goals	Bruce Gossett, 1973	26
Touchdowns (Tot.)	Joe Perry, 1953	13
Points	Ray Wersching, 1984	131

Individual Records—Single Game
Category	Name	Performance
Rushing (Yds.)	Delvin Williams, 10-31-76	194
Passing (Yds.)	Joe Montana, 11-21-82	408
Passing (TDs)	John Brodie, 11-23-65	5
	Steve Spurrier, 11-19-72	5
Receiving (No.)	Bernie Casey, 11-13-66	12
	Dwight Clark, 12-11-82	12
Receiving (Yds.)	Dave Parks, 10-3-65	231
Interceptions	Dave Baker, 12-4-60	4
Field Goals	Ray Wersching, 10-16-83	6
Touchdowns (Tot.)	Billy Kilmer, 10-15-61	4
Points	Gordy Soltau, 10-27-51	26

1984 TEAM STATISTICS

	San Francisco	Opp.
Total First Downs	356	302
Rushing	138	101
Passing	204	173
Penalty	14	28
Third Down: Made/Att.	96/207	75/213
Fourth Down: Made/Att.	5/7	6/21
Total Net Yards	6366	5176
Avg. Per Game	397.9	323.5
Total Plays	1057	1029
Avg. Per Play	6.0	5.0
Net Yards Rushing	2465	1795
Avg. Per Game	154.1	112.2
Total Rushes	534	432
Net Yards Passing	3901	3381
Avg. Per Game	243.8	211.3
Tackled/Yards Lost	27/178	51/363
Gross Yards	4079	3744
Att./Completions	496/312	546/298
Completion Pct.	62.9	54.6
Had Intercepted	10	25
Punts/Avg.	62/40.9	80/40.5
Net Punting Avg.	34.0	32.7
Penalties/Yards Lost	100/884	91/723
Fumbles/Ball Lost	26/12	28/13
Touchdowns	57	24
Rushing	21	10
Passing	32	14
Returns	4	0
Avg. Time of Possession	30:26	29:34

1984 TEAM RECORD
Preseason (2-2)

Date	San Francisco		Opponents	
8/4	13	*Los Angeles Raiders	10	
8/11	20	Denver	21	
8/18	15	San Diego	35	
8/24	17	*Seattle	7	
	65		73	

Regular Season (15-1)

Date	San Francisco		Opp.	Att.
9/2	30	Detroit	27	56,782
9/10	37	*Washington	31	59,707
9/16	30	*New Orleans	20	57,611
9/23	21	Philadelphia	9	62,771
9/30	14	*Atlanta	5	57,990
10/8	31	New York Giants	10	76,112
10/14	17	*Pittsburgh	20	59,110
10/21	34	Houston	21	39,900
10/28	33	Los Angeles Rams	0	65,481
11/4	23	*Cincinnati	17	58,324
11/11	41	Cleveland	7	60,092
11/18	24	*Tampa Bay	17	57,704
11/25	35	New Orleans	3	65,177
12/2	35	Atlanta	17	29,644
12/8	51	*Minnesota	7	56,670
12/14	19	*Los Angeles Rams	16	59,743
	475		227	922,818

*Home Game

Score by Periods

San Francisco	110	157	67	141	—	475
Opponents	29	86	48	64	—	227

Attendance

Home 466,859   Away 455,959   Total 922,818
Single game home record, 61,214 (4 times, 1972)
Single season home record, 466,859 (1984)

1984 INDIVIDUAL STATISTICS

Rushing

	Att.	Yds.	Avg.	LG	TD
Tyler	246	1262	5.1	40	7
Craig	155	649	4.2	28	7
D. Harmon	39	192	4.9	19	1
Ring	38	162	4.3	34	3
Montana	39	118	3.0	15	2
Solomon	6	72	12.0	47	1
Cooper	3	13	4.3	7	0
Monroe	3	13	4.3	7	0
Runager	1	−5	−5.0	−5	0
Cavanaugh	4	−11	−2.8	−1	0
San Francisco	534	2465	4.6	47	21
Opponents	432	1795	4.2	25	10

Passing

	Att.	Comp.	Pct.	Yds.	TD	Int.	Tkld.	Rate
Montana	432	279	64.6	3630	28	10	22/138	102.9
Cavanaugh	61	33	54.1	449	4	0	5/40	99.7
D. Harmon	2	0	0.0	0	0	0	0/0	39.6
D. Clark	1	0	0.0	0	0	0	0/0	39.6
San Fran.	496	312	62.9	4079	32	10	27/178	101.9
Opponents	546	298	54.6	3744	14	25	51/363	65.6

Receiving

	No.	Yds.	Avg.	LG	TD
Craig	71	675	9.5	64t	3
D. Clark	52	880	16.9	80t	6
Cooper	41	459	11.2	26	4
Solomon	40	737	18.4	64t	10
Tyler	28	230	8.2	26t	2
Francis	23	285	12.4	32	2
Nehemiah	18	357	19.8	59t	2
Wilson	17	245	14.4	44	1
Monroe	11	139	12.6	47	1
Frank	7	60	8.6	21	1
Ring	3	10	3.3	15	0
D. Harmon	1	2	2.0	2	0
San Francisco	312	4079	13.1	80t	32
Opponents	298	3744	12.6	61	14

Interceptions

	No.	Yds.	Avg.	LG	TD
Turner	4	51	12.8	21	0
Lott	4	26	6.5	15	0
Shell	3	81	27.0	53t	1
Hicks	3	42	14.0	29	0
McLemore	2	54	27.0	54t	1
Williamson	2	42	21.0	26	0
J. Fahnhorst	2	9	4.5	9	0
Wright	2	0	0.0	0	0
Fuller	1	38	38.0	38	0
Bunz	1	2	2.0	2	0
M. Clark	1	0	0.0	0	0
San Francisco	25	345	13.8	54t	2
Opponents	10	155	15.5	43	0

Punting

	No.	Yds.	Avg.	In 20	LG
Runager	56	2341	41.8	18	59
Orosz	5	195	39.0	1	55
San Francisco	62	2536	40.9	19	59
Opponents	80	3239	40.5	12	58

Punt Returns

	No.	FC	Yds.	Avg.	LG	TD
McLemore	45	11	521	11.6	79t	1
San Francisco	45	11	521	11.6	79t	1
Opponents	30	4	190	6.3	25	0

Kickoff Returns

	No.	Yds.	Avg.	LG	TD
Monroe	27	561	20.8	44	0
D. Harmon	13	357	27.5	51	0
McLemore	3	80	26.7	50	0
Ring	1	27	27.0	27	0
Wilson	1	14	14.0	14	0
Cooper	1	0	0.0	0	0
McIntyre	1	0	0.0	0	0
San Francisco	47	1039	22.1	51	0
Opponents	78	1499	19.2	38	0

Scoring

	TD R	TD P	TD Rt	PAT	FG	Saf	TP
Wersching	0	0	0	56/56	25/35	0	131
Solomon	1	10	0	0/0	0/0	0	66
Craig	7	3	0	0/0	0/0	0	60
Tyler	7	2	0	0/0	0/0	0	54
D. Clark	0	6	0	0/0	0/0	0	36
Cooper	0	4	0	0/0	0/0	0	24
Ring	3	0	0	0/0	0/0	0	18
Francis	0	2	0	0/0	0/0	0	12
McLemore	0	0	2	0/0	0/0	0	12
Montana	2	0	0	0/0	0/0	0	12
Nehemiah	0	2	0	0/0	0/0	0	12
Johnson	0	0	1	0/0	0/0	1	8
Frank	0	1	0	0/0	0/0	0	6
D. Harmon	1	0	0	0/0	0/0	0	6
Monroe	0	1	0	0/0	0/0	0	6
Shell	0	0	1	0/0	0/0	0	6
Wilson	0	1	0	0/0	0/0	0	6
San Fran.	21	32	4	56/57	25/35	1	475
Opponents	10	14	0	24/24	19/25	1	227

FIRST-ROUND SELECTIONS

(If Club had no first-round selection, first player drafted is listed with round in parentheses.)

Year	Player, College, Position
1950	Leo Nomellini, Minnesota, T
1951	Y. A. Tittle, Louisiana State, B
1952	Hugh McElhenny, Washington, B
1953	Harry Babcock, Georgia, E
	Tom Stolhandske, Texas, E
1954	Bernie Faloney, Maryland, B
1955	Dickie Moegle, Rice, B
1956	Earl Morrall, Michigan State, B
1957	John Brodie, Stanford, B
1958	Jim Pace, Michigan, B
	Charlie Krueger, Texas A&M, T
1959	Dave Baker, Oklahoma, B
	Dan James, Ohio State, C
1960	Monty Stickles, Notre Dame, E
1961	Jimmy Johnson, UCLA, CB
	Bernie Casey, Bowling Green, WR
	Bill Kilmer, UCLA, QB
1962	Lance Alworth, Arkansas, WR
1963	Kermit Alexander, UCLA, CB
1964	Dave Parks, Texas Tech, WR
1965	Ken Willard, North Carolina, RB
	George Donnelly, Illinois, DE
1966	Stan Hindman, Mississippi, DE
1967	Steve Spurrier, Florida, QB
	Cas Banaszek, Northwestern, T
1968	Forrest Blue, Auburn, C
1969	Ted Kwalick, Penn State, TE
	Gene Washington, Stanford, WR
1970	Cedrick Hardman, North Texas State, DE
	Bruce Taylor, Boston U., DB
1971	Tim Anderson, Ohio State, DB
1972	Terry Beasley, Auburn, WR
1973	Mike Holmes, Texas Southern, DB
1974	Wilbur Jackson, Alabama, RB
	Bill Sandifer, UCLA, DT
1975	Jimmy Webb, Mississippi State, DT
1976	Randy Cross, UCLA, C (2)
1977	Elmo Boyd, Eastern Kentucky, WR (3)
1978	Ken MacAfee, Notre Dame, TE
	Dan Bunz, Cal State-Long Beach, LB
1979	James Owens, UCLA, WR (2)
1980	Earl Cooper, Rice, RB
	Jim Stuckey, Clemson, DT
1981	Ronnie Lott, Southern California, DB
1982	Bubba Paris, Michigan, T (2)
1983	Roger Craig, Nebraska, RB (2)
1984	Todd Shell, Brigham Young, LB
1985	Jerry Rice, Mississippi Valley State, WR

SAN FRANCISCO 49ERS 1985 VETERAN ROSTER

No.	Name	Pos.	Ht.	Wt.	Birth-date	NFL Exp.	College	Birthplace	Residence	'84 Games/ Starts
68	Ayers, John	G	6-5	265	4/14/53	9	West Texas State	Carrizo Springs, Tex.	Redwood City, Calif.	16/16
76	Board, Dwaine	DE	6-5	248	11/29/56	6	North Carolina A&T	Union Hall, Va.	Redwood City, Calif.	16/16
57	Bunz, Dan	LB	6-4	225	10/7/55	7	Long Beach State	Roseville, Calif.	Loomis, Calif.	16/16
95	Carter, Michael	NT	6-2	281	10/29/60	2	Southern Methodist	Dallas, Tex.	Dallas, Tex.	16/0
6	†Cavanaugh, Matt	QB	6-2	212	10/27/56	8	Pittsburgh	Youngstown, Ohio	Foxboro, Mass.	8/1
87	Clark, Dwight	WR	6-4	215	1/8/57	7	Clemson	Kinston, N.C.	Redwood City, Calif.	16/14
29	Clark, Mario	CB	6-2	195	3/29/54	10	Oregon	Pasadena, Calif.	Pasadena, Calif.	11/6
47	Collier, Tim	CB	6-0	176	5/31/54	9	East Texas State	Dallas, Tex.	San Mateo, Calif.	0*
89	Cooper, Earl	TE	6-2	227	9/17/57	6	Rice	Lexington, Tex.	Houston, Tex.	16/8
33	Craig, Roger	FB	6-0	222	7/10/60	3	Nebraska	Preston, Miss.	Bettendorf, Iowa	16/16
51	Cross, Randy	G	6-3	265	4/25/54	10	UCLA	New York, N.Y.	Redwood City, Calif.	16/16
74	Dean, Fred	DE	6-2	232	2/24/52	11	Louisiana Tech	Arcadia, La.	San Diego, Calif.	5/0
50	Ellison, Riki	LB	6-2	220	8/15/60	3	Southern California	Christchurch, New Zealand	Foster City, Calif.	16/16
55	Fahnhorst, Jim	LB	6-4	230	11/8/58	2	Minnesota	St. Cloud, Minn.	Foster City, Calif.	14/2
71	Fahnhorst, Keith	T	6-6	273	2/6/52	12	Minnesota	St. Cloud, Minn.	St. Paul, Minn.	15/15
54	Ferrari, Ron	LB	6-0	212	7/30/59	4	Illinois	Springfield, Ill.	Moweaqua, Ill.	11/0
81	Francis, Russ	TE	6-6	242	4/3/53	10	Oregon	Seattle, Wash.	Wallingford, Ver.	10/8
86	Frank, John	TE	6-3	225	4/17/62	2	Ohio State	Mt. Lebanon, Pa.	Pittsburgh, Pa.	15/2
49	Fuller, Jeff	S	6-2	216	8/8/62	2	Texas A&M	Dallas, Tex.	Dallas, Tex.	13/1
24	Harmon, Derrick	RB	5-10	202	4/26/63	2	Cornell	New York, N.Y.	Ithaca, N.Y.	16/0
75	Harty, John	NT	6-4	263	12/17/58	4	Iowa	Sioux City, Iowa	Sioux City, Iowa	0*
22	Hicks, Dwight	S	6-1	192	4/5/56	7	Michigan	Mt. Holly, N.J.	Menlo Park, Calif.	16/16
28	†Holmoe, Tom	CB-S	6-2	180	3/7/60	3	Brigham Young	Los Angeles, Calif.	San Mateo, Calif.	16/1
97	Johnson, Gary	NT	6-2	261	8/31/53	11	Grambling	Shreveport, La.	San Diego, Calif.	16/1*
94	Kelcher, Louie	NT	6-5	310	8/23/53	11	Southern Methodist	Beaumont, Tex.	Olivenhain, Calif.	16/0
66	Kennedy, Allan	T	6-7	275	1/8/58	4	Washington State	Vancouver, Canada	San Mateo, Calif.	15/1
42	Lott, Ronnie	S-CB	6-0	199	5/8/59	5	Southern California	Albuquerque, N.M.	Santa Clara, Calif.	12/11
53	†McColl, Milt	LB	6-6	230	8/28/59	5	Stanford	Oak Park, Ill.	Menlo Park, Calif.	16/0
62	McIntyre, Guy	G	6-3	271	2/17/61	2	Georgia	Thomasville, Ga.	Thomasville, Ga.	16/0
43	McLemore, Dana	KR-CB	5-10	183	7/1/60	4	Hawaii	Los Angeles, Calif.	San Mateo, Calif.	16/0
32	Monroe, Carl	RB-KR	5-8	166	2/20/60	3	Utah	Pittsburgh, Pa.	Sunnyvale, Calif.	16/0
16	Montana, Joe	QB	6-2	195	6/11/56	7	Notre Dame	New Eagle, Pa.	Redwood City, Calif.	16/15
52	Montgomery, Blanchard	LB	6-2	236	2/17/61	3	UCLA	Los Angeles, Calif.	Foster City, Calif.	16/0
83	Nehemiah, Renaldo	WR	6-1	183	3/24/59	4	Maryland	Newark, N.J.	Gaithersburg, Md.	16/0
77	Paris, Bubba	T	6-6	295	10/6/60	3	Michigan	Louisville, Ky.	Redwood City, Calif.	16/15
65	Pillers, Lawrence	NT-DE	6-4	250	11/4/52	10	Alcorn A&M	Hazlehurst, Miss.	San Mateo, Calif.	16/7
56	Quillan, Fred	C	6-5	266	1/27/56	8	Oregon	West Palm Beach, Fla.	San Mateo, Calif.	16/16
64	Reynolds, Jack	LB	6-1	232	11/22/47	16	Tennessee	Cincinnati, Ohio	San Salvador, Bahamas	15/14
30	Ring, Bill	RB	5-10	205	12/13/56	5	Brigham Young	Des Moines, Iowa	Redwood City, Calif.	16/1
4	Runager, Max	P	6-1	189	3/24/56	7	South Carolina	Greenwood, S.C.	Orangeburg, S.C.	14/0
61	Sapolu, Jesse	G	6-4	260	3/10/61	2	Hawaii	Laie, Western Samoa	Honolulu, Hawaii	1/0
90	Shell, Todd	LB	6-4	225	6/24/62	2	Brigham Young	Mesa, Ariz.	Mesa, Ariz.	16/0
67	Shields, Billy	T	6-8	279	8/23/53	11	Georgia Tech	Vicksburg, Miss.	San Diego, Calif.	11/1
88	Solomon, Freddie	WR	5-11	188	1/11/53	11	Tampa	Sumter, S.C.	San Carlos, Calif.	14/13
72	Stover, Jeff	NT	6-5	275	5/22/58	4	Oregon	Corning, Calif.	Chico, Calif.	6/2
79	†Stuckey, Jim	DE	6-4	253	6/21/58	6	Clemson	Cayce, S.C.	Redwood City, Calif.	16/7
78	Tuiasosopo, Manu	NT	6-3	252	8/30/57	7	UCLA	Los Angeles, Calif.	Woodinville, Wash.	16/16
58	Turner, Keena	LB	6-2	219	10/22/58	6	Purdue	Chicago, Ill.	San Carlos, Calif.	16/16
26	Tyler, Wendell	RB	5-10	200	5/20/55	8	UCLA	Shreveport, La.	West Covina, Calif.	16/15
99	Walter, Michael	LB	6-3	238	11/30/60	3	Oregon	Salem, Ore.	Eugene, Ore.	16/0
14	Wersching, Ray	K	5-11	210	8/21/50	13	California	Mondsee, Austria	San Carlos, Calif.	16/0
27	Williamson, Carlton	S	6-0	204	6/12/58	5	Pittsburgh	Atlanta, Ga.	Mountain View, Calif.	15/15
85	Wilson, Mike	WR	6-3	210	12/19/58	5	Washington State	Los Angeles, Calif.	San Mateo, Calif.	13/3
21	Wright, Eric	CB	6-1	180	4/18/59	5	Missouri	St. Louis, Mo.	San Carlos, Calif.	16/14

* Collier and Harty missed '84 season due to injury; Johnson played 4 games with San Diego, 12 with San Francisco in '84.

†Option playout; subject to developments.

Also played with 49ers in '84—DE Greg Boyd (2 games), TE Al Dixon (2), C John Macaulay (3), P Tom Orosz (2).

COACHING STAFF

Head Coach, Bill Walsh

Pro Career: Begins seventh season as an NFL head coach. Directed 49ers to NFC championship in 1981 and 1984 and to victories in Super Bowl XVI (26-21 over Cincinnati) and Super Bowl XIX (38-16 over Miami). Started pro coaching career in 1966 as offensive backfield coach for the Oakland Raiders. He then spent eight seasons (1967-75) in Cincinnati, where he was responsible for coaching the Bengals' quarterbacks and receivers. His tenure in Cincinnati was followed by a season with the San Diego Chargers as offensive coordinator. While at Cincinnati he tutored Ken Anderson, who became the first NFL quarterback to lead the league in passing two straight years. At San Diego, he helped develop the talents of quarterback Dan Fouts. No pro playing experience. Career record: 56-41.

Background: End at San Jose State in 1953-54. Started college coaching career at California, where he served under Marv Levy from 1960-62. In 1963, he joined John Ralston's Stanford staff and worked with the defensive backfield for three seasons. Returned to Stanford as head coach in 1977 and directed Cardinals to a two-year record of 17-7, including wins in the Sun and Bluebonnet Bowls. Received his master's degree in history from San Jose State in 1959.

Personal: Born November 30, 1931, in Los Angeles, Calif. He and his wife, Geri, live in Menlo Park, Calif., and have three children—Steve, Craig, and Elizabeth.

Assistant Coaches

Jerry Attaway, conditioning; born January 3, 1946, Susanville, Calif., lives in San Carlos, Calif. Defensive back Yuba, Calif., J.C. 1964-65, Cal-Davis 1967. No pro playing experience. College coach: Cal-Davis 1970-71, Idaho 1972-74, Utah State 1975-77, Southern California 1978-82. Pro coach: Joined 49ers in 1983.

Paul Hackett, quarterbacks-receivers; born July 5, 1947, Burlington, Vt., lives in Redwood City, Calif. Quarterback Cal-Davis 1965-68. No pro playing experience. College coach: Cal-Davis 1970-71, California 1972-75, Southern California 1976-80. Pro coach: Cleveland Browns 1981-82, joined 49ers in 1983.

Norb Hecker, linebackers; born May 26, 1927, Berea, Ohio, lives in San Francisco. End Baldwin-Wallace 1947-50. Pro end-defensive back Los Angeles Rams 1951-53, Toronto Argonauts (CFL) 1954, Washington Redskins 1955-57. College coach: Stanford 1972-78. Pro coach: Hamilton Tiger-Cats (CFL) 1958, Green Bay Packers 1959-65, Atlanta Falcons 1966-68 (head coach), New York Giants 1969-71, joined 49ers in 1979.

Sherman Lewis, running backs, born June 29, 1942, Louisville, Ky., lives in Redwood City, Calif. Running back Michigan State 1961-63. Pro running back Toronto Argonauts (CFL) 1964-65, New York Jets 1966. College coach: Michigan State 1969-82. Pro coach: Joined 49ers in 1983.

Bobb McKittrick, offensive line; born December 29, 1935, Baker, Ore., lives in San Mateo, Calif. Guard Oregon State 1955-57. No pro playing experience. College coach: Oregon State 1961-64, UCLA 1965-70. Pro coach: Los Angeles Rams 1971-72, San Diego Chargers 1974-78, joined 49ers in 1979.

Bill McPherson, defensive line; born October 24, 1931, Santa Clara, Calif., lives in San Jose, Calif. Tackle Santa Clara 1950-52. No pro playing experience. College coach: Santa Clara 1963-74, UCLA 1975-77. Pro coach: Philadelphia Eagles 1978, joined 49ers in 1979.

Ray Rhodes, defensive backfield; born October 20, 1950, Mexia, Tex., lives in Fremont, Calif. Running back-receiver Texas Christian 1969-70, Tulsa 1972-73. Pro defensive back New York Giants 1974-79, San Francisco 49ers 1980. Pro coach: Joined 49ers in 1981.

SAN FRANCISCO 49ERS 1985 FIRST-YEAR ROSTER

Name	Pos.	Ht.	Wt.	Birth-date	College	Birthplace	Residence	How Acq.
Aboulhosn, Hassan (1)	P	6-2	210	5/15/59	North Virginia C.C.	Beirut, Lebanon	Fairfax, Va.	FA
Baker, Keith (1)	WR	5-10	187	6/4/57	Texas Southern	Dallas, Tex.	Dallas, Tex.	FA
Barry, Scott	QB	6-2	190	10/17/62	Cal-Davis	Sacramento, Calif.	Sacramento, Calif.	D6
Brafford, Todd (1)	G	6-5	270	9/2/60	Utah State	Concord, N.C.	El Monte, Calif.	FA
Brown, James	NT	6-3	270	5/9/60	Savannah State	Richmond, Ga.	Augusta, Ga.	FA
Chumley, Donald	NT	6-4	259	3/14/62	Georgia	Heidelburg, Germany	Savannah, Ga.	D12
Collie, Bruce	T	6-6	275	6/27/62	Texas-Arlington	Nuremburg, Germany	San Antonio, Tex.	D5
Freeman, Reese (1)	NT	6-3	265	4/5/62	Northern Colorado	Dorchester, Mass.	Evans, Colo.	FA
Goodman, Vyn	LB	6-2	230	2/22/61	San Jose State	Bakersfield, Calif.	San Jose, Calif.	FA
Huff, Charles	CB-S	5-11	195	2/24/63	Presbyterian State	Statesboro, Ga.	Portal, Ga.	FA
Jones, Don (1)	WR	6-2	200	10/13/60	Texas A&M	Los Angeles, Calif.	Nacogdoches, Tex.	FA
Lumpkin, Joey	LB	6-2	240	2/19/60	Arizona State	Ardmore, Okla.	Scottsdale, Ariz.	FA
McCann, Douglas	S	6-3	205	10/26/62	Santa Clara	Berkeley, Calif.	San Jose, Calif.	FA
Metter, Jeff (1)	LB	6-3	220	3/8/60	Eastern Washington	Seattle, Wash.	Foster City, Calif.	FA
Moore, Brian	C	6-3	280	10/1/61	Cal Poly-SLO	Seattle, Wash.	Danville, Calif.	FA
Moore, Dana	P	5-10	185	9/7/61	Mississippi State	Baton Rouge, La.	Baton Rouge, La.	FA
Moore, Ricky	FB	5-11	236	4/7/63	Alabama	Huntsville, Ala.	Huntsville, Ala.	D3
Morris, Raymond (1)	LB	5-11	240	6/8/61	Texas-El Paso	Crane, Tex.	Odessa, Tex.	FA
Nelson, Byron (1)	T	6-5	280	5/8/62	Arizona	San Diego, Calif.	Phoenix, Ariz.	FA
Price, Eric	CB-S	5-10	185	2/13/63	Stanford	Springfield, Mo.	Palo Alto, Calif.	FA
Rice, Jerry	WR	6-2	200	10/13/62	Mississippi Val. St.	Starkville, Miss.	Crawford, Miss.	D1
Rogers, Shawn (1)	RB	5-11	195	1/2/61	Cal-Davis	Vallejo, Calif.	Davis, Calif.	FA
Selden, William	LB	6-2	220	8/28/62	Santa Clara	Santa Cruz, Calif.	San Jose, Calif.	FA
Smith, Steve	T	6-7	280	1/2/62	Pacific	Modesto, Calif.	Stockton, Calif.	FA
Villa, Steven	QB	6-2	200	11/14/61	Santa Clara	Concord, Calif.	Concord, Calif.	FA
Williams, Gardner (1)	CB-S	6-2	195	12/11/61	St. Mary's, Calif.	Washington, D.C.	Oakland, Calif.	FA
Wood, David	DE	6-4	255	5/12/62	Arizona	Phoenix, Ariz.	Phoenix, Ariz.	D11
Wyman, Mike	NT	6-6	245	3/22/62	Stanford	San Diego, Calif.	Reno, Nev.	FA

Players who report to an NFL team for the first time are designated on rosters as rookies (R). If a player reported to an NFL training camp in a previous year but was not on the active squad for three or more regular season or postseason games, he is listed on the first-year roster and designated by a (1). Thereafter, a player who is on the active squad for three or more regular season or postseason games is credited with an additional year of playing experience.

NOTES

_____
_____
_____
_____
_____
_____
_____
_____
_____
_____
_____
_____
_____
_____
_____
_____
_____
_____
_____
_____

George Seifert, defensive coordinator; born January 22, 1940, San Francisco, Calif., lives in Sunnyvale, Calif. Linebacker Utah 1960-62. No pro playing experience. College coach: Westminster 1965 (head coach), Iowa 1966, Oregon 1967-71, Stanford 1972-74, 1977-79, Cornell 1975-76 (head coach). Pro coach: Joined 49ers in 1980.

Fred von Appen, special teams; born March 22, 1942, Eugene, Ore., lives in Cupertino, Calif. Lineman Linfield College 1960-63. No pro playing experience. College coach: Linfield 1967-68, Arkansas 1969, 1981, UCLA 1970, Virginia Tech 1971, Oregon 1972-76, Stanford 1977-78, 1982. Pro coach: Green Bay Packers 1979-80, joined 49ers in 1983.

National Football Conference Central Division

Team Colors: Florida Orange, White, and Red

One Buccaneer Place
Tampa, Florida 33607
Telephone: (813) 870-2700

Club Officials

Owner: Hugh F. Culverhouse
President: John H. McKay
Vice President: Joy Culverhouse
Vice President-Head Coach: Leeman Bennett
Secretary-Treasurer: Ward Holland
Director of Administration: Herbert M. Gold
Assistant to the Owner: Phil Krueger
Director of Player Personnel: Jim Gruden
Director of Ticket Operations: Terry Wooten
Director of Public Relations: Rick Odioso
Director of Marketing & Advertising:
  Bob Passwaters
Assistant Director-Community Relations:
  Sandy Cottrell
Assistant Director-Media Relations: John Gerdes
Director of Pro Personnel: Erik Widmark
College Personnel: Gary Horton, Leland Kendall,
  Dean Rossi
Controller: Ed Easom
Trainer: Jay Shoop
Assistant Trainer: Scott Anderson
Equipment Manager: Frank Pupello
Assistant Equipment Manager: Carl Melchior

Stadium: Tampa Stadium • **Capacity:** 74,270
  North Dale Mabry
  Tampa, Florida 33607

Playing Surface: Grass

Training Camp: One Buccaneer Place
  Tampa, Florida 33607

1985 SCHEDULE

Preseason

Aug. 10	**Pittsburgh**	8:00
Aug. 17	**Atlanta**	8:00
Aug. 24	at New Orleans	7:00
Aug. 30	**Washington**	8:00

Regular Season

Sept. 8	at Chicago	12:00
Sept. 15	**Minnesota**	4:00
Sept. 22	at New Orleans	12:00
Sept. 29	at Detroit	1:00
Oct. 6	**Chicago**	1:00
Oct. 13	**Los Angeles Rams**	1:00
Oct. 20	at Miami	4:00
Oct. 27	**New England**	1:00
Nov. 3	at New York Giants	1:00
Nov. 10	**St. Louis**	1:00
Nov. 17	at New York Jets	1:00
Nov. 24	**Detroit**	1:00
Dec. 1	at Green Bay	12:00
Dec. 8	at Minnesota	3:00
Dec. 15	**Indianapolis**	1:00
Dec. 22	**Green Bay**	1:00

BUCCANEERS COACHING HISTORY

(45-91-1)

1976-84   John McKay................ 45-91-1

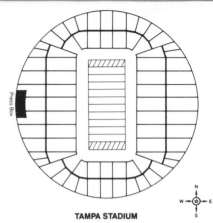

TAMPA STADIUM

RECORD HOLDERS

Individual Records — Career

Category	Name	Performance
Rushing (Yds.)	Ricky Bell, 1977-1981	3,057
Passing (Yds.)	Doug Williams, 1978-1982	12,648
Passing (TDs)	Doug Williams, 1978-1982	73
Receiving (No.)	James Wilder, 1981-84	243
Receiving (Yds.)	Kevin House, 1980-84	3,919
Interceptions	Cedric Brown, 1977-1984	29
Punting (Avg.)	Frank Garcia, 1983-84	42.1
Punt Return (Avg.)	John Holt, 1981-83	7.5
Kickoff Ret. (Avg.)	Isaac Hagins, 1976-1980	21.9
Field Goals	Bill Capece, 1981-83	43
Touchdowns (Tot.)	James Wilder, 1981-84	28
Points	Bill Capece, 1981-83	196

Individual Records — Single Season

Category	Name	Performance
Rushing (Yds.)	James Wilder, 1984	1,544
Passing (Yds.)	Doug Williams, 1981	3,563
Passing (TDs)	Doug Williams, 1980	20
Receiving (No.)	James Wilder, 1984	85
Receiving (Yds.)	Kevin House, 1981	1,176
Interceptions	Cedric Brown, 1981	9
Punting (Avg.)	Larry Swider, 1981	42.7
Punt Return (Avg.)	Danny Reece, 1978	8.9
Kickoff Return (Avg.)	Isaac Hagins, 1977	23.5
Field Goals	Obed Ariri, 1984	19
Touchdowns (Tot.)	James Wilder, 1984	13
Points	Obed Ariri, 1984	95

Individual Records — Single Game

Category	Name	Performance
Rushing (Yds.)	James Wilder, 11-6-83	219
Passing (Yds.)	Doug Williams, 11-16-80	486
Passing (TDs)	Doug Williams, 11-16-80	4
	Doug Williams, 10-4-81	4
	Jack Thompson, 11-27-83	4
Receiving (No.)	James Wilder, 12-12-82	11
	James Wilder, 9-25-83	11
	James Wilder, 12-2-84	11
Receiving (Yds.)	Kevin House, 10-18-81	178
Interceptions	Many times	2
	Last time by Beasley Reece, 11-27-83	
Field Goals	Bill Capece, 10-30-83	4
	Bill Capece, 1-2-83	4
Touchdowns	Morris Owens, 10-24-76	3
Points	Morris Owens, 10-24-76	18

1984 TEAM STATISTICS

	Tampa Bay	Opp.
Total First Downs	344	311
Rushing	114	139
Passing	209	157
Penalty	21	15
Third Down: Made/Att.	94/219	93/212
Fourth Down: Made/Att.	7/17	7/16
Total Net Yards	5321	5474
Avg. Per Game	332.6	342.1
Total Plays	1091	1033
Avg. Per Play	4.9	5.3
Net Yards Rushing	1776	2233
Avg. Per Game	111.0	139.6
Total Rushes	483	511
Net Yards Passing	3545	3241
Avg. Per Game	221.6	202.6
Tackled/Yards Lost	45/362	32/239
Gross Yards	3907	3480
Att./Completions	563/334	490/286
Completion Pct.	59.3	58.4
Had Intercepted	23	18
Punts/Avg.	68/41.9	68/41.0
Net Punting Avg.	34.7	35.3
Penalties/Yards Lost	118/875	136/1078
Fumbles/Ball Lost	36/20	27/14
Touchdowns	40	47
Rushing	17	27
Passing	22	20
Returns	1	0
Avg. Time of Possession	31:17	28:43

1984 TEAM RECORD
Preseason (3-2)

Date	Tampa Bay		Opponents
7/28	0	Seattle	38
8/4	30	*Houston	17
8/11	21	*Cincinnati	13
8/18	21	Atlanta	52
8/24	14	*Miami	13
	86		133

Regular Season (6-10)

Date	Tampa Bay		Opp.	Att.
9/2	14	Chicago	34	58,802
9/9	13	New Orleans	17	54,686
9/16	21	*Detroit	17	44,560
9/23	14	New York Giants	17	72,650
9/30	30	*Green Bay (OT)	27	47,487
10/7	35	*Minnesota	31	47,405
10/14	7	Detroit (OT)	13	44,308
10/21	9	*Chicago	44	60,003
10/28	20	Kansas City	24	38,984
11/4	24	Minnesota	27	54,949
11/11	20	*New York Giants	17	46,534
11/18	17	San Francisco	24	57,704
11/25	33	*Los Angeles Rams	34	42,242
12/2	14	Green Bay	27	46,800
12/9	23	*Atlanta	6	33,808
12/16	41	*New York Jets	21	43,817
	335		380	794,739

*Home Game   (OT) Overtime

Score by Periods

Tampa Bay	57	102	64	109	3	—	335
Opponents	54	108	76	136	6	—	380

Attendance
Home 365,856   Away 428,883   Total 794,739
Single game home record, 72,033 (1-6-80)
Single season home record, 545,980 (1979)

1984 INDIVIDUAL STATISTICS

Rushing

	Att.	Yds.	Avg.	LG	TD
Wilder	407	1544	3.8	37	13
DeBerg	28	59	2.1	14	2
Carver	11	44	4.0	12	0
J. Thompson	5	35	7.0	13	0
Armstrong	10	34	3.4	9	2
Morton	16	27	1.7	8	0
Carter	1	16	16.0	16	0
Dierking	3	14	4.7	9	0
Peoples	1	2	2.0	2	0
Owens	1	1	1.0	1	0
Tampa Bay	483	1776	3.7	37	17
Opponents	511	2233	4.4	51	27

Passing

	Att.	Comp.	Pct.	Yds.	TD	Int.	Tkld.	Rate
DeBerg	509	308	60.5	3554	19	18	35/308	79.3
J. Thompson	52	25	48.1	337	2	5	10/54	42.4
Garcia	1	0	0.0	0	0	0	0/0	39.6
Wilder	1	1	100.0	16	1	0	0/0	158.3
Tampa Bay	563	334	59.3	3907	22	23	45/362	76.4
Opponents	490	286	58.4	3480	20	18	32/239	78.6

Receiving

	No.	Yds.	Avg.	LG	TD
Wilder	85	685	8.1	50	0
House	76	1005	13.2	55	5
Carter	60	816	13.6	74t	5
J. Bell	29	397	13.7	27	4
Giles	24	310	12.9	38	2
T. Bell	22	350	15.9	29	0
Armstrong	22	180	8.2	18	3
Dixon	5	69	13.8	21	0
Carroll	5	50	10.0	17	1
Carver	3	27	9.0	12	0
Owens	2	13	6.5	9	1
Dierking	1	5	5.0	5t	1
Tampa Bay	334	3907	11.7	74t	22
Opponents	286	3480	12.2	77t	20

Interceptions

	No.	Yds.	Avg.	LG	TD
Cotney	5	123	24.6	29	0
Brantley	3	55	18.3	38	0
Castille	3	38	12.7	30	0
Logan	1	27	27.0	27t	1
Holt	1	25	25.0	25	0
Acorn	1	14	14.0	14	0
Brown	1	14	14.0	14	0
Reece	1	12	12.0	12	0
Cannon	1	0	0.0	0	0
Davis	1	0	0.0	0	0
Tampa Bay	18	308	17.1	38	1
Opponents	23	249	10.8	61	0

Punting

	No.	Yds.	Avg.	In 20	LG
Garcia	68	2849	41.9	12	60
Tampa Bay	68	2849	41.9	12	60
Opponents	68	2787	41.0	19	60

Punt Returns

	No.	FC	Yds.	Avg.	LG	TD
Bright	23	1	173	7.5	21	0
Z. Thomas, Den.-T.B.	21	3	125	6.0	15	0
Z. Thomas, T.B.	1	0	7	7.0	7	0
Holt	6	3	17	2.8	8	0
T. Bell	4	1	10	2.5	8	0
Tampa Bay	34	5	207	6.1	21	0
Opponents	36	11	310	8.6	31	0

Kickoff Returns

	No.	Yds.	Avg.	LG	TD
Morton	38	835	22.0	43	0
Z. Thomas, Den.-T.B.	18	351	19.5	33	0
Bright	16	303	18.9	33	0
Owens	8	168	21.0	36	0
Wood	5	43	8.6	16	0
Spradlin	1	5	5.0	5	0
Tampa Bay	68	1354	19.9	43	0
Opponents	67	1336	19.9	47	0

Scoring

	TD R	TD P	TD Rt	PAT	FG	Saf	TP
Ariri	0	0	0	38/40	19/26	0	95
Wilder	13	0	0	0/0	0/0	0	78
Armstrong	2	3	0	0/0	0/0	0	30
Carter	0	5	0	0/0	0/0	0	30
House	0	5	0	0/0	0/0	0	30
J. Bell	0	4	0	0/0	0/0	0	24
DeBerg	2	0	0	0/0	0/0	0	12
Giles	0	2	0	0/0	0/0	0	12
Carroll	0	1	0	0/0	0/0	0	6
Dierking	0	1	0	0/0	0/0	0	6
Logan	0	0	1	0/0	0/0	0	6
Owens	0	1	0	0/0	0/0	0	6
Tampa Bay	17	22	1	38/40	19/26	0	335
Opponents	27	20	0	44/46	18/27	0	380

FIRST-ROUND SELECTIONS

(If Club had no first-round selection, first player drafted is listed with round in parentheses.)

Year	Player, College, Position
1976	Lee Roy Selmon, Oklahoma, DT
1977	Ricky Bell, Southern California, RB
1978	Doug Williams, Grambling, QB
1979	Greg Roberts, Oklahoma, G (2)
1980	Ray Snell, Wisconsin, G
1981	Hugh Green, Pittsburgh, LB
1982	Sean Farrell, Penn State, G
1983	Randy Grimes, Baylor, C (2)
1984	Keith Browner, Southern California, LB (2)
1985	Ron Holmes, Washington, DE

TAMPA BAY BUCCANEERS 1985 VETERAN ROSTER

No.	Name	Pos.	Ht.	Wt.	Birth-date	NFL Exp.	College	Birthplace	Residence	'84 Games/Starts
27	Acorn, Fred	CB	5-10	180	3/17/61	2	Texas	Rotan, Tex.	Tampa, Fla.	16/1
2	Ariri, Obed	K	5-8	170	4/7/56	2	Clemson	Owerri, Nigeria	Tampa, Fla.	16/0
46	†Armstrong, Adger	RB	6-0	225	6/21/57	6	Texas A&M	Houston, Tex.	Houston, Tex.	15/9
82	Bell, Jerry	TE	6-5	230	3/7/59	4	Arizona State	Derby, Conn.	Tampa, Fla.	16/11
83	Bell, Theo	WR	6-0	195	12/21/53	9	Arizona	Bakersfield, Calif.	Tampa, Fla.	15/0
71	Braggs, Byron	DE	6-4	270	10/10/59	5	Alabama	Montgomery, Ala.	Montgomery, Ala.	14/0
52	Brantley, Scot	LB	6-1	230	3/7/59	6	Florida	Chester, S.C.	Lutz, Fla.	16/16
29	†Bright, Leon	RB	5-9	190	5/19/55	5	Florida State	Merritt Island, Fla.	Rockledge, Fla.	12/0
34	†Brown, Cedric	S	6-2	200	5/6/54	9	Kent State	Columbus, Ohio	Tampa, Fla.	9/9
57	Browner, Keith	LB	6-5	240	1/24/62	2	Southern California	Warren, Ohio	Tampa, Fla.	16/10
77	†Bujnoch, Glenn	G	6-6	265	12/20/53	10	Texas A&M	Houston, Tex.	Cincinnati, Ohio	8/3
78	Cannon, John	DE	6-5	260	7/30/60	4	William & Mary	Long Branch, N.J.	Tampa, Fla.	16/16
86	Carroll, Jay	TE	6-4	230	11/8/61	2	Minnesota	Winona, Minn.	Tampa, Fla.	16/2
87	Carter, Gerald	WR	6-1	190	6/19/57	6	Texas A&M	Bryan, Tex.	Bryan, Tex.	16/9
28	Carver, Melvin	RB	5-11	225	7/14/59	4	Nevada-Las Vegas	Pensacola, Fla.	Tampa, Fla.	5/1
23	Castille, Jeremiah	CB	5-10	175	1/15/61	3	Alabama	Columbus, Ga.	Phenix City, Ala.	16/16
33	Cotney, Mark	S	6-0	205	6/26/52	10	Cameron State	Altus, Okla.	Tampa, Fla.	16/9
72	Courson, Steve	G	6-1	270	10/1/55	8	South Carolina	Philadelphia, Pa.	Pittsburgh, Pa.	14/12
31	Curry, Craig	S	6-0	190	7/20/61	2	Texas	Houston, Tex.	Austin, Tex.	5/0
75	Darns, Phil	DE	6-3	245	7/27/59	2	Mississippi Valley State	Tampa, Fla.	Tampa, Fla.	2/0
58	Davis, Jeff	LB	6-0	230	1/26/60	4	Clemson	Greensboro, N.C.	Tampa, Fla.	16/16
17	DeBerg, Steve	QB	6-3	205	1/19/54	9	San Jose State	Oakland, Calif.	Tampa, Fla.	16/13
25	Dierking, Scott	RB	5-11	225	5/24/55	9	Purdue	Great Lakes, Ill.	Chicago, Ill.	8/2
81	Dixon, Dwayne	WR	6-1	205	8/2/62	2	Florida	Gainesville, Fla.	Alachua, Fla.	10/0
62	Farrell, Sean	G	6-3	260	5/25/60	4	Penn State	Southampton, N.Y.	Tampa, Fla.	15/14
44	Ferguson, Vagas	RB	6-0	205	3/6/57	4	Notre Dame	Richmond, Ind.	Rolling Meadows, Ill.	0*
5	Garcia, Frank	P	6-0	205	6/5/57	3	Arizona	Tucson, Ariz.	Tucson, Ariz.	16/0
88	Giles, Jimmie	TE	6-3	240	11/8/54	9	Alcorn State	Greenville, Miss.	Tampa, Fla.	14/14
53	Green, Hugh	LB	6-2	225	7/27/59	5	Pittsburgh	Natchez, Miss.	Tampa, Fla.	8/8
60	Grimes, Randy	C-G	6-4	265	7/20/60	3	Baylor	Tyler, Tex.	Houston, Tex.	10/3
73	Heller, Ron	T	6-6	270	8/25/62	2	Penn State	Farmingdale, N.Y.	Farmingdale, N.Y.	14/14
21	Holt, John	CB	5-11	180	5/14/59	5	West Texas State	Lawton, Okla.	Tampa, Fla.	15/15
89	House, Kevin	WR	6-1	185	12/20/57	6	Southern Illinois	St. Louis, Mo.	Tampa, Fla.	16/16
91	Janatta, John	T	6-7	275	4/10/61	2	Illinois	Chicago, Ill.	Chicago, Ill.	0*
56	Johnson, Cecil	LB	6-2	235	8/9/55	9	Pittsburgh	Miami, Fla.	Tampa, Fla.	8/6
79	Kaplan, Ken	T	6-4	270	1/12/60	2	New Hampshire	Boston, Mass.	Tampa, Fla.	16/2
16	Kiel, Blair	QB	6-0	200	11/29/61	2	Notre Dame	Columbus, Ind.	Tampa, Fla.	10/0
76	Logan, David	NT	6-2	250	10/25/56	7	Pittsburgh	Pittsburgh, Pa.	Pittsburgh, Pa.	16/16
67	Morgan, Karl	NT	6-1	255	2/23/61	2	UCLA	Houma, La.	Houma, La.	13/0
20	†Morton, Michael	RB	5-8	180	2/6/60	4	Nevada-Las Vegas	Birmingham, Ala.	Tampa, Fla.	16/0
26	Owens, James	RB	5-11	200	7/5/55	7	UCLA	Sacramento, Calif.	Tampa, Fla.	4/0
38	Peoples, George	RB	6-0	215	8/25/60	4	Auburn	Tampa, Fla.	Seffner, Fla.	6/0
43	Reece, Beasley	S	6-1	195	3/18/54	10	North Texas State	Waco, Tex.	Tampa, Fla.	16/14
74	Sanders, Gene	T	6-3	285	11/10/56	7	Texas A&M	New Orleans, La.	Tampa, Fla.	16/14
63	Selmon, Lee Roy	DE	6-3	250	10/20/54	10	Oklahoma	Eufaula, Okla.	Tampa, Fla.	16/16
55	Spradlin, Danny	LB	6-1	235	3/3/59	5	Tennessee	Maryville, Tenn.	Maryville, Tenn.	15/0
70	Thomas, Kelly	T	6-6	270	9/9/60	3	Southern California	Lynwood, Calif.	Tampa, Fla.	10/2
41	Thomas, Norris	CB	6-0	180	5/3/54	9	Southern Mississippi	Inverness, Miss.	Pascagoula, Miss.	15/0
84	Thomas, Zach	WR	6-0	185	9/8/60	3	South Carolina State	Rockledge, Fla.	Cocoa, Fla.	14/0*
14	Thompson, Jack	QB	6-3	220	5/18/56	6	Washington State	Pago Pago, Amer. Samoa	Tampa, Fla.	5/3
59	†Thompson, Robert	LB	6-3	230	2/4/60	3	Michigan	Chicago, Ill.	Tampa, Fla.	9/1
51	Washington, Chris	LB	6-4	225	3/6/62	2	Iowa State	Jackson, Miss.	Tampa, Fla.	16/7
32	Wilder, James	RB	6-3	220	5/12/58	5	Missouri	Sikeston, Mo.	Tampa, Fla.	16/16
50	Wilson, Steve	C	6-4	270	5/19/54	10	Georgia	Fort Sill, Okla.	Tampa, Fla.	16/13
85	Witte, Mark	TE	6-3	235	12/3/59	3	North Texas State	Corpus Christi, Tex.	San Marcos, Tex.	16/0

* Ferguson last active with Cleveland in '83; Janatta last active with Chicago in '83; Z. Thomas played 12 games with Denver, 2 with Tampa Bay in '84.

†Option playout; subject to developments.

Also played with Buccaneers in '84—CB-S Randy Clark (2 games), S Maurice Harvey (15), G Noah Jackson (6), DE Brison Manor (6), DE Booker Reese (1), WR Perry Tuttle (3), CB Mike Washington (1), LB Richard Wood (16).

COACHING STAFF

Head Coach,
Leeman Bennett

Pro Career: Became only the second head coach in the 10-year history of the franchise when named to the post on January 23, 1985. Previously head coach of the Atlanta Falcons 1977-82. During that time, Bennett had a record of 47-44 and led the Falcons to postseason playoffs in 1978, 1980, and 1982. NFC coach of the year following 1980 season in which Falcons were 12-4 and NFC Western Division champions. Served seven years as a pro assistant coaching offensive backs with St. Louis Cardinals 1970-71 and Detroit Lions 1972 and receivers with Los Angeles Rams 1973-76. No pro playing experience. Career record: 47-44.

Background: College quarterback and defensive back Kentucky 1958-60. College coach Kentucky 1961-62, 1965, Pittsburgh 1966, Cincinnati 1967-68, and Navy 1969.

Personal: Born June 20, 1938, in Paducah, Kentucky. Leeman and his wife, Pat, live in Tampa and have two sons—Paul and Greg.

Assistant Coaches

Greg Brown, offensive-film assistant; born October 10, 1957, Denver, Colo., lives in Tampa. Defensive back Glendale Community College 1976-77, Texas-El Paso 1978-79. No pro playing experience. Pro coach: Denver Gold (USFL) 1983-84, first year with Buccaneers.

Joe Diange, strength; born April 24, 1956, Massapequa Park, N.Y., lives in Tampa. Linebacker Penn State 1976-77. No pro playing experience. College coach: Penn State 1978-81; Navy 1982-83. Pro coach: Joined Buccaneers in 1984.

Kim Helton, offensive line; born July 28, 1948, Pensacola, Fla., lives in Tampa. Center Florida 1967-69. No pro playing experience. College coach: Florida 1972-78, Miami 1979-82. Pro coach: Joined Buccaneers in 1983.

Don Lawrence, defensive line; born June 4, 1937, Cleveland, Ohio, lives in Tampa. Tackle Notre Dame 1953-55. Pro tackle Washington Redskins 1956-61. College coach: Notre Dame 1963-67, Kansas State 1968-69, Cincinnati 1970, Virginia 1971-73 (head coach), Texas Christian 1974-75, Missouri 1976-77. Pro coach: British Columbia Lions (CFL) 1978-79, Kansas City Chiefs 1980-82, Buffalo Bills 1983-84, first year with Buccaneers.

Vic Rapp, running backs; born December 23, 1935, Marionville, Mo., lives in Tampa. Running back Southwest Missouri State 1954-57. No pro playing experience. College coach: Missouri 1967-71. Pro coach: Edmonton Eskimos (CFL) 1972-76, British Columbia Lions (CFL) 1977-82 (head coach), Houston Oilers 1983, Los Angeles Rams 1984, first year with Buccaneers.

Jimmy Raye, offensive coordinator-quarterbacks; born July 3, 1945, Fayetteville, N.C., lives in Tampa. Quarterback Michigan State 1965-67. Pro defensive back Philadelphia Eagles 1969. College coach: Michigan State 1971-75, Wyoming 1976. Pro coach: San Francisco 49ers 1977, Detroit Lions 1978-79, Atlanta Falcons 1980-82, Los Angeles Rams 1983-84, first year with Buccaneers.

Dick Roach, defensive backs; born August 23, 1937, Rapid City, S.D., lives in Tampa. Defensive back Black Hills State 1952-55. No pro playing experience. College coach: Montana State 1966-69, Oregon State 1970, Wyoming 1971-72, Fresno State 1973, Washington State 1974-75. Pro coach: Montreal Alouettes (CFL) 1976-77, Kansas City Chiefs 1978-80, New England Patriots 1981, Michigan Panthers (USFL) 1983-84, first year with Buccaneers.

Larry Seiple, receivers; born February 14, 1945, Allentown, Pa., lives in Tampa. Punter-tight end Kentucky 1964-66. Pro punter Miami Dolphins 1967-77. College coach: Miami 1979. Pro coach: Detroit Lions 1980-84, first year with Buccaneers.

TAMPA BAY BUCCANEERS 1985 FIRST-YEAR ROSTER

Name	Pos.	Ht.	Wt.	Birth-date	College	Birthplace	Residence	How Acq.
Abbott, Vince (1)	K	5-11	200	5/31/58	Cal State-Fullerton	London, England	Santa Ana, Calif.	FA
Aldredge, Corwyn	TE	6-5	225	9/6/63	Mississippi State	Baton Rouge, La.	Starkville, Miss.	FA
Branton, Gene (1)	WR	6-4	235	11/23/60	Texas Southern	Tampa, Fla.	Tampa, Fla.	D6('83)
Delegal, Lucious	CB-S	6-2	205	2/2/62	Miami	Miami, Fla.	Miami, Fla.	FA
Emerson, Brad	T	6-5	260	6/8/63	Wheaton	Long Beach, Calif.	Santa Barbara, Calif.	FA
Epps, Kelvin	WR	5-10	170	7/24/63	Texas	Dallas, Tex.	Dallas, Tex.	FA
Freeman, Phil	WR	5-11	180	12/9/62	Arizona	St. Paul, Minn.	Los Angeles, Calif.	D8
Gilliard, Mookie	CB-S	6-0	190	11/26/61	South Carolina	Ft. Stewart, Ga.	Hinesville, Ga.	FA
Gunn, Carlton	NT	6-2	305	8/12/60	Carson-Newman	Tampa, Fla.	Tampa, Fla.	FA
Harrell, John	T	6-4	265	12/22/63	Louisiana State	Alexandria, La.	Alexandria, La.	FA
Heaven, Mike	CB-S	5-11	180	12/20/63	Illinois	Boynton, Beach, Fla.	Champaign, Ill.	D4
Hines, Joe (1)	LB	6-0	225	2/14/60	Texas Christian	Newark, N.J.	Newark, N.J.	FA
Holmes, Ron	DE	6-4	255	8/26/63	Washington	Ft. Benning, Ga.	Seattle, Wash.	D1
Howard, Joe	WR	5-9	170	12/21/62	Notre Dame	Washington, D.C.	Washington, D.C.	FA
Igwebuike, Donald	K	5-9	170	12/27/60	Clemson	Anambra, Nigeria	Clemson, S.C.	D10
Jostes, Randy	NT	6-4	270	8/15/61	Missouri	Lincoln, Neb.	St. Charles, Mo.	FA
Kennell, Lonnie (1)	NT	6-2	270	12/8/61	Wichita State	Crescent City, Fla.	Crescent City, Fla.	FA
Magee, Calvin	TE	6-3	235	4/23/63	Southern	New Orleans, La.	New Orleans, La.	FA
Mallory, Rick (1)	G	6-2	265	10/25/56	Washington	Seattle, Wash.	Renton, Wash.	D9('84)
Melka, James	LB	6-1	230	1/15/62	Wisconsin	West Allis, Wis.	West Allis, Wis.	D12a
Miles, Freddie	RB	5-8	195	10/25/62	Florida	Miami, Fla.	Miami, Fla.	FA
Moore, Willie	LB	6-1	235	4/21/62	So. Mississippi	Meridian, Miss.	Meridian, Miss.	FA
Nelson, Sam	TE	6-3	230	6/9/63	Michigan	Ft. Wayne, Ind.	Ft. Wayne, Ind.	FA
Newton, Kelvin (1)	LB	6-1	235	4/20/59	Texas Christian	Beaumont, Tex.	Beaumont, Tex.	FA
Prior, Mike	CB-S	6-0	200	11/14/63	Illinois State	Chicago Heights, Ill.	Chicago Heights, Ill.	D7
Randle, Ervin	LB	6-1	250	10/12/62	Baylor	Hearne, Tex.	Hearne, Tex.	D3
Retherford, David	WR	6-0	180	4/19/61	Purdue	Glendale, Ariz.	Seffner, Fla.	FA
Risher, Alan (1)	QB	6-2	190	5/6/61	Louisiana State	New Orleans, La.	Slidell, La.	FA
Rockford, Jim	CB-S	5-10	180	9/5/61	Oklahoma	Springfield, Ill.	Springfield, Ill.	D12
Rodgers, Jim	CB-S	6-1	195	1/25/62	Washington	Ashland, Ore.	Aloha, Ore.	FA
Rowe, Steve	P	6-5	230	3/19/61	Eastern Kentucky	Louisville, Ky.	Louisville, Ky.	FA
Schulte, Rick	G	6-3	260	11/24/63	Illinois	Chicago, Ill.	Des Plaines, Ill.	FA
Scott, Ed	WR	6-0	190	12/29/62	Idaho State	Berkeley, Calif.	San Diego, Calif.	FA
Sommerfield, Mike	DE	6-4	240	2/1/59	Central Florida	Miami, Fla.	Miami, Fla.	FA
Swafford, Don (1)	T	6-7	280	3/22/57	Florida	Dayton, Ohio	Brooksville, Fla.	D7('79)
Vogel, Paul	LB	6-1	215	2/22/61	South Carolina	New York, N.Y.	Greenville, S.C.	FA
Wilkes, Del	G	6-3	255	12/21/61	South Carolina	Columbia, S.C.	Irmo, S.C.	FA
Williams, Carl	WR	6-2	175	1/21/63	Louisville	Atlanta, Ga.	Atlanta, Ga.	FA
Williams, James	RB	5-10	205	2/27/62	Memphis State	Humboldt, Tenn.	Humboldt, Tenn.	D11
Wright, Jerry	WR	5-11	170	12/9/62	Eastern Illinois	Chicago, Ill.	Chicago, Ill.	FA
Wroten, Tony	TE	6-3	225	10/8/62	Washington	Ft. Dix, N.J.	Renton, Wash.	FA

Players who report to an NFL team for the first time are designated on rosters as rookies (R). If a player reported to an NFL training camp in a previous year but was not on the active squad for three or more regular season or postseason games, he is listed on the first-year roster and designated by a (1). Thereafter, a player who is on the active squad for three or more regular season or postseason games is credited with an additional year of playing experience.

NOTES

_____

_____

_____

_____

_____

_____

_____

_____

_____

_____

_____

_____

Doug Shively, defensive coordinator-linebackers; born March 18, 1938, Lexington, Ky., lives in Tampa. End Kentucky 1955-58. No pro playing experience. College coach: Virginia Tech 1961-66, Kentucky 1967-69, Clemson 1970-72, North Carolina 1973. Pro coach: New Orleans Saints 1974-76, Atlanta Falcons 1977-82, Arizona Wranglers (USFL, head coach) 1983, San Diego Chargers 1984, first year with Buccaneers.

Howard Tippett, special teams-linebackers; born September 23, 1938, Tallassee, Ala., lives in Tampa. Quarterback-safety East Tennessee State 1955-57. No pro playing experience. College coach: Tulane 1963-65, West Virginia 1966, 1971, Houston 1967-70, Mississippi State 1972-73, 1979, Washington State 1976, Oregon 1977-78, UCLA 1980. Pro coach: Jacksonville Sharks (WFL) 1974-75, joined Buccaneers in 1981.

WASHINGTON REDSKINS

National Football Conference Eastern Division

Team Colors: Burgundy and Gold

Redskin Park
P.O. Box 17247
Dulles International Airport
Washington, D.C. 20041
Telephone: (703) 471-9100

Club Officials

Chairman of the Board-Chief Operating Executive:
  Jack Kent Cooke
Executive Vice President: John Kent Cooke
Senior Vice President: Gerard T. Gabrys
Secretary: Robert N. Eisman
Controller: Steven A. Costa
Board of Directors: Jack Kent Cooke, John Kent
  Cooke, James Lacher, William A. Shea, Esq.,
  The Honorable John W. Warner
General Manager: Bobby Beathard
Assistant General Managers: Bobby Mitchell,
  Charles Casserly
Director of Player Personnel: Dick Daniels
Director of Pro Scouting: Kirk Mee
Talent Scouts: Billy Devaney, George Saimes
Director of Public Relations: Charles M. Taylor
Assistant Public Relations Directors: Ronn Levine,
  John C. Konoza
Director of Marketing: Jim Schaus
Director of Stadium Operations: Dale Morris
Director of Photography: Nate Fine
Ticket Manager: Sue Barton
Head Trainer: Lamar (Bubba) Tyer
Assistant Trainers: Joe Kuczo, Keoki Kamau
Equipment Manager: Jay Brunetti

Stadium: Robert F. Kennedy Stadium •
  Capacity: 55,431
    East Capitol Street
    Washington, D.C. 20003

Playing Surface: Grass (PAT)

Training Camp: Dickinson College
                  Carlisle, Pennsylvania 17013

1985 SCHEDULE

Preseason
Aug. 10	at Atlanta	8:00
Aug. 18	at Los Angeles Raiders	1:00
Aug. 23	**New England**	8:00
Aug. 30	at Tampa Bay	8:00

Regular Season
Sept. 9	at Dallas (Monday)	8:00
Sept. 15	**Houston**	1:00
Sept. 22	**Philadelphia**	1:00
Sept. 29	at Chicago	12:00
Oct. 7	**St. Louis** (Monday)	9:00
Oct. 13	**Detroit**	1:00
Oct. 20	at New York Giants	1:00
Oct. 27	at Cleveland	1:00
Nov. 3	at Atlanta	1:00
Nov. 10	**Dallas**	4:00
Nov. 18	**N.Y. Giants** (Monday)	9:00
Nov. 24	at Pittsburgh	1:00
Dec. 1	**San Francisco**	4:00
Dec. 8	at Philadelphia	1:00
Dec. 15	**Cincinnati**	1:00
Dec. 21	at St. Louis (Saturday)	3:00

REDSKINS COACHING HISTORY

Boston 1932-36
(353-318-26)

1932	Lud Wray	4-4-2
1933-34	William (Lone Star) Dietz	11-11-2
1935	Eddie Casey	2-8-1
1936-42	Ray Flaherty*	56-23-3
1943	Arthur (Dutch) Bergman	7-4-1
1944-45	Dudley DeGroot	14-6-1
1946-48	Glen (Turk) Edwards	16-18-1
1949	John (Billick) Whelchel**	2-4-1
1949-51	Herman Ball***	5-15-0
1951	Dick Todd	5-4-0
1952-53	Earl (Curly) Lambeau	10-13-1
1954-58	Joe Kuharich	26-32-2
1959-60	Mike Nixon	4-18-2
1961-65	Bill McPeak	21-46-3
1966-68	Otto Graham	17-22-3
1969	Vince Lombardi	7-5-2
1970	Bill Austin	6-8-0
1971-77	George Allen	69-35-1
1978-80	Jack Pardee	24-24-0
1981-84	Joe Gibbs	47-18-0

*Retired to enter Navy
**Released after seven games in 1949
***Released after three games in 1951

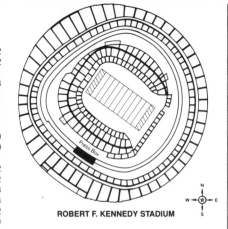

ROBERT F. KENNEDY STADIUM

RECORD HOLDERS
Individual Records—Career

Category	Name	Performance
Rushing (Yds.)	John Riggins, 1976-79, 1981-84	6,795
Passing (Yds.)	Joe Theismann, 1974-1984	23,432
Passing (TDs)	Sonny Jurgensen, 1964-1974	209
Receiving (No.)	Charley Taylor, 1964-1977	649
Receiving (Yds.)	Charley Taylor, 1964-1977	9,140
Interceptions	Brig Owens, 1966-1977	36
Punting (Avg.)	Sammy Baugh, 1937-1952	45.1
Punt Return (Avg.)	Johnny Williams, 1952-53	12.8
Kickoff Return (Avg.)	Bobby Mitchell, 1962-68	28.5
Field Goals	Mark Moseley, 1974-1984	235
Touchdowns (Tot.)	Charley Taylor, 1964-1977	90
Points	Mark Moseley, 1974-1984	1,079

Individual Records—Single Season

Category	Name	Performance
Rushing (Yds.)	John Riggins, 1983	1,347
Passing (Yds.)	Sonny Jurgensen, 1967	3,747
Passing (TDs)	Sonny Jurgensen, 1967	31
Receiving (No.)	Art Monk, 1984	106
Receiving (Yds.)	Bobby Mitchell, 1963	1,436
Interceptions	Dan Sandifer, 1948	13
Punting (Avg.)	Sammy Baugh, 1940	51.4
Punt Return (Avg.)	Johnny Williams, 1952	15.3
Kickoff Return (Avg.)	Mike Nelms, 1981	29.7
Field Goals	Mark Moseley, 1983	33
Touchdowns (Tot.)	John Riggins, 1983	24
Points	Mark Moseley, 1983	161

Individual Records—Single Game

Category	Name	Performance
Rushing (Yds.)	Mike Thomas, 11-21-76	195
Passing (Yds.)	Sammy Baugh, 10-31-48	446
Passing (TDs)	Sammy Baugh, 10-31-43	6
	Sammy Baugh, 11-23-47	6
Receiving (No.)	Clarence Harmon, 12-7-80	12
Receiving (Yds.)	Bobby Mitchell, 11-7-63	218
Interceptions	Sammy Baugh, 11-14-43	4
	Dan Sandifer, 10-31-48	4
Field Goals	Many Times	5
	Last time by Mark Moseley, 10-26-80	5
Touchdowns (Tot.)	Dick James, 12-17-61	4
	Larry Brown, 12-4-73	4
Points	Dick James, 12-17-61	24
	Larry Brown, 12-4-73	24

1984 TEAM STATISTICS

	Washington	Opp.
Total First Downs	339	307
Rushing	154	91
Passing	164	194
Penalty	21	22
Third Down: Made/Att.	107/236	79/211
Fourth Down: Made/Att.	11/15	11/23
Total Net Yards	5350	5361
Avg. Per Game	334.4	335.1
Total Plays	1121	1031
Avg. Per Play	4.8	5.2
Net Yards Rushing	2274	1589
Avg. Per Game	142.1	99.3
Total Rushes	588	390
Net Yards Passing	3076	3772
Avg. Per Game	192.3	235.8
Tackled/Yards Lost	48/341	66/529
Gross Yards	3417	4301
Att./Completions	485/286	575/318
Completion Pct.	59.0	55.3
Had Intercepted	13	21
Punts/Avg.	73/38.8	78/39.9
Net Punting Avg.	34.9	32.1
Penalties/Yards Lost	80/723	84/803
Fumbles/Ball Lost	33/15	32/22
Touchdowns	51	39
Rushing	20	13
Passing	24	25
Returns	7	1
Avg. Time of Possession	32:49	27:11

1984 TEAM RECORD
Preseason (2-2)

Date	Washington		Opponents	
8/4	16	Denver	13	
8/10	20	*Los Angeles Raiders	21	
8/17	27	*New England	31	
8/25	14	New Orleans	9	
	77		74	

Regular Season (11-5)

Date	Washington		Opp.	Att.
9/2	17	*Miami	35	52,683
9/10	31	San Francisco	37	59,707
9/16	30	*New York Giants	14	52,997
9/23	26	New England	10	60,503
9/30	20	*Philadelphia	0	53,064
10/7	35	Indianapolis	7	60,012
10/14	34	*Dallas	14	55,431
10/21	24	St. Louis	26	50,262
10/28	13	New York Giants	37	76,192
11/5	27	*Atlanta	14	51,301
11/11	28	*Detroit	14	50,212
11/18	10	Philadelphia	16	63,117
11/25	41	*Buffalo	14	51,513
11/29	31	Minnesota	17	55,017
12/9	30	Dallas	28	64,286
12/16	29	*St. Louis	27	54,299
	426		310	910,596

*Home Game

Score by Periods

Washington	89	144	108	85	—	426
Opponents	73	70	107	60	—	310

Attendance

Home 421,500   Away 489,096   Total 910,596
Single game home record, 55,431 (10-14-84, 12-30-84)
Single season home record, 427,651 (1979)

1984 INDIVIDUAL STATISTICS

Rushing

	Att.	Yds.	Avg.	LG	TD
Riggins	327	1239	3.8	24	14
Griffin	97	408	4.2	31	0
Theismann	62	314	5.1	27	1
J. Washington	56	192	3.4	12	1
Kane	17	43	2.5	10	0
Wonsley	18	38	2.1	7	4
Monk	2	18	9.0	18	0
Hayes	2	13	6.5	24	0
Moore	3	13	4.3	5	0
Walker	1	2	2.0	2	0
Hart	3	-6	-2.0	-2	0
Washington	588	2274	3.9	31	20
Opponents	390	1589	4.1	39	13

Passing

	Att.	Comp.	Pct.	Yds.	TD	Int.	Tkld.	Rate
Theismann	477	283	59.3	3391	24	13	48/341	86.6
Hart	7	3	42.9	26	0	0	0/0	53.3
J. Washington	1	0	0.0	0	0	0	0/0	39.6
Washington	485	286	59.0	3417	24	13	48/341	85.9
Opponents	575	318	55.3	4301	25	21	66/529	78.6

Receiving

	No.	Yds.	Avg.	LG	TD
Monk	106	1372	12.9	72	7
Muhammad	42	729	17.4	80t	4
Didier	30	350	11.7	44	5
Brown	18	200	11.1	36	3
Warren	18	192	10.7	26	0
Moore	17	115	6.8	18	2
J. Washington	13	74	5.7	12	0
McGrath	10	118	11.8	24	1
Seay	9	111	12.3	19	1
Griffin	8	43	5.4	8	0
Riggins	7	43	6.1	11	0
Walker	5	52	10.4	19	1
Kane	1	7	7.0	7	0
Jones	1	6	6.0	6	0
Garrett	1	5	5.0	5	0
Washington	286	3417	11.9	80t	24
Opponents	318	4301	13.5	83t	25

Interceptions

	No.	Yds.	Avg.	LG	TD
Dean	7	114	16.3	36t	2
Green	5	91	18.2	50	1
Milot	3	42	14.0	27	0
Jordan	2	18	9.0	16	0
Coleman	1	49	49.0	49t	1
R. Smith	1	37	37.0	37	0
A. Washington	1	25	25.0	25	0
Coffey	1	15	15.0	15	0
Washington	21	391	18.6	50	4
Opponents	13	159	12.2	40	0

Punting

	No.	Yds.	Avg.	In 20	LG
Hayes	72	2834	39.4	11	59
Washington	73	2834	38.8	11	59
Opponents	78	3114	39.9	17	64

Punt Returns

	No.	FC	Yds.	Avg.	LG	TD
Nelms	49	1	428	8.7	46	0
Green	2	0	13	6.5	13	0
Coffey	1	0	6	6.0	6	0
Mauti	1	1	2	2.0	2	0
Seay	1	0	-2	-2.0	-2	0
G. Williams	1	0	0	0.0	0	0
Coleman	0	0	27	—	27	0
Washington	55	2	474	8.6	46	0
Opponents	38	16	187	4.9	14	0

Kickoff Returns

	No.	Yds.	Avg.	LG	TD
Nelms	42	860	20.5	36	0
Griffin	9	164	18.2	31	0
Kane	3	43	14.3	31	0
Seay	3	53	17.7	22	0
J. Smith	2	38	19.0	22	0
R. Smith, N.E.-Wash.	1	22	22.0	22	0
Mauti	1	16	16.0	16	0
Washington	60	1174	19.6	36	0
Opponents	73	1404	19.2	89t	1

Scoring

	TD R	TD P	TD Rt	PAT	FG	Saf	TP
Moseley	0	0	0	48/51	24/31	0	120
Riggins	14	0	0	0/0	0/0	0	84
Monk	0	7	0	0/0	0/0	0	42
Didier	0	5	0	0/0	0/0	0	30
Muhammad	0	4	0	0/0	0/0	0	24
Wonsley	4	0	0	0/0	0/0	0	24
Brown	0	3	0	0/0	0/0	0	18
Dean	0	0	2	0/0	0/0	0	12
Moore	0	2	0	0/0	0/0	0	12
Coleman	0	0	1	0/0	0/0	0	6
Grant	0	0	1	0/0	0/0	0	6
Green	0	0	1	0/0	0/0	0	6
Jacoby	0	1	0	0/0	0/0	0	6
Jordan	0	0	1	0/0	0/0	0	6
McGrath	0	1	0	0/0	0/0	0	6
Seay	0	1	0	0/0	0/0	0	6
Theismann	1	0	0	0/0	0/0	0	6
J. Washington	1	0	0	0/0	0/0	0	6
Walker	0	1	0	0/0	0/0	0	6
Washington	20	24	7	48/51	24/31	0	426
Opponents	13	25	1	37/39	13/20	0	310

FIRST-ROUND SELECTIONS

(If Club had no first-round selection, first player drafted is listed with round in parentheses.)

Year	Player, College, Position
1936	Riley Smith, Alabama, B
1937	Sammy Baugh, Texas Christian, B
1938	Andy Farkas, Detroit, B
1939	I.B. Hale, Texas Christian, T
1940	Ed Boell, New York U., B
1941	Forest Evashevski, Michigan, B
1942	Orban (Spec) Sanders, Texas, B
1943	Jack Jenkins, Missouri, B
1944	Mike Micka, Colgate, B
1945	Jim Hardy, Southern California, B
1946	Cal Rossi, UCLA, B*
1947	Cal Rossi, UCLA, B
1948	Harry Gilmer, Alabama, B
	Lowell Tew, Alabama, B
1949	Rob Goode, Texas A&M, B
1950	George Thomas, Oklahoma, B
1951	Leon Heath, Oklahoma, B
1952	Larry Isbell, Baylor, B
1953	Jack Scarbath, Maryland, B
1954	Steve Meilinger, Kentucky, E
1955	Ralph Guglielmi, Notre Dame, B
1956	Ed Vereb, Maryland, B
1957	Don Bosseler, Miami, B
1958	M. Sommer, George Washington, B (2)
1959	Don Allard, Boston College, B
1960	Richie Lucas, Penn State, QB
1961	Norman Snead, Wake Forest, QB
	Joe Rutgens, Illinois, DT
1962	Ernie Davis, Syracuse, RB
1963	Pat Richter, Wisconsin, RB
1964	Charley Taylor, Arizona State, RB-WR
1965	Bob Breitenstein, Tulsa, T (2)
1966	Charlie Gogolak, Princeton, K
1967	Ray McDonald, Idaho, RB
1968	Jim Smith, Oregon, DB
1969	Eugene Epps, Texas-El Paso, DB (2)
1970	Bill Brundige, Colorado, DT (2)
1971	Cotton Speyrer, Texas, WR (2)
1972	Moses Denson, Maryland State, RB (8)
1973	Charles Cantrell, Lamar, G (5)
1974	Jon Keyworth, Colorado, TE (6)
1975	Mike Thomas, Nevada-Las Vegas, RB (6)
1976	Mike Hughes, Baylor, G (5)
1977	Duncan McColl, Stanford, DE (4)
1978	Tony Green, Florida, RB (6)
1979	Don Warren, San Diego State, TE (4)
1980	Art Monk, Syracuse, WR
1981	Mark May, Pittsburgh, T
1982	Vernon Dean, San Diego State, DB (2)
1983	Darrell Green, Texas A&I, DB
1984	Bob Slater, Oklahoma, DT (2)
1985	Tory Nixon, San Diego State, DB (2)

*Choice lost due to ineligibility.

WASHINGTON REDSKINS 1985 VETERAN ROSTER

No.	Name	Pos.	Ht.	Wt.	Birth-date	NFL Exp.	College	Birthplace	Residence	'84 Games/ Starts
67	†Beasley, Tom	DE	6-5	248	8/11/54	8	Virginia Tech	Bluefield, W. Va.	Prosperity, Pa.	13/3
53	Bostic, Jeff	C	6-2	258	9/18/58	6	Clemson	Greensboro, N.C.	Oakton, Va.	8/8
69	Brooks, Perry	DT	6-3	270	12/4/54	8	Southern	Bogalousa, La.	Fairfax, Va.	16/1
87	Brown, Charlie	WR	5-10	179	10/29/58	4	South Carolina State	John's Island, S.C.	Herndon, Va.	9/4
65	†Butz, Dave	DT	6-7	295	6/23/50	13	Purdue	Lafayette, Ala.	Belleville, Ill.	15/15
48	Coffey, Ken	S	6-0	190	11/7/60	3	Southwest Texas State	Rantoul, Ill.	Reston, Va.	12/10
51	Coleman, Monte	LB	6-2	230	11/4/57	7	Central Arkansas	Pine Bluff, Ark.	Herndon, Va.	16/5
54	†Cronan, Peter	LB	6-2	238	1/13/55	8	Boston College	Bourue, Mass.	Framingham, Mass.	3/0
32	Dean, Vernon	CB	5-11	178	5/5/59	4	San Diego State	Los Angeles, Calif.	Reston, Va.	16/14
86	Didier, Clint	TE	6-5	240	4/4/59	4	Portland State	Pasco, Wash.	Eltopia, Wash.	11/2
76	†Donnalley, Rick	C-G	6-2	257	12/11/58	4	North Carolina	Wilmington, Del.	Herndon, Va.	15/8
77	Grant, Darryl	DT	6-1	275	11/22/59	5	Rice	San Antonio, Tex.	Reston, Va.	15/15
28	Green, Darrell	CB	5-8	170	2/15/60	3	Texas A&I	Houston, Tex.	Centerville, Va.	16/16
35	Griffin, Keith	RB	5-8	185	10/26/61	2	Miami	Columbus, Ohio	Fairfax, Va.	16/2
68	Grimm, Russ	G	6-3	275	5/2/59	5	Pittsburgh	Scottsdale, Pa.	Oakton, Va.	16/16
5	Hayes, Jeff	P	5-11	175	8/19/59	4	North Carolina	Elkin, N.C.	Centerville, Va.	16/0
61	Huff, Ken	G	6-4	265	2/21/53	11	North Carolina	Hutchinson, Kan.	Oakton, Va.	15/9
66	Jacoby, Joe	T	6-7	305	7/6/59	5	Louisville	Louisville, Ky.	Oakton, Va.	16/16
82	Jones, Anthony	TE	6-3	248	5/16/60	2	Wichita State	Baltimore, Md.	Reston, Va.	16/0
22	†Jordan, Curtis	S	6-2	205	1/25/54	9	Texas Tech	Lubbock, Tex.	Oakton, Va.	16/14
55	Kaufman, Mel	LB	6-2	218	2/24/58	5	Cal Poly-SLO	Los Angeles, Calif.	Reston, Va.	15/15
63	Kimball, Bruce	G	6-2	260	8/19/56	3	Massachusetts	Beverly, Mass.	Rye, N.H.	8/0
50	Kubin, Larry	LB	6-2	234	2/26/59	4	Penn State	Union, N.J.	Reston, Va.	16/0
12	†Laufenberg, Babe	QB	6-2	195	12/5/59	2	Indiana	Burbank, Calif.	Canoga Park, Calif.	0*
79	Liebenstein, Todd	DE	6-6	255	1/9/60	3	Nevada-Las Vegas	Las Vegas, Nev.	Herndon, Va.	1/1
72	Manley, Dexter	DE	6-3	250	2/2/59	5	Oklahoma State	Houston, Tex.	Reston, Va.	15/14
71	Mann, Charles	DE	6-6	260	4/12/61	3	Nevada-Reno	Sacramento, Calif.	Reston, Va.	15/15
84	†Mauti, Rich	WR	6-0	195	5/24/54	8	Penn State	Hollis Place, N.Y.	Mandeville, La.	16/0
73	May, Mark	T	6-6	295	11/2/59	5	Pittsburgh	Oneonta, N.Y.	Clifton, Va.	16/16
78	McGee, Tony	DE	6-3	249	1/18/49	15	Bishop, Tex.	Battle Creek, Mich.	Centerville, Va.	16/0
83	†McGrath, Mark	WR	5-11	175	12/17/57	4	Montana State	San Diego, Calif.	Seattle, Wash.	13/2
57	Milot, Rich	LB	6-4	237	5/28/57	7	Penn State	Coraopolis, Pa.	Herndon, Va.	14/12
81	Monk, Art	WR	6-3	209	12/5/57	6	Syracuse	White Plains, N.Y.	Arlington, Va.	16/16
30	Moore, Jeff	RB	6-0	196	8/20/56	6	Jackson State	Kosciusko, Miss.	Jackson, Miss.	7/0
3	†Moseley, Mark	K	6-0	204	3/12/48	14	Stephen F. Austin	Laneville, Tex.	Haymarket, Va.	16/0
89	Muhammad, Calvin	WR	6-0	190	12/10/58	4	Texas Southern	Jacksonville, Fla.	Reston, Va.	10/8
29	Murphy, Mark	S	6-4	210	7/13/55	9	Colgate	Fulton, N.Y.	Vienna, Va.	7/2
21	Nelms, Mike	KR-WR	6-1	202	4/8/55	6	Baylor	Ft. Worth, Tex.	Herndon, Va.	16/0
52	Olkewicz, Neal	LB	6-0	233	1/30/57	7	Maryland	Phoenixville, Pa.	Rockville, Md.	16/16
23	Peters, Tony	S	6-1	190	4/28/53	10	Oklahoma	Oklahoma City, Okla.	Chantilly, Va.	8/6
44	†Riggins, John	RB	6-2	240	8/4/49	14	Kansas	Senaca, Kan.	Vienna, Va.	14/14
	t-Rogers, George	RB	6-2	225	12/8/58	5	South Carolina	Duluth, Ga.	Columbia, S.C.	16/16
10	Schroeder, Jay	QB	6-4	215	6/28/61	2	UCLA	Milwaukee, Wis.	Reston, Va.	0*
26	Smith, Ricky	CB	6-0	182	7/20/60	4	Alabama State	Quincy, Fla.	Pensacola, Fla.	12/0*
74	Starke, George	T	6-5	260	7/18/48	13	Columbia	New York, N.Y.	Washington, D.C.	9/7
	Sverchek, Paul	DT	6-3	256	5/9/61	2	Cal Poly-SLO	San Luis Obispo, Calif.	San Luis Obispo, Calif.	3/0*
7	Theismann, Joe	QB	6-0	198	9/9/49	12	Notre Dame	New Brunswick, N.J.	Leesburg, Va.	16/16
62	Towns, Morris	T	6-4	263	1/10/54	9	Missouri	St. Louis, Mo.	Houston, Tex.	4/0
88	Walker, Rick	TE	6-4	235	5/28/55	9	UCLA	Santa Ana, Calif.	McLean, Va.	16/14
85	Warren, Don	TE	6-4	242	5/5/56	7	San Diego State	Bellingham, Wash.	Huntington Beach, Calif.	16/16
24	Washington, Anthony	CB	6-1	204	2/4/58	5	Fresno State	San Francisco, Calif.	Fresno, Calif.	16/2
47	Williams, Greg	S	5-11	185	8/1/59	4	Mississippi State	Greenville, Miss.	Centerville, Va.	16/0
	Williams, Mike	TE	6-4	251	8/27/59	3	Alabama A&M	Lafayette, Ala.	Reston, Va.	1/0
39	Wonsley, Otis	RB	5-10	214	8/13/57	5	Alcorn State	Pascagoula, Miss.	Moss Point, Miss.	16/0

* Laufenberg missed '84 season due to injury; Schroeder active with Washington for 16 games in '84 but did not play; Smith played 1 game with New England, 11 with Washington in '84; Sverchek played 3 games with Minnesota in '84.

†Option playout; subject to developments.

t-Redskins traded for Rogers (New Orleans).

Traded—Running back Joe Washington to Atlanta.

Retired—Jim Hart, 19-year quarterback, 2 games in '84.

Also played with Redskins in '84—LB Stuart Anderson (2 games), TE Walt Arnold (4), CB Brian Carpenter (3), WR Alvin Garrett (3), LB Trey Junkin (12), RB Rick Kane (12), WR Virgil Seay (11), RB Jimmy Smith (1), G-T J.T. Turner (1), LB Jim Youngblood (4).

COACHING STAFF

Head Coach, Joe Gibbs

Pro Career: Enters fifth year as Redskins coach. Led Washington to an 11-5 record in 1984 and a third consecutive playoff berth. Named head coach on January 13, 1981, after spending eight years as an NFL assistant coach and nine years on the college level. Came to Redskins from the San Diego Chargers where he was offensive coordinator in 1979 and 1980. Prior to that, he was offensive coordinator for the Tampa Bay Buccaneers in 1978 and offensive backfield coach for the St. Louis Cardinals from 1973-77. While he was with San Diego, the Chargers won the AFC West title and led the NFL in passing two straight years. No pro playing experience. Career record: 47-18.

Background: Played tight end, linebacker, and guard under Don Coryell at San Diego State in 1961 and 1962 after spending two years at Cerritos, Calif., J.C. 1959-60. Started his college coaching career at San Diego State 1964-66, followed by stints at Florida State 1967-68, Southern California 1969-70, and Arkansas 1971-72.

Personal: Born November 25, 1940, in Mocksville, N.C. Graduated from Santa Fe Springs, Calif., High School. Two-time national racquetball champion and ranked second in the over-35 category in 1978. Joe and his wife, Pat, live in Washington, D.C., and have two sons—J.D. and Coy.

Assistant Coaches

Don Breaux, offensive backs; born August 3, 1940, Jennings, La., lives in Washington, D.C. Quarterback McNeese State 1959-61. Pro quarterback Denver Broncos 1963, San Diego Chargers 1964-65. College coach: Florida State 1966-67, Arkansas 1968-71, 1977-80, Florida 1973-74, Texas 1975-76. Pro coach: Joined Redskins in 1981.

Joe Bugel, assistant head coach-offense; born March 10, 1940, Pittsburgh, Pa., lives in Washington, D.C. Guard Western Kentucky 1960-62. No pro playing experience. College coach: Western Kentucky 1964-68, Navy 1969-72, Iowa State 1973, Ohio State 1974. Pro coach: Detroit Lions 1975-76, Houston Oilers 1977-80, joined Redskins in 1981.

Bill Hickman, administrative assistant; born June 21, 1923, Baltimore, Md., lives in Washington, D.C. Halfback Virginia 1946-48. No pro playing experience. College coach: Virginia 1949, Duke 1950, North Carolina State 1951, Vanderbilt 1953, North Carolina 1966-72. Pro coach: Washington Redskins 1973-77, Los Angeles Rams 1978-80, rejoined Redskins in 1981.

Larry Peccatiello, defensive coordinator; born December 21, 1935, Newark N.J., lives in Washington, D.C. Receiver William & Mary 1955-58. No pro playing experience. College coach: William & Mary 1961-68, Navy 1969-70, Rice 1971. Pro coach: Houston Oilers 1972-75, Seattle Seahawks 1976-80, joined Redskins in 1981.

Richie Petitbon, assistant head coach-defense; born April 18, 1938, New Orleans, La., lives in Washington, D.C. Back Tulane 1955-58. Pro defensive back Chicago Bears 1959-67, Los Angeles Rams 1969-70, Washington Redskins 1971-73. Pro coach: Houston Oilers 1974-77, joined Redskins in 1978.

Jerry Rhome, quarterbacks; born March 6, 1942, Dallas, Tex., lives in Washington, D.C. Quarterback Southern Methodist 1960-61, Tulsa 1963-64. Pro quarterback Dallas Cowboys 1965-68, Cleveland Browns 1969, Houston Oilers 1970, Los Angeles Rams 1971-72. College coach: Tulsa 1973-75. Pro coach: Seattle Seahawks 1976-82, joined Redskins in 1983.

Dan Riley, conditioning; born October 19, 1949, Syracuse, N.Y., lives in Chantilly, Va. No college or pro playing experience. College coach: Army 1973-76, Penn State 1977-81. Pro coach: Joined Redskins in 1982.

WASHINGTON REDSKINS 1985 FIRST-YEAR ROSTER

Name	Pos.	Ht.	Wt.	Birth-date	College	Birthplace	Residence	How Acq.
Allen, Brian(1)	WR	6-1	183	8/6/62	Idaho	San Bernardino, Calif.	Falls Church, Va.	FA
Allen, Marv	LB	6-3	230	4/7/60	Brigham Young	Maywood, Calif.	Hacienda Hts., Calif.	FA
Anderson, Tony	WR	5-10	175	10/4/63	Southern Illinois	Chicago, Ill.	Chicago, Ill.	FA
Branch, Reggie	RB	5-11	227	10/22/62	East Carolina	Sanford, Fla.	Sanford, Fla.	FA
Branion, Joby	CB	5-11	190	3/12/63	Duke	Chicago, Ill	Wareham, Mass.	FA
Cherry, Raphel	CB	6-0	194	12/19/61	Hawaii	Little Rock, Ark.	Los Angeles, Calif.	D5
Coleman, Dan	DT	6-4	265	8/14/62	Murray State	Lansing, Mich.	Murray, Ky.	FA
Dailey, Darnell(1)	LB	6-3	250	9/8/59	Maryland	Baltimore, Md.	Silver Spring, Md.	FA
Dubois, Napoleon	S	6-1	183	2/6/63	Richmond	Gainesville, Fla.	Hawthorne, Fla.	FA
Eernissee, Dan	C	6-3	247	9/25/61	Washington	Seattle, Wash.	Seattle, Wash.	FA
Falter, Rod	S	5-11	195	5/10/63	Kearney State	Creighton, Neb.	Kearney, Neb.	FA
Ford, Kenny	LB	6-3	215	11/23/62	Texas A&M	Wharton, Tex.	Wharton, Tex.	FA
Gary, Andre	WR	6-0	200	8/14/63	Texas-Arlington	Houston, Tex.	Houston, Tex.	FA
Geier, Mitch	G	6-4	283	3/15/62	Troy State	Lancaster, Pa.	Tarpon Springs, Fla.	D9
Hall, Vincent	RB	5-9	174	4/8/63	Mid. Tennessee St.	Scottsboro, Ala.	Murfreesboro, Tenn.	FA
Hamel, Dean	DT	6-3	275	7/7/61	Tulsa	Warren, Mich.	Tulsa, Okla.	D12
Hamilton, Steve(1)	DE	6-4	253	9/28/61	East Carolina	Niagara Falls, N.Y.	Falls Church, Va.	D2a ('84)
Harris, Jamie	WR-KR	5-9	170	3/23/62	Oklahoma State	McKinney, Tex.	Allen, Tex.	D7
Hartman, Tom	T	6-6	280	5/8/62	Virginia Tech	Wilkes-Barre, Pa.	Blacksburg, Va.	FA
Hunter, Tony	RB	5-10	205	2/24/63	Minnesota	Memphis, Tenn.	Memphis, Tenn.	FA
Jackson, Ron	RB	5-11	189	2/26/62	Washington	Anniston, Ala.	Seattle, Wash.	FA
Jones, Greg(1)	RB	5-11	184	7/1/60	Alcorn State	Milwaukee, Wis.	Milwaukee, Wis.	FA
Kafentzis, Kurt	S	6-1	189	12/31/62	Hawaii	Richland, Wash.	Honolulu, Hawaii	FA
Kenealy, Mike	S	6-0	187	4/3/63	Central Michigan	Royal Oaks, Mich.	Royal Oaks, Mich.	FA
Kepano, Tony	G	6-1	258	5/24/63	Georgia Tech	Woodbridge, Va.	Woodbridge, Va.	FA
Kimble, Gary	CB	5-11	184	4/5/63	Sam Houston State	Missouri City, Tex.	Huntsville, Tex.	D11a
Layher, Floyd	T	6-7	285	7/30/62	Pacific	San Jose, Calif.	San Jose, Calif.	FA
Lee, Danzell	TE	6-2	232	3/16/63	Lamar	Corsicana, Tex.	Corsicana, Tex.	D6
Legg, Bill	C	6-3	265	4/9/62	West Virginia	So. Charleston, W. Va.	Poco, W. Va.	FA
McClearn, Mike(1)	T	6-4	273	1/7/61	Temple	Newburgh, N.Y.	Newburgh, N.Y.	FA
McKenzie, Raleigh	G	6-2	262	2/8/63	Tennessee	Knoxville, Tenn.	Knoxville, Tenn.	D11
Mills, David	TE	6-2	225	11/17/61	Brigham Young	Salt Lake City, Utah	Provo, Utah	FA
Moog, Aaron	DE	6-4	260	2/3/62	Nevada-Las Vegas	Loma Linda, Calif.	Ontario, Calif.	FA
Newton, Mike	RB	5-11	227	5/14/62	So. Connecticut	Brooklyn, N.Y.	Brooklyn, N.Y.	FA
Nixon, Tory	CB	5-10	186	2/24/62	San Diego State	Eugene, Ore.	San Diego, Calif.	D2
Orr, Terry	RB	6-3	227	9/27/61	Texas	Savannah, Ga.	Savannah, Ga.	D10
Pegues, Jeff (1)	LB	6-2	236	1/19/62	East Carolina	Laurinburg, N.C.	Reston, Va.	D5 ('84)
Pendergrass, Boris	WR	6-0	175	12/22/63	Rutgers	Bronx, N.Y.	New Brunswick, N.J.	FA
Pendleton, Kirk(1)	WR	6-3	195	4/4/62	Brigham Young	Salt Lake City, Utah	Provo, Utah	FA
Peterson, Ron	T	6-10	300	10/8/63	Nebraska-Omaha	Omaha, Neb.	Omaha, Neb.	FA
Phillips, Joe	WR	5-9	188	4/12/63	Kentucky	Franklin, Ky.	Franklin, Ky.	FA
Pope, Bobby	G	6-3	271	8/19/62	North Carolina	Hickory, N.C.	Hickory, N.C.	FA
Rogers, Gregory	CB	5-8	177	4/19/63	Towson State	Baltimore, Md.	Towson, Md.	FA
Satele, Alvis	LB	6-0	228	4/30/63	Hawaii	Honolulu, Hawaii	Honolulu, Hawaii	FA
Singer, Curt(1)	T	6-5	264	11/4/61	Tennessee	Aliquippa, Pa.	Knoxville, Tenn.	D6 ('84)
Slater, Bob(1)	DT	6-4	265	11/14/60	Oklahoma	Pawhuska, Okla.	Fairfax, Va.	D2 ('84)
Smith, Keith	TE	6-4	240	6/14/61	Texas-El Paso	Bronx, N.Y.	New York, N.Y.	FA
Suelter, Roger	RB	6-0	205	11/14/62	Kearney State	Papillion, Neb.	Kearney, Neb.	FA
Vital, Lionel	RB	5-9	195	7/15/63	Nicholls State	Lafayette, La.	Lopeauville, La.	D7a
Wilburn, Barry	S	6-3	186	12/9/63	Mississippi	Memphis, Tenn.	Memphis, Tenn.	D8
Winn, Bryant	LB	6-3	231	11/7/62	Houston	Memphis, Tenn.	Houston, Tex.	D12a
Wooten, Mike	C	6-3	253	10/23/62	VMI	Roanoke, Va.	Princeton, N.C.	FA
Zalenski, Scott	G	6-5	265	6/12/62	Ohio State	Washington, D.C.	Chagrin Falls, Ohio	FA

Players who report to an NFL team for the first time are designated on rosters as rookies (R). If a player reported to an NFL training camp in a previous year but was not on the active squad for three or more regular season or postseason games, he is listed on the first-year roster and designated by a (1). Thereafter, a player who is on the active squad for three or more regular season or postseason games is credited with an additional year of playing experience.

NOTES

_____
_____
_____
_____
_____
_____

Wayne Sevier, special teams; born July 3, 1941, San Diego, lives in Washington, D.C. Quarterback Chaffey, Calif., J.C. 1960, San Diego State 1961-62. No pro playing experience. College coach: California Western 1968-69. Pro coach: St. Louis Cardinals 1974-75, Atlanta Falcons 1976, San Diego Chargers 1979-80, joined Redskins in 1981.

Warren Simmons, tight ends; born February 25, 1942, Poughkeepsie, N.Y., lives in Washington, D.C. Center San Diego State 1963-65. No pro playing experience. College coach: Cal State-Fullerton 1972-75, Cerritos, Calif., J.C. 1976-80. Pro coach: Joined Redskins in 1981.

Charley Taylor, wide receivers; born September 28, 1942, Grand Prairie, Tex., lives in Reston, Va. Running back Arizona State 1961-63. Pro wide receiver Washington Redskins 1964-76. Pro coach: Joined Redskins in 1982.

LaVern Torgeson, defensive line; born February 28, 1929, LaCrosse, Wash., lives in Washington, D.C. Center-linebacker Washington State 1948-50. Pro linebacker Detroit Lions 1951-54, Washington Redskins 1955-58. Pro coach: Washington Redskins 1959-61, 1971-77, Pittsburgh Steelers 1962-68, Los Angeles Rams 1969-70, 1978-80, rejoined Redskins in 1981.

1984 SEASON IN REVIEW

Trades
Preseason Standings and Results
Regular Season Standings and Results
Week by Week Game Summaries
Pro Football Awards
All-Star Teams
Paid Attendance Breakdown
NFL Paid Attendance
NFL's 10 Biggest Weekends
NFL's 10 Highest Scoring Weekends
Top 10 Televised Sports Events of All Time
Rushing, Passing, and Receiving Leaders
Team and Individual Statistics

Trades

1984 Interconference Trades

Quarterback **Jerry Golsteyn** from Tampa Bay to the L.A. Raiders for defensive back **Irvin Phillips** (5/21).

Guard **Jerry Baker** from Denver to Minnesota for a draft choice (7/3).

Defensive back **Mario Clark** from Buffalo to San Francisco for a draft choice (7/17).

Running back **Robert Alexander** from the L.A. Rams to San Diego for a draft choice (7/24).

Running back **Perry Harrington** from Philadelphia to Cleveland for a draft choice (7/24).

Tackle **Don Swafford** from Cincinnati to Tampa Bay for a draft choice (7/24).

Quarterback **Jeff Christensen** from Cincinnati to the L.A. Rams for a draft choice (7/25).

Guard **Ray Snell** from Tampa Bay to Pittsburgh for guard **Steve Courson** (7/31).

Wide receiver **Preston Dennard** from the L.A. Rams to Buffalo for a draft choice (8/1).

Defensive back **Chris Williams** from Buffalo to the L.A. Rams for a draft choice (8/1).

Defensive back **John Turner** from Minnesota to San Diego for tackle **Billy Shields** (8/11).

Defensive end **Brison Manor** from Denver to Tampa Bay for a draft choice (8/13).

Punter **Dave Finzer** from San Diego to Chicago for a draft choice (8/15).

Linebacker **Terry Tautolo** from Miami to Detroit for past consideration (8/20).

Defensive end **Kenny Neil** and a draft choice from San Diego to San Francisco for a draft choice (8/20).

Center **Rick Donnalley** from Pittsburgh to Washington for a draft choice (8/20).

Wide receiver **Perry Tuttle** from Buffalo to Tampa Bay for a draft choice (8/21).

Defensive end **Gary Burley** from Cincinnati to Atlanta for a draft choice (8/23).

Defensive back **Rod Hill** from Dallas to Buffalo for a draft choice (8/24).

Defensive back **Gerald Small** from Miami to Atlanta for guard **Ron Lee** and a draft choice (8/27).

Defensive back **Rod McSwain** from Atlanta to New England for a draft choice (8/27).

Defensive back **Kenny Hill** from the L.A. Raiders to the N.Y. Giants for a draft choice (8/27).

Defensive back **George Radachowsky** from the L.A. Rams to Indianapolis for a draft choice (8/27).

Tackle **Morris Towns** from the L.A. Raiders to Washington for a draft choice (8/30).

Linebacker **Thomas Howard** from Kansas City to St. Louis for a draft choice (9/1).

Defensive back **Ricky Smith** from New England to Washington for a draft choice (9/11).

Defensive back **Brian Carpenter** from Washington to Buffalo for a draft choice (9/19).

Defensive tackle **Gary Johnson** from San Diego to San Francisco for draft choices (9/29).

Wide receiver **Calvin Muhammad** from the L.A. Raiders to Washington for a draft choice (10/3).

Running back **Earl Campbell** from Houston to New Orleans for a draft choice (10/9).

Linebacker **Brad Van Pelt** from Minnesota to the L.A. Raiders for draft choices (10/9).

1985 Interconference Trades

Running back **Butch Woolfolk** from the N.Y. Giants to Houston for the Oilers' third-round choice in 1985 (3/21). New York selected defensive back **Tyrone Davis** (Clemson).

Houston's first-round choice in 1985 to Minnesota for the Vikings' first-round choice in 1985 (4/23). In a subsequent trade, Minnesota sent Houston's first-round choice to Atlanta for the Falcons' first- and third-round choices in 1985 (4/30). (See NFC Trades).

Quarterback **Scott Brunner** from Denver to Green Bay for a draft choice (4/26).

Buffalo traded the 1985 first-round choice it acquired from Cleveland and its own fourth-round choice in 1986 to Green Bay for the Packers' first- and second-round choices in 1985. Buffalo selected defensive back **Derrick Burroughs** (Memphis State) and wide receiver **Chris Burkett** (Jackson State). Green Bay selected tackle **Ken Ruettgers** (Southern California) (4/30).

San Francisco's first-, second-, and third-round choices in 1985 to New England for the Patriots' first- and third-round choices in 1985. San Francisco selected wide receiver **Jerry Rice** (Mississippi Valley State) and running back **Ricky Moore** (Alabama). New England selected center **Trevor Matich** (Brigham Young), defensive end **Ben Thomas** (Auburn), and defensive back **Audrey McMillian** (Houston) (4/30).

Houston's second-round choice in 1985 to Denver for Tampa Bay's second-round choice in 1985, which was previously acquired by Denver, and the Broncos' fifth-round choice in 1985. Denver selected wide receiver **Vance Johnson** (Arizona). Houston selected defensive end **Richard Byrd** (Southern Mississippi) and kicker **Lee Johnson** (Brigham Young) (4/30).

Kansas City traded the L.A. Rams' fifth-round choice in 1985, which it had acquired, and its own sixth-round draft choice in 1985 to Houston for defensive end **Bob Hamm** and a draft choice. Houston selected linebacker **Frank Bush** (North Carolina State) and linebacker **Joe Krakoski** (Washington) (4/30).

Quarterback **Joe Ferguson** from Buffalo to Detroit for a draft choice (4/30).

Quarterback **Gary Danielson** from Detroit to Cleveland for a draft choice (5/1).

1984 AFC Trades

Defensive back **Derrick Hatchett** from Houston to the L.A. Raiders for past consideration (6/19).

Running back **Pete Johnson** from Cincinnati to San Diego for running back **James Brooks** (6/21).

Rights to kicker **Stu Crum** from the N.Y. Jets to Kansas City for a draft choice (7/17).

Tackle **Bob Cryder** from New England to Seattle for a draft choice (7/31).

Wide receiver **Butch Johnson** from Houston to Denver for a draft choice (8/20).

Punter **Luke Prestridge** from Denver to New England for a draft choice (8/20).

Wide receiver **Greg Hawthorne** from Pittsburgh to New England for a draft choice (8/21).

Running back **Pete Johnson** from San Diego to Miami for the rights to defensive end **Dewey Forte** and a draft choice (9/22).

Defensive back **Lawrence Johnson** from Cleveland to Buffalo for a draft choice (10/9).

Tackle **Steve August** from Seattle to Pittsburgh for a draft choice (10/9).

Rights to linebacker **Ricky Hunley** from Cincinnati to Denver for draft choices (10/9).

Center **Jim Romano** from L.A. Raiders to Houston for draft choices (10/9).

1985 AFC Trades

Quarterback **Mark Herrmann** from Indianapolis to San Diego for a draft choice (4/10).

Cleveland's first- and third-round choices in 1985 to Buffalo for the Bills' first-round choice in the 1985 Supplementary Draft (4/24). In a subsequent trade, Buffalo sent Cleveland's first-round choice to Green Bay in exchange for the Packers' first-round choice (See Interconference Trades).

Linebacker **Charles Jackson** from Kansas City to the N.Y. Jets for the Jets' seventh-round choice in 1985 (4/25). Kansas City sent the Jets' seventh-round choice to Dallas to complete a prior transaction.

Center **Jon Borchardt** from Buffalo to Seattle for a draft choice (4/26).

1984 NFC Trades

Linebacker **Brad Van Pelt** from the New York Giants to Minnesota for running back **Tony Galbreath** (7/12).

Kicker **Jan Stenerud** from Green Bay to Minnesota for a draft choice (7/20).

Linebacker **John Harper** from Atlanta to St. Louis for a draft choice (8/13).

Quarterback **Bob Holly** from Washington to Philadelphia for a draft choice (8/14).

Tight end **Junior Miller** from Atlanta to New Orleans for a draft choice (8/27).

Linebacker **Angelo King** from Dallas to Detroit for a draft choice (8/27).

Defensive tackle **Booker Reese** from Tampa Bay to the L.A. Rams for a draft choice (9/4).

Quarterback **Steve Dils** from Minnesota to the L.A. Rams for a draft choice (9/19).

1985 NFC Trades

Running back **George Rogers** and New Orleans' fifth-, tenth-, and eleventh-round choices in 1985 to Washington for the Redskins' first-round choice in 1985. New Orleans selected linebacker **Alvin Toles** (Tennessee) (4/26). Washington selected running back **Raphel Cherry** (Hawaii), running back **Terry Orr** (Texas), and guard **Raleigh McKenzie** (Tennessee) (4/30).

Minnesota's first-round choice in 1985 to Atlanta for the Falcons' first- and third-round choices in 1985. Atlanta selected tackle **Bill Fralic** (Pittsburgh). Minnesota selected linebacker **Chris Doleman** (Pittsburgh) and linebacker **Tim Meamber** (Washington) (4/30).

Washington's second-round choice in 1985, first-round choice in 1986, and running back **Joe Washington** to Atlanta for the Falcons' second-round choice in 1985 and their second- and sixth-round choices in 1986. Washington selected defensive back **Tory Nixon** (San Diego State) (4/30). Atlanta traded Washington's second-round choice to St. Louis (See following trade).

St. Louis' second-round choice in 1985 to Atlanta for Washington's second-round choice (owned by Atlanta) and the Falcons' fifth-round choice in 1985. Atlanta selected defensive end **Mike Gann** (Notre Dame). St. Louis selected tackle **Scott Bergold** (Wisconsin) and tight end **K.D. Dunn** (Clemson) (4/30).

1984 PRESEASON STANDINGS

American Football Conference

EASTERN DIVISION

	W	L	T	Pct.	Pts.	OP
Miami	3	1	0	.750	95	47
New England	2	2	0	.500	100	105
Buffalo	1	3	0	.250	45	75
Indianapolis	1	3	0	.250	46	109
N.Y. Jets	1	3	0	.250	66	91

CENTRAL DIVISION

	W	L	T	Pct.	Pts.	OP
Cincinnati	3	1	0	.750	94	67
Pittsburgh	3	1	0	.750	80	57
Cleveland	1	3	0	.250	67	92
Houston	1	3	0	.250	96	109

WESTERN DIVISION

	W	L	T	Pct.	Pts.	OP
Seattle*	4	1	0	.800	97	51
Denver	3	1	0	.750	89	49
San Diego	2	2	0	.500	79	96
Kansas City	1	3	0	.250	68	97
L.A. Raiders	1	3	0	.250	68	82

Includes Hall of Fame Game

National Football Conference

EASTERN DIVISION

	W	L	T	Pct.	Pts.	OP
Dallas	3	1	0	.750	96	74
N.Y. Giants	3	1	0	.750	104	69
St. Louis	3	1	0	.750	71	37
Philadelphia	2	2	0	.500	82	66
Washington	2	2	0	.500	77	74

CENTRAL DIVISION

	W	L	T	Pct.	Pts.	OP
Tampa Bay*	3	2	0	.600	86	133
Detroit	2	2	0	.500	72	89
Green Bay	2	2	0	.500	92	85
Chicago	1	3	0	.250	75	68
Minnesota	1	3	0	.250	54	97

WESTERN DIVISION

	W	L	T	Pct.	Pts.	OP
New Orleans	3	1	0	.750	105	74
L.A. Rams	2	2	0	.500	94	76
San Francisco	2	2	0	.500	65	73
Atlanta	1	3	0	.250	92	113

AFC Preseason Records —Team By Team

EASTERN DIVISION

MIAMI (3-1)

24	*Indianapolis	3
29	Minnesota	7
29	L.A. Raiders	23
13	Tampa Bay	14
95		47

NEW ENGLAND (2-2)

20	*N.Y. Giants	48
13	Buffalo	23
31	Washington	27
36	*Kansas City	7
100		105

BUFFALO (1-3)

3	Seattle	7
23	*New England	13
12	*Detroit	17
7	Chicago	38
45		75

INDIANAPOLIS (1-3)

3	Miami	24
26	*N.Y. Giants	20
0	Denver	31
17	Green Bay	34
46		109

N.Y. JETS (1-3)

15	*Cincinnati	21
17	Houston	36
14	N.Y. Giants	20
20	L.A. Raiders	14
66		91

CENTRAL DIVISION

CINCINNATI (3-1)

21	N.Y. Jets	15
13	Tampa Bay	21
25	Chicago	17
35	*Detroit	14
94		67

PITTSBURGH (3-1)

31	Cleveland	14
20	*Philadelphia (OT)	17
20	Dallas	10
9	N.Y. Giants	16
80		57

CLEVELAND (1-3)

14	*Pittsburgh	31
21	L.A. Rams	10
13	Kansas City	31
19	Philadelphia	20
67		92

HOUSTON (1-3)

17	Tampa Bay	30
36	*N.Y. Jets	17
19	*New Orleans	31
24	Dallas	31
96		109

WESTERN DIVISION

SEATTLE (4-1)

38	Tampa Bay (HOF)	0
7	*Buffalo	3
28	Detroit	24
17	*St. Louis	7
7	San Francisco	17
97		51

DENVER (3-1)

13	*Washington	16
21	San Francisco	20
31	*Indianapolis	0
24	Atlanta	13
89		49

SAN DIEGO (2-2)

17	*L.A. Rams	10
13	*Dallas	24
35	*San Francisco	15
14	L.A. Rams	47
79		96

KANSAS CITY (1-3)

20	*New Orleans	34
10	St. Louis	14
31	*Cleveland	13
7	New England	36
68		97

L.A. RAIDERS (1-3)

10	San Francisco	13
21	Washington	20
23	*Miami	29
14	*N.Y. Jets	20
68		82

NFC Preseason Records —Team By Team

EASTERN DIVISION

DALLAS (3-1)

31	*Green Bay	17
24	San Diego	13
10	*Pittsburgh	20
31	*Houston	24
96		74

N.Y. GIANTS (3-1)

48	New England	20
20	Indianapolis	26
20	*N.Y. Jets	14
16	*Pittsburgh	9
104		69

ST. LOUIS (3-1)

19	Chicago	10
14	*Kansas City	10
7	Seattle	17
31	*Minnesota	0
71		37

PHILADELPHIA (2-2)

14	Detroit	17
17	Pittsburgh	20
31	Minnesota	10
20	*Cleveland	19
82		66

WASHINGTON (2-2)

16	Denver	13
20	*L.A. Raiders	21
27	*New England	31
14	New Orleans	9
77		74

CENTRAL DIVISION

TAMPA BAY (3-2)

0	Seattle (HOF)	38
30	*Houston	17
21	*Cincinnati	13
21	Atlanta	52
14	*Miami	13
86		133

DETROIT (2-2)

17	*Philadelphia	14
24	*Seattle	28
17	Buffalo	12
14	Cincinnati	35
72		89

GREEN BAY (2-2)

17	Dallas	31
17	*Chicago	10
24	L.A. Rams	27
34	*Indianapolis	17
92		85

CHICAGO (1-3)

10	*St. Louis	19
10	*Green Bay	17
17	Cincinnati	25
38	Buffalo	7
75		68

MINNESOTA (1-3)

37	*Atlanta	6
7	*Miami	29
10	*Philadelphia	31
0	St. Louis	31
54		97

WESTERN DIVISION

NEW ORLEANS (3-1)

34	Kansas City	20
31	*Atlanta	21
31	Houston	19
9	*Washington	14
105		74

L.A. RAMS (2-2)

10	San Diego	17
10	*Cleveland	21
27	*Green Bay	24
47	*San Diego	14
94		76

SAN FRANCISCO (2-2)

13	*L.A. Raiders	10
20	Denver	21
15	San Diego	35
17	*Seattle	7
65		73

ATLANTA (1-3)

6	Minnesota	37
21	New Orleans	31
52	*Tampa Bay	21
13	*Denver	24
92		113

Denotes Home Game
(OT) Denotes Overtime
(HOF) Denotes Hall of Fame Game

American Football Conference

EASTERN DIVISION

	W	L	T	Pct.	Pts.	OP
Miami	14	2	0	.875	513	298
New England	9	7	0	.563	362	352
N.Y. Jets	7	9	0	.438	332	364
Indianapolis	4	12	0	.250	239	414
Buffalo	2	14	0	.125	250	454

CENTRAL DIVISION

	W	L	T	Pct.	Pts.	OP
Pittsburgh	9	7	0	.563	387	310
Cincinnati	8	8	0	.500	339	339
Cleveland	5	11	0	.313	250	297
Houston	3	13	0	.188	240	437

WESTERN DIVISION

	W	L	T	Pct.	Pts.	OP
Denver	13	3	0	.813	353	241
Seattle*	12	4	0	.750	418	282
L.A. Raiders*	11	5	0	.688	368	278
Kansas City	8	8	0	.500	314	324
San Diego	7	9	0	.438	394	413

National Football Conference

EASTERN DIVISION

	W	L	T	Pct.	Pts.	OP
Washington	11	5	0	.688	426	310
N.Y. Giants*	9	7	0	.563	299	301
St. Louis	9	7	0	.563	423	345
Dallas	9	7	0	.563	308	308
Philadelphia	6	9	1	.406	278	320

CENTRAL DIVISION

	W	L	T	Pct.	Pts.	OP
Chicago	10	6	0	.625	325	248
Green Bay	8	8	0	.500	390	309
Tampa Bay	6	10	0	.375	335	380
Detroit	4	11	1	.281	283	408
Minnesota	3	13	0	.188	276	484

WESTERN DIVISION

	W	L	T	Pct.	Pts.	OP
San Francisco	15	1	0	.938	475	227
L.A. Rams*	10	6	0	.625	346	316
New Orleans	7	9	0	.438	298	361
Atlanta	4	12	0	.250	281	382

Wild Card qualifiers for playoffs
New York Giants clinched Wild Card berth based on 3-1 record vs. St. Louis'
2-2 and Dallas' 1-3. St. Louis finished ahead of Dallas based on better division record
(5-3 to 3-5).

FIRST-ROUND PLAYOFFS
AFC . . . . Seattle 13, Los Angeles Raiders 7, December 22 at Seattle
NFC . . . . New York Giants 16, Los Angeles Rams 13, December 23 at Anaheim
DIVISIONAL PLAYOFFS
AFC . . . . Miami 31, Seattle 10, December 29 at Miami
. . . . Pittsburgh 24, Denver 17, December 30 at Denver
NFC . . . . San Francisco 21, New York Giants 10, December 29 at San Francisco
. . . . Chicago 23, Washington 19, December 30 at Washington
CHAMPIONSHIP GAMES
AFC . . . . Miami 45, Pittsburgh 28, January 6 at Miami
NFC . . . . San Francisco 23, Chicago 0, January 6 at San Francisco
SUPER BOWL XIX . . . . San Francisco (NFC) 38, Miami (AFC) 16, January 20
at Stanford Stadium, Stanford, California
AFC-NFC PRO BOWL . . . . AFC 22, NFC 14, January 27 at Aloha Stadium,
Honolulu, Hawaii

AFC Season Records—Team By Team

BUFFALO (2-14)

17	*New England	21
7	St. Louis	37
17	*Miami	21
26	*N.Y. Jets	28
17	Indianapolis	31
17	*Philadelphia	27
28	Seattle	31
7	*Denver	37
10	*Cleveland	13
10	New England	38
14	*Dallas	3
14	Washington	41
21	*Indianapolis	15
17	N.Y. Jets	21
17	*Miami	35
21	Cincinnati	52
250		454

CINCINNATI (8-8)

17	Denver	20
22	*Kansas City	27
23	N.Y. Jets	43
14	*L.A. Rams	24
17	Pittsburgh	38
13	*Houston	3
14	New England	20
12	*Cleveland	9
31	Houston	13
17	San Francisco	23
22	*Pittsburgh	20
6	*Seattle	26
35	*Atlanta	14
20	Cleveland (OT)	17
24	New Orleans	21
52	*Buffalo	21
339		339

CLEVELAND (5-11)

0	Seattle	33
17	L.A. Rams	20
14	*Denver	24
20	*Pittsburgh	10
6	Kansas City	10
16	*New England	17
20	*N.Y. Jets	24
9	Cincinnati	12
14	*New Orleans	16
13	Buffalo	10
7	*San Francisco	41
23	Atlanta	7
27	*Houston	10
17	*Cincinnati (OT)	20
20	Pittsburgh	23
27	Houston	20
250		297

DENVER (13-3)

20	*Cincinnati	17
0	Chicago	27
24	Cleveland	14
21	*Kansas City	0
16	*L.A. Raiders	13
28	Detroit	7
17	*Green Bay	14
37	Buffalo	7
22	L.A. Raiders (OT)	19
26	*New England	19
16	San Diego	13
42	*Minnesota	21
24	*Seattle	27
13	Kansas City	16
16	*San Diego	13
31	Seattle	14
353		241

HOUSTON (3-13)

14	*L.A. Raiders	24
21	*Indianapolis	35
14	San Diego	31
10	Atlanta	42
10	*New Orleans	27
3	Cincinnati	13
10	Miami	28
21	*San Francisco	34
13	*Cincinnati	31
7	Pittsburgh	35
17	Kansas City	16
31	*N.Y. Jets	20
10	Cleveland	27
23	*Pittsburgh (OT)	20
16	L.A. Rams	27
20	*Cleveland	27
240		437

INDIANAPOLIS (4-12)

14	*N.Y. Jets	23
35	Houston	21
33	*St. Louis	34
7	Miami	44
31	*Buffalo	17
7	*Washington	35
7	Philadelphia	16
17	*Pittsburgh	16
3	Dallas	22
10	*San Diego	38
9	N.Y. Jets	5
17	*New England	50
7	L.A. Raiders	21
15	Buffalo	21
17	*Miami	35
10	New England	16
239		414

KANSAS CITY (8-8)

37	Pittsburgh	27
27	Cincinnati	22
20	*L.A. Raiders	22
0	Denver	21
10	*Cleveland	6
16	*N.Y. Jets	17
31	*San Diego	13
7	N.Y. Jets	28
24	*Tampa Bay	20
0	Seattle	45
16	*Houston	17
7	L.A. Raiders	17
27	N.Y. Giants	28
16	*Denver	13
34	*Seattle	7
42	San Diego	21
314		324

L.A. RAIDERS (11-5)

24	Houston	14
28	*Green Bay	7
22	Kansas City	20
33	*San Diego	30
13	Denver	16
28	*Seattle	14
23	*Minnesota	20
44	San Diego	37
19	*Denver (OT)	22
6	Chicago	17
14	Seattle	17
17	*Kansas City	7
21	*Indianapolis	7
45	Miami	34
24	Detroit	3
7	*Pittsburgh	13
368		278

MIAMI (14-2)

35	Washington	17
28	*New England	7
21	Buffalo	17
44	*Indianapolis	7
36	St. Louis	28
31	Pittsburgh	7
28	*Houston	10
44	New England	24
38	*Buffalo	7
31	N.Y. Jets	17
24	*Philadelphia	23
28	San Diego (OT)	34
28	*N.Y. Jets	17
34	*L.A. Raiders	45
35	Indianapolis	17
28	*Dallas	21
513		298

NEW ENGLAND (9-7)

21	Buffalo	17
7	Miami	28
38	*Seattle	23
10	*Washington	26
28	N.Y. Jets	21
17	Cleveland	16
20	*Cincinnati	14
24	*Miami	44
30	*N.Y. Jets	20
19	Denver	26
38	*Buffalo	10
50	Indianapolis	17
17	Dallas	20
10	*St. Louis	33
17	Philadelphia	27
16	*Indianapolis	10
362		352

N.Y. JETS (7-9)

23	Indianapolis	14
17	*Pittsburgh	23
43	*Cincinnati	23
28	Buffalo	26
21	*New England	28
17	Kansas City	16
24	Cleveland	20
28	*Kansas City	7
20	New England	30
17	*Miami	31
5	*Indianapolis	9
20	Houston	31
17	Miami	28
10	*N.Y. Giants	20
21	*Buffalo	17
21	Tampa Bay	41
332		364

PITTSBURGH (9-7)

27	*Kansas City	37
23	N.Y. Jets	17
24	*L.A. Rams	14
10	Cleveland	20
38	*Cincinnati	17
7	*Miami	31
20	San Francisco	17
16	Indianapolis	17
35	*Atlanta	10
35	*Houston	7
20	Cincinnati	22
24	New Orleans	27
52	*San Diego	24
20	Houston (OT)	23
23	*Cleveland	20
13	L.A. Raiders	7
387		310

SAN DIEGO (7-9)

42	Minnesota	13
17	Seattle	31
31	*Houston	14
30	L.A. Raiders	33
27	*Detroit	24
34	Green Bay	28
13	Kansas City	31
37	*L.A. Raiders	44
0	*Seattle	24
38	Indianapolis	10
13	*Denver	16
34	*Miami (OT)	28
24	Pittsburgh	52
20	*Chicago	7
13	Denver	16
21	*Kansas City	42
394		413

SEATTLE (12-4)

33	*Cleveland	0
31	*San Diego	17
23	New England	38
30	*Chicago	9
20	Minnesota	12
14	L.A. Raiders	28
31	*Buffalo	28
30	Green Bay	24
24	San Diego	0
45	*Kansas City	0
17	*L.A. Raiders	14
26	Cincinnati	6
27	Denver	24
38	*Detroit	17
7	Kansas City	34
14	*Denver	31
418		282

Denotes Home Game
(OT) Denotes Overtime

NFC Season Records—Team by Team

ATLANTA (4-12)

36	New Orleans	28
24	*Detroit (OT)	27
20	Minnesota	27
42	*Houston	10
5	San Francisco	14
30	L.A. Rams	28
7	*N.Y. Giants	19
10	*L.A. Rams	24
10	Pittsburgh	35
14	Washington	27
13	*New Orleans	17
7	*Cleveland	23
14	Cincinnati	35
17	*San Francisco	35
6	Tampa Bay	23
26	*Philadelphia	10
281		**382**

CHICAGO (10-6)

34	*Tampa Bay	14
27	*Denver	0
9	Green Bay	7
9	Seattle	38
14	*Dallas	23
20	*New Orleans	7
21	St. Louis	38
44	Tampa Bay	9
16	*Minnesota	7
17	*L.A. Raiders	6
13	L.A. Rams	29
16	*Detroit	14
34	Minnesota	3
7	San Diego	20
14	*Green Bay	20
30	Detroit	13
325		**248**

DALLAS (9-7)

20	L.A. Rams	13
7	N.Y. Giants	28
23	*Philadelphia	17
20	*Green Bay	6
23	Chicago	14
20	*St. Louis	31
14	Washington	34
30	*New Orleans (OT)	27
22	*Indianapolis	3
7	*N.Y. Giants	19
24	St. Louis	17
3	Buffalo	14
20	*New England	17
26	Philadelphia	10
28	*Washington	30
21	Miami	28
308		**308**

DETROIT (4-11-1)

27	*San Francisco	30
27	Atlanta (OT)	24
17	Tampa Bay	21
28	*Minnesota	29
24	San Diego	27
7	*Denver	28
13	*Tampa Bay (OT)	7
16	Minnesota	14
9	Green Bay	41
23	*Philadelphia (OT)	23
14	Washington	28
14	Chicago	16
31	*Green Bay	28
17	Seattle	38
3	*L.A. Raiders	24
13	*Chicago	30
283		**408**

GREEN BAY (8-8)

24	*St. Louis	23
7	L.A. Raiders	28
7	*Chicago	9
6	Dallas	20
27	Tampa Bay (OT)	30
28	*San Diego	34
14	Denver	17
24	*Seattle	30
41	*Detroit	9
23	New Orleans	13
45	*Minnesota	17
31	*L.A. Rams	6
28	Detroit	31
27	*Tampa Bay	14
20	Chicago	14
38	Minnesota	14
390		**309**

L.A. RAMS (10-6)

13	*Dallas	20
20	*Cleveland	17
14	Pittsburgh	24
24	Cincinnati	14
33	*N.Y. Giants	12
28	*Atlanta	30
28	New Orleans	10
24	Atlanta	10
0	*San Francisco	33
16	St. Louis	13
29	*Chicago	13
6	Green Bay	31
34	Tampa Bay	33
34	*New Orleans	21
27	*Houston	16
16	San Francisco	19
346		**316**

MINNESOTA (3-13)

13	*San Diego	42
17	Philadelphia	19
27	*Atlanta	20
29	Detroit	28
12	*Seattle	20
31	Tampa Bay	35
20	L.A. Raiders	23
14	*Detroit	16
7	Chicago	16
27	*Tampa Bay	24
17	Green Bay	45
21	Denver	42
3	*Chicago	34
17	*Washington	31
7	San Francisco	51
14	*Green Bay	38
276		**484**

NEW ORLEANS (7-9)

28	*Atlanta	36
17	*Tampa Bay	13
20	San Francisco	30
34	*St. Louis	24
27	Houston	10
7	Chicago	20
10	*L.A. Rams	28
27	Dallas (OT)	30
16	Cleveland	14
13	*Green Bay	23
17	Atlanta	13
27	*Pittsburgh	24
3	*San Francisco	35
21	L.A. Rams	34
21	*Cincinnati	24
10	N.Y. Giants	3
298		**361**

N.Y. GIANTS (9-7)

28	*Philadelphia	27
28	*Dallas	7
14	Washington	30
17	*Tampa Bay	14
12	L.A. Rams	33
10	*San Francisco	31
19	Atlanta	7
10	Philadelphia	24
37	*Washington	13
19	Dallas	7
17	Tampa Bay	20
16	*St. Louis	10
28	*Kansas City	27
20	N.Y. Jets	10
21	St. Louis	31
3	*New Orleans	10
299		**301**

PHILADELPHIA (6-9-1)

27	N.Y. Giants	28
19	*Minnesota	17
17	Dallas	23
9	*San Francisco	21
0	Washington	20
27	Buffalo	17
16	*Indianapolis	7
24	*N.Y. Giants	10
14	*St. Louis	34
23	Detroit (OT)	23
23	Miami	24
16	*Washington	10
16	St. Louis	17
10	*Dallas	26
27	*New England	17
10	Atlanta	26
278		**320**

ST. LOUIS (9-7)

23	Green Bay	24
37	*Buffalo	7
34	Indianapolis	33
24	New Orleans	34
28	*Miami	36
31	Dallas	20
38	*Chicago	21
26	*Washington	24
34	*Philadelphia	14
13	*L.A. Rams	16
17	*Dallas	24
10	N.Y. Giants	16
17	*Philadelpia	16
33	New England	10
31	*N.Y. Giants	21
27	Washington	29
423		**345**

SAN FRANCISCO (15-1)

30	Detroit	27
37	*Washington	31
30	*New Orleans	20
21	Philadelphia	9
14	*Atlanta	5
31	N.Y. Giants	10
17	*Pittsburgh	20
34	Houston	21
33	L.A. Rams	0
23	*Cincinnati	17
41	Cleveland	7
24	*Tampa Bay	17
35	New Orleans	3
35	Atlanta	17
51	*Minnesota	7
19	*L.A. Rams	16
475		**227**

TAMPA BAY (6-10)

14	Chicago	34
13	New Orleans	17
21	*Detroit	17
14	N.Y. Giants	17
30	*Green Bay (OT)	27
35	*Minnesota	31
7	Detroit (OT)	13
9	*Chicago	44
20	Kansas City	24
24	Minnesota	27
20	*N.Y. Giants	17
17	San Francisco	24
33	*L.A. Rams	34
14	Green Bay	27
23	*Atlanta	6
41	*N.Y. Jets	21
335		**380**

WASHINGTON (11-5)

17	*Miami	35
31	San Francisco	37
30	*N.Y. Giants	14
26	New England	10
20	*Philadelphia	0
35	Indianapolis	7
34	*Dallas	14
24	St. Louis	26
13	N.Y. Giants	37
27	*Atlanta	14
28	*Detroit	14
10	Philadelphia	16
41	*Buffalo	14
31	Minnesota	17
30	Dallas	28
29	*St. Louis	27
426		**310**

*Denotes Home Game
(OT) Denotes Overtime

Attendances as they appear in the following, and in the club-by-club sections starting on page 24, are turnstile counts and not paid attendance. Paid attendance totals are on page 168.

FIRST WEEK SUMMARY

NFL teams showed no mercy toward each other in scoring an NFL opening weekend-record 658 points. All five AFC West teams were victorious defeating their opponents by a combined score of 156-71. Seattle captured its first-ever opening-day win by blanking Cleveland 33-0. The Browns suffered their first shutout in 102 games dating back to 1977. The Seahawks victory was costly, though, running back Curt Warner was lost for the remainder of the season with a knee injury. Three rookie head coaches' debuts were also spoiled in Week One. The Broncos defeated Sam Wyche's Bengals 20-17 and the Raiders' 24-14 win over the Oilers blemished Hugh Campbell's first NFL game. Les Steckel's Minnesota Vikings could not withstand a 526-yard offensive assault and lost 42-13 to the Chargers. San Diego's Charlie Joiner caught three passes for 52 yards in the game to become only the fourth NFL player to gain more than 10,000 yards receiving in a career. Kansas City quarterback Todd Blackledge won his first NFL start, 37-27 over Pittsburgh, to give the AFC West a clean-sweep (5-0) for the weekend. Two other quarterbacks starting their first NFL games notched wins. Pat Ryan, Jets' backup the past six seasons, guided the New York Jets to a 23-14 triumph over the Colts. Dallas' Gary Hogeboom, after winning the starting job in training camp over Danny White, led the Cowboys to a 20-13 win over the Rams. The victory moved Dallas's Tom Landry (235-134-6) into second place on the NFL's winningest coaches list behind George Halas. New York Giants quarterback Phil Simms returned to the starting lineup after being injured most of the last two seasons, by passing for 409 yards and four touchdowns in the Giants' 28-27 defeat of the Eagles. Miami's second-year quarterback Dan Marino, fired five scoring passes in the Dolphins' 35-17 bombing of the Redskins. The Falcons, still stinging from the loss of running back William Andrews, got some needed help from Gerald Riggs, who ran for a team-record 202 yards in Atlanta's 36-28 victory over New Orleans. New England opened a 21-0 lead and held on to defeat Buffalo 21-17. San Francisco waited until the last four seconds to down Detroit 30-27 on Ray Wersching's 22-yard field goal. Forrest Gregg's return to Green Bay was a winning one, as the Packers edged the Cardinals 24-23. Green Bay joined Denver, Seattle, and the New York Giants as the only home winners in Week One.

SUNDAY, SEPTEMBER 2

Atlanta 36, New Orleans 28—At Louisiana Superdome, attendance 66,652. Gerald Riggs rushed 35 times for a club-record 202 yards and two touchdowns to help the Falcons over the Saints. Riggs, making his first NFL start, scored on a three-yard run in the second quarter and his one-yard blast in the final period put Atlanta ahead 33-21. But in a game which saw the lead change hands six times, it was Tom Pridemore's fumble recovery on the Falcons' 4-yard line with less than three minutes to play that sealed the Atlanta win. The Falcons generated 422 yards total offense compared to the Saints' 268.

Atlanta	5	14	7	10	— 36
New Orleans	7	14	0	7	— 28

Atl — FG Luckhurst 38
Atl — Safety, Bryan tackled Todd in end zone
NO — G. Rogers 3 run (Andersen kick)
Atl — A. Jackson 50 pass from Bartkowski Luckhurst kick)
NO — Young 18 pass from Todd (Andersen kick)
Atl — Riggs 3 run (Luckhurst kick)
NO — G. Rogers 4 run (Andersen kick)
Atl — Bailey 5 pass from Bartkowski (Luckhurst kick)
Atl — Riggs 1 run (Luckhurst kick)
NO — Tice 3 pass from Todd (Andersen kick)
Atl — FG Luckhurst 48

Denver 20, Cincinnati 17—At Mile High Stadium, attendance 74,178. Backup quarterback Gary Kubiak's eight-yard touchdown pass to rookie tight end Clarence Kay with 5:26 remaining lifted the Broncos over the Bengals. Kubiak relieved John Elway, who left the game with a shoulder injury in the third quarter. Denver had jumped to a 13-3 lead on a 25-yard touchdown pass from Elway to Butch Johnson and Gene Lang's one-yard run. Ken Anderson, who completed 25 of 49 passes for 323 yards, rallied the Bengals to a 17-13 lead with 11:42 left in the game, but Denver thwarted two late Cincinnati scoring threats to preserve the win.

Cincinnati	0	3	7	7	— 17
Denver	0	13	0	7	— 20

Cin — FG Breech 46
Den — Johnson 35 pass from Elway (kick failed)
Den — Lang 1 run (Karlis kick)
Cin — Brooks 1 run (Breech kick)
Cin — Kinnebrew 1 run (Breech kick)
Den — Kay 8 pass from Kubiak (Karlis kick)

Kansas City 37, Pittsburgh 27—At Three Rivers Stadium, attendance 56,709. Kansas City capitalized on four Pittsburgh turnovers and Todd Blackledge ran for one score and passed for another to lead the Chiefs to a 37-27 win. Blackledge, making his first NFL start in relief of injured Bill Kenney, ran one-yard for a touchdown to cap the Chiefs' first drive of the season. He added a 22-yard scoring pass to Stephone Paige in the third quarter to put the game out of reach. Two fumble recoveries by the Kansas City defense led to Nick Lowery field goals of 37 and 47 yards. Theotis Brown scored on runs of three and six yards following Deron Cherry's interception and Mike Bell's fumble recovery. Pittsburgh gained 465 total yards, including a club-record 419 net yards passing. John Stallworth caught eight passes for a career-high 167 yards and rookie Louis Lipps added six receptions for 183 yards and two touchdowns.

Kansas City	7	17	13	0	— 37
Pittsburgh	3	14	3	7	— 27

KC — Blackledge 1 run (Lowery kick)
Pitt — FG Anderson 30
KC — FG Lowery 37
KC — Brown 3 run (Lowery kick)
Pitt — Lipps 80 pass from Woodley (Anderson kick)
KC — Brown 6 run (Lowery kick)
Pitt — Stallworth 29 pass from Woodley (Anderson kick)
Pitt — FG Anderson 47
KC — Paige 22 pass from Blackledge (Lowery kick)
KC — FG Lowery 47
KC — FG Lowery 37
Pitt — Lipps 21 pass from Malone (Anderson kick)

Los Angeles Raiders 24, Houston 14—At Astrodome, attendance 49,092. Second-half scoring runs by Marcus Allen, Frank Hawkins, and Jim Plunkett rallied the Raiders to a 24-14 win. Quarterback Warren Moon, seeing his first NFL action, gave the Oilers a 7-0 halftime lead on a 10-yard pass to Mike Holston. Los Angeles took a 13-7 third-quarter lead on one-yard runs by Allen and Hawkins. Plunkett extended the margin to 19-7 with a one-yard plunge early in the fourth quarter. A 28-yard field goal by Chris Bahr and a safety by the Oilers for holding in the end zone finished the Raiders' second-half onslaught.

L.A. Raiders	0	0	13	11	— 24
Houston	0	7	0	7	— 14

Hou — Holston 10 pass from Moon (Kempf kick)
Raiders — Allen 1 run (kick failed)
Raiders — Hawkins 1 run (Bahr kick)
Raiders — Plunkett 1 run (pass failed)
Raiders — FG Bahr 28
Raiders — Safety, holding penalty on Houston in end zone
Hou — McCloskey 5 pass from Moon (Kempf kick)

Miami 35, Washington 17—At Robert F. Kennedy Stadium, attendance 52,683. Dan Marino completed 21 of 28 passes for 311 yards and five touchdowns as the Dolphins rolled over the Redskins in a rematch of Super Bowl XVII. Marino found Mark Duper (six catches for 178 yards) on first-half scoring passes of 26 and 74 yards. He then threw three more scores in the third quarter to give Miami an insurmountable 35-10 lead. Glenn Blackwood and William Judson each had an interception and Lyle Blackwood recovered a Redskins fumble while the Dolphins played error-free football.

Miami	7	7	21	0	— 35
Washington	0	10	0	7	— 17

Mia — Duper 26 pass from Marino (von Schamann kick)
Wash — Riggins 1 run (Moseley kick)
Wash — FG Moseley 32
Mia — Duper 74 pass from Marino (von Schamann kick)
Mia — Jensen 6 pass from Marino (von Schamann kick)
Mia — Clayton 9 pass from Marino (von Schamann kick)
Mia — Jensen 4 pass from Marino (von Schamann kick)
Wash — J. Washington 4 run (Moseley kick)

New England 21, Buffalo 17—At Rich Stadium, attendance 48,528. The Patriots opened a 21-0 second-quarter lead and held off the Bills for the win. Steve Grogan completed a 65-yard touchdown pass to Stephen Starring and a 3-yarder to Derrick Ramsey in the first eight minutes of the game and New England never looked back. Tony Collins scored on a four-yard run midway through the second period to finish the Patriots' scoring. Starring finished with 105 yards on three receptions.

New England	14	7	0	0	— 21
Buffalo	0	3	7	7	— 17

NE — Starring 65 pass from Grogan (Franklin kick)
NE — Ramsey 3 pass from Grogan (Franklin kick)
NE — Collins 4 run (Franklin kick)
Buff — FG Danelo 27
Buff — Dennard 8 pass from Ferguson (Danelo kick)
Buff — Hunter 9 pass from Ferguson (Danelo kick)

New York Jets 23, Indianapolis 14—At Hoosier Dome, attendance 60,398. Pat Ryan, making the first start of his seven-year career, completed 14 of 29 passes for 163 yards to lead the Jets to a 23-14 triumph in the first regular-season game ever played in the Hoosier Dome. Ryan threw two scoring passes to tight end Mickey Shuler (13 and 8 yards) and Pat Leahy kicked a 29-yard field goal to give the Jets a 16-7 third-quarter lead. Frank Middleton's three-yard scoring run early in the fourth quarter brought the Colts back to within two points (16-14). But with only 1:35 left in the game, New York linebacker Greg Buttle returned a fumble four yards for a score to insure the victory. Mark Gastineau had four sacks for the Jets which helped him win AFC defensive player of the week. Freeman McNeil led all rushers in the game with 112 yards on 29 carries.

N.Y. Jets	0	7	9	7	— 23
Indianapolis	0	7	0	7	— 14

Ind — Dickey 3 run (Allegre kick)
NYJ — Shuler 13 pass from Ryan (Leahy kick)
NYJ — FG Leahy 29
NYJ — Shuler 8 pass from Ryan (kick failed)
Ind — Middleton 3 run (Allegre kick)
NYJ — Buttle 4 fumble recovery return (Leahy kick)

New York Giants 28, Philadelphia 27—At Giants Stadium, attendance 71,520. Phil Simms completed 23 of 30 passes for 409 yards and four touchdowns to power the Giants over the Eagles. New York jumped to a 21-6 lead at the half on Simms' scoring passes to Zeke Mowatt (24 yards), Byron Williams (65), and Bobby Johnson (35). Simms also added a 16-yarder to Johnson early in the fourth quarter for a 28-20 advantage. The Eagles cut the score to 28-27 with 5:45 to play but Simms and the Giants' offense, which accounted for 497 total yards, ran out the clock to preserve the win. Johnson finished with eight receptions or 137 yards and Williams had five for 167. Simms' passing yardage total was the second most in Giants history to Y. A. Tittle's 505 in 1962. It also was the most passing yardage ever given up by a Philadelphia defense.

Philadelphia	3	3	14	7	— 27
N.Y. Giants	7	14	0	7	— 28

Phil — FG McFadden 47
NYG — Mowatt 24 pass from Simms (Haji-Sheikh kick)
Phil — FG McFadden 41
NYG — Williams 65 pass from Simms (Haji-Sheikh kick)
NYG — Johnson 35 pass from Simms (Haji-Sheikh kick)
Phil — Montgomery 4 run (McFadden kick)
Phil — Quick 14 pass from Jaworski (McFadden kick)
NYG — Johnson 16 pass from Simms (Haji-Sheikh kick)
Phil — Kraynak recovered block punt in end zone (McFadden kick)

Green Bay 24, St. Louis 23—At Lambeau Field, attendance 53,738. Lynn Dickey passed for one touchdown and ran for another to spearhead the Packers' victory. St. Louis took an early 7-0 lead, but Jessie Clark's one-yard run and Dickey's (16 of 22 for 188 yards) four-yard scoring pass to Paul Coffman put Green Bay ahead 14-7 at the half. Following Dickey's one-yard touchdown run and Eddie Garcia's field goal, the Cardinals cut the deficit to 24-20 on Neil Lomax's 18-yard touchdown pass to Roy Green. Neil O'Donoghue's 48-yard field goal midway through the fourth quarter cut the score to 24-23, but his 45-yard attempt with 2:10 left fell short. James Lofton had seven receptions for 134 yards for the Packers. Lomax completed 25 of 35 passes for 270 yards. St. Louis outgained Green Bay 417 to 266 total yards.

St. Louis	7	0	6	10	— 23
Green Bay	0	14	10	0	— 24

StL — Tilley 14 pass from Lomax (O' Donoghue kick)
GB — Clark 1 run (Garcia kick)
GB — Coffman 4 pass from Dickey (Garcia kick)
GB — Dickey 1 run (Garcia kick)
StL — Anderson 3 run (kick failed)
GB — FG Garcia 38
StL — Green 18 pass from Lomax (O'Donoghue kick)
StL — FG O'Donoghue 48

San Diego 42, Minnesota 13—At Metrodome, attendance 57,276. Dan Fouts directed the Chargers' 526-yard offensive assault by completing 21 of 28 passes for 292 yards and two touchdowns as San Diego blasted Minnesota. Fouts threw a pair of scoring passes to Wes Chandler (20 and 17 yards) in the first quarter. Pete Johnson then added two one-yard touchdown runs to put the Chargers ahead 28-3 early in the third quarter. Charlie Joiner's (three catches for 52 yards) 25-yard scoring reception from tight end Pete Holohan helped him surpass the 10,000-yard career receiving mark. Gill Byrd returned an interception 18 yards for San Diego's final score less than two minutes later. Andre Young also had two interceptions for the Chargers.

San Diego	14	7	21	0	— 42
Minnesota	3	0	7	3	— 13

SD — Chandler 20 pass from Fouts (Benirschke kick)
Minn — FG Stenerud 41
SD — Chandler 17 pass from Fouts (Benirschke kick)

SD — P. Johnson 1 run (Benirschke kick)
SD — P. Johnson 1 run (Benirschke kick)
SD — Joiner 25 pass from Holohan (Benirschke kick)
SD — Byrd 18 interception return (Benirschke kick)
Minn — Browner 63 fumble recovery return (Stenerud kick)
Minn — FG Stenerud 52

San Francisco 30, Detroit 27—At Pontiac Silverdome, attendance 56,782. Ray Wersching's 22-yard field goal with four seconds remaining provided the margin of victory for the 49ers. In a game that saw the lead change five times, San Francisco tied the score twice before Wersching's winning kick. Joe Montana's five-yard touchdown pass to Carl Monroe knotted the game 7-7 in the first quarter and Wersching's career-long 53-yard field goal deadlocked the score 20-20 with 4:31 gone in the final period. Dana McLemore's 55-yard punt return set up Wendell Tyler's nine-yard scoring run with 8:25 remaining for a 27-20 edge, but Detroit's Gary Danielson completed a 49-yard touchdown pass to Leonard Thompson to tie the score again at 27-27.

San Francisco	7	7	3	13	—	30
Detroit	7	6	7	7	—	27

Det — Sims 2 run (Murray kick)
SF — Monroe 5 pass from Montana (Wersching kick)
Det — FG Murray 39
SF — Tyler 2 run (Wersching kick)
Det — FG Murray 43
Det — Jones 2 pass from Danielson (Murray kick)
SF — FG Wersching 42
SF — FG Wersching 53
SF — Tyler 9 run (Wersching kick)
Det — Thompson 49 pass from Danielson (Murray kick)
SF — FG Wersching 22

Chicago 34, Tampa Bay 14—At Soldier Field, attendance 58,789. Interceptions by linebackers Mike Singletary and Al Harris led to a pair of third-quarter touchdowns that enabled the Bears to capture their first opening-day win since 1979. Chicago led 13-7 at halftime when Singletary's interception set up Jim McMahon's 21-yard touchdown pass to Willie Gault. Matt Suhey then scored on a one-yard run following Harris' steal. Anthony Hutchison added a one-yard touchdown run after the Bears had recovered a Tampa Bay fumble in the fourth quarter. The Bears' defense totalled four sacks, two fumble recoveries, and six interceptions.

Tampa Bay	0	7	0	7	—	14
Chicago	3	10	14	7	—	34

Chi — FG B. Thomas 29
TB — Carter 74 pass from Thompson (Ariri kick)
Chi — FG B. Thomas 32
Chi — McMahon 9 run (B. Thomas kick)
Chi — Gault 21 pass from McMahon (B. Thomas kick)
Chi — Suhey 1 run (B. Thomas kick)
Chi — Hutchison 1 run (B. Thomas kick)
TB — Owens 4 pass from DeBerg (Ariri kick)

MONDAY, SEPTEMBER 3

Seattle 33, Cleveland 0—At Kingdome, attendance 59,540. Dave Krieg fired three touchdown passes and Norm Johnson kicked four field goals (22, 50, 41, and 24 yards) to power the Seahawks to their first-ever opening day victory. Krieg connected on scoring passes of 5 yards to Mike Tice and 7 yards to Paul Johns in the first half, and finished the scoring with a 34-yarder to Daryl Turner in the third quarter. Jacob Green recorded three sacks to lead the Seattle defense which had seven sacks overall, three fumble recoveries, two interceptions, and one blocked punt. The Seahawks' win wasn't all sweet though, as second-year running back Curt Warner was lost for the remainder of the season with a knee injury. The Browns, who gained only 120 total yards, failed to score for the first time in 102 games. The last time Cleveland was shut out was when the Rams blanked the Browns 9-0 on November 27, 1977.

Cleveland	0	0	0	0	—	0
Seattle	7	13	13	0	—	33

Sea — Tice 5 pass from Krieg (Johnson kick)
Sea — FG Johnson 22
Sea — Johns 7 pass from Krieg (Johnson kick)
Sea — FG Johnson 50
Sea — FG Johnson 41
Sea — FG Johnson 24
Sea — Turner 34 pass from Krieg (Johnson kick)

Dallas 20, Los Angeles Rams 13—At Anaheim Stadium, attendance 65,403. Gary Hogeboom, making his first NFL start, completed a club-record 33 passes (in 47 attempts) for 343 yards to lead the Cowboys' 20-13 comeback win. Five interceptions of Rams quarterback Vince Ferragamo helped Dallas overcome a 13-0 first-quarter deficit. Dexter Clinkscale's two interceptions led to Hogeboom's 19-yard touchdown pass to Doug Cosbie and Rafael Septien's 31-yard field goal. Septien tied the game 13-13 in the third quarter with a 52-yard field goal after Mike Hegman's interception. Everson Walls' steal set up Tony Dorsett's seven-yard scoring run for the winning margin with 3:56 left. The victory moved Dallas coach Tom Landry (235-134-6) into second place on the NFL's all-time win list behind George Halas.

Dallas	0	7	3	10	—	20
L.A. Rams	13	0	0	0	—	13

Rams — Dickerson 2 run (Lansford kick)
Rams — FG Lansford 31
Rams — FG Lansford 36
Dall — Cosbie 19 pass from Hogeboom (Septien kick)
Dall — FG Septien 31
Dall — FG Septien 52
Dall — Dorsett 7 run (Septien kick)

SECOND WEEK SUMMARY

The haves and the have nots were divided evenly after week two. Seven teams remained undefeated while seven clubs sought win number one. Most surprising among the winners were the New York Giants who recorded their first 2-0 start since 1968. Phils Simms, who completed three scoring passes, led the offense, while Lawrence Taylor inspired the defense in New York's 28-7 win over Dallas. The Raiders also won 28-7 over the Packers, as Los Angeles held Pro Bowl wide receiver James Lofton without a reception for the first time in 67 games. Miami defeated New England for the seventeenth consecutive time in the Orange Bowl. Kansas City survived the heroics of Ken Anderson to outlast Cincinnati 27-22. Chicago's 27-0 shutout of Denver was highlighted by Walter Payton's 179 yards rushing which gave him the NFL record for combined yards (15,517). Franco Harris made his debut in Seattle and rushed for 46 yards (14 carries) to help the Seahawks down San Diego 31-17. Charlie Joiner, who caught four passes for the Chargers, joined a select group of NFL receivers with 600 or more career receptions. San Francisco exploded to a 27-3 halftime lead and survived Washington's furious comeback to down the Redskins 37-31. The Vikings thought they had their first win wrapped up for new coach Les Steckel, but a penalty on the final play of the game gave the Eagles new life. Ron Jaworski's one-yard touchdown pass to John Spagnola with one second left gave Philadelphia a 19-17 win. The Jets got a 97-yard kickoff return for a touchdown from Bobby Humphery in their first home game ever at the Meadowlands, but the Steelers capitalized on three interceptions and two fumble recoveries to win 23-17. Ed Murray's 48-yard field goal in overtime helped Detroit to a 27-24 win over Atlanta. The Cardinals dominated the Bills 37-7 for their first win of the season. The play of Eric Dickerson and LeRoy Irvin propelled the Rams over the winless Browns 20-17. Hokie Gajan led the Saints to their first win, a 17-13 victory over the Buccaneers. Only four visiting teams were victorious in Week Two, including the Colts who beat the Oilers 35-21. (Pittsburgh, Kansas City, and Detroit were the other visiting winners.)

THURSDAY, SEPTEMBER 6

Pittsburgh 23, New York Jets 17—At Giants Stadium, attendance 70,564. David Woodley threw for two touchdowns and Gary Anderson kicked three field goals (32, 43, and 27 yards) to lead the Steelers to their first win. Woodley, who completed 14 of 25 passes for 187 yards, connected on scoring passes of six yards to Louis Lipps and three yards to Weegie Thompson. The Steelers' defense limited the Jets to 168 total yards, had three interceptions, a fumble recovery, and four sacks. New York's Bobby Humphery had a 97-yard kickoff return for a touchdown (second longest in Jets history and first since Burgess Owens' in 1973 against Denver) to mark the Jets' first game in Giants Stadium.

Pittsburgh	7	6	7	3	—	23
N.Y. Jets	0	7	10	0	—	17

Pitt — Lipps 6 pass from Woodley (Anderson kick)
NYJ — Walker 14 pass from Ryan (Leahy kick)
Pitt — FG Anderson 32
Pitt — FG Anderson 43
NYJ — Humphery 97 kickoff return (Leahy kick)
Pitt — Thompson 3 pass from Woodley (Anderson kick)
NYJ — FG Leahy 52
Pitt — FG Anderson 27

SUNDAY, SEPTEMBER 9

St. Louis 37, Buffalo 7—At Busch Memorial Stadium, attendance 35,785. Neil Lomax completed 21 of 29 passes for 265 yards and two touchdowns to lead the Cardinals to their first win. Lomax threw a pair of four-yard touchdowns to Roy Green and Ottis Anderson in the first quarter and St. Louis never looked back. Anderson and Stump Mitchell added scoring runs of two and one yards, respectively, to put the game away. Neil O'Donoghue also added field goals of 23, 21, and 52 yards. The Cardinals dominated the Bills offensively, outgaining Buffalo 486 yards to 171.

Buffalo	0	0	7	0	—	7
St. Louis	17	7	7	6	—	37

StL — FG O'Donoghue 23
StL — Green 4 pass from Lomax (O'Donoghue kick)
StL — Anderson 4 pass from Lomax (O'Donoghue kick)
StL — Anderson 2 run (O'Donoghue kick)
StL — Mitchell 1 run (O'Donoghue kick)
Buff — Dennard 22 pass from Ferguson (Danelo kick)
StL — FG O'Donoghue 21
StL — FG O'Donoghue 52

Los Angeles Rams 20, Cleveland 17—At Anaheim Stadium, attendance 43,043. Mike Lansford's 27-yard field goal with 1:25 to play lifted the Rams over the Browns. Cleveland held a 17-10 third-quarter lead but Vince Ferragamo's five-yard touchdown pass to Ron Brown tied the score with 10:46 left. Eric Dickerson, who gained 102 yards rushing, picked up 48 on six carries on the drive that set up Lansford's winning kick. LeRoy Irvin scored the game's first touchdown on an 81-yard interception return.

Cleveland	7	3	7	0	—	17
L.A. Rams	7	3	0	10	—	20

Rams — Irvin 81 interception return (Lansford kick)
Cle — Pruitt 6 run (Bahr kick)
Rams — FG Lansford 37
Cle — FG Bahr 25
Cle — Newsome 4 pass from McDonald (Bahr kick)
Rams — Brown 5 pass from Ferragamo (Lansford kick)
Rams — FG Lansford 27

Indianapolis 35, Houston 21—At Astrodome, attendance 43,820. Mike Pagel threw for three touchdowns and scored on a one-yard run to power the Colts to their first victory. Pagel completed 15 of 20 passes for 215 yards and had touchdowns of 31 and 14 yards to Ray Butler and 33 yards to Terry Porter. The Colts' Curtis Dickey led all rushers with 22 carries for 84 yards, including a nine-yard touchdown run in the second period. Earl Campbell scored three touchdowns for the Oilers on runs of 2, 15, and 1 yards.

Indianapolis	0	21	7	7	—	35
Houston	7	7	0	7	—	21

Hou — Campbell 2 run (Kempf kick)
Ind — Pagel 1 run (Biasucci kick)
Hou — Campbell 15 run (Kempf kick)
Ind — Dickey 15 run (Biasucci kick)
Ind — Butler 31 pass from Pagel (Biasucci kick)
Ind — Butler 14 pass from Pagel (Biasucci kick)
Hou — Campbell 1 run (Kempf kick)
Ind — Porter 33 pass from Pagel (Biasucci kick)

New York Giants 28, Dallas 7—At Giants Stadium, attendance 75,921. Phil Simms passed for three touchdowns and Lawrence Taylor led an inspired defense as the Giants defeated the Cowboys. New York opened a 21-0 lead in the second quarter on Simms' scoring passes of 62 yards to Byron Williams, 16 yards to Lionel Manuel, and Andy Headen's team-record 81-yard fumble recovery return for a touchdown. Byron Hunt recovered Ron Fellows' fumble of the second-half kickoff on Dallas' 18-yard line, and one play later, Simms hit Zeke Mowatt with an 18-yard touchdown and 28-0 lead. Taylor had 11 tackles, 3 sacks, and forced 2 fumbles to earn NFC defensive player of the week honors.

Dallas	0	0	7	0	—	7
N.Y. Giants	14	7	7	0	—	28

NYG — B. Williams 62 pass from Simms (Haji-Sheikh kick)
NYG — Manuel 16 pass from Simms (Haji-Sheikh kick)
NYG — Headen 81 fumble recovery return (Haji-Sheikh kick)
NYG — Mowatt 18 pass from Simms (Haji-Sheikh kick)
Dall — Cosbie 2 pass from Hogeboom (Septien kick)

Chicago 27, Denver 0—At Soldier Field, attendance 54,335. Walter Payton broke loose for a career-long 72-yard touchdown run and rushed for 179 yards as the Bears defeated the Broncos. Payton also added seven yards receiving to total 15,517 combined yards, breaking Jim Brown's previous mark of 15,459. Chicago led 27-0 at halftime on two Bob Thomas field goals from 38 and 26 yards, Willie Gault's 61-yard scoring reception, and Matt Suhey's four-yard run. Thomas added three extra points for a career total of 547 points, breaking George Blanda's team mark of 541. The Bears' defense had four takeaways and held the Broncos to 130 total yards (53 rushing and 77 passing). The loss was the first shutout suffered by Denver in 88 games.

Denver	0	0	0	0	—	0
Chicago	10	17	0	0	—	27

Chi — FG B. Thomas 38
Chi — Gault 61 pass from McMahon (B. Thomas kick)
Chi — Payton 72 run (B. Thomas kick)
Chi — FG B. Thomas 26
Chi — Suhey 4 run (B. Thomas kick)

Detroit 27, Atlanta 24—At Atlanta-Fulton County Stadium, attendance 49,878. Ed Murray's 48-yard field goal 5:06 into overtime, lifted the Lions to their first win. Billy Sims, who carried 23 times for 140 yards, gave Detroit the lead in the first quarter 7-0 on a nine-yard run. Gary Danielson (21 of 32 for 250 yards) completed 11-yard touchdown passes to Leonard Thompson and David Lewis for a 24-17 third-quarter lead. Steve Bartkowski had a brilliant day for the Falcons, connecting on 24 of 28 passes for 299 yards and two touchdowns, including a 29-yarder to Stacey Bailey in the fourth period which forced overtime.

Detroit	10	7	7	0	3	—	27
Atlanta	0	10	7	7	0	—	24

Det — Sims 9 run (Murray kick)
Det — FG Murray 46
Det — Lewis 11 pass from Danielson (Murray kick)
Atl — Riggs 1 run (Luckhurst kick)
Atl — FG Luckhurst 51
Atl — B. Johnson 45 pass from Bartkowski (Luckhurst kick)
Det — L. Thompson 11 pass from Danielson (Murray kick)
Atl — Bailey 29 pass from Bartkowski (Luckhurst kick)
Det — FG Murray 48

Los Angeles Raiders 28, Green Bay 7—At Memorial Coliseum, attendance 46,269. The Raiders broke open a 7-7 tie at halftime by scoring 21 unanswered points in the second half to beat the Packers 28-7. Los Angeles' running game came alive after halftime with rushing touchdowns by Frank Hawkins (one yard), Marcus Allen (seven), and Derrick Jensen (one). Defensively, the Raiders allowed only 105 passing yards (209 overall) and held James Lofton without a reception and John Jefferson with just three for 19 yards.

Green Bay	0	7	0	0	— 7
L.A. Raiders	7	0	7	14	— 28

Raiders — Christensen 3 pass from Plunkett (Bahr kick)
GB — West 7 pass from Wright (Garcia kick)
Raiders — Hawkins 1 run (Bahr kick)
Raiders — Allen 7 run (Bahr kick)
Raiders — Jensen 1 run (Bahr kick)

Kansas City 27, Cincinnati 22—At Riverfront Stadium, attendance 47,111. Todd Blackledge completed a pair of touchdown passes and Nick Lowery kicked two field goals as the Chiefs outlasted the Bengals. Theotis Brown scored on a five-yard run and Blackledge hooked up with Anthony Hancock on a 46-yard touchdown pass to give the Chiefs a 14-0 second-quarter margin. The Bengals battled back to take a 17-14 lead early in the second half on an 18-yard interception return for a touchdown by Ray Horton, a 2-yard run by Charles Alexander, and Jim Breech's 18-yard field goal. Kansas City put the game away on Carlos Carson's 29-yard scoring catch and Lowery field goals of 52 and 40 yards. Ken Anderson completed 24 of 37 passes for 310 yards as Cincinnati's offense compiled 398 total yards. Kansas City accumulated 323 total yards.

Kansas City	7	7	10	3	— 27
Cincinnati	0	14	3	5	— 22

KC — Brown 5 run (Lowery kick)
KC — Hancock 46 pass from Blackledge (Lowery kick)
Cin — Horton 18 interception return (Breech kick)
Cin — Alexander 2 run (Breech kick)
Cin — FG Breech 18
KC — Carson 29 pass from Blackledge (Lowery kick)
KC — FG Lowery 52
Cin — Safety, ball fumbled out of end zone
Cin — FG Breech 29
KC — FG Lowery 40

Philadelphia 19, Minnesota 17—At Veterans Stadium, attendance 55,942. Ron Jaworski's touchdown pass to John Spagnola on a fourth-and-one play with one second remaining gave the Eagles a 19-17 win. Philadelphia opened a 12-3 lead on Paul McFadden's four field goals (27, 37, 49, and 37 yards), but Minnesota went ahead 17-12 on Alfred Anderson's one-yard touchdown run and his 20-yard scoring pass to quarterback Tommy Kramer. McFadden became the first Eagles kicker to make four field goals in a game since Tom Dempsey in 1971. Wilbert Montgomery (19 carries for 98 yards) became Philadelphia's career rushing leader with 5,867 total yards.

Minnesota	3	0	0	14	— 17
Philadelphia	3	6	3	7	— 19

Minn — FG Stenerud 38
Phil — FG McFadden 27
Phil — FG McFadden 37
Phil — FG McFadden 49
Phil — FG McFadden 37
Minn — Kramer 20 pass from Anderson (Stenerud kick)
Minn — Anderson 1 run (Stenerud kick)
Phil — Spagnola 1 pass from Jaworski (McFadden kick)

Miami 28, New England 7—At Orange Bowl, attendance 66,083. Dan Marino fired a pair of touchdown passes to Mark Clayton within a span of 1:36 of the third quarter to break a 7-7 halftime tie and hand the Patriots their seventeenth consecutive loss in the Orange Bowl. Jim Jensen, playing wide receiver, took a lateral from Marino (16 of 27 for 234 yards) and completed his first NFL touchdown pass, a 35-yarder to Mark Duper, for the Dolphins' first score. Miami's defense had four interceptions, including an 86-yard touchdown return as Mike Kozlowski picked off a pass and ran 26 yards before lateralling to William Judson who went the remaining 60 yards.

New England	0	7	0	0	— 7
Miami	0	7	14	7	— 28

Mia — Duper 35 pass from Jensen (von Schamann kick)
NE — Dawson 9 pass from Grogan (Franklin kick)
Mia — Clayton 38 pass from Marino (von Schamann kick)
Mia — Clayton 15 pass from Marino (von Schamann kick)
Mia — Judson 60 return with lateral from Kozlowski 26 pass interception (von Schamann kick)

Seattle 31, San Diego 17—At Kingdome, attendance 61,314. Dave Krieg ran for two touchdowns and threw for another to lead the Seahawks over the Chargers. Seattle broke a 10-10 halftime tie on Krieg's 37-yard run and went ahead 24-10 on his three-yarder early in the fourth quarter. Krieg gained 61 yards on six carries and completed 18 of 38 passes for 263 yards, including a 22-yard scoring strike to Daryl Turner with 4:34 to play. San Diego's Dan Fouts connected on 23 of 40 passes for 332 yards, including four to Charlie Joiner for 43 yards who became the fourth player in NFL history to catch 600 passes in a career (603). San Diego suffered four interceptions and four fumbles. Franco Harris carried 14 times for 46 yards in his debut for Seattle.

San Diego	10	0	0	7	— 17
Seattle	0	10	7	14	— 31

SD — FG Benirschke 43
SD — Duckworth 61 pass from Fouts (Benirschke kick)
Sea — Lane 1 run (Johnson kick)
Sea — FG Johnson 41
Sea — Krieg 37 run (Johnson kick)
Sea — Krieg 3 run (Johnson kick)
Sea — Turner 22 pass from Krieg (Johnson kick)
SD — Sievers 4 pass from Fouts (Benirschke kick)

New Orleans 17, Tampa Bay 13—At Louisiana Superdome, attendance 54,686. Hokie Gajan's 51-yard reception in the final two minutes of play helped set up his game-winning eight-yard touchdown run as the Saints upended the Buccaneers. Tampa Bay took the early lead on Jack Thompson's two-yard touchdown pass to Adger Armstrong. New Orleans tied the score on a two-yard run by Tyrone Anthony, but Obed Ariri connected on field goals from 48 and 40 yards to put the Buccaneers back on top 13-7. Morten Andersen's 23-yard field goal in the third quarter helped the Saints narrow the margin to 13-10.

Tampa Bay	7	3	3	0	— 13
New Orleans	0	7	3	7	— 17

TB — Armstrong 2 pass from Thompson (Ariri kick)
NO — Anthony 2 run (Andersen kick)
TB — FG Ariri 48
TB — FG Ariri 40
NO — FG Andersen 23
NO — Gajan 8 run (Andersen kick)

MONDAY, SEPTEMBER 10

San Francisco 37, Washington 31—At Candlestick Park, attendance 59,707. Joe Montana accounted for three touchdowns and Ray Wersching kicked three field goals (19, 46, and 38 yards) as the 49ers downed the Redskins in a rematch of the 1983 NFC Championship Game. San Francisco stormed to a 27-0 lead on scoring passes of five yards to Wendell Tyler, 15 yards to Dwight Clark, two Wersching field goals, and Tyler's one-yard run. The 49ers gained 534 total yards, including 381 passing by Montana, who completed 24 of 40 attempts. Montana put the game away with a seven-yard run in the fourth quarter after the Redskins had cut the score to 27-17. Joe Theismann led the Washington comeback by completing 24 of 43 passes for 331 yards and two touchdowns. Redskins wide receiver Art Monk caught 10 of Theismann's passes for 200 yards. San Francisco controlled the ball the final 3:44 to insure victory.

Washington	0	3	14	14	— 31
San Francisco	14	13	0	10	— 37

SF — Tyler 1 run (Wersching kick)
SF — Tyler 5 pass from Montana (Wersching kick)
SF — FG Wersching 19
SF — FG Wersching 46
SF — Clark 15 pass from Montana (Wersching kick)
Wash — FG Moseley 38
Wash — Brown 14 pass from Theismann (Moseley kick)
Wash — Riggins 1 run (Moseley kick)
SF — Montana 7 run (Wersching kick)
Wash — Riggins 1 run (Moseley kick)
SF — FG Wersching 38
Wash — Seay 12 pass from Theismann (Moseley kick)

THIRD WEEK SUMMARY

Comebacks were prevalent this week as no fewer than five teams rallied for exciting victories. New England fell behind Seattle 23-0 before Tony Eason replaced starting quarterback Steve Grogan and ignited a 38-point outburst by throwing for two touchdowns and running for another. Neil Lomax threw a pair of fourth-quarter touchdowns to Roy Green and Neil O'Donoghue kicked a last-second field goal to give St. Louis a 34-33 win over Indianapolis. The Raiders spotted Kansas City a 13-point lead in the first half, but scored 19 unanswered points to edge the Chiefs 22-20. Tampa Bay and Denver both rallied from being behind two touchdowns to record wins. Steve DeBerg relieved starter Jack Thompson and threw for two touchdowns to lead the Buccaneers to their first win of the season, 21-17 over the Lions. John Elway found himself in a similar situation for the Broncos and came up with a similar solution. Elway completed second-period scoring passes to Clint Sampson and Butch Johnson to rally Denver over Cleveland 24-14. Returning players had a direct impact in the outcomes of two games. San Diego's Kellen Winslow ended a one-week retirement by catching 10 passes for 146 yards in the Chargers' 31-14 defeat of the Oilers. It was Houston's NFL-record nineteenth consecutive road loss. In Washington, Vernon Dean celebrated his first start of the season by intercepting three passes, returning one for a touchdown, to help the Redskins win their first game. Dallas upended Philadelphia 23-17 on wide receiver Mike Renfro's 49-yard flea-flicker touchdown pass to Doug Donley. The 49ers survived an injury to Joe Montana to maintain their perfect record as Matt Cavanaugh directed San Francisco's 30-20 win over New Orleans. Vikings rookie head coach Les Steckel won his first game of the year, 27-20 over the Falcons. The Bears' number-one ranked NFL defense held the Packers to 154 total yards as Chicago defeated Green Bay 9-7. Freeman McNeil rushed for 150 yards and Pat Leahy contributed 19 points (five field goals and four extra points) to the Jets' 43-23 victory over the Bengals. Pittsburgh shut down the Rams 24-14 as Sam Washington intercepted two passes for the second straight week. Miami joined the Raiders, Chicago, and San Francisco as the NFL's only undefeated teams with a 21-17 decision over Buffalo on Monday night.

SUNDAY, SEPTEMBER 16

Minnesota 27, Atlanta 20—At Metrodome, attendance 53,955. The Vikings exploded for three third-quarter touchdowns to give Les Steckel his first head coaching victory. Following Jan Stenerud's 22- and club-record 54-yard field goals, Tommy Kramer completed touchdown passes to Leo Lewis (42 yards) and Steve Jordan (21), and Alfred Anderson completed a 43-yard scoring pass to Dwight Collins to open a 27-13 lead. Minnesota gained 414 total yards after compiling only 437 in its first two games.

Atlanta	3	3	7	7	— 20
Minnesota	3	3	21	0	— 27

Atl — FG Luckhurst 33
Minn — FG Stenerud 22
Minn — FG Stenerud 54
Atl — FG Luckhurst 43
Minn — Lewis 42 pass from Kramer (Stenerud kick)
Atl — Bailey 57 pass from Bartkowski (Luckhurst kick)
Minn — Jordan 21 pass from Kramer (Stenerud kick)
Minn — Collins 43 pass from Anderson (Stenerud kick)
Atl — B. Johnson 32 pass from Bartkowski (Luckhurst kick)

Chicago 9, Green Bay 7—At Lambeau Field, attendance 55,942. Bob Thomas provided all the points Chicago needed (three field goals from 18, 49, and 28 yards) and the Bears' defense held the Packers to 154 total yards, as Chicago edged Green Bay. The Packers led 7-6 at the half but Thomas' third field goal with 11:21 left proved decisive. Green Bay's Eddie Garcia tried a 47-yard field goal with 4:54 to go but it was wide. Walter Payton gained 110 yards on 27 carries for the Bears. Chicago played over two quarters without quarterback Jim McMahon who suffered an injured back. It was Green Bay's smallest offensive output since gaining 84 yards against the Jets in 1981.

Chicago	3	3	0	3	— 9
Green Bay	0	7	0	0	— 7

Chi — FG B. Thomas 18
Chi — FG B. Thomas 49
GB — Clark 1 run (Garcia kick)
Chi — FG B. Thomas 28

New York Jets 43, Cincinnati 23—At Giants Stadium, attendance 64,193. Freeman McNeil ran for 150 yards and two touchdowns and Pat Leahy tied a club record for most points in a game (19) as the Jets overwhelmed the Bengals. New York led 23-16 but pulled away with a 20-point fourth-quarter outburst. McNeil scored on runs of 15 and 33 yards. Leahy drilled a career-high five field goals (from 22, 39, 32, 36, and 29 yards) and four extra points to tie Jim Turner's team mark. Pat Ryan completed 20 of 33 passes for 251 yards, including a nine-yard touchdown pass to Mickey Shuler. Kirk Springs returned three kickoffs for 110 yards. The Jets' defense intercepted four passes and recovered two fumbles.

Cincinnati	9	0	7	7	— 23
N.Y. Jets	6	7	10	20	— 43

NYJ — FG Leahy 22
Cin — FG Breech 21
NYJ — FG Leahy 39
Cin — Brooks 3 pass from Anderson (pass failed)
NYJ — McNeil 15 run (Leahy kick)
Cin — Harris 80 pass from Anderson (Breech kick)
NYJ — FG Leahy 32
NYJ — Shuler 9 pass from Ryan (Leahy kick)
NYJ — FG Leahy 36
NYJ — McNeil 33 run (Leahy kick)
NYJ — FG Leahy 29
NYJ — Harper 9 run (Leahy kick)
Cin — Esiason 1 run (Breech kick)

Denver 24, Cleveland 14—at Cleveland Stadium, attendance 61,980. John Elway rallied the Broncos from a 14-0 second-quarter deficit on touchdown passes to Clint Sampson (23 yards) and Butch Johnson (18) to down the Browns 24-14. Elway started the comeback following Dennis Smith's interception with five minutes remaining in the first half. Rich Karlis' 25-yard field goal, four seconds before intermission, gave Denver a 17-14 edge. The Broncos' defense sacked Browns quarterback Paul McDonald seven times and intercepted three passes, including rookie Randy Robbins' 62-yard touchdown return.

Denver	0	17	0	7	— 24
Cleveland	7	7	0	0	— 14

Cle — Pruitt 1 run (Bahr kick)
Cle — Pruitt 2 run (Bahr kick)
Den — Sampson 23 pass from Elway (Karlis kick)
Den — Johnson 18 pass from Elway (Karlis kick)
Den — FG Karlis 25
Den — Robbins 62 interception return (Karlis kick)

Tampa Bay 21, Detroit 17—At Tampa Stadium, attendance 44,560. Steve DeBerg came off the bench to throw two touchdown passes and rally Tampa Bay from a 14-point deficit to a 21-17 win. Trailing 14-0, DeBerg replaced starter Jack Thompson and completed a five-yard scoring pass to Gerald Carter 1:54 before halftime to cut the margin to 14-7. James Wilder's two-yard touchdown run tied the score and capped a 79-yard, 16-play drive. Detroit regained the lead 17-14, but DeBerg brought the Buccaneers back on a seven-play, 81-yard drive climaxed by a five-yard touchdown toss to Jimmie Giles with 3:11 remaining. The victory was the first for Tampa Bay this season.

Detroit	7	7	3	0	—	17
Tampa Bay	0	7	7	7	—	21

Det — Nichols 77 pass from Danielson (Murray kick)
Det — Danielson 4 run (Murray kick)
TB — G. Carter 5 pass from DeBerg (Ariri kick)
TB — Wilder 2 run (Ariri kick)
Det — FG Murray 28
TB — Giles 5 pass from DeBerg (Ariri kick)

San Diego 31, Houston 14—At San Diego Jack Murphy Stadium, attendance 52,266. Kellen Winslow ended his short retirement by catching 10 passes for 146 yards, and Earnest Jackson ran for three touchdowns as the Chargers cruised to a 31-14 victory. San Diego scored on its first four possessions. Jackson's touchdowns came on runs of three, one, and six yards. Pete Johnson added a one-yard plunge. Dan Fouts, who led the San Diego offense which gained 477 total yards, threw for his second straight 300-yard passing game (26 of 37 for 336 yards). Chargers head coach Don Coryell became the seventeenth NFL coach to win 100 games.

Houston	0	7	0	7	—	14
San Diego	14	14	0	3	—	31

SD — Jackson 3 run (Benirschke kick)
SD — Jackson 1 run (Benirschke kick)
SD — P. Johnson 1 run (Benirschke kick)
Hou — Smith 75 pass from Moon (Kempf kick)
SD — Jackson 6 run (Benirschke kick)
SD — FG Benirschke 23
Hou — Mullins 7 pass from Luck (Kempf kick)

Los Angeles Raiders 22, Kansas City 20—At Arrowhead Stadium, attendance 75,111. Chris Bahr's 19-yard field goal with one minute remaining clinched the Raiders' comeback win. Kansas City opened up a 13-0 second-quarter lead on a pair of Nick Lowery field goals and Kevin Ross' 71-yard interception return for a score. The Raiders responded with 19 unanswered points on Bahr field goals of 43 and 24 yards, Jim Plunkett's (28 of 47 for 313 yards) three-yard touchdown pass to Todd Christensen, and Frank Hawkins one-yard run. Herman Heard's five-yard scoring run gave the Chiefs a 20-19 lead with 4:44 left but Plunkett guided the Raiders 73 yards in 13 plays to set up Bahr's winning kick.

L.A. Raiders	0	3	6	13	—	22
Kansas City	3	10	0	7	—	20

KC — FG Lowery 29
KC — Ross 71 interception return (Lowery kick)
KC — FG Lowery 27
Raiders — FG Bahr 43
Raiders — Christensen 3 pass from Plunkett (kick blocked)
Raiders — Hawkins 1 run (Bahr kick)
Raiders — FG Bahr 24
KC — Heard 5 run (Lowery kick)
Raiders — FG Bahr 19

Pittsburgh 24, Los Angeles Rams 14—At Three Rivers Stadium, attendance 58,104. David Woodley passed for two touchdowns and cornerback Sam Washington returned an interception for another to lead the Steelers over the Rams. Woodley, who completed 20 of 30 for 244 yards, hit Bennie Cunningham with a one-yard touchdown pass and 1:15 later Washington followed with a 12-yard interception return for a score and 14-7 halftime lead. Washington picked off two passes for the second week in a row to earn AFC defensive player of the week honors. Los Angeles' Vince Ferragamo suffered a broken finger on his throwing hand in the second period and was replaced by Jeff Kemp, who connected with Drew Hill for a 57-yard touchdown pass. Eric Dickerson was limited to 49 yards rushing on 23 carries.

L.A. Rams	7	0	7	0	—	14
Pittsburgh	0	14	3	7	—	24

Rams — Crutchfield 4 pass from Ferragamo (Lansford kick)
Pitt — Cunningham 1 pass from Woodley (Anderson kick)
Pitt — Washington 12 interception return (Anderson kick)
Pitt — FG Anderson 41
Rams — Drew Hill 57 pass from Kemp (Lansford kick)
Pitt — Lipps 11 pass from Woodley (Anderson kick)

San Francisco 30, New Orleans 20—At Candlestick Park, attendance 57,611. Backup quarterback Matt Cavanaugh replaced injured Joe Montana in the third quarter and rallied the 49ers to a 30-20 win. San Francisco jumped to a 17-0 lead but Ken Stabler replaced New Orleans starter Richard Todd and guided the Saints to a 20-17 advantage after three quarters. Cavanaugh fired a 23-yard touchdown pass to Earl Cooper early in the fourth quarter and Ray Wersching kicked field goals of 22 and 40 yards to secure the victory. The 49ers' defense intercepted five passes and registered two sacks.

New Orleans	0	10	10	0	—	20
San Francisco	7	10	0	13	—	30

SF — Solomon 32 pass from Montana (Wersching kick)
SF — FG Wersching 31
SF — Tyler 3 run (Wersching kick)
NO — Goodlow 8 pass from Stabler (Andersen kick)
NO — FG Andersen 32
NO — Brenner 26 pass from Stabler (Andersen kick)
NO — FG Andersen 41
SF — Cooper 23 pass from Cavanaugh (Wersching kick)
SF — FG Wersching 22
SF — FG Wersching 40

Washington 30, New York Giants 14—At Robert F. Kennedy Stadium, attendance 52,997. Fourth-quarter touchdown returns by Vernon Dean and Curtis Jordan helped the Redskins win their first game. With Washington leading 16-14, Dean returned the second of his three interceptions 36 yards for a touchdown. Jordan, subbing for injured Mark Murphy, took a fumble by New York's Lionel Manuel 29 yards for a score less than six minutes later to put the game out of reach. The victory offset the performance of Giants quarterback Phil Simms, who completed 22 of 45 passes for 347 yards, including six passes for 117 yards to rookie Bobby Johnson. Dean, making his first start of the season, was named NFC defensive player of the week.

N.Y. Giants	7	0	7	0	—	14
Washington	7	6	0	17	—	30

Wash — Riggins 1 run (Moseley kick)
NYG — Carpenter 1 run (Haji-Sheikh kick)
Wash — Riggins 1 run (kick failed)
NYG — Johnson 27 pass from Simms (Haji-Sheikh kick)
Wash — FG Moseley 21
Wash — Dean 36 interception return (Moseley kick)
Wash — Jordan 29 fumble recovery return (Moseley kick)

Dallas 23, Philadelphia 17—At Texas Stadium, attendance 64,521. Gary Hogeboom completed 22 of 40 passes for 320 yards and Rafael Septien kicked three field goals (47, 51, and 30 yards) to lead the Cowboys over the Eagles. Dallas led 16-10 on Septien's three field goals and Hogeboom's 25-yard touchdown pass to Ron Springs. Wide receiver Mike Renfro extended the lead to 23-10 when he threw a 49-yard touchdown pass to receiving mate Doug Donley. Donley totalled five receptions for 122 yards. The Cowboys' offense compiled 447 yards and the defense yielded 299.

Philadelphia	0	10	0	7	—	17
Dallas	3	10	10	0	—	23

Dall — FG Septien 47
Dall — FG Septien 51
Phil — Quick 16 pass from Jaworski (McFadden kick)
Dall — Springs 25 pass from Hogeboom (Septien kick)
Phil — FG McFadden 39
Dall — FG Septien 30
Dall — Donley 49 pass from Renfro (Septien kick)
Phil — Quick 9 pass from Jaworski (McFadden kick)

St. Louis 34, Indianapolis 33—At Hoosier Dome, attendance 60,274. Neil O'Donoghue's 46-yard field goal with seven seconds left climaxed the Cardinals' furious comeback. Neil Lomax and Roy Green combined on fourth-quarter touchdowns of 47 and 56 yards to close the score to 33-31. Lomax completed 16 of 39 passes for 270 yards, including eight to Green for 183 yards. Ottis Anderson rushed for 119 yards on 23 carries and scored St. Louis' first touchdown on a 10-yard run. Carl Birdsong was the unsung hero placing four of six punts inside the Colts' 20-yard line. Phil Smith had a 96-yard kickoff return for a touchdown for Indianapolis.

St. Louis	0	14	3	17	—	34
Indianapolis	7	10	9	7	—	33

Ind — Dickey 10 run (Biasucci kick)
StL — Anderson 10 run (O'Donoghue kick)
StL — L. Smith 25 interception return (O'Donoghue kick)
Ind — Porter 63 pass from Dickey (Biasucci kick)
Ind — FG Biasucci 21
Ind — FG Biasucci 50
StL — FG O'Donoghue 47
Ind — P. Smith 96 kickoff return (kick failed)
StL — Green 47 pass from Lomax (O'Donoghue kick)
Ind — Young 4 pass from Pagel (Biasucci kick)
StL — Green 56 pass from Lomax (O'Donoghue kick)
StL — FG O'Donoghue 46

New England 38, Seattle 23—At Sullivan Stadium, attendance 43,140. Tony Eason replaced Steve Grogan with nine minutes left in the first half and ignited the Patriots' stunning 38-23 win. Down 23-0, Eason ran 25 yards for a touchdown with 35 seconds remaining to cut the Seahawks' halftime advantage to 23-7. Opening the second half, Eason fired a two-yard scoring pass to Derrick Ramsey, and Mosi Tatupu added a one-yard run two possessions later to close the gap to 23-21. Tony Franklin's 32-yard field goal gave New England the lead for good, 24-23, with 6:31 remaining. Tatupu scored on a 10-yard run one minute later and Eason, the AFC's offensive player of the week, rifled a 15-yard touchdown pass to Irving Fryar to complete the scoring.

Seattle	9	14	0	0	—	23
New England	0	7	14	17	—	38

Sea — FG Johnson 42
Sea — Turner 41 pass from Krieg (kick failed)
Sea — Johns 47 punt return (Johnson kick)
Sea — Beasley 25 interception return (Johnson kick)
NE — Eason 25 run (Franklin kick)
NE — Ramsey 2 pass from Eason (Franklin kick)
NE — Tatupu 1 run (Franklin kick)
NE — FG Franklin 32
NE — Tatupu 10 run (Franklin kick)
NE — Fryar 15 pass from Eason (Franklin kick)

MONDAY, SEPTEMBER 17

Miami 21, Buffalo 17—At Rich Stadium, attendance 65,455. Dan Marino completed three touchdown passes as the Dolphins opened an 18-point lead and then held off the Bills' late rally to preserve the victory. Marino (26 of 35 for 296 yards) threw scoring passes in each of the first three quarters to Mark Duper (11 yards), Mark Clayton (12), and Nat Moore (1) for a 21-3 Miami lead. Buffalo closed the gap to 21-17 and had several opportunities to go ahead but fumble recoveries by Don McNeal and Doug Betters ended the Bills' final threats.

Miami	7	7	7	0	—	21
Buffalo	0	3	7	7	—	17

Mia — Duper 11 pass from Marino (von Schamann kick)
Mia — Clayton 12 pass from Marino (von Schamann kick)
Buff — FG Danelo 33
Mia — Moore 1 pass from Marino (von Schamann kick)
Buff — Neal 1 run (Danelo kick)
Buff — Dawkins 37 pass from Ferguson (Danelo kick)

FOURTH WEEK SUMMARY

The teams of the NFC Western division—San Francisco, Los Angeles Rams, Atlanta, and New Orleans—played undefeated football (4-0) this weekend. Matt Cavanaugh, who started in place of injured Joe Montana, completed three touchdown passes in the 49ers' 21-9 win over the Eagles. Jeff Kemp made his first NFL start and fired the go-ahead touchdown pass (a 52-yarder to Ron Brown) for the Rams in their 24-14 win over the Bengals. Saints quarterback Richard Todd returned after a one-week layoff to guide New Orleans over St. Louis 34-24. Todd directed a 450-yard attack, while the Saints' defense limited the Cardinals' explosive offense to 337 total yards. Steve Bartkowski threw three scoring passes to help lead the Falcons' 42-10 triumph over the Oilers. The victory ended Atlanta's two-game losing streak. Pat Ryan of the New York Jets teamed with Wesley Walker for three touchdowns to help the Jets edge Buffalo 28-26. Cleveland's Paul McDonald threw for 222 yards and two touchdowns in the second half to rally the Browns to their first win of the season, 20-10, over the Steelers. Jim Plunkett was sharp in the Raiders' Monday night showdown with the Chargers, but needed Marcus Allen's fourth touchdown of the game, with 45 seconds left, to lift the Raiders to a 33-30 victory. Denver recorded its first shutout in three years by downing Kansas City 21-0. Sammy Winder gained 139 yards on 31 carries to lead the Broncos. The Kingdome hosted the matchup of the week between the number-two and number-three rushers of all time, Chicago's Walter Payton and Seattle's Franco Harris. Payton won the individual contest by rushing for 116 yards to move into second place on the all-time rushing list with 12,091, just ahead of Harris. Seattle won the game, 38-9, as Chicago committed six turnovers in suffering its first loss. Pete Johnson, acquired by Miami the previous Saturday, scored the Dolphins' first rushing touchdown of the season in Miami's 44-7 romp over Indianapolis. Dallas got 10 tackles and 2 quarterback sacks from Randy White in the Cowboys' 20-6 defeat of the Packers. Jan Stenerud kicked five field goals to help Minnesota edge Detroit 29-28. The New York Giants downed Tampa Bay 17-14, thanks to Lawrence Taylor's four sacks and Phil Simms' pair of scoring passes. John Riggins gained 140 yards to become Washington's all-time leading rusher (5,898 yards) and scored his one-hundredth career touchdown on a 13-yard run to help the Redskins over the Patriots 26-10. The 14 NFL games drew 860,005 fans this weekend, the fourth-highest in-house total in league history.

SUNDAY, SEPTEMBER 23

Seattle 38, Chicago 9—At Kingdome, attendance 61,520. Dave Krieg accounted for two second-half touchdowns and the defense scored three more as the Seahawks handed the Bears their first defeat. Seattle capitalized on six Chicago turnovers (three fumbles, three interceptions). The Seahawks led 10-7 at halftime and extended it to 24-7 on Krieg's three-yard scoring run and 55-yard touchdown pass to Eric Lane. Keith Simpson (39 yards) and Terry Jackson (62) returned interceptions for touchdowns and Joe Nash recovered a fumble in the end zone for another score. With his performance, Nash was named AFC defensive player of the week. Walter Payton, who gained 116 yards rushing to raise his career total to 12,091 yards, passed Franco Harris (12,032 yards) to move into second place on the all-time career rushing chart behind Jim Brown (12,312).

Chicago	7	0	0	2	—	9
Seattle	7	3	21	7	—	38

Chi — Suhey 3 pass from Payton (B. Thomas kick)
Sea — Simpson 39 interception return (Johnson kick)
Sea — FG Johnson 27
Sea — Krieg 3 run (Johnson kick)
Sea — Lane 55 pass from Krieg (Johnson kick)
Sea — Nash fumble recovery in end zone (Johnson kick)

Chi — Safety, Seattle holding in end zone
Sea — T. Jackson 62 interception return (Johnson kick)

Miami 44, Indianapolis 7—At Orange Bowl, attendance 55,415. Dan Marino threw a pair of touchdown passes and Woody Bennett ran for two more as the Dolphins blasted the Colts. Marino's 80-yard scoring bomb to Mark Duper (seven catches for 173 yards) snapped a 7-7 tie and triggered Miami's 37-point explosion. Duper added a five-yard touchdown catch for a 23-7 halftime lead. Bennett scored on runs of four and one yards following Don McNeal's 11-yard interception return for a touchdown. Pete Johnson, acquired from the Chargers the day before the game, scored the Dolphins' first rushing touchdown of the season, a one-yarder. Doug Betters accounted for three of Miami's six quarterback sacks.

Indianapolis	0	7	0	0	— 7
Miami	7	16	14	7	— 44

Mia — P. Johnson 1 run (von Schamann kick)
Ind — Young 5 pass from Pagel (Biasucci kick)
Mia — Duper 80 pass from Marino (kick failed)
Mia — FG von Schamann 27
Mia — Duper 5 pass from Marino (von Schamann kick)
Mia — McNeal 11 interception return (von Schamann kick)
Mia — Bennett 4 run (von Schamann kick)
Mia — Bennett 1 run (von Schamann kick)

Dallas 20, Green Bay 6—At Texas Stadium, attendance 64,222. Michael Downs, Everson Walls, and Randy White spearheaded the Dallas defense which held Green Bay to 204 total yards en route to a 20-6 win. Downs had two quarterback sacks and blocked an extra point and Walls had two of the Cowboys' four interceptions. White had 10 tackles and one-and-a-half sacks to win NFC defensive player of the week honors. The Cowboys led 13-0 at halftime on Timmy Newsome's one-yard run and Rafael Septien's pair of field goals from 32 and 42 yards, but it wasn't until Tony Dorsett scored from seven yards out with 46 seconds left, that victory was assured. Danny White's 11 punts set a club record, while Dorsett (8,621) moved into sixth place on the all-time rushing list passing Jim Taylor (8,597).

Green Bay	0	0	6	0	— 6
Dallas	7	6	0	7	— 20

Dall — Newsome 1 run (Septien kick)
Dall — FG Septien 32
Dall — FG Septien 42
GB — Brown 5 interception return (kick blocked)
Dall — Dorsett 7 run (Septien kick)

Atlanta 42, Houston 10—At Atlanta-Fulton County Stadium, attendance 45,248. Steve Bartkowski completed 11 of 13 passes for 195 yards and three touchdowns and Gerald Riggs rushed for 120 yards and two scores to help the Falcons snap a two-game losing streak. Atlanta surged to a 21-0 first-quarter lead on Bartkowski's 23-yard scoring pass to Arthur Cox and Riggs' scoring runs of two and four yards. It was the first time the Falcons had scored a first-quarter touchdown in 13 games. Billy Johnson (25 yards) and Cox (16) caught third-quarter touchdown passes to put the game away.

Houston	0	10	0	0	— 10
Atlanta	21	0	14	7	— 42

Atl — Cox 23 pass from Bartkowski (Luckhurst kick)
Atl — Riggs 2 run (Luckhurst kick)
Atl — Riggs 4 run (Luckhurst kick)
Hou — FG Kempf 22
Hou — Moriarty 2 pass from Moon (Kempf kick)
Atl — B. Johnson 25 pass from Bartkowski (Luckhurst kick)
Atl — Cox 16 pass from Bartkowski (Luckhurst kick)
Atl — J. Johnson 35 interception return (Luckhurst kick)

Denver 21, Kansas City 0—At Mile High Stadium, attendance 74,263. Sammy Winder rushed a career-high 31 times for 139 yards and one touchdown to power the Broncos over the Chiefs. Denver capped back-to-back 80-yard, seven-play scoring drives in the second quarter on Winder's six-yard run and Rick Parros' three-yard blast. Mike Harden's 45-yard interception return for a score sealed the victory. It was the Broncos' first shutout win since blanking the Raiders 17-0 on October 4, 1981, and the Chiefs' first blanking since December 16, 1979 (3-0 vs. Tampa Bay).

Kansas City	0	0	0	0	— 0
Denver	0	14	7	0	— 21

Den — Winder 6 run (Karlis kick)
Den — Parros 3 run (Karlis kick)
Den — Harden 45 interception return (Karlis kick)

Los Angeles Rams 24, Cincinnati 14—At Riverfront Stadium, attendance 45,406. Jeff Kemp completed 13 of 23 passes for 205 yards and one touchdown in his first NFL start to guide the Rams over the Bengals. After Eric Dickerson scored on a six-yard run midway through the second quarter, Kemp hooked up with Ron Brown on a 52-yard touchdown pass to lead 14-7. Mike Lansford's 29-yard field goal increased the Rams margin to 17-7, but Cris Collinsworth's 10-yard scoring catch brought Cincinnati to within 17-14 with 1:49 left. Mike Guman returned the Bengals' ensuing onside kick 43 yards for a touchdown to seal the victory.

L.A. Rams	0	7	7	10	— 24
Cincinnati	0	0	7	7	— 14

Rams — Dickerson 6 run (Lansford kick)
Cin — Kinnebrew 2 run (Breech kick)
Rams — Brown 52 pass from Kemp (Lansford kick)
Rams — FG Lansford 29
Cin — Collinsworth 10 pass from Anderson (Breech kick)
Rams — Guman 43 kickoff return (Lansford kick)

Minnesota 29, Detroit 28—At Pontiac Silverdome, attendance 57,511. Jan Stenerud kicked five field goals (35, 32, 37, 34, and 19 yards) for the fourth time in his career, as the Vikings edged the Lions. Minnesota, which led 16-14 at halftime, recovered three second-half Detroit fumbles to extend its lead. Linebacker Chris Martin returned a fumbled punt eight yards for a touchdown early in the third quarter and Stenerud followed with a pair of field goals. The Vikings' victory offset a fine performance by Lions quarterback Gary Danielson. Danielson completed four touchdown passes, including three to wide receiver Leonard Thompson. Minnesota was led by rookie Alfred Anderson, who gained 120 yards on 19 carries and Leo Lewis, who caught five passes for 101 yards.

Minnesota	7	9	10	3	— 29
Detroit	7	7	7	7	— 28

Minn — White 26 pass from Kramer (Stenerud kick)
Det — Thompson 1 pass from Danielson (Murray kick)
Minn — FG Stenerud 35
Det — Thompson 66 pass from Danielson (Murray kick)
Minn — FG Stenerud 32
Minn — FG Stenerud 37
Minn — Martin 8 fumble recovery return (Stenerud kick)
Det — Jones 10 pass from Danielson (Murray kick)
Minn — FG Stenerud 34
Minn — FG Stenerud 19
Det — Thompson 15 pass from Danielson (Murray kick)

New York Jets 28, Buffalo 26—At Rich Stadium, attendance 48,330. Pat Ryan and Wesley Walker combined for three touchdowns and Freeman McNeil rushed for 112 yards on 24 carries to lead the Jets over the Bills. New York overcame a 10-0 second-quarter deficit on Tony Paige's two-yard run and Ryan touchdown passes of 12 and 44 yards to Walker. Walker also caught a 36-yard touchdown pass in the fourth quarter to total 128 yards on seven receptions.

N.Y. Jets	0	21	0	7	— 28
Buffalo	10	0	9	7	— 26

Buff — FG Danelo 52
Buff — Williams 1 pass from Ferguson (Danelo kick)
NYJ — Paige 2 run (Leahy kick)
NYJ — Walker 12 pass from Ryan (Leahy kick)
NYJ — Walker 44 pass from Ryan (Leahy kick)
Buff — FG Danelo 36
Buff — FG Danelo 27
Buff — FG Danelo 20
NYJ — Walker 36 pass from Ryan (Leahy kick)
Buff — Dawkins 31 pass from Ferguson (Danelo kick)

Cleveland 20, Pittsburgh 10—At Cleveland Stadium, attendance 77,312. Paul McDonald completed 15 of 28 passes for 293 yards, including 222 in the second half, to rally the Browns to their first win. Trailing 7-3 in the third quarter, McDonald hit Boyce Green with a 44-yard scoring pass and Duriel Harris on a three-yarder which gave the Browns the lead for good, 17-10. Matt Bahr converted 18- and 48-yard field goals, while the Cleveland defense, ranked number one in the AFC, held Pittsburgh to 219 total yards. The Browns gained 413 total yards and became the first team to score on the Steelers in the fourth quarter this season.

Pittsburgh	0	7	3	0	— 10
Cleveland	0	0	10	10	— 20

Pitt — Washington 69 interception return (Anderson kick)
Cle — FG Bahr 18
Cle — Green 44 pass from McDonald (Bahr kick)
Pitt — FG Anderson 46
Cle — Harris 3 pass from McDonald (Bahr kick)
Cle — FG Bahr 48

New Orleans 34, St. Louis 24—At Louisiana Superdome, attendance 58,723. Running back Wayne Wilson caught two touchdowns passes as the Saints outlasted the Cardinals. Richard Todd (14 of 29 for 264 yards) threw a 15-yard scoring pass to Hoby Brenner (six receptions for 131 yards) and Hokie Gajan completed a 34-yard touchdown pass on a halfback option play to Wilson for a 20-14 lead in the third quarter. The Cardinals forged ahead 24-20 on Stump Mitchell's second touchdown of the game (a 22-yard run) and Neil O'Donoghue's 39-yard field goal. But St. Louis' lead didn't last long, as Todd found Wilson on a 30-yard scoring pass with 6:07 to play. Frank Wattelet finished the Saints' scoring by returning a fumble 22 yards for a touchdown on the final play of the game. The Saints outgained the Cardinals 450 yards to 337.

St. Louis	0	7	7	10	— 24
New Orleans	10	3	7	14	— 34

NO — FG Andersen 25
NO — W. Wilson 34 pass from Gajan (Andersen kick)
StL — Ferrell 11 pass from Lomax (O'Donoghue kick)
NO — FG Andersen 29
StL — Mitchell 7 run (O'Donoghue kick)
NO — Brenner 15 pass from Todd (Andersen kick)
StL — Mitchell 22 run (O'Donoghue kick)
StL — FG O'Donoghue 39
NO — W. Wilson 30 pass from Todd (Andersen kick)
NO — Wattelet 22 fumble recovery return (Andersen kick)

San Francisco 21, Philadelphia 9—At Veterans Stadium, attendance 62,771. Matt Cavanaugh, replacing injured starter Joe Montana, threw for three touchdowns as the 49ers grounded the Eagles 21-9. Cavanaugh completed 17 of 34 attempts for 252 yards and had scoring passes to Roger Craig (35 yards) and Freddie Solomon (2) in the first half, and Dwight Clark (51) in the second. Paul McFadden provided all the Eagles' scoring on field goals of 35, 32, and 33 yards.

San Francisco	7	7	0	7	— 21
Philadelphia	0	6	3	0	— 9

SF — Craig 35 pass from Cavanaugh (Wersching kick)
Phil — FG McFadden 35
Phil — FG McFadden 32
SF — Solomon 2 pass from Cavanaugh (Wersching kick)
Phil — FG McFadden 33
SF — D. Clark 51 pass from Cavanaugh (Wersching kick)

New York Giants 17, Tampa Bay 14—At Giants Stadium, attendance 72,650. Phil Simms passed for two touchdowns and Lawrence Taylor registered four sacks as the Giants beat the Buccaneers, 17-14. Ali Haji-Sheikh's 34-yard field goal and Simms' 20-yard scoring strike to Bobby Johnson (following a fumble recovery by Jim Burt), gave New York a 10-0 halftime lead. Tampa Bay cut the margin to 10-7 in the third quarter on James Wilder's (24 carries for 112 yards) one-yard run. Simms brought New York back with a 21-yard touchdown pass to Zeke Mowatt for the winning points.

Tampa Bay	0	0	7	7	— 14
N.Y. Giants	0	10	0	7	— 17

NYG — FG Haji-Sheikh 34
NYG — Johnson 20 pass from Simms (Haji-Sheikh kick)
TB — Wilder 1 run (Ariri kick)
NYG — Mowatt 21 pass from Simms (Haji-Sheikh kick)
TB — Armstrong 1 run (Ariri kick)

Washington 26, New England 10—At Sullivan Stadium, attendance 60,503. John Riggins rushed for 140 yards on 33 carries and Mark Moseley kicked four field goals (19, 42, 22, and 27 yards) to lead the Redskins over the Patriots. Washington opened a 20-0 third-quarter lead on Riggins' 100th career touchdown (13-yard run), a pair of Moseley field goals, and Joe Theismann's 15-yard touchdown pass to Charlie Brown. Riggins' rushing total gave him 5,898 career yards with the Redskins, breaking Larry Brown's club record of 5,875. The Redskins' offense controlled the ball for 43:12, while the defense limited the Patriots to a New England record-tying low of 17 yards rushing.

Washington	7	3	13	3	— 26
New England	0	0	7	3	— 10

Wash — Riggins 13 run (Moseley kick)
Wash — FG Moseley 19
Wash — FG Moseley 42
Wash — Brown 15 pass from Theismann (Moseley kick)
NE — Starring 38 pass from Eason (Franklin kick)
Wash — FG Moseley 22
NE — FG Franklin 22
Wash — FG Moseley 27

MONDAY, SEPTEMBER 24

Los Angeles Raiders 33, San Diego 30—At Memorial Coliseum, attendance 76,131. Marcus Allen's fourth touchdown of the game, a one-yard run with 45 seconds remaining, lifted the Raiders over the Chargers. Allen also had scoring runs of one and two yards and caught a 30-yard touchdown pass from Jim Plunkett. Plunkett completed 24 of 33 passes for 363 yards, including eight to Todd Christensen for 120 yards. The win overshadowed the performances of San Diego's Earnest Jackson, who gained 155 yards on 29 carries, and Kellen Winslow, who caught nine passes for 119 yards and a touchdown. Allen's performance earned him AFC offensive player of the week honors.

San Diego	7	3	3	17	— 30
L.A. Raiders	6	7	7	13	— 33

Raiders — FG Bahr 42
SD — Winslow 11 pass from Fouts (Benirschke kick)
Raiders — FG Bahr 36
SD — FG Benirschke 51
Raiders — Allen 1 run (Bahr kick)
Raiders — Allen 30 pass from Plunkett (Bahr kick)
SD — FG Benirschke 33
SD — Jackson 1 run (Benirschke kick)
SD — FG Benirschke 48
SD — Lowe 32 interception return (Benirschke kick)
Raiders — Allen 2 run (kick failed)
Raiders — Allen 1 run (Bahr kick)

FIFTH WEEK SUMMARY

The Denver Broncos controlled the ball the final 4:34 to hand the Raiders their first loss of the season, 16-13, snapping Los Angeles' nine-game win streak. The loss created a three-way tie in the AFC West among those two teams and Seattle, a 20-12 victor at Minnesota. San Francisco and Miami remained the NFL's only undefeated teams. The 49ers got a pair of second-quarter touchdown passes from Joe Montana, and the defense didn't allow a touchdown for the second straight week, which enabled San Francisco to down Atlanta 14-5. The Dolphins' Dan Marino passed for a club-record 429 yards and three touchdowns as Miami defeated St. Louis 36-28. The Dolphins scored on five of their first six possessions to put the game away early. Conversely, two other quarterbacks suffered through the worst of times. In Anaheim, the Rams tallied an NFL-record three safeties, including one on their five sacks of Phil Simms, and held the Giants to just eight yards rushing en route to a 33-12 win. Kansas City snapped a two-week winless streak with a 10-6 triumph over Cleveland. The Chiefs demoralized the Browns' attack by sacking quarterback Paul McDonald 11 times. Walter Payton tied Jim Brown's career mark for 100-yard rushing games (58) by gaining 155 yards (130 in the first half) on 25 carries, but it wasn't enough as the Cowboys defeated Chicago 23-14 to win their third straight game. At Tampa Stadium, Obed Ariri's third field goal with 4:22 left in overtime, brought an end to a see-saw battle and gave the Buccaneers a 30-27 victory over the Packers. James Wilder rushed an NFL record-tying 43 times for 172 yards to help Tampa Bay. Buffalo's Greg Bell and Indianapolis' Randy McMillan battled head to head for rushing honors and while Bell won the battle, McMillan won the war. Bell outgained McMillan 144 to 114, but McMillan's two touchdowns powered the Colts over the Bills. Tony Eason was too much for the Jets to handle as the second-year quarterback accounted for all four Patriots touchdowns in their 28-21 win. Meanwhile, Dwayne Woodruff and Donnie Shell each intercepted two passes in the Steelers' 38-17 victory over the Bengals.

SUNDAY, SEPTEMBER 30

San Francisco 14, Atlanta 5—At Candlestick Park, attendance 57,990. Joe Montana returned to the starting lineup and capped a pair of second-quarter 80-yard drives with scoring passes of 5 yards to Russ Francis and 21 yards to Mike Wilson to lead the 49ers' win. Atlanta moved inside the San Francisco 10-yard line four times but came away with only a field goal. The Falcons outgained the 49ers 418 yards to 310, as Gerald Riggs ran for 136 yards and Steve Bartkowski completed 22 of 41 passes for 267 yards. It was the second straight game in which the San Francisco defense did not allow a touchdown.

Atlanta	3	0	0	2	— 5
San Francisco	0	14	0	0	— 14

Atl — FG Luckhurst 22
SF — Francis 5 pass from Montana (Wersching kick)
SF — Wilson 21 pass from Montana (Wersching kick)
Atl — Safety, Case tackled Runager in end zone

Indianapolis 31, Buffalo 17—At Hoosier Dome, attendance 60,032. Randy McMillan rushed for 114 yards and two second-half touchdowns to rally the Colts over the Bills 31-17. Buffalo led 17-10 before McMillan scored from 10 yards out to tie the game late in the third quarter. He then bolted 31 yards for the go-ahead touchdown early in the final period. The Colts had five sacks and three interceptions, including Mark Kafentzis' 59-yard touchdown return to finish the scoring. Greg Bell gained 144 yards on 29 carries for the Bills.

Buffalo	0	10	7	0	— 17
Indianapolis	7	3	7	14	— 31

Ind — Butler 7 pass from Pagel (Biasucci kick)
Buff — FG Danelo 23
Buff — Dufek 11 run (Danelo kick)
Ind — FG Biasucci 43
Buff — Dennard 4 pass from Dukek (Danelo kick)
Ind — McMillan 10 run (Biasucci kick)
Ind — McMillan 31 run (Biasucci kick)
Ind — Kafentzis 59 interception return (Biasucci kick)

Kansas City 10, Cleveland 6—At Arrowhead Stadium, attendance 40,785. Todd Blackledge's nine-yard scoring pass to Billy Jackson with 11:02 remaining in the game, clinched the Chiefs' victory and snapped a two-game losing streak. The touchdown was Kansas City's first in eight quarters. The Chiefs' defense stifled the Cleveland offense as Bill Maas and Ken McAlister each had three of Kansas City's club-record 11 quarterback sacks (for 78 yards in losses). Deron Cherry's 67-yard interception return in the final minute of play assured the Chiefs' victory.

Cleveland	0	3	3	0	— 6
Kansas City	0	3	0	7	— 10

Cle — FG Bahr 34
KC — FG Lowery 42
Cle — FG Bahr 23
KC — Jackson 9 pass from Blackledge (Lowery kick)

Dallas 23, Chicago 14—At Soldier Field, attendance 63,623. Gary Hogeboom connected on 18 of 29 passes for 265 yards and one touchdown and Rafael Septien kicked three field goals to help the Cowboys win their third straight game. Dallas took a 17-14 halftime lead on Septien's 44-yard field goal, Tony Dorsett's 68-yard screen pass from Hogeboom, and Timmy Newsome's two-yard run. Septien finished the Cowboys' scoring with 32- and 23-yard field goals in the second half, while the Cowboys' defense shut down the Bears' attack. Walter Payton ran for 155 yards (130 in the first half) on 25 carries to tie Jim Brown with 58 career 100-yard games.

Dallas	10	7	3	3	— 23
Chicago	7	7	0	0	— 14

Dall — FG Septien 44
Chi — McMahon 16 run (B. Thomas kick)
Dall — Dorsett 68 pass from Hogeboom (Septien kick)
Chi — Payton 20 run (B. Thomas kick)
Dall — Newsome 2 run (Septien kick)
Dall — FG Septien 32
Dall — FG Septien 23

San Diego 27, Detroit 24—At San Diego Jack Murphy Stadium, attendance 53,509. San Diego opened a 24-7 halftime lead and withstood a furious Detroit rally to record the victory. Dan Fouts (22 of 34 for 268 yards) led the Chargers to scores on four of their first five possessions. Jewerl Thomas' pair of one-yard touchdown runs and Buford McGee's three-yard blast gave San Diego a 24-7 halftime lead. Billy Sims gained 119 yards on 14 carries for the Lions.

Detroit	0	7	14	3	— 24
San Diego	7	17	0	3	— 27

SD — Thomas 1 run (Benirschke kick)
SD — Thomas 1 run (Benirschke kick)
SD — McGee 3 run (Benirschke kick)
Det — Sims 1 run (Murray kick)
SD — FG Benirschke 18
Det — Sims 1 run (Murray kick)
Det — Chadwick 12 run (Murray kick)
SD — FG Benirschke 41
Det — FG Murray 44

Tampa Bay 30, Green Bay 27—At Tampa Stadium, attendance 47,487. Obed Ariri's third field goal of the game, a 48-yarder with 10:32 elapsed in overtime, lifted the Buccaneers over the Packers. Tampa Bay had taken a 27-20 lead on nose tackle Dave Logan's 27-yard interception return for a score, but Green Bay forced overtime with eight seconds left when Gerry Ellis took a lateral from James Lofton and ran 14 yards to cap a 36-yard scoring play. Ariri also connected from 46 and 49 yards out. James Wilder gained 172 yards on an NFL record-tying 43 carries for the Buccaneers.

Green Bay	10	3	7	7	0	— 27
Tampa Bay	7	10	0	10	3	— 30

TB — Wilder 33 run (Ariri kick)
GB — Clark 43 run (Garcia kick)
GB — FG Garcia 41
TB — FG Ariri 46
TB — DeBerg 6 run (Ariri kick)
GB — FG Garcia 51
GB — Coffman 4 pass from Dickey (Garcia kick)
TB — FG Ariri 49
TB — Logan 27 interception return (Ariri kick)
GB — Ellis 14 lateral from Lofton after 22 pass from Dickey (Garcia kick)
TB — FG Ariri 48

Denver 16, Los Angeles Raiders 13—At Mile High Stadium, attendance 74,833. Gerald Willhite's four-yard touchdown run in the third quarter proved decisive as the Broncos snapped the Raiders' nine-game winning streak and moved into a tie for first place in the AFC West. Rich Karlis kept the Broncos close with field goals of 27, 32, and 19 yards, but Denver trailed Los Angeles 10-9 midway through the third period. John Elway drove the Broncos 82 yards in 11 plays for Willhite's winning score. Denver controlled the game, outrushing the Raiders 231 yards to 70.

L.A. Raiders	0	7	3	3	— 13
Denver	0	6	10	0	— 16

Den — FG Karlis 27
Raiders — Christensen 19 pass from Plunkett (Bahr kick)
Den — FG Karlis 32
Den — FG Karlis 19
Raiders — FG Bahr 27
Den — Willhite 4 run (Karlis kick)
Raiders — FG Bahr 50

Miami 36, St. Louis 28—At Busch Memorial Stadium, attendance 46,991. Dan Marino passed for a Miami-record 429 yards (on 24 of 36 passes) and three touchdowns to power the Dolphins over the Cardinals. Miami scored on five of six first-half possessions to lead 26-14 by halftime. Marino, the AFC offensive player of the week, followed a pair of Uwe von Schamann field goals (from 27 and 26 yards) with scoring passes to Joe Rose (26 yards) and Mark Clayton (29). Pete Johnson scored on a one-yard run to conclude the Dolphins' first-half scoring. Tony Nathan caught a 23-yard scoring pass and von Schamann kicked another 27-yard field goal to complete Miami's scoring. Mark Duper caught eight passes for 164 yards and Clayton five for 143. The Dolphins rolled up a club-record 552 yards total offense, and yielded 445.

Miami	6	20	0	10	— 36
St. Louis	0	14	7	7	— 28

Mia — FG von Schamann 27
Mia — FG von Schamann 26
Mia — Rose 26 pass from Marino (kick blocked)
StL — Mitchell 2 run (O'Donoghue kick)
Mia — P. Johnson 1 run (von Schamann kick)
StL — Marsh 22 pass from Lomax (O'Donoghue kick)
Mia — Clayton 29 pass from Marino (von Schamann kick)
StL — Ferrell 11 run (O'Donoghue kick)
Mia — Nathan 23 pass from Marino (von Schamann kick)
Mia — FG von Schamann 27
StL — Mitchell 4 run (O'Donoghue kick)

New England 28, New York Jets 21—At Giants Stadium, attendance 68,978. Tony Eason fired three touchdown passes and ran for another to lead the Patriots over the Jets. Eason completed a club-record 28 of 42 passes for 354 yards. He capped scoring drives of 83, 72, and 94 yards with touchdowns of two yards to Lin Dawson, four yards to Bo Robinson, and 43 yards to Stanley Morgan. His four-yard run with less than a minute to go in the first half, climaxed a 78-yard march and gave New England a 14-14 tie. Ten players caught at least one pass for the Patriots as the offense totalled 476 yards. Linebacker Andre Tippett had two of New England's six sacks. The Jets failed to sack the opposing quarterback for the first time since the opening game of the 1983 season.

New England	7	7	14	0	— 28
N.Y. Jets	7	7	0	7	— 21

NYJ — Walker 12 pass from Ryan (Leahy kick)
NE — Dawson 2 pass from Eason (Franklin kick)
NYJ — Paige 1 run (Leahy kick)
NE — Eason 4 run (Franklin kick)
NE — Robinson 4 pass from Eason (Franklin kick)
NE — Morgan 43 pass from Eason (Franklin kick)
NYJ — Shuler 7 pass from Ryan (Leahy kick)

New Orleans 27, Houston 10—At Astrodome, attendance 43,108. Hokie Gajan ran for two touchdowns and the defense yielded a club-record-low 133 total yards (including 49 passing), as the Saints captured their second straight win 27-10. Gajan had scoring runs of 15 and 37 yards, while Morten Andersen kicked field goals of 23 and 27 yards. Frank Wattelet had a 35-yard interception return for a touchdown.

New Orleans	14	3	0	10	— 27
Houston	0	0	3	7	— 10

NO — Gajan 15 run (Andersen kick)
NO — Wattelet 35 interception return (Andersen kick)
NO — FG Andersen 23
Hou — FG Kempf 25
Hou — Campbell 1 run (Kempf kick)
NO — FG Andersen 27
NO — Gajan 37 run (Andersen kick)

Los Angeles Rams 33, New York Giants 12—At Anaheim Stadium, attendance 53,417. Henry Ellard returned a punt 83 yards for a score and the Rams scored an NFL record three safeties in defeating the Giants 33-12. Dwayne Crutchfield (one-yard run) and David Hill (two-yard pass) added touchdowns and Mike Lansford kicked a pair of field goals (33 and 35 yards) for Los Angeles. The safeties occurred on blocked punts in the end zone by Norwood Vann and Ivory Sully, and a sack of Giants quarterback Phil Simms by Reggie Doss and Jack Youngblood. Youngblood had two of the Rams' five sacks. Los Angeles held New York to eight yards rushing, the second fewest in Rams history.

N.Y. Giants	6	0	0	6	— 12
L.A. Rams	0	17	16	0	— 33

NYG — McConkey recovered kickoff in end zone (kick failed)
Rams — Crutchfield 1 run (Lansford kick)
Rams — Ellard 83 punt return (Lansford kick)
Rams — FG Lansford 33
Rams — Safety, Sully blocked punt out of end zone
Rams — Safety, Doss and Youngblood tackled Simms in end zone
Rams — David Hill 2 pass from Kemp (Lansford kick)
Rams — FG Lansford 35
Rams — Safety, Vann blocked punt out of end zone
NYG — Gray 15 pass from Simms (kick failed)

Washington 20, Philadelphia 0—At Robert F. Kennedy Stadium, attendance 53,064. John Riggins carried 28 times for 104 yards and one touchdown as the Redskins handed the Eagles their third straight defeat. Washington opened a 10-0 lead at halftime on a flea-flicker 51-yard scoring pass from Joe Theismann to Art Monk, and Mark Moseley's 35-yard field goal. Riggins' eight-yard touchdown run put the game out of reach in the third quarter. Theismann rushed for 56 yards to become the first quarterback in Washington history to gain over 1,500 yards in a career. The Redskins' shutout was the team's first since defeating St. Louis 28-0 the final game of the 1982 season.

Philadelphia	0	0	0	0	— 0
Washington	0	10	7	3	— 20

Wash — Monk 51 pass from Theismann (Moseley kick)
Wash — FG Moseley 35
Wash — Riggins 8 run (Moseley kick)
Wash — FG Moseley 29

Seattle 20, Minnesota 12—At Metrodome, attendance 57,171. Dave Krieg fired a 20-yard touchdown pass to Steve Largent on the Seahawks' first possession of the game and Seattle never looked back in defeating Minnesota. Krieg completed 17 of 27 passes for 222 yards, including eight for 130 yards to Largent, who tied Lance Alworth for the fifth-longest pass catch streak in NFL history (96 games). Norm Johnson kicked 41- and 31-yard field goals and Eric Lane scored on a 40-yard run with 1:08 remaining to close out the scoring. Lane gained 113 yards on 14 carries, as Seattle's offense rolled up 409 total yards.

Seattle	7	3	0	10	— 20
Minnesota	3	3	3	3	— 12

Minn—FG Stenerud 43
Sea —Largent 20 pass from Krieg (Johnson kick)
Minn—FG Stenerud 44
Sea —FG Johnson 41
Minn—FG Stenerud 28
Sea —FG Johnson 31
Minn—FG Stenerud 34
Sea —Lane 40 run (Johnson kick)

MONDAY, OCTOBER 1

Pittsburgh 38, Cincinnati 17—At Three Rivers Stadium, attendance 57,098. Dwayne Woodruff and Donnie Shell each returned interceptions for touchdowns as the Steelers handed the Bengals their fifth straight loss. Woodruff's 42-yard interception return for a score gave Pittsburgh a 14-0 first-half lead just 1:08 after rookie Rich Erenberg ran 31 yards for a touchdown. The Bengals closed the gap to 24-17 in the fourth quarter, but the Steelers scored twice within 25 seconds to put the game away. Woodruff's second interception of the game set up Walter Abercrombie's five-yard scoring run. Shell then returned his second theft 52 yards for a touchdown with 4:23 to play. Shell and Woodruff shared AFC defensive player of the week honors as the Pittsburgh defense intercepted five passes and recorded six sacks.

Cincinnati	0	10	0	7	— 17
Pittsburgh	0	14	10	14	— 38

Pitt—Erenberg 31 run (Anderson kick)
Pitt—Woodruff 42 interception return (Anderson kick)
Cin—Jennings 38 pass from Schonert (Breech kick)
Cin—FG Breech 32
Pitt—FG Anderson 31
Pitt—Thompson 23 pass from Woodley (Anderson kick)
Cin—Schonert 1 run (Breech kick)
Pitt—Abercrombie 5 run (Anderson kick)
Pitt—Shell 52 interception return (Anderson kick)

SIXTH WEEK SUMMARY

On the second play of the third quarter, his seventeenth carry in Chicago's 20-7 victory against New Orleans, Walter Payton gained six yards to eclipse Jim Brown's NFL career rushing record of 12,312 yards. Payton, needing 67 yards to break the mark, gained 154 on 32 carries to total 12,400 for his career. His fifty-ninth 100-yard game also gave him sole possession of a record he shared with Brown. Dan Marino returned to his native Pittsburgh and fired two touchdown passes to lead the Dolphins over the Steelers 31-7. St. Louis exploded for 17 consecutive points in the third quarter and Roy Green caught scoring passes of 70 and 45 yards to help beat Dallas 31-20. Joe Theismann completed 85 percent of his passes (17 of 20) and threw for four touchdowns in the Redskins' 35-7 triumph over the Colts. Joe Montana completed three touchdowns in the 49ers' 31-10 defeat of the Giants on Monday night. The Raiders returned to winning form as Marc Wilson responded to his first action since November 6, 1983, by throwing for 309 yards in Los Angeles' 28-14 win over Seattle. Denver kept pace with the Raiders in the AFC West by capitalizing on 10 Detroit turnovers (seven interceptions, three fumble recoveries) to easily beat the Lions 28-7. Ray Clayborn's 85-yard interception return with seven seconds left, preserved the Patriots' 17-16 comeback win over the Browns. Clayborn had not intercepted a pass in his previous 30 games. Boomer Esiason scored the game's only touchdown to lead the Bengals to a 13-3 win over the Oilers and give head coach Sam Wyche his first NFL victory. San Diego's Dan Fouts passed for 376 yards and three scores to out-duel Green Bay's Lynn Dickey, who threw for 384 yards and three touchdowns as well. In the end, the Chargers prevailed 34-28 thanks in part to Kellen Winslow's club-record 15 receptions for 157 yards. Kansas City was edged by the New York Jets 17-16, but Nick Lowery kicked three of three field-goal attempts to become the NFL's all-time career accuracy leader with a percentage of .736 (100 of 131).

SUNDAY, OCTOBER 7

Atlanta 30, Los Angeles Rams 28—At Anaheim Stadium, attendance 47,832. Mick Luckhurst kicked three field goals, including a 37-yarder as time expired, that helped the Falcons record their first road win ever against the Rams. Lynn Cain, starting in place of sidelined Gerald Riggs, rushed for 145 yards on 35 carries and scored three touchdowns (31, 1, and 9 yards). Cain's final touchdown, early in the fourth quarter, put Atlanta ahead 24-21. Los Angeles countered with Eric Dickerson (19 carries for 107 yards), who sprinted 47 yards for a score to cap an 86-yard drive and give the Rams a 28-27 lead with 7:04 to play. Luckhurst also had a 50- and club-record 52-yard field goal. Wide receiver Stacey Bailey caught seven passes for 158 yards.

Atlanta	0	10	7	13	— 30
L.A. Rams	0	7	14	7	— 28

Atl —Cain 31 run (Luckhurst kick)
Atl —FG Luckhurst 52
Rams—Ellard 14 pass from Dils (Lansford kick)
Rams—Dickerson 2 run (Lansford kick)
Atl —Cain 1 run (Luckhurst kick)
Rams—Drew Hill 63 pass from Kemp (Lansford kick)
Atl —Cain 9 run (Luckhurst kick)
Atl —FG Luckhurst 50
Rams—Dickerson 47 run (Lansford kick)
Atl —FG Luckhurst 37

Denver 28, Detroit 7—At Pontiac Silverdome, attendance 55,836. The Broncos capitalized on seven interceptions, three fumble recoveries, and six sacks to upend the Lions. Denver scored twice within 54 seconds in the first quarter on Sammy Winder's one-yard run and defensive end Rulon Jones' five-yard fumble return. Steve Wilson's first of two interceptions with 53 seconds left in the half, set up John Elway's 42-yard touchdown pass to Steve Watson for a 21-7 lead. Ken Woodard's 27-yard interception return for a touchdown midway through the fourth quarter completed the scoring. Elway completed 16 of 22 passes for 210 yards. His favorite target was Watson who caught seven passes for 111 yards.

Denver	14	7	0	7	— 28
Detroit	0	7	0	0	— 7

Den—Winder 1 run (Karlis kick)
Den—Jones 5 fumble recovery return (Karlis kick)
Det —Danielson 2 run (Murray kick)
Den—Watson 42 pass from Elway (Karlis kick)
Den—Woodard 27 interception return (Karlis kick)

Cincinnati 13, Houston 3—At Riverfront Stadium, attendance 43,637. Rookie quarterback Boomer Esiason ran for a touchdown and Jim Breech kicked two field goals to give Cincinnati head coach Sam Wyche his first NFL victory. Esiason, starting in place of injured Ken Anderson, scored on a three-yard run late in the third quarter. Breech's field goals came in the second quarter (33 yards) and the fourth period (22). Ross Browner had two of the Bengals' four sacks as the defense held the Oilers to 235 total yards.

Houston	0	0	3	0	— 3
Cincinnati	0	3	7	3	— 13

Cin —FG Breech 33
Hou—FG Kempf 24
Cin —Esiason 3 run (Breech kick)
Cin —FG Breech 22

Miami 31, Pittsburgh 7—At Three Rivers Stadium, attendance 59,103. Dan Marino fired two second-quarter touchdown passes to help the Dolphins down the Steelers. After a scoreless first quarter, Marino (16 of 24 passes for 226 yards) hooked up with tight ends Bruce Hardy and Joe Rose on scoring passes of 3 and 34 yards, respectively. Nose tackle Bob Baumhower returned a fumble 21 yards for his first NFL touchdown with only 1:14 left before the half to give Miami a 21-0 lead. Uwe von Schamann kicked a 37-yard field goal and Woody Bennett ran one yard for the game's final points. Miami's Mark Clayton had five receptions for 110 yards.

Miami	0	21	3	7	— 31
Pittsburgh	0	0	7	0	— 7

Mia—Hardy 3 pass from Marino (von Schamann kick)
Mia—Rose 34 pass from Marino (von Schamann kick)
Mia—Baumhower 21 fumble recovery return (von Schamann kick)
Mia—FG von Schamann 37
Pitt—Pollard 1 run (Anderson kick)
Mia—Bennett 1 run (von Schamann kick)

Tampa Bay 35, Minnesota 31—At Tampa Stadium, attendance 47,405. Steve DeBerg passed for two touchdowns and James Wilder ran for two more as the Buccaneers rallied for a 35-31 win. Tommy Kramer (27 of 47 for 386 yards) guided the Vikings to leads of 14-0 and 21-7. The Buccaneers came back to tie the score both times on Adger Armstrong's 1-yard run, DeBerg's 7-yard pass to Kevin House, and Wilder's 11-yard run. Tampa Bay grabbed its first lead 28-21 in the third quarter on Gerald Carter's six-yard touchdown catch. Wilder's 10-yard scoring run extended the Buccaneers' lead to 35-24 with 4:50 to play. Minnesota outgained Tampa Bay 543 to 314 total yards. House had seven receptions for 126 yards for Tampa Bay.

Minnesota	14	7	0	10	— 31
Tampa Bay	7	14	7	7	— 35

Minn—Brown 1 run (Stenerud kick)
Minn—Brown 13 pass from Kramer (Stenerud kick)
TB —Armstrong 1 run (Ariri kick)
TB —House 7 pass from DeBerg (Ariri kick)
Minn—Mularkey 1 pass from Kramer (Stenerud kick)
TB —Wilder 11 run (Ariri kick)
TB —Carter 6 pass from DeBerg (Ariri kick)
Minn—FG Stenerud 20
TB —Wilder 10 run (Ariri kick)
Minn—Anderson 6 run (Stenerud kick)

New England 17, Cleveland 16—At Cleveland Stadium, attendance 53,036. Tony Collins' two-yard touchdown run early in the fourth quarter secured the Patriots' comeback win. Following Tony Franklin's 45-yard field goal, the Browns scored 16 unanswered points on three Matt Bahr field goals and Paul McDonald's 16-yard scoring pass to Duriel Harris. Tony Eason rallied the Patriots with a 42-yard touchdown strike to Stephen Starring followed by a 24-yard completion to Starring to set up Collins' winning run. Ray Clayborn sealed the victory with seven seconds remaining by intercepting a pass and returning it 85 yards. It was Clayborn's first interception in 30 games. McDonald was excellent in defeat, completing 23 of 37 passes for 320 yards.

New England	3	0	7	7	— 17
Cleveland	0	9	7	0	— 16

NE —FG Franklin 45
Cle—FG Bahr 24
Cle—FG Bahr 48
Cle—FG Bahr 27
Cle—Harris 16 pass from McDonald (Bahr kick)
NE —Starring 42 pass from Eason (Franklin kick)
NE —Collins 2 run (Franklin kick)

Chicago 20, New Orleans 7—At Soldier Field, attendance 53,752. Walter Payton became the NFL's leading career rusher with 12,400 yards, breaking Jim Brown's mark of 12,312, when he rushed for 154 yards on 32 carries in the Bears' win over the Saints. Chicago trailed 7-6 before Payton scored on a one-yard run to give the Bears a 13-7 halftime edge. Jim McMahon, playing with a broken bone in his throwing hand, completed 10 of 14 passes for 128 yards and threw a 16-yard touchdown pass to Dennis McKinnon in the fourth quarter to secure the victory. Payton's record-breaking run came on the second play of the second half when he gained six yards around left end. It was his 59th 100-yard game, which also broke Brown's career mark of 58. The win snapped the Bears' two-game losing streak.

New Orleans	0	7	0	0	— 7
Chicago	6	7	0	7	— 20

Chi—FG B. Thomas 48
Chi—FG B. Thomas 46
NO—W. Wilson 15 pass from Todd (Andersen kick)
Chi—Payton 1 run (B. Thomas kick)
Chi—McKinnon 16 pass from McMahon (B. Thomas kick)

New York Jets 17, Kansas City 16—At Arrowhead Stadium, attendance 51,843. The Jets rallied from a 9-0 second-quarter deficit to defeat the Chiefs 17-16. Following three field goals by Kansas City's Nick Lowery, Pat Leahy kicked a 37-yard field goal to cut the Chiefs' lead to 9-3. Ron Faurot's fumble recovery set up Tony Paige's one-yard run 31 seconds before halftime which put New York in front for good, 10-9. The Jets extended the lead to 17-9 on their first possession of the second half as Pat Ryan capped a 76-yard drive with a 15-yard touchdown pass to Mickey Shuler. Freeman McNeil gained 107 yards on 19 carries for the Jets. Lowery's three field goals boosted his career total to 100 of 131 (.736) to become the NFL's all-time leader in field goal accuracy.

N.Y. Jets	0	10	7	0	— 17
Kansas City	6	3	0	7	— 16

KC —FG Lowery 31
KC —FG Lowery 42
KC —FG Lowery 21
NYJ—FG Leahy 37
NYJ—Paige 1 run (Leahy kick)
NYJ—Shuler 15 pass from Ryan (Leahy kick)
KC —Scott 1 pass from Blackledge (Lowery kick)

Philadelphia 27, Buffalo 17—At Rich Stadium, attendance 37,555. Ron Jaworski accounted for three touchdowns and Paul McFadden kicked two field goals from 36 and 22 yards to help the Eagles beat the Bills and snap a three-game losing streak. Jaworski completed scoring passes of 15 yards to Tony Woodruff and 4 yards to Vyto Kab. Jaworski put the game out of reach late in the fourth quarter when he scored on a one-yard run. Greg Bell gained 77 yards on 20 carries and scored both Buffalo touchdowns on runs of 12 and 3 yards.

Philadelphia	7	10	3	7	— 27
Buffalo	7	3	0	7	— 17

Buff—Bell 12 run (Danelo kick)
Phil —Woodruff 15 pass from Jaworski (McFadden kick)
Buff—FG Danelo 27
Phil —Kab 4 pass from Jaworski (McFadden kick)
Phil —FG McFadden 36
Phil —FG McFadden 22
Buff—Bell 3 run (Danelo kick)
Phil —Jaworski 1 run (McFadden kick)

St. Louis 31, Dallas 20—At Texas Stadium, attendance 61,438. Neil Lomax completed 19 of 29 passes for 354 yards and three touchdowns to lead the Cardinals to their first win in Texas Stadium in seven years. St. Louis exploded for 17 third-quarter points to put the game out of reach. Lomax opened the scoring with a 20-yard scoring pass to Doug Marsh and set up Stump Mitchell's three-yard run in the second quarter with a 44-yard pass to Roy Green. Green, who caught eight passes for 189 yards, had touchdown receptions of 70 and 45 yards. The Cardinals' offense generated 477 total yards, including 110 rushing by Ottis Anderson.

St. Louis	7	7	17	0	— 31
Dallas	7	6	0	7	— 20

StL —Marsh 20 pass from Lomax (O'Donoghue kick)
Dall —Dorsett 31 run (Septien kick)
Dall —FG Septien 35
StL —Mitchell 3 run (O'Donoghue kick)
Dall —FG Septien 36
StL —FG O'Donoghue 22
StL —Green 70 pass from Lomax (O'Donoghue kick)
StL —Green 45 pass from Lomax (O'Donoghue kick)
Dall —Cornwell 10 pass from D. White (Septien kick)

San Diego 34, Green Bay 28—At Lambeau Field, attendance 54,045. Dan Fouts completed 31 of 50 passes for 376 yards and three touchdowns to lead the Chargers past the Packers. San Diego never trailed after Fouts hit Bobby Duckworth on a 27-yard scoring pass 1:59 into the game. Fouts also threw touchdown passes to Pete Holohan (three yards) and Earnest Jackson (nine). Jackson rushed a club-record 32 times for 93 yards and scored on a one-yard run in the fourth quarter. Kellen Winslow caught a team-record 15 passes for 157 yards, while the Packers' James Lofton had 5 catches for 158 yards. Green Bay's Lynn Dickey completed 25 of 39 passes for 384 yards and three touchdowns.

San Diego	7	7	10	10	— 34
Green Bay	7	7	7	7	— 28

SD — Duckworth 27 pass from Fouts (Benirschke kick)
GB — Coffman 3 pass from Dickey (Garcia kick)
SD — Holohan 3 pass from Fouts (Benirschke kick)
GB — West 29 pass from Dickey (Garcia kick)
SD — Jackson 9 pass from Fouts (Benirschke kick)
GB — Ellis 4 run (Garcia kick)
SD — FG Benirschke 31
SD — Jackson 1 run (Benirschke kick)
GB — Lofton 25 pass from Dickey (Garcia kick)
SD — FG Benirschke 39

Los Angeles Raiders 28, Seattle 14—At Memorial Coliseum, attendance 77,904. Marc Wilson relieved injured Jim Plunkett and fired two touchdown passes to lead the Raiders to victory. Los Angeles opened a 14-0 lead as Marcus Allen's 92-yard reception set up his one-yard touchdown dive and Todd Christensen caught a 24-yard scoring pass. With the game tied 14-14, Wilson (12 of 19 for 309 yards) completed a 58-yard scoring pass to Allen. Rod Martin returned an interception 14 yards for another touchdown, just 19 seconds later, for the game's final score. Allen finished with four receptions for 173 yards as the Raiders outgained the Seahawks 375 yards to 192. Martin was named the AFC's defensive player of the week.

Seattle	0	7	0	7	— 14
L.A. Raiders	0	14	0	14	— 28

Raiders — Allen 1 run (Bahr kick)
Raiders — Christensen 24 pass from Wilson (Bahr kick)
Sea — Largent 27 pass from Kreig (Johnson kick)
Sea — Hughes 2 run (Johnson kick)
Raiders — Allen 58 pass from Wilson (Bahr kick)
Raiders — Martin 14 interception return (Bahr kick)

Washington 35, Indianapolis 7—At Hoosier Dome, attendance 60,012. Joe Theismann and Art Monk hooked up on three touchdown passes as the Redskins kept pace with the first-place Cowboys in the NFC East. Theismann completed 17 of 20 passes for 267 yards and four touchdowns. Monk caught eight passes for 141 yards and had touchdowns of 10, 48, and 16 yards. Mike McGrath's 11-yard touchdown catch in the third quarter finished the scoring. Washington dominated the game offensively, gaining 446 yards to Indianapolis' 186. Vernon Dean had two interceptions and Dave Butz nine tackles to lead the Redskins' defense. Butz's performance earned him NFC defensive player of the week honors.

Washington	7	21	7	0	— 35
Indianapolis	7	0	0	0	— 7

Wash — Monk 10 pass from Theismann (Moseley kick)
Ind — Moore 2 run (Allegre kick)
Wash — Monk 48 pass from Theismann (Moseley kick)
Wash — Riggins 1 run (Moseley kick)
Wash — Monk 16 pass from Theismann (Moseley kick)
Wash — McGrath 11 pass from Theismann (Moseley kick)

MONDAY, OCTOBER 8

San Francisco 31, New York Giants 10—At Giants Stadium, attendance 76,112. Joe Montana threw three touchdown passes and Wendell Tyler rushed for 101 yards on 14 carries as the 49ers defeated the Giants to mark their best start ever. San Francisco exploded to a 21-0 lead just 7:33 into the game as Montana (15 of 24 for 207 yards) fired touchdown passes to Renaldo Nehemiah (59 yards) and John Frank (1), and Dana McLemore scored on a 79-yard punt return. Montana's eight-yard scoring pass to Roger Craig gave the 49ers an insurmountable 28-3 halftime lead. The Giants outgained the 49ers 389 yards to 384. Butch Woolfolk's one-yard run in the fourth period was the first touchdown allowed by the San Francisco defense in 12 quarters.

San Francisco	21	7	3	0	— 31
N.Y. Giants	3	0	0	7	— 10

SF — Nehemiah 59 pass from Montana (Wersching kick)
SF — Frank 1 pass from Montana (Wersching kick)
SF — McLemore 79 punt return (Wersching kick)
NY — FG Haji-Sheikh 20
SF — Craig 8 pass from Montana (Wersching kick)
SF — FG Wersching 37
NY — Woolfolk 1 run (Haji-Sheikh kick)

SEVENTH WEEK SUMMARY

The Steelers came up with the big plays to hand the 49ers their first loss of the season 20-17. San Francisco led by a touchdown before John Stallworth's touchdown reception tied the game and Gary Anderson's 21-yard field goal with 1:42 left helped Pittsburgh over the 49ers. The Rams gained ground on San Francisco with a 28-10 triumph over the Saints. Eric Dickerson rushed for 164 yards for Los Angeles, while Earl Campbell (five carries for 19 yards) saw his first action in a New Orleans uniform. Washington dominated Dallas 34-14 to take sole possession of first place in the NFC East. Joe Theismann passed for three touchdowns for the Redskins and John Riggins bruised his way to 165 yards rushing to become the fifth NFL running back to top the 10,000-yard career mark. The Cardinals and Giants both posted victories to tie with Dallas one game back of Washington. Bill Kenney, sidelined since the last week of the preseason because of an injury, replaced Todd Blackledge midway through the third quarter and directed the Chiefs past the Chargers 31-13. Kenney had one of his first passes returned 99 yards for a touchdown by San Diego's Gill Byrd, but then he settled down to throw for 238 yards and two scores. Gary Danielson came off the bench in similar fashion and threw a 37-yard touchdown pass to Leonard Thompson to give the Lions a 13-7 overtime win over the Buccaneers. Detroit was the only NFC Central winner this week. Green Bay gave away two touchdowns on fumble recoveries in the first 37 seconds of their Monday night game in Denver played in near blizzard conditions. The Broncos tacked on the winning points on Rich Karlis' second-quarter field goal. The weather didn't stop James Lofton from catching 11 passes for 206 yards. The Raiders upended the Vikings 23-20 on a last-second field goal by Chris Bahr. The Cardinals overpowered the Bears 38-21. Tony Eason's pair of second-half touchdowns enabled New England to overcome Cincinnati 20-14. The Jets kept pace with the second-place Patriots in the AFC East by defeating the Browns 24-20, despite Ozzie Newsome's 14 receptions for 191 yards. Miami remained undefeated with a 28-10 decision over Houston.

SUNDAY, OCTOBER 14

Seattle 31, Buffalo 28—At Kingdome, attendance 59,034. Dave Krieg passed for three touchdowns, including a 51-yarder to Steve Largent with 8:07 remaining, to clinch the Seahawks' victory. Seattle jumped out to a 17-0 lead on Krieg scoring passes to Daryl Turner (4 yards) and Largent (10), and Norm Johnson's 25-yard field goal. After the Bills closed to 17-14 in the second quarter, the Seahawks extended their lead to 24-14 on Eric Lane's one-yard run. However, Buffalo took a 28-24 lead with 11:10 left on Joe Ferguson's second touchdown pass. Krieg then drove Seattle 88 yards in six plays for the winning score. Largent caught five passes for 106 yards to move into twelfth place on the all-time reception list with 496.

Buffalo	0	14	7	7	— 28
Seattle	17	0	7	7	— 31

Sea — Turner 4 pass from Krieg (Johnson kick)
Sea — Largent 10 pass from Krieg (Johnson kick)
Sea — FG Johnson 25
Buff — Sanford 46 fumble recovery return (Danelo kick)
Buff — Wilson 65 punt return (Danelo kick)
Sea — Lane 1 run (Johnson kick)
Buff — Franklin 50 pass from Ferguson (Danelo kick)
Buff — Dennard 3 pass from Ferguson (Danelo kick)
Sea — Largent 51 pass from Krieg (Johnson kick)

St. Louis 38, Chicago 21—At Busch Memorial Stadium, attendance 49,554. Neil Lomax completed 14 of 24 passes for 271 yards and Ottis Anderson scored two touchdowns as the Cardinals overpowered the Bears 38-21. Chicago led 21-17 early in the third quarter, but St. Louis rallied for three unanswered touchdowns. Lomax fired a one-yard touchdown pass to Anderson, who earlier had scored on a nine-yard run, and followed with a nine-yard scoring run himself following a blocked punt. Willard Harrell's one-yard blast closed out the scoring. Walter Payton rushed for 100 yards for the sixth straight week. The Bears' offense outgained the Cardinals 370 yards to 354. Roy Green caught six passes for 166 yards for St. Louis.

Chicago	7	7	7	0	— 21
St. Louis	10	7	7	14	— 38

StL — FG O'Donoghue 44
Chi — Gault 28 pass from McMahon (B. Thomas kick)
StL — Love 5 run (O'Donoghue kick)
Chi — Payton 1 run (B. Thomas kick)
StL — Anderson 9 run (O'Donoghue kick)
Chi — Suhey 1 run (B. Thomas kick)
StL — Anderson 1 pass from Lomax (O'Donoghue kick)
StL — Lomax 9 run (O'Donoghue kick)
StL — Harrell 1 run (O'Donoghue kick)

New England 20, Cincinnati 14—At Sullivan Stadium, attendance 48,154. Tony Eason scrambled for two touchdowns and Tony Franklin added a pair of field goals to climax the Patriots' comeback win. New England trailed Cincinnati 14-3 at halftime, before Eason scored on runs of 13 and 25 yards. Franklin kicked a 27-yard field goal with 1:50 left to finish the scoring. Eason completed 11 of 22 passes for 187 yards and ran his string of pass attempts without an interception to a club-record 141. The win marked the Patriots' first three-game win streak since 1980.

Cincinnati	7	7	0	0	— 14
New England	3	0	7	10	— 20

NE — FG Franklin 20
Cin — Harris 34 pass from Esiason (Breech kick)
Cin — Collinsworth 7 pass from Esiason (Breech kick)
NE — Eason 13 run (Franklin kick)
NE — Eason 25 run (Franklin kick)
NE — FG Franklin 27

Philadelphia 16, Indianapolis 7—At Veterans Stadium, attendance 50,277. Paul McFadden kicked three field goals to lead the Eagles to a 16-7 victory over the Colts. Ron Jaworski, who completed 21 of 29 passes for 194 yards, played only the first half but directed three scoring drives which put Philadelphia on top 13-3 by halftime. Jaworski completed a six-yard touchdown pass to Mike Quick and set up McFadden field goals of 34 and 32 yards. McFadden's 33-yarder late in the fourth quarter completed the Eagles scoring. Ken Clarke registered seven tackles and two sacks to earn NFC defensive player of the week honors.

Indianapolis	0	0	0	7	— 7
Philadelphia	7	6	0	3	— 16

Phil — Quick 6 pass from Jaworski (McFadden kick)
Phil — FG McFadden 34
Phil — FG McFadden 32
Ind — McMillan 1 run (Allegre kick)
Phil — FG McFadden 33

Washington 34, Dallas 14—At Robert F. Kennedy Stadium, attendance 55,431. John Riggins became the fifth NFL player to gain 10,000 yards in a career (10,141) when he rushed for 165 yards as the Redskins won their fifth straight. Dallas led 7-0 on Tony Dorsett's 29-yard scoring run, but Washington countered with 34 unanswered points. After linebacker Monte Coleman returned an interception 49 yards for a touchdown, Joe Theismann completed two scoring passes to Clint Didier (eight and three yards) and an 80-yarder to Calvin Muhammad. Mark Moseley kicked field goals of 20 and 22 yards to complete the onslaught. Riggins, the NFC's offensive player of the week, carried the ball on 32 of Washington's 62 plays but failed to score a rushing touchdown for the first time in eight games.

Dallas	7	0	0	7	— 14
Washington	7	10	10	7	— 34

Dall — Dorsett 29 run (Septien kick)
Wash — Coleman 49 interception return (Moseley kick)
Wash — Didier 8 pass from Theismann (Moseley kick)
Wash — FG Moseley 20
Wash — Muhammad 80 pass from Theismann (Moseley kick)
Wash — FG Moseley 22
Wash — Didier 3 pass from Theismann (Moseley kick)
Dall — Dorsett 6 run (Septein kick)

Miami 28, Houston 10—At Orange Bowl, attendance 52,435. Dan Marino completed 25 of 32 pases for 321 yards and three touchdowns as the Dolphins won easily over the Oilers 28-10. Marino connected on 18 of 20 passes for 218 yards in the first half, including a 27-yard touchdown to Mark Clayton. Mark Duper (17 yards) and Nat Moore (32) caught second-half scoring passes, and rookie Joe Carter ran 25 yards for the Dolphins' final score. Carter gained 105 yards on 13 carries to become the first Miami player to rush for over 100 yards since Andra Franklin gained 107 against New England on December 12, 1982. The Dolphins amassed 515 total yards and yielded 239.

Houston	0	0	3	7	— 10
Miami	0	7	7	14	— 28

Mia — Clayton 27 pass from Marino (von Schamann kick)
Mia — Duper 17 pass from Marino (von Schamann kick)
Hou — FG Kempf 49
Mia — Moore 32 pass from Marino (von Schamann kick)
Mia — Carter 25 run (von Schamann kick)
Hou — Dressel 9 pass from Moon (Kempf kick)

Los Angeles Rams 28, New Orleans 10—At Louisiana Superdome, attendance 63,161. Eric Dickerson exploded for 164 yards on 21 carries and Jeff Kemp fired three touchdown passes to highlight the Rams' win. Los Angeles broke the game open with three second-quarter touchdowns. Kemp completed touchdown passes of 25 yards to Drew Hill and 13 yards to Henry Ellard. Nolan Cromwell returned an interception 33 yards for a score which gave the Rams a 21-3 advantage at halftime. Ron Brown's 21-yard scoring reception in the third quarter finished the scoring for Los Angeles.

L.A. Rams	0	21	7	0	— 28
New Orleans	3	0	0	7	— 10

NO — FG Andersen 47
Rams — Drew Hill 25 pass from Kemp (Lansford kick)
Rams — Ellard 13 pass from Kemp (Lansford kick)
Rams — Cromwell 33 interception return (Lansford kick)
Rams — Brown 21 pass from Kemp (Lansford kick)
NO — Gajan 1 run (Andersen kick)

Los Angeles Raiders 23, Minnesota 20—At Memorial Coliseum, attendance 49,276. Chris Bahr's third field goal of the day, a 20-yarder on the game's final play, lifted the Raiders to a 23-20 comeback win. Los Angeles trailed Minnesota 20-13 after three quarters, but Jack Squirek's fumble recovery set up Marcus Allen's one-yard run with 12:52 remaining to give the Raiders a 20-20 tie. Frank Hawkins rushed five times for 29 yards on the drive that set up the winning kick. Los Angeles gained 393 yards and yielded 226.

Minnesota	13	0	7	0	— 20
L.A. Raiders	7	3	3	10	— 23

Raiders — Christensen 34 pass from Wilson (Bahr kick)
Minn — Jones 70 pass from Kramer (Stenerud kick)
Minn — Rice 3 run (kick blocked)
Raiders — FG Bahr 22
Raiders — FG Bahr 24
Minn — Mularkey 2 pass from Kramer (Stenerud kick)
Raiders — Allen 1 run (Bahr kick)
Raiders — FG Bahr 20

New York Giants 19, Atlanta 7—At Atlanta-Fulton County Stadium, attendance 50,268. Rob Carpenter scored two touchdowns and Ali Haji-Sheikh kicked a pair of field goals to help the Giants snap a two-game losing streak. Carpenter scored on a one-yard run and a nine-yard reception. Haji-Sheikh was successful on field goals from 41 and 34 yards. Phil Simms completed 16 of 25 passes for 247 yards, including four to Lionel Manuel for 120 yards. The New York defense had three interceptions, one fumble recovery, and four sacks, and held Atlanta scoreless on four downs from the Giants' 1-yard line in the first quarter.

N.Y. Giants	6	10	0	3	— 19
Atlanta	0	0	7	0	— 7

NYG—Carpenter 1 run (kick failed)
NYG—Carpenter 9 pass from Simms (Haji-Sheikh kick)
NYG—FG Haji-Sheikh 41
Atl —Riggs 1 run (Luckhurst kick)
NYG—FG Haji-Sheikh 34

New York Jets 24, Cleveland 20—At Cleveland Stadium, attendance 55,673. Tony Paige's one-yard touchdown run with 5:39 remaining lifted the Jets over the Browns. Johnny Hector's 64-yard run set up the Jets' first touchdown—Freeman McNeil's three-yard touchdown plunge 2:04 into the game. McNeil converted Barry Bennett's fumble recovery into an eight-yard scoring run in the second quarter to give the Jets a 17-14 halftime edge. Cleveland took the lead on a pair of Matt Bahr field goals before Pat Ryan mounted New York's winning 80-yard drive. Ozzie Newsome gained 191 yards on a Browns-record 14 receptions.

N.Y. Jets	7	10	0	7	— 24
Cleveland	7	7	3	3	— 20

NYJ—McNeil 3 run (Leahy kick)
Cle —Pruitt 1 run (Bahr kick)
NYJ—FG Leahy 30
NYJ—McNeil 8 run (Leahy kick)
Cle —Pruitt 1 run (Bahr kick)
Cle —FG Bahr 49
Cle —FG Bahr 18
NYJ—Paige 1 run (Leahy kick)

Pittsburgh 20, San Francisco 17—At Candlestick Park, attendance 59,110. Bryan Hinkle's 43-yard interception return set up Gary Anderson's 21-yard field goal with 1:42 to play as the Steelers knocked the 49ers from the ranks of the unbeaten. Pittsburgh held a 10-7 halftime lead, but San Francisco went ahead 17-10 early in the fourth quarter on Ray Wersching's 30-yard field goal and Wendell Tyler's seven-yard run. Mark Malone, starting in place of the injured David Woodley, threw a six-yard touchdown pass to John Stallworth with 3:21 left to tie the score. San Francisco had a chance to tie the game with seven seconds remaining but Wersching's 37-yard field goal attempt was wide. Pittsburgh's Frank Pollard gained over 100 yards rushing for the first time in his career (24 carries for 105 yards).

Pittsburgh	7	3	0	10	— 20
San Francisco	0	7	0	10	— 17

Pitt—Erenberg 2 run (Anderson kick)
Pitt—FG Anderson 48
SF —Montana 7 run (Wersching kick)
SF —FG Wersching 30
SF —Tyler 7 run (Wersching kick)
Pitt—Stallworth 6 pass from Malone (Anderson kick)
Pitt—FG Anderson 21

Kansas City 31, San Diego 13—At Arrowhead Stadium, attendance 62,233. Bill Kenney replaced starter Todd Blackledge early in the second half and completed two touchdown passes to spark the Chiefs' win. Kenney, playing for the first time this season because of a broken thumb, threw scoring passes to Stephone Paige (18 yards) and Ed Beckman (5) to give Kansas City a commanding 24-13 fourth-quarter edge. Herman Heard's 69-yard scoring run with 4:37 to play put the game out of reach. Kenney, who completed 13 of 22 passes, contributed 238 yards to the Chiefs' 506-yard offensive assault. Gill Byrd had a 99-yard interception return for the Chargers.

San Diego	3	3	7	0	— 13
Kansas City	10	0	7	14	— 31

KC—Lacy 24 run (Lowery kick)
SD—FG Ricardo 38
KC—FG Lowery 22
SD—FG Ricardo 42
SD—Byrd 99 interception return (Ricardo kick)
KC—Paige 18 pass from Kenney (Lowery kick)
KC—Beckman 5 pass from Kenney (Lowery kick)
KC—Heard 69 run (Lowery kick)

Detroit 13, Tampa Bay 7—At Pontiac Silverdome, attendance 44,308. Gary Danielson completed a 37-yard touchdown pass to Leonard Thompson 4:34 into overtime to give the Lions their second overtime win this season. William Gay's fumble recovery on Detroit's 41-yard line set up the decisive four-play, 59-yard drive. Tampa Bay's Steve DeBerg completed a team-record 86.2 percent (25 completions in 29 attempts) of his passes for 272 yards. DeBerg drove the Buccaneers into scoring position on the final play in regulation, but Obed Ariri's 42-yard field goal attempt sailed wide left.

Tampa Bay	7	0	0	0	0	— 7
Detroit	0	7	0	0	6	— 13

TB —House 25 pass from DeBerg (Ariri kick)
Det—Danielson 18 run (Murray kick)
Det—Thompson 37 pass from Danielson

MONDAY, OCTOBER 15

Denver 17, Green Bay 14—At Mile High Stadium, attendance 62,546. The Broncos scored on two fumble recoveries in the first 37 seconds of the game and held on to defeat the Packers in a heavy snowstorm. Steve Foley returned the first fumble 22 yards for a score on Green Bay's first play from scrimmage. Louis Wright scored on the second fumble recovery from 27 yards on the Packers' first play following the Broncos' second kickoff. Rich Karlis' 30-yard field goal in the first minute of the second quarter provided Denver's margin of victory. Green Bay rallied in the second half behind the passing of Lynn Dickey, who completed 27 of 37 passes for 371 yards. James Lofton, who brought the Packers back to within three points in the fourth quarter (17-14) with a 54-yard scoring catch, had career bests for receptions (11) and yards (206). Karl Mecklenburg's fumble recovery with 3:08 left sealed the win. The Packers outgained the Broncos in total yardage (423 to 193).

Green Bay	0	0	7	7	— 14
Denver	14	3	0	0	— 17

Den—Foley 22 fumble recovery return (Karlis kick)
Den—L. Wright 27 fumble recovery return (Karlis kick)
Den—FG Karlis 30
GB —Ellis 5 run (Garcia kick)
GB —Lofton 54 pass from Dickey (Garcia kick)

EIGHTH WEEK SUMMARY

At the season's midpoint, the AFC Western Division and NFC Eastern Division boasted all 10 teams with records of .500 or better. In the NFC East, the Cowboys looked like sure losers, but came away with a 30-27 overtime victory against the Saints. New Orleans held a 27-6 fourth-quarter lead before Dallas scored three touchdowns in a ten-and-a-half minute span to tie the score 27-27. Rafael Septien's 41-yard field goal completed the greatest comeback in Cowboys history. Neil O'Donoghue's 21-yard field goal with three seconds remaining helped the Cardinals over the Redskins 26-24 to deadlock the two teams, along with the Cowboys, in a three-way tie for first place in the division. The Eagles' third straight victory, 24-10 over the Giants, evened both teams' records at 4-4. In the AFC West, the Chargers and the Raiders tangled in the game of the week. Los Angeles opened a 34-20 lead but needed Marc Wilson's fifth touchdown pass of the game, a 51-yarder to Malcolm Barnwell, to beat San Diego 44-37. Dan Fouts passed for 410 yards, including 107 to Kellen Winslow before the latter was lost for the season with torn knee ligaments. The Broncos joined the Raiders atop the AFC West with a 37-7 defeat of the Bills. Seattle stayed one game off the pace as Terry Jackson's interception with 24 seconds left secured the Seahawks' 30-24 triumph over the Packers. Pat Ryan of the Jets fired three touchdown passes to lead New York to a 28-7 win over Kansas City. The loss evened the Chiefs record at 4-4, while the Jets stayed two games behind the undefeated Dolphins, who cruised past the Patriots 44-24. Indianapolis scored the most improbable victory of the weekend, 17-16 over Pittsburgh, as Ray Butler raced 20 yards with a deflected pass to complete a 54-yard touchdown play with 34 seconds left. Cleveland's Steve Cox kicked a 60-yard field goal, second longest in NFL history, but four field goals by Cincinnati's Jim Breech brought the Bengals a 12-9 win. Warren Moon (356 yards passing and two touchdowns) and Joe Montana (353 yards passing and three scores) hooked up in a passing duel as the 49ers won over the Oilers 34-21. Billy Sims became the Lions' all-time leading ground gainer in Detroit's 16-14 defeat of Minnesota. Jim McMahon's three touchdown passes powered the Bears over the Buccaneers 44-9.

SUNDAY, OCTOBER 21

Chicago 44, Tampa Bay 9—At Tampa Stadium, attendance 60,003. Jim McMahon passed for 219 yards and three touchdowns and Walter Payton ran for two more scores as the Bears handed the Buccaneers their first home defeat. Payton, who was held to less than 100 yards rushing for the second time this season (20 carries for 72 yards), scored on first-quarter runs of eight and three yards. Dennis McKinnon caught a 32-yard touchdown pass to give Chicago a 20-3 lead at the half. McMahon continued his hot passing in the second half, throwing scoring passes of 10 yards to Willie Gault and 49 yards to Brad Anderson. Dennis Gentry's five-yard run completed the Bears' scoring. Richard Dent had three of the Bears' six sacks.

Chicago	14	6	7	17	— 44
Tampa Bay	0	3	0	6	— 9

Chi—Payton 8 run (B. Thomas kick)
Chi—Payton 3 run (B. Thomas kick)
TB —FG Ariri 46
Chi—McKinnon 32 pass from McMahon (kick failed)
Chi—Gault 10 pass from McMahon (B. Thomas kick)
Chi—FG B. Thomas 49
TB —Carter 4 pass from DeBerg (kick failed)
Chi—Anderson 49 pass from McMahon (B. Thomas kick)
Chi—Gentry 5 run (B. Thomas kick)

Cincinnati 12, Cleveland 9—At Riverfront Stadium, attendance 50,667. Jim Breech kicked his fourth field goal of the game, a 33-yarder as time expired, to help the Bengals defeat the Browns. Breech earlier connected on field goals from 24, 23, and 25 yards out. Cleveland also scored all its points via field goals. Matt Bahr was good from 50 and 47 yards, while Steve Cox kicked a 60-yarder, the second longest in NFL history.

Cleveland	3	3	0	3	— 9
Cincinnati	3	3	0	6	— 12

Cin—FG Breech 24
Cle—FG Bahr 50
Cin—FG Breech 23
Cle—FG Cox 60
Cin—FG Breech 25
Cle—FG Bahr 47
Cin—FG Breech 33

Denver 37, Buffalo 7—At Rich Stadium, attendance 31,204. Denver quarterbacks John Elway and Gary Kubiak combined for three touchdown passes and Rich Karlis kicked three field goals (45, 45, and 40 yards) to lead the Broncos over the Bills. Elway completed touchdown passes to Clarence Kay (3 yards) and Steve Watson (52) before leaving in the second quarter with a bruised shoulder. Kubiak came on and scrambled three yards for a score and threw a 14-yard scoring pass to Sammy Winder for Denver's final points. The Broncos' defense forced five turnovers (four interceptions and one fumble recovery) and had six sacks.

Denver	3	20	7	7	— 37
Buffalo	0	0	0	7	— 7

Den—FG Karlis 45
Den—Kay 3 pass from Elway (Karlis kick)
Den—Watson 52 pass from Elway (Karlis kick)
Den—FG Karlis 45
Den—FG Karlis 40
Den—Kubiak 3 run (Karlis kick)
Den—Winder 14 pass from Kubiak (Karlis kick)
Buff—Brookins 70 pass from Kofler (Danelo kick)

Detroit 16, Minnesota 14—At Metrodome, attendance 59,953. Ed Murray kicked a 41-yard field goal with 49 seconds left to lead the Lions over the Vikings. Detroit trailed Minnesota 14-0 at halftime before Billy Sims scored on a one-yard run early in the third quarter to get the Lions back into the game. Murray followed with field goals of 44 and 41 yards to bring Detroit within 14-13. Sims carried 22 times for 103 yards to become the Lions' all-time leading rusher with 5,106 yards. Alvin Hall's last-minute interception secured the victory.

Detroit	0	0	10	6	— 16
Minnesota	7	7	0	0	— 14

Minn—Nelson 7 pass from Kramer (Stenerud kick)
Minn—Brown 2 run (Stenerud kick)
Det —Sims 1 run (Murray kick)
Det —FG Murray 44
Det —FG Murray 41
Det —FG Murray 41

New York Jets 28, Kansas City 7—At Giants Stadium, attendance 66,782. Pat Ryan threw three touchdown passes and the defense limited the Chiefs to 205 total yards to help the Jets over the Chiefs 28-7. Ryan completed 21 of 31 for 260 yards and had first-half scoring passes of 44 yards to Bobby Humphery and 16 yards to Mickey Shuler. Mark Gastineau's fumble recovery in the end zone extended New York's lead to 21-0. Cedric Minter's 39-yard scoring catch in the final period finished the scoring. The Jets recorded four sacks and allowed just 84 yards passing.

Kansas City	0	0	0	7	— 7
N.Y. Jets	7	7	7	7	— 28

NYJ—Humphery 44 pass from Ryan (Leahy kick)
NYJ—Shuler 16 pass from Ryan (Leahy kick)
NYJ—Gastineau fumble recovery in end zone (Ryan run)
KC —Lacy 7 pass from Kenney (Lowery kick)
NYJ—Minter 39 pass from Ryan (Leahy kick)

Los Angeles Raiders 44, San Diego 37—At San Diego Jack Murphy Stadium, attendance 57,442. Marc Wilson completed 24 of 37 passes for 332 yards and five touchdowns to lead the Raiders' victory. Los Angeles opened a 34-20 lead by scoring 20 points in a seven-minute span of the third quarter. Wilson threw scoring passes of one yard to Derrick Jensen and 20 yards to Dokie Williams, and Chris Bahr kicked field goals of 42 and 33 yards to account for the 20 points. Wilson also completed touchdown passes of 10 yards to Marcus Allen and 45 and 51 yards to Malcolm Barnwell. The Chargers scored 17 points in the final quarter to make the game close, but Ted Watts' interception in the end zone helped the Raiders hold on. Dan Fouts hit on 24 of 45 passes for 410 yards and three touchdowns as the teams combined for 962 total yards (Raiders 498; Chargers 464).

L.A. Raiders	7	7	20	10	— 44
San Diego	7	13	0	17	— 37

SD —Jackson 5 run (Ricardo kick)
Raiders—Allen 10 pass from Wilson (Bahr kick)
SD —Chandler 22 pass from Fouts (kick failed)
SD —Jackson 32 run (Ricardo kick)
Raiders—Barnwell 45 pass from Wilson (Bahr kick)
Raiders—FG Bahr 42
Raiders—Jensen 1 pass from Wilson (Bahr kick)
Raiders—FG Bahr 33
Raiders—Williams 20 pass from Wilson (Bahr kick)
SD —FG Ricardo 29
Raiders—Barnwell 51 pass from Wilson (Bahr kick)
SD —Winslow 5 pass from Fouts (Ricardo kick)

Raiders—FG Bahr 32
SD —Duckworth 50 pass from Fouts (Ricardo kick)

Miami 44, New England 24—At Sullivan Stadium, attendance 60,711. Dan Marino threw for four touchdowns and led Miami's 552-yard offensive assault as the Dolphins snapped the Patriots' three-game win streak. Miami scored on seven of nine possessions, including their last five. Marino (24 of 39 for 316 yards) completed scoring passes to Nat Moore (19 and 15 yards), Dan Johnson (5), and Mark Clayton (15) to increase his season total to 24, breaking Bob Griese's club-record of 22 set in 1977. Pete Johnson scored on runs of one and three yards and Uwe von Schamann kicked a 28-yard field goal to finish the Dolphins' scoring. Miami's season-high 236 yards rushing included 92 yards on 14 carries by rookie Joe Carter. The Patriots accumulated 408 yards total offense, including 313 yards passing by Tony Eason. New England also became the first team to score on the Dolphins in the first quarter this season.

Miami	3	13	14	14	— 44
New England	3	7	7	7	— 24

Mia—FG von Schamann 28
NE —FG Franklin 48
Mia—P. Johnson 1 run (von Schamann kick)
NE —Weathers 14 pass from Eason (Franklin kick)
Mia—Moore 19 pass from Marino (kick failed)
Mia—D. Johnson 5 pass from Marino (von Schamann kick)
NE —Morgan 76 pass from Eason (Franklin kick)
Mia—Clayton 15 pass from Marino (von Schamann kick)
NE —Ramsey 5 pass from Eason (Franklin kick)
Mia—Moore 15 pass from Marino (von Schamann kick)
Mia—P. Johnson 3 run (von Schamann kick)

Dallas 30, New Orleans 27—At Texas Stadium, attendance 50,966. Rafael Septien's 41-yard field goal 3:42 into overtime concluded the biggest comeback in Cowboys history. Dallas trailed New Orleans 27-6 entering the fourth quarter before Tony Dorsett's three-yard touchdown run put the Cowboys back on track. Danny White, in relief of starting quarterback Gary Hogeboom, threw a 12-yard scoring pass to Mike Renfro with 3:59 left. Jim Jeffcoat's fumble recovery in the end zone for a touchdown with 2:53 remaining tied the game and forced the overtime.

New Orleans	0	17	10	0	0	— 27
Dallas	3	3	0	21	3	— 30

Dall—FG Septien 37
NO —Young 36 pass from Todd (Andersen kick)
Dall—FG Septien 27
NO —Gajan 62 run (Andersen kick)
NO —FG Andersen 49
NO —FG Andersen 50
NO —Winston 43 interception return (Andersen kick)
Dall—Dorsett 3 run (Septien kick)
Dall—Renfro 12 pass from D. White (Septien kick)
Dall—Jeffcoat fumble recovery in end zone (Septien kick)
Dall—FG Septien 41

Philadelphia 24, New York Giants 10—At Veterans Stadium, attendance 64,677. Ron Jaworski threw for 287 yards and three touchdowns to help the Eagles down the Giants and even their record at 4-4. The teams were deadlocked 10-10 at the end of the third quarter, when Philadelphia capitalized on Jerry Robinson's fumble recovery and Ray Ellis' interception. Jaworski turned both turnovers into touchdown passes of 11 yards to Mel Hoover and 37 yards to Tony Woodruff. The latter gave Philadelphia a 24-10 lead with 1:04 to play and helped the Eagles to their third straight win for the first time since 1981. Jaworski also had an 83-yard touchdown to rookie Kenny Jackson to open the scoring. The Giants fell to 4-4.

N.Y. Giants	0	7	3	0	— 10
Philadelphia	7	3	0	14	— 24

Phil —Jackson 83 pass from Jaworski (McFadden kick)
NYG—Carpenter 1 run (Haji-Sheikh kick)
Phil —FG McFadden 45
NYG—FG Haji-Sheikh 31
Phil —Hoover 11 pass from Jaworski (McFadden kick)
Phil —Woodruff 37 pass from Jaworski (McFadden kick)

Indianapolis 17, Pittsburgh 16—At Hoosier Dome, attendance 60,026. Wide receiver Ray Butler grabbed a deflected pass on the dead run to complete a 54-yard touchdown with 34 seconds left and lift the Colts over the Steelers. The play started when Mike Pagel's pass was almost intercepted by Sam Washington, who bobbled the ball into Butler's hands at the Pittsburgh 40-yard line. The Steelers had taken a 16-10 lead on Louis Lipps' 62-yard touchdown reception and three field goals by Gary Anderson, including a 53-yarder that broke Lou Michaels previous club record (50 yards) set in 1963. Pittsburgh generated 405 yards total offense while the defense had six sacks, including three by linebacker Mike Merriweather.

Pittsburgh	3	10	0	3	— 16
Indianapolis	0	0	0	17	— 17

Pitt—FG Anderson 53
Pitt—Lipps 62 pass from Woodley (Anderson kick)
Pitt—FG Anderson 25
Ind—FG Allegre 41
Ind—Moore 8 run (Allegre kick)
Pitt—FG Anderson 43
Ind—Butler 54 pass from Pagel (Allegre kick)

San Francisco 34, Houston 21—At Astrodome, attendance 39,900. Joe Montana completed touchdown passes of 11 yards to Russ Francis, 26 yards to Wendell Tyler, and 80 yards to Dwight Clark to lead the 49ers over the Oilers. San Francisco opened a 20-7 lead early in the third quarter on two Montana scoring passes and Ray Wersching field goals of 26 and 22 yards. Houston narrowed the margin to 20-14, but Roger Craig scored on a five-yard run with 7:50 remaining to put the game out of reach 27-14. Montana finished with 25 completions in 35 attempts for 353 yards, including five to Clark for 127. Tyler contributed 108 yards rushing (on 23 carries) of 49ers' 517 total yards.

San Francisco	10	7	3	14	— 34
Houston	0	7	7	7	— 21

SF —Francis 11 pass from Montana (Wersching kick)
SF —FG Wersching 26
Hou—Moriarty 1 run (Kempf kick)
SF —Tyler 26 pass from Montana (Wersching kick)
SF —FG Wersching 22
Hou—Smith 45 pass from Moon (Kempf kick)
SF —Craig 5 run (Wersching kick)
Hou—Williams 29 pass from Moon (Kempf kick)
SF —D. Clark 80 pass from Montana (Wersching kick)

Seattle 30, Green Bay 24—At Milwaukee County Stadium, attendance 52,286. Dave Krieg passed for two touchdowns and Norm Johnson kicked field goals from 29, 39, and 45 yards, as the Seahawks held on to defeat the Packers. Krieg (22 of 35 for 310 yards) found Steve Largent with a 31-yard first-quarter scoring pass to tie the score at 7-7. After a pair of Johnson field goals, Terry Taylor's interception set up Eric Lane's one-yard run to give Seattle a 20-17 halftime edge. Krieg hit Daryl Turner with a 25-yard scoring pass to extend the lead to 27-17. Terry Jackson's interception in the end zone with 24 seconds left, preserved the win. Largent caught seven passes for 129 yards to go over the 500 mark in career receptions (503). The Packers compiled over 400 yards total offense (404) for the third straight week, but suffered their seventh straight defeat.

Seattle	7	13	7	3	— 30
Green Bay	17	0	7	0	— 24

GB —Lofton 79 pass from Dickey (Del Greco kick)
Sea—Largent 31 pass from Krieg (Johnson kick)
GB —Lofton 20 pass from Dickey (Del Greco kick)
GB —FG Del Greco 42
Sea—FG Johnson 29
Sea—FG Johnson 39
Sea—Lane 1 run (Johnson kick)
Sea—Turner 25 pass from Krieg (Johnson kick)
GB —Ellis 8 pass from Dickey (Del Greco kick)
Sea—FG Johnson 45

St. Louis 26, Washington 24—At Busch Memorial Stadium, attendance 50,262. Neil O'Donoghue's 21-yard field goal with three seconds remaining climaxed the Cardinals' comeback win. Trailing 21-10, St. Louis rallied behind Neil Lomax touchdown passes to Doug Marsh (19 yards) and Roy Green (83), but a missed extra point by O'Donoghue kept Washington in front, 24-23. O'Donoghue's 40-yard field goal attempt with 2:53 left sailed wide, but Lomax's 21-yard completion to Pat Tilley put the Cardinals in range for O'Donoghue's winning kick. Lomax completed 20 of 38 passes for 361 yards, including a 38-yard touchdown completion to Green (six receptions for 163 yards) to open the scoring. St. Louis gained 456 total yards and yielded 296.

Washington	7	0	14	3	— 24
St. Louis	7	3	7	9	— 26

StL —Green 38 pass from Lomax (O'Donoghue kick)
Wash—Didier 3 pass from Theismann (Moseley kick)
StL —FG O'Donoghue 29
Wash—Riggins 2 run (Moseley kick)
Wash—Walker 7 pass from Theismann (Moseley kick)
StL —Marsh 19 pass from Lomax (O'Donoghue kick)
Wash—FG Moseley 39
StL —Green 83 pass from Lomax (kick failed)
StL —FG O'Donoghue 21

MONDAY, OCTOBER 22

Los Angeles Rams 24, Atlanta 10—At Atlanta-Fulton County Stadium, attendance 52,681. Henry Ellard scored two touchdowns and set up another, and Eric Dickerson ran for 145 yards on 24 carries to lead the Rams' win. Los Angeles exploded for 21 second-quarter points to take control. Ellard, the NFL's leading punt returner, scored on a 69-yard return, a nine-yard pass from Jeff Kemp, and set up Dickerson's 10-yard touchdown run with a 29-yard punt return. Ellard totalled 104 yards on three returns, while Kemp completed 14 of 19 passes for 129 yards.

L.A. Rams	0	21	0	3	— 24
Atlanta	0	3	0	7	— 10

Rams—Dickerson 10 run (Lansford kick)
Rams—Ellard 9 pass from Kemp (Lansford kick)
Atl —FG Luckhurst 39
Rams—Ellard 69 punt return (Lansford kick)
Rams—FG Lansford 18
Atl —Bailey 18 pass from Bartkowski (Luckhurst kick)

NINTH WEEK SUMMARY

The Broncos won a 22-19 shootout over the Raiders to claim sole possession of first place in the AFC West. Los Angeles led 19-6 before Broncos backup quarterback Gary Kubiak's second touchdown pass, in the game's final minute, tied the score. Rich Karlis' 35-yard field goal on the final play of overtime lifted Denver to the victory. Seattle used three touchdown passes from Dave Krieg to Steve Largent to hand San Diego their first shutout in five years 24-0. Largent marked his 100th consecutive game with at least one reception, while Kenny Easley set a club record with three interceptions. In San Francisco, the 49ers' 33-0 mauling of the Rams marked Los Angeles' worst defeat since 1963. Danny White threw two scoring passes in his first start of the year to guide Dallas to a 22-3 win over Indianapolis. The Cardinals stayed in step with the Cowboys atop the NFC East by upending the Eagles 34-14. The Giants' 37-13 defeat of the Redskins tightened the NFC East race. Joe Morris scored three touchdowns for New York and the defense confined Washington to 79 yards rushing. The Giants' victory snapped a six-game losing streak to the Redskins. The running of Frank Pollard (111 yards on 14 carries) and the passing of Mark Malone (three touchdowns) propelled the Steelers past the Falcons 35-10. Larry Kinnebrew's four touchdown runs produced a victory for the Bengals over the Oilers 31-13. Chicago dominated Minnesota on both offense and defense, but had to struggle to win 16-7. The Bears set a team record with 11 sacks and Walter Payton crossed the 1,000-yard barrier for the NFL record-tying eighth season. The Packers won their second game in convincing fashion, 41-9 over the Lions, who were playing without running back Billy Sims. Lynn Dickey threw four scoring passes and Eddie Lee Ivery totalled 116 yards rushing on only nine carries for Green Bay. Two new head coaches experienced contrasting debuts. Morten Andersen's career-long 53-yard field goal on the last play of the game gave New Orleans a 16-14 win and Cleveland's Marty Schottenheimer his first loss as the Browns' head coach. The Patriots rallied from a 20-3 deficit to upend the Jets 30-20 for Raymond Berry's first head coaching win. Kansas City and Tampa Bay combined for an NFL-record 100 pass attempts in the Chiefs' 24-20 win. Dan Marino eclipsed Bob Griese's 16-year old team record for passing yards in a season in the Dolphins' 38-7 victory over the Bills.

SUNDAY, OCTOBER 28

Pittsburgh 35, Atlanta 10—At Three Rivers Stadium, attendance 55,971. Dwayne Woodruff returned a fumble 65 yards for a score just 33 seconds into the game as the Steelers downed the Falcons. Mark Malone combined with John Stallworth on scoring passes of 20 and 31 yards. Rich Erenberg caught a seven-yarder from Malone in the fourth quarter. Frank Pollard gained 111 yards on 14 carries and scored on a five-yard run following an interception by Woodruff.

Atlanta	0	3	0	7	— 10
Pittsburgh	7	7	14	7	— 35

Pitt—Woodruff 65 fumble recovery return (Anderson kick)
Pitt—Stallworth 20 pass from Malone (Anderson kick)
Atl —FG Luckhurst 40
Pitt—Pollard 5 run (Anderson kick)
Pitt—Stallworth 31 pass from Malone (Anderson kick)
Pitt—Erenberg 7 pass from Malone (Anderson kick)
Atl —Bailey 9 pass from Moroski (Luckhurst kick)

Miami 38, Buffalo 7—At Orange Bowl, attendance 58,824. Dan Marino completed three touchdown passes for the third straight week to lead the Dolphins over the Bills. Miami built a 24-0 first-half lead on Marino scoring passes of 7 and 65 yards to Mark Clayton (three catches for 106 yards) and 10 yards to Dan Johnson, and Uwe von Schamann's 22-yard field goal. Marino connected on 19 of 28 passes for 282 yards, which raised his season total to 2,672 yards, breaking Bob Griese's 1968 club record of 2,473. Woody Bennett and Pete Johnson added one-yard touchdown runs in the second half to complete the scoring. The Dolphins outgained the Bills 493 to 273. Miami's defense had one interception, three fumble recoveries, and five sacks.

Buffalo	0	0	0	7	— 7
Miami	7	17	0	14	— 38

Mia —Clayton 7 pass from Marino (von Schamann kick)
Mia —D. Johnson 10 pass from Marino (von Schamann kick)
Mia —FG von Schamann 22
Mia —Clayton 65 pass from Marino (von Schamann kick)
Mia —Bennett 1 run (von Schamann kick)
Mia —P. Johnson 1 run (von Schamann kick)
Buff—Dennard 5 pass from Kofler (Danelo kick)

Cincinnati 31, Houston 13—At Astrodome, attendance 34,010. Ken Anderson, starting for the first time since Week Five, completed 18 of 24 passes for 154 yards, including 13 straight at one point, to propel the Bengals over the Oilers. Running back Larry Kinnebrew also scored four touchdowns to lead Cincinnati. Houston led 7-0, but Cincinnati countered with 31 unanswered points. Kinnebrew scored on runs of one and three yards in the first half to give the Bengals a 17-7 halftime lead. He then added a one-yard scoring run and 11-yard touchdown reception in the second half. Cincinnati rushed for a season-high 219 yards.

Cincinnati	0	17	7	7	— 31
Houston	7	0	0	6	— 13

Hou—Moriarty 1 run (Kempf kick)
Cin —Kinnebrew 1 run (Breech kick)

Cin —Kinnebrew 3 run (Breech kick)
Cin —FG Breech 34
Cin —Kinnebrew 11 pass from Anderson (Breech kick)
Cin —Kinnebrew 1 run (Breech kick)
Hou—Luck 4 run (pass failed)

Dallas 22, Indianapolis 3—At Texas Stadium, attendance 58,724. Danny White made his first start of the season a successful one, passing for 262 yards and two touchdowns to highlight the Cowboys' win. White, who completed 21 of 32 passes, threw a pair of second-quarter scoring passes to Tony Hill (38 yards) and Doug Cosbie (5) for a 13-0 lead. Rafael Septien added three field goals in the second half to complete the Dallas assault. Hill caught eight passes for 125 yards and Tony Dorsett topped the 100-yard rushing mark (104) for the first time in 12 games. The Cowboys' defense held the Colts to 73 yards rushing, 82 passing, and had four turnovers (two interceptions and two fumble recoveries).

Indianapolis	0	0	0	3	— 3
Dallas	0	13	3	6	— 22

Dall—Hill 38 pass from D. White (Septien kick)
Dall—Cosbie 5 pass from D. White (kick failed)
Dall—FG Septien 19
Dall—FG Septien 19
Dall—FG Septien 24
Ind —FG Allegre 52

Denver 22, Los Angeles Raiders 19—At Memorial Coliseum, attendance 91,020. Rich Karlis' 35-yard field goal as time expired in overtime lifted the Broncos past the Raiders into sole possession of first place in the AFC West. Denver capitalized on seven Los Angeles turnovers (three interceptions and four fumble recoveries), including Roger Jackson's 23-yard interception return to the Raiders' 22-yard line to set up Karlis' winning kick. Gary Kubiak started in place of injured John Elway and forced the extra period with a 12-yard touchdown pass to Steve Watson with 24 seconds left in regulation. The tying score was set up by Rulon Jones' fumble recovery at the Broncos' 16-yard line with 2:16 to play. Kubiak completed 21 of 34 for 206 yards. Sammy Winder rushed a club-record 34 times for 126 yards. Steve Foley's fumble recovery at the Broncos' 7 thwarted the Raiders most serious bid to win in overtime.

Denver	0	6	0	13	3	— 22
L.A. Raiders	9	3	7	0	0	— 19

Raiders—Safety, Martin tackled Kubiak in end zone
Raiders—Allen 36 pass from Wilson (Bahr kick)
Raiders—FG Bahr 44
Den —FG Karlis 41
Den —FG Karlis 24
Raiders—Allen 1 run (Bahr kick)
Den —Kay 4 pass from Kubiak (pass failed)
Den —Watson 12 pass from Kubiak (Karlis kick)
Den —FG Karlis 35

Green Bay 41, Detroit 9—At Lambeau Field, attendance 54,289. Lynn Dickey threw for four touchdowns, Eddie Lee Ivery rushed for 116 yards, and Tom Flynn intercepted two passes to help the Packers end a seven-game losing streak. Dickey (17 of 25 for 248 yards) hit Paul Coffman on a pair of touchdowns (20 and 3 yards) and found offensive lineman Blake Moore on a three-yarder for a commanding 28-9 halftime advantage. James Lofton caught a six-yard scoring pass in the third quarter and Al Del Greco's 45- and 34-yard field goals completed the scoring. It was Ivery's first action of the season.

Detroit	3	6	0	0	— 9
Green Bay	14	14	10	3	— 41

GB —Clark 1 run (Del Greco kick)
GB —Coffman 20 pass from Dickey (Del Greco kick)
Det—FG Murray 46
Det—FG Murray 37
GB —Coffman 3 pass from Dickey (Del Greco kick)
Det—FG Murray 41
GB —Moore 3 pass from Dickey (Del Greco kick)
GB —Lofton 6 pass from Dickey (Del Greco kick)
GB —FG Del Greco 45
GB —FG Del Greco 34

Chicago 16, Minnesota 7—At Soldier Field, attendance 57,517. Walter Payton passed the 1,000-yard rushing mark for an NFL record-tying eighth time in his career and the Chicago defense registered a team-record 11 sacks as the Bears defeated the Vikings. Following Matt Suhey's two-yard touchdown run, Jim McMahon threw an 18-yard scoring pass to Dennis McKinnon and Bob Thomas converted a 19-yard field goal to give Chicago a 16-0 lead at halftime. Payton rushed for 54 yards to total 1,001 for the season, tying Franco Harris' NFL record. Richard Dent had two-and-a-half sacks to lead the defense.

Minnesota	0	0	0	7	— 7
Chicago	6	10	0	0	— 16

Chi —Suhey 2 run (kick failed)
Chi —McKinnon 18 pass from McMahon (B. Thomas kick)
Chi —FG B. Thomas 19
Minn—Lewis 22 pass from Wilson (Stenerud kick)

New Orleans 16, Cleveland 14—At Cleveland Stadium, attendance 52,489. Morten Andersen kicked a career-long 53-yard field goal on the game's final play to snap the Saints' three-game winless streak. Richard Todd, who completed 21 of 27 passes for 294 yards, opened the scoring with a two-yard touchdown pass to Hokie Gajan. Todd then set up Andersen's second field goal of the game, a 21-yarder, with a 41-yard pass to Tyrone Young to cut Cleveland's lead to 14-13 with 3:05 remaining. Todd's 36-yard completion to Lindsay Scott set up the winning kick. The loss spoiled the head coaching debut of the Browns' Marty Schottenheimer.

New Orleans	0	10	0	6	— 16
Cleveland	0	7	7	0	— 14

NO —Gajan 2 pass from Todd (Andersen kick)
Cle —Newsome 5 pass from McDonald (Bahr kick)
NO —FG Andersen 26
Cle —Newsome 5 pass from McDonald (Bahr kick)
NO —FG Andersen 21
NO —FG Andersen 53

New England 30, New York Jets 20—At Sullivan Stadium, attendance 60,513. Craig James' 25-yard touchdown run ignited a 24-point second-half outburst as the Patriots rallied to defeat the Jets. The victory made Raymond Berry's head coaching debut a successful one. New York dominated the first half, leading 20-6, but James' score cut the margin to 20-16 going into the fourth period. Tony Eason's (23 of 35 for 273 yards) five-yard touchdown pass to Stephen Starring gave New England the lead for good with 10:53 to play 23-20. Tony Collins then scored on a four-yard run with 2:53 left to cap an 89-yard, 10-play drive and put the game away. The Patriots' victory overshadowed the performances of the Jets' Freeman McNeil, who rushed for 110 yards, and Mark Gastineau, who had three sacks.

N.Y. Jets	10	10	0	0	— 20
New England	0	6	10	14	— 30

NYJ —FG Leahy 46
NYJ —Klever 7 pass from O'Brien (Leahy kick)
NE —FG Franklin 20
NYJ —FG Leahy 18
NYJ —Barber 2 run (Leahy kick)
NE —FG Franklin 27
NE —FG Franklin 47
NE —C. James 25 run (Franklin kick)
NE —Starring 5 pass from Eason (Franklin kick)
NE —Collins 4 run (Franklin kick)

St. Louis 34, Philadelphia 14—At Veterans Stadium, attendance 54,310. Neil Lomax passed for two touchdowns and Stump Mitchell ran for a pair as the Cardinals snapped the Eagles' three-game win streak. Lomax completed 77 percent of his passes (20 of 26) for 286 yards. His first scoring pass, an eight-yarder to Pat Tilley, gave St. Louis the lead for good 17-14. Lomax extended the Cardinals' lead to 24-14 with a 24-yard touchdown pass to Doug Marsh in the third quarter. Mitchell scored on two one-yard plunges. The second followed Wayne Smith's interception and climaxed a 95-yard drive. Philadelphia's Mike Quick caught six passes for 170 yards, including a 90-yarder for a touchdown.

St. Louis	0	17	7	10	— 34
Philadelphia	7	7	0	0	— 14

Phil —Kab 2 pass from Jaworski (McFadden kick)
StL —Mitchell 1 run (O' Donoghue kick)
Phil —Quick 90 pass from Jaworski (McFadden kick)
StL —FG O'Donoghue 28
StL —Tilley 8 pass from Lomax (O'Donoghue kick)
StL —Marsh 24 pass from Lomax (O'Donoghue kick)
StL —Mitchell 1 run (O'Donoghue kick)
StL —FG O'Donoghue 47

San Francisco 33, Los Angeles Rams 0—At Anaheim Stadium, attendance 65,481. Joe Montana passed for 365 yards and three touchdowns to help the 49ers open a three-game lead in the NFC West. Montana completed 21 of 31 passes, including 13 straight in the second quarter. He had touchdown passes of 64 yards to Roger Craig and 6 yards to Freddie Solomon that enabled San Francisco to open a 19-0 halftime advantage. Dwight Clark added a 44-yard touchdown catch in the final period to complete the scoring. The 49ers outgained the Rams 472 yards to 206, and held Eric Dickerson to just 38 yards rushing. It was the Rams worst defeat since 1963 (Chicago beat Los Angeles 52-14) and team's first shutout since 1981 (against Pittsburgh).

San Francisco	3	16	7	7	— 33
L.A. Rams	0	0	0	0	— 0

SF —FG Wersching 46
SF —FG Wersching 46
SF —Craig 64 pass from Montana (pass failed)
SF —Solomon 6 pass from Montana (Wersching kick)
SF —Craig 6 run (Wersching kick)
SF —D. Clark 44 pass from Montana (Wersching kick)

Kansas City 24, Tampa Bay 20—At Arrowhead Stadium, attendance 41,710. Bill Kenney passed for 332 yards and two touchdowns to lead the Chiefs to a 24-20 win over the Buccaneers. Following Ken Lacy's two-yard second-quarter touchdown run, Kenney connected with Lacy on a five-yard scoring pass early in the third period to give Kansas City a 14-13 lead. Henry Marshall caught a 27-yard scoring pass early in the fourth quarter and Kevin Ross' 21-yard interception return helped set up Nick Lowery's 47-yard field goal which finished the scoring. Kenney (26 of 46) and Tampa Bay quarterback Steve DeBerg (29 of 54) combined for a single-game NFL-record 100 passing attempts.

Tampa Bay	0	7	6	7	— 20
Kansas City	0	7	7	10	— 24

KC —Lacy 2 run (Lowery kick)
TB —House 7 pass from DeBerg (Ariri kick)
KC —Lacy 5 pass from Kenney (Lowery kick)
TB —FG Ariri 34
TB —FG Ariri 25
KC —Marshall 27 pass from Kenney (Lowery kick)
KC —FG Lowery 47
TB —Dierking 5 pass from DeBerg (Ariri kick)

New York Giants 37, Washington 13—At Giants Stadium, attendance 76,192. Joe Morris ran for three touchdowns and Phil Simms passed for two more as the Giants halted a six-game losing streak to the Redskins. Simms directed New York's 424-yard attack by completing 18 of 29 passes for 339 yards. He opened the scoring with a 22-yard touchdown completion to Earnest Gray (seven catches, 128 yards) and finished the onslaught with an eight-yard pass to Bobby Johnson. Morris scored on runs of two, one, and five yards and gained 68 of the Giants' season-high 130 yards rushing. Monte Coleman had two-and-a-half of the Redskins' seven sacks.

Washington	0	6	0	7	— 13
N.Y. Giants	14	9	7	7	— 37

NYG —Gray 22 pass from Simms (Haji-Sheikh kick)
NYG —Morris 2 run (Haji-Sheikh kick)
NYG —Morris 1 run (kick failed)
NYG —FG Haji-Sheikh 19
Wash —FG Moseley 23
Wash —FG Moseley 33
NYG —Morris 5 run (Haji-Sheikh kick)
NYG —Johnson 8 pass from Simms (Haji-Sheikh kick)
Wash —Moore 4 pass from Theismann (Moseley kick)

MONDAY, OCTOBER 29

Seattle 24, San Diego 0—At San Diego Jack Murphy Stadium, attendance 53,974. Dave Krieg threw three touchdown passes to Steve Largent and Kenny Easley had a club-record three interceptions as the Seahawks handed the Chargers their first shutout in five years. Krieg completed 23 of 29 passes for 282 yards and connected on scoring strikes of 11, 13, and 16 yards to Largent. Largent had four catches for 51 yards to mark his 100th straight game with at least one reception. The Seattle defense held San Diego to 201 total yards and registered six sacks. The Chargers failed to score for the first time since October 7, 1979, when they lost to the Broncos 7-0.

Seattle	7	10	7	0	— 24
San Diego	0	0	0	0	— 0

Sea —Largent 11 pass from Krieg (Johnson kick)
Sea —FG Johnson 42
Sea —Largent 13 pass from Krieg (Johnson kick)
Sea —Largent 16 pass from Krieg (Johnson kick)

TENTH WEEK SUMMARY

The NFC East became a true gridlock situation, where the Giants, Cowboys, Cardinals, and Redskins were tied for the lead with 6-4 records. New York completed its first season-sweep of Dallas since 1963 as Ali Haji-Sheikh's four field goals were the difference in the 19-7 win. The Cardinals were beating the Rams 13-3 at the half, but dropped a 16-13 decision as Los Angeles' Eric Dickerson became the second 1,000-yard rusher this season with 208 yards on 21 carries. John Riggins' 100 yards rushing and two touchdowns powered Washington over Atlanta 27-14. Philadelphia trailed the top four teams in the NFC East by a game-and-a-half after tying Detroit 23-23. The 49ers, managed to maintain a three-game lead in the NFC West, despite Joe Montana's four interceptions. Montana's touchdown pass to Freddie Solomon in the final two minutes helped San Francisco to a 23-17 triumph over Cincinnati. NFC Central leader Chicago marked its best start since 1963 with a physical 17-6 win over the Los Angeles Raiders. The Seahawks returned an NFL-record four of six interceptions for touchdowns to destroy the Chiefs 45-0. The Seahawks' victory marked Seattle's second consecutive shutout. Denver preserved its AFC Western Division lead, but had to stage a comeback to do so. Dennis Smith's 64-yard fumble recovery return for a score with 1:45 left rallied the Broncos over the Patriots 26-19. The Dolphins found themselves behind the Jets 17-14 at halftime, but Dan Marino (422 yards passing) helped Miami score the game's final 17 points for a 31-17 win. Pittsburgh handed Houston its twenty-third consecutive road loss 35-7. Cleveland's Marty Schottenheimer celebrated his first victory as a head coach, 13-10 over Buffalo. Minnesota trimmed Tampa Bay 27-24 on Jan Stenerud's 53-yard field goal with two seconds to play. The Chargers halted a three-game losing streak by downing the Colts 38-10. Charlie Joiner caught nine passes in the game to move into second place in NFL career receptions with 635. Paul Coffman, who caught two touchdown passes for the second consecutive week, helped the Packers beat the Saints 23-13.

SUNDAY, NOVEMBER 4

San Francisco 23, Cincinnati 17—At Candlestick Park, attendance 58,324. Joe Montana hit Freddie Solomon with a four-yard touchdown pass with 1:39 remaining to give the 49ers a 23-17 win. Carlton Williamson then intercepted a pass with 35 seconds left to secure the victory. Montana completed 27 of 42 passes for 301 yards, but his career-high four interceptions helped the Bengals get out to a 17-7 halftime lead. Ray Wersching kicked three second-half field goals from 29, 35, and 24 yards to cut the Bengals' lead to 17-16. Dwight Clark caught seven passes for 124 yards, including a 39-yarder to help set up Solomon's winning touchdown. Gary Johnson had two of the 49ers' six sacks.

Cincinnati	3	14	0	0	—	17
San Francisco	0	7	3	13	—	23

Cin — FG Breech 39
SF — Cooper 15 pass from Montana (Wersching kick)
Cin — Kinnebrew 6 run (Breech kick)
Cin — Collinsworth 7 pass from Anderson (Breech kick)
SF — FG Wersching 29
SF — FG Wersching 35
SF — FG Wersching 24
SF — Solomon 4 pass from Montana (Wersching kick)

Cleveland 13, Buffalo 10—At Rich Stadium, attendance 33,343. Earnest Byner picked up a fumble and raced 55 yards for the game-winning touchdown with 7:30 remaining to give the Browns a 13-10 comeback victory. The play started when Paul McDonald completed a pass to Willis Adams who fumbled, and Byner recovered. Despite a steady downpour, Browns running back Boyce Green established career highs with 29 carries for 156 yards. Buffalo linebacker Chris Keating also scored on a fumble recovery from 34 yards in the second quarter.

Cleveland	3	3	0	7	—	13
Buffalo	0	7	3	0	—	10

Cle — FG Bahr 28
Buff — Keating 34 fumble recovery return (Nelson kick)
Cle — FG Bahr 36
Buff — FG Nelson 42
Cle — Byner 55 fumble recovery return (Bahr kick)

Green Bay 23, New Orleans 13—At Louisiana Superdome, attendance 57,426. Paul Coffman caught two touchdown passes for the second straight week and Al Del Greco kicked three field goals to lead the Packers over the Saints. Tom Flynn's second-quarter fumble recovery set up Lynn Dickey's 33-yard scoring completion to Coffman. Coffman also caught a five-yard touchdown pass in the third period. Del Greco was good on field goals from 41, 34, and 41 yards out. Green Bay rushed for over 200 yards (207) for the first time since November 23, 1980, when the Packers gained 246 yards against Minnesota.

Green Bay	0	10	10	3	—	23
New Orleans	7	3	0	3	—	13

NO — W. Wilson 1 run (Andersen kick)
GB — FG Del Greco 41
GB — Coffman 33 pass from Dickey (Del Greco kick)
NO — FG Andersen 35
GB — Coffman 5 pass from Dickey (Del Greco kick)
GB — FG Del Greco 34
NO — FG Andersen 46
GB — FG Del Greco 41

Pittsburgh 35, Houston 7—At Three Rivers Stadium, attendance 48,892. Mark Malone completed three touchdown passes to John Stallworth and ran for another to lead the Steelers over the Oilers. The game was played in a driving rain. Malone's 13-yard bootleg run for a score, along with Stallworth touchdown catches of 43 and 17 yards, gave Pittsburgh a 21-0 halftime lead. Stallworth (four catches, 109 yards) added a 39-yarder in the third quarter to finish the first three-touchdown afternoon of his career. Twenty seconds later, Bryan Hinkle returned a fumble 21 yards for the Steelers' final points.

Houston	0	0	7	0	—	7
Pittsburgh	7	14	14	0	—	35

Pitt — Stallworth 43 pass from Malone (Anderson kick)
Pitt — Malone 13 run (Anderson kick)
Pitt — Stallworth 17 pass from Malone (Anderson kick)
Pitt — Stallworth 39 pass from Malone (Anderson kick)
Pitt — Hinkle 21 fumble recovery return (Anderson kick)
Hou — J. Williams 5 pass from Luck (Cooper kick)

Seattle 45, Kansas City 0—At Kingdome, attendance 61,396. The Seahawks intercepted six passes and returned four for touchdowns (an NFL record) en route to their second straight shutout victory and third this season. AFC defensive player of the week Dave Brown returned interceptions 90 and 58 yards for scores. Keith Simpson and Kenny Easley brought back interceptions 76 and 58 yards for touchdowns, respectively. Terry Taylor returned two more interceptions 43 yards as Seattle set another NFL mark with 325 interception return yards. Dave Krieg completed 12 of 20 passes for 138 yards and had touchdowns of 11 yards to Dan Doornink and 2 yards to Mike Tice. The Seahawks set club marks for interceptions and largest margin of victory.

Kansas City	0	0	0	0	—	0
Seattle	3	28	7	7	—	45

Sea — FG Johnson 29
Sea — Brown 90 interception return (Johnson kick)
Sea — Simpson 76 interception return (Johnson kick)
Sea — Doornink 11 pass from Krieg (Johnson kick)
Sea — Tice 2 pass from Krieg (Johnson kick)
Sea — Brown 58 interception return (Johnson kick)
Sea — Easley 58 interception return (Johnson kick)

Chicago 17, Los Angeles Raiders 6—At Soldier Field, attendance 59,858. Walter Payton ran for 111 yards and two touchdowns as the Bears shut down the Raiders 17-6. Payton ran 18 yards for a score in the first quarter to complete a 76-yard drive. He then scored following Leslie Frazier's interception on an eight-yard run early in the second period to give Chicago a 14-0 lead. The Bears' defense held the Raiders to 181 total yards and intercepted three passes, recovered two fumbles, and recorded nine sacks, including four-and-a-half by the NFC's defensive player of the week Richard Dent. Chicago's 7-3 record marked its best start since 1963.

L.A. Raiders	0	3	3	0	—	6
Chicago	7	7	0	3	—	17

Chi — Payton 18 run (B. Thomas kick)
Chi — Payton 8 run (B. Thomas kick)
Raiders — FG Bahr 44
Raiders — FG Bahr 40
Chi — FG B. Thomas 29

Los Angeles Rams 16, St. Louis 13—At Busch Memorial Stadium, attendance 50,950. Eric Dickerson rushed for a career-high 208 yards on 21 carries and Mike Lansford kicked three field goals to lead the Rams over the Cardinals. St. Louis opened a 13-3 lead on a pair of Neil O'Donoghue field goals and Neil Lomax's (34 of 52 for 341 yards) 53-yard touchdown pass to Roy Green (five receptions for 105 yards). Jeff Kemp's 52-yard scoring pass to Ron Brown cut the margin to 13-10. Fumble recoveries by Reggie Doss and Greg Meisner set up the tying (27 yards) and winning (32) field goals by Lansford. The Rams allowed 362 yards and controlled the ball for only 22:05. Jack Youngblood had three of Los Angeles' six sacks and blocked the Cardinals' 48-yard field goal attempt on the game's final play.

L.A. Rams	3	0	10	3	—	16
St. Louis	3	10	0	0	—	13

Rams — FG Lansford 33
StL — FG O'Donoghue 49
StL — Green 53 pass from Lomax (O'Donoghue kick)
StL — FG O'Donoghue 43
Rams — Brown 52 pass from Kemp (Lansford kick)
Rams — FG Lansford 27
Rams — FG Lansford 32

Miami 31, New York Jets 17—At Giants Stadium, attendance 72,655. Dan Marino completed 23 of 42 passes for 422 yards and two touchdowns to rally the Dolphins over the Jets. New York led 17-14, but Miami scored two touchdowns and a field goal in the final 7:45 for the win. Marino drove the Dolphins 80 yards in four plays for the go-ahead touchdown, a 47-yard pass to Mark Clayton. Uwe von Schamann kicked a 30-yard field goal and Pete Johnson scored on a two-yard run in the final four minutes to seal the victory. Mark Duper caught seven passes for 155 yards and Nat Moore added 105 yards on five receptions as Miami generated 507 total yards. Freeman McNeil topped the 100-yard rushing mark (132 yards on 20 carries) for the twelfth time in his career, breaking Matt Snell's previous Jets record of 11.

Miami	7	0	7	17	—	31
N.Y. Jets	7	3	0	7	—	17

Mia — Moore 37 pass from Marino (von Schamann kick)
NYJ — Walker 33 pass from Ryan (Leahy kick)
NYJ — FG Leahy 32
Mia — Bennett 3 run (von Schamann kick)
NYJ — McNeil 6 run (Leahy kick)
Mia — Clayton 47 pass from Marino (von Schamann kick)
Mia — FG von Schamann 30
Mia — P. Johnson 2 run (von Schamann kick)

Denver 26, New England 19—At Mile High Stadium, attendance 74,908. Dennis Smith's 64-yard fumble recovery return for a touchdown with 1:45 to play lifted the Broncos over the Patriots. Denver trailed New England 19-12 when John Elway completed a five-yard touchdown pass to Butch Johnson (nine catches, 156 yards) to tie the score with 4:03 left. Elway completed 26 of 40 passes for 315 yards. He also threw scoring passes of 17 and 35 yards, respectively, to Johnson and Steve Watson (eight receptions for 134 yards). Patriots quarterback Tony Eason connected on 21 of 38 passes for 313 yards, including eight to Stanley Morgan for 122 yards. Craig James rushed for 120 yards on 20 carries in his first start for New England. Steve Foley's interception in the closing moments ended New England's final threat.

New England	3	3	7	6	—	19
Denver	0	6	6	14	—	26

NE — FG Franklin 30
NE — FG Franklin 40
Den — Watson 35 pass from Elway (kick failed)
NE — Weathers 15 pass from Eason (Franklin kick)
Den — Johnson 17 pass from Elway (kick failed)
NE — FG Franklin 47
NE — FG Franklin 19
Den — Johnson 5 pass from Elway (Karlis kick)
Den — D. Smith 64 fumble recovery return (Karlis kick)

New York Giants 19, Dallas 7—At Texas Stadium, attendance 60,235. Phil Simms passed for one touchdown and Ali Haji-Sheikh converted four of four field goal attempts (40, 38, 23, and 27 yards) as the Giants completed their first season-sweep of the Cowboys since 1963. New York scored 13 unanswered points in the second half to reverse Dallas' 7-6 halftime advantage. Simms (16 of 37 for 244 yards) hooked up with Lionel Manuel (five catches for 102 yards) on a nine-yard scoring pass to give the Giants a 13-7 lead. Haji-Sheikh kicked two field goals in the fourth quarter to put the game away. Leonard Marshall had two-and-a-half of New York's five sacks.

N.Y. Giants	6	0	7	6	—	19
Dallas	0	7	0	0	—	7

NYG — FG Haji-Sheikh 40
NYG — FG Haji-Sheikh 38
Dall — Hill 30 pass from Hogeboom (Septien kick)
NYG — Manuel 9 pass from Simms (Haji-Sheikh kick)
NYG — FG Haji-Sheikh 23
NYG — FG Haji-Sheikh 27

Detroit 23, Philadelphia 23—At Pontiac Silverdome, attendance 59,141. Ed Murray's 21-yard field goal attempt 4:44 into overtime hit the right upright and bounced back, forcing the Lions to settle for their first tie in 11 years. Philadelphia's Paul McFadden kicked a 40-yard field goal with three seconds left in regulation to tie the score, but the Eagles could not mount a serious threat in the extra period. Mike Quick caught five passes for 110 yards for Philadelphia, including a 68-yard touchdown pass. McFadden became the first Eagles player to kick a pair of 50-yard field goals (52 and 51) in the same game. The Lions last tie game came against the Packers (13-13) on September 23, 1973.

Philadelphia	3	3	7	10	0	—	23
Detroit	7	10	0	6	0	—	23

Det — Jones 4 pass from Danielson (Murray kick)
Phil — FG McFadden 52
Det — Danielson 22 pass from Jones (Murray kick)
Det — FG Murray 32
Phil — FG McFadden 51
Phil — Quick 68 pass from Jaworski (McFadden kick)
Det — FG Murray 33
Phil — Haddix 2 run (McFadden kick)
Det — FG Murray 18
Phil — FG McFadden 40

San Diego 38, Indianapolis 10—At Hoosier Dome, attendance 60,143. Dan Fouts passed for 283 yards and three touchdowns and the San Diego defense intercepted four passes to help the Chargers end a three-game losing streak. Fouts completed 27 of 38 passes, including a seven-yard scoring throw to Charlie Joiner for a 17-7 halftime lead. Fouts' fourth-quarter touchdown passes to Wes Chandler (20 yards) and Buford McGee (2) put the game out of reach. Joiner caught nine passes for 119 yards to move into second place in NFL career catches (635) and yards (10,466). Tim Fox, Gill Byrd, John Turner, and Linden King intercepted passes for San Diego.

San Diego	7	10	7	14	—	38
Indianapolis	0	7	3	0	—	10

SD — Jackson 2 run (Benirschke kick)
SD — FG Benirschke 23
Ind — Butler 74 pass from Herrmann (Allegre kick)
SD — Joiner 7 pass from Fouts (Benirschke kick)
SD — Morris 1 run (Benirschke kick)
Ind — FG Allegre 54
SD — Chandler 20 pass from Fouts (Benirschke kick)
SD — McGee 2 pass from Fouts (Benirschke kick)

Minnesota 27, Tampa Bay 24—At Metrodome, attendance 54,949. Jan Stenerud's 53-yard field goal with two seconds left lifted the Vikings over the Buccaneers and snapped Minnesota's five-game losing streak. Wade Wilson (24 of 36 for 236 yards) moved the Vikings 47 yards in the final minute to set up the winning kick. Earlier, Wilson's three-yard touchdown completion to Ted Brown put Minnesota ahead 24-17 with 6:07 to go, but Steve DeBerg's 11-yard scoring pass to Kevin House tied the score with 1:03 to play. James Wilder was the only Tampa Bay player to run the ball, carrying 30 times for 146 yards and two touchdowns.

Tampa Bay	7	7	0	10	—	24
Minnesota	3	7	7	10	—	27

TB — Wilder 6 run (Ariri kick)
Minn — FG Stenerud 30
TB — Wilder 2 run (Ariri kick)
Minn — Jordan 4 run (Stenerud kick)
Minn — Nelson 5 run (Stenerud kick)
TB — FG Ariri 29
Minn — Brown 3 pass from Wilson (Stenerud kick)
TB — House 11 pass from DeBerg (Ariri kick)
Minn — FG Stenerud 53

MONDAY, NOVEMBER 5

Washington 27, Atlanta 14—At Robert F. Kennedy Stadium, attendance 51,301. Joe Theismann and John Riggins each accounted for two touchdowns to help the Redskins snap a two-game losing streak. Following a scoreless first quarter, Theismann and Riggins each scored on one-yard runs to give Washington a 14-7 halftime lead. Atlanta rallied to tie the game 14-14, but Neal Olkewicz recovered a fumble to set up Riggins' second one-yard touchdown, the 105th of his career. Theismann's seven-yard scoring pass to Calvin Muhammad sealed the victory. Gerald Riggs (134 yards rushing on 27 attempts) became the first running back to gain over 100 yards against the Redskins this season.

Atlanta	0	7	7	0 —	14
Washington	0	14	6	7 —	27

Wash — Riggins 1 run (Moseley kick)
Wash — Theismann 1 run (Moseley kick)
Atl — Riggs 1 run (Luckhurst kick)
Atl — Riggs 10 run (Luckhurst kick)
Wash — Riggins 1 run (kick failed)
Wash — Muhammad 7 pass from Theismann (Moseley kick)

ELEVENTH WEEK SUMMARY

It's rare when the Raiders lose three straight games, and even rarer still when they lose on Monday night, but both happened when the Seahawks beat the defending NFL champions 17-14. Seattle scored all its points in the third quarter to hand Los Angeles only its third Monday night defeat in 25 appearances. Sammy Winder's touchdown run with 38 seconds left helped the Broncos stay one game ahead of the field in the AFC West with a 16-13 win over the Chargers. Larry Kinnebrew performed similar heroics to keep Cincinnati's playoff hopes alive. Kinnebrew's scoring run in the last minute gave the Bengals a 22-20 triumph over the Steelers. Houston snapped the longest road losing streak in NFL history—23 games—by edging Kansas City 17-16 as Larry Moriarty rushed for 117 yards. Miami allowed Philadelphia to open a 14-0 lead but rallied to a 24-23 victory when Doug Betters blocked the Eagles' potential game-tying extra point. The Patriots scored 28 unanswered points to sail past the Bills 38-10. The Colts held the Jets without a touchdown for the first time since October 25, 1981, to post a 9-5 win. Dallas and Washington scored victories to remain tied for the NFC Eastern Division lead. Two touchdowns by Ron Springs powered the Cowboys past the Cardinals 24-17. Two Redskins running backs replaced John Riggins to lead Washington past Detroit 28-14. Otis Wonsley (three touchdowns) and Keith Griffin (114 yards rushing) replaced the ailing Riggins as the Lions suffered their ninth straight loss to the Redskins. John McKay's announcement that he would retire at the end of the season inspired the Buccaneers to a 20-17 victory over the Giants. Eric Dickerson became the first running back to gain over 100 yards (149) against the Bears in the last 12 games as the Rams rallied for a 29-13 win. Los Angeles remained three games back of division-leader San Francisco as Joe Montana orchestrated a 468-yard attack to dominate Cleveland 41-7. A pair of Hoby Brenner touchdown receptions helped the Saints beat the Falcons 17-14. Lynn Dickey's four touchdown passes led the Packers over the Vikings 45-17.

SUNDAY, NOVEMBER 11

New England 38, Buffalo 10—At Sullivan Stadium, attendance 43,313. Tony Collins' pair of one-yard touchdown runs within a three-minute span broke the game open and ignited the Patriots' win. With the score tied 10-10 in the third quarter, Collins scored his first touchdown with 2:50 left and his second came on the last play of the quarter to give the Patriots a 24-10 lead. Tony Eason completed two of his three touchdown passes in the fourth period—24 yards to Stanley Morgan and 7 yards to Cedric Jones—to put the game out of reach. The aggressive New England defense had three interceptions, one fumble recovery, and eight sacks.

Buffalo	7	0	3	0 —	10
New England	0	10	14	14 —	38

Buff — Dennard 68 pass from Ferguson (Nelson kick)
NE — Jones 17 pass from Eason (Franklin kick)
NE — FG Franklin 21
Buff — FG Nelson 34
NE — Collins 1 run (Franklin kick)
NE — Collins 1 run (Franklin kick)
NE — Morgan 24 pass from Eason (Franklin kick)
NE — Jones 7 pass from Eason (Franklin kick)

Los Angeles Rams 29, Chicago 13—At Anaheim Stadium, attendance 62,021. Eric Dickerson ran for 149 yards, including 98 in the second half, as the Rams scored 23 unanswered points to defeat the Bears. Chicago led 13-6 at the half, before Henry Ellard caught a 63-yard touchdown pass from Jeff Kemp to cut the margin to 13-12. Dickerson then scored on a one-yard run to conclude a 95-yard drive. Gary Green's fumble recovery set up Dickerson's four-yard run just 79 seconds later. Dickerson became the first running back in the last 12 games to gain over 100 yards rushing against the Bears. Walter Payton caught seven passes (for 78 yards) to total 361 career receptions, breaking Johnny Morris' previous club record of 356.

Chicago	7	6	0	0 —	13
L.A. Rams	0	6	6	17 —	29

Chi — Fuller 1 run (B. Thomas kick)
Chi — FG B. Thomas 20
Rams — FG Lansford 21
Rams — FG Lansford 45
Chi — FG B. Thomas 52
Rams — Ellard 63 pass from Kemp (kick failed)
Rams — Dickerson 1 run (Lansford kick)
Rams — Dickerson 4 run (Lansford kick)
Rams — FG Lansford 29

Indianapolis 9, New York Jets 5—At Giants Stadium, attendance 51,066. Raul Allegre kicked three field goals and the defense registered six sacks and allowed only 143 total yards to help the Colts break a two-game losing streak. Allegre was good on field goals from 44, 46, and 25 yards. Leo Wisniewski (three sacks) and Donnell Thompson (two) helped hold New York, playing without Freeman McNeil, without a touchdown for the first time since October 25, 1981, when the Jets lost to Seattle 19-3.

Indianapolis	3	3	0	3 —	9
N.Y. Jets	0	2	3	0 —	5

Ind — FG Allegre 44
NYJ — Safety, ball snapped out of end zone
Ind — FG Allegre 46
NYJ — FG Leahy 27
Ind — FG Allegre 25

Dallas 24, St. Louis 17—At Busch Memorial Stadium, attendance 48,721. Victor Scott's interception set up Gary Hogeboom's 26-yard touchdown pass to Ron Springs with 9:03 left to carry the Cowboys over the Cardinals. Dallas opened a 17-7 halftime lead on Springs' 1-yard run, James Jones' 8-yard reception, and Rafael Septien's 35-yard field goal. St. Louis rallied to score 10 unanswered points in the third quarter to tie the score 17-17. Neil Lomax completed 27 of 52 passes for 388 yards to set a Cardinals record for passing yardage in a season (3,383). St. Louis led Dallas in first downs (25 to 16) and total yards (435 to 250), but gave up five sacks, and lost two interceptions and four fumbles.

Dallas	7	10	0	7 —	24
St. Louis	0	7	10	0 —	17

Dall — Springs 1 run (Septien kick)
StL — Tilley 15 pass from Lomax (O'Donoghue kick)
Dall — J. Jones 8 pass from Hogeboom (Septien kick)
Dall — FG Septien 35
StL — Love 1 pass from Lomax (O'Donoghue kick)
StL — FG O'Donoghue 30
Dall — Springs 26 pass from Hogeboom (Septien kick)

Denver 16, San Diego 13—At San Diego Jack Murphy Stadium, attendance 53,162. Sammy Winder's one-yard touchdown run with 38 seconds remaining helped the Broncos down the Chargers. San Diego took a 13-6 lead early in the fourth quarter before Rich Karlis' third field goal of the day, a 37-yarder, cut the margin to 13-9. John Elway completed four of six passes in the 77-yard winning drive, including completions of 19 yards to Butch Johnson and 15 yards to Ray Alexander. The Chargers had an opportunity to send the game into overtime, but Rolf Benirschke's 46-yard field goal attempt was wide left with two seconds remaining.

Denver	3	3	0	10 —	16
San Diego	7	3	0	3 —	13

Den — FG Karlis 44
SD — Joiner 25 pass from Fouts (Benirschke kick)
Den — FG Karlis 45
SD — FG Benirschke 49
SD — FG Benirschke 43
Den — FG Karlis 37
Den — Winder 1 run (Karlis kick)

Washington 28, Detroit 14—At Robert F. Kennedy Stadium, attendance 50,212. Rookie Keith Griffin, subbing for the injured John Riggins, gained 114 yards on 32 carries and Otis Wonsley ran for three scores to help the Redskins down the Lions for the ninth straight time. Following Joe Theismann's seven-yard touchdown pass to Jeff Moore, Wonsley scored on a pair of one-yard runs and added a three-yarder in the third quarter for a 28-0 Washington lead. The Lions closed the gap to 28-14, but the Redskins' defense stopped Detroit three times in Washington territory in the final period. Dexter Manley had three-and-a-half of the Redskins' five sacks.

Detroit	0	0	14	0 —	14
Washington	14	7	7	0 —	28

Wash — Moore 7 pass from Theismann (Moseley kick)
Wash — Wonsley 1 run (Moseley kick)
Wash — Wonsley 1 run (Moseley kick)
Wash — Wonsley 3 run (Moseley kick)
Det — J. Jones 1 run (Murray kick)
Det — Rubick 19 pass from Danielson (Murray kick)

Houston 17, Kansas City 16—At Arrowhead Stadium, attendance 44,464. Warren Moon's one-yard touchdown plunge and Joe Cooper's 44-yard field goal with 1:34 left helped Houston hold off the Chiefs and clinched the Oilers' first win. Moon completed a two-yard touchdown pass to Jamie Williams in the second quarter, which, coupled with his scoring run, gave Houston a 14-9 edge with 12:29 remaining. Larry Moriarty gained 117 yards on 29 carries and Tim Smith had 107 yards on eight receptions for the Oilers. It was Houston's first road victory since 1981, ending an NFL record of 23 straight road defeats.

Houston	0	7	0	10 —	17
Kansas City	3	3	3	7 —	16

KC — FG Lowery 31
Hou — Williams 2 pass from Moon (Cooper kick)
KC — FG Lowery 38
KC — FG Lowery 33
Hou — Moon 1 run (Cooper kick)
Hou — FG Cooper 44
KC — Marshall 4 pass from Blackledge (Lowery kick)

Green Bay 45, Minnesota 17—At Milwaukee County Stadium, attendance 52,931. Lynn Dickey threw for 303 yards and four touchdowns as the Packers rolled over the Vikings 45-17. The teams were tied 17-17 early in the third period when Green Bay caught fire and scored 28 straight points. Dickey threw touchdown passes to Jessie Clark (18 and 2 yards) and James Lofton (63). Gerry Ellis' (10 carries, 107 yards) six-yard scoring run capped the explosion. Dickey finished with 22 completions in 40 attempts to lead the Packers' 513-yard assault. Lofton had four receptions for 119 yards.

Minnesota	0	10	7	0 —	17
Green Bay	7	10	14	14 —	45

GB — Coffman 7 pass from Dickey (Del Greco kick)
GB — FG Del Greco 24
Minn — FG Stenerud 39
Minn — Jordan 14 pass from Wilson (Stenerud kick)
GB — West 2 run (Del Greco kick)
Minn — Anderson 28 pass from Wilson (Stenerud kick)
GB — Clark 18 pass from Dickey (Del Greco kick)
GB — Clark 2 pass from Dickey (Del Greco kick)
GB — Lofton 63 pass from Dickey (Del Greco kick)
GB — Ellis 6 run (Del Greco kick)

New Orleans 17, Atlanta 13—At Atlanta-Fulton County Stadium, attendance 40,590. Richard Todd and Hoby Brenner combined for two touchdowns as the Saints defeated the Falcons 17-13. Todd's 37-yard scoring pass to Brenner helped open a 10-0 New Orleans advantage, but Atlanta came back to tie the score by halftime. After the Falcons gained a 13-10 edge late in the third quarter, Todd threw a 17-yard pass to Brenner, with 12:11 remaining, for the decisive score.

New Orleans	10	0	0	7 —	17
Atlanta	0	10	3	0 —	13

NO — Brenner 37 pass from Todd (Andersen kick)
NO — FG Andersen 47
Atl — Riggs 1 run (Luckhurst kick)
Atl — FG Luckhurst 39
Atl — FG Luckhurst 24
NO — Brenner 17 pass from Todd (Andersen kick)

Tampa Bay 20, New York Giants 17—At Tampa Stadium, attendance 46,534. James Wilder, who became the second Tampa Bay player ever to gain over 1,000 yards rushing in a season, helped the Buccaneers end a four-game losing streak by beating the Giants 20-17. Wilder rushed for 99 yards to total 1,062 for the season. The Giants led 10-3 early in the third quarter before Steve DeBerg and Kevin House connected on a 10-yard scoring pass to tie the score 10-10. House's 42-yard reception set up Wilder's one-yard run midway through the fourth quarter. Later, House's 26-yard catch helped position the Buccaneers for Obed Ariri's 20-yard field goal and 20-10 lead. House gained 89 yards on four receptions.

N.Y. Giants	3	0	7	7 —	17
Tampa Bay	0	3	7	10 —	20

NYG — FG Haji-Sheikh 41
TB — FG Ariri 37
NYG — Mowatt 23 pass from Simms (Haji-Sheikh kick)
TB — House 10 pass from DeBerg (Ariri kick)
TB — Wilder 1 run (Ariri kick)
TB — FG Ariri 20
NYG — Johnson 11 pass from Simms (Haji-Sheikh kick)

Miami 24, Philadelphia 23—At Orange Bowl, attendance 70,227. Doug Betters blocked an extra-point attempt that would have tied the score with 1:52 left to preserve the Dolphins' victory. Philadelphia led for most of three quarters before Miami struck for a pair of touchdowns within a span of 3:44 in the second half. Woody Bennett ran two yards for a touchdown with 2:07 left in the third quarter to close the score to 17-14. Pete Johnson scored from one-yard out 1:37 into the final period following an interception by Paul Lankford that put the Dolphins out in front for the first time all day, 21-17. Ron Jaworski passed for three Philadelphia touchdowns, but Uwe von Schamann's 27-yard field goal proved the difference for Miami.

Philadelphia	14	0	3	6 —	23
Miami	0	7	7	10 —	24

Phil — Quick 19 pass from Jaworski (McFadden kick)
Phil — Woodruff 13 pass from Jaworski (McFadden kick)
Mia — Nathan 11 pass from Marino (von Schamann kick)
Phil — FG McFadden 45
Mia — Bennett 2 run (von Schamann kick)
Mia — P. Johnson 1 run (von Schamann kick)
Mia — FG von Schamann 27
Phil — Hoover 38 pass from Jaworski (kick blocked)

Cincinnati 22, Pittsburgh 20—At Riverfront Stadium, attendance 52,497. Larry Kinnebrew's three-yard touchdown run with 35 seconds remaining lifted the Bengals over the Steelers. Pittsburgh led 13-3 at halftime, but Cincinnati scored 12 unanswered points in the third quarter. Jim Breech kicked a pair of field goals from 42 and 28 yards, and James Brooks ran 24 yards for a touchdown to give the Bengals a 15-13 advantage. Turk Schonert replaced starter Ken Anderson (bruised shoulder) in the third quarter and guided Cincinnati 49 yards to the winning score. Pittsburgh's John Stallworth caught seven passes for 76 yards to total 1,004 yards for the season and become the first Steeler to have three 1,000-yard seasons. It was Mark Malone's first loss in four starts for Pittsburgh this year.

Pittsburgh	0	13	0	7	— 20
Cincinnati	3	0	12	7	— 22

Cin — FG Breech 21
Pitt — FG Anderson 47
Pitt — Malone 1 run (Anderson kick)
Pitt — FG Anderson 21
Cin — Brooks 24 run (run failed)
Cin — FG Breech 42
Cin — FG Breech 28
Pitt — Lipps 36 run (Anderson kick)
Cin — Kinnebrew 3 run (Breech kick)

San Francisco 41, Cleveland 7—At Cleveland Stadium, attendance 60,092. Joe Montana completed two touchdown passes to Freddie Solomon and Roger Craig ran for two more to spearhead the 49ers' win. San Francisco opened a 13-0 lead on Ray Wersching field goals of 47 and 26 yards and Craig's 20-yard run. After Craig's second touchdown, a two-yard run, Solomon (five receptions for 105 yards) hauled in a 60-yard pass from Montana on the last play of the third quarter. Montana and Solomon opened the fourth period scoring with a two-yard touchdown pass. Bill Ring's five-yard touchdown run completed San Francisco's 468-yard offensive assault. Montana, despite playing in a heavy rain, completed 24 of 30 passes for 263 yards.

San Francisco	6	7	14	14	— 41
Cleveland	0	0	0	7	— 7

SF — FG Wersching 47
SF — FG Wersching 26
SF — Craig 20 run (Wersching kick)
SF — Craig 2 run (Wersching kick)
SF — Solomon 60 pass from Montana (Wersching kick)
SF — Solomon 2 pass from Montana (Wersching kick)
SF — Ring 5 run (Wersching kick)
Cle — Davis 18 pass from McDonald (Bahr kick)

MONDAY, NOVEMBER 12
Seattle 17, Los Angeles Raiders 14—At Kingdome, attendance 64,001. Dave Krieg engineered Seattle's 17-point third-quarter blitz by passing for two touchdowns as the Seahawks sent the Raiders to their third loss ever on Monday night. Norm Johnson's 27-yard field goal initiated the Seahawks' comeback following Shelton Robinson's fumble recovery. Los Angeles held Seattle to 46 total yards in the first half, before Krieg got on track hitting Byron Walker and Daryl Turner on touchdown passes of 8 and 20 yards, respectively. The Seattle defense registered four sacks, three interceptions, three fumble recoveries, and stopped two last-gasp scoring attempts by the Raiders in the final 4:26 to insure victory.

L.A. Raiders	0	7	0	7	— 14
Seattle	0	0	17	0	— 17

Raiders — Allen 1 run (Bahr kick)
Sea — FG Johnson 27
Sea — Walker 8 pass from Krieg (Johnson kick)
Sea — Turner 20 pass from Krieg (Johnson kick)
Raiders — Allen 1 run (Bahr kick)

TWELFTH WEEK SUMMARY

The San Francisco 49ers became the first team to clinch a playoff berth with a 24-17 win over Tampa Bay. Fred Dean, who ended his contract holdout and returned to action for the first time this season, and Wendell Tyler, who became the fourth 1,000-yard rusher in 49ers history, led San Francisco to the victory. Two streaks came to a halt this weekend. San Diego dropped Miami 34-28 in overtime to end the Dolphins' 16-game unbeaten string. Miami had a 14-point lead at one point during the game, but Dan Fouts' fourth touchdown pass tied the score and sent the game into overtime. Buford McGee's 25-yard scoring run on San Diego's first extra-period possession gave San Diego the win. Conversely, the Bills snapped a 12-game losing streak by surprising the Cowboys 14-3. Greg Bell ran 85 yards for a score on Buffalo's first play from scrimmage and the defense became the first team in five years to hold Dallas without a touchdown. Washington's John Riggins became the oldest player in NFL history to gain over 1,000 yards rushing in a season, but it wasn't enough as the Eagles beat the Redskins 16-10. The Giants seized the opportunity to join the Cowboys and Redskins in a three-way tie for first in the NFC East by defeating the Cardinals 16-10. Chicago's Bob Thomas kicked a 19-yard field goal with two seconds left to give the Bears a 16-14 win over the Lions. The Packers continued to show improvement in their 31-6 victory over the Los Angeles Rams. Eddie Lee Ivery scored three times in his first start of the season as the Packers won their fourth straight game for the first time since 1978. John Elway completed five touchdown passes to help keep the Broncos atop the AFC West with a 42-21 thrashing of the Vikings. Seattle kept pace with Denver, capitalizing on five Bengals turnovers to down Cincinnati 26-6. The Raiders ended a three-week dry spell with a 17-7 victory over the Chiefs. Rod Martin returned a fumble 77 yards for a score to help the Raiders end their winless streak. The Browns parlayed 11 sacks, two interceptions, and a pair of fumble recoveries into a 23-7 triumph over the Falcons. Tony Eason threw for four touchdowns, three to tight end Derrick Ramsey, as New England blasted Indianapolis 50-17. The Oilers' Warren Moon completed three scoring passes to help Houston beat the Jets 31-21.

New Orleans scored its first win in eight tries on Monday night by defeating Pittsburgh 27-24.

SUNDAY, NOVEMBER 18
Cleveland 23, Atlanta 7—At Atlanta-Fulton County Stadium, attendance 28,280. The Browns' defense had 11 sacks, two interceptions, and a pair of fumble recoveries to help Cleveland beat the Falcons 23-7. Paul McDonald threw a 43-yard scoring pass to Bruce Davis and Matt Bahr's 46-yard field goal gave Cleveland a 13-7 lead at the half. Bahr kicked second-half field goals of 46 and 20 yards and Ozzie Newsome caught a 16-yard touchdown pass to finish the scoring. Clay Matthews had three-and-a-half sacks to lead the defense.

Cleveland	10	3	0	10	— 23
Atlanta	7	0	0	0	— 7

Atl — Bailey 20 pass from Bartkowski (Luckhurst kick)
Cle — Davis 43 pass from McDonald (Bahr kick)
Cle — FG Bahr 27
Cle — FG Bahr 46
Cle — Newsome 16 pass from McDonald (Bahr kick)
Cle — FG Bahr 20

Buffalo 14, Dallas 3—At Rich Stadium, attendance 74,391. Rookie Greg Bell rushed for 206 yards on 27 carries and scored two touchdowns to lead the Bills to their first win of the season, snapping a 12-game losing streak. Buffalo took a 7-0 lead on the first play from scrimmage on Bell's 85-yard touchdown run, the longest ever against Dallas. Bell, the AFC offensive player of the week, also caught a three-yard touchdown pass from Joe Ferguson in the fourth quarter. The Bills' defense completely shut down the Cowboys' offense, marking the first time since October 28, 1979 (against Pittsburgh), that Dallas had not scored a touchdown in a game.

Dallas	0	3	0	0	— 3
Buffalo	7	0	0	7	— 14

Buff — Bell 85 run (Nelson kick)
Dall — FG Septien 20
Buff — Bell 3 pass from Ferguson (Nelson kick)

Chicago 16, Detroit 14—At Soldier Field, attendance 54,911. Bob Thomas' third field goal of the game, a 19-yarder with two seconds remaining, lifted the Bears over the Lions. Chicago led 10-7 at halftime on Steve Fuller's one-yard touchdown pass to Pat Dunsmore and Thomas' 24-yard field goal, but Detroit took a 14-10 edge into the final period. Thomas then kicked a 52-yard field goal to cut the deficit to one point. Fuller helped set up the winning kick with a 27-yard pass to Emery Moorehead.

Detroit	0	7	7	0	— 14
Chicago	7	3	0	6	— 16

Chi — Dunsmore 1 pass from Fuller (B. Thomas kick)
Chi — FG B. Thomas 24
Det — J. Jones 1 run (Murray kick)
Det — Chadwick 7 pass from Danielson (Murray kick)
Chi — FG B. Thomas 52
Chi — FG B. Thomas 19

Los Angeles Raiders 17, Kansas City 7—At Memorial Coliseum, attendance 48,575. Rod Martin returned one fumble for a touchdown and caused another to set up the Raiders' second score as Los Angeles broke a three-game losing streak. Martin raced 77 yards with Bill Kenney's fumble in the first quarter to give the Raiders a 7-0 lead. Howie Long's fumble recovery set up Marc Wilson's 12-yard touchdown pass to Dokie Williams for a 14-0 lead just 13 seconds before halftime. Los Angeles ate up 12:31 of the clock in the second half en route to Chris Bahr's 22-yard field goal. The Chiefs avoided the shutout when Kenney hit Malcolm Scott on a three-yard touchdown pass with 1:41 remaining.

Kansas City	0	0	0	7	— 7
L.A. Raiders	7	7	0	3	— 17

Raiders — Martin 77 fumble recovery return (Bahr kick)
Raiders — Williams 12 pass from Wilson (Bahr kick)
Raiders — FG Bahr 22
KC — Scott 3 pass from Kenney (Lowery kick)

Green Bay 31, Los Angeles Rams 6—At Milwaukee County Stadium, attendance 52,031. Eddie Lee Ivery ran for three touchdowns and Tim Lewis had a club-record 99-yard interception return for another score as the Packers won their fourth straight game for the first time since 1978. Ivery, making his first start of the season, scored on a pair of one-yard runs in the first half to give Green Bay a 14-6 advantage. The Packers shut out the Rams in the second half and scored 10 points in the third quarter on Al Del Greco's 21-yard field goal and Ivery's two-yard run. James Lofton caught six passes for 129 yards. Los Angeles' Eric Dickerson gained 132 yards on 25 carries.

L.A. Rams	3	3	0	0	— 6
Green Bay	0	14	10	7	— 31

Rams — FG Lansford 21
GB — Ivery 1 run (Del Greco kick)
Rams — FG Lansford 50
GB — Ivery 1 run (Del Greco kick)
GB — FG Del Greco 21
GB — Ivery 2 run (Del Greco kick)
GB — T. Lewis 99 interception return (Del Greco kick)

San Diego 34, Miami 28—At San Diego Jack Murphy Stadium, attendance 53,041. Buford McGee's 25-yard touchdown run 3:17 into overtime helped San Diego snap Miami's 16-game regular-season win streak. The Dolphins led 21-14 at halftime, but Dan Fouts threw two of his four scoring passes in the fourth quarter to send the game into overtime. Fouts threw for 380 yards and set club records with 37 completions and 56 attempts. He completed touchdown passes to Charlie Joiner (19 yards) and Eric Sievers (3), the latter with just 51 seconds remaining. Sievers' touchdown climaxed a 91-yard, 19-play drive that consumed 10 minutes of the final period. Sievers caught a personal-high 12 passes for 119 yards. Dan Marino (28 of 41 for 338 yards) moved Miami within field-goal range in the closing seconds, but Uwe von Schamann's 44-yard attempt sailed wide left.

Miami	0	21	7	0	0	— 28
San Diego	7	7	0	14	6	— 34

SD — Sievers 3 pass from Fouts (Benirschke kick)
Mia — Clayton 12 pass from Marino (von Schamann kick)
Mia — P. Johnson 1 run (von Schamann kick)
SD — Joiner 4 pass from Fouts (Benirschke kick)
Mia — Bennett 4 pass from Marino (von Schamann kick)
Mia — P. Johnson 3 run (von Schamann kick)
SD — Joiner 19 pass from Fouts (Benirschke kick)
SD — Sievers 3 pass from Fouts (Benirschke kick)
SD — McGee 25 run (no PAT attempted)

Denver 42, Minnesota 21—At Mile High Stadium, attendance 74,716. John Elway completed 16 of 19 passes for 218 yards and five touchdowns to lead the Broncos to their club-record tenth straight win. Following Gerald Willhite's 13-yard scoring run, Elway threw touchdown passes to Sammy Winder (8 yards), Steve Watson (26), Butch Johnson (19), and Ray Alexander (12) for a 35-7 lead at the half. Elway left the game in the third quarter after completing a 13-yard scoring pass to Watson, who caught five passes for 123 yards. The Denver defense held Minnesota in check with three interceptions, two fumble recoveries, and five sacks.

Minnesota	0	7	0	14	— 21
Denver	21	14	7	0	— 42

Den — Willhite 13 run (Karlis kick)
Den — Winder 8 pass from Elway (Karlis kick)
Den — Watson 26 pass from Elway (Karlis kick)
Minn — Brown 21 pass from Kramer (Stenerud kick)
Den — Johnson 19 pass from Elway (Karlis kick)
Den — Alexander 12 pass from Elway (Karlis kick)
Den — Watson 13 pass from Elway (Karlis kick)
Minn — Brown 1 run (Stenerud kick)
Minn — Rice 9 lateral from Senser after 6 pass from Wilson (Stenerud kick)

New England 50, Indianapolis 17—At Hoosier Dome, attendance 60,009. Tony Eason completed a club-record 29 of 42 passes for 291 yards and four touchdowns as the Patriots easily beat the Colts. Eason hit Derrick Ramsey with three first-half scoring passes from 4, 26, and 23 yards. Tony Franklin's 28-yard field goal three second before halftime put New England on top 26-10. Second-half touchdowns by Stanley Morgan (a 12-yard reception) and Mosi Tatupu (1- and 20-yard runs) gave the Patriots their highest single-game point total since they defeated the Colts 50-21 on November 18, 1979. Art Schlichter passed for 188 yards in his first career start for the Colts.

New England	16	10	7	17	— 50
Indianapolis	0	10	0	7	— 17

NE — Ramsey 4 pass from Eason (Franklin kick)
NE — Safety, R. James tackled Middleton in end zone
NE — Ramsey 26 pass from Eason (Franklin kick)
Ind — Schlichter 13 run (Allegre kick)
NE — Ramsey 23 pass from Eason (Franklin kick)
Ind — FG Allegre 35
NE — FG Franklin 28
NE — Morgan 12 pass from Eason (Franklin kick)
NE — FG Franklin 40
NE — Tatupu 1 run (Franklin kick)
Ind — Henry 13 pass from Schlichter (Allegre kick)
NE — Tatupu 20 run (Franklin kick)

Houston 31, New York Jets 20—At Astrodome, attendance 40,141. Warren Moon completed three touchdown passes to spark the Oilers' comeback victory. Trailing 13-0, Moon helped Houston explode for 31 unanswered points. He threw touchdown passes to Tim Smith (5 and 14 yards) and Herkie Walls (10). Larry Moriarty rushed for over 100 yards for the second straight week (138 yards on 23 carries). His 51-yard touchdown sprint secured the win.

N.Y. Jets	10	3	0	7	— 20
Houston	0	10	14	7	— 31

NYJ — Barber 12 run (Leahy kick)
NYJ — FG Leahy 19
NYJ — FG Leahy 26
Hou — Smith 5 pass from Moon (Cooper kick)
Hou — FG Cooper 44
Hou — Smith 14 pass from Moon (Cooper kick)
Hou — Walls 10 pass from Moon (Cooper kick)
Hou — Moriarty 51 run (Cooper kick)
NYJ — Paige 3 run (Leahy kick)

New York Giants 16, St. Louis 10—At Giants Stadium, attendance 73,428. Ali Haji-Sheikh kicked three field goals and the Giants' defense forced six turnovers to defeat St. Louis 16-10. St. Louis led 7-0 before third-quarter field goals of 34, 39, and 45 yards by Haji-Sheikh gave New

York the lead for good 9-7. Phil Simms connected with Lionel Manuel on an 11-yard touchdown pass with 5:53 left for the Giants' final points. The Cardinals' Ottis Anderson rushed 24 times for 111 yards and caught six passes for 112. Mark Haynes had two of the Giants' four interceptions, while rookie Gary Reasons had an interception and a fumble recovery.

St. Louis	0	7	0	3	—	10
N.Y. Giants	0	0	9	7	—	16

StL — Lomax 1 run (O'Donoghue kick)
NYG — FG Haji-Sheikh 34
NYG — FG Haji-Sheikh 39
NYG — FG Haji-Sheikh 45
NYG — Manuel 11 pass from Simms (Haji-Sheikh kick)
StL — FG O'Donoghue 20

Seattle 26, Cincinnati 6—At Riverfront Stadium, attendance 50,280. Seattle scored 17 points in the first half and never looked back in registering a team-record sixth straight win. Zach Dixon scored twice for Seattle on runs of two and one yards. Steve Largent caught a 12-yard touchdown pass to tie Alfred Jenkins for the fourth-longest consecutive game pass-catching streak in league history, 103 games. Jeff Bryant had two of Seattle's four sacks and tackled Cincinnati quarterback Turk Schonert in the end zone in the fourth quarter for a safety. The Seahawks also intercepted two passes and recovered three fumbles to total 55 takeaways for the season.

Seattle	7	10	0	9	—	26
Cincinnati	0	3	3	0	—	6

Sea — Dixon 2 run (Johnson kick)
Sea — Largent 12 pass from Krieg (Johnson kick)
Cin — FG Breech 30
Sea — FG Johnson 25
Cin — FG Breech 33
Sea — Safety, J. Bryant tackled Schonert in end zone
Sea — Dixon 1 run (Johnson kick)

San Francisco 24, Tampa Bay 17—At Candlestick Park, attendance 57,704. Wendell Tyler rushed for 97 yards to become only the fourth 1,000-yard rusher in San Francisco history (1,008) as the 49ers downed the Buccaneers 24-17. Keena Turner's second-quarter interception set up Roger Craig's two-yard touchdown run. Freddie Solomon scored on a three-yard sweep to give the 49ers a 14-10 halftime lead. Tyler's one-yard touchdown run preceded Ray Wersching's 39-yard field goal, which finished the scoring. Fred Dean, appearing in his first game of the season, sacked Steve DeBerg in the closing minutes to end the Buccaneers' final scoring threat.

Tampa Bay	0	10	0	7	—	17
San Francisco	0	14	7	3	—	24

SF — Craig 2 run (Wersching kick)
TB — FG Ariri 27
SF — Solomon 3 run (Wersching kick)
TB — Giles 9 pass from DeBerg (Ariri kick)
SF — Tyler 1 run (Wersching kick)
TB — Carter 9 pass from DeBerg (Ariri kick)
SF — FG Wersching 39

Philadelphia 16, Washington 10—At Veterans Stadium, attendance 63,117. Two rookies, Andre Waters and Paul McFadden, helped account for all the Eagles' points in a 16-10 victory. McFadden kicked three field goals (43, 34, and 41 yards) and Waters returned a kickoff 89 yards for the deciding touchdown with 5:08 left in the third quarter to down the Redskins. Philadelphia's defense forced three interceptions and recovered three fumbles. John Riggins rushed for 92 yards (on 26 carries) to become the oldest NFL player, at 35 years four months, to gain 1,000 yards rushing (1,046) in a season.

Washington	0	7	3	0	—	10
Philadelphia	3	3	10	0	—	16

Phil — FG McFadden 43
Wash — Didier 3 pass from Theismann (Moseley kick)
Phil — FG McFadden 34
Phil — FG McFadden 41
Wash — FG Moseley 33
Phil — Waters 89 kickoff return (McFadden kick)

MONDAY, NOVEMBER 19

New Orleans 27, Pittsburgh 24—At Louisiana Superdome, attendance 66,005. Fourth-quarter touchdowns by Junior Miller and Dennis Winston led the Saints to their first-ever Monday night win in eight appearances. Richard Todd fired his second scoring pass, a 21-yarder to Miller, and Winston returned an interception 47 yards for a touchdown 1:34 later, to give New Orleans a 27-17 lead with 6:24 remaining. Louis Lipps closed the Saints' lead to 27-24 with 1:17 left when he caught a 25-yard touchdown for the Steelers. His 76-yard punt return for a score was the team's first since 1974. John Stallworth's fifty-second career touchdown catch, a 14-yarder, broke Lynn Swann's club record of 51. Bruce Clark had two fumble recoveries, one interception, and one sack for New Orleans.

Pittsburgh	0	14	0	10	—	24
New Orleans	3	10	0	14	—	27

NO — FG Andersen 27
Pitt — Lipps 76 punt return (Anderson kick)
Pitt — Stallworth 14 pass from Malone (Anderson kick)
NO — FG Andersen 32
NO — Hardy 28 pass from Todd (Andersen kick)
Pitt — FG Anderson 21
NO — Miller 21 pass from Todd (Andersen kick)
NO — Winston 47 interception return (Andersen kick)
Pitt — Lipps 25 pass from Campbell (Anderson kick)

THIRTEENTH WEEK SUMMARY

With three weeks remaining in the season, only three teams had division titles clinched, and 18 were still in contention for the playoffs. Miami wrapped up the AFC East when Dallas defeated New England 20-17 on Thanksgiving Day, but the Dolphins beat the Jets 28-17 on Sunday just to make sure. The Cowboys win insured them of their twentieth winning season and a share of the NFC East lead. The Giants also retained a piece of the NFC East top spot but it wasn't easy. New York trailed Kansas City 27-14 before Phil Simms completed two touchdown passes in the final eight minutes as the Giants edged the Chiefs 28-27. The Redskins joined the Cowboys and Giants in first place with a 41-14 win over the Bills as Joe Theismann became the team's all-time passing yardage leader. The Bears secured the NFC Central title, their first championship of any kind since 1963, with a 34-3 trouncing of the Vikings. Chicago's defense limited Minnesota to 161 total yards, while Walter Payton scampered for 117. San Francisco claimed the NFC West crown by downing New Orleans 35-3. The Cardinals and Rams provided thrilling finishes. Neil O'Donoghue's 44-yard field goal with eight seconds left gave St. Louis a 17-16 triumph over Philadelphia. Los Angeles' Eric Dickerson ran for 124 yards and two touchdowns in the fourth quarter in Tampa Bay to rally the Rams from a 26-17 deficit to a 34-33 victory. Gary Jeter's blocked extra point in the first quarter proved to be the difference. Mark Malone's four touchdown passes helped Pittsburgh score its most points in 16 years under Chuck Noll in a 52-24 blitzing of San Diego. Charlie Joiner of the Chargers caught six passes to become the NFL's all-time leading receiver with 651 receptions. The Bengals kept their slim playoff hopes alive with a 35-14 victory over the Falcons. The Browns, losers in four previous home dates, defeated the Oilers 27-10. Seattle's 27-24 victory over Denver gave the Seahawks a share of the lead in the AFC West. Dave Krieg completed 30 of 44 passes for 406 yards, including an 80-yard touchdown pass to Daryl Turner on the game's first play. The loss snapped the Broncos' club-record 10-game winning streak. Detroit gained 518 total yards and controlled the ball for nearly three quarters in its 31-28 win over the Packers. The Colts fell to the Raiders 21-7.

THURSDAY, NOVEMBER 22

Detroit 31, Green Bay 28—At Pontiac Silverdome, attendance 63,698. The Lions, behind the passing of Gary Danielson, overcame a 14-0 deficit and defeated the Packers 31-28. The victory snapped a two-game Detroit losing streak. Danielson completed 24 of 33 passes for 305 yards. He threw touchdown passes of 10 and 21 yards to David Lewis and 21 yards to Jeff Chadwick. Green Bay led 21-17 at halftime, but Bobby Watkins' interception set up James Jones' go-ahead one-yard touchdown run with 13:52 left. Detroit controlled the ball for 44:47 minutes and totalled 518 yards on offense to end Green Bay's four-game unbeaten string.

Green Bay	14	7	0	7	—	28
Detroit	0	17	7	7	—	31

GB — Ellis 40 run (Del Greco kick)
GB — Coffman 44 pass from Dickey (Del Greco kick)
Det — Lewis 10 pass from Danielson (Murrary kick)
GB — Ivery 7 pass from Dickey (Del Greco kick)
Det — Lewis 21 pass from Danielson (Murray kick)
Det — FG Murray 32
Det — J. Jones 1 run (Murray kick)
Det — Chadwick 21 pass from Danielson (Murray kick)
GB — Epps 4 pass from Wright (Del Greco kick)

Dallas 20, New England 17—At Texas Stadium, attendance 55,341. Rafael Septien's 23-yard field goal with four seconds left insured the Cowboys of their twentieth consecutive winning season. Dallas got out to a 17-3 lead on Michael Downs' 27-yard interception return for a score, Tony Hill's (eight receptions for 125 yards) nine-yard touchdown catch, and Septien's 28-yard field goal. New England scored two fourth-quarter touchdowns on a one-yard pass from Tony Eason to Derrick Ramsey and a one-yard run by Eason to tie the score 17-17 with 1:58 remaining. Danny White, returning from a two-week layoff, drove Dallas 55 yards in 10 plays to set up the decisive kick. The Cowboys registered 10 sacks, including three by Randy White and two by Bill Bates. Craig James gained 112 yards on 19 carries for New England.

New England	3	0	0	14	—	17
Dallas	7	3	7	3	—	20

Dall — Downs 27 interception return (Septien kick)
NE — FG Franklin 29
Dall — FG Septien 28
Dall — Hill 9 pass from White (Septien kick)
NE — Ramsey 1 pass from Eason (Franklin kick)
NE — Eason 1 run (Franklin kick)
Dall — FG Septien 23

SUNDAY, NOVEMBER 25

Cincinnati 35, Atlanta 14—At Riverfront Stadium, attendance 44,678. The Bengals opened a 28-0 lead en route to a 35-14 win over the Falcons. Turk Schonert, who completed 20 of 23 passes for 288 yards, hit Cris Collinsworth (six catches for 134 yards) on a 57-yard touchdown bomb on the fourth play of the game to ignite the scoring spree. Larry Kinnebrew scored on a one-yard run and Robert Jackson returned an interception 28 yards for another score just 24 seconds later to give Cincinnati a 21-0 halftime lead. Rodney Holman's fumble recovery set up Charles Alexander's one-yard run. Collinsworth added a 20-yard touchdown catch late in the game to finish the Bengals' scoring.

Atlanta	0	0	14	0	—	14
Cincinnati	14	7	7	7	—	35

Cin — Collinsworth 57 pass from Schonert (Breech kick)
Cin — Kinnebrew 1 run (Breech kick)
Cin — Jackson 28 interception return (Breech kick)
Cin — Alexander 1 run (Breech kick)
Atl — Riggs 6 run (Luckhurst kick)
Atl — Riggs 2 run (Luckhurst kick)
Cin — Collinsworth 20 pass from Schonert (Breech kick)

Washington 41, Buffalo 14—At Robert F. Kennedy Stadium, attendance 51,513. Joe Theismann threw for two touchdowns to lead the Redskins over the Bills. Washington scored on its first four possessions. Theismann completed scoring passes of 11 yards to Art Monk and 18 yards to Charlie Brown, Mark Moseley kicked a 38-yard field goal, and John Riggins scored on a two-yard run. Theismann completed 26 of 33 passes for 311 yards to raise his career yardage total to 22,706, breaking Sonny Jurgensen's club mark of 22,585. Art Monk caught a personal-best 11 passes for 104 yards to total a club-record 82 catches for the year. The Washington offense generated 421 yards total offense. The Redskins' defense limited the Bills to 85 yards rushing and 86 net passing yards and had seven sacks.

Buffalo	0	7	7	0	—	14
Washington	17	10	7	7	—	41

Wash — Monk 11 pass from Theismann (Moseley kick)
Wash — FG Moseley 38
Wash — Riggins 2 run (Moseley kick)
Wash — Brown 18 pass from Theismann (Moseley kick)
Buff — Franklin 8 pass from Ferguson (Nelson kick)
Wash — FG Moseley 51
Buff — Dennard 36 pass from Ferguson (Nelson kick)
Wash — Dean 11 interception return (Moseley kick)
Wash — Wonsley 3 run (Moseley kick)

Chicago 34, Minnesota 3—At Metrodome, attendance 56,881. Steve Fuller threw a pair of touchdown passes and Walter Payton ran for 117 yards and one score to lead the Bears to their first division title since 1963. Fuller completed a 30-yard scoring pass to Willie Gault in the first quarter and connected with Emery Moorehead on a 13-yarder 24 seconds before halftime. Todd Bell intercepted two passes, returning one 36 yards for a touchdown in the third period. Bob Thomas kicked two field goals (45 and 37 yards) and Payton's two-yard scoring run finished the scoring. Chicago gained 399 total yards while yielding 161 (90 rushing, 71 passing).

Chicago	7	10	17	0	—	34
Minnesota	3	0	0	0	—	3

Minn — FG Stenerud 19
Chi — Gault 30 pass from Fuller (B. Thomas kick)
Chi — FG B. Thomas 45
Chi — Moorehead 13 pass from Fuller (B. Thomas kick)
Chi — FG B. Thomas 37
Chi — Bell 36 interception return (B. Thomas kick)
Chi — Payton 2 run (B. Thomas kick)

Los Angeles Raiders 21, Indianapolis 7—At Memorial Coliseum, attendance 40,289. Marc Wilson passed for two touchdowns and ran for a third as the Raiders downed the Colts. Wilson followed James Davis' fumble recovery with a seven-yard scoring pass to Todd Christensen. Dave Casper caught his first pass of the season, a one-yarder, for a touchdown and a 14-0 halftime lead. Wilson finished an 80-yard, 14-play drive with a 14-yard run to put the game away early in the final period. Marcus Allen carried 18 times for 110 yards. The Raiders' defense limited the Colts to 77 yards rushing, 81 passing, and just four first downs in the first three quarters. Mike Davis and Howie Long each had two of Los Angeles' six sacks.

Indianapolis	0	0	7	0	—	7
L.A. Raiders	7	7	0	7	—	21

Raiders — Christensen 7 pass from Wilson (Bahr kick)
Raiders — Casper 1 pass from Wilson (Bahr kick)
Ind — McMillan 1 run (Allegre kick)
Raiders — Wilson 14 run (Bahr kick)

Cleveland 27, Houston 10—At Cleveland Stadium, attendance 46,077. Cleveland's Paul McDonald completed a career-high three touchdown passes to help snap Houston's two-game win streak. McDonald opened the scoring by hitting Brian Brennan on a 14-yard pass. He then followed Hanford Dixon's second-quarter interception with a 12-yard touchdown pass to Ozzie Newsome (10 receptions for 102 yards) for a 17-7 lead. Brennan's seven-yard scoring catch in the final period finished the scoring. Matt Bahr kicked field goals of 18 and 29 yards, the latter set up by an Al Gross interception.

Houston	7	0	0	3	— 10
Cleveland	7	13	0	7	— 27

Cle —Brennan 14 pass from McDonald (Bahr kick)
Hou —Bostic 25 fumble recovery return (Cooper kick)
Cle —FG Bahr 18
Cle —Newsome 12 pass from McDonald (Bahr kick)
Cle —FG Bahr 29
Hou —FG Cooper 39
Cle —Brennan 7 pass from McDonald (Bahr kick)

New York Giants 28, Kansas City 27—At Giants Stadium, attendance 74,383. Phil Simms rallied the Giants from a 27-14 deficit by throwing two touchdown passes in the final 7:30 to edge the Chiefs 28-27. Simms first hit Bobby Johnson on a 22-yard touchdown pass, and then found Zeke Mowatt for the game-winning points on a three-yard scoring pass with 2:22 to play. Mark Haynes' fumble recovery stopped Kansas City's final threat and sealed the win. Simms directed New York's 471-yard attack and finished with 24 completions in 41 attempts for 343 yards, including seven to Mowatt for 126.

Kansas City	0	17	0	10	— 27
N.Y. Giants	0	7	7	14	— 28

KC —Paige 26 pass from Kenney (Lowery kick)
NYG —Carpenter 1 run (Haji-Sheikh kick)
KC —FG Lowery 41
KC —Scott 8 pass from Kenney (Lowery kick)
NYG —Carpenter 1 run (Haji-Sheikh kick)
KC —FG Lowery 52
KC —Carson 34 pass from Kenney (Lowery kick)
NYG —Johnson 22 pass from Simms (Haji-Sheikh kick)
NYG —Mowatt 3 pass from Simms (Haji-Sheikh kick)

Los Angeles Rams 34, Tampa Bay 33—At Tampa Stadium, attendance 42,242. Eric Dickerson ran for 191 yards and three touchdowns and helped ignite the Rams' 17-point fourth-quarter rally, en route to a 34-33 win. Los Angeles trailed 16-10 when Dickerson's second two-yard scoring run put the Rams out in front 17-16. Tampa Bay came back to lead 26-17, before Dickerson scored on a 33-yard run. He also set up Jeff Kemp's one-yard quarterback sneak for a touchdown with a 51-yard run. Mike Lansford's second field goal, a 27-yarder, gave the Rams a 34-26 lead with 5:35 left. LeRoy Irvin's interception in the closing seconds secured the victory. Gary Jeter's blocked extra point in the first quarter proved the difference.

L.A. Rams	0	10	7	17	— 34
Tampa Bay	9	7	10	7	— 33

TB —FG Ariri 26
TB —Wilder 1 run (kick blocked)
Rams —Dickerson 2 run (Lansford kick)
TB —J. Bell 16 pass from DeBerg (Ariri kick)
Rams —FG Lansford 35
Rams —Dickerson 2 run (Lansford kick)
TB —FG Ariri 24
TB —Armstrong 6 pass from DeBerg (Ariri kick)
Rams —Kemp 1 run (Lansford kick)
Rams —Dickerson 33 run (Lansford kick)
Rams —FG Lansford 27
TB —Wilder 1 run (Ariri kick)

St. Louis 17, Philadelphia 16—At Busch Memorial Stadium, attendance 39,858. Neil O'Donoghue's 44-yard field goal with eight seconds remaining lifted the Cardinals over the Eagles. Neil Lomax connected on a pair of touchdown passes to Stump Mitchell (24 yards) and Pat Tilley (19) to give St. Louis a 14-6 lead entering the fourth quarter. But Joe Pisarcik, filling in for Ron Jaworski who suffered a broken leg in the first quarter, rallied Philadelphia to a 16-14 margin with 1:50 to play. Lomax completed an 11-yard pass to Roy Green and scrambled for 14 yards to set up O'Donoghue's winning kick.

Philadelphia	0	6	0	10	— 16
St. Louis	7	0	7	3	— 17

StL —Mitchell 24 pass from Lomax (O'Donoghue kick)
Phil —FG McFadden 31
Phil —FG McFadden 43
StL —Tilley 19 pass from Lomax (O'Donoghue kick)
Phil —Quick 16 pass from Pisarcik (McFadden kick)
Phil —FG McFadden 32
StL —FG O'Donoghue 44

Pittsburgh 52, San Diego 21—At Three Rivers Stadium, attendance 55,856. Mark Malone completed four touchdown passes, including three to John Stallworth, to help the Steelers snap a two-game losing streak. Pittsburgh built a 24-3 lead on Gary Anderson's club-record 55-yard field goal, Malone scoring passes to Louis Lipps (15 yards) and Stallworth (30), and Frank Pollard's first of two two-yard runs. After San Diego closed to within 24-17, Malone (18 of 22 for 253 yards) put the game out of reach with touchdown passes of 5 and 45 yards to Stallworth (seven catches for 116 yards). Malone finished the scoring with a one-yard run. It was the most points scored by the Steelers in 16 years under Chuck Noll. The Chargers' Charlie Joiner caught six passes (70 yards) to raise his career total to 651 and become the NFL's all-time leading receiver, surpassing Hall of Famer Charley Taylor (649).

San Diego	0	10	7	7	— 24
Pittsburgh	3	21	21	7	— 52

Pitt —FG Anderson 55
Pitt —Lipps 15 pass from Malone (Anderson kick)
Pitt —Pollard 2 run (Anderson kick)
SD —FG Benirschke 29
Pitt —Stallworth 30 pass from Malone (Anderson kick)
SD —James 59 punt return (Benirschke kick)
SD —Chandler 63 pass from Luther (Benirschke kick)
Pitt —Pollard 2 run (Anderson kick)
Pitt —Stallworth 5 pass from Malone (Anderson kick)
Pitt —Stallworth 45 pass from Malone (Anderson kick)
Pitt —Malone 1 run (Anderson kick)
SD —Joiner 25 pass from Luther (Benirschke kick)

San Francisco 35, New Orleans 3—At Louisiana Superdome, attendance 65,177. Joe Montana passed for two scores, Wendell Tyler rushed for over 100 yards, and rookie linebacker Todd Shell led the defense, as the 49ers clinched the NFC West title. San Francisco led 7-3 at halftime, but blew the game open in the third quarter on Montana touchdown passes, just 1:44 apart, to Earl Cooper (19 yards) and Freddie Solomon (28) for a 21-3 edge. Shell, who had two of the 49ers' eight sacks, scored on a 53-yard interception return. Bill Ring added a one-yard run to complete the scoring. Tyler gained 117 yards on 15 carries. The San Francisco offense outgained New Orleans 407 yards to 201.

San Francisco	0	7	14	14	— 35
New Orleans	0	3	0	0	— 3

SF —Craig 1 run (Wersching kick)
NO—FG Andersen 27
SF —Cooper 19 pass from Montana (Wersching kick)
SF —Solomon 28 pass from Montana (Wersching kick)
SF —Shell 53 interception return (Wersching kick)
SF —Ring 1 run (Wersching kick)

Seattle 27, Denver 24—At Mile High Stadium, attendance 74,922. Dave Krieg completed 30 of 44 passes for 406 yards and three touchdowns, and Steve Largent gained 191 yards on 12 receptions, to lead the Seahawks to a 27-24 victory and a share of the lead in the AFC West. Krieg connected with rookie Daryl Turner on an 80-yard bomb on the game's first play. He later added a six-yarder to David Hughes in the third quarter and a three-yarder to Largent in the final period to break a 17-17 tie. The Broncos' final chance to extend their 10-game win streak ended when Rich Karlis' 25-yard field goal attempt with 39 seconds left hit the right upright and bounced away.

Seattle	7	3	7	10	— 27
Denver	3	7	7	7	— 24

Sea—Turner 80 pass from Krieg (Johnson kick)
Den—FG Karlis 27
Sea—FG Johnson 33
Den—Johnson 19 pass from Elway (Karlis kick)
Sea—Hughes 6 pass from Krieg (Johnson kick)
Den—Lang 2 run (Karlis kick)
Sea—Largent 3 pass from Krieg (Johnson kick)
Sea—FG Johnson 28
Den—Lang 9 pass from Elway (Karlis kick)

MONDAY, NOVEMBER 26

Miami 28, New York Jets 17—At Orange Bowl, attendance 74,884. Dan Marino completed four touchdown passes to tie the NFL single-season record for scoring passes and lead the Dolphins over the Jets. New York took an early 7-0 lead before Marino (19 of 31 for 192 yards) countered with touchdown completions to Mark Clayton (five yards) and Bruce Hardy (one) for a 14-10 Miami lead. Third-quarter scoring receptions by Dan Johnson (7 yards) and Hardy (12) gave Marino 36 for the season, tying the NFL record held by Y. A. Tittle and George Blanda. The Dolphins' win overshadowed the record-breaking performance of Freeman McNeil, who surpassed the Jets' single-season rushing record of 1,005 (by John Riggins), by running for 116 yards to total 1,028.

N.Y. Jets	7	3	7	0	— 17
Miami	0	14	14	0	— 28

NYJ—McNeil 28 pass from O'Brien (Leahy kick)
Mia —Clayton 5 pass from Marino (von Schamann kick)
NYJ—FG Leahy 30
Mia —Hardy 1 pass from Marino (von Schamann kick)
Mia —D. Johnson 7 pass from Marino (von Schamann kick)
NYJ—Paige 1 run (Leahy kick)
Mia —Hardy 12 pass from Marino (von Schamann kick)

FOURTEENTH WEEK SUMMARY

A pair of overtime decisions helped create a serious title race in the AFC Central Division. Cincinnati came back to tie Cleveland 17-17 on tackle-eligible Anthony Muñoz's one-yard touchdown catch. The victory moved the Bengals to within one game of division-leading Pittsburgh when Jim Breech's 35-yard field goal (4:34 into overtime) was good. The Steelers suffered the uncommon fate of losing in overtime. Joe Cooper's 30-yard field goal with 5:53 elapsed in overtime, lifted the Oilers to a 23-20 win. It was the one-hundredth overtime game in regular-season play since the rule was adopted in 1974, and the Steelers' first loss in seven contests. In the AFC West, Seattle got some help from Kansas City and took over sole possession of first place. Dave Krieg completed a club-record five touchdown passes to lead the Seahawks to a 38-17 win over the Lions. The Broncos fell a game behind Seattle, when the Chiefs' Nick Lowery kicked three fourth-quarter field goals to give Kansas City a 16-13 triumph. The win snapped the Chiefs' four-game losing streak. Seattle, winners of a team-record eight in a row, clinched a playoff berth when St. Louis defeated New England 33-10. The Cardinals' victory tied St. Louis with the Cowboys, Giants, and Redskins for first place in the NFC East. Dallas committed six turnovers, but its defense registered seven sacks and held Philadelphia to 173 yards en route to a 26-10 win. The Giants won the Battle of the Meadowlands by downing the Jets 20-10, while the Redskins opened a 31-0 lead and hung on to defeat the Vikings 31-17. San Francisco clinched the home-field advantage throughout the playoffs with its 35-17 victory over Atlanta. The 49ers' defense created six turnovers to help San Francisco over the Falcons. Dan Marino threw for 470 yards and four touchdowns but it wasn't enough as the Raiders defeated Miami 45-34. Los Angeles' Mike Haynes returned an interception 97 yards for a score to lead the Raiders. Eric Dickerson gained 149 yards to lead the Rams over the Saints 34-21. Lynn Dickey rallied the Packers from a 14-0 deficit to a 27-14 victory over the Buccaneers. San Diego surprised Chicago 20-7 on Monday night as Bobby Duckworth scored on an 88-yard touchdown pass. Fourteen teams remained in contention for Super Bowl XIX.

THURSDAY, NOVEMBER 29

Washington 31, Minnesota 17—At Metrodome, attendance 55,017. Joe Theismann completed a 68-yard touchdown pass to Calvin Muhammad on the first play of the game and the Redskins never looked back in downing the Vikings. Washington cruised to a 31-0 halftime lead on Clint Didier's four-yard touchdown reception, Joe Jacoby's fumble recovery in the end zone, Darryl Grant's 22-yard fumble return for a score, and Mark Moseley's 30-yard field goal. Theismann completed 19 of 24 passes for 223 yards, including 13 in a row in the second half. Muhammad caught five passes for 115 yards. Minnesota's Leo Lewis had seven receptions for 130 yards and two scores.

Washington	17	14	0	0	— 31
Minnesota	0	0	10	7	— 17

Wash—Muhammad 68 pass from Theismann (Moseley kick)
Wash—FG Moseley 30
Wash—Didier 4 pass from Theismann (Moseley kick)
Wash—Jacoby fumble recovery in end zone (Moseley kick)
Wash—Grant 22 fumble recovery return (Moseley kick)
Minn —FG Stenerud 31
Minn —Lewis 14 pass from Manning (Stenerud kick)
Minn —Lewis 8 pass from Manning (Stenerud kick)

SUNDAY, DECEMBER 2

Cincinnati 20, Cleveland 17—At Cleveland Stadium, attendance 51,774. Jim Breech connected on a 35-yard field goal 4:34 into overtime to lift the Bengals over the Browns. Cincinnati trailed 17-7 midway through the third quarter, but a 22-yard field goal by Breech and a one-yard touchdown pass from Boomer Esiason to tackle-eligible Anthony Muñoz with one second left in regulation, sent the game into overtime. John Simmons recovered a blocked punt to set up Breech's first field goal and his 30-yard punt return set up Breech's game winner.

Cincinnati	7	0	10	0	3	— 20
Cleveland	0	10	0	7	0	— 17

Cin—Jennings 15 pass from Schonert (Breech kick)
Cle—FG Bahr 24
Cle—Brennan 21 pass from McDonald (Bahr kick)
Cle—Pruitt 1 run (Bahr kick)
Cin—FG Breech 22
Cin—Muñoz 1 pass from Esiason (Breech kick)
Cin—FG Breech 35

Buffalo 21, Indianapolis 15—At Rich Stadium, attendance 20,693. The Bills scored on three consecutive first-quarter possessions and hung on to defeat the Colts. Fred Smerlas started the first-period explosion with a fumble recovery on the Indianapolis 35-yard line that led to Greg Bell's seven-yard touchdown run. Joe Dufek, replacing Joe Ferguson, then completed scoring passes on Buffalo's next two drives. Dufek capped an 89-yard march with an 18-yard completion to Tony Hunter and combined with Byron Franklin on a 64-yard bomb to give the Bills a 21-9 halftime lead.

Indianapolis	0	9	3	3	— 15
Buffalo	21	0	0	0	— 21

Buff—Bell 7 run (Nelson kick)
Buff—Hunter 18 pass from Dufek (Nelson kick)
Buff—Franklin 64 pass from Dufek (Nelson kick)
Ind —Safety, Wilson tackled in end zone
Ind —Middleton 14 pass from Schlichter (Allegre kick)
Ind —FG Allegre 28
Ind —FG Allegre 21

Dallas 26, Philadelphia 10—At Veterans Stadium, attendance 66,322. Dennis Thurman's 38-yard interception return for a touchdown 6:46 into the game, gave Dallas a lead it never relinquished in defeating Philadelphia 26-10. Danny White connected with Ron Springs on a 57-yard touchdown pass and 13 seconds later John Dutton tackled

Joe Pisarcik in the end zone for a safety and 16-3 Cowboys lead. Timmy Newsome ran eight yards for a touchdown and Michael Downs' interception set up Rafael Septien's 32-yard field goal to close out the Cowboys' scoring. Dallas won the game despite six turnovers (five interceptions, one fumble). The defense held Philadelphia to 173 total yards, recorded seven sacks, and had two fumble recoveries.

Dallas	7	0	16	3	—	26
Philadelphia	0	3	0	7	—	10

Dall—Thurman 38 interception return (Septien kick)
Phil—FG McFadden 23
Dall—Springs 57 pass from D. White (Septien kick)
Dall—Safety, Dutton tackled Pisarcik in end zone
Dall—Newsome 8 run (Septien kick)
Phil—Kab 2 pass from Pisarcik (McFadden kick)
Dall—FG Septein 32

Kansas City 16, Denver 13—At Arrowhead Stadium, attendance 38,494. Nick Lowery kicked three fourth-quarter field goals, including a 42-yarder with 1:56 remaining, to give the Chiefs a 16-13 comeback win. Denver led 10-0 before Bill Kenney concluded an 86-yard drive with a 24-yard scoring pass to Carlos Carson (seven catches for 126 yards). Carson's touchdown cut the margin to 10-7 eight seconds before halftime. Lowery field goals of 46 and 28 yards preceded his game winner. The victory snapped Kansas City's four-game losing streak. Rich Karlis' last-second field-goal attempt from 42 yards, hit an upright and bounced back for the second week in a row.

Denver	7	3	3	0	—	13
Kansas City	0	7	0	9	—	16

Den —Watson 48 pass from Elway (Karlis kick)
Den —FG Karlis 22
KC —Carson 24 pass from Kenney (Lowery kick)
Den —FG Karlis 37
KC —FG Lowery 46
KC —FG Lowery 28
KC —FG Lowery 42

Seattle 38, Detroit 17—At Kingdome, attendance 62,441. Dave Krieg completed a club-record five touchdown passes to beat Detroit and move Seattle into sole possession of first place in the AFC West. In the first half, Krieg connected with Steve Largent (eight receptions for 104 yards) for touchdowns of 3 and 13 yards. His four-yard pass to Daryl Turner, 36 seconds before halftime, gave the Seahawks the lead for good 21-17. Turner also caught a 51-yard bomb in the fourth quarter. Mike Tice's five-yard touchdown catch completed Seattle's 17-point explosion in the final period. Krieg finished with 27 completions in 38 attempts for 294 yards. The Seahawks notched their club-record eighth win in a row and second consecutive playoff berth.

Detroit	3	14	0	0	—	17
Seattle	7	14	0	17	—	38

Sea —Largent 3 pass from Krieg (Johnson kick)
Det —FG Murray 45
Det —Jenkins 25 run (Murray kick)
Sea —Largent 13 pass from Krieg (Johnson kick)
Det —J. Jones 15 pass from Danielson (Murray kick)
Sea —Turner 4 pass from Krieg (Johnson kick)
Sea —Turner 51 pass from Krieg (Johnson kick)
Sea —FG Johnson 36
Sea —Tice 5 pass from Krieg (Johnson kick)

Los Angeles Raiders 45, Miami 34—At Orange Bowl, attendance 71,222. Marcus Allen rushed for 155 yards (20 carries) and three touchdowns and Mike Haynes had a team-record 97-yard interception return for a score to lead the Raiders over the Dolphins. Los Angeles opened a 24-13 lead on Haynes' touchdown, Allen's 11-yard run, and Marc Wilson's seven-yard scoring pass to Dave Casper. Miami overtook the Raiders 27-24 in the third quarter on a pair of Dan Marino touchdown passes to Mark Clayton (64 and 11 yards). Los Angeles went ahead for good on Dokie Williams' 75-yard touchdown catch and Allen scoring runs of 6 and 52 yards, the latter with 1:43 left to clinch the win. Marino set club records for completions (35), attempts (57), and yards (470). His four touchdown passes gave him an NFL-record 40 for the season. Haynes also had a 54-yard interception return to total a team-record 151 interception return yards.

L.A. Raiders	7	10	7	21	—	45
Miami	7	6	14	7	—	34

Raiders —Haynes 97 interception return (Bahr kick)
Mia —Cefalo 4 pass from Marino (von Schamann kick)
Mia —Nathan 6 run (kick blocked)
Raiders —Allen 11 run (Bahr kick)
Raiders —FG Bahr 44
Raiders —Casper 7 pass from Wilson (Bahr kick)
Mia —Clayton 64 pass from Marino (von Schamann kick)
Mia —Clayton 11 pass from Marino (von Schamann kick)
Raiders —Williams 75 pass from Wilson (Bahr kick)
Raiders —Allen 6 run (Bahr kick)
Mia —Duper 9 pass from Marino (von Schamann kick)
Raiders —Allen 52 run (Bahr kick)

Los Angeles Rams 34, New Orleans 21—At Anaheim Stadium, attendance 49,348. Eric Dickerson carried 33 times for 149 yards and a touchdown and Henry Ellard caught two scoring passes to lead the Rams to victory. Los Angeles built a 24-0 second-quarter lead on LeRoy Irvin's 51-yard interception return, Dickerson's seven-yard run, Ellard's 16-yard touchdown reception, and Mike Lansford's 25-yard field goal. The Saints closed the score to 27-21 on three touchdown passes by Dave Wilson, but Jeff Kemp's 34-yard scoring pass to Ellard secured the win. The Rams' defense limited the Saints to 224 total yards and registered four interceptions, one fumble recovery, and five sacks, including two-and-a-half by Reggie Doss.

New Orleans	0	7	0	14	—	21
L.A. Rams	14	10	3	7	—	34

Rams —Irvin 51 interception return (Lansford kick)
Rams —Dickerson 7 run (Lansford kick)
Rams —Ellard 16 pass from Kemp (Lansford kick)
Rams —FG Lansford 25
NO —Scott 14 pass from Wilson (Andersen kick)
Rams —FG Lansford 30
NO —Young 3 pass from Wilson (Andersen kick)
NO —Goodlow 8 pass from Wilson (Andersen kick)
Rams —Ellard 34 pass from Kemp (Lansford kick)

New York Giants 20, New York Jets 10—At Giants Stadium, attendance 74,975. The Giants compiled a season-high 169 yards rushing and Ali Haji-Sheikh kicked two field goals from 48 and 30 yards to defeat the Jets 20-10. Rob Carpenter's one-yard touchdown run ended an 80-yard drive and Joe Morris (17 carries, 83 yards) scored from eight yards out to give the Giants a 17-0 lead late in the third quarter. Mark Haynes' interception at the goal line stopped the Jets' final scoring threat with about four minutes to play. Ken O'Brien completed 28 of 41 passes for 351 yards for the Jets, including 11 to Mickey Shuler for 127 yards.

N.Y. Giants	0	10	7	3	—	20
N.Y. Jets	0	0	3	7	—	10

NYG —Carpenter 1 run (Haji-Sheikh kick)
NYG —FG Haji-Sheikh 48
NYG —Morris 8 run (Haji-Sheikh kick)
NYJ —FG Leahy 43
NYG —FG Haji-Sheikh 30
NYJ —Jones 32 pass from O'Brien (Leahy kick)

Houston 23, Pittsburgh 20—At Astrodome, attendance 39,781. Joe Cooper kicked a 30-yard field goal 5:53 into overtime, to give the Oilers a 23-20 win and hand the Steelers their first-ever loss in overtime play. Warren Moon, who completed 27 of 45 passes for 303 yards, helped Houston to a 13-3 halftime lead with a five-yard pass to Chris Dressel. Stanley Edwards' five-yard run put the Oilers in front by a touchdown again after Pittsburgh had tied the score 13-13 on Mark Malone's five-yard scoring pass to Weegie Thompson. Malone's seven-yard touchdown pass to Louis Lipps in the fourth quarter sent the game into overtime. Houston won the toss to start overtime and drove 63 yards to set up Cooper's winning kick. Houston's John James punted seven times to total 1,078 career punts, breaking Jerrel Wilson's NFL record of 1,072. The Oilers outgained the Steelers 424 total yards to 272.

Pittsburgh	3	0	10	7	0	—	20
Houston	3	10	0	7	3	—	23

Pitt —FG Anderson 32
Hou —FG Cooper 19
Hou —FG Cooper 38
Hou —Dressel 5 pass from Moon (Cooper kick)
Pitt —Thompson 5 pass from Malone (Anderson kick)
Pitt —FG Anderson 24
Hou —Edwards 5 run (Cooper kick)
Pitt —Lipps 7 pass from Malone (Anderson kick)
Hou —FG Cooper 30

St. Louis 33, New England 10—At Sullivan Stadium, attendance 53,558. The Cardinals converted two turnovers into 10 first-half points to help them roll over the Patriots 33-10. Neil Lomax drove St. Louis 72 yards on the game's opening drive and completed a one-yard touchdown pass to Doug Marsh. Thomas Howard returned a fumble 29 yards for a score on New England's first possession. Benny Perrin's fumble recovery led to Neil O'Donoghue's 36-yard field goal and 17-3 second-quarter lead. Ottis Anderson rushed for 136 yards on 30 carries and his two-yard touchdown run gave the Cardinals a commanding 27-3 halftime lead. Anderson crossed the 1,000-yard mark for the fifth time in his career (1,059).

St. Louis	14	13	0	6	—	33
New England	3	0	7	0	—	10

StL —Marsh 1 pass from Lomax (O'Donoghue kick)
StL —Howard 29 fumble recovery return (O'Donoghue kick)
NE —FG Franklin 19
StL —FG O'Donoghue 36
StL —FG O'Donoghue 33
StL —Anderson 2 run (O'Donoghue kick)
NE —Dawson 11 pass from Eason (Franklin kick)
StL —Mitchell 3 run (kick failed)

San Francisco 35, Atlanta 17—At Atlanta-Fulton County Stadium, attendance 29,644. The 49ers' defense created six turnovers (three interceptions and three fumble recoveries) and converted two into touchdowns to clinch the home-field advantage throughout the playoffs. Joe Montana threw a pair of first-half touchdowns to Freddie Solomon (64 yards) and Dwight Clark (6). Gary Johnson returned a fumble 34 yards for his third career score to give the 49ers a 21-10 halftime lead. Dana McLemore returned an interception 54 yards for a touchdown in the third quarter and Keena Turner's interception set up Roger Craig's five-yard fourth-quarter scoring run. The Falcons outgained the 49ers 414 total yards to 290, as Gerald Riggs rushed for 133 yards and Alfred Jackson caught 11 passes for a club-record 193 yards.

San Francisco	7	14	7	7	—	35
Atlanta	3	7	7	0	—	17

Atl —FG Luckhurst 32
SF —Solomon 64 pass from Montana (Wersching kick)
SF —D. Clark 6 pass from Montana (Wersching kick)
Atl —Riggs 2 run (Luckhurst kick)
SF —Johnson 34 fumble recovery return (Wersching kick)
Atl —Jackson 48 pass from Moroski (Luckhurst kick)
SF —McLemore 54 interception return (Wersching kick)
SF —Craig 5 run (Wersching kick)

Green Bay 27, Tampa Bay 14—At Lambeau Field, attendance 46,800. Lynn Dickey ran for one touchdown and passed for another to rally the Packers over the Buccaneers. Tampa Bay built a 14-0 lead before Eddie Lee Ivery's four-yard touchdown run and Dickey's one-yard plunge tied the game. Four minutes later, Dickey threw a 10-yard touchdown pass to Ray Crouse for the game-winning score. Ivery's two-yard scoring run with 3:11 remaining secured the win.

Tampa Bay	0	7	7	0	—	14
Green Bay	0	0	7	20	—	27

TB —Armstrong 16 pass from Wilder (Ariri kick)
TB —J. Bell 9 pass from DeBerg (Ariri kick)
GB —Ivery 4 run (Del Greco kick)
GB —Dickey 1 run (Del Greco kick)
GB —Crouse 10 pass from Dickey (kick failed)
GB —Ivery 2 run (Del Greco kick)

MONDAY, DECEMBER 3

San Diego 20, Chicago 7—At San Diego Jack Murphy Stadium, attendance 45,470. Bobby Duckworth's 88-yard touchdown reception and Lee Williams' 66-yard interception return for a score lifted the Chargers over the Bears. San Diego led the defensive struggle 6-0 at halftime on a pair of Rolf Benirschke field goals from 48 and 27 yards. Walter Payton's (92 yards on 23 carries) 10-yard run gave Chicago a 7-6 lead entering the fourth quarter. Duckworth (three catches for 179 yards) caught the decisive touchdown from Ed Luther, starting in place of injured Dan Fouts. Williams' interception return added an insurance score with 1:15 remaining. Rusty Lisch quarterbacked the Bears most of the way in relief of injured Steve Fuller, and could not mount a serious scoring drive. The Bears were forced to punt 11 times.

Chicago	0	0	7	0	—	7
San Diego	0	6	0	14	—	20

SD —FG Benirschke 48
SD —FG Benirschke 27
Chi —Payton 10 run (B. Thomas kick)
SD —Duckworth 88 pass from Luther (Benirschke kick)
SD —L. Williams 66 interception return (Benirschke kick)

FIFTEENTH WEEK SUMMARY

As the final week of the season approached, four playoff berths remained unclaimed and 13 teams continued in contention for Super Bowl XIX. Eric Dickerson's record-setting day kept the Rams' wild card playoff hopes alive. Dickerson ran for 215 yards to total 2,007 yards for the season, breaking O.J. Simpson's NFL record of 2,003 yards set in 1973, as Los Angeles defeated Houston 27-16. The Raiders, 24-3 winners over the Lions on Monday night, secured a playoff spot for the third straight year when the Eagles beat the Patriots 27-17 on Sunday. Pittsburgh kept hold of its one-game lead in the AFC Central when Gary Anderson kicked a 34-yard field goal with five seconds left to lift the Steelers over the Browns 23-20. It was Cleveland's fifteenth consecutive loss in Three Rivers Stadium. The AFC Western Division had co-leaders for the second time in three weeks when Kansas City surprised Seattle 34-7 and Denver edged San Diego 16-13. The spoiler Chiefs intercepted six passes to halt the Seahawks' eight-game winning streak. Rich Karlis' 28-yard field goal with just over two minutes to play helped the Broncos gain a share of the top spot in the AFC West. Washington took command in the NFC East by defeating Dallas 30-28. The Redskins trailed the Cowboys 21-6 at halftime before mounting a furious comeback. John Riggins, who carried the ball just three times the previous two games, rushed for 111 yards and scored the decisive one-yard touchdown with 6:34 left. The Cardinals' 31-21 triumph over the Giants created a three-way tie (with Dallas) for second place in the division. Walter Payton ran for 175 yards and played briefly at quarterback, but Rich Campbell's last minute touchdown pass lifted the Packers over the Bears 20-14. Tampa Bay snapped a three-game losing streak by downing Atlanta 23-6, as James Wilder became the seventh NFL player to amass over 2,000 yards from scrimmage in a season. The Jets broke a six-game winless string with a 21-17 win over the Bills. The Bengals 24-21 defeat of the Saints kept Cincinnati's hopes for a playoff berth alive. San Francisco scored on 9 of 11 possessions to total its most points since 1965 in a 51-7 thrashing of Minnesota. Four second-half scoring passes by Dan Marino helped the Dolphins come back from a 17-7 deficit and win 35-17 over the Colts.

SATURDAY, DECEMBER 8

New York Jets 21, Buffalo 17—At Giants Stadium, attendance 45,378. Ken O'Brien's 39-yard touchdown pass to Wesley Walker ignited a second-half comeback as the Jets downed the Bills to break a six-game losing streak. New York trailed 17-7 at halftime before Walker's touchdown with 39 seconds left in the third quarter, cut the margin to three points. Tony Paige ran three yards for the decisive score with 10:47 to play.

Buffalo	7	10	0	0	— 17
N.Y. Jets	7	0	7	7	— 21

Buff —David 36 run with blocked punt (Nelson kick)
NYJ —Minter 6 run (Leahy kick)
Buff —Bell 3 run (Nelson kick)
Buff —FG Nelson 47
NYJ —Walker 39 pass from O'Brien (Leahy kick)
NYJ —Paige 3 run (Leahy kick)

San Francisco 51, Minnesota 7—At Candlestick Park, attendance 56,670. The 49ers scored on 9 of 11 possessions to dominate the Vikings 51-7. Joe Montana, playing only the first half, completed 15 of 21 passes for 246 yards. He threw touchdowns to Dwight Clark (44 yards), Freddie Solomon (3), and Renaldo Nehemiah (59). Wendell Tyler scored on a five-yard run and Ray Wersching's first of three field goals, a 41-yarder, gave San Francisco a 31-7 halftime lead. Derrick Harmon (3-yard run) and Bill Ring (15) added fourth-quarter touchdowns to complete the romp. It was the most points scored by the 49ers since they scored 52 against Chicago on September 19, 1965.

Minnesota	0	7	0	0	— 7
San Francisco	14	17	6	14	— 51

SF —D. Clark 44 pass from Montana (Wersching kick)
SF —Solomon 3 pass from Montana (Wersching kick)
Minn —Nelson 5 run (Stenerud kick)
SF —Tyler 5 run (Wersching kick)
SF —Nehemiah 59 pass from Montana (Wersching kick)
SF —FG Wersching 41
SF —FG Wersching 25
SF —FG Wersching 38
SF —Harmon 3 run (Wersching kick)
SF —Ring 15 run (Wersching kick)

SUNDAY, DECEMBER 9

Tampa Bay 23, Atlanta 6—At Tampa Stadium, attendance 33,808. James Wilder became the seventh NFL player to amass over 2,000 yards from scrimmage in a season and Obed Ariri kicked three field goals to help the Buccaneers snap a three-game losing streak. Wilder gained 125 yards on 28 carries and caught two passes for 22 yards to total 2,066 yards. He also scored on a one-yard run in the third quarter. Ariri was good on field goals from 30 yards (first quarter), 36 (second quarter), and 28 (fourth period). Steve DeBerg's two-yard run, capping a 16-play, 94-yard drive, gave Tampa Bay the lead for good 13-6.

Atlanta	0	6	0	0	— 6
Tampa Bay	3	10	7	3	— 23

TB —FG Ariri 30
TB —DeBerg 2 run (Ariri kick)
Atl —FG Luckhurst 33
Atl —FG Luckhurst 49
TB —FG Ariri 36
TB —Wilder 1 run (Ariri kick)
TB —FG Ariri 28

Cincinnati 24, New Orleans 21—At Louisiana Superdome, attendance 40,855. Ken Anderson, sidelined because of an injury the past three weeks, celebrated his return to action by throwing two touchdown passes in the Bengals' 24-21 win. Entering in the second quarter, Anderson (18 of 26 for 191 yards) completed scoring drives of 78 and 63 yards with passes of 27 yards to James Brooks and 15 yards to Stanford Jennings. The victory overshadowed the play of Saints quarterback Dave Wilson, who completed 20 of 32 passes for 325 yards and three touchdowns, but was sacked six times by Cincinnati's defense.

Cincinnati	0	3	14	7	— 24
New Orleans	0	7	7	7	— 21

Cin —FG Breech 35
NO —Brenner 54 pass from D. Wilson (Andersen kick)
Cin —Brooks 27 pass from Anderson (Breech kick)
Cin —Jennings 15 pass from Anderson (Breech kick)
NO —Brenner 35 pass from D. Wilson (Andersen kick)
Cin —Jennings 1 run (Breech kick)
NO —Goodlow 5 pass from D. Wilson (Andersen kick)

Pittsburgh 23, Cleveland 20—At Three Rivers Stadium, attendance 55,825. Gary Anderson's third field goal of the game, a 34-yarder with five seconds remaining, helped the Steelers over the Browns. Pittsburgh built a 17-6 lead on Mark Malone's 61-yard touchdown bomb to Louis Lipps, Frank Pollard's one-yard run, and Anderson's 40-yard field goal. Cleveland rallied for a 20-20 tie on a Paul McDonald touchdown run with 8:49 to play, but could not escape its fifteenth consecutive loss in Three Rivers Stadium.

Cleveland	3	10	0	7	— 20
Pittsburgh	7	10	3	3	— 23

Cle —FG Bahr 29
Pitt —Lipps 61 pass from Malone (Anderson kick)
Pitt —FG Anderson 40
Cle —FG Bahr 49
Pitt —Pollard 1 run (Anderson kick)
Cle —Feacher 16 pass from McDonald (Bahr kick)
Pitt —FG Anderson 22
Cle —McDonald 3 run (Bahr kick)
Pitt —FG Anderson 34

Green Bay 20, Chicago 14—At Soldier Field, attendance 59,374. Third-string Packers quarterback Rich Campbell threw a 43-yard touchdown pass to Phillip Epps with 34 seconds remaining to defeat the Bears. Campbell replaced injured Green Bay starter Randy Wright late in the first half and threw a three-yard scoring pass to Ed West for a 7-0 halftime margin. Walter Payton's two-yard touchdown pass to Matt Suhey tied the score, but Del Rodgers returned the ensuing kickoff 97 yards to give Green Bay a 13-7 lead. Payton, who took a turn at quarterback, rushed 35 times for 175 yards and scored on a seven-yard run to give the Bears a 14-13 edge. The Packers forced five turnovers, including two interceptions by Tom Flynn, and totalled five sacks, three by Mike Douglass.

Green Bay	0	7	6	7	— 20
Chicago	0	0	7	7	— 14

GB—West 3 pass from Campbell (Del Greco kick)
Chi—Suhey 2 pass from Payton (B. Thomas kick)
GB—Rodgers 97 kickoff return (pass failed)
Chi—Payton 7 run (B. Thomas kick)
GB—Epps 43 pass from Campbell (Del Greco kick)

Los Angeles Rams 27, Houston 16—At Anaheim Stadium, attendance 49,092. Eric Dickerson carried 27 times for 215 yards to total 2,007 yards for the season, breaking O.J. Simpson's NFL record of 2,003 set in 1973. Dickerson's seven-yard touchdown run in the first quarter helped the Rams to a 20-13 halftime lead and his six-yard scoring run in the final period secured the win after the Oilers had closed the gap to 20-16. Jeff Kemp opened the Rams' scoring with a 57-yard touchdown pass to Drew Hill. Mike Lansford converted his first two field-goal attempts, from 35 and 19 yards, for a club-record 13 in a row. Jack Youngblood's team-record 201 consecutive games played came to an end when a back injury sidelined the defensive end.

Houston	3	10	3	0	— 16
L.A. Rams	17	3	0	7	— 27

Rams—Drew Hill 57 pass from Kemp (Lansford kick)
Hou —FG Cooper 21
Rams—Dickerson 7 run (Lansford kick)
Rams—FG Lansford 35
Hou —FG Cooper 42
Hou —Moriarty 4 run (Cooper kick)
Rams—FG Lansford 19
Hou —FG Cooper 18
Rams—Dickerson 6 run (Lansford kick)

Miami 35, Indianapolis 17—At Hoosier Dome, attendance 60,411. Dan Marino brought the Dolphins back from a 17-7 halftime deficit by throwing for four touchdowns in the second half and for over 400 yards for the second week in a row. Marino (29 of 41 for 404 yards) completed second-half scoring passes to Nat Moore (2 yards), Bruce Hardy (2), Jimmy Cefalo (25), and Mark Clayton (7). Clayton, who caught nine passes for 127 yards, raised his season total to 69 receptions, breaking Jim Clancy's club mark of 67 set in 1967.

Miami	7	0	14	14	— 35
Indianapolis	7	10	0	0	— 17

Ind —Butler 5 pass from Pagel (Allegre kick)
Mia—Bennett 2 run (von Schamann kick)
Ind —FG Allegre 52
Ind —McMillan 6 run (Allegre kick)
Mia—Moore 2 pass from Marino (von Schamann kick)
Mia—Hardy 2 pass from Marino (von Schamann kick)
Mia—Cefalo 25 pass from Marino (von Schamann kick)
Mia—Clayton 7 pass from Marino (von Schamann kick)

Philadelphia 27, New England 17—At Veterans Stadium, attendance 41,581. Joe Pisarcik ran for two touchdowns to lead the Eagles to a 27-17 win and knock the Patriots out of playoff contention. Pisarcik scored first- and fourth-quarter touchdowns on runs of one and three yards, respectively. Wilbert Montgomery's (19 carries for 100 yards) 10-yard scoring run gave Philadelphia a 17-10 halftime lead. Paul McFadden, who was good on field goals from 50 and 46 yards and had three extra points, totalled a team season-record kick-scoring mark of 112 points.

New England	10	0	7	0	— 17
Philadelphia	7	10	3	7	— 27

NE —FG Franklin 24
Phil—Pisarcik 1 run (McFadden kick)
NE —Morgan 9 pass from Eason (Franklin kick)
Phil—FG McFadden 50
Phil—Montgomery 10 run (McFadden kick)
Phil—FG McFadden 46
NE —Jones fumble recovery in end zone (Franklin kick)
Phil—Pisarcik 3 run (McFadden kick)

St. Louis 31, New York Giants 21—At Busch Memorial Stadium, attendance 49,973. Neil Lomax became the sixth quarterback in NFL history to pass for over 4,000 yards in a season (4,151) as the Cardinals downed the Giants to remain in playoff contention. Lomax (23 of 33 for 300 yards and three touchdowns) connected on touchdowns to Pat Tilley (4 yards), Stump Mitchell (44), and Roy Green (35), but the stubborn Giants remained tied with the Cardinals after three quarters of play 21-21. Ottis Anderson's 12-yard run with 12:17 left gave St. Louis the lead for good 28-21. Joe Morris gained 107 yards in 16 carries to become the first Giants running back to top the 100-yard rushing mark this season. Thomas Howard had two interceptions for the Cardinals.

N.Y. Giants	7	0	14	0	— 21
St. Louis	0	14	7	10	— 31

NYG—Manuel 5 pass from Simms (Haji-Sheikh kick)
StL —Tilley 4 pass from Lomax (O'Donoghue kick)
StL —Mitchell 44 pass from Lomax (O'Donoghue kick)
NYG—Mowatt 18 pass from Simms (Haji-Sheikh kick)
StL —Green 35 pass from Lomax (O'Donoghue kick)
NYG—Carpenter 1 run (Haji-Sheikh kick)
StL —Anderson 12 run (O'Donoghue kick)
StL —FG O'Donoghue 34

Denver 16, San Diego 13—At Mile High Stadium, attendance 74,867. Rich Karlis' third field goal of the game, a 28-yarder with 2:08 left, helped the Broncos snap a two-game losing streak and move into a tie for first place in the AFC West. Following Karlis field goals of 30 and 50 yards, Denver took a 13-6 lead on Sammy Winder's four-yard touchdown run. The Broncos overcame three turnovers, which led to all of San Diego's points, as the defense held the Chargers on two goal-line stands and allowed only 234 total yards. Rulon Jones had two sacks for the Broncos.

San Diego	6	0	0	7	— 13
Denver	0	6	7	3	— 16

SD —FG Benirschke 42
SD —FG Benirschke 41
Den—FG Karlis 30
Den—FG Karlis 50
Den—Winder 4 run (Karlis kick)
SD —McGee 4 pass from Luther (Benirschke kick)
Den—FG Karlis 28

Kansas City 34, Seattle 7—At Arrowhead Stadium, attendance 34,855. Bill Kenney threw a pair of touchdown passes and the Kansas City defense intercepted six passes as the Chiefs ended the Seahawks' eight-game unbeaten streak. The teams traded touchdowns in the first quarter before Nick Lowery's 29-yard field goal gave Kansas City the lead for good 10-7. Fifty-seven seconds later, Scott Radecic returned an interception 19 yards for a 17-7 edge. Kenney, who completed 18 of 37 passes for 312 yards, threw scoring passes to Henry Marshall (26 yards) and Carlos Carson (25). Lowery's second field goal, a 22-yarder, finished the scoring. Marshall had eight catches for 166 yards.

Seattle	7	0	0	0	— 7
Kansas City	7	17	7	3	— 34

KC —Heard 2 run (Lowery kick)
Sea—Turner 49 pass from Krieg (Johnson kick)
KC —FG Lowery 29
KC —Radecic 19 interception return (Lowery kick)
KC —Marshall 26 pass from Kenney (Lowery kick)
KC —Carson 25 pass from Kenney (Lowery kick)
KC —FG Lowery 22

Washington 30, Dallas 28—At Texas Stadium, attendance 64,286. John Riggins' one-yard touchdown run with 6:34 left capped the Redskins' 30-28 comeback win. The Cowboys opened a 21-6 lead on three Danny White (22 of 42 for 327 yards) touchdown passes. The Redskins countered in the third quarter with 17 unanswered points to lead 23-21 on Darrell Green's 32-yard interception return for a score, Calvin Muhammad's 22-yard touchdown reception, and Mark Moseley's 21-yard field goal. Dallas regained the lead (28-23) 1:26 later as White found Tony Hill on a 43-yard scoring pass. Riggins finished with 111 yards on 24 carries. The Redskins suffered eight sacks and registered five.

Washington	0	6	17	7	— 30
Dallas	7	14	0	7	— 28

Dall —Donley 6 pass from D. White (Septien kick)
Wash—FG Moseley 31
Dall —Cosbie 2 pass from D. White (Septien kick)
Wash—FG Moseley 34
Dall —Renfro 60 pass from D. White (Septien kick)
Wash—Green 32 interception return (Moseley kick)
Wash—Muhammad 22 pass from Theismann (Moseley kick)
Wash—FG Moseley 21
Dall —Hill 43 pass from D. White (Septien kick)
Wash—Riggins 1 run (Moseley kick)

MONDAY, DECEMBER 10

Los Angeles Raiders 24, Detroit 3—At Pontiac Silverdome, attendance 66,710. The Raiders combined the passing of Marc Wilson and Jim Plunkett with stingy defense to down the Lions. Wilson completed 11 of 19 for 194 yards, including a 12-yard touchdown pass to Todd Christensen. Plunkett, making his first appearance since October 7, connected on three of four passes for 102 yards and had a 73-yard scoring bomb to Marcus Allen. Cle Montgomery returned a punt 69 yards for a score in the fourth quarter. Bill Pickel had three-and-a-half of the Raiders' eight quarterback sacks. Los Angeles was assured a playoff berth for the third straight year when New England lost to Philadelphia.

L.A. Raiders	0	7	3	14 —	24
Detroit	0	3	0	0 —	3

Raiders — Christensen 12 pass from Wilson (Bahr kick)
Det — FG Murray 48
Raiders — FG Bahr 37
Raiders — Montgomery 69 punt return (Bahr kick)
Raiders — Allen 73 pass from Plunkett (Bahr kick)

SIXTEENTH WEEK SUMMARY

Going into the NFL's final weekend, four of the five NFC East teams had legitimate postseason opportunities. The elongated weekend (Friday through Monday) came down to the wire with the Redskins and Giants advancing and the Cardinals and Cowboys being left out. Washington won its third consecutive NFC East crown by defeating St. Louis 29-27, despite St. Louis quarterback Neil Lomax's 468-yard, two touchdown performance. The Cardinals' loss opened the playoff door for the Rams for the second year under John Robinson. Los Angeles was a 19-16 loser to the 49ers on Friday night. Dallas lost a 28-21 thriller to Miami on Monday night to eliminate itself from the playoffs for the first time since 1974. Losses by the Cardinals and Cowboys enabled the Giants, 10-3 losers to the Saints on Saturday, to sneak into the playoffs by virtue of a better divisional record versus St. Louis and Dallas. Denver captured the AFC West title for the first time since 1978 with a 31-14 win over Seattle. Pittsburgh claimed the AFC Central crown by defeating the Raiders 13-7. Two other teams came close but narrowly missed making the playoffs. Cincinnati's Ken Anderson threw for three scores in his first start since November 11, and led the Bengals to their eighth win in their last 11 games, 52-21 over the Bills. Green Bay recorded its seventh win in the last eight games 38-14 over Minnesota. Kansas City finished with a three-game win streak defeating San Diego 42-21. The Chargers lost all eight games with AFC West foes. The Falcons ended a nine-game winless string by downing the Eagles 26-10. The Patriots halted a month-long drought with a 16-10 triumph over the Colts. John McKay finished his coaching career in winning style as the Buccaneers easily beat the Jets 41-21. Quarterback Greg Landry, playing in his first NFL game in three years, accounted for two touchdowns to lead the Bears over the Lions 30-13. Earnest Byner's 188 yards rushing helped Cleveland down Houston 27-20. Several NFL records did not survive the season. San Francisco became the first team to win 15 regular-season games. Art Monk, who caught 11 passes for 136 yards in Washington's win over St. Louis, set an NFL mark with 106 catches. Miami's Dan Marino became the first player to pass for over 5,000 yards in a season (5,084), and his 48 touchdown passes was also a league mark. Dolphins receiver Mark Clayton caught a record 18 touchdowns. The Bears' defense, with 12 sacks against the Lions, totalled 72 for the year, the most since the Raiders 67 in 1967. For the second season in a row the AFC-NFC interconference series ended in a 26-26 tie.

FRIDAY, DECEMBER 14

San Francisco 19, Los Angeles Rams 16—At Candlestick Park, attendance 59,743. Joe Montana threw for two touchdowns as the 49ers became the first-ever NFL team to win 15 regular-season games. San Francisco built a 14-3 first-quarter lead on Montana scoring passes of 47 yards to Freddie Solomon and 1-yard to Earl Cooper. After Ray Wersching kicked a 38-yard field goal to open the second period, Los Angeles ran off 13 straight points to cut the margin to 17-16. But Gary Johnson sacked Jeff Kemp in the end zone for a safety with 1:06 left for the 49ers final margin of victory. Eric Dickerson was held to under 100 yards (98) for only the fourth time this season, but the Rams clinched their second straight Wild Card playoff berth under John Robinson when the Redskins defeated the Cardinals on Sunday.

L.A. Rams	3	10	0	3 —	16
San Francisco	14	3	0	2 —	19

Rams — FG Lansford 41
SF — Solomon 47 pass from Montana (Wersching kick)
SF — Cooper 1 pass from Montana (Wersching kick)
SF — FG Wersching 38
Rams — Dickerson 4 run (Lansford kick)
Rams — FG Lansford 28
Rams — FG Lansford 42
SF — Safety, Johnson tackled Kemp in end zone

SATURDAY, DECEMBER 15

Denver 31, Seattle 14—At Kingdome, attendance 64,411. John Elway accounted for two touchdowns and the defense forced two key turnovers to lead the Broncos to their first division title since 1978. Elway's one-yard run and Rich Karlis' 34-yard field goal gave Denver a 10-7 first-half margin it never relinquished. Tony Lilly recovered Seattle's fumble on the second-half kickoff to set up Elway's 14-yard touchdown pass to Jim Wright. Steve Foley's 40-yard interception return for score late in the third quarter put Denver ahead 24-7. Rick Parros' four-yard touchdown run finished the scoring. The Seahawks outgained the Broncos 385 yards to 291 behind the passing of Dave Krieg, who completed 30 of 50 passes for 334 yards and two touchdowns.

Denver	10	0	14	7 —	31
Seattle	0	7	7	0 —	14

Den — Elway 1 run (Karlis kick)
Den — FG Karlis 34
Sea — Doornink 4 pass from Krieg (Johnson kick)
Den — J. Wright 14 pass from Elway (Karlis kick)
Den — Foley 40 interception return (Karlis kick)
Sea — Young 14 pass from Krieg (Johnson kick)
Den — Parros 4 run (Karlis kick)

New Orleans 10, New York Giants 3—At Giants Stadium, attendance 63,739. The Saints scored on their first possession of the game and the defense held the Giants to 189 total yards to lead the victory. Dave Wilson completed a two-yard touchdown pass to Hokie Gajan to conclude a 13-play, 72-yard drive, and Morten Andersen kicked a 37-yard field goal for the Saints' points. New Orleans recorded seven sacks, including two each by Whitney Paul and Frank Warren. Interceptions by Bobby Johnson and Frank Wattelet in the closing minutes halted New York's final scoring threats. Phil Simms passed for 127 yards to become the eighth player in NFL history to top the 4,000-yard mark for a season (4,044). The Giants earned a Wild Card playoff spot when St. Louis and Dallas both lost.

New Orleans	7	0	0	3 —	10
N.Y. Giants	0	3	0	0 —	3

NO — Gajan 2 pass from Wilson (Andersen kick)
NYG — FG Haji-Sheikh 37
NO — FG Andersen 37

SUNDAY, DECEMBER 16

Cincinnati 52, Buffalo 21—At Riverfront Stadium, attendance 55,771. Ken Anderson threw three touchdown passes in his first start since November 11, as the Bengals routed the Bills. Anderson completed 17 of 23 passes for 206 yards and guided Cincinnati to a 28-7 halftime lead behind scoring passes to Cris Collinsworth (12 yards), Rodney Holman (11), and Steve Kreider (11). Larry Kinnebrew (1 yard) and Stanford Jennings (20) added rushing touchdowns for the Bengals. Fourth-quarter interception returns for scores of 43 yards by John Simmons and 57 yards by Jeff Griffin completed Cincinnati's scoring.

Buffalo	7	0	7	7 —	21
Cincinnati	7	21	3	21 —	52

Buff — Bell 5 run (Nelson kick)
Cin — Collinsworth 12 pass from Anderson (Breech kick)
Cin — Kinnebrew 1 run (Breech kick)
Cin — Holman 11 pass from Anderson (Breech kick)
Cin — Kreider 11 pass from Anderson (Breech kick)
Cin — FG Breech 36
Buff — Franklin 16 pass from Dufek (Nelson kick)
Cin — Jennings 20 run (Breech kick)
Cin — Simmons 43 interception return (Breech kick)
Cin — J. Griffin 57 interception return (Breech kick)
Buff — Bell 1 run (Nelson kick)

Chicago 30, Detroit 13—At Pontiac Silverdome, attendance 53,252. Greg Landry, signed as a free agent by the Bears on December 5, passed for one touchdown and ran for another to power Chicago over Detroit. Landry, who was seeing his first NFL action in three years, scored on a one-yard run in the second quarter and connected with Willie Gault on a 55-yard scoring pass in the fourth period. Bob Thomas was successful on all of his three field goal attempts (30, 35, and 42 yards). Calvin Thomas opened the Bears' scoring with a one-yard touchdown run. The Chicago defense registered 12 sacks (100 yards lost) to total an NFL-record 72 for the season.

Chicago	0	14	3	13 —	30
Detroit	3	3	0	7 —	13

Det — FG Murray 52
Chi — C. Thomas 1 run (B. Thomas kick)
Det — FG Murray 45
Chi — Landry 1 run (B. Thomas kick)
Chi — FG B. Thomas 30
Chi — FG B. Thomas 35
Chi — Gault 55 pass from Landry (B. Thomas kick)
Chi — FG B. Thomas 42
Det — Jones 4 pass from Hipple (Murray kick)

Cleveland 27, Houston 20—At Astrodome, attendance 33,676. Rookie Earnest Byner broke loose for 188 yards rushing and two touchdowns to lead the Browns to a 27-20 win over the Oilers. Byner scored on runs of 2 and 15 yards. He also set up Matt Bahr's 29-yard second-quarter field goal with a 54-yard run. Houston tied the score in the third period 17-17, but Johnny Davis' two-yard touchdown run 4:19 into the final period put the Browns ahead to stay. Bahr's 29-yard field goal with 2:43 to play provided insurance. The Oilers' Warren Moon completed 19 of 31 passes for 306 yards.

Cleveland	7	3	7	10 —	27
Houston	0	7	10	3 —	20

Cle — Byner 2 run (Bahr kick)
Cle — FG Bahr 29
Hou — Moriarty 4 run (Cooper kick)
Hou — FG Cooper 33
Cle — Byner 15 run (Bahr kick)
Hou — Moriarty 4 run (Cooper kick)
Cle — Davis 2 run (Bahr kick)
Hou — FG Cooper 26
Cle — FG Bahr 29

New England 16, Indianapolis 10—At Sullivan Stadium, attendance 22,383. Tony Franklin kicked three field goals and Craig James ran for a career-high 138 yards on 30 carries to lead the Patriots to their first win in four weeks. New England opened a 13-0 lead on Tony Eason's three-yard touchdown pass to Lin Dawson and Franklin field goals of 21 and 34 yards. The Colts closed the deficit to 13-10 and moved into position to tie the game, but Julius Adams blocked Raul Allegre's 42-yard field goal attempt with 4:53 remaining. Indianapolis played the game under interim coach Hal Hunter after Frank Kush had resigned earlier in the week.

Indianapolis	0	0	10	0 —	10
New England	3	10	0	3 —	16

NE — FG Franklin 21
NE — Dawson 3 pass from Eason (Franklin kick)
NE — FG Franklin 34
Ind — FG Allegre 25
Ind — Henry 19 pass from Schlichter (Allegre kick)
NE — FG Franklin 36

Green Bay 38, Minnesota 14—At Metrodome, attendance 51,197. Lynn Dickey passed for two touchdowns and ran for another to lead the Packers to their seventh victory in their last eight games. Dickey completed 16 of 20 passes for 198 yards in only one half of play. He threw scoring passes of 21 yards to Phillip Epps and 2 yards to Ed West. Dickey lunged for a one-yard touchdown with 52 seconds left in the first half to give Green Bay a 31-0 lead. The Packers compiled 448 total yards, while allowing 241.

Green Bay	10	21	7	0 —	38
Minnesota	0	0	7	7 —	14

GB — Epps 21 pass from Dickey (Del Greco kick)
GB — FG Del Greco 30
GB — Ivery 5 run (Del Greco kick)
GB — West 2 pass from Dickey (Del Greco kick)
GB — Dickey 1 run (Del Greco kick)
Minn — Nelson 4 run (Stenerud kick)
GB — Lofton 26 pass from Campbell (Del Greco kick)
Minn — Teal 53 interception return (Stenerud kick)

Kansas City 42, San Diego 21—At San Diego Jack Murphy Stadium, attendance 40,221. Bill Kenney passed for three touchdowns in two quarters of play to help the Chiefs finish the season with a three-game win streak. Kenney completed 17 of 23 passes for 245 yards. He followed Billy Jackson's three-yard touchdown run with scoring passes to Walt Arnold (4 yards), Henry Marshall (8), and Stephone Paige (65) for a 28-0 halftime lead. Kenney was replaced by Todd Blackledge in the second half. Blackledge engineered two scoring drives climaxed by Herman Heard's three-yard run and Theotis Brown's two-yard plunge. San Diego outgained Kansas City 443 to 399 yards.

Kansas City	14	14	14	0 —	42
San Diego	0	0	7	14 —	21

KC — Jackson 3 run (Lowery kick)
KC — Arnold 4 pass from Kenney (Lowery kick)
KC — Marshall 8 pass from Kenney (Lowery kick)
KC — Paige 65 pass from Kenney (Lowery kick)
KC — Heard 3 run (Lowery kick)
KC — Brown 2 run (Lowery kick)
SD — Chandler 15 pass from Luther (Benirschke kick)
SD — McGee 2 run (Benirschke kick)
SD — McGee 3 run (Benirschke kick)

Tampa Bay 41, New York Jets 21—At Tampa Stadium, attendance 43,817. Steve DeBerg completed three touchdown passes and James Wilder ran for a pair of scores as the Buccaneers gave retiring coach John McKay a winning farewell. DeBerg connected on 26 of 34 passes for 280 yards. He threw touchdown passes to Jerry Bell (3 and 18 yards) and Jay Carroll (4), whose first NFL touchdown gave the Buccaneers a 34-7 lead with 12:10 to play. Wilder rushed 31 times for 103 yards and scored on runs of six and four yards. Tampa Bay's offense gave up five sacks, including two by Mark Gastineau, who ended the season as the league leader with 22.

N.Y. Jets	0	7	0	14 —	21
Tampa Bay	10	7	3	21 —	41

TB — FG Ariri 37
TB — Wilder 6 run (Ariri kick)
TB — J. Bell 3 pass from DeBerg (Ariri kick)
NYJ — Dennison 5 pass from O'Brien (Leahy kick)
TB — FG Ariri 35
TB — J. Bell 18 pass from DeBerg (Ariri kick)
TB — Carroll 4 pass from DeBerg (Ariri kick)
NYJ — Paige 3 pass from O'Brien (Leahy kick)
TB — Wilder 4 run (Ariri kick)
NYJ — Hector 2 run (Leahy kick)

Atlanta 26, Philadelphia 10—At Atlanta-Fulton County Stadium, attendance 15,582. Mick Luckhurst kicked four field goals (from 38, 29, 27, and 34 yards) and rookie quarterback David Archer passed for one touchdown and set up another to help the Falcons snap a nine-game losing streak. Archer's first NFL completion was a 16-yard scoring pass to Arthur Cox late in the second quarter following Fulton Kuykendall's fumble recovery. Archer (12 of 18 for 197 yards) also set up Gerald Riggs' two-yard touchdown run by completing passes of 15 and 34 yards to Stacey Bailey. Bailey had eight receptions for 140 yards.

Philadelphia	3	0	7	0	— 10
Atlanta	3	10	7	6	— 26

Phil — FG McFadden 20
Atl — FG Luckhurst 38
Atl — FG Luckhurst 29
Atl — Cox 16 pass from Archer (Luckhurst kick)
Atl — Riggs 2 run (Luckhurst kick)
Phil — Quick 15 pass from Pisarcik (McFadden kick)
Atl — FG Luckhurst 27
Atl — FG Luckhurst 34

Pittsburgh 13, Los Angeles Raiders 7—At Memorial Coliseum, attendance 83,056. Walter Abercrombie ran for 111 yards on 28 carries and the defense shut down the Raiders' offense, to help the Steelers to clinch the AFC Central Division title. In addition to his rushing effort, Abercrombie's 59-yard pass reception set up Frank Pollard's one-yard fourth-quarter touchdown run. Pollard's score gave Pittsburgh a 10-0 lead. Gary Anderson also kicked field goals from 26 and 37 yards for the Steelers. Donnie Shell's second interception of the game at the Pittsburgh 46-yard line with 2:24 left, insured the Steelers' victory. Pittsburgh ran up 365 yards total offense to the Raiders 188.

Pittsburgh	3	0	0	10	— 13
L.A. Raiders	0	0	0	7	— 7

Pitt — FG Anderson 26
Pitt — Pollard 1 run (Anderson kick)
Pitt — FG Anderson 37
Raiders — Williams 2 pass from Plunkett (Bahr kick)

Washington 29, St. Louis 27—At Robert F. Kennedy Stadium, attendance 54,299. Mark Moseley's 37-yard field goal with 1:33 left lifted the Redskins to the NFC Eastern Division title and eliminated the Cardinals from the playoffs. Washington took a 23-7 halftime lead on a pair of Joe Theismann touchdown passes to Art Monk (23 and 12 yards), John Riggins' five-yard scoring run, and Moseley's first of three field goals from 21 yards. Neil Lomax rallied St. Louis in the second half by completing 25 of 28 passes for 314 yards, including an 18-yard scoring pass to Roy Green with 6:15 remaining. That score gave the Cardinals their first lead of the day 27-26. Monk, who caught 11 passes for 136 yards to total an NFL-record 106 for the season, had two catches for 27 yards on the drive that helped set up Moseley's decisive kick. Lomax finished with 468 yards on 37 of 46 completions, while Theismann hit on 20 of 35 passes for 298 yards.

St. Louis	0	7	10	10	— 27
Washington	6	17	3	3	— 29

Wash — Monk 23 pass from Theismann (kick failed)
Wash — Monk 12 pass from Theismann (Moseley kick)
StL — Lomax 1 run (O'Donoghue kick)
Wash — Riggins 5 run (Moseley kick)
Wash — FG Moseley 21
StL — FG O'Donoghue 30
StL — Green 75 pass from Lomax (O'Donoghue kick)
Wash — FG Moseley 37
StL — FG O'Donoghue 34
StL — Green 18 pass from Lomax (O'Donoghue kick)
Wash — FG Moseley 37

MONDAY, DECEMBER 17

Miami 28, Dallas 21—At Orange Bowl, attendance 74,139. Dan Marino became the first NFL player ever to pass for over 5,000 yards (5,084) in a season as the Dolphins eliminated the Cowboys from the playoffs for the first time since 1974. Marino (23 of 40 for 340 yards and four touchdowns) connected with Mark Clayton (41 yards) and Bruce Hardy (3) for a 14-0 third-quarter lead. Dallas rallied to tie the score, but Marino and Clayton teamed up again on a 39-yard touchdown pass for a 21-14 edge. Tony Hill's spectacular 66-yard touchdown catch 44 seconds later deadlocked the game once more, but Clayton's (four catches for 150 yards) NFL-record eighteenth touchdown reception of the year, a 63-yarder with 51 seconds remaining, insured the Dolphins the home field advantage throughout the playoffs.

Dallas	0	0	7	14	— 21
Miami	0	7	7	14	— 28

Mia — Clayton 41 pass from Marino (von Schamann kick)
Mia — Hardy 3 pass from Marino (von Schamann kick)
Dall — Newsome 1 run (Septien kick)
Dall — Newsome 4 run (Septien kick)
Mia — Clayton 39 pass from Marino (von Schamann kick)
Dall — Hill 66 pass from D. White Septien kick)
Mia — Clayton 63 pass from Marino (von Schamann kick)

SEVENTEENTH WEEK

SATURDAY, DECEMBER 22, 1984
AFC FIRST-ROUND PLAYOFF GAME

Seattle 13, Los Angeles Raiders 7—At Kingdome, attendance 62,049. The Seahawks combined a strong running attack and an aggressive defense to defeat the Raiders in the first round of the AFC playoffs. Seattle gained 205 yards on the ground, including 126 by Dan Doornink on 29 carries. The Seahawks' defense held the Raiders to 240 yards (105 rushing and 135 passing) and sacked Jim Plunkett six times, including two-and-a-half by Jacob Green. Seattle safeties Kenny Easley and John Harris each had an interception and cornerback Keith Simpson recovered a fumble. Dave Krieg completed 4 of 10 passes for 70 yards for the Seahawks and threw a 26-yard touchdown to Daryl Turner. Norm Johnson added field goals of 35 and 44 yards to finish the Seahawks' scoring. The Raiders only touchdown came on a 46-yard pass from Plunkett to Marcus Allen.

L.A. Raiders	0	0	0	7	— 7
Seattle	0	7	3	3	— 13

Sea — Turner 26 pass from Krieg (Johnson kick)
Sea — FG Johnson 35
Sea — FG Johnson 44
Raiders — Allen 46 pass from Plunkett (Bahr kick)

SUNDAY, DECEMBER 23, 1984
NFC FIRST-ROUND PLAYOFF GAME

New York Giants 16, Los Angeles Rams 13—At Anaheim Stadium, attendance 67,037. A ball-control offense, which held a 34:04 to 25:57 time of possession advantage, and a stingy defense, which limited the Rams to 214 total yards, sparked New York's first-round victory over Los Angeles. New York's Ali Haji-Sheikh was three-for-three in field goal tries, connecting from 37, 39, and 36 yards. Giants quarterback Phil Simms completed 22 of 31 passes for 179 yards. Zeke Mowatt was Simms' favorite target with seven receptions for 73 yards. The Rams' Eric Dickerson, carried the ball 23 times for 107 yards, and had a 14-yard touchdown run.

N.Y. Giants	10	0	6	0	— 16
L.A. Rams	0	3	7	3	— 13

NYG — FG Haji-Sheikh 37
NYG — Carpenter 1 run (Haji-Sheikh kick)
Rams — FG Lansford 38
NYG — FG Haji-Sheikh 39
Rams — Dickerson 14 run (Lansford kick)
NYG — FG Haji-Sheikh 36
Rams — FG Lansford 22

EIGHTEENTH WEEK

SATURDAY, DECEMBER 29, 1984
AFC DIVISIONAL PLAYOFF GAME

Miami 31, Seattle 10—At Orange Bowl, attendance 73,469. Miami advanced to the AFC Championship Game for the second time in three years with a 31-10 victory over Seattle. Leading 14-10, the Dolphins exploded for two scores in the final five minutes of the third period to pull away from the Seahawks. Dan Marino completed a three-yard touchdown pass to Bruce Hardy to give Miami a 21-10 lead. On Miami's next possession, Marino hit Mark Clayton with a 33-yard scoring pass to put the Dolphins ahead 28-10. Uwe von Schamann then added a 37-yard field goal to complete Miami's scoring. Marino (21 of 34 for 262 yards), who threw an NFL-record 48 touchdown passes during the regular season, completed three against the Seahawks.

Seattle	0	10	0	0	— 10
Miami	7	7	14	3	— 31

Mia — Nathan 14 run (von Schamann kick)
Sea — FG Johnson 27
Mia — Cefalo 34 pass from Marino (von Schamann kick)
Sea — Largent 56 pass from Krieg (Johnson kick)
Mia — Hardy 3 pass from Marino (von Schamann kick)
Mia — Clayton 33 pass from Marino (von Schamann kick)
Mia — FG von Schamann 37

SATURDAY, DECEMBER 29, 1984
NFC DIVISIONAL PLAYOFF GAME

San Francisco 21, New York Giants 10—At Candlestick Park, attendance 60,303. NFC Western Division champion San Francisco jumped to a 14-0 first-period lead over the NFC Wild Card representative New York Giants and then held on for a 21-10 win. Joe Montana connected with Dwight Clark for a 21-yard touchdown pass and Russ Francis for a 9-yard score to give the 49ers their quick lead. The Giants closed the score to 14-10 on Ali Haji-Sheikh's 46-yard field goal and Harry Carson's 14-yard pass interception return for a touchdown. The 49ers took control of the game on Freddie Solomon's 29-yard scoring catch with 10:51 gone in the second period. Montana completed 25 of 39 passes for 309 yards and three touchdowns, and had three interceptions. Clark caught nine passes for 112 yards and Solomon four for 94 yards.

N.Y. Giants	0	10	0	0	— 10
San Francisco	14	7	0	0	— 21

SF — Clark 21 pass from Montana (Wersching kick)
SF — Francis 9 pass from Montana (Wersching kick)
NYG — FG Haji-Sheikh 46
NYG — Carson 14 interception return (Haji-Sheikh kick)
SF — Solomon 29 pass from Montana (Wersching kick)

SUNDAY, DECEMBER 30, 1984
AFC DIVISIONAL PLAYOFF

Pittsburgh 24, Denver 17—At Mile High Stadium, attendance 74,981. Pittsburgh advanced to the AFC Championship Game for the first time since 1979 with a 24-17 victory over Denver. Frank Pollard's two-yard scoring run with 1:59 remaining clinched the Steelers' victory. The winning touchdown was set up by Eric Williams, who intercepted John Elway's pass at the Denver 30-yard line and returned it to the 2. Three plays later, Pollard scored. Pittsburgh led 10-7 at halftime, but the Broncos went ahead 17-10 after intermission on a 21-yard field goal by Rich Karlis and a 20-yard scoring pass from Elway to Steve Watson. The Steelers tied the score 17-17 on a 10-yard pass from Mark Malone to Louis Lipps with 3:19 left in the third period. Pollard rushed for 99 yards on 16 carries and Walter Abercrombie added 75 on 17 attempts. Malone completed 17 of 28 passes for 224 yards. Lipps caught five for 86.

Pittsburgh	0	10	7	7	— 24
Denver	7	0	10	0	— 17

Den — Wright 9 pass from Elway (Karlis kick)
Pitt — FG Anderson 28
Pitt — Pollard 1 run (Anderson kick)
Den — FG Karlis 21
Den — Watson 20 pass from Elway (Karlis kick)
Pitt — Lipps 10 pass from Malone (Anderson kick)
Pitt — Pollard 2 run (Anderson kick)

SUNDAY, DECEMBER 30, 1984
NFC DIVISIONAL PLAYOFF

Chicago 23, Washington 19—At Robert F. Kennedy Stadium, attendance 55,431. NFC Central Division titlist Chicago held on and defeated NFC Eastern champion Washington 23-19. The victory was the first playoff win for the Bears since 1963. Chicago took a 10-3 lead over the Redskins when Walter Payton, who rushed for 104 yards on 24 carries, threw a 19-yard touchdown pass to Pat Dunsmore with two minutes to play in the first half. Chicago went ahead 16-3 on Willie Gault's 75-yard scoring catch 26 seconds into the third period. The Redskins closed the gap to 16-10, but Dennis McKinnon's 16-yard touchdown reception finished the Bears' scoring. Steve Fuller completed 9 of 15 passes for 211 yards and two touchdowns. The Chicago defense had seven sacks, led by Richard Dent with three.

Chicago	0	10	13	0	— 23
Washington	3	0	14	2	— 19

Wash — FG Moseley 25
Chi — FG B. Thomas 34
Chi — Dunsmore 19 pass from Payton (B. Thomas kick)
Chi — Gault 75 pass from Fuller (kick failed)
Wash — Riggins 1 run (Moseley kick)
Chi — McKinnon 16 pass from Fuller (B. Thomas kick)
Wash — Riggins 1 run (Moseley kick)
Wash — Safety, Finzer stepped out of end zone

NINETEENTH WEEK

SUNDAY, JANUARY 6, 1985
AFC CHAMPIONSHIP GAME

Miami 45, Pittsburgh 28—At Orange Bowl, attendance 76,029. Dan Marino completed four touchdown passes to lead Miami over Pittsburgh and into Super Bowl XIX. Trailing 14-10 with 1:30 remaining in the second period, Marino connected with Mark Duper on a 41-yard pass and Tony Nathan ran for a two-yard score to give Miami a 24-14 halftime lead. On the Dolphins' first possession of the third period, Marino threw Duper a 36-yard touchdown pass to boost the Dolphins lead to 31-14. Pittsburgh pulled to within 31-21 with 7:55 remaining in the third period on a 19-yard pass from Mark Malone to John Stallworth, but the Dolphins responded with two more scores to take a commanding 45-21 lead. Marino completed 21 of 32 for an AFC Championship Game-record 421 yards. His four touchdowns also were an AFC title game record. Duper caught five passes for 148 yards and Nathan hauled in eight for 114. Miami's 435 yards passing set an NFL postseason playoff game record, surpassing the 415 by San Diego versus Miami in a 1981 AFC divisional game. Miami's 569 total yards and Pittsburgh's 455 set an AFC Championship Game record for most net yards (1,024) by two teams.

Pittsburgh	7	7	7	7	— 28
Miami	7	17	14	7	— 45

Mia — Clayton 40 pass from Marino (von Schamann kick)
Pitt — Erenberg 7 run (Anderson kick)
Mia — FG von Schamann 26
Pitt — Stallworth 65 pass from Malone (Anderson kick)
Mia — Duper 41 pass from Marino (von Schamann kick)
Mia — Nathan 2 run (von Schamann kick)
Mia — Duper 36 pass from Marino (von Schamann kick)
Pitt — Stallworth 19 pass from Malone (Anderson kick)
Mia — Bennett 1 run (von Schamann kick)
Mia — Moore 6 pass from Marino (von Schamann kick)
Pitt — Capers 29 pass from Malone (Anderson kick)

San Francisco 23, Chicago 0—At Candlestick Park, attendance 61,040. NFC Western Division champion San Francisco gained its second Super Bowl berth in the last four seasons with a 23-0 win over NFC Central Division titlist Chicago. The outcome represented the first shutout in the NFC Championship Game since the Los Angeles Rams blanked Tampa Bay 9-0 in 1979. The 49ers managed only a 6-0 halftime lead on a pair of Ray Wersching field goals. In the second half, the 49ers increased their lead to 13-0 on Wendell Tyler's nine-yard scoring run. In the fourth quarter, Joe Montana threw a 10-yard touchdown pass to Freddie Solomon to complete an eight-play, 88-yard drive. Wersching's 34-yard field goal with 1:57 remaining in the game finished the scoring. Montana completed 18 of 34 passes for 233 yards and one touchdown, and had two interceptions. He was sacked by the Bears three times, while the 49ers had nine sacks. Chicago's Walter Payton carried 22 times for 92 yards. The Bears' Gary Fencik had two key interceptions which stopped San Francisco threats.

Chicago	0	0	0	0 —	0
San Francisco	3	3	7	10 —	23

SF — FG Wersching 21
SF — FG Wersching 22
SF — Tyler 9 run (Wersching kick)
SF — Solomon 10 pass from Montana (Wersching kick)
SF — FG Wersching 34

TWENTIETH WEEK
SUNDAY, JANUARY 20, 1985
SUPER BOWL XIX
STANFORD, CALIFORNIA

San Francisco 38, Miami 16—At Stanford Stadium, attendance 84,059. The San Francisco 49ers captured their second Super Bowl title with a dominating offense and a defense which tamed Miami's explosive passing attack. The Dolphins held a 10-7 lead at the end of the first period, which represented the most points scored by two teams in an opening quarter of a Super Bowl. However, the 49ers used excellent field position in the second period to build a 28-16 halftime lead. Roger Craig set a Super Bowl record by scoring three touchdowns on pass receptions of 8 and 16 yards, and a run of two yards. San Francisco's Joe Montana was voted the game's most valuable player. He joins Green Bay's Bart Starr and Pittsburgh's Terry Bradshaw as the only two-time Super Bowl most valuable players. Montana completed 24 of 35 passes for a Super Bowl record 331 yards and three touchdowns, and rushed five times for 59 yards, including a six-yard touchdown. Craig had 58 yards on 15 carries and seven catches for 77 yards. Wendell Tyler rushed 13 times for 65 yards and caught four passes for 70 yards. Dwight Clark had six receptions for 77 yards, while Russ Francis had five catches for 60 yards. San Francisco's 537 total net yards bettered the previous Super Bowl record of 429 yards by Oakland in 1977. The 49ers also held a time of possession advantage over the Dolphins of 37:11 to 22:49. On defense, the 49ers had four sacks of Miami's Dan Marino, who had not been sacked during the two previous playoff games and had been sacked only 13 times during the 1984 regular season. The 38 points scored by San Francisco tied the Super Bowl record by the Los Angeles Raiders in their 38-9 win over Washington in Game XVIII last season.

Miami	10	6	0	0 —	16
San Francisco	7	21	10	0 —	38

Mia — FG von Schamann 37
SF — Monroe 33 pass from Montana (Wersching kick)
Mia — D. Johnson 2 pass from Marino (von Schamann kick)
SF — Craig 8 pass from Montana (Wersching kick)
SF — Montana 6 run (Wersching kick)
SF — Craig 2 run (Wersching kick)
Mia — FG von Schamann 31
Mia — FG von Schamann 30
SF — FG Wersching 27
SF — Craig 16 pass from Montana (Wersching kick)

TWENTY-FIRST WEEK
SUNDAY, JANUARY 27, 1985
AFC-NFC PRO BOWL
HONOLULU, HAWAII

AFC 22, NFC 14—At Aloha Stadium, attendance 50,385. Defensive end Art Still of the Kansas City Chiefs recovered a fumble and returned it 83 yards for a touchdown to clinch the AFC's victory over the NFC. Still's touchdown came in the fourth period with the AFC trailing 14-12 and was one of several outstanding defensive plays in a Pro Bowl dominated by two record-breaking defenses. Both teams combined for a Pro Bowl-record 17 sacks, including four by New York Jets defensive end Mark Gastineau, who was named the game's outstanding player. The AFC's first score came on a safety when Gastineau tackled Rams running back Eric Dickerson in the end zone. The AFC's second score, a six-yard pass from Miami's Dan Marino to Los Angeles Raiders running back Marcus Allen, was set up by a partial block of a punt by Seahawks linebacker Fredd Young. The NFC leads the series that started in 1970 9-6.

AFC	0	9	0	13 —	22
NFC	0	0	7	7 —	14

AFC — Safety, Dickerson tackled in end zone by Gastineau
AFC — Allen 6 pass from Marino (Johnson kick)
NFC — Lofton 13 pass from Montana (Stenerud kick)
NFC — Payton 1 run (Stenerud kick)
AFC — FG Johnson 33
AFC — Still 83 fumble recovery return (Johnson kick)
AFC — FG Johnson 22

1984 Professional Football Awards

	NFL	AFC	NFC
Professional Football Writers Association			
Most Valuable Player	Dan Marino		
Rookie of the Year	Louis Lipps		
Coach of the Year		Chuck Knox	Bill Walsh
Associated Press			
Most Valuable Player	Dan Marino		
Offensive Player-of-the-Year	Dan Marino		
Defensive Player-of-the-Year	Kenny Easley		
Rookie of the Year—Offense	Louis Lipps		
Rookie of the Year—Defense	Bill Maas		
Coach of the Year	Chuck Knox		
United Press International			
Player of the Year		Mark Gastineau	Eric Dickerson
Rookie of the Year		Louis Lipps	Paul McFadden
Coach of the Year		Chuck Knox	Bill Walsh
Newspaper Enterprise Association			
Jim Thorpe Trophy—MVP	Dan Marino		
Rookie of the Year	Louis Lipps		
George Halas Trophy—Defensive Player of the Year	Mike Haynes		
The Sporting News			
Player of the Year	Dan Marino		
Rookie of the Year	Louis Lipps		
Coach of the Year	Chuck Knox		
Pro Football Weekly			
Offensive Most Valuable Player	Dan Marino		
Defensive Most Valuable Player	Kenny Easley		
Offensive Rookie of the Year	Louis Lipps		
Defensive Rookie of the Year	Tom Flynn		
Comeback Player of the Year	John Stallworth		
Coach of the Year	Dan Reeves		
Football News			
Coach of the Year		Dan Reeves	Bill Walsh
Player of the Year		Dan Marino	Joe Montana
Rookie of the Year	Louis Lipps		
AFC-NFC Pro Bowl			
Player of the Game (Dan McGuire Award)	Mark Gastineau		
Maxwell Club			
Player of the Year (Bert Bell Trophy)	Dan Marino		
College and Pro Football Newsweekly			
Player of the Year	Dan Marino		
Coach of the Year	Dan Reeves		
Football Digest			
Player of the Year	Dan Marino		
Coach of the Year	Chuck Knox		
Offensive Rookie of the Year	Greg Bell		
Defensive Rookie of the Year	Rick Bryan		

AFC-NFC Players-of-the-Week

	AFC Offense	AFC Defense	NFC Offense	NFC Defense
Week 1	Dan Marino, Mia.	Mark Gastineau, NYJ	Gerald Riggs, Atl.	Gary Fencik, Chi.
Week 2	Mike Pagel, Ind.	Mike Bell, KC	Walter Payton, Chi.	Lawrence Taylor, NYG
Week 3	Tony Eason, NE	Sam Washington, Pitt.	Steve DeBerg, TB	Vernon Dean, Wash.
Week 4	Marcus Allen, Raiders	Joe Nash, Sea.	Jan Stenerud, Minn.	Randy White, Dall.
Week 5	Dan Marino, Mia.	Donnie Shell, Pitt. Dwayne Woodruff, Pitt.	James Wilder, TB	Jack Youngblood, Rams
Week 6	Dan Fouts, SD	Rod Martin, Raiders	Neil Lomax, St. L.	Dave Butz, Wash.
Week 7	Ozzie Newsome, Clev.	Steve Foley, Den.	John Riggins, Wash.	Ken Clarke, Phil.
Week 8	Marc Wilson, Raiders	Mark Gastineau, NYJ	Joe Montana, SF	Mike Cofer, Det.
Week 9	Larry Kinnebrew, Cin. Gary Kubiak, Den.	Kenny Easley, Sea.	Phil Simms, NYG	Tom Flynn, GB
Week 10	John Elway, Den.	Dave Brown, Sea.	Eric Dickerson, Rams	Richard Dent, Chi.
Week 11	Larry Moriarty, Hou.	Ronnie Lippett, NE	Lynn Dickey, GB	Jim Wilks, NO
Week 12	Greg Bell, Buff.	Clay Matthews, Clev.	Ottis Anderson, St. L.	Bruce Clark, NO
Week 13	Dave Krieg, Sea.	Mike Merriweather, Pitt.	Gary Danielson, Det.	E.J. Junior, St. L.
Week 14	Dan Marino, Mia.	Mike Haynes, Raiders	Alfred Jackson, Atl.	Randy White, Dall.
Week 15	Henry Marshall, KC	Russell Carter, NYJ	Eric Dickerson, Rams	Darrell Green, Wash.
Week 16	Mark Clayton, Mia.	Donnie Shell, Pitt.	Neil Lomax, St. L. Art Monk, Wash.	Steve McMichael, Chi.

ALL-PRO TEAMS

1984 PFWA ALL-PRO TEAM
Selected by Professional Football Writers Association

OFFENSE

Roy Green, St. Louis	Wide Receiver
Art Monk, Washington	Wide Receiver
Ozzie Newsome, Cleveland	Tight End
Keith Fahnhorst, San Francisco	Tackle
Joe Jacoby, Washington	Tackle
Russ Grimm, Washington	Guard
John Hannah, New England	Guard
Dwight Stephenson, Miami	Center
Dan Marino, Miami	Quarterback
Eric Dickerson, Los Angeles Rams	Running Back
Walter Payton, Chicago	Running Back
Norm Johnson, Seattle	Kicker
Louis Lipps, Pittsburgh	Punt Returner
Bobby Humphery, New York Jets	Kick Returner

DEFENSE

Mark Gastineau, New York Jets	Defensive End
Howie Long, Los Angeles Raiders	Defensive End
Randy White, Dallas	Defensive Tackle
E. J. Junior, St. Louis	Inside Linebacker
Mike Singletary, Chicago	Inside Linebacker
Rod Martin, Los Angeles Raiders	Outside Linebacker
Lawrence Taylor, New York Giants	Outside Linebacker
Lester Hayes, Los Angeles Raiders	Cornerback
Mike Haynes, Los Angeles Raiders	Cornerback
Michael Downs, Dallas	Safety
Kenny Easley, Seattle	Safety
Reggie Roby, Miami	Punter

1984 NEA ALL-PRO TEAM
Selected by Newspaper Enterprise Association

OFFENSE

Roy Green, St. Louis	Wide Receiver
James Lofton, Green Bay	Wide Receiver
Ozzie Newsome, Cleveland	Tight End
Keith Fahnhorst, San Francisco	Tackle
Anthony Muñoz, Cincinnati	Tackle
Russ Grimm, Washington	Guard
John Hannah, New England	Guard
Dwight Stephenson, Miami	Center
Dan Marino, Miami	Quarterback
Eric Dickerson, Los Angeles Rams	Running Back
Walter Payton, Chicago	Running Back
Jan Stenerud, Minnesota	Kicker

DEFENSE

Mark Gastineau, New York Jets	Defensive End
Howie Long, Los Angeles Raiders	Defensive End
Dan Hampton, Chicago	Defensive Tackle
Randy White, Dallas	Defensive Tackle
Clay Matthews, Cleveland	Outside Linebacker
Lawrence Taylor, New York Giants	Outside Linebacker
E. J. Junior, St. Louis	Inside Linebacker
Mike Singletary, Chicago	Inside Linebacker
Mark Haynes, New York Giants	Cornerback
Mike Haynes, Los Angeles Raiders	Cornerback
Wes Hopkins, Philadelphia	Safety
Kenny Easley, Seattle	Safety
Reggie Roby, Miami	Punter

1984 ASSOCIATED PRESS ALL-PRO TEAM

OFFENSE

Roy Green, St. Louis	Wide Receiver
Art Monk, Washington	Wide Receiver
Ozzie Newsome, Cleveland	Tight End
Keith Fahnhorst, San Francisco	Tackle
Joe Jacoby, Washington	Tackle
Russ Grimm, Washington	Guard
Ed Newman, Miami	Guard
Dwight Stephenson, Miami	Center
Dan Marino, Miami	Quarterback
Eric Dickerson, Los Angeles Rams	Running Back
Walter Payton, Chicago	Running Back
Norm Johnson, Seattle	Kicker
Henry Ellard, Los Angeles Rams	Kick Returner

DEFENSE

Mark Gastineau, New York Jets	Defensive End
Howie Long, Los Angeles Raiders	Defensive End
Dan Hampton, Chicago	Defensive Tackle
Randy White, Dallas	Defensive Tackle
Joe Nash, Seattle	Nose Tackle
Rod Martin, Los Angeles Raiders	Outside Linebacker
Lawrence Taylor, New York Giants	Outside Linebacker
E. J. Junior, St. Louis	Inside Linebacker
Mike Singletary, Chicago	Inside Linebacker
Mark Haynes, New York Giants	Cornerback
Mike Haynes, Los Angeles Raiders	Cornerback
Deron Cherry, Kansas City	Safety
Kenny Easley, Seattle	Safety
Reggie Roby, Miami	Punter

1984 ALL-NFL TEAM
Selected by Associated Press, Newspaper Enterprise Association, and Professional Football Writers Association

OFFENSE

Roy Green, St. Louis (AP, NEA, PFWA)	Wide Receiver
Art Monk, Washington (AP, PFWA)	Wide Receiver
James Lofton, Green Bay (NEA)	Wide Receiver
Ozzie Newsome, Cleveland (AP, NEA, PFWA)	Tight End
Keith Fahnhorst, San Francisco (AP, NEA, PFWA)	Tackle
Joe Jacoby, Washington (AP, PFWA)	Tackle
Anthony Muñoz, Cincinnati (NEA)	Tackle
Russ Grimm, Washington (AP, NEA, PFWA)	Guard
John Hannah, New England (NEA, PFWA)	Guard
Ed Newman, Miami (AP)	Guard
Dwight Stephenson, Miami (AP, NEA, PFWA)	Center
Dan Marino, Miami (AP, NEA, PFWA)	Quarterback
Eric Dickerson, Los Angeles Rams (AP, NEA, PFWA)	Running Back
Walter Payton, Chicago (AP, NEA, PFWA)	Running Back
Norm Johnson, Seattle (AP, PFWA)	Kicker
Jan Stenerud, Minnesota (NEA)	Kicker
Henry Ellard, Los Angeles Rams (AP)	Kick Returner
Bobby Humphery, New York Jets (PFWA)	Kick Returner
Louis Lipps, Pittsburgh (PFWA)	Punt Returner

DEFENSE

Mark Gastineau, New York Jets (AP, NEA, PFWA)	Defensive End
Howie Long, Los Angeles Raiders (AP, NEA, PFWA)	Defensive End
Randy White, Dallas (AP, NEA, PFWA)	Defensive Tackle
Dan Hampton, Chicago (AP, NEA)	Defensive Tackle
Joe Nash, Seattle (AP)	Nose Tackle
E. J. Junior, St. Louis (AP, NEA, PFWA)	Inside Linebacker
Mike Singletary, Chicago (AP, NEA, PFWA)	Inside Linebacker
Lawrence Taylor, New York Giants (AP, NEA, PFWA)	Outside Linebacker
Rod Martin, Los Angeles Raiders (AP, PFWA)	Outside Linebacker
Clay Matthews, Cleveland (NEA)	Outside Linebacker
Mike Haynes, Los Angeles Raiders (AP, NEA, PFWA)	Cornerback
Mark Haynes, New York Giants (AP, NEA)	Cornerback
Lester Hayes, Los Angeles Raiders (PFWA)	Cornerback
Kenny Easley, Seattle (AP, NEA, PFWA)	Safety
Deron Cherry, Kansas City (AP)	Safety
Michael Downs, Dallas (PFWA)	Safety
Wes Hopkins, Philadelphia (NEA)	Safety
Reggie Roby, Miami (AP, NEA, PFWA)	Punter

1984 ALL-AFC TEAM
Selected by United Press International

OFFENSE

Mark Duper, Miami . . . . Wide Receiver
John Stallworth, Pittsburgh . . . . Wide Receiver
Ozzie Newsome, Cleveland . . . . Tight End
Henry Lawrence, Los Angeles Raiders . . . . Tackle
Anthony Muñoz, Cincinnati . . . . Tackle
John Hannah, New England . . . . Guard
Ed Newman, Miami . . . . Guard
Dwight Stephenson, Miami . . . . Center
Dan Marino, Miami . . . . Quarterback
Marcus Allen, Los Angeles Raiders . . . . Running Back
Freeman McNeil, New York Jets . . . . Running Back
Norm Johnson, Seattle . . . . Kicker

DEFENSE

Mark Gastineau, New York Jets . . . . Defensive End
Howie Long, Los Angeles Raiders . . . . Defensive End
Joe Nash, Seattle . . . . Nose Tackle
Rod Martin, Los Angeles Raiders . . . . Outside Linebacker
Mike Merriweather, Pittsburgh . . . . Outside Linebacker
Tom Cousineau, Cleveland . . . . Inside Linebacker
Steve Nelson, New England . . . . Inside Linebacker
Lester Hayes, Los Angeles Raiders . . . . Cornerback
Mike Haynes, Los Angeles Raiders . . . . Cornerback
Deron Cherry, Kansas City . . . . Safety
Kenny Easley, Seattle . . . . Safety
Reggie Roby, Miami . . . . Punter

1984 ALL-NFC TEAM
Selected by United Press International

OFFENSE

Roy Green, St. Louis . . . . Wide Receiver
Art Monk, Washington . . . . Wide Receiver
Paul Coffman, Green Bay . . . . Tight End
Keith Fahnhorst, San Francisco . . . . Tackle
Joe Jacoby, Washington . . . . Tackle
Randy Cross, San Francisco . . . . Guard
Russ Grimm, Washington . . . . Guard
Fred Quillan, San Francisco . . . . Center
Joe Montana, San Francisco . . . . Quarterback
Eric Dickerson, Los Angeles Rams . . . . Running Back
Walter Payton, Chicago . . . . Running Back
Jan Stenerud, Minnesota . . . . Kicker

DEFENSE

Richard Dent, Chicago . . . . Defensive End
Lee Roy Selmon, Tampa Bay . . . . Defensive End
Randy White, Dallas . . . . Nose Tackle
Rickey Jackson, New Orleans . . . . Outside Linebacker
Lawrence Taylor, New York Giants . . . . Outside Linebacker
E. J. Junior, St. Louis . . . . Inside Linebacker
Mike Singletary, Chicago . . . . Inside Linebacker
Mark Haynes, New York Giants . . . . Cornerback
Everson Walls, Dallas . . . . Cornerback
Michael Downs, Dallas . . . . Safety
Dwight Hicks, San Francisco . . . . Safety
Bucky Scribner, Green Bay . . . . Punter

1984 ALL-ROOKIE TEAM
Selected by Professional Football Writers Association

OFFENSE

Louis Lipps, Pittsburgh . . . . Wide Receiver
Daryl Turner, Seattle . . . . Wide Receiver
Clarence Kay, Denver . . . . Tight End
Dean Steinkuhler, Houston . . . . Tackle
Ron Heller, Tampa Bay . . . . Tackle
Brian Blados, Cincinnati . . . . Guard
Ron Solt, Indianapolis . . . . Guard
Jim Sweeney, New York Jets . . . . Center
Warren Moon, Houston . . . . Quarterback
Alfred Anderson, Minnesota . . . . Running Back
Greg Bell, Buffalo . . . . Running Back
Paul McFadden, Philadelphia . . . . Kicker

DEFENSE

Alphonso Carreker, Green Bay . . . . Defensive End
Blaise Winter, Indianapolis . . . . Defensive End
Bill Maas, Kansas City . . . . Nose Tackle
Eugene Lockhart, Dallas . . . . Inside Linebacker
Gary Reasons, New York Giants . . . . Inside Linebacker
Carl Banks, New York Giants . . . . Outside Linebacker
Keith Browner, Tampa Bay . . . . Outside Linebacker
Frank Minnifield, Cleveland . . . . Cornerback
Kevin Ross, Kansas City . . . . Cornerback
Tom Flynn, Green Bay . . . . Safety
Don Rogers, Cleveland . . . . Safety
Brian Hansen, New Orleans . . . . Punter

1984 Paid Attendance Breakdown

	Games	Attendance	Average
AFC Preseason	11	473,453	43,041
NFC Preseason	11	562,381	51,126
AFC-NFC Preseason, Interconference	35	1,725,551	49,301
NFL Preseason Total	**57**	**2,761,385**	**48,445**
AFC Regular Season	86	5,124,275	59,585
NFC Regular Season	86	5,219,911	60,697
AFC-NFC Regular Season, Interconference	52	3,053,926	58,729
NFL Regular Season Total	**224**	**13,398,112**	**59,813**
AFC First-Round Playoff	1		
(Los Angeles Raiders-Seattle)		64,291	
AFC Divisional Playoffs	2		
(Seattle-Miami)		74,291	
(Pittsburgh-Denver)		74,502	
AFC Championship Game	1		
(Pittsburgh-Miami)		74,588	
NFC First-Round Playoff	1		
(New York Giants-Los Angeles Rams)		66,919	
NFC Divisional Playoffs	2		
(New York Giants-San Francisco)		60,373	
(Chicago-Washington)		54,450	
NFC Championship Game	1		
(Chicago-San Francisco)		61,336	
Super Bowl XIX at Stanford, California	1		
(Miami-San Francisco)		84,059	
AFC-NFC Pro Bowl at Honolulu, Hawaii	1	50,385	
NFL Postseason Total	**10**	**665,194**	**66,519**
NFL All Games	**291**	**16,824,691**	**57,817**

NFL Paid Attendance

Year	Regular Season	Average	Postseason	Super Bowl
1984	13,398,112 (224 games)	59,813	665,194 (10)	84,059
1983	13,277,222 (224 games)	59,273	675,513 (10)	72,932
1982*	7,367,438 (126 games)	58,472	1,033,153 (16)	103,667
1981	13,606,990 (224 games)	60,745	637,763 (10)	81,270
1980	13,392,230 (224 games)	59,787	624,430 (10)	75,500
1979	13,182,039 (224 games)	58,848	630,326 (10)	103,985
1978	12,771,800 (224 games)	57,017	624,388 (10)	79,641
1977	11,018,632 (196 games)	56,218	534,925 (8)	75,804
1976	11,070,543 (196 games)	56,482	492,884 (8)	103,438
1975	10,213,193 (182 games)	56,116	475,919 (8)	80,187
1974	10,236,322 (182 games)	56,244	438,664 (8)	80,997
1973	10,730,933 (182 games)	58,961	525,433 (8)	71,882
1972	10,445,827 (182 games)	57,395	483,345 (8)	90,182
1971	10,076,035 (182 games)	55,363	483,891 (8)	81,023
1970	9,533,333 (182 games)	52,381	458,493 (8)	79,204
1969	6,096,127 (112 games) NFL	54,430	162,279 (3)	80,562
	2,843,373 (70 games) AFL	40,620	167,088 (3)	
1968	5,882,313 (112 games) NFL	52,521	215,902 (3)	75,377
	2,635,004 (70 games) AFL	37,643	114,438 (2)	
1967	5,938,924 (112 games) NFL	53,026	166,208 (3)	75,546
	2,295,697 (63 games) AFL	36,439	53,330 (1)	
1966	5,337,044 (105 games) NFL	50,829	74,152 (1)	61,946**
	2,160,369 (63 games) AFL	34,291	42,080 (1)	
1965	4,634,021 (98 games) NFL	47,286	100,304 (2)	
	1,782,384 (56 games) AFL	31,828	30,361 (1)	
1964	4,563,049 (98 games) NFL	46,562	79,544 (1)	
	1,447,875 (56 games) AFL	25,855	40,242 (1)	
1963	4,163,643 (98 games) NFL	42,486	45,801 (1)	
	1,208,697 (56 games) AFL	21,584	63,171 (2)	
1962	4,003,421 (98 games) NFL	40,851	64,892 (1)	
	1,147,302 (56 games) AFL	20,487	37,981 (1)	
1961	3,986,159 (98 games) NFL	40,675	39,029 (1)	
	1,002,657 (56 games) AFL	17,904	29,556 (1)	
1960	3,128,296 (78 games) NFL	40,106	67,325 (1)	
	926,156 (56 games) AFL	16,538	32,183 (1)	
1959	3,140,000 (72 games)	43,617	57,545 (1)	
1958	3,006,124 (72 games)	41,752	123,659 (2)	
1957	2,836,318 (72 games)	39,393	119,579 (2)	
1956	2,551,263 (72 games)	35,434	56,836 (1)	
1955	2,521,836 (72 games)	35,026	85,693 (1)	
1954	2,190,571 (72 games)	30,425	43,827 (1)	
1953	2,164,585 (72 games)	30,064	54,577 (1)	
1952	2,052,126 (72 games)	28,502	97,507 (2)	
1951	1,913,019 (72 games)	26,570	57,522 (1)	
1950	1,977,753 (78 games)	25,356	136,647 (3)	
1949	1,391,735 (60 games)	23,196	27,980 (1)	
1948	1,525,243 (60 games)	25,421	36,309 (1)	
1947	1,837,437 (60 games)	30,624	66,268 (2)	
1946	1,732,135 (55 games)	31,493	58,346 (1)	
1945	1,270,401 (50 games)	25,408	32,178 (1)	
1944	1,019,649 (50 games)	20,393	46,016 (1)	
1943	969,128 (50 games)	19,383	71,315 (2)	
1942	887,920 (55 games)	16,144	36,006 (1)	
1941	1,108,615 (55 games)	20,157	55,870 (2)	
1940	1,063,025 (55 games)	19,328	36,034 (1)	
1939	1,071,200 (55 games)	19,476	32,279 (1)	
1938	937,197 (55 games)	17,040	48,120 (1)	
1937	963,039 (55 games)	17,510	15,878 (1)	
1936	816,007 (54 games)	15,111	29,545 (1)	
1935	638,178 (53 games)	12,041	15,000 (1)	
1934	492,684 (60 games)	8,211	35,059 (1)	

*Players 57-day strike reduced 224-game schedule to 126 games.

**Only Super Bowl that did not sell out.

NFL's 10 Biggest Weekends

(Turnstile Count)

Weekend	Games	Attendance
October 12-13, 1980	14	875,466
September 5-6-7, 1981	14	865,699
September 12-13, 1982	14	862,954
September 23-24, 1984	14	860,208
September 16, 19-20, 1982	14	850,358
September 23-24, 1979	14	848,777
November 2-3, 1980	14	844,884
November 1-2, 1981	14	842,978
September 27-28, 1981	14	841,514
October 2-3, 1983	14	841,329

NFL's 10 Highest Scoring Weekends

Point Total	Date	Weekend
761	October 9-10, 1983	6th
732	November 9-10, 1980	10th
725	November 24, 27-28, 1983	13th
696	October 2-3, 1983	5th
676	September 21-22, 1980	3rd
675	October 23-24, 1983	8th
667	November 22-23, 1981	12th
667	November 22, 25-26, 1984	13th
661	October 25-26, 1981	8th
658	September 2-3, 1984	1st

Top 10 Televised Sports Events

Program	Date	Network	Rating	Share
Super Bowl XVI	1/24/82	CBS	49.1	73.0
Super Bowl XVII	1/30/83	NBC	48.6	69.0
Super Bowl XII	1/15/78	CBS	47.2	67.0
Super Bowl XIII	1/21/79	NBC	47.1	74.0
Super Bowl XVIII	1/22/84	CBS	46.4	71.0
Super Bowl XIX	1/20/85	ABC	46.4	63.0
Super Bowl XIV	1/20/80	CBS	46.3	67.0
Super Bowl XI	1/9/77	NBC	44.4	73.0
Super Bowl XV	1/25/81	NBC	44.4	63.0
Super Bowl VI	1/16/72	CBS	44.2	74.0

Ten Best Rushing Performances, 1984

	Attempts	Yards	TD
1. Eric Dickerson L.A. Rams vs. Houston, December 9	27	215	2
2. Eric Dickerson L.A. Rams vs. St. Louis, November 4	21	208	0
3. Greg Bell Buffalo vs. Dallas, November 18	27	206	1
4. Gerald Riggs Atlanta vs. New Orleans, September 2	35	202	2
5. Eric Dickerson L.A. Rams vs. Tampa Bay, November 25	28	191	3
6. Earnest Byner Cleveland vs. Houston, December 16	21	188	2
7. Walter Payton Chicago vs. Denver, September 9	20	179	1
8. Eric Dickerson L.A. Rams vs. New Orleans, October 14	20	175	0
Walter Payton Chicago vs. Green Bay, December 9	35	175	1
10. James Wilder Tampa Bay vs. Green Bay, September 30	43	172	1

100-Yard Rushing Performances, 1984

First Week
Gerald Riggs, Atlanta	202 yards vs. New Orleans
Eric Dickerson, L.A. Rams	138 yards vs. Dallas
Freeman McNeil, N.Y. Jets	112 yards vs. Indianapolis
George Rogers, New Orleans	102 yards vs. Atlanta

Second Week
Walter Payton, Chicago	179 yards vs. Denver
Billy Sims, Detroit	140 yards vs. Atlanta
Alfred Anderson, Minnesota	105 yards vs. Philadelphia
Eric Dickerson, L.A. Rams	102 yards vs. Cleveland

Third Week
Freeman McNeil, N.Y. Jets	150 yards vs. Cincinnati
Curtis Dickey, Indianapolis	121 yards vs. St. Louis
Ottis Anderson, St. Louis	119 yards vs. Indianapolis
Walter Payton, Chicago	110 yards vs. Green Bay
Tony Collins, New England	107 yards vs. Seattle

Fourth Week
Earnest Jackson, San Diego	155 yards vs. L.A. Raiders
John Riggins, Washington	140 yards vs. New England
Sammy Winder, Denver	139 yards vs. Kansas City
Alfred Anderson, Minnesota	120 yards vs. Detroit
Gerald Riggs, Atlanta	120 yards vs. Houston
Walter Payton, Chicago	116 yards vs. Seattle
Wendell Tyler, San Francisco	113 yards vs. Philadelphia
Freeman McNeil, N.Y. Jets	112 yards vs. Buffalo
James Wilder, Tampa Bay	112 yards vs. N.Y. Giants

Fifth Week
James Wilder, Tampa Bay	172 yards vs. Green Bay
Walter Payton, Chicago	155 yards vs. Dallas
Greg Bell, Buffalo	144 yards vs. Indianapolis
Gerald Riggs, Atlanta	136 yards vs. San Francisco
Eric Dickerson, L.A. Rams	120 yards vs. N.Y. Giants
Billy Sims, Detroit	119 yards vs. San Diego
Randy McMillan, Indianapolis	114 yards vs. Buffalo
Eric Lane, Seattle	113 yards vs. Minnesota
Stump Mitchell, St. Louis	109 yards vs. Miami
John Riggins, Washington	104 yards vs. Philadelphia

Sixth Week
Walter Payton, Chicago	154 yards vs. New Orleans
Lynn Cain, Atlanta	145 yards vs. L.A. Rams
Ottis Anderson, St. Louis	110 yards vs. Dallas
Eric Dickerson, L.A. Rams	107 yards vs. Atlanta
Freeman McNeil, N.Y. Jets	107 yards vs. Kansas City
Wendell Tyler, San Francisco	101 yards vs. N.Y. Giants

Seventh Week
Eric Dickerson, L.A. Rams	175 yards vs. New Orleans
John Riggins, Washington	165 yards vs. Dallas
Greg Bell, Buffalo	113 yards vs. Seattle
Joe Carter, Miami	105 yards vs. Houston
Frank Pollard, Pittsburgh	105 yards vs. San Francisco
Walter Payton, Chicago	100 yards vs. St. Louis
Billy Sims, Detroit	100 yards vs. Tampa Bay

Eighth Week
Eric Dickerson, L.A. Rams	145 yards vs. Atlanta
Wendell Tyler, San Francisco	108 yards vs. Houston
Marcus Allen, L.A. Raiders	107 yards vs. San Diego
Billy Sims, Detroit	103 yards vs. Minnesota

Ninth Week
Sammy Winder, Denver	126 yards vs. L.A. Raiders
Eddie Lee Ivery, Green Bay	116 yards vs. Detroit
Frank Pollard, Pittsburgh	111 yards vs. Atlanta
Freeman McNeil, N.Y. Jets	110 yards vs. New England
Tony Dorsett, Dallas	104 yards vs. Indianapolis

Tenth Week
Eric Dickerson, L.A. Rams	208 yards vs. St. Louis
Boyce Green, Cleveland	156 yards vs. Buffalo
James Wilder, Tampa Bay	146 yards vs. Minnesota
Gerald Riggs, Atlanta	134 yards vs. Washington
Freeman McNeil, N.Y. Jets	132 yards vs. Miami
Craig James, New England	120 yards vs. Denver
Walter Payton, Chicago	111 yards vs. L.A. Raiders
John Riggins, Washington	100 yards vs. Atlanta

Eleventh Week
Eric Dickerson, L.A. Rams	149 yards vs. Chicago
Larry Moriarty, Houston	117 yards vs. Kansas City
Keith Griffin, Washington	114 yards vs. Detroit
Gerry Ellis, Green Bay	107 yards vs. Minnesota

Twelfth Week
Greg Bell, Buffalo	206 yards vs. Dallas
Larry Moriarty, Houston	138 yards vs. N.Y. Jets
Eric Dickerson, L.A. Rams	132 yards vs. Green Bay
Earnest Jackson, San Diego	124 yards vs. Miami
Boyce Green, Cleveland	121 yards vs. Atlanta
Larry Kinnebrew, Cincinnati	119 yards vs. Seattle
Ottis Anderson, St. Louis	111 yards vs. N.Y. Giants

Thirteenth Week
Eric Dickerson, L.A. Rams	191 yards vs. Tampa Bay
Walter Payton, Chicago	117 yards vs. Minnesota
Wendell Tyler, San Francisco	117 yards vs. New Orleans
Freeman McNeil, N.Y. Jets	116 yards vs. Miami
Craig James, New England	112 yards vs. Dallas
Marcus Allen, L.A. Raiders	110 yards vs. Indianapolis
Walter Abercrombie, Pittsburgh	109 yards vs. San Diego

Fourteenth Week
Marcus Allen, L.A. Raiders	155 yards vs. Miami
Eric Dickerson, L.A. Rams	149 yards vs. New Orleans
Ottis Anderson, St. Louis	136 yards vs. New England
Gerald Riggs, Atlanta	133 yards vs. San Francisco
Tony Dorsett, Dallas	110 yards vs. Philadelphia

Fifteenth Week
Eric Dickerson, L.A. Rams	215 yards vs. Houston
Walter Payton, Chicago	175 yards vs. Green Bay
James Wilder, Tampa Bay	125 yards vs. Atlanta
John Riggins, Washington	111 yards vs. Dallas
Joe Morris, N.Y. Giants	107 yards vs. St. Louis
Earnest Byner, Cleveland	103 yards vs. Pittsburgh
Larry Moriarty, Houston	102 yards vs. L.A. Rams
Wilbert Montgomery, Phil.	100 yards vs. New England

Sixteenth Week
Earnest Byner, Cleveland	188 yards vs. Houston
Craig James, New England	138 yards vs. Indianapolis
Walter Abercrombie, Pittsburgh	111 yards vs. L.A. Raiders
James Wilder, Tampa Bay	103 yards vs. N.Y. Jets

Times 100 or More
Dickerson 12; Payton 9; McNeil 7; Riggins, Riggs, Wilder 5; O. Anderson, Sims, Tyler 4; Allen, Bell, James, Moriarty 3; Abercrombie, A. Anderson, Byner, Dorsett, Green, Jackson, Pollard, Winder 2.

Ten Best Passing Yardage Performances, 1984

	Att.	Comp.	Yards	TD
1. Dan Marino Miami vs. L.A. Raiders, December 2	57	35	470	4
2. Neil Lomax St. Louis vs. Washington, December 16	46	37	468	2
3. Dan Marino Miami vs. St. Louis, September 30	36	24	429	3
4. Dan Marino Miami vs. N.Y. Jets, November 4	42	23	422	2
5. Dan Fouts San Diego vs. L.A. Raiders, October 21	45	24	410	3
6. Phil Simms N.Y. Giants vs. Philadelphia, September 2	30	23	409	4
7. Dave Krieg Seattle vs. Denver, November 25	44	30	406	3
8. Dan Marino Miami vs. Indianapolis, December 9	41	29	404	4
9. Neil Lomax St. Louis vs. Dallas, November 11	52	27	388	2
10. Tommy Kramer Minnesota vs. Tampa Bay, October 7	47	27	386	2

300-Yard Passing Performances, 1984

First Week
Phil Simms, N.Y. Giants — 409 yards vs. Philadelphia
Gary Hogeboom, Dallas — 343 yards vs. L.A. Rams
Ken Anderson, Cincinnati — 323 yards vs. Denver
Dan Marino, Miami — 311 yards vs. Washington

Second Week
Joe Montana, San Francisco — 381 yards vs. Washington
Warren Moon, Houston — 365 yards vs. Indianapolis
Dan Fouts, San Diego — 332 yards vs. Seattle
Joe Theismann, Washington — 331 yards vs. San Francisco
Ken Anderson, Cincinnati — 310 yards vs. Kansas City

Third Week
Phil Simms, N.Y. Giants — 347 yards vs. Washington
Dan Fouts, San Diego — 336 yards vs. Houston
Gary Hogeboom, Dallas — 320 yards vs. Philadelphia
Ken Anderson, Cincinnati — 316 yards vs. N.Y. Jets
Jim Plunkett, L.A. Raiders — 313 yards vs. Kansas City

Fourth Week
Jim Plunkett, L.A. Raiders — 363 yards vs. San Diego
Joe Ferguson, Buffalo — 340 yards vs. N.Y. Jets

Fifth Week
Dan Marino, Miami — 429 yards vs. St. Louis
Tony Eason, New England — 354 yards vs. N.Y. Jets
Neil Lomax, St. Louis — 308 yards vs. Miami

Sixth Week
Tommy Kramer, Minnesota — 386 yards vs. Tampa Bay
Lynn Dickey, Green Bay — 384 yards vs. San Diego
Dan Fouts, San Diego — 376 yards vs. Green Bay
Neil Lomax, St. Louis — 354 yards vs. Dallas
Paul McDonald, Cleveland — 320 yards vs. New England
Marc Wilson, L.A. Raiders — 309 yards vs. Seattle

Seventh Week
Lynn Dickey, Green Bay — 371 yards vs. Denver
Dan Marino, Miami — 321 yards vs. Houston

Eighth Week
Dan Fouts, San Diego — 410 yards vs. L.A. Raiders
Lynn Dickey, Green Bay — 364 yards vs. Seattle
Neil Lomax, St. Louis — 361 yards vs. Washington
Warren Moon, Houston — 356 yards vs. San Francisco
Joe Montana, San Francisco — 353 yards vs. Houston
Marc Wilson, L.A. Raiders — 332 yards vs. San Diego
Dan Marino, Miami — 316 yards vs. New England
Tony Eason, New England — 313 yards vs. Miami
Dave Krieg, Seattle — 310 yards vs. Green Bay
Paul McDonald, Cleveland — 300 yards vs. Cincinnati

Ninth Week
Joe Montana, San Francisco — 365 yards vs. L.A. Rams
Ron Jaworski, Philadelphia — 340 yards vs. St. Louis
Phil Simms, N.Y. Giants — 339 yards vs. Washington
Bill Kenney, Kansas City — 332 yards vs. Tampa Bay

Tenth Week
Dan Marino, Miami — 422 yards vs. N.Y. Jets
Neil Lomax, St. Louis — 341 yards vs. L.A. Rams
John Elway, Denver — 315 yards vs. New England
Tony Eason, New England — 313 yards vs. Denver
Joe Montana, San Francisco — 301 yards vs. Cincinnati

Eleventh Week
Neil Lomax, St. Louis — 388 yards vs. Dallas
Lynn Dickey, Green Bay — 303 yards vs. Minnesota

Twelfth Week
Dan Fouts, San Diego — 380 yards vs. Miami
Dan Marino, Miami — 338 yards vs. San Diego
Steve DeBerg, Tampa Bay — 316 yards vs. San Francisco

Thirteenth Week
Dave Krieg, Seattle — 406 yards vs. Denver
Phil Simms, N.Y. Giants — 343 yards vs. Kansas City
Steve DeBerg, Tampa Bay — 322 yards vs. L.A. Rams
Joe Theismann, Washington — 311 yards vs. Buffalo
Gary Danielson, Detroit — 305 yards vs. Green Bay

Fourteenth Week
Dan Marino, Miami — 470 yards vs. L.A. Raiders
Ken O'Brien, N.Y. Jets — 351 yards vs. N.Y. Giants
Warren Moon, Houston — 303 yards vs. Pittsburgh

Fifteenth Week
Dan Marino, Miami — 404 yards vs. Indianapolis
Danny White, Dallas — 327 yards vs. Washington
Dave Wilson, New Orleans — 325 yards vs. Cincinnati
Bill Kenney, Kansas City — 312 yards vs. Seattle
Neil Lomax, St. Louis — 300 yards vs. N.Y. Giants

Sixteenth Week
Neil Lomax, St. Louis — 468 yards vs. Washington
Dan Marino, Miami — 340 yards vs. Dallas
Dave Krieg, Seattle — 334 yards vs. Denver
Joe Pisarcik, Philadelphia — 334 yards vs. Atlanta
Ed Luther, San Diego — 333 yards vs. Kansas City
Warren Moon, Houston — 306 yards vs. Cleveland

Times 300 or more
Marino 9; Lomax 7; Fouts 5; Dickey, Montana, Moon, Simms 4; Anderson, Eason, Krieg 3; DeBerg, Hogeboom, Kenney, McDonald, Plunkett, Theismann, Wilson 2.

Ten Best Receiving Yardage Performances, 1984

	Yards	No.	TD
1. James Lofton Green Bay vs. Denver, October 15	206	11	1
2. Art Monk Washington vs. San Francisco, Sept. 10	200	10	0
3. Roy Green St. Louis vs. Washington, December 16	196	8	2
4. Alfred Jackson Atlanta vs. San Francisco, December 2	193	11	1
5. Steve Largent Seattle vs. Denver, November 25	191	12	1
Ozzie Newsome Cleveland vs. N.Y. Jets, October 14	191	14	0
7. Roy Green St. Louis vs. Dallas, October 7	189	8	2
8. Roy Green St. Louis vs. Indianapolis, September 16	183	8	2
Louis Lipps Pittsburgh vs. Kansas City, September 2	183	6	2
10. Bobby Duckworth San Diego vs. Chicago, December 3	179	3	1

100-Yard Receiving Performances, 1984
(Number in parentheses is receptions.)

First Week

Louis Lipps, Pittsburgh	183 yards (6) vs. Kansas City
Mark Duper, Miami	178 yards (6) vs. Washington
John Stallworth, Pittsburgh	167 yards (8) vs. Kansas City
Byron Williams, N.Y. Giants	167 yards (5) vs. Philadelphia
Mike Quick, Philadelphia	147 yards (8) vs. N.Y. Giants
Cris Collinsworth, Cincinnati	141 yards (10) vs. Denver
Doug Donley, Dallas	137 yards (9) vs. L.A. Rams
Bobby Johnson, N.Y. Giants	137 yards (8) vs. Philadelphia
James Lofton, Green Bay	134 yards (7) vs. St. Louis
Bobby Duckworth, San Diego	115 yards (4) vs. Minnesota
Stephen Starring, New England	105 yards (3) vs. Buffalo

Second Week

Art Monk, Washington	200 yards (10) vs. San Francisco
Pete Holohan, San Diego	133 yards (6) vs. Seattle
Billy Johnson, Atlanta	116 yards (8) vs. Detroit
Anthony Hancock, Kansas City	109 yards (3) vs. Cincinnati
Dwight Clark, San Francisco	105 yards (5) vs. Washington
Tim Smith, Houston	102 yards (6) vs. Indianapolis

Third Week

Roy Green, St. Louis	183 yards (8) vs. Indianapolis
Tim Smith, Houston	159 yards (5) vs. San Diego
Drew Hill, L.A. Rams	152 yards (4) vs. Pittsburgh
M.L. Harris, Cincinnati	148 yards (4) vs. N.Y. Jets
Kellen Winslow, San Diego	146 yards (10) vs. Houston
Malcolm Barnwell, L.A. Raiders	129 yards (8) vs. Kansas City
Doug Donley, Dallas	122 yards (5) vs. Philadelphia
Tracy Porter, Indianapolis	120 yards (4) vs. St. Louis
Bobby Johnson, N.Y. Giants	117 yards (6) vs. Washington
Paul Johns, Seattle	105 yards (8) vs. New England
Duriel Harris, Cleveland	104 yards (5) vs. Denver
Stacey Bailey, Atlanta	102 yards (4) vs. Minnesota
John Stallworth, Pittsburgh	100 yards (6) vs. L.A. Rams

Fourth Week

Mark Duper, Miami	173 yards (7) vs. Indianapolis
Henry Marshall, Kansas City	148 yards (8) vs. Denver
Hoby Brenner, New Orleans	131 yards (6) vs. St. Louis
Wesley Walker, N.Y. Jets	128 yards (7) vs. Buffalo
Todd Christensen, L.A. Raiders	120 yards (8) vs. San Diego
Kellen Winslow, San Diego	119 yards (9) vs. L.A. Raiders
Doug Cosbie, Dallas	103 yards (7) vs. Green Bay
Leo Lewis, Minnesota	101 yards (5) vs. Detroit

Fifth Week

Mark Duper, Miami	164 yards (8) vs. St. Louis
Mark Clayton, Miami	143 yards (5) vs. St. Louis
Steve Largent, Seattle	130 yards (8) vs. Minnesota
John Stallworth, Pittsburgh	119 yards (6) vs. Cincinnati
Earnest Gray, N.Y. Giants	112 yards (9) vs. L.A. Rams

Sixth Week

Roy Green, St. Louis	189 yards (8) vs. Dallas
Marcus Allen, L.A. Raiders	173 yards (4) vs. Seattle
Stacey Bailey, Atlanta	158 yards (7) vs. L.A. Rams
James Lofton, Green Bay	158 yards (5) vs. San Diego
Kellen Winslow, San Diego	157 yards (15) vs. Green Bay
Art Monk, Washington	141 yards (8) vs. Indianapolis
Kevin House, Tampa Bay	126 yards (7) vs. Minnesota
Duriel Harris, Cleveland	136 yards (8) vs. New England
Steve Watson, Denver	111 yards (7) vs. Detroit
Mark Clayton, Miami	110 yards (5) vs. Pittsburgh
Mike Jones, Minnesota	110 yards (6) vs. Tampa Bay
Paul Coffman, Green Bay	104 yards (8) vs. San Diego

Seventh Week

James Lofton, Green Bay	206 yards (11) vs. Denver
Ozzie Newsome, Cleveland	191 yards (14) vs. N.Y. Jets
Roy Green, St. Louis	166 yards (6) vs. Chicago
Carlos Carson, Kansas City	165 yards (7) vs. San Diego
Tony Hill, Dallas	134 yards (9) vs. Washington
Mike Jones, Minnesota	132 yards (5) vs. L.A. Raiders
Lionel Manuel, N.Y. Giants	120 yards (4) vs. Atlanta
Steve Largent, Seattle	106 yards (5) vs. Buffalo
Calvin Muhammad, Washington	104 yards (5) vs. Dallas
Stanley Morgan, New England	102 yards (3) vs. Cincinnati

Eighth Week

Roy Green, St. Louis	163 yards (6) vs. Washington
James Lofton, Green Bay	162 yards (5) vs. Seattle
Steve Largent, Seattle	129 yards (7) vs. Green Bay
Dwight Clark, San Francisco	127 yards (5) vs. Houston
Mark Nichols, Detroit	117 yards (5) vs. Minnesota
Stanley Morgan, New England	114 yards (3) vs. Miami
Gerald Carter, Tampa Bay	109 yards (10) vs. Chicago
Kellen Winslow, San Diego	107 yards (8) vs. L.A. Raiders
Tim Smith, Houston	101 yards (6) vs. San Francisco
John Stallworth, Pittsburgh	101 yards (5) vs. Indianapolis

Ninth Week

Mike Quick, Philadelphia	170 yards (6) vs. St. Louis
Carlos Carson, Kansas City	131 yards (7) vs. Tampa Bay
Earnest Gray, N.Y. Giants	128 yards (7) vs. Washington
Tony Hill, Dallas	125 yards (8) vs. Indianapolis
Mark Clayton, Miami	106 yards (3) vs. Buffalo
Art Monk, Washington	104 yards (4) vs. N.Y. Giants
Tyrone Young, New Orleans	101 yards (4) vs. Cleveland
Kevin House, Tampa Bay	100 yards (10) vs. Kansas City

Tenth Week

Butch Johnson, Denver	156 yards (9) vs. New England
Mark Duper, Miami	155 yards (7) vs. N.Y. Jets
Steve Watson, Denver	134 yards (8) vs. New England
Ken Jenkins, Detroit	128 yards (8) vs. Philadelphia
Dwight Clark, San Francisco	124 yards (7) vs. Cincinnati
Stanley Morgan, New England	122 yards (8) vs. Denver
Charlie Joiner, San Diego	119 yards (9) vs. Indianapolis
Mike Quick, Philadelphia	110 yards (5) vs. Detroit
John Stallworth, Pittsburgh	109 yards (4) vs. Houston
Roy Green, St. Louis	105 yards (5) vs. L.A. Rams
Nat Moore, Miami	105 yards (5) vs. N.Y. Jets
Lionel Manuel, N.Y. Giants	102 yards (5) vs. Dallas

Eleventh Week

James Lofton, Green Bay	119 yards (4) vs. Minnesota
Tim Smith, Houston	107 yards (8) vs. Kansas City
Calvin Muhammad, Washington	105 yards (7) vs. Detroit
Freddie Solomon, San Francisco	105 yards (5) vs. Cleveland

Twelfth Week

Gerald Carter, Tampa Bay	166 yards (9) vs. San Francisco
James Lofton, Green Bay	129 yards (6) vs. L.A. Rams
Steve Watson, Denver	123 yards (5) vs. Minnesota
Eric Sievers, San Diego	119 yards (12) vs. Miami
Ottis Anderson, St. Louis	112 yards (6) vs. N.Y. Giants
Derrick Ramsey, New England	104 yards (8) vs. Indianapolis

Thirteenth Week

Steve Largent, Seattle	191 yards (12) vs. Denver
Carlos Carson, Kansas City	153 yards (5) vs. N.Y. Giants
Cris Collinsworth, Cincinnati	134 yards (6) vs. Atlanta
Zeke Mowatt, N.Y. Giants	126 yards (7) vs. Kansas City
Tony Hill, Dallas	125 yards (8) vs. New England
Louis Lipps, Pittsburgh	118 yards (7) vs. San Diego
John Stallworth, Pittsburgh	116 yards (7) vs. San Diego
Mark Nichols, Detroit	108 yards (4) vs. Green Bay
Mike Quick, Philadelphia	107 yards (8) vs. St. Louis
Wes Chandler, San Diego	105 yards (4) vs. Pittsburgh

| Art Monk, Washington | 104 yards (11) vs. Buffalo |
| Ozzie Newsome, Cleveland | 102 yards (10) vs. Houston |

Fourteenth Week

Alfred Jackson, Atlanta	193 yards (11) vs. San Francisco
Bobby Duckworth, San Diego	179 yards (3) vs. Chicago
Mark Clayton, Miami	177 yards (9) vs. L.A. Raiders
Leo Lewis, Minnesota	130 yards (7) vs. Washington
Mickey Shuler, N.Y. Jets	127 yards (11) vs. N.Y. Giants
Carlos Carson, Kansas City	126 yards (7) vs. Denver
Dokie Williams, L.A. Raiders	122 yards (2) vs. Miami
Calvin Muhammad, Washington	115 yards (5) vs. Minnesota
John Spagnola, Philadelphia	114 yards (11) vs. Dallas
John Stallworth, Pittsburgh	113 yards (6) vs. Houston
Tim Smith, Houston	108 yards (7) vs. Pittsburgh
Kevin House, Tampa Bay	105 yards (6) vs. Green Bay
Steve Largent, Seattle	104 yards (8) vs. Detroit
Lam Jones, N.Y. Jets	103 yards (4) vs. N.Y. Giants

Fifteenth Week

Henry Marshall, Kansas City	166 yards (8) vs. Seattle
Mark Clayton, Miami	127 yards (9) vs. Indianapolis
Renaldo Nehemiah, San Fran.	125 yards (6) vs. Minnesota
Tony Hill, Dallas	119 yards (7) vs. Washington
Hoby Brenner, New Orleans	101 yards (3) vs. Cincinnati
Stanley Morgan, New England	101 yards (5) vs. Philadelphia

Sixteenth Week

Roy Green, St. Louis	196 yards (8) vs. Washington
Tim Smith, Houston	167 yards (7) vs. Cleveland
Mark Clayton, Miami	150 yards (4) vs. Dallas
Stacey Bailey, Atlanta	140 yards (8) vs. Philadelphia
Art Monk, Washington	136 yards (11) vs. St. Louis
Mike Quick, Philadelphia	135 yards (7) vs. Atlanta
Ottis Anderson, St. Louis	124 yards (12) vs. Washington
Tony Hill, Dallas	115 yards (6) vs. Miami
Calvin Muhammad, Washington	110 yards (5) vs. St. Louis

Times 100 or More

Stallworth 7; Clayton, Green, Lofton, T. Smith 6; T. Hill, Largent, Monk, Quick 5; Carson, Duper, Morgan, Muhammad, Winslow 4; Bailey, Clark, House, Watson 3; O. Anderson, Brenner, Carter, Collinsworth, Donley, Duckworth, Gray, Harris, Johnson, M. Jones, Lewis, Lipps, Manuel, Marshall, Newsome, Nichols 2.

AMERICAN FOOTBALL CONFERENCE OFFENSE

	Buff.	Cin.	Clev.	Den.	Hou.	Ind.	K.C.	Raid.	Mia.	N.E.	N.Y.J.	Pitt.	S.D.	Sea.
First Downs	263	339	295	299	284	254	295	301	387	315	310	302	374	287
Rushing	98	135	89	121	95	114	88	114	115	104	118	117	106	94
Passing	149	179	180	152	164	117	178	162	243	186	176	167	240	171
Penalty	16	25	26	26	25	23	29	25	29	25	16	18	28	22
Rushes	398	540	489	508	433	510	408	516	484	482	504	574	456	495
Net Yds. Gained	1643	2179	1696	2076	1656	2025	1527	1886	1918	2032	2189	2179	1654	1645
Avg. Gain	4.1	4.0	3.5	4.1	3.8	4.0	3.7	3.7	4.0	4.2	4.3	3.8	3.6	3.3
Avg. Yds. per Game	102.7	136.2	106.0	129.8	103.5	126.6	95.4	117.9	119.9	127.0	136.8	136.2	103.4	102.8
Passes Attempted	588	496	495	475	487	411	593	491	572	500	488	443	662	497
Completed	298	306	273	263	282	206	305	266	367	292	272	240	401	283
% Completed	50.7	61.7	55.2	55.4	57.9	50.1	51.4	54.2	64.2	58.4	55.7	54.2	60.6	56.9
Total Yds. Gained	3252	3659	3490	3116	3610	2543	3869	3718	5146	3685	3341	3519	4928	3751
Times Sacked	60	45	55	35	49	58	33	54	14	66	52	35	36	42
Yds. Lost	554	358	358	257	382	436	301	360	128	454	382	278	285	328
Net Yds. Gained	2698	3301	3132	2859	3228	2107	3568	3358	5018	3231	2959	3241	4643	3423
Avg. Yds. per Game	168.6	206.3	195.8	178.7	201.8	131.7	223.0	209.9	313.6	201.9	184.9	202.6	290.2	213.9
Net Yds. per Pass Play	4.16	6.10	5.69	5.61	6.02	4.49	5.70	6.16	8.56	5.71	5.48	6.78	6.65	6.35
Yds. Gained per Comp.	10.91	11.96	12.78	11.85	12.80	12.34	12.69	13.98	14.02	12.62	12.28	14.66	12.29	13.25
Combined Net Yds. Gained	4341	5480	4828	4935	4884	4132	5095	5244	6936	5263	5148	5420	6297	5068
% Total Yds. Rushing	37.8	39.8	35.1	42.1	33.9	49.0	30.0	36.0	27.7	38.6	42.5	40.2	26.3	32.5
% Total Yds. Passing	62.2	60.2	64.9	57.9	66.1	51.0	70.0	64.0	72.3	61.4	57.5	59.8	73.7	67.5
Avg. Yds. per Game	271.3	342.5	301.8	308.4	305.3	258.3	318.4	327.8	433.5	328.9	321.8	338.8.	393.6	316.8
Ball Control Plays	1046	1081	1039	1018	969	979	1034	1061	1070	1048	1044	1052	1154	1034
Avg. Yds. per Play	4.2	5.1	4.6	4.8	5.0	4.2	4.9	4.9	6.5	5.0	4.9	5.2	5.5	4.9
Avg. Time of Poss.	28:43	30:50	30:53	28:56	28:02	27:24	27:25	29:26	30:18	29:51	30:02	30:33	31:43	30:46
Third Down Efficiency	35.4	44.1	39.0	32.5	33.2	29.9	32.7	35.9	51.5	39.6	41.5	40.3	47.1	37.8
Had Intercepted	30	22	23	17	15	22	22	28	18	14	21	25	21	26
Yds. Opp. Returned	416	364	518	189	214	423	683	300	377	237	207	371	180	333
Ret. by Opp. for TD	4	2	3	0	2	2	7	2	1	3	0	1	0	3
Punts	90	67	76	96	88	98	98	91	51	92	75	70	66	95
Yds. Punted	3696	2832	3213	3850	3482	4383	4397	3809	2281	3904	2935	2883	2773	3567
Avg. Yds. per Punt	41.1	42.3	42.3	40.1	39.6	44.7	44.9	41.9	44.7	42.4	39.1	41.2	42.0	37.5
Punt Returns	33	38	40	41	26	38	42	67	39	48	35	61	33	44
Yds. Returned	297	473	322	318	152	278	346	667	365	430	324	696	212	484
Avg. Yds. per Return	9.0	12.4	8.1	7.8	5.8	7.3	8.2	10.0	9.4	9.0	9.3	11.4	6.4	11.0
Returned for TD	1	0	0	0	0	0	0	1	0	0	0	1	1	1
Kickoff Returns	76	61	61	45	69	69	56	56	44	63	65	54	63	54
Yds. Returned	1422	1155	1157	897	1352	1331	1061	1216	799	1246	1498	1026	1319	1007
Avg. Yds. per Return	18.7	18.9	19.0	19.9	19.6	19.3	18.9	21.7	18.2	19.8	23.0	19.0	20.9	18.6
Returned for TD	0	0	0	0	0	1	0	0	0	0	1	0	0	0
Penalties	121	85	111	78	99	95	98	143	67	86	96	112	112	128
Yds. Penalized	997	693	928	636	813	798	801	1209	527	674	779	948	1023	1179
Fumbles	31	32	31	36	36	35	34	42	26	29	26	40	35	24
Lost	14	17	16	17	16	16	15	20	10	15	13	15	17	13
Out of Bounds	6	2	1	1	1	5	3	2	0	2	1	2	4	3
Own Rec. for TD	0	0	1	0	0	0	0	0	0	1	0	0	0	0
Opp. Rec. by	21	15	15	24	11	13	11	14	12	8	18	10	17	25
Opp. Rec. for TD	2	0	0	4	1	0	0	1	1	0	2	2	0	1
Total Points Scored	250	339	250	353	240	239	314	368	513	362	332	387	394	418
Total TDs	31	39	25	42	28	28	35	44	70	42	40	45	48	51
TDs Rushing	9	18	10	12	13	13	12	19	18	15	17	13	18	10
TDs Passing	18	17	14	22	14	13	21	21	49	26	20	25	25	32
TDs on Ret. and Rec.	4	4	1	8	1	2	2	4	3	1	3	7	5	9
Extra Points	31	37	25	38	27	27	35	40	66	42	39	45	46	50
Safeties	0	1	0	0	0	1	0	2	0	1	1	0	0	1
Field Goals Made	11	22	25	21	15	14	23	20	9	22	17	24	20	20
Field Goals Attempted	21	31	35	28	19	23	33	27	19	28	24	32	29	24
% Successful	52.4	71.0	71.4	75.0	78.9	60.9	69.7	74.1	47.4	78.6	70.8	75.0	69.0	83.3

AMERICAN FOOTBALL CONFERENCE DEFENSE

	Buff.	Cin.	Clev.	Den.	Hou.	Ind.	K.C.	Raid.	Mia.	N.E.	N.Y.J.	Pitt.	S.D.	Sea.
First Downs	345	322	270	311	345	343	335	297	314	311	341	282	322	288
Rushing	134	115	103	90	158	124	121	107	130	109	117	87	109	99
Passing	186	191	145	206	168	194	192	147	172	182	198	167	189	160
Penalty	25	16	22	15	19	25	22	43	12	20	26	28	24	29
Rushes	531	477	494	435	596	559	523	517	458	498'	497	454	457	475
Net Yds. Gained	2106	1868	1945	1664	2789	2007	1980	1892	2155	1886	2064	1617	1851	1789
Avg. Gain	4.0	3.9	3.9	3.8	4.7	3.6	3.8	3.7	4.7	3.8	4.2	3.6	4.1	3.8
Avg. Yds. per Game	131.6	116.8	121.6	104.0	174.3	125.4	123.8	118.3	134.7	117.9	129.0	101.1	115.7	111.8
Passes Attempted	495	517	458	631	447	515	586	508	551	513	511	515	531	521
Completed	300	302	261	346	271	298	332	254	310	283	312	299	323	265
% Completed	60.6	58.4	57.0	54.8	60.6	57.9	56.7	50.0	56.3	55.2	61.1	58.1	60.8	50.9
Total Yds. Gained	3667	3689	3049	4453	3446	3890	4009	3268	3604	3666	3862	3689	4303	3572
Times Sacked	26	40	43	57	32	42	50	64	42	55	44	47	33	55
Yds. Lost	191	298	353	430	267	320	364	516	339	452	360	390	218	398
Net Yds. Gained	3476	3391	2696	4023	3179	3570	3645	2752	3265	3214	3502	3299	4085	3174
Avg. Yds. per Game	217.3	211.9	168.5	251.4	198.7	223.1	227.8	172.0	204.1	200.9	218.9	206.2	255.3	198.4
Net Yds. per Pass Play	6.67	6.09	5.38	5.85	6.64	6.41	5.73	4.81	5.51	5.66	6.31	5.87	7.24	5.51
Yds. Gained per Comp.	12.22	12.22	11.68	12.87	12.72	13.05	12.08	12.87	11.63	12.95	12.38	12.34	13.32	13.48
Combined Net Yds. Gained	5582	5259	4641	5687	5968	5577	5625	4644	5420	5100	5566	4916	5936	4963
% Total Yds. Rushing	37.7	35.5	41.9	29.3	46.7	36.0	35.2	40.7	39.8	37.0	37.1	32.9	31.2	36.0
% Total Yds. Passing	62.3	64.5	58.1	70.7	53.3	64.0	64.8	59.3	60.2	63.0	62.9	67.1	68.8	64.0
Avg. Yds. per Game	348.9	328.7	290.1	355.4	373.0	348.6	351.6	290.3	338.8	318.8	347.9	307.3	371.0	310.2
Ball Control Plays	1052	1034	995	1123	1075	1116	1159	1089	1051	1066	1052	1016	1021	1051
Avg. Yds. per Play	5.3	5.1	4.7	5.1	5.6	5.0	4.9	4.3	5.2	4.8	5.3	4.8	5.8	4.7
Third Down Efficiency	42.9	40.6	39.6	35.4	47.7	42.6	36.6	30.1	41.1	39.7	39.7	32.9	42.1	34.0
Intercepted by	16	25	20	31	13	18	30	20	24	17	15	31	19	38
Yds. Returned by	233	368	236	510	139	190	465	339	478	210	152	433	499	697
Returned for TD	0	4	0	4	0	1	2	2	2	0	0	4	4	7
Punts	72	67	77	81	64	80	91	117	83	83	67	90	73	83
Yds. Punted	2812	2771	3123	3361	2702	3363	3642	5071	3476	3347	2854	3818	2890	3345
Avg. Yds. per Punt	39.1	41.4	40.6	41.5	42.2	42.0	40.0	43.3	41.9	40.3	42.6	42.4	39.6	40.3
Punt Returns	52	38	43	44	60	62	60	34	17	45	37	37	43	32
Yds. Returned	597	310	489	335	618	600	461	345	138	442	242	351	399	205
Avg. Yds. per Return	11.5	8.2	11.4	7.6	10.3	9.7	7.7	10.1	8.1	9.8	6.5	9.5	9.3	6.4
Returned for TD	0	0	0	0	0	0	0	0	0	1	0	1	0	1
Kickoff Returns	44	69	52	55	51	42	64	61	66	73	48	61	72	67
Yds. Returned	958	1446	1159	1181	986	849	1354	1063	1368	1373	1030	1338	1437	1116
Avg. Yds. per Return	21.8	21.0	22.3	21.5	19.3	20.2	21.2	17.4	20.7	18.8	21.5	21.9	20.0	16.7
Returned for TD	0	1	0	0	0	0	0	0	0	0	0	0	0	0
Penalties	87	90	108	104	105	98	108	121	93	87	87	107	108	114
Yds. Penalized	734	743	765	891	876	813	951	1061	772	773	723	945	905	883
Fumbles	36	27	34	44	24	29	18	28	23	33	34	30	34	47
Lost	21	15	15	24	11	13	11	14	12	8	18	11	17	25
Out of Bounds	1	2	0	3	1	2	1	5	1	4	2	2	3	3
Own Rec. for TD	1	0	0	0	0	0	0	0	0	0	0	0	0	0
Opp. Rec. by	14	16	16	17	16	16	15	20	10	15	13	15	17	13
Opp. Rec. for TD	0	0	2	0	1	1	2	0	0	2	0	1	1	1
Total Points Scored	454	339	297	241	437	414	324	278	298	352	364	310	413	282
Total TDs	56	39	30	26	53	50	38	33	39	42	41	35	51	34
TDs Rushing	19	21	10	10	27	16	10	12	16	11	16	12	23	11
TDs Passing	32	15	15	16	23	31	19	19	22	25	24	19	27	18
TDs on Ret. and Rec.	5	3	5	0	3	3	9	2	1	6	1	4	1	5
Extra Points	56	37	30	26	51	47	37	29	37	37	40	34	50	34
Safeties	1	1	0	1	1	2	1	0	0	0	0	0	0	1
Field Goals Made	20	22	29	19	22	21	19	17	9	21	26	22	19	14
Field Goals Attempted	28	27	33	33	30	23	27	21	17	31	37	28	25	22
% Successful	71.4	81.5	87.9	57.6	73.3	91.3	70.4	81.0	52.9	67.7	70.3	78.6	76.0	63.6

NATIONAL FOOTBALL CONFERENCE OFFENSE

	Atl.	Chi.	Dall.	Det.	G.B.	Rams	Minn.	N.O.	N.Y.G.	Phil.	St.L.	S.F.	T.B.	Wash.
First Downs	292	297	323	306	315	258	289	298	310	280	345	356	344	339
Rushing	123	164	93	118	120	140	111	131	97	83	129	138	114	154
Passing	151	115	202	170	168	100	150	137	198	176	200	204	209	164
Penalty	18	18	28	18	27	18	28	30	15	21	16	14	21	21
Rushes	489	674	469	446	461	541	444	523	493	381	488	534	483	588
Net Yds. Gained	1994	2974	1714	2017	2019	2864	1844	2171	1660	1338	2088	2465	1776	2274
Avg. Gain	4.1	4.4	3.7	4.5	4.4	5.3	4.2	4.2	3.4	3.5	4.3	4.6	3.7	3.9
Avg. Yds. per Game	124.6	185.9	107.1	126.1	126.2	179.0	115.3	135.7	103.8	83.6	130.5	154.1	111.0	142.1
Passes Attempted	478	390	604	531	506	358	533	476	535	606	566	496	563	485
Completed	294	226	322	298	281	176	281	246	288	331	347	312	334	286
% Completed	61.5	57.9	53.3	56.1	55.5	49.2	52.7	51.7	53.8	54.6	61.3	62.9	59.3	59.0
Total Yds. Gained	3546	2695	3995	3787	3740	2382	3337	3198	4066	3823	4634	4079	3907	3417
Times Sacked	67	36	48	61	42	32	64	45	55	60	49	27	45	48
Yds. Lost	496	232	389	486	310	240	465	361	434	463	377	178	362	341
Net Yds. Gained	3050	2463	3606	3301	3430	2142	2872	2837	3632	3360	4257	3901	3545	3076
Avg. Yds. per Game	190.6	153.9	225.4	206.3	214.4	133.9	179.5	177.3	227.0	210.0	266.1	243.8	221.6	192.3
Net Yds. per Pass Play	5.60	5.78	5.53	5.58	6.26	5.49	4.81	5.45	6.16	5.05	6.92	7.46	5.83	5.77
Yds. Gained per Comp.	12.06	11.92	12.41	12.71	13.31	13.53	11.88	13.00	14.12	11.55	13.35	13.07	11.70	11.95
Combined Net Yds. Gained	5044	5437	5320	5318	5449	5006	4716	5008	5292	4698	6345	6366	5321	5350
% Total Yds. Rushing	39.5	54.7	32.2	37.9	37.1	57.2	39.1	43.4	31.4	28.5	32.9	38.7	33.4	42.5
% Total Yds. Passing	60.5	45.3	67.8	62.1	62.9	42.8	60.9	56.6	68.6	71.5	67.1	61.3	66.6	57.5
Avg. Yds. per Game	315.3	339.8	332.5	332.4	340.6	312.9	294.8	313.0	330.8	293.6	396.6	397.9	332.6	334.4
Ball Control Plays	1034	1100	1121	1038	1009	931	1041	1044	1083	1047	1103	1057	1091	1121
Avg. Yds. per Play	4.9	4.9	4.7	5.1	5.4	5.4	4.5	4.8	4.9	4.5	5.8	6.0	4.9	4.8
Avg. Time of Poss.	30:14	35:08	29:00	29:43	26:48	28:22	28:14	30:13	30:44	29:30	32:43	30:26	31:17	32:49
Third Down Efficiency	35.3	41.2	34.9	39.1	36.6	33.3	34.7	39.7	36.6	33.2	41.4	46.4	42.9	45.3
Had Intercepted	20	15	26	22	30	17	25	28	18	17	16	10	23	13
Yds. Opp. Returned	304	241	382	251	317	240	344	420	222	211	219	155	249	159
Ret. by Opp. for TD	2	3	4	1	2	2	2	3	1	1	0	0	0	0
Punts	70	85	108	76	85	74	82	70	94	92	68	62	68	73
Yds. Punted	2855	3328	4123	3164	3596	2866	3473	3020	3598	3880	2594	2536	2849	2834
Avg. Yds. per Punt	40.8	39.2	38.2	41.6	42.3	38.7	42.4	43.1	38.3	42.2	38.1	40.9	41.9	38.8
Punt Returns	41	63	54	36	48	40	31	33	55	40	47	45	34	55
Yds. Returned	264	558	446	241	351	489	217	268	368	250	399	521	207	474
Avg. Yds. per Return	6.4	8.9	8.3	6.7	7.3	12.2	7.0	8.1	6.7	6.3	8.5	11.6	6.1	8.6
Returned for TD	0	0	0	0	0	2	0	0	0	0	0	1	0	0
Kickoff Returns	70	49	63	74	67	58	86	72	61	59	74	47	68	60
Yds. Returned	1367	896	1199	1347	1362	1244	1775	1465	1117	1156	1563	1039	1354	1174
Avg. Yds. per Return	19.5	18.3	19.0	18.2	20.3	21.4	20.6	20.3	18.3	19.6	21.1	22.1	19.9	19.6
Returned for TD	0	0	0	0	1	1	0	0	0	1	0	0	0	0
Penalties	125	114	100	138	110	93	90	101	79	77	109	100	118	80
Yds. Penalized	1011	851	947	1165	915	830	762	849	703	632	904	884	875	723
Fumbles	39	31	35	36	17	31	39	22	17	23	32	26	36	33
Lost	21	16	17	14	7	18	16	13	9	16	20	12	20	15
Out of Bounds	0	4	4	1	0	2	1	0	0	0	2	1	0	2
Own Rec. for TD	0	0	0	0	0	0	0	0	0	0	0	0	0	1
Opp. Rec. by	20	13	16	11	15	22	17	10	16	11	12	12	14	21
Opp. Rec. for TD	0	0	1	0	0	0	2	1	1	0	1	1	0	2
Total Points Scored	281	325	308	283	390	346	276	298	299	278	423	475	335	426
Total TDs	31	37	34	32	51	38	31	34	36	27	51	57	40	51
TDs Rushing	16	22	12	13	18	16	10	9	12	6	21	21	17	20
TDs Passing	14	14	19	19	30	16	18	21	22	19	28	32	22	24
TDs on Ret. and Rec.	1	1	3	0	3	6	3	4	2	2	2	4	1	7
Extra Points	31	35	33	31	48	37	30	34	32	26	48	56	38	48
Safeties	2	1	1	0	0	3	0	0	0	0	0	1	0	0
Field Goals Made	20	22	23	20	12	25	20	20	17	30	23	25	19	24
Field Goals Attempted	27	28	29	27	21	33	23	27	33	37	35	35	26	31
% Successful	74.1	78.6	79.3	74.1	57.1	75.8	87.0	74.1	51.5	81.1	65.7	71.4	73.1	77.4

NATIONAL FOOTBALL CONFERENCE DEFENSE

	Atl.	Chi.	Dall.	Det.	G.B.	Rams	Minn.	N.O.	N.Y.G.	Phil.	St.L.	S.F.	T.B.	Wash.
First Downs	317	216	283	328	323	309	342	298	296	307	292	302	311	307
Rushing	131	72	106	120	136	108	144	134	107	123	108	101	139	91
Passing	162	122	155	177	166	179	182	142	174	171	157	173	157	194
Penalty	24	22	22	31	21	22	16	22	15	13	27	28	15	22
Rushes	538	378	510	519	545	449	547	549	474	556	442	432	511	390
Net Yds. Gained	2153	1377	2226	1808	2145	1600	2573	2461	1818	2189	1923	1795	2233	1589
Avg. Gain	4.0	3.6	4.4	3.5	3.9	3.6	4.7	4.5	3.8	3.9	4.4	4.2	4.4	4.1
Avg. Yds. per Game	134.6	86.1	139.1	113.0	134.1	100.0	160.8	153.8	113.6	136.8	120.2	112.2	139.6	99.3
Passes Attempted	443	435	527	466	551	566	490	422	529	492	494	546	490	575
Completed	262	198	250	288	315	346	319	239	288	262	251	298	286	318
% Completed	59.1	45.5	47.4	61.8	57.2	61.1	65.1	56.6	54.4	53.3	50.8	54.6	58.4	55.3
Total Yds. Gained	3413	3069	3200	3782	3470	3964	3954	2873	3736	3506	3574	3744	3480	4301
Times Sacked	38	72	57	37	44	43	25	55	48	60	55	51	32	66
Yds. Lost	287	583	390	271	324	298	175	420	361	456	403	363	239	529
Net Yds. Gained	3126	2486	2810	3511	3146	3666	3779	2453	3375	3050	3171	3381	3241	3772
Avg. Yds. per Game	195.4	155.4	175.6	219.4	196.6	229.1	236.2	153.3	210.9	190.6	198.2	211.3	202.6	235.8
Net Yds. per Pass Play	6.50	4.90	4.81	6.98	5.29	6.02	7.34	5.14	5.85	5.53	5.78	5.66	6.21	5.88
Yds. Gained per Comp.	13.03	15.50	12.80	13.13	11.02	11.46	12.39	12.02	12.97	13.38	14.24	12.56	12.17	13.53
Combined Net Yds. Gained	5279	3863	5036	5319	5291	5266	6352	4914	5193	5239	5094	5176	5474	5361
% Total Yds. Rushing	40.8	35.6	44.2	34.0	40.5	30.4	40.5	50.1	35.0	41.8	37.8	34.7	40.8	29.6
% Total Yds. Passing	59.2	64.4	55.8	66.0	59.5	69.6	59.5	49.9	65.0	58.2	62.2	65.3	59.2	70.4
Avg. Yds. per Game	329.9	241.4	314.8	332.4	330.7	329.1	397.0	307.1	324.6	327.4	318.4	323.5	342.1	335.1
Ball Control Plays	1019	885	1094	1022	1140	1058	1062	1026	1051	1108	991	1029	1033	1031
Avg. Yds. per Play	5.2	4.4	4.6	5.2	4.6	5.0	6.0	4.8	4.9	4.7	5.1	5.0	5.3	5.2
Third Down Efficiency	44.3	26.4	33.6	45.4	36.6	39.1	45.5	37.7	37.5	41.7	34.8	35.2	43.9	37.4
Intercepted by	12	21	28	14	27	17	11	13	19	20	21	25	18	21
Yds. Returned by	147	290	297	87	338	399	120	213	182	287	163	345	308	401
Returned for TD	1	1	2	0	2	3	1	3	0	0	1	2	1	4
Punts	60	100	99	73	89	71	68	84	92	89	81	80	68	78
Yds. Punted	2497	4160	4236	2921	3643	2949	2777	3492	3677	3497	3157	3239	2787	3114
Avg. Yds. per Punt	41.6	41.6	42.8	40.0	40.9	41.5	40.8	41.6	40.0	39.3	39.0	40.5	41.0	39.9
Punt Returns	42	41	55	49	46	35	49	47	50	58	27	30	36	38
Yds. Returned	450	249	230	516	368	196	435	550	479	486	239	190	310	187
Avg. Yds. per Return	10.7	6.1	4.2	10.5	8.0	5.6	8.9	11.7	9.6	8.4	8.9	6.3	8.6	4.9
Returned for TD	1	0	0	1	0	0	0	1	2	0	0	0	0	0
Kickoff Returns	48	68	65	60	73	74	59	45	55	69	85	78	67	73
Yds. Returned	1053	1443	1310	1250	1171	1288	1281	916	1088	1298	1549	1499	1336	1404
Avg. Yds. per Return	21.9	21.2	20.2	20.8	16.0	17.4	21.7	20.4	19.8	18.8	18.2	19.2	19.9	19.2
Returned for TD	0	1	0	0	0	0	0	0	0	0	1	0	0	1
Penalties	93	86	95	107	145	115	113	119	93	96	75	91	136	84
Yds. Penalized	820	698	868	978	1129	871	1047	1025	699	904	578	723	1078	803
Fumbles	36	33	35	28	33	42	35	28	24	32	20	28	27	32
Lost	20	13	16	11	15	22	18	10	16	11	12	13	14	22
Out of Bounds	0	2	2	0	2	3	2	1	0	6	0	1	0	1
Own Rec. for TD	0	0	0	0	0	0	1	0	0	1	0	0	0	0
Opp. Rec. by	21	16	17	13	7	17	15	13	9	16	20	12	20	15
Opp. Rec. for TD	2	1	1	2	2	0	1	1	1	0	1	0	0	0
Total Points Scored	382	248	308	408	309	316	484	361	301	320	345	227	380	310
Total TDs	48	29	36	48	34	36	59	41	35	36	39	24	47	39
TDs Rushing	16	10	8	17	14	15	20	13	10	12	11	10	27	13
TDs Passing	27	14	23	27	16	18	35	23	20	22	26	14	20	25
TDs on Ret. and Rec.	5	5	5	4	4	3	4	5	5	2	2	0	0	1
Extra Points	46	26	35	48	33	32	58	41	34	36	36	24	44	37
Safeties	0	0	0	0	0	1	0	1	3	1	0	1	0	0
Field Goals Made	16	16	19	24	24	22	24	24	17	22	25	19	18	13
Field Goals Attempted	30	22	28	29	31	31	28	33	26	35	38	25	27	20
% Successful	53.3	72.7	67.9	82.8	77.4	71.0	85.7	72.7	65.4	62.9	65.8	76.0	66.7	65.0

AFC, NFC, AND NFL SUMMARY

	AFC Offense Total	AFC Offense Average	AFC Defense Total	AFC Defense Average	NFC Offense Total	NFC Offense Average	NFC Defense Total	NFC Defense Average	NFL Total	NFL Average
First Downs	4305	307.5	4426	316.1	4352	310.9	4231	302.2	8657	309.2
Rushing	1508	107.7	1603	114.5	1715	122.5	1620	115.7	3223	115.1
Passing	2464	176.0	2497	178.4	2344	167.4	2311	165.1	4808	171.7
Penalty	333	23.8	326	23.3	293	20.9	300	21.4	626	22.4
Rushes	6797	485.5	6971	497.9	7014	501.0	6840	488.6	13,811	493.3
Net Yds. Gained	26,305	1878.9	27,613	1972.4	29,198	2085.6	27,890	1992.1	55,503	1982.3
Avg. Gain	—	3.9	—	4.0	—	4.2	—	4.1	—	4.0
Avg. Yds. per Game	—	117.4	—	123.3	—	130.3	—	124.5	—	123.9
Passes Attempted	7198	514.1	7299	521.4	7127	509.1	7026	501.9	14,325	511.6
Completed	4054	289.6	4156	296.9	4022	287.3	3920	280.0	8076	288.4
% Completed	—	56.3	—	56.9	—	56.4	—	55.8	—	56.4
Total Yds. Gained	51,627	3687.6	52,167	3726.2	50,606	3614.7	50,066	3576.1	102,233	3651.2
Times Sacked	634	45.3	630	45.0	679	48.5	683	48.8	1313	46.9
Yds. Lost	4861	347.2	4896	349.7	5134	366.7	5099	364.2	9995	357.0
Net Yds. Gained	46,766	3340.4	47,271	3376.5	45,472	3248.0	44,967	3211.9	92,238	3294.2
Avg. Yds. per Game	—	208.8	—	211.0	—	203.0	—	200.7	—	205.9
Net Yds. per Pass Play	—	5.97	—	5.96	—	5.83	—	5.83	—	5.90
Yds. Gained per Comp.	—	12.73	—	12.55	—	12.58	—	12.77	—	12.66
Combined Net Yds. Gained	73,071	5219.4	74,884	5348.9	74,670	5333.6	72,857	5204.1	147,741	5276.5
% Total Yds. Rushing	—	36.00	—	36.87	—	39.10	—	38.28	—	37.57
% Total Yds. Passing	—	64.00	—	63.13	—	60.90	—	61.72	—	62.43
Avg. Yds. per Game	—	326.2	—	334.3	—	333.3	—	325.3	—	329.8
Ball Control Plays	14,629	1044.9	14,900	1064.3	14,820	1058.6	14,549	1039.2	29,449	1051.8
Avg. Plays per Play	—	5.0	—	5.0	—	5.0	—	5.0	—	5.0
Third Down Efficiency	—	38.6	—	38.8	—	38.7	—	38.5	—	38.7
Interceptions	304	21.7	317	22.6	280	20.0	267	19.1	584	20.9
Yds. Returned	4812	343.7	4949	353.5	3714	265.3	3577	255.5	8526	304.5
Returned for TD	30	2.1	30	2.1	21	1.5	21	1.5	51	1.8
Punts	1153	82.4	1128	80.6	1107	79.1	1132	80.9	2260	80.7
Yds. Punted	48,005	3428.9	46,575	3326.8	44,716	3194.0	46,146	3296.1	92,721	3311.5
Avg. Yds. per Punt	—	41.6	—	41.3	—	40.4	—	40.8	—	41.0
Punt Returns	585	41.8	604	43.1	622	44.4	603	43.1	1207	43.1
Yds. Returned	5364	383.1	5532	395.1	5053	360.9	4885	348.9	10,417	372.0
Avg. Yds. per Return	—	9.2	—	9.2	—	8.1	—	8.1	—	8.6
Returned for TD	5	0.4	3	0.2	3	0.2	5	0.4	8	0.3
Kickoff Returns	836	59.7	825	58.9	908	64.9	919	65.6	1744	62.3
Yds. Returned	16,486	1177.6	16,658	1189.9	18,058	1289.9	17,886	1277.6	34,544	1233.7
Avg. Yds. per Return	—	19.7	—	20.2	—	19.9	—	19.5	—	19.8
Returned for TD	2	0.1	2	0.1	3	0.2	3	0.2	5	0.2
Penalties	1431	102.2	1417	101.2	1434	102.4	1448	103.4	2865	102.3
Yds. Penalized	12,005	857.5	11,835	845.4	12,051	860.8	12,221	872.9	24,056	859.1
Fumbles	457	32.6	441	31.5	417	29.8	433	30.9	874	31.2
Lost	214	15.3	215	15.4	214	15.3	213	15.2	428	15.3
Out of Bounds	33	2.4	30	2.1	17	1.2	20	1.4	50	1.8
Own Rec. for TD	2	0.1	1	0.1	1	0.1	2	0.1	3	0.1
Opp. Rec.	214	15.3	213	15.2	210	15.0	211	15.1	424	15.1
Opp. Rec. for TD	14	1.0	11	0.8	9	0.6	12	0.9	23	0.8
Total Points Scored	4759	339.9	4803	343.1	4743	338.8	4699	335.6	9502	339.4
Total TDs	568	40.6	567	40.5	550	39.3	551	39.4	1118	39.9
TDs Rushing	197	14.1	214	15.3	213	15.2	196	14.0	410	14.6
TDs Passing	317	22.6	305	21.8	298	21.3	310	22.1	615	22.0
TDs on Ret. and Rec.	54	3.9	48	3.4	39	2.8	45	3.2	93	3.3
Extra Points	548	39.1	545	38.9	527	37.6	530	37.9	1075	38.4
Safeties	7	0.5	8	0.6	8	0.6	7	0.5	15	0.5
Field Goals Made	263	18.8	280	20.0	300	21.4	283	20.2	563	20.1
Field Goals Attempted	373	26.6	382	27.3	412	29.4	403	28.8	785	28.0
% Successful	—	70.5	—	73.3	—	72.8	—	70.2	—	71.7

CLUB LEADERS

	Offense	Defense
First Downs	Mia. 387	Chi. 216
Rushing	Chi. 164	Chi. 72
Passing	Mia. 243	Chi. 122
Penalty	N.O. 30	Mia. 12
Rushes	Chi. 674	Chi. 378
Net Yds. Gained	Chi. 2974	Chi. 1377
Avg. Gain	Rams 5.3	Det. 3.5
Passes Attempted	S.D. 662	N.O. 422
Completed	S.D. 401	Chi. 198
% Completed	Mia. 64.2	Chi. 45.5
Total Yds. Gained	Mia. 5146	N.O. 2873
Times Sacked	Mia. 14	Chi. 72
Yds. Lost	Mia. 128	Chi. 583
Net Yds. Gained	Mia. 5018	N.O. 2453
Net Yds. per Pass Play	Mia. 8.56	Raid. & Dal. 4.81
Yds. Gained per Comp.	Pitt. 14.66	G.B. 11.02
Combined Net Yds. Gained	Mia. 6936	Chi. 3863
% Total Yds. Rushing	Rams 57.2	Den. 29.3
% Total Yds. Passing	S.D. 73.7	N.O. 49.9
Ball Control Plays	S.D. 1154	Chi. 885
Avg. Yds. per Play	Mia. 6.5	Raiders 4.3
Avg. Time of Poss.	Chi. 35:08	—
Third Down Efficiency	Mia. 51.5	Chi. 26.4
Interceptions	—	Sea. 38
Yds. Returned	—	Sea. 697
Returned for TD	—	Sea. 7
Punts	Dall. 108	—
Yds. Punted	K.C. 4397	—
Avg. Yds. per Punt	K.C. 44.9	—
Punt Returns	Raiders 67	Mia. 17
Yds. Returned	Pitt. 696	Mia. 138
Avg. Yds. per Return	Cin. 12.4	Dall. 4.2
Returned for TD	Rams 2	—
Kickoff Returns	Minn. 86	Ind. 42
Yds. Returned	Minn. 1775	Ind. 849
Avg. Yds. per Return	N.Y.J. 23.0	G.B. 16.0
Returned for TD	Five with 1	—
Total Points Scored	Mia. 513	S.F. 227
Total TDs	Mia. 70	S.F. 24
TDs Rushing	Chi. 22	Dall. 8
TDs Passing	Mia. 49	Chi. & S.F. 14
TDs on Ret. and Rec.	Sea. 9	Three with 0
Extra Points	Mia. 66	S.F. 24
Safeties	Rams 3	—
Field Goals Made	Phil. 30	Mia. 9
Field Goals Attempted	Phil. 37	Mia. 17
% Successful	Minn. 87.0	Mia. 52.9

CLUB RANKINGS BY YARDS

	Offense			Defense		
Team	Total	Rush	Pass	Total	Rush	Pass
Atlanta	19	15	20	15	21	7
Buffalo	27	26	25	23	19	19
Chicago	7	*1	26	*1	*1	2
Cincinnati	5	6t	13t	13	11	18
Cleveland	24	21	18	2	15	3
Dallas	11	20	6	7	24	5
Denver	22	10	23	25	5	27
Detroit	12	14	13t	17	8	21
Green Bay	6	13	9	16	20	8
Houston	23	23	17	27	28	11
Indianapolis	28	12	28	22	17	22
Kansas City	17	27	7	24	16	23
Los Angeles Raiders	15	17	12	3	13	4
Los Angeles Rams	21	2	27	14	3	24
Miami	*1	16	*1	19	22	14
Minnesota	25	18	22	28	27	26
New England	14	11	16	9	12	12
New Orleans	20	8	24	4	26	*1
New York Giants	13	22	5	11	9	16
New York Jets	16	5	21	21	18	20
Philadelphia	26	28	11	12	23	6
Pittsburgh	8	6t	15	5	4	15
St. Louis	3	9	3	8	14	9
San Diego	4	24	2	26	10	28
San Francisco	2	3	4	10	7	17
Seattle	18	25	10	6	6	10
Tampa Bay	10	19	8	20	25	13
Washington	9	4	19	18	2	25

t—Tie for position

*—League leader

NFL TAKEAWAYS AND GIVEAWAYS

	Takeaways			Giveaways			Net Diff.
	Int.	Fum.	Total	Int.	Fum.	Total	
Seattle	38	25	63	26	13	39	24
Denver	31	24	55	17	17	34	21
San Francisco	25	13	38	10	12	22	16
Washington	21	22	43	13	15	28	15
Miami	24	12	36	18	10	28	8
New York Giants	19	16	35	18	9	27	8
Green Bay	27	15	42	30	7	37	5
Kansas City	30	11	41	22	15	37	4
Los Angeles Rams	17	22	39	17	18	35	4
Chicago	21	13	34	15	16	31	3
Pittsburgh	31	11	42	25	15	40	2
Cincinnati	25	15	40	22	17	39	1
Dallas	28	16	44	26	17	43	1
New York Jets	15	18	33	21	13	34	− 1
Philadelphia	20	11	31	17	16	33	− 2
San Diego	19	17	36	21	17	38	− 2
St. Louis	21	12	33	16	20	36	− 3
Cleveland	20	15	35	23	16	39	− 4
New England	17	8	25	14	15	29	− 4
Buffalo	16	21	37	30	14	44	− 7
Houston	13	11	24	15	16	31	− 7
Indianapolis	18	13	31	22	16	38	− 7
Atlanta	12	20	32	20	21	41	− 9
Detroit	14	11	25	22	14	36	− 11
Tampa Bay	18	14	32	23	20	43	− 11
Minnesota	11	18	29	25	16	41	− 12
Los Angeles Raiders	20	14	34	28	20	48	− 14
New Orleans	13	10	23	28	13	41	− 18

SCORING

POINTS

Kickers
- NFC: 131—Ray Wersching, San Francisco
- AFC: 117—Gary Anderson, Pittsburgh

Non-kickers
- AFC: 108—Marcus Allen, Los Angeles Raiders
- 108—Mark Clayton, Miami
- NFC: 84—Eric Dickerson, Los Angeles Rams
- 84—John Riggins, Washington

TOUCHDOWNS
- AFC: 18—Marcus Allen, Los Angeles Raiders (13-rush, 5-pass)
- 18—Mark Clayton, Miami (18-pass)
- NFC: 14—Eric Dickerson, Los Angeles Rams (14-rush)
- 14—John Riggins, Washington (14-rush)

EXTRA POINTS
- AFC: 66—Uwe von Schamann, Miami (70 attempts)
- NFC: 56—Ray Wersching, San Francisco (56 attempts)

FIELD GOALS
- NFC: 30—Paul McFadden, Philadelphia (37 attempts)
- AFC: 24—Gary Anderson, Pittsburgh (32 attempts)
- 24—Matt Bahr, Cleveland (32 attempts)

MOST POINTS, GAME
- AFC: 24—Marcus Allen, Los Angeles Raiders vs. San Diego, September 24 (4 TD)
- 24—Larry Kinnebrew, Cincinnati vs. Houston, October 28 (4 TD)
- NFC: 18—Lynn Cain, Atlanta vs. Los Angeles Rams, October 7 (3 TD)
- 18—Eric Dickerson, Los Angeles Rams vs. Tampa Bay, November 25 (3 TD)
- 18—Eddie Lee Ivery, Green Bay vs. Los Angeles Rams, November 18 (3 TD)
- 18—Art Monk, Washington vs. Indianapolis, October 7 (3 TD)
- 18—Joe Morris, New York Giants vs. Washington, October 28 (3 TD)
- 18—Leonard Thompson, Detroit vs. Minnesota, September 23 (3 TD)
- 18—Otis Wonsley, Washington vs. Detroit, November 11 (3 TD)

TEAM LEADERS
- AFC: BUFFALO: 48, Greg Bell; CINCINNATI: 103, Jim Breech; CLEVELAND: 97, Matt Bahr; DENVER: 101, Rich Karlis; HOUSTON: 46, Joe Cooper; INDIANAPOLIS: 47, Raul Allegre; KANSAS CITY: 104, Nick Lowery; LOS ANGELES RAIDERS: 108, Marcus Allen; MIAMI: 108, Mark Clayton; NEW ENGLAND: 108, Tony Franklin; NEW YORK JETS: 89, Pat Leahy; PITTSBURGH: 117, Gary Anderson; SAN DIEGO: 92, Rolf Benirschke; SEATTLE: 110, Norm Johnson.
- NFC: ATLANTA: 91, Mick Luckhurst; CHICAGO: 101, Bob Thomas; DALLAS: 102, Rafael Septien; DETROIT: 91, Ed Murray; GREEN BAY: 61, Al Del Greco; LOS ANGELES RAMS: 112, Mike Lansford; MINNESOTA: 90, Jan Stenerud; NEW ORLEANS: 94, Morten Andersen; NEW YORK GIANTS: 83, Ali Haji-Sheikh; PHILADELPHIA: 116, Paul McFadden; ST. LOUIS: 117, Neil O'Donoghue; SAN FRANCISCO: 131, Ray Wersching; TAMPA BAY: 95, Obed Ariri; WASHINGTON: 120, Mark Moseley.

TEAM CHAMPIONS
- AFC: 513—Miami
- NFC: 475—San Francisco

AFC SCORING—TEAM

	TD	TDR	TDP	TD Misc.	PAT	PAT Att.	FG	FG Att.	SAF	TP
Miami	70	18	49	3	66	70	9	19	0	513
Seattle	51	10	32	9	50	51	20	24	1	418
San Diego	48	18	25	5	46	47	20	29	0	394
Pittsburgh	45	13	25	7	45	45	24	32	0	387
L.A. Raiders	44	19	21	4	40	42	20	27	2	368
New England	42	15	26	1	42	42	22	28	1	362
Denver	42	12	22	8	38	42	21	28	0	353
Cincinnati	39	18	17	4	37	39	22	31	1	339
N.Y. Jets	40	17	20	3	39	40	17	24	1	332
Kansas City	35	12	21	2	35	35	23	33	0	314
Buffalo	31	9	18	4	31	31	11	21	0	250
Cleveland	25	10	14	1	25	25	25	35	0	250
Houston	28	13	14	1	27	28	15	19	0	240
Indianapolis	28	13	13	2	27	28	14	23	1	239
AFC Total	568	197	317	54	548	567	263	373	7	4759
AFC Average	40.6	14.1	22.6	3.9	39.1	40.5	18.8	26.6	0.5	339.9

NFC SCORING—TEAM

	TD	TDR	TDP	TD Misc.	PAT	PAT Att.	FG	FG Att.	SAF	TP
San Francisco	57	21	32	4	56	57	25	35	1	475
Washington	51	20	24	7	48	51	24	31	0	426
St. Louis	51	21	28	2	48	51	23	35	0	423
Green Bay	51	18	30	3	48	51	12	21	0	390
L.A. Rams	38	16	16	6	37	38	25	33	3	346
Tampa Bay	40	17	22	1	38	40	19	26	0	335
Chicago	37	22	14	1	35	37	22	28	1	325
Dallas	34	12	19	3	33	34	23	29	1	308
N.Y. Giants	36	12	22	2	32	36	17	33	0	299
New Orleans	34	9	21	4	34	34	20	27	0	298
Detroit	32	13	19	0	31	31	20	27	0	283
Atlanta	31	16	14	1	31	31	20	27	2	281
Philadelphia	27	6	19	2	26	27	30	37	0	278
Minnesota	31	10	18	3	30	31	20	23	0	276
NFC Total	550	213	298	39	527	549	300	412	8	4743
NFC Average	39.3	15.2	21.3	2.8	37.6	39.2	21.4	29.4	0.6	338.8
League Total	1118	410	615	93	1075	1116	563	785	15	9502
League Avg.	39.9	14.6	22.0	3.3	38.4	39.9	20.1	28.0	0.5	339.4

NFL TOP 10 SCORERS —TOUCHDOWNS

	TD	TDR	TDP	TD Misc.	TP
Allen, Marcus, L.A. Raiders	18	13	5	0	108
Clayton, Mark, Miami	18	0	18	0	108
Dickerson, Eric, L.A. Rams	14	14	0	0	84
Riggins, John, Washington	14	14	0	0	84
Riggs, Gerald, Atlanta	13	13	0	0	78
Wilder, James, Tampa Bay	13	13	0	0	78
Green, Roy, St. Louis	12	0	12	0	72
Johnson, Pete, S.D.-Miami	12	12	0	0	72
Largent, Steve, Seattle	12	0	12	0	72
Five players tied with	11				66

NFL TOP 10 SCORERS — KICKING

	PAT	PAT Att.	FG	FG Att.	TP
Wersching, Ray, San Francisco	56	56	25	35	131
Moseley, Mark, Washington	48	51	24	31	120
Anderson, Gary, Pittsburgh	45	45	24	32	117
O'Donoghue, Neil, St. Louis	48	51	23	35	117
McFadden, Paul, Philadelphia	26	27	30	37	116
Lansford, Mike, L.A. Rams	37	38	25	33	112
Johnson, Norm, Seattle	50	51	20	24	110
Franklin, Tony, New England	42	42	22	28	108
Lowery, Nick, Kansas City	35	35	23	33	104
Breech, Jim, Cincinnati	37	37	22	31	103

AFC SCORING—INDIVIDUAL

KICKERS

	PAT	PAT Att.	FG	FG Att.	TP
Anderson, Gary, Pittsburgh	45	45	24	32	117
Johnson, Norm, Seattle	50	51	20	24	110
Franklin, Tony, New England	42	42	22	28	108
Lowery, Nick, Kansas City	35	35	23	33	104
Breech, Jim, Cincinnati	37	37	22	31	103
Karlis, Rich, Denver	38	41	21	28	101
Bahr, Chris, L.A. Raiders	40	42	20	27	100
Bahr, Matt, Cleveland	25	25	24	32	97
von Schamann, Uwe, Miami	66	70	9	19	93
Benirschke, Rolf, San Diego	41	41	17	26	92
Leahy, Pat, N.Y. Jets	38	39	17	24	89
Allegre, Raul, Indianapolis	14	14	11	18	47
Cooper, Joe, Houston	13	13	11	13	46
Danelo, Joe, Buffalo	17	17	8	16	41
Kempf, Florian, Houston	14	14	4	6	26
Nelson, Chuck, Buffalo	14	14	3	5	23
Biasucci, Dean, Indianapolis	13	14	3	5	22
Ricardo, Benny, San Diego	5	6	3	3	14
Cox, Steve, Cleveland	0	0	1	3	3

NON-KICKERS

	TD	TDR	TDP	TD Misc.	TP
Allen, Marcus, L.A. Raiders	18	13	5	0	108
Clayton, Mark, Miami	18	0	18	0	108
Johnson, Pete, S.D.-Miami	12	12	0	0	72
Largent, Steve, Seattle	12	0	12	0	72
Lipps, Louis, Pittsburgh	11	1	9	1	66
Stallworth, John, Pittsburgh	11	0	11	0	66
Kinnebrew, Larry, Cincinnati	10	9	1	0	60
Turner, Daryl, Seattle	10	0	10	0	60
Jackson, Earnest, San Diego	9	8	1	0	54
Bell, Greg, Buffalo	8	7	1	0	48
Bennett, Woody, Miami	8	7	1	0	48
Duper, Mark, Miami	8	0	8	0	48
Paige, Tony, N.Y. Jets	8	7	1	0	48
Christensen, Todd, L.A. Raiders	7	0	7	0	42
Dennard, Preston, Buffalo	7	0	7	0	42
Moriarty, Larry, Houston	7	6	1	0	42
Ramsey, Derrick, New England	7	0	7	0	42
Walker, Wesley, N.Y. Jets	7	0	7	0	42
Watson, Steve, Denver	7	0	7	0	42
Butler, Raymond, Indianapolis	6	0	6	0	36

	TD	TDR	TDP	TD Misc.	TP
Chandler, Wes, San Diego	6	0	6	0	36
Collinsworth, Cris, Cincinnati	6	0	6	0	36
Johnson, Butch, Denver	6	0	6	0	36
Joiner, Charlie, San Diego	6	0	6	0	36
McGee, Buford, San Diego	6	4	2	0	36
McNeil, Freeman, N.Y. Jets	6	5	1	0	36
Moore, Nat, Miami	6	0	6	0	36
Pollard, Frank, Pittsburgh	6	6	0	0	36
Pruitt, Mike, Cleveland	6	6	0	0	36
Shuler, Mickey, N.Y. Jets	6	0	6	0	36
Winder, Sammy, Denver	6	4	2	0	36
Collins, Anthony, New England	5	5	0	0	30
Eason, Tony, New England	5	5	0	0	30
Hardy, Bruce, Miami	5	0	5	0	30
Jennings, Stanford, Cincinnati	5	2	3	0	30
Lane, Eric, Seattle	5	4	1	0	30
McMillan, Randy, Indianapolis	5	5	0	0	30
Morgan, Stanley, New England	5	0	5	0	30
Newsome, Ozzie, Cleveland	5	0	5	0	30
Brooks, James, Cincinnati	4	2	2	0	24
Brown, Theotis, Kansas City	4	4	0	0	24
Carson, Carlos, Kansas City	4	0	4	0	24
Dawson, Lin, New England	4	0	4	0	24
Duckworth, Bobby, San Diego	4	0	4	0	24
Franklin, Byron, Buffalo	4	0	4	0	24
Heard, Herman, Kansas City	4	4	0	0	24
Lacy, Kenneth, Kansas City	4	2	2	0	24
Marshall, Henry, Kansas City	4	0	4	0	24
Paige, Stephone, Kansas City	4	0	4	0	24
Smith, Tim, Houston	4	0	4	0	24
Starring, Stephen, New England	4	0	4	0	24
Tatupu, Mosi, New England	4	4	0	0	24
Williams, Dokie, L.A. Raiders	4	0	4	0	24
Brennan, Brian, Cleveland	3	0	3	0	18
Byner, Earnest, Cleveland	3	2	0	1	18
Dickey, Curtis, Indianapolis	3	3	0	0	18
Erenberg, Rich, Pittsburgh	3	2	1	0	18
Hawkins, Frank, L.A. Raiders	3	3	0	0	18
Johnson, Dan, Miami	3	0	3	0	18
Jones, Cedric, New England	3	0	2	1	18
Kay, Clarence, Denver	3	0	3	0	18
Krieg, Dave, Seattle	3	3	0	0	18
Lang, Gene, Denver	3	2	1	0	18
Malone, Mark, Pittsburgh	3	3	0	0	18
Nathan, Tony, Miami	3	1	2	0	18
Scott, Willie, Kansas City	3	0	3	0	18
Sievers, Eric, San Diego	3	0	3	0	18
Thompson, Weegie, Pittsburgh	3	0	3	0	18
Tice, Mike, Seattle	3	0	3	0	18
Williams, Jamie, Houston	3	0	3	0	18
Martin, Rod, L.A. Raiders	2	0	0	2	*14
Alexander, Charles, Cincinnati	2	2	0	0	12
Barber, Marion, N.Y. Jets	2	2	0	0	12
Barnwell, Malcolm, L.A. Raiders	2	0	2	0	12
Brown, Dave, Seattle	2	0	0	2	12
Byrd, Gill, San Diego	2	0	0	2	12
Casper, Dave, L.A. Raiders	2	0	2	0	12
Cefalo, Jimmy, Miami	2	0	2	0	12
Davis, Bruce, Cleveland	2	0	2	0	12
Dawkins, Julius, Buffalo	2	0	2	0	12
Dixon, Zachary, Seattle	2	2	0	0	12
Doornink, Dan, Seattle	2	0	2	0	12
Dressel, Chris, Houston	2	0	2	0	12
Easley, Ken, Seattle	2	0	0	2	12
Esiason, Boomer, Cincinnati	2	2	0	0	12
Foley, Steve, Denver	2	0	0	2	12
Harris, M.L., Cincinnati	2	0	2	0	12
Henry, Bernard, Indianapolis	2	0	2	0	12
Hughes, David, Seattle	2	1	1	0	12
Humphery, Bobby, N.Y. Jets	2	0	1	1	12
Hunter, Tony, Buffalo	2	0	2	0	12
Jackson, Billy, Kansas City	2	1	1	0	12
Jensen, Derrick, L.A. Raiders	2	1	1	0	12
Jensen, Jim, Miami	2	0	2	0	12
Johns, Paul, Seattle	2	0	1	1	12
Middleton, Frank, Indianapolis	2	1	1	0	12
Minter, Cedric, N.Y. Jets	2	1	1	0	12
Moore, Alvin, Indianapolis	2	2	0	0	12
Parros, Rick, Denver	2	2	0	0	12
Porter, Tracy, Indianapolis	2	0	2	0	12
Rose, Joe, Miami	2	0	2	0	12
Simpson, Keith, Seattle	2	0	0	2	12
Thomas, Jewerl, San Diego	2	0	0	2	12
Washington, Sam, Pittsburgh	2	0	0	2	12
Weathers, Clarence, New England	2	0	2	0	12
Willhite, Gerald, Denver	2	2	0	0	12
Winslow, Kellen, San Diego	2	0	2	0	12
Woodruff, Dwayne, Pittsburgh	2	0	0	2	12
Young, Dave, Indianapolis	2	0	2	0	12
Abercrombie, Walter, Pittsburgh	1	1	0	0	6
Alexander, Ray, Denver	1	0	1	0	6
Arnold, Walt, Wash.-Kansas City	1	0	1	0	6
Baumhower, Bob, Miami	1	0	0	1	6
Beckman, Ed, Kansas City	1	0	1	0	6
Blackledge, Todd, Kansas City	1	1	0	0	6
Bostic, Keith, Houston	1	0	0	1	6
Brookins, Mitchell, Buffalo	1	0	1	0	6
Buttle, Greg, N.Y. Jets	1	0	0	1	6
Carter, Joe, Miami	1	1	0	0	6
Cunningham, Bennie, Pittsburgh	1	0	1	0	6
David, Stan, Buffalo	1	0	0	1	6
Davis, Johnny, Cleveland	1	1	0	0	6
Dennison, Glenn, N.Y. Jets	1	0	1	0	6
Dufek, Joe, Buffalo	1	1	0	0	6
Edwards, Stan, Houston	1	1	0	0	6
Elway, John, Denver	1	1	0	0	6
Feacher, Ricky, Cleveland	1	0	1	0	6
Fryar, Irving, New England	1	0	1	0	6
Gastineau, Mark, N.Y. Jets	1	0	0	1	6
Green, Boyce, Cleveland	1	0	1	0	6
Griffin, James, Cincinnati	1	0	0	1	6
Hancock, Anthony, Kansas City	1	0	1	0	6
Harden, Mike, Denver	1	0	0	1	6
Harper, Bruce, N.Y. Jets	1	1	0	0	6
Haynes, Mike, L.A. Raiders	1	0	0	1	6
Hector, Johnny, N.Y. Jets	1	1	0	0	6
Hinkle, Bryan, Pittsburgh	1	0	0	1	6
Holman, Rodney, Cincinnati	1	0	1	0	6
Holohan, Pete, San Diego	1	0	1	0	6
Holston, Michael, Houston	1	0	1	0	6
Horton, Ray, Cincinnati	1	0	0	1	6
Jackson, Robert, Cincinnati	1	0	0	1	6
Jackson, Terry, Seattle	1	0	0	1	6
James, Craig, New England	1	1	0	0	6
James, Lionel, San Diego	1	0	0	1	6
Jones, Lam, N.Y. Jets	1	0	1	0	6
Jones, Rulon, Denver	1	0	0	1	6
Judson, William, Miami	1	0	0	1	6
Kafentzis, Mark, Indianapolis	1	0	0	1	6
Keating, Chris, Buffalo	1	0	0	1	6
Klever, Rocky, N.Y. Jets	1	0	1	0	6
Kreider, Steve, Cincinnati	1	0	1	0	6
Kubiak, Gary, Denver	1	1	0	0	6
Lowe, Woodrow, San Diego	1	0	0	1	6
Luck, Oliver, Houston	1	1	0	0	6
McCloskey, Mike, Houston	1	0	1	0	6
McDonald, Paul, Cleveland	1	1	0	0	6
McNeal, Don, Miami	1	0	0	1	6
Montgomery, Cleotha, L.A. Raiders	1	0	0	1	6
Moon, Warren, Houston	1	1	0	0	6
Morris, Wayne, San Diego	1	1	0	0	6
Mullins, Eric, Houston	1	0	0	1	6
Munoz, Anthony, Cincinnati	1	0	1	0	6
Nash, Joe, Seattle	1	0	0	1	6
Neal, Speedy, Buffalo	1	1	0	0	6
Pagel, Mike, Indianapolis	1	1	0	0	6
Plunkett, Jim, L.A. Raiders	1	1	0	0	6
Radecic, Scott, Kansas City	1	0	0	1	6
Robbins, Randy, Denver	1	0	0	1	6
Robinson, Bo, New England	1	0	1	0	6
Ross, Kevin, Kansas City	1	0	0	1	6
Sampson, Clinton, Denver	1	0	1	0	6
Sanford, Lucius, Buffalo	1	0	0	1	6
Schlichter, Art, Indianapolis	1	1	0	0	6
Schonert, Turk, Cincinnati	1	1	0	0	6
Shell, Donnie, Pittsburgh	1	0	0	1	6
Simmons, John, Cincinnati	1	0	0	1	6
Smith, Dennis, Denver	1	0	0	1	6
Smith, Phil, Indianapolis	1	0	0	1	6
Walker, Byron, Seattle	1	0	1	0	6
Walls, Herkie, Houston	1	0	1	0	6
Williams, Lee, San Diego	1	0	0	1	6
Williams, Van, Buffalo	1	0	1	0	6
Wilson, Don, Buffalo	1	0	0	1	6
Wilson, Marc, L.A. Raiders	1	1	0	0	6
Woodard, Ken, Denver	1	0	0	1	6
Wright, James, Denver	1	0	1	0	6
Wright, Louis, Denver	1	0	0	1	6
Young, Charle, Seattle	1	0	1	0	6
Bryant, Jeff, Seattle	0	0	0	0	*2
Humiston, Mike, Indianapolis	0	0	0	0	*2
James, Roland, New England	0	0	0	0	*2
Ryan, Pat, N.Y. Jets	0	0	0	0	#1

*indicates safety (also 1 each Cin., Raiders, Jets)
#indicates extra point scored.

NFC SCORING—INDIVIDUAL

KICKERS	PAT	PAT Att.	FG	FG Att.	TP
Wersching, Ray, San Francisco	56	56	25	35	131
Moseley, Mark, Washington	48	51	24	31	120
O'Donoghue, Neil, St. Louis	48	51	23	35	117
McFadden, Paul, Philadelphia	26	27	30	37	116
Lansford, Mike, L.A. Rams	37	38	25	33	112
Septien, Rafael, Dallas	33	34	23	29	102
Thomas, Bob, Chicago	35	37	22	28	101
Ariri, Obed, Tampa Bay	38	40	19	26	95
Andersen, Morten, New Orleans	34	34	20	27	94
Luckhurst, Mick, Atlanta	31	31	20	27	91
Murray, Ed, Detroit	31	31	20	27	91
Stenerud, Jan, Minnesota	30	31	20	23	90
Haji-Sheikh, Ali, N.Y. Giants	32	35	17	33	83
Del Greco, Al, Green Bay	34	34	9	12	61
Garcia, Eddie, Green Bay	14	15	3	9	23

NON-KICKERS	TD	TDR	TDP	TD Misc.	TP
Dickerson, Eric, L.A. Rams	14	14	0	0	84
Riggins, John, Washington	14	14	0	0	84
Riggs, Gerald, Atlanta	13	13	0	0	78
Wilder, James, Tampa Bay	13	13	0	0	78
Green, Roy, St. Louis	12	0	12	0	72
Mitchell, Stump, St. Louis	11	9	2	0	66
Payton, Walter, Chicago	11	11	0	0	66
Solomon, Freddie, San Francisco	11	1	10	0	66
Craig, Roger, San Francisco	10	7	3	0	60
Coffman, Paul, Green Bay	9	0	9	0	54
Quick, Mike, Philadelphia	9	0	9	0	54
Tyler, Wendell, San Francisco	9	7	2	0	54
Anderson, Ottis, St. Louis	8	6	2	0	48
Carpenter, Rob, N.Y. Giants	8	7	1	0	48
Ellard, Henry, L.A. Rams	8	0	6	2	48
Jones, James, Detroit	8	3	5	0	48
Dorsett, Tony, Dallas	7	6	1	0	42
Gajan, Hokie, New Orleans	7	5	2	0	42
Ivery, Eddie Lee, Green Bay	7	6	1	0	42
Johnson, Bob, N.Y. Giants	7	0	7	0	42
Lofton, James, Green Bay	7	0	7	0	42
Monk, Art, Washington	7	0	7	0	42
Bailey, Stacey, Atlanta	6	0	6	0	36
Brenner, Hoby, New Orleans	6	0	6	0	36
Brown, Ted, Minnesota	6	3	3	0	36
Clark, Dwight, San Francisco	6	0	6	0	36
Clark, Jessie, Green Bay	6	4	2	0	36
Ellis, Gerry, Green Bay	6	4	2	0	36
Gault, Willie, Chicago	6	0	6	0	36
Mowatt, Zeke, N.Y. Giants	6	0	6	0	36
Suhey, Matt, Chicago	6	4	2	0	36
Thompson, Leonard, Detroit	6	0	6	0	36
Armstrong, Adger, Tampa Bay	5	2	3	0	30
Carter, Gerald, Tampa Bay	5	0	5	0	30
Didier, Clint, Washington	5	0	5	0	30
Hill, Tony, Dallas	5	0	5	0	30
House, Kevin, Tampa Bay	5	0	5	0	30
Marsh, Doug, St. Louis	5	0	5	0	30
Newsome, Tim, Dallas	5	5	0	0	30
Sims, Billy, Detroit	5	5	0	0	30
Tilley, Pat, St. Louis	5	0	5	0	30
West, Ed, Green Bay	5	1	4	0	30
Bell, Jerry, Tampa Bay	4	0	4	0	24
Brown, Ron, L.A. Rams	4	0	4	0	24
Campbell, Earl, Houston-N.O.	4	4	0	0	24
Cooper, Earl, San Francisco	4	0	4	0	24
Cosbie, Doug, Dallas	4	0	4	0	24
Danielson, Gary, Detroit	4	3	1	0	24
Hill, Drew, L.A. Rams	4	0	4	0	24
Lewis, Leo, Minnesota	4	0	4	0	24
Manuel, Lionel, N.Y. Giants	4	0	4	0	24
Morris, Joe, N.Y. Giants	4	4	0	0	24
Muhammad, Calvin, Washington	4	0	4	0	24
Nelson, Darrin, Minnesota	4	3	1	0	24
Springs, Ron, Dallas	4	1	3	0	24
Wilson, Wayne, New Orleans	4	1	3	0	24
Wonsley, Otis, Washington	4	4	0	0	24
Anderson, Alfred, Minnesota	3	2	1	0	18
Brown, Charlie, Washington	3	0	3	0	18
Cain, Lynn, Atlanta	3	3	0	0	18
Chadwick, Jeff, Detroit	3	1	2	0	18
Cox, Arthur, Atlanta	3	0	3	0	18
Dickey, Lynn, Green Bay	3	3	0	0	18
Epps, Phillip, Green Bay	3	0	3	0	18
Goodlow, Eugene, New Orleans	3	0	3	0	18
Johnson, Billy, Atlanta	3	0	3	0	18
Jordan, Steve, Minnesota	3	1	2	0	18
Kab, Vyto, Philadelphia	3	0	3	0	18
Lewis, David, Detroit	3	0	3	0	18
Lomax, Neil, St. Louis	3	3	0	0	18
McKinnon, Dennis, Chicago	3	0	3	0	18
Ring, Bill, San Francisco	3	3	0	0	18
Woodruff, Tony, Philadelphia	3	0	3	0	18
Young, Tyrone, New Orleans	3	0	3	0	18
Crutchfield, Dwayne, L.A. Rams	2	1	1	0	12
DeBerg, Steve, Tampa Bay	2	2	0	0	12
Dean, Vernon, Washington	2	0	0	2	12
Donley, Doug, Dallas	2	0	2	0	12
Ferrell, Earl, St. Louis	2	1	1	0	12
Francis, Russ, San Francisco	2	0	2	0	12
Giles, Jimmie, Tampa Bay	2	0	2	0	12
Gray, Earnest, N.Y. Giants	2	0	2	0	12
Harris, Duriel, Cleveland-Dallas	2	0	2	0	12
Hoover, Mel, Philadelphia	2	0	2	0	12
Irvin, LeRoy, L.A. Rams	2	0	0	2	12
Jackson, Alfred, Atlanta	2	0	2	0	12
Love, Randy, St. Louis	2	1	1	0	12
McLemore, Dana, San Francisco	2	0	0	2	12
McMahon, Jim, Chicago	2	2	0	0	12
Montana, Joe, San Francisco	2	2	0	0	12
Montgomery, Wilbert, Philadelphia	2	2	0	0	12
Moore, Jeff, Washington	2	0	2	0	12
Mularkey, Mike, Minnesota	2	0	2	0	12
Nehemiah, Renaldo, San Francisco	2	0	2	0	12
Pisarcik, Joe, Philadelphia	2	2	0	0	12
Renfro, Mike, Dallas	2	0	2	0	12
Rice, Allen, Minnesota	2	1	1	0	12
Rogers, George, New Orleans	2	2	0	0	12
Wattelet, Frank, New Orleans	2	0	0	2	12
Williams, Byron, N.Y. Giants	2	0	2	0	12
Winston, Dennis, New Orleans	2	0	0	2	12
Johnson, Gary, S.D.-S.F.	1	0	0	1	*8
Anderson, Brad, Chicago	1	0	1	0	6
Anthony, Tyrone, New Orleans	1	1	0	0	6
Bell, Todd, Chicago	1	0	0	1	6
Brown, Robert, Green Bay	1	0	0	1	6
Browner, Joey, Minnesota	1	0	0	1	6
Carroll, Jay, Tampa Bay	1	0	1	0	6
Coleman, Monte, Washington	1	0	0	1	6
Collins, Dwight, Minnesota	1	0	1	0	6
Cornwell, Fred, Dallas	1	0	1	0	6
Cromwell, Nolan, L.A. Rams	1	0	0	1	6
Crouse, Ray, Green Bay	1	0	1	0	6
Dierking, Scott, Tampa Bay	1	0	1	0	6
Downs, Mike, Dallas	1	0	0	1	6
Dunsmore, Pat, Chicago	1	0	1	0	6
Frank, John, San Francisco	1	0	1	0	6
Fuller, Steve, Chicago	1	1	0	0	6
Gentry, Dennis, Chicago	1	1	0	0	6
Grant, Darryl, Washington	1	0	0	1	6
Green, Darrell, Washington	1	0	0	1	6
Guman, Mike, L.A. Rams	1	0	0	1	6
Haddix, Michael, Philadelphia	1	1	0	0	6
Hardy, Larry, New Orleans	1	0	1	0	6
Harmon, Derrick, San Francisco	1	1	0	0	6
Harrell, Willard, St. Louis	1	1	0	0	6
Headen, Andy, N.Y. Giants	1	0	0	1	6
Hill, David, L.A. Rams	1	0	1	0	6
Howard, Thomas, St. Louis	1	0	0	1	6
Hutchison, Anthony, Chicago	1	1	0	0	6
Jackson, Jeff, Atlanta	1	0	0	1	6
Jackson, Kenny, Philadelphia	1	0	1	0	6
Jacoby, Joe, Washington	1	0	0	1	6
Jaworski, Ron, Philadelphia	1	1	0	0	6
Jeffcoat, Jim, Dallas	1	0	0	1	6
Jenkins, Ken, Detroit	1	1	0	0	6
Jones, James, Dallas	1	0	1	0	6
Jones, Mike, Minnesota	1	0	1	0	6
Jordan, Curtis, Washington	1	0	0	1	6
Kemp, Jeff, L.A. Rams	1	1	0	0	6
Kramer, Tommy, Minnesota	1	1	0	0	6
Kraynak, Rich, Philadelphia	1	0	0	1	6
Landry, Greg, Chicago	1	1	0	0	6
Lewis, Tim, Green Bay	1	0	0	1	6
Logan, Dave, Tampa Bay	1	0	0	1	6
Martin, Chris, Minnesota	1	0	0	1	6
McConkey, Phil, N.Y. Giants	1	0	0	1	6
McGrath, Mark, Washington	1	0	1	0	6
Miller, Junior, New Orleans	1	0	1	0	6
Monroe, Carl, San Francisco	1	0	1	0	6
Moore, Blake, Green Bay	1	0	1	0	6
Moorehead, Emery, Chicago	1	0	1	0	6
Nichols, Mark, Detroit	1	0	1	0	6
Owens, James, Tampa Bay	1	0	1	0	6
Rodgers, Del, Green Bay	1	0	0	1	6
Rubick, Rob, Detroit	1	0	1	0	6
Scott, Lindsay, New Orleans	1	0	1	0	6
Seay, Virgil, Washington	1	0	1	0	6

	TD	TDR	TDP	TD Misc.	TP
Shell, Todd, San Francisco	1	0	0	1	6
Smith, Leonard, St. Louis	1	0	0	1	6
Spagnola, John, Philadelphia	1	0	1	0	6
Teal, Willie, Minnesota	1	0	0	1	6
Theismann, Joe, Washington	1	1	0	0	6
Thomas, Calvin, Chicago	1	1	0	0	6
Thurman, Dennis, Dallas	1	0	0	1	6
Tice, John, New Orleans	1	0	1	0	6
Walker, Rick, Washington	1	0	1	0	6
Washington, Joe, Washington	1	1	0	0	6
Waters, Andre, Philadelphia	1	0	0	1	6
White, Sammy, Minnesota	1	0	1	0	6
Wilson, Mike, San Francisco	1	0	1	0	6
Woolfolk, Butch, N.Y. Giants	1	1	0	0	6
Bryan, Rick, Atlanta	0	0	0	0	*2
Case, Scott, Atlanta	0	0	0	0	*2
Dutton, John, Dallas	0	0	0	0	*2
Sully, Ivory, L.A. Rams	0	0	0	0	*2
Vann, Norwood, L.A. Rams	0	0	0	0	*2

*indicates safety (also 1 each; Chi., Rams)

FIELD GOALS

BEST PERCENTAGE
NFC: .870—Jan Stenerud, Minnesota (20 made, 23 attempts)
AFC: .833—Norm Johnson, Seattle (20 made, 24 attempts)
MADE
NFC: 30—Paul McFadden, Philadelphia
AFC: 24—Gary Anderson, Pittsburgh
24—Matt Bahr, Cleveland
ATTEMPTS
NFC: 37—Paul McFadden, Philadelphia
AFC: 33—Nick Lowery, Kansas City
AVERAGE YARDS MADE
NFC: 40.2—Ed Murray, Detroit
AFC: 38.5—Raul Allegre, Indianapolis
LONGEST
AFC: 60—Steve Cox, Cleveland vs. Cincinnati, October 21
NFC: 54—Jan Stenerud, Minnesota vs. Atlanta, September 16

AFC FIELD GOALS—TEAM

	Made	Att.	Pct.	Long
Seattle	20	24	.833	50
Houston	15	19	.789	49
New England	22	28	.786	48
Denver	21	28	.750	50
Pittsburgh	24	32	.750	55
Los Angeles Raiders	20	27	.741	50
Cleveland	25	35	.714	60
Cincinnati	22	31	.710	48
New York Jets	17	24	.708	52
Kansas City	23	33	.697	52
San Diego	20	29	.690	51
Indianapolis	14	23	.609	54
Buffalo	11	21	.524	52
Miami	9	19	.474	37
AFC Totals	263	373	—	60
AFC Average	18.8	26.6	.705	—

NFC FIELD GOALS—TEAM

	Made	Att.	Pct.	Long
Minnesota	20	23	.870	54
Philadelphia	30	37	.811	52
Dallas	23	29	.793	52
Chicago	22	28	.786	52
Washington	24	31	.774	51
Los Angeles Rams	25	33	.758	50
Atlanta	20	27	.741	52
Detroit	20	27	.741	52
New Orleans	20	27	.741	53
Tampa Bay	19	26	.731	49
San Francisco	25	35	.714	53
St. Louis	23	35	.657	52
Green Bay	12	21	.571	51
New York Giants	17	33	.515	48
NFC Totals	300	412	—	54
NFC Average	21.4	29.4	.728	—
League Totals	563	785	—	60
League Average	20.1	28.0	.717	—

AFC FIELD GOALS—INDIVIDUAL

	1-19	20-29	30-39	40-49	50 & Over	Totals	Avg. Yds. Att.	Avg. Yds. Made	Avg. Yds. Miss	Long
Johnson, Norm	0-0	9-10	4-4	6-7	1-3	20-24	35.5	33.9	43.8	50
Seattle	—	.900	1.000	.857	.333	.833				
Franklin, Tony	2-2	10-10	4-7	6-8	0-1	22-28	33.3	30.7	42.7	48
New England	1.000	1.000	.571	.750	.000	.786				
Anderson, Gary	0-0	8-9	6-9	8-11	2-3	24-32	36.7	35.3	41.0	55
Pittsburgh	—	.889	.667	.727	.667	.750				
Bahr, Matt	3-3	12-12	2-7	6-9	1-1	24-32	33.8	32.3	38.3	50
Cleveland	1.000	1.000	.286	.667	1.000	.750				
Karlis, Rich	1-1	6-7	7-8	6-9	1-3	21-28	36.0	34.1	41.4	50
Denver	1.000	.857	.875	.667	.333	.750				
Bahr, Chris	1-1	7-7	4-7	7-11	1-1	20-27	35.3	33.7	40.0	50
L.A. Raiders	1.000	1.000	.571	.636	1.000	.741				
Breech, Jim	0-0	9-10	10-12	3-4	0-5	22-31	35.0	31.4	43.8	48
Cincinnati	—	.900	.833	.750	.000	.710				
Leahy, Pat	2-2	5-6	7-8	2-5	1-3	17-24	35.3	32.2	42.6	52
N.Y. Jets	1.000	.833	.875	.400	.333	.708				
Lowery, Nick	0-0	7-7	6-11	8-10	2-5	23-33	38.2	36.3	42.6	52
Kansas City	—	1.000	.545	.800	.400	.697				
Benirschke, Rolf	1-1	4-6	3-4	8-11	1-4	17-26	39.4	37.0	44.0	51
San Diego	1.000	.667	.750	.727	.250	.654				
Allegre, Raul	0-0	4-4	1-2	3-6	3-6	11-18	42.1	38.5	47.9	54
Indianapolis	—	1.000	.500	.500	.500	.611				
Danelo, Joe	0-0	5-5	2-4	0-4	1-3	8-16	36.6	30.6	42.6	52
Buffalo	—	1.000	.500	.000	.333	.500				
von Schamann, Uwe	0-0	7-7	2-5	0-4	0-3	9-19	36.8	27.9	44.9	37
Miami	—	1.000	.400	.000	.000	.474				
Non-Qualifiers (Fewer than 16 attempts or average of one per game)										
Ricardo, Benny	0-0	1-1	1-1	1-1	0-0	3-3	36.3	36.3	—	42
San Diego	—	1.000	1.000	1.000	—	1.000				
Cooper, Joe	2-2	2-2	4-4	3-5	0-0	11-13	33.7	32.1	42.5	44
Houston	1.000	1.000	1.000	.600	—	.846				
Kempf, Florian	0-0	3-3	0-1	1-2	0-0	4-6	32.7	30.0	38.0	49
Houston	—	1.000	.000	.500	—	.667				
Biasucci, Dean	0-0	1-1	0-0	1-1	1-3	3-5	44.2	38.0	53.5	50
Indianapolis	—	1.000	—	1.000	.333	.600				
Nelson, Chuck	0-0	0-0	1-2	2-3	0-0	3-5	40.6	41.0	40.0	47
Buffalo	—	—	.500	.667	—	.600				
Cox, Steve	0-0	0-0	0-0	0-0	1-3	1-3	58.7	60.0	58.0	60
Cleveland	—	—	—	—	.333	.333				
AFC Totals	12-12	100-107	64-96	71-111	16-47	263-373	36.5	33.7	43.1	60
	1.000	.935	.667	.640	.340	.705				
League Totals	25-25	178-192	173-231	150-248	37-89	563-785	36.8	34.4	43.0	60
	1.000	.927	.749	.605	.416	.717				

NFC FIELD GOALS — INDIVIDUAL

	1-19	20-29	30-39	40-49	50 & Over	Totals	Avg. Yds. Att.	Avg. Yds. Made	Avg. Yds. Miss	Long
Stenerud, Jan	2-2	3-3	9-9	3-5	3-4	20-23	37.0	35.3	48.3	54
Minnesota	1.000	1.000	1.000	.600	.750	.870				
McFadden, Paul	0-0	4-5	13-16	10-12	3-4	30-37	38.2	37.7	40.4	52
Philadelphia	—	.800	.813	.833	.750	.811				
Septien, Rafael	2-2	6-7	9-9	4-8	2-3	23-29	35.2	33.0	43.7	52
Dallas	1.000	.857	1.000	.500	.667	.793				
Thomas, Bob	3-3	6-7	5-6	6-9	2-3	22-28	36.2	34.9	41.0	52
Chicago	1.000	.857	.833	.667	.667	.786				
Moseley, Mark	1-1	9-10	12-13	1-5	1-2	24-31	33.1	30.6	41.7	51
Washington	1.000	.900	.923	.200	.500	.774				
Lansford, Mike	2-2	9-9	10-13	3-7	1-2	25-33	33.9	31.4	41.8	50
L.A. Rams	1.000	1.000	.769	.429	.500	.758				
Andersen, Morten	0-0	9-9	4-5	5-10	2-3	20-27	37.1	34.9	43.7	53
New Orleans	—	1.000	.800	.500	.667	.741				
Luckhurst, Mick	0-0	4-4	9-10	4-9	3-4	20-27	39.9	37.9	45.6	52
Atlanta	—	1.000	.900	.444	.750	.741				
Murray, Ed	1-1	1-2	5-7	12-13	1-4	20-27	40.6	40.2	42.0	52
Detroit	1.000	.500	.714	.923	.250	.741				
Ariri, Obed	0-0	7-7	6-7	6-10	0-2	19-26	37.6	35.0	44.7	49
Tampa Bay	—	1.000	.857	.600	.000	.731				
Wersching, Ray	1-1	8-8	8-11	7-13	1-2	25-35	37.0	34.5	43.3	53
San Francisco	1.000	1.000	.727	.538	.500	.714				
O'Donoghue, Neil	0-0	7-7	7-9	8-16	1-3	23-35	38.6	35.7	44.2	52
St. Louis	—	1.000	.778	.500	.333	.657				
Haji-Sheikh, Ali	1-1	3-3	8-13	5-12	0-4	17-33	38.8	34.2	43.8	48
N.Y. Giants	1.000	1.000	.615	.417	.000	.515				
Non-Qualifiers (Fewer than 16 attempts or average of one per game)										
Del Greco, Al	0-0	2-2	3-4	4-5	0-1	9-12	37.3	34.7	45.3	45
Green Bay	—	1.000	.750	.800	.000	.750				
Garcia, Eddie	0-0	0-2	1-3	1-3	1-1	3-9	39.0	43.3	36.8	51
Green Bay	—	.000	.333	.333	1.000	.333				
NFC Totals	13-13	78-85	109-135	79-137	21-42	300-412	37.2	35.0	43.0	54
	1.000	.918	.807	.577	.500	.728				
League Totals	25-25	178-192	173-231	150-248	37-89	563-785	36.8	34.4	43.0	60
	1.000	.927	.749	.605	.416	.717				

RUSHING

INDIVIDUAL CHAMPIONS
NFC: 2,105—Eric Dickerson, Los Angeles Rams
AFC: 1,179—Earnest Jackson, San Diego

YARDS PER ATTEMPT
NFC: 6.0—Hokie Gajan, New Orleans
AFC: 5.0—Joe Carter, Miami

TOUCHDOWNS
NFC: 14—Eric Dickerson, Los Angeles Rams
14—John Riggins, Washington
AFC: 13—Marcus Allen, Los Angeles Raiders

ATTEMPTS
NFC: 407—James Wilder, Tampa Bay
AFC: 296—Earnest Jackson, San Diego
296—Sammy Winder, Denver

LONGEST
AFC: 85 yards—Greg Bell, Buffalo vs. Dallas, November 18 (TD)
NFC: 81 yards—Billy Sims, Detroit vs. San Diego, September 30

MOST YARDS, GAME
NFC: 215 yards—Eric Dickerson, Los Angeles Rams vs. Houston, December 9 (27 attempts)
AFC: 206 yards—Greg Bell, Buffalo vs. Dallas, November 18 (27 attempts)

TEAM LEADERS
AFC: BUFFALO: 1100, Greg Bell; CINCINNATI: 623, Larry Kinnebrew; CLEVELAND: 673, Boyce Green; DENVER: 1153, Sammy Winder; HOUSTON: 785, Larry Moriarty; INDIANAPOLIS: 705, Randy McMillan; KANSAS CITY: 684, Herman Heard; LOS ANGELES RAIDERS: 1168, Marcus Allen; MIAMI: 606, Woody Bennett; NEW ENGLAND: 790, Craig James; NEW YORK JETS: 1070, Freeman McNeil; PITTSBURGH: 851, Frank Pollard; SAN DIEGO: 1179, Earnest Jackson; SEATTLE: 327, David Hughes.

NFC: ATLANTA: 1486, Gerald Riggs; CHICAGO: 1684, Walter Payton; DALLAS: 1189, Tony Dorsett; DETROIT: 687, Billy Sims; GREEN BAY: 581, Gerry Ellis; LOS ANGELES RAMS: 2105, Eric Dickerson; MINNESOTA: 773, Alfred Anderson; NEW ORLEANS: 914, George Rogers; NEW YORK GIANTS: 795, Rob Carpenter; PHILADELPHIA: 789, Wilbert Montgomery; ST. LOUIS: 1174, Ottis Anderson; SAN FRANCISCO: 1262, Wendell Tyler; TAMPA BAY: 1544, James Wilder; WASHINGTON: 1239, John Riggins.

TEAM CHAMPIONS (NET YARDS)
NFC: 2,974—Chicago
AFC: 2,189—New York Jets

AFC RUSHING—TEAM

	Att.	Yards	Avg.	Long	TD
N.Y. Jets	504	2189	4.3	64	17
Cincinnati	540	2179	4.0	33	18
Pittsburgh	574	2179	3.8	52	13
Denver	508	2076	4.1	52	12
New England	482	2032	4.2	73	15
Indianapolis	510	2025	4.0	31t	13
Miami	484	1918	4.0	35	18
L.A. Raiders	516	1886	3.7	52t	19
Cleveland	489	1696	3.5	54	10
Houston	433	1656	3.8	51t	13
San Diego	456	1654	3.6	32t	18
Seattle	495	1645	3.3	40t	10
Buffalo	398	1643	4.1	85t	9
Kansas City	408	1527	3.7	69t	12
AFC Total	6797	26305	—	85t	197
AFC Average	485.5	1878.9	3.9	—	14.1

NFC RUSHING—TEAM

	Att.	Yards	Avg.	Long	TD
Chicago	674	2974	4.4	72t	22
L.A. Rams	541	2864	5.3	66	16
San Francisco	534	2465	4.6	47	21
Washington	588	2274	3.9	31	20
New Orleans	523	2171	4.2	62t	9
St. Louis	488	2088	4.3	39	21
Green Bay	461	2019	4.4	50	18
Detroit	446	2017	4.5	81	13
Atlanta	489	1994	4.1	57	16
Minnesota	444	1844	4.2	39	10
Tampa Bay	483	1776	3.7	37	17
Dallas	469	1714	3.7	31t	12
N.Y. Giants	493	1660	3.4	28	12
Philadelphia	381	1338	3.5	27	6
NFC Total	7014	29198	—	81	213
NFC Average	501.0	2085.6	4.2	—	15.2
League Total	13811	55503	—	85t	410
League Average	493.3	1982.3	4.0	—	14.6

NFL TOP 10 RUSHERS

	Att.	Yards	Avg.	Long	TD
Dickerson, Eric, L.A. Rams	379	2105	5.6	66	14
Payton, Walter, Chicago	381	1684	4.4	72t	11
Wilder, James, Tampa Bay	407	1544	3.8	37	13
Riggs, Gerald, Atlanta	353	1486	4.2	57	13
Tyler, Wendell, San Francisco	246	1262	5.1	40	7
Riggins, John, Washington	327	1239	3.8	24	14
Dorsett, Tony, Dallas	302	1189	3.9	31t	6
Jackson, Earnest, San Diego	296	1179	4.0	32t	8
Anderson, Ottis, St. Louis	289	1174	4.1	24	6
Allen, Marcus, L.A. Raiders	275	1168	4.2	52t	13

AFC RUSHING—INDIVIDUAL

	Att.	Yards	Avg.	Long	TD
Jackson, Earnest, San Diego	296	1179	4.0	32t	8
Allen, Marcus, L.A. Raiders	275	1168	4.2	52t	13
Winder, Sammy, Denver	296	1153	3.9	24	4
Bell, Greg, Buffalo	262	1100	4.2	85t	7
McNeil, Freeman, N.Y. Jets	229	1070	4.7	53	5
Pollard, Frank, Pittsburgh	213	851	4.0	52	6
James, Craig, New England	160	790	4.9	73	1
Moriarty, Larry, Houston	189	785	4.2	51t	6
McMillan, Randy, Indianapolis	163	705	4.3	31t	5
Heard, Herman, Kansas City	165	684	4.1	69t	4
Green, Boyce, Cleveland	202	673	3.3	29	0
Kinnebrew, Larry, Cincinnati	154	623	4.0	23	9
Abercrombie, Walter, Pittsburgh	145	610	4.2	31	1
Bennett, Woody, Miami	144	606	4.2	23	7
Nathan, Tony, Miami	118	558	4.7	22	1
Tatupu, Mosi, New England	133	553	4.2	20t	4
Collins, Anthony, New England	138	550	4.0	21	5
Hector, Johnny, N.Y. Jets	124	531	4.3	64	1
Dickey, Curtis, Indianapolis	131	523	4.0	30	3
Pruitt, Mike, Cleveland	163	506	3.1	14	6
Carter, Joe, Miami	100	495	5.0	35	1
Alexander, Charles, Cincinnati	132	479	3.6	22	2
Byner, Earnest, Cleveland	72	426	5.9	54	2
Erenberg, Rich, Pittsburgh	115	405	3.5	31t	2
Brooks, James, Cincinnati	103	396	3.8	33	2
Jennings, Stanford, Cincinnati	79	379	4.8	20t	2
Hawkins, Frank, L.A. Raiders	108	376	3.5	17	3
Willhite, Gerald, Denver	77	371	4.8	52	2
Brown, Theotis, Kansas City	97	337	3.5	25	4
Hughes, David, Seattle	94	327	3.5	14	1
Lane, Eric, Seattle	80	299	3.7	40t	4
Middleton, Frank, Indianapolis	92	275	3.0	20	1
Edwards, Stan, Houston	60	267	4.5	20	1
King, Kenny, L.A. Raiders	67	254	3.8	18	0
Elway, John, Denver	56	237	4.2	21	1
McGee, Buford, San Diego	67	226	3.4	30	4
Jackson, Billy, Kansas City	50	225	4.5	16	1
Doornink, Dan, Seattle	57	215	3.8	25	0
Moon, Warren, Houston	58	211	3.6	31	1
Parros, Rick, Denver	46	208	4.5	25	2
Johnson, Pete, S.D.-Miami	87	205	2.4	9	12
Morris, Randall, Seattle	58	189	3.3	16	0
Krieg, Dave, Seattle	46	186	4.0	37t	3
Neal, Speedy, Buffalo	49	175	3.6	10	1
Harris, Franco, Seattle	68	170	2.5	16	0
Lacy, Kenneth, Kansas City	46	165	3.6	24t	2
Eason, Tony, New England	40	154	3.9	25t	5
Dixon, Zachary, Seattle	52	149	2.9	17	2
Pagel, Mike, Indianapolis	26	149	5.7	23	1
Barber, Marion, N.Y. Jets	31	148	4.8	18	2
Schlichter, Art, Indianapolis	19	145	7.6	22	1
Minter, Cedric, N.Y. Jets	34	136	4.0	14	1
Paige, Tony, N.Y. Jets	35	130	3.7	24	7
Moore, Alvin, Indianapolis	38	127	3.3	18	2
James, Lionel, San Diego	25	115	4.6	20	0
Wonsley, George, Indianapolis	37	111	3.0	13	0
Blackledge, Todd, Kansas City	18	102	5.7	26	1
Ferguson, Joe, Buffalo	19	102	5.4	20	0
Ryan, Pat, N.Y. Jets	23	92	4.0	16	0
Corley, Anthony, Pittsburgh	18	89	4.9	23	0
Veals, Elton, Pittsburgh	31	87	2.8	9	0
Moore, Booker, Buffalo	24	84	3.5	21	0
Kofler, Matt, Buffalo	10	80	8.0	19	0
Schonert, Turk, Cincinnati	13	77	5.9	17	1
Luck, Oliver, Houston	10	75	7.5	18	1
Franklin, Andra, Miami	20	74	3.7	12	0
Wilson, Stanley, Cincinnati	17	74	4.4	9	0
Lipps, Louis, Pittsburgh	3	71	23.7	36t	1
Anderson, Ken, Cincinnati	11	64	5.8	14	0
Esiason, Boomer, Cincinnati	19	63	3.3	9	2
White, Charles, Cleveland	24	62	2.6	8	0
Bryant, Cullen, Seattle	20	58	2.9	8	0
Wilson, Marc, L.A. Raiders	30	56	1.9	14t	1

	Att.	Yards	Avg.	Long	TD
Muncie, Chuck, San Diego	14	51	3.6	11	0
Williams, Van, Buffalo	18	51	2.8	7	0
Harper, Bruce, N.Y. Jets	10	48	4.8	16	1
Thomas, Jewerl, San Diego	14	43	3.1	9	2
Lang, Gene, Denver	8	42	5.3	15	2
Malone, Mark, Pittsburgh	25	42	1.7	13t	3
Warner, Curt, Seattle	10	40	4.0	9	0
Clayton, Mark, Miami	3	35	11.7	30	0
O'Brien, Ken, N.Y. Jets	16	29	1.8	7	0
Brewer, Chris, Denver	10	28	2.8	8	0
Brookins, Mitchell, Buffalo	2	27	13.5	16	0
Kubiak, Gary, Denver	9	27	3.0	17	1
Dufek, Joe, Buffalo	9	22	2.4	13	1
Joyner, Willie, Houston	14	22	1.6	9	0
Walls, Herkie, Houston	4	20	5.0	20	0
Paige, Stephone, Kansas City	3	19	6.3	9	0
Gillespie, Fernandars, Pittsburgh	7	18	2.6	9	0
Davis, Johnny, Cleveland	3	15	5.0	8	1
Plunkett, Jim, L.A. Raiders	16	14	0.9	9	1
Woodley, David, Pittsburgh	11	14	1.3	7	0
Grogan, Steve, New England	7	12	1.7	1	0
Gunter, Micheal, Kansas City	15	12	0.8	4	0
Holt, Harry, Cleveland	1	12	12.0	12	0
Morris, Wayne, San Diego	5	12	2.4	5	1
Farley, John, Cincinnati	7	11	1.6	5	0
Luther, Ed, San Diego	4	11	2.8	7	0
Largent, Steve, Seattle	2	10	5.0	6	0
Collinsworth, Cris, Cincinnati	1	7	7.0	7	0
Humm, David, L.A. Raiders	2	7	3.5	9	0
Myles, Jesse, Denver	5	7	1.4	2	0
Davis, Bruce, Cleveland	1	6	6.0	6	0
Hunter, Tony, Buffalo	1	6	6.0	6	0
Verser, David, Cincinnati	2	5	2.5	3	0
Young, Charle, Seattle	1	5	5.0	5	0
Dennison, Glenn, N.Y. Jets	1	4	4.0	4	0
McDonald, Paul, Cleveland	22	4	0.2	10	1
Willis, Chester, L.A. Raiders	5	4	0.8	2	0
Jensen, Derrick, L.A. Raiders	3	3	1.0	2	1
Johnson, Butch, Denver	1	3	3.0	3	0
Martin, Mike, Cincinnati	1	3	3.0	3	0
McCall, Joe, L.A. Raiders	1	3	3.0	3	0
Moore, Nat, Miami	1	3	3.0	3	0
Riddick, Robb, Buffalo	3	3	1.0	6	0
Montgomery, Cleotha, L.A. Raiders	1	1	1.0	1	0
Ricks, Lawrence, Kansas City	2	1	0.5	1	0
Walker, Wesley, N.Y. Jets	1	1	1.0	1	0
Arnold, Jim, Kansas City	1	0	0.0	0	0
Colquitt, Craig, Pittsburgh	1	0	0.0	0	0
Mullins, Eric, Houston	1	0	0.0	0	0
Pruitt, Greg, L.A. Raiders	8	0	0.0	3	0
Spencer, Todd, Pittsburgh	1	0	0.0	0	0
Stark, Rohn, Indianapolis	2	0	0.0	0	0
Cooper, Joe, Houston	1	−2	−2.0	−2	0
Harris, M.L., Cincinnati	1	−2	−2.0	−2	0
Osiecki, Sandy, Kansas City	1	−2	−2.0	−2	0
Capers, Wayne, Pittsburgh	1	−3	−3.0	−3	0
Zorn, Jim, Seattle	7	−3	−0.4	7	0
Avellini, Bob, Chicago-N.Y. Jets	3	−5	−1.7	0	0
Campbell, Scott, Pittsburgh	3	−5	−1.7	0	0
Strock, Don, Miami	2	−5	−2.5	0	0
Franklin, Byron, Buffalo	1	−7	−7.0	−7	0
Marino, Dan, Miami	28	−7	−0.3	10	0
Carson, Carlos, Kansas City	1	−8	−8.0	−8	0
Kenney, Bill, Kansas City	9	−8	−0.9	1	0
Walker, Dwight, Cleveland	1	−8	−8.0	−8	0
Smith, Phil, Indianapolis	2	−10	−5.0	−3	0
Fryar, Irving, New England	2	−11	−5.5	0	0
Starring, Stephen, New England	2	−16	−8.0	0	0
Fouts, Dan, San Diego	12	−29	−2.4	3	0

t indicates touchdown
Leader based on most yards gained.

NFC RUSHING—INDIVIDUAL

	Att.	Yards	Avg.	Long	TD
Dickerson, Eric, L.A. Rams	379	2105	5.6	66	14
Payton, Walter, Chicago	381	1684	4.4	72t	11
Wilder, James, Tampa Bay	407	1544	3.8	37	13
Riggs, Gerald, Atlanta	353	1486	4.2	57	13
Tyler, Wendell, San Francisco	246	1262	5.1	40	7
Riggins, John, Washington	327	1239	3.8	24	14
Dorsett, Tony, Dallas	302	1189	3.9	31t	6
Anderson, Ottis, St. Louis	289	1174	4.1	24	6
Rogers, George, New Orleans	239	914	3.8	28	2
Carpenter, Rob, N.Y. Giants	250	795	3.2	22	7
Montgomery, Wilbert, Phil.	201	789	3.9	27	2
Anderson, Alfred, Minnesota	201	773	3.8	23	2

Name	Att.	Yards	Avg.	Long	TD
Sims, Billy, Detroit	130	687	5.3	81	5
Craig, Roger, San Francisco	155	649	4.2	28	7
Gajan, Hokie, New Orleans	102	615	6.0	62t	5
Ellis, Gerry, Green Bay	123	581	4.7	50	4
Ivery, Eddie Lee, Green Bay	99	552	5.6	49	6
Jones, James, Detroit	137	532	3.9	34	3
Morris, Joe, N.Y. Giants	133	510	3.8	28	4
Campbell, Earl, Houston-N.O.	146	468	3.2	22	4
Brown, Ted, Minnesota	98	442	4.5	19	3
Mitchell, Stump, St. Louis	81	434	5.4	39	9
Suhey, Matt, Chicago	124	424	3.4	21	4
Griffin, Keith, Washington	97	408	4.2	31	0
Nelson, Darrin, Minnesota	80	406	5.1	39	3
Clark, Jessie, Green Bay	87	375	4.3	43t	4
Jenkins, Ken, Detroit	78	358	4.6	25t	1
Crutchfield, Dwayne, L.A. Rams	73	337	4.6	36	1
Theismann, Joe, Washington	62	314	5.1	27	1
Cain, Lynn, Atlanta	77	276	3.6	31t	3
McMahon, Jim, Chicago	39	276	7.1	30	2
Newsome, Tim, Dallas	66	268	4.1	30	5
Oliver, Hubert, Philadelphia	72	263	3.7	17	0
Wilson, Wayne, New Orleans	74	261	3.5	36	1
Redden, Barry, L.A. Rams	45	247	5.5	35	0
Danielson, Gary, Detroit	41	218	5.3	40	3
Ferrell, Earl, St. Louis	44	203	4.6	25	1
Springs, Ron, Dallas	68	197	2.9	16	1
Harmon, Derrick, San Francisco	39	192	4.9	19	1
Washington, Joe, Washington	56	192	3.4	12	1
Thomas, Calvin, Chicago	40	186	4.7	37	1
Lomax, Neil, St. Louis	35	184	5.3	20	3
Crouse, Ray, Green Bay	53	169	3.2	14	0
Ring, Bill, San Francisco	38	162	4.3	34	3
Simms, Phil, N.Y. Giants	42	162	3.9	21	0
Kemp, Jeff, L.A. Rams	34	153	4.5	23	1
Huckleby, Harlan, Green Bay	35	145	4.1	23	0
Haddix, Michael, Philadelphia	48	130	2.7	21	1
Lisch, Rusty, Chicago	18	121	6.7	31	0
Montana, Joe, San Francisco	39	118	3.0	15	2
Todd, Richard, New Orleans	28	111	4.0	15	0
Anthony, Tyrone, New Orleans	20	105	5.3	19	1
Moroski, Mike, Atlanta	21	98	4.7	17	0
Galbreath, Tony, N.Y. Giants	22	97	4.4	11	0
Rodgers, Del, Green Bay	25	94	3.8	15	0
Woolfolk, Butch, N.Y. Giants	40	92	2.3	17	1
Bussey, Dexter, Detroit	32	91	2.8	18	0
Love, Randy, St. Louis	25	90	3.6	13	1
Fuller, Steve, Chicago	15	89	5.9	26	1
Williams, Mike, Philadelphia	33	83	2.5	8	0
Lofton, James, Green Bay	10	82	8.2	26	0
Gentry, Dennis, Chicago	21	79	3.8	28	1
Solomon, Freddie, San Francisco	6	72	12.0	47	1
Jordan, Donald, Chicago	11	70	6.4	29	0
DeBerg, Steve, Tampa Bay	28	59	2.1	14	2
Rice, Allen, Minnesota	14	58	4.1	16	1
D'Addio, Dave, Detroit	7	46	6.6	14	0
Jones, Mike, Minnesota	4	45	11.3	36	0
Carver, Mel, Tampa Bay	11	44	4.0	12	0
Kane, Rick, Washington	17	43	2.5	10	0
Manning, Archie, Minnesota	11	42	3.8	16	0
Hardy, Andre, Philadelphia	14	41	2.9	10	0
Hutchison, Anthony, Chicago	14	39	2.8	6	1
Archer, David, Atlanta	6	38	6.3	12	0
Wonsley, Otis, Washington	18	38	2.1	7	4
Thompson, Jack, Tampa Bay	5	35	7.0	13	0
Armstrong, Adger, Tampa Bay	10	34	3.4	9	2
Bartkowski, Steve, Atlanta	15	34	2.3	8	0
Witkowski, John, Detroit	7	33	4.7	10	0
Wilson, Wade, Minnesota	9	30	3.3	12	0
Morton, Michael, Tampa Bay	16	27	1.7	8	0
Nichols, Mark, Detroit	3	27	9.0	13	0
Brown, Ron, L.A. Rams	2	25	12.5	16	0
Waddy, Billy, Minnesota	3	24	8.0	11	0
White, Danny, Dallas	6	21	3.5	8	0
Hogeboom, Gary, Dallas	15	19	1.3	11	0
Pisarcik, Joe, Philadelphia	7	19	2.7	16	2
Jaworski, Ron, Philadelphia	5	18	3.6	10	1
Monk, Art, Washington	2	18	9.0	18	0
Hodge, Floyd, Atlanta	2	17	8.5	9	0
Carter, Gerald, Tampa Bay	1	16	16.0	16	0
Stamps, Sylvester, Atlanta	3	15	5.0	8	0
Dierking, Scott, Tampa Bay	3	14	4.7	9	0
Martin, Robbie, Detroit	1	14	14.0	14	0
Cooper, Earl, San Francisco	3	13	4.3	7	0
Hayes, Jeff, Washington	2	13	6.5	24	0
Jones, James, Dallas	8	13	1.6	6	0
Monroe, Carl, San Francisco	3	13	4.3	7	0
Moore, Jeff, Washington	3	13	4.3	5	0
Chadwick, Jeff, Detroit	1	12	12.0	12t	1
McKinnon, Dennis, Chicago	2	12	6.0	21	0
Coleman, Greg, Minnesota	2	11	5.5	13	0
Lewis, Leo, Minnesota	2	11	5.5	6	0
Wright, Randy, Green Bay	8	11	1.4	5	0
Kramer, Tommy, Minnesota	15	9	0.6	14	0
Machurek, Mike, Detroit	1	9	9.0	9	0
Benson, Cliff, Atlanta	3	8	2.7	6	0
Johnson, Billy, Atlanta	3	8	2.7	11	0
Wilson, Tim, New Orleans	2	8	4.0	5	0
Austin, Cliff, Atlanta	4	7	1.8	3	0
Harrell, Willard, St. Louis	6	7	1.2	4	1
Hill, Tony, Dallas	1	7	7.0	7	0
Pridemore, Tom, Atlanta	1	7	7.0	7	0
Dickey, Lynn, Green Bay	18	6	0.3	9	3
Harrington, Perry, St. Louis	3	6	2.0	5	0
Donley, Doug, Dallas	2	5	2.5	6	0
Goodlow, Eugene, New Orleans	1	5	5.0	5	0
McIvor, Rick, St. Louis	3	5	1.7	6	0
Jordan, Steve, Minnesota	1	4	4.0	4t	1
Hipple, Eric, Detroit	2	3	1.5	2	0
Nelson, David, Minnesota	1	3	3.0	3	0
Campbell, Rich, Green Bay	2	2	1.0	5	0
Cephous, Frank, N.Y. Giants	3	2	0.7	2	0
Guman, Mike, L.A. Rams	1	2	2.0	2	0
Manuel, Lionel, N.Y. Giants	3	2	0.7	11	0
Peoples, George, Tampa Bay	1	2	2.0	2	0
Walker, Rick, Washington	1	2	2.0	2	0
West, Ed, Green Bay	1	2	2.0	2t	1
Landry, Greg, Chicago	2	1	0.5	1t	1
Owens, James, Tampa Bay	1	1	1.0	1	0
Baschnagel, Brian, Chicago	1	0	0.0	0	0
Ferragamo, Vince, L.A. Rams	4	0	0.0	2	0
Finzer, David, Chicago	2	0	0.0	5	0
Giacomarro, Ralph, Atlanta	1	0	0.0	0	0
Stabler, Ken, New Orleans	1	−1	−1.0	−1	0
Moorehead, Emery, Chicago	1	−2	−2.0	−2	0
Duckett, Kenny, New Orleans	1	−3	−3.0	−3	0
Ellard, Henry, L.A. Rams	3	−5	−1.7	5	0
Marsh, Doug, St. Louis	1	−5	−5.0	−5	0
Quick, Mike, Philadelphia	1	−5	−5.0	−5	0
Runager, Max, San Francisco	1	−5	−5.0	−5	0
Smith, Waddell, Dallas	1	−5	−5.0	−5	0
Black, Mike, Detroit	3	−6	−2.0	4	0
Hart, Jim, Washington	3	−6	−2.0	−2	0
Thompson, Leonard, Detroit	3	−7	−2.3	4	0
Wilson, Dave, New Orleans	3	−7	−2.3	−2	0
Green, Roy, St. Louis	1	−10	−10.0	−10	0
Cavanaugh, Matt, San Francisco	4	−11	−2.8	−1	0
Collins, Dwight, Minnesota	3	−14	−4.7	1	0
Hansen, Brian, New Orleans	2	−27	−13.5	−12	0

t indicates touchdown
Leader based on most yards gained.

PASSING

INDIVIDUAL CHAMPIONS (RATING POINTS)
AFC: 108.9—Dan Marino, Miami
NFC: 102.9—Joe Montana, San Francisco
ATTEMPTS
AFC: 564—Dan Marino, Miami
NFC: 560—Neil Lomax, St. Louis
COMPLETIONS
AFC: 362—Dan Marino, Miami
NFC: 345—Neil Lomax, St. Louis
COMPLETION PERCENTAGE
NFC: 67.3—Steve Bartkowski, Atlanta (269 attempts, 181 completions)
AFC: 64.2—Dan Marino, Miami (564 attempts, 362 completions)
YARDS
AFC: 5,084—Dan Marino, Miami
NFC: 4,614—Neil Lomax, St. Louis
MOST YARDS, GAME
AFC: 470—Dan Marino, Miami vs. Los Angeles Raiders, December 2 (57 attempts, 35 completions)
NFC: 468—Neil Lomax, St. Louis vs. Washington, December 16 (46 attempts, 37 completions)
YARDS PER ATTEMPT
AFC: 9.01—Dan Marino, Miami (564 attempts, 5,084 yards)
NFC: 8.40—Joe Montana, San Francisco (432 attempts, 3,630 yards)

TOUCHDOWN PASSES
AFC: 48—Dan Marino, Miami
NFC: 28—Neil Lomax, St. Louis
28—Joe Montana, San Francisco
MOST TOUCHDOWNS, GAME
AFC: 5—John Elway, Denver vs. Minnesota, November 18
5—Dave Krieg, Seattle vs. Detroit, December 2
5—Dan Marino, Miami vs. Washington, September 2
5—Marc Wilson, Los Angeles Raiders vs. San Diego, October 21
NFC: 4—Gary Danielson, Detroit vs. Minnesota, September 23
4—Lynn Dickey, Green Bay vs. Detroit, October 28
4—Lynn Dickey, Green Bay vs. Minnesota, November 11
4—Phil Simms, New York Giants vs. Philadelphia, September 2
4—Joe Theismann, Washington vs. Indianapolis, October 7
4—Danny White, Dallas vs. Washington, December 9
LONGEST
AFC: 92 yards—Marc Wilson (to Marcus Allen), Los Angeles Raiders vs. Seattle, October 7
NFC: 90 yards—Ron Jaworski (to Mike Quick), Philadelphia vs. St. Louis, October 28 (TD)
LOWEST PERCENTAGE INTERCEPTED
AFC: 1.9—Tony Eason, New England (431 attempts, 8 intercepted)
NFC: 2.3—Joe Montana, San Francisco (432 attempts, 10 intercepted)
TEAM CHAMPIONS
AFC: 5,018—Miami
NFC: 4,257—St. Louis

AFC PASSING —TEAM

	Att.	Comp.	Pct. Comp.	Gross Yards	Tkd.	Yards Lost	Net Yards	TD	Pct. TD	Long	Had Int.	Pct. Int.	Avg. Yds. Att.	Avg. Yds. Comp.
Miami	572	367	64.2	5146	14	128	5018	49	8.6	80t	18	3.1	9.00	14.02
San Diego	662	401	60.6	4928	36	285	4643	25	3.8	88t	21	3.2	7.44	12.29
Kansas City	593	305	51.4	3869	33	301	3568	21	3.5	65t	22	3.7	6.52	12.69
Seattle	497	283	56.9	3751	42	328	3423	32	6.4	80t	26	5.2	7.55	13.25
Los Angeles Raiders	491	266	54.2	3718	54	360	3358	21	4.3	92	28	5.7	7.57	13.98
Cincinnati	496	306	61.7	3659	45	358	3301	17	3.4	80t	22	4.4	7.38	11.96
Pittsburgh	443	240	54.2	3519	35	278	3241	25	5.6	80t	25	5.6	7.94	14.66
New England	500	292	58.4	3685	66	454	3231	26	5.2	76t	14	2.8	7.37	12.62
Houston	487	282	57.9	3610	49	382	3228	14	2.9	76	15	3.1	7.41	12.80
Cleveland	495	273	55.2	3490	55	358	3132	14	2.8	64	23	4.6	7.05	12.78
New York Jets	488	272	55.7	3341	52	382	2959	20	4.1	49	21	4.3	6.85	12.28
Denver	475	263	55.4	3116	35	257	2859	22	4.6	73	17	3.6	6.56	11.85
Buffalo	588	298	50.7	3252	60	554	2698	18	3.1	70t	30	5.1	5.53	10.91
Indianapolis	411	206	50.1	2543	58	436	2107	13	3.2	74t	22	5.4	6.19	12.34
AFC Total	7198	4054	—	51,627	634	4861	46,766	317	—	88t	304	—	—	—
AFC Average	514.1	289.6	56.3	3,687.6	45.3	347.2	3,340.4	22.6	4.4	—	21.7	4.2	7.17	12.73

NFC PASSING —TEAM

	Att.	Comp.	Pct. Comp.	Gross Yards	Tkd.	Yards Lost	Net Yards	TD	Pct. TD	Long	Had Int.	Pct. Int.	Avg. Yds. Att.	Avg. Yds. Comp.
St. Louis	566	347	61.3	4634	49	377	4257	28	4.9	83t	16	2.8	8.19	13.35
San Francisco	496	312	62.9	4079	27	178	3901	32	6.5	80t	10	2.0	8.22	13.07
New York Giants	535	288	53.8	4066	55	434	3632	22	4.1	65t	18	3.4	7.60	14.12
Dallas	604	322	53.3	3995	48	389	3606	19	3.1	68t	26	4.3	6.61	12.41
Tampa Bay	563	334	59.3	3907	45	362	3545	22	3.9	74t	23	4.1	6.94	11.70
Green Bay	506	281	55.5	3740	42	310	3430	30	5.9	79t	30	5.9	7.39	13.31
Philadelphia	606	331	54.6	3823	60	463	3360	19	3.1	90t	17	2.8	6.31	11.55
Detroit	531	298	56.1	3787	61	486	3301	19	3.6	77t	22	4.1	7.13	12.71
Washington	485	286	59.0	3417	48	341	3076	24	4.9	80t	13	2.7	7.05	11.95
Atlanta	478	294	61.5	3546	67	496	3050	14	2.9	61	20	4.2	7.42	12.06
Minnesota	533	281	52.7	3337	64	465	2872	18	3.4	70t	25	4.7	6.26	11.88
New Orleans	476	246	51.7	3198	45	361	2837	21	4.4	74	28	5.9	6.72	13.00
Chicago	390	226	57.9	2695	36	232	2463	14	3.6	61t	15	3.8	6.91	11.92
Los Angeles Rams	358	176	49.2	2382	32	240	2142	16	4.5	68	17	4.7	6.65	13.53
NFC Total	7127	4022	—	50,606	679	5134	45,472	298	—	90t	280	—	—	—
NFC Average	509.1	287.3	56.4	3,614.7	48.5	366.7	3,248.0	21.3	4.2	—	20.0	3.9	7.10	12.58
League Total	14325	8076	—	102,233	1313	9995	92,238	615	—	90t	584	—	—	—
League Average	511.6	288.4	56.4	3,651.2	46.9	357.0	3,294.2	22.0	4.3	—	20.9	4.1	7.14	12.66

Leader based on net yards.

NFL TOP 10 INDIVIDUAL QUALIFIERS

	Att.	Comp.	Pct. Comp.	Yards	Avg. Gain	TD	Pct. TD	Long	Int.	Pct. Int.	Rating Points
Marino, Dan, Miami	564	362	64.2	5084	9.01	48	8.5	80t	17	3.0	108.9
Montana, Joe, San Francisco	432	279	64.6	3630	8.40	28	6.5	80t	10	2.3	102.9
Eason, Tony, New England	431	259	60.1	3228	7.49	23	5.3	76t	8	1.9	93.4
Lomax, Neil, St. Louis	560	345	61.6	4614	8.24	28	5.0	83t	16	2.9	92.5
Bartkowski, Steve, Atlanta	269	181	67.3	2158	8.02	11	4.1	61	10	3.7	89.7
Theismann, Joe, Washington	477	283	59.3	3391	7.11	24	5.0	80t	13	2.7	86.6
Dickey, Lynn, Green Bay	401	237	59.1	3195	7.97	25	6.2	79t	19	4.7	85.6
Fouts, Dan, San Diego	507	317	62.5	3740	7.38	19	3.7	61t	17	3.4	83.4
Krieg, Dave, Seattle	480	276	57.5	3671	7.65	32	6.7	80t	24	5.0	83.3
Danielson, Gary, Detroit	410	252	61.5	3076	7.50	17	4.1	77t	15	3.7	83.1

AFC PASSING — INDIVIDUAL QUALIFIERS

	Att.	Comp.	Pct. Comp.	Yards	Avg. Gain	TD	Pct. TD	Long	Int.	Pct. Int.	Rating Points
Marino, Dan, Miami	564	362	64.2	5084	9.01	48	8.5	80t	17	3.0	108.9
Eason, Tony, New England	431	259	60.1	3228	7.49	23	5.3	76t	8	1.9	93.4
Fouts, Dan, San Diego	507	317	62.5	3740	7.38	19	3.7	61t	17	3.4	83.4
Krieg, Dave, Seattle	480	276	57.5	3671	7.65	32	6.7	80t	24	5.0	83.3
Anderson, Ken, Cincinnati	275	175	63.6	2107	7.66	10	3.6	80t	12	4.4	81.0
Kenney, Bill, Kansas City	282	151	53.5	2098	7.44	15	5.3	65t	10	3.5	80.7
Moon, Warren, Houston	450	259	57.6	3338	7.42	12	2.7	76	14	3.1	76.9
Elway, John, Denver	380	214	56.3	2598	6.84	18	4.7	73	15	3.9	76.8
Malone, Mark, Pittsburgh	272	147	54.0	2137	7.86	16	5.9	61t	17	6.3	73.4
Ryan, Pat, N.Y. Jets	285	156	54.7	1939	6.80	14	4.9	44t	14	4.9	72.0
Wilson, Marc, L.A. Raiders	282	153	54.3	2151	7.63	15	5.3	92	17	6.0	71.7
McDonald, Paul, Cleveland	493	271	55.0	3472	7.04	14	2.8	64	23	4.7	67.3
Ferguson, Joe, Buffalo	344	191	55.5	1991	5.79	12	3.5	68t	17	4.9	63.5
Blackledge, Todd, Kansas City	294	147	50.0	1707	5.81	6	2.0	46t	11	3.7	59.2

Non-Qualifiers	Att.	Comp.	Pct. Comp.	Yards	Avg. Gain	TD	Pct. TD	Long	Int.	Pct. Int.	Rating Points
Luck, Oliver, Houston	36	22	61.1	256	7.11	2	5.6	37	1	2.8	89.6
Kubiak, Gary, Denver	75	44	58.7	440	5.87	4	5.3	41	1	1.3	87.6
Luther, Ed, San Diego	151	83	55.0	1163	7.70	5	3.3	88t	3	2.0	82.7
Woodley, David, Pittsburgh	156	85	54.5	1273	8.16	8	5.1	80t	7	4.5	79.9
Schonert, Turk, Cincinnati	117	78	66.7	945	8.08	4	3.4	57t	7	6.0	77.8
O'Brien, Ken, N.Y. Jets	203	116	57.1	1402	6.91	6	3.0	49	7	3.4	74.0
Pagel, Mike, Indianapolis	212	114	53.8	1426	6.73	8	3.8	54t	8	3.8	71.8
Campbell, Scott, Pittsburgh	15	8	53.3	109	7.27	1	6.7	25t	1	6.7	71.3
Plunkett, Jim, L.A. Raiders	198	108	54.5	1473	7.44	6	3.0	73t	10	5.1	67.6
Esiason, Boomer, Cincinnati	102	51	50.0	530	5.20	3	2.9	36	3	2.9	62.9
Dufek, Joe, Buffalo	150	74	49.3	829	5.53	4	2.7	64t	8	5.3	52.9
Avellini, Bob, Chicago-N.Y. Jets	53	30	56.6	288	5.43	0	0.0	50	3	5.7	48.3
Grogan, Steve, New England	68	32	47.1	444	6.53	3	4.4	65t	6	8.8	46.4
Schlichter, Art, Indianapolis	140	62	44.3	702	5.01	3	2.1	54	7	5.0	46.2
Herrmann, Mark, Indianapolis	56	29	51.8	352	6.29	1	1.8	74t	6	10.7	37.8
Kofler, Matt, Buffalo	93	33	35.5	432	4.65	2	2.2	70t	5	5.4	35.8
Osiecki, Sandy, Kansas City	17	7	41.2	64	3.76	0	0.0	19	1	5.9	27.6
Stankavage, Scott, Denver	18	4	22.2	58	3.22	0	0.0	16	1	5.6	17.4
Zorn, Jim, Seattle	17	7	41.2	80	4.71	0	0.0	21	2	11.8	16.4
Less than 10 attempts											
Allen, Marcus, L.A. Raiders	4	1	25.0	38	9.50	0	0.0	38	0	0.0	66.7
Clayton, Mark, Miami	1	0	0.0	0	0.00	0	0.0	0	1	100.0	0.0
Cox, Steve, Cleveland	1	1	100.0	16	16.00	0	0.0	16	0	0.0	118.8
Dickey, Curtis, Indianapolis	1	1	100.0	63	63.00	1	100.0	63t	0	0.0	158.3
Flick, Tom, Cleveland	1	1	100.0	2	2.00	0	0.0	2	0	0.0	79.2
Holohan, Pete, San Diego	2	1	50.0	25	12.50	1	50.0	25t	0	0.0	135.4
Humm, David, L.A. Raiders	7	4	57.1	56	8.00	0	0.0	21	1	14.3	43.5
James, Lionel, San Diego	2	0	0.0	0	0.00	0	0.0	0	1	50.0	0.0
Jensen, Jim, Miami	1	1	100.0	35	35.00	1	100.0	35t	0	0.0	158.3
Kerrigan, Mike, New England	1	1	100.0	13	13.00	0	0.0	13	0	0.0	118.8
McInally, Pat, Cincinnati	2	2	100.0	77	38.50	0	0.0	43	0	0.0	118.8
Moore, Alvin, Indianapolis	1	0	0.0	0	0.00	0	0.0	0	0	0.0	39.6
Moriarty, Larry, Houston	1	1	100.0	16	16.00	0	0.0	16	0	0.0	118.8
Morris, Randall, Seattle	0	0	—	0	—	0	—	0	0	—	0.0
Mosley, Mike, Buffalo	1	0	0.0	0	0.00	0	0.0	0	0	0.0	39.6
Stark, Rohn, Indianapolis	1	0	0.0	0	0.00	0	0.0	0	1	100.0	0.0
Strock, Don, Miami	6	4	66.7	27	4.50	0	0.0	12	0	0.0	76.4
Willhite, Gerald, Denver	2	1	50.0	20	10.00	0	0.0	20	0	0.0	85.4

t indicates touchdown.

NFC PASSING — INDIVIDUAL QUALIFIERS

	Att.	Comp.	Pct. Comp.	Yards	Avg. Gain	TD	Pct. TD	Long	Int.	Pct. Int.	Rating Points
Montana, Joe, San Francisco	432	279	64.6	3630	8.40	28	6.5	80t	10	2.3	102.9
Lomax, Neil, St. Louis	560	345	61.6	4614	8.24	28	5.0	83t	16	2.9	92.5
Bartkowski, Steve, Atlanta	269	181	67.3	2158	8.02	11	4.1	61	10	3.7	89.7
Theismann, Joe, Washington	477	283	59.3	3391	7.11	24	5.0	80t	13	2.7	86.6
Dickey, Lynn, Green Bay	401	237	59.1	3195	7.97	25	6.2	79t	19	4.7	85.6
Danielson, Gary, Detroit	410	252	61.5	3076	7.50	17	4.1	77t	15	3.7	83.1
DeBerg, Steve, Tampa Bay	509	308	60.5	3554	6.98	19	3.7	55	18	3.5	79.3
Kemp, Jeff, L.A. Rams	284	143	50.4	2021	7.12	13	4.6	63t	7	2.5	78.7
Simms, Phil, N.Y. Giants	533	286	53.7	4044	7.59	22	4.1	65t	18	3.4	78.1
Jaworski, Ron, Philadelphia	427	234	54.8	2754	6.45	16	3.7	90t	14	3.3	73.5
White, Danny, Dallas	233	126	54.1	1580	6.78	11	4.7	66t	11	4.7	71.5
Kramer, Tommy, Minnesota	236	124	52.5	1678	7.11	9	3.8	70t	10	4.2	70.6
Hogeboom, Gary, Dallas	367	195	53.1	2366	6.45	7	1.9	68t	14	3.8	63.7
Todd, Richard, New Orleans	312	161	51.6	2178	6.98	11	3.5	74	19	6.1	60.6

Non-Qualifiers	Att.	Comp.	Pct. Comp.	Yards	Avg. Gain	TD	Pct. TD	Long	Int.	Pct. Int.	Rating Points
Fuller, Steve, Chicago	78	53	67.9	595	7.63	3	3.8	31	0	0.0	103.3
Cavanaugh, Matt, San Francisco	61	33	54.1	449	7.36	4	6.6	51t	0	0.0	99.7
McMahon, Jim, Chicago	143	85	59.4	1146	8.01	8	5.6	61t	2	1.4	97.8
Archer, David, Atlanta	18	11	61.1	181	10.06	1	5.6	34	1	5.6	90.3
Wilson, Dave, New Orleans	93	51	54.8	647	6.96	7	7.5	54t	4	4.3	83.9
Pisarcik, Joe, Philadelphia	176	96	54.5	1036	5.89	3	1.7	40	3	1.7	70.6
Landry, Greg, Chicago	20	11	55.0	199	9.95	1	5.0	55t	3	15.0	66.5
Manning, Archie, Minnesota	94	52	55.3	545	5.80	2	2.1	56	3	3.2	66.1
Hipple, Eric, Detroit	38	16	42.1	246	6.47	1	2.6	40	1	2.6	62.0
Witkowski, John, Detroit	34	13	38.2	210	6.18	0	0.0	39	0	0.0	59.7

	Att.	Comp.	Pct. Comp.	Yards	Avg. Gain	TD	Pct. TD	Long	Int.	Pct. Int.	Rating Points
Moroski, Mike, Atlanta	191	102	53.4	1207	6.32	2	1.0	48t	9	4.7	56.8
Wilson, Wade, Minnesota	195	102	52.3	1019	5.23	5	2.6	38	11	5.6	52.5
Campbell, Rich, Green Bay	38	16	42.1	218	5.74	3	7.9	43t	5	13.2	47.8
Thompson, Jack, Tampa Bay	52	25	48.1	337	6.48	2	3.8	74t	5	9.6	42.4
Stabler, Ken, New Orleans	70	33	47.1	339	4.84	2	2.9	29	5	7.1	41.3
Lisch, Rusty, Chicago	85	43	50.6	413	4.86	0	0.0	23	6	7.1	35.1
Wright, Randy, Green Bay	62	27	43.5	310	5.00	2	3.2	56	6	9.7	30.4
Ferragamo, Vince, L.A. Rams	66	29	43.9	317	4.80	2	3.0	68	8	12.1	29.2
Machurek, Mike, Detroit	43	14	32.6	193	4.49	0	0.0	48	6	14.0	8.3
Less than 10 attempts											
Anderson, Alfred, Minnesota	7	3	42.9	95	13.57	2	28.6	43t	1	14.3	89.9
Baschnagel, Brian, Chicago	2	1	50.0	7	3.50	0	0.0	7	0	0.0	58.3
Clark, Dwight, San Francisco	1	0	0.0	0	0.00	0	0.0	0	0	0.0	39.6
Coleman, Greg, Minnesota	1	0	0.0	0	0.00	0	0.0	0	0	0.0	39.6
Dickerson, Eric, L.A. Rams	1	0	0.0	0	0.00	0	0.0	0	1	100.0	0.0
Dils, Steve, Minnesota-L.A. Rams	7	4	57.1	44	6.29	1	14.3	14t	1	14.3	75.9
Dorsett, Tony, Dallas	1	0	0.0	0	0.00	0	0.0	0	1	100.0	0.0
Ellis, Gerry, Green Bay	4	1	25.0	†7	4.25	0	0.0	17	0	0.0	44.8
Gajan, Hokie, New Orleans	1	1	100.0	34	34.00	1	100.0	34t	0	0.0	158.3
Galbreath, Tony, N.Y. Giants	1	1	100.0	13	13.00	0	0.0	13	0	0.0	118.8
Garcia, Frank, Tampa Bay	1	0	0.0	0	0.00	0	0.0	0	0	0.0	39.6
Harmon, Derrick, San Francisco	2	0	0.0	0	0.00	0	0.0	0	0	0.0	39.6
Hart, Jim, Washington	7	3	42.9	26	3.71	0	0.0	13	0	0.0	53.3
Jenkins, Ken, Detroit	1	0	0.0	0	0.00	0	0.0	0	0	0.0	39.6
Jones, James, Detroit	5	3	60.0	62	12.40	1	20.0	27	0	0.0	143.3
May, Dean, Philadelphia	1	1	100.0	33	33.00	0	0.0	33	0	0.0	118.8
McIvor, Rick, St. Louis	4	0	0.0	0	0.00	0	0.0	0	0	0.0	39.6
Mitchell, Stump, St. Louis	1	1	100.0	20	20.00	0	0.0	20	0	0.0	118.8
Montgomery, Wilbert, Philadelphia	2	0	0.0	0	0.00	0	0.0	0	0	0.0	39.6
Payton, Walter, Chicago	8	3	37.5	47	5.88	2	25.0	42	1	12.5	57.8
Perrin, Benny, St. Louis	1	1	100.0	0	0.00	0	0.0	0	0	0.0	79.2
Renfro, Mike, Dallas	2	1	50.0	49	24.50	1	50.0	49t	0	0.0	135.4
Rutledge, Jeff, N.Y. Giants	1	1	100.0	9	9.00	0	0.0	9	0	0.0	104.2
Scribner, Bucky, Green Bay	1	0	0.0	0	0.00	0	0.0	0	0	0.0	39.6
Springs, Ron, Dallas	1	0	0.0	0	0.00	0	0.0	0	0	0.0	39.6
Suhey, Matt, Chicago	1	0	0.0	0	0.00	0	0.0	0	0	0.0	39.6
Washington, Joe, Washington	1	0	0.0	0	0.00	0	0.0	0	0	0.0	39.6
Wilder, James, Tampa Bay	1	1	100.0	16	16.00	1	100.0	16t	0	0.0	158.3

t indicates touchdown.

PASS RECEIVING

INDIVIDUAL CHAMPIONS
NFC: 106—Art Monk, Washington
AFC: 89—Ozzie Newsome, Cleveland

RECEPTIONS, GAME
AFC: 15—Kellen Winslow, San Diego at Green Bay, October 7 (157 yards)
NFC: 12—Ottis Anderson, St. Louis at Washington, December 16 (124 yards)

YARDS
NFC: 1,555—Roy Green, St. Louis
AFC: 1,395—John Stallworth, Pittsburgh

YARDS, GAME
NFC: 206—James Lofton, Green Bay at Denver, October 15 (11 receptions)
AFC: 191—Steve Largent, Seattle at Denver, November 25 (12 receptions)
191—Ozzie Newsome, Cleveland at New York Jets, October 14 (14 receptions)

YARDS PER RECEPTION
NFC: 22.0—James Lofton, Green Bay (62 receptions, 1,361 yards)
AFC: 20.4—Daryl Turner, Seattle (35 receptions, 715 yards)

TOUCHDOWNS
AFC: 18—Mark Clayton, Miami
NFC: 12—Roy Green, St. Louis

LONGEST
AFC: 92 yards—Marcus Allen (from Marc Wilson), Los Angeles Raiders vs. Seattle, October 7
NFC: 90 yards—Mike Quick (from Ron Jaworski), Philadelphia vs. St. Louis, October 28 (TD)

TEAM LEADERS, RECEPTIONS
AFC: BUFFALO: 69, Byron Franklin; CINCINNATI: 65, Cris Collinsworth; CLEVELAND: 89, Ozzie Newsome; DENVER: 69, Steve Watson; HOUSTON: 69, Tim Smith; INDIANAPOLIS: 43, Raymond Butler; KANSAS CITY: 62, Henry Marshall; LOS ANGELES RAIDERS: 80, Todd Christensen; MIAMI: 73, Mark Clayton; NEW ENGLAND: 66, Derrick Ramsey; NEW YORK JETS: 68, Mickey Shuler; PITTSBURGH: 80, John Stallworth; SAN DIEGO: 61, Charlie Joiner; SEATTLE: 74, Steve Largent.
NFC: ATLANTA: 67, Stacey Bailey; CHICAGO: 45, Walter Payton; DALLAS: 60, Doug Cosbie; DETROIT: 77, James Jones; GREEN BAY: 62, James Lofton; LOS ANGELES RAMS: 34, Henry Ellard; MINNESOTA: 47, Leo Lewis; NEW ORLEANS: 35, Hokie Gajan; NEW YORK GI-ANTS: 48, Bob Johnson and Zeke Mowatt; PHILADELPHIA: 65, John Spagnola; ST. LOUIS: 78, Roy Green; SAN FRANCISCO: 71, Roger Craig; TAMPA BAY: 85, James Wilder; WASHINGTON: 106, Art Monk.

NFL TOP 10 PASS RECEIVERS

	No.	Yards	Avg.	Long	TD
Monk, Art, Washington	106	1372	12.9	72	7
Newsome, Ozzie, Cleveland	89	1001	11.2	52	5
Wilder, James, Tampa Bay	85	685	8.1	50	0
Stallworth, John, Pittsburgh	80	1395	17.4	51	11
Christensen, Todd, L.A. Raiders	80	1007	12.6	38	7
Green, Roy, St. Louis	78	1555	19.9	83t	12
Jones, James, Detroit	77	662	8.6	39	5
House, Kevin, Tampa Bay	76	1005	13.2	55	5
Largent, Steve, Seattle	74	1164	15.7	65	12
Clayton, Mark, Miami	73	1389	19.0	65t	18

NFL TOP 10 PASS RECEIVERS BY YARDS

	Yards	No.	Avg.	Long	TD
Green, Roy, St. Louis	1555	78	19.9	83t	12
Stallworth, John, Pittsburgh	1395	80	17.4	51	11
Clayton, Mark, Miami	1389	73	19.0	65t	18
Monk, Art, Washington	1372	106	12.9	72	7
Lofton, James, Green Bay	1361	62	22.0	79t	7
Duper, Mark, Miami	1306	71	18.4	80t	8
Watson, Steve, Denver	1170	69	17.0	73	7
Largent, Steve, Seattle	1164	74	15.7	65	12
Smith, Tim, Houston	1141	69	16.5	75t	4
Bailey, Stacey, Atlanta	1138	67	17.0	61	6

AFC PASS RECEIVING—INDIVIDUAL

	No.	Yards	Avg.	Long	TD
Newsome, Ozzie, Cleveland	89	1001	11.2	52	5
Stallworth, John, Pittsburgh	80	1395	17.4	51	11
Christensen, Todd, L.A. Raiders	80	1007	12.6	38	7
Largent, Steve, Seattle	74	1164	15.7	65	12
Clayton, Mark, Miami	73	1389	19.0	65t	18
Duper, Mark, Miami	71	1306	18.4	80t	8
Watson, Steve, Denver	69	1170	17.0	73	7
Smith, Tim, Houston	69	1141	16.5	75t	4
Franklin, Byron, Buffalo	69	862	12.5	64t	4
Shuler, Mickey, N.Y. Jets	68	782	11.5	49	6
Ramsey, Derrick, New England	66	792	12.0	34	7
Collinsworth, Cris, Cincinnati	64	989	15.5	57t	6
Allen, Marcus, L.A. Raiders	64	758	11.8	92	5
Marshall, Henry, Kansas City	62	912	14.7	37	4
Joiner, Charlie, San Diego	61	793	13.0	41	6
Nathan, Tony, Miami	61	579	9.5	26	2
Carson, Carlos, Kansas City	57	1078	18.9	57	4
Holohan, Pete, San Diego	56	734	13.1	51	1
Winslow, Kellen, San Diego	55	663	12.1	33	2
Chandler, Wes, San Diego	52	708	13.6	63t	6
Harris, M.L., Cincinnati	48	759	15.8	80t	2
Starring, Stephen, New England	46	657	14.3	65t	4
Lipps, Louis, Pittsburgh	45	860	19.1	80t	9
Barnwell, Malcolm, L.A. Raiders	45	851	18.9	51t	2
Winder, Sammy, Denver	44	288	6.5	21	2
Butler, Raymond, Indianapolis	43	664	15.4	74t	6
Moore, Nat, Miami	43	573	13.3	37t	6
Johnson, Butch, Denver	42	587	14.0	49	6
Walker, Wesley, N.Y. Jets	41	623	15.2	44t	7
Williams, Jamie, Houston	41	545	13.3	32	3
Sievers, Eric, San Diego	41	438	10.7	32	3
Dressel, Chris, Houston	40	378	9.5	42	2
Porter, Tracy, Indianapolis	39	590	15.1	63t	2
Dawson, Lin, New England	39	427	10.9	27	4
Jackson, Earnest, San Diego	39	222	5.7	21	1
Morgan, Stanley, New England	38	709	18.7	76t	5
Erenberg, Rich, Pittsburgh	38	358	9.4	25	1
Brown, Theotis, Kansas City	38	236	6.2	17	0
Turner, Daryl, Seattle	35	715	20.4	80t	10
Brennan, Brian, Cleveland	35	455	13.0	52	3
Jennings, Stanford, Cincinnati	35	346	9.9	43	3
Johnson, Dan, Miami	34	426	12.5	42	3
Bell, Greg, Buffalo	34	277	8.1	37	1
Brooks, James, Cincinnati	34	268	7.9	27t	2
Young, Charle, Seattle	33	337	10.2	31	1
Hunter, Tony, Buffalo	33	331	10.0	30	2
Moore, Booker, Buffalo	33	172	5.2	14	0
Jones, Lam, N.Y. Jets	32	470	14.7	37	1
Doornink, Dan, Seattle	31	365	11.8	32	2
Moriarty, Larry, Houston	31	206	6.6	24	1
Paige, Stephone, Kansas City	30	541	18.0	65t	4
Dennard, Preston, Buffalo	30	417	13.9	68t	7
Alexander, Charles, Cincinnati	29	203	7.0	22	0
Hardy, Bruce, Miami	28	257	9.2	19	5
Scott, Willie, Kansas City	28	253	9.0	27	3
Branch, Cliff, L.A. Raiders	27	401	14.9	47	2
Willhite, Gerald, Denver	27	298	11.0	63	0
Duckworth, Bobby, San Diego	25	715	28.6	88t	4
McNeil, Freeman, N.Y. Jets	25	294	11.8	32	1
Heard, Herman, Kansas City	25	223	8.9	17	0
Riddick, Robb, Buffalo	23	276	12.0	38	0
James, Lionel, San Diego	23	206	9.0	31	0
Williams, Dokie, L.A. Raiders	22	509	23.1	75t	4
Feacher, Ricky, Cleveland	22	382	17.4	64	1
Holston, Michael, Houston	22	287	13.0	28	0
Bouza, Matt, Indianapolis	22	270	12.3	22	0
James, Craig, New England	22	159	7.2	16	0
Hughes, David, Seattle	22	121	5.5	25	1
Dawkins, Julius, Buffalo	21	295	14.0	37t	1
Adams, Willis, Cleveland	21	261	12.4	24	0
Holman, Rodney, Cincinnati	21	239	11.4	27	1
Pollard, Frank, Pittsburgh	21	186	8.9	18	0
Holt, Harry, Cleveland	20	261	13.1	36	0
Kreider, Steve, Cincinnati	20	243	12.2	27	1
Hector, Johnny, N.Y. Jets	20	182	9.1	26	0
Edwards, Stan, Houston	20	151	7.6	20	0
Gaffney, Derrick, N.Y. Jets	19	285	15.0	29	0
Bryant, Steve, Houston	19	278	14.6	28	0
Jones, Cedric, New England	19	244	12.8	22	2
McMillan, Randy, Indianapolis	19	201	10.6	44	0
Kinnebrew, Larry, Cincinnati	19	159	8.4	22	1
Brookins, Mitchell, Buffalo	18	318	17.7	70t	1
Walls, Herkie, Houston	18	291	16.2	76	1
Cefalo, Jimmy, Miami	18	185	10.3	25t	2
Thompson, Weegie, Pittsburgh	17	291	17.1	59	3
Johns, Paul, Seattle	17	207	12.2	32	1
Sawyer, John, Denver	17	122	7.2	25	0

	No.	Yards	Avg.	Long	TD
Bendross, Jesse, San Diego	16	213	13.3	29	0
Tatupu, Mosi, New England	16	159	9.9	24	0
Dennison, Glenn, N.Y. Jets	16	141	8.8	20	1
Kay, Clarence, Denver	16	136	8.5	21	3
Abercrombie, Walter, Pittsburgh	16	135	8.4	59	0
Collins, Anthony, New England	16	100	6.3	19	0
Middleton, Frank, Indianapolis	15	112	7.5	16	1
Jackson, Billy, Kansas City	15	101	6.7	11	1
Humphery, Bobby, N.Y. Jets	14	206	14.7	44t	1
Young, Dave, Indianapolis	14	164	11.7	28	2
Dickey, Curtis, Indianapolis	14	135	9.6	33	1
King, Kenny, L.A. Raiders	14	99	7.1	15	0
Walker, Byron, Seattle	13	236	18.2	41	1
Jensen, Jim, Miami	13	139	10.7	20	2
Lacy, Kenneth, Kansas City	13	87	6.7	20	2
Rose, Joe, Miami	12	195	16.3	34t	2
Curtis, Isaac, Cincinnati	12	135	11.3	22	0
Green, Boyce, Cleveland	12	124	10.3	44t	1
Sherwin, Tim, Indianapolis	11	169	15.4	26	0
Fryar, Irving, New England	11	164	14.9	26	1
Martin, Mike, Cincinnati	11	164	14.9	42	0
Henry, Bernard, Indianapolis	11	139	12.6	19t	2
Byner, Earnest, Cleveland	11	118	10.7	26	0
Wright, James, Denver	11	118	10.7	21	1
Lane, Eric, Seattle	11	101	9.2	55t	1
Arnold, Walt, Wash.-K.C.	11	95	8.6	15	1
Egloff, Ron, San Diego	11	92	8.4	17	0
Hancock, Anthony, Kansas City	10	217	21.7	46t	1
Walker, Dwight, Cleveland	10	122	12.2	25	0
Minter, Cedric, N.Y. Jets	10	109	10.9	39t	1
Barber, Marion, N.Y. Jets	10	79	7.9	17	0
McCloskey, Mike, Houston	9	152	16.9	51	1
Sampson, Clinton, Denver	9	123	13.7	25	1
McGee, Buford, San Diego	9	76	8.4	43	2
Neal, Speedy, Buffalo	9	76	8.4	18	0
Morris, Randall, Seattle	9	61	6.8	18	0
Moore, Alvin, Indianapolis	9	52	5.8	12	0
Wonsley, George, Indianapolis	9	47	5.2	17	0
Alexander, Ray, Denver	8	132	16.5	41	1
Weathers, Clarence, New England	8	115	14.4	29	2
Tice, Mike, Seattle	8	90	11.3	30	3
Castor, Chris, Seattle	8	89	11.1	21	0
Smith, J.T., Kansas City	8	69	8.6	16	0
Barnett, Buster, Buffalo	8	67	8.4	18	0
Carter, Joe, Miami	8	53	6.6	15	0
Hawthorne, Greg, New England	7	127	18.1	26	0
Davis, Bruce, Cleveland	7	119	17.0	43t	2
Skansi, Paul, Seattle	7	85	12.1	27	0
Capers, Wayne, Pittsburgh	7	81	11.6	19	0
Hawkins, Frank, L.A. Raiders	7	51	7.3	15	0
Brammer, Mark, Buffalo	7	49	7.0	12	0
Beckman, Ed, Kansas City	7	44	6.3	9	1
Verser, David, Cincinnati	6	113	18.8	28	0
Mullins, Eric, Houston	6	85	14.2	25	1
Bennett, Woody, Miami	6	44	7.3	20	1
Paige, Tony, N.Y. Jets	6	31	5.2	10	1
Parros, Rick, Denver	6	25	4.2	9	0
Metzelaars, Pete, Seattle	5	80	16.0	25	0
Harper, Bruce, N.Y. Jets	5	71	14.2	28	0
Kolodziejski, Chris, Pittsburgh	5	59	11.8	22	0
Williams, Van, Buffalo	5	46	9.2	32	1
Pruitt, Mike, Cleveland	5	29	5.8	9	0
White, Charles, Cleveland	5	29	5.8	17	0
Morris, Wayne, San Diego	5	20	4.0	9	0
Roaches, Carl, Houston	4	69	17.3	24	0
Cunningham, Bennie, Pittsburgh	4	64	16.0	29	1
Mosley, Mike, Buffalo	4	38	9.5	17	0
Muncie, Chuck, San Diego	4	38	9.5	20	0
Robinson, Bo, New England	4	32	8.0	17	1
Casper, Dave, L.A. Raiders	4	29	7.3	13	2
White, Craig, Buffalo	4	28	7.0	11	0
Lang, Gene, Denver	4	24	6.0	9t	1
Summers, Don, Denver	3	32	10.7	16	0
Klever, Rocky, N.Y. Jets	3	29	9.7	13	1
Bryant, Cullen, Seattle	3	20	6.7	11	0
Nelson, Darrell, Pittsburgh	2	31	15.5	19	0
Sohn, Kurt, N.Y. Jets	2	28	14.0	16	0
Sweeney, Calvin, Pittsburgh	2	25	12.5	16	0
Myles, Jesse, Denver	2	22	11.0	12	0
Scales, Dwight, Seattle	2	22	11.0	11	0
Brewer, Chris, Denver	2	20	10.0	16	0
Wilson, Stanley, Cincinnati	2	15	7.5	11	0
Kern, Don, Cincinnati	2	14	7.0	9	0
Pruitt, Greg, L.A. Raiders	2	12	6.0	8	0
Farley, John, Cincinnati	2	11	5.5	10	0
Johnson, Pete, San Diego	2	7	3.5	7	0
Dixon, Zachary, Seattle	2	6	3.0	6	0
Young, Glen, Cleveland	1	47	47.0	47	0

	No.	Yards	Avg.	Long	TD
Pratt, Bob, Seattle	1	30	30.0	30	0
Kubiak, Gary, Denver	1	20	20.0	20	0
Bolden, Rickey, Cleveland	1	19	19.0	19	0
Warner, Curt, Seattle	1	19	19.0	19	0
Stracka, Tim, Cleveland	1	15	15.0	15	0
Little, David, Kansas City	1	13	13.0	13	0
Gillespie, Fernandars, Pittsburgh	1	12	12.0	12	0
Bruckner, Nick, N.Y. Jets	1	11	11.0	11	0
Gissinger, Andy, San Diego	1	3	3.0	3	0
Harris, Franco, Seattle	1	3	3.0	3	0
Logan, Dave, Denver	1	3	3.0	3	0
Jensen, Derrick, L.A. Raiders	1	1	1.0	1t	1
Muñoz, Anthony, Cincinnati	1	1	1.0	1t	1
Fouts, Dan, San Diego	1	0	0.0	0	0
McDonald, Paul, Cleveland	1	−4	−4.0	−4	0
Studdard, Dave, Denver	1	−4	−4.0	−4	0

t indicates touchdown
Leader based on most passes caught.

AFC TOP 25 PASS RECEIVERS BY YARDS

	Yards	No.	Avg.	Long	TD
Stallworth, John, Pittsburgh	1395	80	17.4	51	11
Clayton, Mark, Miami	1389	73	19.0	65t	18
Duper, Mark, Miami	1306	71	18.4	80t	8
Watson, Steve, Denver	1170	69	17.0	73	7
Largent, Steve, Seattle	1164	74	15.7	65	12
Smith, Tim, Houston	1141	69	16.5	75t	4
Carson, Carlos, Kansas City	1078	57	18.9	57	4
Christensen, Todd, L.A. Raiders	1007	80	12.6	38	7
Newsome, Ozzie, Cleveland	1001	89	11.2	52	5
Collinsworth, Cris, Cincinnati	989	64	15.5	57t	6
Marshall, Henry, Kansas City	912	62	14.7	37	4
Franklin, Byron, Buffalo	862	69	12.5	64t	4
Lipps, Louis, Pittsburgh	860	45	19.1	80t	9
Barnwell, Malcolm, L.A. Raiders	851	45	18.9	51t	2
Joiner, Charlie, San Diego	793	61	13.0	41	6
Ramsey, Derrick, New England	792	66	12.0	34	7
Shuler, Mickey, N.Y. Jets	782	68	11.5	49	6
Harris, M.L., Cincinnati	759	48	15.8	80t	2
Allen, Marcus, L.A. Raiders	758	64	11.8	92	5
Holohan, Pete, San Diego	734	56	13.1	51	1
Duckworth, Bobby, San Diego	715	25	28.6	88t	4
Turner, Daryl, Seattle	715	35	20.4	80t	10
Morgan, Stanley, New England	709	38	18.7	76t	5
Chandler, Wes, San Diego	708	52	13.6	63t	6
Butler, Raymond, Indianapolis	664	43	15.4	74t	6

NFC PASS RECEIVING — INDIVIDUAL

	No.	Yards	Avg.	Long	TD
Monk, Art, Washington	106	1372	12.9	72	7
Wilder, James, Tampa Bay	85	685	8.1	50	0
Green, Roy, St. Louis	78	1555	19.9	83t	12
Jones, James, Detroit	77	662	8.6	39	5
House, Kevin, Tampa Bay	76	1005	13.2	55	5
Craig, Roger, San Francisco	71	675	9.5	64t	3
Anderson, Ottis, St. Louis	70	611	8.7	57	2
Bailey, Stacey, Atlanta	67	1138	17.0	61	6
Spagnola, John, Philadelphia	65	701	10.8	34	1
Lofton, James, Green Bay	62	1361	22.0	79t	7
Quick, Mike, Philadelphia	61	1052	17.2	90t	9
Carter, Gerald, Tampa Bay	60	816	13.6	74t	5
Cosbie, Doug, Dallas	60	789	13.2	36	4
Montgomery, Wilbert, Philadelphia	60	501	8.4	28	0
Hill, Tony, Dallas	58	864	14.9	66t	5
Clark, Dwight, San Francisco	52	880	16.9	80t	6
Tilley, Pat, St. Louis	52	758	14.6	42	5
Jackson, Alfred, Atlanta	52	731	14.1	50t	2
Dorsett, Tony, Dallas	51	459	9.0	68t	1
Thompson, Leonard, Detroit	50	773	15.5	66t	6
Johnson, Bob, N.Y. Giants	48	795	16.6	45	7
Mowatt, Zeke, N.Y. Giants	48	698	14.5	34	6
Lewis, Leo, Minnesota	47	830	17.7	56	4
Springs, Ron, Dallas	46	454	9.9	57t	3
Brown, Ted, Minnesota	46	349	7.6	35	3
Payton, Walter, Chicago	45	368	8.2	31	0
Coffman, Paul, Green Bay	43	562	13.1	44t	9
Muhammad, Calvin, Washington	42	729	17.4	80t	4
Suhey, Matt, Chicago	42	312	7.4	23	2
Riggs, Gerald, Atlanta	42	277	6.6	21	0
Cooper, Earl, San Francisco	41	459	11.2	26	4
Solomon, Freddie, San Francisco	40	737	18.4	64t	10
Marsh, Doug, St. Louis	39	608	15.6	47	5
Jones, Mike, Minnesota	38	591	15.6	70t	1
Gray, Earnest, N.Y. Giants	38	529	13.9	31	2
Jordan, Steve, Minnesota	38	414	10.9	26	2
Chadwick, Jeff, Detroit	37	540	14.6	46	2
Galbreath, Tony, N.Y. Giants	37	357	9.6	37	0
Ellis, Gerry, Green Bay	36	312	8.7	22	2

	No.	Yards	Avg.	Long	TD
Renfro, Mike, Dallas	35	583	16.7	60t	2
Gajan, Hokie, New Orleans	35	288	8.2	51	2
Nichols, Mark, Detroit	34	744	21.9	77t	1
Ellard, Henry, L.A. Rams	34	622	18.3	63t	6
Gault, Willie, Chicago	34	587	17.3	61t	6
Cox, Arthur, Atlanta	34	329	9.7	23t	3
Manuel, Lionel, N.Y. Giants	33	619	18.8	53	4
Harris, Duriel, Cleveland-Dallas	33	521	15.8	43	2
Groth, Jeff, New Orleans	33	487	14.8	31	0
Wilson, Wayne, New Orleans	33	314	9.5	34t	3
Haddix, Michael, Philadelphia	33	231	7.0	22	0
Donley, Doug, Dallas	32	473	14.8	49t	2
Oliver, Hubert, Philadelphia	32	142	4.4	21	0
Hill, David, L.A. Rams	31	300	9.7	26	1
Sims, Billy, Detroit	31	239	7.7	20	0
Woodruff, Tony, Philadelphia	30	484	16.1	38	3
Didier, Clint, Washington	30	350	11.7	44	5
Young, Tyrone, New Orleans	29	597	20.6	74	3
Moorehead, Emery, Chicago	29	497	17.1	50	1
McKinnon, Dennis, Chicago	29	431	14.9	32t	3
Bell, Jerry, Tampa Bay	29	397	13.7	27	4
Clark, Jessie, Green Bay	29	234	8.1	20	2
Brenner, Hoby, New Orleans	28	554	19.8	57	6
Tyler, Wendell, San Francisco	28	230	8.2	26t	2
Nelson, Darrin, Minnesota	27	162	6.0	17	1
Epps, Phillip, Green Bay	26	435	16.7	56	3
Jackson, Kenny, Philadelphia	26	398	15.3	83t	1
Jefferson, John, Green Bay	26	339	13.0	33	0
Mitchell, Stump, St. Louis	26	318	12.2	44t	2
Newsome, Tim, Dallas	26	263	10.1	29	0
Benson, Cliff, Atlanta	26	244	9.4	30	0
Ferrell, Earl, St. Louis	26	218	8.4	21	1
Carpenter, Rob, N.Y. Giants	26	209	8.0	19	1
Williams, Byron, N.Y. Giants	24	471	19.6	65t	2
Johnson, Billy, Atlanta	24	371	15.5	45t	3
Giles, Jimmie, Tampa Bay	24	310	12.9	38	2
Hodge, Floyd, Atlanta	24	234	9.8	26	0
Brown, Ron, L.A. Rams	23	478	20.8	54	4
Francis, Russ, San Francisco	23	285	12.4	32	2
Bell, Theo, Tampa Bay	22	350	15.9	29	0
Goodlow, Eugene, New Orleans	22	281	12.8	23	3
Armstrong, Adger, Tampa Bay	22	180	8.2	18	3
White, Sammy, Minnesota	21	399	19.0	47	1
Scott, Lindsay, New Orleans	21	278	13.2	37	1
Jenkins, Ken, Detroit	21	246	11.7	68	0
Dickerson, Eric, L.A. Rams	21	139	6.6	19	0
Guman, Mike, L.A. Rams	19	161	8.5	29	0
Ivery, Eddie Lee, Green Bay	19	141	7.4	18	1
Nehemiah, Renaldo, San Francisco	18	357	19.8	59t	2
Brown, Charlie, Washington	18	200	11.1	36	3
Warren, Don, Washington	18	192	10.7	26	0
Wilson, Mike, San Francisco	17	245	14.4	44	1
LaFleur, Greg, St. Louis	17	198	11.6	23	0
Moore, Jeff, Washington	17	115	6.8	18	2
Anderson, Alfred, Minnesota	17	102	6.0	28t	1
Lewis, David, Detroit	16	236	14.8	58	3
Senser, Joe, Minnesota	15	110	7.3	26	0
Hill, Drew, L.A. Rams	14	390	27.9	68	4
Rubick, Rob, Detroit	14	188	13.4	29	1
Mularkey, Mike, Minnesota	14	134	9.6	26	2
Harrell, Willard, St. Louis	14	106	7.6	15	0
Washington, Joe, Washington	13	74	5.7	12	0
Morris, Joe, N.Y. Giants	12	124	10.3	26	0
Anthony, Tyrone, New Orleans	12	113	9.4	32	0
Cain, Lynn, Atlanta	12	87	7.3	18	0
Rogers, George, New Orleans	12	76	6.3	15	0
Collins, Dwight, Minnesota	11	143	13.0	43t	1
Monroe, Carl, San Francisco	11	139	12.6	47	1
Pittman, Danny, St. Louis	10	145	14.5	50	0
McGrath, Mark, Washington	10	118	11.8	24	1
Seay, Virgil, Washington	9	111	12.3	19	1
Dunsmore, Pat, Chicago	9	106	11.8	25	1
Kab, Vyto, Philadelphia	9	102	11.3	26	3
Crouse, Ray, Green Bay	9	93	10.3	25	1
Saldi, Jay, Chicago	9	90	10.0	20	0
Grant, Otis, L.A. Rams	9	64	7.1	15	0
Bussey, Dexter, Detroit	9	63	7.0	19	0
Woolfolk, Butch, N.Y. Giants	9	53	5.9	13	0
Thomas, Calvin, Chicago	9	39	4.3	9	0
McConkey, Phil, N.Y. Giants	8	154	19.3	39	0
Miller, Junior, New Orleans	8	81	10.1	22	1
Huckleby, Harlan, Green Bay	8	65	8.1	13	0
Griffin, Keith, Washington	8	43	5.4	8	0
Farmer, George, L.A. Rams	7	75	10.7	23	0
Frank, John, San Francisco	7	60	8.6	21	1
Jones, James, Dallas	7	57	8.1	19	1
Williams, Mike, Philadelphia	7	47	6.7	15	0
Riggins, John, Washington	7	43	6.1	11	0

	No.	Yards	Avg.	Long	TD
Barber, Mike, L.A. Rams	7	42	6.0	11	0
Love, Randy, St. Louis	7	33	4.7	16	1
Hoover, Mel, Philadelphia	6	143	23.8	44	2
Landrum, Mike, Atlanta	6	66	11.0	30	0
Tice, John, New Orleans	6	55	9.2	17	1
West, Ed, Green Bay	6	54	9.0	29t	4
Baschnagel, Brian, Chicago	6	53	8.8	17	0
Dixon, Dwayne, Tampa Bay	5	69	13.8	21	0
Mack, Cedric, St. Louis	5	61	12.2	22	0
Rodgers, Del, Green Bay	5	56	11.2	22	0
Walker, Rick, Washington	5	52	10.4	19	1
Carroll, Jay, Tampa Bay	5	50	10.0	17	1
Rice, Allen, Minnesota	4	59	14.8	24	1
McDonald, James, L.A. Rams	4	55	13.8	22	0
Hardy, Larry, New Orleans	4	50	12.5	28t	1
Stamps, Sylvester, Atlanta	4	48	12.0	31	0
Redden, Barry, L.A. Rams	4	39	9.8	6	0
Childs, Henry, Green Bay	4	32	8.0	17	0
Gentry, Dennis, Chicago	4	29	7.3	13	0
Lewis, Gary, Green Bay	4	29	7.3	15	0
Anderson, Brad, Chicago	3	77	25.7	49t	1
Mandley, Pete, Detroit	3	38	12.7	19	0
Campbell, Earl, Houston-N.O.	3	27	9.0	15	0
Carver, Mel, Tampa Bay	3	27	9.0	12	0
Duckett, Kenny, New Orleans	3	24	8.0	11	0
Goode, John, St. Louis	3	23	7.7	10	0
McCall, Reese, Detroit	3	15	5.0	7	0
Ring, Bill, San Francisco	3	10	3.3	15	0
Mullady, Tom, N.Y. Giants	2	35	17.5	22	0
Krenk, Mitch, Chicago	2	31	15.5	24	0
Cornwell, Fred, Dallas	2	23	11.5	13	1
Garrity, Gregg, Pitt.-Philadelphia	2	22	11.0	12	0
Hardy, Andre, Philadelphia	2	22	11.0	13	0
Cassidy, Ron, Green Bay	2	16	8.0	10	0
Owens, James, Tampa Bay	2	13	6.5	9	0
Crutchfield, Dwayne, L.A. Rams	2	11	5.5	7	1
McMahon, Jim, Chicago	1	42	42.0	42	0
Danielson, Gary, Detroit	1	22	22.0	22t	1
Kramer, Tommy, Minnesota	1	20	20.0	20t	1
LeCount, Terry, Minnesota	1	14	14.0	14	0
Cameron, Jack, Chicago	1	13	13.0	13	0
Simms, Phil, N.Y. Giants	1	13	13.0	13	0
D'Addio, Dave, Detroit	1	12	12.0	12	0
Hasselbeck, Don, Minnesota	1	10	10.0	10	0
Martin, Robbie, Detroit	1	9	9.0	9	0
Taylor, Lenny, Green Bay	1	8	8.0	8	0
Cabral, Brian, Chicago	1	7	7.0	7	0
Carmichael, Harold, Dallas	1	7	7.0	7	0
Curran, Willie, Atlanta	1	7	7.0	7	0
Hutchison, Anthony, Chicago	1	7	7.0	7	0
Kane, Rick, Washington	1	7	7.0	7	0
Matthews, Allama, Atlanta	1	7	7.0	7	0
Smith, Waddell, Dallas	1	7	7.0	7	0
Tuttle, Perry, T.B.-Atlanta	1	7	7.0	7	0
Faulkner, Chris, L.A. Rams	1	6	6.0	6	0
Jones, Anthony, Washington	1	6	6.0	6	0
Jordan, Donald, Chicago	1	6	6.0	6	0
Phillips, Kirk, Dallas	1	6	6.0	6	0
Dierking, Scott, Tampa Bay	1	5	5.0	5t	1
Garrett, Alvin, Washington	1	5	5.0	5	0
Mistler, John, Buffalo-N.Y. Giants	1	5	5.0	5	0
Belcher, Kevin, N.Y. Giants	1	4	4.0	4	0
Moore, Blake, Green Bay	1	3	3.0	3t	1
Harmon, Derrick, San Francisco	1	2	2.0	2	0
Pozderac, Phil, Dallas	1	1	1.0	1	0

t indicates touchdown
Leader based on most passes caught.

NFC TOP 25 PASS RECEIVERS BY YARDS

	Yards	No.	Avg.	Long	TD
Green, Roy, St. Louis	1555	78	19.9	83t	12
Monk, Art, Washington	1372	106	12.9	72	7
Lofton, James, Green Bay	1361	62	22.0	79t	7
Bailey, Stacey, Atlanta	1138	67	17.0	61	6
Quick, Mike, Philadelphia	1052	61	17.2	90t	9
House, Kevin, Tampa Bay	1005	76	13.2	55	5
Clark, Dwight, San Francisco	880	52	16.9	80t	6
Hill, Tony, Dallas	864	58	14.9	66t	5
Lewis, Leo, Minnesota	830	47	17.7	56	4
Carter, Gerald, Tampa Bay	816	60	13.6	74t	5
Johnson, Bob, N.Y. Giants	795	48	16.6	45	7
Cosbie, Doug, Dallas	789	60	13.2	36	4
Thompson, Leonard, Detroit	773	50	15.5	66t	6
Tilley, Pat, St. Louis	758	52	14.6	42	5
Nichols, Mark, Detroit	744	34	21.9	77t	1
Solomon, Freddie, San Francisco	737	40	18.4	64t	10
Jackson, Alfred, Atlanta	731	52	14.1	50t	2
Muhammad, Calvin, Washington	729	42	17.4	80t	4

	Yards	No.	Avg.	Long	TD
Spagnola, John, Philadelphia	701	65	10.8	34	1
Mowatt, Zeke, N.Y. Giants	698	48	14.5	34	6
Wilder, James, Tampa Bay	685	85	8.1	50	0
Craig, Roger, San Francisco	675	71	9.5	64t	3
Jones, James, Detroit	662	77	8.6	39	5
Ellard, Henry, L.A. Rams	622	34	18.3	63t	6
Manuel, Lionel, N.Y. Giants	619	33	18.8	53	4

INTERCEPTIONS

INDIVIDUAL CHAMPIONS
  AFC: 10—Ken Easley, Seattle
  NFC: 9—Tom Flynn, Green Bay
MOST INTERCEPTIONS, GAME
  NFC: 3—Vernon Dean, Washington vs. New York Giants, September 16 (61 yards)
         Tom Flynn, Green Bay vs. Detroit, October 28 (23 yards)
  AFC: 3—Kenny Easley, Seattle vs. San Diego, October 29 (33 yards)
YARDAGE
  AFC: 220—Mike Haynes, Los Angeles Raiders (6 interceptions)
  NFC: 166—LeRoy Irvin, Los Angeles Rams (5 interceptions)
LONGEST
  AFC: 99 yards—Gill Byrd, San Diego vs. Kansas City, October 14 (TD)
  NFC: 99 yards—Tim Lewis, Green Bay vs. Los Angeles Rams, November 18 (TD)
TOUCHDOWNS
  AFC: 2—Dave Brown, Seattle
       2—Gill Byrd, San Diego
       2—Ken Easley, Seattle
       2—Keith Simpson, Seattle
       2—Sam Washington, Pittsburgh
  NFC: 2—Vernon Dean, Washington
       2—LeRoy Irvin, Los Angeles Rams
       2—Dennis Winston, New Orleans
MOST TOUCHDOWNS, GAME
  AFC: 2—Dave Brown, Seattle vs. Kansas City, November 4
  NFC: 1—By 18 players
TEAM LEADERS
  AFC: BUFFALO: 5, Charles Romes; CINCINNATI: 4, Louis Breeden, Robert Jackson, and Bobby Kemp; CLEVELAND: 5, Hanford Dixon and Al Gross; DENVER: 6, Steve Foley and Mike Harden; HOUSTON: 4, Willie Tullis; INDIANAPOLIS: 6, Eugene Daniel; KANSAS CITY: 7, Deron Cherry; LOS ANGELES RAIDERS: 6, Mike Haynes; MIAMI: 6, Glenn Blackwood; NEW ENGLAND: 3, Ray Clayborn and Ronnie Lippett; NEW YORK JETS: 4, Russell Carter; PITTSBURGH: 7, Donnie Shell; SAN DIEGO: 4, Gill Byrd; SEATTLE: 10, Kenny Easley.
  NFC: ATLANTA: 5, Kenny Johnson; CHICAGO: 5, Gary Fencik and Leslie Frazier; DALLAS: 7, Mike Downs; DETROIT: 6, Bobby Watkins; GREEN BAY: 9, Tom Flynn; LOS ANGELES RAMS: 5, LeRoy Irvin; MINNESOTA: 3, Rufus Bess; NEW ORLEANS: 4, Dave Waymer; NEW YORK GIANTS: 7, Mark Haynes; PHILADELPHIA: 7, Ray Ellis; ST. LOUIS: 5, Lionel Washington; SAN FRANCISCO: 4, Ronnie Lott and Keena Turner; TAMPA BAY: 5, Mark Cotney; WASHINGTON: 7, Vernon Dean.
TEAM CHAMPIONS
  AFC: 38—Seattle
  NFC: 28—Dallas

AFC INTERCEPTIONS—TEAM

	No.	Yards	Avg.	Long	TD
Seattle	38	697	18.3	90t	7
Denver	31	510	16.5	63	4
Pittsburgh	31	433	14.0	69t	4
Kansas City	30	465	15.5	71t	2
Cincinnati	25	368	14.7	70	4
Miami	24	478	19.9	86t	2
Los Angeles Raiders	20	339	17.0	97t	2
Cleveland	20	236	11.8	47	0
San Diego	19	499	26.3	99t	4
Indianapolis	18	190	10.6	59t	1
New England	17	210	12.4	85	0
Buffalo	16	233	14.6	55	0
New York Jets	15	152	10.1	28	0
Houston	13	139	10.7	26	0
AFC Total	317	4949	—	99t	30
AFC Average	22.6	353.5	15.6	—	2.1

NFC INTERCEPTIONS—TEAM

	No.	Yards	Avg.	Long	TD
Dallas	28	297	10.6	43	2
Green Bay	27	338	12.5	99t	2
San Francisco	25	345	13.8	54t	2
Washington	21	401	19.1	50	4
Chicago	21	290	13.8	61	1
St. Louis	21	163	7.8	25t	1
Philadelphia	20	287	14.4	33	0
New York Giants	19	182	9.6	29	0
Tampa Bay	18	308	17.1	38	1

	No.	Yards	Avg.	Long	TD
Los Angeles Rams	17	399	23.5	81t	3
Detroit	14	87	6.2	36	0
New Orleans	13	213	16.4	47t	3
Atlanta	12	147	12.3	35t	1
Minnesota	11	120	10.9	53t	1
NFC Total	267	3577	—	99t	21
NFC Average	19.1	255.5	13.4	—	1.5
League Total	584	8526	—	99t	51
League Average	20.9	304.5	14.6	—	1.8

NFL TOP 10 INTERCEPTORS

	No.	Yards	Avg.	Long	TD
Easley, Ken, Seattle	10	126	12.6	58t	2
Flynn, Tom, Green Bay	9	106	11.8	31	0
Brown, Dave, Seattle	8	179	22.4	90t	2
Lewis, Tim, Green Bay	7	151	21.6	99t	1
Downs, Mike, Dallas	7	126	18.0	27t	1
Ellis, Ray, Philadelphia	7	119	17.0	31	0
Dean, Vernon, Washington	7	114	16.3	36t	2
Haynes, Mark, N.Y. Giants	7	90	12.9	22	0
Cherry, Deron, Kansas City	7	140	20.0	67	0
Shell, Donnie, Pittsburgh	7	61	8.7	52t	1

AFC INTERCEPTIONS—INDIVIDUAL

	No.	Yards	Avg.	Long	TD
Easley, Ken, Seattle	10	126	12.6	58t	2
Brown, Dave, Seattle	8	179	22.4	90t	2
Cherry, Deron, Kansas City	7	140	20.0	67	0
Shell, Donnie, Pittsburgh	7	61	8.7	52t	1
Haynes, Mike, L.A. Raiders	6	220	36.7	97t	1
Blackwood, Glenn, Miami	6	169	28.2	50	0
Washington, Sam, Pittsburgh	6	138	23.0	69t	2
Ross, Kevin, Kansas City	6	124	20.7	71t	1
Foley, Steve, Denver	6	97	16.2	40t	1
Harden, Mike, Denver	6	79	13.2	45t	1
Harris, John, Seattle	6	79	13.2	29	0
Daniel, Eugene, Indianapolis	6	25	4.2	18	0
Romes, Charles, Buffalo	5	130	26.0	55	0
Gross, Al, Cleveland	5	103	20.6	47	0
Woodruff, Dwayne, Pittsburgh	5	56	11.2	42t	1
Dixon, Hanford, Cleveland	5	31	6.2	18	0
Byrd, Gill, San Diego	4	157	39.3	99t	2
Simpson, Keith, Seattle	4	138	34.5	76t	2
Judson, William, Miami	4	121	30.3	60t	1
Breeden, Louis, Cincinnati	4	96	24.0	70	0
Jackson, Terry, Seattle	4	78	19.5	62t	1
Wilson, Steve, Denver	4	59	14.8	22	0
Lewis, Albert, Kansas City	4	57	14.3	31	0
Tullis, Willie, Houston	4	48	12.0	22	0
McElroy, Vann, L.A. Raiders	4	42	10.5	31	0
Jackson, Robert, Cincinnati	4	32	8.0	28t	1
Kemp, Bobby, Cincinnati	4	27	6.8	14	0
Carter, Russell, N.Y. Jets	4	26	6.5	19	0
Clayborn, Ray, New England	3	102	34.0	85	0
Hinkle, Bryan, Pittsburgh	3	77	25.7	43	0
Randle, Tate, Indianapolis	3	66	22.0	54	0
Taylor, Terry, Seattle	3	63	21.0	37	0
Lowe, Woodrow, San Diego	3	61	20.3	32t	1
Williams, Eric, Pittsburgh	3	49	16.3	44	0
Horton, Ray, Cincinnati	3	48	16.0	48t	1
Freeman, Steve, Buffalo	3	45	15.0	45	0
McNeal, Don, Miami	3	41	13.7	30	1
Smith, Billy Ray, San Diego	3	41	13.7	21	0
Blackwood, Lyle, Miami	3	29	9.7	15	0
Lankford, Paul, Miami	3	25	8.3	22	0
Hartwig, Carter, Houston	3	23	7.7	19	0
Lippett, Ronnie, New England	3	23	7.7	13	0
Krauss, Barry, Indianapolis	3	20	6.7	18	0
Smith, Dennis, Denver	3	13	4.3	10	0
Carpenter, Brian, Wash.-Buffalo	3	11	3.7	11	0
Burroughs, Jim, Indianapolis	3	9	3.0	6	0
Mecklenburg, Karl, Denver	2	105	52.5	63	0
Robbins, Randy, Denver	2	62	31.0	62t	1
Radecic, Scott, Kansas City	2	54	27.0	35	1
Ray, Darrol, N.Y. Jets	2	54	27.0	28	0
King, Linden, San Diego	2	52	26.0	37	0
Simmons, John, Cincinnati	2	43	21.5	43t	1
Turner, John, San Diego	2	43	21.5	43	0
Marion, Fred, New England	2	39	19.5	26	0
McAlister, Ken, Kansas City	2	33	16.5	22	0
Williams, Reggie, Cincinnati	2	33	16.5	33	0
Martin, Rod, L.A. Raiders	2	31	15.5	17	1
Young, Andre, San Diego	2	31	15.5	31	0
Busick, Steve, Denver	2	21	10.5	16	0
Burruss, Lloyd, Kansas City	2	16	8.0	16	0
Lynn, Johnny, N.Y. Jets	2	16	8.0	16	0
James, Roland, New England	2	14	7.0	14	0
Griffin, Ray, Cincinnati	2	13	6.5	13	0
Schroy, Ken, N.Y. Jets	2	13	6.5	13	0
Daniels, Calvin, Kansas City	2	11	5.5	11	0
Davis, Mike, L.A. Raiders	2	11	5.5	11	0
Cousineau, Tom, Cleveland	2	9	4.5	9	0
Merriweather, Mike, Pittsburgh	2	9	4.5	8	0
Buttle, Greg, N.Y. Jets	2	5	2.5	5	0
Gibson, Ernest, New England	2	4	2.0	4	0
Johnson, Eddie, Cleveland	2	3	1.5	3	0
Sanford, Rick, New England	2	2	1.0	2	0
Woods, Rick, Pittsburgh	2	0	0.0	0	0
Hill, Greg, Kansas City	2	−1	−0.5	0	0
Williams, Lee, San Diego	1	66	66.0	66t	1
Kafentzis, Mark, Indianapolis	1	59	59.0	59t	1
Griffin, James, Cincinnati	1	57	57.0	57t	1
Brown, Bud, Miami	1	53	53.0	53	0
Rogers, Don, Cleveland	1	39	39.0	39	0
Fox, Tim, San Diego	1	36	36.0	36	0
Brown, Chris, Pittsburgh	1	31	31.0	31	0
Woodard, Ken, Denver	1	27	27.0	27t	1
Brown, Steve, Houston	1	26	26.0	26	0
Kozlowski, Mike, Miami	1	26	26.0	26	0
Minnifield, Frank, Cleveland	1	26	26.0	26	0
Mullen, Davlin, N.Y. Jets	1	25	25.0	25	0
Smerlas, Fred, Buffalo	1	25	25.0	25	0
Dombroski, Paul, New England	1	23	23.0	23	0
Jackson, Roger, Denver	1	23	23.0	23	0
Eason, Bo, Houston	1	20	20.0	20	0
Gaines, Greg, Seattle	1	18	18.0	18	0
Perry, Rod, Cleveland	1	17	17.0	17	0
Jackson, Charles, Kansas City	1	16	16.0	16	0
Barnes, Jeff, L.A. Raiders	1	15	15.0	15	0
Cameron, Glenn, Cincinnati	1	15	15.0	15	0
Kush, Rod, Buffalo	1	15	15.0	15	0
Scholtz, Bruce, Seattle	1	15	15.0	15	0
Blanton, Jerry, Kansas City	1	14	14.0	14	0
Ryan, Jim, Denver	1	13	13.0	13	0
Springs, Kirk, N.Y. Jets	1	13	13.0	13	0
Cole, Robin, Pittsburgh	1	12	12.0	12	0
Gregor, Bob, San Diego	1	12	12.0	12	0
Lyday, Allen, Houston	1	12	12.0	12	0
Van Pelt, Brad, L.A. Raiders	1	9	9.0	9	0
Banks, Chip, Cleveland	1	8	8.0	8	0
Davis, James, L.A. Raiders	1	8	8.0	8	0
Glasgow, Nesby, Indianapolis	1	8	8.0	8	0
Duhe, A.J., Miami	1	7	7.0	7	0
Smith, Lucious, Buffalo	1	7	7.0	7	0
Sowell, Robert, Miami	1	7	7.0	7	0
Comeaux, Darren, Denver	1	5	5.0	5	0
Lilly, Tony, Denver	1	5	5.0	5	0
Turner, Jim, Cincinnati	1	4	4.0	4	0
Blackmon, Don, New England	1	3	3.0	3	0
Davis, Preston, Indianapolis	1	3	3.0	3	0
Hayes, Lester, L.A. Raiders	1	3	3.0	3	0
Allen, Patrick, Houston	1	2	2.0	2	0
Brazile, Robert, Houston	1	2	2.0	2	0
Abraham, Robert, Houston	1	1	1.0	1	0
Bryant, Jeff, Seattle	1	1	1.0	1	0
Kremer, Ken, Kansas City	1	1	1.0	1	0
Wright, Louis, Denver	1	1	1.0	1	0
Bellinger, Rodney, Buffalo	1	0	0.0	0	0
Brudzinski, Bob, Miami	1	0	0.0	0	0
Clayton, Harvey, Pittsburgh	1	0	0.0	0	0
Clifton, Kyle, N.Y. Jets	1	0	0.0	0	0
Johnson, Lawrence, Cleveland	1	0	0.0	0	0
McKinney, Odis, L.A. Raiders	1	0	0.0	0	0
Nelson, Steve, New England	1	0	0.0	0	0
Rockins, Chris, Cleveland	1	0	0.0	0	0
Schuh, Jeff, Cincinnati	1	0	0.0	0	0
Talley, Darryl, Buffalo	1	0	0.0	0	0
Watts, Ted, L.A. Raiders	1	0	0.0	0	0
Thompson, Ted, Houston	0	5	—	5	0

t indicates touchdown
Leader based on most interceptions.

NFC INTERCEPTIONS—INDIVIDUAL

	No.	Yards	Avg.	Long	TD
Flynn, Tom, Green Bay	9	106	11.8	31	0
Lewis, Tim, Green Bay	7	151	21.6	99t	1
Downs, Mike, Dallas	7	126	18.0	27t	1
Ellis, Ray, Philadelphia	7	119	17.0	31	0
Dean, Vernon, Washington	7	114	16.3	36t	2
Haynes, Mark, N.Y. Giants	7	90	12.9	22	0
Watkins, Bobby, Detroit	6	0	0.0	0	0
Irvin, LeRoy, L.A. Rams	5	166	33.2	81t	2

	No.	Yards	Avg.	Long	TD
Cotney, Mark, Tampa Bay	5	123	24.6	29	0
Hopkins, Wes, Philadelphia	5	107	21.4	33	0
Fencik, Gary, Chicago	5	102	20.4	61	0
Green, Darrell, Washington	5	101	20.2	50	1
Frazier, Leslie, Chicago	5	89	17.8	33	0
Thurman, Dennis, Dallas	5	81	16.2	43	1
Johnson, Kenny, Atlanta	5	75	15.0	28	0
Washington, Lionel, St. Louis	5	42	8.4	18	0
Turner, Keena, San Francisco	4	51	12.8	21	0
Bell, Todd, Chicago	4	46	11.5	36t	1
Smith, Wayne, St. Louis	4	35	8.8	23	0
Foules, Elbert, Philadelphia	4	27	6.8	20	0
Lott, Ronnie, San Francisco	4	26	6.5	15	0
Perrin, Benny, St. Louis	4	22	5.5	22	0
Waymer, Dave, New Orleans	4	9	2.3	9	0
Green, Gary, L.A. Rams	3	88	29.3	60	0
Shell, Todd, San Francisco	3	81	27.0	53t	1
Brantley, Scot, Tampa Bay	3	55	18.3	38	0
Cromwell, Nolan, L.A. Rams	3	54	18.0	33t	1
Hicks, Dwight, San Francisco	3	42	14.0	29	0
Milot, Rich, Washington	3	42	14.0	27	0
Castille, Jeremiah, Tampa Bay	3	38	12.7	30	0
Lee, Mark, Green Bay	3	33	11.0	14	0
Clinkscale, Dextor, Dallas	3	32	10.7	23	0
Anderson, John, Green Bay	3	24	8.0	22	0
Graham, William, Detroit	3	22	7.3	15	0
Walls, Everson, Dallas	3	12	4.0	12	0
Bess, Rufus, Minnesota	3	7	2.3	7	0
Williams, Perry, N.Y. Giants	3	7	2.3	7	0
Fellows, Ron, Dallas	3	3	1.0	3	0
Hegman, Mike, Dallas	3	3	1.0	3	0
Winston, Dennis, New Orleans	2	90	45.0	47t	2
Hall, Alvin, Detroit	2	64	32.0	36	0
McLemore, Dana, San Francisco	2	54	27.0	54t	1
Wattelet, Frank, New Orleans	2	52	26.0	35t	1
Collins, Jim, L.A. Rams	2	43	21.5	40	0
Williamson, Carlton, San Francisco	2	42	21.0	26	0
Smith, Leonard, St. Louis	2	31	15.5	25t	1
Kinard, Terry, N.Y. Giants	2	29	14.5	29	0
Reasons, Gary, N.Y. Giants	2	26	13.0	26	0
Butler, Bobby, Atlanta	2	25	12.5	25	0
Johnson, Johnnie, L.A. Rams	2	21	10.5	21	0
Swain, John, Minnesota	2	20	10.0	11	0
Jordan, Curtis, Washington	2	18	9.0	16	0
Fahnhorst, Jim, San Francisco	2	9	4.5	9	0
Richardson, Mike, Chicago	2	7	3.5	7	0
Edwards, Herman, Philadelphia	2	0	0.0	0	0
Griffin, Jeff, St. Louis	2	0	0.0	0	0
McNorton, Bruce, Detroit	2	0	0.0	0	0
Pridemore, Tom, Atlanta	2	0	0.0	0	0
Wright, Eric, San Francisco	2	0	0.0	0	0
Howard, Thomas, St. Louis	2	−4	−2.0	1	0
Teal, Willie, Minnesota	1	53	53.0	53t	1
Coleman, Monte, Washington	1	49	49.0	49t	1
Fuller, Jeff, San Francisco	1	38	38.0	38	0
Smith, Ricky, N.E.-Washington	1	37	37.0	37	0
Jackson, Jeff, Atlanta	1	35	35.0	35t	1
Harris, Al, Chicago	1	34	34.0	34	0
Lockhart, Eugene, Dallas	1	32	32.0	32	0
Newsome, Vince, L.A. Rams	1	31	31.0	31	0
Wilson, Brenard, Philadelphia	1	28	28.0	28	0
Logan, Dave, Tampa Bay	1	27	27.0	27t	1
Holt, John, Tampa Bay	1	25	25.0	25	0
Washington, Anthony, Washington	1	25	25.0	25	0
Browner, Joey, Minnesota	1	20	20.0	20	0
Studwell, Scott, Minnesota	1	20	20.0	20	0
Heflin, Victor, St. Louis	1	19	19.0	19	0
Junior, E.J., St. Louis	1	18	18.0	18	0
Kovach, Jim, New Orleans	1	16	16.0	16	0
Poe, Johnnie, New Orleans	1	16	16.0	16	0
Coffey, Ken, Washington	1	15	15.0	15	0
Acorn, Fred, Tampa Bay	1	14	14.0	14	0
Brown, Cedric, Tampa Bay	1	14	14.0	14	0
Hunt, Byron, N.Y. Giants	1	14	14.0	14	0
Jackson, Rickey, New Orleans	1	14	14.0	14	0
Reece, Beasley, Tampa Bay	1	12	12.0	12	0
Britt, James, Atlanta	1	10	10.0	10	0
Clark, Bruce, New Orleans	1	9	9.0	9	0
Duerson, Dave, Chicago	1	9	9.0	9	0
Hood, Estus, Green Bay	1	8	8.0	8	0
Cumby, George, Green Bay	1	7	7.0	7	0
Currier, Bill, N.Y. Giants	1	7	7.0	7	0
Johnson, Bobby, New Orleans	1	7	7.0	7	0
Carson, Harry, N.Y. Giants	1	6	6.0	6	0
Wilkes, Reggie, Philadelphia	1	6	6.0	6	0
Brown, Robert, Green Bay	1	5	5.0	5t	1

	No.	Yards	Avg.	Long	TD
Scott, Victor, Dallas	1	5	5.0	5	0
Headen, Andy, N.Y. Giants	1	4	4.0	4	0
Murphy, Mark, Green Bay	1	4	4.0	8	0
Singletary, Mike, Chicago	1	4	4.0	4	0
Bates, Bill, Dallas	1	3	3.0	3	0
Bunz, Dan, San Francisco	1	2	2.0	2	0
Small, Gerald, Atlanta	1	2	2.0	2	0
Fantetti, Ken, Detroit	1	1	1.0	1	0
Cannon, John, Tampa Bay	1	0	0.0	0	0
Clark, Mario, San Francisco	1	0	0.0	0	0
Davis, Jeff, Tampa Bay	1	0	0.0	0.	0
Dickerson, Anthony, Dallas	1	0	0.0	0	0
Hannon, Tom, Minnesota	1	0	0.0	0	0
Lee, Carl, Minnesota	1	0	0.0	0	0
McLeod, Mike, Green Bay	1	0	0.0	0	0
McNeill, Fred, Minnesota	1	0	0.0	0	0
Schmidt, Terry, Chicago	1	0	0.0	0	0
Gayle, Shaun, Chicago	1	−1	−1.0	−1	0
Taylor, Lawrence, N.Y. Giants	1	−1	−1.0	−1	0
Owens, Mel, L.A. Rams	1	−4	−4.0	−4	0

t indicates touchdown
Leader based on most interceptions.

PUNTING

INDIVIDUAL CHAMPIONS
  AFC: 44.9 — Jim Arnold, Kansas City (98 punts, 4,397 yards)
  NFC: 43.8 — Brian Hansen, New Orleans (63 punts, 3,020 yards)
NET AVERAGE
  AFC: 38.1 — Reggie Roby, Miami (51 punts, 1,943 net yards)
  NFC: 36.6 — Greg Coleman, Minnesota (82 punts, 2,998 net yards)
LONGEST
  AFC: 89 yards — Luke Prestridge, New England vs. Miami, October 21
  NFC: 87 yards — David Finzer, Chicago vs. New Orleans, October 7
MOST PUNTS
  AFC: 98 — Jim Arnold, Kansas City
    98 — Rohn Stark, Indianapolis
  NFC: 92 — Mike Horan, Philadelphia
MOST PUNTS, GAME
  AFC: 11 — Rich Camarillo, New England vs. Dallas, November 22
  NFC: 11 — David Finzer, Chicago vs. San Diego, December 3
    11 — Danny White, Dallas vs. Green Bay, September 23
TEAM CHAMPIONS
  AFC: 44.9 — Kansas City
  NFC: 43.1 — New Orleans

AFC PUNTING — TEAM

	Total Punts	Gross Yards	Long	Gross Avg.	TB	Blk.	Opp. Ret.	Ret. Yards	In 20	Net Avg.
Kansas City	98	4397	63	44.9	13	0	60	461	22	37.5
Miami	51	2281	69	44.7	10	0	17	138	15	38.1
Indianapolis	98	4383	72	44.7	7	0	62	600	21	37.2
New England	92	3904	89	42.4	12	0	45	442	20	35.0
Cleveland	76	3213	69	42.3	8	2	43	489	16	33.7
Cincinnati	67	2832	61	42.3	8	0	38	310	19	35.3
San Diego	66	2773	60	42.0	3	0	43	399	11	35.1
L.A. Raiders	91	3809	63	41.9	12	0	34	345	25	35.4
Pittsburgh	70	2883	62	41.2	5	0	37	351	21	34.7
Buffalo	90	3696	63	41.1	8	2	52	597	16	32.7
Denver	96	3850	83	40.1	6	0	44	335	16	35.4
Houston	88	3482	55	39.6	5	0	60	618	20	31.4
N.Y. Jets	75	2935	64	39.1	8	1	37	242	19	33.8
Seattle	95	3567	60	37.5	10	0	32	205	24	33.3
AFC Total	1153	48005	89	—	115	5	604	5532	265	—
AFC Average	82.4	3428.9	—	41.6	8.2	0.4	43.1	395.1	18.9	34.8

NFC PUNTING — TEAM

	Total Punts	Gross Yards	Long	Gross Avg.	TB	Blk.	Opp. Ret.	Ret. Yards	In 20	Net Avg.
New Orleans	70	3020	66	43.1	7	1	47	550	9	33.3
Minnesota	82	3473	62	42.4	2	0	49	435	16	36.6
Green Bay	85	3596	61	42.3	12	0	46	368	18	35.2
Philadelphia	92	3880	69	42.2	6	0	58	486	21	35.6
Tampa Bay	68	2849	60	41.9	9	0	36	310	12	34.7
Detroit	76	3164	63	41.6	8	0	49	516	13	32.7
San Francisco	62	2536	59	40.9	12	1	30	190	19	34.0
Atlanta	70	2855	58	40.8	6	2	42	450	12	32.6
Chicago	85	3328	87	39.2	4	2	41	249	26	35.3
Washington	73	2834	59	38.8	5	1	38	187	11	34.9
L.A. Rams	74	2866	58	38.7	9	0	35	196	21	33.6
N.Y. Giants	94	3598	54	38.3	10	4	50	479	22	31.1
Dallas	108	4123	54	38.2	11	0	55	230	25	34.0
St. Louis	68	2594	59	38.1	8	1	27	239	19	32.3
NFC Total	1107	44716	87	—	109	12	603	4885	244	—
NFC Average	79.1	3194.0	—	40.4	7.8	0.9	43.1	348.9	17.4	34.0
League Total	2260	92721	89	—	224	17	1207	10417	509	—
League Average	80.7	3311.5	—	41.0	8.0	0.6	43.1	372.0	18.2	34.4

NFL TOP 10 PUNTERS

	Net Punts	Gross Yards	Long	Gross Avg.	Total Punts	TB	Blk.	Opp. Ret.	Ret. Yards	In 20	Net Avg.
Arnold, Jim, Kansas City	98	4397	63	44.9	98	13	0	60	461	22	37.5
Roby, Reggie, Miami	51	2281	69	44.7	51	10	0	17	138	15	38.1
Stark, Rohn, Indianapolis	98	4383	72	44.7	98	7	0	62	600	21	37.2
Hansen, Brian, New Orleans	69	3020	66	43.8	70	7	1	47	550	9	33.3
Cox, Steve, Cleveland	74	3213	69	43.4	76	8	2	43	489	16	33.7
Prestridge, Luke, New England	44	1884	89	42.8	44	5	0	21	228	8	35.4
Coleman, Greg, Minnesota	82	3473	62	42.4	82	2	0	49	435	16	36.6
Scribner, Bucky, Green Bay	85	3596	61	42.3	85	12	0	46	368	18	35.2
McInally, Pat, Cincinnati	67	2832	61	42.3	67	8	0	38	310	19	35.3
Horan, Mike, Philadelphia	92	3880	69	42.2	92	6	0	58	486	21	35.6

AFC PUNTING — INDIVIDUAL

	Net Punts	Gross Yards	Long	Gross Avg.	Total Punts	TB	Blk.	Opp. Ret.	Ret. Yards	In 20	Net Avg.
Arnold, Jim, Kansas City	98	4397	63	44.9	98	13	0	60	461	22	37.5
Roby, Reggie, Miami	51	2281	69	44.7	51	10	0	17	138	15	38.1
Stark, Rohn, Indianapolis	98	4383	72	44.7	98	7	0	62	600	21	37.2
Cox, Steve, Cleveland	74	3213	69	43.4	76	8	2	43	489	16	33.7
Prestridge, Luke, New England	44	1884	89	42.8	44	5	0	21	228	8	35.4
McInally, Pat, Cincinnati	67	2832	61	42.3	67	8	0	38	310	19	35.3
Camarillo, Rich, New England	48	2020	61	42.1	48	7	0	24	214	12	34.7
Buford, Maury, San Diego	66	2773	60	42.0	66	3	0	43	399	11	35.1
Kidd, John, Buffalo	88	3696	63	42.0	90	8	2	52	597	16	32.7
Guy, Ray, L.A. Raiders	91	3809	63	41.9	91	12	0	34	345	25	35.4
Colquitt, Craig, Pittsburgh	70	2883	62	41.2	70	5	0	37	351	21	34.7
Norman, Chris, Denver	96	3850	83	40.1	96	6	0	44	335	16	35.4
Ramsey, Chuck, N.Y. Jets	74	2935	64	39.7	75	8	1	37	242	19	33.8
James, John, Houston	88	3482	55	39.6	88	5	0	60	618	20	31.4
West, Jeff, Seattle	95	3567	60	37.5	95	10	0	32	205	24	33.3

Leader based on gross average, minimum 40 punts.

NFC PUNTING — INDIVIDUAL

	Net Punts	Gross Yards	Long	Gross Avg.	Total Punts	TB	Blk.	Opp. Ret.	Ret. Yards	In 20	Net Avg.
Hansen, Brian, New Orleans	69	3020	66	43.8	70	7	1	47	550	9	33.3
Coleman, Greg, Minnesota	82	3473	62	42.4	82	2	0	49	435	16	36.6
Scribner, Bucky, Green Bay	85	3596	61	42.3	85	12	0	46	368	18	35.2
Horan, Mike, Philadelphia	92	3880	69	42.2	92	6	0	58	486	21	35.6
Giacomarro, Ralph, Atlanta	68	2855	58	42.0	70	6	2	42	450	12	32.6
Garcia, Frank, Tampa Bay	68	2849	60	41.9	68	9	0	36	310	12	34.7
Runager, Max, San Francisco	56	2341	59	41.8	57	12	0	26	176	18	33.8
Black, Mike, Detroit	76	3164	63	41.6	76	8	0	49	516	13	32.7
Finzer, David, Chicago	83	3328	87	40.1	85	4	2	41	249	26	35.3
Jennings, Dave, N.Y. Giants	90	3598	54	40.0	93	10	3	50	479	22	31.4
Hayes, Jeff, Washington	72	2834	59	39.4	73	5	1	38	187	11	34.9
Misko, John, L.A. Rams	74	2866	58	38.7	74	9	0	35	196	21	33.6
Birdsong, Carl, St. Louis	67	2594	59	38.7	68	8	1	27	239	19	32.3
White, Danny, Dallas	82	3151	54	38.4	82	8	0	38	156	21	34.6
Non-Qualifiers											
Warren, John, Dallas	21	799	48	38.0	21	3	0	13	47	3	33.0
Miller, Jim, Dallas	5	173	41	34.6	5	0	0	4	27	1	29.2
Orosz, Tom, San Francisco	5	195	55	39.0	5	0	0	4	14	1	36.2
Haji-Sheikh, Ali, N.Y. Giants	0	0	0	—	1	0	1	0	0	0	0.0

Leader based on gross average, minimum 40 punts.

PUNT RETURNS

INDIVIDUAL CHAMPIONS (AVERAGE)
AFC: 15.7—Mike Martin, Cincinnati
NFC: 13.4—Henry Ellard, Los Angeles Rams

YARDAGE
AFC: 656—Louis Lipps, Pittsburgh (53 returns)
NFC: 521—Dana McLemore, San Francisco (45 returns)

MOST YARDS, GAME
AFC: 152—Cleotha Montgomery, Los Angeles Raiders vs. Detroit, December 10 (9 returns)
NFC: 104—Henry Ellard, Los Angeles Rams vs. Atlanta, October 22 (3 returns)

RETURNS
NFC: 57—Jeff Fisher, Chicago
AFC: 53—Louis Lipps, Pittsburgh
53—Greg Pruitt, Los Angeles Raiders

MOST RETURNS, GAME
AFC: 9—Cleotha Montgomery, Los Angeles Raiders vs. Detroit, December 10 (152 yards)
NFC: 8—Jeff Fisher, Chicago vs. Detroit, December 16 (103 yards)
8—Phil McConkey, New York Giants vs. Dallas, November 4 (38 yards)

FAIR CATCHES
NFC: 19—Evan Cooper, Philadelphia
AFC: 16—Greg Pruitt, Los Angeles Raiders

LONGEST
NFC: 83 yards—Henry Ellard, Los Angeles Rams vs. New York Giants, September 30 (TD)
AFC: 76 yards—Louis Lipps, Pittsburgh vs. New Orleans, November 19 (TD)

TOUCHDOWNS
NFC: 2—Henry Ellard, Los Angeles Rams vs. New York Giants, September 30 (83 yards), Los Angeles Rams vs. Atlanta, October 22 (69 yards)
AFC: 1—Lionel James, San Diego vs. Pittsburgh, November 25 (58 yards)
1—Paul Johns, Seattle vs. New England, September 16 (47 yards)
1—Louis Lipps, Pittsburgh vs. New Orleans, November 19 (76 yards)
1—Cleotha Montgomery, Los Angeles Raiders vs. Detroit, December 10 (69 yards)
1—Don Wilson, Buffalo vs. Seattle, October 14 (65 yards)

TEAM CHAMPIONS
AFC: 12.4—Cincinnati
NFC: 12.2—Los Angeles Rams

AFC PUNT RETURNS—TEAM

	No.	FC	Yards	Avg.	Long	TD
Los Angeles Raiders	67	17	667	10.0	69t	1
Pittsburgh	61	2	696	11.4	76t	1
New England	48	15	430	9.0	55	0
Seattle	44	11	484	11.0	47t	1
Kansas City	42	15	346	8.2	27	0
Denver	41	12	318	7.8	35	0
Cleveland	40	13	322	8.1	19	0
Miami	39	27	365	9.4	37	0
Cincinnati	38	11	473	12.4	55	0
Indianapolis	38	12	278	7.3	35	0
New York Jets	35	12	324	9.3	33	0
Buffalo	33	8	297	9.0	65t	1
San Diego	33	12	212	6.4	58t	1
Houston	26	8	152	5.8	18	0
AFC Total	585	175	5364	—	76t	5
AFC Average	41.8	12.5	383.1	9.2	—	0.4

NFC PUNT RETURNS—TEAM

	No.	FC	Yards	Avg.	Long	TD
Chicago	63	11	558	8.9	28	0
Washington	55	2	474	8.6	46	0
New York Giants	55	18	368	6.7	31	0
Dallas	54	15	446	8.3	18	0
Green Bay	48	16	351	7.3	39	0
St. Louis	47	5	399	8.5	39	0
San Francisco	45	11	521	11.6	79t	1
Atlanta	41	4	264	6.4	37	0
Los Angeles Rams	40	4	489	12.2	83t	2

	No.	FC	Yards	Avg.	Long	TD
Philadelphia	40	19	250	6.3	16	0
Detroit	36	11	241	6.7	23	0
Tampa Bay	34	5	207	6.1	21	0
New Orleans	33	18	268	8.1	61	0
Minnesota	31	10	217	7.0	21	0
NFC Total	622	149	5053	—	83t	3
NFC Average	44.4	10.6	360.9	8.1	—	0.2
League Total	1207	324	10417	—	83t	8
League Average	43.1	11.6	372.0	8.6	—	0.3

NFL TOP 10 PUNT RETURNERS

	No.	FC	Yards	Avg.	Long	TD
Martin, Mike, Cincinnati	24	5	376	15.7	55	0
Ellard, Henry, L.A. Rams	30	3	403	13.4	83t	2
Lipps, Louis, Pittsburgh	53	2	656	12.4	76t	1
McLemore, Dana, San Francisco	45	11	521	11.6	79t	1
Willhite, Gerald, Denver	20	9	200	10.0	35	0
Fryar, Irving, New England	36	10	347	9.6	55	0
Wilson, Don, Buffalo	33	8	297	9.0	65t	1
Pruitt, Greg, L.A. Raiders	53	16	473	8.9	38	0
Springs, Kirk, N.Y. Jets	28	10	247	8.8	33	0
Mitchell, Stump, St. Louis	38	3	333	8.8	39	0

AFC PUNT RETURNS—INDIVIDUAL

	No.	FC	Yards	Avg.	Long	TD
Martin, Mike, Cincinnati	24	5	376	15.7	55	0
Lipps, Louis, Pittsburgh	53	2	656	12.4	76t	1
Willhite, Gerald, Denver	20	9	200	10.0	35	0
Fryar, Irving, New England	36	10	347	9.6	55	0
Wilson, Don, Buffalo	33	8	297	9.0	65t	1
Pruitt, Greg, L.A. Raiders	53	16	473	8.9	38	0
Springs, Kirk, N.Y. Jets	28	0	247	8.8	33	0
Smith, J.T., Kansas City	39	14	332	8.5	27	0
Walker, Fulton, Miami	21	14	169	8.0	33	0
Brennan, Brian, Cleveland	25	10	199	8.0	19	0
James, Lionel, San Diego	30	9	208	6.9	58t	1
Anderson, Larry, Indianapolis	27	7	182	6.7	19	0
Roaches, Carl, Houston	26	8	152	5.8	18	0
Non-Qualifiers						
Skansi, Paul, Seattle	16	2	145	9.1	16	0
Easley, Ken, Seattle	16	5	194	12.1	42	0
Montgomery, Cle., L.A. Raiders	14	1	194	13.9	69t	1
Simmons, John, Cincinnati	12	6	98	8.2	30	0
Johns, Paul, Seattle	11	4	140	12.7	47t	1
Starring, Stephen, New England	10	1	73	7.3	16	0
Clayton, Mark, Miami	8	2	79	9.9	22	0
Glasgow, Nesby, Indianapolis	7	2	79	11.3	35	0
Woods, Rick, Pittsburgh	6	0	40	6.7	14	0
Walker, Dwight, Cleveland	6	3	50	8.3	13	0
Bird, Steve, St.L.-San Diego	6	0	60	10.0	17	0
Heflin, Vince, Miami	6	1	76	12.7	37	0
Kozlowski, Mike, Miami	4	4	41	10.3	20	0
Minter, Cedric, N.Y. Jets	4	2	44	11.0	18	0
Hancock, Anthony, Kansas City	3	1	14	4.7	7	0
Bouza, Matt, Indianapolis	3	3	17	5.7	11	0
Horton, Ray, Cincinnati	2	0	−1	−0.5	1	0
Bruckner, Nick, N.Y. Jets	2	0	25	12.5	20	0
Clayton, Harvey, Pittsburgh	1	0	0	0.0	0	0
Henderson, Reuben, San Diego	1	2	0	0.0	0	0
Long, Terry, Pittsburgh	1	0	0	0.0	0	0
Padjen, Gary, Indianapolis	1	0	0	0.0	0	0
Smith, Lucious, Buff.-San Diego	1	0	0	0.0	0	0
Wilson, Steve, Denver	1	0	0	0.0	0	0
Gibson, Ernest, New England	1	0	3	3.0	3	0
Dixon, Zachary, Seattle	1	0	5	5.0	5	0
Weathers, Clarence, New England	1	0	7	7.0	7	0
Mullen, Davlin, N.Y. Jets	1	0	8	8.0	8	0
Blackwood, Glenn, Miami	0	4	0	—	0	0
Blackwood, Lyle, Miami	0	2	0	—	0	0
Chandler, Wes, San Diego	0	1	0	—	0	0
James, Roland, New England	0	2	0	—	0	0
Sanford, Rick, New England	0	2	0	—	0	0

t indicates touchdown
Leader based on average return, minimum 20 returns.

NFC PUNT RETURNS—INDIVIDUAL

	No.	FC	Yards	Avg.	Long	TD
Ellard, Henry, L.A. Rams	30	3	403	13.4	83t	2
McLemore, Dana, San Francisco	45	11	521	11.6	79t	1
Mitchell, Stump, St. Louis	38	3	333	8.8	39	0
Fields, Jitter, New Orleans	27	6	236	8.7	61	0
Nelms, Mike, Washington	49	1	428	8.7	46	0
Fisher, Jeff, Chicago	57	11	492	8.6	28	0
Martin, Robbie, Detroit	25	8	210	8.4	23	0
Allen, Gary, Dallas	54	15	446	8.3	18	0

	No.	FC	Yards	Avg.	Long	TD
Nelson, Darrin, Minnesota	23	9	180	7.8	21	0
Bright, Leon, Tampa Bay	23	1	173	7.5	21	0
Epps, Phillip, Green Bay	29	10	199	6.9	39	0
McConkey, Phil, N.Y. Giants	46	15	306	6.7	31	0
Cooper, Evan, Philadelphia	40	19	250	6.3	16	0
Thomas, Zack, Denver-Tampa Bay	21	3	125	6.0	15	0
Non-Qualifiers						
Flynn, Tom, Green Bay	15	4	128	8.5	20	0
Johnson, Billy, Atlanta	15	1	152	10.1	37	0
Johnson, Kenny, Atlanta	10	1	79	7.9	14	0
Curran, Willie, Atlanta	9	1	21	2.3	10	0
Harris, Duriel, Clev.-Dallas	9	0	73	8.1	13	0
Irvin, LeRoy, L.A. Rams	9	0	83	9.2	22	0
Seay, Virgil, Wash.-Atlanta	8	1	10	1.3	7	0
Manuel, Lionel, N.Y. Giants	8	3	62	7.8	22	0
Hall, Alvin, Detroit	7	1	30	4.3	11	0
Holt, John, T.B.	6	3	17	2.8	8	0
Groth, Jeff, New Orleans	6	12	32	5.3	9	0
McKinnon, Dennis, Chicago	5	0	62	12.4	18	0
Bell, Theo, Tampa Bay	4	1	10	2.5	8	0
Pittman, Danny, St. Louis	4	1	10	2.5	5	0
Hayes, Gary, Green Bay	4	0	24	6.0	10	0
Lewis, Leo, Minnesota	4	1	31	7.8	13	0
Mandley, Pete, Detroit	2	2	0	0.0	0	0
Bess, Rufus, Minnesota	2	0	9	4.5	7	0
Green, Darrell, Washington	2	0	13	6.5	13	0
Waddy, Billy, Minnesota	1	0	−3	−3.0	−3	0
Johnson, Demetrious, Detroit	1	0	0	0.0	0	0
Kinard, Terry, N.Y. Giants	1	0	0	0.0	0	0
Teal, Willie, Minnesota	1	0	0	0.0	0	0
Williams, Greg, Washington	1	0	0	0.0	0	0
Jenkins, Ken, Detroit	1	0	1	1.0	1	0
Mauti, Rich, Washington	1	1	2	2.0	2	0
Johnson, Johnnie, L.A. Rams	1	1	3	3.0	3	0
Duerson, Dave, Chicago	1	0	4	4.0	4	0
Coffey, Ken, Washington	1	0	6	6.0	6	0
Green, Roy, St. Louis	0	1	0	—	0	0
Murphy, Mark, Green Bay	0	2	0	—	0	0
Coleman, Monte, Washington	0	0	27	—	27	0

t indicates touchdown
Leader based on average return, minimum 20 returns.

KICKOFF RETURNS

INDIVIDUAL CHAMPIONS (AVERAGE)
AFC: 30.7—Bobby Humphery, New York Jets
NFC: 23.0—Barry Redden, Los Angeles Rams
YARDAGE
AFC: 959—Lionel James, San Diego (43 returns)
NFC: 891—Darrin Nelson, Minnesota (39 returns)
MOST YARDS, GAME
AFC: 179—Van Williams, Buffalo vs. New England, November 11
(7 returns)
NFC: 168—Darrin Nelson, Minnesota vs. Chicago, November 25
(7 returns)
RETURNS
AFC: 43—Lionel James, San Diego
NFC: 42—Mike Nelms, Washington
MOST RETURNS, GAME
AFC: 7—Rich Erenberg, Pittsburgh vs. Kansas City, September 2
(174 yards)
7—David Hughes, Seattle vs. New England, September 16
(134 yards)
7—Van Williams, Buffalo vs. New England, November 11
(179 yards)
7—Darrin Nelson, Minnesota vs. Chicago, November 25
(168 yards)
LONGEST
NFC: 97 yards—Del Rodgers, Green Bay vs. Chicago, December 9 (TD)
AFC: 97 yards—Bobby Humphery, New York Jets vs. Pittsburgh, September 6 (TD)
TOUCHDOWNS
AFC: 1—Bobby Humphery, New York Jets vs. Pittsburgh, September 2
(97 yards)
1—Phil Smith, Indianapolis vs. St. Louis, September 16 (96 yards)
NFC: 1—Mike Guman, Los Angeles Rams vs. Cincinnati, September 23
(43 yards)
1—Del Rodgers, Green Bay vs. Chicago, December 9 (97 yards)
1—Andre Waters, Philadelphia vs. Washington, November 18
(89 yards)
TEAM CHAMPIONS
AFC: 23.0—New York Jets
NFC: 22.1—San Francisco

AFC KICKOFF RETURNS—TEAM

	No.	Yards	Avg.	Long	TD
New York Jets	65	1498	23.0	97t	1
Buffalo	76	1422	18.7	65	0
Houston	69	1352	19.6	49	0

	No.	Yards	Avg.	Long	TD
Indianapolis	69	1331	19.3	96t	1
San Diego	63	1319	20.9	55	0
New England	63	1246	19.8	46	0
Los Angeles Raiders	56	1216	21.7	62	0
Cleveland	61	1157	19.0	40	0
Cincinnati	61	1155	18.9	46	0
Kansas City	56	1061	18.9	45	0
Pittsburgh	54	1026	19.0	47	0
Seattle	54	1007	18.6	38	0
Denver	45	897	19.9	40	0
Miami	44	799	18.2	41	0
AFC Total	836	16486	—	97t	2
AFC Average	59.7	1177.6	19.7	—	0.1

NFC KICKOFF RETURNS—TEAM

	No.	Yards	Avg.	Long	TD
Minnesota	86	1775	20.6	47	0
St. Louis	74	1563	21.1	56	0
New Orleans	72	1465	20.3	64	0
Atlanta	70	1367	19.5	50	0
Green Bay	67	1362	20.3	97t	1
Tampa Bay	68	1354	19.9	43	0
Detroit	74	1347	18.2	46	0
Los Angeles Rams	58	1244	21.4	43t	1
Dallas	63	1199	19.0	34	0
Washington	60	1174	19.6	36	0
Philadelphia	59	1156	19.6	89	1
New York Giants	61	1117	18.3	52	0
San Francisco	47	1039	22.1	51	0
Chicago	49	896	18.3	40	0
NFC Total	908	18058	—	97t	3
NFC Average	64.9	1289.9	19.9	—	0.2
League Total	1744	34544	—	97t	5
League Average	62.3	1233.7	19.8	—	0.2

NFL TOP 10 KICKOFF RETURNERS

	No.	Yards	Avg.	Long	TD
Humphery, Bobby, N.Y. Jets	22	675	30.7	97t	1
Williams, Dokie, L.A. Raiders	24	621	25.9	62	0
Anderson, Larry, Indianapolis	22	525	23.9	69	0
Redden, Barry, L.A. Rams	23	530	23.0	40	0
Mitchell, Stump, St. Louis	35	804	23.0	56	0
Nelson, Darrin, Minnesota	39	891	22.8	47	0
Springs, Kirk, N.Y. Jets	23	521	22.7	73	0
Roaches, Carl, Houston	30	679	22.6	49	0
James, Lionel, San Diego	43	959	22.3	55	0
Anthony, Tyrone, New Orleans	22	490	22.3	64	0

AFC KICKOFF RETURNS—INDIVIDUAL

	No.	Yards	Avg.	Long	TD
Humphery, Bobby, N.Y. Jets	22	675	30.7	97t	1
Williams, Dokie, L.A. Raiders	24	621	25.9	62	0
Anderson, Larry, Indianapolis	22	525	23.9	69	0
Springs, Kirk, N.Y. Jets	23	521	22.7	73	0
Roaches, Carl, Houston	30	679	22.6	49	0
James, Lionel, San Diego	43	959	22.3	55	0
Collins, Anthony, New England	25	544	21.8	46	0
Montgomery, Cle, L.A. Raiders	26	555	21.3	42	0
Walker, Fulton, Miami	29	617	21.3	41	0
Williams, Van, Buffalo	39	820	21.0	65	0
Jennings, Stanford, Cincinnati	22	452	20.5	46	0
Erenberg, Rich, Pittsburgh	28	575	20.5	47	0
Smith, Phil, Indianapolis	32	651	20.3	96t	1
Paige, Stephone, Kansas City	27	544	20.1	45	0
Williams, Jon, New England	23	461	20.0	29	0
Byner, Earnest, Cleveland	22	415	18.9	28	0
Dixon, Zachary, Seattle	25	446	17.8	36	0
Wilson, Don, Buffalo	34	576	16.9	36	0
Non-Qualifiers					
Lang, Gene, Denver	19	404	21.3	38	0
Smith, J.T., Kansas City	19	391	20.6	39	0
Martin, Mike, Cincinnati	19	386	20.3	44	0
Spencer, Todd, Pittsburgh	18	373	20.7	40	0
Davis, Bruce, Cleveland	18	369	20.5	40	0
Hughes, David, Seattle	17	348	20.5	38	0
Walls, Herkie, Houston	15	289	19.3	29	0
McGee, Buford, San Diego	14	315	22.5	35	0
Allen, Patrick, Houston	11	210	19.1	23	0
Bird, Steve, St. Louis-San Diego	11	205	18.6	28	0
Minter, Cedric, N.Y. Jets	10	224	22.4	52	0
Heflin, Vince, Miami	9	130	14.4	26	0
Morris, Randall, Seattle	8	153	19.1	34	0
Brown, Preston, Cleveland	8	136	17.0	27	0
Brooks, James, Cincinnati	7	144	20.6	37	0
Farley, John, Cincinnati	6	93	15.5	32	0
Young, Glen, Cleveland	5	134	26.8	36	0
Fryar, Irving, New England	5	95	19.0	22	0
Williams, Richard, Atlanta-Houston	5	84	16.8	21	0
Ricks, Lawrence, Kansas City	5	83	16.6	21	0
White, Charles, Cleveland	5	80	16.0	23	0
Kafentzis, Mark, Indianapolis	5	69	13.8	22	0
Willhite, Gerald, Denver	4	109	27.3	40	0
Wonsley, George, Indianapolis	4	52	13.0	20	0
Veals, Elton, Pittsburgh	4	40	10.0	18	0
Joyner, Willie, Houston	3	57	19.0	24	0
Bryant, Cullen, Seattle	3	53	17.7	21	0
Verser, David, Cincinnati	3	46	15.3	23	0
Lee, Keith L., New England	3	43	14.3	17	0
Robinson, Bo, New England	3	38	12.7	14	0
Brown, Steve, Houston	3	17	5.7	17	0
Pruitt, Greg, L.A. Raiders	3	16	5.3	13	0
Paige, Tony, N.Y. Jets	3	7	2.3	7	0
Mullen, Davlin, N.Y. Jets	2	34	17.0	23	0
Hancock, Anthony, Kansas City	2	32	16.0	17	0
Dennison, Rick, Denver	2	27	13.5	16	0
Kozlowski, Mike, Miami	2	23	11.5	12	0
Egloff, Ron, San Diego	2	20	10.0	11	0
Moore, Alvin, Indianapolis	2	19	9.5	10	0
Clayton, Mark, Miami	2	15	7.5	14	0
Jones, Cedric, New England	1	20	20.0	20	0
Bruckner, Nick, N.Y. Jets	1	17	17.0	17	0
Thompson, Ted, Houston	1	16	16.0	16	0
Bell, Greg, Buffalo	1	15	15.0	15	0
Corley, Anthony, Pittsburgh	1	15	15.0	15	0
Simmons, John, Cincinnati	1	15	15.0	15	0
Hawthorne, Greg, New England	1	14	14.0	14	0
Hill, Eddie, Miami	1	14	14.0	14	0
Willis, Chester, L.A. Raiders	1	13	13.0	13	0
Gillespie, Fernandars, Pittsburgh	1	12	12.0	12	0
Harris, M.L., Cincinnati	1	12	12.0	12	0
Nicolas, Scott, Cleveland	1	12	12.0	12	0
Brown, Chris, Pittsburgh	1	11	11.0	11	0
Jensen, Derrick, L.A. Raiders	1	11	11.0	11	0
Middleton, Frank, Indianapolis	1	11	11.0	11	0
Contz, Bill, Cleveland	1	10	10.0	10	0
Jackson, Earnest, San Diego	1	10	10.0	10	0
Davidson, Chy, N.Y. Jets	1	9	9.0	9	0
Scott, Willie, Kansas City	1	9	9.0	9	0
Tatupu, Mosi, New England	1	9	9.0	9	0
Harris, John, Seattle	1	7	7.0	7	0
Kinnebrew, Larry, Cincinnati	1	7	7.0	7	0
David, Stan, Buffalo	1	6	6.0	6	0
Gaffney, Derrick, N.Y. Jets	1	6	6.0	6	0
Banker, Ted, N.Y. Jets	1	5	5.0	5	0
White, Craig, Buffalo	1	5	5.0	5	0
Harden, Mike, Denver	1	4	4.0	4	0
Carson, Carlos, Kansas City	1	2	2.0	2	0
Hathaway, Steve, Indianapolis	1	2	2.0	2	0
Sherwin, Tim, Indianapolis	1	2	2.0	2	0
Smith, Aaron, Denver	1	2	2.0	2	0
Holt, Harry, Cleveland	1	1	1.0	1	0
Catano, Mark, Pittsburgh	1	0	0.0	0	0
Cherry, Deron, Kansas City	1	0	0.0	0	0
Duhe, A.J., Miami	1	0	0.0	0	0
Gofourth, Derrel, San Diego	1	0	0.0	0	0
McKinney, Odis, L.A. Raiders	1	0	0.0	0	0
Radachowsky, George, Ind.	1	0	0.0	0	0
Shuler, Mickey, N.Y. Jets	1	0	0.0	0	0
Williams, Gary, Cincinnati	1	0	0.0	0	0
Williams, Jamie, Houston	1	0	0.0	0	0

t indicates touchdown
Leader based on average return, minimum 20 returns.

NFC KICKOFF RETURNS—INDIVIDUAL

	No.	Yards	Avg.	Long	TD
Redden, Barry, L.A. Rams	23	530	23.0	40	0
Mitchell, Stump, St. Louis	35	804	23.0	56	0
Nelson, Darrin, Minnesota	39	891	22.8	47	0
Anthony, Tyrone, New Orleans	22	490	22.3	64	0
Morton, Michael, Tampa Bay	38	835	22.0	43	0
Rodgers, Del, Green Bay	39	843	21.6	97t	1
Anderson, Alfred, Minnesota	30	639	21.3	41	0
Hill, Drew, L.A. Rams	26	543	20.9	40	0
Monroe, Carl, San Francisco	27	561	20.8	44	0
Nelms, Mike, Washington	42	860	20.5	36	0
Allen, Gary, Dallas	33	666	20.2	34	0
McSwain, Chuck, Dallas	20	403	20.2	32	0
Hayes, Joe, Philadelphia	22	441	20.0	44	0
Duckett, Kenny, New Orleans	29	580	20.0	39	0
McConkey, Phil, N.Y. Giants	28	541	19.3	33	0
Cameron, Jack, Chicago	26	485	18.7	40	0
Mandley, Pete, Detroit	22	390	17.7	32	0

Non-Qualifiers	No.	Yards	Avg.	Long	TD
Stamps, Sylvester, Atlanta	19	452	23.8	50	0
Hall, Alvin, Detroit	19	385	20.3	46	0
Johnson, Kenny, Atlanta	19	359	18.9	27	0
Fields, Jitter, New Orleans	19	356	18.7	31	0
Jenkins, Ken, Detroit	18	396	22.0	32	0
Thomas, Zack, Denver-Tampa Bay	18	351	19.5	33	0
Cooper, Evan, Philadelphia	17	299	17.6	48	0
Bright, Leon, Tampa Bay	16	303	18.9	33	0
Pittman, Danny, St. Louis	14	319	22.8	43	0
Huckleby, Harlan, Green Bay	14	261	18.6	54	0
Woolfolk, Butch, N.Y. Giants	14	232	16.6	27	0
Harmon, Derrick, San Francisco	13	357	27.5	51	0
Waters, Andre, Philadelphia	13	319	24.5	89t	1
Harrell, Willard, St. Louis	13	231	17.8	28	0
Epps, Phillip, Green Bay	12	232	19.3	47	0
Curran, Willie, Atlanta	11	219	19.9	42	0
Gentry, Dennis, Chicago	11	209	19.0	33	0
Martin, Robbie, Detroit	10	144	14.4	23	0
Cephous, Frank, N.Y. Giants	9	178	19.8	30	0
Griffin, Keith, Washington	9	164	18.2	31	0
Tate, Rodney, Atlanta	9	148	16.4	31	0
Owens, James, Tampa Bay	8	168	21.0	36	0
Fellows, Ron, Dallas	6	94	15.7	23	0
Morris, Joe, N.Y. Giants	6	69	11.5	14	0
Seay, Virgil, Washington-Atlanta	5	108	21.6	28	0
Jordan, Donald, Chicago	5	62	12.4	22	0
Wood, Richard, Tampa Bay	5	43	8.6	16	0
Duerson, Dave, Chicago	4	95	23.8	26	0
Austin, Cliff, Atlanta	4	77	19.3	23	0
Meade, Mike, Detroit	4	32	8.0	15	0
McLemore, Dana, San Francisco	3	80	26.7	50	0
Waddy, Billy, Minnesota	3	64	21.3	31	0
Bess, Rufus, Minnesota	3	47	15.7	19	0
Kane, Rick, Washington	3	43	14.3	31	0
Everett, Major, Philadelphia	3	40	13.3	18	0
Rice, Allen, Minnesota	3	34	11.3	13	0
Pleasant, Mike, L.A. Rams	2	48	24.0	29	0
Johnson, Billy, Atlanta	2	39	19.5	21	0
Smith, Jimmy, Washington	2	38	19.0	22	0
Bell, Todd, Chicago	2	33	16.5	17	0
Irvin, LeRoy, L.A. Rams	2	33	16.5	22	0
Salonen, Brian, Dallas	2	30	15.0	22	0
Smith, Greg, Minnesota	2	26	13.0	15	0
Ellis, Ray, Philadelphia	2	25	12.5	15	0
Ellard, Henry, L.A. Rams	2	24	12.0	12	0
Rouse, Curtis, Minnesota	2	22	11.0	15	0
Turner, Maurice, Minnesota	2	21	10.5	14	0
McLaughlin, Jim, N.Y. Giants	2	18	9.0	11	0
Granger, Norm, Dallas	2	6	3.0	5	0
Daniel, Kenny, N.Y. Giants	1	52	52.0	52	0
Guman, Mike, L.A. Rams	1	43	43.0	43t	1
Lewis, Leo, Minnesota	1	31	31.0	31	0
Hill, Ken, N.Y. Giants	1	27	27.0	27	0
Ring, Bill, San Francisco	1	27	27.0	27	0
Wilson, Wayne, New Orleans	1	23	23.0	23	0
Smith, Ricky, New England-Wash.	1	22	22.0	22	0
Crutchfield, Dwayne, L.A. Rams	1	20	20.0	20	0
Hardy, Andre, Philadelphia	1	20	20.0	20	0
Jones, Daryll, Green Bay	1	19	19.0	19	0
Green, Roy, St. Louis	1	18	18.0	18	0
Mauti, Rich, Washington	1	16	16.0	16	0
Wilson, Tim, New Orleans	1	16	16.0	16	0
Gaison, Blane, Atlanta	1	15	15.0	15	0
Wilson, Mike, San Francisco	1	14	14.0	14	0
Gault, Willie, Chicago	1	12	12.0	12	0
Strauthers, Thomas, Philadelphia	1	12	12.0	12	0
Prather, Guy, Green Bay	1	7	7.0	7	0
Spradlin, Danny, Tampa Bay	1	5	5.0	5	0
Matthews, Allama, Atlanta	1	3	3.0	3	0
Sully, Ivory, L.A. Rams	1	3	3.0	3	0
Love, Randy, St. Louis	1	1	1.0	1	0
Cooper, Earl, San Francisco	1	0	0.0	0	0
D'Addio, Dave, Detroit	1	0	0.0	0	0
Ferrell, Earl, St. Louis	1	0	0.0	0	0
Malancon, Rydell, Atlanta	1	0	0.0	0	0
McIntyre, Guy, San Francisco	1	0	0.0	0	0
Nelson, David, Minnesota	1	0	0.0	0	0
Tyrrell, Tim, Atlanta	1	0	0.0	0	0

t indicates touchdown

Leader based on average return, minimum 20 returns.

AFC FUMBLES — TEAM

	Fum.	Own Rec.	Fum. *O.B.	TD	Opp. Rec.	Yds.	TD	Tot. Rec.
Seattle	24	8	3	0	25	−21	1	33
New York Jets	26	12	1	0	18	68	2	30
Miami	26	16	0	0	12	60	1	28
New England	29	12	2	1	8	0	0	20
Buffalo	31	11	6	0	21	104	2	32
Cleveland	31	14	1	1	15	112	0	29
Cincinnati	32	13	2	0	15	0	0	28
Kansas City	34	16	3	0	11	−41	0	27
Indianapolis	35	14	5	0	13	−28	0	27
San Diego	35	14	4	0	17	19	0	31
Denver	36	18	1	0	24	117	4	42
Houston	36	19	1	0	11	18	1	30
Pittsburgh	40	23	2	0	10	104	2	33
Los Angeles Raiders	42	20	2	0	14	84	1	34
AFC Totals	457	210	33	2	214	596	14	424
AFC Average	32.6	15.0	2.4	0.1	15.3	42.6	1.0	30.3

NFC FUMBLES — TEAM

	Fum.	Own Rec.	Fum. *O.B.	TD	Opp. Rec.	Yds.	TD	Tot. Rec.
New York Giants	17	8	0	0	16	88	1	24
Green Bay	17	10	0	0	15	−5	0	25
New Orleans	22	9	0	0	10	20	1	19
Philadelphia	23	7	0	0	11	0	0	18
San Francisco	26	13	1	0	12	45	1	25
Chicago	31	11	4	0	13	−2	0	24
Los Angeles Rams	31	11	2	0	22	36	0	33
St. Louis	32	10	2	0	12	56	1	22
Washington	33	16	2	1	21	62	2	37
Dallas	35	14	4	0	16	18	1	30
Detroit	36	21	1	0	11	−20	0	32
Tampa Bay	36	16	0	0	14	11	0	30
Atlanta	39	18	0	0	20	12	0	38
Minnesota	39	22	1	0	17	57	2	39
NFC Totals	417	186	17	1	210	378	9	396
NFC Average	29.8	13.3	1.2	0.1	15.0	27.0	0.6	28.3
League Totals	874	396	50	3	424	974	23	820
League Average	31.2	14.1	1.8	0.1	15.1	34.8	0.8	29.3

*Fumbled out of bounds.
Total yards include all fumble yardage (aborted plays, own & opp. recoveries). Fumbled through the end zone, ball awarded to opponents: Cincinnati (awarded to Pittsburgh), Detroit (awarded to Minnesota), Indianapolis (awarded to New York Jets), Minnesota (awarded to Washington), Los Angeles Rams (awarded to San Francisco).

AFC FUMBLES — INDIVIDUAL

	Fum.	Own Rec.	Opp. Rec.	Yds.	Tot. Rec.
Adams, Willis, Cleveland	1	0	0	0	0
Alexander, Charles, Cincinnati	2	0	0	0	0
Allen, Marcus, L.A. Raiders	8	2	1	0	3
Alzado, Lyle, L.A. Raiders	0	0	1	0	1
Anderson, Ken, Cincinnati	1	0	0	0	0
Anderson, Larry, Indianapolis	4	0	0	0	0
Arnold, Jim, Kansas City	1	2	0	−9	2
Avellini, Bob, Chicago-N.Y. Jets	2	0	0	0	0
Azelby, Joe, Buffalo	0	0	1	0	1
Baab, Mike, Cleveland	1	0	0	−11	0
Bailey, Don, Indianapolis	2	0	1	−27	1
Baker, Jesse, Houston	0	0	1	0	1
Banks, Chip, Cleveland	0	0	3	17	3
Barber, Marion, N.Y. Jets	3	1	0	0	1
Barnes, Jeff, L.A. Raiders	0	0	1	0	1
Barnett, Buster, Buffalo	0	1	0	0	1
Barnwell, Malcolm, L.A. Raiders	1	1	0	0	1
Baumhower, Bob, Miami	0	0	2	23	2
Bell, Greg, Buffalo	5	3	0	0	3
Bell, Mark E., Indianapolis	0	1	0	0	1
Bell, Mike, Kansas City	1	0	2	0	2
Bendross, Jesse, San Diego	1	0	0	0	0
Bennett, Barry, N.Y. Jets	0	0	4	6	4
Bennett, Woody, Miami	4	2	0	0	2
Betters, Doug, Miami	0	0	1	0	1
Bingham, Craig, Pittsburgh	0	0	1	0	1
Bingham, Gregg, Houston	0	0	1	7	1
Bingham, Guy, N.Y. Jets	0	0	1	0	1
Bird, Steve, St. Louis-San Diego	1	0	0	0	0
Blackledge, Todd, Kansas City	8	4	0	−3	4
Blackwood, Glenn, Miami	0	0	1	0	1
Blackwood, Lyle, Miami	0	0	2	0	2
Blanton, Jerry, Kansas City	0	0	1	0	1
Bolden, Rickey, Cleveland	1	0	0	0	0
Bostic, Keith, Houston	0	0	2	25	2
Bouza, Matt, Indianapolis	1	0	0	0	0
Bowser, Charles, Miami	0	0	1	0	1
Bowyer, Walt, Denver	0	0	1	0	1
Branch, Cliff, L.A. Raiders	0	2	0	2	2
Brazile, Robert, Houston	0	0	1	0	1
Breeden, Louis, Cincinnati	1	0	0	0	0
Brennan, Brian, Cleveland	1	0	0	0	0

Name	Fum.	Own Rec.	Opp. Rec.	Yds.	Tot. Rec.
Brewer, Chris, Denver	1	0	1	0	1
Brooks, James, Cincinnati	4	0	0	0	0
Brown, Chris, Pittsburgh	0	0	1	0	1
Brown, Dave, Seattle	0	0	1	0	1
Brown, Steve, Houston	1	0	1	0	1
Brown, Theotis, Kansas City	2	0	0	0	0
Browner, Ross, Cincinnati	0	0	1	0	1
Bruckner, Nick, N.Y. Jets	0	1	0	0	1
Bryan, Bill, Denver	1	0	0	0	0
Bryant, Cullen, Seattle	0	1	0	0	1
Bryant, Jeff, Seattle	0	0	2	0	2
Bryant, Steve, Houston	1	0	0	0	0
Burruss, Lloyd, Kansas City	0	0	1	0	1
Busick, Steve, Denver	0	0	1	0	1
Buttle, Greg, N.Y. Jets	0	0	2	4	2
Byner, Earnest, Cleveland	3	2	0	55	2
Camp, Reggie, Cleveland	0	0	1	0	1
Campbell, Scott, Pittsburgh	1	1	0	0	1
Capers, Wayne, Pittsburgh	1	2	0	2	2
Carpenter, Brian, Washington-Buffalo	0	0	2	0	2
Carson, Carlos, Kansas City	0	1	1	0	2
Carter, Joe, Miami	3	2	0	0	2
Carter, Rubin, Denver	0	0	2	0	2
Cefalo, Jimmy, Miami	1	0	0	0	0
Christensen, Todd, L.A. Raiders	1	0	1	0	1
Clayton, Harvey, Pittsburgh	0	0	1	0	1
Clayton, Mark, Miami	2	1	0	0	1
Clifton, Kyle, N.Y. Jets	0	0	1	0	1
Cole, Robin, Pittsburgh	0	0	1	8	1
Collins, Anthony, New England	3	0	0	0	0
Collins, Glen, Cincinnati	0	0	1	0	1
Collinsworth, Cris, Cincinnati	0	1	0	0	1
Comeaux, Darren, Denver	0	0	1	0	1
Condon, Tom, Kansas City	0	1	0	0	1
Corley, Anthony, Pittsburgh	0	2	0	0	2
Cousineau, Tom, Cleveland	0	0	2	0	2
Curtis, Isaac, Cincinnati	1	0	0	0	0
Dalby, Dave, L.A. Raiders	0	1	0	0	1
Daniels, Calvin, Kansas City	0	0	2	0	2
Davis, Bruce, Cleveland	2	0	0	0	0
Davis, James, L.A. Raiders	0	1	1	0	2
Davis, Mike, L.A. Raiders	0	0	1	0	1
Dawkins, Julius, Buffalo	0	1	0	0	1
Dawson, Lin, New England	0	1	0	0	1
DeLamielleure, Joe, Cleveland	0	1	0	0	1
Dennard, Preston, Buffalo	1	0	0	0	0
Dennison, Rick, Denver	0	1	0	0	1
Dickey, Curtis, Indianapolis	6	1	0	0	1
Dieken, Doug, Cleveland	0	1	0	0	1
Dixon, Hanford, Cleveland	0	0	1	0	1
Dixon, Zachary, Seattle	1	0	0	0	0
Dressel, Chris, Houston	1	0	0	0	0
Duckworth, Bobby, San Diego	1	0	0	0	0
Dufek, Don, Seattle	0	0	1	0	1
Dufek, Joe, Buffalo	1	0	0	0	0
Duper, Mark, Miami	0	1	0	0	1
Easley, Ken, Seattle	0	0	1	0	1
Eason, Bo, Houston	0	0	1	0	1
Eason, Tony, New England	7	2	0	-5	2
Edwards, Eddie, Cincinnati	0	0	3	-2	3
Edwards, Stan, Houston	2	0	0	0	0
Ehin, Chuck, San Diego	0	0	1	0	1
Elway, John, Denver	14	5	0	-10	5
Erenberg, Rich, Pittsburgh	3	3	0	0	3
Esiason, Boomer, Cincinnati	4	2	0	-2	2
Farley, John, Cincinnati	1	1	0	0	1
Farren, Paul, Cleveland	0	1	0	0	1
Faurot, Ron, N.Y. Jets	0	0	1	0	1
Ferguson, Joe, Buffalo	8	2	0	-26	2
Ferguson, Keith, San Diego	0	0	1	0	1
Fields, Joe, N.Y. Jets	0	1	0	0	1
Flick, Tom, Cleveland	1	0	0	0	0
Foley, Steve, Denver	0	0	2	22	2
Foster, Roy, Miami	0	1	0	0	1
Fouts, Dan, San Diego	8	1	0	0	1
Fox, Tim, San Diego	0	0	1	0	1
Franklin, Byron, Buffalo	4	0	0	0	0
Freeman, Steve, Buffalo	0	0	1	0	1
Fryar, Irving, New England	4	1	0	0	1
Gaffney, Derrick, N.Y. Jets	0	1	0	0	1
Garnett, Scott, Denver	0	0	1	0	1
Gary, Keith, Pittsburgh	0	0	1	6	1
Gastineau, Mark, N.Y. Jets	0	0	1	0	1
Gibson, Ernest, New England	0	0	1	0	1
Gillespie, Fernandars, Pittsburgh	1	2	0	0	2
Glasgow, Nesby, Indianapolis	1	0	1	3	1
Golden, Tim, New England	0	1	0	0	1
Golic, Bob, Cleveland	0	0	1	18	1
Green, Boyce, Cleveland	3	2	0	0	2
Green, Jacob, Seattle	0	0	4	0	4
Green, Mike, San Diego	0	0	1	0	1
Greene, Ken, San Diego	0	0	2	0	2
Griffin, James, Cincinnati	0	2	0	0	2
Griffin, Ray, Cincinnati	0	0	1	0	1
Grogan, Steve, New England	4	2	0	-3	2
Gross, Al, Cleveland	0	0	2	28	2
Hamm, Bob, Houston	0	0	1	0	1
Hancock, Anthony, Kansas City	1	1	0	0	1
Harden, Mike, Denver	1	0	2	0	2
Harris, John, Seattle	0	0	1	0	1
Harris, M.L., Cincinnati	2	1	0	0	1
Hartwig, Carter, Houston	0	0	1	0	1
Haslett, Jim, Buffalo	0	0	3	10	3
Hathaway, Steve, Indianapolis	0	0	1	0	1
Hawkins, Frank, L.A. Raiders	3	1	0	0	1
Heard, Herman, Kansas City	5	3	0	0	3
Hector, Johnny, N.Y. Jets	2	0	0	0	0
Heflin, Vince, Miami	1	0	0	0	0
Henderson, Reuben, San Diego	1	0	0	0	0
Hill, Greg, Kansas City	1	0	0	0	0
Hinkle, Bryan, Pittsburgh	0	0	2	21	2
Holle, Eric, Kansas City	0	0	1	2	1
Holman, Rodney, Cincinnati	1	0	1	0	1
Holohan, Pete, San Diego	0	1	1	19	2
Holston, Michael, Houston	0	1	0	0	1
Horton, Ray, Cincinnati	0	0	1	0	1
Hughes, David, Seattle	4	2	1	0	3
Humiston, Mike, Indianapolis	0	0	2	0	2
Humm, David, L.A. Raiders	2	1	0	0	1
Humphery, Bobby, N.Y. Jets	2	2	0	0	2
Hunter, Tony, Buffalo	1	1	0	0	1
Jackson, Billy, Kansas City	2	0	1	0	1
Jackson, Earnest, San Diego	3	2	0	0	2
Jackson, Robert, Cincinnati	0	1	2	0	3
Jackson, Robert E., Cleveland	0	1	0	0	1
Jackson, Tom, Denver	0	0	1	0	1
James, Craig, New England	4	0	0	0	0
James, Lionel, San Diego	9	4	0	0	4
James, Roland, New England	0	0	1	0	1
Jennings, Stanford, Cincinnati	3	2	0	-4	2
Johns, Paul, Seattle	2	0	0	0	0
Johnson, Butch, Denver	1	0	0	0	0
Johnson, Ken, Buffalo	0	0	1	0	1
Johnson, Mike, Houston	0	0	1	0	1
Johnson, Pete, San Diego-Miami	1	2	0	0	2
Joiner, Tim, Houston	0	1	0	0	1
Jones, Cedric, New England	1	1	0	0	1
Jones, Lam, N.Y. Jets	1	0	0	0	0
Jones, Rulon, Denver	0	0	2	5	2
Judie, Ed, Miami	0	1	0	0	1
Judson, William, Miami	0	0	2	37	2
Kafentzis, Mark, Indianapolis	1	0	0	0	0
Kauahi, Kani, Seattle	0	0	2	0	2
Kay, Clarence, Denver	1	0	0	0	0
Keating, Chris, Buffalo	0	0	1	34	1
Kemp, Bobby, Cincinnati	1	0	1	0	1
Kenney, Bill, Kansas City	8	3	0	-34	3
King, Kenny, L.A. Raiders	3	1	0	0	1
King, Linden, San Diego	1	0	2	0	2
Kinnebrew, Larry, Cincinnati	4	0	0	0	0
Klecko, Joe, N.Y. Jets	0	0	2	0	2
Kofler, Matt, Buffalo	1	1	0	0	1
Krauss, Barry, Indianapolis	1	0	2	-5	2
Kreider, Steve, Cincinnati	1	0	0	0	0
Krieg, Dave, Seattle	11	3	0	-24	3
Krumrie, Tim, Cincinnati	0	0	1	8	1
Kubiak, Gary, Denver	1	0	0	0	0
Kush, Rod, Buffalo	1	0	1	0	1
Lacy, Kenneth, Kansas City	2	0	0	0	0
Lane, Eric, Seattle	1	1	2	0	3
Lang, Gene, Denver	0	1	0	6	1
Lanier, Ken, Denver	0	1	0	0	1
Lankford, Paul, Miami	0	0	1	0	1
Largent, Steve, Seattle	1	0	0	0	0
Lilly, Tony, Denver	1	0	1	3	1
Lippett, Ronnie, New England	1	0	1	0	1
Lipps, Louis, Pittsburgh	8	2	0	0	2
Long, Howie, L.A. Raiders	0	0	2	4	2
Long, Terry, Pittsburgh	1	0	0	0	0
Lowe, Woodrow, San Diego	1	0	0	0	0
Luck, Oliver, Houston	2	2	0	0	2
Luther, Ed, San Diego	2	0	0	0	0
Lynn, Johnny, N.Y. Jets	0	0	0	2	0
Malone, Mark, Pittsburgh	4	2	0	0	2
Marino, Dan, Miami	6	2	0	-3	2
Marion, Fred, New England	0	1	0	0	1
Marshall, Henry, Kansas City	2	0	0	0	0

Name	Fum.	Own Rec.	Opp. Rec.	Yds.	Tot. Rec.
Martin, Mike, Cincinnati	4	2	0	0	2
Martin, Rod, L.A. Raiders	0	0	1	77	1
Marve, Eugene, Buffalo	0	0	3	0	3
Marvin, Mickey, L.A. Raiders	0	1	0	0	1
Matthews, Clay, Cleveland	0	0	1	0	1
Maxwell, Vernon, Indianapolis	0	0	2	0	2
McAlister, Ken, Kansas City	0	1	0	0	1
McDonald, Paul, Cleveland	16	5	0	−5	5
McElroy, Vann, L.A. Raiders	0	1	3	12	4
McGee, Buford, San Diego	1	1	0	0	1
McKinney, Odis, L.A. Raiders	1	1	0	0	1
McKnight, Dennis, San Diego	0	2	0	0	2
McMillan, Randy, Indianapolis	1	0	0	0	0
McNeal, Don, Miami	0	0	2	5	2
McNeil, Freeman, N.Y. Jets	4	1	0	0	1
McPherson, Miles, San Diego	0	0	1	0	1
McSwain, Rod, New England	0	0	1	0	1
Mecklenburg, Karl, Denver	0	0	1	0	1
Mehl, Lance, N.Y. Jets	0	0	1	0	1
Merriweather, Mike, Pittsburgh	0	0	1	0	1
Metzelaars, Pete, Seattle	1	0	0	0	0
Middleton, Frank, Indianapolis	2	2	0	0	2
Minnifield, Frank, Cleveland	0	0	2	10	2
Minter, Cedric, N.Y. Jets	1	0	0	0	0
Montgomery, Cleotha, L.A. Raiders	1	1	0	0	1
Moon, Warren, Houston	17	7	0	−1	7
Moore, Alvin, Indianapolis	3	0	0	0	0
Moore, Booker, Buffalo	4	1	0	0	1
Moore, Nat, Miami	2	0	0	0	0
Moriarty, Larry, Houston	5	2	0	−3	2
Morris, Randall, Seattle	2	1	0	0	1
Morris, Wayne, San Diego	0	1	0	0	1
Muncie, Chuck, San Diego	1	0	0	0	0
Muñoz, Anthony, Cincinnati	0	1	0	0	1
Nash, Joe, Seattle	0	0	3	0	3
Nathan, Tony, Miami	3	1	0	0	1
Nicolas, Scott, Cleveland	0	0	1	0	1
Norman, Chris, Denver	1	1	0	0	1
O'Brien, Ken, N.Y. Jets	4	2	0	0	2
Odom, Clifton, Indianapolis	0	0	1	0	1
Owens, Dennis, New England	0	0	1	0	1
Padjen, Gary, Indianapolis	1	0	0	0	0
Pagel, Mike, Indianapolis	4	1	0	0	1
Paige, Tony, N.Y. Jets	1	0	0	0	0
Petersen, Ted, Cleveland-Indianapolis	0	1	0	0	1
Plunkett, Jim, L.A. Raiders	2	1	0	0	1
Pollard, Frank, Pittsburgh	9	2	0	0	2
Porter, Tracy, Indianapolis	2	1	0	0	1
Pruitt, Greg, L.A. Raiders	9	2	0	0	2
Pruitt, Mike, Cleveland	1	1	0	0	1
Puzzuoli, Dave, Cleveland	0	0	1	0	1
Radachowsky, George, Indianapolis	1	0	0	0	0
Randle, Tate, Indianapolis	0	1	1	0	2
Ray, Darrol, N.Y. Jets	0	0	0	52	0
Razzano, Rick, Cincinnati	0	0	1	0	1
Riddick, Robb, Buffalo	1	0	0	0	0
Roaches, Carl, Houston	1	1	0	0	1
Robbins, Randy, Denver	0	0	1	0	1
Robinson, Bo, New England	0	1	0	0	1
Robinson, Shelton, Seattle	0	0	4	3	4
Romano, Jim, L.A. Raiders-Houston	1	0	0	−11	0
Romes, Charles, Buffalo	0	0	1	0	1
Ross, Kevin, Kansas City	0	0	1	0	1
Rudolph, Ben, N.Y. Jets	0	0	1	0	1
Ryan, Jim, Denver	0	0	1	0	1
Ryan, Pat, N.Y. Jets	4	1	0	0	1
Sampson, Clinton, Denver	1	0	0	0	0
Sanford, Lucius, Buffalo	0	0	2	46	2
Sawyer, John, Denver	0	2	0	0	2
Schlichter, Art, Indianapolis	4	3	0	1	3
Scholtz, Bruce, Seattle	0	0	1	0	1
Schonert, Turk, Cincinnati	2	0	0	0	0
Schroy, Ken, N.Y. Jets	0	0	2	0	2
Shuler, Mickey, N.Y. Jets	1	0	0	0	0
Sievers, Eric, San Diego	1	0	1	0	1
Simpkins, Ron, Cincinnati	0	0	1	0	1
Simpson, Keith, Seattle	0	0	2	0	2
Smerlas, Fred, Buffalo	0	0	2	0	2
Smith, Aaron, Denver	1	0	0	0	0
Smith, Billy Ray, San Diego	0	0	3	0	3
Smith, Dennis, Denver	0	0	1	64	1
Smith, J.T., Kansas City	1	0	0	0	0
Smith, Lucious, Buffalo-San Diego	1	0	0	0	0
Smith, Phil, Indianapolis	1	0	0	0	0
Smith, Tim, Houston	0	1	0	0	1
Snell, Ray, Pittsburgh	0	1	0	0	1
Solt, Ron, Indianapolis	0	1	0	0	1
Sowell, Robert, Miami	0	1	0	0	1
Spencer, Todd, Pittsburgh	5	2	0	0	2
Springs, Kirk, N.Y. Jets	3	1	1	4	2
Squirek, Jack, L.A. Raiders	0	0	1	0	1
Stallworth, John, Pittsburgh	1	0	0	0	0
Stankavage, Scott, Denver	0	1	0	0	1
Stark, Rohn, Indianapolis	0	1	0	0	1
Starring, Stephen, New Orleans	1	1	0	8	1
Stensrud, Mike, Houston	0	0	1	0	1
Stephenson, Dwight, Miami	0	1	0	0	1
Still, Art, Kansas City	0	0	1	3	1
Strock, Don, Miami	1	0	0	−2	0
Summers, Don, Denver	0	1	0	0	1
Talley, Darryl, Buffalo	0	0	1	0	1
Tatupu, Mosi, New England	4	1	0	0	1
Thomas, Jewerl, San Diego	1	1	0	0	1
Thomas, Rodell, Miami	0	1	0	0	1
Thompson, Weegie, Pittsburgh	1	0	0	0	0
Tongue, Marco, Buffalo	0	0	1	0	1
Townsend, Andre, Denver	0	0	1	0	1
Tullis, Willie, Houston	1	1	0	0	1
Turner, Jim, Cincinnati	0	0	1	0	1
Turner, John, San Diego	0	0	1	0	1
Utt, Ben, Indianapolis	0	1	0	0	1
Veals, Elton, Pittsburgh	0	1	0	0	1
Waldemore, Stan, N.Y. Jets	0	1	0	0	1
Walker, Dwight, Cleveland	1	0	0	0	0
Walker, Fulton, Miami	2	0	0	0	0
Wilkerson, Doug, San Diego	0	1	0	0	1
Willhite, Gerald, Denver	3	1	1	0	2
Williams, Ed, New England	0	0	1	0	1
Williams, Eric, Pittsburgh	0	1	0	6	1
Williams, Eric, San Diego	0	0	1	0	1
Williams, Jamie, Houston	2	1	0	0	1
Williams, Lester, New England	0	0	1	0	1
Williams, Toby, New England	0	0	1	0	1
Williams, Van, Buffalo	1	1	0	0	1
Willis, Keith, Pittsburgh	0	0	1	0	1
Wilson, Don, Buffalo	3	0	1	40	1
Wilson, Marc, L.A. Raiders	11	3	0	−11	3
Wilson, Steve, Denver	1	0	1	0	1
Winder, Sammy, Denver	5	2	0	0	2
Winslow, Kellen, San Diego	1	0	0	0	0
Winter, Blaise, Indianapolis	0	0	1	0	1
Wisniewski, Leo, Indianapolis	0	0	1	0	1
Woodley, David, Pittsburgh	5	2	0	−4	2
Woodring, John, N.Y. Jets	0	0	1	0	1
Woodruff, Dwayne, Pittsburgh	0	0	1	65	1
Wright, Louis, Denver	0	0	2	27	2
Young, Andre, San Diego	1	0	1	0	1
Young, Charle, Seattle	1	0	0	0	0

Yards includes aborted plays, own recoveries, and opponent recoveries.

Touchdowns: Bob Baumhower, Miami; Keith Bostic, Houston; Greg Buttle, New York Jets; Earnest Byner, Cleveland; Steve Foley, Denver; Mark Gastineau, New York Jets; Bryan Hinkle, Pittsburgh; Cedric Jones, New England; Rulon Jones, Denver; Chris Keating, Buffalo; Rod Martin, Los Angeles Raiders; Joe Nash, Seattle; Lucius Sanford, Buffalo; Dennis Smith, Denver; Dwayne Woodruff, Pittsburgh; and Louis Wright, Denver; 1 each.

Includes both offensive and defensive recoveries for touchdowns.

NFC FUMBLES—INDIVIDUAL

Name	Fum.	Own Rec.	Opp. Rec.	Yds.	Tot. Rec.
Albritton, Vince, Dallas	0	1	1	0	2
Allen, Gary, Dallas	2	1	0	0	1
Allerman, Kurt, St. Louis	0	0	1	2	1
Anderson, Alfred, Minnesota	8	2	0	0	2
Anderson, John, Green Bay	0	0	1	0	1
Anderson, Ottis, St. Louis	8	1	0	0	1
Andrews, George, L.A. Rams	0	0	4	9	4
Anthony, Tyrone, New Orleans	1	1	0	0	1
Archer, David, Atlanta	1	0	0	0	0
Armstrong, Adger, Tampa Bay	1	1	0	0	1
Ayers, John, San Francisco	0	1	0	0	1
Bailey, Stacey, Atlanta	1	0	0	0	0
Baker, Ron, Philadelphia	0	1	0	0	1
Banks, Carl, N.Y. Giants	0	0	1	0	1
Barber, Mike, L.A. Rams	1	0	0	0	0
Bartkowski, Steve, Atlanta	7	4	0	−11	4
Baschnagel, Brian, Chicago	1	2	0	0	2
Bates, Bill, Dallas	0	0	1	0	1
Beasley, Tom, Washington	0	0	1	0	1
Bell, Jerry, Tampa Bay	0	1	0	0	1
Bell, Theo, Tampa Bay	1	0	0	0	0
Bell, Todd, Chicago	0	0	2	4	2
Bess, Rufus, Minnesota	1	1	1	0	2
Black, Mike, Detroit	0	0	1	0	1
Blair, Matt, Minnesota	0	0	1	0	1
Board, Dwaine, San Francisco	0	0	1	0	1

	Fum.	Own Rec.	Opp. Rec.	Yds.	Tot. Rec.
Bostic, Jeff, Washington	0	1	1	0	2
Brantley, Scot, Tampa Bay	0	0	2	0	2
Bright, Leon, Tampa Bay	2	1	0	0	1
Brown, Greg, Philadelphia	0	0	1	0	1
Brown, Ted, Minnesota	2	0	0	0	0
Browner, Joey, Minnesota	0	0	3	63	3
Browner, Keith, Tampa Bay	0	0	1	0	1
Burt, Jim, N.Y. Giants	0	0	2	0	2
Butler, Bobby, Atlanta	0	0	1	10	1
Butz, Dave, Washington	0	0	1	0	1
Cain, Lynn, Atlanta	2	0	0	0	0
Campbell, Earl, Houston-New Orleans	2	2	0	1	2
Campbell, Rich, Green Bay	1	0	0	0	0
Cannon, John, Tampa Bay	0	0	1	0	1
Carpenter, Rob, N.Y. Giants	2	1	0	0	1
Carroll, Jay, Tampa Bay	0	0	1	0	1
Carson, Harry, N.Y. Giants	0	0	1	0	1
Carter, Gerald, Tampa Bay	1	0	1	0	1
Carver, Mel, Tampa Bay	1	0	0	0	0
Castille, Jeremiah, Tampa Bay	0	0	2	16	2
Clark, Bruce, New Orleans	0	0	2	5	2
Clark, Jessie, Green Bay	2	0	0	0	0
Clark, Mario, San Francisco	0	0	1	0	1
Clark, Randy, St. Louis	0	1	1	0	2
Clinkscale, Dextor, Dallas	0	0	2	0	2
Cofer, Mike, Detroit	0	0	1	0	1
Coffey, Ken, Washington	0	0	1	0	1
Coffman, Paul, Green Bay	1	1	0	0	1
Coleman, Monte, Washington	0	0	1	0	1
Collins, Jim, L.A. Rams	1	0	2	17	2
Cooper, Earl, San Francisco	0	1	0	0	1
Cosbie, Doug, Dallas	1	0	0	0	0
Cotney, Mark, Tampa Bay	0	0	2	3	2
Covert, Jim, Chicago	0	2	0	0	2
Cox, Arthur, Atlanta	1	0	0	0	0
Craig, Roger, San Francisco	3	1	0	0	1
Cromwell, Nolan, L.A. Rams	0	0	1	0	1
Croudip, David, L.A. Rams	0	0	2	0	2
Crutchfield, Dwayne, L.A. Rams	1	0	0	0	0
Cumby, George, Green Bay	0	0	2	0	2
Curran, Willie, Atlanta	2	1	0	0	1
Curry, Buddy, Atlanta	0	0	1	4	1
Danielson, Gary, Detroit	7	2	0	-5	2
Davis, Jeff, Tampa Bay	0	0	1	0	1
DeBerg, Steve, Tampa Bay	15	2	0	-8	2
Dean, Vernon, Washington	0	0	1	6	1
Dent, Richard, Chicago	0	0	1	0	1
Dickerson, Anthony, Dallas	0	0	1	0	1
Dickerson, Eric, L.A. Rams	14	4	0	15	4
Dickey, Lynn, Green Bay	3	1	0	-11	1
Dodge, Kirk, Detroit	0	0	1	0	1
Dorsett, Tony, Dallas	12	1	0	-21	1
Doss, Reggie, L.A. Rams	0	0	1	0	1
Douglass, Mike, Green Bay	0	1	1	0	2
Downs, Mike, Dallas	0	0	2	28	2
Duda, Mark, St. Louis	0	0	1	0	1
Ekern, Carl, L.A. Rams	0	0	1	0	1
Ellard, Henry, L.A. Rams	4	2	0	0	2
Ellis, Gerry, Green Bay	2	0	0	0	0
Ellis, Ray, Philadelphia	1	0	1	0	1
Elshire, Neil, Minnesota	0	0	1	0	1
English, Doug, Detroit	0	0	1	0	1
Epps, Phillip, Green Bay	1	1	0	0	1
Farrell, Sean, Tampa Bay	0	2	0	0	2
Fellows, Ron, Dallas	3	0	1	12	1
Fencik, Gary, Chicago	1	1	0	0	1
Ferrell, Earl, St. Louis	3	0	0	0	0
Fields, Jitter, New Orleans	2	1	0	0	1
Fisher, Jeff, Chicago	4	1	0	0	1
Flynn, Tom, Green Bay	1	0	3	3	3
Francis, Russ, San Francisco	1	2	0	0	2
Frye, David, Atlanta	0	0	2	0	2
Gaison, Blane, Atlanta	0	0	1	0	1
Gary, Russell, New Orleans	0	0	1	5	1
Gault, Willie, Chicago	1	0	0	0	0
Gay, William, Detroit	0	0	2	30	2
Giacomarro, Ralph, Atlanta	1	1	0	0	1
Graham, William, Detroit	0	0	2	0	2
Granger, Norm, Dallas	0	0	1	0	1
Grant, Darryl, Washington	0	0	4	22	4
Greco, Don, Detroit	0	1	0	0	1
Green, Gary, Rams	0	0	1	0	1
Green, Roy, St. Louis	1	0	0	0	0
Griffin, Keith, Washington	7	0	0	0	0
Grimm, Russ, Washington	0	2	0	0	2
Guman, Mike, L.A. Rams	0	0	1	0	1
Haddix, Michael, Philadelphia	2	0	0	0	0
Haines, John, Minnesota	0	0	1	6	1

	Fum.	Own Rec.	Opp. Rec.	Yds.	Tot. Rec.
Hall, Alvin, Detroit	3	1	0	0	1
Hallstrom, Ron, Green Bay	0	2	0	1	2
Hampton, Dan, Chicago	0	0	3	0	3
Harmon, Derrick, San Francisco	1	1	1	0	2
Harris, Eric, L.A. Rams	0	0	1	0	1
Harris, Roy, Atlanta	0	0	1	0	1
Harrison, Dennis, Philadelphia	0	0	1	0	1
Hartenstine, Mike, Chicago	0	0	2	0	2
Hasselbeck, Don, Minnesota	0	0	1	0	1
Hayes, Jeff, Washington	2	1	0	0	1
Hayes, Joe, Philadelphia	2	1	0	0	1
Haynes, Mark, N.Y. Giants	0	0	2	12	2
Headen, Andy, N.Y. Giants	0	0	1	81	1
Hegman, Mike, Dallas	0	0	1	0	1
Hicks, Dwight, San Francisco	1	1	2	6	3
Hill, David, L.A. Rams	2	1	0	0	1
Hoage, Terry, New Orleans	0	0	1	0	1
Hodge, Floyd, Atlanta	1	0	0	0	0
Hogeboom, Gary, Dallas	8	4	0	-3	4
Holloway, Randy, Minnesota-St. Louis	0	0	3	0	3
Holt, John, Tampa Bay	0	0	1	0	1
Hopkins, Wes, Philadelphia	0	0	3	0	3
House, Kevin, Tampa Bay	0	1	0	0	1
Howard, Thomas, St. Louis	0	0	1	29	1
Huckleby, Harlan, Green Bay	1	1	0	0	1
Huff, Ken, Washington	0	3	0	0	3
Hunt, Byron, N.Y. Giants	0	0	2	0	2
Irwin, Tim, Minnesota	0	1	0	2	1
Ivery, Eddie Lee, Green Bay	1	0	0	0	0
Jackson, Alfred, Atlanta	0	1	0	0	1
Jackson, Jeff, Atlanta	0	1	0	0	1
Jackson, Rickey, New Orleans	1	1	3	4	4
Jacoby, Joe, Washington	0	1	0	0	1
Jaworski, Ron, Philadelphia	5	2	0	0	2
Jeffcoat, Jim, Dallas	0	0	1	0	1
Jenkins, Ken, Detroit	0	1	0	0	1
Johnson, Billy, Atlanta	1	0	0	0	0
Johnson, Demetrious, Detroit	0	0	1	0	1
Johnson, Dennis, Minnesota	0	0	1	0	1
Johnson, Gary, San Diego-San Francisco	0	0	3	36	3
Johnson, Kenny, Atlanta	2	0	0	0	0
Jones, A.J., L.A. Rams	0	0	1	0	1
Jones, Daryll, Green Bay	0	1	2	0	3
Jones, Ed, Dallas	0	0	2	0	2
Jones, James, Detroit	6	3	0	-21	3
Jones, Mike, Minnesota	1	2	0	0	2
Jones, Terry, Green Bay	0	0	1	0	1
Jordan, Curtis, Washington	0	0	1	29	1
Jordan, Donald, Chicago	1	1	2	0	3
Jordan, Steve, Minnesota	0	0	1	0	1
Junkin, Trey, Buffalo-Washington	0	0	1	0	1
Kane, Rick, Washington	3	0	0	0	0
Kaufman, Mel, Washington	0	0	1	0	1
Kemp, Jeff, L.A. Rams	8	3	0	-16	3
Kinard, Terry, N.Y. Giants	1	0	1	0	1
Korte, Steve, New Orleans	0	1	0	0	1
Kramer, Tommy, Minnesota	10	3	0	-5	3
Kuykendall, Fulton, Atlanta	0	0	2	9	2
Landrum, Mike, Atlanta	0	1	0	0	1
Latimer, Al, Detroit	0	0	1	0	1
Lee, Carl, Minnesota	0	0	1	0	1
Lee, Larry, Detroit	2	1	0	-24	1
Lee, Mark, Green Bay	0	0	2	0	2
Lewis, David, Detroit	2	2	0	0	2
Lewis, Leo, Minnesota	1	3	0	0	3
Lisch, Rusty, Chicago	5	1	0	-6	1
Lockhart, Eugene, Dallas	0	0	1	0	1
Lofton, James, Green Bay	1	0	0	0	0
Lomax, Neil, St. Louis	11	2	0	-5	2
Love, Randy, St. Louis	1	0	0	0	0
Mandley, Pete, Detroit	2	2	0	0	2
Manley, Dexter, Washington	0	0	1	0	1
Mann, Charles, Washington	0	0	1	0	1
Manning, Archie, Minnesota	4	2	0	0	2
Manuel, Lionel, N.Y. Giants	2	0	0	0	0
Martin, Chris, Minnesota	0	0	1	8	1
Martin, George, N.Y. Giants	0	0	1	0	1
Martin, Robbie, Detroit	5	3	1	0	4
McConkey, Phil, N.Y. Giants	2	1	0	0	1
McKinnon, Dennis, Chicago	1	0	0	0	0
McLaughlin, Jim, N.Y. Giants	0	0	1	0	1
McLemore, Dana, San Francisco	1	0	0	0	0
McLeod, Mike, Green Bay	0	0	1	0	1
McMahon, Jim, Chicago	1	0	0	0	0
McNeill, Fred, Minnesota	0	0	2	0	2
McSwain, Chuck, Dallas	2	0	0	0	0
Meade, Mike, Detroit	1	0	0	0	0
Meisner, Greg, L.A. Rams	0	0	1	0	1

	Fum.	Own Rec.	Opp. Rec.	Yds.	Tot. Rec.
Mitchell, Stump, St. Louis	6	2	0	0	2
Monk, Art, Washington	1	0	0	0	0
Monroe, Carl, San Francisco	2	0	0	0	0
Montana, Joe, San Francisco	4	2	0	−3	2
Montgomery, Blanchard, San Francisco	0	1	0	0	1
Montgomery, Wilbert, Philadelphia	5	1	0	0	1
Moore, Jeff, Washington	1	0	0	0	0
Moroski, Mike, Atlanta	6	2	0	0	2
Morris, Joe, N.Y. Giants	1	0	0	0	0
Morton, Michael, Tampa Bay	3	2	0	0	2
Muhammad, Calvin, Washington	1	1	1	0	2
Mularkey, Mike, Minnesota	1	1	0	0	1
Murphy, Mark, Green Bay	1	0	1	2	1
Nelms, Mike, Washington	1	0	0	0	0
Nelson, Darrin, Minnesota	4	3	0	0	3
Newsome, Tim, Dallas	3	0	0	0	0
Nichols, Mark, Detroit	0	1	0	0	1
Noga, Falaniko, St. Louis	0	0	1	0	1
Oliver, Hubert, Philadelphia	0	1	0	0	1
Olkewicz, Neal, Washington	0	0	2	0	2
Owens, Mel, L.A. Rams	0	0	2	0	2
Paris, Bubba, San Francisco	0	1	0	0	1
Payton, Walter, Chicago	5	1	0	0	1
Perrin, Benny, St. Louis	0	0	2	16	2
Peters, Tony, Washington	0	0	1	0	1
Pillers, Lawrence, San Francisco	0	0	1	0	1
Pisarcik, Joe, Philadelphia	4	0	0	0	0
Pittman, Danny, St. Louis	1	1	0	0	1
Pitts, Mike, Atlanta	0	0	2	0	2
Prather, Guy, Green Bay	0	0	1	0	1
Pridemore, Tom, Atlanta	0	0	2	0	2
Provence, Andrew, Atlanta	0	0	1	0	1
Rade, John, Atlanta	0	0	1	0	1
Rafferty, Tom, Dallas	0	2	0	0	2
Reasons, Gary, N.Y. Giants	0	0	3	0	3
Reed, Doug, L.A. Rams	0	0	1	2	1
Reichenbach, Mike, Philadelphia	0	1	1	0	2
Rice, Allen, Minnesota	1	2	0	0	2
Richards, Howard, Dallas	0	1	0	0	1
Richardson, Al, Atlanta	0	0	3	0	3
Richardson, Mike, Chicago	0	0	1	0	1
Riggins, John, Washington	7	0	0	0	0
Riggs, Gerald, Atlanta	11	2	0	0	2
Roberts, William, N.Y. Giants	0	1	0	0	1
Robinson, Jerry, Philadelphia	0	0	1	0	1
Rodgers, Del, Green Bay	1	0	0	0	0
Rogers, George, New Orleans	2	1	0	0	1
Rohrer, Jeff, Dallas	1	0	1	5	1
Rouse, Curtis, Minnesota	0	1	0	0	1
Saldi, Jay, Chicago	2	0	0	0	0
Salonen, Brian, Dallas	0	1	0	0	1
Sams, Ron, Minnesota	1	0	0	−17	0
Scott, Lindsay, New Orleans	1	0	0	0	0
Scott, Victor, Dallas	0	1	1	0	2
Scully, John, Atlanta	0	1	0	0	1
Selmon, Lee Roy, Tampa Bay	0	0	2	0	2
Sharpe, Luis, St. Louis	0	1	0	0	1
Shell, Todd, San Francisco	0	0	1	0	1
Simms, Phil, N.Y. Giants	8	4	0	−5	4
Sims, Billy, Detroit	6	2	0	0	2
Singletary, Mike, Chicago	0	0	1	0	1
Smith, Don, Atlanta	0	0	2	0	2
Smith, Jimmy, Wash.-Raiders-G.B.	0	0	1	0	1
Smith, Leonard, St.Louis	0	0	1	0	1
Smith, Wayne, St. Louis	0	1	2	12	3
Spagnola, John, Philadelphia	2	0	0	0	0
Springs, Ron, Dallas	1	0	0	0	0
Stabler, Ken, New Orleans	1	0	0	0	0
Stamps, Sylvester, Atlanta	2	0	0	0	0
Stieve, Terry, St. Louis	0	1	0	2	1
Suhey, Matt, Chicago	6	2	0	0	2
Sully, Ivory, L.A. Rams	0	0	1	0	1
Swain, John, Minnesota	0	0	1	0	1
Tate, Rodney, Atlanta	1	1	0	0	1
Teal, Willie, Minnesota	1	0	0	0	0
Theismann, Joe, Washington	7	6	0	5	6
Thielemann, R.C., Atlanta	0	1	0	0	1
Thomas, Calvin, Chicago	1	0	1	0	1
Thomas, Zack, Denver-Tampa Bay	3	2	0	0	2
Thompson, Jack, Tampa Bay	1	1	0	0	1
Thompson, Leonard, Detroit	1	1	0	0	1
Thurman, Dennis, Dallas	0	1	0	0	1
Tilley, Pat, St. Louis	1	0	0	0	0
Todd, Richard, New Orleans	9	3	0	−16	3
Tuiasosopo, Manu, San Francisco	0	0	2	6	2
Tyler, Wendell, San Francisco	13	2	0	0	2
Tyrrell, Tim, Atlanta	0	1	2	0	3
Vann, Norwood, L.A. Rams	0	0	2	0	2

	Fum.	Own Rec.	Opp. Rec.	Yds.	Tot. Rec.
Waddy, Billy, Minnesota	1	1	0	0	1
Walker, Rick, Washington	0	1	0	0	1
Washington, Anthony, Washington	0	0	1	0	1
Washington, Joe, Washington	3	0	0	0	0
Washington, Lionel, St. Louis	0	0	1	0	1
Waters, Andre, Philadelphia	1	0	1	0	1
Wattelet, Frank, New Orleans	0	1	1	22	2
West, Ed, Green Bay	0	1	0	0	1
White, Danny, Dallas	2	1	0	−3	1
White, Sammy, Minnesota	1	0	0	0	0
Wilder, James, Tampa Bay	10	4	0	0	4
Wilks, Jim, New Orleans	0	0	1	0	1
Williams, Greg, Washington	0	0	1	0	1
Williams, Jimmy, Detroit	0	0	1	0	1
Williams, Joel, Philadelphia	0	0	2	0	2
Williams, Mike, Philadelphia	1	0	0	0	0
Williams, Perry, N.Y. Giants	0	0	1	0	1
Wilson, Dave, New Orleans	2	0	0	0	0
Wilson, Steve, Tampa Bay	1	0	0	0	0
Wilson, Wade, Minnesota	2	0	0	0	0
Wilson, Wayne, New Orleans	2	0	0	0	0
Winston, Dennis, New Orleans	0	0	1	0	1
Witkowski, John, Detroit	1	0	0	0	0
Witte, Mark, Tampa Bay	0	1	0	0	1
Woolfolk, Butch, N.Y. Giants	1	1	0	0	1
Wright, Randy, Green Bay	1	1	0	0	1
Young, Tyrone, New Orleans	1	0	0	0	0
Youngblood, Jack, L.A. Rams	0	0	1	9	1

Yards includes aborted plays, own recoveries, and opponent recoveries.

Touchdowns: Joey Browner, Minnesota; Darryl Grant, Washington; Andy Headen, New York Giants; Thomas Howard, St. Louis; Joe Jacoby, Washington; Jim Jeffcoat, Dallas; Gary Johnson, San Diego-San Francisco; Curtis Jordan, Washington; Chris Martin, Minnesota; and Frank Wattelet, New Orleans; 1 each.

Includes both offensive and defensive recoveries for touchdowns.

SACKS

INDIVIDUAL CHAMPIONS
AFC: 22 —Mark Gastineau, New York Jets
NFC: 17.5—Richard Dent, Chicago
TEAM CHAMPIONS
NFC: 72—Chicago
AFC: 64—Los Angeles Raiders

AFC SACKS—TEAM

	Sacks	Yards
Los Angeles Raiders	64	516
Denver	57	430
New England	55	452
Seattle	55	398
Kansas City	50	364
Pittsburgh	47	390
New York Jets	44	360
Cleveland	43	353
Miami	42	339
Indianapolis	42	320
Cincinnati	40	298
San Diego	33	218
Houston	32	267
Buffalo	26	191

NFC SACKS—TEAM

	Sacks	Yards
Chicago	72	583
Washington	66	529
Philadelphia	60	456
Dallas	57	390
New Orleans	55	420
St. Louis	55	403
San Francisco	51	363
New York Giants	48	361
Green Bay	44	324
Los Angeles Rams	43	298
Atlanta	38	287
Detroit	37	271
Tampa Bay	32	239
Minnesota	25	175

NFL TOP 10 INDIVIDUAL LEADERS IN SACKS

	Total
Gastineau, Mark, N.Y. Jets	22.0
Tippett, Andre, New England	18.5
Dent, Richard, Chicago	17.5
Brown, Greg, Philadelphia	16.0
Merriweather, Mike, Pittsburgh	15.0
Bryant, Jeff, Seattle	14.5
Still, Art, Kansas City	14.5
Betters, Doug, Miami	14.0
Camp, Reggie, Cleveland	14.0
Greer, Curtis, St. Louis	14.0

AFC SACKS—INDIVIDUAL

Gastineau, Mark, N.Y. Jets	22.0
Tippett, Andre, New England	18.5
Merriweather, Mike, Pittsburgh	15.0
Bryant, Jeff, Seattle	14.5
Still, Art, Kansas City	14.5
Betters, Doug, Miami	14.0
Camp, Reggie, Cleveland	14.0
Bell, Mike, Kansas City	13.5
Green, Jacob, Seattle	13.0
Pickel, Bill, L.A. Raiders	12.5
Long, Howie, L.A. Raiders	12.0
Matthews, Clay, Cleveland	12.0
Cooks, Johnie, Indianapolis	11.5
Baker, Jesse, Houston	11.0
Jones, Rulon, Denver	11.0
Martin, Rod, L.A. Raiders	11.0
Bowser, Charles, Miami	9.0
Edwards, Eddie, Cincinnati	9.0
Williams, Reggie, Cincinnati	9.0
Maxwell, Vernon, Indianapolis	8.5
Browner, Ross, Cincinnati	8.0
Ferguson, Keith, San Diego	8.0
Chavous, Barney, Denver	7.5
Fanning, Mike, Seattle	7.0
Mecklenburg, Karl, Denver	7.0
Nash, Joe, Seattle	7.0
Nelson, Edmund, Pittsburgh	7.0
Townsend, Greg, L.A. Raiders	7.0
Wisniewski, Leo, Indianapolis	7.0
Owens, Dennis, New England	6.5
Alzado, Lyle, L.A. Raiders	6.0
Jackson, Tom, Denver	6.0
Williams, Toby, New England	6.0
Davis, Mike, L.A. Raiders	5.5
Hinkle, Bryan, Pittsburgh	5.5
Blackmon, Don, New England	5.0
Krumrie, Tim, Cincinnati	5.0
Maas, Bill, Kansas City	5.0
Mehl, Lance, N.Y. Jets	5.0
Talley, Darryl, Buffalo	5.0
Townsend, Andre, Denver	5.0
Willis, Keith, Pittsburgh	5.0
Baldwin, Keith, Cleveland	4.5
Daniels, Calvin, Kansas City	4.5
Robinson, Fred, San Diego	4.5
Stensrud, Mike, Houston	4.5
Adams, Julius, New England	4.0
Bennett, Barry, N.Y. Jets	4.0
Bokamper, Kim, Miami	4.0
Gary, Keith, Pittsburgh	4.0
Hairston, Carl, Cleveland	4.0
King, Linden, San Diego	4.0
McAlister, Ken, Kansas City	4.0
Nelson, Steve, New England	4.0
Thompson, Donnell, Indianapolis	4.0
Gaines, Greg, Seattle	3.5
Haslett, Jim, Buffalo	3.5
Johnson, Ken, Buffalo	3.5
Sims, Kenneth, New England	3.5
Sochia, Brian, Houston	3.5
Bowyer, Walt, Denver	3.0
Brudzinski, Bob, Miami	3.0
Carter, Rubin, Denver	3.0
Carter, Russell, N.Y. Jets	3.0
Charles, Mike, Miami	3.0
Collins, Glen, Cincinnati	3.0
Dennison, Rick, Denver	3.0
Klecko, Joe, N.Y. Jets	3.0
Lowe, Woodrow, San Diego	3.0
McNanie, Sean, Buffalo	3.0
Odom, Clifton, Indianapolis	3.0
Ryan, Jim, Denver	3.0
Smith, Billy Ray, San Diego	3.0
Woodard, Ken, Denver	3.0
Banks, Chip, Cleveland	2.5
Goodman, John, Pittsburgh	2.5
Kremer, Ken, Kansas City	2.5
Millen, Matt, L.A. Raiders	2.5
Riley, Avon, Houston	2.5
Ackerman, Rick, S.D.-Raiders	2.0
Barnett, Bill, Miami	2.0
Baumhower, Bob, Miami	2.0
Bingham, Gregg, Houston	2.0
Bostic, Keith, Houston	2.0
Bracelin, Greg, Indianapolis	2.0
Brazile, Robert, Houston	2.0
Cole, Robin, Pittsburgh	2.0
Ehin, Chuck, San Diego	2.0
Faurot, Ron, N.Y. Jets	2.0
Frazier, Guy, Cincinnati	2.0
Freeman, Steve, Buffalo	2.0
Golic, Bob, Cleveland	2.0
Hamm, Bob, Houston	2.0
Henson, Luther, New England	2.0
Keating, Chris, Buffalo	2.0
Kush, Rod, Buffalo	2.0
Lindstrom, Dave, Kansas City	2.0
Lyons, Marty, N.Y. Jets	2.0
Puzzuoli, Dave, Cleveland	2.0
Rogers, Doug, New England	2.0
Schuh, Jeff, Cincinnati	2.0
Simpson, Keith, Seattle	2.0
Smerlas, Fred, Buffalo	2.0
Squirek, Jack, L.A. Raiders	2.0
White, Brad, Indianapolis	2.0
Williams, Ben, Buffalo	2.0
Williams, Eric, Pittsburgh	2.0
Winter, Blaise, Indianapolis	2.0
Baldwin, Tom, N.Y. Jets	1.5
Edwards, Randy, Seattle	1.5
Elko, Bill, San Diego	1.5
Franks, Elvis, Cleveland	1.5
Nelson, Bob, L.A. Raiders	1.5
Rudolph, Ben, N.Y. Jets	1.5
Williams, Lester, New England	1.5
Barnes, Jeff, L.A. Raiders	1.0
Benson, Charles, Miami	1.0
Brown, Mark, Miami	1.0
Busick, Steve, Denver	1.0
Butler, Keith, Seattle	1.0
Cameron, Glenn, Cincinnati	1.0
Clayton, Harvey, Pittsburgh	1.0
Comeaux, Darren, Denver	1.0
David, Stan, Buffalo	1.0
Dawson, Mike, Kansas City	1.0
Duhe, A. J., Miami	1.0
Dunn, Gary, Pittsburgh	1.0
Eason, Bo, Houston	1.0
Foster, Jerome, Houston	1.0
Fox, Tim, San Diego	1.0
Garnett, Scott, Denver	1.0
Green, Mike, San Diego	1.0
Greene, Ken, San Diego	1.0
Harris, John, Seattle	1.0
Horton, Ray, Cincinnati	1.0
Jackson, Michael, Seattle	1.0
Jones, Sean, L.A. Raiders	1.0
Krauss, Barry, Indianapolis	1.0
Lewis, Albert, Kansas City	1.0
Little, David, Pittsburgh	1.0
Mangiero, Dino, Seattle	1.0
Manor, Brison, T.B.-Denver	1.0
Marion, Fred, New England	1.0
McKinney, Odis, L.A. Raiders	1.0
Moyer, Paul, Seattle	1.0
Parker, Steve, Indianapolis	1.0
Rhone, Earnest, Miami	1.0
Robbins, Randy, Denver	1.0
Smith, Dennis, Denver	1.0
Spani, Gary, Kansas City	1.0
Thomas, Rodell, Miami	1.0
Williams, Lee, San Diego	1.0
Young, Andre, San Diego	1.0
Young, Fredd, Seattle	1.0
Blanton, Jerry, Kansas City	0.5
Holle, Eric, Kansas City	0.5
Johnson, Eddie, Cleveland	0.5
Johnson, Mike, Houston	0.5
McGrew, Larry, New England	0.5
Rembert, Johnny, New England	0.5
Robinson, Shelton, Seattle	0.5
Wilson, Steve, Denver	0.5

NFC SACKS—INDIVIDUAL

Dent, Richard, Chicago	17.5
Brown, Greg, Philadelphia	16.0
Greer, Curtis, St. Louis	14.0
Manley, Dexter, Washington	13.5
White, Randy, Dallas	12.5
Harrison, Dennis, Philadelphia	12.0
Jackson, Rickey, New Orleans	12.0
Hampton, Dan, Chicago	11.5
Jeffcoat, Jim, Dallas	11.5
Taylor, Lawrence, N.Y. Giants	11.5
Clark, Bruce, New Orleans	10.5
Clarke, Ken, Philadelphia	10.5
Coleman, Monte, Washington	10.5
Baker, Al, St. Louis	10.0
Board, Dwaine, San Francisco	10.0
Gay, William, Detroit	10.0
McMichael, Steve, Chicago	10.0
Junior, E. J., St. Louis	9.5
Paul, Whitney, New Orleans	9.5
Youngblood, Jack, L.A. Rams	9.5
Douglass, Mike, Green Bay	9.0
Doss, Reggie, L.A. Rams	8.5
Green, Curtis, Detroit	8.5
Merrill, Casey, N.Y. Giants	8.5
Grant, Darryl, Washington	8.0
Jones, Ed, Dallas	8.0
Selmon, Lee Roy, Tampa Bay	8.0
Wilks, Jim, New Orleans	7.5
Burt, Jim, N.Y. Giants	7.0
Cofer, Mike, Detroit	7.0
Hartenstine, Mike, Chicago	7.0
Johnson, Ezra, Green Bay	7.0
Mann, Charles, Washington	7.0
Holloway, Randy, Minn.-St. Louis	6.5
Marshall, Leonard, N.Y. Giants	6.5
Wilson, Otis, Chicago	6.5
Andrews, George, L.A. Rams	6.0
Geathers, James, New Orleans	6.0
Smith, Don, Atlanta	6.0
Brooks, Perry, Washington	5.5
Galloway, David, St. Louis	5.5
Kaufman, Mel, Washington	5.5
Logan, Dave, Tampa Bay	5.5
Martin, George, N.Y. Giants	5.5
Pitts, Mike, Atlanta	5.5
Bates, Bill, Dallas	5.0
Brown, Robert, Green Bay	5.0
Burley, Gary, Atlanta	5.0
Darby, Byron, Philadelphia	5.0
English, Doug, Detroit	5.0
Johnson, Gary, S.D.-San Fran.	5.0
Washington, Chris, Tampa Bay	5.0
Bell, Todd, Chicago	4.5
Butz, Dave, Washington	4.5
McGee, Tony, Washington	4.5
Carter, Michael, San Francisco	4.0
Dean, Fred, San Francisco	4.0
Green, Hugh, Tampa Bay	4.0
Johnson, Charlie, Minnesota	4.0
Jones, Terry, Green Bay	4.0
McColl, Milt, San Francisco	4.0
Milot, Rich, Washington	4.0
Tuiasosopo, Manu, San Fran.	4.0
Warren, Frank, New Orleans	4.0
Anderson, John, Green Bay	3.5
Cannon, John, Tampa Bay	3.5
Downs, Mike, Dallas	3.5
Elshire, Neil, Minnesota	3.5
Hegman, Mike, Dallas	3.5
Mays, Stafford, St. Louis	3.5
Meisner, Greg, L.A. Rams	3.5
Owens, Mel, L.A. Rams	3.5
Richardson, Al, Atlanta	3.5
Singletary, Mike, Chicago	3.5
Armstrong, Harvey, Philadelphia	3.0
Banks, Carl, N.Y. Giants	3.0
Carreker, Alphonso, Green Bay	3.0
Cobb, Garry, Detroit	3.0
DeJurnett, Charles, L.A. Rams	3.0
Duda, Mark, St. Louis	3.0
Duerson, Dave, Chicago	3.0
Griggs, Anthony, Philadelphia	3.0
Martin, Charles, Green Bay	3.0
Nelson, Lee, St. Louis	3.0
Scott, Randy, Green Bay	3.0
Stuckey, Jim, San Francisco	3.0
Cumby, George, Green Bay	2.5
Dutton, John, Dallas	2.5
Keys, Tyrone, Chicago	2.5
Lockhart, Eugene, Dallas	2.5
Provence, Andrew, Atlanta	2.5
Beasley, Tom, Washington	2.0
Benson, Thomas, Atlanta	2.0
Browner, Keith, Tampa Bay	2.0
Bryan, Rick, Atlanta	2.0
Cotney, Mark, Tampa Bay	2.0
Dickerson, Anthony, Dallas	2.0
Ellison, Riki, San Francisco	2.0
Frye, David, Atlanta	2.0
Green, Gary, L.A. Rams	2.0
Grooms, Elois, St. Louis	2.0
Haines, John, Minnesota	2.0
Harris, Al, Chicago	2.0
Harris, Bob, St. Louis	2.0
Jackson, Jeff, Atlanta	2.0
Lewis, Reggie, New Orleans	2.0
Moore, Derland, New Orleans	2.0
Murphy, Mark, Green Bay	2.0
Pillers, Lawrence, San Francisco	2.0
Sally, Jerome, N.Y. Giants	2.0
Shell, Todd, San Francisco	2.0
Strauthers, Thomas, Philadelphia	2.0
Turner, Keena, San Francisco	2.0
Waechter, Henry, Ind.-Chicago	2.0
Wilcher, Mike, L.A. Rams	2.0
Wilkes, Reggie, Philadelphia	2.0
Williams, Jimmy, Detroit	2.0
Yeates, Jeff, Atlanta	2.0
Fantetti, Ken, Detroit	1.5
Fuller, Jeff, San Francisco	1.5
Hopkins, Wes, Philadelphia	1.5
Schulz, Jody, Philadelphia	1.5
Stover, Jeff, San Francisco	1.5
Williams, Joel, Philadelphia	1.5
Albritton, Vince, Dallas	1.0
Benish, Dan, Atlanta	1.0
Bess, Rufus, Minnesota	1.0
Blair, Matt, Minnesota	1.0
Brantley, Scot, Tampa Bay	1.0
Browner, Joey, Minnesota	1.0
Bunz, Dan, San Francisco	1.0
Clark, Mario, San Francisco	1.0
Clinkscale, Dextor, Dallas	1.0
Cobb, Robert, Minnesota	1.0
Ekern, Carl, L.A. Rams	1.0
Fencik, Gary, Chicago	1.0
Ferrari, Ron, San Francisco	1.0
Harris, Roy, Atlanta	1.0
Headen, Andy, N.Y. Giants	1.0
Hill, Ken, N.Y. Giants	1.0
Humphrey, Donnie, Green Bay	1.0
Hunt, Byron, N.Y. Giants	1.0
Jeter, Gary, L.A. Rams	1.0
Johnson, Kenny, Atlanta	1.0
Kovach, Jim, New Orleans	1.0
Kuykendall, Fulton, Atlanta	1.0
Lott, Ronnie, San Francisco	1.0
Martin, Chris, Minnesota	1.0
Martin, Doug, Minnesota	1.0
McNeill, Fred, Minnesota	1.0
Mularkey, Mike, Minnesota	1.0
Mullaney, Mark, Minnesota	1.0
Neill, Bill, Green Bay	1.0
Newsome, Vince, L.A. Rams	1.0
Olkewicz, Neal, Washington	1.0
Osborne, Jim, Chicago	1.0
Reasons, Gary, N.Y. Giants	1.0
Reed, Doug, L.A. Rams	1.0
Robinson, Jerry, Philadelphia	1.0
Sendlein, Robin, Minnesota	1.0
Smerek, Don, Dallas	1.0
Smith, Leonard, St. Louis	1.0
Thurman, Dennis, Dallas	1.0
Tuinei, Mark, Dallas	1.0
Walter, Mike, San Francisco	1.0
Williamson, Carlton, San Fran.	1.0
Arbubakrr, Hasson, Minnesota	0.5
Collins, Jim, L.A. Rams	0.5
Curry, Buddy, Atlanta	0.5
Harris, Eric, L.A. Rams	0.5
Winston, Dennis, New Orleans	0.5

HISTORY

Pro Football Hall of Fame

Chronology

Past NFL Standings

All-Time Team vs. Team Results

Super Bowl Game Summaries

Playoff Game Summaries

AFC-NFC Pro Bowl Game Summaries

AFC-NFC Interconference Games

Monday Night Results

History of Overtime Games

Number-One Draft Choices

PRO FOOTBALL HALL OF FAME

The Professional Football Hall of Fame is located in Canton, Ohio, site of the organizational meeting on September 17, 1920, from which the National Football League evolved. The NFL recognized Canton as the Hall of Fame site on April 27, 1961. Canton area individuals, foundations, and companies donated almost $400,000 in cash and services to provide funds for the construction of the original two-building complex, which was dedicated on September 7, 1963. The original Hall of Fame complex was almost doubled in size with the completion of a $620,000 expansion project that was dedicated on May 10, 1971. A second expansion project was completed on November 20, 1978. It features three exhibition areas and a theater twice the size of the original one.

The Hall represents the sport of pro football in many ways—through three large and colorful exhibition galleries, in the twin enshrinement halls, with numerous fan-participation electronic devices, a research library, and an NFL gift shop.

In recent years, the Pro Football Hall of Fame has become an extremely popular tourist attraction. At the end of 1984, a total of 3,700,063 fans had visited the Pro Football Hall of Fame.

New members of the Pro Football Hall of Fame are elected annually by a 29-member National Board of Selectors, made up of media representatives from every league city and the president of the Pro Football Writers Association. Between three and six new members are elected each year. An affirmative vote of approximately 80 percent is needed for election.

Any fan may nominate any eligible player or contributor simply by writing to the Pro Football Hall of Fame. Players must be retired five years to be eligible, while a coach need only to be retired with no time limit specified. Contributors (administrators, owners, et al.) may be elected while they are still active.

The charter class of 17 enshrinees was elected in 1963 and the honor roll now stands at 128 with the election of a five-man class in 1985. That class consists of Frank Gatski, Joe Namath, Pete Rozelle, O.J. Simpson, and Roger Staubach.

Roster of Members

HERB ADDERLEY
Defensive back. 6-1, 200. Born in Philadelphia, Pennsylvania, June 8, 1939. Michigan State. Inducted in 1980. 1961-69 Green Bay Packers, 1970-72 Dallas Cowboys.

LANCE ALWORTH
Wide receiver. 6-0, 184. Born in Houston, Texas, August 3, 1940. Arkansas. Inducted in 1978. 1962-70 San Diego Chargers, 1971-72 Dallas Cowboys.

DOUG ATKINS
Defensive end. 6-8, 275. Born in Humboldt, Tennessee, May 8, 1930. Tennessee. Inducted in 1982. 1953-54 Cleveland Browns, 1955-66 Chicago Bears, 1967-69 New Orleans Saints.

MORRIS (RED) BADGRO
End. 6-0, 190. Born in Orilla, Washington, December 1, 1902. Southern California. Inducted in 1981. 1927 New York Yankees, 1930-35 New York Giants, 1936 Brooklyn Dodgers.

CLIFF BATTLES
Halfback. 6-1, 201. Born in Akron, Ohio, May 1, 1910. Died April 27, 1981. West Virginia Wesleyan. Inducted in 1968. 1932 Boston Braves, 1933-36 Boston Redskins, 1937 Washington Redskins.

SAMMY BAUGH
Quarterback. 6-2, 180. Born in Temple, Texas, March 17, 1914. Texas Christian. Inducted in 1963. 1937-52 Washington Redskins.

CHUCK BEDNARIK
Center-linebacker. 6-3, 230. Born in Bethlehem, Pennsylvania, May 1, 1925. Pennsylvania. Inducted in 1967. 1949-62 Philadelphia Eagles.

BERT BELL
Commissioner. Team owner. Born in Philadelphia, Pennsylvania, February 25, 1895. Died October 11, 1959. Pennsylvania. Inducted in 1963. 1933-1940 Philadelphia Eagles, 1941-42 Pittsburgh Steelers, 1943 Phil-Pitt, 1944-46 Pittsburgh Steelers. Commissioner, 1946-59.

BOBBY BELL
Linebacker. 6-4, 225. Born in Shelby, North Carolina, June 17, 1940. Minnesota. Inducted in 1983. 1963-74 Kansas City Chiefs.

RAYMOND BERRY
End. 6-2, 187. Born in Corpus Christi, Texas, February 27, 1933. Southern Methodist. Inducted in 1973. 1955-67 Baltimore Colts.

CHARLES W. BIDWILL, SR.
Team owner. Born in Chicago, Illinois, September 16, 1895. Died April 19, 1947. Loyola of Chicago. Inducted in 1967. 1933-43 Chicago Cardinals, 1944 Card-Pitt, 1945-47 Chicago Cardinals.

GEORGE BLANDA
Quarterback-kicker. 6-2, 215. Born in Youngwood, Pennsylvania, September 17, 1927. Kentucky. Inducted in 1981. 1949-58 Chicago Bears, 1960-66 Houston Oilers, 1967-75 Oakland Raiders.

JIM BROWN
Fullback. 6-2, 232. Born in St. Simons, Georgia, February 17, 1936. Syracuse. Inducted in 1971. 1957-65 Cleveland Browns.

PAUL BROWN
Coach. Born in Norwalk, Ohio, September 7, 1908. Miami, Ohio. Inducted in 1967. 1946-49 Cleveland Browns (AAFC), 1950-62 Cleveland Browns, 1968-75 Cincinnati Bengals.

ROOSEVELT BROWN
Offensive tackle. 6-3, 255. Born in Charlottesville, Virginia, October 20, 1932. Morgan State. Inducted in 1975. 1953-65 New York Giants.

WILLIE BROWN
Defensive back. 6-1, 210. Born in Yazoo City, Mississippi, December 2, 1940. Grambling. Inducted in 1984. 1963-66 Denver Broncos, 1967-78 Oakland Raiders.

DICK BUTKUS
Linebacker. 6-3, 245. Born in Chicago, Illinois, December 9, 1942. Illinois. Inducted in 1979. 1965-73 Chicago Bears.

TONY CANADEO
Halfback. 5-11, 195. Born in Chicago, Illinois, May 5, 1919. Gonzaga. Inducted in 1974. 1941-44, 1946-52 Green Bay Packers.

JOE CARR
NFL president. Born in Columbus, Ohio, October 22, 1880. Died May 20, 1939. Did not attend college. Inducted in 1963. President, 1921-39 National Football League.

GUY CHAMBERLIN
End. Coach. 6-2, 210. Born in Blue Springs, Nebraska, January 16, 1894. Died April 4, 1967. Nebraska. Inducted in 1965. 1920 Decatur Staleys, 1921 Chicago Staleys, 1922-23 Canton Bulldogs, 1924 Cleveland Bulldogs, 1925-26 Frankford Yellowjackets, 1927-28 Chicago Cardinals.

JACK CHRISTIANSEN
Defensive back. 6-1, 185. Born in Sublette, Kansas, December 20, 1928. Colorado State. Inducted in 1970. 1951-58 Detroit Lions.

EARL (DUTCH) CLARK
Quarterback. 6-0, 185. Born in Fowler, Colorado, October 11, 1906. Died August 5, 1978. Colorado College. Inducted in 1963. 1931-32 Portsmouth Spartans, 1934-38 Detroit Lions.

GEORGE CONNOR
Tackle-linebacker. 6-3, 240. Born in Chicago, Illinois, January 1, 1925. Holy Cross, Notre Dame. Inducted in 1975. 1948-55 Chicago Bears.

JIMMY CONZELMAN
Quarterback. Coach. Team owner. 6-0, 180. Born in St. Louis, Missouri, March 6, 1898. Died July 31, 1970. Washington, Missouri. Inducted in 1964. 1920 Decatur Staleys, 1921-22 Rock Island, Ill., Independents, 1923-24 Milwaukee Badgers; owner-coach, 1925-26 Detroit Panthers; player-coach 1927-29, coach 1930 Providence Steamroller; coach, 1940-42 Chicago Cardinals, 1946-48 Chicago Cardinals.

WILLIE DAVIS
Defensive end. 6-3, 245. Born in Lisbon, Louisiana, July 24, 1934. Grambling. Inducted in 1981. 1958-59 Cleveland Browns, 1960-69 Green Bay Packers.

ART DONOVAN
Defensive tackle. 6-3, 265. Born in Bronx, New York, June 5, 1925. Boston College. Inducted in 1968. 1950 Baltimore Colts, 1951 New York Yanks, 1952 Dallas Texans, 1953-61 Baltimore Colts.

JOHN (PADDY) DRISCOLL
Quarterback. 5-11, 160. Born in Evanston, Illinois, January 11, 1896. Died June 29, 1968. Northwestern. Inducted in 1965. 1920 Decatur Staleys, 1920-25 Chicago Cardinals, 1926-29 Chicago Bears. Head coach, 1956-57 Chicago Bears.

BILL DUDLEY
Halfback. 5-10, 176. Born in Bluefield, Virginia, December 24, 1921. Virginia. Inducted in 1966. 1942 Pittsburgh Steelers, 1945-46 Pittsburgh Steelers, 1947-49 Detroit Lions, 1950-51, 1953 Washington Redskins.

GLEN (TURK) EDWARDS
Tackle. 6-2, 260. Born in Mold, Washington, September 28, 1907. Died January 10, 1973. Washington State. Inducted in 1969. 1932 Boston Braves, 1933-36 Boston Redskins, 1937-40 Washington Redskins.

WEEB EWBANK
Coach. Born in Richmond, Indiana, May 6, 1907. Miami, Ohio. Inducted in 1978. 1954-62 Baltimore Colts, 1963-73 New York Jets.

TOM FEARS
End. 6-2, 215. Born in Los Angeles, California, December 3, 1923. Santa Clara, UCLA. Inducted in 1970. 1948-56 Los Angeles Rams.

RAY FLAHERTY
Coach. Born in Spokane, Washington, September 1, 1904. Gonzaga. Inducted in 1976. 1926 Los Angeles Wildcats (AFL), 1927 New York Yankees, 1928-29, 1931-35 New York Giants. Coach, 1936 Boston Redskins, 1937-1942 Washington Redskins, 1946-48 New York Yankees (AAFC), 1949 Chicago Hornets (AAFC).

LEN FORD
End. 6-5, 260. Born in Washington, D.C., February 18, 1926. Died March 14, 1972. Michigan. Inducted in 1976. 1948-49 Los Angeles Dons (AAFC), 1950-57 Cleveland Browns, 1958 Green Bay Packers.

DAN FORTMANN
Guard. 6-0, 207. Born in Pearl River, New York, April 11, 1916. Colgate. Inducted in 1965. 1936-43 Chicago Bears.

FRANK GATSKI
Center. 6-3, 240. Born in Farmington, West Virginia, March 13, 1922. Marshall, Auburn. Inducted in 1985. 1946-49 Cleveland Browns (AAFC), 1950-56 Cleveland Browns, 1957 Detroit Lions.

BILL GEORGE
Linebacker. 6-2, 230. Born in Waynesburg, Pennsylvania, October 27, 1930. Wake Forest. Inducted in 1974. 1952-65 Chicago Bears, 1966 Los Angeles Rams.

FRANK GIFFORD
Halfback. 6-1, 195. Born in Santa Monica, California, August 16, 1930. Southern California. Inducted in 1977. 1952-60, 1962-64 New York Giants.

SID GILLMAN
Coach. Born in Minneapolis, Minnesota, October 26, 1911. Ohio State. Inducted in 1983. 1955-59 Los Angeles Rams, 1960-69 San Diego Chargers, 1973-74 Houston Oilers.

OTTO GRAHAM
Quarterback. 6-1, 195. Born in Waukegan, Illinois, December 6, 1921. Northwestern. Inducted in 1965. 1946-49 Cleveland Browns (AAFC), 1950-55 Cleveland Browns.

RED GRANGE
Halfback. 6-0, 185. Born in Forksville, Pennsylvania, June 13, 1903. Illinois. Inducted in 1963. 1925 Chicago Bears, 1926 New York Yankees (AFL), 1927 New York Yankees, 1929-34 Chicago Bears.

FORREST GREGG
Tackle. 6-4, 250. Born in Sulphur Springs, Texas, October 18, 1933. Southern Methodist. Inducted in 1977. 1956, 1958-70 Green Bay Packers, 1971 Dallas Cowboys.

LOU GROZA
Tackle-kicker. 6-3, 250. Born in Martin's Ferry, Ohio, January 25, 1924. Ohio State. Inducted in 1974. 1946-49 Cleveland Browns (AAFC), 1950-59, 1961-67 Cleveland Browns.

JOE GUYON
Halfback. 6-1, 180. Born in Mahnomen, Minnesota, November 26, 1892. Died November 27, 1971. Carlisle, Georgia Tech. Inducted in 1966. 1920 Canton Bulldogs, 1921 Cleveland Indians, 1922-23 Oorang Indians, 1924 Rock Island, Ill., Independents, 1924-25 Kansas City Cowboys, 1927 New York Giants.

GEORGE HALAS
End. Coach. Team Owner. Born in Chicago, Illinois, February 2, 1895. Died October 31, 1983. Illinois. Inducted in 1963. 1920 Decatur Staleys, 1921 Chicago Staleys, 1922-29 Chicago Bears; coach, 1933-42, 1946-55, 1958-67 Chicago Bears.

ED HEALEY
Tackle. 6-3, 220. Born in Indian Orchard, Massachusetts, December 28, 1894. Died December 9, 1978. Dartmouth. Inducted in 1964. 1920-22 Rock Island, Ill., Independents, 1922-27 Chicago Bears.

MEL HEIN
Center. 6-2, 225. Born in Redding, California, August 22, 1909. Washington State. Inducted in 1963. 1931-45 New York Giants.

WILBUR (PETE) HENRY
Tackle. 6-0, 250. Born in Mansfield, Ohio, October 31, 1897. Died February 7, 1952. Washington & Jefferson. Inducted in 1963. 1920-23 Canton Bulldogs, 1925-26 Canton Bulldogs, 1927 New York Giants, 1927-28 Pottsville Maroons.

ARNIE HERBER
Quarterback. 6-1, 200. Born in Green Bay, Wisconsin, April 2, 1910. Died October 14, 1969. Wisconsin, Regis College. Inducted in 1966. 1930-40 Green Bay Packers, 1944-45 New York Giants.

BILL HEWITT
End. 5-11, 191. Born in Bay City, Michigan, October 8, 1909. Died January 14, 1947. Michigan. Inducted in 1971. 1932-36 Chicago Bears, 1937-39 Philadelphia Eagles, 1943 Phil-Pitt.

CLARKE HINKLE
Fullback. 5-11, 201. Born in Toronto, Ohio, April 10, 1912. Bucknell. Inducted in 1964. 1932-41 Green Bay Packers.

ELROY (CRAZYLEGS) HIRSCH
Halfback-end. 6-2, 190. Born in Wausau, Wisconsin, June 17, 1923. Wisconsin, Michigan. Inducted in 1968. 1946-48 Chicago Rockets (AAFC), 1949-57 Los Angeles Rams.

CAL HUBBARD
Tackle. 6-5, 250. Born in Keytesville, Missouri, October 11, 1900. Died October 17, 1977. Centenary, Geneva. Inducted in 1963. 1927-28 New York Giants, 1929-33, 1935 Green Bay Packers, 1936 New York Giants, 1936 Pittsburgh Pirates.

SAM HUFF
Linebacker. 6-1, 230. Born in Morgantown, West Virginia, October 4, 1934. West Virginia. Inducted in 1982. 1956-63 New York Giants, 1964-67, 1969 Washington Redskins.

LAMAR HUNT
Team owner. Born in El Dorado, Arkansas, August 2, 1932. Southern Methodist. Inducted in 1972. 1960-62 Dallas Texans, 1963-85 Kansas City Chiefs.

DON HUTSON
End. 6-1, 180. Born in Pine Bluff, Arkansas, January 31, 1913. Alabama. Inducted in 1963. 1935-45 Green Bay Packers.

DAVID (DEACON) JONES
Defensive end. 6-5, 250. Born in Eatonville, Florida, December 9, 1938. South Carolina State. Inducted 1980. 1961-71 Los Angeles Rams, 1972-73 San Diego Chargers, 1974 Washington Redskins.

SONNY JURGENSEN
Quarterback. 6-0, 203. Born in Wilmington, North Carolina, August 23, 1934. Duke. Inducted in 1983. 1957-63 Philadelphia Eagles, 1964-74 Washington Redskins.

WALT KIESLING
Guard. Coach. 6-2, 245. Born in St. Paul, Minnesota, March 27, 1903. Died March 2, 1962. St. Thomas (Minnesota). Inducted in 1966. 1926-27 Duluth Eskimos, 1928 Pottsville Maroons, 1929-33 Chicago Cardinals, 1934 Chicago Bears, 1935-36 Green Bay Packers, 1937-38 Pittsburgh Pirates; coach, 1939-42 Pittsburgh Steelers; co-coach, 1943 Phil-Pitt, 1944 Card-Pitt; coach, 1954-56 Pittsburgh Steelers.

FRANK (BRUISER) KINARD
Tackle. 6-1, 210. Born in Pelahatchie, Mississippi, October 23, 1914. Mississippi. Inducted in 1971. 1938-44 Brooklyn Dodgers-Tigers, 1946-47 New York Yankees (AAFC).

EARL (CURLY) LAMBEAU
Coach. Born in Green Bay, Wisconsin, April 9, 1898. Died June 1, 1965. Notre Dame. Inducted in 1963. 1919-49 Green Bay Packers, 1950-51 Chicago Cardinals, 1952-53 Washington Redskins.

DICK (NIGHT TRAIN) LANE
Defensive back. 6-2, 210. Born in Austin, Texas, April 16, 1928. Scottsbluff Junior College. Inducted in 1974. 1952-53 Los Angeles Rams, 1954-59 Chicago Cardinals, 1960-65 Detroit Lions.

YALE LARY
Defensive back-punter. 5-11, 189. Born in Fort Worth, Texas, November 24, 1930. Texas A&M. Inducted in 1979. 1952-53, 1956-64 Detroit Lions.

DANTE LAVELLI
End. 6-0, 199. Born in Hudson, Ohio, February 23, 1923. Ohio State. Inducted in 1975. 1946-49 Cleveland Browns (AAFC), 1950-56 Cleveland Browns.

BOBBY LAYNE
Quarterback. 6-2, 190. Born in Santa Anna, Texas, December 19, 1926. Texas. Inducted in 1967. 1948 Chicago Bears, 1949 New York Bulldogs, 1950-58 Detroit Lions, 1958-62 Pittsburgh Steelers.

ALPHONSE (TUFFY) LEEMANS
Fullback. 6-0, 200. Born in Superior, Wisconsin, November 12, 1912. Died January 19, 1979. George Washington. Inducted in 1978. 1936-43 New York Giants.

BOB LILLY
Defensive tackle. 6-5, 260. Born in Olney, Texas, July 24, 1939. Texas Christian. Inducted in 1980. 1961-74 Dallas Cowboys.

VINCE LOMBARDI
Coach. Born in Brooklyn, New York, June 11, 1913. Died September 3, 1970. Fordham. Inducted in 1971. 1959-67 Green Bay Packers, 1969 Washington Redskins.

SID LUCKMAN
Quarterback. 6-0, 195. Born in Brooklyn, New York, November 21, 1916. Columbia. Inducted in 1965. 1939-50 Chicago Bears.

ROY (LINK) LYMAN
Tackle. 6-2, 252. Born in Table Rock, Nebraska, November 30, 1898. Died December 28, 1972. Nebraska. Inducted in 1964. 1922-23, 1925 Canton Bulldogs, 1924 Cleveland Bulldogs, 1925 Frankford Yellowjackets, 1926-28, 1930-31, 1933-34 Chicago Bears.

TIM MARA
Team owner. Born in New York, New York, July 29, 1887. Died February 17, 1959. Did not attend college. Inducted in 1963. 1925-59 New York Giants.

GINO MARCHETTI
Defensive end. 6-4, 245. Born in Antioch, California, January 2, 1927. San Francisco. Inducted in 1972. 1952 Dallas Texans, 1953-64, 1966 Baltimore Colts.

GEORGE PRESTON MARSHALL
Team owner. Born in Grafton, West Virginia, October 11, 1897. Died August 9, 1969. Randolph-Macon. Inducted in 1963. 1932 Boston Braves, 1933-36 Boston Redskins, 1937-69 Washington Redskins.

OLLIE MATSON
Halfback. 6-2, 220. Born in Trinity, Texas, May 1, 1930. San Francisco. Inducted in 1972. 1952, 1954-58 Chicago Cardinals, 1959-62 Los Angeles Rams, 1963 Detroit Lions, 1964-66 Philadelphia Eagles.

GEORGE McAFEE
Halfback. 6-0, 177. Born in Ironton, Ohio, March 13, 1918. Duke. Inducted in 1966. 1940-41, 1945-50 Chicago Bears.

MIKE McCORMACK
Offensive tackle. 6-4, 248. Born in Chicago, Illinois, June 21, 1930. Kansas. Inducted in 1984. 1951 New York Yankees, 1954-62 Cleveland Browns.

HUGH McELHENNY
Halfback. 6-1, 198. Born in Los Angeles, California, December 31, 1928. Washington. Inducted in 1970. 1952-60 San Francisco 49ers, 1961-62 Minnesota Vikings, 1963 New York Giants, 1964 Detroit Lions.

JOHNNY BLOOD (McNALLY)
Halfback. 6-0, 185. Born in New Richmond, Wisconsin, November 27, 1903. St. John's (Minnesota). Inducted in 1963. 1925-26 Milwaukee Badgers, 1926-27 Duluth Eskimos, 1928 Pottsville Maroons, 1929-33 Green Bay Packers, 1934 Pittsburgh Pirates, 1935-36 Green Bay Packers. Player-coach, 1937-39 Pittsburgh Pirates.

MIKE MICHALSKE
Guard. 6-0, 209. Born in Cleveland, Ohio, April 24, 1903. Penn State. Inducted in 1964. 1926 New York Yankees (AFL), 1927-28 New York Yankees, 1929-35, 1937 Green Bay Packers.

WAYNE MILLNER
End. 6-0, 191. Born in Roxbury, Massachusetts, January 31, 1913. Died November 19, 1976. Notre Dame. Inducted in 1968. 1936 Boston Redskins, 1937-41, 1945 Washington Redskins.

BOBBY MITCHELL
Running back-wide receiver. 6-0, 195. Born in Hot Springs, Arkansas, June 6, 1935. Illinois. Inducted in 1983. 1958-61 Cleveland Browns, 1962-68 Washington Redskins.

RON MIX
Tackle. 6-4, 250. Born in Los Angeles, California, March 10, 1938. Southern California. Inducted in 1979. 1960-69 San Diego Chargers, 1971 Oakland Raiders.

LENNY MOORE
Back. 6-1, 198. Born in Reading, Pennsylvania, November 25, 1933. Penn State. Inducted in 1975. 1956-67 Baltimore Colts.

MARION MOTLEY
Fullback. 6-1, 238. Born in Leesburg, Georgia, June 5, 1920. South Carolina State, Nevada. Inducted in 1968. 1946-49 Cleveland Browns (AAFC), 1950-53 Cleveland Browns, 1955 Pittsburgh Steelers.

GEORGE MUSSO
Defensive and offensive guard. 6-2, 270. Born in Collinsville, Illinois. April 8, 1910. Milliken. Inducted in 1982. 1933-44 Chicago Bears.

BRONKO NAGURSKI
Fullback. 6-2, 225. Born in Rainy River, Ontario, Canada, November 3, 1908. Minnesota. Inducted in 1963. 1930-37, 1943 Chicago Bears.

JOE NAMATH
Quarterback. 6-2, 200. Born in Beaver Falls, Pennsylvania, May 31, 1943. Alabama. Inducted in 1985. 1965-76 New York Jets, 1977 Los Angeles Rams.

EARLE (GREASY) NEALE
Coach. Born in Parkersburg, West

Virginia, November 5, 1891. Died November 2, 1973. West Virginia Wesleyan. Inducted in 1969. 1941-42, 1944-50 Philadelphia Eagles, co-coach Phil-Pitt 1943.

ERNIE NEVERS
Fullback. 6-1, 205. Born in Willow River, Minnesota, June 11, 1903. Died May 3, 1976. Stanford. Inducted in 1963. 1926-27 Duluth Eskimos, 1929-31 Chicago Cardinals.

RAY NITSCHKE
Linebacker. 6-3, 235. Born in Elmwood Park, Illinois, December 29, 1936. Illinois. Inducted in 1978. 1958-72 Green Bay Packers.

LEO NOMELLINI
Defensive tackle. 6-3, 264. Born in Lucca, Italy, June 19, 1924. Minnesota. Inducted in 1969. 1950-63 San Francisco 49ers.

MERLIN OLSEN
Defensive tackle. 6-5, 270. Born in Logan, Utah, September 14, 1940. Utah State. Inducted in. 1982. 1962-76 Los Angeles Rams.

JIM OTTO
Center. 6-2, 255. Born in Wausau, Wisconsin, January 5, 1938. Miami. Inducted in 1980. 1960-74 Oakland Raiders.

STEVE OWEN
Tackle. Coach. 6-0, 235. Born in Cleo Springs, Oklahoma, April 21, 1898. Died May 17, 1964. Phillips. Inducted in 1966. 1924-25 Kansas City Cowboys, 1926-30 New York Giants; coach, 1931-53 New York Giants.

CLARENCE (ACE) PARKER
Quarterback. 5-11, 168. Born in Portsmouth, Virginia, May 17, 1912. Duke. Inducted in 1972. 1937-41 Brooklyn Dodgers, 1945 Boston Yanks, 1946 New York Yankees (AAFC).

JIM PARKER
Guard-tackle. 6-3, 273. Born in Macon, Georgia, April 3, 1934. Ohio State. Inducted in 1973. 1957-67 Baltimore Colts.

JOE PERRY
Fullback. 6-0, 200. Born in Stevens, Arkansas, January 27, 1927. Compton Junior College. Inducted in 1969. 1948-49 San Francisco 49ers (AAFC), 1950-60, 1963 San Francisco 49ers, 1961-62 Baltimore Colts.

PETE PIHOS
End. 6-1, 210. Born in Orlando, Florida, October 22, 1923. Indiana. Inducted in 1970. 1947-55 Philadelphia Eagles.

HUGH (SHORTY) RAY
Supervisor of officials. Born in Highland Park, Illinois, September 21, 1884. Died September 16, 1956. Illinois. Inducted in 1966.

DAN REEVES
Team owner. Born in New York, New York, June 30, 1912. Died April 15, 1971. Georgetown. Inducted in 1967. 1941-45 Cleveland Rams, 1946-71 Los Angeles Rams.

JIM RINGO
Center. 6-1, 235. Born in Orange, New Jersey, November 21, 1932. Syracuse. Inducted in 1981. 1953-63

Green Bay Packers, 1964-67 Philadelphia Eagles.

ANDY ROBUSTELLI
Defensive end. 6-0, 230. Born in Stamford, Connecticut, December 6, 1925. Arnold College. Inducted in 1971. 1951-55 Los Angeles Rams, 1956-64 New York Giants.

ART ROONEY
Team owner. Born in Coulterville, Pennsylvania, January 27, 1901. Georgetown, Duquesne. Inducted in 1964. 1933-40 Pittsburgh Pirates, 1941-42, 1949-85, Pittsburgh Steelers, 1943 Phil-Pitt; 1944 Card-Pitt.

PETE ROZELLE
Commissioner. Born in South Gate, California, March 1, 1926. San Francisco. Inducted in 1985. Commissioner 1960-85.

GALE SAYERS
Running back. 6-0, 200. Born in Wichita, Kansas, May 30, 1943. Kansas. Inducted in 1977. 1965-71 Chicago Bears.

JOE SCHMIDT
Linebacker. 6-0, 222. Born in Pittsburgh, Pennsylvania, January 19, 1932. Pittsburgh. Inducted in 1973. 1953-65 Detroit Lions.

O.J. SIMPSON
Running back. 6-1, 212. Born in San Francisco, California, July 9, 1947. Southern California. Inducted in 1985. 1969-77 Buffalo Bills, 1978-79 San Francisco 49ers.

BART STARR
Quarterback. 6-1, 200. Born in Montgomery, Alabama, January 9, 1934. Alabama. Inducted in 1977. 1956-71 Green Bay Packers; coach, 1975-83 Green Bay Packers.

ROGER STAUBACH
Quarterback. 6-3, 202. Born in Cincinnati, Ohio, February 5, 1942. Navy. Inducted in 1985. 1969-79 Dallas Cowboys.

ERNIE STAUTNER
Defensive tackle. 6-2, 235. Born in Calm, Bavaria, Germany, April 20, 1925. Boston College. Inducted in 1969. 1950-63 Pittsburgh Steelers.

KEN STRONG
Halfback. 5-11, 210. Born in New Haven, Connecticut, August 6, 1906. Died October 5, 1979. New York University. Inducted in 1967. 1929-32 Staten Island Stapletons, 1936-37 New York Yanks (AFL), 1933-35, 1939, 1944-47 New York Giants.

JOE STYDAHAR
Tackle. 6-4, 230. Born in Kaylor, Pennsylvania, March 3, 1912. Died March 23, 1977. West Virginia. Inducted in 1967. 1936-42, 1945-46 Chicago Bears.

CHARLEY TAYLOR
Wide receiver-running back. 6-3, 210. Born in Grand Prairie, Texas, September 28, 1941. Arizona State. Inducted in 1984. 1964-75, 1977 Washington Redskins.

JIM TAYLOR
Fullback. 6-0, 216. Born in Baton Rouge, Louisiana, September 20, 1935. Louisiana State. Inducted in 1976. 1958-66 Green Bay Packers,

1967 New Orleans Saints.

JIM THORPE
Halfback. 6-1, 190. Born in Prague, Oklahoma, May 28, 1888. Died March 28, 1953. Carlisle. Inducted in 1963. 1920 Canton Bulldogs, 1921 Cleveland Indians, 1922-23 Oorang Indians, 1923 Toledo Maroons, 1924 Rock Island, Ill., Independents, 1925 New York Giants, 1926 Canton Bulldogs, 1928 Chicago Cardinals.

Y. A. TITTLE
Quarterback. 6-0, 200. Born in Marshall, Texas, October 24, 1926. Louisiana State. Inducted in 1971. 1948-49 Baltimore Colts (AAFC), 1950 Baltimore Colts, 1951-60 San Francisco 49ers, 1961-64 New York Giants.

GEORGE TRAFTON
Center. 6-2, 235. Born in Chicago, Illinois, December 6, 1896. Died September 5, 1971. Notre Dame. Inducted in 1964. 1920 Decatur Staleys, 1921 Chicago Staleys, 1922-32 Chicago Bears.

CHARLEY TRIPPI
Halfback. 6-0, 185. Born in Pittston, Pennsylvania, December 14, 1922. Georgia. Inducted in 1968. 1947-55 Chicago Cardinals.

EMLEN TUNNELL
Safety. 6-1, 200. Born in Bryn Mawr, Pennsylvania, March 29, 1925. Died July 23, 1975. Toledo, Iowa. Inducted in 1967. 1948-58 New York Giants, 1959-61 Green Bay Packers.

CLYDE (BULLDOG) TURNER
Center. 6-2, 235. Born in Sweetwater, Texas, November 10, 1919. Hardin-Simmons. Inducted in 1966. 1940-52 Chicago Bears.

JOHNNY UNITAS
Quarterback. 6-1, 195. Born in Pittsburgh, Pennsylvania, May 7, 1933. Louisville. Inducted in 1979. 1956-72 Baltimore Colts, 1973 San Diego Chargers.

NORM VAN BROCKLIN
Quarterback. 6-1, 190. Born in Eagle Butte, South Dakota, March 15, 1926. Died May 1, 1983. Oregon. Inducted in 1971. 1949-57 Los Angeles Rams, 1958-60 Philadelphia Eagles.

STEVE VAN BUREN
Halfback. 6-1, 200. Born in La Ceiba, Honduras, December 28, 1920. Louisiana State. Inducted in 1965. 1944-51 Philadelphia Eagles.

PAUL WARFIELD
Wide receiver. 6-0, 188. Born in Warren, Ohio, November 28, 1942. Ohio State. Inducted in 1983. 1964-69, 1976-77 Cleveland Browns, 1970-74 Miami Dolphins, 1975 Memphis Grizzlies (WFL).

BOB WATERFIELD
Quarterback. 6-2, 200. Born in Elmira, New York, July 26, 1920. Died April 25, 1983. UCLA. Inducted in 1965. 1945 Cleveland Rams, 1946-52 Los Angeles Rams.

ARNIE WEINMEISTER
Defensive tackle. 6-4, 235. Born in Rhein, Saskatchewan, Canada, March 23, 1923. Washington. Inducted in 1984. 1948-49 New York Yankees (AAFC), 1950-53 New York Giants.

BILL WILLIS
Guard. 6-2, 215. Born in Columbus, Ohio, October 5, 1921. Ohio State. Inducted in 1977. 1946-49 Cleveland Browns (AAFC), 1950-53 Cleveland Browns.

LARRY WILSON
Defensive back. 6-0, 190. Born in Rigby, Idaho, March 24, 1938. Utah. Inducted in 1978. 1960-72 St. Louis Cardinals.

ALEX WOJCIECHOWICZ
Center. 6-0, 235. Born in South River, New Jersey, August 12, 1915. Fordham. Inducted in 1968. 1938-46 Detroit Lions, 1946-50 Philadelphia Eagles.

1892 Rutgers and Princeton had played a college soccer football game, the first ever, in 1869. Rugby had gained favor over soccer, however, and from it rugby football, then football, had evolved among American colleges. It was also played by athletic clubs. Intensive competition existed between two Pittsburgh clubs, Allegheny Athletic Association and Pittsburgh Athletic Club. William (Pudge) Heffelfinger, former star at Yale, brought in by AAA, paid $500 to play in game against PAC, becoming first person known to have been paid openly to play football, Nov. 12. AAA won 4-0 when Heffelfinger picked up PAC fumble and ran for touchdown, which then counted four points.

1898 Morgan AC founded on Chicago's South Side, later became Chicago Normals, Racine (a Chicago street) Cardinals, Chicago Cardinals, and St. Louis Cardinals, oldest continuing operation in pro football.

1899 Duquesne Country and Athletic Club, or Pittsburgh Duquesnes, included large payroll signing players returning from Spanish-American War, sought help from Pittsburgh sportsman William C. Temple. He bought football team from athletic club, became first known individual club owner.

1901 Temple and Barney Dreyfuss of baseball Pirates formed new team and urged cross-state rivalry with Philadelphia.

1902 Philadelphia Athletics, managed by Connie Mack, and Nationals or Phillies formed football teams. Athletics won first night football game, 39-0 over Kanaweola AC at Elmira, N.Y., Nov. 21.

Athletics claimed pro championship after winning two, losing one against Phillies and going 1-1-1 against Pittsburgh Pros. Pitcher Rube Waddell played for Athletics, pitcher Christy Matthewson was fullback for Pittsburgh in one game.

"World Series," actually four-team tournament, played among Athletics, New York Knickerbockers, Watertown, N.Y., Red and Blacks, and Syracuse AC, was played in Madison Square Garden. Philadelphia and Syracuse played first indoor football game before 3,000, Dec. 28. Syracuse, with Pop Warner at guard, won game 6-0, went on to win tournament.

1903 Franklin (Pa.) AC won second and last "World Series" of pro football over Philadelphia, Watertown, and Orange, N.J., AC.

Pro football declined in Pittsburgh area. Some PAC players hired by Massillon, Ohio, Tigers, making Massillon first openly professional team in Ohio. Emphasis shifted there from Pennsylvania.

1904 Ohio had at least eight pro teams. Attempt failed to form league to end cutthroat bidding for players, write rules for all.

1905 Canton Bulldogs turned professional.

1906 Archrivals Massillon and Canton played twice, Massillon won both. Because of betting scandal, Canton manager Blondy Wallace left in disgrace, interest in pro football in two cities declined.

1913 Jim Thorpe, former football star for Carlisle Indian School and hero of 1912 Olympics, played season for Pine Village Pros in Indiana.

1915 Canton revived name "Bulldogs" and signed Thorpe for $250 a game.

1916 With Thorpe starring, Canton won 10 straight, most by lopsided scores, was acclaimed pro football champion of world.

1919 George Calhoun, Curly Lambeau organized Green Bay Packers. Indian Packing Company provided equipment, name "Packers." They had 10-1 record against other company teams.

1920 Pro football was in state of confusion, teams were loosely organized, players moved freely among teams, there was no system for recruiting players. A league in which all followed the same rules was needed. Meeting was held among interested teams in August, second meeting was held in Canton and American Professional Football Association, forerunner of National Football League, formed Sept. 17. Teams were from five states—Akron Pros, Canton Bulldogs, Cleveland Indians, Dayton Triangles, Massillon Tigers from Ohio; Hammond Pros, Muncie Flyers from Indiana; Racine Cardinals, Rock Island Independents, Decatur Staleys, represented by George Halas, from Illinois; Rochester, N.Y., Jeffersons; and "Wisconsin."

Capitalizing on his fame, Thorpe was chosen league president, Stan Cofall of Massillon vice president. Membership fee of $100 arrived at to give aura of respectability. No team ever paid it. Massillon and Muncie did not field teams. Buffalo All-Americans, Chicago Tigers, Columbus, Ohio, Panhandles, and Detroit Tigers joined league later in year. League operated sporadically, teams played as many non-members as members, either no standings kept or have since been lost. Akron, Buffalo, Canton all claimed championship, hastily arranged series of games, one of them between Buffalo and Canton at Polo Grounds, New York City, failed to settle issue of championship.

First recorded player deal sale of Bob Nash, tackle and end for Akron, to Buffalo for $300, five percent of gate receipts.

1921 APFA reorganized at Akron, Joe Carr of Panhandles named president, Apr. 30. Carl Storck of Dayton named secretary-treasurer. Carr established league headquarters at Columbus.

Chicago Tigers, beaten by Racine Cardinals in 1920 game for "rights" to Chicago, dropped out, so did Hammond.

J.E. Clair of Acme Packing Company granted franchise for Green Bay Packers, Aug. 27. Cincinnati Celts also joined league.

Thorpe moved from Canton to Cleveland Indians.

A. E. Staley turned Decatur Staleys over to George Halas, who moved them to Cubs Park in Chicago, promising to keep the name "Staleys" one more year.

Five teams that dropped out had records stricken from standings—Evansville, Hammond, Louisville, Minneapolis, and Muncie.

Chicago Staleys claimed league championship with 10-1-1 record. Buffalo, 9-1-2, claimed Chicago included nonleague games in record,

but Carr ruled for Staleys.

1922 Packers disciplined for using college players under assumed names, Clair turned franchise back to league, Jan. 28. Curly Lambeau promised to obey rules, used $50 of own money to buy back franchise, June 24. Bad weather, low attendance plagued Packers, merchants raised $2,500, public non-profit corporation set up to operate team with Lambeau as manager, coach.

APFA changed name to National Football League, June 24. Staleys became Chicago Bears.

Thorpe, other Indian players formed Oorang Indians in Marion, Ohio, sponsored by Oorang dog kennels.

1923 Oorang folded with 1-10 record, Thorpe moved to Toledo Maroons. Player-coach Halas of Chicago recovered fumble by Thorpe in game against Oorang, ran 98 yards for touchdown.

1924 Frankford Yellowjackets of Philadelphia awarded franchise, that city entered league for first time. League champion Canton moved to Cleveland to play before larger crowds to meet rising payroll.

1925 Tim Mara and Billy Gibson awarded franchise for New York City for $500. Detroit Panthers, coached by Jimmy Conzelman, Pottsville, Pa., Maroons; Providence R.I., Steam Roller also entered league. New team in Canton took name "Bulldogs."

University of Illinois season ended and Red Grange signed contract to play for Chicago Bears immediately, Nov. 22. Crowd of 38,000 watched Grange and Bears in traditional Thanksgiving game against Cardinals. Barnstorming tour began in which Bears played seven games in 11 days in St. Louis, Philadelphia, New York, then cities in South and West. Crowd of 70,000 watched game against Giants at Polo Grounds, helping assure future of NFL franchise in New York.

Pottsville defeated Chicago Cardinals for what they thought was NFL championship, but week later played "Notre Dame All Stars" in Philadelphia. Frankford protested, saying "territorial rights" had been impinged upon. Carr upheld protest, cancelled Pottsville franchise, ordered Cardinals to play two more games. They did, won both, were proclaimed NFL champions.

1926 Grange's manager, C.C. Pyle, asked Bears for five-figure salary for Grange, one-third ownership of team. Bears refused, lost Grange. Pyle leased Yankee Stadium in New York City, petitioned for NFL franchise, was refused, started first American Football League. It lasted one season, included Grange's New York Yankees, eight other teams. AFL champion Philadelphia Quakers played postseason game against NFL New York Giants, lost 31-0.

Halas pushed through rule prohibiting any team from signing player whose college class had not graduated, Feb. 6.

NFL membership swelled to 22, frustrating AFL growth. Paddy Driscoll of Cardinals moved to rival Bears. Ole Haugsrud, operator of Duluth, Minn., Eskimos, gained NFL franchise, signed Ernie Nevers of Stanford, giving NFL gate attraction

to rival Grange. Thirteen-member Eskimos, "Iron Men of the North," played 28 exhibition or league games, 26 on road.

1927 AFL folded, NFL shrank to 12 teams. Akron, Canton, Columbus left NFL. New York Yankees and Grange joined NFL. Grange suffered knee injury. New York Giants won first NFL championship, scoring five consecutive shutouts at one point.

1928 Grange left football, appeared in movie and on vaudeville circuit. Duluth disbanded, Nevers quit pro football, played baseball, was assistant coach at Stanford.

1929 Chris O'Brien sold Chicago Cardinals to David Jones, July 27. NFL added fourth official, field judge, July 28. Cardinals became first pro team to go to out-of-town training camp, Coldwater, Mich., Aug. 21. Dayton played final season, last of original Ohio teams to leave league.

Grange, Nevers returned to NFL. Nevers scored 40 points for Cardinals against Bears, Nov. 28, six touchdowns rushing, four extra points. Grange returned to Bears.

Packers signed back Johnny Blood (McNally), tackle Cal Hubbard, guard Mike Michalske, and won first NFL championship.

1930 Portsmouth, Ohio, Spartans joined NFL. Defunct Dayton franchise bought by John Dwyer, became Brooklyn Dodgers. Bears, Cardinals played exhibition for unemployment relief funds, indoors at Chicago Stadium, layer of dirt covering arena floor. New York Giants, "Notre Dame All-Stars" coached by Knute Rockne, played charity exhibition before 55,000 at Polo Grounds.

Halas retired as player, resigned as coach of Bears in favor of Ralph Jones.

Packers won second straight NFL championship.

1931 Pro football shrank to 10 teams. Carr fined Bears, Packers, Portsmouth $1,000 each for using players whose college classes had not graduated, July 11.

Playing career of Al Nesser, last of six brothers to play in NFL, ended when Cleveland Indians disbanded.

Green Bay won third straight NFL championship.

1932 George P. Marshall, Vincent Bendix, Jay O'Brien, M. Dorland Doyle awarded franchise for Boston, July 9. Named team "Braves" after baseball team using same park.

NFL membership dropped to eight, lowest in history. First playoff in NFL history arranged between Bears and Spartans. Moved indoors to Chicago Stadium because of blizzard conditions in city. Arena allowed only 80-yard field that came right to walls. For safety, goal posts moved from end to goal lines, inbounds lines or hashmarks drawn 10 yards from sidelines for ball to be put in play. Bears won 9-0, Dec. 18, scoring touchdown disputed by Spartans who claimed Bronko Nagurski threw jump pass to Red Grange from point less than five yards behind the line of scrimmage, violating existing passing rule.

1933 NFL made significant changes in rules of football first time. Innovations of 1932 indoor playoffs—inbounds lines or hashmarks 10 yards from sidelines, goal posts on goal lines—became rules, Feb. 25.

Following resolution by George P. Marshall, NFL divided into two five-team divisions, winners to meet in annual championship playoff, July 8.

Franchise was awarded to Art Rooney and A. McCool for Pittsburgh, July 8; team was named "Pirates." Inactive Frankford franchise declared forfeited, Philadelphia franchise awarded to Bert Bell, Lud Wray, July 9; named team "Eagles." Boston changed name to "Redskins." George Halas bought out Ed (Dutch) Sternaman, became sole owner of Chicago Bears, reinstated himself as head coach. David Jones sold Cardinals to Charles W. Bidwill, Cincinnati Reds joined league.

Eastern Division champion New York Giants met Western Division champion Bears at Wrigley Field in first NFL championship game, Dec. 17. Bears won 23-21.

1934 Bears played scoreless tie against collegians in first Chicago All-Star Game before 79,432 at Soldier Field, Aug. 31.

NFL legalized forward passes anywhere behind line of scrimmage.

G.A. (Dick) Richards purchased Portsmouth Spartans, moved them to Detroit, June 30; they took name "Lions." Cincinnati Reds franchise moved during season, became St. Louis Gunners.

Player waiver rule adopted, Dec. 10.

Grange retired from football.

1935 Bell of Philadelphia proposed, NFL adopted annual draft of college players, to begin in 1936, with team finishing last in standings having first choice each round of draft, May 19.

Cincinnati Reds-St. Louis Gunners franchise died.

Inbounds lines or hashmarks moved nearer center of field, 15 yards from sidelines.

1936 No franchise shifts for first time since formation of NFL and for first time all teams played same number of games.

Last place previous year, Philadelphia Eagles made Jay Berwanger, University of Chicago back, first choice in first NFL draft, Feb. 8. Eagles later traded negotiation rights to him to Bears. He never played pro football.

Rival league was formed, became second to call itself American Football League. It included six teams, Boston Shamrocks won championship.

1937 Cleveland returned to NFL. Homer Marshman was granted a franchise, Feb. 12; he named new team "Rams." Marshall moved Redskins to Washington, Feb. 13.

Los Angeles Bulldogs had 8-0 record in American Football League; six-team league folded.

1938 Fifteen-yard penalty adopted for roughing passer.

Hugh (Shorty) Ray became technical advisor on rules and officiating in NFL. Marshall, Los Angeles newspaper officials established Pro Bowl game between NFL champion, team of all-stars.

1939 New York Giants defeated Pro All-Stars 13-10 in first Pro Bowl game at Wrigley Field, Los Angeles, Jan. 15.

Carr, NFL president since 1921, died in Columbus, May 20. Carl Storck named successor, May 25.

National Broadcasting Company camera beamed Brooklyn Dodgers-Philadelphia Eagles game from Ebbets Field back to studios of network, handful of sets then in New York City,

first NFL game to be televised.

1940 Clipping penalty reduced from 25 to 15 yards, all distance penalties enforced from spot on field of play limited to half distance to goal, Apr. 12.

Pittsburgh changed nickname from Pirates to Steelers.

Rival league formed, became third to call itself American Football League. It included six teams, Columbus, Ohio, Bullies won championship.

Art Rooney sold Pittsburgh to Alexis Thompson, Dec. 9, and later purchased part-interest in Philadelphia.

Bears, playing T-formation with man-in-motion, defeated Washington 73-0 in NFL championship, Dec. 8. It was first championship game carried on network radio, broadcast by Red Barber to 120 stations of Mutual Broadcasting System, which paid $2,500 for rights.

1941 Elmer Layden, head coach, athletic director at Notre Dame, named first commissioner of NFL, March 1. Moved league headquarters to Chicago. Carl Storck resigned as president-secretary, Apr. 5.

Co-owners Bell, Rooney of Eagles transferred them to Alexis Thompson in exchange for Pittsburgh franchise. Homer Marshman, associates sold Cleveland Rams to Daniel F. Reeves, Fred Levy, Jr., June 1.

Playoffs were provided for in case of ties in division races. Sudden death overtime provided for in case playoff was tied after four quarters.

Columbus won championship of five-team American Football League; it folded.

Bears defeated Green Bay 33-14 in first divisional playoff in NFL history, winning Western Division championship, Dec. 14.

1942 Players departing for service in World War II reduced rosters of NFL teams. Halas left Bears for armed forces, was replaced by co-coaches Hunk Anderson, Luke Johnsos.

1943 Cleveland Rams, with co-owners Lt. Daniel F. Reeves, Maj. Fred Levy, Jr., in service, granted permission to suspend operations for one season, April 6. Levy transferred his stock in team to Reeves, Apr. 16.

NFL adopted free substitution, Apr. 7. Abbreviated wartime rosters, however, prevented its effects from taking place immediately.

Philadelphia, Pittsburgh granted permission to merge, became Phil-Pitt, June 19. They divided home games between two cities, Greasy Neale, Walt Kiesling were co-coaches. Merger automatically dissolved last day of season, Dec. 5.

Ted Collins granted franchise for Boston to become active in 1944.

1944 Collins, who had wanted franchise in Yankee Stadium in New York, named new team in Boston "Yanks." Cleveland resumed operations. Brooklyn Dodgers changed name to "Tigers."

Cardinals, Pittsburgh requested by league to merge for one year under name, Card-Pitt, Apr. 21. Merger automatically dissolved last day of season, Dec. 3.

Coaching from bench legalized, Apr. 20.

1945 Inbounds lines or hashmarks moved nearer center of field, 20 yards from sidelines. Players required to wear long stockings, Apr. 9.

Boston Yanks, Brooklyn Tigers merger as "Yanks," Apr. 10.

Halas rejoined Bears after service with U.S. Navy in Pacific. Returned to head coaching.

After Japanese surrender ending World War II, count showed NFL service roster, limited to men who played in league games, totaled 638, 21 of whom had died.

1946 Layden resigned as commissioner, replaced by Bell, co-owner of Pittsburgh Steelers, Jan. 11. Bell moved league headquarters from Chicago to Philadelphia suburb of Bala Cynwyd.

Free substitution withdrawn, substitutions limited to no more than three men at time. Forward passes made automatically incomplete upon striking goal posts, Jan. 11.

NFL champion Cleveland given permission to transfer to Los Angeles, Jan. 12. NFL became coast-to-coast league first time.

Rival league, All-America Football Conference, formed. Four of its eight teams were in same population centers as NFL teams — Brooklyn Dodgers, New York Yankees, Chicago Rockets, Los Angeles Dons. Cleveland Browns won AAFC championship.

Backs Frank Filchock and Merle Hapes of the Giants questioned about attempt by New York man to fix championship game vs. Chicago; Commissioner Bell suspended Hapes, permitted Filchock to play. He played well but Chicago won 24-14.

1947 Bell's contract as commissioner was renewed for five years, Jan. 1; same day NFL Constitution amended imposing major penalty for anyone not reporting offer of bribe, attempt to fix game, or any other infraction of rules having to do with gambling.

NFL added fifth official, back judge. Sudden death readopted for championship games, Jan. 24.

"Bonus" draft choice made for first time; one team each year would get special bonus choice before first round began.

Halfback Fred Gehrke of Los Angeles Rams painted horns on Rams' helmets, first helmet emblems in pro football.

AAFC again had eight teams, Cleveland Browns won second championship.

1948 Plastic head protectors prohibited. Flexible artificial tee permitted at kickoff. Officials besides referee equipped with whistles, not horns, Jan. 14.

Fred Mandel sold Lions to syndicate headed by D. Lyle Fife, Jan. 15.

Cleveland Browns won third straight championship of eight-team AAFC.

1949 Thompson sold NFL champion Philadelphia Eagles to syndicate headed by James P. Clark, Jan. 15.

Commissioner Bell, vice president and treasurer Dennis Shea, given 10-year contracts, Jan. 20.

Free substitution adopted for one year, Jan. 20.

Boston Yanks became New York Bulldogs, shared Polo Grounds with Giants.

Cleveland won fourth straight championship of AAFC, reduced to seven teams. Bell announced merger agreement Dec. 9 in which three AAFC teams — Cleveland, San Francisco 49ers, Baltimore Colts — would enter NFL in 1950.

1950 Free substitution restored, way opened for two-platoon era, specialization in pro football, Jan. 23.

Name "National Football League" returned after about three months as "National-American Football League." American, National conferences replaced Eastern, Western divisions, Mar. 3.

New York Bulldogs became "Yanks," divided players of former AAFC Yankees with Giants. Special allocation draft held in which 13 teams drafted remaining AAFC players, with special consideration for Baltimore, 15 choices compared to 10 for other teams.

Los Angeles Rams became first NFL team to contract to have all its games televised. Arrangement covered both home and away games, sponsor agreed to make up difference in home game income if lower than year before (cost sponsor $307,000). Washington also arranged to televise games, other teams made deals to put selected games on television.

For first time in history deadlocks occurred, playoffs were necessary in both conferences (divisions). Cleveland defeated Giants in American, Los Angeles defeated Bears in National. In one of the most exciting championship games, Cleveland defeated Los Angeles 30-28, Dec. 24.

1951 Pro Bowl game, dormant since 1942, revived under new format matching all-stars of each conference at Los Angeles Memorial Coliseum. American Conference defeated National 28-27, Jan. 14.

Abraham Watner returned Baltimore Colts franchise to league, was voted $50,000 for Colts' players, Jan. 18.

Rule passed that no tackle, guard, or center eligible for forward pass, Jan. 18.

DuMont Network paid $75,000 for rights to championship game, televised coast-to-coast for first time, Los Angeles defeated Cleveland 24-17, Dec. 23.

1952 Ted Collins sold New York Yanks' franchise to NFL, Jan. 19. New franchise awarded to Dallas Texans, first NFL team in Texas, Jan. 24. Yanks had been, in order, Boston Yanks, New York Bulldogs, New York Yanks. Texans, won 1, lost 11, folded, last NFL team to become extinct.

Pittsburgh Steelers abandoned single wing for T formation, last pro team to do so.

Los Angeles reversed television policy, aired only road games.

1953 Baltimore re-entered NFL. League awarded holdings of defunct Dallas franchise to group headed by Carroll Rosenbloom that formed team with name "Colts," same as former franchise, Jan. 23.

Names of American, National Conferences changed to Eastern, Western Conferences, Jan. 24.

Thorpe died, Mar. 28.

Arthur McBride sold Cleveland to syndicate headed by Dave R. Jones, June 10.

NFL policy of blacking out television of home games upheld by Judge Allan K. Grim of U.S. District Court in Philadelphia, Nov. 12.

1954 Bell given new 12-year contract.

1955 Sudden death overtime rule used for first time, on experimental basis in preseason game between Los Angeles, New York at Portland, Ore., Aug. 28. Los Angeles won 23-17 three minutes into overtime.

Runners could advance ball, even by crawling along ground, until stopped, sometimes leading to rough play. As result, rules changed so ball declared dead immediately if player touched ground with any part of body except hands or feet while in grasp of opponent.

Quarterback Otto Graham played last game for Cleveland, 38-14 victory over Los Angeles for NFL championship.

NBC replaced DuMont as network for title game, paying rights fee of $100,000.

1956 Halas retired as coach of Bears, replaced by Paddy Driscoll. Giants moved from Polo Grounds to Yankee Stadium.

Grabbing opponent's facemask made illegal, with exception of ball carrier's. "Loudspeaker coaching" from sidelines prohibited. Brown ball with white stripes replaced white with black stripes for night games. Language of "dead ball rule" improved, stipulating ball dead when runner contacted by defensive player and touched ground with any part of body except hands and feet.

CBS became first to broadcast some NFL regular season games to selected television markets across nation.

Hugh (Shorty) Ray, former NFL rules advisor and rules author, died.

1957 Pete Rozelle named general manager of Los Angeles. Anthony J. Morabito, founder, co-owner of 49ers died of heart attack during game against Bears, Oct. 28. Then NFL record crowd, 102,368, saw 49ers-Rams game at Los Angeles Memorial Coliseum, Nov. 10. Detroit Lions came from 20 points down for playoff victory over 49ers 31-27, Dec. 22.

1958 "Bonus" draft choice eliminated, Jan. 29.

Halas reinstated himself as Bears coach for third time; others were in 1933, 1946.

Jim Brown of Cleveland gained NFL-record 1,527 yards rushing.

Baltimore, coached by Weeb Ewbank, defeated New York 23-17 in first sudden death NFL championship game, Alan Ameche scoring for Colts after 8 minutes, 15 seconds of overtime, Dec. 28.

1959 Tim Mara, co-founder of Giants, died, Feb. 17.

Lamar Hunt announced intentions to form second pro football league. Hunt representing Dallas, others representing Denver, Houston, Los Angeles, Minneapolis-St. Paul, New York City held first meeting of league at Chicago, Aug. 14. Made plans to begin play in 1960. Eight days later at second meeting announced name of organization would be "American Football League." Buffalo became seventh AFL team, Oct. 28, Boston eighth, Nov. 22. First AFL draft held, Nov. 22. Joe Foss named AFL commissioner, Nov. 30. Second draft held, Dec. 2.

NFL commissioner Bell died of heart attack suffered at Franklin Field, Philadelphia, during last two minutes of game between Eagles-Pittsburgh, Oct. 11. Treasurer Austin Gunsel named President in office of Commissioner until January, 1960, annual meeting, Oct. 14.

1960 Pete Rozelle elected NFL commissioner on twenty-third ballot, succeeding Bell, Jan. 26.

Hunt, founder of AFL, elected president for 1960, Jan. 26. Oakland become eighth AFL team, Jan. 30. Eastern, Western divisions set up,

Jan. 30. Five-year contact signed with American Broadcasting Company for network televising of selected games, June 9.

AFL adopted two-point option on points after touchdown, one point if successful kick, two for successful run or pass across goal line from 2-yard line, Jan. 28.

NFL awarded Dallas 1960 franchise, Minnesota 1961 franchise, expanding to 14 teams, Jan. 28. They took nicknames "Cowboys," "Vikings."

"No-tampering" verbal pact, relative to players' contracts, agreed to between NFL, AFL, Feb. 9.

Chicago Cardinals transferred to St. Louis, Mar. 13.

Boston Patriots defeated Bills 28-7 at Buffalo in first AFL preseason game before 16,000, July 30. Denver Broncos defeated Patriots 13-10 at Boston in first AFL regular season game before 21,597, Sept. 9.

1961 Houston Oilers defeated Los Angeles Chargers 24-16 for first AFL championship before 32,183 at Houston, Jan. 1.

Detroit defeated Cleveland 17-16 in first Playoff Bowl, or Bert Bell Benefit Bowl, between second-place teams in each conference in Miami, Jan. 7.

End Willard Dewveall of Bears played out his option, joined Houston of AFL, first player to deliberately move from one league to other, Jan. 14.

Ed McGah, Wayne Valley, Robert Osborne bought out their partners in ownership of Oakland Raiders, Jan. 17. Chargers transferred to San Diego, Feb. 10. Dave R. Jones sold Cleveland to group headed by Arthur B. Modell, Mar. 22. Howsam brothers sold Denver to group headed by Calvin Kunz, Gerry Phipps, May 26.

NBC awarded two-year contract for radio and television rights to NFL championship game for $615,000 annually, $300,000 of which was to go directly into NFL Player Benefit Plan, Apr. 5.

Canton, where league that became NFL had been formed in 1920, chosen site of Pro Football Hall of Fame, Apr. 27.

Bill legalizing single network television contracts by professional sports leagues introduced in Congress by Rep. Emanuel Celler passed House, Senate, signed into law by President John F. Kennedy, Sept. 30.

Green Bay won first NFL championship since 1944, defeating New York 37-0, Dec. 31.

1962 West defeated East 47-27 in first AFL All-Star Game before 20,973 in San Diego, Jan. 7.

NFL prohibited grabbing any player's facemask, Jan. 9.

Commissioners Rozelle of NFL, Foss of AFL given new five-year contracts, Jan. 8, 9.

NFL entered into single network agreement with CBS for telecasting all regular season games for $4,650,000 annually, Jan. 10.

Judge Roszel Thompson of U.S. District Court, Baltimore, ruled against AFL in antitrust suit against NFL, May 21. AFL had charged monopoly, conspiracy in areas of expansion, television, player signings. Case lasted two and a half years, trial lasted two months.

McGah, Valley acquired controlling interest in Oakland, May 24. AFL assumed financial responsibility for

New York Titans, Nov. 8. Dan Reeves purchased partners' stock in Los Angeles Rams, becoming majority owner, Dec. 27.

Dallas defeated Oilers 20-17 for AFL championship at Houston after 17 minutes, 54 seconds of sudden death overtime on 25-yard field goal by Tommy Brooker, Dec. 23. Game lasted record 77 minutes, 54 seconds.

Judge Edward Weinfeld of U.S. District Court, New York City, upheld legality of NFL's television blackout within 75-mile radius of home games, denied injunction sought by persons who had demanded championship between Giants, Green Bay be televised in New York City area, Dec. 28.

1963 AFL's guarantee for visiting teams during regular season increased from $20,000 to $30,000, Jan. 10.

Hunt's Dallas Texans transferred to Kansas City, becoming "Chiefs," Feb. 8. New York Titans sold to five-member syndicate headed by David (Sonny) Werblin, name changed to "Jets," Mar. 28.

Commissioner Rozelle suspended indefinitely Paul Hornung, Green Bay halfback, Alex Karras, Detroit defensive tackle, for placing bets on their own teams and on other games; also fined five other Detroit players $2,000 each for betting on one game in which they did not participate, and the Detroit Lions Football Co. $2,000 on each of two counts for failure to report promptly information and for lack of sideline supervision.

AFL allowed New York, Oakland to select players from other franchises in hopes of giving league more competitive balance, May 11.

NBC awarded exclusive network broadcasting rights for 1963 AFL championship game for $926,000, May 23.

U.S. Fourth Circuit Court of Appeals reaffirmed lower court's finding for NFL in $10-million suit brought by AFL, ending three and a half years of litigation, Nov. 21.

Boston defeated Buffalo 26-8 in first divisional playoff in AFL history before 33,044 in Buffalo, Dec. 28.

Chicago defeated New York 14-10 for NFL championship, record sixth and last title for Halas in his thirty-sixth season as Bears' coach, Dec. 29.

1964 William Clay Ford, their president since 1961, purchased Detroit, Jan. 10. Group representing late James P. Clark sold Philadelphia to group headed by Jerry Wolman, Jan. 21. Carroll Rosenbloom, majority owner since 1953, acquired complete ownership of Baltimore, Jan. 23.

CBS submitted winning bid of $14.1 million per year for NFL regular season television rights for 1964, 1965, Jan. 24. CBS acquired rights to 1964, 1965 NFL championship games for $1.8 million per game, Apr. 17. AFL signed five-year, $36-million television contract with NBC to begin with 1965 season, assuring each team approximately $900,000 a year from television rights, Jan. 29.

Paul Hornung of Green Bay, Alex Karras of Detroit reinstated by Rozelle, Mar. 16.

Paul Brown departed Cleveland after 17 years as their head coach, Blanton Collier replaced him.

AFL commissioner Foss given new three-year contract commencing in 1965, May 22.

New York defeated Denver 30-6 before then AFL-record crowd of 46,665 in first game at Shea Stadium, Sept. 12.

Pete Gogolak of Cornell signed contract with Buffalo, becoming first soccer-style kicker in pro football.

1965 NFL teams pledged not to sign college seniors until completion of all their games, including bowl games, empowered commissioner to discipline clubs up to as much as loss of entire draft list for violation of pledge, Feb. 15.

NFL added sixth official, line judge, Feb. 19. Color of officials' penalty flags changed from white to bright gold, Apr. 5.

Atlanta awarded NFL franchise for 1966, with Rankin Smith as owner, June 30. Miami awarded AFL franchise for 1966, with Joe Robbie, Danny Thomas as owners, Aug. 16.

Green Bay defeated Baltimore 13-10 in sudden death Western Conference playoff game, Don Chandler kicking 25-yard field goal for Packers after 13 minutes, 39 seconds of overtime, Dec. 26.

CBS acquired rights to NFL regular season games in 1966, 1967, plus option for 1968, for $18.8 million per year, Dec. 29.

1966 AFL-NFL war reached its peak, leagues spent combined total of $7 million to sign 1966 draft choices. NFL signed 75 percent of its 232 draftees, AFL 46 percent of its 181. Of 111 common draft choices, 79 joined NFL, 28 joined AFL, four went unsigned.

Rights to NFL 1966, 1967 championship games sold to CBS for $2 million per game, Feb. 14.

Joe Foss resigned as AFL commissioner, Apr. 7. Al Davis, head coach, general manager of Oakland Raiders, named to replace him, Apr. 8.

Goal posts offset from goal line, colored bright gold, with uprights 20 feet above crossbar made standard in NFL, May 16.

Merger announced; NFL, AFL entered into agreement to form combined league of 24 teams, expanding to 26 in 1968, June 8. Rozelle named commissioner. Leagues agreed to play separate schedules until 1970, but would meet, starting in 1967, in world championship game (Super Bowl) and play each other in preseason games.

Davis rejoined Oakland Raiders, Milt Woodard named president of AFL, July 25.

Barron Hilton sold San Diego to group headed by Eugene Klein, Sam Schulman, Aug. 25.

Congress approved merger, passing special legislation exempting agreement itself from anti-trust action, Oct. 21.

New Orleans awarded NFL franchise to begin play in 1967, Nov. 1.

NFL realigned for 1967-69 seasons into Capitol, Century divisions in Eastern Conference, Central, Coastal divisions in Western Conference, Dec. 2. New Orleans, New York agreed to switch divisions in 1968, return to 1967 alignment in 1969.

Rights to Super Bowl for four years sold to CBS and NBC for $9.5 million, Dec. 13.

1967 Green Bay Packers of NFL defeated Kansas City of AFL 35-10 at Los Angeles in first Super Bowl, Jan. 15. Winning share for Packers was $15,000 each, losing share for Chiefs $7,500 each.

"Sling-shot" goal post, six-foot-wide border around field made standard in NFL, Feb. 22.

Baltimore made Bubba Smith, Michigan State defensive lineman, first choice in first combined AFL-NFL draft, Mar. 14.

AFL awarded franchise to Cincinnati, to begin play in 1968, with Paul Brown as part-owner, general manager, head coach, May 24.

Arthur B. Modell, president of the Cleveland Browns, elected president of the NFL, May 28.

AFL team defeated NFL team for first time, Denver beat Detroit 13-7 in preseason game, Aug. 5.

Green Bay defeated Dallas 21-17 for NFL championship on last-minute one-yard quarterback sneak by Bart Starr in 13-below temperature at Green Bay, Dec. 31.

George Halas retired fourth and last time as head coach of Chicago Bears at age 73.

1968 Green Bay defeated Oakland 33-14 in Super Bowl II at Miami, game had first $3-million gate in pro football history, Jan. 14.

Lombardi resigned as head coach of Packers, remained as general manager.

Sonny Werblin sold his shares in New York Jets to partners Don Lillis, Leon Hess, Townsend Martin, Phil Iselin, May 21. Lillis assumed presidency of Jets, May 21. Lillis died, July 23. Iselin appointed president, Aug. 6.

Ewbank became first coach to win titles in both NFL, AFL, his Jets defeated Oakland 27-23 for AFL championship, Dec. 29.

1969 AFL established format of interdivisional playoffs with winner in one division playing runner-up in other, for 1969 only, Jan. 11.

AFL team won Super Bowl for first time; Jets defeated Baltimore 16-7 at Miami, Jan. 12.

Lombardi became part-owner, executive vice president, head coach of Washington Redskins.

NFL and AFL scrapped preseason experiment "Pressure Point" run or pass one-point conversion tried in 1969, Mar. 20.

Wolman sold Philadelphia Eagles to Leonard Tose, May 1.

Baltimore, Cleveland, Pittsburgh agreed to join AFL teams to form 13-team American Football Conference, remaining NFL teams to form National Football Conference in NFL in 1970, May 17. AFC teams voted to realign in Eastern, Central, Western divisions.

Monday night football set for 1970; ABC acquired rights to televise 13 NFL regular season Monday night games in 1970, 1971, 1972.

George P. Marshall, president emeritus of Redskins, died at 72, Aug. 9.

1970 Kansas City defeated Minnesota 23-7 in Super Bowl IV at New Orleans, Jan. 11. Gross receipts of approximately $3.8 million largest ever for one-day team sports event, television audience largest ever for one-day sports event.

NFC realigned into Eastern, Central, Western divisions, Jan. 16.

CBS acquired rights to televise all NFC games, except Monday night games, in 1970-73, including divisional playoffs and NFC championship, also rights to Super Bowl in 1972, 1974, AFC-NFC Pro Bowl in 1971, 1973, Jan. 26.

NBC acquired rights to televise all AFC games, except Monday night games, in 1970-73, including divisional playoffs and AFC championship, also rights to Super Bowl in 1971, 1973, AFC-NFC Pro Bowl in 1972, 1974, Jan. 26.

Art Modell resigned as president of NFL, Mar. 12. Milt Woodard resigned as president of AFL, Mar. 13. Lamar Hunt elected president of AFC, George S. Halas, Sr., elected president of NFC, Mar. 19.

Merged league adopted rules changes putting names on backs of players' jerseys, making Wilson brand official football of league, making point after touchdown worth one point, making scoreboard clock official timing device of game, Mar. 18.

Players Negotiating Committee, NFL Players Association announced four-year agreement guaranteeing approximately $4,535,000 annually to player pension, insurance benefits, Aug. 3. Owners also agreed to contribute $250,000 annually to improve or implement such items as disability payments, widows' benefits, maternity benefits, dental benefits. Agreement also provided for increased preseason game and per diem payments averaging approximately $2,600,000 annually.

Lombardi, part-owner, executive vice president, head coach of Redskins, died at 57, Sept. 3.

Tom Dempsey of New Orleans Saints kicked game-winning NFL-record 63-yard field goal against Detroit Lions, Nov. 8.

1971 Baltimore defeated Dallas 16-13 on Jim O'Brien's 32-yard field goal with five seconds to go in Super Bowl V at Miami, Jan. 17. NBC telecast was viewed in estimated 23,980,000 homes, largest audience ever for one-day sports event.

NFC defeated AFC 27-6 in first AFC-NFC Pro Bowl at Los Angeles, Jan. 24.

Boston Patriots changed name to New England Patriots, Mar. 25.

Rules change adopted making sole criteria for determining intentional grounding whether passer was making deliberate attempt to prevent loss of yardage, Mar. 25.

Reeves, president, general manager of Rams, died at 58, Apr. 15.

Miami defeated Kansas City 27-24 in sudden death in AFC divisional playoff game, Garo Yepremian kicking 37-yard field goal for Dolphins after 22 minutes, 40 seconds of overtime, game lasting 82 minutes, 40 seconds in all, longest in history, Dec. 25.

1972 Dallas defeated Miami 24-3 in Super Bowl VI at Miami, Jan. 16. CBS telecast was viewed in estimated 27,450,000 homes, top-rated one-day telecast ever.

Inbounds lines or hashmarks moved nearer center of field, 23 yards, 1 foot, 9 inches from sidelines, Mar. 23. Exception made to the rule allowing team in possession on its own 15 yard line or within put ball in play at spot 20 yards from nearest sideline so it could punt without direct conflict with goal post, May 24.

Method of determining won-lost percentage in standings changed, May 24. Tie games, previously not counted in standings, made equal to half-game won and half-game lost.

Hunt, Halas, reelected presidents of AFC, NFC, May 25.

Robert Irsay purchased Los Angeles, tranferred ownership to Carroll Rosenbloom in exchange for Baltimore, July 13.

William V. Bidwill purchased stock of brother Charles (Stormy) Bidwill, became sole owner, president of St. Louis Cardinals, Sept. 2.

National District Attorneys Association endorsed position of professional leagues in opposing proposed legalization of gambling in professional team sports, Sept. 28.

1973 Rozelle announced all Super Bowl VII tickets sold, game would be telecast in Los Angeles, site of game, on experimental basis, Jan. 3.

Miami defeated Washington 14-7 in Super Bowl VII at Los Angeles, completing undefeated 17-0 record for 1972 season, Jan. 14. NBC telecast viewed by approximately 75,000,000 people. Although all 90,182 tickets had been sold and temperature reached 84 degrees on clear, sunny day, 8,476 ticket buyers did not attend game that was first ever televised locally.

AFC defeated NFC 33-28 in Pro Bowl in Dallas, first time since 1951 game played outside Los Angeles, Jan. 21.

Jersey numbering system adopted, 1-19 for quarterbacks, specialists; 20-49, running, defensive backs; 50-59, centers, linebackers; 60-79, defensive linemen, interior offensive linemen except centers; 80-89, wide receivers, tight ends, Apr. 5. Players who had been in NFL in 1972 could continue to use old numbers.

Dan Rooney of Pittsburgh appointed chairman of Expansion Committee, Apr. 6.

NFL Charities non-profit organization created to derive income from monies generated by licensing of NFL trademarks and names, June 26; would support education, charitable activities, supply economic support to persons formerly associated with professional football no longer able to support themselves.

Congress adopted for three years experimental legislation requiring any NFL game that had been declared a sellout 72 hours prior to kick-off to be made available for local telecast, Sept. 14. Legislation provided for annual review to be made by Federal Communications Commission.

1974 Miami defeated Minnesota 24-7 in Super Bowl VIII at Houston, second straight Super Bowl championship for Miami, Jan. 13. CBS telecast viewed by approximately 75 million people.

Rival league formed; World Football League held organizational meeting, Jan. 14.

Rozelle given 10-year contract effective January 1, 1973, Feb. 27.

Tampa awarded franchise to begin play in 1976, Apr. 24. NFL announced one more franchise would be awarded to become operative in 1976.

Sweeping rules changes adopted as recommended by Competition Committee to add action, tempo to game: sudden death for preseason, regular season games, limited to one 15-minute overtime; goal posts moved from goal line to end lines; kickoffs to be made from 35 not 40 yard line; after missed field goals ball to be returned to line of scrimmage or 20 yard line, whichever is farthest from goal line; restrictions placed on members of punting team to open up return possibilities; roll-blocking, cutting of wide receivers eliminated; extent of downfield contact defender can have with eligible receivers restricted; penalty for offensive holding, illegal use of hands, tripping reduced from 15 yards to 10 yards when occurs within three yards of line of scrimmage; wide receivers blocking back toward ball within three yards of line of scrimmage prevented from blocking below the waist, Apr. 25.

Toronto Northmen of World Football League signed Larry Csonka, Jim Kiick, Paul Warfield of Miami, Mar. 31.

Seattle awarded NFL franchise to begin play in 1976, June 4. Lloyd W. Nordstrom, president of Seattle Seahawks, Hugh F. Culverhouse, president of Tampa Bay Buccaneers, sign franchise agreement, Dec. 5.

Birmingham Americans defeated Florida Blazers 22-21 in WFL World Bowl, winning championship of the 12-team league, Dec.5.

1975 Pittsburgh defeated Minnesota 16-6 in Super Bowl IX at New Orleans, Steelers' first championship since entering NFL in 1933. NBC telecast was viewed by approximately 78 million people.

Rules changed making incomplete pass into end zone on fourth down with line of scrimmage inside 20 returned to line of scrimmage instead of 20; double shift on or inside opponent's 20 permitted provided it has been shown three times in game instead of three times in quarter; penalty for ineligible receiver downfield reduced from 15 to 10 yards, Mar. 19.

Divisional winners with highest won-lost percentage made home teams for playoffs, surviving winners with highest percentage made home teams for championship games, June 26.

World Football League folded, Oct. 22.

1976 Pittsburgh defeated Dallas 21-17 in Super Bowl X in Miami; Steelers joined Green Bay, Miami as two-time winners of Super Bowl, CBS telecast viewed by estimated 80 million people, largest television audience in history.

Lloyd Nordstrom, president of Seattle, died at 66, Jan. 20. His brother Elmer succeeded him as majority representative of the team.

Veteran player allocation held to stock Seattle, Tampa Bay franchises with 39 players each, Mar. 30-31. College draft held, with Seattle, Tampa Bay getting eight extra choices each, Apr. 8-9.

Steelers defeated College All-Stars 24-0 in storm-shortened final Chicago All-Star Game, July 23. St. Louis defeated San Diego 20-10 in preseason game before 38,000 in Korakuen Stadium, Tokyo, in first NFL game outside North America, Aug. 16.

1977 Oakland defeated Minnesota 32-14 before record crowd of 100,421 in Super Bowl XI at Pasadena, Jan. 9. Paid attendance was pro-record 103,438. NBC telecast was viewed by 81.9 million people, largest ever to view sports event. Victory was fifth straight for AFC in Super Bowl.

Players Association, NFL Management Council ratified collective bargaining agreement extending until July 15, 1982, covering five football seasons while continuing pension plan — including years 1974, 1975 and 1976 — with contributions totaling more than $55 million. Total cost of agreement estimated at $107 million. Agreement called for college draft at least through 1986, contained no-strike, no-suit clause, established 43-man active player limit, reducing pension vesting to four years, provided for increases in minimum salaries, preseason and postseason pay, improved insurance, medical, dental benefits, modified previous practices in player movement and control. Reaffirmed NFL commissioner's disciplinary authority. Additionally, agreement called for NFL member clubs to make payments totaling $16 million the next 10 years to settle various legal disputes, Feb. 25.

NFL regular season paid attendance was record 11,070,543.

San Francisco 49ers sold to Edward J. DeBartolo, Jr., Mar. 28.

Sixteen-game regular season, four-game preseason adopted to begin in 1978, Mar. 29. Second wild card team adopted for playoffs beginning in 1978, wild card teams to play each other with winners advancing to round of eight postseason series along with six division winners.

Defender permitted to contact eligible receiver either in three-yard zone at or beyond line of scrimmage or once beyond that zone, but not both, Mar. 31. Wide receivers prohibited from clipping anywhere, even in legal clipping zone. Penalty of loss of coin toss option in addition to 15-yard penalty provided if team does not arrive on field for warmup at least 15 minutes prior to scheduled kickoff.

Seattle Seahawks permanently aligned in AFC Western Division, Tampa Bay in NFC Central Division, Mar. 31.

NFL decided to experiment with seventh official in selected preseason games, Apr. 1.

Rules changes made it illegal to strike an opponent above shoulders (head slap) during initial charge of a defensive lineman; made it illegal for an offensive lineman to thrust his hands to an opponent's neck, face, or head; made it illegal for a back who lines up inside the tight end to break to the outside and then cut back inside to deliver a block below the waist of an opponent. Also, if a punting team commits a foul before its opponent takes possession and the receiving team subsequently commits a foul, the penalties offset each other and the down is replayed, June 14-15.

Commissioner Rozelle confirmed that agreements were negotiated with the three television networks — ABC, CBS, and NBC — to televise all NFL regular season and postseason games, plus selected preseason games, for four years beginning with the 1978 season. ABC was awarded rights to 16 Monday night, four prime time (with possible expansion to six during the last three years of the contract), the AFC-NFC Pro Bowl, and the AFC-NFC Hall of Fame games. CBS received rights to all NFC regular season and postseason games (except those in the ABC package) and Super Bowls XIV (1980) and XVI (1982). NBC received rights to all AFC regular season and postseason games (except those in the ABC package) and Super Bowls XIII (1979) and XV (1981). Industry sources considered it the largest single television package ever negotiated, October.

Chicago's Walter Payton set a single-game rushing record with 275 yards (40 carries) against Minnesota, Nov. 20.

Cincinnati defeated Kansas City 27-7 at Arrowhead Stadium in the NFL's 5,000th game in recorded history, Dec. 4.

1978 Dallas defeated Denver 27-10 in Super Bowl XII, held indoors for the first time, at the Louisiana Superdome in New Orleans, Jan. 15. CBS telecast viewed by 102,010,000 people, meaning the game was watched by more viewers than any other show of any kind in the history of televison. Dallas's win was first NFC victory in last six Super Bowls.

According to Harris Sports Survey, 70 percent of the nation's sports fans say they follow football, compared to 54 percent who follow baseball. As far as fans' favorite sport, football increased its lead as the country's favorite to 26 to 16 percent over baseball, Jan. 19.

NFL regular season paid attendance was 11,018,632. In addition, during five years of TV blackout legislation, percent of capacity in NFL attendance has declined from record level of 95.5 percent in 1973 to 87.8 percent in 1977. NFL had over 1.5 million unsold seats in 1977, compared to fewer than one-half million in 1973.

Added seventh official, side judge, Mar. 14.

Study on the use of instant replay as an officiating aid to be made during seven nationally televised preseason games in 1978, Mar. 16.

Rules changes adopted permitting defender to maintain contact on receivers within a five-yard zone beyond scrimmage line, but restricted contact on receivers beyond that point; further clarified the pass blocking rule interpretation to permit extended arms and open hands, Mar. 17.

The NFL played for the first time in Mexico City with the Saints defeating the Eagles, 14-7, in a preseason game before a sellout crowd, Aug. 5.

1979 Pittsburgh defeated Dallas 35-31 in Super Bowl XIII to become the first team ever to win three Super Bowls, Jan. 21. Super Bowl XIII was the top-ranked TV sporting event of all time, according to figures compiled by A.C. Nielsen Co. The NBC telecast was viewed in 35,090,000 homes, which bettered the previous record of Super Bowl XII with 34,410,000.

Bolstered by the expansion of the regular season schedule from 14 to 16 weeks, the NFL paid attendance exceeded 12 million (12,771,800) for the first time. The per-game average of 57,017 was the third highest in league history and best since 1973.

Rules changes emphasized additional player safety: prohibited players on the receiving team from blocking below the waist during kickoffs, punts, and field goal attempts; prohibited wearing of torn or altered equipment and exposed pads that may be hazardous; extended the zone in which there can be no crackback blocks from three yards on either side of the line of scrimmage to five yards in order to provide a greater measure of protection; permitted free activation of three players from the injured reserve list after the final cutdown to 45 players, Mar. 16.

Commissioner Pete Rozelle announced that the 1980 AFC-NFC Pro Bowl Game would be played at Aloha Stadium in Honolulu, Hawaii. This would mark the first time in the 30-year history of the Pro Bowl that the game would be played in a non-NFL city.

Carroll D. Rosenbloom, president of the Rams, died at 72, April 2.

1980 Nielsen figures showed that the CBS telecast of Super Bowl XIV between Pittsburgh and Los Angeles was the most watched sports event of all time. It was viewed in 35,330,000 homes.

Rules changes adopted placed greater restrictions on contact in the area of the head, neck, and face. Under the heading of "Personal Foul," players have been prohibited from directly striking, swinging, or clubbing on the head, neck, or face. Starting in 1980, a penalty may be called for such contact to the head, neck, or face whether or not the initial contact is made below the neck area.

The NFL entered into an agreement with the National Athletic Injury/Illness Reporting System (NAIRS) to proceed with developing a program to study injuries.

CBS, with a record bid of $12 million, won the national radio rights to 26 National Football League regular season games and all 10 postseason games for the 1980 through 1983 seasons.

NFL regular season attendance of nearly 13.4 million set a record for the second year in a row; 1979's total was 13.2 million. Average paid attendance for the 224-game 1980 regular season was 59,787, highest in the league's 61-year history. The previous high was 58,961 for 182 games in 1973. NFL games in 1980 were played before 92.4 percent of total stadium capacity.

Television ratings in 1980 were the second-best in NFL history, trailing only the combined ratings of the 1976 season.

1981 The Oakland Raiders became the first wild card team to win the Super Bowl by defeating Philadelphia 27-10 at the Louisiana Superdome in New Orleans, Jan. 25. The Raiders finished second to San Diego in the AFC Western Division. In the playoffs they beat Houston at Oakland and Cleveland and San Diego on the road to advance to the Super Bowl.

The 1980 season concluded with a record Aloha Stadium crowd viewing the NFC's win over the AFC in the annual AFC-NFC Pro Bowl game in Honolulu, Feb. 1. It was the second straight sellout of the game in Honolulu.

Industrialist Edgar F. Kaiser, Jr., purchased the Denver Broncos from Gerald and Allan Phipps, Feb.26.

1982 The 1981 NFL regular season paid attendance of 13,606,990 for an average of 60,745 was the highest in the league's 62-year history. It also was the first time the season average exceeded 60,000. NFL games in 1981 were played before 93.8 percent of total stadium capacity.

NFL signed a five-year contract with the three TV networks (ABC, CBS, NBC) to televise all NFL regular and postseason games starting with the 1982 season.

The San Francisco-Cincinnati Super Bowl XVI game on January 24 achieved the highest rating of any televised sports event. The game was watched by a record 110,230,000 viewers in this country for a rating of 49.1.

1983 The 1982 season was reduced from a 16-game schedule to 9 as the result of the 57-day players' strike. Because of the shortened season, the league adopted for the 1982 playoffs a format of 16 teams competing in a Super Bowl Tournament. NFC number-one seed Washington eventually defeated AFC number-two seed Miami, 27-17, in Super Bowl XVII at the Rose Bowl to mark only the second time the NFC had won consecutive Super Bowls.

Despite the players' strike, the average paid attendance in 1982 was 58,472, the fifth-highest in league history, compared to 1981's record average of 60,745.

Super Bowl XVII was the second-highest rated live television program of all time and gave the NFL a sweep of the top 10 live programs in TV history. Super Bowl XVII was viewed in over 40 million homes, the largest total ever for a live telecast.

1984 The Los Angeles Raiders-Washington Redskins Super Bowl XVIII game on Jan. 22 achieved a 46.4 television rating to become the eleventh-highest-rated TV program of all time and fifth-highest Super Bowl.

An 11-man group headed by H.R. Bright purchased the Dallas Cowboys from Clint Murchison, Jr., March 20. Club President Tex Schramm was designated as managing general partner.

Businessman Patrick Bowlen purchased a majority interest in the Denver Broncos from Edgar Kaiser, March 21.

At their May 23-25 meetings in Washington, D.C., owners awarded Super Bowl XXI to the Los Angeles area to be played at the Rose Bowl in Pasadena and Super Bowl XXII to San Diego to be played in Jack Murphy Stadium.

Real estate developer Alex G. Spanos purchased a majority interest in the San Diego Chargers from Eugene V. Klein, Aug. 28.

Houston defeated Pittsburgh 23-20 to mark the 100th overtime game in regular season play since the rule was adopted in 1974, Dec. 2.

National Football League paid attendance exceeded 13 million for the fifth consecutive complete season when 13,398,112 attended NFL games for an average of 59,813, the second-highest in league history. Teams averaged 42.4 points per game, the second-highest total since the 1970 merger.

According to a CBS Sports/New York Times survey, 53 percent of the nation's sports fans said they most enjoy watching football, compared to 18 percent for baseball, Dec. 2-4.

1985 Super Bowl XIX, in which San Francisco defeated Miami 38-16, was viewed on television by more people than any other live event in history. President Ronald Reagan, who took his second oath of office before tossing the coin for Super Bowl XIX, was one of 115,936,000 viewers who watched a portion of the Jan. 20 game. The game drew a 46.4 rating and a 63 percent share. In addition, six million viewed the game live in the United Kingdom and close to that figure in Italy. Super Bowl XIX had a direct economic impact of $113.5 million on the San Francisco Bay Area.

NBC Radio and the NFL entered into a two-year agreement granting NBC the radio rights to a 37-game package in each of the next two NFL seasons, Mar. 6. The package included 27 regular season games and 10 postseason games.

Super Bowl XXIII was awarded to the Miami area to be played at the proposed Dolphins Stadium and Super Bowl XXIV will be played at the Superdome in New Orleans it was announced at the NFL annual meeting in Phoenix, Mar. 10-15.

Norman Braman, in partnership with Edward Leibowitz, bought the Philadelphia Eagles from Leonard Tose, Apr. 29.

Bruce Smith, Virginia Tech defensive lineman, selected by Buffalo, was the first player chosen in the fiftieth NFL draft, Apr. 30.

The group headed by Tom Benson, Jr., was conditionally approved to purchase the New Orleans Saints from John W. Mecom, Jr., May 9. Benson and Mecom announced final sale, June 3.

1984

AMERICAN CONFERENCE

EASTERN DIVISION

	W	L	T	Pct.	Pts.	OP
Miami	14	2	0	.875	513	298
New England	9	7	0	.563	362	352
N.Y. Jets	7	9	0	.438	332	364
Indianapolis	4	12	0	.250	239	414
Buffalo	2	14	0	.125	250	454

CENTRAL DIVISION

	W	L	T	Pct.	Pts.	OP
Pittsburgh	9	7	0	.563	387	310
Cincinnati	8	8	0	.500	339	339
Cleveland	5	11	0	.313	250	297
Houston	3	13	0	.188	240	437

WESTERN DIVISION

	W	L	T	Pct.	Pts.	OP
Denver	13	3	0	.813	353	241
Seattle*	12	4	0	.750	418	282
L.A. Raiders*	11	5	0	.688	368	278
Kansas City	8	8	0	.500	314	324
San Diego	7	9	0	.438	394	413

NATIONAL CONFERENCE

EASTERN DIVISION

	W	L	T	Pct.	Pts.	OP
Washington	11	5	0	.688	426	310
N.Y. Giants*	9	7	0	.563	299	301
St. Louis	9	7	0	.563	423	345
Dallas	9	7	0	.563	308	308
Philadelphia	6	9	1	.406	278	320

CENTRAL DIVISION

	W	L	T	Pct.	Pts.	OP
Chicago	10	6	0	.625	325	248
Green Bay	8	8	0	.500	390	309
Tampa Bay	6	10	0	.375	335	380
Detroit	4	11	1	.281	283	408
Minnesota	3	13	0	.188	276	484

WESTERN DIVISION

	W	L	T	Pct.	Pts.	OP
San Francisco	15	1	0	.938	475	227
L.A. Rams*	10	6	0	.625	346	316
New Orleans	7	9	0	.438	298	361
Atlanta	4	12	0	.250	281	382

*Wild Card qualifiers for playoffs

New York Giants clinched Wild Card berth based on 3-1 record vs. St. Louis's 2-2 and Dallas's 1-3. St. Louis finished ahead of Dallas based on better division record (5-3 to 3-5).

First round playoff: SEATTLE 13, Los Angeles Raiders 7
Divisional playoffs: MIAMI 31, Seattle 10, Pittsburgh 24, DENVER 17
AFC championship: MIAMI 45, Pittsburgh 28
First round playoff: New York Giants 16, LOS ANGELES RAMS 13
Divisional playoffs: SAN FRANCISCO 21, New York Giants 10, Chicago 23, WASHINGTON 10
NFC championship: SAN FRANCISCO 23, Chicago 0
Super Bowl XIX: San Francisco (NFC) 38, Miami (AFC) 16, at Stanford Stadium, Stanford, Calif.

In the Past Standings section, home teams in playoff games are indicated by capital letters.

1983

AMERICAN CONFERENCE

EASTERN DIVISION

	W	L	T	Pct.	Pts.	OP
Miami	12	4	0	.750	389	250
New England	8	8	0	.500	274	289
Buffalo	8	8	0	.500	283	351
Baltimore	7	9	0	.438	264	354
N.Y. Jets	7	9	0	.438	313	331

CENTRAL DIVISION

	W	L	T	Pct.	Pts.	OP
Pittsburgh	10	6	0	.625	355	303
Cleveland	9	7	0	.563	356	342
Cincinnati	7	9	0	.438	346	302
Houston	2	14	0	.125	288	460

WESTERN DIVISION

	W	L	T	Pct.	Pts.	OP
L.A. Raiders	12	4	0	.750	442	338
Seattle*	9	7	0	.563	403	397
Denver*	9	7	0	.563	302	327
San Diego	6	10	0	.375	358	462
Kansas City	6	10	0	.375	386	367

NATIONAL CONFERENCE

EASTERN DIVISION

	W	L	T	Pct.	Pts.	OP
Washington	14	2	0	.875	541	332
Dallas*	12	4	0	.750	479	360
St. Louis	8	7	1	.531	374	428
Philadelphia	5	11	0	.313	233	322
N.Y. Giants	3	12	1	.219	267	347

CENTRAL DIVISION

	W	L	T	Pct.	Pts.	OP
Detroit	9	7	0	.563	347	286
Green Bay	8	8	0	.500	429	439
Chicago	8	8	0	.500	311	301
Minnesota	8	8	0	.500	316	348
Tampa Bay	2	14	0	.125	241	380

WESTERN DIVISION

	W	L	T	Pct.	Pts.	OP
San Francisco	10	6	0	.625	432	293
L.A. Rams*	9	7	0	.563	361	344
New Orleans	8	8	0	.500	319	337
Atlanta	7	9	0	.438	370	389

*Wild Card qualifiers for playoffs

Seattle and Denver gained Wild Card berths over Cleveland because of their victories over the Browns.

First round playoff: SEATTLE 31, Denver 7
Divisional playoffs: Seattle 27, MIAMI 20, LOS ANGELES RAIDERS 38, Pittsburgh 10
AFC championship: LOS ANGELES RAIDERS 30, Seattle 14
First round playoff: Los Angeles Rams 24, DALLAS 17
Divisional playoffs: SAN FRANCISCO 24, Detroit 23, WASHINGTON 51, L.A. Rams 7
NFC championship: WASHINGTON 24, San Francisco 21
Super Bowl XVIII: Los Angeles Raiders (AFC) 38, Washington (NFC) 9, at Tampa Stadium, Tampa, Fla.

1982

AMERICAN CONFERENCE

	W	L	T	Pct.	Pts.	OP
L.A. Raiders	8	1	0	.889	260	200
Miami	7	2	0	.778	198	131
Cincinnati	7	2	0	.778	232	177
Pittsburgh	6	3	0	.667	204	146
San Diego	6	3	0	.667	288	221
N.Y. Jets	6	3	0	.667	245	166
New England	5	4	0	.556	143	157
Cleveland	4	5	0	.444	140	182
Buffalo	4	5	0	.444	150	154
Seattle	4	5	0	.444	127	147
Kansas City	3	6	0	.333	176	184
Denver	2	7	0	.222	148	226
Houston	1	8	0	.111	136	245
Baltimore	0	8	1	.056	113	236

NATIONAL CONFERENCE

	W	L	T	Pct.	Pts.	OP
Washington	8	1	0	.889	190	128
Dallas	6	3	0	.667	226	145
Green Bay	5	3	1	.611	226	169
Minnesota	5	4	0	.556	187	198
Atlanta	5	4	0	.556	183	199
St. Louis	5	4	0	.556	135	170
Tampa Bay	5	4	0	.556	158	178
Detroit	4	5	0	.444	181	176
New Orleans	4	5	0	.444	129	160
N.Y. Giants	4	5	0	.444	164	160
San Francisco	3	6	0	.333	209	206
Chicago	3	6	0	.333	141	174
Philadelphia	3	6	0	.333	191	195
L.A. Rams	2	7	0	.222	200	250

As the result of a 57-day players' strike, the 1982 NFL regular season schedule was reduced from 16 weeks to 9. At the conclusion of the regular season, the NFL conducted a 16-team postseason Super Bowl Tournament. Eight teams from each conference were seeded 1-8 based on their records during the season.

Miami finished ahead of Cincinnati based on better conference record (6-1 to 6-2). Pittsburgh won common games tie-breaker with San Diego (3-1 to 2-1) after New York Jets were eliminated from three-way tie based on conference record (Pittsburgh and San Diego 5-3 vs. Jets 2-3). Cleveland finished ahead of Buffalo and Seattle based on better conference record (4-3 to 3-3 to 3-5). Minnesota (4-1), Atlanta (4-3), St. Louis (5-4), Tampa Bay (3-3) seeds were determined by best won-lost record in conference games. Detroit finished ahead of New Orleans and the New York Giants based on better conference record (4-4 to 3-5 to 3-5).

First round playoff: MIAMI 28, New England 13
LOS ANGELES RAIDERS 27, Cleveland 10
New York Jets 44, CINCINNATI 17
San Diego 31, PITTSBURGH 28
Second round playoff: New York Jets 17, LOS ANGELES RAIDERS 14
MIAMI 34, San Diego 13
AFC championship: MIAMI 14, New York Jets 0
First round playoff: WASHINGTON 31, Detroit 7
GREEN BAY 41, St. Louis 16
MINNESOTA 30, Atlanta 24
DALLAS 30, Tampa Bay 17
Second round playoff: WASHINGTON 21, Minnesota 7
DALLAS 37, Green Bay 26
NFC championship: WASHINGTON 31, Dallas 17
Super Bowl XVII: Washington (NFC) 27, Miami (AFC) 17, at Rose Bowl, Pasadena, Calif.

1981

AMERICAN CONFERENCE

EASTERN DIVISION

	W	L	T	Pct.	Pts.	OP
Miami	11	4	1	.719	345	275
N.Y. Jets*	10	5	1	.656	355	287
Buffalo*	10	6	0	.625	311	276
Baltimore	2	14	0	.125	259	533
New England	2	14	0	.125	322	370

CENTRAL DIVISION

	W	L	T	Pct.	Pts.	OP
Cincinnati	12	4	0	.750	421	304
Pittsburgh	8	8	0	.500	356	297
Houston	7	9	0	.438	281	355
Cleveland	5	11	0	.313	276	375

WESTERN DIVISION

	W	L	T	Pct.	Pts.	OP
San Diego	10	6	0	.625	478	390
Denver	10	6	0	.625	321	289
Kansas City	9	7	0	.563	343	290
Oakland	7	9	0	.438	273	343
Seattle	6	10	0	.375	322	388

NATIONAL CONFERENCE

EASTERN DIVISION

	W	L	T	Pct.	Pts.	OP
Dallas	12	4	0	.750	367	277
Philadelphia*	10	6	0	.625	368	221
N.Y. Giants*	9	7	0	.563	295	257
Washington	8	8	0	.500	347	349
St. Louis	7	9	0	.438	315	408

CENTRAL DIVISION

	W	L	T	Pct.	Pts.	OP
Tampa Bay	9	7	0	.563	315	268
Detroit	8	8	0	.500	397	322
Green Bay	8	8	0	.500	324	361
Minnesota	7	9	0	.438	325	369
Chicago	6	10	0	.375	253	324

WESTERN DIVISION

	W	L	T	Pct.	Pts.	OP
San Francisco	13	3	0	.813	357	250
Atlanta	7	9	0	.438	426	355
Los Angeles	6	10	0	.375	303	351
New Orleans	4	12	0	.250	207	378

*Wild Card qualifiers for playoffs

San Diego won AFC Western title over Denver on the basis of a better division record (6-2 to 5-3). Buffalo won a Wild Card playoff berth over Denver as the result of a 9-7 victory in head-to-head competition.

First round playoff: Buffalo 31, NEW YORK JETS 27
Divisional playoffs: San Diego 41, MIAMI 38, sudden death overtime; CINCINNATI 28, Buffalo 21
AFC championship: CINCINNATI 27, San Diego 7
First round playoff: New York Giants 27, PHILADELPHIA 21
Divisional playoffs: DALLAS 38, Tampa Bay 0, SAN FRANCISCO 38, New York Giants 24
NFC championship: SAN FRANCISCO 28, Dallas 27
Super Bowl XVI: San Francisco (NFC) 26, Cincinnati (AFC) 21, at Silverdome, Pontiac, Mich.

1980

AMERICAN CONFERENCE
EASTERN DIVISION

	W	L	T	Pct.	Pts.	OP
Buffalo	11	5	0	.688	320	260
New England	10	6	0	.625	441	325
Miami	8	8	0	.500	266	305
Baltimore	7	9	0	.438	355	387
N.Y. Jets	4	12	0	.250	302	395

CENTRAL DIVISION

	W	L	T	Pct.	Pts.	OP
Cleveland	11	5	0	.688	357	310
Houston*	11	5	0	.688	295	251
Pittsburgh	9	7	0	.563	352	313
Cincinnati	6	10	0	.375	244	312

WESTERN DIVISION

	W	L	T	Pct.	Pts.	OP
San Diego	11	5	0	.688	418	327
Oakland*	11	5	0	.688	364	306
Kansas City	8	8	0	.500	319	336
Denver	8	8	0	.500	310	323
Seattle	4	12	0	.250	291	408

NATIONAL CONFERENCE
EASTERN DIVISION

	W	L	T	Pct.	Pts.	OP
Philadelphia	12	4	0	.750	384	222
Dallas*	12	4	0	.750	454	311
Washington	6	10	0	.375	261	293
St. Louis	5	11	0	.313	299	350
N.Y. Giants	4	12	0	.250	249	425

CENTRAL DIVISION

	W	L	T	Pct.	Pts.	OP
Minnesota	9	7	0	.563	317	308
Detroit	9	7	0	.563	334	272
Chicago	7	9	0	.438	304	264
Tampa Bay	5	10	1	.344	271	341
Green Bay	5	10	1	.344	231	371

WESTERN DIVISION

	W	L	T	Pct.	Pts.	OP
Atlanta	12	4	0	.750	405	272
Los Angeles*	11	5	0	.688	424	289
San Francisco	6	10	0	.375	320	415
New Orleans	1	15	0	.063	291	487

*Wild Card qualifiers for playoffs

Philadelphia won division title over Dallas on the basis of best net points in division games (plus 84 net points to plus 50). Minnesota won division title because of a better conference record than Detroit (8-4 to 9-5). Cleveland won division title because of a better conference record than Houston (8-4 to 7-5). San Diego won division title over Oakland on the basis of best net points in division games (plus 60 net points to plus 37).

First round playoff: OAKLAND 27, Houston 7
Divisional playoffs: SAN DIEGO 20, Buffalo 14; Oakland 14, CLEVELAND 12
AFC championship: Oakland 34, SAN DIEGO 27
First round playoff: DALLAS 34, Los Angeles 13
Divisional playoffs: PHILADELPHIA 31, Minnesota 16; Dallas 30, ATLANTA 27
NFC championship: PHILADELPHIA 20, Dallas 7
Super Bowl XV: Oakland (AFC) 27, Philadelphia (NFC) 10, at Louisiana Superdome, New Orleans, La.

1979

AMERICAN CONFERENCE
EASTERN DIVISION

	W	L	T	Pct.	Pts.	OP
Miami	10	6	0	.625	341	257
New England	9	7	0	.563	411	326
N.Y. Jets	8	8	0	.500	337	383
Buffalo	7	9	0	.438	268	279
Baltimore	5	11	0	.313	271	351

CENTRAL DIVISION

	W	L	T	Pct.	Pts.	OP
Pittsburgh	12	4	0	.750	416	262
Houston*	11	5	0	.688	362	331
Cleveland	9	7	0	.563	359	352
Cincinnati	4	12	0	.250	337	421

WESTERN DIVISION

	W	L	T	Pct.	Pts.	OP
San Diego	12	4	0	.750	411	246
Denver*	10	6	0	.625	289	262
Seattle	9	7	0	.563	378	372
Oakland	9	7	0	.563	365	337
Kansas City	7	9	0	.438	238	262

NATIONAL CONFERENCE
EASTERN DIVISION

	W	L	T	Pct.	Pts.	OP
Dallas	11	5	0	.688	371	313
Philadelphia*	11	5	0	.688	339	282
Washington	10	6	0	.625	348	295
N.Y. Giants	6	10	0	.375	237	323
St. Louis	5	11	0	.313	307	358

CENTRAL DIVISION

	W	L	T	Pct.	Pts.	OP
Tampa Bay	10	6	0	.625	273	237
Chicago*	10	6	0	.625	306	249
Minnesota	7	9	0	.438	259	337
Green Bay	5	11	0	.313	246	316
Detroit	2	14	0	.125	219	365

WESTERN DIVISION

	W	L	T	Pct.	Pts.	OP
Los Angeles	9	7	0	.563	323	309
New Orleans	8	8	0	.500	370	360
Atlanta	6	10	0	.375	300	388
San Francisco	2	14	0	.125	308	416

*Wild Card qualifiers for playoffs

Dallas won division title because of a better conference record than Philadelphia (10-2 to 9-3). Tampa Bay won division title because of a better division record than Chicago (6-2 to 5-3). Chicago won a wild card berth over Washington on the basis of best net points in all games (plus 57 net points to plus 53).

First round playoff: HOUSTON 13, Denver 7
Divisional playoffs: Houston 17, SAN DIEGO 14; PITTSBURGH 34, Miami 14
AFC championship: PITTSBURGH 27, Houston 13
First round playoff: PHILADELPHIA 27, Chicago 17
Divisional playoffs: TAMPA BAY 24, Philadelphia 17; Los Angeles 21, DALLAS 19
NFC championship: Los Angeles 9, TAMPA BAY 0
Super Bowl XIV: Pittsburgh (AFC) 31, Los Angeles (NFC) 19, at Rose Bowl, Pasadena, Calif.

1978

AMERICAN CONFERENCE
EASTERN DIVISION

	W	L	T	Pct.	Pts.	OP
New England	11	5	0	.688	358	286
Miami*	11	5	0	.688	372	254
N.Y. Jets	8	8	0	.500	359	364
Buffalo	5	11	0	.313	302	354
Baltimore	5	11	0	.313	239	421

CENTRAL DIVISION

	W	L	T	Pct.	Pts.	OP
Pittsburgh	14	2	0	.875	356	195
Houston*	10	6	0	.625	283	298
Cleveland	8	8	0	.500	334	356
Cincinnati	4	12	0	.250	252	284

WESTERN DIVISION

	W	L	T	Pct.	Pts.	OP
Denver	10	6	0	.625	282	198
Oakland	9	7	0	.563	311	283
Seattle	9	7	0	.563	345	358
San Diego	9	7	0	.563	355	309
Kansas City	4	12	0	.250	243	327

NATIONAL CONFERENCE
EASTERN DIVISION

	W	L	T	Pct.	Pts.	OP
Dallas	12	4	0	.750	384	208
Philadelphia*	9	7	0	.563	270	250
Washington	8	8	0	.500	273	283
St. Louis	6	10	0	.375	248	296
N.Y. Giants	6	10	0	.375	264	298

CENTRAL DIVISION

	W	L	T	Pct.	Pts.	OP
Minnesota	8	7	1	.531	294	306
Green Bay	8	7	1	.531	249	269
Detroit	7	9	0	.438	290	300
Chicago	7	9	0	.438	253	274
Tampa Bay	5	11	0	.313	241	259

WESTERN DIVISION

	W	L	T	Pct.	Pts.	OP
Los Angeles	12	4	0	.750	316	245
Atlanta*	9	7	0	.563	240	290
New Orleans	7	9	0	.438	281	298
San Francisco	2	14	0	.125	219	350

*Wild Card qualifiers for playoffs

New England won division title on the basis of a better division record than Miami (6-2 to 5-3). Minnesota won division title because of a better head-to-head record against Green Bay (1-0-1).

First round playoff: Houston 17, MIAMI 9
Divisional playoffs: Houston 31, NEW ENGLAND 14; PITTSBURGH 33, Denver 10
AFC championship: PITTSBURGH 34, Houston 5
First round playoff: ATLANTA 14, Philadelphia 13
Divisional playoffs: DALLAS 27, Atlanta 20; LOS ANGELES 34, Minnesota 10
NFC championship: Dallas 28, LOS ANGELES 0
Super Bowl XIII: Pittsburgh (AFC) 35, Dallas (NFC) 31, at Orange Bowl, Miami, Fla.

1977

AMERICAN CONFERENCE
EASTERN DIVISION

	W	L	T	Pct.	Pts.	OP
Baltimore	10	4	0	.714	295	221
Miami	10	4	0	.714	313	197
New England	9	5	0	.643	278	217
N.Y. Jets	3	11	0	.214	191	300
Buffalo	3	11	0	.214	160	313

CENTRAL DIVISION

	W	L	T	Pct.	Pts.	OP
Pittsburgh	9	5	0	.643	283	243
Houston	8	6	0	.571	299	230
Cincinnati	8	6	0	.571	238	235
Cleveland	6	8	0	.429	269	267

WESTERN DIVISION

	W	L	T	Pct.	Pts.	OP
Denver	12	2	0	.857	274	148
Oakland*	11	3	0	.786	351	230
San Diego	7	7	0	.500	222	205
Seattle	5	9	0	.357	282	373
Kansas City	2	12	0	.143	225	349

NATIONAL CONFERENCE
EASTERN DIVISION

	W	L	T	Pct.	Pts.	OP
Dallas	12	2	0	.857	345	212
Washington	9	5	0	.643	196	189
St. Louis	7	7	0	.500	272	287
Philadelphia	5	9	0	.357	220	207
N.Y. Giants	5	9	0	.357	181	265

CENTRAL DIVISION

	W	L	T	Pct.	Pts.	OP
Minnesota	9	5	0	.643	231	227
Chicago*	9	5	0	.643	255	253
Detroit	6	8	0	.429	183	252
Green Bay	4	10	0	.286	134	219
Tampa Bay	2	12	0	.143	103	223

WESTERN DIVISION

	W	L	T	Pct.	Pts.	OP
Los Angeles	10	4	0	.714	302	146
Atlanta	7	7	0	.500	179	129
San Francisco	5	9	0	.357	220	260
New Orleans	3	11	0	.214	232	336

*Wild Card qualifier for playoffs

Baltimore won division title on the basis of a better conference record than Miami (9-3 to 8-4). Chicago won a wild card berth over Washington on the basis of best net points in conference games (plus 48 net points to plus 4).

Divisional playoffs: DENVER 34, Pittsburgh 21; Oakland 37, BALTIMORE 31, sudden death overtime
AFC championship: DENVER 20, Oakland 17
Divisional playoffs: DALLAS 37, Chicago 7, Minnesota 14, LOS ANGELES 7
NFC championship: DALLAS 23, Minnesota 6
Super Bowl XII: Dallas (NFC) 27, Denver (AFC) 10, at Louisiana Superdome, New Orleans, La.

1976

AMERICAN CONFERENCE
EASTERN DIVISION

	W	L	T	Pct.	Pts.	OP
Baltimore	11	3	0	.786	417	246
New England*	11	3	0	.786	376	236
Miami	6	8	0	.429	263	264
N.Y. Jets	3	11	0	.214	169	383
Buffalo	2	12	0	.143	245	363

CENTRAL DIVISION

	W	L	T	Pct.	Pts.	OP
Pittsburgh	10	4	0	.714	342	138
Cincinnati	10	4	0	.714	335	210
Cleveland	9	5	0	.643	267	287
Houston	5	9	0	.357	222	273

WESTERN DIVISION

	W	L	T	Pct.	Pts.	OP
Oakland	13	1	0	.929	350	237
Denver	9	5	0	.643	315	206
San Diego	6	8	0	.429	248	285
Kansas City	5	9	0	.357	290	376
Tampa Bay	0	14	0	.000	125	412

NATIONAL CONFERENCE
EASTERN DIVISION

	W	L	T	Pct.	Pts.	OP
Dallas	11	3	0	.786	296	194
Washington*	10	4	0	.714	291	217
St. Louis	10	4	0	.714	309	267
Philadelphia	4	10	0	.286	165	286
N.Y. Giants	3	11	0	.214	170	250

CENTRAL DIVISION

	W	L	T	Pct.	Pts.	OP
Minnesota	11	2	1	.821	305	176
Chicago	7	7	0	.500	253	216
Detroit	6	8	0	.429	262	220
Green Bay	5	9	0	.357	218	299

WESTERN DIVISION

	W	L	T	Pct.	Pts.	OP
Los Angeles	10	3	1	.750	351	190
San Francisco	8	6	0	.571	270	190
Atlanta	4	10	0	.286	172	312
New Orleans	4	10	0	.286	253	346
Seattle	2	12	0	.143	229	429

*Wild Card qualifier for playoffs

Baltimore won division title on the basis of a better division record than New England (7-1 to 6-2). Pittsburgh won division title because of a two-game sweep over Cincinnati. Washington won wild card berth over St. Louis because of a two-game sweep over Cardinals.

Divisional playoffs: OAKLAND 24, New England 21; Pittsburgh 40, BALTIMORE 14
AFC championship: OAKLAND 24, Pittsburgh 7
Divisional playoffs: MINNESOTA 35, Washington 20; Los Angeles 14, DALLAS 12
NFC championship: MINNESOTA 24, Los Angeles 13
Super Bowl XI: Oakland (AFC) 32, Minnesota (NFC) 14, at Rose Bowl, Pasadena, Calif.

1975

AMERICAN CONFERENCE

EASTERN DIVISION

	W	L	T	Pct.	Pts.	OP
Baltimore	10	4	0	.714	395	269
Miami	10	4	0	.714	357	222
Buffalo	8	6	0	.571	420	355
New England	3	11	0	.214	258	358
N.Y. Jets	3	11	0	.214	258	433

CENTRAL DIVISION

	W	L	T	Pct.	Pts.	OP
Pittsburgh	12	2	0	.857	373	162
Cincinnati*	11	3	0	.786	340	246
Houston	10	4	0	.714	293	226
Cleveland	3	11	0	.214	218	372

WESTERN DIVISION

	W	L	T	Pct.	Pts.	OP
Oakland	11	3	0	.786	375	255
Denver	6	8	0	.429	254	307
Kansas City	5	9	0	.357	282	341
San Diego	2	12	0	.143	189	345

NATIONAL CONFERENCE

EASTERN DIVISION

	W	L	T	Pct.	Pts.	OP
St. Louis	11	3	0	.786	356	276
Dallas*	10	4	0	.714	350	268
Washington	8	6	0	.571	325	276
N.Y. Giants	5	9	0	.357	216	306
Philadelphia	4	10	0	.286	225	302

CENTRAL DIVISION

	W	L	T	Pct.	Pts.	OP
Minnesota	12	2	0	.857	377	180
Detroit	7	7	0	.500	245	262
Chicago	4	10	0	.286	191	379
Green Bay	4	10	0	.286	226	285

WESTERN DIVISION

	W	L	T	Pct.	Pts.	OP
Los Angeles	12	2	0	.857	312	135
San Francisco	5	9	0	.357	255	286
Atlanta	4	10	0	.286	240	289
New Orleans	2	12	0	.143	165	360

Wild Card qualifier for playoffs
Baltimore won division title on the basis of a two-game sweep over Miami.
Divisional playoffs: PITTSBURGH 28, Baltimore 10; OAKLAND 31, Cincinnati 28
AFC championship: PITTSBURGH 16, Oakland 10
Divisional playoffs: LOS ANGELES 35, St. Louis 23; Dallas 17, MINNESOTA 14
NFC championship: Dallas 37, LOS ANGELES 7
Super Bowl X: Pittsburgh (AFC) 21, Dallas (NFC) 17, at Orange Bowl, Miami, Fla.

1974

AMERICAN CONFERENCE

EASTERN DIVISION

	W	L	T	Pct.	Pts.	OP
Miami	11	3	0	.786	327	216
Buffalo*	9	5	0	.643	264	244
New England	7	7	0	.500	348	289
N.Y. Jets	7	7	0	.500	279	300
Baltimore	2	12	0	.143	190	329

CENTRAL DIVISION

	W	L	T	Pct.	Pts.	OP
Pittsburgh	10	3	1	.750	305	189
Cincinnati	7	7	0	.500	283	259
Houston	7	7	0	.500	236	282
Cleveland	4	10	0	.286	251	344

WESTERN DIVISION

	W	L	T	Pct.	Pts.	OP
Oakland	12	2	0	.857	355	228
Denver	7	6	1	.536	302	294
Kansas City	5	9	0	.357	233	293
San Diego	5	9	0	.357	212	285

NATIONAL CONFERENCE

EASTERN DIVISION

	W	L	T	Pct.	Pts.	OP
St. Louis	10	4	0	.714	285	218
Washington*	10	4	0	.714	320	196
Dallas	8	6	0	.571	297	235
Philadelphia	7	7	0	.500	242	217
N.Y. Giants	2	12	0	.143	195	299

CENTRAL DIVISION

	W	L	T	Pct.	Pts.	OP
Minnesota	10	4	0	.714	310	195
Detroit	7	7	0	.500	256	270
Green Bay	6	8	0	.429	210	206
Chicago	4	10	0	.286	152	279

WESTERN DIVISION

	W	L	T	Pct.	Pts.	OP
Los Angeles	10	4	0	.714	263	181
San Francisco	6	8	0	.429	226	236
New Orleans	5	9	0	.357	166	263
Atlanta	3	11	0	.214	111	271

Wild Card qualifier for playoffs
St. Louis won division title because of a two-game sweep over Washington.
Divisional playoffs: OAKLAND 28, Miami 26; PITTSBURGH 32, Buffalo 14
AFC championship: Pittsburgh 24, OAKLAND 13
Divisional playoffs: MINNESOTA 30, St. Louis 14; LOS ANGELES 19, Washington 10
NFC championship: MINNESOTA 14, Los Angeles 10
Super Bowl IX: Pittsburgh (AFC) 16, Minnesota (NFC) 6, at Tulane Stadium, New Orleans, La.

1973

AMERICAN CONFERENCE

EASTERN DIVISION

	W	L	T	Pct.	Pts.	OP
Miami	12	2	0	.857	343	150
Buffalo	9	5	0	.643	259	230
New England	5	9	0	.357	258	300
Baltimore	4	10	0	.286	226	341
N.Y. Jets	4	10	0	.286	240	306

CENTRAL DIVISION

	W	L	T	Pct.	Pts.	OP
Cincinnati	10	4	0	.714	286	231
Pittsburgh*	10	4	0	.714	347	210
Cleveland	7	5	2	.571	234	255
Houston	1	13	0	.071	199	447

WESTERN DIVISION

	W	L	T	Pct.	Pts.	OP
Oakland	9	4	1	.679	292	175
Denver	7	5	2	.571	354	296
Kansas City	7	5	2	.571	231	192
San Diego	2	11	1	.179	188	386

NATIONAL CONFERENCE

EASTERN DIVISION

	W	L	T	Pct.	Pts.	OP
Dallas	10	4	0	.714	382	203
Washington*	10	4	0	.714	325	198
Philadelphia	5	8	1	.393	310	393
St. Louis	4	9	1	.321	286	365
N.Y. Giants	2	11	1	.179	226	362

CENTRAL DIVISION

	W	L	T	Pct.	Pts.	OP
Minnesota	12	2	0	.857	296	168
Detroit	6	7	1	.464	271	247
Green Bay	5	7	2	.429	202	259
Chicago	3	11	0	.214	195	334

WESTERN DIVISION

	W	L	T	Pct.	Pts.	OP
Los Angeles	12	2	0	.857	388	178
Atlanta	9	5	0	.643	318	224
New Orleans	5	9	0	.357	163	312
San Francisco	5	9	0	.357	262	319

Wild Card qualifier for playoffs
Cincinnati won division title on the basis of a better conference record than Pittsburgh (8-3 to 7-4). Dallas won division title on the basis of a better point differential vs. Washington (net 13 points).
Divisional playoffs: OAKLAND 33, Pittsburgh 14; MIAMI 34, Cincinnati 16
AFC championship: MIAMI 27, Oakland 10
Divisional playoffs: MINNESOTA 27, Washington 20; DALLAS 27, Los Angeles 16
NFC championship: Minnesota 27, DALLAS 10
Super Bowl VIII: Miami (AFC) 24, Minnesota (NFC) 7, at Rice Stadium, Houston, Tex.

1972

AMERICAN CONFERENCE

EASTERN DIVISION

	W	L	T	Pct.	Pts.	OP
Miami	14	0	0	1.000	385	171
N.Y. Jets	7	7	0	.500	367	324
Baltimore	5	9	0	.357	235	252
Buffalo	4	9	1	.321	257	377
New England	3	11	0	.214	192	446

CENTRAL DIVISION

	W	L	T	Pct.	Pts.	OP
Pittsburgh	11	3	0	.786	343	175
Cleveland*	10	4	0	.714	268	249
Cincinnati	8	6	0	.571	299	229
Houston	1	13	0	.071	164	380

WESTERN DIVISION

	W	L	T	Pct.	Pts.	OP
Oakland	10	3	1	.750	365	248
Kansas City	8	6	0	.571	287	254
Denver	5	9	0	.357	325	350
San Diego	4	9	1	.321	264	344

NATIONAL CONFERENCE

EASTERN DIVISION

	W	L	T	Pct.	Pts.	OP
Washington	11	3	0	.786	336	218
Dallas*	10	4	0	.714	319	240
N.Y. Giants	8	6	0	.571	331	247
St. Louis	4	9	1	.321	193	303
Philadelphia	2	11	1	.179	145	352

CENTRAL DIVISION

	W	L	T	Pct.	Pts.	OP
Green Bay	10	4	0	.714	304	226
Detroit	8	5	1	.607	339	290
Minnesota	7	7	0	.500	301	252
Chicago	4	9	1	.321	225	275

WESTERN DIVISION

	W	L	T	Pct.	Pts.	OP
San Francisco	8	5	1	.607	353	249
Atlanta	7	7	0	.500	269	274
Los Angeles	6	7	1	.464	291	286
New Orleans	2	11	1	.179	215	361

Wild Card qualifier for playoffs
Divisional playoffs: PITTSBURGH 13, Oakland 7; MIAMI 20, Cleveland 14
AFC championship: Miami 21, PITTSBURGH 17
Divisional playoffs: Dallas 30, SAN FRANCISCO 28; WASHINGTON 16, Green Bay 3
NFC championship: WASHINGTON 26, Dallas 3
Super Bowl VII: Miami (AFC) 14, Washington (NFC) 7, at Memorial Coliseum, Los Angeles, Calif.

1971

AMERICAN CONFERENCE

EASTERN DIVISION

	W	L	T	Pct.	Pts.	OP
Miami	10	3	1	.769	315	174
Baltimore*	10	4	0	.714	313	140
New England	6	8	0	.429	238	325
N.Y. Jets	6	8	0	.429	212	299
Buffalo	1	13	0	.071	184	394

CENTRAL DIVISION

	W	L	T	Pct.	Pts.	OP
Cleveland	9	5	0	.643	285	273
Pittsburgh	6	8	0	.429	246	292
Houston	4	9	1	.308	251	330
Cincinnati	4	10	0	.286	284	265

WESTERN DIVISION

	W	L	T	Pct.	Pts.	OP
Kansas City	10	3	1	.769	302	208
Oakland	8	4	2	.667	344	278
San Diego	6	8	0	.429	311	341
Denver	4	9	1	.308	203	275

NATIONAL CONFERENCE

EASTERN DIVISION

	W	L	T	Pct.	Pts.	OP
Dallas	11	3	0	.786	406	222
Washington*	9	4	1	.692	276	190
Philadelphia	6	7	1	.462	221	302
St. Louis	4	9	1	.308	231	279
N.Y. Giants	4	10	0	.286	228	362

CENTRAL DIVISION

	W	L	T	Pct.	Pts.	OP
Minnesota	11	3	0	.786	245	139
Detroit	7	6	1	.538	341	286
Chicago	6	8	0	.429	185	276
Green Bay	4	8	2	.333	274	298

WESTERN DIVISION

	W	L	T	Pct.	Pts.	OP
San Francisco	9	5	0	.643	300	216
Los Angeles	8	5	1	.615	313	260
Atlanta	7	6	1	.538	274	277
New Orleans	4	8	2	.333	266	347

Wild Card qualifier for playoffs
Divisional playoffs: Miami 27, KANSAS CITY 24, sudden death overtime; Baltimore 20, CLEVELAND 3
AFC championship: MIAMI 21, Baltimore 0
Divisional playoffs: Dallas 20, MINNESOTA 12; SAN FRANCISCO 24, Washington 20
NFC championship: DALLAS 14, San Francisco 3
Super Bowl VI: Dallas (NFC) 24, Miami (AFC) 3, at Tulane Stadium, New Orleans, La.

1970

AMERICAN CONFERENCE

EASTERN DIVISION

	W	L	T	Pct.	Pts.	OP
Baltimore	11	2	1	.846	321	234
Miami*	10	4	0	.714	297	228
N.Y. Jets	4	10	0	.286	255	286
Buffalo	3	10	1	.231	204	337
Boston Patriots	2	12	0	.143	149	361

CENTRAL DIVISION

	W	L	T	Pct.	Pts.	OP
Cincinnati	8	6	0	.571	312	255
Cleveland	7	7	0	.500	286	265
Pittsburgh	5	9	0	.357	210	272
Houston	3	10	1	.231	217	352

WESTERN DIVISION

	W	L	T	Pct.	Pts.	OP
Oakland	8	4	2	.667	300	293
Kansas City	7	5	2	.583	272	244
San Diego	5	6	3	.455	282	278
Denver	5	8	1	.385	253	264

NATIONAL CONFERENCE

EASTERN DIVISION

	W	L	T	Pct.	Pts.	OP
Dallas	10	4	0	.714	299	221
N.Y. Giants	9	5	0	.643	301	270
St. Louis	8	5	1	.615	325	228
Washington	6	8	0	.429	297	314
Philadelphia	3	10	1	.231	241	332

CENTRAL DIVISION

	W	L	T	Pct.	Pts.	OP
Minnesota	12	2	0	.857	335	143
Detroit*	10	4	0	.714	347	202
Chicago	6	8	0	.429	256	261
Green Bay	6	8	0	.429	196	293

WESTERN DIVISION

	W	L	T	Pct.	Pts.	OP
San Francisco	10	3	1	.769	352	267
Los Angeles	9	4	1	.692	325	202
Atlanta	4	8	2	.333	206	261
New Orleans	2	11	1	.154	172	347

Wild Card qualifier for playoffs
Divisional playoffs: BALTIMORE 17, Cincinnati 0; OAKLAND 21, Miami 14
AFC championship: BALTIMORE 27, Oakland 17
Divisional playoffs: DALLAS 5, Detroit 0; San Francisco 17, MINNESOTA 14
NFC championship: Dallas 17, SAN FRANCISCO 10
Super Bowl V: Baltimore (AFC) 16, Dallas (NFC) 13, at Orange Bowl, Miami, Fla.

1969 NFL

EASTERN CONFERENCE	W	L	T	Pct.	Pts.	OP	WESTERN CONFERENCE	W	L	T	Pct.	Pts.	OP
Capitol Division							**Coastal Division**						
Dallas	11	2	1	.846	369	223	Los Angeles	11	3	0	.786	320	243
Washington	7	5	2	.583	307	319	Baltimore	8	5	1	.615	279	268
New Orleans	5	9	0	.357	311	393	Atlanta	6	8	0	.429	276	268
Philadelphia	4	9	1	.308	279	377	San Francisco	4	8	2	.333	277	319
Century Division	W	L	T	Pct.	Pts.	OP	**Central Division**	W	L	T	Pct.	Pts.	OP
Cleveland	10	3	1	.769	351	300	Minnesota	12	2	0	.857	379	133
N.Y. Giants	6	8	0	.429	264	298	Detroit	9	4	1	.692	259	188
St. Louis	4	9	1	.308	314	389	Green Bay	8	6	0	.571	269	221
Pittsburgh	1	13	0	.071	218	404	Chicago	1	13	0	.071	210	339

Conference championships: Cleveland 38, DALLAS 14; MINNESOTA 23, Los Angeles 20
NFL championship: MINNESOTA 27, Cleveland 7
Super Bowl IV: Kansas City (AFL) 23, Minnesota (NFL) 7, at Tulane Stadium, New Orleans, La.

1969 AFL

EASTERN DIVISION	W	L	T	Pct.	Pts.	OP	WESTERN DIVISION	W	L	T	Pct.	Pts.	OP
N.Y. Jets	10	4	0	.714	353	269	Oakland	12	1	1	.923	377	242
Houston	6	6	2	.500	278	279	Kansas City	11	3	0	.786	359	177
Boston Patriots	4	10	0	.286	266	316	San Diego	8	6	0	.571	288	276
Buffalo	4	10	0	.286	230	359	Denver	5	8	1	.385	297	344
Miami	3	10	1	.231	233	332	Cincinnati	4	9	1	.308	280	367

Divisional Playoffs: Kansas City 13, N.Y. JETS 6; OAKLAND 56, Houston 7
AFL championship: Kansas City 17, OAKLAND 7

1968 NFL

EASTERN CONFERENCE	W	L	T	Pct.	Pts.	OP	WESTERN CONFERENCE	W	L	T	Pct.	Pts.	OP
Capitol Division							**Coastal Division**						
Dallas	12	2	0	.857	431	186	Baltimore	13	1	0	.929	402	144
N.Y. Giants	7	7	0	.500	294	325	Los Angeles	10	3	1	.769	312	200
Washington	5	9	0	.357	249	358	San Francisco	7	6	1	.538	303	310
Philadelphia	2	12	0	.143	202	351	Atlanta	2	12	0	.143	170	389
Century Division	W	L	T	Pct.	Pts.	OP	**Central Division**	W	L	T	Pct.	Pts.	OP
Cleveland	10	4	0	.714	394	273	Minnesota	8	6	0	.571	282	242
St. Louis	9	4	1	.692	325	289	Chicago	7	7	0	.500	250	333
New Orleans	4	9	1	.308	246	327	Green Bay	6	7	1	.462	281	227
Pittsburgh	2	11	1	.154	244	397	Detroit	4	8	2	.333	207	241

Conference championships: CLEVELAND 31, Dallas 20; BALTIMORE 24, Minnesota 14
NFL championship: Baltimore 34, CLEVELAND 0
Super Bowl III: N.Y. Jets (AFL) 16, Baltimore (NFL) 7, at Orange Bowl, Miami, Fla.

1968 AFL

EASTERN DIVISION	W	L	T	Pct.	Pts.	OP	WESTERN DIVISION	W	L	T	Pct.	Pts.	OP
N.Y. Jets	11	3	0	.786	419	280	Oakland	12	2	0	.857	453	233
Houston	7	7	0	.500	303	248	Kansas City	12	2	0	.857	371	170
Miami	5	8	1	.385	276	355	San Diego	9	5	0	.643	382	310
Boston Patriots	4	10	0	.286	229	406	Denver	5	9	0	.357	255	404
Buffalo	1	12	1	.077	199	367	Cincinnati	3	11	0	.214	215	329

Western Division playoff: OAKLAND 41, Kansas City 6
AFL championship: N.Y. JETS 27, Oakland 23

1967 NFL

EASTERN CONFERENCE	W	L	T	Pct.	Pts.	OP	WESTERN CONFERENCE	W	L	T	Pct.	Pts.	OP
Capitol Division							**Coastal Division**						
Dallas	9	5	0	.643	342	268	Los Angeles	11	1	2	.917	398	196
Philadelphia	6	7	1	.462	351	409	Baltimore	11	1	2	.917	394	198
Washington	5	6	3	.455	347	353	San Francisco	7	7	0	.500	273	337
New Orleans	3	11	0	.214	233	379	Atlanta	1	12	1	.077	175	422
Century Division	W	L	T	Pct.	Pts.	OP	**Central Division**	W	L	T	Pct.	Pts.	OP
Cleveland	9	5	0	.643	334	297	Green Bay	9	4	1	.692	332	209
N.Y. Giants	7	7	0	.500	369	379	Chicago	7	6	1	.538	239	218
St. Louis	6	7	1	.462	333	356	Detroit	5	7	2	.417	260	259
Pittsburgh	4	9	1	.308	281	320	Minnesota	3	8	3	.273	233	294

Los Angeles won division title on the basis of advantage in points (58-34) in two games vs. Baltimore.
Conference championships: DALLAS 52, Cleveland 14; GREEN BAY 28, Los Angeles 7
NFL championship: GREEN BAY 21, Dallas 17
Super Bowl II: Green Bay (NFL) 33, Oakland (AFL) 14, at Orange Bowl, Miami, Fla.

1967 AFL

EASTERN DIVISION	W	L	T	Pct.	Pts.	OP	WESTERN DIVISION	W	L	T	Pct.	Pts.	OP
Houston	9	4	1	.692	258	199	Oakland	13	1	0	.929	468	233
N.Y. Jets	8	5	1	.615	371	329	Kansas City	9	5	0	.643	408	254
Buffalo	4	10	0	.286	237	285	San Diego	8	5	1	.615	360	352
Miami	4	10	0	.286	219	407	Denver	3	11	0	.214	256	409
Boston Patriots	3	10	1	.231	280	389							

AFL championship: OAKLAND 40, Houston 7

1966 NFL

EASTERN CONFERENCE	W	L	T	Pct.	Pts.	OP	WESTERN CONFERENCE	W	L	T	Pct.	Pts.	OP
Dallas	10	3	1	.769	445	239	Green Bay	12	2	0	.857	335	163
Cleveland	9	5	0	.643	403	259	Baltimore	9	5	0	.643	314	226
Philadelphia	9	5	0	.643	326	340	Los Angeles	8	6	0	.571	289	212
St. Louis	8	5	1	.615	264	265	San Francisco	6	6	2	.500	320	325
Washington	7	7	0	.500	351	355	Chicago	5	7	2	.417	234	272
Pittsburgh	5	8	1	.385	316	347	Detroit	4	9	1	.308	206	317
Atlanta	3	11	0	.214	204	437	Minnesota	4	9	1	.308	292	304
N.Y. Giants	1	12	1	.077	263	501							

NFL championship: Green Bay 34, DALLAS 27
Super Bowl I: Green Bay (NFL) 35, Kansas City (AFL) 10, at Memorial Coliseum, Los Angeles, Calif.

1966 AFL

EASTERN DIVISION	W	L	T	Pct.	Pts.	OP	WESTERN DIVISION	W	L	T	Pct.	Pts.	OP
Buffalo	9	4	1	.692	358	255	Kansas City	11	2	1	.846	448	276
Boston Patriots	8	4	2	.677	315	283	Oakland	8	5	1	.615	315	288
N.Y. Jets	6	6	2	.500	322	312	San Diego	7	6	1	.538	335	284
Houston	3	11	0	.214	335	396	Denver	4	10	0	.286	196	381
Miami	3	11	0	.214	213	362							

AFL championship: Kansas City 31, BUFFALO 7

1965 NFL

EASTERN CONFERENCE	W	L	T	Pct.	Pts.	OP	WESTERN CONFERENCE	W	L	T	Pct.	Pts.	OP
Cleveland	11	3	0	.786	363	325	Green Bay	10	3	1	.769	316	224
Dallas	7	7	0	.500	325	280	Baltimore	10	3	1	.769	389	284
N.Y. Giants	7	7	0	.500	270	338	Chicago	9	5	0	.643	409	275
Washington	6	8	0	.429	257	301	San Francisco	7	6	1	.538	421	402
Philadelphia	5	9	0	.357	363	359	Minnesota	7	7	0	.500	383	403
St. Louis	5	9	0	.357	296	309	Detroit	6	7	1	.462	257	295
Pittsburgh	2	12	0	.143	202	397	Los Angeles	4	10	0	.286	269	328

Western Conference playoff: GREEN BAY 13, Baltimore 10, sudden death overtime
NFL championship: GREEN BAY 23, Cleveland 12

1965 AFL

EASTERN DIVISION	W	L	T	Pct.	Pts.	OP	WESTERN DIVISION	W	L	T	Pct.	Pts.	OP
Buffalo	10	3	1	.769	313	226	San Diego	9	2	3	.818	340	227
N.Y. Jets	5	8	1	.385	285	303	Oakland	8	5	1	.615	298	239
Boston Patriots	4	8	2	.333	244	302	Kansas City	7	5	2	.583	322	285
Houston	4	10	0	.286	298	429	Denver	4	10	0	.286	303	392

AFL championship: Buffalo 23, SAN DIEGO 0

1964 NFL

EASTERN CONFERENCE	W	L	T	Pct.	Pts.	OP	WESTERN CONFERENCE	W	L	T	Pct.	Pts.	OP
Cleveland	10	3	1	.769	415	293	Baltimore	12	2	0	.857	428	225
St. Louis	9	3	2	.750	357	331	Green Bay	8	5	1	.615	342	245
Philadelphia	6	8	0	.429	312	313	Minnesota	8	5	1	.615	355	296
Washington	6	8	0	.429	307	305	Detroit	7	5	2	.583	280	260
Dallas	5	8	1	.385	250	289	Los Angeles	5	7	2	.417	283	339
Pittsburgh	5	9	0	.357	253	315	Chicago	5	9	0	.357	260	379
N.Y. Giants	2	10	2	.167	241	399	San Francisco	4	10	0	.286	236	330

NFL championship: CLEVELAND 27, Baltimore 0

1964 AFL

EASTERN DIVISION	W	L	T	Pct.	Pts.	OP	WESTERN DIVISION	W	L	T	Pct.	Pts.	OP
Buffalo	12	2	0	.857	400	242	San Diego	8	5	1	.615	341	300
Boston Patriots	10	3	1	.769	365	297	Kansas City	7	7	0	.500	366	306
N.Y. Jets	5	8	1	.385	278	315	Oakland	5	7	2	.417	303	350
Houston	4	10	0	.286	310	355	Denver	2	11	1	.154	240	438

AFL championship: BUFFALO 20, San Diego 7

1963 NFL

EASTERN CONFERENCE	W	L	T	Pct.	Pts.	OP	WESTERN CONFERENCE	W	L	T	Pct.	Pts.	OP
N.Y. Giants	11	3	0	.786	448	280	Chicago	11	1	2	.917	301	144
Cleveland	10	4	0	.714	343	262	Green Bay	11	2	1	.846	369	206
St. Louis	9	5	0	.643	341	283	Baltimore	8	6	0	.571	316	285
Pittsburgh	7	4	3	.636	321	295	Detroit	5	8	1	.385	326	265
Dallas	4	10	0	.286	305	378	Minnesota	5	8	1	.385	309	390
Washington	3	11	0	.214	279	398	Los Angeles	5	9	0	.357	210	350
Philadelphia	2	10	2	.167	242	381	San Francisco	2	12	0	.143	198	391

NFL championship: CHICAGO 14, N.Y. Giants 10

1963 AFL

EASTERN DIVISION	W	L	T	Pct.	Pts.	OP	WESTERN DIVISION	W	L	T	Pct.	Pts.	OP
Boston Patriots	7	6	1	.538	327	257	San Diego	11	3	0	.786	399	255
Buffalo	7	6	1	.538	304	291	Oakland	10	4	0	.714	363	282
Houston	6	8	0	.429	302	372	Kansas City	5	7	2	.417	347	263
N.Y. Jets	5	8	1	.385	249	399	Denver	2	11	1	.154	301	473

Eastern Division playoff: Boston 26, BUFFALO 8
AFL championship: SAN DIEGO 51, Boston 10

1962 NFL

EASTERN CONFERENCE

	W	L	T	Pct.	Pts.	OP
N.Y. Giants	12	2	0	.857	398	283
Pittsburgh	9	5	0	.643	312	363
Cleveland	7	6	1	.538	291	257
Washington	5	7	2	.417	305	376
Dallas Cowboys	5	8	1	.385	398	402
St. Louis	4	9	1	.308	287	361
Philadelphia	3	10	1	.231	282	356

WESTERN CONFERENCE

	W	L	T	Pct.	Pts.	OP
Green Bay	13	1	0	.929	415	148
Detroit	11	3	0	.786	315	177
Chicago	9	5	0	.643	321	287
Baltimore	7	7	0	.500	293	288
San Francisco	6	8	0	.429	282	331
Minnesota	2	11	1	.154	254	410
Los Angeles	1	12	1	.077	220	334

NFL championship: Green Bay 16, N.Y. GIANTS 7

1962 AFL

EASTERN DIVISION

	W	L	T	Pct.	Pts.	OP
Houston	11	3	0	.786	387	270
Boston Patriots	9	4	1	.692	346	295
Buffalo	7	6	1	.538	309	272
N.Y. Titans	5	9	0	.357	278	423

WESTERN DIVISION

	W	L	T	Pct.	Pts.	OP
Dallas Texans	11	3	0	.786	389	233
Denver	7	7	0	.500	353	334
San Diego	4	10	0	.286	314	392
Oakland	1	13	0	.071	213	370

AFL championship: Dallas Texans 20, HOUSTON 17, sudden death overtime

1961 NFL

EASTERN CONFERENCE

	W	L	T	Pct.	Pts.	OP
N.Y. Giants	10	3	1	.769	368	220
Philadelphia	10	4	0	.714	361	297
Cleveland	8	5	1	.615	319	270
St. Louis	7	7	0	.500	279	267
Pittsburgh	6	8	0	.429	295	287
Dallas Cowboys	4	9	1	.308	236	380
Washington	1	12	1	.077	174	392

WESTERN CONFERENCE

	W	L	T	Pct.	Pts.	OP
Green Bay	11	3	0	.786	391	223
Detroit	8	5	1	.615	270	258
Baltimore	8	6	0	.571	302	307
Chicago Bears	8	6	0	.571	326	302
San Francisco	7	6	1	.538	346	272
Los Angeles	4	10	0	.286	263	333
Minnesota	3	11	0	.214	285	407

NFL championship: GREEN BAY 37, N.Y. Giants 0

1961 AFL

EASTERN DIVISION

	W	L	T	Pct.	Pts.	OP
Houston	10	3	1	.769	513	242
Boston Patriots	9	4	1	.692	413	313
N.Y. Titans	7	7	0	.500	301	390
Buffalo	6	8	0	.429	294	342

WESTERN DIVISION

	W	L	T	Pct.	Pts.	OP
San Diego	12	2	0	.857	396	219
Dallas Texans	6	8	0	.429	334	343
Denver	3	11	0	.214	251	432
Oakland	2	12	0	.143	237	458

AFL championship: Houston 10, SAN DIEGO 3

1960 NFL

EASTERN CONFERENCE

	W	L	T	Pct.	Pts.	OP
Philadelphia	10	2	0	.833	321	246
Cleveland	8	3	1	.727	362	217
N.Y. Giants	6	4	2	.600	271	261
St. Louis	6	5	1	.545	288	230
Pittsburgh	5	6	1	.455	240	275
Washington	1	9	2	.100	178	309

WESTERN CONFERENCE

	W	L	T	Pct.	Pts.	OP
Green Bay	8	4	0	.667	332	209
Detroit	7	5	0	.583	239	212
San Francisco	7	5	0	.583	208	205
Baltimore	6	6	0	.500	288	234
Chicago	5	6	1	.455	194	299
L.A. Rams	4	7	1	.364	265	297
Dall. Cowboys	0	11	1	.000	177	369

NFL championship: PHILADELPHIA 17, Green Bay 13

1960 AFL

EASTERN CONFERENCE

	W	L	T	Pct.	Pts.	OP
Houston	10	4	0	.714	379	285
N.Y. Titans	7	7	0	.500	382	399
Buffalo	5	8	1	.385	296	303
Boston	5	9	0	.357	286	349

WESTERN CONFERENCE

	W	L	T	Pct.	Pts.	OP
L.A. Chargers	10	4	0	.714	373	336
Dall. Texans	8	6	0	.571	362	253
Oakland	6	8	0	.429	319	388
Denver	4	9	1	.308	309	393

AFL championship: HOUSTON 24, L.A. Chargers 16

1959

EASTERN CONFERENCE

	W	L	T	Pct.	Pts.	OP
N.Y. Giants	10	2	0	.833	284	170
Cleveland	7	5	0	.583	270	214
Philadelphia	7	5	0	.583	268	278
Pittsburgh	6	5	1	.545	257	216
Washington	3	9	0	.250	185	350
Chi. Cardinals	2	10	0	.167	234	324

WESTERN CONFERENCE

	W	L	T	Pct.	Pts.	OP
Baltimore	9	3	0	.750	374	251
Chi. Bears	8	4	0	.667	252	196
Green Bay	7	5	0	.583	248	246
San Francisco	7	5	0	.583	255	237
Detroit	3	8	1	.273	203	275
Los Angeles	2	10	0	.167	242	315

NFL championship: BALTIMORE 31, N.Y. Giants 16

1958

EASTERN CONFERENCE

	W	L	T	Pct.	Pts.	OP
N.Y. Giants	9	3	0	.750	246	183
Cleveland	9	3	0	.750	302	217
Pittsburgh	7	4	1	.636	261	230
Washington	4	7	1	.364	214	268
Chi. Cardinals	2	9	1	.182	261	356
Philadelphia	2	9	1	.182	235	306

WESTERN CONFERENCE

	W	L	T	Pct.	Pts.	OP
Baltimore	9	3	0	.750	381	203
Chi. Bears	8	4	0	.667	298	230
Los Angeles	8	4	0	.667	344	278
San Francisco	6	6	0	.500	257	324
Detroit	4	7	1	.364	261	276
Green Bay	1	10	1	.091	193	382

Eastern Conference playoff: N.Y. GIANTS 10, Cleveland 0
NFL championship: Baltimore 23, N.Y. GIANTS 17, sudden death overtime

1957

EASTERN CONFERENCE

	W	L	T	Pct.	Pts.	OP
Cleveland	9	2	1	.818	269	172
N.Y. Giants	7	5	0	.583	254	211
Pittsburgh	6	6	0	.500	161	178
Washington	5	6	1	.455	251	230
Philadelphia	4	8	0	.333	173	230
Chi. Cardinals	3	9	0	.250	200	299

WESTERN CONFERENCE

	W	L	T	Pct.	Pts.	OP
Detroit	8	4	0	.667	251	231
San Francisco	8	4	0	.667	260	264
Baltimore	7	5	0	.583	303	235
Los Angeles	6	6	0	.500	307	278
Chi. Bears	5	7	0	.417	203	211
Green Bay	3	9	0	.250	218	311

Western Conference playoff: Detroit 31, SAN FRANCISCO 27
NFL championship: DETROIT 59, Cleveland 14

1956

EASTERN CONFERENCE

	W	L	T	Pct.	Pts.	OP
N.Y. Giants	8	3	1	.727	264	197
Chi. Cardinals	7	5	0	.583	240	182
Washington	6	6	0	.500	183	225
Cleveland	5	7	0	.417	167	177
Pittsburgh	5	7	0	.417	217	250
Philadelphia	3	8	1	.273	143	215

WESTERN CONFERENCE

	W	L	T	Pct.	Pts.	OP
Chi. Bears	9	2	1	.818	363	246
Detroit	9	3	0	.750	300	188
San Francisco	5	6	1	.455	233	284
Baltimore	5	7	0	.417	270	322
Green Bay	4	8	0	.333	264	342
Los Angeles	4	8	0	.333	291	307

NFL championship: N.Y. GIANTS 47, Chi. Bears 7

1955

EASTERN CONFERENCE

	W	L	T	Pct.	Pts.	OP
Cleveland	9	2	1	.818	349	218
Washington	8	4	0	.667	246	222
N.Y. Giants	6	5	1	.545	267	223
Chi. Cardinals	4	7	1	.364	224	252
Philadelphia	4	7	1	.364	248	231
Pittsburgh	4	8	0	.333	195	285

WESTERN CONFERENCE

	W	L	T	Pct.	Pts.	OP
Los Angeles	8	3	1	.727	260	231
Chi. Bears	8	4	0	.667	294	251
Green Bay	6	6	0	.500	258	276
Baltimore	5	6	1	.455	214	239
San Francisco	4	8	0	.333	216	298
Detroit	3	9	0	.250	230	275

NFL championship: Cleveland 38, LOS ANGELES 14

1954

EASTERN CONFERENCE

	W	L	T	Pct.	Pts.	OP
Cleveland	9	3	0	.750	336	162
Philadelphia	7	4	1	.636	284	230
N.Y. Giants	7	5	0	.583	293	184
Pittsburgh	5	7	0	.417	219	263
Washington	3	9	0	.250	207	432
Chi. Cardinals	2	10	0	.167	183	347

WESTERN CONFERENCE

	W	L	T	Pct.	Pts.	OP
Detroit	9	2	1	.818	337	189
Chi. Bears	8	4	0	.667	301	279
San Francisco	7	4	1	.636	313	251
Los Angeles	6	5	1	.545	314	285
Green Bay	4	8	0	.333	234	251
Baltimore	3	9	0	.250	131	279

NFL championship: CLEVELAND 56, Detroit 10

1953

EASTERN CONFERENCE

	W	L	T	Pct.	Pts.	OP
Cleveland	11	1	0	.917	348	162
Philadelphia	7	4	1	.636	352	215
Washington	6	5	1	.545	208	215
Pittsburgh	6	6	0	.500	211	263
N.Y. Giants	3	9	0	.250	179	277
Chi. Cardinals	1	10	1	.091	190	337

WESTERN CONFERENCE

	W	L	T	Pct.	Pts.	OP
Detroit	10	2	0	.833	271	205
San Francisco	9	3	0	.750	372	237
Los Angeles	8	3	1	.727	366	236
Chi. Bears	3	8	1	.273	218	262
Baltimore	3	9	0	.250	182	350
Green Bay	2	9	1	.182	200	338

NFL championship: DETROIT 17, Cleveland 16

1952

AMERICAN CONFERENCE

	W	L	T	Pct.	Pts.	OP
Cleveland	8	4	0	.667	310	213
N.Y. Giants	7	5	0	.583	234	231
Philadelphia	7	5	0	.583	252	271
Pittsburgh	5	7	0	.417	300	273
Chi. Cardinals	4	8	0	.333	172	221
Washington	4	8	0	.333	240	287

NATIONAL CONFERENCE

	W	L	T	Pct.	Pts.	OP
Detroit	9	3	0	.750	344	192
Los Angeles	9	3	0	.750	349	234
San Francisco	7	5	0	.583	285	221
Green Bay	6	6	0	.500	295	312
Chi. Bears	5	7	0	.417	245	326
Dallas Texans	1	11	0	.083	182	427

National Conference playoff: DETROIT 31, Los Angeles 21
NFL championship: Detroit 17, CLEVELAND 7

1951

AMERICAN CONFERENCE

	W	L	T	Pct.	Pts.	OP
Cleveland	11	1	0	.917	331	152
N.Y. Giants	9	2	1	.818	254	161
Washington	5	7	0	.417	183	296
Pittsburgh	4	7	1	.364	183	235
Philadelphia	4	8	0	.333	234	264
Chi. Cardinals	3	9	0	.250	210	287

NATIONAL CONFERENCE

	W	L	T	Pct.	Pts.	OP
Los Angeles	8	4	0	.667	392	261
Detroit	7	4	1	.636	336	259
San Francisco	7	4	1	.636	255	205
Chi. Bears	7	5	0	.583	286	282
Green Bay	3	9	0	.250	254	375
N.Y. Yanks	1	9	2	.100	241	382

NFL championship: LOS ANGELES 24, Cleveland 17

1950

AMERICAN CONFERENCE

	W	L	T	Pct.	Pts.	OP
Cleveland	10	2	0	.833	310	144
N.Y. Giants	10	2	0	.833	268	150
Philadelphia	6	6	0	.500	254	141
Pittsburgh	6	6	0	.500	180	195
Chi. Cardinals	5	7	0	.417	233	287
Washington	3	9	0	.250	232	326

NATIONAL CONFERENCE

	W	L	T	Pct.	Pts.	OP
Los Angeles	9	3	0	.750	466	309
Chi. Bears	9	3	0	.750	279	207
N.Y. Yanks	7	5	0	.583	366	367
Detroit	6	6	0	.500	321	285
Green Bay	3	9	0	.250	244	406
San Francisco	3	9	0	.250	213	300
Baltimore	1	11	0	.083	213	462

American Conference playoff: CLEVELAND 8, N.Y. Giants 3
National Conference playoff: LOS ANGELES 24, Chi. Bears 14
NFL championship: CLEVELAND 30, Los Angeles 28

1949

EASTERN DIVISION

	W	L	T	Pct.	Pts.	OP
Philadelphia	11	1	0	.917	364	134
Pittsburgh	6	5	1	.545	224	214
N.Y. Giants	6	6	0	.500	287	298
Washington	4	7	1	.364	268	339
N.Y. Bulldogs	1	10	1	.091	153	365

WESTERN DIVISION

	W	L	T	Pct.	Pts.	OP
Los Angeles	8	2	2	.800	360	239
Chi. Bears	9	3	0	.750	332	218
Chi. Cardinals	6	5	1	.545	360	301
Detroit	4	8	0	.333	237	259
Green Bay	2	10	0	.167	114	329

NFL championship: Philadelphia 14, LOS ANGELES 0

1948

EASTERN DIVISION

	W	L	T	Pct.	Pts.	OP
Philadelphia	9	2	1	.818	376	156
Washington	7	5	0	.583	291	287
N.Y. Giants	4	8	0	.333	297	388
Pittsburgh	4	8	0	.333	200	243
Boston	3	9	0	.250	174	372

WESTERN DIVISION

	W	L	T	Pct.	Pts.	OP
Chi. Cardinals	11	1	0	.917	395	226
Chi. Bears	10	2	0	.833	375	151
Los Angeles	6	5	1	.545	327	269
Green Bay	3	9	0	.250	154	290
Detroit	2	10	0	.167	200	407

NFL championship: PHILADELPHIA 7, Chi. Cardinals 0

1947

EASTERN DIVISION	W	L	T	Pct.	Pts.	OP	WESTERN DIVISION	W	L	T	Pct.	Pts.	OP
Philadelphia	8	4	0	.667	308	242	Chi. Cardinals	9	3	0	.750	306	231
Pittsburgh	8	4	0	.667	240	259	Chi. Bears	8	4	0	.667	363	241
Boston	4	7	1	.364	168	256	Green Bay	6	5	1	.545	274	210
Washington	4	8	0	.333	295	367	Los Angeles	6	6	0	.500	259	214
N.Y. Giants	2	8	2	.200	190	309	Detroit	3	9	0	.250	231	305

Eastern Division playoff: Philadelphia 21, PITTSBURGH 0
NFL championship: CHI. CARDINALS 28, Philadelphia 21

1946

EASTERN DIVISION	W	L	T	Pct.	Pts.	OP	WESTERN DIVISION	W	L	T	Pct.	Pts.	OP
N.Y. Giants	7	3	1	.700	236	162	Chi. Bears	8	2	1	.800	289	193
Philadelphia	6	5	0	.545	231	220	Los Angeles	6	4	1	.600	277	257
Washington	5	5	1	.500	171	191	Green Bay	6	5	0	.545	148	158
Pittsburgh	5	5	1	.500	136	117	Chi. Cardinals	6	5	0	.545	260	198
Boston	2	8	1	.200	189	273	Detroit	1	10	0	.091	142	310

NFL championship: Chi. Bears 24, N.Y. GIANTS 14

1945

EASTERN DIVISION	W	L	T	Pct.	Pts.	OP	WESTERN DIVISION	W	L	T	Pct.	Pts.	OP
Washington	8	2	0	.800	209	121	Cleveland	9	1	0	.900	244	136
Philadelphia	7	3	0	.700	272	133	Detroit	7	3	0	.700	195	194
N.Y. Giants	3	6	1	.333	179	198	Green Bay	6	4	0	.600	258	173
Boston	3	6	1	.333	123	211	Chi. Bears	3	7	0	.300	192	235
Pittsburgh	2	8	0	.200	79	220	Chi. Cardinals	1	9	0	.100	98	228

NFL championship: CLEVELAND 15, Washington 14

1944

EASTERN DIVISION	W	L	T	Pct.	Pts.	OP	WESTERN DIVISION	W	L	T	Pct.	Pts.	OP
N.Y. Giants	8	1	1	.889	206	75	Green Bay	8	2	0	.800	238	141
Philadelphia	7	1	2	.875	267	131	Chi. Bears	6	3	1	.667	258	172
Washington	6	3	1	.667	169	180	Detroit	6	3	1	.667	216	151
Boston	2	8	0	.200	82	233	Cleveland	4	6	0	.400	188	224
Brooklyn	0	10	0	.000	69	166	Card-Pitt	0	10	0	.000	108	328

NFL championship: Green Bay 14, N.Y. GIANTS 7

1943

EASTERN DIVISION	W	L	T	Pct.	Pts.	OP	WESTERN DIVISION	W	L	T	Pct.	Pts.	OP
Washington	6	3	1	.667	229	137	Chi. Bears	8	1	1	.889	303	157
N.Y. Giants	6	3	1	.667	197	170	Green Bay	7	2	1	.778	264	172
Phil-Pitt	5	4	1	.556	225	230	Detroit	3	6	1	.333	178	218
Brooklyn	2	8	0	.200	65	234	Chi. Cardinals	0	10	0	.000	95	238

Eastern Division playoff: Washington 28, N.Y. GIANTS 0
NFL championship: CHI. BEARS 41, Washington 21

1942

EASTERN DIVISION	W	L	T	Pct.	Pts.	OP	WESTERN DIVISION	W	L	T	Pct.	Pts.	OP
Washington	10	1	0	.909	227	102	Chi. Bears	11	0	0	1.000	376	84
Pittsburgh	7	4	0	.636	167	119	Green Bay	8	2	1	.800	300	215
N.Y. Giants	5	5	1	.500	155	139	Cleveland	5	6	0	.455	150	207
Brooklyn	3	8	0	.273	100	168	Chi. Cardinals	3	8	0	.273	98	209
Philadelphia	2	9	0	.182	134	239	Detroit	0	11	0	.000	38	263

NFL championship: WASHINGTON 14, Chi. Bears 6

1941

EASTERN DIVISION	W	L	T	Pct.	Pts.	OP	WESTERN DIVISION	W	L	T	Pct.	Pts.	OP
N.Y. Giants	8	3	0	.727	238	114	Chi. Bears	10	1	0	.909	396	147
Brooklyn	7	4	0	.636	158	127	Green Bay	10	1	0	.909	258	120
Washington	6	5	0	.545	176	174	Detroit	4	6	1	.400	121	195
Philadelphia	2	8	1	.200	119	218	Chi. Cardinals	3	7	1	.300	127	197
Pittsburgh	1	9	1	.100	103	276	Cleveland	2	9	0	.182	116	244

Western Division playoff: CHI. BEARS 33, Green Bay 14
NFL championship: CHI. BEARS 37, N.Y. Giants 9

1940

EASTERN DIVISION	W	L	T	Pct.	Pts.	OP	WESTERN DIVISION	W	L	T	Pct.	Pts.	OP
Washington	9	2	0	.818	245	142	Chi. Bears	8	3	0	.727	238	152
Brooklyn	8	3	0	.727	186	120	Green Bay	6	4	1	.600	238	155
N.Y. Giants	6	4	1	.600	131	133	Detroit	5	5	1	.500	138	153
Pittsburgh	2	7	2	.222	60	178	Cleveland	4	6	1	.400	171	191
Philadelphia	1	10	0	.091	111	211	Chi. Cardinals	2	7	2	.222	139	222

NFL championship: Chi. Bears 73, WASHINGTON 0

1939

EASTERN DIVISION	W	L	T	Pct.	Pts.	OP	WESTERN DIVISION	W	L	T	Pct.	Pts.	OP
N.Y. Giants	9	1	1	.900	168	85	Green Bay	9	2	0	.818	233	153
Washington	8	2	1	.800	242	94	Chi. Bears	8	3	0	.727	298	157
Brooklyn	4	6	1	.400	108	219	Detroit	6	5	0	.545	145	150
Philadelphia	1	9	1	.100	105	200	Cleveland	5	5	1	.500	195	164
Pittsburgh	1	9	1	.100	114	216	Chi. Cardinals	1	10	0	.091	84	254

NFL championship: GREEN BAY 27, N.Y. Giants 0

1938

EASTERN DIVISION	W	L	T	Pct.	Pts.	OP	WESTERN DIVISION	W	L	T	Pct.	Pts.	OP
N.Y. Giants	8	2	1	.800	194	79	Green Bay	8	3	0	.727	223	118
Washington	6	3	2	.667	148	154	Detroit	7	4	0	.636	119	108
Brooklyn	4	4	3	.500	131	161	Chi. Bears	6	5	0	.545	194	148
Philadelphia	5	6	0	.455	154	164	Cleveland	4	7	0	.364	131	215
Pittsburgh	2	9	0	.182	79	169	Chi. Cardinals	2	9	0	.182	111	168

NFL championship: N.Y. GIANTS 23, Green Bay 17

1937

EASTERN DIVISION	W	L	T	Pct.	Pts.	OP	WESTERN DIVISION	W	L	T	Pct.	Pts.	OP
Washington	8	3	0	.727	195	120	Chi. Bears	9	1	1	.900	201	100
N.Y. Giants	6	3	2	.667	128	109	Green Bay	7	4	0	.636	220	122
Pittsburgh	4	7	0	.364	122	145	Detroit	7	4	0	.636	180	105
Brooklyn	3	7	1	.300	82	174	Chi. Cardinals	5	5	1	.500	135	165
Philadelphia	2	8	1	.200	86	177	Cleveland	1	10	0	.091	75	207

NFL championship: Washington 28, CHI. BEARS 21

1936

EASTERN DIVISION	W	L	T	Pct.	Pts.	OP	WESTERN DIVISION	W	L	T	Pct.	Pts.	OP
Boston	7	5	0	.583	149	110	Green Bay	10	1	1	.909	248	118
Pittsburgh	6	6	0	.500	98	187	Chi. Bears	9	3	0	.750	222	94
N.Y. Giants	5	6	1	.455	115	163	Detroit	8	4	0	.667	235	102
Brooklyn	3	8	1	.273	92	161	Chi. Cardinals	3	8	1	.273	74	143
Philadelphia	1	11	0	.083	51	206							

NFL championship: Green Bay 21, Boston 6, at Polo Grounds, N.Y.

1935

EASTERN DIVISION	W	L	T	Pct.	Pts.	OP	WESTERN DIVISION	W	L	T	Pct.	Pts.	OP
N.Y. Giants	9	3	0	.750	180	96	Detroit	7	3	2	.700	191	111
Brooklyn	5	6	1	.455	90	141	Green Bay	8	4	0	.667	181	96
Pittsburgh	4	8	0	.333	100	209	Chi. Bears	6	4	2	.600	192	106
Boston	2	8	1	.200	65	123	Chi. Cardinals	6	4	2	.600	99	97
Philadelphia	2	9	0	.182	60	179							

NFL championship: DETROIT 26, N.Y. Giants 7
One game between Boston and Philadelphia was canceled.

1934

EASTERN DIVISION	W	L	T	Pct.	Pts.	OP	WESTERN DIVISION	W	L	T	Pct.	Pts.	OP
N.Y. Giants	8	5	0	.615	147	107	Chi. Bears	13	0	0	1.000	286	86
Boston	6	6	0	.500	107	94	Detroit	10	3	0	.769	238	59
Brooklyn	4	7	0	.364	61	153	Green Bay	7	6	0	.538	156	112
Philadelphia	4	7	0	.364	127	85	Chi. Cardinals	5	6	0	.455	80	84
Pittsburgh	2	10	0	.167	51	206	St. Louis	1	2	0	.333	27	61
							Cincinnati	0	8	0	.000	10	243

NFL championship: N.Y. GIANTS 30, Chi. Bears 13

1933

EASTERN DIVISION	W	L	T	Pct.	Pts.	OP	WESTERN DIVISION	W	L	T	Pct.	Pts.	OP
N.Y. Giants	11	3	0	.786	244	101	Chi. Bears	10	2	1	.833	133	82
Brooklyn	5	4	1	.556	93	54	Portsmouth	6	5	0	.545	128	87
Boston	5	5	2	.500	103	97	Green Bay	5	7	1	.417	170	107
Philadelphia	3	5	1	.375	77	158	Cincinnati	3	6	1	.333	38	110
Pittsburgh	3	6	2	.333	67	208	Chi. Cardinals	1	9	1	.100	52	101

NFL championship: CHI. BEARS 23, N.Y. Giants 21

1932

	W	L	T	Pct.
Chicago Bears	7	1	6	.875
Green Bay Packers	10	3	1	.769
Portsmouth, O., Spartans	6	2	4	.750
Boston Braves	4	4	2	.500
New York Giants	4	6	2	.400
Brooklyn Dodgers	3	9	0	.250
Chicago Cardinals	2	6	2	.250
Stapleton Stapes	2	7	3	.222

1931

	W	L	T	Pct.
Green Bay Packers	12	2	0	.857
Portsmouth, O., Spartans	11	3	0	.786
Chicago Bears	8	5	0	.615
Chicago Cardinals	5	4	0	.556
New York Giants	7	6	1	.538
Providence Steamroller	4	4	3	.500
Stapleton Stapes	4	6	1	.400
Cleveland Indians	2	8	0	.200
Brooklyn Dodgers	2	12	0	.143
Frankford Yellowjackets	1	6	1	.143

1930

	W	L	T	Pct.
Green Bay Packers	10	3	1	.769
New York Giants	13	4	0	.765
Chicago Bears	9	4	1	.692
Brooklyn Dodgers	7	4	1	.636
Providence Steamroller	6	4	1	.600
Stapleton Stapes	5	5	2	.500
Chicago Cardinals	5	6	2	.455
Portsmouth, O., Spartans	5	6	3	.455
Frankford Yellowjackets	4	14	1	.222
Minneapolis Red Jackets	1	7	1	.125
Newark Tornadoes	1	10	1	.091

1929

	W	L	T	Pct.
Green Bay Packers	12	0	1	1.000
New York Giants	13	1	1	.929
Frankford Yellowjackets	9	4	5	.692
Chicago Cardinals	6	6	1	.500
Boston Bulldogs	4	4	0	.500
Orange, N.J., Tornadoes	3	4	4	.429
Stapleton Stapes	3	4	3	.429
Providence Steamroller	4	6	2	.400
Chicago Bears	4	9	2	.308
Buffalo Bisons	1	7	1	.125
Minneapolis Red Jackets	1	9	0	.100
Dayton Triangles	0	6	0	.000

1928

	W	L	T	Pct.
Providence Steamroller	8	1	2	.889
Frankford Yellowjackets	11	3	2	.786
Detroit Wolverines	7	2	1	.778
Green Bay Packers	6	4	3	.600
Chicago Bears	7	5	1	.583
New York Giants	4	7	2	.364
New York Yankees	4	8	1	.333
Pottsville, Pa., Maroons	2	8	0	.200
Chicago Cardinals	1	5	0	.167
Dayton Triangles	0	7	0	.000

1927

	W	L	T	Pct.
New York Giants	11	1	1	.917
Green Bay Packers	7	2	1	.778
Chicago Bears	9	3	2	.750
Cleveland Bulldogs	8	4	1	.667
Providence Steamroller	8	5	1	.615
New York Yankees	7	8	1	.467
Frankford Yellowjackets	6	9	0	.400
Pottsville, Pa., Maroons	5	8	0	.385
Chicago Cardinals	3	7	1	.300
Dayton Triangles	1	6	1	.143
Duluth Eskimos	1	8	0	.111
Buffalo Bisons	0	5	0	.000

1926

	W	L	T	Pct.
Frankford Yellowjackets	14	1	1	.933
Chicago Bears	12	1	3	.923
Pottsville, Pa., Maroons	10	2	1	.833
Kansas City Cowboys	8	3	1	.727
Green Bay Packers	7	3	3	.700
Los Angeles Buccaneers	6	3	1	.667
New York Giants	8	4	1	.667
Duluth Eskimos	6	5	2	.545
Buffalo Rangers	4	4	2	.500
Chicago Cardinals	5	6	1	.455
Providence Steamroller	5	7	0	.417
Detroit Panthers	4	6	2	.400
Hartford Blues	3	7	0	.300
Brooklyn Lions	3	8	0	.273
Milwaukee Badgers	2	7	0	.222
Akron, Ohio, Indians	1	4	3	.200
Dayton Triangles	1	4	1	.200
Racine, Wis., Legion	1	4	0	.200
Columbus Tigers	1	6	0	.143
Canton, Ohio, Bulldogs	1	9	3	.100
Hammond, Ind., Pros	0	4	0	.000
Louisville Colonels	0	4	0	.000

1925

	W	L	T	Pct.
Cnicago Cardinals	11	2	1	.846
Pottsville, Pa., Maroons	10	2	0	.833
Detroit Panthers	8	2	2	.800
New York Giants	8	4	0	.667
Akron, Ohio, Indians	4	2	2	.667
Frankford Yellowjackets	13	7	0	.650
Chicago Bears	9	5	3	.643
Rock Island Independents	5	3	3	.625
Green Bay Packers	8	5	0	.615
Providence Steamroller	6	5	1	.545
Canton, Ohio, Bulldogs	4	4	0	.500
Cleveland Bulldogs	5	8	1	.385
Kansas City Cowboys	2	5	1	.286
Hammond, Ind., Pros	1	3	0	.250
Buffalo Bisons	1	6	2	.143
Duluth Kelleys	0	3	0	.000
Rochester Jeffersons	0	6	1	.000
Milwaukee Badgers	0	6	0	.000
Dayton Triangles	0	7	1	.000
Columbus Tigers	0	9	0	.000

1924

	W	L	T	Pct.
Cleveland Bulldogs	7	1	1	.875
Chicago Bears	6	1	4	.857
Frankford Yellowjackets	11	2	1	.846
Duluth Kelleys	5	1	0	.833
Rock Island Independents	6	2	2	.750
Green Bay Packers	8	4	0	.667
Buffalo Bisons	6	4	0	.600
Racine, Wis., Legion	4	3	3	.571
Chicago Cardinals	5	4	1	.556
Columbus Tigers	4	4	0	.500
Hammond, Ind., Pros	2	2	1	.500
Milwaukee Badgers	5	8	0	.385
Dayton Triangles	2	7	0	.222
Kansas City Cowboys	2	7	0	.222
Akron, Ohio, Indians	1	6	0	.143
Kenosha, Wis., Maroons	0	5	1	.000
Minneapolis Marines	0	6	0	.000
Rochester Jeffersons	0	7	0	.000

1923

	W	L	T	Pct.
Canton, Ohio, Bulldogs	11	0	1	1.000
Chicago Bears	9	2	1	.818
Green Bay Packers	7	2	1	.778
Milwaukee Badgers	7	2	3	.778
Cleveland Indians	3	1	3	.750
Chicago Cardinals	8	4	0	.667
Duluth Kelleys	4	3	0	.571
Buffalo All-Americans	5	4	3	.556
Columbus Tigers	5	4	1	.556
Racine, Wis., Legion	4	4	2	.500
Toledo Maroons	2	3	2	.400
Rock Island Independents	2	3	3	.400
Minneapolis Marines	2	5	2	.286
St. Louis All-Stars	1	4	2	.200
Hammond, Ind., Pros	1	5	1	.167
Dayton Triangles	1	6	1	.143
Akron, Ohio, Indians	1	6	0	.143
Oorang Indians	1	10	0	.091
Rochester Jeffersons	0	2	0	.000
Louisville Brecks	0	3	0	.000

1922

	W	L	T	Pct.
Canton, Ohio, Bulldogs	10	0	2	1.000
Chicago Bears	9	3	0	.750
Chicago Cardinals	8	3	0	.727
Toledo Maroons	5	2	2	.714
Rock Island Independents	4	2	1	.667
Dayton Triangles	4	3	1	.571
Green Bay Packers	4	3	3	.571
Racine, Wis., Legion	5	4	1	.556
Akron, Ohio, Pros	3	4	2	.429
Buffalo All-Americans	3	4	1	.429
Milwaukee Badgers	2	4	3	.333
Oorang Indians	2	6	0	.250
Minneapolis Marines	1	3	0	.250
Evansville Crimson Giants	0	2	0	.000
Louisville Brecks	0	3	0	.000
Rochester Jeffersons	0	3	1	.000
Hammond, Ind., Pros	0	4	1	.000
Columbus Panhandles	0	7	0	.000

1921

	W	L	T	Pct.
Chicago Staleys	10	1	1	.909
Buffalo All-Americans	9	1	2	.900
Akron, Ohio, Pros	7	2	1	.778
Green Bay Packers	6	2	2	.750
Canton, Ohio, Bulldogs	4	3	3	.571
Dayton Triangles	4	3	1	.571
Rock Island Independents	5	4	1	.556
Chicago Cardinals	2	3	2	.400
Cleveland Indians	2	6	0	.250
Rochester Jeffersons	2	6	0	.250
Detroit Heralds	1	7	1	.125
Columbus Panhandles	0	6	0	.000
Cincinnati Celts	0	8	0	.000

ATLANTA vs. BUFFALO
Series tied, 2-2
1973—Bills, 17-6 (A)
1977—Bills, 3-0 (B)
1980—Falcons, 30-14 (B)
1983—Falcons, 31-14 (A)
(Points—Falcons 67, Bills 48)

ATLANTA vs. CHICAGO
Falcons lead series, 9-4
1966—Bears, 23-6 (C)
1967—Bears, 23-14 (A)
1968—Falcons, 16-13 (C)
1969—Falcons, 48-31 (A)
1970—Bears, 23-14 (A)
1972—Falcons, 37-21 (C)
1973—Falcons, 46-6 (A)
1974—Falcons, 13-10 (A)
1976—Falcons, 10-0 (C)
1977—Falcons, 16-10 (C)
1978—Bears, 13-7 (C)
1980—Falcons, 28-17 (A)
1983—Falcons, 20-17 (C)
(Points—Falcons 275, Bears 207)

ATLANTA vs. CINCINNATI
Bengals lead series, 4-1
1971—Falcons, 9-6 (C)
1975—Bengals, 21-14 (A)
1978—Bengals, 37-7 (A)
1981—Bengals, 30-28 (A)
1984—Bengals, 35-14 (C)
(Points—Bengals 129, Falcons 72)

ATLANTA vs. CLEVELAND
Browns lead series, 6-1
1966—Browns, 49-17 (A)
1968—Browns, 30-7 (C)
1971—Falcons, 31-14 (C)
1976—Browns, 20-17 (A)
1978—Browns, 24-16 (A)
1981—Browns, 28-17 (C)
1984—Browns, 23-7 (A)
(Points—Browns 188, Falcons 112)

ATLANTA vs. DALLAS
Cowboys lead series, 7-1
1966—Cowboys, 47-14 (A)
1967—Cowboys, 37-7 (D)
1969—Cowboys, 24-17 (A)
1970—Cowboys, 13-0 (D)
1974—Cowboys, 24-0 (A)
1976—Falcons, 17-10 (A)
1978—*Cowboys, 27-20 (D)
1980—*Cowboys, 30-27 (A)
(Points—Cowboys 212, Falcons 102)
*NFC Divisional Playoff

ATLANTA vs. DENVER
Falcons lead series, 3-2
1970—Broncos, 24-10 (D)
1972—Falcons, 23-20 (A)
1975—Falcons, 35-21 (A)
1979—Broncos, 20-17 (A) OT
1982—Falcons, 34-27 (D)
(Points—Falcons 119, Broncos 112)

ATLANTA vs. DETROIT
Lions lead series, 11-4
1966—Lions, 28-10 (D)
1967—Lions, 24-3 (D)
1968—Lions, 24-7 (A)
1969—Lions, 27-21 (D)
1971—Lions, 41-38 (D)
1972—Lions, 26-23 (A)
1973—Lions, 31-6 (D)
1975—Lions, 17-14 (A)
1976—Lions, 24-10 (D)
1977—Falcons, 17-6 (A)
1978—Lions, 14-0 (A)
1979—Lions, 24-23 (D)
1980—Falcons, 43-28 (A)
1983—Falcons, 30-14 (D)
1984—Lions, 27-24 (A) OT
(Points—Lions 341, Falcons 283)

ATLANTA vs. GREEN BAY
Packers lead series, 8-6
1966—Packers, 56-3 (Mil)
1967—Packers, 23-0 (Mil)
1968—Packers, 38-7 (A)
1969—Packers, 28-10 (GB)
1970—Packers, 27-24 (GB)
1971—Falcons, 28-21 (A)
1972—Falcons, 10-9 (Mil)
1974—Packers, 10-3 (A)
1975—Packers, 22-13 (GB)
1976—Packers, 24-20 (A)
1979—Falcons, 25-7 (A)
1981—Falcons, 31-17 (GB)
1982—Packers, 38-7 (A)
1983—Falcons, 47-41 (A) OT
(Points—Packers 354, Falcons 235)

ATLANTA vs. HOUSTON
Falcons lead series, 4-1
1972—Falcons, 20-10 (A)
1976—Oilers, 20-14 (H)

1978—Falcons, 20-14 (A)
1981—Falcons, 31-27 (H)
1984—Falcons, 42-10 (A)
(Points—Falcons 127, Oilers 81)

ATLANTA vs. *INDIANAPOLIS
Colts lead series, 8-0
1966—Colts, 19-7 (A)
1967—Colts, 38-31 (B)
Colts, 49-7 (A)
1968—Colts, 28-20 (A)
Colts, 44-0 (B)
1969—Colts, 21-14 (A)
Colts, 13-6 (B)
1974—Colts, 17-7 (A)
(Points—Colts 229, Falcons 92)
*Franchise in Baltimore prior to 1984

ATLANTA vs. KANSAS CITY
Chiefs lead series, 1-0
1972—Chiefs, 17-14 (A)

ATLANTA vs. *L.A. RAIDERS
Raiders lead series, 3-1
1971—Falcons, 24-13 (A)
1975—Raiders, 37-34 (O) OT
1979—Raiders, 50-19 (O)
1982—Raiders, 38-14 (A)
(Points—Raiders 138, Falcons 91)
*Franchise in Oakland prior to 1982

ATLANTA vs. L.A. RAMS
Rams lead series, 27-7-2
1966—Rams, 19-14 (A)
1967—Rams, 31-3 (A)
Rams, 20-3 (LA)
1968—Rams, 27-14 (LA)
Rams, 17-10 (A)
1969—Rams, 17-7 (LA)
Rams, 38-6 (A)
1970—Tie, 10-10 (A)
Rams, 17-7 (LA)
1971—Tie, 20-20 (LA)
Rams, 24-16 (A)
1972—Falcons, 31-3 (A)
Rams, 20-7 (LA)
1973—Rams, 31-0 (LA)
Falcons, 15-13 (A)
1974—Rams, 21-0 (LA)
Rams, 30-7 (A)
1975—Rams, 22-7 (LA)
Rams, 16-7 (A)
1976—Rams, 30-14 (A)
Rams, 59-0 (LA)
1977—Falcons, 17-6 (A)
Rams, 23-7 (LA)
1978—Rams, 10-0 (LA)
Falcons, 15-7 (A)
1979—Rams, 20-14 (LA)
Rams, 34-13 (A)
1980—Falcons, 13-10 (A)
Rams, 20-17 (LA) OT
1981—Rams, 37-35 (A)
Rams, 21-16 (LA)
1982—Rams, 34-17 (A)
1983—Rams, 27-21 (LA)
Rams, 36-13 (A)
1984—Rams, 30-28 (LA)
Rams, 24-10 (A)
(Points—Rams 805, Falcons 453)

ATLANTA vs. MIAMI
Dolphins lead series, 4-0
1970—Dolphins, 20-7 (A)
1974—Dolphins, 42-7 (M)
1980—Dolphins, 20-17 (A)
1983—Dolphins, 31-24 (M)
(Points—Dolphins 113, Falcons 55)

ATLANTA vs. MINNESOTA
Vikings lead series, 9-5
1966—Falcons, 20-13 (M)
1967—Falcons, 21-20 (A)
1968—Vikings, 47-7 (M)
1969—Vikings, 10-3 (A)
1970—Vikings, 37-7 (A)
1971—Vikings, 24-7 (M)
1973—Falcons, 20-14 (A)
1974—Vikings, 23-10 (M)
1975—Vikings, 38-0 (A)
1977—Vikings, 14-7 (A)
1980—Vikings, 24-23 (M)
1981—Falcons, 31-30 (A)
1982—*Vikings, 30-24 (M)
1984—Vikings, 27-20 (M)
(Points—Vikings 344, Falcons 207)
*NFC First Round Playoff

ATLANTA vs. NEW ENGLAND
Series tied, 2-2
1972—Patriots, 21-20 (NE)
1977—Patriots, 16-10 (A)
1980—Falcons, 37-21 (NE)
1983—Falcons, 24-13 (A)
(Points—Falcons 91, Patriots 71)

ATLANTA vs. NEW ORLEANS
Falcons lead series, 21-11

1967—Saints, 27-24 (NO)
1969—Falcons, 45-17 (A)
1970—Falcons, 14-3 (NO)
Falcons, 32-14 (A)
1971—Falcons, 28-6 (A)
Falcons, 24-20 (NO)
1972—Falcons, 21-14 (NO)
Falcons, 36-20 (A)
1973—Falcons, 62-7 (NO)
Falcons, 14-10 (A)
1974—Saints, 14-13 (NO)
Saints, 13-3 (A)
1975—Falcons, 14-7 (A)
Saints, 23-7 (NO)
1976—Saints, 30-0 (NO)
Falcons, 23-20 (A)
1977—Saints, 21-20 (NO)
Falcons, 35-7 (A)
1978—Falcons, 20-17 (NO)
Falcons, 20-17 (A)
1979—Falcons, 40-34 (NO) OT
Falcons, 37-6 (A)
1980—Falcons, 41-14 (NO)
Falcons, 31-13 (A)
1981—Falcons, 27-0 (A)
Falcons, 41-10 (NO)
1982—Falcons, 35-0 (A)
Saints, 35-6 (NO)
1983—Saints, 19-17 (A)
Falcons, 27-10 (NO)
1984—Falcons, 36-28 (NO)
Saints, 17-13 (A)
(Points—Falcons 758, Saints 541)

ATLANTA vs. N.Y. GIANTS
Falcons lead series, 6-5
1966—Falcons, 27-16 (NY)
1968—Falcons, 24-21 (A)
1971—Giants, 21-17 (A)
1974—Falcons, 14-7 (New Haven)
1977—Falcons, 17-3 (A)
1978—Falcons, 23-20 (A)
1979—Giants, 24-3 (NY)
1981—Giants, 27-24 (A) OT
1982—Giants, 16-14 (NY)
1983—Giants, 16-13 (A) OT
1984—Giants, 19-7 (A)
(Points—Giants 188, Falcons 185)

ATLANTA vs. N.Y. JETS
Falcons lead series, 2-1
1973—Falcons, 28-20 (NY)
1980—Jets, 14-7 (A)
1983—Falcons, 27-21 (NY)
(Points—Falcons 62, Jets 55)

ATLANTA vs. PHILADELPHIA
Falcons lead series, 6-5-1
1966—Eagles, 23-10 (P)
1967—Eagles, 38-7 (A)
1969—Falcons, 27-3 (P)
1970—Tie, 13-13 (P)
1973—Falcons, 44-27 (P)
1976—Eagles, 14-13 (A)
1978—*Falcons, 14-13 (A)
1979—Falcons, 14-10 (P)
1980—Falcons, 20-17 (P)
1981—Eagles, 16-13 (P)
1983—Eagles, 28-24 (A)
1984—Eagles, 26-10 (A)
(Points—Falcons 225, Eagles 212)
*NFC First Round Playoff

ATLANTA vs. PITTSBURGH
Steelers lead series, 6-1
1966—Steelers, 57-33 (A)
1968—Steelers, 41-21 (A)
1970—Falcons, 27-16 (A)
1974—Steelers, 24-17 (P)
1978—Steelers, 31-7 (P)
1981—Steelers, 34-20 (A)
1984—Steelers, 35-10 (P)
(Points—Steelers 238, Falcons 135)

ATLANTA vs. ST. LOUIS
Cardinals lead series, 6-3
1966—Falcons, 16-10 (A)
1968—Cardinals, 17-12 (StL)
1971—Cardinals, 26-9 (A)
1973—Cardinals, 32-10 (A)
1975—Cardinals, 23-20 (StL)
1978—Cardinals, 42-21 (StL)
1980—Falcons, 33-27 (StL) OT
1981—Falcons, 41-20 (A)
1982—Cardinals, 23-20 (A)
(Points—Falcons 220, Falcons 182)

ATLANTA vs. SAN DIEGO
Falcons lead series, 2-0
1973—Falcons, 41-0 (SD)
1979—Falcons, 28-26 (SD)
(Points—Falcons 69, Chargers 26)

ATLANTA vs. SAN FRANCISCO
49ers lead series, 19-17
1966—49ers, 44-7 (A)
1967—49ers, 38-7 (SF)

49ers, 34-28 (A)
1968—49ers, 28-13 (SF)
49ers, 14-12 (A)
1969—49ers, 24-12 (A)
Falcons, 21-7 (SF)
1970—Falcons, 21-20 (A)
49ers, 24-20 (SF)
1971—Falcons, 20-17 (A)
49ers, 24-3 (SF)
1972—49ers, 49-14 (A)
49ers, 20-0 (SF)
1973—49ers, 13-9 (A)
Falcons, 17-3 (SF)
1974—49ers, 16-10 (A)
49ers, 27-0 (SF)
1975—Falcons, 17-3 (SF)
Falcons, 31-9 (A)
1976—49ers, 15-0 (SF)
Falcons, 21-16 (A)
1977—Falcons, 7-0 (SF)
49ers, 10-3 (A)
1978—Falcons, 20-17 (SF)
Falcons, 21-10 (A)
1979—Falcons, 20-15 (SF)
Falcons, 31-21 (A)
1980—Falcons, 20-17 (SF)
Falcons, 35-10 (A)
1981—Falcons, 34-17 (A)
49ers, 17-14 (SF)
1982—Falcons, 17-7 (SF)
1983—49ers, 24-20 (A)
Falcons, 28-24 (A)
1984—49ers, 14-5 (SF)
49ers, 35-17 (A)
(Points—49ers 676, Falcons 582)

ATLANTA vs. SEATTLE
Seahawks lead series, 2-0
1976—Seahawks, 30-13 (S)
1979—Seahawks, 31-28 (A)
(Points—Seahawks 61, Falcons 41)

ATLANTA vs. TAMPA BAY
Buccaneers lead series, 3-2
1977—Falcons, 17-0 (TB)
1978—Buccaneers, 14-9 (TB)
1979—Falcons, 17-14 (A)
1981—Buccaneers, 24-23 (TB)
1984—Buccaneers, 23-6 (TB)
(Points—Buccaneers 75, Falcons 72)

ATLANTA vs. WASHINGTON
Redskins lead series, 8-2-1
1966—Redskins, 33-20 (W)
1967—Tie, 20-20 (A)
1969—Redskins, 27-20 (W)
1972—Redskins, 24-13 (W)
1975—Redskins, 30-27 (A)
1977—Redskins, 10-6 (W)
1978—Falcons, 20-17 (A)
1979—Redskins, 16-7 (A)
1980—Falcons, 10-6 (A)
1983—Redskins, 37-21 (W)
1984—Redskins, 27-14 (W)
(Points—Redskins 247, Falcons 178)

BUFFALO vs. ATLANTA
Series tied, 2-2;
See Atlanta vs. Buffalo

BUFFALO vs. CHICAGO
Bears lead series, 2-1
1970—Bears, 31-13 (C)
1974—Bills, 16-6 (B)
1979—Bears, 7-0 (B)
(Points—Bears 44, Bills 29)

BUFFALO vs. CINCINNATI
Bengals lead series, 7-5
1968—Bengals, 34-23 (C)
1969—Bills, 16-13 (B)
1970—Bengals, 43-14 (B)
1973—Bengals, 16-13 (B)
1975—Bengals, 33-24 (C)
1978—Bills, 5-0 (B)
1979—Bills, 51-24 (B)
1980—Bills, 14-0 (C)
1981—Bengals, 27-24 (C) OT
*Bengals, 28-21 (C)
1983—Bills, 10-6 (C)
1984—Bengals, 52-21 (C)
(Points—Bengals 276, Bills 236)
*AFC Divisional Playoff

BUFFALO vs. CLEVELAND
Browns lead series, 4-2
1972—Browns, 27-10 (C)
1974—Bills, 15-10 (C)
1977—Browns, 27-16 (B)
1978—Browns, 41-20 (C)
1981—Bills, 22-13 (B)
1984—Browns, 13-10 (B)
(Points—Browns 131, Bills 93)

BUFFALO vs. DALLAS
Cowboys lead series, 3-1
1971—Cowboys, 49-37 (B)

1976—Cowboys, 17-10 (D)
1981—Cowboys, 27-14 (D)
1984—Bills, 14-3 (B)
(Points—Cowboys 96, Bills 75)

BUFFALO vs. DENVER
Bills lead series, 13-9-1
1960—Broncos, 27-21 (B)
Tie, 38-38 (D)
1961—Broncos, 22-10 (B)
Bills, 23-10 (D)
1962—Broncos, 23-20 (B)
Bills, 45-38 (D)
1963—Bills, 30-28 (D)
Bills, 27-17 (B)
1964—Bills, 30-13 (D)
Bills, 30-19 (D)
1965—Bills, 30-15 (D)
Bills, 31-13 (B)
1966—Bills, 38-21 (B)
1967—Bills, 17-16 (D)
Broncos, 21-20 (B)
1968—Broncos, 34-32 (D)
1969—Bills, 41-28 (B)
1970—Broncos, 25-10 (B)
1975—Bills, 38-14 (B)
1977—Broncos, 26-6 (D)
1979—Broncos, 19-16 (B)
1981—Bills, 9-7 (B)
1984—Broncos, 37-7 (B)
(Points—Bills 569, Broncos 511)

BUFFALO vs. DETROIT
Series tied, 1-1-1
1972—Tie, 21-21 (B)
1976—Lions, 27-14 (D)
1979—Bills, 20-17 (D)
(Points—Lions 65, Bills 55)

BUFFALO vs. GREEN BAY
Bills lead series, 2-1
1974—Bills, 27-7 (GB)
1979—Bills, 19-12 (B)
1982—Packers, 33-21 (Mil)
(Points—Bills 67, Packers 52)

BUFFALO vs. HOUSTON
Oilers lead series, 17-8
1960—Bills, 25-24 (B)
Oilers, 31-23 (H)
1961—Bills, 22-12 (H)
Oilers, 28-16 (B)
1962—Oilers, 28-23 (B)
Oilers, 17-14 (H)
1963—Oilers, 31-20 (H)
Oilers, 28-14 (H)
1964—Bills, 48-17 (H)
Bills, 24-10 (B)
1965—Oilers, 19-17 (B)
Bills, 29-18 (H)
1966—Bills, 27-20 (B)
Bills, 42-20 (H)
1967—Oilers, 20-3 (B)
Oilers, 10-3 (H)
1968—Oilers, 30-7 (B)
Oilers, 35-6 (H)
1969—Oilers, 17-3 (B)
Oilers, 28-14 (H)
1971—Oilers, 20-14 (B)
1974—Oilers, 21-9 (B)
1976—Oilers, 13-3 (B)
1978—Oilers, 17-10 (H)
1983—Bills, 30-13 (B)
(Points—Oilers 527, Bills 446)

BUFFALO vs. *INDIANAPOLIS
Series tied, 14-14-1
1970—Tie, 17-17 (Balt)
Colts, 20-14 (Buff)
1971—Colts, 43-0 (Buff)
Colts, 24-0 (Balt)
1972—Colts, 17-0 (Buff)
Colts, 35-7 (Balt)
1973—Bills, 31-13 (Buff)
Bills, 24-17 (Balt)
1974—Bills, 27-14 (Balt)
Bills, 6-0 (Buff)
1975—Bills, 38-31 (Balt)
Colts, 42-35 (Buff)
1976—Colts, 31-13 (Buff)
Colts, 58-20 (Balt)
1977—Colts, 17-14 (Balt)
Colts, 31-13 (Buff)
1978—Bills, 24-17 (Buff)
Bills, 21-14 (Balt)
1979—Bills, 31-13 (Balt)
Colts, 14-13 (Buff)
1980—Colts, 17-12 (Buff)
Colts, 28-24 (Balt)
1981—Bills, 35-3 (Balt)
Bills, 23-17 (Buff)
1982—Bills, 20-0 (Buff)
1983—Bills, 28-23 (Buff)
Bills, 30-7 (Balt)
1984—Colts, 31-17 (I)
Bills, 21-15 (Buff)
(Points—Colts 609, Bills 558)
*Franchise in Baltimore prior to 1984

BUFFALO vs. *KANSAS CITY
Bills lead series, 14-11-1
1960—Texans, 45-28 (B)
Texans, 24-7 (D)
1961—Bills, 27-24 (B)
Bills, 30-20 (D)
1962—Texans, 41-21 (D)
Bills, 23-14 (B)
1963—Tie, 27-27 (B)
Bills, 35-26 (KC)
1964—Bills, 34-17 (B)
Bills, 35-22 (KC)
1965—Bills, 23-7 (KC)
Bills, 34-25 (B)
1966—Chiefs, 42-20 (B)
Bills, 29-14 (KC)
**Chiefs, 31-7 (B)
1967—Chiefs, 23-13 (KC)
1968—Chiefs, 18-7 (B)
1969—Chiefs, 29-7 (B)
Chiefs, 22-19 (KC)
1971—Chiefs, 22-9 (KC)
1973—Bills, 23-14 (B)
1976—Bills, 50-17 (B)
1978—Bills, 28-13 (B)
Chiefs, 14-10 (KC)
1982—Bills, 14-9 (B)
1983—Bills, 14-9 (KC)
(Points—Chiefs 574, Bills 569)
*Franchise in Dallas prior to 1963 and known as Texans
**AFL Championship

BUFFALO vs. *L.A. RAIDERS
Raiders lead series, 12-11
1960—Bills, 38-9 (B)
Raiders, 20-7 (O)
1961—Raiders, 31-22 (B)
Bills, 26-21 (O)
1962—Bills, 14-6 (B)
Bills, 10-6 (O)
1963—Raiders, 35-17 (O)
Bills, 12-0 (B)
1964—Bills, 23-20 (B)
Raiders, 16-13 (O)
1965—Bills, 17-12 (B)
Bills, 17-14 (O)
1966—Bills, 31-10 (O)
1967—Raiders, 24-20 (B)
Raiders, 28-21 (O)
1968—Raiders, 48-6 (B)
Raiders, 13-10 (O)
1969—Raiders, 50-21 (O)
1972—Raiders, 28-16 (O)
1974—Bills, 21-20 (B)
1977—*Raiders, 34-13 (O)
1980—Bills, 24-7 (B)
1983—Raiders, 27-24 (B)
(Points—Raiders 479, Bills 423)
*Franchise in Oakland prior to 1982

BUFFALO vs. L.A. RAMS
Rams lead series, 3-1
1970—Rams, 19-0 (B)
1974—Rams, 19-14 (LA)
1980—Bills, 10-7 (B) OT
1983—Rams, 41-17 (LA)
(Points—Rams 86, Bills 41)

BUFFALO vs. MIAMI
Dolphins lead series, 30-7-1
1966—Bills, 58-24 (B)
Bills, 29-0 (M)
1967—Bills, 35-13 (B)
Dolphins, 17-14 (M)
1968—Tie, 14-14 (M)
Dolphins, 21-17 (B)
1969—Dolphins, 24-6 (M)
Bills, 28-3 (B)
1970—Dolphins, 33-14 (B)
Dolphins, 45-7 (M)
1971—Dolphins, 29-14 (B)
Dolphins, 34-0 (M)
1972—Dolphins, 24-23 (M)
Dolphins, 30-16 (B)
1973—Dolphins, 27-6 (M)
Dolphins, 17-0 (B)
1974—Dolphins, 24-16 (B)
Dolphins, 35-28 (M)
1975—Dolphins, 35-30 (M)
Dolphins, 31-21 (B)
1976—Dolphins, 30-21 (B)
Dolphins, 45-27 (M)
1977—Dolphins, 13-0 (B)
Dolphins, 31-24 (M)
1978—Dolphins, 31-24 (M)
Dolphins, 25-24 (B)
1979—Dolphins, 9-7 (B)
Dolphins, 17-7 (M)
1980—Bills, 17-7 (B)
Dolphins, 17-14 (M)
1981—Bills, 31-21 (B)
Dolphins, 16-6 (M)
1982—Dolphins, 9-7 (B)
Dolphins, 27-10 (M)
1983—Dolphins, 12-0 (B)

Bills, 38-35 (M) OT
1984—Dolphins, 21-17 (B)
Dolphins, 38-7 (M)
(Points—Dolphins 884, Bills 647)

BUFFALO vs. MINNESOTA
Vikings lead series, 3-1
1971—Vikings, 19-0 (M)
1975—Vikings, 35-13 (B)
1979—Vikings, 10-3 (M)
1982—Bills, 23-22 (B)
(Points—Vikings 86, Bills 39)

BUFFALO vs. *NEW ENGLAND
Patriots lead series, 26-23-1
1960—Bills, 13-0 (B)
Bills, 38-14 (Buff)
1961—Patriots, 23-21 (Buff)
Patriots, 52-21 (B)
1962—Tie, 28-28 (Buff)
Patriots, 21-10 (B)
1963—Bills, 28-21 (Buff)
Patriots, 17-7 (B)
**Patriots, 26-8 (Buff)
1964—Patriots, 36-28 (Buff)
Bills, 24-14 (B)
1965—Bills, 24-7 (Buff)
Bills, 23-7 (B)
1966—Patriots, 20-10 (Buff)
Patriots, 14-3 (B)
1967—Patriots, 23-0 (Buff)
Bills, 44-16 (B)
1968—Patriots, 16-7 (Buff)
Patriots, 23-6 (B)
1969—Bills, 23-16 (Buff)
Patriots, 35-21 (B)
1970—Bills, 45-10 (B)
Patriots, 14-10 (Buff)
1971—Patriots, 38-33 (NE)
Bills, 27-20 (Buff)
1972—Bills, 38-14 (Buff)
Bills, 27-24 (NE)
1973—Bills, 31-13 (NE)
Bills, 37-13 (Buff)
1974—Bills, 30-28 (Buff)
Bills, 29-28 (NE)
1975—Bills, 45-31 (Buff)
Bills, 34-14 (NE)
1976—Patriots, 26-22 (Buff)
Patriots, 20-10 (NE)
1977—Bills, 24-14 (NE)
Patriots, 20-7 (Buff)
1978—Patriots, 14-10 (Buff)
Patriots, 26-24 (NE)
1979—Patriots, 26-6 (Buff)
Bills, 16-13 (NE) OT
1980—Bills, 31-13 (Buff)
Patriots, 24-2 (NE)
1981—Bills, 20-17 (Buff)
Bills, 19-10 (NE)
1982—Patriots, 30-19 (NE)
1983—Patriots, 31-0 (Buff)
Patriots, 21-7 (NE)
1984—Patriots, 21-17 (B)
Patriots, 38-10 (NE)
(Points—Patriots 1,040, Bills 1,017)
*Franchise in Boston prior to 1971
**Division Playoff

BUFFALO vs. NEW ORLEANS
Bills lead series, 2-1
1973—Saints, 13-0 (NO)
1980—Bills, 35-26 (NO)
1983—Bills, 27-21 (B)
(Points—Bills 62, Saints 60)

BUFFALO vs. N.Y. GIANTS
Giants lead series, 2-1
1970—Giants, 20-6 (NY)
1975—Giants, 17-14 (B)
1978—Bills, 41-17 (B)
(Points—Bills 61, Giants 54)

BUFFALO vs. *N.Y. JETS
Bills lead series, 26-23
1960—Titans, 27-3 (NY)
Titans, 17-13 (B)
1961—Bills, 41-31 (B)
Titans, 21-14 (NY)
1962—Titans, 17-6 (B)
Bills, 20-3 (NY)
1963—Bills, 45-14 (B)
Bills, 19-10 (NY)
1964—Bills, 34-24 (B)
Bills, 20-7 (NY)
1965—Bills, 33-21 (B)
Jets, 14-12 (NY)
1966—Bills, 33-23 (NY)
Bills, 14-3 (B)
1967—Bills, 20-17 (B)
Jets, 20-10 (NY)
1968—Bills, 37-35 (B)
Jets, 25-21 (NY)
1969—Jets, 33-19 (NY)
Jets, 16-6 (NY)
1970—Bills, 34-31 (B)
Bills, 10-6 (NY)
1971—Jets, 28-17 (NY)

Jets, 20-7 (B)
1972—Jets, 41-24 (B)
Jets, 41-3 (NY)
1973—Bills, 9-7 (B)
Bills, 34-14 (NY)
1974—Bills, 16-12 (B)
Jets, 20-10 (NY)
1975—Bills, 42-14 (B)
Bills, 24-23 (NY)
1976—Jets, 17-14 (B)
Jets, 19-14 (B)
1977—Jets, 24-19 (B)
Bills, 14-10 (NY)
1978—Jets, 21-20 (B)
Jets, 45-14 (NY)
1979—Bills, 46-31 (B)
Bills, 14-12 (NY)
1980—Bills, 20-10 (B)
Bills, 31-24 (NY)
1981—Bills, 31-0 (B)
Jets, 33-14 (NY)
**Bills, 31-27 (NY)
1983—Jets, 34-10 (B)
Bills, 24-17 (NY)
1984—Jets, 28-26 (B)
Jets, 21-17 (NY)
(Points—Bills 1,009, Jets 1,008)
*Jets known as Titans prior to 1963
**AFC First Round Playoff

BUFFALO vs. PHILADELPHIA
Eagles lead series, 2-1
1973—Bills, 27-26 (B)
1981—Eagles, 20-14 (B)
1984—Eagles, 27-17 (B)
(Points—Eagles 73, Bills 58)

BUFFALO vs. PITTSBURGH
Steelers lead series, 5-3
1970—Steelers, 23-10 (P)
1972—Steelers, 38-21 (B)
1974—*Steelers, 32-14 (P)
1975—Bills, 30-21 (P)
1978—Steelers, 28-17 (B)
1979—Steelers, 28-0 (P)
1980—Bills, 28-13 (B)
1982—Bills, 13-0 (B)
(Points—Steelers 183, Bills 133)
*AFC Divisional Playoff

BUFFALO vs. ST. LOUIS
Cardinals lead series, 3-1
1971—Cardinals, 28-23 (B)
1975—Bills, 32-14 (StL)
1981—Cardinals, 24-0 (StL)
1984—Cardinals, 37-7 (StL)
(Points—Cardinals 103, Bills 62)

BUFFALO vs. *SAN DIEGO
Chargers lead series, 15-9-2
1960—Chargers, 24-10 (B)
Bills, 32-3 (LA)
1961—Chargers, 19-11 (B)
Chargers, 28-10 (SD)
1962—Bills, 35-10 (B)
Bills, 40-20 (SD)
1963—Chargers, 14-10 (SD)
Chargers, 23-13 (B)
1964—Bills, 30-3 (B)
Bills, 27-24 (SD)
**Bills, 20-7 (B)
1965—Chargers, 34-3 (B)
Tie, 20-20 (SD)
**Bills, 23-0 (SD)
1966—Chargers, 27-7 (SD)
Tie, 17-17 (B)
1967—Chargers, 37-17 (B)
1968—Chargers, 21-6 (SD)
1969—Chargers, 45-6 (SD)
1971—Chargers, 20-3 (SD)
1973—Chargers, 34-7 (SD)
1976—Chargers, 34-13 (B)
1979—Chargers, 27-19 (SD)
1980—Bills, 26-24 (SD)
***Chargers, 20-14 (SD)
1981—Bills, 28-27 (SD)
(Points—Chargers 562, Bills 447)
*Franchise in Los Angeles prior to 1961
**AFL Championship
***AFC Divisional Playoff

BUFFALO vs. SAN FRANCISCO
Bills lead series, 2-1
1972—Bills, 27-20 (B)
1980—Bills, 18-13 (SF)
1983—49ers, 23-10 (B)
(Points—49ers 56, Bills 55)

BUFFALO vs. SEATTLE
Seahawks lead series, 2-0
1977—Seahawks, 56-17 (S)
1984—Seahawks, 31-28 (S)
(Points—Seahawks 87, Bills 45)

BUFFALO vs. TAMPA BAY
Buccaneers lead series, 2-1
1976—Bills, 14-9 (TB)
1978—Buccaneers, 31-10 (TB)
1982—Buccaneers, 24-23 (TB)
(Points—Buccaneers 64, Bills 47)

223

BUFFALO vs. WASHINGTON
Series tied 2-2
1972—Bills, 24-17 (W)
1977—Redskins, 10-0 (B)
1981—Bills, 21-14 (B)
1984—Redskins, 41-14 (W)
(Points—Redskins 82, Bills 59)

CHICAGO vs. ATLANTA
Falcons lead series, 9-4;
See Atlanta vs. Chicago
CHICAGO vs. BUFFALO
Bears lead series, 2-1;
See Buffalo vs. Chicago
CHICAGO vs. CINCINNATI
Bengals lead series, 2-0;
1972—Bengals, 13-3 (Chi)
1980—Bengals, 17-14 (Chi) OT
(Points—Bengals 30, Bears 17)
CHICAGO vs. CLEVELAND
Browns lead series, 6-2
1951—Browns, 42-21 (Cle)
1954—Browns, 39-10 (Chi)
1960—Browns, 42-0 (Cle)
1961—Bears, 17-14 (Chi)
1967—Browns, 24-0 (Cle)
1969—Browns, 28-24 (Chi)
1972—Bears, 17-0 (Cle)
1980—Browns, 27-21 (Cle)
(Points—Browns 216, Bears 110)
CHICAGO vs. DALLAS
Cowboys lead series, 8-3
1960—Bears, 17-7 (C)
1962—Bears, 34-33 (D)
1964—Cowboys, 24-10 (C)
1968—Cowboys, 34-3 (C)
1971—Bears, 23-19 (C)
1973—Cowboys, 20-17 (C)
1976—Cowboys, 31-21 (D)
1977—*Cowboys, 37-7 (D)
1979—Cowboys, 24-20 (D)
1981—Cowboys, 10-9 (D)
1984—Cowboys, 23-14 (C)
(Points—Cowboys 262, Bears 175)
*NFC Divisional Playoff
CHICAGO vs. DENVER
Bears lead series, 4-3
1971—Broncos, 6-3 (D)
1973—Bears, 33-14 (D)
1976—Broncos, 28-14 (C)
1978—Broncos, 16-7 (D)
1981—Bears, 35-24 (C)
1983—Bears, 31-14 (C)
1984—Bears, 27-0 (C)
(Points—Bears 150, Broncos 102)
CHICAGO vs. *DETROIT
Bears lead series, 62-44-5
1930—Spartans, 7-6 (P)
Bears, 14-6 (C)
1931—Bears, 9-6 (C)
Spartans, 3-0 (P)
1932—Tie, 13-13 (C)
Tie, 7-7 (P)
**Bears, 9-0 (C)
1933—Bears, 17-14 (C)
Bears, 17-7 (P)
1934—Bears, 19-16 (D)
Bears, 10-7 (C)
1935—Tie, 20-20 (C)
Lions, 14-2 (D)
1936—Bears, 12-10 (C)
Lions, 13-7 (D)
1937—Bears, 28-20 (C)
Bears, 13-0 (D)
1938—Lions, 13-7 (C)
Lions, 14-7 (D)
1939—Lions, 10-0 (C)
Bears, 23-13 (D)
1940—Bears, 7-0 (C)
Lions, 17-14 (D)
1941—Bears, 49-0 (C)
Bears, 24-7 (D)
1942—Bears, 16-0 (C)
Bears, 42-0 (D)
1943—Bears, 27-21 (D)
Bears, 35-14 (D)
1944—Tie, 21-21 (C)
Lions, 41-21 (D)
1945—Lions, 16-10 (D)
Lions, 35-28 (C)
1946—Bears, 42-6 (C)
Bears, 45-24 (D)
1947—Bears, 33-24 (C)
Bears, 34-14 (D)
1948—Bears, 28-0 (C)
Bears, 42-14 (D)
1949—Bears, 27-24 (C)
Bears, 28-7 (D)
1950—Bears, 35-21 (D)
Bears, 6-3 (C)
1951—Bears, 28-23 (D)
Lions, 41-28 (C)
1952—Bears, 24-23 (C)
Lions, 45-21 (D)

1953—Lions, 20-16 (C)
Lions, 13-7 (D)
1954—Lions, 48-23 (D)
Bears, 28-24 (C)
1955—Bears, 24-14 (D)
Bears, 21-20 (C)
1956—Lions, 42-10 (D)
Bears, 38-21 (C)
1957—Bears, 27-7 (D)
Lions, 21-13 (C)
1958—Lions, 20-7 (D)
Bears, 21-16 (C)
1959—Bears, 24-14 (D)
Bears, 25-14 (C)
1960—Bears, 28-7 (C)
Lions, 36-0 (D)
1961—Bears, 31-17 (D)
Lions, 16-15 (C)
1962—Lions, 11-3 (D)
Bears, 3-0 (C)
1963—Bears, 37-21 (D)
Bears, 24-14 (C)
1964—Lions, 10-0 (C)
Bears, 27-24 (D)
1965—Bears, 38-10 (C)
Bears, 17-10 (D)
1966—Lions, 14-3 (D)
Tie, 10-10 (C)
1967—Bears, 14-3 (C)
Bears, 27-13 (D)
1968—Lions, 42-0 (D)
Bears, 28-10 (C)
1969—Lions, 13-7 (D)
Lions, 20-3 (C)
1970—Lions, 28-14 (D)
Lions, 16-10 (C)
1971—Bears, 28-23 (D)
Lions, 28-3 (C)
1972—Lions, 38-24 (C)
Lions, 14-0 (D)
1973—Lions, 30-7 (C)
Lions, 40-7 (D)
1974—Bears, 17-9 (C)
Lions, 34-17 (D)
1975—Lions, 27-7 (D)
Bears, 25-21 (C)
1976—Bears, 10-3 (C)
Lions, 14-10 (D)
1977—Bears, 30-20 (C)
Bears, 31-14 (D)
1978—Bears, 19-0 (C)
Lions, 21-17 (D)
1979—Bears, 35-7 (C)
Lions, 20-0 (D)
1980—Bears, 24-7 (C)
Bears, 23-17 (D) OT
1981—Lions, 48-17 (D)
Lions, 23-7 (C)
1982—Lions, 17-10 (D)
Bears, 20-17 (C)
1983—Lions, 31-17 (D)
Lions, 38-17 (C)
1984—Bears, 16-14 (D)
Bears, 30-13 (C)
(Points—Bears 2,041, Lions 1,886)
*Franchise in Portsmouth prior to 1934
and known as the Spartans
**Championship
*CHICAGO vs. GREEN BAY
Bears lead series, 68-55-6
1921—Staleys, 20-0 (C)
1923—Bears, 3-0 (GB)
1924—Bears, 3-0 (C)
1925—Packers, 14-10 (GB)
Bears, 21-0 (C)
1926—Tie, 6-6 (GB)
Bears, 19-13 (C)
Tie, 3-3 (C)
1927—Bears, 7-6 (GB)
Bears, 14-6 (C)
1928—Tie, 12-12 (GB)
Packers, 16-6 (C)
Packers, 6-0 (C)
1929—Packers, 23-0 (GB)
Packers, 14-0 (C)
Packers, 25-0 (C)
1930—Packers, 7-0 (GB)
Packers, 13-12 (C)
Bears, 21-0 (C)
1931—Packers, 7-0 (GB)
Packers, 6-2 (C)
Bears, 7-6 (C)
1932—Tie, 0-0 (GB)
Packers, 2-0 (C)
Bears, 9-0 (C)
1933—Bears, 14-7 (GB)
Bears, 10-7 (C)
Bears, 7-6 (C)
1934—Bears, 24-10 (GB)
Bears, 27-14 (C)
1935—Packers, 7-0 (GB)
Packers, 17-14 (C)
1936—Bears, 30-3 (GB)

Packers, 21-10 (C)
1937—Bears, 14-2 (GB)
Packers, 24-14 (C)
1938—Bears, 2-0 (GB)
Packers, 24-17 (C)
1939—Packers, 21-16 (GB)
Bears, 30-27 (C)
1940—Bears, 41-10 (GB)
Bears, 14-7 (C)
1941—Bears, 25-17 (GB)
Bears, 16-14 (C)
**Bears, 33-14 (C)
1942—Bears, 44-28 (GB)
Bears, 38-7 (C)
1943—Tie, 21-21 (GB)
Bears, 21-7 (C)
1944—Packers, 42-28 (GB)
Bears, 21-0 (C)
1945—Packers, 31-21 (GB)
Bears, 28-24 (C)
1946—Bears, 30-7 (GB)
Bears, 10-7 (C)
1947—Packers, 29-20 (GB)
Bears, 20-17 (C)
1948—Bears, 45-7 (GB)
Bears, 7-6 (C)
1949—Bears, 17-0 (GB)
Bears, 24-3 (C)
1950—Packers, 31-21 (GB)
Bears, 28-14 (C)
1951—Bears, 31-20 (GB)
Bears, 24-13 (C)
1952—Bears, 24-14 (GB)
Packers, 41-28 (C)
1953—Bears, 17-13 (GB)
Tie, 21-21 (C)
1954—Bears, 10-3 (GB)
Bears, 28-23 (C)
1955—Packers, 24-3 (GB)
Bears, 52-31 (C)
1956—Bears, 37-21 (GB)
Bears, 38-14 (C)
1957—Packers, 21-17 (GB)
Bears, 21-14 (C)
1958—Bears, 34-20 (GB)
Bears, 24-10 (C)
1959—Packers, 9-6 (GB)
Bears, 28-17 (C)
1960—Bears, 17-14 (GB)
Packers, 41-13 (C)
1961—Packers, 24-0 (GB)
Packers, 31-28 (C)
1962—Packers, 49-0 (GB)
Packers, 38-7 (C)
1963—Bears, 10-3 (GB)
Bears, 26-7 (C)
1964—Packers, 23-12 (GB)
Packers, 17-3 (C)
1965—Packers, 23-14 (GB)
Bears, 31-10 (C)
1966—Packers, 17-0 (C)
Packers, 13-6 (GB)
1967—Packers, 13-10 (GB)
Packers, 17-13 (C)
1968—Bears, 13-10 (GB)
Packers, 28-27 (C)
1969—Packers, 17-0 (GB)
Packers, 21-3 (C)
1970—Packers, 20-19 (GB)
Bears, 35-17 (C)
1971—Packers, 17-14 (C)
Packers, 31-10 (GB)
1972—Packers, 20-17 (GB)
Packers, 23-17 (C)
1973—Bears, 31-17 (GB)
Packers, 21-0 (C)
1974—Bears, 10-9 (C)
Packers, 20-3 (Mil)
1975—Bears, 27-14 (C)
Packers, 28-7 (GB)
1976—Bears, 24-13 (C)
Bears, 16-10 (GB)
1977—Bears, 26-0 (C)
Bears, 21-10 (C)
1978—Packers, 24-14 (GB)
Bears, 14-0 (C)
1979—Bears, 6-3 (C)
Bears, 15-14 (GB)
1980—Packers, 12-6 (GB) OT
Bears, 61-7 (C)
1981—Packers, 16-9 (C)
Packers, 21-17 (GB)
1983—Packers, 31-28 (GB)
Bears, 23-21 (C)
1984—Bears, 9-7 (C)
Packers, 20-14 (C)
(Points—Bears 2,144, Packers 1,911)
*Bears known as Staleys prior to 1922
**Division Playoff
CHICAGO vs. HOUSTON
Oilers lead series, 2-1
1973—Bears, 35-14 (C)
1977—Oilers, 47-0 (H)

1980—Oilers, 10-6 (C)
(Points—Oilers 71, Bears 41)
CHICAGO vs. *INDIANAPOLIS
Colts lead series, 21-13
1953—Colts, 13-9 (B)
Colts, 16-14 (C)
1954—Bears, 28-9 (C)
Bears, 28-13 (B)
1955—Colts, 23-17 (B)
Bears, 38-10 (C)
1956—Colts, 28-21 (B)
Bears, 58-27 (C)
1957—Colts, 21-10 (B)
Colts, 29-14 (C)
1958—Colts, 51-38 (B)
Colts, 17-0 (C)
1959—Bears, 26-21 (B)
Colts, 21-7 (C)
1960—Colts, 42-7 (B)
Colts, 24-20 (C)
1961—Bears, 24-10 (C)
Bears, 21-20 (B)
1962—Bears, 35-15 (C)
Bears, 57-0 (C)
1963—Bears, 10-3 (C)
Bears, 17-7 (B)
1964—Colts, 52-0 (B)
Colts, 40-24 (C)
1965—Colts, 26-21 (C)
Bears, 13-0 (B)
1966—Bears, 27-17 (C)
Colts, 21-16 (B)
1967—Colts, 24-3 (C)
1968—Colts, 28-7 (B)
1969—Colts, 24-21 (C)
1970—Colts, 21-20 (B)
1975—Colts, 35-7 (C)
1983—Colts, 22-19 (B) OT
(Points—Colts 730, Bears 677)
*Franchise in Baltimore prior to 1984
CHICAGO vs. KANSAS CITY
Bears lead series, 2-1
1973—Chiefs, 19-7 (KC)
1977—Bears, 28-27 (C)
1981—Bears, 16-13 (KC) OT
(Points—Chiefs 59, Bears 51)
CHICAGO vs. *L.A. RAIDERS
Raiders lead series, 3-2
1972—Raiders, 28-21 (O)
1976—Raiders, 28-27 (C)
1978—Raiders, 25-19 (C) OT
1981—Bears, 23-6 (O)
1984—Bears, 17-6 (C)
(Points—Bears 107, Raiders 93)
*Franchise in Oakland prior to 1982
CHICAGO vs. *L.A. RAMS
Bears lead series, 42-27-3
1937—Bears, 20-2 (Clev)
Bears, 15-7 (C)
1938—Rams, 14-7 (C)
Rams, 23-21 (Clev)
1939—Rams, 30-21 (Clev)
Bears, 35-21 (C)
1940—Bears, 21-14 (Clev)
Bears, 47-25 (C)
1941—Bears, 48-21 (Clev)
Bears, 31-13 (C)
1942—Bears, 21-7 (Clev)
Bears, 47-0 (C)
1944—Rams, 19-7 (Clev)
Bears, 28-21 (C)
1945—Rams, 17-0 (Clev)
Rams, 41-21 (C)
1946—Tie, 28-28 (C)
Bears, 27-21 (LA)
1947—Bears, 41-21 (LA)
Rams, 17-14 (C)
1948—Bears, 42-21 (C)
Bears, 21-6 (LA)
1949—Rams, 31-16 (C)
Rams, 27-24 (LA)
1950—Rams, 24-20 (LA)
Bears, 24-14 (C)
**Rams, 24-14 (LA)
1951—Rams, 42-17 (C)
1952—Rams, 31-7 (LA)
Rams, 40-24 (C)
1953—Rams, 38-24 (LA)
Bears, 24-21 (C)
1954—Rams, 42-38 (LA)
Bears, 24-13 (C)
1955—Bears, 31-20 (LA)
Bears, 24-3 (C)
1956—Bears, 35-24 (LA)
Bears, 30-21 (C)
1957—Bears, 34-26 (C)
Bears, 16-10 (LA)
1958—Bears, 31-10 (C)
Rams, 41-35 (LA)
1959—Bears, 28-21 (C)
Bears, 26-21 (LA)
1960—Bears, 34-27 (C)
Tie, 24-24 (LA)
1961—Bears, 21-17 (LA)

Bears, 28-24 (C)
1962—Bears, 27-23 (LA)
Bears, 30-14 (C)
1963—Bears, 52-14 (LA)
Bears, 6-0 (C)
1964—Bears, 38-17 (C)
Bears, 34-24 (C)
1965—Rams, 30-28 (LA)
Bears, 31-6 (C)
1966—Bears, 31-17 (LA)
Bears, 17-10 (C)
1967—Rams, 28-17 (C)
1968—Bears, 17-16 (LA)
1969—Rams, 9-7 (C)
1971—Rams, 17-3 (LA)
1972—Tie, 13-13 (C)
1973—Rams, 26-0 (C)
1975—Rams, 38-10 (LA)
1976—Rams, 20-12 (LA)
1977—Bears, 24-23 (C)
1979—Bears, 27-23 (C)
1981—Rams, 24-7 (C)
1982—Bears, 34-26 (LA)
1983—Rams, 21-14 (LA)
1984—Rams, 29-13 (LA)
(Points—Bears 1,700, Rams 1,501)
*Franchise in Cleveland prior to 1946
**Conference Playoff
CHICAGO vs. MIAMI
Dolphins lead series, 3-0
1971—Dolphins, 34-3 (M)
1975—Dolphins, 46-13 (C)
1979—Dolphins, 31-16 (M)
(Points—Dolphins 111, Bears 32)
CHICAGO vs. MINNESOTA
Vikings lead series, 25-20-2
1961—Vikings, 37-13 (M)
Bears, 52-35 (C)
1962—Bears, 13-0 (M)
Bears, 31-30 (C)
1963—Bears, 28-7 (M)
Tie, 17-17 (C)
1964—Bears, 34-28 (M)
Vikings, 41-14 (C)
1965—Bears, 45-37 (M)
Vikings, 24-17 (C)
1966—Bears, 13-10 (M)
Bears, 41-28 (C)
1967—Bears, 17-7 (M)
Tie, 10-10 (C)
1968—Bears, 27-17 (M)
Bears, 26-24 (C)
1969—Vikings, 31-0 (C)
Vikings, 31-14 (M)
1970—Vikings, 24-0 (C)
Vikings, 16-13 (M)
1971—Bears, 20-17 (M)
Vikings, 27-10 (C)
1972—Vikings, 13-10 (C)
Vikings, 23-10 (M)
1973—Vikings, 22-13 (C)
Vikings, 31-13 (M)
1974—Vikings, 11-7 (M)
Vikings, 17-0 (C)
1975—Vikings, 28-3 (M)
Vikings, 13-9 (C)
1976—Vikings, 20-19 (M)
Bears, 14-13 (C)
1977—Vikings, 22-16 (M) OT
Bears, 10-7 (C)
1978—Vikings, 24-20 (C)
Vikings, 17-14 (M)
1979—Bears, 26-7 (C)
Vikings, 30-27 (M)
1980—Vikings, 34-14 (C)
Vikings, 13-7 (M)
1981—Vikings, 24-21 (M)
Bears, 10-9 (C)
1982—Vikings, 35-7 (M)
1983—Vikings, 23-14 (C)
Bears, 19-13 (M)
1984—Bears, 16-7 (C)
Bears, 34-3 (M)
(Points—Vikings 954, Bears 811)
CHICAGO vs. NEW ENGLAND
Patriots lead series, 2-1
1973—Patriots, 13-10 (C)
1979—Patriots, 27-7 (C)
1982—Bears, 26-13 (C)
(Points—Patriots 53, Bears 43)
CHICAGO vs. NEW ORLEANS
Bears lead series, 7-4
1968—Bears, 23-17 (NO)
1970—Bears, 24-3 (NO)
1971—Bears, 35-14 (C)
1973—Saints, 21-16 (NO)
1974—Bears, 24-10 (C)
1975—Bears, 42-17 (NO)
1977—Saints, 42-24 (C)
1980—Bears, 22-3 (C)
1982—Saints, 10-0 (C)
1983—Saints, 34-31 (NO) OT
1984—Bears, 20-7 (C)

(Points—Bears 261, Saints 178)
CHICAGO vs. N.Y. GIANTS
Bears lead series, 26-16-2
1925—Bears, 19-7 (NY)
Giants, 9-0 (C)
1926—Bears, 7-0 (C)
1927—Giants, 13-7 (NY)
1928—Bears, 13-0 (C)
1929—Giants, 26-14 (C)
Giants, 34-0 (NY)
Giants, 14-9 (C)
1930—Giants, 12-0 (C)
Bears, 12-0 (NY)
1931—Bears, 6-0 (C)
Bears, 12-6 (NY)
Giants, 25-6 (C)
1932—Bears, 28-8 (NY)
Bears, 6-0 (C)
1933—Bears, 14-10 (C)
Giants, 3-0 (NY)
*Bears, 23-21 (C)
1934—Bears, 27-7 (C)
Bears, 10-9 (NY)
*Giants, 30-13 (NY)
1935—Bears, 20-3 (NY)
Giants, 3-0 (C)
1936—Bears, 25-7 (NY)
1937—Tie, 3-3 (NY)
1939—Giants, 16-13 (NY)
1940—Bears, 37-21 (NY)
1941—*Bears, 37-9 (C)
1942—Bears, 26-7 (NY)
1943—Bears, 56-7 (NY)
1946—Giants, 14-0 (NY)
*Bears, 24-14 (NY)
1948—Bears, 35-14 (C)
1949—Bears, 35-28 (NY)
1956—Tie, 17-17 (NY)
*Giants, 47-7 (NY)
1962—Giants, 26-24 (C)
1963—*Bears, 14-10 (C)
1965—Bears, 35-14 (NY)
1967—Bears, 34-7 (C)
1969—Giants, 28-24 (NY)
1970—Bears, 24-16 (NY)
1974—Bears, 16-13 (C)
1977—Bears, 12-9 (NY) OT
(Points—Bears 737, Giants 574)
*NFL Championship
CHICAGO vs. N.Y. JETS
Series tied, 1-1
1974—Jets, 23-21 (C)
1979—Bears, 23-13 (C)
(Points—Bears 44, Jets 36)
CHICAGO vs. PHILADELPHIA
Bears lead series, 19-4-1
1933—Tie, 3-3 (P)
1935—Bears, 39-0 (C)
1936—Bears, 17-0 (P)
Bears, 28-7 (P)
1938—Bears, 28-6 (P)
1939—Bears, 27-14 (C)
1941—Bears, 49-14 (P)
1942—Bears, 45-14 (C)
1944—Bears, 28-7 (P)
1946—Bears, 21-14 (C)
1947—Bears, 40-7 (C)
1948—Eagles, 12-7 (P)
1949—Bears, 38-21 (C)
1955—Bears, 17-10 (C)
1961—Eagles, 16-14 (P)
1963—Bears, 16-7 (C)
1968—Bears, 29-16 (P)
1970—Bears, 20-16 (C)
1972—Bears, 21-12 (P)
1975—Bears, 15-13 (C)
1979—*Eagles, 27-17 (P)
1980—Eagles, 17-14 (P)
1983—Bears, 7-6 (P)
Bears, 17-14 (C)
(Points—Bears 557, Eagles 273)
*NFC First Round Playoff
CHICAGO vs. *PITTSBURGH
Bears lead series, 13-4-1
1934—Bears, 28-0 (P)
1935—Bears, 23-7 (P)
1936—Bears, 27-9 (P)
Bears, 26-6 (C)
1937—Bears, 7-0 (P)
1939—Bears, 32-0 (P)
1941—Bears, 34-7 (C)
1945—Bears, 28-7 (P)
1947—Bears, 49-7 (C)
1949—Bears, 30-21 (C)
1958—Steelers, 24-10 (P)
1959—Bears, 27-21 (C)
1963—Tie, 17-17 (P)
1967—Steelers, 41-13 (P)
1969—Bears, 38-7 (C)
1971—Bears, 17-15 (C)
1975—Steelers, 34-3 (P)
1980—Steelers, 38-3 (P)
(Points—Bears 412, Steelers 261)

*Steelers known as Pirates prior to 1941
***CHICAGO vs. **ST. LOUIS**
Bears lead series, 50-25-6
(NP denotes Normal Park;
Wr denotes Wrigley Field;
Co denotes Comiskey Park;
So denotes Soldier Field;
all Chicago)
1920—Cardinals, 7-6 (NP)
Staleys, 10-0 (Wr)
1921—Tie, 0-0 (Wr)
1922—Cardinals, 6-0 (Co)
Cardinals, 9-0 (Co)
1923—Bears, 3-0 (Wr)
1924—Bears, 6-0 (Wr)
Bears, 21-0 (Co)
1925—Cardinals, 9-0 (Co)
Tie, 0-0 (Wr)
1926—Bears, 16-0 (Wr)
Bears, 10-0 (So)
Tie, 0-0 (Wr)
1927—Bears, 9-0 (NP)
Cardinals, 3-0 (Wr)
1928—Bears, 15-0 (NP)
Bears, 34-0 (Wr)
1929—Tie, 0-0 (Wr)
Cardinals, 40-6 (Co)
1930—Cardinals, 32-6 (Co)
Bears, 6-0 (Wr)
1931—Bears, 26-13 (Wr)
Bears, 18-7 (Wr)
1932—Tie, 0-0 (Wr)
Bears, 34-0 (Wr)
1933—Bears, 12-9 (Wr)
Bears, 22-6 (Wr)
1934—Bears, 20-0 (Wr)
Bears, 17-6 (Wr)
1935—Tie, 7-7 (Wr)
Bears, 13-0 (Wr)
1936—Bears, 7-3 (Wr)
Cardinals, 14-7 (Wr)
1937—Bears, 16-7 (Wr)
Bears, 42-28 (Wr)
1938—Bears, 16-13 (So)
Bears, 34-28 (Wr)
1939—Bears, 44-7 (Wr)
Bears, 48-7 (Co)
1940—Cardinals, 21-7 (Co)
Bears, 31-23 (Wr)
1941—Bears, 53-7 (Wr)
Bears, 34-24 (Co)
1942—Bears, 41-14 (Wr)
Bears, 21-7 (Co)
1943—Bears, 20-0 (Wr)
Bears, 35-24 (Co)
1945—Cardinals, 16-7 (Wr)
Bears, 28-20 (Co)
1946—Bears, 34-17 (Co)
Cardinals, 35-28 (Wr)
1947—Cardinals, 31-7 (Co)
Cardinals, 30-21 (Wr)
1948—Bears, 28-17 (Co)
Cardinals, 24-21 (Wr)
1949—Cardinals, 17-7 (Co)
Bears, 52-21 (Wr)
1950—Bears, 27-6 (Wr)
Cardinals, 20-10 (Co)
1951—Cardinals, 28-14 (Co)
Cardinals, 24-14 (Wr)
1952—Cardinals, 21-10 (Co)
Bears, 10-7 (Wr)
1953—Cardinals, 24-17 (Wr)
1954—Bears, 29-7 (Co)
1955—Cardinals, 53-14 (Co)
1956—Bears, 10-3 (Wr)
1957—Cardinals, 14-6 (Co)
1958—Bears, 30-14 (Wr)
1959—Bears, 31-7 (So)
1965—Bears, 34-13 (Wr)
1966—Cardinals, 24-17 (StL)
1967—Bears, 30-3 (Wr)
1969—Cardinals, 20-17 (StL)
1972—Bears, 27-10 (StL)
1975—Cardinals, 34-20 (So)
1977—Cardinals, 16-13 (StL)
1978—Bears, 17-10 (So)
1979—Bears, 42-6 (So)
1982—Cardinals, 10-7 (So)
1984—Cardinals, 38-21 (StL)
(Points—Bears 1,517, Cardinals 977)
*Franchise in Decatur prior to 1921; Bears known as Staleys prior to 1922
**Franchise in Chicago prior to 1960
CHICAGO vs. SAN DIEGO
Chargers lead series, 4-1
1970—Chargers, 20-7 (C)
1974—Chargers, 28-21 (SD)
1978—Chargers, 40-7 (SD)
1981—Bears, 20-17 (C) OT
1984—Chargers, 20-7 (SD)
(Points—Chargers 125, Bears 62)
CHICAGO vs. SAN FRANCISCO
Series tied, 23-23-1

1950—Bears, 32-20 (SF)
Bears, 17-0 (C)
1951—Bears, 13-7 (C)
1952—49ers, 40-16 (C)
Bears, 20-17 (SF)
1953—49ers, 35-28 (C)
49ers, 24-14 (SF)
1954—49ers, 31-24 (SF)
Bears, 31-27 (C)
1955—49ers, 20-19 (C)
Bears, 34-23 (SF)
1956—Bears, 31-7 (C)
Bears, 38-21 (SF)
1957—49ers, 21-17 (C)
49ers, 21-17 (SF)
1958—Bears, 28-6 (C)
Bears, 27-14 (SF)
1959—49ers, 20-17 (SF)
Bears, 14-3 (C)
1960—Bears, 27-10 (C)
49ers, 25-7 (SF)
1961—Bears, 31-0 (C)
49ers, 41-31 (SF)
1962—Bears, 30-14 (C)
49ers, 34-27 (C)
1963—49ers, 20-14 (SF)
Bears, 27-7 (C)
1964—49ers, 31-21 (SF)
Bears, 23-21 (C)
1965—49ers, 52-24 (SF)
Bears, 61-20 (C)
1966—Tie, 30-30 (C)
49ers, 41-14 (SF)
1967—Bears, 28-14 (SF)
1968—Bears, 27-19 (C)
1969—49ers, 42-21 (SF)
1970—49ers, 37-16 (C)
1971—49ers, 13-0 (SF)
1972—49ers, 34-21 (C)
1974—49ers, 34-0 (C)
1975—49ers, 31-3 (SF)
1976—Bears, 19-12 (SF)
1978—Bears, 16-13 (SF)
1979—Bears, 28-27 (SF)
1981—49ers, 28-17 (SF)
1983—Bears, 13-3 (C)
1984—*49ers, 23-0 (SF)
(Points—49ers 1,033, Bears 1,013)
*NFC Championship
CHICAGO vs. SEATTLE
Seahawks lead series, 3-1
1976—Bears, 34-7 (S)
1978—Seahawks, 31-29 (C)
1982—Seahawks, 20-14 (S)
1984—Seahawks, 38-9 (C)
(Points—Seahawks 96, Bears 86)
CHICAGO vs. TAMPA BAY
Bears lead series, 10-4
1977—Bears, 10-0 (TB)
1978—Buccaneers, 33-19 (TB)
Bears, 14-3 (C)
1979—Buccaneers, 17-13 (C)
Bears, 14-0 (TB)
1980—Bears, 23-0 (C)
Bears, 14-13 (TB)
1981—Bears, 28-17 (C)
Buccaneers, 20-10 (TB)
1982—Buccaneers, 26-23 (TB) OT
1983—Bears, 17-10 (C)
Bears, 27-0 (TB)
1984—Bears, 34-14 (C)
Bears, 44-9 (TB)
(Points—Bears 290, Buccaneers 162)
CHICAGO vs. *WASHINGTON
Bears lead series, 19-11-1
1932—Tie, 7-7 (B)
1933—Bears, 7-0 (C)
Redskins, 10-0 (B)
1934—Bears, 21-0 (B)
1935—Bears, 30-14 (B)
1936—Bears, 26-0 (B)
1937—**Redskins, 28-21 (C)
1938—Bears, 31-7 (C)
1940—Redskins, 7-3 (W)
**Bears, 73-0 (W)
1941—Bears, 35-21 (C)
1942—**Redskins, 14-6 (W)
1943—Redskins, 21-7 (W)
**Bears, 41-21 (W)
1945—Redskins, 28-21 (W)
1946—Bears, 24-20 (C)
1947—Bears, 56-20 (W)
1948—Bears, 48-13 (C)
1949—Bears, 31-21 (W)
1951—Bears, 27-0 (C)
1953—Bears, 27-24 (W)
1957—Redskins, 14-3 (C)
1964—Redskins, 27-20 (W)
1968—Redskins, 38-28 (C)
1971—Bears, 16-15 (C)
1974—Redskins, 42-0 (W)
1976—Bears, 33-7 (C)
1978—Bears, 14-10 (W)

1980—Bears, 35-21 (C)
1981—Redskins, 24-7 (C)
1984—***Bears, 23-19 (W)
(Points—Bears 721, Redskins 493)
*Franchise in Boston prior to 1937 and known as Braves prior to 1933
**NFL Championship
***NFC Divisional Playoff

CINCINNATI vs. ATLANTA
Bengals lead series, 4-1;
See Atlanta vs. Cincinnati

CINCINNATI vs. BUFFALO
Bengals lead series, 7-5;
See Buffalo vs. Cincinnati

CINCINNATI vs. CHICAGO
Bengals lead series, 2-0;
See Chicago vs. Cincinnati

CINCINNATI vs. CLEVELAND
Bengals lead series, 15-14
1970—Browns, 30-27 (Cle)
    Bengals, 14-10 (Cin)
1971—Browns, 27-24 (Cin)
    Browns, 31-27 (Cle)
1972—Browns, 27-6 (Cle)
    Browns, 27-24 (Cin)
1973—Browns, 17-10 (Cle)
    Bengals, 34-17 (Cin)
1974—Bengals, 33-7 (Cin)
    Bengals, 34-24 (Cle)
1975—Bengals, 24-17 (Cin)
    Browns, 35-23 (Cle)
1976—Bengals, 45-24 (Cle)
    Bengals, 21-6 (Cin)
1977—Browns, 13-3 (Cin)
    Bengals, 10-7 (Cle)
1978—Bengals, 13-10 (Cle) OT
    Bengals, 48-16 (Cin)
1979—Browns, 28-27 (Cle)
    Bengals, 16-12 (Cin)
1980—Browns, 31-7 (Cle)
    Browns, 27-24 (Cin)
1981—Bengals, 20-17 (Cle)
    Bengals, 41-21 (Cle)
1982—Bengals, 23-10 (Cin)
1983—Browns, 17-7 (Clev)
    Bengals, 28-21 (Cin)
1984—Bengals, 12-9 (Cin)
    Bengals, 20-17 (Clev) OT
(Points—Bengals 639, Browns 561)

CINCINNATI vs. DALLAS
Cowboys lead series, 2-0
1973—Cowboys, 38-10 (D)
1979—Cowboys, 38-13 (D)
(Points—Cowboys 76, Bengals 23)

CINCINNATI vs. DENVER
Broncos lead series, 8-6
1968—Bengals, 24-10 (C)
    Broncos, 10-7 (D)
1969—Broncos, 30-23 (C)
    Broncos, 27-16 (D)
1971—Bengals, 24-10 (D)
1972—Bengals, 21-10 (C)
1973—Broncos, 28-10 (D)
1975—Bengals, 17-16 (D)
1976—Bengals, 17-7 (C)
1977—Broncos, 24-13 (C)
1979—Broncos, 10-0 (D)
1981—Bengals, 38-21 (C)
1983—Broncos, 24-17 (D)
1984—Broncos, 20-17 (D)
(Points—Broncos 247, Bengals 244)

CINCINNATI vs. DETROIT
Lions lead series, 2-1
1970—Lions, 38-3 (D)
1974—Lions, 23-19 (C)
1983—Bengals, 17-9 (C)
(Points—Lions 70, Bengals 39)

CINCINNATI vs. GREEN BAY
Bengals lead series, 3-2
1971—Packers, 20-17 (GB)
1976—Bengals, 28-7 (C)
1977—Bengals, 17-7 (Mil)
1980—Packers, 14-9 (GB)
1983—Bengals, 34-14 (C)
(Points—Bengals 105, Packers 62)

CINCINNATI vs. HOUSTON
Bengals lead series, 19-12-1
1968—Oilers, 27-17 (C)
1969—Tie, 31-31 (H)
1970—Oilers, 20-13 (C)
    Bengals, 30-20 (H)
1971—Oilers, 10-6 (H)
    Bengals, 28-13 (C)
1972—Bengals, 30-7 (C)
    Bengals, 61-17 (H)
1973—Bengals, 24-10 (C)
    Bengals, 27-24 (H)
1974—Oilers, 34-21 (C)
    Oilers, 20-3 (H)
1975—Bengals, 21-19 (H)
    Bengals, 23-19 (C)
1976—Bengals, 27-7 (H)

    Bengals, 31-27 (C)
1977—Bengals, 13-10 (C) OT
    Oilers, 21-16 (H)
1978—Bengals, 28-13 (C)
    Oilers, 17-10 (H)
1979—Oilers, 30-27 (C) OT
    Oilers, 42-21 (H)
1980—Bengals, 13-10 (C)
    Oilers, 23-3 (H)
1981—Oilers, 17-10 (H)
    Bengals, 34-21 (C)
1982—Bengals, 27-6 (C)
    Bengals, 35-27 (H)
1983—Bengals, 55-14 (H)
    Bengals, 38-10 (C)
1984—Bengals, 13-3 (C)
    Bengals, 31-13 (H)
(Points—Bengals 764, Oilers 585)

CINCINNATI vs. *INDIANAPOLIS
Colts lead series, 5-4
1970—**Colts, 17-0 (B)
1972—Colts, 20-19 (C)
1974—Bengals, 24-14 (B)
1976—Colts, 28-27 (B)
1979—Colts, 38-28 (B)
1980—Bengals, 34-33 (C)
1981—Bengals, 41-19 (B)
1982—Bengals, 20-17 (B)
1983—Colts, 34-31 (C)
(Points—Bengals 224, Colts 220)
*Franchise in Baltimore prior to 1984
**AFC Divisional Playoff

CINCINNATI vs. KANSAS CITY
Chiefs lead series, 8-7
1968—Chiefs, 13-3 (KC)
    Chiefs, 16-9 (C)
1969—Bengals, 24-19 (C)
    Chiefs, 42-22 (KC)
1970—Chiefs, 27-19 (C)
1972—Bengals, 23-16 (KC)
1973—Bengals, 14-6 (C)
1974—Bengals, 33-6 (C)
1976—Bengals, 27-24 (KC)
1977—Bengals, 27-7 (KC)
1978—Chiefs, 24-23 (C)
1979—Chiefs, 10-7 (C)
1980—Bengals, 20-6 (KC)
1983—Chiefs, 20-15 (KC)
1984—Bengals, 27-22 (C)
(Points—Bengals 288, Chiefs 263)

CINCINNATI vs. *L.A. RAIDERS
Raiders lead series, 11-4
1968—Raiders, 31-10 (C)
    Raiders, 34-0 (C)
1969—Bengals, 31-17 (C)
    Raiders, 37-17 (O)
1970—Bengals, 31-21 (C)
1971—Bengals, 31-27 (O)
1972—Raiders, 20-14 (C)
1974—Raiders, 30-27 (O)
1975—Bengals, 14-10 (C)
    **Raiders, 31-28 (C)
1976—Raiders, 35-20 (O)
1978—Raiders, 34-21 (C)
1980—Raiders, 28-17 (O)
1982—Bengals, 31-17 (C)
1983—Raiders, 20-10 (C)
(Points—Raiders 396, Bengals 298)
*Franchise in Oakland prior to 1982
**AFC Divisional Playoff

CINCINNATI vs. L.A. RAMS
Bengals lead series, 3-2
1972—Rams, 15-12 (LA)
1976—Bengals, 20-12 (C)
1978—Bengals, 20-19 (LA)
1981—Bengals, 24-10 (C)
1984—Rams, 24-14 (C)
(Points—Bengals 90, Rams 80)

CINCINNATI vs. MIAMI
Dolphins lead series, 7-3
1968—Dolphins, 24-22 (C)
    Bengals, 38-21 (M)
1969—Bengals, 27-21 (C)
1971—Dolphins, 23-13 (C)
1973—*Dolphins, 34-16 (M)
1974—Bengals, 24-3 (M)
1977—Bengals, 23-17 (C)
1978—Dolphins, 21-0 (M)
1980—Dolphins, 17-16 (M)
1983—Dolphins, 38-14 (M)
(Points—Dolphins 240, Bengals 172)
*AFC Divisional Playoff

CINCINNATI vs. MINNESOTA
Series tied, 2-2
1973—Bengals, 27-0 (C)
1977—Vikings, 42-10 (M)
1980—Bengals, 14-0 (C)
1983—Vikings, 20-14 (M)
(Points—Bengals 65, Vikings 62)

CINCINNATI vs. *NEW ENGLAND
Patriots lead series, 5-3
1968—Patriots, 33-14 (B)
1969—Patriots, 25-14 (C)

1970—Bengals, 45-7 (C)
1972—Bengals, 31-7 (NE)
1975—Bengals, 27-10 (C)
1978—Patriots, 20-18 (C)
1979—Patriots, 20-14 (C)
1984—Patriots, 20-14 (NE)
(Points—Bengals 162, Patriots 132)
*Franchise in Boston prior to 1971

CINCINNATI vs. NEW ORLEANS
Bengals lead series 3-2
1970—Bengals, 26-6 (C)
1975—Bengals, 21-0 (NO)
1978—Saints, 20-18 (C)
1981—Saints, 17-7 (NO)
1984—Bengals, 24-21 (NO)
(Points—Bengals 96, Saints 64)

CINCINNATI vs. N.Y. GIANTS
Bengals lead series, 2-0
1972—Bengals, 13-10 (C)
1977—Bengals, 30-13 (C)
(Points—Bengals 43, Giants 23)

CINCINNATI vs. N.Y. JETS
Jets lead series, 6-3
1968—Jets, 27-14 (NY)
1969—Jets, 21-7 (C)
    Jets, 40-7 (NY)
1971—Jets, 35-21 (NY)
1973—Bengals, 20-14 (C)
1976—Bengals, 42-3 (NY)
1981—Bengals, 31-30 (NY)
1982—*Jets, 44-17 (C)
1984—Jets, 43-23 (NY)
(Points—Jets 257, Bengals 182)
*AFC First Round Playoff

CINCINNATI vs. PHILADELPHIA
Bengals lead series, 4-0
1971—Bengals, 37-14 (C)
1975—Bengals, 31-0 (P)
1979—Bengals, 37-13 (C)
1982—Bengals, 18-14 (P)
(Points—Bengals 123, Eagles 41)

CINCINNATI vs. PITTSBURGH
Steelers lead series, 17-12
1970—Steelers, 21-10 (P)
    Bengals, 34-7 (C)
1971—Steelers, 21-10 (P)
    Steelers, 21-13 (C)
1972—Bengals, 15-10 (C)
    Steelers, 40-17 (P)
1973—Bengals, 19-7 (C)
    Steelers, 20-13 (P)
1974—Bengals, 17-10 (C)
    Steelers, 27-3 (P)
1975—Steelers, 30-24 (C)
    Steelers, 35-14 (P)
1976—Steelers, 23-6 (P)
    Steelers, 7-3 (C)
1977—Steelers, 20-14 (P)
    Bengals, 17-10 (C)
1978—Steelers, 28-3 (C)
    Steelers, 7-6 (P)
1979—Bengals, 34-10 (C)
    Steelers, 37-17 (P)
1980—Bengals, 30-28 (C)
    Bengals, 17-16 (P)
1981—Bengals, 34-7 (C)
    Bengals, 17-10 (P)
1982—Steelers, 26-20 (P) OT
1983—Steelers, 24-14 (C)
    Bengals, 23-10 (P)
1984—Steelers, 38-17 (P)
    Bengals, 22-20 (C)
(Points—Steelers 570, Bengals 483)

CINCINNATI vs. ST. LOUIS
Bengals lead series, 2-0
1973—Bengals, 42-24 (C)
1979—Bengals, 34-28 (C)
(Points—Bengals 76, Cardinals 52)

CINCINNATI vs. SAN DIEGO
Chargers lead series, 9-7
1968—Chargers, 29-13 (SD)
    Chargers, 31-10 (C)
1969—Bengals, 34-20 (C)
    Chargers, 21-14 (SD)
1970—Bengals, 17-14 (SD)
1971—Bengals, 31-0 (C)
1973—Bengals, 20-13 (SD)
1974—Chargers, 20-17 (C)
1975—Bengals, 47-17 (C)
1977—Chargers, 24-3 (SD)
1978—Chargers, 22-13 (SD)
1979—Bengals, 26-24 (C)
1980—Chargers, 31-14 (C)
1981—Bengals, 40-17 (SD)
    *Bengals, 27-7 (C)
1982—Chargers, 50-34 (SD)
(Points—Bengals 358, Chargers 342)
*AFC Championship

CINCINNATI vs. SAN FRANCISCO
49ers lead series, 4-1
1974—Bengals, 21-3 (SF)
1978—49ers, 28-12 (SF)
1981—49ers, 21-3 (C)
    *49ers, 26-21 (Detroit)

1984—49ers, 23-17 (SF)
(Points—49ers 101, Bengals 74)
*Super Bowl XVI

CINCINNATI vs. SEATTLE
Bengals lead series, 3-1
1977—Bengals, 42-20 (C)
1981—Bengals, 27-21 (C)
1982—Bengals, 24-10 (C)
1984—Seahawks, 26-6 (C)
(Points—Bengals 99, Seahawks 77)

CINCINNATI vs. TAMPA BAY
Bengals lead series, 2-1
1976—Bengals, 21-0 (C)
1980—Buccaneers, 17-12 (C)
1983—Bengals, 23-17 (TB)
(Points—Bengals 56, Buccaneers 34)

CINCINNATI vs. WASHINGTON
Redskins lead series, 2-1
1970—Redskins, 20-0 (W)
1974—Bengals, 28-17 (C)
1979—Redskins, 28-14 (W)
(Points—Redskins 65, Bengals 42)

CLEVELAND vs. ATLANTA
Browns lead series, 6-1;
See Atlanta vs. Cleveland

CLEVELAND vs. BUFFALO
Browns lead series, 4-2;
See Buffalo vs. Cleveland

CLEVELAND vs. CHICAGO
Browns lead series, 6-2;
See Chicago vs. Cleveland

CLEVELAND vs. CINCINNATI
Browns lead series, 15-14;
See Cincinnati vs. Cleveland

CLEVELAND vs. DALLAS
Browns lead series, 15-8
1960—Browns, 48-7 (D)
1961—Browns, 25-7 (C)
    Browns, 38-17 (D)
1962—Browns, 19-10 (C)
    Cowboys, 45-21 (D)
1963—Browns, 41-24 (D)
    Browns, 27-17 (C)
1964—Browns, 27-6 (C)
    Browns, 20-16 (D)
1965—Browns, 23-17 (C)
    Browns, 24-17 (D)
1966—Browns, 30-21 (C)
    Cowboys, 26-14 (D)
1967—Cowboys, 21-14 (C)
    *Cowboys, 52-14 (D)
1968—Cowboys, 28-7 (C)
    *Browns, 31-20 (C)
1969—Browns, 42-10 (C)
    *Browns, 38-14 (D)
1970—Cowboys, 6-2 (C)
1974—Cowboys, 41-17 (D)
1979—Browns, 26-7 (C)
1982—Cowboys, 31-14 (D)
(Points—Browns 562, Cowboys 460)
*Conference Championship

CLEVELAND vs. DENVER
Broncos lead series, 8-3
1970—Browns, 27-13 (C)
1971—Broncos, 27-0 (C)
1972—Browns, 27-20 (D)
1974—Browns, 23-21 (C)
1975—Broncos, 16-15 (D)
1976—Broncos, 44-13 (D)
1978—Browns, 19-7 (C)
1980—Browns, 19-16 (C)
1981—Broncos, 23-20 (D) OT
1983—Broncos, 27-6 (D)
1984—Broncos, 24-14 (C)
(Points—Broncos 253, Browns 168)

CLEVELAND vs. DETROIT
Lions lead series, 12-3
1952—*Lions, 17-6 (D)
    *Lions, 17-7 (C)
1953—*Lions, 17-16 (D)
1954—Lions, 14-10 (C)
    *Browns, 56-10 (C)
1957—Lions, 20-7 (D)
    *Lions, 59-14 (D)
1958—Lions, 30-10 (C)
1963—Lions, 38-10 (D)
1964—Browns, 37-21 (C)
1967—Lions, 31-14 (D)
1969—Lions, 28-21 (C)
1970—Lions, 41-24 (C)
1975—Lions, 21-10 (D)
1983—Browns, 31-26 (D)
(Points—Lions 390, Browns 273)
*NFL Championship

CLEVELAND vs. GREEN BAY
Packers lead series, 7-5
1953—Browns, 27-0 (Mil)
1955—Browns, 41-10 (C)
1956—Browns, 24-7 (Mil)
1961—Packers, 49-17 (C)
1964—Packers, 28-21 (Mil)
1965—*Packers, 23-12 (GB)

1966—Packers, 21-20 (C)
1967—Packers, 55-7 (Mil)
1969—Browns, 20-7 (C)
1972—Packers, 26-10 (C)
1980—Browns, 26-21 (C)
1983—Packers, 35-21 (Mil)
(Points—Packers 282, Browns 246)
*NFL Championship

CLEVELAND vs. HOUSTON
Browns lead series, 18-11
1970—Browns, 28-14 (C)
       Browns, 21-10 (H)
1971—Browns, 31-0 (C)
       Browns, 37-24 (H)
1972—Browns, 23-17 (H)
       Browns, 20-0 (H)
1973—Browns, 42-13 (C)
       Browns, 23-13 (H)
1974—Browns, 20-7 (C)
       Oilers, 28-24 (H)
1975—Oilers, 40-10 (C)
       Oilers, 21-10 (H)
1976—Browns, 21-7 (H)
       Browns, 13-10 (C)
1977—Browns, 24-23 (H)
       Oilers, 19-15 (C)
1978—Oilers, 16-13 (C)
       Oilers, 14-10 (H)
1979—Oilers, 31-10 (H)
       Browns, 14-7 (C)
1980—Browns, 16-7 (C)
       Browns, 17-14 (H)
1981—Oilers, 9-3 (C)
       Oilers, 17-13 (H)
1982—Browns, 20-14 (H)
1983—Browns, 25-19 (C) OT
       Oilers, 34-27 (H)
1984—Browns, 27-10 (C)
       Browns, 27-20 (H)
(Points—Browns 575, Oilers 467)

CLEVELAND vs. *INDIANAPOLIS
Browns lead series, 10-5
1956—Colts, 21-7 (C)
1959—Browns, 38-31 (B)
1962—Colts, 36-14 (C)
1964—**Browns, 27-0 (C)
1968—Browns, 30-20 (B)
       **Colts, 34-0 (C)
1971—Browns, 14-13 (B)
       ***Colts, 20-3 (C)
1973—Browns, 24-14 (C)
1975—Colts, 21-7 (B)
1978—Browns, 45-24 (B)
1979—Browns, 13-10 (C)
1980—Browns, 28-27 (B)
1981—Browns, 42-28 (C)
1983—Browns, 41-23 (C)
(Points—Browns 333, Colts 322)
*Franchise in Baltimore prior to 1984
**NFL Championship
***AFC Divisional Playoff

CLEVELAND vs. KANSAS CITY
Chiefs lead series, 5-4-1
1971—Chiefs, 13-7 (KC)
1972—Chiefs, 31-7 (C)
1973—Tie, 20-20 (KC)
1975—Browns, 40-14 (C)
1976—Chiefs, 39-14 (KC)
1977—Browns, 44-7 (C)
1978—Chiefs, 17-3 (KC)
1979—Browns, 27-24 (KC)
1980—Browns, 20-13 (C)
1984—Chiefs, 10-6 (KC)
(Points—Browns 188, Chiefs 188)

CLEVELAND vs. *L.A.RAIDERS
Raiders lead series, 8-1
1970—Raiders, 23-20 (O)
1971—Raiders, 34-20 (C)
1973—Browns, 7-3 (O)
1974—Raiders, 40-24 (C)
1975—Raiders, 38-17 (O)
1977—Raiders, 26-10 (C)
1979—Raiders, 19-14 (O)
1980—**Raiders, 14-12 (C)
1982—***Raiders, 27-10 (LA)
(Points—Raiders 224, Browns 134)
*Franchise in Oakland prior to 1982
**AFC Divisional Playoff
***AFC First Round Playoff

CLEVELAND vs. L.A. RAMS
Browns lead series, 8-7
1950—*Browns, 30-28 (C)
1951—Browns, 38-23 (LA)
       *Rams, 24-17 (LA)
1952—Browns, 37-7 (C)
1955—*Browns, 38-14 (LA)
1957—Rams, 45-31 (LA)
1958—Browns, 30-27 (LA)
1963—Browns, 20-6 (C)
1965—Rams, 42-7 (LA)
1968—Rams, 24-6 (C)
1973—Rams, 30-17 (LA)
1977—Rams, 9-0 (C)

1978—Browns, 30-19 (C)
1981—Rams, 27-16 (LA)
1984—Rams, 20-17 (LA)
(Points—Browns 348, Rams 331)
*NFL Championship

CLEVELAND vs. MIAMI
Browns lead series, 3-2
1970—Browns, 28-0 (M)
1972—*Dolphins, 20-14 (M)
1973—Dolphins, 17-9 (C)
1976—Browns, 17-13 (C)
1979—Browns, 30-24 (C) OT
(Points—Browns 98, Dolphins 74)
*AFC Divisional Playoff

CLEVELAND vs. MINNESOTA
Vikings lead series, 7-1
1965—Vikings, 27-17 (C)
1967—Browns, 14-10 (C)
1969—Vikings, 51-3 (M)
       *Vikings, 27-7 (M)
1973—Vikings, 26-3 (M)
1975—Vikings, 42-10 (C)
1980—Vikings, 28-23 (M)
1983—Vikings, 27-21 (C)
(Points—Vikings 238, Browns 98)
*NFL Championship

CLEVELAND vs. NEW ENGLAND
Browns lead series, 5-2
1971—Browns, 27-7 (C)
1974—Browns, 21-14 (NE)
1977—Browns, 30-27 (C) OT
1980—Patriots, 34-17 (NE)
1982—Browns, 10-7 (C)
1983—Browns, 30-0 (NE)
1984—Patriots, 17-16 (C)
(Points—Browns 151, Patriots 106)

CLEVELAND vs. NEW ORLEANS
Browns lead series, 8-1
1967—Browns, 42-7 (NO)
1968—Browns, 24-10 (NO)
       Browns, 35-17 (C)
1969—Browns, 27-17 (NO)
1971—Browns, 21-17 (NO)
1975—Browns, 17-16 (C)
1978—Browns, 24-16 (NO)
1981—Browns, 20-17 (C)
1984—Saints 16-14 (C)
(Points—Browns 224, Saints 133)

CLEVELAND vs. N.Y. GIANTS
Browns lead series, 25-16-2
1950—Giants, 6-0 (C)
       Giants, 17-13 (NY)
       *Browns, 8-3 (C)
1951—Browns, 14-13 (C)
       Browns, 10-0 (NY)
1952—Giants, 17-9 (C)
       Giants, 37-34 (NY)
1953—Browns, 7-0 (NY)
       Browns, 62-14 (C)
1954—Browns, 24-14 (C)
       Browns, 16-7 (NY)
1955—Browns, 24-14 (C)
       Tie, 35-35 (NY)
1956—Giants, 21-9 (C)
       Browns, 24-7 (NY)
1957—Browns, 6-3 (C)
       Browns, 34-28 (NY)
1958—Giants, 21-17 (NY)
       Giants, 13-10 (NY)
       *Giants, 10-0 (NY)
1959—Browns, 10-6 (C)
       Giants, 48-7 (NY)
1960—Giants, 17-13 (C)
       Browns, 48-34 (NY)
1961—Giants, 37-21 (C)
       Tie, 7-7 (NY)
1962—Browns, 17-7 (C)
       Giants, 17-13 (NY)
1963—Browns, 35-24 (C)
       Giants, 33-6 (NY)
1964—Browns, 42-20 (C)
       Browns, 52-20 (NY)
1965—Browns, 38-14 (NY)
       Browns, 34-21 (C)
1966—Browns, 28-7 (NY)
       Browns, 49-40 (C)
1967—Giants, 38-34 (NY)
       Browns, 24-14 (C)
1968—Browns, 45-10 (C)
1969—Browns, 28-17 (C)
       Giants, 27-14 (NY)
1973—Browns, 12-10 (C)
1977—Browns, 21-7 (NY)
(Points—Browns 950, Giants 759)
*Conference Playoff

CLEVELAND vs. N.Y. JETS
Browns lead series, 7-2
1970—Browns, 31-21 (NY)
1972—Browns, 26-10 (NY)
1976—Browns, 38-17 (C)
1978—Browns, 37-34 (C) OT
1979—Browns, 25-22 (NY) OT
1980—Browns, 17-14 (C)

1981—Jets, 14-13 (C)
1983—Browns, 10-7 (C)
1984—Jets, 24-20 (C)
(Points—Browns 217, Jets 163)

CLEVELAND vs. PHILADELPHIA
Browns lead series, 29-11-1
1950—Browns, 35-10 (P)
       Browns, 13-7 (C)
1951—Browns, 20-17 (C)
       Browns, 24-9 (NY)
1952—Browns, 49-7 (C)
       Eagles, 28-20 (C)
1953—Eagles, 37-13 (C)
       Eagles, 42-27 (P)
1954—Eagles, 28-10 (P)
       Browns, 6-0 (C)
1955—Browns, 21-17 (C)
       Eagles, 33-17 (P)
1956—Browns, 16-0 (P)
       Browns, 17-14 (C)
1957—Browns, 24-7 (C)
       Eagles, 17-7 (P)
1958—Browns, 28-14 (C)
       Browns, 21-14 (P)
1959—Browns, 28-7 (C)
       Browns, 28-21 (P)
1960—Browns, 41-24 (P)
       Eagles, 31-29 (C)
1961—Eagles, 27-20 (C)
       Browns, 45-24 (C)
1962—Eagles, 35-7 (P)
       Tie, 14-14 (C)
1963—Browns, 37-7 (C)
       Browns, 23-17 (P)
1964—Browns, 28-20 (P)
       Browns, 38-24 (C)
1965—Browns, 35-17 (P)
       Browns, 38-34 (C)
1966—Browns, 27-7 (C)
       Eagles, 33-21 (P)
1967—Eagles, 28-24 (P)
1968—Browns, 47-13 (C)
1969—Browns, 27-20 (P)
1972—Browns, 27-17 (P)
1976—Browns, 24-3 (P)
1979—Browns, 24-19 (P)
1982—Eagles, 24-21 (P)
(Points—Browns 1,045, Eagles 743)

CLEVELAND vs. PITTSBURGH
Browns lead series, 40-30
1950—Browns, 30-17 (P)
       Browns, 45-7 (C)
1951—Browns, 17-0 (C)
       Browns, 28-0 (P)
1952—Browns, 21-20 (P)
       Browns, 29-28 (C)
1953—Browns, 34-16 (C)
       Browns, 20-16 (P)
1954—Steelers, 55-27 (P)
       Browns, 42-7 (C)
1955—Browns, 41-14 (C)
       Browns, 30-7 (P)
1956—Browns, 14-10 (P)
       Steelers, 24-16 (C)
1957—Browns, 23-12 (P)
       Browns, 24-0 (C)
1958—Browns, 45-12 (P)
       Browns, 27-10 (C)
1959—Steelers, 17-7 (P)
       Steelers, 21-20 (C)
1960—Browns, 28-20 (C)
       Steelers, 14-10 (P)
1961—Browns, 30-28 (C)
       Steelers, 17-13 (P)
1962—Browns, 41-14 (P)
       Browns, 35-14 (C)
1963—Browns, 35-23 (C)
       Steelers, 9-7 (P)
1964—Steelers, 23-7 (C)
       Browns, 30-17 (P)
1965—Browns, 24-19 (C)
       Browns, 42-21 (P)
1966—Browns, 41-10 (C)
       Steelers, 16-6 (P)
1967—Browns, 21-10 (C)
       Browns, 34-14 (P)
1968—Browns, 31-24 (C)
       Browns, 45-24 (P)
1969—Browns, 42-31 (C)
       Browns, 24-3 (P)
1970—Browns, 15-7 (C)
       Steelers, 28-9 (P)
1971—Browns, 27-17 (C)
       Browns, 26-9 (P)
1972—Browns, 26-24 (C)
       Steelers, 30-0 (P)
1973—Browns, 33-6 (C)
       Browns, 21-16 (P)
1974—Steelers, 20-16 (P)
       Steelers, 26-16 (C)
1975—Steelers, 42-6 (C)
       Steelers, 31-17 (P)
1976—Steelers, 31-14 (P)

       Browns, 18-16 (C)
1977—Steelers, 28-14 (C)
       Steelers, 35-31 (P)
1978—Steelers, 15-9 (P) OT
       Steelers, 34-14 (C)
1979—Steelers, 51-35 (C)
       Steelers, 33-30 (P) OT
1980—Browns, 27-26 (C)
       Steelers, 16-13 (P)
1981—Steelers, 13-7 (P)
       Steelers, 32-10 (C)
1982—Browns, 10-9 (C)
       Steelers, 37-21 (P)
1983—Steelers, 44-17 (P)
       Browns, 30-17 (C)
1984—Browns, 20-10 (C)
       Steelers, 23-20 (P)
(Points—Browns 1,594, Steelers 1,414)

CLEVELAND vs. *ST. LOUIS
Browns lead series, 30-9-3
1950—Browns, 34-24 (Cle)
       Browns, 10-7 (Chi)
1951—Browns, 34-17 (Chi)
       Browns, 49-28 (Cle)
1952—Browns, 28-13 (Cle)
       Browns, 10-0 (Chi)
1953—Browns, 27-7 (Chi)
       Browns, 27-16 (Cle)
1954—Browns, 31-7 (Cle)
       Browns, 35-3 (Chi)
1955—Browns, 26-20 (Chi)
       Browns, 35-24 (Cle)
1956—Cardinals, 9-7 (Chi)
       Cardinals, 24-7 (Cle)
1957—Browns, 17-7 (Chi)
       Browns, 31-0 (Cle)
1958—Browns, 35-28 (Cle)
       Browns, 38-24 (Chi)
1959—Browns, 34-7 (Chi)
       Browns, 17-7 (Cle)
1960—Browns, 28-27 (Chi)
       Tie, 17-17 (StL)
1961—Browns, 20-17 (C)
       Browns, 21-10 (StL)
1962—Browns, 34-7 (StL)
       Browns, 38-14 (C)
1963—Cardinals, 20-14 (C)
       Browns, 24-10 (StL)
1964—Tie, 33-33 (C)
       Cardinals, 28-19 (StL)
1965—Cardinals, 49-13 (C)
       Browns, 27-24 (StL)
1966—Cardinals, 34-28 (C)
       Browns, 38-10 (StL)
1967—Browns, 20-16 (C)
       Browns, 20-16 (StL)
1968—Cardinals, 27-21 (C)
       Cardinals, 27-16 (StL)
1969—Tie, 21-21 (C)
       Browns, 27-21 (StL)
1974—Cardinals, 29-7 (StL)
1979—Browns, 38-20 (StL)
(Points—Browns 1,056, Cardinals 749)
*Franchise in Chicago (Chi) prior to 1960

CLEVELAND vs. SAN DIEGO
Chargers lead series, 5-3-1
1970—Chargers, 27-10 (C)
1972—Browns, 21-17 (SD)
1973—Tie, 16-16 (C)
1974—Chargers, 36-35 (SD)
1976—Browns, 21-17 (C)
1977—Chargers, 37-14 (SD)
1981—Chargers, 44-14 (C)
1982—Chargers, 30-13 (C)
1983—Browns, 30-24 (SD) OT
(Points—Chargers 248, Browns 174)

CLEVELAND vs. SAN FRANCISCO
Browns lead series, 8-4
1950—Browns, 34-14 (C)
1951—49ers, 24-10 (SF)
1953—Browns, 23-21 (C)
1955—Browns, 38-3 (SF)
1959—49ers, 21-20 (C)
1962—Browns, 13-10 (SF)
1968—Browns, 33-21 (SF)
1970—49ers, 34-31 (SF)
1974—Browns, 7-0 (C)
1978—Browns, 24-7 (C)
1981—Browns, 15-12 (SF)
1984—49ers, 41-7 (C)
(Points—Browns 255, 49ers 208)

CLEVELAND vs. SEATTLE
Seahawks lead series, 6-2
1977—Seahawks, 20-19 (S)
1978—Seahawks, 47-24 (S)
1979—Seahawks, 29-24 (C)
1980—Browns, 27-3 (S)
1981—Seahawks, 42-21 (S)
1982—Browns, 21-7 (S)
1983—Seahawks, 24-9 (C)
1984—Seahawks, 33-0 (S)
(Points—Seahawks 205, Browns 145)

CLEVELAND vs. TAMPA BAY

Browns lead series, 3-0
1976—Browns, 24-7 (TB)
1980—Browns, 34-27 (TB)
1983—Browns, 20-0 (C)
(Points—Browns 78, Buccaneers 34)

CLEVELAND vs. WASHINGTON
Browns lead series, 31-7-1
1950—Browns, 20-14 (C)
    Browns, 45-21 (W)
1951—Browns, 45-0 (C)
1952—Browns, 19-15 (C)
    Browns, 48-24 (W)
1953—Browns, 30-14 (W)
    Browns, 27-3 (C)
1954—Browns, 62-3 (C)
    Browns, 34-14 (W)
1955—Redskins, 27-17 (C)
    Browns, 24-14 (W)
1956—Browns, 20-9 (W)
    Redskins, 20-17 (C)
1957—Browns, 21-17 (C)
    Tie, 30-30 (W)
1958—Browns, 20-10 (W)
    Browns, 21-14 (C)
1959—Browns, 34-7 (C)
    Browns, 31-17 (W)
1960—Browns, 31-10 (W)
    Browns, 27-16 (C)
1961—Browns, 31-7 (C)
    Browns, 17-6 (W)
1962—Browns, 17-16 (C)
    Redskins, 17-9 (W)
1963—Browns, 37-14 (C)
    Browns, 27-20 (W)
1964—Browns, 27-13 (W)
    Browns, 34-24 (C)
1965—Browns, 17-7 (W)
    Browns, 24-16 (C)
1966—Browns, 38-14 (W)
    Browns, 14-3 (C)
1967—Browns, 42-37 (C)
1968—Browns, 24-21 (W)
1969—Browns, 27-23 (C)
1971—Browns, 20-13 (W)
1975—Redskins, 23-7 (C)
1979—Redskins, 13-9 (C)
(Points—Browns 1,032, Redskins 598)

DALLAS vs. ATLANTA
Cowboys lead series, 7-1;
See Atlanta vs. Dallas
DALLAS vs. BUFFALO
Cowboys lead series, 3-1;
See Buffalo vs. Dallas
DALLAS vs. CHICAGO
Cowboys lead series, 8-3;
See Chicago vs. Dallas
DALLAS vs. CINCINNATI
Cowboys lead series, 2-0;
See Cincinnati vs. Dallas
DALLAS vs. CLEVELAND
Browns lead series, 15-8;
See Cleveland vs. Dallas
DALLAS vs. DENVER
Cowboys lead series, 3-1
1973—Cowboys, 22-10 (Den)
1977—Cowboys, 14-6 (Dal)
    *Cowboys, 27-10 (New Orleans)
1980—Broncos, 41-20 (Den)
(Points—Cowboys 83, Broncos 67)
*Super Bowl XII
DALLAS vs. DETROIT
Cowboys lead series, 6-2
1960—Lions, 23-14 (Det)
1963—Cowboys, 17-14 (Dal)
1968—Cowboys, 59-13 (Dal)
1970—*Cowboys, 5-0 (Dal)
1972—Cowboys, 28-24 (Dal)
1975—Cowboys, 36-10 (Det)
1977—Cowboys, 37-0 (Dal)
1981—Lions, 27-24 (Det)
(Points—Cowboys 220, Lions 111)
*NFC Divisional Playoff
DALLAS vs. GREEN BAY
Packers lead series, 8-5
1960—Packers, 41-7 (GB)
1964—Packers, 45-21 (D)
1965—Packers, 13-3 (Mil)
1966—*Packers, 34-27 (D)
1967—*Packers, 21-17 (GB)
1968—Packers, 28-17 (D)
1970—Cowboys, 16-3 (D)
1972—Packers, 16-13 (Mil)
1975—Packers, 19-17 (D)
1978—Cowboys, 42-14 (Mil)
1980—Cowboys, 28-7 (Mil)
1982—**Cowboys, 37-26 (D)
1984—Cowboys, 20-6 (D)
(Points—Packers 273, Cowboys 265)
*NFL Championship
**NFC Second Round Playoff
DALLAS vs. HOUSTON
Cowboys lead series, 3-1

1970—Cowboys, 52-10 (D)
1974—Cowboys, 10-0 (H)
1979—Oilers, 30-24 (D)
1982—Cowboys, 37-7 (H)
(Points—Cowboys 123, Oilers 47)
DALLAS vs. *INDIANAPOLIS
Cowboys lead series, 6-3
1960—Colts, 45-7 (D)
1967—Colts, 23-17 (B)
1969—Cowboys, 27-10 (D)
1970—**Colts, 16-13 (Miami)
1972—Cowboys, 21-0 (B)
1976—Cowboys, 30-27 (D)
1978—Cowboys, 38-0 (D)
1981—Cowboys, 37-13 (B)
1984—Cowboys, 22-3 (D)
(Points—Cowboys 212, Colts 137)
*Franchise in Baltimore prior to 1984
**Super Bowl V
DALLAS vs. KANSAS CITY
Cowboys lead series, 2-1
1970—Cowboys, 27-16 (KC)
1975—Chiefs, 34-31 (D)
1983—Cowboys, 41-21 (D)
(Points—Cowboys 99, Chiefs 71)
DALLAS vs. *L.A. RAIDERS
Raiders lead series, 2-1
1974—Raiders, 27-23 (O)
1980—Cowboys, 19-13 (O)
1983—Raiders, 40-38 (D)
(Points—Raiders 80, Cowboys 80)
*Franchise in Oakland prior to 1982
DALLAS vs. L.A. RAMS
Cowboys lead series, 10-9
1960—Rams, 38-13 (D)
1962—Cowboys, 27-17 (LA)
1967—Rams, 35-13 (D)
1969—Rams, 24-23 (LA)
1971—Cowboys, 28-21 (D)
1973—Rams, 37-31 (LA)
    *Cowboys, 27-16 (D)
1975—Cowboys, 18-7 (D)
    **Cowboys, 37-7 (LA)
1976—*Rams, 14-12 (D)
1978—Rams, 27-14 (LA)
    **Cowboys, 28-0 (LA)
1979—Cowboys, 30-6 (D)
    *Rams, 21-19 (D)
1980—Rams, 38-14 (LA)
    ***Cowboys, 34-13 (D)
1981—Cowboys, 29-17 (D)
1983—***Rams, 24-17 (D)
1984—Cowboys, 20-13 (LA)
(Points—Cowboys 434, Rams 375)
*NFC Divisional Playoff
**NFC Championship
***NFC First Round Playoff
DALLAS vs. MIAMI
Dolphins lead series, 3-2
1971—*Cowboys, 24-3 (New Orleans)
1973—Dolphins, 14-7 (D)
1978—Dolphins, 23-16 (M)
1981—Cowboys, 28-27 (M)
1984—Dolphins, 28-21 (M)
(Points—Cowboys 96, Dolphins 95)
*Super Bowl VI
DALLAS vs. MINNESOTA
Cowboys lead series, 10-5
1961—Cowboys, 21-7 (D)
    Cowboys, 28-0 (M)
1966—Cowboys, 28-17 (D)
1968—Cowboys, 20-7 (M)
1970—Vikings, 54-13 (M)
1971—*Cowboys, 20-12 (M)
1973—**Vikings, 27-10 (D)
1974—Vikings, 23-21 (D)
1975—*Cowboys, 17-14 (M)
1977—Cowboys, 16-10 (M) OT
    **Cowboys, 23-6 (D)
1978—Vikings, 21-10 (M)
1979—Cowboys, 36-20 (M)
1982—Vikings, 31-27 (M)
1983—Cowboys, 37-24 (M)
(Points—Cowboys 327, Vikings 273)
*NFC Divisional Playoff
**NFC Championship
DALLAS vs. NEW ENGLAND
Cowboys lead series, 5-0
1971—Cowboys, 44-21 (D)
1975—Cowboys, 34-31 (NE)
1978—Cowboys, 17-10 (D)
1981—Cowboys, 35-21 (NE)
1984—Cowboys, 20-17 (D)
(Points—Cowboys 150, Patriots 100)
DALLAS vs. NEW ORLEANS
Cowboys lead series, 11-1
1967—Cowboys, 14-10 (D)
    Cowboys, 27-10 (NO)
1968—Cowboys, 17-3 (NO)
1969—Cowboys, 21-17 (NO)
    Cowboys, 33-17 (D)
1971—Saints, 24-14 (NO)
1973—Cowboys, 40-3 (D)

1976—Cowboys, 24-6 (NO)
1978—Cowboys, 27-7 (D)
1982—Cowboys, 21-7 (D)
1983—Cowboys, 21-20 (D)
1984—Cowboys, 30-27 (D) OT
(Points—Cowboys 289, Saints 151)
DALLAS vs. N.Y. GIANTS
Cowboys lead series, 30-13-2
1960—Tie, 31-31 (NY)
1961—Giants, 31-10 (D)
    Cowboys, 17-16 (NY)
1962—Giants, 41-10 (D)
    Giants, 41-31 (NY)
1963—Giants, 37-21 (NY)
    Giants, 34-27 (D)
1964—Tie, 13-13 (D)
    Cowboys, 31-21 (NY)
1965—Cowboys, 31-2 (D)
    Cowboys, 38-20 (NY)
1966—Cowboys, 52-7 (D)
    Cowboys, 17-7 (NY)
1967—Cowboys, 38-24 (D)
    Cowboys, 28-10 (NY)
1968—Giants, 27-21 (D)
    Cowboys, 28-10 (NY)
1969—Cowboys, 25-3 (D)
1970—Cowboys, 28-10 (D)
    Giants, 23-20 (NY)
1971—Cowboys, 20-13 (D)
    Cowboys, 42-14 (NY)
1972—Cowboys, 23-14 (NY)
    Giants, 23-3 (D)
1973—Cowboys, 45-28 (D)
    Cowboys, 23-10 (New Haven)
1974—Giants, 14-6 (D)
    Cowboys, 21-7 (New Haven)
1975—Cowboys, 13-7 (NY)
    Cowboys, 14-3 (D)
1976—Cowboys, 24-14 (NY)
    Cowboys, 9-3 (D)
1977—Cowboys, 41-21 (D)
    Cowboys, 24-10 (NY)
1978—Cowboys, 34-24 (NY)
    Cowboys, 24-3 (D)
1979—Cowboys, 16-14 (NY)
    Cowboys, 28-7 (D)
1980—Cowboys, 24-3 (D)
    Giants, 38-35 (NY)
1981—Cowboys, 18-10 (D)
    Giants, 13-10 (NY) OT
1983—Cowboys, 28-13 (D)
    Cowboys, 38-20 (NY)
1984—Giants, 28-7 (NY)
    Giants, 19-7 (D)
(Points—Cowboys 1,066, Giants 771)
DALLAS vs. N.Y. JETS
Cowboys lead series, 3-0
1971—Cowboys, 52-10 (D)
1975—Cowboys, 31-21 (NY)
1978—Cowboys, 30-7 (NY)
(Points—Cowboys 113, Jets 38)
DALLAS vs. PHILADELPHIA
Cowboys lead series, 33-16
1960—Eagles, 27-25 (D)
1961—Eagles, 43-7 (D)
    Eagles, 35-13 (P)
1962—Cowboys, 41-19 (D)
    Eagles, 28-14 (P)
1963—Eagles, 24-21 (P)
    Cowboys, 27-20 (D)
1964—Eagles, 17-14 (D)
    Eagles, 24-14 (P)
1965—Eagles, 35-24 (P)
    Cowboys, 21-19 (D)
1966—Cowboys, 56-7 (D)
    Eagles, 24-23 (P)
1967—Eagles, 21-14 (P)
    Cowboys, 38-17 (D)
1968—Cowboys, 45-13 (P)
    Cowboys, 34-14 (D)
1969—Cowboys, 38-7 (P)
    Cowboys, 49-14 (D)
1970—Cowboys, 17-7 (P)
    Cowboys, 21-17 (D)
1971—Cowboys, 42-7 (P)
    Cowboys, 20-7 (D)
1972—Cowboys, 28-6 (D)
    Cowboys, 28-7 (P)
1973—Eagles, 30-16 (P)
    Cowboys, 31-10 (D)
1974—Eagles, 13-10 (P)
    Cowboys, 31-24 (D)
1975—Cowboys, 20-17 (P)
    Cowboys, 27-17 (D)
1976—Cowboys, 27-7 (D)
    Cowboys, 26-7 (P)
1977—Cowboys, 16-10 (P)
    Cowboys, 24-14 (D)
1978—Cowboys, 14-7 (D)
    Cowboys, 31-13 (P)
1979—Eagles, 31-21 (D)
    Cowboys, 24-17 (P)
1980—Eagles, 17-10 (P)
    Cowboys, 35-27 (D)

*Eagles, 20-7 (P)
1981—Cowboys, 17-14 (P)
    Cowboys, 21-10 (D)
1982—Eagles, 24-20 (D)
1983—Cowboys, 37-7 (D)
    Cowboys, 27-20 (P)
1984—Cowboys, 23-17 (D)
    Cowboys, 26-10 (P)
(Points—Cowboys 1,215, Eagles 842)
*NFC Championship
DALLAS vs. PITTSBURGH
Steelers lead series, 12-10
1960—Steelers, 35-28 (D)
1961—Cowboys, 27-24 (D)
    Steelers, 37-7 (P)
1962—Steelers, 30-28 (D)
    Cowboys, 42-27 (P)
1963—Steelers, 27-21 (D)
    Steelers, 24-19 (D)
1964—Steelers, 23-17 (P)
    Cowboys, 17-14 (D)
1965—Steelers, 22-13 (P)
    Cowboys, 24-17 (D)
1966—Cowboys, 52-21 (D)
    Cowboys, 20-7 (P)
1967—Cowboys, 24-21 (P)
1968—Cowboys, 28-7 (D)
1969—Cowboys, 10-7 (P)
1972—Cowboys, 17-13 (D)
1975—*Steelers, 21-17 (Miami)
1977—Steelers, 28-13 (P)
1978—**Steelers, 35-31 (Miami)
1979—Steelers, 14-3 (P)
1982—Cowboys, 36-28 (D)
(Points—Steelers 490, Cowboys 486)
*Super Bowl X
**Super Bowl XIII
DALLAS vs. ST. LOUIS
Cowboys lead series, 28-16-1
1960—Cardinals, 12-10 (StL)
1961—Cardinals, 31-17 (D)
    Cardinals, 31-13 (StL)
1962—Cardinals, 28-24 (D)
    Cardinals, 52-20 (StL)
1963—Cardinals, 34-7 (D)
    Cowboys, 28-24 (StL)
1964—Cardinals, 16-6 (D)
    Cowboys, 31-13 (StL)
1965—Cardinals, 20-13 (StL)
    Cowboys, 27-13 (D)
1966—Tie, 10-10 (StL)
    Cowboys, 31-17 (D)
1967—Cowboys, 46-21 (D)
1968—Cowboys, 27-10 (StL)
1969—Cowboys, 24-3 (D)
1970—Cardinals, 20-7 (StL)
    Cardinals, 38-0 (D)
1971—Cowboys, 16-13 (StL)
    Cowboys, 31-12 (D)
1972—Cowboys, 33-24 (D)
    Cowboys, 27-6 (StL)
1973—Cowboys, 45-10 (D)
    Cowboys, 30-3 (StL)
1974—Cardinals, 31-28 (StL)
    Cowboys, 17-14 (D)
1975—Cowboys, 37-31 (D) OT
    Cardinals, 31-17 (StL)
1976—Cardinals, 21-17 (StL)
    Cowboys, 19-14 (D)
1977—Cowboys, 30-24 (StL)
    Cardinals, 24-17 (D)
1978—Cowboys, 21-12 (D)
    Cowboys, 24-21 (StL) OT
1979—Cowboys, 22-21 (StL)
    Cowboys, 22-13 (D)
1980—Cowboys, 27-24 (StL)
    Cowboys, 31-21 (D)
1981—Cowboys, 30-17 (D)
    Cardinals, 20-17 (StL)
1982—Cowboys, 24-7 (StL)
1983—Cowboys, 34-17 (StL)
    Cowboys, 35-17 (D)
1984—Cardinals, 31-20 (D)
    Cowboys, 24-17 (StL)
(Points—Cowboys 1,036, Cardinals 889)
DALLAS vs. SAN DIEGO
Cowboys lead series, 2-1
1972—Cowboys, 34-28 (SD)
1980—Cowboys, 42-31 (D)
1983—Chargers, 24-23 (SD)
(Points—Cowboys 99, Chargers 83)
DALLAS vs. SAN FRANCISCO
Cowboys lead series, 8-7-1
1960—49ers, 26-14 (D)
1963—49ers, 31-24 (SF)
1965—Cowboys, 39-31 (D)
1967—49ers, 24-16 (SF)
1969—Tie, 24-24 (D)
1970—*Cowboys, 17-10 (SF)
1971—*Cowboys, 14-3 (D)
1972—49ers, 31-10 (D)
    **Cowboys, 30-28 (SF)
1974—Cowboys, 20-14 (D)

1977—Cowboys, 42-35 (SF)
1979—Cowboys, 21-13 (SF)
1980—Cowboys, 59-14 (D)
1981—49ers, 42-14 (SF)
    *49ers, 28-27 (SF)
1983—49ers, 42-17 (SF)
(Points—49ers 399, Cowboys 388)
*NFC Championship
**NFC Divisional Playoff
DALLAS vs. SEATTLE
Cowboys lead series, 3-0
1976—Cowboys, 28-13 (S)
1980—Cowboys, 51-7 (D)
1983—Cowboys, 35-10 (S)
(Points—Cowboys 114, Seahawks 30)
DALLAS vs. TAMPA BAY
Cowboys lead series, 6-0
1977—Cowboys, 23-7 (D)
1980—Cowboys, 28-17 (D)
1981—*Cowboys, 38-0 (D)
1982—Cowboys, 14-9 (D)
    **Cowboys, 30-17 (D)
1983—Cowboys, 27-24 (D) OT
(Points—Cowboys 160, Buccaneers 74)
*NFC Divisional Playoff
**NFC First Round Playoff
DALLAS vs. WASHINGTON
Cowboys lead series, 28-20-2
1960—Redskins, 26-14 (W)
1961—Tie, 28-28 (D)
    Redskins, 34-24 (W)
1962—Tie, 35-35 (D)
    Cowboys, 38-10 (W)
1963—Redskins, 21-17 (W)
    Cowboys, 35-20 (D)
1964—Cowboys, 24-18 (D)
    Cowboys, 28-16 (W)
1965—Cowboys, 27-7 (D)
    Redskins, 34-31 (W)
1966—Cowboys, 31-30 (W)
    Redskins, 34-31 (D)
1967—Cowboys, 17-14 (W)
    Cowboys, 27-20 (D)
1968—Cowboys, 44-24 (W)
    Cowboys, 29-20 (D)
1969—Cowboys, 41-28 (W)
    Cowboys, 20-10 (D)
1970—Cowboys, 45-21 (W)
    Cowboys, 34-0 (D)
1971—Redskins, 20-16 (D)
    Cowboys, 13-0 (W)
1972—Redskins, 24-20 (W)
    Cowboys, 34-24 (D)
    *Redskins, 26-3 (W)
1973—Redskins, 14-7 (W)
    Cowboys, 27-7 (D)
1974—Redskins, 28-21 (W)
    Cowboys, 24-23 (D)
1975—Redskins, 30-24 (W) OT
    Cowboys, 31-10 (D)
1976—Cowboys, 20-7 (W)
    Redskins, 27-14 (D)
1977—Cowboys, 34-16 (D)
    Cowboys, 14-7 (W)
1978—Redskins, 9-5 (W)
    Cowboys, 37-10 (D)
1979—Redskins, 34-20 (W)
    Cowboys, 35-34 (D)
1980—Cowboys, 17-3 (W)
    Cowboys, 14-10 (D)
1981—Cowboys, 26-10 (W)
    Cowboys, 24-10 (D)
1982—Cowboys, 24-10 (W)
    *Redskins, 31-17 (W)
1983—Cowboys, 31-30 (W)
    Redskins, 31-10 (D)
1984—Redskins, 34-14 (W)
    Redskins, 30-28 (D)
(Points—Cowboys 1,205, Redskins 1,018)
*NFC Championship

DENVER vs. ATLANTA
Falcons lead series, 3-2;
See Atlanta vs. Denver
DENVER vs. BUFFALO
Bills lead series, 13-9-1;
See Buffalo vs. Denver
DENVER vs. CHICAGO
Bears lead series, 4-3;
See Chicago vs. Denver
DENVER vs. CINCINNATI
Broncos lead series, 8-6;
See Cincinnati vs. Denver
DENVER vs. CLEVELAND
Broncos lead series, 8-3;
See Cleveland vs. Denver
DENVER vs. DALLAS
Cowboys lead series, 3-1;
See Dallas vs. Denver
DENVER vs. DETROIT
Broncos lead series, 3-2
1971—Lions, 24-20 (Den)
1974—Broncos, 31-27 (Det)

1978—Lions, 17-14 (Det)
1981—Broncos, 27-21 (Den)
1984—Broncos, 28-7 (Det)
(Points—Broncos 120, Lions 96)
DENVER vs. GREEN BAY
Broncos lead series, 3-1
1971—Packers, 34-13 (Mil)
1975—Broncos, 23-13 (D)
1978—Broncos, 16-3 (D)
1984—Broncos, 17-14 (D)
(Points—Broncos 69, Packers 64)
DENVER vs. HOUSTON
Oilers lead series, 18-9-1
1960—Oilers, 45-25 (D)
    Oilers, 20-10 (H)
1961—Oilers, 55-14 (D)
    Oilers, 45-14 (H)
1962—Broncos, 20-10 (D)
    Oilers, 34-17 (H)
1963—Oilers, 20-14 (H)
    Oilers, 33-24 (D)
1964—Oilers, 38-17 (D)
    Oilers, 34-15 (H)
1965—Broncos, 28-17 (D)
    Broncos, 31-21 (H)
1966—Oilers, 45-7 (H)
    Broncos, 40-38 (D)
1967—Oilers, 10-6 (H)
    Oilers, 20-18 (D)
1968—Oilers, 38-17 (H)
1969—Oilers, 24-21 (H)
    Tie, 20-20 (D)
1970—Oilers, 31-21 (H)
1972—Oilers, 30-17 (D)
1973—Broncos, 48-20 (H)
1974—Broncos, 37-14 (D)
1976—Oilers, 17-3 (H)
1977—Broncos, 24-14 (H)
1979—*Oilers, 13-7 (H)
1980—Oilers, 20-16 (D)
1983—Broncos, 26-14 (H)
(Points—Oilers 727, Broncos 570)
*AFC First Round Playoff
DENVER vs. *INDIANAPOLIS
Broncos lead series, 5-1
1974—Broncos, 17-6 (B)
1977—Broncos, 27-13 (D)
1978—Colts, 7-6 (B)
1981—Broncos, 28-10 (D)
1983—Broncos, 17-10 (B)
    Broncos, 21-19 (D)
(Points—Broncos 116, Colts 65)
*Franchise in Baltimore prior to 1984
DENVER vs. *KANSAS CITY
Chiefs lead series, 33-16
1960—Texans, 17-14 (D)
    Texans, 34-7 (Da)
1961—Texans, 19-12 (D)
    Texans, 49-21 (Da)
1962—Texans, 24-3 (D)
    Texans, 17-10 (Da)
1963—Chiefs, 59-7 (D)
    Chiefs, 52-21 (KC)
1964—Broncos, 33-27 (D)
    Chiefs, 49-39 (KC)
1965—Chiefs, 31-23 (D)
    Chiefs, 45-35 (KC)
1966—Chiefs, 37-10 (KC)
    Chiefs, 56-10 (D)
1967—Chiefs, 52-9 (KC)
    Chiefs, 38-24 (D)
1968—Chiefs, 34-2 (KC)
    Chiefs, 30-7 (D)
1969—Chiefs, 26-13 (D)
    Chiefs, 31-17 (KC)
1970—Broncos, 26-13 (D)
    Chiefs, 16-0 (KC)
1971—Chiefs, 16-3 (D)
    Chiefs, 28-10 (KC)
1972—Chiefs, 45-24 (D)
    Chiefs, 24-21 (KC)
1973—Chiefs, 16-14 (KC)
    Broncos, 14-10 (D)
1974—Broncos, 17-14 (KC)
    Chiefs, 42-34 (D)
1975—Broncos, 37-33 (D)
    Chiefs, 26-13 (KC)
1976—Broncos, 35-26 (KC)
    Broncos, 17-16 (D)
1977—Broncos, 23-7 (D)
    Broncos, 14-7 (KC)
1978—Broncos, 23-17 (KC) OT
    Broncos, 24-3 (D)
1979—Broncos, 24-10 (KC)
    Broncos, 20-3 (D)
1980—Chiefs, 23-17 (D)
    Chiefs, 31-14 (KC)
1981—Chiefs, 28-14 (KC)
    Broncos, 16-13 (D)
1982—Chiefs, 37-16 (D)
1983—Chiefs, 27-24 (D)
    Chiefs, 48-17 (KC)
1984—Broncos, 21-0 (D)

Chiefs, 16-13 (KC)
(Points—Chiefs 1,319, Broncos 865)
*Franchise in Dallas prior to 1963 and
known as Texans
DENVER vs. *L.A. RAIDERS
Raiders lead series, 34-14-2
1960—Broncos, 31-14 (D)
    Raiders, 48-10 (O)
1961—Raiders, 33-19 (O)
    Raiders, 27-24 (D)
1962—Broncos, 44-7 (D)
    Broncos, 23-6 (O)
1963—Raiders, 26-10 (D)
    Raiders, 35-31 (O)
1964—Raiders, 40-7 (O)
    Tie, 20-20 (D)
1965—Raiders, 28-20 (D)
    Raiders, 24-13 (O)
1966—Raiders, 17-3 (D)
    Raiders, 28-10 (O)
1967—Raiders, 51-0 (O)
    Raiders, 21-17 (D)
1968—Raiders, 43-7 (D)
    Raiders, 33-27 (O)
1969—Raiders, 24-14 (D)
    Raiders, 41-10 (O)
1970—Raiders, 35-23 (O)
    Raiders, 24-19 (D)
1971—Raiders, 27-16 (D)
    Raiders, 21-13 (O)
1972—Broncos, 30-23 (O)
    Raiders, 37-20 (D)
1973—Tie, 23-23 (D)
    Raiders, 21-17 (O)
1974—Raiders, 28-17 (D)
    Broncos, 20-17 (O)
1975—Raiders, 42-17 (D)
    Raiders, 17-10 (O)
1976—Raiders, 17-10 (D)
    Raiders, 19-6 (O)
1977—Broncos, 30-7 (D)
    Raiders, 24-14 (D)
    **Broncos, 20-17 (D)
1978—Broncos, 14-6 (D)
    Broncos, 21-6 (O)
1979—Raiders, 27-3 (O)
    Raiders, 14-10 (D)
1980—Raiders, 9-3 (O)
    Raiders, 24-21 (D)
1981—Broncos, 9-7 (D)
    Broncos, 17-0 (O)
1982—Raiders, 27-10 (LA)
1983—Raiders, 22-7 (D)
    Raiders, 22-20 (LA)
1984—Broncos, 16-13 (D)
    Broncos, 22-19 (LA) OT
(Points—Raiders 1,158, Broncos 821)
*Franchise in Oakland prior to 1982
**AFC Championship
DENVER vs. L.A. RAMS
Series tied, 2-2
1972—Broncos, 16-10 (LA)
1974—Rams, 17-10 (D)
1979—Rams, 13-9 (D)
1982—Broncos, 27-24 (LA)
(Points—Rams 64, Broncos 62)
DENVER vs. MIAMI
Dolphins lead series, 4-2-1
1966—Dolphins, 24-7 (M)
    Broncos, 17-7 (D)
1967—Dolphins, 35-21 (M)
1968—Broncos, 21-14 (D)
1969—Dolphins, 27-24 (M)
1971—Tie, 10-10 (D)
1975—Dolphins, 14-13 (M)
(Points—Dolphins 131, Broncos 113)
DENVER vs. MINNESOTA
Series tied, 2-2
1972—Vikings, 23-20 (D)
1978—Vikings, 12-9 (M) OT
1981—Broncos, 19-17 (D)
1984—Broncos, 42-21 (D)
(Points—Broncos 90, Vikings 73)
DENVER vs. *NEW ENGLAND
Patriots lead series, 12-11
1960—Broncos, 13-10 (B)
    Broncos, 31-24 (D)
1961—Patriots, 45-17 (B)
    Patriots, 28-24 (D)
1962—Patriots, 41-16 (B)
    Patriots, 33-29 (D)
1963—Broncos, 14-10 (D)
    Patriots, 40-21 (B)
1964—Patriots, 39-10 (D)
    Patriots, 12-7 (B)
1965—Broncos, 27-10 (B)
    Patriots, 28-20 (D)
1966—Patriots, 24-10 (D)
    Broncos, 17-10 (B)
1967—Broncos, 26-21 (D)
1968—Patriots, 20-17 (D)
    Broncos, 35-14 (B)
1969—Broncos, 35-7 (D)

1972—Broncos, 45-21 (D)
1976—Patriots, 38-14 (NE)
1979—Broncos, 45-10 (D)
1980—Patriots, 23-14 (NE)
1984—Broncos, 26-19 (D)
(Points—Patriots 527, Broncos 513)
*Franchise in Boston prior to 1971
DENVER vs. NEW ORLEANS
Broncos lead series, 3-0
1970—Broncos, 31-6 (NO)
1974—Broncos, 33-17 (D)
1979—Broncos, 10-3 (D)
(Points—Broncos 74, Saints 26)
DENVER vs. N. Y. GIANTS
Broncos lead series, 2-1
1972—Giants, 29-17 (NY)
1976—Broncos, 14-13 (D)
1980—Broncos, 14-9 (NY)
(Points—Giants 51, Broncos 45)
DENVER vs. *N. Y. JETS
Series tied, 10-10-1
1960—Titans, 28-24 (NY)
    Titans, 30-27 (D)
1961—Titans, 35-28 (NY)
    Broncos, 27-10 (D)
1962—Titans, 32-10 (NY)
    Titans, 46-45 (D)
1963—Tie, 35-35 (NY)
    Jets, 14-9 (D)
1964—Jets, 30-6 (NY)
    Broncos, 20-16 (D)
1965—Broncos, 16-13 (D)
    Jets, 45-10 (NY)
1966—Jets, 16-7 (D)
1967—Jets, 38-24 (NY)
    Broncos, 33-24 (NY)
1968—Broncos, 21-13 (NY)
1969—Broncos, 21-19 (D)
1973—Broncos, 40-28 (NY)
1976—Broncos, 46-3 (D)
1978—Jets, 31-28 (D)
1980—Broncos, 31-24 (D)
(Points—Broncos 530, Jets 508)
*Jets known as Titans prior to 1963
DENVER vs. PHILADELPHIA
Eagles lead series, 3-1
1971—Eagles, 17-16 (P)
1975—Broncos, 25-10 (D)
1980—Eagles, 27-6 (P)
1983—Eagles, 13-10 (P)
(Points—Eagles 67, Broncos 57)
DENVER vs. PITTSBURGH
Broncos lead series, 6-5-1
1970—Broncos, 16-13 (D)
1971—Broncos, 22-10 (P)
1973—Broncos, 23-13 (P)
1974—Tie, 35-35 (D) OT
1975—Steelers, 20-9 (P)
1977—Broncos, 21-7 (D)
    *Broncos, 34-21 (D)
1978—Steelers, 21-17 (D)
    Steelers, 33-10 (P)
1979—Steelers, 42-7 (P)
1983—Broncos, 14-10 (P)
1984—*Steelers, 24-17 (D)
(Points—Steelers 249, Broncos 225)
*AFC Divisional Playoff
DENVER vs. ST. LOUIS
Broncos lead series, 1-0-1
1973—Tie, 17-17 (StL)
1977—Broncos, 7-0 (D)
(Points—Broncos 24, Cardinals 17)
DENVER vs. *SAN DIEGO
Chargers lead series, 26-23-1
1960—Chargers, 23-19 (D)
    Chargers, 41-33 (LA)
1961—Chargers, 37-0 (SD)
    Chargers, 19-16 (D)
1962—Broncos, 30-21 (D)
    Broncos, 23-20 (SD)
1963—Broncos, 50-34 (D)
    Chargers, 58-20 (SD)
1964—Chargers, 42-14 (SD)
    Chargers, 31-20 (D)
1965—Chargers, 34-31 (SD)
    Chargers, 33-21 (D)
1966—Chargers, 24-17 (SD)
    Broncos, 20-17 (D)
1967—Chargers, 38-21 (SD)
    Chargers, 24-20 (SD)
1968—Chargers, 55-24 (SD)
    Chargers, 47-23 (D)
1969—Broncos, 13-0 (D)
    Chargers, 45-24 (SD)
1970—Chargers, 24-21 (SD)
    Tie, 17-17 (D)
1971—Broncos, 20-16 (D)
    Chargers, 45-17 (SD)
1972—Chargers, 37-14 (SD)
    Broncos, 38-13 (D)
1973—Broncos, 30-19 (D)
    Broncos, 42-28 (SD)
1974—Broncos, 27-7 (D)

Chargers, 17-0 (SD)
1975—Broncos, 27-17 (SD)
Broncos, 13-10 (D) OT
1976—Broncos, 26-0 (D)
Broncos, 17-0 (SD)
1977—Broncos, 17-14 (SD)
Broncos, 17-9 (D)
1978—Broncos, 27-14 (D)
Chargers, 23-0 (SD)
1979—Broncos, 7-0 (D)
Chargers, 17-7 (SD)
1980—Chargers, 30-13 (D)
Broncos, 20-13 (SD)
1981—Broncos, 42-24 (D)
Chargers, 34-17 (SD)
1982—Chargers, 23-3 (D)
Chargers, 30-20 (SD)
1983—Broncos, 14-6 (D)
Chargers, 31-7 (SD)
1984—Broncos, 16-13 (SD)
Broncos, 16-13 (D)
(Points—Chargers 1,187, Broncos 991)
*Franchise in Los Angeles prior to 1961

DENVER vs. SAN FRANCISCO
Series tied, 2-2
1970—49ers, 19-14 (SF)
1973—49ers, 36-34 (D)
1979—Broncos, 38-28 (SF)
1982—Broncos, 24-21 (D)
(Points—Broncos 110, 49ers 104)

DENVER vs. SEATTLE
Broncos lead series, 9-7
1977—Broncos, 24-13 (S)
1978—Broncos, 28-7 (D)
Broncos, 20-17 (S) OT
1979—Broncos, 37-34 (D)
Seahawks, 28-23 (S)
1980—Broncos, 36-20 (D)
Broncos, 25-17 (S)
1981—Seahawks, 13-10 (S)
Broncos, 23-13 (D)
1982—Seahawks, 17-10 (D)
Seahawks, 13-11 (S)
1983—Seahawks, 27-19 (S)
Broncos, 38-27 (D)
*Seahawks, 31-7 (S)
1984—Seahawks, 27-24 (D)
Broncos, 31-14 (S)
(Points—Broncos 366, Seahawks 318)
*AFC First Round Playoff

DENVER vs. TAMPA BAY
Broncos lead series, 2-0
1976—Broncos, 48-13 (D)
1981—Broncos, 24-7 (TB)
(Points—Broncos 72, Buccaneers 20)

DENVER vs. WASHINGTON
Redskins lead series, 2-1
1970—Redskins, 19-3 (D)
1974—Redskins, 30-3 (W)
1980—Broncos, 20-17 (D)
(Points—Redskins 66, Broncos 26)

DETROIT vs. ATLANTA
Lions lead series, 11-4;
See Atlanta vs. Detroit

DETROIT vs. BUFFALO
Series tied, 1-1-1;
See Buffalo vs. Detroit

DETROIT vs. CHICAGO
Bears lead series, 62-44-5;
See Chicago vs. Detroit

DETROIT vs. CINCINNATI
Lions lead series, 2-1;
See Cincinnati vs. Detroit

DETROIT vs. CLEVELAND
Lions lead series, 12-3;
See Cleveland vs. Detroit

DETROIT vs. DALLAS
Cowboys lead series, 6-2;
See Dallas vs. Detroit

DETROIT vs. DENVER
Broncos lead series, 3-2;
See Denver vs. Detroit

*DETROIT vs. GREEN BAY
Packers lead series, 55-47-7
1930—Packers, 47-13 (GB)
Tie, 6-6 (P)
1932—Packers, 15-10 (GB)
Spartans, 19-0 (P)
1933—Packers, 17-0 (GB)
Spartans, 7-0 (P)
1934—Lions, 3-0 (GB)
Packers, 3-0 (D)
1935—Packers, 13-9 (GB)
Packers, 31-7 (GB)
Lions, 20-10 (D)
1936—Packers, 20-18 (GB)
Packers, 26-17 (D)
1937—Packers, 26-6 (GB)
Lions, 14-13 (D)
1938—Lions, 17-7 (GB)
Packers, 28-7 (D)
1939—Packers, 26-7 (GB)

Packers, 12-7 (D)
1940—Lions, 23-14 (GB)
Packers, 50-7 (D)
1941—Packers, 23-0 (GB)
Packers, 24-7 (D)
1942—Packers, 38-7 (Mil)
Packers, 28-7 (D)
1943—Packers, 35-14 (GB)
Packers, 27-6 (D)
1944—Packers, 27-6 (GB)
Packers, 14-0 (D)
1945—Packers, 57-21 (Mil)
Lions, 14-3 (D)
1946—Packers, 10-7 (Mil)
Packers, 9-0 (D)
1947—Packers, 34-17 (GB)
Packers, 35-14 (D)
1948—Packers, 33-21 (GB)
Lions, 24-20 (D)
1949—Packers, 16-14 (GB)
Lions, 21-7 (D)
1950—Lions, 45-7 (GB)
Lions, 24-21 (D)
1951—Lions, 24-17 (GB)
Lions, 52-35 (D)
1952—Lions, 52-17 (GB)
Lions, 48-24 (D)
1953—Lions, 14-7 (GB)
Lions, 34-15 (D)
1954—Lions, 21-17 (GB)
Lions, 28-24 (D)
1955—Packers, 20-17 (GB)
Lions, 24-10 (D)
1956—Lions, 20-16 (GB)
Packers, 24-20 (D)
1957—Lions, 24-14 (GB)
Lions, 18-6 (D)
1958—Tie, 13-13 (GB)
Lions, 24-14 (D)
1959—Packers, 28-10 (GB)
Packers, 24-17 (D)
1960—Packers, 28-9 (GB)
Lions, 23-10 (D)
1961—Lions, 17-13 (Mil)
Packers, 17-9 (D)
1962—Packers, 9-7 (GB)
Lions, 26-14 (D)
1963—Packers, 31-10 (Mil)
Tie, 13-13 (D)
1964—Packers, 14-10 (D)
Packers, 30-7 (GB)
1965—Packers, 31-21 (D)
Lions, 12-7 (GB)
1966—Packers, 23-14 (GB)
Packers, 31-7 (D)
1967—Tie, 17-17 (GB)
Packers, 27-17 (D)
1968—Lions, 23-17 (GB)
Tie, 14-14 (D)
1969—Packers, 28-17 (D)
Lions, 16-10 (GB)
1970—Lions, 40-0 (GB)
Lions, 20-0 (D)
1971—Lions, 31-28 (D)
Tie, 14-14 (Mil)
1972—Packers, 24-23 (D)
Packers, 33-7 (GB)
1973—Tie, 13-13 (GB)
Lions, 34-0 (D)
1974—Packers, 21-19 (Mil)
Lions, 19-17 (D)
1975—Lions, 30-16 (Mil)
Lions, 13-10 (D)
1976—Packers, 24-14 (GB)
Lions, 27-6 (D)
1977—Lions, 10-6 (D)
Packers, 10-9 (GB)
1978—Packers, 13-7 (D)
Packers, 35-14 (Mil)
1979—Packers, 24-16 (Mil)
Packers, 18-13 (D)
1980—Lions, 29-7 (Mil)
Lions, 24-3 (D)
1981—Lions, 31-27 (D)
Packers, 31-17 (GB)
1982—Lions, 30-10 (GB)
Lions, 27-24 (D)
1983—Lions, 38-14 (D)
Lions, 23-20 (Mil) OT
1984—Packers, 41-9 (GB)
Lions, 31-28 (D)
(Points—Packers 2,059, Lions 1,866)
*Franchise in Portsmouth prior to 1934
and known as the Spartans

DETROIT vs. HOUSTON
Oilers lead series, 2-1
1971—Lions, 31-7 (D)
1975—Oilers, 24-8 (H)
1983—Oilers, 27-17 (H)
(Points—Oilers 58, Lions 56)

DETROIT vs. *INDIANAPOLIS
Series tied, 16-16-2
1953—Lions, 27-17 (B)

Lions, 17-7 (D)
1954—Lions, 35-0 (D)
Lions, 27-3 (B)
1955—Colts, 28-13 (B)
Lions, 24-14 (D)
1956—Lions, 31-14 (B)
Lions, 27-3 (D)
1957—Colts, 34-14 (B)
Lions, 31-27 (D)
1958—Colts, 28-15 (B)
Colts, 40-14 (D)
1959—Colts, 21-9 (B)
Colts, 31-24 (D)
1960—Lions, 30-17 (D)
Lions, 20-15 (B)
1961—Lions, 16-15 (B)
Colts, 17-14 (D)
1962—Lions, 29-20 (B)
Lions, 21-14 (D)
1963—Colts, 25-21 (D)
Colts, 24-21 (B)
1964—Colts, 34-0 (D)
Lions, 31-14 (B)
1965—Colts, 31-7 (B)
Tie, 24-24 (D)
1966—Colts, 45-14 (B)
Lions, 20-14 (D)
1967—Colts, 41-7 (B)
Colts, 27-10 (D)
1969—Tie, 17-17 (B)
1973—Colts, 29-27 (D)
1977—Lions, 13-10 (B)
1980—Colts, 10-9 (D)
(Points—Colts 710, Lions 659)
*Franchise in Baltimore prior to 1984

DETROIT vs. KANSAS CITY
Series tied, 2-2
1971—Lions, 32-21 (D)
1975—Chiefs, 24-21 (KC) OT
1980—Chiefs, 20-17 (KC)
1981—Lions, 27-10 (D)
(Points—Lions 97, Chiefs 75)

DETROIT vs. *L.A. RAIDERS
Raiders lead series, 3-2
1970—Lions, 28-14 (D)
1974—Raiders, 35-13 (O)
1978—Raiders, 29-17 (O)
1981—Lions, 16-0 (D)
1984—Raiders, 24-3 (D)
(Points—Raiders 102, Lions 77)
*Franchise in Oakland prior to 1982

DETROIT vs. *L.A. RAMS
Rams lead series, 36-34-1
1937—Lions, 28-0 (C)
Lions, 27-7 (D)
1938—Rams, 21-17 (C)
Lions, 6-0 (D)
1939—Lions, 15-7 (D)
Rams, 14-3 (C)
1940—Lions, 6-0 (D)
Rams, 24-0 (C)
1941—Lions, 17-7 (D)
Lions, 14-0 (C)
1942—Rams, 14-0 (D)
Rams, 27-7 (C)
1944—Rams, 20-17 (D)
Rams, 26-14 (C)
1945—Rams, 28-21 (D)
1946—Rams, 35-14 (LA)
Rams, 41-20 (D)
1947—Rams, 27-13 (D)
Rams, 28-17 (LA)
1948—Rams, 44-7 (LA)
Rams, 34-27 (D)
1949—Rams, 27-24 (LA)
Rams, 21-10 (D)
1950—Rams, 30-28 (D)
Rams, 65-24 (LA)
1951—Rams, 27-21 (D)
Lions, 24-22 (LA)
1952—Lions, 17-14 (LA)
Lions, 24-16 (D)
**Lions, 31-21 (D)
1953—Rams, 31-19 (D)
Rams, 37-24 (LA)
1954—Lions, 21-3 (D)
Lions, 27-24 (LA)
1955—Rams, 17-10 (D)
Rams, 24-13 (LA)
1956—Lions, 24-21 (D)
Lions, 16-7 (LA)
1957—Lions, 10-7 (D)
Rams, 35-17 (LA)
1958—Rams, 42-28 (D)
Lions, 41-24 (LA)
1959—Lions, 17-7 (LA)
Lions, 23-17 (D)
1960—Rams, 48-35 (LA)
Lions, 12-10 (D)
1961—Lions, 14-13 (LA)
Lions, 28-10 (LA)
1962—Lions, 13-10 (LA)
Lions, 12-3 (LA)
1963—Lions, 23-2 (LA)

Rams, 28-21 (D)
1964—Tie, 17-17 (LA)
Lions, 37-17 (D)
1965—Lions, 20-0 (D)
Lions, 31-7 (LA)
1966—Rams, 14-7 (D)
Rams, 23-3 (LA)
1967—Rams, 31-7 (D)
1968—Rams, 10-7 (LA)
1969—Lions, 28-0 (D)
1970—Lions, 28-23 (LA)
1971—Rams, 21-13 (D)
1972—Rams, 34-17 (LA)
1974—Rams, 16-13 (LA)
1975—Rams, 20-0 (D)
1976—Rams, 20-17 (D)
1980—Lions, 41-20 (LA)
1981—Rams, 20-13 (LA)
1982—Rams, 19-14 (LA)
1983—Rams, 21-10 (LA)
(Points—Rams 1,366, Lions 1,298)
*Franchise in Cleveland prior to 1946
**Conference Playoff

DETROIT vs. MIAMI
Dolphins lead series, 2-0
1973—Dolphins, 34-7 (M)
1979—Dolphins, 28-10 (D)
(Points—Dolphins 62, Lions 17)

DETROIT vs. MINNESOTA
Vikings lead series, 29-16-2
1961—Lions, 37-10 (M)
Lions, 13-7 (D)
1962—Lions, 17-6 (M)
Lions, 37-23 (D)
1963—Lions, 28-10 (D)
Vikings, 34-31 (M)
1964—Lions, 24-20 (M)
Tie, 23-23 (D)
1965—Lions, 31-29 (M)
Vikings, 29-7 (D)
1966—Lions, 32-31 (M)
Vikings, 28-16 (D)
1967—Tie, 10-10 (M)
Lions, 14-3 (D)
1968—Vikings, 24-10 (M)
Vikings, 13-6 (D)
1969—Vikings, 24-10 (M)
Vikings, 27-0 (D)
1970—Vikings, 30-17 (D)
Vikings, 24-20 (M)
1971—Vikings, 16-13 (D)
Vikings, 29-10 (M)
1972—Vikings, 34-10 (M)
Vikings, 16-14 (D)
1973—Vikings, 23-9 (D)
Vikings, 28-7 (M)
1974—Vikings, 7-6 (D)
Lions, 20-16 (M)
1975—Vikings, 25-19 (M)
Lions, 17-10 (D)
1976—Lions, 10-9 (D)
Vikings, 31-23 (M)
1977—Vikings, 14-7 (M)
Vikings, 30-21 (D)
1978—Vikings, 17-7 (M)
Lions, 45-14 (D)
1979—Vikings, 13-10 (D)
Vikings, 14-7 (M)
1980—Lions, 27-7 (D)
Vikings, 34-0 (M)
1981—Vikings, 26-24 (M)
Lions, 45-7 (D)
1982—Vikings, 34-31 (D)
1983—Vikings, 20-17 (M)
Lions, 13-2 (D)
1984—Vikings, 29-28 (D)
Lions, 16-14 (M)
(Points—Vikings 925, Lions 838)

DETROIT vs. NEW ENGLAND
Lions lead series, 2-1
1971—Lions, 34-7 (NE)
1976—Lions, 30-10 (D)
1979—Patriots, 24-17 (NE)
(Points—Lions 81, Patriots 41)

DETROIT vs. NEW ORLEANS
Series tied, 4-4-1
1968—Tie, 20-20 (D)
1970—Saints, 19-17 (NO)
1972—Lions, 27-14 (D)
1973—Saints, 20-13 (NO)
1974—Lions, 19-14 (D)
1976—Saints, 17-16 (NO)
1977—Lions, 23-19 (D)
1979—Saints, 17-7 (NO)
1980—Lions, 24-13 (D)
(Points—Lions 166, Saints 153)

*DETROIT vs. N.Y. GIANTS
Lions lead series, 18-11-1
1930—Giants, 19-6 (P)
1931—Spartans, 14-6 (P)
Giants, 14-0 (NY)
1932—Spartans, 7-0 (P)
Spartans, 6-0 (NY)

1933—Spartans, 17-7 (P)
    Giants, 13-10 (NY)
1934—Lions, 9-0 (D)
1935—**Lions, 26-7 (D)
1936—Giants, 14-7 (NY)
    Lions, 38-0 (D)
1937—Lions, 17-0 (NY)
1939—Lions, 18-14 (D)
1941—Giants, 20-13 (NY)
1943—Tie, 0-0 (D)
1945—Lions, 35-14 (NY)
1947—Lions, 35-7 (D)
1949—Lions, 45-21 (NY)
1953—Lions, 27-16 (NY)
1955—Giants, 24-19 (D)
1958—Giants, 19-17 (D)
1962—Lions, 17-14 (NY)
1964—Lions, 26-3 (D)
1967—Lions, 30-7 (NY)
1969—Lions, 24-0 (D)
1972—Lions, 30-16 (D)
1974—Lions, 20-19 (D)
1976—Lions, 24-10 (NY)
1982—Giants, 13-6 (D)
1983—Lions, 15-9 (D)
(Points—Lions 520, Giants 344)
*Franchise in Portsmouth prior to 1934
and known as the Spartans
**NFL Championship

DETROIT vs. N.Y. JETS
Jets lead series, 2-1
1972—Lions, 37-20 (D)
1979—Jets, 31-10 (NY)
1982—Jets, 28-13 (D)
(Points—Jets 79, Lions 60)

***DETROIT vs. PHILADELPHIA**
Lions lead series, 11-9-2
1933—Spartans, 25-0 (P)
1934—Lions, 10-0 (P)
1935—Lions, 35-0 (D)
1936—Lions, 23-0 (D)
1938—Eagles, 21-7 (D)
1940—Lions, 21-0 (P)
1941—Lions, 21-17 (D)
1945—Lions, 28-24 (D)
1948—Eagles, 45-21 (P)
1949—Eagles, 22-14 (D)
1951—Lions, 28-10 (P)
1954—Tie, 13-13 (D)
1957—Lions, 27-16 (P)
1960—Eagles, 28-10 (P)
1961—Eagles, 27-24 (D)
1965—Lions, 35-28 (P)
1968—Eagles, 12-0 (D)
1971—Eagles, 23-20 (D)
1974—Eagles, 28-17 (D)
1977—Lions, 17-13 (D)
1979—Eagles, 44-7 (P)
1984—Tie, 23-23 (D) OT
(Points—Lions 426, Eagles 394)
*Franchise in Portsmouth prior to 1934
and known as the Spartans

***DETROIT vs. *PITTSBURGH**
Lions lead series, 13-8-1
1934—Lions, 40-7 (D)
1936—Lions, 28-3 (D)
1937—Lions, 7-3 (D)
1938—Lions, 16-7 (D)
1940—Pirates, 10-7 (D)
1942—Steelers, 35-7 (D)
1946—Lions, 17-7 (D)
1947—Steelers, 17-10 (P)
1948—Lions, 17-14 (D)
1949—Steelers, 14-7 (P)
1950—Lions, 10-7 (D)
1952—Lions, 31-6 (P)
1953—Lions, 38-21 (D)
1955—Lions, 31-28 (P)
1956—Lions, 45-7 (D)
1959—Tie, 10-10 (P)
1962—Lions, 45-7 (D)
1966—Steelers, 17-3 (P)
1967—Steelers, 24-14 (D)
1969—Steelers, 16-13 (P)
1973—Steelers, 24-10 (P)
1983—Lions, 45-3 (D)
(Points—Lions 451, Steelers 287)
*Steelers known as Pirates prior to 1941

***DETROIT vs. **ST. LOUIS**
Lions lead series, 25-15-5
1930—Tie, 0-0 (P)
    Cardinals, 23-0 (C)
1931—Cardinals, 20-19 (C)
1932—Tie, 7-7 (P)
1933—Spartans, 7-6 (P)
1934—Lions, 6-0 (D)
    Lions, 17-13 (C)
1935—Tie, 10-10 (D)
    Lions, 7-6 (C)
1936—Lions, 39-0 (D)
    Lions, 14-7 (C)
1937—Lions, 16-7 (C)
    Lions, 16-7 (D)
1938—Lions, 10-0 (D)

    Lions, 7-3 (C)
1939—Lions, 21-3 (D)
    Lions, 17-3 (C)
1940—Tie, 0-0 (Buffalo)
    Lions, 43-14 (C)
1941—Tie, 14-14 (C)
    Lions, 21-3 (D)
1942—Cardinals, 13-0 (C)
    Cardinals, 7-0 (D)
1943—Lions, 35-17 (D)
    Lions, 7-0 (C)
1945—Lions, 10-0 (C)
    Lions, 26-0 (D)
1946—Cardinals, 34-14 (C)
    Cardinals, 36-14 (D)
1947—Cardinals, 45-21 (C)
    Cardinals, 17-7 (D)
1948—Cardinals, 56-20 (D)
    Cardinals, 28-14 (D)
1949—Lions, 24-7 (C)
    Cardinals, 42-19 (D)
1959—Lions, 45-21 (D)
1961—Lions, 45-14 (StL)
1967—Cardinals, 38-28 (StL)
1969—Lions, 20-0 (D)
1970—Lions, 16-3 (D)
1973—Lions, 20-16 (StL)
1975—Cardinals, 24-13 (D)
1978—Cardinals, 21-14 (StL)
1980—Lions, 20-7 (D)
    Cardinals, 24-23 (StL)
(Points—Lions 746, Cardinals 626)
*Franchise in Portsmouth prior to 1934
and known as the Spartans
**Franchise in Chicago prior to 1960

DETROIT vs. SAN DIEGO
Lions lead series, 3-2
1972—Lions, 34-20 (D)
1977—Lions, 20-0 (D)
1978—Lions, 31-14 (D)
1981—Chargers, 28-23 (SD)
1984—Chargers, 27-24 (SD)
(Points—Lions 132, Chargers 89)

DETROIT vs. SAN FRANCISCO
Lions lead series, 25-23-1
1950—Lions, 24-7 (D)
    49ers, 28-27 (SF)
1951—49ers, 20-10 (D)
    49ers, 21-17 (SF)
1952—49ers, 17-3 (D)
    49ers, 28-0 (SF)
1953—Lions, 24-21 (D)
    Lions, 14-10 (SF)
1954—49ers, 37-31 (SF)
    Lions, 48-7 (D)
1955—49ers, 27-24 (D)
    49ers, 38-21 (SF)
1956—Lions, 20-17 (D)
    Lions, 17-13 (SF)
1957—49ers, 35-31 (SF)
    Lions, 31-10 (D)
    *Lions, 31-27 (SF)
1958—49ers, 24-21 (SF)
    Lions, 35-21 (D)
1959—49ers, 34-13 (D)
    49ers, 33-7 (SF)
1960—49ers, 14-10 (SF)
    Lions, 24-0 (SF)
1961—49ers, 49-0 (D)
    Tie, 20-20 (SF)
1962—Lions, 45-24 (D)
    Lions, 38-24 (SF)
1963—Lions, 26-3 (D)
    49ers, 45-7 (SF)
1964—Lions, 26-17 (SF)
    Lions, 24-7 (D)
1965—49ers, 27-21 (D)
    49ers, 17-14 (SF)
1966—49ers, 27-24 (SF)
    49ers, 41-14 (D)
1967—Lions, 45-3 (SF)
1968—49ers, 14-7 (D)
1969—Lions, 26-14 (SF)
1970—Lions, 28-7 (D)
1971—49ers, 31-27 (SF)
1973—Lions, 30-20 (D)
1974—Lions, 17-13 (D)
1975—Lions, 28-17 (SF)
1977—49ers, 28-7 (D)
1978—Lions, 33-14 (D)
1980—Lions, 17-13 (D)
1981—Lions, 24-17 (D)
1983—**49ers, 24-23 (SF)
1984—49ers, 30-27 (D)
(Points—Lions 1,119, 49ers 997)
*Conference Playoff
**NFC Divisional Playoff

DETROIT vs. SEATTLE
Seahawks lead series, 2-1
1976—Lions, 41-14 (S)
1978—Seahawks, 28-16 (S)
1984—Seahawks, 38-17 (S)
(Points—Seahawks 80, Lions 74)

DETROIT vs. TAMPA BAY
Lions lead series, 8-6
1977—Lions, 16-7 (D)
1978—Lions, 15-7 (TB)
    Lions, 34-23 (D)
1979—Buccaneers, 31-16 (TB)
    Buccaneers, 16-14 (D)
1980—Lions, 24-10 (TB)
    Lions, 27-14 (D)
1981—Buccaneers, 28-10 (TB)
    Lions, 20-17 (D)
1982—Buccaneers, 23-21 (TB)
1983—Lions, 11-0 (TB)
    Lions, 23-20 (D)
1984—Buccaneers, 21-17 (TB)
    Lions, 13-7 (D) OT
(Points—Lions 258, Buccaneers 227)

***DETROIT vs. **WASHINGTON**
Redskins lead series, 18-8
1932—Spartans, 10-0 (B)
1933—Spartans, 13-0 (B)
1934—Lions, 24-0 (D)
1935—Redskins, 17-7 (B)
    Lions, 14-0 (D)
1938—Redskins, 7-5 (D)
1939—Redskins, 31-7 (W)
1940—Redskins, 20-14 (D)
1942—Redskins, 15-3 (D)
1943—Redskins, 42-20 (W)
1946—Redskins, 17-16 (W)
1947—Lions, 38-21 (D)
1948—Redskins, 46-21 (W)
1951—Lions, 35-17 (D)
1956—Redskins, 18-17 (W)
1965—Lions, 14-10 (D)
1968—Redskins, 14-3 (W)
1970—Redskins, 31-10 (W)
1973—Redskins, 20-0 (D)
1976—Redskins, 20-7 (W)
1978—Redskins, 21-19 (D)
1979—Redskins, 27-24 (D)
1981—Redskins, 33-31 (W)
1982—***Redskins, 31-7 (W)
1983—Redskins, 38-17 (W)
1984—Redskins, 28-14 (W)
(Points—Redskins 514, Lions 400)
*Franchise in Portsmouth prior to 1934
and known as the Spartans.
**Franchise in Boston prior to 1937
***NFC First Round Playoff

GREEN BAY vs. ATLANTA
Packers lead series, 8-6;
See Atlanta vs. Green Bay
GREEN BAY vs. BUFFALO
Bills lead series, 2-1;
See Buffalo vs. Green Bay
GREEN BAY vs. CHICAGO
Bears lead series, 68-55-6;
See Chicago vs. Green Bay
GREEN BAY vs. CINCINNATI
Bengals lead series, 3-2;
See Cincinnati vs. Green Bay
GREEN BAY vs. CLEVELAND
Packers lead series, 7-5;
See Cleveland vs. Green Bay
GREEN BAY vs. DALLAS
Packers lead series, 8-5;
See Dallas vs. Green Bay
GREEN BAY vs. DENVER
Broncos lead series, 3-1;
See Denver vs. Green Bay
GREEN BAY vs. DETROIT
Packers lead series, 55-47-7;
See Detroit vs. Green Bay
GREEN BAY vs. HOUSTON
Series tied, 2-2
1972—Packers, 23-10 (H)
1977—Oilers, 16-10 (GB)
1980—Oilers, 22-3 (GB)
1983—Packers, 41-38 (H) OT
***GREEN BAY vs. *INDIANAPOLIS**
Packers lead series, 18-16-1
1953—Packers, 37-14 (GB)
    Packers, 35-24 (B)
1954—Packers, 7-6 (B)
    Packers, 24-13 (Mil)
1955—Colts, 24-20 (Mil)
    Colts, 14-10 (B)
1956—Packers, 38-33 (Mil)
    Colts, 28-21 (B)
1957—Colts, 45-17 (Mil)
    Packers, 24-21 (B)
1958—Colts, 24-17 (Mil)
    Colts, 56-0 (B)
1959—Colts, 38-21 (B)
    Colts, 28-24 (Mil)
1960—Colts, 35-21 (GB)
    Colts, 38-24 (B)
1961—Packers, 45-7 (GB)
    Colts, 45-21 (B)
1962—Packers, 17-6 (B)
    Packers, 17-13 (GB)
1963—Packers, 31-20 (GB)

    Packers, 34-20 (B)
1964—Colts, 21-20 (GB)
    Colts, 24-21 (B)
1965—Packers, 20-17 (Mil)
    Packers, 42-27 (B)
    **Packers, 13-10 (GB) OT
1966—Packers, 24-3 (Mil)
    Packers, 14-10 (B)
1967—Colts, 13-10 (B)
1968—Colts, 16-3 (GB)
1969—Colts, 14-6 (B)
1970—Colts, 13-10 (Mil)
1974—Packers, 20-13 (B)
1982—Tie, 20-20 (B) OT
(Points—Packers 742, Colts 739)
*Franchise in Baltimore prior to 1984
**Conference Playoff

GREEN BAY vs. KANSAS CITY
Series tied, 1-1-1
1966—*Packers, 35-10 (Los Angeles)
1973—Tie, 10-10 (Mil)
1977—Chiefs, 20-10 (KC)
(Points—Packers 55, Chiefs 40)
*Super Bowl I

***GREEN BAY vs. *L.A. RAIDERS**
Raiders lead series, 4-1
1967—**Packers, 33-14 (Miami)
1972—Raiders, 20-14 (GB)
1976—Raiders, 18-14 (O)
1978—Raiders, 28-3 (GB)
1984—Raiders, 28-7 (LA)
(Points—Raiders 108, Packers 71)
*Franchise in Oakland prior to 1982
**Super Bowl II

***GREEN BAY vs. *L.A. RAMS**
Rams lead series, 38-34-2
1937—Packers, 35-10 (C)
    Packers, 35-7 (GB)
1938—Packers, 26-17 (GB)
    Packers, 28-7 (C)
1939—Rams, 27-24 (GB)
    Packers, 7-6 (C)
1940—Packers, 31-14 (GB)
    Tie, 13-13 (C)
1941—Packers, 24-7 (Mil)
    Packers, 17-14 (C)
1942—Packers, 45-28 (GB)
    Packers, 30-12 (C)
1944—Packers, 30-21 (GB)
    Packers, 42-7 (C)
1945—Rams, 27-14 (GB)
    Rams, 20-7 (C)
1946—Rams, 21-17 (Mil)
    Rams, 38-17 (LA)
1947—Packers, 17-14 (Mil)
    Packers, 30-10 (LA)
1948—Packers, 16-0 (GB)
    Rams, 24-10 (LA)
1949—Rams, 48-7 (GB)
    Rams, 35-7 (LA)
1950—Rams, 45-14 (Mil)
    Rams, 51-14 (LA)
1951—Rams, 28-0 (Mil)
    Rams, 42-14 (LA)
1952—Rams, 30-28 (Mil)
    Rams, 45-27 (LA)
1953—Rams, 38-20 (Mil)
    Rams, 33-17 (LA)
1954—Packers, 35-17 (Mil)
    Rams, 35-27 (LA)
1955—Packers, 30-28 (Mil)
    Rams, 31-17 (LA)
1956—Packers, 42-17 (Mil)
    Rams, 49-21 (LA)
1957—Rams, 31-27 (Mil)
    Rams, 42-17 (LA)
1958—Rams, 20-7 (GB)
    Rams, 34-20 (LA)
1959—Rams, 45-6 (Mil)
    Packers, 38-20 (LA)
1960—Rams, 33-31 (Mil)
    Packers, 35-2 (LA)
1961—Packers, 35-17 (GB)
    Packers, 24-17 (LA)
1962—Packers, 41-10 (GB)
    Packers, 20-17 (LA)
1963—Packers, 42-10 (GB)
    Packers, 31-14 (LA)
1964—Packers, 24-24 (Mil)
    Tie, 24-24 (LA)
1965—Packers, 6-3 (Mil)
    Rams, 21-10 (LA)
1966—Packers, 24-13 (GB)
    Packers, 27-23 (LA)
1967—Packers, 27-24 (LA)
    **Packers, 28-7 (Mil)
1968—Rams, 16-14 (Mil)
1969—Rams, 34-21 (LA)
1970—Rams, 31-21 (GB)
1971—Rams, 30-13 (LA)
1973—Rams, 24-7 (LA)
1974—Packers, 17-6 (Mil)

1975—Rams, 22-5 (LA)
1977—Rams, 24-6 (Mil)
1978—Rams, 31-14 (LA)
1980—Rams, 51-21 (LA)
1981—Rams, 35-23 (LA)
1982—Packers, 35-23 (Mil)
1983—Packers, 27-24 (Mil)
1984—Packers, 31-6 (Mil)
(Points—Rams 1,749, Packers 1,624)
*Franchise in Cleveland prior to 1946
**Conference Championship

GREEN BAY vs. MIAMI
Dolphins lead series, 3-0
1971—Dolphins, 27-6 (Mia)
1975—Dolphins, 31-7 (Mia)
1979—Dolphins, 27-7 (Mia)
(Points—Dolphins 85, Packers 20)

GREEN BAY vs. MINNESOTA
Vikings lead series, 24-22-1
1961—Packers, 33-7 (Minn)
      Packers, 28-10 (Mil)
1962—Packers, 34-7 (GB)
      Packers, 48-21 (Minn)
1963—Packers, 37-28 (Minn)
      Packers, 28-7 (GB)
1964—Vikings, 24-23 (GB)
      Packers, 42-13 (Minn)
1965—Packers, 38-13 (Minn)
      Packers, 24-19 (GB)
1966—Vikings, 20-17 (GB)
      Packers, 28-16 (Minn)
1967—Vikings, 10-7 (GB)
      Packers, 30-27 (Minn)
1968—Vikings, 26-13 (Mil)
      Vikings, 14-10 (Minn)
1969—Vikings, 19-7 (Mil)
      Vikings, 9-7 (Mil)
1970—Packers, 13-10 (Mil)
      Vikings, 10-3 (Minn)
1971—Vikings, 24-13 (GB)
      Vikings, 3-0 (Minn)
1972—Vikings, 27-13 (GB)
      Packers, 23-7 (Minn)
1973—Vikings, 11-3 (GB)
      Vikings, 31-7 (GB)
1974—Vikings, 32-17 (GB)
      Packers, 19-7 (Minn)
1975—Vikings, 28-17 (GB)
      Vikings, 24-3 (Minn)
1976—Vikings, 17-10 (Mil)
      Vikings, 20-9 (Minn)
1977—Vikings, 19-7 (Minn)
      Vikings, 13-6 (GB)
1978—Vikings, 21-7 (Minn)
      Tie, 10-10 (GB) OT
1979—Vikings, 27-21 (Min) OT
      Packers, 19-7 (Mil)
1980—Packers, 16-3 (GB)
      Packers, 25-13 (Minn)
1981—Vikings, 30-13 (Mil)
      Packers, 35-23 (Minn)
1982—Packers, 26-7 (Mil)
1983—Vikings, 20-17 (GB) OT
      Packers, 29-21 (Minn)
1984—Packers, 45-17 (Mil)
      Packers, 38-14 (Minn)
(Points—Packers 918, Vikings 786)

GREEN BAY vs. NEW ENGLAND
Series tied, 1-1
1973—Patriots, 33-24 (NE)
1979—Packers, 27-14 (GB)
(Points—Packers 51, Patriots 47)

GREEN BAY vs. NEW ORLEANS
Packers lead series, 9-2
1968—Packers, 29-7 (Mil)
1971—Saints, 29-21 (Mil)
1972—Packers, 30-20 (NO)
1973—Packers, 30-10 (Mil)
1975—Saints, 20-19 (NO)
1976—Packers, 32-27 (Mil)
1977—Packers, 24-20 (NO)
1978—Packers, 28-17 (Mil)
1979—Packers, 28-19 (Mil)
1981—Packers, 35-7 (NO)
1984—Packers, 23-13 (NO)
(Points—Packers 299, Saints 189)

GREEN BAY vs. N.Y. GIANTS
Packers lead series, 24-18-2
1928—Giants, 6-0 (GB)
      Packers, 7-0 (NY)
1929—Packers, 20-6 (NY)
1930—Packers, 14-7 (GB)
      Giants, 13-6 (NY)
1931—Packers, 27-7 (GB)
      Packers, 14-10 (NY)
1932—Packers, 13-0 (GB)
      Giants, 6-0 (NY)
1933—Giants, 10-7 (Mil)
      Giants, 17-6 (NY)
1934—Packers, 20-6 (Mil)
      Giants, 17-3 (NY)
1935—Packers, 16-7 (GB)
1936—Packers, 26-14 (NY)

1937—Giants, 10-0 (NY)
1938—Giants, 15-3 (NY)
      *Giants, 23-17 (NY)
1939—*Packers, 27-0 (Mil)
1940—Packers, 7-3 (NY)
1942—Tie, 21-21 (NY)
1943—Packers, 35-21 (NY)
1944—Giants, 24-0 (NY)
      *Packers, 14-7 (NY)
1945—Packers, 23-14 (NY)
1947—Tie, 24-24 (NY)
1948—Giants, 49-3 (Mil)
1949—Giants, 30-10 (GB)
1952—Packers, 17-3 (NY)
1957—Giants, 31-17 (GB)
1959—Giants, 20-3 (NY)
1961—Packers, 20-17 (Mil)
      *Packers, 37-0 (GB)
1962—*Packers, 16-7 (NY)
1967—Packers, 48-21 (Mil)
1969—Packers, 20-10 (Mil)
1971—Giants, 42-40 (GB)
1973—Packers, 16-14 (New Haven)
1975—Packers, 40-14 (Mil)
1980—Giants, 27-21 (NY)
1981—Packers, 27-14 (NY)
      Packers, 26-24 (Mil)
1982—Packers, 27-19 (NY)
1983—Packers, 27-3 (NY)
(Points—Packers 737, Giants 661)
*NFL Championship

GREEN BAY vs. N.Y. JETS
Jets lead series, 3-1
1973—Packers, 23-7 (Mil)
1979—Jets, 27-22 (GB)
1981—Jets, 28-3 (NY)
1982—Jets, 15-13 (NY)
(Points—Jets 77, Packers 61)

GREEN BAY vs. PHILADELPHIA
Packers lead series, 17-5
1933—Packers, 35-9 (GB)
      Packers, 10-0 (P)
1934—Packers, 19-6 (GB)
1935—Packers, 13-6 (P)
1937—Packers, 37-7 (Mil)
1939—Packers, 23-16 (P)
1940—Packers, 27-20 (GB)
1942—Packers, 7-0 (P)
1946—Packers, 19-7 (P)
1947—Eagles, 28-14 (P)
1951—Packers, 37-24 (GB)
1952—Packers, 12-10 (Mil)
1954—Packers, 37-14 (P)
1958—Packers, 38-35 (GB)
1960—*Eagles, 17-13 (P)
1962—Packers, 49-0 (P)
1968—Packers, 30-13 (GB)
1970—Packers, 30-17 (Mil)
1974—Eagles, 36-14 (P)
1976—Packers, 28-13 (GB)
1978—Eagles, 10-3 (P)
1979—Eagles, 21-10 (GB)
(Points—Packers 505, Eagles 309)
*NFL Championship

GREEN BAY vs. *PITTSBURGH
Packers lead series, 16-10
1933—Packers, 47-0 (GB)
1935—Packers, 27-0 (GB)
      Packers, 34-14 (P)
1936—Packers, 42-10 (Mil)
1938—Packers, 20-0 (GB)
1940—Packers, 24-3 (Mil)
1941—Packers, 54-7 (P)
1942—Packers, 24-21 (Mil)
1946—Packers, 17-7 (GB)
1947—Steelers, 18-17 (Mil)
1948—Steelers, 38-7 (P)
1949—Steelers, 30-7 (Mil)
1951—Packers, 35-33 (Mil)
      Steelers, 28-7 (P)
1953—Steelers, 31-14 (P)
1954—Steelers, 21-20 (GB)
1957—Steelers, 27-10 (P)
1960—Packers, 19-13 (P)
1963—Packers, 33-14 (Mil)
1965—Packers, 41-9 (P)
1967—Steelers, 24-17 (GB)
1969—Packers, 38-34 (P)
1970—Packers, 20-12 (P)
1975—Steelers, 16-13 (Pit)
1980—Steelers, 22-20 (P)
1983—Steelers, 25-21 (GB)
(Points—Packers 645, Steelers 440)
*Steelers known as Pirates prior to 1941

GREEN BAY vs. *ST. LOUIS
Packers lead series, 38-20-4
1921—Tie, 3-3 (C)
1922—Cardinals, 16-3 (C)
1924—Cardinals, 3-0 (C)
1925—Packers, 9-6 (C)
1926—Cardinals, 13-7 (GB)
      Packers, 3-0 (C)
1927—Packers, 13-0 (GB)

Tie, 6-6 (C)
1928—Packers, 20-0 (GB)
1929—Packers, 9-2 (GB)
      Packers, 7-6 (C)
      Packers, 12-0 (C)
1930—Packers, 14-0 (GB)
      Cardinals, 13-6 (C)
1931—Packers, 26-7 (GB)
      Cardinals, 21-13 (C)
1932—Packers, 15-7 (GB)
      Packers, 19-9 (C)
1933—Packers, 14-6 (C)
1934—Packers, 15-0 (GB)
      Cardinals, 9-0 (Mil)
      Cardinals, 6-0 (C)
1935—Cardinals, 7-6 (GB)
      Cardinals, 3-0 (Mil)
      Cardinals, 9-7 (C)
1936—Packers, 10-7 (GB)
      Packers, 24-0 (Mil)
      Tie, 0-0 (C)
1937—Cardinals, 14-7 (GB)
      Packers, 34-13 (Mil)
1938—Packers, 28-7 (Mil)
      Packers, 24-22 (Buffalo)
1939—Packers, 14-10 (GB)
      Packers, 27-20 (Mil)
1940—Packers, 31-6 (Mil)
      Packers, 28-7 (C)
1941—Packers, 14-13 (Mil)
      Packers, 17-9 (GB)
1942—Packers, 17-13 (C)
      Packers, 55-24 (GB)
1943—Packers, 28-7 (C)
      Packers, 35-14 (Mil)
1945—Packers, 33-14 (GB)
1946—Packers, 19-7 (C)
      Cardinals, 24-6 (GB)
1947—Cardinals, 14-10 (GB)
      Cardinals, 21-20 (C)
1948—Cardinals, 17-7 (Mil)
      Cardinals, 42-7 (C)
1949—Cardinals, 39-17 (Mil)
      Cardinals, 41-21 (C)
1955—Packers, 31-14 (GB)
1956—Cardinals, 24-21 (C)
1962—Packers, 17-0 (Mil)
1963—Packers, 30-7 (StL)
1967—Packers, 31-23 (StL)
1969—Packers, 45-28 (GB)
1971—Tie, 16-16 (StL)
1973—Packers, 25-21 (GB)
1976—Cardinals, 29-0 (StL)
1982—**Packers, 41-16 (GB)
1984—Packers, 24-23 (GB)
(Points—Packers 1,041, Cardinals 758)
*Franchise in Chicago prior to 1960
**NFC First Round Playoff

GREEN BAY vs. SAN DIEGO
Packers lead series, 3-1
1970—Packers, 22-20 (SD)
1974—Packers, 34-0 (GB)
1978—Packers, 24-3 (SD)
1984—Chargers, 34-28 (GB)
(Points—Packers 108, Chargers 57)

GREEN BAY vs. SAN FRANCISCO
49ers lead series, 22-20-1
1950—Packers, 25-21 (GB)
      49ers, 30-14 (SF)
1951—49ers, 31-19 (SF)
1952—49ers, 24-14 (SF)
1953—49ers, 37-7 (Mil)
      49ers, 48-14 (SF)
1954—49ers, 23-17 (Mil)
      49ers, 35-0 (SF)
1955—Packers, 27-21 (Mil)
      Packers, 28-7 (SF)
1956—49ers, 17-16 (GB)
      49ers, 38-20 (SF)
1957—49ers, 24-14 (Mil)
      49ers, 27-20 (SF)
1958—49ers, 33-12 (Mil)
      49ers, 48-21 (SF)
1959—Packers, 21-20 (GB)
      Packers, 36-14 (SF)
1960—Packers, 41-14 (Mil)
      Packers, 13-0 (SF)
1961—Packers, 30-10 (GB)
      49ers, 22-21 (SF)
1962—Packers, 31-13 (Mil)
      Packers, 31-21 (SF)
1963—Packers, 28-10 (Mil)
      Packers, 21-17 (SF)
1964—Packers, 24-14 (Mil)
      49ers, 24-14 (SF)
1965—Packers, 27-10 (GB)
      Tie, 24-24 (SF)
1966—49ers, 21-20 (SF)
      Packers, 20-7 (Mil)
1967—Packers, 13-0 (GB)
1968—49ers, 27-20 (SF)
1969—Packers, 14-7 (Mil)
1970—49ers, 26-10 (SF)

1972—Packers, 34-24 (Mil)
1973—49ers, 20-6 (SF)
1974—49ers, 7-6 (SF)
1976—49ers, 26-14 (GB)
1977—Packers, 16-14 (Mil)
1980—Packers, 23-16 (Mil)
1981—49ers, 13-3 (Mil)
(Points—49ers 885, Packers 829)

GREEN BAY vs. SEATTLE
Packers lead series, 3-1
1976—Packers, 27-20 (Mil)
1978—Packers, 45-28 (Mil)
1981—Packers, 34-24 (GB)
1984—Seahawks, 30-24 (Mil)
(Points—Packers 130, Seahawks 102)

GREEN BAY vs. TAMPA BAY
Series tied, 6-6-1
1977—Packers, 13-0 (TB)
1978—Packers, 9-7 (GB)
      Packers, 17-7 (TB)
1979—Buccaneers, 21-10 (GB)
      Buccaneers, 21-3 (TB)
1980—Tie, 14-14 (TB) OT
      Buccaneers, 20-17 (Mil)
1981—Buccaneers, 21-10 (GB)
      Buccaneers, 37-3 (TB)
1983—Packers, 55-14 (GB)
      Packers, 12-9 (TB) OT
1984—Buccaneers, 30-27 (TB) OT
      Packers, 27-14 (GB)
(Points—Packers 217, Buccaneers 215)

GREEN BAY vs. *WASHINGTON
Packers lead series, 14-11-1
1932—Packers, 21-0 (B)
1933—Tie, 7-7 (GB)
      Redskins, 20-7 (B)
1934—Packers, 10-0 (B)
1936—Packers, 31-2 (GB)
      Packers, 7-3 (B)
      **Packers, 21-6 (New York)
1937—Redskins, 14-6 (W)
1939—Packers, 24-14 (W)
1941—Packers, 22-17 (W)
1943—Redskins, 33-7 (W)
1946—Packers, 20-7 (W)
1947—Packers, 27-10 (Mil)
1948—Redskins, 23-7 (W)
1949—Packers, 30-0 (W)
1950—Packers, 35-21 (Mil)
1952—Packers, 35-20 (Mil)
1958—Redskins, 37-21 (W)
1959—Packers, 21-0 (GB)
1968—Packers, 27-7 (W)
1972—Redskins, 21-16 (W)
      ***Redskins, 16-3 (W)
1974—Redskins, 17-6 (GB)
1977—Redskins, 10-9 (W)
1979—Redskins, 38-21 (W)
1983—Packers, 48-47 (GB)
(Points—Packers 459, Redskins 420)
*Franchise in Boston prior to 1937 and
known as Braves prior to 1933
**NFL Championship
***NFC Divisional Playoff

HOUSTON vs. ATLANTA
Falcons lead series, 4-1;
See Atlanta vs. Houston
HOUSTON vs. BUFFALO
Oilers lead series, 17-8;
See Buffalo vs. Houston
HOUSTON vs. CHICAGO
Oilers lead series, 2-1;
See Chicago vs. Houston
HOUSTON vs. CINCINNATI
Bengals lead series, 19-12-1;
See Cincinnati vs. Houston
HOUSTON vs. CLEVELAND
Browns lead series, 18-11;
See Cleveland vs. Houston
HOUSTON vs. DALLAS
Cowboys lead series, 3-1;
See Dallas vs. Houston
HOUSTON vs. DENVER
Oilers lead series, 18-9-1;
See Denver vs. Houston
HOUSTON vs. DETROIT
Oilers lead series, 2-1;
See Detroit vs. Houston
HOUSTON vs. GREEN BAY
Series tied, 2-2;
See Green Bay vs. Houston
HOUSTON vs. *INDIANAPOLIS
Colts lead series, 4-3
1970—Colts, 24-20 (H)
1973—Oilers, 31-27 (B)
1976—Colts, 38-14 (B)
1979—Oilers, 28-16 (B)
1980—Oilers, 21-16 (H)
1983—Colts, 20-10 (B)
1984—Colts, 35-21 (H)
(Points—Colts 176, Oilers 145)
*Franchise in Baltimore prior to 1984

HOUSTON vs. *KANSAS CITY
Chiefs lead series, 20-11
1960—Oilers, 20-10 (H)
Texans, 24-0 (D)
1961—Texans, 26-21 (D)
Oilers, 38-7 (H)
1962—Texans, 31-7 (H)
Oilers, 14-6 (D)
**Texans, 20-17 (H) OT
1963—Chiefs, 28-7 (KC)
Oilers, 28-7 (H)
1964—Chiefs, 28-7 (KC)
Chiefs, 28-19 (H)
1965—Chiefs, 52-21 (KC)
Oilers, 38-36 (H)
1966—Chiefs, 48-23 (KC)
1967—Chiefs, 25-20 (H)
Oilers, 24-19 (KC)
1968—Chiefs, 26-21 (H)
Chiefs, 24-10 (KC)
1969—Chiefs, 24-0 (KC)
1970—Chiefs, 24-9 (KC)
1971—Chiefs, 20-16 (H)
1973—Chiefs, 38-14 (KC)
1974—Chiefs, 17-7 (H)
1975—Oilers, 17-13 (KC)
1977—Oilers, 34-20 (H)
1978—Oilers, 20-17 (KC)
1979—Oilers, 20-6 (H)
1980—Oilers, 21-20 (KC)
1981—Chiefs, 23-10 (KC)
1983—Chiefs, 13-10 (H) OT
1984—Oilers, 17-16 (KC)
(Points—Chiefs 697, Oilers 529)
*Franchise in Dallas prior to 1963 and known as Texans
**AFL Championship

HOUSTON vs. *L.A. RAIDERS
Raiders lead series, 21-10
1960—Oilers, 37-22 (O)
Raiders, 14-13 (H)
1961—Oilers, 55-0 (H)
Oilers, 47-16 (O)
1962—Oilers, 28-20 (O)
Oilers, 32-17 (H)
1963—Raiders, 24-13 (H)
Raiders, 52-49 (O)
1964—Oilers, 42-28 (H)
Raiders, 20-10 (O)
1965—Raiders, 21-17 (O)
Raiders, 33-21 (H)
1966—Oilers, 31-0 (H)
Raiders, 38-23 (O)
1967—Raiders, 19-7 (H)
**Raiders, 40-7 (O)
1968—Raiders, 24-15 (H)
1969—Raiders, 21-17 (O)
***Raiders, 56-7 (O)
1971—Raiders, 41-21 (O)
1972—Raiders, 34-0 (H)
1973—Raiders, 17-6 (H)
1975—Oilers, 27-26 (O)
1976—Raiders, 14-13 (H)
1977—Raiders, 34-29 (O)
1978—Raiders, 21-17 (O)
1979—Oilers, 31-17 (H)
1980—****Raiders, 27-7 (O)
1981—Oilers, 17-16 (H)
1983—Raiders, 20-6 (LA)
1984—Raiders, 24-14 (H)
(Points—Raiders 756, Oilers 659)
*Franchise in Oakland prior to 1982
**AFL Championship
***Inter-Divisional Playoff
****AFC First Round Playoff

HOUSTON vs. L.A. RAMS
Rams lead series, 3-1
1973—Rams, 31-26 (H)
1978—Rams, 10-6 (H)
1981—Oilers, 27-20 (LA)
1984—Rams, 27-16 (LA)
(Points—Rams 88, Oilers 75)

HOUSTON vs. MIAMI
Series tied, 9-9
1966—Dolphins, 20-13 (H)
Dolphins, 29-28 (M)
1967—Oilers, 17-14 (H)
Oilers, 41-10 (M)
1968—Oilers, 24-10 (M)
Dolphins, 24-7 (H)
1969—Oilers, 22-10 (H)
Oilers, 32-7 (M)
1970—Dolphins, 20-10 (H)
1972—Dolphins, 34-13 (M)
1975—Oilers, 20-19 (H)
1977—Dolphins, 27-7 (M)
1978—Oilers, 35-30 (H)
*Oilers, 17-9 (H)
1979—Oilers, 9-6 (M)
1981—Dolphins, 16-10 (H)
1983—Dolphins, 24-17 (H)
1984—Dolphins, 28-10 (M)
(Points—Dolphins 337, Oilers 332)
*AFC First Round Playoff

HOUSTON vs. MINNESOTA
Vikings lead series, 2-1
1974—Vikings, 51-10 (M)
1980—Oilers, 20-16 (H)
1983—Vikings, 34-14 (M)
(Points—Vikings 101, Oilers 44)

HOUSTON vs. *NEW ENGLAND
Patriots lead series 14-13-1
1960—Oilers, 24-10 (B)
Oilers, 37-21 (H)
1961—Tie, 31-31 (B)
Oilers, 27-15 (H)
1962—Patriots, 34-21 (B)
Oilers, 21-17 (H)
1963—Patriots, 45-3 (B)
Patriots, 46-28 (H)
1964—Patriots, 25-24 (B)
Patriots, 34-17 (H)
1965—Oilers, 31-10 (H)
Patriots, 42-14 (B)
1966—Patriots, 27-21 (B)
Patriots, 38-14 (H)
1967—Patriots, 18-7 (B)
Oilers, 27-6 (H)
1968—Oilers, 16-0 (B)
Oilers, 45-17 (H)
1969—Patriots, 24-0 (B)
Oilers, 27-23 (H)
1971—Patriots, 28-20 (NE)
1973—Patriots, 32-0 (H)
1975—Oilers, 7-0 (NE)
1978—Oilers, 26-23 (NE)
**Oilers, 31-14 (NE)
1980—Oilers, 38-34 (H)
1981—Patriots, 38-10 (NE)
1982—Patriots, 29-21 (NE)
(Points—Patriots 681, Oilers 588)
*Franchise in Boston prior to 1971
**AFC Divisional Playoff

HOUSTON vs. NEW ORLEANS
Oilers lead series, 2-2-1
1971—Tie, 13-13 (H)
1976—Oilers, 31-26 (NO)
1978—Oilers, 17-12 (NO)
1981—Saints, 27-24 (H)
1984—Saints, 27-10 (H)
(Points—Saints 105, Oilers 95)

HOUSTON vs. N.Y. GIANTS
Giants lead series, 2-0
1973—Giants, 34-14 (NY)
1982—Giants, 17-14 (NY)
(Points—Giants 51, Oilers 28)

HOUSTON vs. *N.Y. JETS
Oilers lead series, 15-10-1
1960—Oilers, 27-21 (H)
Oilers, 42-28 (NY)
1961—Oilers, 49-13 (H)
Oilers, 48-21 (NY)
1962—Oilers, 56-17 (H)
Oilers, 44-10 (NY)
1963—Jets, 24-17 (NY)
Oilers, 31-27 (H)
1964—Jets, 24-21 (NY)
Oilers, 33-17 (H)
1965—Oilers, 27-21 (H)
Jets, 41-14 (NY)
1966—Jets, 52-13 (NY)
Oilers, 24-0 (H)
1967—Tie, 28-28 (NY)
1968—Jets, 20-14 (H)
Jets, 26-7 (NY)
1969—Jets, 26-17 (NY)
Jets, 34-26 (H)
1972—Oilers, 26-20 (H)
1974—Oilers, 27-22 (NY)
1977—Oilers, 20-0 (H)
1979—Oilers, 27-24 (H) OT
1980—Jets, 31-28 (NY) OT
1981—Jets, 33-17 (NY)
1984—Oilers, 31-20 (H)
(Points—Oilers 714, Jets 600)
*Jets known as Titans prior to 1963

HOUSTON vs. PHILADELPHIA
Eagles lead series, 3-0
1972—Eagles, 18-17 (H)
1979—Eagles, 26-20 (H)
1982—Eagles, 35-14 (P)
(Points—Eagles 79, Oilers 51)

HOUSTON vs. PITTSBURGH
Steelers lead series, 22-9
1970—Oilers, 19-7 (P)
Steelers, 7-3 (H)
1971—Steelers, 23-16 (P)
Oilers, 29-3 (H)
1972—Steelers, 24-7 (P)
Steelers, 9-3 (H)
1973—Steelers, 36-7 (H)
Steelers, 33-7 (P)
1974—Steelers, 13-7 (H)
Oilers, 13-10 (P)
1975—Steelers, 24-17 (H)
Steelers, 32-9 (H)
1976—Steelers, 32-16 (P)
Steelers, 21-0 (H)
1977—Oilers, 27-10 (H)
Steelers, 27-10 (P)
1978—Oilers, 24-17 (P)
Steelers, 13-3 (H)
*Steelers, 34-5 (P)
1979—Steelers, 38-7 (P)
Oilers, 20-17 (H)
*Steelers, 27-13 (P)
1980—Steelers, 31-17 (P)
Oilers, 6-0 (H)
1981—Steelers, 26-13 (P)
Oilers, 21-20 (H)
1982—Steelers, 24-10 (H)
1983—Steelers, 40-28 (H)
Steelers, 17-10 (P)
1984—Oilers, 23-20 (H) OT
(Points—Steelers 670, Oilers 397)
*AFC Championship

HOUSTON vs. ST. LOUIS
Cardinals lead series, 3-0
1970—Cardinals, 44-0 (StL)
1974—Cardinals, 31-27 (H)
1979—Cardinals, 24-17 (H)
(Points—Cardinals 99, Oilers 44)

HOUSTON vs. *SAN DIEGO
Chargers lead series, 16-11-1
1960—Oilers, 38-28 (H)
Chargers, 24-21 (LA)
**Oilers, 24-16 (H)
1961—Chargers, 34-24 (SD)
Oilers, 33-13 (H)
**Oilers, 10-3 (SD)
1962—Oilers, 42-17 (SD)
Oilers, 33-27 (H)
1963—Chargers, 27-0 (SD)
Chargers, 20-14 (H)
1964—Chargers, 27-21 (SD)
Chargers, 20-17 (H)
1965—Chargers, 31-14 (SD)
Chargers, 37-26 (H)
1966—Chargers, 28-22 (H)
1967—Chargers, 13-3 (SD)
Oilers, 24-17 (H)
1968—Chargers, 30-14 (SD)
1969—Chargers, 21-17 (H)
1970—Tie, 31-31 (SD)
1971—Oilers, 49-33 (H)
1972—Chargers, 34-20 (SD)
1974—Oilers, 21-14 (H)
1975—Oilers, 33-17 (H)
1976—Chargers, 30-27 (SD)
1978—Chargers, 45-24 (H)
1979—***Oilers, 17-14 (SD)
1984—Chargers, 31-14 (SD)
(Points—Chargers 682, Oilers 633)
*Franchise in Los Angeles prior to 1961
**AFL Championship
***AFC Divisional Playoff

HOUSTON vs. SAN FRANCISCO
49ers lead series, 3-2
1970—49ers, 30-20 (H)
1975—Oilers, 27-13 (SF)
1978—Oilers, 20-19 (H)
1981—49ers, 28-6 (SF)
1984—49ers, 34-21 (H)
(Points—49ers 124, Oilers 94)

HOUSTON vs. SEATTLE
Oilers lead series, 3-2
1977—Oilers, 22-10 (S)
1979—Seahawks, 34-14 (S)
1980—Seahawks, 26-7 (H)
1981—Oilers, 35-17 (H)
1982—Oilers, 23-21 (H)
(Points—Seahawks 108, Oilers 101)

HOUSTON vs. TAMPA BAY
Oilers lead series, 2-1
1976—Oilers, 20-0 (H)
1980—Oilers, 20-14 (H)
1983—Buccaneers, 33-24 (TB)
(Points—Oilers 64, Buccaneers 47)

HOUSTON vs. WASHINGTON
Oilers lead series, 2-1
1971—Redskins, 22-13 (W)
1975—Oilers, 13-10 (H)
1979—Oilers, 29-27 (W)
(Points—Redskins 59, Oilers 55)

INDIANAPOLIS vs. ATLANTA
Colts lead series, 8-0;
See Atlanta vs. Indianapolis
INDIANAPOLIS vs. BUFFALO
Series tied, 14-14-1;
See Buffalo vs. Indianapolis
INDIANAPOLIS vs. CHICAGO
Colts lead series, 21-13;
See Chicago vs. Indianapolis
INDIANAPOLIS vs. CINCINNATI
Colts lead series, 5-4;
See Cincinnati vs. Indianapolis
INDIANAPOLIS vs. CLEVELAND
Browns lead series, 10-5;

See Cleveland vs. Indianapolis
INDIANAPOLIS vs. DALLAS
Cowboys lead series, 6-3;
See Dallas vs. Indianapolis
INDIANAPOLIS vs. DENVER
Broncos lead series, 5-1;
See Denver vs. Indianapolis
INDIANAPOLIS vs. DETROIT
Series tied, 16-16-2;
See Detroit vs. Indianapolis
INDIANAPOLIS vs. GREEN BAY
Packers lead series, 18-16-1;
See Green Bay vs. Indianapolis
INDIANAPOLIS vs. HOUSTON
Colts lead series, 4-3;
See Houston vs. Indianapolis
*INDIANAPOLIS vs. KANSAS CITY
Chiefs lead series, 5-3
1970—Chiefs, 44-24 (B)
1972—Chiefs, 24-10 (KC)
1975—Colts, 28-14 (B)
1977—Colts, 17-6 (KC)
1979—Chiefs, 14-0 (KC)
Chiefs, 10-7 (B)
1980—Colts, 31-24 (KC)
Chiefs, 38-28 (B)
(Points—Chiefs 174, Colts 145)
*Franchise in Baltimore prior to 1984

*INDIANAPOLIS vs **L.A. RAIDERS
Raiders lead series, 4-2
1970—***Colts, 27-17 (B)
1971—Colts, 37-14 (O)
1973—Raiders, 34-21 (B)
1975—Raiders, 31-20 (B)
1977—****Raiders, 37-31 (B) OT
1984—Raiders, 21-7 (LA)
(Points—Raiders 154, Colts 143)
*Franchise in Baltimore prior to 1984
**Franchise in Oakland prior to 1982
***AFC Championship
****AFC Divisional Playoff

*INDIANAPOLIS vs. L.A. RAMS
Colts lead series, 20-14-2
1953—Rams, 21-13 (B)
Rams, 45-2 (LA)
1954—Rams, 48-0 (B)
Colts, 22-21 (LA)
1955—Tie, 17-17 (B)
Rams, 20-14 (LA)
1956—Colts, 56-21 (B)
Rams, 31-7 (LA)
1957—Colts, 31-14 (B)
Rams, 37-21 (LA)
1958—Colts, 34-7 (B)
Rams, 30-28 (LA)
1959—Colts, 35-21 (B)
Colts, 45-26 (LA)
1960—Colts, 31-17 (B)
Rams, 10-3 (LA)
1961—Colts, 27-24 (B)
Rams, 34-17 (LA)
1962—Colts, 30-27 (B)
Colts, 14-2 (LA)
1963—Rams, 17-16 (LA)
Colts, 19-16 (B)
1964—Colts, 35-20 (B)
Colts, 24-7 (LA)
1965—Colts, 35-20 (B)
Colts, 20-17 (LA)
1966—Colts, 17-3 (LA)
Rams, 23-7 (B)
1967—Tie, 24-24 (B)
Rams, 34-10 (LA)
1968—Colts, 27-10 (B)
Colts, 28-24 (LA)
1969—Rams, 27-20 (B)
Colts, 13-7 (LA)
1971—Colts, 24-17 (B)
1975—Rams, 24-13 (LA)
(Points—Colts 779, Rams 763)
*Franchise in Baltimore prior to 1984

*INDIANAPOLIS vs. MIAMI
Dolphins lead series, 22-9
1970—Colts, 35-0 (B)
Dolphins, 34-17 (M)
1971—Dolphins, 17-14 (M)
Colts, 14-3 (B)
**Dolphins, 21-0 (M)
1972—Dolphins, 23-0 (B)
Dolphins, 16-0 (M)
1973—Dolphins, 44-0 (M)
Colts, 16-3 (B)
1974—Dolphins, 17-7 (M)
Dolphins, 17-16 (B)
1975—Colts, 33-17 (M)
Colts, 10-7 (B) OT
1976—Colts, 28-14 (B)
Colts, 17-16 (M)
1977—Colts, 45-28 (B)
Dolphins, 17-6 (M)
1978—Dolphins, 42-0 (B)
Dolphins, 26-8 (M)
1979—Dolphins, 19-0 (M)

Dolphins, 28-24 (B)
1980—Colts, 30-17 (M)
Dolphins, 24-14 (B)
1981—Colts, 31-28 (B)
Dolphins, 27-10 (M)
1982—Dolphins, 24-20 (M)
Dolphins, 34-7 (B)
1983—Dolphins, 21-7 (B)
Dolphins, 37-0 (M)
1984—Dolphins, 44-7 (M)
Dolphins, 35-17 (I)
(Points—Dolphins 703, Colts 430)
*Franchise in Baltimore prior to 1984
**AFC Championship

*INDIANAPOLIS vs. MINNESOTA
Colts lead series, 12-5-1
1961—Colts, 34-33 (B)
Vikings, 28-20 (M)
1962—Colts, 34-7 (M)
Colts, 42-17 (B)
1963—Colts, 37-34 (M)
Colts, 41-10 (B)
1964—Vikings, 34-24 (M)
Colts, 17-14 (B)
1965—Colts, 35-16 (B)
Colts, 41-21 (M)
1966—Colts, 38-23 (M)
Colts, 20-17 (B)
1967—Tie, 20-20 (M)
1968—Colts, 21-9 (B)
**Colts, 24-14 (B)
1969—Vikings, 52-14 (M)
1971—Vikings, 10-3 (B)
1982—Vikings, 13-10 (M)
(Points—Colts 475, Vikings 372)
*Franchise in Baltimore prior to 1984
*Conference Championship

*INDIANAPOLIS vs. **NEW ENGLAND
Colts lead series, 15-14
1970—Colts, 14-6 (Bos)
Colts, 27-3 (Balt)
1971—Colts, 23-3 (NE)
Patriots, 21-17 (Balt)
1972—Colts, 24-17 (NE)
Colts, 31-0 (Balt)
1973—Patriots, 24-16 (NE)
Colts, 18-13 (Balt)
1974—Patriots, 42-3 (NE)
Patriots, 27-17 (Balt)
1975—Patriots, 21-10 (NE)
Colts, 34-21 (Balt)
1976—Colts, 27-13 (NE)
Patriots, 21-14 (Balt)
1977—Patriots, 17-3 (NE)
Colts, 30-24 (Balt)
1978—Colts, 34-27 (NE)
Patriots, 35-14 (Balt)
1979—Colts, 31-26 (Balt)
Patriots, 50-21 (NE)
1980—Patriots, 37-21 (Balt)
Patriots, 47-21 (NE)
1981—Colts, 29-28 (NE)
Colts, 23-21 (Balt)
1982—Patriots, 24-13 (Balt)
1983—Colts, 29-23 (NE) OT
Colts, 12-7 (B)
1984—Patriots, 50-17 (I)
Colts, 16-10 (NE)
(Points—Patriots 664, Colts 583)
*Franchise in Baltimore prior to 1984
**Franchise in Boston prior to 1971

*INDIANAPOLIS vs. NEW ORLEANS
Colts lead series, 3-0
1967—Colts, 30-10 (B)
1969—Colts, 30-10 (NO)
1973—Colts, 14-10 (B)
(Points—Colts 74, Saints 30)
*Franchise in Baltimore prior to 1984

*INDIANAPOLIS vs. N.Y. GIANTS
Colts lead series, 7-3
1954—Colts, 20-14 (B)
1955—Giants, 17-7 (NY)
1958—Colts, 24-21 (NY)
**Colts, 23-17 (NY) OT
1959—**Colts, 31-16 (B)
1963—Giants, 37-28 (B)
1968—Colts, 26-0 (NY)
1971—Colts, 31-7 (NY)
1975—Colts, 21-0 (NY)
1979—Colts, 31-7 (NY)
(Points—Colts 239, Giants 139)
*Franchise in Baltimore prior to 1984
**NFL Championship

*INDIANAPOLIS vs. N.Y. JETS
Colts lead series, 16-14
1968—**Jets 16-7 (Miami)
1970—Colts, 29-22 (NY)
Colts, 35-20 (B)
1971—Colts, 22-0 (B)
Colts, 14-13 (NY)
1972—Jets, 44-34 (B)
Jets, 24-20 (NY)
1973—Jets, 34-10 (B)

Jets, 20-17 (NY)
1974—Colts, 35-20 (NY)
Jets, 45-38 (B)
1975—Colts, 45-28 (NY)
Colts, 52-19 (B)
1976—Colts, 20-0 (NY)
Colts, 33-16 (B)
1977—Colts, 20-12 (NY)
Colts, 33-12 (B)
1978—Jets, 33-10 (B)
Jets, 24-16 (NY)
1979—Colts, 10-8 (B)
Jets, 30-17 (NY)
1980—Colts, 17-14 (NY)
Colts, 35-21 (B)
1981—Jets, 41-14 (B)
Jets, 25-0 (NY)
1982—Jets, 37-0 (NY)
1983—Colts, 17-14 (NY)
Jets, 10-6 (B)
1984—Jets, 23-14 (I)
Colts, 9-5 (NY)
(Points—Jets 630, Colts 629)
*Franchise in Baltimore prior to 1984
**Super Bowl III

*INDIANAPOLIS vs. PHILADELPHIA
Series tied, 5-5
1953—Eagles, 45-14 (P)
1965—Colts, 34-24 (B)
1967—Colts, 38-6 (P)
1969—Colts, 24-20 (B)
1970—Colts, 29-10 (B)
1974—Eagles, 30-10 (P)
1978—Eagles, 17-14 (B)
1981—Colts, 38-13 (P)
1983—Colts, 22-21 (P)
1984—Eagles, 16-7 (P)
(Points—Eagles 227, Colts 205)
*Franchise in Baltimore prior to 1984

*INDIANAPOLIS vs. PITTSBURGH
Steelers lead series, 8-4
1957—Steelers, 19-13 (B)
1968—Colts, 41-7 (P)
1971—Colts, 34-21 (B)
1974—Steelers, 30-0 (B)
1975—**Steelers, 28-10 (P)
1976—**Steelers, 40-14 (B)
1977—Colts, 31-21 (B)
1978—Steelers, 35-13 (P)
1979—Steelers, 17-13 (P)
1980—Steelers, 20-17 (B)
1983—Steelers, 24-13 (B)
1984—Colts, 17-16 (I)
(Points—Steelers 278, Colts 216)
*Franchise in Baltimore prior to 1984
**AFC Divisional Playoff

*INDIANAPOLIS vs. ST. LOUIS
Cardinals lead series 5-4
1961—Colts, 16-0 (B)
1964—Colts, 47-27 (B)
1968—Colts, 27-0 (B)
1972—Cardinals, 10-3 (B)
1976—Cardinals, 24-17 (StL)
1978—Colts, 30-17 (StL)
1980—Cardinals, 17-10 (B)
1981—Cardinals, 35-24 (B)
1984—Cardinals, 34-33 (I)
(Points—Colts 207, Cardinals 164)
*Franchise in Baltimore prior to 1984

*INDIANAPOLIS vs. SAN DIEGO
Chargers lead series, 4-2
1970—Colts, 16-14 (SD)
1972—Chargers, 23-20 (B)
1976—Colts, 37-21 (SD)
1981—Chargers, 43-14 (B)
1982—Chargers, 44-26 (SD)
1984—Chargers, 38-10 (I)
(Points—Chargers 183, Colts 123)
*Franchise in Baltimore prior to 1984

*INDIANAPOLIS vs. SAN FRANCISCO
Colts lead series, 21-14
1953—49ers, 38-21 (B)
49ers, 45-14 (SF)
1954—Colts, 17-13 (B)
49ers, 10-7 (SF)
1955—Colts, 26-14 (B)
49ers, 35-24 (SF)
1956—49ers, 20-17 (B)
49ers, 30-17 (SF)
1957—Colts, 27-21 (B)
49ers, 17-13 (SF)
1958—Colts, 35-27 (B)
49ers, 21-12 (SF)
1959—Colts, 45-14 (B)
Colts, 34-14 (SF)
1960—49ers, 30-22 (B)
49ers, 34-10 (SF)
1961—Colts, 20-17 (B)
Colts, 27-24 (SF)
1962—49ers, 21-13 (B)
Colts, 22-3 (SF)
1963—Colts, 20-14 (SF)
Colts, 20-3 (B)

1964—Colts, 37-7 (B)
Colts, 14-3 (SF)
1965—Colts, 27-24 (B)
Colts, 34-28 (SF)
1966—Colts, 36-14 (B)
Colts, 30-14 (SF)
1967—Colts, 41-7 (B)
Colts, 26-9 (SF)
1968—Colts, 27-10 (B)
Colts, 42-14 (SF)
1969—49ers, 24-21 (B)
49ers, 20-17 (SF)
1972—49ers, 24-21 (SF)
(Points—Colts 836, 49ers 663)
*Franchise in Baltimore prior to 1984

*INDIANAPOLIS vs. SEATTLE
Colts lead series, 2-0
1977—Colts, 29-14 (S)
1978—Colts, 17-14 (S)
(Points—Colts 46, Seahawks 28)
*Franchise in Baltimore prior to 1984

*INDIANAPOLIS vs. TAMPA BAY
Series tied, 1-1
1976—Colts, 42-17 (B)
1979—Buccaneers, 29-26 (B) OT
(Points—Colts 68, Buccaneers 46)
*Franchise in Baltimore prior to 1984

*INDIANAPOLIS vs. WASHINGTON
Colts lead series, 15-6
1953—Colts, 27-17 (B)
1954—Redskins, 24-21 (W)
1955—Redskins, 14-13 (B)
1956—Colts, 19-17 (B)
1957—Colts, 21-17 (W)
1958—Colts, 35-10 (B)
1959—Redskins, 27-24 (W)
1960—Colts, 20-0 (B)
1961—Colts, 27-6 (W)
1962—Colts, 34-21 (B)
1963—Colts, 36-20 (W)
1964—Colts, 45-17 (B)
1965—Colts, 38-7 (W)
1966—Colts, 37-10 (B)
1967—Colts, 17-13 (W)
1969—Colts, 41-17 (B)
1973—Redskins, 22-14 (W)
1977—Colts, 10-3 (B)
1978—Colts, 21-17 (B)
1981—Redskins, 38-14 (W)
1984—Redskins, 35-7 (I)
(Points—Colts 521, Redskins 352)
*Franchise in Baltimore prior to 1984

KANSAS CITY vs. ATLANTA
Chiefs lead series, 1-0;
See Atlanta vs. Kansas City
KANSAS CITY vs. BUFFALO
Bills lead series, 14-11-1;
See Buffalo vs. Kansas City
KANSAS CITY vs. CHICAGO
Bears lead series, 2-1;
See Chicago vs. Kansas City
KANSAS CITY vs. CINCINNATI
Chiefs lead series, 8-7;
See Cincinnati vs. Kansas City
KANSAS CITY vs. CLEVELAND
Chiefs lead series, 5-4-1;
See Cleveland vs. Kansas City
KANSAS CITY vs. DALLAS
Cowboys lead series, 2-1;
See Dallas vs. Kansas City
KANSAS CITY vs. DENVER
Chiefs lead series, 33-16;
See Denver vs. Kansas City
KANSAS CITY vs. DETROIT
Series tied, 2-2;
See Detroit vs. Kansas City
KANSAS CITY vs. GREEN BAY
Series tied, 1-1-1;
See Green Bay vs. Kansas City
KANSAS CITY vs. HOUSTON
Chiefs lead series, 20-11;
See Houston vs. Kansas City
KANSAS CITY vs. INDIANAPOLIS
Chiefs lead series, 5-3;
See Indianapolis vs. Kansas City
*KANSAS CITY vs. **L.A. RAIDERS
Raiders lead series, 29-20-2
1960—Texans, 34-16 (D)
Raiders, 20-19 (D)
1961—Texans, 42-35 (O)
Texans, 43-11 (D)
1962—Texans, 26-16 (O)
Texans, 35-7 (D)
1963—Raiders, 10-7 (O)
Raiders, 22-7 (KC)
1964—Chiefs, 21-9 (O)
Chiefs, 42-7 (KC)
1965—Raiders, 37-10 (O)
Chiefs, 14-7 (KC)
1966—Chiefs, 32-10 (O)
Raiders, 34-13 (KC)
1967—Raiders, 23-21 (O)

Raiders, 44-22 (KC)
1968—Chiefs, 24-10 (KC)
Raiders, 38-21 (O)
***Raiders, 41-6 (O)
1969—Raiders, 27-24 (KC)
Raiders, 10-6 (O)
****Chiefs, 17-7 (O)
1970—Tie, 17-17 (KC)
Raiders, 20-6 (O)
1971—Tie, 20-20 (O)
Chiefs, 16-14 (KC)
1972—Chiefs, 27-14 (KC)
Raiders, 26-3 (O)
1973—Chiefs, 16-3 (KC)
Raiders, 37-7 (O)
1974—Raiders, 27-7 (O)
Raiders, 7-6 (KC)
1975—Chiefs, 42-10 (KC)
Raiders, 28-20 (O)
1976—Raiders, 24-21 (KC)
Raiders, 21-10 (O)
1977—Raiders, 37-28 (KC)
Raiders, 21-20 (O)
1978—Raiders, 28-6 (O)
Raiders, 20-10 (KC)
1979—Chiefs, 35-7 (KC)
Chiefs, 24-21 (O)
1980—Raiders, 27-14 (KC)
Chiefs, 31-17 (O)
1981—Chiefs, 27-0 (KC)
Chiefs, 28-17 (O)
1982—Chiefs, 21-16 (KC)
1983—Raiders, 21-20 (LA)
Raiders, 28-20 (KC)
1984—Raiders, 22-20 (KC)
Raiders, 17-7 (LA)
(Points—Raiders 1,013, Chiefs 1,010)
*Franchise in Dallas prior to 1963 and known as Texans
**Franchise in Oakland prior to 1982
***Division Playoff
****AFL Championship

KANSAS CITY vs. L.A. RAMS
Rams lead series, 2-0
1973—Rams, 23-13 (KC)
1982—Rams, 20-14 (LA)
(Points—Rams 43, Chiefs 27)

KANSAS CITY vs. MIAMI
Chiefs lead series, 7-5
1966—Chiefs, 34-16 (KC)
Chiefs, 19-18 (M)
1967—Chiefs, 24-0 (M)
Chiefs, 41-0 (M)
1968—Chiefs, 48-3 (M)
1969—Chiefs, 17-10 (KC)
1971—*Dolphins, 27-24 (KC) OT
1972—Dolphins, 20-10 (KC)
1974—Dolphins, 9-3 (M)
1976—Chiefs, 20-17 (M) OT
1981—Dolphins, 17-7 (KC)
1983—Dolphins, 14-6 (M)
(Points—Chiefs 253, Dolphins 151)
*AFC Divisional Playoff

KANSAS CITY vs. MINNESOTA
Series tied, 2-2
1969—*Chiefs, 23-7 (New Orleans)
1970—Vikings, 27-10 (M)
1974—Vikings, 35-15 (KC)
1981—Chiefs, 10-6 (M)
(Points—Vikings 75, Chiefs 58)
*Super Bowl IV

*KANSAS CITY vs. **NEW ENGLAND
Chiefs lead series, 11-7-3
1960—Patriots, 42-14 (B)
Texans, 34-0 (D)
1961—Patriots, 18-17 (D)
Patriots, 28-21 (B)
1962—Texans, 42-28 (D)
Texans, 27-7 (B)
1963—Tie, 24-24 (B)
Chiefs, 35-3 (KC)
1964—Patriots, 24-7 (B)
Patriots, 31-24 (KC)
1965—Chiefs, 27-17 (KC)
Tie, 10-10 (B)
1966—Chiefs, 43-24 (B)
Tie, 27-27 (KC)
1967—Chiefs, 33-10 (B)
1968—Chiefs, 31-17 (KC)
1969—Chiefs, 31-0 (B)
1970—Chiefs, 23-10 (KC)
1973—Chiefs, 10-7 (NE)
1977—Patriots, 21-17 (NE)
1981—Patriots, 33-17 (NE)
(Points—Chiefs 514, Patriots 381)
*Franchise located in Dallas prior to 1963 and known as Texans
**Franchise in Boston prior to 1971

KANSAS CITY vs. NEW ORLEANS
Saints lead series 2-1
1972—Chiefs, 20-17 (NO)
1976—Saints, 27-17 (KC)
1982—Saints, 27-17 (NO)
(Points—Saints 71, Chiefs 54)

KANSAS CITY vs. N.Y. GIANTS
Giants lead series, 4-1
1974—Giants, 33-27 (KC)
1978—Giants, 26-10 (NY)
1979—Giants, 21-17 (KC)
1983—Chiefs, 38-17 (KC)
1984—Giants, 28-27 (NY)
(Points—Giants 125, Chiefs 119)
*KANSAS CITY vs. **N.Y. JETS
Chiefs lead series, 13-11
1960—Titans, 37-35 (D)
　　　Titans, 41-35 (NY)
1961—Titans, 28-7 (NY)
　　　Texans, 35-24 (D)
1962—Texans, 20-17 (D)
　　　Texans, 52-31 (NY)
1963—Jets, 17-0 (NY)
　　　Chiefs, 48-0 (KC)
1964—Jets, 27-14 (NY)
　　　Chiefs, 24-7 (KC)
1965—Jets, 14-10 (NY)
　　　Jets, 13-10 (KC)
1966—Chiefs, 32-24 (NY)
1967—Chiefs, 42-18 (KC)
　　　Chiefs, 21-7 (NY)
1968—Jets, 20-19 (KC)
1969—Chiefs, 34-16 (NY)
　　　***Chiefs, 13-6 (NY)
1971—Jets, 13-10 (NY)
1974—Chiefs, 24-16 (KC)
1975—Jets, 30-24 (KC)
1982—Chiefs, 37-13 (KC)
1984—Jets, 17-16 (KC)
　　　Jets, 28-7 (NY)
(Points—Chiefs 573, Jets 460)
*Franchise in Dallas prior to 1963 and known as Texans
**Jets known as Titans prior to 1963
***Inter-Divisional Playoff
KANSAS CITY vs. PHILADELPHIA
Eagles lead series, 1-0
1972—Eagles, 21-20 (KC)
KANSAS CITY vs. PITTSBURGH
Steelers lead series, 8-4
1970—Chiefs, 31-14 (P)
1971—Chiefs, 38-16 (KC)
1972—Steelers, 16-7 (P)
1974—Steelers, 34-24 (KC)
1975—Steelers, 28-3 (P)
1976—Steelers, 45-0 (KC)
1978—Steelers, 27-24 (P)
1979—Steelers, 30-3 (KC)
1980—Chiefs, 21-16 (P)
1981—Chiefs, 37-33 (KC)
1982—Steelers, 35-14 (P)
1984—Chiefs, 37-27 (P)
(Points—Steelers 326, Chiefs 234)
KANSAS CITY vs. ST. LOUIS
Chiefs lead series, 3-0-1
1970—Tie, 6-6 (KC)
1974—Chiefs, 17-13 (StL)
1980—Chiefs, 21-13 (StL)
1983—Chiefs, 38-14 (KC)
(Points—Chiefs 82, Cardinals 46)
*KANSAS CITY vs. **SAN DIEGO
Chargers lead series, 25-23-1
1960—Chargers, 21-20 (LA)
　　　Texans, 17-0 (D)
1961—Chargers, 26-10 (D)
　　　Chargers, 24-14 (SD)
1962—Chargers, 32-28 (SD)
　　　Texans, 26-17 (D)
1963—Chargers, 24-10 (SD)
　　　Chargers, 38-17 (SD)
1964—Chargers, 28-14 (KC)
　　　Chiefs, 49-6 (SD)
1965—Tie, 10-10 (SD)
　　　Chiefs, 31-7 (KC)
1966—Chiefs, 24-14 (KC)
　　　Chiefs, 27-17 (SD)
1967—Chargers, 45-31 (SD)
　　　Chargers, 17-16 (KC)
1968—Chiefs, 27-20 (KC)
　　　Chiefs, 40-3 (SD)
1969—Chiefs, 27-9 (KC)
　　　Chiefs, 27-3 (KC)
1970—Chiefs, 26-14 (KC)
　　　Chargers, 31-13 (SD)
1971—Chargers, 21-14 (KC)
　　　Chiefs, 31-10 (KC)
1972—Chiefs, 26-14 (SD)
　　　Chargers, 27-17 (KC)
1973—Chiefs, 19-0 (SD)
　　　Chiefs, 33-6 (KC)
1974—Chiefs, 24-14 (SD)
　　　Chargers, 14-7 (KC)
1975—Chiefs, 12-10 (SD)
　　　Chargers, 28-20 (KC)
1976—Chargers, 30-16 (KC)
　　　Chiefs, 23-20 (SD)
1977—Chiefs, 23-7 (KC)
　　　Chiefs, 21-16 (SD)
1978—Chargers, 29-23 (SD) OT

Chiefs, 23-0 (KC)
1979—Chargers, 20-14 (KC)
　　　Chargers, 28-7 (SD)
1980—Chargers, 24-7 (KC)
　　　Chargers, 20-7 (SD)
1981—Chargers, 42-31 (KC)
　　　Chargers, 22-20 (SD)
1982—Chiefs, 19-12 (KC)
1983—Chargers, 17-14 (KC)
　　　Chargers, 41-38 (SD)
1984—Chargers, 31-13 (KC)
　　　Chiefs, 42-21 (SD)
(Points—Chiefs 1,050, Chargers 928)
*Franchise in Dallas prior to 1963 and known as Texans
**Franchise in Los Angeles prior to 1961
KANSAS CITY vs. SAN FRANCISCO
49ers lead series, 2-1
1971—Chiefs, 26-17 (SF)
1975—49ers, 20-3 (KC)
1982—49ers, 26-13 (KC)
(Points—49ers 63, Chiefs 42)
KANSAS CITY vs. SEATTLE
Chiefs lead series, 7-6
1977—Seahawks, 34-31 (KC)
1978—Seahawks, 13-10 (KC)
　　　Seahawks, 23-19 (S)
1979—Chiefs, 24-6 (S)
　　　Chiefs, 37-21 (KC)
1980—Seahawks, 17-16 (KC)
　　　Chiefs, 31-30 (S)
1981—Chiefs, 20-14 (S)
　　　Chiefs, 40-13 (KC)
1983—Chiefs, 17-13 (KC)
　　　Seahawks, 51-48 (S) OT
1984—Seahawks, 45-0 (S)
　　　Chiefs, 34-7 (KC)
(Points—Chiefs 327, Seahawks 287)
KANSAS CITY vs. TAMPA BAY
Chiefs lead series, 3-2
1976—Chiefs, 28-19 (TB)
1978—Buccaneers, 30-13 (KC)
1979—Buccaneers, 3-0 (TB)
1981—Chiefs, 19-10 (KC)
1984—Chiefs, 24-20 (KC)
(Points—Chiefs 84, Buccaneers 82)
KANSAS CITY vs. WASHINGTON
Chiefs lead series, 2-1
1971—Chiefs, 27-20 (KC)
1976—Chiefs, 33-30 (W)
1983—Redskins, 27-12 (W)
(Points—Redskins 77, Chiefs 72)

L.A. RAIDERS vs. ATLANTA
Raiders lead series, 3-1;
See Atlanta vs. L.A. Raiders
L.A. RAIDERS vs. BUFFALO
Raiders lead series, 12-11;
See Buffalo vs. L.A. Raiders
L.A. RAIDERS vs. CHICAGO
Raiders lead series, 3-2;
See Chicago vs. L.A. Raiders
L.A. RAIDERS vs. CINCINNATI
Raiders lead series, 11-4;
See Cincinnati vs. L.A. Raiders
L.A. RAIDERS vs. CLEVELAND
Raiders lead series, 8-1;
See Cleveland vs. L.A. Raiders
L.A. RAIDERS vs. DALLAS
Raiders lead series, 2-1;
See Dallas vs. L.A. Raiders
L.A. RAIDERS vs. DENVER
Raiders lead series, 34-14-2;
See Denver vs. L.A. Raiders
L.A. RAIDERS vs. DETROIT
Raiders lead series, 3-2;
See Detroit vs. L.A. Raiders
L.A. RAIDERS vs. GREEN BAY
Raiders lead series, 4-1;
See Green Bay vs. L.A. Raiders
L.A. RAIDERS vs. HOUSTON
Raiders lead series, 21-10;
See Houston vs. L.A. Raiders
L.A. RAIDERS vs. INDIANAPOLIS
Raiders lead series, 4-2;
See Indianapolis vs. L.A. Raiders
L.A. RAIDERS vs. KANSAS CITY
Raiders lead series, 29-20-2;
See Kansas City vs. L.A. Raiders
*L.A. RAIDERS vs. L.A. RAMS
Raiders lead series, 3-1
1972—Raiders, 45-17 (O)
1977—Rams, 20-14 (LA)
1979—Raiders, 24-17 (LA)
1982—Raiders, 37-31 (LA Raiders)
(Points—Raiders 120, Rams 85)
*Franchise in Oakland prior to 1982
*L.A. RAIDERS vs. MIAMI
Raiders lead series, 14-3-1
1966—Raiders, 23-14 (M)
　　　Raiders, 21-10 (O)
1967—Raiders, 31-17 (O)
1968—Raiders, 47-21 (M)

1969—Raiders, 20-17 (O)
　　　Tie, 20-20 (M)
1970—Dolphins, 20-13 (M)
　　　**Raiders, 21-14 (O)
1973—Raiders, 12-7 (O)
　　　***Dolphins, 27-10 (M)
1974—Raiders, 28-26 (O)
1975—Raiders, 31-21 (M)
1978—Dolphins, 23-6 (M)
1979—Raiders, 13-3 (O)
1980—Raiders, 16-10 (O)
1981—Raiders, 33-17 (M)
1983—Raiders, 27-14 (LA)
1984—Raiders, 45-34 (M)
(Points—Raiders 417, Dolphins 315)
*Franchise in Oakland prior to 1982
**AFC Divisional Playoff
***AFC Championship
*L.A. RAIDERS vs. MINNESOTA
Raiders lead series, 5-1
1973—Vikings, 24-16 (M)
1976—**Raiders, 32-14 (Pasadena)
1977—Raiders, 35-13 (O)
1978—Raiders, 27-20 (O)
1981—Raiders, 36-10 (M)
1984—Raiders, 23-20 (LA)
(Points—Raiders 169, Vikings 101)
*Franchise in Oakland prior to 1982
**Super Bowl XI
*L.A. RAIDERS vs. **NEW ENGLAND
Series tied, 11-11-1
1960—Raiders, 27-14 (O)
　　　Patriots, 34-28 (B)
1961—Patriots, 20-17 (B)
　　　Patriots, 35-21 (O)
1962—Patriots, 26-16 (B)
　　　Raiders, 20-0 (O)
1963—Patriots, 20-14 (O)
　　　Patriots, 20-14 (B)
1964—Patriots, 17-14 (O)
　　　Tie, 43-43 (B)
1965—Raiders, 24-10 (B)
　　　Raiders, 30-21 (O)
1966—Patriots, 24-21 (B)
1967—Raiders, 35-7 (O)
　　　Raiders, 48-14 (B)
1968—Raiders, 41-10 (O)
1969—Raiders, 38-23 (B)
1971—Patriots, 20-6 (NE)
1974—Raiders, 41-26 (O)
1976—Patriots, 48-17 (NE)
　　　***Raiders, 24-21 (O)
1978—Patriots, 21-14 (O)
1981—Raiders, 27-17 (O)
(Points—Raiders 580, Patriots 491)
*Franchise in Oakland prior to 1982
**Franchise in Boston prior to 1971
***AFC Divisional Playoff
*L.A. RAIDERS vs. NEW ORLEANS
Raiders lead series, 2-0-1
1971—Tie, 21-21 (NO)
1975—Raiders, 48-10 (O)
1979—Raiders, 42-35 (NO)
(Points—Raiders 111, Saints 66)
*Franchise in Oakland prior to 1982
*L.A. RAIDERS vs. N.Y. GIANTS
Raiders lead series, 3-0
1973—Raiders, 42-0 (O)
1980—Raiders, 33-17 (NY)
1983—Raiders, 27-12 (LA)
(Points—Raiders 102, Giants 29)
*Franchise in Oakland prior to 1982
*L.A. RAIDERS vs. **N.Y. JETS
Series tied, 11-11-2
1960—Raiders, 28-27 (NY)
　　　Titans, 31-28 (O)
1961—Titans, 14-6 (O)
　　　Titans, 23-12 (NY)
1962—Titans, 28-17 (O)
　　　Titans, 31-21 (NY)
1963—Jets, 10-7 (NY)
　　　Raiders, 49-26 (O)
1964—Jets, 35-13 (NY)
　　　Raiders, 35-26 (O)
1965—Tie, 24-24 (NY)
　　　Raiders, 24-14 (O)
1966—Raiders, 24-21 (NY)
　　　Tie, 28-28 (O)
1967—Jets, 27-14 (NY)
　　　Raiders, 38-29 (O)
1968—Raiders, 43-32 (O)
　　　***Jets, 27-23 (NY)
1969—Raiders, 27-14 (NY)
1970—Raiders, 14-13 (NY)
1972—Raiders, 24-16 (O)
1977—Raiders, 28-27 (NY)
1979—Jets, 28-19 (NY)
1982—****Jets, 17-14 (LA)
(Points—Jets 568, Raiders 560)
*Franchise in Oakland prior to 1982
**Jets known as Titans prior to 1963
***AFL Championship
****AFC Second Round Playoff

*L.A. RAIDERS vs. PHILADELPHIA
Raiders lead series, 3-1
1971—Raiders, 34-10 (O)
1976—Raiders, 26-7 (P)
1980—Eagles, 10-7 (P)
　　　**Raiders, 27-10 (NO)
(Points—Raiders 94, Eagles 37)
*Franchise in Oakland prior to 1982
**Super Bowl XV
*L.A. RAIDERS vs. PITTSBURGH
Raiders lead series, 9-6
1970—Raiders, 31-14 (O)
1972—Steelers, 34-28 (P)
　　　**Steelers, 13-7 (P)
1973—Raiders, 17-9 (O)
　　　**Raiders, 33-14 (O)
1974—Raiders, 17-0 (P)
　　　***Steelers, 24-13 (O)
1975—***Steelers, 16-10 (P)
1976—Raiders, 31-28 (O)
　　　***Raiders, 24-7 (O)
1977—Raiders, 16-7 (P)
1980—Raiders, 45-34 (O)
1981—Raiders, 30-27 (O)
1983—**Raiders, 38-10 (LA)
1984—Steelers, 13-7 (LA)
(Points—Raiders 339, Steelers 258)
*Franchise in Oakland prior to 1982
**AFC Divisional Playoff
***AFC Championship
*L.A. RAIDERS vs. ST. LOUIS
Series tied, 1-1
1973—Raiders, 17-10 (StL)
1983—Cardinals, 34-24 (LA)
(Points—Cardinals 44, Raiders 41)
*Franchise in Oakland prior to 1982
*L.A. RAIDERS vs. **SAN DIEGO
Raiders lead series, 32-17-2
1960—Chargers, 52-28 (LA)
　　　Chargers, 41-17 (O)
1961—Chargers, 44-0 (SD)
　　　Chargers, 41-10 (O)
1962—Chargers, 42-33 (O)
　　　Chargers, 31-21 (SD)
1963—Chargers, 34-33 (SD)
　　　Raiders, 41-27 (O)
1964—Chargers, 31-17 (O)
　　　Raiders, 21-20 (SD)
1965—Chargers, 17-6 (O)
　　　Chargers, 24-14 (SD)
1966—Chargers, 29-20 (O)
　　　Raiders, 41-19 (SD)
1967—Raiders, 51-10 (O)
　　　Raiders, 41-21 (SD)
1968—Chargers, 23-14 (O)
　　　Raiders, 34-27 (SD)
1969—Raiders, 24-12 (SD)
　　　Raiders, 21-16 (O)
1970—Tie, 27-27 (SD)
　　　Raiders, 20-17 (O)
1971—Raiders, 34-0 (SD)
　　　Raiders, 34-33 (O)
1972—Tie, 17-17 (O)
　　　Raiders, 21-19 (SD)
1973—Raiders, 27-17 (SD)
　　　Raiders, 31-3 (O)
1974—Raiders, 14-10 (SD)
　　　Raiders, 17-10 (O)
1975—Raiders, 6-0 (O)
　　　Raiders, 25-0 (SD)
1976—Raiders, 27-17 (SD)
　　　Raiders, 24-0 (O)
1977—Raiders, 24-0 (O)
　　　Chargers, 12-7 (SD)
1978—Raiders, 21-20 (O)
　　　Chargers, 27-23 (SD)
1979—Raiders, 30-10 (O)
　　　Raiders, 45-22 (O)
1980—Chargers, 30-24 (SD) OT
　　　Raiders, 38-24 (O)
　　　***Raiders, 34-27 (SD)
1981—Chargers, 55-21 (O)
　　　Chargers, 23-10 (SD)
1982—Raiders, 28-24 (LA)
　　　Raiders, 41-34 (SD)
1983—Raiders, 42-10 (LA)
　　　Raiders, 30-14 (LA)
1984—Raiders, 33-30 (LA)
　　　Raiders, 44-37 (SD)
(Points—Raiders 1,287, Chargers 1,149)
*Franchise in Oakland prior to 1982
**Franchise in Los Angeles prior to 1961
***AFC Championship
*L.A. RAIDERS vs. SAN FRANCISCO
Raiders lead series, 3-1
1970—49ers, 38-7 (O)
1974—Raiders, 35-24 (SF)
1979—Raiders, 23-10 (O)
1982—Raiders, 23-17 (SF)
(Points—49ers 89, Raiders 88)
*Franchise in Oakland prior to 1982
*L.A. RAIDERS vs. SEATTLE
Series tied, 8-8

235

1977—Raiders, 44-7 (O)
1978—Seahawks, 27-7 (S)
Seahawks, 17-16 (O)
1979—Seahawks, 27-10 (S)
Seahawks, 29-24 (O)
1980—Raiders, 33-14 (O)
Raiders, 19-17 (S)
1981—Raiders, 20-10 (O)
Raiders, 32-31 (S)
1982—Raiders, 28-23 (LA)
1983—Seahawks, 38-36 (S)
Seahawks, 34-21 (LA)
**Raiders, 30-14 (LA)
1984—Raiders, 28-14 (LA)
Seahawks, 17-14 (S)
***Seahawks, 13-7 (S)
(Points—Raiders 369, Seahawks 332)
*Franchise in Oakland prior to 1982
**AFC Championship
***AFC First Round Playoff
L.A. RAIDERS vs. TAMPA BAY
Raiders lead series, 2-0
1976—Raiders, 49-16 (O)
1981—Raiders, 18-16 (O)
(Points—Raiders 67, Buccaneers 32)
*Franchise in Oakland prior to 1982
L.A. RAIDERS vs. WASHINGTON
Raiders lead series, 4-1
1970—Raiders, 34-20 (O)
1975—Raiders, 26-23 (W) OT
1980—Raiders, 24-21 (O)
1983—Redskins, 37-35 (W)
**Raiders, 38-9 (Tampa)
(Points—Raiders 157, Redskins 110)
*Franchise in Oakland prior to 1982
**Super Bowl XVIII

L.A. RAMS vs. ATLANTA
Rams lead series, 27-7-2;
See Atlanta vs. L.A. Rams
L.A. RAMS vs. BUFFALO
Rams lead series, 3-1;
See Buffalo vs. L.A. Rams
L.A. RAMS vs. CHICAGO
Bears lead series, 42-27-3;
See Chicago vs. L.A. Rams
L.A. RAMS vs. CINCINNATI
Bengals lead series, 3-2;
See Cincinnati vs. L.A. Rams
L.A. RAMS vs. CLEVELAND
Browns lead series, 8-7;
See Cleveland vs. L.A. Rams
L.A. RAMS vs. DALLAS
Cowboys lead series, 10-9;
See Dallas vs. L.A. Rams
L.A. RAMS vs. DENVER
Series tied 2-2;
See Denver vs. L.A. Rams
L.A. RAMS vs. DETROIT
Rams lead series, 36-34-1;
See Detroit vs. L.A. Rams
L.A. RAMS vs. GREEN BAY
Rams lead series, 38-34-2;
See Green Bay vs. L.A. Rams
L.A. RAMS vs. HOUSTON
Rams lead series, 3-1;
See Houston vs. L.A. Rams
L.A. RAMS vs. INDIANAPOLIS
Colts lead series, 20-14-2;
See Indianapolis vs. L.A. Rams
L.A. RAMS vs. KANSAS CITY
Rams lead series, 2-0;
See Kansas City vs. L.A. Rams
L.A. RAMS VS. L.A. RAIDERS
Raiders lead series, 3-1;
See L.A. Raiders vs. L.A. Rams
L.A. RAMS vs. MIAMI
Dolphins lead series, 3-1
1971—Dolphins, 20-14 (LA)
1976—Rams, 31-28 (M)
1980—Dolphins, 35-14 (LA)
1983—Dolphins, 30-14 (M)
(Points—Dolphins 113, Rams 73)
L.A. RAMS vs. MINNESOTA
Vikings lead series, 15-11-2
1961—Rams, 31-17 (LA)
Vikings, 42-21 (M)
1962—Vikings, 38-14 (LA)
Tie, 24-24 (M)
1963—Rams, 27-24 (LA)
Vikings, 21-13 (M)
1964—Rams, 22-13 (LA)
Vikings, 34-13 (M)
1965—Vikings, 38-35 (LA)
Vikings, 24-13 (M)
1966—Vikings, 35-7 (M)
Rams, 21-6 (LA)
1967—Rams, 39-3 (LA)
1968—Rams, 31-3 (M)
1969—Vikings, 20-13 (LA)
*Vikings, 23-20 (M)
1970—Vikings, 13-3 (M)
1972—Vikings, 45-41 (LA)

1973—Vikings, 10-9 (M)
1974—Rams, 20-17 (LA)
**Vikings, 14-10 (M)
1976—Tie, 10-10 (M) OT
**Vikings, 24-13 (M)
1977—Rams, 35-3 (LA)
***Vikings, 14-7 (LA)
1978—Rams, 34-17 (M)
***Rams, 34-10 (LA)
1979—Rams, 27-21 (LA) OT
(Points—Rams 587, Vikings 563)
*Conference Championship
**NFC Championship
***NFC Divisional Playoff
L.A. RAMS vs. NEW ENGLAND
Patriots lead series, 2-1
1974—Patriots, 20-14 (NE)
1980—Rams, 17-14 (NE)
1983—Patriots, 21-7 (LA)
(Points—Patriots 55, Rams 38)
L.A. RAMS vs. NEW ORLEANS
Rams lead series, 22-8
1967—Rams 27-13 (NO)
1969—Rams, 36-17 (LA)
1970—Rams, 30-17 (NO)
Rams, 34-16 (LA)
1971—Saints, 24-20 (NO)
Rams, 45-28 (LA)
1972—Rams, 34-14 (LA)
Saints, 19-16 (NO)
1973—Rams, 29-7 (LA)
Rams, 24-13 (NO)
1974—Rams, 24-0 (LA)
Saints, 20-7 (NO)
1975—Rams, 38-14 (LA)
Rams, 14-7 (NO)
1976—Rams, 16-10 (NO)
Rams, 33-14 (LA)
1977—Rams, 14-7 (LA)
Saints, 27-26 (NO)
1978—Rams, 26-20 (NO)
Saints, 10-3 (LA)
1979—Rams, 35-17 (NO)
Saints, 29-14 (LA)
1980—Rams, 45-31 (LA)
Rams, 27-7 (NO)
1981—Rams, 23-17 (NO)
Saints, 21-13 (LA)
1983—Rams, 30-27 (LA)
Rams, 26-24 (NO)
1984—Rams, 28-10 (NO)
Rams, 34-21 (LA)
(Points—Rams 765, Saints 507)
L.A. RAMS vs. N.Y. GIANTS
Rams lead series, 16-7
1938—Giants, 28-0 (NY)
1940—Rams, 13-0 (NY)
1941—Giants, 49-14 (NY)
1945—Rams, 21-17 (NY)
1946—Rams, 31-21 (NY)
1947—Rams, 34-10 (LA)
1948—Rams, 52-37 (NY)
1953—Rams, 21-7 (LA)
1954—Rams, 17-16 (NY)
1959—Giants, 23-21 (LA)
1961—Giants, 24-14 (NY)
1966—Rams, 55-14 (LA)
1968—Rams, 24-21 (LA)
1970—Rams, 31-3 (NY)
1973—Rams, 40-6 (LA)
1976—Rams, 24-10 (LA)
1978—Rams, 20-17 (NY)
1979—Giants, 20-14 (LA)
1980—Rams, 28-7 (NY)
1981—Giants, 10-7 (NY)
1983—Rams, 16-6 (NY)
1984—Rams, 33-12 (LA)
**Giants, 16-13 (LA)
(Points—Rams 543, Giants 374)
*Franchise in Cleveland prior to 1946
**NFC First Round Playoff
L.A. RAMS vs. N.Y. JETS
Series tied, 2-2
1970—Jets, 31-20 (LA)
1974—Rams, 20-13 (NY)
1980—Rams, 38-13 (LA)
1983—Jets, 27-24 (NY) OT
(Points—Rams 102, Jets 84)
L.A. RAMS vs. PHILADELPHIA
Rams lead series, 14-9-1
1937—Rams, 21-3 (P)
1939—Rams, 35-13 (Colorado Springs)
1940—Rams, 21-13 (C)
1942—Rams, 24-14 (Akron)
1944—Eagles, 26-13 (P)
1945—Eagles, 28-14 (P)
1946—Eagles, 25-14 (LA)
1947—Eagles, 14-7 (P)
1948—Tie, 28-28 (LA)
1949—Eagles, 38-14 (P)
*Eagles, 14-0 (LA)
1950—Eagles, 56-20 (P)
1955—Rams, 23-21 (P)

1956—Rams, 27-7 (LA)
1957—Rams, 17-13 (LA)
1959—Eagles, 23-20 (P)
1964—Rams, 20-10 (LA)
1967—Rams, 33-17 (LA)
1969—Rams, 23-17 (P)
1972—Rams, 34-3 (P)
1975—Rams, 42-3 (P)
1977—Rams, 20-0 (LA)
1978—Rams, 16-14 (P)
1983—Eagles, 13-9 (P)
(Points—Rams 495, Eagles 413)
*Franchise in Cleveland prior to 1946
**NFL Championship
L.A. RAMS vs. **PITTSBURGH
Rams lead series, 12-4-2
1938—Rams, 28-14 (New Orleans)
1939—Tie, 14-14 (C)
1941—Rams, 17-14 (Akron)
1947—Rams, 48-7 (P)
1948—Rams, 31-14 (LA)
1949—Tie, 7-7 (LA)
1952—Rams, 28-14 (LA)
1955—Rams, 27-26 (LA)
1956—Steelers, 30-13 (P)
1961—Rams, 24-14 (LA)
1964—Rams, 26-14 (P)
1968—Rams, 45-10 (LA)
1971—Rams, 23-14 (P)
1975—Rams, 10-3 (LA)
1978—Rams, 10-7 (LA)
1979—***Steelers, 31-19 (Pasadena)
1981—Steelers, 24-0 (P)
1984—Steelers, 24-14 (P)
(Points—Rams 369, Steelers 274)
*Franchise in Cleveland prior to 1946
**Steelers known as Pirates prior to 1941
***Super Bowl XIV
L.A. RAMS vs. **ST. LOUIS
Rams lead series, 19-15-2
1937—Cardinals, 6-0 (Clev)
Cardinals, 13-7 (Chi)
1938—Cardinals, 7-6 (Clev)
Cardinals, 31-17 (Chi)
1939—Rams, 24-0 (Chi)
Rams, 14-0 (Clev)
1940—Rams, 26-14 (Clev)
Cardinals, 17-7 (Chi)
1941—Rams, 10-6 (Clev)
Cardinals, 7-0 (Chi)
1942—Cardinals, 7-0 (Chi)
Rams, 7-3 (Clev)
1945—Rams, 21-0 (Clev)
Rams, 35-21 (Chi)
1946—Cardinals, 34-10 (Chi)
Rams, 17-14 (LA)
1947—Rams, 27-7 (LA)
Cardinals, 17-10 (Chi)
1948—Cardinals, 27-22 (LA)
Cardinals, 27-24 (Chi)
1949—Tie, 28-28 (Chi)
Cardinals, 31-27 (LA)
1951—Rams, 45-21 (LA)
1953—Tie, 24-24 (Chi)
1954—Rams, 28-17 (LA)
1958—Rams, 20-14 (Chi)
1960—Cardinals, 43-21 (LA)
1965—Rams, 27-3 (StL)
1968—Rams, 24-13 (StL)
1970—Rams, 34-13 (LA)
1972—Cardinals, 24-14 (StL)
1975—***Rams, 35-23 (LA)
1976—Cardinals, 30-28 (LA)
1979—Rams, 21-0 (LA)
1980—Rams, 21-13 (StL)
1984—Rams, 16-13 (StL)
(Points—Rams 697, Cardinals 568)
*Franchise in Cleveland prior to 1946
**Franchise in Chicago prior to 1960
***NFC Divisional Playoff
L.A. RAMS vs. SAN DIEGO
Rams lead series, 2-1
1970—Rams, 37-10 (LA)
1975—Rams, 13-10 (SD) OT
1979—Chargers, 40-16 (LA)
(Points—Rams 66, Chargers 60)
L.A. RAMS vs. SAN FRANCISCO
Rams lead series, 43-25-2
1950—Rams, 35-14 (SF)
Rams, 28-21 (LA)
1951—49ers, 44-17 (SF)
Rams, 23-16 (LA)
1952—Rams, 35-9 (LA)
Rams, 34-21 (SF)
1953—49ers, 31-30 (LA)
49ers, 31-27 (LA)
1954—Tie, 24-24 (LA)
Rams, 42-34 (SF)
1955—Rams, 23-14 (SF)
Rams, 27-14 (LA)
1956—49ers, 33-30 (SF)
Rams, 30-6 (LA)
1957—49ers, 23-20 (SF)

Rams, 37-24 (LA)
1958—Rams, 33-3 (SF)
Rams, 56-7 (LA)
1959—49ers, 34-0 (SF)
49ers, 24-16 (LA)
1960—49ers, 13-9 (SF)
49ers, 23-7 (LA)
1961—49ers, 35-0 (SF)
Rams, 17-7 (LA)
1962—Rams, 28-14 (SF)
49ers, 24-17 (LA)
1963—Rams, 28-21 (LA)
Rams, 21-17 (SF)
1964—Rams, 42-14 (LA)
49ers, 28-7 (SF)
1965—49ers, 45-21 (LA)
49ers, 30-27 (SF)
1966—Rams, 34-3 (LA)
49ers, 21-13 (SF)
1967—Rams, 27-24 (LA)
Rams, 17-7 (SF)
1968—Rams, 24-10 (LA)
Tie, 20-20 (SF)
1969—Rams, 27-21 (SF)
Rams, 41-30 (LA)
1970—49ers, 20-6 (LA)
Rams, 30-13 (SF)
1971—Rams, 20-13 (SF)
Rams, 17-6 (LA)
1972—Rams, 31-7 (LA)
Rams, 26-16 (SF)
1973—Rams, 40-20 (SF)
Rams, 31-13 (LA)
1974—Rams, 37-14 (LA)
Rams, 15-13 (SF)
1975—Rams, 23-14 (SF)
49ers, 24-23 (LA)
1976—49ers, 16-0 (LA)
Rams, 23-3 (SF)
1977—Rams, 34-14 (LA)
Rams, 23-10 (SF)
1978—Rams, 27-10 (LA)
Rams, 31-28 (SF)
1979—Rams, 27-24 (LA)
Rams, 26-20 (SF)
1980—Rams, 48-26 (LA)
Rams, 31-17 (SF)
1981—49ers, 20-17 (SF)
49ers, 33-31 (LA)
1982—49ers, 30-24 (LA)
Rams, 21-20 (SF)
1983—Rams, 10-7 (SF)
49ers, 45-35 (LA)
1984—49ers, 33-0 (LA)
49ers, 19-16 (SF)
(Points—Rams 1,714, 49ers 1,385)
L.A. RAMS vs. SEATTLE
Rams lead series, 2-0
1976—Rams, 45-6 (LA)
1979—Rams, 24-0 (S)
(Points—Rams 69, Seahawks 6)
L.A. RAMS vs. TAMPA BAY
Rams lead series, 4-2
1977—Rams, 31-0 (LA)
1978—Rams, 26-23 (LA)
1979—Buccaneers, 21-6 (TB)
*Rams, 9-0 (TB)
1980—Buccaneers, 10-9 (TB)
1984—Rams, 34-33 (TB)
(Points—Rams 115, Buccaneers 87)
*NFC Championship
L.A. RAMS vs. WASHINGTON
Redskins lead series, 14-5-1
1937—Redskins, 16-7 (C)
1938—Redskins, 37-13 (W)
1941—Redskins, 17-13 (W)
1942—Redskins, 33-14 (W)
1944—Redskins, 14-10 (W)
1945—*Rams, 15-14 (C)
1948—Rams, 41-13 (W)
1949—Rams, 53-27 (LA)
1951—Redskins, 31-21 (W)
1962—Redskins, 20-14 (W)
1963—Redskins, 37-14 (LA)
1967—Tie, 28-28 (LA)
1969—Rams, 24-13 (W)
1971—Redskins, 38-24 (LA)
1974—Redskins, 23-17 (LA)
***Rams, 19-10 (LA)
1977—Redskins, 17-14 (W)
1981—Redskins, 30-7 (LA)
1983—Redskins, 42-20 (LA)
***Redskins, 51-7 (W)
(Points—Redskins 511, Rams 375)
*Franchise in Cleveland prior to 1946
**NFL Championship
***NFC Divisional Playoff

MIAMI vs. ATLANTA
Dolphins lead series, 4-0;
See Atlanta vs. Miami
MIAMI vs. BUFFALO
Dolphins lead series, 30-7-1;

See Buffalo vs. Miami
MIAMI vs. CHICAGO
Dolphins lead series, 3-0;
See Chicago vs. Miami
MIAMI vs. CINCINNATI
Dolphins lead series, 7-3;
See Cincinnati vs. Miami
MIAMI vs. CLEVELAND
Browns lead series, 3-2;
See Cleveland vs. Miami
MIAMI vs. DALLAS
Dolphins lead series, 3-2;
See Dallas vs. Miami
MIAMI vs. DENVER
Dolphins lead series, 4-2-1;
See Denver vs. Miami
MIAMI vs. DETROIT
Dolphins lead series, 2-0;
See Detroit vs. Miami
MIAMI vs. GREEN BAY
Dolphins lead series, 3-0;
See Green Bay vs. Miami
MIAMI vs. HOUSTON
Series tied, 9-9;
See Houston vs. Miami
MIAMI vs. INDIANAPOLIS
Dolphins lead series, 22-9;
See Indianapolis vs. Miami
MIAMI vs. KANSAS CITY
Chiefs lead series, 7-5;
See Kansas City vs. Miami
MIAMI vs. L.A. RAIDERS
Raiders lead series, 14-3-1;
See L.A. Raiders vs. Miami
MIAMI vs. L.A. RAMS
Dolphins lead series, 3-1;
See L.A. Rams vs. Miami
MIAMI vs. MINNESOTA
Dolphins lead series, 4-1
1972—Dolphins, 16-14 (Minn)
1973—*Dolphins, 24-7 (Houston)
1976—Vikings, 29-7 (Mia)
1979—Dolphins, 27-12 (Minn)
1982—Dolphins, 22-14 (Mia)
(Points—Dolphins 96, Vikings 76)
*Super Bowl VIII
MIAMI vs. *NEW ENGLAND
Dolphins lead series, 24-13
1966—Patriots, 20-14 (M)
1967—Patriots, 41-10 (B)
        Dolphins, 41-32 (M)
1968—Dolphins, 34-10 (B)
        Dolphins, 38-7 (M)
1969—Dolphins, 17-16 (B)
        Patriots, 38-23 (Tampa)
1970—Patriots, 27-14 (B)
        Dolphins, 37-20 (M)
1971—Dolphins, 41-3 (M)
        Patriots, 34-13 (NE)
1972—Dolphins, 52-0 (M)
        Dolphins, 37-21 (NE)
1973—Dolphins, 44-23 (M)
        Dolphins, 30-14 (NE)
1974—Patriots, 34-24 (NE)
        Dolphins, 34-27 (M)
1975—Patriots, 22-14 (NE)
        Dolphins, 20-7 (M)
1976—Patriots, 30-14 (NE)
        Dolphins, 10-3 (M)
1977—Dolphins, 17-5 (M)
        Patriots, 14-10 (NE)
1978—Patriots, 33-24 (NE)
        Dolphins, 23-3 (M)
1979—Patriots, 28-13 (NE)
        Dolphins, 39-24 (M)
1980—Patriots, 34-0 (NE)
        Dolphins, 16-13 (M) OT
1981—Dolphins, 30-27 (NE) OT
        Dolphins, 24-14 (M)
1982—Patriots, 3-0 (NE)
        **Dolphins, 28-13 (M)
1983—Dolphins, 34-24 (M)
        Patriots, 17-6 (NE)
1984—Dolphins, 28-7 (M)
        Dolphins, 44-24 (NE)
(Points—Dolphins 905, Patriots 704)
*Franchise in Boston prior to 1971
**AFC First Round Playoff
MIAMI vs. NEW ORLEANS
Dolphins lead series, 3-1
1970—Dolphins, 21-10 (M)
1974—Dolphins, 21-0 (NO)
1980—Dolphins, 21-16 (M)
1983—Saints, 17-7 (NO)
(Points—Dolphins 70, Saints 43)
MIAMI vs. N.Y. GIANTS
Dolphins lead series, 1-0
1972—Dolphins, 23-13 (NY)
MIAMI vs. N.Y. JETS
Dolphins lead series, 21-17-1
1966—Jets, 19-14 (M)
        Jets, 30-13 (NY)
1967—Jets, 29-7 (NY)

Jets, 33-14 (M)
1968—Jets, 35-17 (NY)
        Jets, 31-7 (M)
1969—Jets, 34-31 (NY)
        Jets, 27-9 (M)
1970—Dolphins, 20-6 (NY)
        Dolphins, 16-10 (M)
1971—Jets, 14-10 (M)
        Dolphins, 30-14 (NY)
1972—Dolphins, 27-17 (NY)
        Dolphins, 28-24 (M)
1973—Dolphins, 31-3 (M)
        Dolphins, 24-14 (NY)
1974—Dolphins, 21-17 (M)
        Jets, 17-14 (NY)
1975—Dolphins, 43-0 (NY)
        Dolphins, 27-7 (M)
1976—Dolphins, 16-0 (M)
        Dolphins, 27-7 (NY)
1977—Dolphins, 21-17 (M)
        Dolphins, 14-10 (NY)
1978—Jets, 33-20 (NY)
        Jets, 24-13 (M)
1979—Jets, 33-27 (NY)
        Jets, 27-24 (M)
1980—Jets, 17-14 (NY)
        Jets, 24-17 (M)
1981—Tie, 28-28 (M) OT
        Jets, 16-15 (NY)
1982—Dolphins, 45-28 (NY)
        Dolphins, 20-19 (M)
        *Dolphins, 14-0 (M)
1983—Dolphins, 32-14 (NY)
        Dolphins, 34-14 (M)
1984—Dolphins, 31-17 (NY)
        Dolphins, 28-17 (M)
(Points—Dolphins 843, Jets 726)
*AFC Championship
MIAMI vs. PHILADELPHIA
Dolphins lead series, 3-2
1970—Eagles, 24-17 (P)
1975—Dolphins, 24-16 (M)
1978—Eagles, 17-3 (P)
1981—Dolphins, 13-10 (M)
1984—Dolphins, 24-23 (M)
(Points—Eagles 90, Dolphins 81)
MIAMI vs. PITTSBURGH
Dolphins lead series, 6-3
1971—Dolphins, 24-21 (M)
1972—*Dolphins, 21-17 (P)
1973—Dolphins, 30-26 (M)
1976—Steelers, 14-3 (P)
1979—**Steelers, 34-14 (P)
1980—Steelers, 23-10 (P)
1981—Dolphins, 30-10 (M)
1984—Dolphins, 31-7 (P)
        *Dolphins, 45-28 (M)
(Points—Dolphins 208, Steelers 180)
*AFC Championship
**AFC Divisional Playoff
MIAMI vs. ST. LOUIS
Dolphins lead series, 5-0
1972—Dolphins, 31-10 (M)
1977—Dolphins, 55-14 (StL)
1978—Dolphins, 24-10 (M)
1981—Dolphins, 20-7 (StL)
1984—Dolphins, 36-28 (StL)
(Points—Dolphins 166, Cardinals 69)
MIAMI vs. SAN DIEGO
Chargers lead series, 8-5
1966—Chargers, 44-10 (SD)
1967—Chargers, 24-0 (SD)
        Dolphins, 41-24 (M)
1968—Chargers, 34-28 (SD)
1969—Chargers, 21-14 (M)
1972—Dolphins, 24-10 (M)
1974—Dolphins, 28-21 (SD)
1977—Chargers, 14-13 (M)
1978—Dolphins, 28-21 (SD)
1980—Chargers, 27-24 (M) OT
1981—*Chargers, 41-38 (M) OT
1982—**Dolphins, 34-13 (M)
1984—Chargers, 34-28 (SD) OT
(Points—Chargers 328, Dolphins 310)
*AFC Divisional Playoff
**AFC Second Round Playoff
MIAMI vs. SAN FRANCISCO
Dolphins lead series, 4-1
1973—Dolphins, 21-13 (M)
1977—Dolphins, 19-15 (SF)
1980—Dolphins, 17-13 (M)
1983—Dolphins, 20-17 (SF)
1984—*49ers, 38-16 (Stanford)
(Points—49ers 96, Dolphins 93)
*Super Bowl XIX
MIAMI vs. SEATTLE
Dolphins lead series, 3-1
1977—Dolphins, 31-13 (M)
1979—Dolphins, 19-10 (M)
1983—*Seahawks, 27-20 (M)
1984—*Dolphins, 31-10 (M)
(Points—Dolphins 101, Seahawks 60)
*AFC Divisional Playoff

MIAMI vs. TAMPA BAY
Series tied, 1-1
1976—Dolphins, 23-20 (TB)
1982—Buccaneers, 23-17 (TB)
(Points—Buccaneers 43, Dolphins 40)
MIAMI vs. WASHINGTON
Dolphins lead series, 4-2
1972—*Dolphins, 14-7 (Los Angeles)
1974—Redskins, 20-17 (W)
1978—Dolphins, 16-0 (W)
1981—Dolphins, 13-10 (M)
1982—**Redskins, 27-17 (Pasadena)
1984—Dolphins, 35-17 (W)
(Points—Dolphins 112, Redskins 81)
*Super Bowl VII
**Super Bowl XVII

MINNESOTA vs. ATLANTA
Vikings lead series, 9-5;
See Atlanta vs. Minnesota
MINNESOTA vs. BUFFALO
Vikings lead series, 3-1;
See Buffalo vs. Minnesota
MINNESOTA vs. CHICAGO
Vikings lead series, 25-20-2;
See Chicago vs. Minnesota
MINNESOTA vs. CINCINNATI
Series tied, 2-2;
See Cincinnati vs. Minnesota
MINNESOTA vs. CLEVELAND
Vikings lead series, 7-1;
See Cleveland vs. Minnesota
MINNESOTA vs. DALLAS
Cowboys lead series, 10-5;
See Dallas vs. Minnesota
MINNESOTA vs. DENVER
Series tied, 2-2;
See Denver vs. Minnesota
MINNESOTA vs. DETROIT
Vikings lead series, 29-16-2;
See Detroit vs. Minnesota
MINNESOTA vs. GREEN BAY
Vikings lead series, 24-22-1;
See Green Bay vs. Minnesota
MINNESOTA vs. HOUSTON
Vikings lead series, 2-1;
See Houston vs. Minnesota
MINNESOTA vs. INDIANAPOLIS
Colts lead series, 12-5-1;
See Indianapolis vs. Minnesota
MINNESOTA vs. KANSAS CITY
Series tied, 2-2;
See Kansas City vs. Minnesota
MINNESOTA vs. L.A. RAIDERS
Raiders lead series, 5-1;
See L.A. Raiders vs. Minnesota
MINNESOTA vs. L.A. RAMS
Vikings lead series, 15-11-2;
See L.A. Rams vs. Minnesota
MINNESOTA vs. MIAMI
Dolphins lead series, 4-1;
See Miami vs. Minnesota
MINNESOTA vs. *NEW ENGLAND
Patriots lead series, 2-1
1970—Vikings, 35-14 (B)
1974—Patriots, 17-14 (M)
1979—Patriots, 27-23 (NE)
(Points—Vikings 72, Patriots 58)
*Franchise in Boston prior to 1971
MINNESOTA vs. NEW ORLEANS
Vikings lead series, 8-3
1968—Saints, 20-17 (NO)
1970—Vikings, 26-0 (M)
1971—Vikings, 23-10 (NO)
1972—Vikings, 37-6 (M)
1974—Vikings, 29-9 (M)
1975—Vikings, 20-7 (NO)
1976—Vikings, 40-9 (NO)
1978—Saints, 31-24 (NO)
1980—Vikings, 23-20 (NO)
1981—Vikings, 20-10 (M)
1983—Saints, 17-16 (NO)
(Points—Vikings 275, Saints 139)
MINNESOTA vs. N.Y. GIANTS
Vikings lead series, 6-1
1964—Vikings, 30-21 (NY)
1965—Vikings, 40-14 (M)
1967—Vikings, 27-24 (M)
1969—Giants, 24-23 (NY)
1971—Vikings, 17-10 (NY)
1973—Vikings, 31-7 (New Haven)
1976—Vikings, 24-7 (M)
(Points—Vikings 192, Giants 107)
MINNESOTA vs. N.Y. JETS
Jets lead series, 3-1
1970—Jets, 20-10 (NY)
1975—Vikings, 29-21 (M)
1979—Jets, 14-7 (NY)
1982—Jets 42-14 (M)
(Points—Jets 97, Vikings 60)
MINNESOTA vs. PHILADELPHIA
Vikings lead series, 8-3
1962—Vikings, 31-21 (M)

1963—Vikings, 34-13 (P)
1968—Vikings, 24-17 (P)
1971—Vikings, 13-0 (P)
1973—Vikings, 28-21 (P)
1976—Vikings, 31-12 (P)
1978—Vikings, 28-27 (M)
1980—Eagles, 42-7 (M)
        *Eagles, 31-16 (P)
1981—Vikings, 35-23 (M)
1984—Eagles, 19-17 (M)
(Points—Vikings 264, Eagles 226)
*NFC Divisional Playoff
MINNESOTA vs. PITTSBURGH
Vikings lead series, 5-4
1962—Steelers, 39-31 (P)
1964—Vikings, 30-10 (M)
1967—Vikings, 41-27 (P)
1969—Vikings, 52-14 (M)
1972—Steelers, 23-10 (P)
1974—*Steelers, 16-6 (New Orleans)
1976—Vikings, 17-6 (M)
1980—Steelers, 23-17 (M)
1983—Vikings, 17-14 (P)
(Points—Vikings 221, Steelers 172)
*Super Bowl IX
MINNESOTA vs. ST. LOUIS
Cardinals lead series, 7-3
1963—Cardinals, 56-14 (M)
1967—Cardinals, 34-24 (M)
1969—Vikings, 27-10 (StL)
1972—Cardinals, 19-17 (M)
1974—Vikings, 28-24 (StL)
        *Vikings, 30-14 (M)
1977—Cardinals, 27-7 (M)
1979—Cardinals, 37-7 (StL)
1981—Cardinals, 30-17 (StL)
1983—Cardinals, 41-31 (StL)
(Points—Cardinals 292, Vikings 202)
*NFC Divisional Playoff
MINNESOTA vs. SAN DIEGO
Chargers lead series, 3-2
1971—Chargers, 30-14 (SD)
1975—Vikings, 28-13 (M)
1978—Chargers, 13-7 (M)
1981—Vikings, 33-31 (SD)
1984—Chargers, 42-13 (M)
(Points—Chargers 129, Vikings 95)
MINNESOTA vs. SAN FRANCISCO
Series tied, 12-12-1
1961—49ers, 38-24 (M)
        49ers, 38-28 (SF)
1962—49ers, 21-7 (SF)
        49ers, 35-12 (M)
1963—Vikings, 24-20 (SF)
        Vikings, 45-14 (M)
1964—Vikings, 27-22 (SF)
        Vikings, 24-7 (M)
1965—Vikings, 42-41 (SF)
        49ers, 45-24 (M)
1966—Tie, 20-20 (SF)
        Vikings, 28-3 (SF)
1967—49ers, 27-21 (M)
1968—Vikings, 30-20 (SF)
1969—Vikings, 10-7 (M)
1970—*49ers, 17-14 (M)
1971—49ers, 13-9 (M)
1972—49ers, 20-17 (SF)
1973—Vikings, 17-13 (SF)
1975—Vikings, 27-17 (M)
1976—49ers, 20-16 (SF)
1977—Vikings, 28-27 (M)
1979—Vikings, 28-22 (M)
1983—49ers, 48-17 (M)
1984—49ers, 51-7 (SF)
(Points—49ers 606, Vikings 546)
*NFC Divisional Playoff
MINNESOTA vs. SEATTLE
Seahawks lead series, 2-1
1976—Vikings, 27-21 (M)
1978—Seahawks, 29-28 (S)
1984—Seahawks, 20-12 (M)
(Points—Seahawks 70, Vikings 67)
MINNESOTA vs. TAMPA BAY
Vikings lead series, 9-5
1977—Vikings, 9-3 (TB)
1978—Buccaneers, 16-10 (M)
        Vikings, 24-7 (TB)
1979—Buccaneers, 12-10 (M)
        Vikings, 23-22 (TB)
1980—Vikings, 38-30 (M)
        Vikings, 21-10 (TB)
1981—Buccaneers, 21-13 (TB)
        Vikings, 25-10 (M)
1982—Vikings, 17-10 (M)
1983—Vikings, 19-16 (TB) OT
        Buccaneers, 17-12 (M)
1984—Buccaneers, 35-31 (TB)
        Vikings, 27-24 (M)
(Points—Vikings 279, Buccaneers 233)
MINNESOTA vs. WASHINGTON
Vikings lead series, 5-4
1968—Vikings, 27-14 (M)
1970—Vikings, 19-10 (W)
1972—Redskins, 24-21 (M)

1973—*Vikings, 27-20 (M)
1975—Redskins, 31-30 (W)
1976—*Vikings 35-20 (M)
1980—Vikings, 39-14 (W)
1982—**Redskins, 21-7 (W)
1984—Redskins, 31-17 (M)
(Points—Vikings 222, Redskins 185)
*NFC Divisional Playoff
**NFC Second Round Playoff

NEW ENGLAND vs. ATLANTA
Series tied, 2-2;
See Atlanta vs. New England
NEW ENGLAND vs. BUFFALO
Patriots lead series, 26-23-1;
See Buffalo vs. New England
NEW ENGLAND vs. CHICAGO
Patriots lead series, 2-1;
See Chicago vs. New England
NEW ENGLAND vs. CINCINNATI
Patriots lead series, 5-3;
See Cincinnati vs. New England
NEW ENGLAND vs. CLEVELAND
Browns lead series, 5-2;
See Cleveland vs. New England
NEW ENGLAND vs. DALLAS
Cowboys lead series, 5-0;
See Dallas vs. New England
NEW ENGLAND vs. DENVER
Patriots lead series, 12-11;
See Denver vs. New England
NEW ENGLAND vs. DETROIT
Lions lead series, 2-1;
See Detroit vs. New England
NEW ENGLAND vs. GREEN BAY
Series tied, 1-1;
See Green Bay vs. New England
NEW ENGLAND vs. HOUSTON
Patriots lead series, 14-13-1;
See Houston vs. New England
NEW ENGLAND vs. INDIANAPOLIS
Colts lead series, 15-14;
See Indianapolis vs. New England
NEW ENGLAND vs. KANSAS CITY
Chiefs lead series, 11-7-3;
See Kansas City vs. New England
NEW ENGLAND vs. L.A. RAIDERS
Series tied, 11-11-1;
See L.A. Raiders vs. New England
NEW ENGLAND vs. L.A. RAMS
Patriots lead series, 2-1;
See L.A. Rams vs. New England
NEW ENGLAND vs. MIAMI
Dolphins lead series, 24-13;
See Miami vs. New England
NEW ENGLAND vs. MINNESOTA
Patriots lead series, 2-1;
See Minnesota vs. New England
NEW ENGLAND vs. NEW ORLEANS
Patriots lead series, 4-0
1972—Patriots, 17-10 (NO)
1976—Patriots, 27-6 (NE)
1980—Patriots, 38-27 (NO)
1983—Patriots, 7-0 (NE)
(Points—Patriots 89, Saints 43)
*NEW ENGLAND vs. N.Y. GIANTS
Series tied, 1-1
1970—Giants, 16-0 (B)
1974—Patriots, 28-20 (New Haven)
(Points—Giants 36, Patriots 28)
*Franchise in Boston prior to 1971
*NEW ENGLAND vs. **N.Y. JETS
Jets lead series, 28-20-1
1960—Patriots, 28-24 (NY)
Patriots, 38-21 (B)
1961—Titans, 21-20 (B)
Titans, 37-30 (NY)
1962—Patriots, 43-14 (NY)
Patriots, 24-17 (B)
1963—Patriots, 38-14 (B)
Jets, 31-24 (NY)
1964—Patriots, 26-10 (B)
Jets, 35-14 (NY)
1965—Jets, 30-20 (B)
Patriots, 27-23 (NY)
1966—Tie, 24-24 (B)
Jets, 38-28 (NY)
1967—Jets, 30-23 (NY)
Jets, 29-24 (B)
1968—Jets, 47-31 (Birmingham)
Jets, 48-14 (NY)
1969—Jets, 23-14 (B)
Jets, 23-17 (NY)
1970—Jets, 31-21 (B)
Jets, 17-3 (NY)
1971—Patriots, 20-0 (NE)
Jets, 13-6 (NY)
1972—Jets, 41-13 (NE)
Jets, 34-10 (NY)
1973—Jets, 9-7 (NE)
Jets, 33-13 (NY)
1974—Patriots, 24-0 (NY)
Jets, 21-16 (NE)

1975—Jets, 36-7 (NY)
Jets, 30-28 (NE)
1976—Patriots, 41-7 (NE)
Patriots, 38-24 (NY)
1977—Jets, 30-27 (NY)
Patriots, 24-13 (NE)
1978—Patriots, 55-21 (NE)
Patriots, 19-17 (NY)
1979—Patriots, 56-3 (NE)
Jets, 27-26 (NY)
1980—Patriots, 21-11 (NY)
Patriots, 34-21 (NE)
1981—Jets, 28-24 (NY)
Jets, 17-6 (NE)
1982—Jets, 31-7 (NE)
1983—Patriots, 23-13 (NE)
Jets, 26-3 (NY)
1984—Patriots, 28-21 (NY)
Patriots, 30-20 (NE)
Points—Patriots 1,137, Jets 1,134)
*Franchise in Boston prior to 1971
**Jets known as Titans prior to 1963
NEW ENGLAND vs. PHILADELPHIA
Eagles lead series, 3-2
1973—Eagles, 24-23 (P)
1977—Patriots, 14-6 (NE)
1978—Patriots, 24-14 (NE)
1981—Eagles, 13-3 (P)
1984—Eagles, 27-17 (P)
(Points—Eagles 84, Patriots 81)
NEW ENGLAND vs. PITTSBURGH
Steelers lead series, 5-2
1972—Steelers, 33-3 (P)
1974—Steelers, 21-17 (NE)
1976—Patriots, 30-27 (P)
1979—Steelers, 16-13 (NE) OT
1981—Steelers, 27-21 (P) OT
1982—Steelers, 37-14 (P)
1983—Patriots, 28-23 (P)
(Points—Steelers 184, Patriots 126)
*NEW ENGLAND vs. ST. LOUIS
Cardinals lead series, 4-1
1970—Cardinals, 31-0 (StL)
1975—Cardinals, 24-17 (StL)
1978—Patriots, 16-6 (StL)
1981—Cardinals, 27-20 (NE)
1984—Cardinals, 33-10 (NE)
(Points—Cardinals 121, Patriots 63)
*Franchise in Boston prior to 1971
*NEW ENGLAND vs. **SAN DIEGO
Patriots lead series, 13-12-2
1960—Patriots, 35-0 (LA)
Chargers, 45-16 (B)
1961—Chargers, 38-27 (B)
Patriots, 41-0 (SD)
1962—Patriots, 24-20 (B)
Patriots, 20-14 (SD)
1963—Chargers, 17-13 (SD)
Chargers, 7-6 (B)
***Chargers, 51-10 (SD)
1964—Chargers, 33-28 (SD)
Chargers, 26-17 (B)
1965—Tie, 10-10 (B)
Patriots, 22-6 (SD)
1966—Chargers, 24-0 (SD)
Patriots, 35-17 (B)
1967—Chargers, 28-14 (SD)
Tie, 31-31 (SD)
1968—Chargers, 27-17 (B)
1969—Chargers, 13-10 (B)
Chargers, 28-18 (SD)
1970—Chargers, 16-14 (B)
1973—Patriots, 30-14 (NE)
1975—Patriots, 33-19 (SD)
1977—Patriots, 24-20 (SD)
1978—Patriots, 28-23 (NE)
1979—Patriots, 27-21 (NE)
1983—Patriots, 37-21 (NE)
(Points—Patriots 592, Chargers 564)
*Franchise in Boston prior to 1971
**Franchise in Los Angeles prior to 1961
***AFL Championship
NEW ENGLAND vs. SAN FRANCISCO
49ers lead series, 3-1
1971—49ers, 27-10 (SF)
1975—Patriots, 24-16 (NE)
1980—49ers, 21-17 (NE)
1983—49ers, 33-13 (NE)
(Points—49ers 97, Patriots 64)
NEW ENGLAND vs. SEATTLE
Patriots lead series, 4-1
1977—Patriots, 31-0 (NE)
1980—Patriots, 37-31 (S)
1982—Patriots, 16-0 (S)
1983—Seahawks, 24-6 (NE)
1984—Patriots, 38-23 (NE)
(Points—Patriots 128, Seahawks 78)
NEW ENGLAND vs. TAMPA BAY
Patriots lead series, 1-0
1976—Patriots, 31-14 (TB)
NEW ENGLAND vs. WASHINGTON
Redskins lead series, 3-1
1972—Patriots, 24-23 (NE)

1978—Redskins, 16-14 (NE)
1981—Redskins, 24-22 (W)
1984—Redskins, 26-10 (NE)
(Points—Redskins 89, Patriots 70)

NEW ORLEANS vs. ATLANTA
Falcons lead series, 21-11;
See Atlanta vs. New Orleans
NEW ORLEANS vs. BUFFALO
Bills lead series, 2-1;
See Buffalo vs. New Orleans
NEW ORLEANS vs. CHICAGO
Bears lead series, 7-4;
See Chicago vs. New Orleans
NEW ORLEANS vs. CINCINNATI
Bengals lead series, 3-2;
See Cincinnati vs. New Orleans
NEW ORLEANS vs. CLEVELAND
Browns lead series, 8-1;
See Cleveland vs. New Orleans
NEW ORLEANS vs. DALLAS
Cowboys lead series, 11-1;
See Dallas vs. New Orleans
NEW ORLEANS vs. DENVER
Broncos lead series, 3-0;
See Denver vs. New Orleans
NEW ORLEANS vs. DETROIT
Series tied, 4-4-1;
See Detroit vs. New Orleans
NEW ORLEANS vs. GREEN BAY
Packers lead series, 9-2;
See Green Bay vs. New Orleans
NEW ORLEANS vs. HOUSTON
Series tied, 2-2-1;
See Houston vs. New Orleans
NEW ORLEANS vs. INDIANAPOLIS
Colts lead series, 3-0;
See Indianapolis vs. New Orleans
NEW ORLEANS vs. KANSAS CITY
Saints lead series, 2-1;
See Kansas City vs. New Orleans
NEW ORLEANS vs. L.A. RAIDERS
Raiders lead series, 2-0-1;
See L.A. Raiders vs. New Orleans
NEW ORLEANS vs. L.A. RAMS
Rams lead series, 22-8;
See L.A. Rams vs. New Orleans
NEW ORLEANS vs. MIAMI
Dolphins lead series, 3-1;
See Miami vs. New Orleans
NEW ORLEANS vs. MINNESOTA
Vikings lead series, 8-3;
See Minnesota vs. New Orleans
NEW ORLEANS vs. NEW ENGLAND
Patriots lead series, 4-0;
See New England vs. New Orleans
NEW ORLEANS vs. N.Y. GIANTS
Series tied, 5-5
1967—Giants, 27-21 (NY)
1968—Giants, 38-21 (NY)
1969—Saints, 25-24 (NY)
1970—Saints, 14-10 (NO)
1972—Giants, 45-21 (NY)
1975—Saints, 28-14 (NY)
1978—Saints, 28-17 (NO)
1979—Saints, 24-14 (NO)
1981—Giants, 20-7 (NY)
1984—Saints, 10-3 (NY)
(Points—Giants 226, Saints 185)
NEW ORLEANS vs. N.Y. JETS
Jets lead series, 3-1
1972—Jets, 18-17 (NY)
1977—Jets, 16-13 (NO)
1980—Saints, 21-20 (NY)
1983—Jets, 31-28 (NO)
(Points—Jets 85, Saints 79)
NEW ORLEANS vs. PHILADELPHIA
Eagles lead series, 8-5
1967—Saints, 31-24 (NO)
Eagles, 48-21 (P)
1968—Eagles, 29-17 (P)
1969—Eagles, 13-10 (P)
Saints, 26-17 (NO)
1972—Saints, 21-3 (NO)
1974—Saints, 14-10 (NO)
1977—Eagles, 28-7 (P)
1978—Eagles, 24-17 (NO)
1979—Eagles, 26-14 (NO)
1980—Eagles, 34-21 (NO)
1981—Eagles, 21-3 (NO)
1983—Saints, 20-17 (P) OT
(Points—Eagles 304, Saints 233)
NEW ORLEANS vs. PITTSBURGH
Series tied 4-4
1967—Steelers, 14-10 (NO)
1968—Saints, 16-12 (P)
Saints, 24-14 (NO)
1969—Saints, 27-24 (NO)
1974—Steelers, 28-7 (NO)
1978—Steelers, 20-14 (P)
1981—Steelers, 20-6 (NO)
1984—Saints, 27-24 (NO)
(Points—Steelers 156, Saints 131)

NEW ORLEANS vs. ST. LOUIS
Cardinals lead series, 8-4
1967—Cardinals, 31-20 (StL)
1968—Cardinals, 21-20 (NO)
Cardinals, 31-17 (StL)
1969—Saints, 51-42 (StL)
1970—Cardinals, 24-17 (StL)
1974—Saints, 14-0 (NO)
1977—Cardinals, 49-31 (StL)
1980—Cardinals, 40-7 (NO)
1981—Cardinals, 30-3 (StL)
1982—Cardinals, 21-7 (NO)
1983—Saints, 28-17 (NO)
1984—Saints, 34-24 (NO)
(Points—Cardinals 330, Saints 249)
NEW ORLEANS vs. SAN DIEGO
Chargers lead series, 3-0
1973—Chargers, 17-14 (SD)
1977—Chargers, 14-0 (NO)
1979—Chargers, 35-0 (NO)
(Points—Chargers 66, Saints 14)
NEW ORLEANS vs. SAN FRANCISCO
49ers lead series, 21-8-2
1967—49ers, 27-13 (SF)
1969—Saints, 43-38 (NO)
1970—Tie, 20-20 (SF)
49ers, 38-27 (NO)
1971—49ers, 38-20 (NO)
Saints, 26-20 (SF)
1972—49ers, 37-2 (NO)
Tie, 20-20 (SF)
1973—49ers, 40-0 (SF)
Saints, 16-10 (NO)
1974—49ers, 17-13 (NO)
49ers, 35-21 (SF)
1975—49ers, 35-21 (SF)
49ers, 16-6 (NO)
1976—49ers, 33-3 (NO)
49ers, 27-7 (NO)
1977—49ers, 10-7 (NO) OT
49ers, 20-17 (SF)
1978—Saints, 14-7 (SF)
Saints, 24-13 (NO)
1979—Saints, 30-21 (SF)
Saints, 31-20 (NO)
1980—49ers, 26-23 (NO)
49ers, 38-35 (SF) OT
1981—49ers, 21-14 (SF)
49ers, 21-17 (NO)
1982—Saints, 23-20 (SF)
1983—49ers, 32-13 (NO)
49ers, 27-0 (SF)
1984—49ers, 30-20 (SF)
49ers, 35-3 (NO)
(Points—49ers 792, Saints 529)
NEW ORLEANS vs. SEATTLE
Series tied, 1-1
1976—Saints, 51-27 (S)
1979—Seahawks, 38-24 (S)
(Points—Saints 75, Seahawks 65)
NEW ORLEANS vs. TAMPA BAY
Saints lead series, 4-3
1977—Buccaneers, 33-14 (NO)
1978—Saints, 17-10 (TB)
1979—Saints, 42-14 (TB)
1981—Buccaneers, 31-14 (NO)
1982—Buccaneers, 13-10 (NO)
1983—Saints, 24-21 (TB)
1984—Saints, 17-13 (NO)
(Points—Saints 138, Buccaneers 135)
NEW ORLEANS vs. WASHINGTON
Redskins lead series, 7-4
1967—Redskins, 30-10 (NO)
Saints, 30-14 (W)
1968—Redskins, 37-17 (NO)
1969—Redskins, 26-20 (NO)
Redskins, 17-14 (W)
1971—Redskins, 24-14 (W)
1973—Saints, 19-3 (NO)
1975—Redskins, 41-3 (W)
1979—Redskins, 14-10 (W)
1980—Redskins, 22-14 (W)
1982—Redskins, 27-10 (NO)
(Points—Redskins 231, Saints 185)

N.Y. GIANTS vs. ATLANTA
Falcons lead series, 6-5;
See Atlanta vs. N.Y. Giants
N.Y. GIANTS vs. BUFFALO
Giants lead series, 2-1;
See Buffalo vs. N.Y. Giants
N.Y. GIANTS vs. CHICAGO
Bears lead series, 26-16-2;
See Chicago vs. N.Y. Giants
N.Y. GIANTS vs. CINCINNATI
Bengals lead series, 2-0;
See Cincinnati vs. N.Y. Giants
N.Y. GIANTS vs. CLEVELAND
Browns lead series, 25-16-2;
See Cleveland vs. N.Y. Giants
N.Y. GIANTS vs. DALLAS
Cowboys lead series, 30-13-2;
See Dallas vs. N.Y. Giants

N.Y. GIANTS vs. DENVER
Broncos lead series, 2-1;
See Denver vs. N.Y. Giants
N.Y. GIANTS vs. DETROIT
Lions lead series, 18-11-1;
See Detroit vs. N.Y. Giants
N.Y. GIANTS vs. GREEN BAY
Packers lead series, 24-18-2;
See Green Bay vs. N.Y. Giants
N.Y. GIANTS vs. HOUSTON
Giants lead series, 2-0;
See Houston vs. N.Y. Giants
N.Y. GIANTS vs. INDIANAPOLIS
Colts lead series, 7-3;
See Indianapolis vs. N.Y. Giants
N.Y. GIANTS vs. KANSAS CITY
Giants lead series, 4-1;
See Kansas City vs. N.Y. Giants
N.Y. GIANTS vs. L.A. RAIDERS
Raiders lead series, 3-0;
See L.A. Raiders vs. N.Y. Giants
N.Y. GIANTS vs. L.A. RAMS
Rams lead series, 16-7;
See L.A. Rams vs. N.Y. Giants
N.Y. GIANTS vs. MIAMI
Dolphins lead series, 1-0;
See Miami vs. N.Y. Giants
N.Y. GIANTS vs. MINNESOTA
Vikings lead series, 6-1;
See Minnesota vs. N.Y. Giants
N.Y. GIANTS vs. NEW ENGLAND
Series tied, 1-1;
See New England vs. N.Y. Giants
N.Y. GIANTS vs. NEW ORLEANS
Series tied, 5-5;
See New Orleans vs. N.Y. Giants
N.Y. GIANTS vs. N.Y. JETS
Series tied, 2-2
1970—Giants, 22-10 (NYJ)
1974—Jets, 26-20 (New Haven) OT
1981—Jets, 26-7 (NYG)
1984—Giants, 20-10 (NYJ)
(Points—Jets 72, Giants 69)
N.Y. GIANTS vs. PHILADELPHIA
Giants lead series, 54-45-2
1933—Giants, 56-0 (NY)
    Giants, 20-14 (NY)
1934—Giants, 17-0 (NY)
    Eagles, 6-0 (P)
1935—Giants, 10-0 (NY)
    Giants, 21-14 (P)
1936—Eagles, 10-7 (P)
    Giants, 21-17 (NY)
1937—Giants, 16-7 (P)
    Giants, 21-0 (NY)
1938—Eagles, 14-10 (P)
    Giants, 17-7 (NY)
1939—Giants, 13-3 (P)
    Giants, 27-10 (NY)
1940—Giants, 20-14 (P)
    Giants, 17-7 (NY)
1941—Giants, 24-0 (P)
    Giants, 16-0 (NY)
1942—Giants, 35-17 (NY)
    Giants, 14-0 (NY)
1944—Eagles, 24-17 (NY)
    Tie, 21-21 (P)
1945—Eagles, 38-17 (P)
    Giants, 28-21 (NY)
1946—Eagles, 24-14 (P)
    Giants, 45-17 (NY)
1947—Eagles, 23-0 (P)
    Eagles, 41-24 (NY)
1948—Eagles, 45-0 (P)
    Eagles, 35-14 (NY)
1949—Eagles, 24-3 (NY)
    Eagles, 17-3 (P)
1950—Giants, 7-3 (NY)
    Giants, 9-7 (P)
1951—Giants, 26-24 (NY)
    Giants, 23-7 (P)
1952—Giants, 31-7 (P)
    Eagles, 14-10 (NY)
1953—Eagles, 30-7 (P)
    Giants, 37-28 (NY)
1954—Giants, 27-14 (NY)
    Eagles, 29-14 (P)
1955—Eagles, 27-17 (NY)
    Giants, 31-7 (NY)
1956—Giants, 20-3 (NY)
    Giants, 21-7 (P)
1957—Giants, 24-20 (P)
    Giants, 13-0 (NY)
1958—Eagles, 27-24 (P)
    Giants, 24-10 (NY)
1959—Eagles, 49-21 (P)
    Giants, 24-7 (NY)
1960—Eagles, 17-10 (NY)
    Eagles, 31-23 (P)
1961—Giants, 38-21 (NY)
    Giants, 28-24 (P)
1962—Giants, 29-13 (P)
    Giants, 19-14 (NY)
1963—Giants, 37-14 (P)
    Giants, 42-14 (NY)
1964—Eagles, 38-7 (P)
    Eagles, 23-17 (NY)
1965—Giants, 16-14 (P)
    Eagles, 35-27 (NY)
1966—Eagles, 35-17 (P)
    Eagles, 31-3 (NY)
1967—Giants, 44-7 (NY)
1968—Eagles, 34-25 (P)
    Giants, 7-6 (NY)
1969—Eagles, 23-20 (NY)
1970—Eagles, 30-23 (NY)
    Eagles, 23-20 (P)
1971—Eagles, 23-7 (P)
    Eagles, 41-28 (NY)
1972—Giants, 27-12 (NY)
    Giants, 62-10 (NY)
1973—Tie, 23-23 (NY)
1974—Eagles, 35-7 (P)
    Eagles, 20-7 (New Haven)
1975—Giants, 23-14 (P)
    Eagles, 13-10 (NY)
1976—Eagles, 20-7 (P)
    Eagles, 10-0 (NY)
1977—Eagles, 28-10 (NY)
    Eagles, 17-14 (P)
1978—Eagles, 19-17 (NY)
    Eagles, 20-3 (P)
1979—Eagles, 23-17 (P)
    Eagles, 17-13 (NY)
1980—Eagles, 35-3 (P)
    Eagles, 31-16 (NY)
1981—Eagles, 24-10 (NY)
    Giants, 20-10 (P)
    *Giants, 27-21 (P)
1982—Giants, 23-7 (NY)
    Giants, 26-24 (P)
1983—Eagles, 17-13 (NY)
    Giants, 23-0 (P)
1984—Giants, 28-27 (NY)
    Eagles, 24-10 (P)
(Points—Giants 1,944, Eagles 1,798)
*NFC First Round Playoff
N.Y. GIANTS vs. *PITTSBURGH
Giants lead series, 40-26-3
1933—Giants, 23-2 (P)
    Giants, 27-3 (NY)
1934—Giants, 14-12 (P)
    Giants, 17-7 (NY)
1935—Giants, 42-7 (P)
    Giants, 13-0 (NY)
1936—Pirates, 10-7 (P)
1937—Giants, 10-7 (P)
    Giants, 17-0 (NY)
1938—Giants, 27-14 (P)
    Pirates, 13-10 (NY)
1939—Giants, 14-7 (P)
    Giants, 23-7 (NY)
1940—Tie, 10-10 (P)
    Giants, 12-0 (NY)
1941—Giants, 37-10 (P)
    Giants, 28-7 (NY)
1942—Steelers, 13-10 (P)
    Steelers, 17-9 (NY)
1945—Giants, 34-6 (P)
    Steelers, 21-7 (NY)
1946—Giants, 17-14 (P)
    Giants, 7-0 (NY)
1947—Steelers, 38-21 (NY)
    Steelers, 24-7 (P)
1948—Giants, 34-27 (NY)
    Steelers, 38-28 (P)
1949—Steelers, 28-7 (P)
    Steelers, 21-17 (NY)
1950—Giants, 18-7 (P)
    Steelers, 17-6 (NY)
1951—Tie, 13-13 (P)
    Giants, 14-0 (NY)
1952—Steelers, 63-7 (P)
1953—Steelers, 24-14 (P)
    Steelers, 14-10 (NY)
1954—Giants, 30-6 (P)
    Giants, 24-3 (NY)
1955—Steelers, 30-23 (P)
    Steelers, 19-17 (NY)
1956—Giants, 38-10 (NY)
    Giants, 17-14 (P)
1957—Giants, 35-0 (NY)
    Steelers, 21-10 (P)
1958—Giants, 17-6 (NY)
    Steelers, 31-10 (P)
1959—Giants, 21-16 (P)
    Steelers, 14-9 (NY)
1960—Steelers, 19-17 (P)
    Giants, 27-24 (NY)
1961—Giants, 17-14 (P)
    Giants, 42-21 (NY)
1962—Giants, 31-27 (P)
    Steelers, 20-17 (NY)
1963—Steelers, 31-0 (P)
    Giants, 33-17 (NY)
1964—Steelers, 27-24 (NY)
    Steelers, 44-17 (NY)
1965—Giants, 23-13 (P)
    Steelers, 35-10 (NY)
1966—Tie, 34-34 (P)
    Steelers, 47-28 (NY)
1967—Giants, 27-24 (P)
    Giants, 28-20 (NY)
1968—Giants, 34-20 (P)
1969—Giants, 10-7 (NY)
    Giants, 21-17 (P)
1971—Steelers, 17-13 (P)
1976—Steelers, 27-0 (NY)
(Points—Giants 1,342, Steelers 1,149)
*Steelers known as Pirates prior to 1941
N.Y. GIANTS vs. *ST. LOUIS
Giants lead series, 51-31-2
1926—Giants, 20-0 (NY)
1927—Giants, 28-7 (NY)
1929—Giants, 24-21 (NY)
1930—Giants, 25-12 (NY)
    Giants, 13-7 (C)
1935—Cardinals, 14-13 (NY)
1936—Giants, 14-6 (NY)
1938—Giants, 6-0 (NY)
1939—Giants, 17-7 (NY)
1941—Cardinals, 10-7 (NY)
1942—Giants, 21-7 (NY)
1943—Giants, 24-13 (NY)
1946—Giants, 28-24 (NY)
1947—Giants, 35-31 (NY)
1948—Cardinals, 63-35 (NY)
1949—Giants, 41-38 (C)
1950—Cardinals, 17-3 (C)
    Giants, 51-21 (NY)
1951—Giants, 28-17 (NY)
    Giants, 10-0 (C)
1952—Cardinals, 24-23 (NY)
    Giants, 28-6 (C)
1953—Giants, 21-7 (NY)
    Giants, 23-20 (C)
1954—Giants, 41-10 (C)
    Giants, 31-17 (NY)
1955—Cardinals, 28-17 (C)
    Giants, 10-0 (NY)
1956—Cardinals, 35-27 (C)
    Giants, 23-10 (NY)
1957—Giants, 27-14 (NY)
    Giants, 28-21 (C)
1958—Giants, 37-7 (Buffalo)
    Cardinals, 23-6 (NY)
1959—Giants, 9-3 (NY)
    Giants, 30-20 (Minn)
1960—Giants, 35-14 (StL)
    Cardinals, 20-13 (NY)
1961—Cardinals, 21-10 (NY)
    Giants, 24-9 (StL)
1962—Giants, 31-14 (StL)
    Giants, 31-28 (NY)
1963—Giants, 38-21 (NY)
    Cardinals, 24-17 (NY)
1964—Giants, 34-17 (NY)
    Tie, 10-10 (StL)
1965—Giants, 14-10 (NY)
    Giants, 28-15 (StL)
1966—Cardinals, 24-19 (StL)
    Cardinals, 20-17 (NY)
1967—Giants, 37-20 (StL)
    Giants, 37-14 (NY)
1968—Cardinals, 28-21 (NY)
1969—Cardinals, 42-17 (StL)
    Giants, 49-6 (NY)
1970—Giants, 35-17 (NY)
    Giants, 34-17 (StL)
1971—Giants, 21-20 (StL)
    Cardinals, 24-7 (NY)
1972—Giants, 27-21 (NY)
    Giants, 13-7 (StL)
1973—Cardinals, 35-27 (StL)
    Giants, 24-13 (New Haven)
1974—Cardinals, 23-21 (New Haven)
    Cardinals, 26-14 (StL)
1975—Cardinals, 26-14 (StL)
    Cardinals, 20-13 (NY)
1976—Cardinals, 27-21 (StL)
    Cardinals, 17-14 (NY)
1977—Cardinals, 28-0 (StL)
    Giants, 27-7 (NY)
1978—Cardinals, 20-10 (StL)
    Giants, 17-0 (NY)
1979—Cardinals, 27-14 (StL)
    Cardinals, 29-20 (StL)
1980—Giants, 41-35 (NY)
    Cardinals, 23-7 (StL)
1981—Giants, 34-14 (NY)
    Giants, 20-10 (StL)
1982—Cardinals, 24-21 (StL)
1983—Tie, 20-20 (StL) OT
    Cardinals, 10-6 (NY)
1984—Giants, 16-10 (NY)
    Cardinals, 31-21 (StL)
(Points—Giants 1,865, Cardinals 1,498)
*Franchise in Chicago prior to 1960
N.Y. GIANTS vs. SAN DIEGO
Series tied, 2-2
1971—Giants, 35-17 (NY)
1975—Giants, 35-24 (NY)
1980—Chargers, 44-7 (SD)
1983—Chargers, 41-34 (NY)
(Points—Chargers 126, Giants 111)
N.Y. GIANTS vs. SAN FRANCISCO
Giants lead series, 9-7
1952—Giants, 23-14 (NY)
1956—Giants, 38-21 (SF)
1957—49ers, 27-17 (NY)
1960—Giants, 21-19 (SF)
1963—Giants, 48-14 (NY)
1968—49ers, 26-10 (NY)
1972—Giants, 23-17 (SF)
1975—Giants, 26-23 (SF)
1977—Giants, 20-17 (NY)
1978—Giants, 27-10 (NY)
1979—Giants, 32-16 (NY)
1980—49ers, 12-0 (SF)
1981—49ers, 17-10 (SF)
    *49ers, 38-24 (SF)
1984—49ers, 31-10 (NY)
    *49ers, 21-10 (SF)
(Points—Giants 339, 49ers 323)
*NFC Divisional Playoff
N.Y. GIANTS vs. SEATTLE
Giants lead series, 3-1
1976—Giants, 28-16 (NY)
1980—Giants, 27-21 (S)
1981—Giants, 32-0 (S)
1983—Seahawks, 17-12 (NY)
(Points—Giants 99, Seahawks 54)
N.Y. GIANTS vs. TAMPA BAY
Giants lead series, 5-3
1977—Giants, 10-0 (TB)
1978—Giants, 19-13 (TB)
    Giants, 17-14 (NY)
1979—Giants, 17-14 (NY)
    Buccaneers, 31-3 (TB)
1980—Buccaneers, 30-13 (TB)
1984—Giants, 17-14 (NY)
    Buccaneers, 20-17 (TB)
(Points—Buccaneers 136, Giants 113)
N.Y. GIANTS vs. *WASHINGTON
Giants lead series, 57-45-3
1932—Braves, 14-6 (B)
    Tie, 0-0 (NY)
1933—Redskins, 21-20 (B)
    Giants, 7-0 (NY)
1934—Giants, 16-13 (B)
    Giants, 3-0 (NY)
1935—Giants, 20-12 (B)
    Giants, 17-6 (NY)
1936—Giants, 7-0 (B)
    Redskins, 14-0 (NY)
1937—Redskins, 13-3 (W)
    Redskins, 49-14 (NY)
1938—Giants, 10-7 (W)
    Giants, 36-0 (NY)
1939—Tie, 0-0 (W)
    Giants, 9-7 (NY)
1940—Redskins, 21-7 (W)
    Giants, 21-7 (NY)
1941—Giants, 17-10 (W)
    Giants, 20-13 (NY)
1942—Giants, 14-7 (W)
    Redskins, 14-7 (NY)
1943—Redskins, 14-10 (NY)
    Giants, 31-7 (W)
    **Redskins, 28-0 (NY)
1944—Giants, 16-13 (NY)
    Giants, 31-0 (W)
1945—Redskins, 24-14 (NY)
    Redskins, 17-0 (W)
1946—Redskins, 24-14 (W)
    Giants, 31-0 (NY)
1947—Redskins, 28-20 (W)
    Giants, 35-10 (NY)
1948—Redskins, 41-10 (NY)
    Redskins, 28-21 (NY)
1949—Giants, 45-35 (W)
    Giants, 23-7 (NY)
1950—Giants, 21-17 (W)
    Giants, 24-21 (NY)
1951—Giants, 35-14 (W)
    Giants, 28-14 (NY)
1952—Giants, 14-10 (W)
    Redskins, 27-17 (NY)
1953—Redskins, 13-9 (W)
    Redskins, 24-21 (NY)
1954—Giants, 51-21 (W)
    Giants, 24-7 (NY)
1955—Giants, 35-7 (NY)
    Giants, 27-20 (W)
1956—Redskins, 33-7 (W)
    Giants, 28-14 (NY)
1957—Giants, 24-20 (W)
    Redskins, 31-14 (NY)
1958—Giants, 21-14 (W)
    Giants, 30-0 (NY)
1959—Giants, 45-14 (W)
    Giants, 24-10 (NY)
1960—Tie, 24-24 (NY)
    Giants, 17-3 (W)

1961—Giants, 24-21 (W)
    Giants, 53-0 (NY)
1962—Giants, 49-34 (NY)
    Giants, 42-24 (NY)
1963—Giants, 24-14 (W)
    Giants, 44-14 (NY)
1964—Giants, 13-10 (NY)
    Redskins, 36-21 (W)
1965—Redskins, 23-7 (NY)
    Giants, 27-10 (W)
1966—Giants, 13-10 (NY)
    Redskins, 72-41 (W)
1967—Redskins, 38-34 (W)
1968—Giants, 48-21 (NY)
    Giants, 13-10 (W)
1969—Giants, 20-14 (W)
1970—Giants, 35-33 (NY)
    Giants, 27-24 (W)
1971—Redskins, 30-3 (NY)
    Giants, 23-7 (W)
1972—Redskins, 23-16 (NY)
    Redskins, 27-13 (NY)
1973—Redskins, 21-3 (New Haven)
    Redskins, 27-24 (W)
1974—Redskins, 13-10 (New Haven)
    Giants, 24-3 (W)
1975—Redskins, 49-13 (W)
    Redskins, 21-13 (NY)
1976—Redskins, 19-17 (W)
    Giants, 12-9 (NY)
1977—Giants, 20-17 (NY)
    Giants, 17-6 (W)
1978—Giants, 17-6 (NY)
    Redskins, 16-13 (W) OT
1979—Redskins, 27-0 (NY)
    Giants, 14-6 (NY)
1980—Redskins, 23-21 (NY)
    Redskins, 16-13 (NY)
1981—Giants, 17-7 (W)
    Redskins, 30-27 (NY) OT
1982—Redskins, 27-17 (NY)
    Redskins, 15-14 (W)
1983—Redskins, 33-17 (NY)
    Redskins, 31-22 (W)
1984—Redskins, 30-14 (W)
    Giants, 37-13 (NY)
(Points—Giants 2,042, Redskins 1,861)
*Franchise in Boston prior to 1937 and
known as Braves prior to 1933
**Division Playoff

N.Y. JETS vs. ATLANTA
Falcons lead series, 2-1;
See Atlanta vs. N.Y. Jets
N.Y. JETS vs. BUFFALO
Bills lead series, 26-23;
See Buffalo vs. N.Y. Jets
N.Y. JETS vs. CHICAGO
Series tied, 1-1;
See Chicago vs. N.Y. Jets
N.Y. JETS vs. CINCINNATI
Jets lead series, 6-3;
See Cincinnati vs. N.Y. Jets
N.Y. JETS vs. CLEVELAND
Browns lead series, 7-2;
See Cleveland vs. N.Y. Jets
N.Y. JETS vs. DALLAS
Cowboys lead series, 3-0;
See Dallas vs. N.Y. Jets
N.Y. JETS vs. DENVER
Series tied, 10-10-1;
See Denver vs. N.Y. Jets
N.Y. JETS vs. DETROIT
Jets lead series, 2-1;
See Detroit vs. N.Y. Jets
N.Y. JETS vs. GREEN BAY
Jets lead series, 3-1;
See Green Bay vs. N.Y. Jets
N.Y. JETS vs. HOUSTON
Oilers lead series, 15-10-1;
See Houston vs. N.Y. Jets
N.Y. JETS vs. INDIANAPOLIS
Colts lead series, 16-14;
See Indianapolis vs. N.Y. Jets
N.Y. JETS vs. KANSAS CITY
Chiefs lead series, 13-11;
See Kansas City vs. N.Y. Jets
N.Y. JETS vs. L.A. RAIDERS
Series tied, 11-11-2;
See L.A. Raiders vs. N.Y. Jets
N.Y. JETS vs. L.A. RAMS
Series tied, 2-2;
See L.A. Rams vs. N.Y. Jets
N.Y. JETS vs. MIAMI
Dolphins lead series, 21-17-1;
See Miami vs. N.Y. Jets
N.Y. JETS vs. MINNESOTA
Jets lead series, 3-1;
See Minnesota vs. N.Y. Jets
N.Y. JETS vs. NEW ENGLAND
Jets lead series, 28-20-1;
See New England vs. N.Y. Jets
N.Y. JETS vs. NEW ORLEANS

Jets lead series, 3-1;
See New Orleans vs. N.Y. Jets
N.Y. JETS vs. N.Y. GIANTS
Series tied, 2-2;
See N.Y. Giants vs. N.Y. Jets
N.Y. JETS vs. PHILADELPHIA
Eagles lead series, 3-0
1973—Eagles, 24-23 (P)
1977—Eagles, 27-0 (P)
1978—Eagles, 17-9 (P)
(Points—Eagles 68, Jets 32)
N.Y. JETS vs. PITTSBURGH
Steelers lead series, 8-0
1970—Steelers, 21-17 (P)
1973—Steelers, 26-14 (P)
1975—Steelers, 20-7 (NY)
1977—Steelers, 23-20 (NY)
1978—Steelers, 28-17 (NY)
1981—Steelers, 38-10 (P)
1983—Steelers, 34-7 (NY)
1984—Steelers, 23-17 (NY)
(Points—Steelers 213, Jets 109)
N.Y. JETS vs. ST. LOUIS
Cardinals lead series, 2-1
1971—Cardinals, 17-10 (StL)
1975—Cardinals 37-6 (NY)
1978—Jets, 23-10 (NY)
(Points—Cardinals 64, Jets 39)
*N.Y. JETS vs. **SAN DIEGO
Chargers lead series, 14-7-1
1960—Chargers, 21-7 (NY)
    Chargers, 50-43 (LA)
1961—Chargers, 25-10 (NY)
    Chargers, 48-13 (SD)
1962—Chargers, 40-14 (SD)
    Titans, 23-3 (NY)
1963—Chargers, 24-20 (SD)
    Chargers, 53-7 (NY)
1964—Tie, 17-17 (NY)
    Chargers, 38-3 (SD)
1965—Chargers, 34-9 (NY)
    Chargers, 38-7 (SD)
1966—Jets, 17-16 (NY)
    Chargers, 42-27 (SD)
1967—Jets, 42-31 (SD)
1968—Jets, 23-20 (NY)
    Jets, 37-15 (SD)
1969—Chargers, 34-27 (SD)
1971—Chargers, 49-21 (SD)
1974—Jets, 27-14 (NY)
1975—Chargers, 24-16 (SD)
1983—Jets, 41-29 (SD)
(Points—Chargers 665, Jets 451)
*Jets known as Titans prior to 1963
**Franchise in Los Angeles prior to 1961
N.Y. JETS vs. SAN FRANCISCO
49ers lead series, 3-1
1971—49ers, 24-21 (NY)
1976—49ers, 17-6 (SF)
1980—49ers, 37-27 (NY)
1983—Jets, 27-13 (SF)
(Points—49ers 91, Jets 81)
N.Y. JETS vs. SEATTLE
Seahawks lead series, 7-0
1977—Seahawks, 17-0 (NY)
1978—Seahawks, 24-17 (NY)
1979—Seahawks, 30-7 (S)
1980—Seahawks, 27-17 (NY)
1981—Seahawks, 19-3 (NY)
    Seahawks, 27-23 (S)
1983—Seahawks, 17-10 (NY)
(Points—Seahawks 161, Jets 77)
N.Y. JETS vs. TAMPA BAY
Jets lead series, 2-1
1976—Jets, 34-0 (NY)
1982—Jets, 32-17 (NY)
1984—Buccaneers, 41-21 (TB)
(Points—Jets 87, Buccaneers 58)
N.Y. JETS vs. WASHINGTON
Redskins lead series, 3-0
1972—Redskins, 35-17 (NY)
1976—Redskins, 37-16 (NY)
1978—Redskins, 23-3 (W)
(Points—Redskins 95, Jets 36)

PHILADELPHIA vs. ATLANTA
Falcons lead series, 6-5-1;
See Atlanta vs. Philadelphia
PHILADELPHIA vs. BUFFALO
Eagles lead series, 2-1;
See Buffalo vs. Philadelphia
PHILADELPHIA vs. CHICAGO
Bears lead series, 19-4-1;
See Chicago vs. Philadelphia
PHILADELPHIA vs. CINCINNATI
Bengals lead series, 4-0;
See Cincinnati vs. Philadelphia
PHILADELPHIA vs. CLEVELAND
Browns lead series, 29-11-1;
See Cleveland vs. Philadelphia
PHILADELPHIA vs. DALLAS
Cowboys lead series, 33-16;
See Dallas vs. Philadelphia

PHILADELPHIA vs. DENVER
Eagles lead series, 3-1;
See Denver vs. Philadelphia
PHILADELPHIA vs. DETROIT
Lions lead series, 12-9-2;
See Detroit vs. Philadelphia
PHILADELPHIA vs. GREEN BAY
Packers lead series, 17-5;
See Green Bay vs. Philadelphia
PHILADELPHIA vs. HOUSTON
Eagles lead series, 3-1;
See Houston vs. Philadelphia
PHILADELPHIA vs. INDIANAPOLIS
Series tied, 5-5;
See Indianapolis vs. Philadelphia
PHILADELPHIA vs. KANSAS CITY
Eagles lead series, 1-0;
See Kansas City vs. Philadelphia
PHILADELPHIA vs. L.A. RAIDERS
Raiders lead series, 3-1;
See L.A. Raiders vs. Philadelphia
PHILADELPHIA vs. L.A. RAMS
Rams lead series, 14-9-1;
See L.A. Rams vs. Philadelphia
PHILADELPHIA vs. MIAMI
Dolphins lead series, 3-2;
See Miami vs. Philadelphia
PHILADELPHIA vs. MINNESOTA
Vikings lead series, 8-3;
See Minnesota vs. Philadelphia
PHILADELPHIA vs. NEW ENGLAND
Eagles lead series, 3-2;
See New England vs. Philadelphia
PHILADELPHIA vs. NEW ORLEANS
Eagles lead series, 8-5;
See New Orleans vs. Philadelphia
PHILADELPHIA vs. N.Y. GIANTS
Giants lead series, 54-45-2;
See N.Y. Giants vs. Philadelphia
PHILADELPHIA vs. N.Y. JETS
Eagles lead series, 3-0;
See N.Y. Jets vs. Philadelphia
PHILADELPHIA vs. *PITTSBURGH
Eagles lead series, 42-25-3
1933—Eagles, 25-6 (Phila)
1934—Eagles, 17-0 (Pitt)
    Pirates, 9-7 (Phila)
1935—Pirates, 17-7 (Phila)
    Eagles, 17-6 (Pitt)
1936—Pirates, 17-0 (Pitt)
    Pirates, 6-0 (Johnstown, Pa.)
1937—Pirates, 27-14 (Pitt)
    Pirates, 16-7 (Pitt)
1938—Eagles, 27-7 (Buffalo)
    Eagles, 14-7 (Charleston, W. Va)
1939—Pirates, 17-14 (Phila)
    Pirates, 24-12 (Pitt)
1940—Pirates, 7-3 (Pitt)
    Eagles, 7-0 (Pitt)
1941—Eagles, 10-7 (Pitt)
    Tie, 7-7 (Phila)
1942—Eagles, 24-14 (Pitt)
    Steelers, 14-0 (Phila)
1945—Eagles, 45-3 (Pitt)
    Eagles, 30-6 (Phila)
1946—Steelers, 10-7 (Pitt)
    Eagles, 10-7 (Phila)
1947—Steelers, 35-24 (Pitt)
    Eagles, 21-0 (Phila)
    **Eagles, 21-0 (Pitt)
1948—Eagles, 34-7 (Pitt)
    Eagles, 17-0 (Phila)
1949—Eagles, 38-7 (Pitt)
    Eagles, 34-17 (Phila)
1950—Eagles, 17-10 (Pitt)
    Steelers, 9-7 (Phila)
1951—Eagles, 34-13 (Pitt)
    Steelers, 17-13 (Phila)
1952—Eagles, 31-25 (Pitt)
    Eagles, 26-21 (Phila)
1953—Eagles, 23-17 (Phila)
    Eagles, 35-7 (Pitt)
1954—Eagles, 24-22 (Phila)
    Steelers, 17-7 (Phila)
1955—Steelers, 13-7 (Pitt)
    Eagles, 24-0 (Phila)
1956—Eagles, 35-21 (Pitt)
    Eagles, 14-7 (Phila)
1957—Eagles, 6-0 (Pitt)
    Eagles, 7-6 (Phila)
1958—Steelers, 24-3 (Pitt)
    Steelers, 31-24 (Phila)
1959—Eagles, 28-24 (Phila)
    Steelers, 31-0 (Pitt)
1960—Eagles, 34-7 (Phila)
    Steelers, 27-21 (Pitt)
1961—Eagles, 21-16 (Phila)
    Eagles, 35-24 (Pitt)
1962—Steelers, 13-7 (Pitt)
    Steelers, 26-17 (Phila)
1963—Tie, 21-21 (Pitt)
    Tie, 20-20 (Pitt)
1964—Eagles, 21-7 (Phila)

    Eagles, 34-10 (Pitt)
1965—Steelers, 20-14 (Phila)
    Eagles, 47-13 (Pitt)
1966—Eagles, 31-14 (Pitt)
    Eagles, 27-23 (Phila)
1967—Eagles, 34-24 (Phila)
1968—Steelers, 6-3 (Pitt)
1969—Eagles, 41-27 (Phila)
1970—Eagles, 30-20 (Phila)
1974—Steelers, 27-0 (Pitt)
1979—Eagles, 17-14 (Phila)
(Points—Eagles 1,330, Steelers 967)
*Steelers known as Pirates prior to 1941
**Division Playoff
PHILADELPHIA vs. *ST. LOUIS
Cardinals lead series, 40-32-4
1935—Cardinals, 12-3 (C)
1936—Cardinals, 13-0 (C)
1937—Tie, 6-6 (P)
1938—Eagles, 7-0 (Erie, Pa.)
1941—Eagles, 21-14 (P)
1945—Eagles, 21-6 (P)
1947—Cardinals, 45-21 (P)
    **Cardinals, 28-21 (C)
1948—Cardinals, 21-14 (P)
    **Eagles, 7-0 (P)
1949—Eagles, 28-3 (P)
1950—Eagles, 45-7 (C)
    Cardinals, 14-10 (P)
1951—Eagles, 17-14 (C)
1952—Eagles, 10-7 (P)
    Cardinals, 28-22 (C)
1953—Eagles, 56-17 (C)
    Eagles, 38-0 (P)
1954—Eagles, 35-16 (C)
    Eagles, 30-14 (P)
1955—Tie, 24-24 (C)
    Eagles, 27-3 (P)
1956—Cardinals, 20-6 (P)
    Cardinals, 28-17 (C)
1957—Eagles, 38-21 (P)
    Cardinals, 31-27 (C)
1958—Tie, 21-21 (C)
    Eagles, 49-21 (P)
1959—Eagles, 28-24 (Minn)
    Eagles, 27-17 (P)
1960—Eagles, 31-27 (P)
    Eagles, 20-6 (StL)
1961—Cardinals, 30-27 (P)
    Eagles, 20-7 (StL)
1962—Cardinals, 27-21 (P)
    Cardinals, 45-35 (StL)
1963—Cardinals, 28-24 (P)
    Cardinals, 38-14 (StL)
1964—Cardinals, 38-13 (P)
    Cardinals, 36-34 (StL)
1965—Eagles, 34-27 (P)
    Eagles, 28-24 (StL)
1966—Eagles, 16-13 (StL)
    Cardinals, 41-10 (P)
1967—Cardinals, 48-14 (StL)
1968—Cardinals, 45-17 (P)
1969—Eagles, 34-30 (P)
1970—Cardinals, 35-20 (P)
    Cardinals, 23-14 (StL)
1971—Eagles, 37-20 (StL)
    Eagles, 19-7 (P)
1972—Tie, 6-6 (P)
    Cardinals, 24-23 (StL)
1973—Cardinals, 34-23 (P)
    Eagles, 27-24 (StL)
1974—Cardinals, 7-3 (StL)
    Cardinals, 13-3 (P)
1975—Cardinals, 31-20 (StL)
    Cardinals, 24-23 (P)
1976—Cardinals, 33-14 (StL)
    Cardinals, 17-14 (P)
1977—Cardinals, 21-17 (P)
    Cardinals, 21-16 (StL)
1978—Cardinals, 16-10 (P)
    Eagles, 14-10 (StL)
1979—Eagles, 24-20 (P)
    Eagles, 16-13 (P)
1980—Cardinals, 24-14 (StL)
    Eagles, 17-3 (P)
1981—Eagles, 52-10 (StL)
    Eagles, 38-0 (P)
1982—Cardinals, 23-20 (P)
1983—Cardinals, 14-11 (P)
    Cardinals, 31-7 (StL)
1984—Cardinals, 34-14 (P)
    Eagles, 17-16 (StL)
(Points—Eagles 1,597, Cardinals 1,543)
*Franchise in Chicago prior to 1960
**NFL Championship
PHILADELPHIA vs. SAN DIEGO
Series tied, 1-1
1974—Eagles, 13-7 (SD)
1980—Chargers, 22-21 (SD)
(Points—Eagles 34, Chargers 29)
PHILADELPHIA vs. SAN FRANCISCO
49ers lead series, 9-4-1
1951—Eagles, 21-14 (P)

1953—49ers, 31-21 (SF)
1956—Tie, 10-10 (P)
1958—49ers, 30-24 (P)
1959—49ers, 24-14 (SF)
1964—49ers, 28-24 (P)
1966—Eagles, 35-34 (SF)
1967—49ers, 28-27 (P)
1969—49ers, 14-13 (SF)
1971—49ers, 31-3 (P)
1973—49ers, 38-28 (SF)
1975—Eagles, 27-17 (P)
1983—Eagles, 22-17 (SF)
1984—49ers, 21-9 (P)
(Points—49ers 337, Eagles 278)
PHILADELPHIA vs. SEATTLE
Eagles lead series, 2-0
1976—Eagles, 27-10 (P)
1980—Eagles, 27-20 (S)
(Points—Eagles 54, Seahawks 30)
PHILADELPHIA vs. TAMPA BAY
Eagles lead series, 2-1
1977—Eagles, 13-3 (P)
1979—*Buccaneers, 24-17 (TB)
1981—Eagles, 20-10 (P)
(Points—Eagles 50, Buccaneers 37)
*NFC Divisional Playoff
PHILADELPHIA vs. *WASHINGTON
Redskins lead series, 56-38-5
1934—Redskins, 6-0 (B)
        Redskins, 14-7 (P)
1935—Eagles, 7-6 (B)
1936—Redskins, 26-3 (P)
        Redskins, 17-7 (B)
1937—Eagles, 14-0 (W)
        Redskins, 10-7 (P)
1938—Redskins, 26-23 (P)
        Redskins, 20-14 (W)
1939—Redskins, 7-0 (P)
        Redskins, 7-6 (W)
1940—Redskins, 34-17 (P)
        Redskins, 13-6 (W)
1941—Redskins, 21-17 (P)
        Redskins, 20-14 (W)
1942—Redskins, 14-10 (P)
        Redskins, 30-27 (W)
1944—Tie, 31-31 (P)
        Eagles, 37-7 (W)
1945—Redskins, 24-14 (W)
        Eagles, 16-0 (P)
1946—Eagles, 28-24 (W)
        Redskins, 27-10 (P)
1947—Eagles, 45-42 (P)
        Eagles, 38-14 (W)
1948—Eagles, 45-0 (W)
        Eagles, 42-21 (P)
1949—Eagles, 49-14 (P)
        Eagles, 44-21 (W)
1950—Eagles, 35-3 (P)
        Eagles, 33-0 (W)
1951—Redskins, 27-23 (P)
        Eagles, 35-21 (W)
1952—Eagles, 38-20 (P)
        Redskins, 27-21 (W)
1953—Tie, 21-21 (P)
        Redskins, 10-0 (W)
1954—Eagles, 49-21 (W)
        Eagles, 41-33 (P)
1955—Eagles, 31-30 (P)
        Redskins, 34-21 (W)
1956—Eagles, 13-9 (P)
        Redskins, 19-17 (W)
1957—Eagles, 21-12 (P)
        Redskins, 42-7 (W)
1958—Redskins, 24-14 (P)
        Redskins, 20-0 (W)
1959—Eagles, 30-23 (P)
        Eagles, 34-14 (W)
1960—Eagles, 19-13 (P)
        Eagles, 38-28 (W)
1961—Eagles, 14-7 (P)
        Eagles, 27-24 (W)
1962—Redskins, 27-21 (P)
        Eagles, 37-14 (W)
1963—Eagles, 37-24 (W)
        Redskins, 13-10 (P)
1964—Redskins, 35-20 (W)
        Redskins, 21-10 (P)
1965—Redskins, 23-21 (P)
        Eagles, 21-14 (W)
1966—Redskins, 27-13 (P)
        Eagles, 37-28 (W)
1967—Eagles, 35-24 (P)
        Tie, 35-35 (W)
1968—Redskins, 17-14 (P)
        Redskins, 16-10 (W)
1969—Tie, 28-28 (W)
        Redskins, 34-29 (P)
1970—Redskins, 33-21 (P)
        Redskins, 24-6 (W)
1971—Tie, 7-7 (W)
        Redskins, 20-13 (P)
1972—Redskins, 14-0 (W)
        Redskins, 23-7 (P)

1973—Redskins, 28-7 (P)
        Redskins, 38-20 (W)
1974—Redskins, 27-20 (P)
        Redskins, 26-7 (W)
1975—Eagles, 26-10 (P)
        Eagles, 26-3 (W)
1976—Redskins, 20-17 (P) OT
        Redskins, 24-0 (W)
1977—Redskins, 23-17 (W)
        Redskins, 17-14 (P)
1978—Redskins, 35-30 (W)
        Eagles, 17-10 (P)
1979—Eagles, 28-17 (P)
        Redskins, 17-7 (W)
1980—Eagles, 24-14 (P)
        Eagles, 24-0 (W)
1981—Eagles, 36-13 (P)
        Redskins, 15-13 (W)
1982—Redskins, 37-34 (P) OT
        Redskins, 13-9 (W)
1983—Redskins, 23-13 (P)
        Redskins, 28-24 (W)
1984—Redskins, 20-0 (W)
        Eagles, 16-10 (P)
(Points—Eagles 2,020, Redskins 1,948)
*Franchise in Boston prior to 1937

PITTSBURGH vs. ATLANTA
Steelers lead series, 6-1;
See Atlanta vs. Pittsburgh
PITTSBURGH vs. BUFFALO
Steelers lead series, 5-3;
See Buffalo vs. Pittsburgh
PITTSBURGH vs. CHICAGO
Bears lead series, 13-4-1;
See Chicago vs. Pittsburgh
PITTSBURGH vs. CINCINNATI
Steelers lead series, 17-12;
See Cincinnati vs. Pittsburgh
PITTSBURGH vs. CLEVELAND
Browns lead series, 40-30;
See Cleveland vs. Pittsburgh
PITTSBURGH vs. DALLAS
Steelers lead series, 12-10;
See Dallas vs. Pittsburgh
PITTSBURGH vs. DENVER
Broncos lead series, 6-5-1;
See Denver vs. Pittsburgh
PITTSBURGH vs. DETROIT
Lions lead series, 13-8-1;
See Detroit vs. Pittsburgh
PITTSBURGH vs. GREEN BAY
Packers lead series, 16-10;
See Green Bay vs. Pittsburgh
PITTSBURGH vs. HOUSTON
Steelers lead series, 22-9;
See Houston vs. Pittsburgh
PITTSBURGH vs. INDIANAPOLIS
Steelers lead series, 8-4;
See Indianapolis vs. Pittsburgh
PITTSBURGH vs. KANSAS CITY
Steelers lead series, 8-4;
See Kansas City vs. Pittsburgh
PITTSBURGH vs. L.A. RAIDERS
Raiders lead series, 9-6;
See L.A. Raiders vs. Pittsburgh
PITTSBURGH vs. L.A. RAMS
Rams lead series, 12-4-2;
See L.A. Rams vs. Pittsburgh
PITTSBURGH vs. MIAMI
Dolphins lead series, 6-3;
See Miami vs. Pittsburgh
PITTSBURGH vs. MINNESOTA
Vikings lead series, 5-4;
See Minnesota vs. Pittsburgh
PITTSBURGH vs. NEW ENGLAND
Steelers lead series, 5-2;
See New England vs. Pittsburgh
PITTSBURGH vs. NEW ORLEANS
Series tied, 4-4;
See New Orleans vs. Pittsburgh
PITTSBURGH vs. N.Y. GIANTS
Giants lead series, 40-26-3;
See N.Y. Giants vs. Pittsburgh
PITTSBURGH vs. N.Y. JETS
Steelers lead series, 8-0;
See N.Y. Jets vs. Pittsburgh
PITTSBURGH vs. PHILADELPHIA
Eagles lead series, 42-25-3;
See Philadelphia vs. Pittsburgh
*PITTSBURGH vs. **ST. LOUIS
Steelers lead series, 28-20-3
1933—Pirates, 14-13 (C)
1935—Pirates, 17-13 (P)
1936—Cardinals, 14-6 (C)
1937—Cardinals, 13-7 (P)
1939—Cardinals, 10-0 (P)
1940—Tie, 7-7 (P)
1942—Steelers, 19-3 (P)
1945—Steelers, 23-0 (P)
1946—Steelers, 14-7 (P)
1948—Cardinals, 24-7 (P)
1950—Steelers, 28-17 (C)

        Steelers, 28-7 (P)
1951—Steelers, 28-14 (C)
        Steelers, 17-14 (P)
1952—Steelers, 34-28 (C)
        Steelers, 21-17 (P)
1953—Steelers, 31-28 (P)
        Steelers, 21-17 (C)
1954—Cardinals, 17-14 (C)
        Steelers, 20-17 (P)
1955—Steelers, 14-7 (P)
        Cardinals, 27-13 (C)
1956—Cardinals, 14-7 (P)
        Cardinals, 38-27 (C)
1957—Steelers, 29-20 (P)
        Steelers, 27-2 (C)
1958—Steelers, 27-20 (C)
        Steelers, 38-21 (P)
1959—Cardinals, 45-24 (C)
        Steelers, 35-20 (P)
1960—Steelers, 27-14 (P)
        Cardinals, 38-7 (StL)
1961—Steelers, 30-27 (P)
        Cardinals, 20-0 (StL)
1962—Steelers, 26-17 (StL)
        Steelers, 19-7 (P)
1963—Steelers, 23-10 (P)
        Cardinals, 24-23 (StL)
1964—Cardinals, 34-30 (StL)
        Cardinals, 21-20 (P)
1965—Cardinals, 20-7 (P)
        Cardinals, 21-17 (P)
1966—Steelers, 30-9 (P)
        Cardinals, 6-3 (StL)
1967—Cardinals, 28-14 (P)
        Tie, 14-14 (StL)
1968—Tie, 28-28 (StL)
        Cardinals, 20-10 (P)
1969—Cardinals, 27-14 (P)
        Cardinals, 47-10 (StL)
1972—Steelers, 25-19 (StL)
1979—Steelers, 24-21 (StL)
(Points — Steelers 984, Cardinals 942)
*Steelers known as Pirates prior to 1941
**Franchise in Chicago prior to 1960
PITTSBURGH vs. SAN DIEGO
Steelers lead series, 8-3
1971—Steelers, 21-17 (P)
1972—Steelers, 24-2 (SD)
1973—Steelers, 38-21 (P)
1975—Steelers, 37-0 (SD)
1976—Steelers, 23-0 (P)
1977—Steelers, 10-9 (SD)
1979—Chargers, 35-7 (SD)
1980—Chargers, 26-17 (SD)
1982—*Chargers, 31-28 (P)
1983—Steelers, 26-3 (P)
1984—Steelers, 52-24 (P)
(Points—Steelers 283, Chargers 168)
*AFC First Round Playoff
PITTSBURGH vs. SAN FRANCISCO
Series tied, 6-6
1951—49ers, 28-24 (P)
1952—Steelers, 24-7 (SF)
1954—49ers, 31-3 (SF)
1958—49ers, 23-20 (SF)
1961—Steelers, 20-10 (SF)
1965—49ers, 27-17 (SF)
1968—49ers, 45-28 (P)
1973—Steelers, 37-14 (SF)
1977—Steelers, 27-0 (P)
1978—Steelers, 24-7 (SF)
1981—49ers, 17-14 (P)
1984—Steelers, 20-17 (SF)
(Points—Steelers 258, 49ers 226)
PITTSBURGH vs. SEATTLE
Steelers lead series, 3-2
1977—Steelers, 30-20 (P)
1978—Steelers, 21-10 (P)
1981—Seahawks, 24-21 (S)
1982—Seahawks, 16-0 (S)
1983—Steelers, 27-21 (S)
(Points—Steelers 99, Seahawks 91)
PITTSBURGH vs. TAMPA BAY
Steelers lead series, 3-0
1976—Steelers, 42-0 (P)
1980—Steelers, 24-21 (TB)
1983—Steelers, 17-12 (P)
(Points—Steelers 83, Buccaneers 33)
*PITTSBURGH vs. **WASHINGTON
Redskins lead series, 39-27-3
1933—Redskins, 21-6 (P)
        Pirates, 16-14 (B)
1934—Redskins, 7-0 (P)
        Redskins, 39-0 (B)
1935—Pirates, 6-0 (P)
        Redskins, 13-3 (B)
1936—Pirates, 10-0 (P)
        Redskins, 30-0 (B)
1937—Redskins, 34-20 (P)
        Pirates, 21-13 (P)
1938—Redskins, 7-0 (P)
        Redskins, 15-0 (W)
1939—Redskins, 44-14 (W)
        Redskins, 21-14 (P)

        Steelers, 28-7 (P)
1940—Redskins, 40-10 (P)
        Redskins, 37-10 (W)
1941—Redskins, 24-20 (P)
        Redskins, 23-3 (W)
1942—Redskins, 28-14 (W)
        Redskins, 14-0 (P)
1945—Redskins, 14-0 (W)
        Redskins, 24-0 (W)
1946—Tie, 14-14 (W)
        Steelers, 14-7 (W)
1947—Redskins, 27-26 (W)
        Steelers, 21-14 (P)
1948—Redskins, 17-14 (W)
        Steelers, 10-7 (P)
1949—Redskins, 27-14 (P)
        Redskins, 27-14 (W)
1950—Steelers, 26-7 (P)
        Redskins, 24-7 (W)
1951—Steelers, 22-7 (P)
        Steelers, 20-10 (W)
1952—Redskins, 28-24 (P)
        Steelers, 24-23 (W)
1953—Redskins, 17-9 (P)
        Steelers, 14-13 (W)
1954—Steelers, 37-7 (P)
        Redskins, 17-14 (W)
1955—Redskins, 23-14 (P)
        Redskins, 28-17 (W)
1956—Steelers, 30-13 (P)
        Steelers, 23-0 (W)
1957—Steelers, 28-7 (P)
        Redskins, 10-3 (W)
1958—Steelers, 24-16 (P)
        Tie, 14-14 (W)
1959—Redskins, 23-17 (P)
        Steelers, 27-6 (W)
1960—Tie, 27-27 (W)
        Steelers, 22-10 (P)
1961—Steelers, 20-0 (P)
        Steelers, 30-14 (W)
1962—Steelers, 23-21 (P)
        Steelers, 27-24 (W)
1963—Steelers, 38-27 (P)
        Steelers, 34-28 (W)
1964—Redskins, 30-0 (P)
        Steelers, 14-7 (W)
1965—Redskins, 31-3 (P)
        Redskins, 35-14 (W)
1966—Redskins, 33-27 (P)
        Redskins, 24-10 (W)
1967—Redskins, 15-10 (P)
1968—Redskins, 16-13 (W)
1969—Redskins, 14-7 (W)
1973—Steelers, 21-16 (P)
1979—Redskins, 38-7 (P)
(Points—Redskins 1,289, Steelers 1,051)
*Steelers known as Pirates prior to 1941
**Franchise in Boston prior to 1937

ST. LOUIS vs. ATLANTA
Cardinals lead series, 6-3;
See Atlanta vs. St. Louis
ST. LOUIS vs. BUFFALO
Cardinals lead series, 3-1;
See Buffalo vs. St. Louis
ST. LOUIS vs. CHICAGO
Bears lead series, 50-25-6;
See Chicago vs. St. Louis
ST. LOUIS vs. CINCINNATI
Bengals lead series, 2-0;
See Cincinnati vs. St. Louis
ST. LOUIS vs. CLEVELAND
Browns lead series, 30-9-3;
See Cleveland vs. St. Louis
ST. LOUIS vs. DALLAS
Cowboys lead series, 28-16-1;
See Dallas vs. St. Louis
ST. LOUIS vs. DENVER
Broncos lead series, 1-0-1;
See Denver vs. St. Louis
ST. LOUIS vs. DETROIT
Lions lead series, 25-15-5;
See Detroit vs. St. Louis
ST. LOUIS vs. GREEN BAY
Packers lead series, 38-20-4;
See Green Bay vs. St. Louis
ST. LOUIS vs. HOUSTON
Cardinals lead series, 3-0;
See Houston vs. St. Louis
ST. LOUIS vs. INDIANAPOLIS
Cardinals lead series, 5-4;
See Indianapolis vs. St. Louis
ST. LOUIS vs. KANSAS CITY
Chiefs lead series, 3-0-1;
See Kansas City vs. St. Louis
ST. LOUIS vs. L.A. RAIDERS
Series tied, 1-1;
See L.A. Raiders vs. St. Louis
ST. LOUIS vs. L.A. RAMS
Rams lead series, 19-15-2;
See L.A. Rams vs. St. Louis
ST. LOUIS vs. MIAMI
Dolphins lead series, 5-0;

See Miami vs. St. Louis
ST. LOUIS vs. MINNESOTA
Cardinals lead series, 7-3;
See Minnesota vs. St. Louis
ST. LOUIS vs. NEW ENGLAND
Cardinals lead series, 4-1;
See New England vs. St. Louis
ST. LOUIS vs. NEW ORLEANS
Cardinals lead series, 8-4;
See New Orleans vs. St. Louis
ST. LOUIS vs. N.Y. GIANTS
Giants lead series, 51-31-2;
See N.Y. Giants vs. St. Louis
ST. LOUIS vs. N.Y. JETS
Cardinals lead series, 2-1;
See N.Y. Jets vs. St. Louis
ST. LOUIS vs. PHILADELPHIA
Cardinals lead series, 40-32-4;
See Philadelphia vs. St. Louis
ST. LOUIS vs. PITTSBURGH
Steelers lead series, 28-20-3;
See Pittsburgh vs. St. Louis
ST. LOUIS vs. SAN DIEGO
Chargers lead series, 2-1;
1971—Chargers, 20-17 (SD)
1976—Chargers, 43-24 (SD)
1983—Cardinals, 44-14 (StL)
(Points—Cardinals 85, Chargers 77)
*ST. LOUIS vs. SAN FRANCISCO
Cardinals lead series, 7-6
1951—Cardinals, 27-21 (SF)
1957—Cardinals, 20-10 (SF)
1962—49ers, 24-17 (SF)
1964—Cardinals, 23-13 (SF)
1968—49ers, 35-17 (SF)
1971—49ers, 26-14 (StL)
1974—Cardinals, 34-9 (SF)
1976—Cardinals, 23-20 (StL) OT
1978—Cardinals, 16-10 (SF)
1979—Cardinals, 13-10 (StL)
1980—49ers, 24-21 (SF) OT
1982—49ers, 31-20 (StL)
1983—49ers, 42-27 (StL)
(Points—49ers 275, Cardinals 272)
*Team in Chicago prior to 1960
ST. LOUIS vs. SEATTLE
Cardinals lead series, 2-0
1976—Cardinals, 30-24 (S)
1983—Cardinals, 33-28 (StL)
(Points—Cardinals 63, Seahawks 52)
ST. LOUIS vs. TAMPA BAY
Buccaneers lead series, 2-1
1977—Buccaneers, 17-7 (TB)
1981—Buccaneers, 20-10 (TB)
1983—Cardinals, 34-27 (TB)
(Points—Buccaneers 64, Cardinals 51)
*ST. LOUIS vs. **WASHINGTON
Redskins lead series, 47-32-2
1932—Cardinals, 9-0 (B)
       Braves, 8-6 (C)
1933—Redskins, 10-0 (C)
       Tie, 0-0 (B)
1934—Redskins, 9-0 (B)
1935—Cardinals, 6-0 (B)
1936—Redskins, 13-10 (B)
1937—Cardinals, 21-14 (W)
1939—Redskins, 28-7 (W)
1940—Redskins, 28-21 (W)
1942—Redskins, 28-0 (W)
1943—Redskins, 13-7 (W)
1945—Redskins, 24-21 (W)
1947—Redskins, 45-21 (W)
1949—Cardinals, 38-7 (C)
1950—Cardinals, 38-28 (W)
1951—Redskins, 7-3 (C)
       Redskins, 20-17 (W)
1952—Cardinals, 23-7 (C)
       Cardinals, 17-6 (W)
1953—Redskins, 24-13 (C)
       Redskins, 28-17 (W)
1954—Cardinals, 38-16 (C)
       Redskins, 37-20 (W)
1955—Cardinals, 24-10 (W)
       Redskins, 31-0 (C)
1956—Cardinals, 31-3 (W)
       Redskins, 17-14 (C)
1957—Redskins, 37-14 (C)
       Cardinals, 44-14 (W)
1958—Cardinals, 37-10 (C)
       Redskins, 45-31 (W)
1959—Cardinals, 49-21 (C)
       Redskins, 23-14 (W)
1960—Cardinals, 44-7 (StL)
       Cardinals, 26-14 (W)
1961—Cardinals, 24-0 (W)
       Cardinals, 38-24 (StL)
1962—Redskins, 24-14 (W)
       Tie, 17-17 (StL)
1963—Cardinals, 21-7 (W)
       Cardinals, 24-20 (StL)
1964—Cardinals, 23-17 (W)
       Cardinals, 38-24 (StL)
1965—Cardinals, 37-16 (W)

Redskins, 24-20 (StL)
1966—Cardinals, 23-7 (StL)
       Redskins, 26-20 (W)
1967—Cardinals, 27-21 (W)
1968—Cardinals, 41-14 (StL)
1969—Redskins, 33-17 (W)
1970—Cardinals, 27-17 (StL)
       Redskins, 28-27 (W)
1971—Redskins, 24-17 (StL)
       Redskins, 20-0 (W)
1972—Cardinals, 24-10 (W)
       Redskins, 33-3 (StL)
1973—Cardinals, 34-27 (StL)
       Redskins, 31-13 (W)
1974—Cardinals, 17-10 (W)
       Cardinals, 23-20 (StL)
1975—Redskins, 27-17 (W)
       Cardinals, 20-17 (StL) OT
1976—Redskins, 20-10 (W)
       Redskins, 16-10 (StL)
1977—Redskins, 24-14 (W)
       Redskins, 26-20 (StL)
1978—Redskins, 28-10 (StL)
       Cardinals, 27-17 (W)
1979—Redskins, 17-7 (StL)
       Redskins, 30-28 (W)
1980—Redskins, 23-0 (W)
       Redskins, 31-7 (StL)
1981—Cardinals, 40-30 (StL)
       Redskins, 42-21 (W)
1982—Redskins, 12-7 (StL)
       Redskins, 28-0 (W)
1983—Redskins, 38-14 (StL)
       Redskins, 45-7 (W)
1984—Cardinals, 26-24 (StL)
       Redskins, 29-27 (W)
(Points—Redskins 1,680, Cardinals 1,532)
*Team in Chicago prior to 1960
**Team in Boston prior to 1937 and known as Braves prior to 1933

SAN DIEGO vs. ATLANTA
Falcons lead series, 2-0;
See Atlanta vs. San Diego
SAN DIEGO vs. BUFFALO
Chargers lead series, 15-9-2;
See Buffalo vs. San Diego
SAN DIEGO vs. CHICAGO
Chargers lead series, 4-1;
See Chicago vs. San Diego
SAN DIEGO vs. CINCINNATI
Chargers lead series, 9-7;
See Cincinnati vs. San Diego
SAN DIEGO vs. CLEVELAND
Chargers lead series, 5-3-1;
See Cleveland vs. San Diego
SAN DIEGO vs. DALLAS
Cowboys lead series, 2-1;
See Dallas vs. San Diego
SAN DIEGO vs. DENVER
Chargers lead series, 26-23-1;
See Denver vs. San Diego
SAN DIEGO vs. DETROIT
Lions lead series, 3-2;
See Detroit vs. San Diego
SAN DIEGO vs. GREEN BAY
Packers lead series, 3-1;
See Green Bay vs. San Diego
SAN DIEGO vs. HOUSTON
Chargers lead series, 16-11-1;
See Houston vs. San Diego
SAN DIEGO vs. INDIANAPOLIS
Chargers lead series, 4-2;
See Indianapolis vs. San Diego
SAN DIEGO vs. KANSAS CITY
Chargers lead series, 25-23-1;
See Kansas City vs. San Diego
SAN DIEGO vs. L.A. RAIDERS
Raiders lead series, 32-17-2;
See L.A. Raiders vs. San Diego
SAN DIEGO vs. L.A. RAMS
Rams lead series, 2-1;
See L.A. Rams vs. San Diego
SAN DIEGO vs. MIAMI
Chargers lead series, 8-5;
See Miami vs. San Diego
SAN DIEGO vs. MINNESOTA
Chargers lead series, 3-2;
See Minnesota vs. San Diego
SAN DIEGO vs. NEW ENGLAND
Patriots lead series, 13-12-2;
See New England vs. San Diego
SAN DIEGO vs. NEW ORLEANS
Chargers lead series, 3-0;
See New Orleans vs. San Diego
SAN DIEGO vs. N.Y. GIANTS
Series tied, 2-2;
See N.Y. Giants vs. San Diego
SAN DIEGO vs. N.Y. JETS
Chargers lead series, 14-7-1;
See N.Y. Jets vs. San Diego
SAN DIEGO vs. PHILADELPHIA
Series tied, 1-1;
See Philadelphia vs. San Diego

SAN DIEGO vs. PITTSBURGH
Steelers lead series, 8-3;
See Pittsburgh vs. San Diego
SAN DIEGO vs. ST. LOUIS
Chargers lead series, 2-1;
See St. Louis vs. San Diego
SAN DIEGO vs. SAN FRANCISCO
Chargers lead series, 3-1
1972—49ers, 34-3 (SF)
1976—Chargers, 13-7 (SD) OT
1979—Chargers, 31-9 (SD)
1982—Chargers, 41-37 (SF)
(Points—Chargers, 88, 49ers 87)
SAN DIEGO vs. SEATTLE
Chargers lead series, 9-4
1977—Chargers, 30-28 (S)
1978—Chargers, 24-20 (S)
       Chargers, 37-10 (SD)
1979—Chargers, 33-16 (S)
       Chargers, 20-10 (SD)
1980—Chargers, 34-13 (S)
       Chargers, 21-14 (SD)
1981—Chargers, 24-10 (SD)
       Seahawks, 44-23 (S)
1983—Seahawks, 34-31 (S)
       Chargers, 28-21 (SD)
1984—Seahawks, 31-17 (S)
       Seahawks, 24-0 (SD)
(Points—Chargers 322, Seahawks 275)
SAN DIEGO vs. TAMPA BAY
Chargers lead series, 2-0
1976—Chargers, 23-0 (TB)
1981—Chargers, 24-23 (TB)
(Points—Chargers 47, Buccaneers 23)
SAN DIEGO vs. WASHINGTON
Redskins lead series, 3-0
1973—Redskins, 38-0 (W)
1980—Redskins, 40-17 (W)
1983—Redskins, 27-24 (SD)
(Points—Redskins 105, Chargers 41)

SAN FRANCISCO vs. ATLANTA
49ers lead series, 19-17;
See Atlanta vs. San Francisco
SAN FRANCISCO vs. BUFFALO
Bills lead series, 2-1;
See Buffalo vs. San Francisco
SAN FRANCISCO vs. CHICAGO
Series tied, 23-23-1;
See Chicago vs. San Francisco
SAN FRANCISCO vs. CINCINNATI
49ers lead series, 4-1;
See Cincinnati vs. San Francisco
SAN FRANCISCO vs. CLEVELAND
Browns lead series, 8-4;
See Cleveland vs. San Francisco
SAN FRANCISCO vs. DALLAS
Cowboys lead series, 8-7-1;
See Dallas vs. San Francisco
SAN FRANCISCO vs. DENVER
Series tied, 2-2;
See Denver vs. San Francisco
SAN FRANCISCO vs. DETROIT
Lions lead series, 25-23-1;
See Detroit vs. San Francisco
SAN FRANCISCO vs. GREEN BAY
49ers lead series, 22-20-1;
See Green Bay vs. San Francisco
SAN FRANCISCO vs. HOUSTON
49ers lead series, 3-2;
See Houston vs. San Francisco
SAN FRANCISCO vs. INDIANAPOLIS
Colts lead series, 21-14;
See Indianapolis vs. San Francisco
SAN FRANCISCO vs. KANSAS CITY
49ers lead series, 2-1;
See Kansas City vs. San Francisco
SAN FRANCISCO vs. L.A RAIDERS
Raiders lead series, 3-1;
See L.A. Raiders vs. San Francisco
SAN FRANCISCO vs. L.A. RAMS
Rams lead series, 43-25-2;
See L.A. Rams vs. San Francisco
SAN FRANCISCO vs. MIAMI
Dolphins lead series, 4-1;
See Miami vs. San Francisco
SAN FRANCISCO vs. MINNESOTA
Series tied, 12-12-1;
See Minnesota vs. San Francisco
SAN FRANCISCO vs. NEW ENGLAND
49ers lead series, 3-1;
See New England vs. San Francisco
SAN FRANCISCO vs. NEW ORLEANS
49ers lead series, 21-8-2;
See New Orleans vs. San Francisco
SAN FRANCISCO vs. N.Y. GIANTS
Giants lead series, 9-7;
See N.Y. Giants vs. San Francisco
SAN FRANCISCO vs. N.Y. JETS
49ers lead series, 3-1;
See N.Y. Jets vs. San Francisco
SAN FRANCISCO vs. PHILADELPHIA
49ers lead series, 9-4-1;
See Philadelphia vs. San Francisco

SAN FRANCISCO vs. PITTSBURGH
Series tied, 6-6;
See Pittsburgh vs. San Francisco
SAN FRANCISCO vs. ST. LOUIS
Cardinals lead series, 7-6;
See St. Louis vs. San Francisco
SAN FRANCISCO vs. SAN DIEGO
Chargers lead series, 3-1;
See San Diego vs. San Francisco
SAN FRANCISCO vs. SEATTLE
Series tied, 1-1
1976—49ers, 37-21 (S)
1979—Seahawks, 35-24 (SF)
(Points—49ers 61, Seahawks 56)
SAN FRANCISCO vs. TAMPA BAY
49ers lead series, 5-1
1977—49ers, 20-10 (SF)
1978—49ers, 6-3 (SF)
1979—49ers, 23-7 (SF)
1980—Buccaneers, 24-23 (SF)
1983—49ers, 35-21 (SF)
1984—49ers, 24-17 (SF)
(Points—49ers 131, Buccaneers 82)
SAN FRANCISCO vs. WASHINGTON
49ers lead series, 7-6-1
1952—49ers, 23-17 (W)
1954—49ers, 41-7 (SF)
1955—Redskins, 7-0 (W)
1961—49ers, 35-3 (SF)
1967—Redskins, 31-28 (W)
1969—Tie, 17-17 (SF)
1970—49ers, 26-17 (SF)
1971—*49ers, 24-20 (SF)
1973—Redskins, 33-9 (W)
1976—Redskins, 24-21 (SF)
1978—Redskins, 38-20 (W)
1981—49ers, 30-17 (W)
1983—**Redskins, 24-21 (W)
1984—Redskins, 37-31 (SF)
(Points—49ers 332, Redskins 286)
*NFC Divisional Playoff
**NFC Championship

SEATTLE vs. ATLANTA
Seahawks lead series, 2-0;
See Atlanta vs. Seattle
SEATTLE vs. BUFFALO
Seahawks lead series, 2-0;
See Buffalo vs. Seattle
SEATTLE vs. CHICAGO
Seahawks lead series, 3-1;
See Chicago vs. Seattle
SEATTLE vs. CINCINNATI
Bengals lead series, 3-1;
See Cincinnati vs. Seattle
SEATTLE vs. CLEVELAND
Seahawks lead series, 6-2;
See Cleveland vs. Seattle
SEATTLE vs. DALLAS
Cowboys lead series, 3-0;
See Dallas vs. Seattle
SEATTLE vs. DENVER
Broncos lead series, 9-7;
See Denver vs. Seattle
SEATTLE vs. DETROIT
Seahawks lead series, 2-1;
See Detroit vs. Seattle
SEATTLE vs. GREEN BAY
Packers lead series, 3-1;
See Green Bay vs. Seattle
SEATTLE vs. HOUSTON
Oilers lead series, 3-2;
See Houston vs. Seattle
SEATTLE vs. INDIANAPOLIS
Colts lead series, 2-0;
See Indianapolis vs. Seattle
SEATTLE vs. KANSAS CITY
Chiefs lead series, 7-6;
See Kansas City vs. Seattle
SEATTLE vs. L.A. RAIDERS
Series tied, 8-8;
See L.A. Raiders vs. Seattle
SEATTLE vs. L.A. RAMS
Rams lead series, 2-0;
See L.A. Rams vs. Seattle
SEATTLE vs. MIAMI
Dolphins lead series, 3-1;
See Miami vs. Seattle
SEATTLE vs. MINNESOTA
Seahawks lead series, 2-1;
See Minnesota vs. Seattle
SEATTLE vs. NEW ENGLAND
Patriots lead series, 4-1;
See New England vs. Seattle
SEATTLE vs. NEW ORLEANS
Series tied, 1-1;
See New Orleans vs. Seattle
SEATTLE vs. N.Y. GIANTS
Giants lead series, 3-1;
See N.Y. Giants vs. Seattle
SEATTLE vs. N.Y. JETS
Seahawks lead series, 7-0;
See N.Y. Jets vs. Seattle

SEATTLE vs. PHILADELPHIA
Eagles lead series, 2-0;
See Philadelphia vs. Seattle
SEATTLE vs. PITTSBURGH
Steelers lead series, 3-2;
See Pittsburgh vs. Seattle
SEATTLE vs. ST. LOUIS
Cardinals lead series, 2-0;
See St. Louis vs. Seattle
SEATTLE vs. SAN DIEGO
Chargers lead series, 9-4;
See San Diego vs. Seattle
SEATTLE vs. SAN FRANCISCO
Series tied, 1-1;
See San Francisco vs. Seattle
SEATTLE vs. TAMPA BAY
Seahawks lead series, 2-0
1976—Seahawks, 13-10 (TB)
1977—Seahawks, 30-23 (S)
(Points—Seahawks 43, Buccaneers 33)
SEATTLE vs. WASHINGTON
Redskins lead series, 2-1
1976—Redskins, 31-7 (W)
1980—Seahawks, 14-0 (W)
1983—Redskins, 27-17 (S)
(Points—Redskins 58, Seahawks 38)

TAMPA BAY vs. ATLANTA
Buccaneers lead series, 3-2;
See Atlanta vs. Tampa Bay
TAMPA BAY vs. BUFFALO
Buccaneers lead series, 2-1;
See Buffalo vs. Tampa Bay
TAMPA BAY vs. CHICAGO
Bears lead series, 10-4;
See Chicago vs. Tampa Bay
TAMPA BAY vs. CINCINNATI
Bengals lead series, 2-1;
See Cincinnati vs. Tampa Bay
TAMPA BAY vs. CLEVELAND
Browns lead series, 3-0;
See Cleveland vs. Tampa Bay
TAMPA BAY vs. DALLAS
Cowboys lead series, 6-0;
See Dallas vs. Tampa Bay
TAMPA BAY vs. DENVER
Broncos lead series, 2-0;
See Denver vs. Tampa Bay
TAMPA BAY vs. DETROIT
Lions lead series, 8-6;
See Detroit vs. Tampa Bay
TAMPA BAY vs. GREEN BAY
Series tied, 6-6-1;
See Green Bay vs. Tampa Bay
TAMPA BAY vs. HOUSTON
Oilers lead series, 2-1;
See Houston vs. Tampa Bay
TAMPA BAY vs. INDIANAPOLIS
Series tied, 1-1;
See Indianapolis vs. Tampa Bay
TAMPA BAY vs. KANSAS CITY
Chiefs lead series, 3-2;
See Kansas City vs. Tampa Bay
TAMPA BAY vs. L.A RAIDERS
Raiders lead series, 2-0;
See L.A. Raiders vs. Tampa Bay
TAMPA BAY vs. L.A. RAMS
Rams lead series, 4-2;
See L.A. Rams vs. Tampa Bay
TAMPA BAY vs. MIAMI
Series tied, 1-1;
See Miami vs. Tampa Bay
TAMPA BAY vs. MINNESOTA
Vikings lead series, 9-5;
See Minnesota vs. Tampa Bay
TAMPA BAY vs. NEW ENGLAND
Patriots lead series, 1-0;
See New England vs. Tampa Bay
TAMPA BAY vs. NEW ORLEANS
Saints lead series, 4-3;
See New Orleans vs. Tampa Bay
TAMPA BAY vs. N.Y. GIANTS
Giants lead series, 5-3;
See N.Y. Giants vs. Tampa Bay
TAMPA BAY vs. N.Y. JETS
Jets lead series, 2-1;
See N.Y. Jets vs. Tampa Bay
TAMPA BAY vs. PHILADELPHIA
Eagles lead series, 2-1;
See Philadelphia vs. Tampa Bay
TAMPA BAY vs. PITTSBURGH
Steelers lead series, 3-0;
See Pittsburgh vs. Tampa Bay
TAMPA BAY vs. ST. LOUIS
Buccaneers lead series, 2-1;
See St. Louis vs. Tampa Bay
TAMPA BAY vs. SAN DIEGO
Chargers lead series, 2-0;
See San Diego vs. Tampa Bay
TAMPA BAY vs. SAN FRANCISCO
49ers lead series, 5-1;
See San Francisco vs. Tampa Bay
TAMPA BAY vs. SEATTLE
Seahawks lead series, 2-0;
See Seattle vs. Tampa Bay
TAMPA BAY vs. WASHINGTON
Redskins lead series, 2-0
1977—Redskins, 10-0 (TB)
1982—Redskins, 21-13 (TB)
(Points—Redskins 31, Buccaneers 13)

WASHINGTON vs. ATLANTA
Redskins lead series, 8-2-1;
See Atlanta vs. Washington
WASHINGTON vs. BUFFALO
Series tied 2-2;
See Buffalo vs. Washington
WASHINGTON vs. CHICAGO
Bears lead series, 19-11-1;
See Chicago vs. Washington
WASHINGTON vs. CINCINNATI
Redskins lead series, 2-1;
See Cincinnati vs. Washington
WASHINGTON vs. CLEVELAND
Browns lead series, 31-7-1;
See Cleveland vs. Washington
WASHINGTON vs. DALLAS
Cowboys lead series, 28-20-2;
See Dallas vs. Washington
WASHINGTON vs. DENVER
Redskins lead series, 2-1;
See Denver vs. Washington
WASHINGTON vs. DETROIT
Redskins lead series, 18-8;
See Detroit vs. Washington
WASHINGTON vs. GREEN BAY
Packers lead series, 14-11-1;
See Green Bay vs. Washington
WASHINGTON vs. HOUSTON
Oilers lead series, 2-1;
See Houston vs. Washington
WASHINGTON vs. INDIANAPOLIS
Colts lead series, 15-6;
See Indianapolis vs. Washington
WASHINGTON vs. KANSAS CITY
Chiefs lead series, 2-1;
See Kansas City vs. Washington
WASHINGTON vs. L.A. RAIDERS
Raiders lead series, 4-1;
See L.A. Raiders vs. Washington
WASHINGTON vs. L.A. RAMS
Redskins lead series, 14-5-1;
See L.A. Rams vs. Washington
WASHINGTON vs. MIAMI
Dolphins lead series, 4-2;
See Miami vs. Washington
WASHINGTON vs. MINNESOTA
Vikings lead series, 5-4;
See Minnesota vs. Washington
WASHINGTON vs. NEW ENGLAND
Redskins lead series, 3-1;
See New England vs. Washington
WASHINGTON vs. NEW ORLEANS
Redskins lead series, 7-4;
See New Orleans vs. Washington
WASHINGTON vs. N.Y. GIANTS
Giants lead series, 57-45-3;
See N.Y. Giants vs. Washington
WASHINGTON vs. N.Y. JETS
Redskins lead series, 3-0;
See N.Y. Jets vs. Washington
WASHINGTON vs. PHILADELPHIA
Redskins lead series, 56-38-5;
See Philadelphia vs. Washington
WASHINGTON vs. PITTSBURGH
Redskins lead series, 39-27-3;
See Pittsburgh vs. Washington
WASHINGTON vs. ST. LOUIS
Redskins lead series, 47-32-2;
See St. Louis vs. Washington
WASHINGTON vs. SAN DIEGO
Redskins lead series, 3-0;
See San Diego vs. Washington
WASHINGTON vs. SAN FRANCISCO
49ers lead series, 7-6-1;
See San Francisco vs. Washington
WASHINGTON vs. SEATTLE
Redskins lead series, 2-1;
See Seattle vs. Washington
WASHINGTON vs. TAMPA BAY
Redskins lead series, 2-0;
See Tampa Bay vs. Washington

RESULTS

Game	Date	Winner	Loser	Site	Attendance
XIX	1-20-85	SanFrancisco(NFC)38	Miami (AFC) 16	Stanford	84,059
XVIII	1-22-84	L.A. Raiders (AFC) 38	Washington (NFC) 9	Tampa	72,920
XVII	1-30-83	Washington (NFC) 27	Miami (AFC) 17	Pasadena	103,667
XVI	1-24-82	SanFrancisco(NFC)26	Cincinnati (AFC) 21	Pontiac	81,270
XV	1-25-81	Oakland (AFC) 27	Philadelphia (NFC) 10	New Orleans	76,135
XIV	1-20-80	Pittsburgh (AFC) 31	Los Angeles (NFC) 19	Pasadena	103,985
XIII	1-21-79	Pittsburgh (AFC) 35	Dallas (NFC) 31	Miami	79,484
XII	1-15-78	Dallas (NFC) 27	Denver (AFC) 10	New Orleans	75,583
XI	1- 9-77	Oakland (AFC) 32	Minnesota (NFC) 14	Pasadena	103,438
X	1-18-76	Pittsburgh (AFC) 21	Dallas (NFC) 17	Miami	80,187
IX	1-12-75	Pittsburgh (AFC) 16	Minnesota (NFC) 6	New Orleans	80,997
VIII	1-13-74	Miami (AFC) 24	Minnesota (NFC) 7	Houston	71,882
VII	1-14-73	Miami (AFC) 14	Washington (NFC) 7	Los Angeles	90,182
VI	1-16-72	Dallas (NFC) 24	Miami (AFC) 3	New Orleans	81,023
V	1-17-71	Baltimore (AFC) 16	Dallas (NFC) 13	Miami	79,204
IV	1-11-70	Kansas City (AFL) 23	Minnesota (NFL) 7	New Orleans	80,562
III	1-12-69	N.Y. Jets (AFL) 16	Baltimore (NFL) 7	Miami	75,389
II	1-14-68	Green Bay (NFL) 33	Oakland (AFL) 14	Miami	75,546
I	1-15-67	Green Bay (NFL) 35	Kansas City (AFL) 10	Los Angeles	61,946

SUPER BOWL COMPOSITE STANDINGS

	W	L	Pct	Pts.	OP
Pittsburgh Steelers	4	0	1.000	103	73
Green Bay Packers	2	0	1.000	68	24
San Francisco 49ers	2	0	1.000	64	37
New York Jets	1	0	1.000	16	7
Oakland/L.A. Raiders	3	1	.750	111	66
Baltimore Colts	1	1	.500	23	29
Kansas City Chiefs	1	1	.500	33	42
Dallas Cowboys	2	3	.400	112	85
Miami Dolphins	2	3	.400	74	103
Washington Redskins	1	2	.333	43	69
Cincinnati Bengals	0	1	.000	21	26
Denver Broncos	0	1	.000	10	27
Los Angeles Rams	0	1	.000	19	31
Philadelphia Eagles	0	1	.000	10	27
Minnesota Vikings	0	4	.000	34	95

PAST SUPER BOWL MOST VALUABLE PLAYERS

(Selected by Sport Magazine)

Super Bowl I	— Bart Starr, Green Bay
Super Bowl II	— Bart Starr, Green Bay
Super Bowl III	— Joe Namath, New York Jets
Super Bowl IV	— Len Dawson, Kansas City
Super Bowl V	— Chuck Howley, Dallas
Super Bowl VI	— Roger Staubach, Dallas
Super Bowl VII	— Jake Scott, Miami
Super Bowl VIII	— Larry Csonka, Miami
Super Bowl IX	— Franco Harris, Pittsburgh
Super Bowl X	— Lynn Swann, Pittsburgh
Super Bowl XI	— Fred Biletnikoff, Oakland
Super Bowl XII	— Randy White and Harvey Martin, Dallas
Super Bowl XIII	— Terry Bradshaw, Pittsburgh
Super Bowl XIV	— Terry Bradshaw, Pittsburgh
Super Bowl XV	— Jim Plunkett, Oakland
Super Bowl XVI	— Joe Montana, San Francisco
Super Bowl XVII	— John Riggins, Washington
Super Bowl XVIII	— Marcus Allen, Los Angeles Raiders
Super Bowl XIX	— Joe Montana, San Francisco

SUPER BOWL XIX

Stanford Stadium, Stanford, California   January 20, 1985
Attendance: 84,059

SAN FRANCISCO 38, MIAMI 16—The San Francisco 49ers captured their second Super Bowl title with a dominating offense and a defense that tamed Miami's explosive passing attack. The Dolphins held a 10-7 lead at the end of the first period, which represented the most points scored by two teams in an opening quarter of a Super Bowl. However, the 49ers used excellent field position in the second period to build a 28-16 halftime lead. Running back Roger Craig set a Super Bowl record by scoring three touchdowns on pass receptions of 8 and 16 yards and a run of 2 yards. San Francisco's Joe Montana was voted the game's most valuable player. He joins Green Bay's Bart Starr and Pittsburgh's Terry Bradshaw as the only two-time Super Bowl most valuable players. Montana completed 24 of 35 passes for a Super Bowl-record 331 yards and three touchdowns, and rushed five times for 59 yards, including a six-yard touchdown. Craig had 58 yards on 15 carries and caught seven passes for 77 yards. Wendell Tyler rushed 13 times for 65 yards and had four catches for 70 yards. Dwight Clark had six receptions for 77 yards, while Russ Francis had five for 60. San Francisco's 537 total net yards bettered the previous Super Bowl record of 429 yards by Oakland in Super Bowl XI. The 49ers also held a time of possession advantage over the Dolphins of 37:11 to 22:49.

On defense, the 49ers had four sacks of Miami's Dan Marino, who had not been sacked during the two previous playoff games and had been sacked only 13 times during the 1984 regular season. The 38 points scored by San Francisco tied the Super Bowl record set by the Los Angeles Raiders in their 38-9 win over Washington in Game XVIII last season.

Miami (16)	Offense	San Francisco (38)
Mark Duper	WR	Dwight Clark
Jon Giesler	LT	Bubba Paris
Roy Foster	LG	John Ayers
Dwight Stephenson	C	Fred Quillan
Ed Newman	RG	Randy Cross
Cleveland Green	RT	Keith Fahnhorst
Bruce Hardy	TE	Russ Francis
Mark Clayton	WR	Freddie Solomon
Dan Marino	QB	Joe Montana
Tony Nathan	RB	Wendell Tyler
Woody Bennett	RB	Roger Craig
	Defense	
Doug Betters	LE	Lawrence Pillers
Bob Baumhower	NT	Manu Tuiasosopo
Kim Bokamper	RE	Dwaine Board
Bob Brudzinski	LOLB	Dan Bunz
Jay Brophy	LILB	Riki Ellison
Mark Brown	RILB	Jack Reynolds
Charles Bowser	ROLB	Keena Turner
Don McNeal	LCB	Ronnie Lott
William Judson	RCB	Eric Wright
Glenn Blackwood	SS	Carlton Williamson
Lyle Blackwood	FS	Dwight Hicks

SUBSTITUTIONS

Miami— Offense: K—Uwe von Schamann. P—Reggie Roby. QB—Don Strock. RB—Joe Carter, Eddie Hill. TE—Dan Johnson, Joe Rose. WR—Jimmy Cefalo, Vince Heflin, Jim Jensen, Nat Moore. KR—Fulton Walker. G—Steve Clark, Ronnie Lee, Jeff Toews. Defense: E—Bill Barnett, Charles Benson. T—Mike Charles. LB—A.J. Duhe, Earnie Rhone, Jackie Shipp, Sanders Shiver. CB—Paul Lankford, Robert Sowell. S—Bud Brown, Mike Kozlowski. DNP: FB—Pete Johnson.

San Francisco—Offense: K—Ray Wersching. P—Max Runager. RB—Derrick Harmon, Carl Monroe, Bill Ring. TE—Earl Cooper. WR—Renaldo Nehemiah, Mike Wilson. KR—Dana McLemore. T—Allan Kennedy, Billy Shields. G—Guy McIntyre. Defense: E—Fred Dean, Jim Stuckey. T—Michael Carter, Gary Johnson, Louie Kelcher, Jeff Stover. LB—Milt McColl, Blanchard Montgomery, Todd Shell, Mike Walter. CB—Tom Holmoe. S—Jeff Fuller. DNP: QB—Matt Cavanaugh, TE—John Frank, CB—Mario Clark.

OFFICIALS

Referee—Pat Haggerty. Umpire: Tom Hensley. Head Linesman: Leo Miles. Line Judge: Ray Dodez. Back Judge: Tom Kelleher. Side Judge: Bill Quinby. Field Judge: Bob Lewis.

SCORING

Miami (AFC)	10	6	0	0 — 16	
San Francisco (NFC)	7	21	10	0 — 38	

Mia —FG von Schamann 37
SF —Monroe 33 pass from Montana (Wersching kick)
Mia —D. Johnson 2 pass from Marino (von Schamann kick)
SF —Craig 8 pass from Montana (Wersching kick)
SF —Montana 6 run (Wersching kick)
SF —Craig 2 run (Wersching kick)
Mia —FG von Schamann 31
Mia —FG von Schamann 30
SF —FG Wersching 27
SF —Craig 16 pass from Montana (Wersching kick)

TEAM STATISTICS

	Miami	San Francisco
Total First Downs	19	31
First Downs Rushing	2	16
First Downs Passing	17	15
First Downs Penalty	0	0
Total Net Yardage	314	537
Total Offensive Plays	63	76
Average Gain per Offensive Play	5.0	7.1
Rushes	9	40
Yards Gained Rushing (net)	25	211
Average Yards per Rush	2.8	5.3
Passes Attempted	50	35
Passes Completed	29	24
Had Intercepted	2	0
Times Tackled Attempting to Pass	4	1
Yards Lost Attempting to Pass	29	5
Yards Gained Passing (net)	289	326
Punts	6	3
Average Distance	39.3	32.7
Punt Returns	2	5

Punt Return Yardage	15	51
Kickoff Returns	7	4
Kickoff Return Yardage	140	40
Interception Return Yardage	0	0
Total Return Yardage	155	91
Fumbles	1	2
Own Fumbles Recovered	1	0
Opponent Fumbles Recovered	2	0
Penalties	1	2
Yards Penalized	10	10
Total Points Scored	16	38
Touchdowns	1	5
Touchdowns Rushing	0	2
Touchdowns Passing	1	3
Touchdown Returns	0	0
Extra Points	1	5
Field Goals	3	1
Field Goals Attempted	3	1
Third Down Efficiency	4/12	6/11
Fourth Down Efficiency	0/0	0/1
Time of Possession	22:49	37:11

INDIVIDUAL STATISTICS

RUSHING

Miami	Att.	Yds.	LG	TD
Nathan	5	18	16	0
Bennett	3	7	7	0
Marino	1	0	0	0

San Fran.	Att.	Yds.	LG	TD
Tyler	13	65	9	0
Montana	5	59	19	1
Craig	15	58	10	1
Harmon	5	20	7	0
Solomon	1	5	5	0
Cooper	1	4	4	0

PASSING

Miami	Att.	Comp.	Yds.	TD	Int.
Marino	50	29	318	1	2

San Fran.	Att.	Comp.	Yds.	TD	Int.
Montana	35	24	331	3	0

RECEIVING

Miami	No.	Yds.	LG	TD
Nathan	10	83	25	0
Clayton	6	92	27	0
Rose	6	73	30	0
D. Johnson	3	28	21	1
Moore	2	17	9	0
Cefalo	1	14	14	0
Duper	1	11	11	0

San Fran.	No.	Yds.	LG	TD
Craig	7	77	20	2
D. Clark	6	77	33	0
Francis	5	60	19	0
Tyler	4	70	40	0
Monroe	1	33	33t	1
Solomon	1	14	14	0

INTERCEPTIONS

Miami	No.	Yds.	LG	TD
None				

San Fran.	No.	Yds.	LG	TD
Williamson	1	0	0	0
Wright	1	0	0	0

PUNTING

Miami	No.	Avg.	LG	Blk.
Roby	6	39.3	51	0

San Fran.	No.	Avg.	LG	Blk.
Runager	3	32.7	35	0

PUNT RETURNS

Miami	No.	FC	Yds.	LG	TD
Walker	2	0	15	9	0

San Fran.	No.	FC	Yds.	LG	TD
McLemore	5	0	51	28	0

KICKOFF RETURNS

Miami	No.	Yds.	LG	TD
Walker	4	93	28	0
Hardy	2	31	16	0
Hill	1	16	16	0

San Fran.	No.	Yds.	LG	TD
Harmon	2	24	23	0
Monroe	1	16	16	0
McIntyre	1	0	0	0

SUPER BOWL XVIII

Tampa Stadium, Tampa, Florida   January 22, 1984
Attendance: 72,920

LOS ANGELES RAIDERS 38, WASHINGTON 9—The Los Angeles Raiders dominated the Washington Redskins from the beginning in Super Bowl XVIII and achieved the most lopsided victory in Super Bowl history, surpassing Green Bay's 35-10 win over Kansas City in Super Bowl I. The Raiders took a 7-0 lead 4:52 into the game when Derrick Jensen blocked a Jeff Hayes punt and recovered it in the end zone for a touchdown. With 9:14 remaining in the first half, Raiders quarterback Jim Plunkett threw a 12-yard touchdown pass to wide receiver Cliff Branch to complete a three-play, 65-yard drive. Washington cut the Raiders' lead to 14-3 on a 24-yard field goal by Mark Moseley. With seven seconds left in the first half, Raiders linebacker Jack Squirek intercepted a Joe Theismann pass at the Redskins' 5-yard line and ran it in for a touchdown to give Los Angeles a 21-3 halftime lead. In the third period, running back Marcus Allen, who rushed for a Super Bowl record 191 yards on 20 carries, increased the Raiders' lead to 35-3 on touchdown runs of 5 and 74 yards, the latter erasing the previous Super Bowl record of 58 yards set by Baltimore's Tom Matte in Game III. Allen was named the game's most valuable player. The victory over Washington raised Raiders coach Tom Flores' playoff record to 8-1, including a 27-10 win against Philadelphia in Super Bowl XV. The 38 points scored by the Raiders was the highest point total by a Super Bowl team. The previous high was 35 points by Green Bay in Game I.

SCORING

Washington (NFC)	0	3	6	0	— 9
L.A. Raiders (AFC)	7	14	14	3	— 38

Raiders—Jensen recovered blocked punt in end zone (Bahr kick)
Raiders—Branch 12 pass from Plunkett (Bahr kick)
Wash   —FG Moseley 24
Raiders—Squirek 5 interception return (Bahr kick)
Wash   —Riggins 1 run (kick blocked)
Raiders—Allen 5 run (Bahr kick)
Raiders—Allen 74 run (Bahr kick)
Raiders—FG Bahr 21

SUPER BOWL XVII

Rose Bowl, Pasadena, California   January 30, 1983
Attendance: 103,667

WASHINGTON 27, MIAMI 17—Fullback John Riggins' Super Bowl record 166 yards on 38 carries sparked Washington to a 27-17 victory over AFC champion Miami. It was Riggins' fourth straight 100-yard rushing game during the play-offs, also a record. The win marked Washington's first NFL title since 1942, and was only the second time in Super Bowl history NFC teams scored consecutive victories (Green Bay did it in Super Bowls I and II and San Francisco won Super Bowl XVI). The Redskins, under second-year head coach Joe Gibbs, used a balanced offense that accounted for 400 total yards (a Super Bowl record 276 yards rushing and 124 passing), second in Super Bowl history to 429 yards by Oakland in Super Bowl XI. The Dolphins built a 17-10 lead on a 76-yard touchdown pass from quarterback David Woodley to wide receiver Jimmy Cefalo 6:49 into the first period, a 20-yard field goal by Uwe von Schamann with 6:00 left in the half, and a Super Bowl record 98-yard kickoff return by Fulton Walker with 1:38 remaining. Washington had tied the score at 10-10 with 1:51 left on a four-yard touchdown pass from Joe Theismann to wide receiver Alvin Garrett. Mark Moseley started the Redskins' scoring with a 31-yard field goal late in the first period, and added a 20-yarder midway through the third period to cut the Dolphins' lead to 17-13. Riggins, who was voted the game's most valuable player, gave Washington its first lead of the game with 10:01 left when he ran 43 yards off left tackle for a touchdown on a fourth-and-one situation. Wide receiver Charlie Brown caught a six-yard scoring pass from Theismann with 1:55 left to complete the scoring. The Dolphins managed only 176 yards (142 in first half). Theismann completed 15 of 23 passes for 143 yards, two touchdowns, and had two interceptions. For Miami, Woodley was 4 of 14 for 97 yards, with one touchdown, and one interception. Don Strock was 0 for 3 in relief.

SCORING

Miami (AFC)	7	10	0	0	— 17
Washington (NFC)	0	10	3	14	— 27

Mia   —Cefalo 76 pass from Woodley (von Schamann kick)
Wash—FG Moseley 31
Mia   —FG von Schamann 20
Wash—Garrett 4 pass from Theismann (Moseley kick)
Mia   —Walker 98 kickoff return (von Schamann kick)
Wash—FG Moseley 20
Wash—Riggins 43 run (Moseley kick)
Wash—Brown 6 pass from Theismann (Moseley kick)

SUPER BOWL XVI

Pontiac Silverdome, Pontiac, Michigan   January 24, 1982
Attendance: 81,270

SAN FRANCISCO 26, CINCINNATI 21—Ray Wersching's Super Bowl record-tying four field goals and Joe Montana's controlled passing helped lift the San Francisco 49ers to their first NFL championship with a 26-21 victory over Cincinnati. The 49ers built a game-record 20-0 halftime lead via Montana's one-yard touchdown run, which capped an 11-play, 68-yard drive; fullback Earl Cooper's 11-yard scoring pass from Montana, which climaxed a Super Bowl record 92-yard drive on 12 plays; and Wersching's 22- and 26-yard field goals. The Bengals rebounded in the second half, closing the gap to 20-14 on quarterback Ken Anderson's five-yard run and Dan Ross's four-yard reception from Anderson, who established Super Bowl passing records for completions (25) and completion percentage (73.5 percent on 25 of 34). Wersching added early fourth-period field goals of 40 and 23 yards to increase the 49ers' lead to 26-14. The Bengals managed to score on an Anderson-to-Ross three-yard pass with only 16 seconds remaining. Ross set a Super Bowl record with 11 receptions for 104 yards. Montana, the game's most valuable player, completed 14 of 22 passes for 157 yards. Cincinnati compiled 356 yards to San Francisco's 275, which marked the first time in Super Bowl history that the team that gained the most yards from scrimmage lost the game.

San Francisco (NFC)	7	13	0	6	— 26
Cincinnati (AFC)	0	0	7	14	— 21

SF —Montana 1 run (Wersching kick)
SF —Cooper 11 pass from Montana (Wersching kick)
SF —FG Wersching 22
SF —FG Wersching 26
Cin—Anderson 5 run (Breech kick)
Cin—Ross 4 pass from Anderson (Breech kick)
SF —FG Wersching 40
SF —FG Wersching 23
Cin—Ross 3 pass from Anderson (Breech kick)

SUPER BOWL XV

Louisiana Superdome, New Orleans, Louisiana   January 25, 1981
Attendance: 76,135

OAKLAND 27, PHILADELPHIA 10—Jim Plunkett threw three touchdown passes, including an 80-yarder to Kenny King, as the Raiders became the first wild card team to win the Super Bowl. Plunkett's touchdown bomb to King—the longest play in Super Bowl history—gave Oakland a decisive 14-0 lead with nine seconds left in the first period. Linebacker Rod Martin had set up Oakland's first touchdown, a two-yard reception by Cliff Branch, with a 16-yard interception return to the Eagles' 32 yard line. The Eagles never recovered from that early deficit, managing only a Tony Franklin field goal (30 yards) and an eight-yard touchdown pass from Ron Jaworski to Keith Krepfle the rest of the game. Plunkett, who became a starter in the sixth game of the season, completed 13 of 21 for 261 yards and was named the game's most valuable player. Oakland won 9 of 11 games with Plunkett starting, but that was good enough only for second place in the AFC West, although they tied division winner San Diego with an 11-5 record. The Raiders, who had previously won Super Bowl XI over Minnesota, had to win three playoff games to get to the championship game. Oakland defeated Houston 27-7 at home followed by road victories over Cleveland, 14-12 and San Diego, 34-27. Oakland's Mark van Eeghen was the game's leading rusher with 80 yards on 19 carries. Philadelphia's Wilbert Montgomery led all receivers with six receptions for 91 yards. Branch had five for 67 and Harold Carmichael of Philadelphia five for 83. Martin finished the game with three interceptions, a Super Bowl record.

Oakland (AFC)	14	0	10	3 — 27
Philadelphia (NFC)	0	3	0	7 — 10

Oak—Branch 2 pass from Plunkett (Bahr kick)
Oak—King 80 pass from Plunkett (Bahr kick)
Phil—FG Franklin 30
Oak—Branch 29 pass from Plunkett (Bahr kick)
Oak—FG Bahr 46
Phil—Krepfle 8 pass from Jaworski (Franklin kick)
Oak—FG Bahr 35

SUPER BOWL XIV

Rose Bowl, Pasadena, California   January 20, 1980
Attendance: 103,985

PITTSBURGH 31, LOS ANGELES 19—Terry Bradshaw completed 14 of 21 passes for 309 yards and set two passing records as the Steelers became the first team to win four Super Bowls. Despite three interceptions by the Rams, Bradshaw kept his poise and brought the Steelers from behind in the second half. Trailing 13-10 at halftime, Pittsburgh went ahead 17-13 when Bradshaw hit Lynn Swann with a 47-yard touchdown pass after 2:48 of the third quarter. On the Rams' next possession Vince Ferragamo, who completed 15 of 25 passes for 212 yards, responded with a 50-yard pass to Billy Waddy that moved Los Angeles from its own 26 to the Steelers' 24. On the following play, Lawrence McCutcheon connected with Ron Smith on a halfback option pass that gave the Rams a 19-17 lead. On Pittsburgh's initial possession of the final period, Bradshaw lofted a 73-yard scoring pass to John Stallworth to put the Steelers in front to stay, 24-19. Franco Harris scored on a one-yard run later in the quarter to seal the verdict. A 45-yard pass from Bradshaw to Stallworth was the key play in the drive to Harris's score. Bradshaw, the game's most valuable player for the second straight year, set career Super Bowl records for most touchdown passes (nine) and most passing yards (932). Larry Anderson gave the Steelers excellent field position throughout the game with five kickoff returns for a record 162 yards.

Los Angeles (NFC)	7	6	6	0 — 19
Pittsburgh (AFC)	3	7	7	14 — 31

Pitt—FG Bahr 41
LA—Bryant 1 run (Corral kick)
Pitt—Harris 1 run (Bahr kick)
LA—FG Corral 31
LA—FG Corral 45
Pitt—Swann 47 pass from Bradshaw (Bahr kick)
LA—Smith 24 pass from McCutcheon (kick failed)
Pitt—Stallworth 73 pass from Bradshaw (Bahr kick)
Pitt—Harris 1 run (Bahr kick)

SUPER BOWL XIII

Orange Bowl, Miami, Florida   January 21, 1979
Attendance: 79,484

PITTSBURGH 35, DALLAS 31—Terry Bradshaw threw a record four touchdown passes to lead the Steelers to victory. The Steelers became the first team to win three Super Bowls, mostly because of Bradshaw's accurate arm. Bradshaw, voted the game's most valuable player, completed 17 of 30 passes for 318 yards, a personal high. Three of those passes went for touchdowns—two to John Stallworth and the third, with 26 seconds remaining in the second period, to Rocky Bleier. The Cowboys scored twice before intermission on Roger Staubach's 39-yard pass to Tony Hill and a 37-yard run by linebacker Mike Hegman, who stole the ball from Bradshaw. The Steelers broke open the contest with two touchdowns in a span of 19 seconds midway through the final period. Franco Harris rambled 22 yards up the middle to give the Steelers a 28-17 lead with 7:10 left. Pittsburgh got the ball right back when Randy White fumbled the kickoff and Dennis Winston recovered for the Steelers. On first down, Bradshaw hit Lynn Swann with an 18-yard scoring pass to boost the Steelers' lead to 35-17 with 6:51 to play. The Cowboys refused to let the Steelers run away with the contest. Staubach connected with Billy Joe DuPree on a seven-yard scoring pass with 2:23 left. Then the Cowboys recovered an onside kick and Staubach took them in for another score, passing four yards to Butch Johnson with 22 seconds remaining. Bleier recovered another onside kick with 17 seconds left to seal the victory for the Steelers.

Pittsburgh (AFC)	7	14	0	14 — 35
Dallas (NFC)	7	7	3	14 — 31

Pitt—Stallworth 28 pass from Bradshaw (Gerela kick)
Dall—Hill 39 pass from Staubach (Septien kick)
Dall—Hegman 37 fumble recovery return (Septien kick)
Pitt—Stallworth 75 pass from Bradshaw (Gerela kick)
Pitt—Bleier 7 pass from Bradshaw (Gerela kick)
Dall—FG Septien 27
Pitt—Harris 22 run (Gerela kick)
Pitt—Swann 18 pass from Bradshaw (Gerela kick)
Dall—DuPree 7 pass from Staubach (Septien kick)

Dall—B. Johnson 4 pass from Staubach (Septien kick)

SUPER BOWL XII

Louisiana Superdome, New Orleans, Louisiana   January 15, 1978
Attendance: 75,583

DALLAS 27, DENVER 10—The Cowboys evened their Super Bowl record at 2-2 by defeating Denver before a sellout crowd of 75,583, plus 102,010,000 television viewers, the largest audience ever to watch a sporting event. Dallas converted two interceptions into 10 points and Efren Herrera added a 35-yard field goal for a 13-0 halftime advantage. In the third period Craig Morton engineered a drive to the Cowboys' 30 and Jim Turner's 47-yard field goal made the score 13-3. After an exchange of punts, Butch Johnson made a spectacular diving catch in the end zone to complete a 45-yard pass from Roger Staubach and put the Cowboys ahead 20-3. Following Rick Upchurch's 67-yard kickoff return, Norris Weese guided the Broncos to a touchdown to cut the Dallas lead to 20-10. Dallas clinched the victory when running back Robert Newhouse threw a 29-yard touchdown pass to Golden Richards with 7:04 remaining in the game. It was the first pass thrown by Newhouse since 1975. Harvey Martin and Randy White, who were named co-most valuable players, led the Cowboys' defense, which recovered four fumbles and intercepted four passes.

Dallas (NFC)	10	3	7	7 — 27
Denver (AFC)	0	0	10	0 — 10

Dall—Dorsett 3 run (Herrera kick)
Dall—FG Herrera 35
Dall—FG Herrera 43
Den—FG Turner 47
Dall—Johnson 45 pass from Staubach (Herrera kick)
Den—Lytle 1 run (Turner kick)
Dall—Richards 29 pass from Newhouse (Herrera kick)

SUPER BOWL XI

Rose Bowl, Pasadena, California   January 9, 1977
Attendance: 103,438

OAKLAND 32, MINNESOTA 14—The Raiders won their first NFL championship before a record Super Bowl crowd plus 81 million television viewers, the largest audience ever to watch a sporting event. The Raiders gained a record-breaking 429 yards, including running back Clarence Davis's 137 yards rushing, and wide receiver Fred Biletnikoff made four key receptions, which earned him the game's most valuable player trophy. Oakland scored on three successive possessions in the second quarter to build a 16-0 halftime lead. Errol Mann's 24-yard field goal opened the scoring, then the AFC champions put together drives of 64 and 35 yards, scoring on a one-yard pass from Ken Stabler to Dave Casper and a one-yard run by Pete Banaszak. The Raiders increased their lead to 19-0 on a 40-yard field goal in the third quarter, but Minnesota responded with a 12-play, 58-yard drive late in the period, with Fran Tarkenton passing eight yards to wide receiver Sammy White to cut the deficit to 19-7. Two fourth quarter interceptions clinched the title for the Raiders. One set up Banaszak's second touchdown run, the other resulted in cornerback Willie Brown's Super Bowl record 75-yard interception return.

Oakland (AFC)	0	16	3	13 — 32
Minnesota (NFC)	0	0	7	7 — 14

Oak—FG Mann 24
Oak—Casper 1 pass from Stabler (Mann kick)
Oak—Banaszak 1 run (kick failed)
Oak—FG Mann 40
Minn—S. White 8 pass from Tarkenton (Cox kick)
Oak—Banaszak 2 run (Mann kick)
Oak—Brown 75 interception return (kick failed)
Minn—Voigt 13 pass from Lee (Cox kick)

SUPER BOWL X

Orange Bowl, Miami, Florida   January 18, 1976
Attendance: 80,187

PITTSBURGH 21, DALLAS 17—The Steelers won the Super Bowl for the second year in a row on Terry Bradshaw's 64-yard touchdown pass to Lynn Swann and an aggressive defense that snuffed out a late rally by the Cowboys with an end zone interception on the final play of the game. In the fourth quarter Pittsburgh ran on fourth down and gave up the ball on the Cowboys' 39 with 1:22 to play. Staubach ran and passed for two first downs but his last desperation pass was picked off by Glen Edwards. Dallas's scoring was the result of two touchdown passes by Staubach, one to Drew Pearson for 29 yards and the other to Percy Howard for 34 yards. Toni Fritsch had a 36-yard field goal. The Steelers scored on two touchdown passes by Bradshaw, one to Randy Grossman for seven yards and the long bomb to Swann. Roy Gerela had 36- and 18-yard field goals. Reggie Harrison blocked a punt through the end zone for a safety. Swann set a Super Bowl record by gaining 161 yards on his four receptions.

Dallas (NFC)	7	3	0	7 — 17
Pittsburgh (AFC)	7	0	0	14 — 21

Dall—D. Pearson 29 pass from Staubach (Fritsch kick)
Pitt—Grossman 7 pass from Bradshaw (Gerela kick)
Dall—FG Fritsch 36
Pitt—Safety, Harrison blocked Hoopes's punt through end zone
Pitt—FG Gerela 36
Pitt—FG Gerela 18
Pitt—Swann 64 pass from Bradshaw (kick failed)
Dall—P. Howard 34 pass from Staubach (Fritsch kick)

SUPER BOWL IX

Tulane Stadium, New Orleans, Louisiana   January 12, 1975
Attendance: 80,997

PITTSBURGH 16, MINNESOTA 6—AFC champion Pittsburgh, in its initial Super Bowl appearance, and NFC champion Minnesota, making a third bid for its first Super Bowl title, struggled through a first half in which the only score was produced by the Steelers' defense when Dwight White downed Vikings' quarterback Fran Tarkenton in the end zone for a safety 7:49 into the second period. The Steelers forced another break and took advantage on the second half kickoff when Minnesota's Bill Brown fumbled and Marv Kellum recovered for Pittsburgh on the Vikings' 30. After Rocky Bleier failed to gain on first down, Franco Harris carried three consecutive times for 24 yards, a loss of 3, and a 12-yard touchdown for a 9-0 lead. Though its offense was completely stymied by Pittsburgh's defense, Minnesota managed to move into a threatening position after 4:27 of the final period when Matt Blair blocked Bobby Walden's punt and Terry Brown recovered the ball in the end zone for a touchdown. Fred Cox's kick failed and the Steelers led 9-6. Pittsburgh wasted no time putting the victory away. The Steelers took the ensuing kickoff and marched 66 yards in 11 plays, climaxed by Terry Bradshaw's four-yard scoring pass to Larry Brown with 3:31 left. Pittsburgh's defense permitted Minnesota only 119 yards total offense, including a Super Bowl low of 17 yards rushing. The Steelers, meanwhile, gained 333 yards, including Harris's record 158 yards on 34 carries.

Pittsburgh (AFC)	0	2	7	7	— 16
Minnesota (NFC)	0	0	0	6	— 6

Pitt—Safety, White downed Tarkenton in end zone
Pitt—Harris 12 run (Gerela kick)
Minn—T. Brown recovered blocked punt in end zone (kick failed)
Pitt—L. Brown 4 pass from Bradshaw (Gerela kick)

SUPER BOWL VIII

Rice Stadium, Houston, Texas   January 13, 1974
Attendance: 71,882

MIAMI 24, MINNESOTA 7—The defending NFL champion Dolphins, representing the AFC for the third straight year, scored the first two times they had possession on marches of 62 and 56 yards in the first period while the Miami defense limited the Vikings to only seven plays. Larry Csonka climaxed the initial 10-play drive with a five-yard touchdown bolt through right guard after 5:27 had elapsed. Four plays later, Miami began another 10-play scoring drive, which ended with Jim Kiick bursting one yard through the middle for another touchdown after 13:38 of the period. Garo Yepremian added a 28-yard field goal midway in the second period for a 17-0 Miami lead. Minnesota then drove from its 20 to a second-and-two situation on the Miami 7 yard line with 1:18 left in the half. But on two plays, Miami limited Oscar Reed to one yard. On fourth-and-one from the 6, Reed went over right tackle, but Dolphins middle linebacker Nick Buoniconti jarred the ball loose and Jake Scott recovered for Miami to halt the Minnesota threat. The Vikings were unable to muster enough offense in the second half to threaten the Dolphins. Csonka rushed 33 times for a Super Bowl record 145 yards. Bob Griese of Miami completed six of seven passes for 73 yards.

Minnesota (NFC)	0	0	0	7	— 7
Miami (AFC)	14	3	7	0	— 24

Mia—Csonka 5 run (Yepremian kick)
Mia—Kiick 1 run (Yepremian kick)
Mia—FG Yepremian 28
Mia—Csonka 2 run (Yepremian kick)
Minn—Tarkenton 4 run (Cox kick)

SUPER BOWL VII

Memorial Coliseum, Los Angeles, California   January 14, 1973
Attendance: 90,182

MIAMI 14, WASHINGTON 7—The Dolphins played virtually perfect football in the first half as their defense permitted the Redskins to cross midfield only once and their offense turned good field position into two touchdowns. On its third possession, Miami opened its first scoring drive from the Dolphins' 37 yard line. An 18-yard pass from Bob Griese to Paul Warfield preceded by three plays Griese's 28-yard touchdown pass to Howard Twilley. After Washington moved from its 17 to the Miami 48 with two minutes remaining in the first half, Dolphins linebacker Nick Buoniconti intercepted a Billy Kilmer pass at the Miami 41 and returned it to the Washington 27. Jim Kiick ran for three yards, Larry Csonka for three, Griese passed to Jim Mandich for 19, and Kiick gained one to the 1 yard line. With 18 seconds left until intermission, Kiick scored from the 1. Washington's only touchdown came with 7:07 left in the game and resulted from a misplayed field goal attempt and fumble by Garo Yepremian, with the Redskins' Mike Bass picking the ball out of the air and running 49 yards for the score.

Miami (AFC)	7	7	0	0	— 14
Washington (NFC)	0	0	0	7	— 7

Mia—Twilley 28 pass from Griese (Yepremian kick)
Mia—Kiick 1 run (Yepremian kick)
Wash—Bass 49 fumble recovery return (Knight kick)

SUPER BOWL VI

Tulane Stadium, New Orleans, Louisiana   January 16, 1972
Attendance: 81,023

DALLAS 24, MIAMI 3—The Cowboys rushed for a record 252 yards and their defense limited the Dolphins to a low of 185 yards while not permitting a touchdown for the first time in Super Bowl history. Dallas converted Chuck Howley's recovery of Larry Csonka's first fumble of the season into a 3-0 advantage and

led at halftime 10-3. After Dallas received the second half kickoff, Duane Thomas led a 71-yard march in eight plays for a 17-3 margin. Howley intercepted Bob Griese's pass at the 50 and returned it to the Miami 9 early in the fourth period, and three plays later Roger Staubach passed seven yards to Mike Ditka for the final touchdown. Thomas rushed for 95 yards and Walt Garrison gained 74. Staubach, voted the game's most valuable player, completed 12 of 19 passes for 119 yards and two touchdowns.

Dallas (NFC)	3	7	7	7	— 24
Miami (AFC)	0	3	0	0	— 3

Dall—FG Clark 9
Dall—Alworth 7 pass from Staubach (Clark kick)
Mia—FG Yepremian 31
Dall—D. Thomas 3 run (Clark kick)
Dall—Ditka 7 pass from Staubach (Clark kick)

SUPER BOWL V

Orange Bowl, Miami, Florida   January 17, 1971
Attendance: 79,204

BALTIMORE 16, DALLAS 13—A 32-yard field goal by first-year kicker Jim O'Brien brought the Baltimore Colts a victory over the Dallas Cowboys in the final five seconds of Super Bowl V. The game between the champions of the AFC and NFC was played on artificial turf for the first time. Dallas led 13-6 at the half but interceptions by Rick Volk and Mike Curtis set up a Baltimore touchdown and O'Brien's decisive kick in the fourth period. Earl Morrall relieved an injured Johnny Unitas late in the first half, although Unitas completed the Colts' only scoring pass. It caromed off receiver Eddie Hinton's finger tips, off Dallas defensive back Mel Renfro, and finally settled into the grasp of John Mackey, who went 45 yards to score on a 75-yard play.

Baltimore (AFC)	0	6	0	10	— 16
Dallas (NFC)	3	10	0	0	— 13

Dall—FG Clark 14
Dall—FG Clark 30
Balt—Mackey 75 pass from Unitas (kick blocked)
Dall—Thomas 7 pass from Morton (Clark kick)
Balt—Nowatzke 2 run (O'Brien kick)
Balt—FG O'Brien 32

SUPER BOWL IV

Tulane Stadium, New Orleans, Louisiana   January 11, 1970
Attendance: 80,562

KANSAS CITY 23, MINNESOTA 7—The AFL squared the Super Bowl at two games apiece with the NFL, building a 16-0 halftime lead behind Len Dawson's superb quarterbacking and a powerful defense. Dawson, the fourth consecutive quarterback to be chosen the Super Bowl's top player, called an almost flawless game, completing 12 of 17 passes and hitting Otis Taylor on a 46-yard play for the final Chiefs touchdown. The Kansas City defense limited Minnesota's strong rushing game to 67 yards and had three interceptions and two fumble recoveries. The crowd of 80,562 set a Super Bowl record, as did the gross receipts of $3,817,872.69.

Minnesota (NFL)	0	0	7	0	— 7
Kansas City (AFL)	3	13	7	0	— 23

KC—FG Stenerud 48
KC—FG Stenerud 32
KC—FG Stenerud 25
KC—Garrett 5 run (Stenerud kick)
Minn—Osborn 4 run (Cox kick)
KC—Taylor 46 pass from Dawson (Stenerud kick)

SUPER BOWL III

Orange Bowl, Miami, Florida   January 12, 1969
Attendance: 75,389

NEW YORK JETS 16, BALTIMORE 7—Jets quarterback Joe Namath "guaranteed" victory on the Thursday before the game, then went out and led the AFL to its first Super Bowl victory over a Baltimore team that had lost only once in 16 games all season. Namath, chosen the outstanding player, completed 17 of 28 passes for 206 yards and directed a steady attack that dominated the NFL champions after the Jets' defense had intercepted Colts quarterback Earl Morrall three times in the first half. The Jets had 337 total yards, including 121 yards rushing by Matt Snell. Johnny Unitas, who had missed most of the season with a sore elbow, came off the bench and led Baltimore to its only touchdown late in the fourth quarter after New York led 16-0.

New York Jets (AFL)	0	7	6	3	— 16
Baltimore (NFL)	0	0	0	7	— 7

NYJ—Snell 4 run (Turner kick)
NYJ—FG Turner 32
NYJ—FG Turner 30
NYJ—FG Turner 9
Balt—Hill 1 run (Michaels kick)

SUPER BOWL II

Orange Bowl, Miami, Florida   January 14, 1968
Attendance: 75,546

GREEN BAY 33, OAKLAND 14—Green Bay, after winning its third consecutive NFL championship, won the Super Bowl title for the second straight year 33-14 over the AFL champion Raiders in a game that drew the first $3 million dollar gate in football history. Bart Starr again was chosen the game's most valuable player as he completed 13 of 24 passes for 202 yards and one touchdown and directed a Packers attack that was in control all the way after building a 16-7 halftime lead. Don Chandler kicked four field goals and all-pro cornerback Herb Adderley capped the Green Bay scoring with a 60-yard run with an interception. The game marked the last for Vince Lombardi as Packers coach, ending nine years at Green Bay in which he won six Western Conference championships, five NFL championships, and two Super Bowls.

Green Bay (NFL)	3	13	10	7	— 33
Oakland (AFL)	0	7	0	7	— 14

GB —FG Chandler 39
GB —FG Chandler 20
GB —Dowler 62 pass from Starr (Chandler kick)
Oak—Miller 23 pass from Lamonica (Blanda kick)
GB —FG Chandler 43
GB —Anderson 2 run (Chandler kick)
GB —FG Chandler 31
GB —Adderley 60 interception return (Chandler kick)
Oak—Miller 23 pass from Lamonica (Blanda kick)

SUPER BOWL I

Memorial Coliseum, Los Angeles, California   January 15, 1967
Attendance: 61,946

GREEN BAY 35, KANSAS CITY 10—The Green Bay Packers opened the Super Bowl series by defeating Kansas City's American Football League champions 35-10 behind the passing of Bart Starr, the receiving of Max McGee, and a key interception by all-pro safety Willie Wood. Green Bay broke open the game with three second-half touchdowns, the first of which was set up by Wood's 40-yard return of an interception to the Chiefs' 5 yard line. McGee, filling in for ailing Boyd Dowler after having caught only three passes all season, caught seven from Starr for 138 yards and two touchdowns. Elijah Pitts ran for two other scores. The Chiefs' 10 points came in the second quarter, the only touchdown on a seven-yard pass from Len Dawson to Curtis McClinton. Starr completed 16 of 23 passes for 250 yards and two touchdowns and was chosen the most valuable player. The Packers collected $15,000 per man and the Chiefs $7,500—the largest single-game shares in the history of team sports.

Kansas City (AFL)	0	10	0	0	— 10
Green Bay (NFL)	7	7	14	7	— 35

GB—McGee 37 pass from Starr (Chandler kick)
KC—McClinton 7 pass from Dawson (Mercer kick)
GB—Taylor 14 run (Chandler kick)
KC—FG Mercer 31
GB—Pitts 5 run (Chandler kick)
GB—McGee 13 pass from Starr (Chandler kick)
GB—Pitts 1 run (Chandler kick)

AFC Championship Game

Includes AFL Championship Games (1960-69)

RESULTS

Season	Date	Winner (Share)	Loser (Share)	Score	Site	Attendance
1984	Jan. 6	Miami ($18,000)	Pittsburgh ($18,000)	45-28	Miami	76,029
1983	Jan. 8	L.A. Raiders ($18,000)	Seattle ($18,000)	30-14	Los Angeles	91,445
1982	Jan. 23	Miami ($18,000)	N.Y. Jets ($18,000)	14-0	Miami	67,396
1981	Jan. 10	Cincinnati ($9,000)	San Diego ($9,000)	27-7	Cincinnati	46,302
1980	Jan. 11	Oakland ($9,000)	San Diego ($9,000)	34-27	San Diego	52,675
1979	Jan. 6	Pittsburgh ($9,000)	Houston ($9,000)	27-13	Pittsburgh	50,475
1978	Jan. 7	Pittsburgh ($9,000)	Houston ($9,000)	34-5	Pittsburgh	50,725
1977	Jan. 1	Denver ($9,000)	Oakland ($9,000)	20-17	Denver	75,044
1976	Dec. 26	Oakland ($8,500)	Pittsburgh ($5,500)	24-7	Oakland	53,821
1975	Jan. 4	Pittsburgh ($8,500)	Oakland ($5,500)	16-10	Pittsburgh	50,609
1974	Dec. 29	Pittsburgh ($8,500)	Oakland ($5,500)	24-13	Oakland	53,800
1973	Dec. 30	Miami ($8,500)	Oakland ($5,500)	27-10	Miami	79,325
1972	Dec. 31	Miami ($8,500)	Pittsburgh ($5,500)	21-17	Pittsburgh	50,845
1971	Jan. 2	Miami ($8,500)	Baltimore ($5,500)	21-0	Miami	76,622
1970	Jan. 3	Baltimore ($8,500)	Oakland ($5,500)	27-17	Baltimore	54,799
1969	Jan. 4	Kansas City ($7,755)	Oakland ($6,252)	17-7	Oakland	53,564
1968	Dec. 29	N.Y. Jets ($7,007)	Oakland ($5,349)	27-23	New York	62,627
1967	Dec. 31	Oakland ($6,321)	Houston ($4,996)	40-7	Oakland	53,330
1966	Jan. 1	Kansas City ($5,309)	Buffalo ($3,799)	31-7	Buffalo	42,080
1965	Dec. 26	Buffalo ($5,189)	San Diego ($3,447)	23-0	San Diego	30,361
1964	Dec. 26	Buffalo ($2,668)	San Diego ($1,738)	20-7	Buffalo	40,242
1963	Jan. 5	San Diego ($2,498)	Boston ($1,596)	51-10	San Diego	30,127
1962	Dec. 23	Dallas ($2,206)	Houston ($1,471)	20-17*	Houston	37,981
1961	Dec. 24	Houston ($1,792)	San Diego ($1,111)	10-3	San Diego	29,556
1960	Jan. 1	Houston ($1,025)	Los Angeles ($718)	24-16	Houston	32,183

Sudden death overtime.

AFC CHAMPIONSHIP GAME COMPOSITE STANDINGS

	W	L	Pct.	Pts.	OP
Miami Dolphins	5	0	1.000	128	55
Kansas City Chiefs*	3	0	1.000	68	31
Cincinnati Bengals	1	0	1.000	27	7
Denver Broncos	1	0	1.000	20	17
Buffalo Bills	2	1	.667	50	38
Pittsburgh Steelers	4	3	.571	153	131
Baltimore Colts	1	1	.500	27	38
New York Jets	1	1	.500	27	37
Oakland/L.A. Raiders	4	7	.364	225	213
Houston Oilers	2	4	.333	76	140
San Diego Chargers**	1	6	.143	111	148
New England Patriots***	0	1	.000	10	51
Seattle Seahawks	0	1	.000	14	30

One game played when franchise was in Dallas (Texans). (Won 20-17)
**One game played when franchise was in Los Angeles. (Lost 24-16)*
***Game played when franchise was in Boston. (Lost 51-10)*

1984 AMERICAN FOOTBALL CONFERENCE CHAMPIONSHIP GAME

Orange Bowl, Miami, Florida   January 6, 1985
Attendance: 76,029

MIAMI 45, PITTSBURGH 28—Dan Marino completed four touchdown passes to lead Miami over Pittsburgh and into Super Bowl XIX. Trailing 14-10 with 1:30 remaining in the second period, Marino connected with Mark Duper on a 41-yard pass and Tony Nathan ran for a two-yard score to give Miami a 24-14 half-time lead. On Miami's first possession of the third period, Marino completed a 36-yard touchdown pass to Duper to boost the Dolphins lead to 31-14. Pittsburgh pulled to within 31-21 with 7:55 remaining in the third period, on a 19-yard pass from Mark Malone to John Stallworth, but the Dolphins responded with two more scores to take a commanding 45-21 lead. Marino completed 21 of 32 for an AFC Championship Game-record 421 yards. His four touchdowns also were an AFC title game record. Duper caught five passes for 148 yards and Nathan hauled in eight for 114. Miami's 435 passing yards set an NFL postseason playoff game record, surpassing the 415 by San Diego versus Miami in a 1981 AFC divisional game. Miami's 569 total yards and Pittsburgh's 455 set an AFC Championship Game record for most net yards (1,024) by two teams. Miami advanced into its second Super Bowl in three years. In Super Bowl XVII, the Dolphins lost to Washington, 27-17.

Pittsburgh Steelers (28)	Offense	Miami Dolphins (45)
John Stallworth	WR	Mark Duper
Pete Rostosky	LT	Jon Giesler
Craig Wolfley	LG	Roy Foster
Mike Webster	C	Dwight Stephenson
Terry Long	RG	Ed Newman
Tunch Ilkin	RT	Cleveland Green
Bennie Cunningham	TE	Bruce Hardy
Louis Lipps	WR	Mark Clayton
Mark Malone	QB	Dan Marino
Walter Abercrombie	RB	Tony Nathan
Frank Pollard	RB	Woody Bennett
	Defense	
John Goodman	LE	Doug Betters
Gary Dunn	NT	Bob Baumhower
Edmund Nelson	RE	Kim Bokamper
Mike Merriweather	LOLB	Bob Brudzinski
David Little	LILB	Jay Brophy
Robin Cole	RILB	Mark Brown
Bryan Hinkle	ROLB	Charles Bowser
Dwayne Woodruff	LCB	Don McNeal
Sam Washington	RCB	William Judson
Donnie Shell	SS	Glenn Blackwood
Eric Williams	FS	Lyle Blackwood

SUBSTITUTIONS

Pittsburgh—Offense: K—Gary Anderson. P—Craig Colquitt. RB—Anthony Corley, Rich Erenberg, Scoop Gillespie, Elton Veals. TE—Darrell Nelson. WR—Wayne Capers, Calvin Sweeney, Weegie Thompson. G—Randy Rasmussen. Defense: E—Mark Catano, Keith Gary, Keith Willis. LB—Craig Bingham, Bob Kohrs, Jack Lambert, Todd Seabaugh. CB—Chris Brown, Harvey Clayton. S—Ron Johnson, Robert Williams, Rick Woods. DNP: QB—Scott Campbell, David Woodley. T—Steve August. G—Blake Wingle.
Miami—Offense: K—Uwe von Schamann. P—Reggie Roby. QB—Don Strock. RB—Eddie Hill, Pete Johnson. TE—Dan Johnson, Joe Rose. WR—Jimmy Cefalo, Vince Heflin, Jim Jensen, Nat Moore. KR—Fulton Walker. G—Steve Clark, Ronnie Lee, Jeff Toews. Defense: E—Bill Barnett, Charles Benson. T—Mike Charles. LB—A.J. Duhe, Earnie Rhone, Jackie Shipp, Sanders Shiver. CB—Paul Lankford, Robert Sowell. S—Bud Brown, Mike Kozlowski. DNP: RB—Joe Carter.

OFFICIALS

Referee—Jerry Markbreit. Umpire—Al Conway. Head Linesman—Sid Semon. Line Judge—Walt Peters. Back Judge—Ben Tompkins. Side Judge—Gil Mace. Field Judge—Don Hakes.

SCORING

Pittsburgh	7	7	7	7 — 28	
Miami	7	17	14	7 — 45	

Mia— Clayton 40 pass from Marino (von Schamann kick)
Pitt — Erenberg 7 run (Anderson kick)
Mia— FG von Schamann 26
Pitt — Stallworth 65 pass from Malone (Anderson kick)
Mia— Duper 41 pass from Marino (von Schamann kick)
Mia— Nathan 2 run (von Schamann kick)
Mia— Duper 36 pass from Marino (von Schamann kick)
Pitt — Stallworth 19 pass from Malone (Anderson kick)
Mia— Bennett 1 run (von Schamann kick)
Mia— Moore 6 pass from Marino (von Schamann kick)
Pitt — Capers 29 pass from Malone (Anderson kick)

TEAM STATISTICS

	Pittsburgh	Miami
Total First Downs	22	28
First Downs Rushing	8	10
First Downs Passing	14	18
First Downs Penalty	0	0
Total Net Yardage	455	569
Total Offensive Plays	68	71
Average Gain per Offensive Play	6.7	8.0
Rushes	32	38
Yards Gained Rushing (net)	143	134
Average Yards per Rush	4.5	3.5
Passes Attempted	36	33
Passes Completed	20	22
Had Intercepted	3	1
Times Tackled Attempting to Pass	0	0
Yards Lost Attempting to Pass	0	0
Yards Gained Passing (net)	312	435
Punts	3	2
Average Distance	43.7	42.5
Punt Returns	1	3
Punt Return Yardage	7	12
Kickoff Returns	5	3
Kickoff Return Yardage	106	62
Interception Return Yardage	18	42
Total Return Yardage	131	116

Fumbles	2	1
Own Fumbles Recovered	1	0
Opponent Fumbles Recovered	1	1
Penalties	3	3
Yards Penalized	30	25
Total Points Scored	28	45
Touchdowns	4	6
Touchdowns Rushing	1	2
Touchdowns Passing	3	4
Touchdown Returns	0	0
Extra Points	4	6
Field Goals	0	1
Field Goals Attempted	1	2
3rd Down Efficiency	6/11	4/11
4th Down Efficiency	0/1	0/1
Time of Possession	27:27	32:33

INDIVIDUAL STATISTICS

RUSHING

Pittsburgh	Att.	Yds.	LG	TD
Abercrombie	15	68	20	0
Pollard	11	48	9	0
Erenberg	6	27	7t	1
Miami	**Att.**	**Yds.**	**LG**	**TD**
Nathan	19	64	16	1
P. Johnson	10	39	12	0
Bennett	8	33	17	1
Strock	1	−2	−2	0

PASSING

Pitt.	Att.	Comp.	Yds.	TD	Int.
Malone	36	20	312	3	3
Miami	**Att.**	**Comp.**	**Yds.**	**TD**	**Int.**
Marino	32	21	421	4	1
Nathan	1	1	14	0	0

RECEIVING

Pittsburgh	No.	Yds.	LG	TD
Erenberg	5	59	24	0
Stallworth	4	111	65t	2
Lipps	3	45	33	0
Sweeney	3	42	20	0
Pollard	3	13	7	0
Capers	1	29	29t	1
Abercrombie	1	13	13	0
Miami	**No.**	**Yds.**	**LG**	**TD**
Nathan	8	114	30	0
Duper	5	148	41t	2
Clayton	4	95	40t	1
Moore	2	34	28	1
Hardy	2	16	14	0
Rose	1	28	28	0

INTERCEPTIONS

Pittsburgh	No.	Yds.	LG	TD
Shell	1	18	18	0
Miami	**No.**	**Yds.**	**LG**	**TD**
Judson	1	34	34	0
G. Blackwood	1	4	4	0
L. Blackwood	1	4	4	0

NFC Championship Game

Includes NFL Championship Games (1933-69)

RESULTS

Season	Date	Winner (Share)	Loser (Share)	Score	Site	Attendance
1984	Jan. 6	San Francisco ($18,000)	Chicago ($18,000)	23-0	San Francisco	61,336
1983	Jan. 8	Washington ($18,000)	San Francisco ($18,000)	24-21	Washington	55,363
1982	Jan. 22	Washington ($18,000)	Dallas ($18,000)	31-17	Washington	55,045
1981	Jan. 10	San Francisco ($9,000)	Dallas ($9,000)	28-27	San Francisco	60,525
1980	Jan. 11	Philadelphia ($9,000)	Dallas ($9,000)	20-7	Philadelphia	71,522
1979	Jan. 6	Los Angeles ($9,000)	Tampa Bay ($9,000)	9-0	Tampa Bay	72,033
1978	Jan. 7	Dallas ($9,000)	Los Angeles ($9,000)	28-0	Los Angeles	71,086
1977	Jan. 1	Dallas ($9,000)	Minnesota ($9,000)	23-6	Dallas	64,293
1976	Dec. 26	Minnesota ($8,500)	Los Angeles ($5,500)	24-13	Minnesota	48,379
1975	Jan. 4	Dallas ($8,500)	Los Angeles ($5,500)	37-7	Los Angeles	88,919
1974	Dec. 29	Minnesota ($8,500)	Los Angeles ($5,500)	14-10	Minnesota	48,444
1973	Dec. 30	Minnesota ($8,500)	Dallas ($5,500)	27-10	Dallas	64,422
1972	Dec. 31	Washington ($8,500)	Dallas ($5,500)	26-3	Washington	53,129
1971	Jan. 2	Dallas ($8,500)	San Francisco ($5,500)	14-3	Dallas	63,409
1970	Jan. 3	Dallas ($8,500)	San Francisco ($5,500)	17-10	San Francisco	59,364
1969	Jan. 4	Minnesota ($7,930)	Cleveland ($5,118)	27-7	Minnesota	46,503
1968	Dec. 29	Baltimore ($9,306)	Cleveland ($5,963)	34-0	Cleveland	78,410
1967	Dec. 31	Green Bay ($7,950)	Dallas ($5,299)	21-17	Green Bay	50,861
1966	Jan. 1	Green Bay ($9,813)	Dallas ($6,527)	34-27	Dallas	74,152
1965	Jan. 2	Green Bay ($7,819)	Cleveland ($5,288)	23-12	Green Bay	50,777
1964	Dec. 27	Cleveland ($8,052)	Baltimore ($5,571)	27-0	Cleveland	79,544
1963	Dec. 29	Chicago ($5,899)	New York ($4,218)	14-10	Chicago	45,801
1962	Dec. 30	Green Bay ($5,888)	New York ($4,166)	16-7	New York	64,892
1961	Dec. 31	Green Bay ($5,195)	New York ($3,339)	37-0	Green Bay	39,029
1960	Dec. 26	Philadelphia ($5,116)	Green Bay ($3,105)	17-13	Philadelphia	67,325
1959	Dec. 27	Baltimore ($4,674)	New York ($3,083)	31-16	Baltimore	57,545
1958	Dec. 28	Baltimore ($4,718)	New York ($3,111)	23-17*	New York	64,185
1957	Dec. 29	Detroit ($4,295)	Cleveland ($2,750)	59-14	Detroit	55,263
1956	Dec. 30	New York ($3,779)	Chi. Bears ($2,485)	47-7	New York	56,836
1955	Dec. 26	Cleveland ($3,508)	Los Angeles ($2,316)	38-14	Los Angeles	85,693
1954	Dec. 26	Cleveland ($2,478)	Detroit ($1,585)	56-10	Cleveland	43,827
1953	Dec. 27	Detroit ($2,424)	Cleveland ($1,654)	17-16	Detroit	54,577
1952	Dec. 28	Detroit ($2,274)	Cleveland ($1,712)	17-7	Cleveland	50,934
1951	Dec. 23	Los Angeles ($2,108)	Cleveland ($1,483)	24-17	Los Angeles	57,522
1950	Dec. 24	Cleveland ($1,113)	Los Angeles ($686)	30-28	Cleveland	29,751
1949	Dec. 18	Philadelphia ($1,094)	Los Angeles ($739)	14-0	Los Angeles	27,980
1948	Dec. 19	Philadelphia ($1,540)	Chi. Cardinals ($874)	7-0	Philadelphia	36,309
1947	Dec. 28	Chi. Cardinals ($1,132)	Philadelphia ($754)	28-21	Chicago	30,759
1946	Dec. 15	Chi. Bears ($1,975)	New York ($1,295)	24-14	New York	58,346

1945	Dec. 16	Cleveland ($1,469)	Washington ($902)	15-14	Cleveland	32,178
1944	Dec. 17	Green Bay ($1,449)	New York ($814)	14-7	New York	46,016
1943	Dec. 26	Chi. Bears ($1,146)	Washington ($765)	41-21	Chicago	34,320
1942	Dec. 13	Washington ($965)	Chi. Bears ($637)	14-6	Washington	36,006
1941	Dec. 21	Chi. Bears ($430)	New York ($288)	37-9	Chicago	13,341
1940	Dec. 8	Chi. Bears ($873)	Washington ($606)	73-0	Washington	36,034
1939	Dec. 10	Green Bay ($703.97)	New York ($455.57)	27-0	Milwaukee	32,279
1938	Dec. 11	New York ($504.45)	Green Bay ($368.81)	23-17	New York	48,120
1937	Dec. 12	Washington ($225.90)	Chi. Bears ($127.78)	28-21	Chicago	15,870
1936	Dec. 13	Green Bay ($250)	Boston ($180)	21-6	New York	29,545
1935	Dec. 15	Detroit ($313.35)	New York ($200.20)	26-7	Detroit	15,000
1934	Dec. 9	New York ($621)	Chi. Bears ($414.02)	30-13	New York	35,059
1933	Dec. 17	Chi. Bears ($210.34)	New York ($140.22)	23-21	Chicago	26,000

Sudden death overtime.

NFC CHAMPIONSHIP GAME COMPOSITE STANDINGS

	W	L	Pct.	Pts.	OP
Green Bay Packers	8	2	.800	223	116
Detroit Lions	4	1	.800	129	100
Minnesota Vikings	4	1	.800	98	63
Philadelphia Eagles	4	1	.800	79	48
Baltimore Colts	3	1	.750	88	60
Washington Redskins*	5	4	.556	164	218
Chicago Bears	6	5	.545	259	217
St. Louis Cardinals**	1	1	.500	28	28
Dallas Cowboys	5	7	.417	227	213
San Francisco 49ers	2	3	.400	85	82
Cleveland Browns	4	7	.364	224	253
Los Angeles Rams***	3	7	.300	120	216
New York Giants	3	11	.214	208	309
Tampa Bay Buccaneers	0	1	.000	0	9

*One game played when franchise was in Boston. (Lost 21-6)
**Both games played when franchise was in Chicago. (Won 28-21, lost 7-0)
***One game played when franchise was in Cleveland. (Won 15-14)

1984 NATIONAL FOOTBALL CONFERENCE CHAMPIONSHIP GAME

Candlestick Park, San Francisco, California   January 6, 1985
Attendance: 61,336

SAN FRANCISCO 23, CHICAGO 0 — NFC Western Division champion San Francisco gained its second Super Bowl berth in the last four seasons with a 23-0 win over NFC Central Division titlist Chicago. The outcome represented the first shutout in an NFC Championship Game since the Los Angeles Rams blanked Tampa Bay 9-0 in 1979. The 49ers managed only a 6-0 halftime lead on a pair of Ray Wersching field goals. Despite the score, Chicago held a first half time of possession advantage of 16:12 to 13:48. In the second half, the 49ers increased their lead to 13-0 on Wendell Tyler's nine-yard scoring run. In the fourth quarter, Joe Montana threw a 10-yard touchdown pass to Freddie Solomon to conclude an eight-play, 88-yard drive. Wersching's 34-yard field goal with 1:57 remaining in the game finished the scoring. Montana completed 18 of 34 passes for 233 yards and one touchdown, and had two interceptions. He was sacked by the Bears three times, while the 49ers had nine sacks. Chicago's Walter Payton carried 22 times for 92 yards. The Bears' Gary Fencik had two key interceptions which stopped San Francisco threats.

Chicago Bears (0)	Offense	San Francisco 49ers (23)
Willie Gault	WR	Dwight Clark
Jim Covert	LT	Bubba Paris
Mark Bortz	LG	John Ayers
Jay Hilgenberg	C	Fred Quillan
Kurt Becker	RG	Randy Cross
Keith Van Horne	RT	Keith Fahnhorst
Emery Moorehead	TE	Russ Francis
Dennis McKinnon	WR	Freddie Solomon
Steve Fuller	QB	Joe Montana
Walter Payton	RB	Roger Craig
Matt Suhey	RB	Wendell Tyler
	Defense	
Mike Hartenstine	LE	Lawrence Pillers
Steve McMichael	LT-NT	Manu Tuiasosopo
Dan Hampton	RT-RE	Dwaine Board
Richard Dent	RE-LOLB	Dan Bunz
Otis Wilson	LLB-LILB	Riki Ellison
Mike Singletary	MLB-RILB	Jack Reynolds
Al Harris	RLB-ROLB	Keena Turner
Mike Richardson	LCB	Ronnie Lott
Leslie Frazier	RCB	Eric Wright
Todd Bell	SS	Carlton Williamson
Gary Fencik	FS	Dwight Hicks

SUBSTITUTIONS

Chicago—Offense: K—Bob Thomas. P—Dave Finzer. RB—Anthony Hutchison, Calvin Thomas. TE—Pat Dunsmore, Mitch Krenk, Jay Saldi. WR—Brad Anderson, Brian Baschnagel, Jack Cameron. KR—Dennis Gentry. T—Andy Frederick. G—Rob Fada. C—Tom Andrews. Defense: E—Tyrone Keys. T—Jim Osborne, Henry Waechter. LB—Brian Cabral, Wilbur Marshall, Dan Rains, Ron Rivera. CB—Jeff Fisher, Terry Schmidt. S—Dave Duerson, Kevin Potter. DNP: QB—Greg Landry, Rusty Lisch.
San Francisco—Offense: K—Ray Wersching. P—Max Runager. QB—Matt Cavanaugh. RB—Derrick Harmon, Carl Monroe, Bill Ring. TE—Earl Cooper, John Frank. WR—Renaldo Nehemiah, Mike Wilson. KR—Dana McLemore. T—Allan Kennedy, Billy Shields. G—Guy McIntyre. Defense: E—Fred Dean, Jim Stuckey. T—Michael Carter, Gary Johnson, Louie Kelcher, Jeff Stover. LB—Milt McColl, Blanchard Montgomery, Todd Shell, Mike Walter. CB—Tom Holmoe. S—Jeff Fuller. DNP: CB—Mario Clark.

OFFICIALS

Referee: Jerry Seeman. Umpire: Gordon Wells. Head Linesman: Jerry Bergman. Line Judge: Bill Reynolds. Back Judge: Al Jury. Side Judge: Dave Parry. Field Judge: Don Orr.

SCORING

Chicago	0	0	0	0 —	0
San Francisco	3	3	7	10 —	23

SF—FG Wersching 21
SF—FG Wersching 22
SF—Tyler 9 run (Wersching kick)
SF—Solomon 10 pass from Montana (Wersching kick)
SF—FG Wersching 34

TEAM STATISTICS

	Chicago	San Francisco
Total First Downs	13	25
First Downs Rushing	9	9
First Downs Passing	3	14
First Downs Penalty	1	2
Total Net Yardage	186	387
Total Offensive Plays	63	67
Average Gain per Offensive Play	3.0	5.8
Rushes	32	29
Yards Gained Rushing (net)	149	159
Average Yards per Rush	4.7	5.5
Passes Attempted	22	35
Passes Completed	13	19
Had Intercepted	1	2
Times Tackled Attempting to Pass	9	3
Yards Lost Attempting to Pass	50	8
Yards Gained Passing (net)	37	228
Punts	7	3
Average Distance	43.1	39.0
Punt Returns	2	4
Punt Return Yardage	12	69
Kickoff Returns	4	1
Kickoff Return Yardage	67	15
Interception Return Yardage	5	0
Total Return Yardage	84	84
Fumbles	1	1
Own Fumbles Recovered	0	1
Opponent Fumbles Recovered	0	0
Penalties	7	3
Yards Penalized	50	20
Total Points Scored	0	23
Touchdowns	0	2
Touchdowns Rushing	0	1
Touchdowns Passing	0	1
Touchdown Returns	0	0
Extra Points	0	2
Field Goals	0	3
Field Goals Attempted	0	3
3rd Down Efficiency	5/16	4/11
4th Down Efficiency	1/2	0/0
Time of Possession	31:53	28:07

INDIVIDUAL STATISTICS
RUSHING

Chicago	Att.	Yds.	LG	TD
Payton	22	92	20	0
Fuller	6	39	23	0
Suhey	3	16	15	0
C. Thomas	1	2	2	0

San Fran.	Att.	Yds.	LG	TD
Tyler	10	68	25	1
Craig	8	44	39	0
Montana	5	22	9	0
Harmon	3	18	14	0
Ring	2	5	3	0
Cavanaugh	1	2	2	0

PASSING

Chicago	Att.	Comp.	Yds.	TD	Int.
Fuller	22	13	87	0	1

San Fran.	Att.	Comp.	Yds.	TD	Int.
Montana	34	18	233	1	2
Cavanaugh	1	1	3	0	0

RECEIVING

Chicago	No.	Yds.	LG	TD
Suhey	4	11	7	0
McKinnon	3	48	21	0
Payton	3	11	5	0
Moorehead	2	14	8	0
Dunsmore	1	3	3	0

San Fran.	No.	Yds.	LG	TD
Solomon	7	73	15	1
D. Clark	4	83	38	0
Wilson	2	25	14	0
Tyler	2	22	16	0
Francis	2	20	12	0
Nehemiah	1	10	10	0
Harmon	1	3	3	0

INTERCEPTIONS

Chicago	No.	Yds.	LG	TD
Fencik	2	5	5	0

San Fran.	No.	Yds.	LG	TD
Hicks	1	0	0	0

AFC Divisional Playoffs
Includes Second-Round Playoff Games (1982), AFL Inter-Divisional Playoff Games (1969), and special playoff games to break ties for AFL Division Championships (1963, 1968)

RESULTS

Season	Date	Winner	Loser	Site	Attendance
1984	Dec. 30	Pittsburgh 24	Denver 17	Denver	74,981
	Dec. 29	Miami 31	Seattle 10	Miami	73,469
1983	Jan. 1	L.A. Raiders 38	Pittsburgh 10	Los Angeles	90,380
	Dec. 31	Seattle 27	Miami 20	Miami	74,136
1982	Jan. 16	Miami 34	San Diego 13	Miami	71,383
	Jan. 15	N.Y. Jets 17	L.A. Raiders 14	Los Angeles	90,038
1981	Jan. 3	Cincinnati 28	Buffalo 21	Cincinnati	55,420
	Jan. 2	*San Diego 41	Miami 38	Miami	73,735
1980	Jan. 4	Oakland 14	Cleveland 12	Cleveland	78,245
	Jan. 3	San Diego 20	Buffalo 14	San Diego	52,253
1979	Dec. 30	Pittsburgh 34	Miami 14	Pittsburgh	50,214
	Dec. 29	Houston 17	San Diego 14	San Diego	51,192
1978	Dec. 31	Houston 31	New England 14	New England	60,753
	Dec. 30	Pittsburgh 33	Denver 10	Pittsburgh	50,230
1977	Dec. 24	*Oakland 37	Baltimore 31	Baltimore	59,925
	Dec. 24	Denver 34	Pittsburgh 21	Denver	75,059
1976	Dec. 19	Pittsburgh 40	Baltimore 14	Baltimore	59,296
	Dec. 18	Oakland 24	New England 21	Oakland	53,050
1975	Dec. 28	Oakland 31	Cincinnati 28	Oakland	53,030
	Dec. 27	Pittsburgh 28	Baltimore 10	Pittsburgh	49,557
1974	Dec. 22	Pittsburgh 32	Buffalo 14	Pittsburgh	49,841
	Dec. 21	Oakland 28	Miami 26	Oakland	53,023
1973	Dec. 23	Miami 34	Cincinnati 16	Miami	78,928
	Dec. 22	Oakland 33	Pittsburgh 14	Oakland	52,646
1972	Dec. 24	Miami 20	Cleveland 14	Miami	78,916
	Dec. 23	Pittsburgh 13	Oakland 7	Pittsburgh	50,327
1971	Dec. 26	Baltimore 20	Cleveland 3	Cleveland	70,734
	Dec. 25	*Miami 27	Kansas City 24	Kansas City	45,822
1970	Dec. 27	Oakland 21	Miami 14	Oakland	52,594
	Dec. 26	Baltimore 17	Cincinnati 0	Baltimore	49,694
1969	Dec. 21	Oakland 56	Houston 7	Oakland	53,539
	Dec. 20	Kansas City 13	N.Y. Jets 6	New York	62,977
1968	Dec. 22	Oakland 41	Kansas City 6	Oakland	53,605
1963	Dec. 28	Boston 26	Buffalo 8	Buffalo	33,044

*Sudden death overtime.

1984 AFC DIVISIONAL PLAYOFFS

Orange Bowl, Miami, Florida   December 29, 1984
Attendance: 73,469

MIAMI 31, SEATTLE 10—The Miami Dolphins advanced to the AFC Championship Game for the second time in three years with a 31-10 victory over Seattle. Leading 14-10, the Dolphins exploded for two scores in the final five minutes of the third period to pull away from the Seahawks. Dan Marino completed a three-yard touchdown pass to Bruce Hardy to give Miami a 21-10 lead. On Miami's next possession, Marino hit Mark Clayton with a 33-yard scoring pass to put the Dolphins ahead 28-10. Uwe von Schamann then added a 37-yard field goal to complete Miami's scoring. Marino completed 21 of 34 for 262 yards and three touchdowns.

Seattle	0	10	0	0 — 10	
Miami	7	7	14	3 — 31	

Mia—Nathan 14 run (von Schamann kick)
Sea—FG Johnson 27
Mia—Cefalo 34 pass from Marino (von Schamann kick)
Sea—Largent 56 pass from Krieg (Johnson kick)
Mia—Hardy 3 pass from Marino (von Schamann kick)
Mia—Clayton 33 pass from Marino (von Schamann kick)
Mia—FG von Schamann 37

Mile High Stadium, Denver, Colorado   December 30, 1984
Attendance: 74,981

PITTSBURGH 24, DENVER 17—Pittsburgh advanced to the AFC Championship Game for the first time since 1979 with a 24-17 victory over Denver. Frank Pollard's two-yard scoring run with 1:59 remaining clinched the Steelers' victory. The winning touchdown was set up by Eric Williams, who intercepted John Elway's pass at the Denver 30-yard line and returned it to the 2. Three plays later, Pollard scored. Pittsburgh led 10-7 at halftime, but the Broncos went ahead 17-10 in the third quarter on a 21-yard field goal by Rich Karlis and a 20-yard scoring pass from Elway to Steve Watson. The Steelers tied the score 17-17 on a 10-yard pass from Mark Malone to Louis Lipps. Pollard rushed for 99 yards on 16 carries and Walter Abercrombie added 75 on 17 attempts. Malone completed 17 of 28 passes for 224 yards. Lipps caught five for 86.

Pittsburgh	0	10	7	7 — 24	
Denver	7	0	10	0 — 17	

Den—Wright 9 pass from Elway (Karlis kick)
Pitt—FG Anderson 28
Pitt—Pollard 1 run (Anderson kick)
Den—FG Karlis 21
Den—Watson 20 pass from Elway (Karlis kick)
Pitt—Lipps 10 pass from Malone (Anderson kick)
Pitt—Pollard 2 run (Anderson kick)

NFC Divisional Playoffs

Includes Second-Round Playoff Games (1982), NFL Conference Championship Games (1967-69), and special playoff games to break ties for NFL Division or Conference Championships (1941, 1943, 1947, 1950, 1952, 1957, 1958, 1965)

RESULTS

Season	Date	Winner	Loser	Site	Attendance
1984	Dec. 30	Chicago 23	Washington 19	Washington	55,431
	Dec. 29	San Francisco 21	N.Y. Giants 10	San Francisco	60,303
1983	Jan. 1	Washington 51	L.A. Rams 7	Washington	54,440
	Dec. 31	San Francisco 24	Detroit 23	San Francisco	59,979
1982	Jan. 16	Dallas 37	Green Bay 26	Dallas	63,972
	Jan. 15	Washington 21	Minnesota 7	Washington	54,593
1981	Jan. 3	San Francisco 38	N.Y. Giants 24	San Francisco	58,360
	Jan. 2	Dallas 38	Tampa Bay 0	Dallas	64,848
1980	Jan. 4	Dallas 30	Atlanta 27	Atlanta	59,793
	Jan. 3	Philadelphia 31	Minnesota 16	Philadelphia	70,178
1979	Dec. 30	Los Angeles 21	Dallas 19	Dallas	64,792
	Dec. 29	Tampa Bay 24	Philadelphia 17	Tampa Bay	71,402
1978	Dec. 31	Los Angeles 34	Minnesota 10	Los Angeles	70,436
	Dec. 30	Dallas 27	Atlanta 20	Dallas	63,406
1977	Dec. 26	Dallas 37	Chicago 7	Dallas	63,260
	Dec. 26	Minnesota 14	Los Angeles 7	Los Angeles	70,203
1976	Dec. 19	Los Angeles 14	Dallas 12	Dallas	63,283
	Dec. 18	Minnesota 35	Washington 20	Minnesota	47,466
1975	Dec. 28	Dallas 17	Minnesota 14	Minnesota	48,050
	Dec. 27	Los Angeles 35	St. Louis 23	Los Angeles	73,459
1974	Dec. 22	Los Angeles 19	Washington 10	Los Angeles	77,925
	Dec. 21	Minnesota 30	St. Louis 14	Minnesota	48,150
1973	Dec. 23	Dallas 27	Los Angeles 16	Dallas	63,272
	Dec. 22	Minnesota 27	Washington 20	Minnesota	48,040
1972	Dec. 24	Washington 16	Green Bay 3	Washington	52,321
	Dec. 23	Dallas 30	San Francisco 28	San Francisco	59,746
1971	Dec. 26	San Francisco 24	Washington 20	San Francisco	45,327
	Dec. 25	Dallas 20	Minnesota 12	Minnesota	47,307
1970	Dec. 27	San Francisco 17	Minnesota 14	Minnesota	45,103
	Dec. 26	Dallas 5	Detroit 0	Dallas	69,613
1969	Dec. 28	Cleveland 38	Dallas 14	Dallas	69,321
	Dec. 27	Minnesota 23	Los Angeles 20	Minnesota	47,900
1968	Dec. 22	Baltimore 24	Minnesota 14	Baltimore	60,238
	Dec. 21	Cleveland 31	Dallas 20	Cleveland	81,497
1967	Dec. 24	Dallas 52	Cleveland 14	Dallas	70,786
	Dec. 23	Green Bay 28	Los Angeles 7	Milwaukee	49,861
1965	Dec. 26	*Green Bay 13	Baltimore 10	Green Bay	50,484
1958	Dec. 21	N.Y. Giants 10	Cleveland 0	New York	61,274
1957	Dec. 22	Detroit 31	San Francisco 27	San Francisco	60,118
1952	Dec. 21	Detroit 31	Los Angeles 21	Detroit	47,645
1950	Dec. 17	Los Angeles 24	Chi. Bears 14	Los Angeles	83,501
	Dec. 17	Cleveland 8	N.Y. Giants 3	Cleveland	33,054
1947	Dec. 21	Philadelphia 21	Pittsburgh 0	Pittsburgh	35,729
1943	Dec. 19	Washington 28	N.Y. Giants 10	New York	42,800
1941	Dec. 14	Chi. Bears 33	Green Bay 14	Chicago	43,425

*Sudden death overtime.

1984 NFC DIVISIONAL PLAYOFFS

Candlestick Park, San Francisco, California — December 29, 1984
Attendance: 60,303

SAN FRANCISCO 21, NEW YORK GIANTS 10—NFC West champion San Francisco jumped to a 14-0 first-period lead over the NFC Wild Card representative New York Giants and held on for a 21-10 win. Joe Montana connected with Dwight Clark for a 21-yard touchdown pass and Russ Francis for a nine-yard score to give the 49ers a quick 14-0 lead. The Giants closed the score to 14-10 on an Ali Haji-Sheikh 46-yard field goal and Harry Carson's 14-yard pass interception return for a touchdown. The 49ers took control of the game on Freddie Solomon's 29-yard scoring catch with 10:51 gone in the second period.

N.Y. Giants	0	10	0	0 — 10	
San Francisco	14	7	0	0 — 21	

SF — Clark 21 pass from Montana (Wersching kick)
SF — Francis 9 pass from Montana (Wersching kick)
NYG— FG Haji-Sheikh 46
NYG— Carson 14 interception return (Haji-Sheikh kick)
SF — Solomon 29 pass from Montana (Wersching kick)

Robert F. Kennedy Stadium, Washington, D.C. — December 30, 1984
Attendance: 55,431

CHICAGO 23, WASHINGTON 19—NFC Central Division titlist Chicago held on and defeated NFC Eastern champion Washington 23-19. The victory was the Bears' first playoff win since 1963. The Bears took a 10-3 lead when Walter Payton threw a 19-yard touchdown pass to Pat Dunsmore with two minutes to play in the first half. Chicago went ahead 16-3 on Willie Gault's 75-yard scoring catch 26 seconds into the third period. The Redskins closed the gap to 16-10, but Dennis McKinnon's 16-yard touchdown reception put the game out-of-reach.

Chicago	0	10	13	0 — 23	
Washington	3	0	14	2 — 19	

Wash — FG Moseley 25
Chi — FG B. Thomas 34
Chi — Dunsmore 19 pass from Payton (B. Thomas kick)
Chi — Gault 75 pass from Fuller (kick failed)
Wash — Riggins 1 run (Moseley kick)
Chi — McKinnon 16 pass from Fuller (B. Thomas kick)
Wash — Riggins 1 run (Moseley kick)
Wash — Safety, Finzer stepped out of end zone

AFC First-Round Playoff Games

RESULTS

Season	Date	Winner	Loser	Site	Attendance
1984	Dec. 22	Seattle 13	L.A. Raiders 7	Seattle	62,049
1983	Dec. 24	Seattle 31	Denver 7	Seattle	64,275
1982	Jan. 9	N.Y. Jets 44	Cincinnati 17	Cincinnati	57,560
	Jan. 9	San Diego 31	Pittsburgh 28	Pittsburgh	53,546
	Jan. 8	L.A. Raiders 27	Cleveland 10	Los Angeles	56,555
	Jan. 8	Miami 28	New England 13	Miami	68,842
1981	Dec. 27	Buffalo 31	N.Y. Jets 27	New York	57,050
1980	Dec. 28	Oakland 27	Houston 7	Oakland	53,333
1979	Dec. 23	Houston 13	Denver 7	Houston	48,776
1978	Dec. 24	Houston 17	Miami 9	Miami	72,445

1984 AFC FIRST-ROUND PLAYOFF GAME

Kingdome, Seattle, Washington — December 22, 1984
Attendance: 62,049

SEATTLE 13, LOS ANGELES RAIDERS 7—The Seahawks combined a strong running attack and an aggressive defense to defeat the Raiders in the first round of the AFC playoffs. Seattle gained 205 yards on the ground, including 126 by Dan Doornink on 29 carries. The Seahawks' defense held the Raiders to 240 yards (105 rushing and 135 passing) and sacked Jim Plunkett six times, including two-and-a-half by Jacob Green. Seattle safeties Kenny Easley and John Harris each had an interception and cornerback Keith Simpson recovered a fumble. Seattle's Dave Krieg completed 4 of 10 passes for 70 yards and threw a 26-yard touchdown to Daryl Turner. Norm Johnson added field goals of 35 and 44 yards to finish the Seahawks scoring. The Raiders only touchdown came on a 46-yard pass from Plunkett to Marcus Allen.

L.A. Raiders	0	0	0	7 — 7	
Seattle	0	7	3	3 — 13	

Sea — Turner 26 pass from Krieg (Johnson kick)
Sea — FG Johnson 35
Sea — FG Johnson 44
Raiders — Allen 46 pass from Plunkett (Bahr kick)

NFC First-Round Playoff Games

RESULTS

Season	Date	Winner	Loser	Site	Attendance
1984	Dec. 23	N.Y. Giants 16	L.A. Rams 13	Anaheim	67,037
1983	Dec. 26	L.A. Rams 24	Dallas 17	Dallas	62,118
1982	Jan. 9	Dallas 30	Tampa Bay 17	Dallas	65,042
	Jan. 9	Minnesota 30	Atlanta 24	Minnesota	60,560
	Jan. 8	Green Bay 41	St. Louis 16	Green Bay	54,282
	Jan. 8	Washington 31	Detroit 7	Washington	55,045
1981	Dec. 27	N.Y. Giants 27	Philadelphia 21	Philadelphia	71,611
1980	Dec. 28	Dallas 34	Los Angeles 13	Dallas	63,052
1979	Dec. 23	Philadelphia 27	Chicago 17	Philadelphia	69,397
1978	Dec. 24	Atlanta 14	Philadelphia 13	Atlanta	59,403

Anaheim Stadium, Anaheim, California — December 23, 1984
Attendance: 67,037

NEW YORK GIANTS 16, LOS ANGELES RAMS 13—A ball-control offense, which held a 34:03 to 25:57 time of possession advantage, and a stingy defense which limited the Rams to 214 total yards, sparked New York's first-round victory over Los Angeles. New York's Ali Haji-Sheikh was three-for-three in field goal tries, connecting from 37, 39, and 36 yards. The Giants' Phil Simms completed 22 of 31 passes for 179 yards. Zeke Mowatt was Simms' favorite target with seven receptions for 73 yards. The Rams' Eric Dickerson carried 23 times for 107 yards and had a 14-yard touchdown run.

N.Y. Giants	10	0	6	0 — 16	
L.A. Rams	0	3	7	3 — 13	

NYG — FG Haji-Sheikh 37
NYG — Carpenter 1 run (Haji-Sheikh kick)
Rams — FG Lansford 38
NYG — FG Haji-Sheikh 39
Rams — Dickerson 14 run (Lansford kick)
NYG — FG Haji-Sheikh 36
Rams — FG Lansford 22

AFC-NFC PRO BOWL SUMMARIES

NFC leads series, 9-6

RESULTS

Year	Date	Winner	Loser	Site	Attendance
1985	Jan. 27	AFC 22	NFC 14	Honolulu	50,385
1984	Jan. 29	NFC 45	AFC 3	Honolulu	50,445
1983	Feb. 6	NFC 20	AFC 19	Honolulu	49,883
1982	Jan. 31	AFC 16	NFC 13	Honolulu	50,402
1981	Feb. 1	NFC 21	AFC 7	Honolulu	50,360
1980	Jan. 27	NFC 37	AFC 27	Honolulu	49,800
1979	Jan. 29	NFC 13	AFC 7	Los Angeles	46,281
1978	Jan. 23	NFC 14	AFC 13	Tampa	51,337
1977	Jan. 17	AFC 24	NFC 14	Seattle	64,752
1976	Jan. 26	NFC 23	AFC 20	New Orleans	30,546
1975	Jan. 20	NFC 17	AFC 10	Miami	26,484
1974	Jan. 20	AFC 15	NFC 13	Kansas City	66,918
1973	Jan. 21	AFC 33	NFC 28	Dallas	37,091
1972	Jan. 23	AFC 26	NFC 13	Los Angeles	53,647
1971	Jan. 24	NFC 27	AFC 6	Los Angeles	48,222

1985 AFC-NFC PRO BOWL

Aloha Stadium, Honolulu, Hawaii   January 27, 1985
Attendance: 50,385

AFC 22, NFC 14—Defensive end Art Still of the Kansas City Chiefs recovered a fumble and returned it 83 yards for a touchdown to clinch the AFC's victory over the NFC. Still's touchdown came in the fourth period with the AFC trailing 14-12 and was one of several outstanding defensive plays in a Pro Bowl dominated by two record-breaking defenses. Both teams combined for a Pro Bowl-record 17 sacks, including four by New York Jets defensive end Mark Gastineau, who was named the game's outstanding player. The AFC's first score came on a safety when Gastineau tackled running back Eric Dickerson of the Los Angeles Rams in the end zone. The AFC's second score, a six-yard pass from Miami's Dan Marino to Los Angeles Raiders running back Marcus Allen, was set up by a partial block of a punt by Seahawks linebacker Fredd Young. The NFC leads the series 9-6, since it started in 1970.

AFC (22)	Offense	NFC (14)
Mark Duper (Miami)	WR	Roy Green (St. Louis)
Anthony Muñoz (Cincinnati)	LT	Joe Jacoby (Washington)
John Hannah (New England)	LG	Russ Grimm (Washington)
Dwight Stephenson (Miami)	C	Fred Quillan (San Francisco)
Ed Newman (Miami)	RG	Randy Cross (San Francisco)
Brian Holloway (New England)	RT	Mike Kenn (Atlanta)
Ozzie Newsome (Cleveland)	TE	Paul Coffman (Green Bay)
John Stallworth (Pittsburgh)	WR	James Lofton (Green Bay)
Dan Marino (Miami)	QB	Joe Montana (San Francisco)
Marcus Allen (L.A. Raiders)	RB	Eric Dickerson (L.A. Rams)
Sammy Winder (Denver)	RB	Walter Payton (Chicago)
	Defense	
Mark Gastineau (N.Y. Jets)	LE	Richard Dent (Chicago)
Joe Nash (Seattle)	NT	Dan Hampton (Chicago)
Howie Long (L.A. Raiders)	RE	Lee Roy Selmon (Tampa Bay)
Mike Merriweather (Pittsburgh)	LOLB	Lawrence Taylor (N.Y. Giants)
Steve Nelson (New England)	LILB	Mike Singletary (Chicago)
Robin Cole (Pittsburgh)	RILB	E. J. Junior (St. Louis)
Rod Martin (L.A. Raiders)	ROLB	Rickey Jackson (New Orleans)
Lester Hayes (L.A. Raiders)	LCB	Ronnie Lott (San Francisco)
Dave Brown (Seattle)	RCB	Darrell Green (Washington)
Kenny Easley (Seattle)	SS	Todd Bell (Chicago)
Vann McElroy (L.A. Raiders)	FS	Dwight Hicks (San Francisco)

HEAD COACHES

AFC—Chuck Noll (Pittsburgh)
NFC—Mike Ditka (Chicago)

SUBSTITUTIONS

AFC—Offense: K—Norm Johnson (Seattle). P—Reggie Roby (Miami). QB—Dave Krieg (Seattle). RB—Greg Bell (Buffalo), Earnest Jackson (San Diego). TE—Todd Christensen (L.A. Raiders). WR—Mark Clayton (Miami), Steve Largent (Seattle). KR—Louis Lipps (Pittsburgh). C—Mike Webster (Pittsburgh). T—Henry Lawrence (L.A. Raiders). G—Mike Munchak (Houston). Defense: E—Art Still (Kansas City). NT—Joe Klecko (N.Y. Jets). OLB—Andre Tippett (New England). ILB—A.J. Duhe (Miami). S—Deron Cherry (Kansas City). SPT—Fredd Young (Seattle). DNP—CB-Mike Haynes (L.A. Raiders).
NFC—Offense: K—Jan Stenerud (Minnesota). P—Brian Hansen (New Orleans). QB—Neil Lomax (St. Louis). RB—Wendell Tyler (San Francisco), James Wilder (Tampa Bay). TE—Doug Cosbie (Dallas). WR—Art Monk (Washington), Mike Quick (Philadelphia). KR—Henry Ellard (L.A. Rams). C—Doug Smith (L.A. Rams). T—Keith Fahnhorst (San Francisco). G—Kent Hill (L.A. Rams). Defense: E—Bruce Clark (New Orleans). NT—Randy White (Dallas). OLB—Keena Turner (San Francisco). ILB—Harry Carson (N.Y. Giants). CB—Eric Wright (San Francisco). S—Carlton Williamson (San Francisco). SPT—Bill Bates (Dallas).

OFFICIALS

Referee: Chuck Heberling. Umpire: Ben Montgomery. Line Judge: Dan Wilford. Linesman: Terry Gierke. Back Judge: Bill Swanson. Field Judge: Charley Musser. Side Judge: Duwayne Gandy.

SCORING

AFC	0	9	0	13 —	22
NFC	0	0	7	7 —	14

AFC—Safety, Gastineau tackled Dickerson in end zone
AFC—Allen 6 pass from Marino (Johnson kick)
NFC—Lofton 13 pass from Montana (Stenerud kick)
NFC—Payton 1 run (Stenerud kick)
AFC—FG Johnson 33
AFC—Still 83 fumble recovery return (Johnson kick)
AFC—FG Johnson 22

TEAM STATISTICS

	AFC	NFC
Total First Downs	11	22
First Downs Rushing	4	11
First Downs Passing	7	11
First Downs Penalty	0	0
Total Net Yardage	204	426
Total Offensive Plays	64	81
Average Gain per Offensive Play	3.2	5.3
Rushes	24	39
Net Yards Gained Rushing	89	191
Average Yards per Rush	3.7	4.9
Passes Attempted	32	33
Passes Completed	14	21
Had Intercepted	0	1
Times Tackled Attempting to Pass	8	9
Yards Lost Attempting to Pass	56	69
Net Yards Gained Passing	115	235
Punts	10	6
Average Distance per Punt	44.3	36.5
Punt Returns	4	7
Punt Return Yardage	33	72
Kickoff Returns	4	2
Kickoff Return Yardage	79	58
Interception Return Yardage	0	0
Total Return Yardage	112	130
Fumbles	1	5
Own Fumbles Recovered	0	1
Opponent Fumbles Recovered	4	1
Penalties	6	2
Yards Penalized	30	20
Total Points Scored	22	14
Touchdowns	2	2
Touchdowns Rushing	0	1
Touchdowns Passing	1	1
Touchdown Returns	1	0
Extra Points	2	2
Field Goals	2	0
Field Goals Attempted	2	2
Safeties	1	0
Third Down Efficiency	4/16	9/18
Fourth Down Efficiency	0/0	0/0
Time of Possession	24:01	35:59

INDIVIDUAL STATISTICS

RUSHING

AFC	Att.	Yds.	LG	TD
Jackson	5	36	23	0
Allen	8	26	14	0
Winder	7	12	6	0
Krieg	2	9	9	0
Bell	1	8	8	0
Marino	1	-2	-2	0
NFC	**Att.**	**Yds.**	**LG**	**TD**
Payton	11	76	20	1
Wilder	7	43	14	0
Dickerson	9	32	9	0
Tyler	7	22	11	0
Montana	1	9	9	0
Lomax	4	9	4	0

PASSING

AFC	Att.	Comp.	Yds.	TD	Int.
Marino	21	10	139	1	0
Krieg	10	4	32	0	0
Allen	1	0	0	0	0
NFC	**Att.**	**Comp.**	**Yds.**	**TD**	**Int.**
Lomax	19	11	192	0	1
Montana	14	10	112	1	0

RECEIVING

AFC	No.	Yds.	LG	TD
Allen	5	82	56	1
Clayton	2	29	19	0
Duper	2	29	15	0
Largent	1	14	14	0
Stallworth	1	10	10	0
Lipps	1	4	4	0
Christensen	1	3	3	0
Jackson	1	0	0	0
NFC	**No.**	**Yds.**	**LG**	**TD**
Quick	3	88	48	0
Payton	3	54	36	0
Monk	3	49	28	0
Lofton	3	33	13t	0
Coffman	3	27	18	0
Wilder	2	22	16	0
Tyler	2	16	16	0
Cosbie	2	15	11	0

INTERCEPTIONS

AFC	No.	Yds.	LG	TD
Cherry	1	0	0	0
NFC	**No.**	**Yds.**	**LG**	**TD**
None				

1984 AFC-NFC PRO BOWL

Aloha Stadium, Honolulu, Hawaii
January 29, 1984
Attendance: 50,445

NFC 45, AFC 3—The NFC won its sixth Pro Bowl in the last seven seasons, 45-3 over the AFC. The NFC was led by the passing of most valuable player Joe Theismann of Washington, who completed 21 of 27 passes for 242 yards and three touchdowns. Theismann set Pro Bowl records for completions and touchdown passes. The NFC established Pro Bowl marks for most points scored and fewest points allowed. Running back William Andrews of Atlanta had six carries for 43 yards and caught four passes for 49 yards, including scoring receptions of 16 and 2 yards. Los Angeles Rams rookie Eric Dickerson gained 46 yards on 11 carries, including a 14-yard touchdown run, and had 45 yards on five catches. Rams safety Nolan Cromwell had a 44-yard interception return for a touchdown early in the third period to give the NFC a commanding 24-3 lead. Green Bay wide receiver James Lofton caught an eight-yard touchdown pass, while tight end teammate Paul Coffman had a six-yard scoring catch.

NFC	3	14	14	14 — 45
AFC	0	3	0	0 — 3

NFC—FG Haji-Sheikh 23
NFC—Andrews 16 pass from Theismann (Haji-Sheikh kick)
NFC—Andrews 2 pass from Montana (Haji-Sheikh kick)
AFC—FG Anderson 43
NFC—Cromwell 44 interception return (Haji-Sheikh kick)
NFC—Lofton 8 pass from Theismann (Haji-Sheikh kick)
NFC—Coffman 6 pass from Theismann (Haji-Sheikh kick)
NFC—Dickerson 14 run (Haji-Sheikh kick)

1983 AFC-NFC PRO BOWL

Aloha Stadium, Honolulu, Hawaii
Sunday, February 6, 1983
Attendance: 49,883

NFC 20, AFC 19—Danny White threw an 11-yard touchdown pass to John Jefferson with 35 seconds remaining to give the NFC a 20-19 victory over the AFC. White, who completed 14 of 26 passes for 162 yards, kept the winning 65-yard drive alive with a 14-yard completion to Jefferson on a fourth-and-seven play at the AFC 25. The AFC was ahead 12-10 at halftime and increased the lead to 19-10 in the third period, when Marcus Allen scored on a one-yard run. Dan Fouts, who attempted 30 passes, set Pro Bowl records for most completions (17) and yards (274). John Stallworth was the AFC's leading receiver with seven catches for 67 yards. William Andrews topped the NFC with five receptions for 48 yards. Fouts and Jefferson were voted co-winners of the player of the game award.

AFC	9	3	7	0 — 19
NFC	0	10	10	0 — 20

AFC—Walker 34 pass from Fouts (Benirschke kick)
AFC—Safety, Still tackled Theismann in end zone
NFC—Andrews 3 run (Moseley kick)
NFC—FG Moseley 35
AFC—FG Benirschke 29
AFC—Allen 1 run (Benirschke kick)
NFC—FG Moseley 41
NFC—Jefferson 11 pass from D. White (Moseley kick)

1982 AFC-NFC PRO BOWL

Aloha Stadium, Honolulu, Hawaii
Sunday, January 31, 1982
Attendance: 50,402

AFC 16, NFC 13—Nick Lowery kicked a 23-yard field goal with three seconds remaining to give the AFC a 16-13 victory over the NFC. Lowery's kick climaxed a 69-yard drive directed by quarterback Dan Fouts. The NFC gained a 13-13 tie with 2:43 to go when Tony Dorsett ran four yards for a touchdown. In the drive to the game-winning field goal, Fouts completed three passes, including a 23-yarder to San Diego teammate Kellen Winslow that put the ball on the NFC's 5 yard line. Two plays later, Lowery kicked the field goal. Winslow, who caught six passes for 86 yards, was named co-player of the game along with NFC defensive end Lee Roy Selmon.

NFC	0	6	0	7 — 13
AFC	0	0	13	3 — 16

NFC—Giles 4 pass from Montana (kick blocked)
AFC—Muncie 2 run (kick failed)
AFC—Campbell 1 run (Lowery kick)
NFC—Dorsett 4 run (Septien kick)
AFC—FG Lowery 23

1981 AFC-NFC PRO BOWL

Aloha Stadium, Honolulu, Hawaii
February 1, 1981
Attendance: 50,360

NFC 21, AFC 7—Ed Murray kicked four field goals and Steve Bartkowski fired a 55-yard scoring pass to Alfred Jenkins to lead the NFC to its fourth straight victory over the AFC and a 7-4 edge in the series. Murray was named the game's most valuable player and missed tying Garo Yepremian's Pro Bowl record of five goals when a 37-yard attempt hit the crossbar with 22 seconds remaining. The AFC's only score came on a nine-yard pass from Brian Sipe to Stanley Morgan in the second period. Bartkowski completed 9 of 21 passes for 173 yards, while Sipe connected on 10 of 15 for 142 yards. Ottis Anderson led all rushers with 70 yards on 10 carries. Earl Campbell, the NFL's leading rusher in 1980, was limited to 24 yards on eight attempts.

AFC	0	7	0	0 — 7
NFC	3	6	0	12 — 21

NFC—FG Murray 31
AFC—Morgan 9 pass from Sipe (J. Smith kick)
NFC—FG Murray 31
NFC—FG Murray 34
NFC—Jenkins 55 pass from Bartkowski (Murray kick)
NFC—FG Murray 36
NFC—Safety (Team)

1980 AFC-NFC PRO BOWL

Aloha Stadium, Honolulu, Hawaii
January 27, 1980
Attendance: 49,800

NFC 37, AFC 27—Running back Chuck Muncie ran for two touchdowns and threw a 25-yard option pass for another score to give the NFC its third consecutive victory over the AFC. Muncie, who was selected the game's most valuable player, snapped a 3-3 tie on a one-yard touchdown run at 1:41 of the second quarter, then scored on an 11-yard run in the fourth quarter for the NFC's final touchdown. Two scoring records were set in the game—37 points by the NFC, eclipsing the 33 by the AFC in 1973, and the 64 points by both teams, surpassing the 61 scored in 1973.

NFC	3	20	7	7 — 37
AFC	3	7	10	7 — 27

NFC—FG Moseley 37
AFC—FG Fritsch 19
NFC—Muncie 1 run (Moseley kick)
AFC—Pruitt 1 pass from Bradshaw (Fritsch kick)
NFC—D. Hill 13 pass from Manning (kick failed)
NFC—T. Hill 25 pass from Muncie (Moseley kick)
NFC—Henry 86 punt return (Moseley kick)
AFC—Campbell 2 run (Fritsch kick)
NFC—Muncie 11 run (Moseley kick)
AFC—Campbell 1 run (Fritsch kick)

1979 AFC-NFC PRO BOWL

Memorial Coliseum, Los Angeles, California
January 29, 1979
Attendance: 46,281

NFC 13, AFC 7—Roger Staubach completed 9 of 15 passes for 125 yards, including the winning touchdown on a 19-yard strike to Dallas Cowboys teammate Tony Hill in the third period. The winning drive began at the AFC's 45 yard line after a shanked punt. Staubach hit Ahmad Rashad with passes of 15 and 17 yards to set up Hill's decisive catch. The victory gave the NFC a 5-4 advantage in Pro Bowl games. Rashad, who accounted for 89 yards on five receptions, was named the player of the game. The AFC led 7-6 at halftime on Bob Griese's eight-yard scoring toss to Steve Largent late in the second quarter. Largent finished the game with five receptions for 75 yards. The NFC scored first as Archie Manning marched his team 70 yards in 11 plays, capped by Wilbert Montgomery's two-yard touchdown run. The AFC's Earl Campbell was the game's leading rusher with 66 yards on 12 carries.

AFC	0	7	0	0 — 7
NFC	0	6	7	0 — 13

NFC—Montgomery 2 run (kick failed)
AFC—Largent 8 pass from Griese (Yepremian kick)
NFC—T. Hill 19 pass from Staubach (Corral kick)

1978 AFC-NFC PRO BOWL

Tampa Stadium, Tampa, Florida
January 23, 1978
Attendance: 51,337

NFC 14, AFC 13—Walter Payton, the NFL's leading rusher in 1977, sparked a second-half comeback to give the NFC a 14-13 win and tie the series between the two conferences at four victories each. Payton, who was the game's most valuable player, gained 77 yards on 13 carries and scored the tying touchdown on a one-yard burst with 7:37 left in the game. Efren Herrera kicked the winning extra point. The AFC dominated the first half of the game, taking a 13-0 lead on field goals of 21 and 39 yards by Toni Linhart and a 10-yard touchdown pass from Ken Stabler to Oakland teammate Cliff Branch. On the NFC's first possession of the second half, Pat Haden put together the first touchdown drive after Eddie Brown returned Ray Guy's punt to the AFC 46 yard line. Haden connected on all four of his passes on that drive, finally hitting Terry Metcalf with a four-yard scoring toss. The NFC continued to rally and, with Jim Hart at quarterback, moved 63 yards in 12 plays for the go-ahead score. During the winning drive, Hart completed five of six passes for 38 yards and Payton picked up 20 more on the ground.

AFC	3	10	0	0 — 13
NFC	0	0	7	7 — 14

AFC—FG Linhart 21
AFC—Branch 10 pass from Stabler (Linhart kick)
AFC—FG Linhart 39
NFC—Metcalf 4 pass from Haden (Herrera kick)
NFC—Payton 1 run (Herrera kick)

1977 AFC-NFC PRO BOWL

Kingdome, Seattle, Washington · January 17, 1977

Attendance: 64,752

AFC 24, NFC 14—O. J. Simpson's three-yard touchdown burst at 7:03 of the first quarter gave the AFC a lead it would not surrender, the victory breaking a two-game NFC win streak and giving the American Conference stars a 4-3 series lead. The AFC took a 17-7 lead midway through the second period on the first of two Ken Anderson touchdown passes, a 12-yarder to Charlie Joiner. But the NFC mounted a 73-yard drive capped by Lawrence McCutcheon's one-yard touchdown plunge to pull within three of the AFC, 17-14, at the half. Following a scoreless third quarter, player of the game Mel Blount thwarted a possible NFC score when he intercepted Jim Hart's pass in the end zone. Less than three minutes later, Blount again picked off a Hart pass, returning it 16 yards to the NFC 27. That set up Anderson's 27-yard touchdown strike to Cliff Branch for the final score.

NFC	0	14	0	0 — 14
AFC	10	7	0	7 — 24

AFC—Simpson 3 run (Linhart kick)
AFC—FG Linhart 31
NFC—Thomas 15 run (Bakken kick)
AFC—Joiner 12 pass from Anderson (Linhart kick)
NFC—McCutcheon 1 run (Bakken kick)
AFC—Branch 27 pass from Anderson (Linhart kick)

1976 AFC-NFC PRO BOWL

Superdome, New Orleans, Louisiana · January 26, 1976

Attendance: 30,546

NFC 23, AFC 20—Mike Boryla, a late substitute who did not enter the game until 5:39 remained, lifted the National Football Conference to a 23-20 victory over the American Football Conference with two touchdown passes in the final minutes. It was the second straight NFC win, squaring the series at 3-3. Until Boryla started firing the ball the AFC was in control, leading 20-9 at the half. Boryla entered the game after Billy Johnson had raced 90 yards with a punt to make the score 20-9 in favor of the AFC. He floated a 14-yard pass to Terry Metcalf and later fired an eight-yarder to Mel Gray for the winner.

AFC	0	13	0	7 — 20
NFC	0	0	9	14 — 23

AFC—FG Stenerud 20
AFC—FG Stenerud 35
AFC—Burrough 64 pass from Pastorini (Stenerud kick)
NFC—FG Bakken 42
NFC—Foreman 4 pass from Hart (kick blocked)
AFC—Johnson 90 punt return (Stenerud kick)
NFC—Metcalf 14 pass from Boryla (Bakken kick)
NFC—Gray 8 pass from Boryla (Bakken kick)

1975 AFC-NFC PRO BOWL

Orange Bowl, Miami, Florida · January 20, 1975

Attendance: 26,484

NFC 17, AFC 10—Los Angeles quarterback James Harris, who took over the NFC offense after Jim Hart of St. Louis suffered a laceration above his right eye in the second period, threw a pair of touchdown passes early in the fourth period to pace the NFC to its second victory in the five-game Pro Bowl series. The NFC win snapped a three-game AFC victory string. Harris, who was named the player of the game, connected with St. Louis's Mel Gray for an eight-yard touchdown 2:03 into the final period. One minute and 24 seconds later, following a recovery by Washington's Ken Houston of a fumble by Franco Harris of Pittsburgh, Harris tossed another eight-yard scoring pass to Washington's Charley Taylor for the decisive points.

NFC	0	3	0	14 — 17
AFC	0	0	10	0 — 10

NFC—FG Marcol 33
AFC—Warfield 32 pass from Griese (Gerela kick)
AFC—FG Gerela 33
NFC—Gray 8 pass from J. Harris (Marcol kick)
NFC—Taylor 8 pass from J. Harris (Marcol kick)

1974 AFC-NFC PRO BOWL

Arrowhead, Kansas City, Missouri · January 20, 1974

Attendance: 66,918

AFC 15, NFC 13—Miami's Garo Yepremian kicked his fifth consecutive field goal without a miss from the 42 yard line with 21 seconds remaining to give the AFC its third straight victory since the NFC won the inaugural game following the 1970 season. The field goal by Yepremian, who was voted the game's outstanding player, offset a 21-yard field goal by Atlanta's Nick Mike-Mayer that had given the NFC a 13-12 advantage with 1:41 remaining. The only touchdown in the game was scored by the NFC on a 14-yard pass from Roman Gabriel to Lawrence McCutcheon.

NFC	0	10	0	3 — 13
AFC	3	3	3	6 — 15

AFC—FG Yepremian 16
NFC—FG Mike-Mayer 27
NFC—McCutcheon 14 pass from Gabriel (Mike-Mayer kick)
AFC—FG Yepremian 37
AFC—FG Yepremian 27
AFC—FG Yepremian 41
NFC—FG Mike-Mayer 21
AFC—FG Yepremian 42

1973 AFC-NFC PRO BOWL

Texas Stadium, Irving, Texas · January 21, 1973

Attendance: 37,091

AFC 33, NFC 28—Paced by the rushing and receiving of player of the game O.J. Simpson, the AFC erased a 14-0 first period deficit and built a commanding 33-14 lead midway through the fourth period before the NFC managed two touchdowns in the final minute of play. Simpson rushed for 112 yards and caught three passes for 58 more to gain unanimous recognition in the balloting for player of the game. John Brockington scored three touchdowns for the NFC.

AFC	0	10	10	13 — 33
NFC	14	0	0	14 — 28

NFC—Brockington 1 run (Marcol kick)
NFC—Brockington 3 pass from Kilmer (Marcol kick)
AFC—Simpson 7 run (Gerela kick)
AFC—FG Gerela 18
AFC—FG Gerela 22
AFC—Hubbard 11 run (Gerela kick)
AFC—O. Taylor 5 pass from Lamonica (kick failed)
AFC—Bell 12 interception return (Gerela kick)
NFC—Brockington 1 run (Marcol kick)
NFC—Kwalick 12 pass from Snead (Marcol kick)

1972 AFC-NFC PRO BOWL

Memorial Coliseum, Los Angeles, California · January 23, 1972

Attendance: 53,647

AFC 26, NFC 13—Four field goals by Jan Stenerud of Kansas City, including a 6-6 tie-breaker from 48 yards, helped lift the AFC from a 6-0 deficit to a 19-6 advantage early in the fourth period. The AFC defense picked off three interceptions. Stenerud was selected as the outstanding offensive player and his Kansas City teammate, linebacker Willie Lanier, was the game's outstanding defensive player.

AFC	0	3	13	10 — 26
NFC	0	6	0	7 — 13

NFC—Grim 50 pass from Landry (kick failed)
AFC—FG Stenerud 25
AFC—FG Stenerud 23
AFC—FG Stenerud 48
AFC—Morin 5 pass from Dawson (Stenerud kick)
AFC—FG Stenerud 42
NFC—V. Washington 2 run (Knight kick)
AFC—F. Little 6 run (Stenerud kick)

1971 AFC-NFC PRO BOWL

Memorial Coliseum, Los Angeles, California · January 24, 1971

Attendance: 48,222

NFC 27, AFC 6—Mel Renfro of Dallas broke open the first meeting between the American Football Conference and National Football Conference all-pro teams as he returned a pair of punts 82 and 56 yards for touchdowns in the final period to provide the NFC with a 27-6 victory over the AFC. Renfro was voted the game's outstanding back and linebacker Fred Carr of Green Bay the outstanding lineman.

AFC	0	3	3	0 — 6
NFC	0	3	10	14 — 27

AFC—FG Stenerud 37
NFC—FG Cox 13
NFC—Osborn 23 pass from Brodie (Cox kick)
NFC—FG Cox 35
AFC—FG Stenerud 16
NFC—Renfro 82 punt return (Cox kick)
NFC—Renfro 56 punt return (Cox kick)

Regular Season Interconference Records, 1970-1984

American Football Conference

Eastern Division
	W	L	T	Pct.
Miami	40	8	0	.833
New York Jets	20	26	0	.435
New England	20	27	0	.426
Indianapolis	17	24	1	.417
Buffalo	18	28	1	.394

Central Division
	W	L	T	Pct.
Pittsburgh	33	14	0	.702
Cincinnati	29	19	0	.604
Cleveland	25	24	0	.510
Houston	17	31	1	.357

Western Division
	W	L	T	Pct.
Los Angeles Raiders	37	12	1	.750
Seattle	14	10	0	.583
Denver	27	24	1	.529
San Diego	24	23	0	.511
Kansas City	17	22	2	.439

National Football Conference

Eastern Division
	W	L	T	Pct.
Dallas	35	14	0	.714
Philadelphia	27	20	0	.574
Washington	25	21	0	.543
St. Louis	21	21	2	.500
New York Giants	16	23	0	.410

Central Division
	W	L	T	Pct.
Minnesota	25	26	0	.490
Detroit	20	25	1	.446
Tampa Bay	9	13	0	.409
Green Bay	17	29	2	.375
Chicago	16	31	0	.340

Western Division
	W	L	T	Pct.
Los Angeles Rams	28	22	0	.560
San Francisco	23	28	0	.451
Atlanta	19	30	0	.388
New Orleans	11	35	2	.250

Interconference Victories, 1970-1984

Regular Season
	AFC	NFC	Tie
1970	12	27	1
1971	15	23	2
1972	20	19	1
1973	19	19	2
1974	23	17	0
1975	23	17	0
1976	16	12	0
1977	19	9	0
1978	31	21	0
1979	36	16	0
1980	33	19	0
1981	24	28	0
1982	15	14	1
1983	26	26	0
1984	26	26	0
Total	338	293	7

Preseason
	AFC	NFC	Tie
1970	21	28	1
1971	28	28	3
1972	27	25	4
1973	23	35	2
1974	35	25	0
1975	30	26	1
1976	30	31	0
1977	38	25	0
1978	20	19	0
1979	25	18	0
1980	22	20	1
1981	18	19	0
1982	25	16	0
1983	15	24	0
1984	16	19	0
Total	373	358	12

AFC VS. NFC (REGULAR SEASON), 1970-1984

	1970	1971	1972	1973	1974	1975	1976	1977	1978	1979	1980	1981	1982	1983	1984	Totals
Miami	2-1	3-0	3-0	3-0	2-1	3-0	0-2	2-0	3-1	4-0	4-0	3-1	1-1	3-1	4-0	40-8
L.A. Raiders	1-2	1-1-1	3-0	2-1	3-0	3-0	3-0	1-1	4-0	4-0	2-2	2-2	3-0	2-2	3-1	37-12-1
Pittsburgh	0-3	1-2	2-1	3-0	3-0	2-1	1-1	2-0	3-1	3-1	4-0	3-1	1-0	2-2	3-1	33-14
Cincinnati	1-2	1-2	2-1	2-1	2-1	3-0	2-0	2-1	2-2	2-2	2-2	2-2	1-0	3-1	2-2	29-19
Denver	2-2	1-3	1-3	0-3-1	2-2	2-1	2-0	1-1	2-2	3-1	3-1	3-1	2-1	0-2	3-1	27-24-1
Cleveland	0-3	2-1	1-2	1-2	1-2	1-3	2-0	1-1	4-0	3-1	3-1	0-2	2-2	1-3		25-24
San Diego	1-2	2-1	0-3	1-2	1-2	0-3	2-0	1-1	2-2	3-1	2-2	2-2	1-0	2-2	4-0	24-23
N.Y. Jets	2-1	0-3	1-2	0-3	2-1	0-3	0-2	1-1	1-3	3-1	1-3	2-0	4-0	3-1	0-2	20-26
New England	0-3	0-3	3-0	2-1	3-0	1-2	1-1	2-0	3-1	3-1	1-3	0-4	0-1	2-2	0-4	20-27
Buffalo	0-3	0-3	2-0-1	2-1	2-1	1-2	0-2	1-1	1-1	2-2	3-1	1-3	1-2	1-3	1-3	18-28-1
Kansas City	2-1	2-1	2-1	1-1-1	1-2	2-1	1-1	1-1	0-2	0-2	2-0	2-2	0-3	2-2	1-1	17-22-2
Indianapolis	3-0	2-1	0-3	2-1	1-2	1-2	0-2	1-1	2-2	1-1	1-1	0-4	0-1-1	2-1	0-4	17-24-1
Houston	0-3	0-2-1	0-3	0-3	0-3	3-0	2-0	2-0	2-2	2-2	4-0	1-3	0-3	1-3	0-4	17-31-1
Seattle								1-0	3-1	3-1	1-3	0-2	1-0	1-3	4-0	14-10
Tampa Bay														0-1		0-1
TOTALS	12-27-1	15-23-2	20-19-1	19-19-2	23-17	23-17	16-12	19-9	31-21	36-16	33-19	24-28	15-14-1	26-26	26-26	338-293-7

NFC VS. AFC (REGULAR SEASON), 1970-1984

	1970	1971	1972	1973	1974	1975	1976	1977	1978	1979	1980	1981	1982	1983	1984	Totals
Dallas	3-0	3-0	3-0	2-1	2-1	2-1	2-0	1-1	3-1	1-3	3-1	4-0	2-1	2-2	2-2	35-14
L.A. Rams	2-1	1-2	1-2	3-0	3-1	3-0	1-1	2-0	2-2	2-2	2-2	1-3	1-2	1-3	3-1	28-22
Philadelphia	1-2	1-2	2-1	2-1	2-1	0-3	0-2	1-1	3-1	2-2	3-1	3-1	2-1	1-1	3-1	27-20
Washington	2-1	1-2	1-2	2-1	2-1	1-2	1-1	1-1	2-2	2-2	1-3	2-2		4-0	3-1	25-21
Minnesota	2-1	2-1	1-2	2-1	2-1	4-0	2-0	1-1	1-3	1-3	1-3	1-3	1-3	4-0	0-4	25-26
San Francisco	4-0	2-1	2-1	1-2	0-3	1-2	1-1	0-2	1-3	0-4	2-2	3-1	1-3	2-2	3-1	23-28
St. Louis	2-0-1	2-1	1-2	0-2-1	2-1	2-1	1-1	0-2	0-4	1-3	1-3	3-1		3-1	3-1	21-21-2
Detroit	3-0	4-0	2-0-1	0-3	1-2	1-2	2-0	2-0	2-2	0-4	0-2	2-2	0-1	1-3	0-4	20-25-1
Atlanta	1-2	3-0	2-2	2-1	0-3	1-2	0-2	0-2	1-3	1-3	2-2	1-3	1-1	3-1	1-3	19-30
Green Bay	2-1	2-1	2-1	1-1-1	2-1	0-3	0-2	0-3	2-2	1-3	1-3	1-1	1-1-1	2-2	0-4	17-29-2
N.Y. Giants	3-0	1-2	1-2	1-2	1-2	2-1	0-2	0-2	1-1	1-1	1-3	1-1	1-0	0-4	2-0	16-23
Chicago	1-2	1-2	1-2	2-2	0-3	0-3	0-2	1-1	0-4	2-2	0-4	4-0	1-1	1-1	2-2	16-31
New Orleans	0-3	0-1-2	0-3	1-2	0-3	0-3	1-2	0-2	1-3	0-4	1-3	2-2	1-0	1-3	3-1	11-35-2
Tampa Bay								0-1	2-0	2-0	1-3	0-4	2-1	1-3	1-1	9-13
Seattle						1-0										0-1
TOTALS	27-12-1	23-15-2	19-20-1	19-19-2	17-23	17-23	12-16	9-19	21-31	16-36	19-33	28-24	14-15-1	26-26	26-26	293-338-7

1984 Interconference Games
(Home Team in capital letters)

AFC 26, NFC 26

AFC Victories
Miami 35, WASHINGTON 17
San Diego 42, MINNESOTA 13
L.A. RAIDERS 28, Green Bay 7
PITTSBURGH 24, L.A. Rams 14
SEATTLE 38, Chicago 9
SAN DIEGO 27, Detroit 24
Miami 36, ST. LOUIS 28
Seattle 20, MINNESOTA 12
Denver 28, DETROIT 7
San Diego 34, GREEN BAY 28
L.A. RAIDERS 23, Minnesota 20
Pittsburgh 20, SAN FRANCISCO 17
DENVER 17, Green Bay 14
Seattle 30, GREEN BAY 24
PITTSBURGH 35, Atlanta 10
KANSAS CITY 24, Tampa Bay 20
MIAMI 24, Philadelphia 23
Cleveland 23, ATLANTA 7
BUFFALO 14, Dallas 3
DENVER 42, Minnesota 21
CINCINNATI 35, Atlanta 14
SEATTLE 38, Detroit 17
SAN DIEGO 20, Chicago 7
Cincinnati 24, NEW ORLEANS 21
L.A. Raiders 24, DETROIT 3
MIAMI 28, Dallas 21

NFC Victories
ST. LOUIS 37, Buffalo 7
L.A. RAMS 20, Cleveland 17
CHICAGO 27, Denver 0
St. Louis 34, INDIANAPOLIS 33
ATLANTA 42, Houston 10
L.A. RAMS 24, Cincinnati 14
WASHINGTON 26, New England 10
New Orleans 27, HOUSTON 10
Philadelphia 27, BUFFALO 17
Washington 35, INDIANAPOLIS 7
PHILADELPHIA 16, Indianapolis 7
San Francisco 34, HOUSTON 21
DALLAS 22, Indianapolis 3
New Orleans 16, CLEVELAND 14
SAN FRANCISCO 23, Cincinnati 17
CHICAGO 17, L.A. Raiders 6
San Francisco 41, CLEVELAND 7
NEW ORLEANS 27, Pittsburgh 24
DALLAS 20, New England 17
WASHINGTON 41, Buffalo 14
N.Y. GIANTS 28, Kansas City 27
N.Y. Giants 20, N.Y. JETS 10
St. Louis 33, NEW ENGLAND 10
L.A. RAMS 27, Houston 16
PHILADELPHIA 27, New England 17
TAMPA BAY 41, N.Y. Jets 21

Monday Night Football, 1970–1984

(Home Team in capitals, games listed in chronological order.)

1984
Dallas 20, LOS ANGELES RAMS 13
SAN FRANCISCO 37, Washington 31
Miami 21, BUFFALO 17
LOS ANGELES RAIDERS 33, San Diego 30
PITTSBURGH 38, Cincinnati 17
San Francisco 31, NEW YORK GIANTS 10
DENVER 17, Green Bay 14
Los Angeles Rams 24, ATLANTA 10
Seattle 24, SAN DIEGO 0
WASHINGTON 27, Atlanta 14
SEATTLE 17, Los Angeles Raiders 14
NEW ORLEANS 27, Pittsburgh 24
MIAMI 28, New York Jets 17
SAN DIEGO 20, Chicago 7
Los Angeles Raiders 24, DETROIT 3
MIAMI 28, Dallas 21

1983
Dallas 31, WASHINGTON 30
San Diego 17, KANSAS CITY 14
LOS ANGELES RAIDERS 27, Miami 14
NEW YORK GIANTS 27, Green Bay 3
New York Jets 34, BUFFALO 10
Pittsburgh 24, CINCINNATI 14
GREEN BAY 48, Washington 47
ST. LOUIS 20, New York Giants 20 (OT)
Washington 27, SAN DIEGO 24
DETROIT 15, New York Giants 9
Los Angeles Rams 36, ATLANTA 13
New York Jets 31, NEW ORLEANS 28
MIAMI 38, Cincinnati 14
DETROIT 13, Minnesota 2
Green Bay 12, TAMPA BAY 9 (OT)
SAN FRANCISCO 42, Dallas 17

1982
Pittsburgh 36, DALLAS 28
Green Bay 27, NEW YORK GIANTS 19
LOS ANGELES RAIDERS 28, San Diego 24
TAMPA BAY 23, Miami 17
New York Jets 28, DETROIT 13
Dallas 37, HOUSTON 7
SAN DIEGO 50, Cincinnati 34
MIAMI 27, Buffalo 10
MINNESOTA 31, Dallas 27

1981
San Diego 44, CLEVELAND 14
Oakland 36, MINNESOTA 10
Dallas 35, NEW ENGLAND 21
Los Angeles 24, CHICAGO 7
PHILADELPHIA 16, Atlanta 13
BUFFALO 31, Miami 21
DETROIT 48, Chicago 17
PITTSBURGH 26, Houston 13
DENVER 19, Minnesota 17
DALLAS 27, Buffalo 14
SEATTLE 44, San Diego 23
ATLANTA 31, Minnesota 30
MIAMI 13, Philadelphia 10
OAKLAND 30, Pittsburgh 27
LOS ANGELES 21, Atlanta 16
SAN DIEGO 23, Oakland 10

1980
Dallas 17, WASHINGTON 3
Houston 16, CLEVELAND 7
PHILADELPHIA 35, New York Giants 3
NEW ENGLAND 23, Denver 14
CHICAGO 23, Tampa Bay 0
DENVER 20, Washington 17
Oakland 45, PITTSBURGH 34
NEW YORK JETS 17, Miami 14
CLEVELAND 27, Chicago 21
HOUSTON 38, New England 34
Oakland 19, SEATTLE 17
Los Angeles 27, NEW ORLEANS 7
OAKLAND 9, Denver 3

MIAMI 16, New England 13 (OT)
LOS ANGELES 38, Dallas 14
SAN DIEGO 26, Pittsburgh 17

1979
Pittsburgh 16, NEW ENGLAND 13 (OT)
Atlanta 14, PHILADELPHIA 10
WASHINGTON 27, New York Giants 0
CLEVELAND 26, Dallas 7
GREEN BAY 27, New England 14
OAKLAND 13, Miami 3
NEW YORK JETS 14, Minnesota 7
PITTSBURGH 42, Denver 7
Seattle 31, ATLANTA 28
Houston 9, MIAMI 6
Philadelphia 31, DALLAS 21
LOS ANGELES 20, Atlanta 14
SEATTLE 30, New York Jets 7
Oakland 42, NEW ORLEANS 35
HOUSTON 20, Pittsburgh 17
SAN DIEGO 17, Denver 7

1978
DALLAS 38, Baltimore 0
MINNESOTA 12, Denver 9 (OT)
Baltimore 34, NEW ENGLAND 27
Minnesota 24, CHICAGO 20
WASHINGTON 9, Dallas 5
MIAMI 21, Cincinnati 0
DENVER 16, Chicago 7
Houston 24, PITTSBURGH 17
ATLANTA 15, Los Angeles 7
BALTIMORE 21, Washington 17
Oakland 34, CINCINNATI 21
HOUSTON 35, Miami 30
Pittsburgh 24, SAN FRANCISCO 7
SAN DIEGO 40, Chicago 7
Cincinnati 20, LOS ANGELES 19
MIAMI 23, New England 3

1977
PITTSBURGH 27, San Francisco 0
CLEVELAND 30, New England 27 (OT)
Oakland 37, KANSAS CITY 28
CHICAGO 24, Los Angeles 23
PITTSBURGH 20, Cincinnati 14
LOS ANGELES 35, Minnesota 3
ST. LOUIS 28, New York Giants 0
BALTIMORE 10, Washington 3
St. Louis 24, DALLAS 17
WASHINGTON 10, Green Bay 9
OAKLAND 34, Buffalo 13
MIAMI 16, Baltimore 6
Dallas 42, SAN FRANCISCO 35

1976
Miami 30, BUFFALO 21
Oakland 24, KANSAS CITY 21
Washington 20, PHILADELPHIA 17 (OT)
MINNESOTA 17, Pittsburgh 6
San Francisco 16, LOS ANGELES 0
NEW ENGLAND 41, New York Jets 7
WASHINGTON 20, St. Louis 10
BALTIMORE 38, Houston 14
CINCINNATI 20, Los Angeles 12
DALLAS 17, Buffalo 10
Baltimore 17, MIAMI 16
SAN FRANCISCO 20, Minnesota 16
OAKLAND 35, Cincinnati 20

1975
Oakland 31, MIAMI 21
DENVER 23, Green Bay 13
Dallas 36, DETROIT 10
WASHINGTON 27, St. Louis 17
New York Giants 17, BUFFALO 14
Minnesota 13, CHICAGO 9
Los Angeles 42, PHILADELPHIA 3
Kansas City 34, DALLAS 31
CINCINNATI 33, Buffalo 24

Pittsburgh 32, HOUSTON 9
MIAMI 20, New England 7
OAKLAND 17, Denver 10
SAN DIEGO 24, New York Jets 16

1974
BUFFALO 21, Oakland 20
PHILADELPHIA 13, Dallas 10
WASHINGTON 30, Denver 3
MIAMI 21, New York Jets 17
DETROIT 17, San Francisco 13
CHICAGO 10, Green Bay 9
PITTSBURGH 24, Atlanta 17
Los Angeles 15, SAN FRANCISCO 13
Minnesota 28, ST. LOUIS 24
Kansas City 42, DENVER 34
Pittsburgh 28, NEW ORLEANS 7
MIAMI 24, Cincinnati 3
Washington 23, LOS ANGELES 17

1973
GREEN BAY 23, New York Jets 7
DALLAS 40, New Orleans 3
DETROIT 31, Atlanta 6
WASHINGTON 14, Dallas 7
Miami 17, CLEVELAND 9
DENVER 23, Oakland 23
BUFFALO 23, Kansas City 14
PITTSBURGH 21, Washington 16
KANSAS CITY 19, Chicago 7
ATLANTA 20, Minnesota 14
SAN FRANCISCO 20, Green Bay 6
MIAMI 30, Pittsburgh 26
LOS ANGELES 40, New York Giants 6

1972
Washington 24, MINNESOTA 21
Kansas City 20, NEW ORLEANS 17
New York Giants 27, PHILADELPHIA 12
Oakland 34, HOUSTON 0
Green Bay 24, DETROIT 23
CHICAGO 13, Minnesota 10
DALLAS 28, Detroit 24
Baltimore 24, NEW ENGLAND 17
Cleveland 21, SAN DIEGO 17
WASHINGTON 24, Atlanta 13
MIAMI 31, St. Louis 10
Los Angeles 26, SAN FRANCISCO 16
OAKLAND 24, New York Jets 16

1971
Minnesota 16, DETROIT 13
ST. LOUIS 17, New York Jets 10
Oakland 34, CLEVELAND 20
DALLAS 20, New York Giants 13
KANSAS CITY 38, Pittsburgh 16
MINNESOTA 10, Baltimore 3
GREEN BAY 14, Detroit 14
BALTIMORE 24, Los Angeles 17
SAN DIEGO 20, St. Louis 17
ATLANTA 28, Green Bay 21
MIAMI 34, Chicago 3
Kansas City 26, SAN FRANCISCO 17
Washington 38, LOS ANGELES 24

1970
CLEVELAND 31, New York Jets 21
Kansas City 44, BALTIMORE 24
DETROIT 28, Chicago 14
Green Bay 22, SAN DIEGO 20
OAKLAND 34, Washington 20
MINNESOTA 13, Los Angeles 3
PITTSBURGH 21, Cincinnati 10
Baltimore 13, GREEN BAY 10
St. Louis 38, DALLAS 0
PHILADELPHIA 23, New York Giants 20
Miami 20, ATLANTA 7
Cleveland 21, HOUSTON 10
Detroit 28, LOS ANGELES 23

Monday Night Won-Loss Records, 1970-1984

	Total	1984	1983	1982	1981	1980	1979	1978	1977	1976	1975	1974	1973	1972	1971	1970
Buffalo	3-9	0-1	0-1	0-1	1-1				0-1	0-2	0-2	1-0	1-0			
Cincinnati	3-10	0-1	0-2	0-1				1-2	0-1	1-1	1-0	0-1				0-1
Cleveland	6-4				0-1	1-1	1-0		1-0				0-1	1-0	0-1	2-0	
Denver	5-8-1	1-0			1-0	1-2	0-2	1-1			1-1	0-2	0-0-1				
Houston	6-6			0-1	0-1	2-0	2-0	2-0		0-1	0-1			0-1		0-1	
Indianapolis	8-4							2-1	1-1	2-0				1-0	1-1	1-1	
Kansas City	7-4		0-1						0-1	0-1	1-0	1-0	1-1	1-0	2-0	1-0	
L.A. Raiders	22-3-1	2-1	1-0	1-0	2-1	3-0	2-0	1-0	2-0	2-0	2-0	0-1	0-0-1	2-0	1-0	1-0
Miami	19-9	3-0	1-1	1-1	1-1	1-1	0-2	2-1	1-0	1-1	1-1	2-0	2-0	1-0	1-0	1-0
New England	2-10				0-1	1-2	0-2	0-2	0-1	1-0	0-1			0-1		
New York Jets	5-9	0-1	2-0	1-0		1-0	1-1			0-1	0-1	0-1	0-1	0-1	0-1	0-1
Pittsburgh	14-9	1-1	1-0	1-0	1-1	0-2	2-1	1-1	2-0	0-1	1-0	2-0	1-1		0-1	1-0
San Diego	10-7	1-2	1-1	1-1	2-1	1-0	1-0	1-0			1-0			0-1	1-0	0-1
Seattle	5-1	2-0			1-0	0-1	2-0									
Atlanta	5-11	0-2	0-1		1-2		1-2	1-0				0-1	1-1	0-1	1-0	0-1
Chicago	4-11	0-1			0-2	1-1		0-3	1-0		0-1	1-0	0-1	1-0	0-1	0-1
Dallas	13-13	1-1	1-1	1-2	2-0	1-1	0-2	1-1	1-1	1-0	1-1	0-1	1-1	1-0	1-0	0-1
Detroit	7-6-1	0-1	2-0	0-1	1-0						0-1	1-0	1-0	0-2	0-1-1	2-0
Green Bay	7-8-1	0-1	2-1	1-0			1-0		0-1		0-1	0-1	1-1	1-0	0-1-1	1-1
L.A. Rams	12-11	1-1	1-0		2-0	2-0	1-0	0-2	1-1	0-2	1-0	1-1	1-0	1-0	0-2	0-2
Minnesota	9-10		0-1	1-0	0-3		0-1	2-0	0-1	1-1	1-0	1-0	0-1	0-2	2-0	1-0
New Orleans	1-6	1-0	0-1			0-1	0-1				0-1	0-1	0-1			
New York Giants	3-9-1	0-1	1-1-1	0-1		0-1	0-1		0-1		1-0		0-1	1-0	0-1	0-1
Philadelphia	5-5				1-1	1-0	1-1			0-1	0-1	1-0		0-1		1-0
St. Louis	4-5-1		0-0-1						2-0	0-1	0-1	0-1		0-1	1-1	1-0
San Francisco	6-7	2-0	1-0				0-1	0-2	2-0			0-2	1-0	0-1	0-1	
Tampa Bay	1-2		0-1	1-0	0-1											
Washington	14-9	1-1	1-2		0-2	1-0	1-1	1-1	1-1	2-0	1-0	2-0	1-1	2-0	1-0	0-1

Monday Night Syndrome

1984

Of the 15 winning teams:	6 won the next week	Of the 30 NFL teams:	14 won the next week
	9 lost the next week		16 lost the next week
	0 tied the next week		0 tied the next week
Of the 15 losing teams:	8 won the next week		
	7 lost the next week		
	0 tied the next week		

1970-84

Of the 199 winning teams:	109 won the next week	Of the 404 NFL teams:	217 won the next week
	87 lost the next week		183 lost the next week
	3 tied the next week		4 tied the next week
Of the 199 losing teams:	103 won the next week		
	95 lost the next week		
	1 tied the next week		
Of the 6 tying teams:	5 won the next week		
	1 lost the next week		
	0 tied the next week		

Thursday-Sunday Night Football, 1978-1984

(Home Team in capitals, games listed in chronological order.)

1984
Pittsburgh 23, NEW YORK JETS 17 (Thur.)
Denver 24, CLEVELAND 14 (Sun.)
DALLAS 30, New Orleans 27 (Sun.)
Washington 31, MINNESOTA 17 (Thur.)

1983
San Francisco 48, MINNESOTA 17 (Thur.)
CLEVELAND 17, Cincinnati 7 (Thur.)
L.A. Raiders 40, DALLAS 38 (Sun.)
L.A. Raiders 42, SAN DIEGO 10 (Thur.)

1982
BUFFALO 23, Minnesota 22 (Thur.)
SAN FRANCISCO 30, L.A. Rams 24 (Thur.)
ATLANTA 17, San Francisco 7 (Sun.)

1981
MIAMI 30, Pittsburgh 10 (Thur.)
Philadelphia 20, BUFFALO 14 (Thur.)
DALLAS 29, Los Angeles 17 (Sun.)
HOUSTON 17, Cleveland 13 (Thur.)

1980
TAMPA BAY 10, Los Angeles 9 (Thur.)
DALLAS 42, San Diego 31 (Sun.)
San Diego 27, MIAMI 24 (OT) (Thur.)
HOUSTON 6, Pittsburgh 0 (Thur.)

1979
Los Angeles 13, DENVER 9 (Thur.)
DALLAS 30, Los Angeles 6 (Sun.)
OAKLAND 45, San Diego 22 (Thur.)
MIAMI 39, New England 24 (Thur.)

1978
New England 21, OAKLAND 14 (Sun.)
Minnesota 21, DALLAS 10 (Thur.)
LOS ANGELES 10, Pittsburgh 7 (Sun.)
Denver 21, OAKLAND 6 (Sun.)

History of Overtime Games

Preseason

Aug. 28, 1955	Los Angeles 23, New York Giants 17, at Portland, Oregon
Aug. 24, 1962	Denver 27, Dallas Texans 24, at Fort Worth, Texas
Aug. 10, 1974	San Diego 20, New York Jets 14, at San Diego
Aug. 17, 1974	Pittsburgh 33, Philadelphia 30, at Philadelphia
Aug. 17, 1974	Dallas 19, Houston 13, at Dallas
Aug. 17, 1974	Cincinnati 13, Atlanta 7, at Atlanta
Sept. 6, 1974	Buffalo 23, New York Giants 17, at Buffalo
Aug. 9, 1975	Baltimore 23, Denver 20, at Denver
Aug. 30, 1975	New England 20, Green Bay 17, at Milwaukee
Sept. 13, 1975	Minnesota 14, San Diego 14, at San Diego
Aug. 1, 1976	New England 21, New York Giants 7, at New England
Aug. 2, 1976	Kansas City 9, Houston 3, at Kansas City
Aug. 20, 1976	New Orleans 26, Baltimore 20, at Baltimore
Sept. 4, 1976	Dallas 26, Houston 20, at Dallas
Aug. 13, 1977	Seattle 23, Dallas 17, at Seattle
Aug. 28, 1977	New England 13, Pittsburgh 10, at New England
Aug. 28, 1977	New York Giants 24, Buffalo 21, at East Rutherford, N.J.
Aug. 2, 1979	Seattle 12, Minnesota 9, at Minnesota
Aug. 4, 1979	Los Angeles 20, Oakland 14, at Los Angeles
Aug. 24, 1979	Denver 20, New England 17, at Denver
Aug. 23, 1980	Tampa Bay 20, Cincinnati 14, at Tampa Bay
Aug. 5, 1981	San Francisco 27, Seattle 24, at Seattle
Aug. 29, 1981	New Orleans 20, Detroit 17, at New Orleans
Aug. 28, 1982	Miami 17, Kansas City 17, at Kansas City
Sept. 3, 1982	Miami 16, New York Giants 13, at Miami
Aug. 6, 1983	L.A. Raiders 26, San Francisco 23, at Los Angeles
Aug. 6, 1983	Atlanta 13, Washington 10, at Atlanta
Aug. 13, 1983	St. Louis 27, Chicago 24, at St. Louis
Aug. 18, 1983	New York Jets 20, Cincinnati 17, at Cincinnati
Aug. 27, 1983	Chicago 20, Kansas City 17, at Chicago
Aug. 11, 1984	Pittsburgh 20, Philadelphia 17, at Pittsburgh

Regular Season

Sept. 22, 1974—Pittsburgh 35, Denver 35, at Denver; Steelers win toss. Gilliam's pass intercepted and returned by Rowser to Denver's 42. Turner misses 41-yard field goal. Walden punts and Greer returns to Broncos' 39. Van Heusen punts and Edwards returns to Steelers' 16. Game ends with Steelers on own 26.

Nov. 10, 1974—New York Jets 26, New York Giants 20, at New Haven, Conn.; Giants win toss. Gogolak misses 42-yard field goal. Namath passes to Boozer for five yards and touchdown at 6:53.

Sept. 28, 1975—Dallas 37, St. Louis 31, at Dallas; Cardinals win toss. Hart's pass intercepted and returned by Jordan to Cardinals' 37. Staubach passes to DuPree for three yards and touchdown at 7:53.

Oct. 12, 1975—Los Angeles 13, San Diego 10, at San Diego; Chargers win toss. Partee punts to Rams' 14. Dempsey kicks 22-yard field goal at 9:27.

Nov. 2, 1975—Washington 30, Dallas 24, at Washington; Cowboys win toss. Staubach's pass intercepted and returned by Houston to Cowboys' 35. Kilmer runs one yard for touchdown at 6:34.

Nov. 16, 1975—St. Louis 20, Washington 17, at St. Louis; Cardinals win toss. Bakken kicks 37-yard field goal at 7:00.

Nov. 23, 1975—Kansas City 24, Detroit 21, at Kansas City; Lions win toss. Chiefs take over on downs at own 38. Stenerud kicks 26-yard field goal at 6:44.

Nov. 23, 1975—Oakland 26, Washington 23, at Washington; Redskins win toss. Bragg punts to Raiders' 42. Blanda kicks 27-yard field goal at 7:13.

Nov. 30, 1975—Denver 13, San Diego 10, at Denver; Broncos win toss. Turner kicks 25-yard field goal at 4:13.

Nov. 30, 1975—Oakland 37, Atlanta 34, at Oakland; Falcons win toss. James punts to Raiders' 16. Guy punts and Herron returns to Falcons' 41. Nick Mike-Mayer misses 45-yard field goal. Guy punts into Falcons' end zone. James punts to Raiders' 39. Blanda kicks 36-yard field goal at 15:00.

Dec. 14, 1975—Baltimore 10, Miami 7, at Baltimore; Dolphins win toss. Seiple punts to Colts' 4. Linhart kicks 31-yard field goal at 12:44.

Sept. 19, 1976—Minnesota 10, Los Angeles 10, at Minnesota; Vikings win toss. Tarkenton's pass intercepted by Monte Jackson and returned to Minnesota 16. Allen blocks Dempsey's 30-yard field goal attempt, ball rolls into end zone for touchback. Clabo punts and Scribner returns to Rams' 20. Rusty Jackson punts to Vikings' 35. Tarkenton's pass intercepted by Kay at Rams' 1, no return. Game ends with Rams on own 3.

*Sept. 27, 1976—Washington 20, Philadelphia 17, at Philadelphia; Eagles win toss. Jones punts and E. Brown loses one yard on return to Redskins' 40. Bragg punts 51 yards into end zone for touchback. Jones punts and E. Brown returns to Redskins' 42. Bragg punts and Marshall returns to Eagles' 41. Boryla's pass intercepted by Dusek at Redskins' 37, no return. Bragg punts and Bradley returns. Philadelphia holding penalty moves ball back to Eagles' 8. Boryla pass intercepted by E. Brown and returned to Eagles' 22. Moseley kicks 29-yard field goal at 12:49.

Oct. 17, 1976—Kansas City 20, Miami 17, at Miami; Chiefs win toss. Wilson punts into end zone for touchback. Bulaich fumbles into Kansas City end zone, Collier recovers for touchdown. Stenerud kicks 34-yard field goal at 14:48.

Oct. 31, 1976—St. Louis 23, San Francisco 20, at St. Louis; Cardinals win toss. Joyce punts and Leonard fumbles on return, Jones recovers at 49ers' 43. Bakken kicks 21-yard field goal at 6:42.

Dec. 5, 1976—San Diego 13, San Francisco 7, at San Diego; Chargers win toss. Morris runs 13 yards for touchdown at 5:12.

Sept. 18, 1977—Dallas 16, Minnesota 10, at Minnesota; Vikings win toss. Dallas starts on Vikings' 47 after a punt early in the overtime period. Staubach scores seven plays later on a four-yard run at 6:14.

*Sept. 26, 1977—Cleveland 30, New England 27, at Cleveland; Browns win toss. Sipe throws a 22-yard pass to Logan at Patriots' 19. Cockroft kicks 35-yard field goal at 4:45.

Oct. 16, 1977—Minnesota 22, Chicago 16, at Minnesota; Bears win toss. Parsons punts 53 yards to Vikings' 18. Minnesota drives to Bears' 11. On a first-and-10, Vikings fake a field goal and holder Krause hits Voigt with a touchdown pass at 6:45.

Oct. 30, 1977—Cincinnati 13, Houston 10, at Cincinnati; Bengals win toss. Bahr kicks a 22-yard field goal at 5:51.

Nov. 13, 1977—San Francisco 10, New Orleans 7, at New Orleans; Saints win toss. Saints fail to move ball and Blanchard punts to 49ers' 41. Wersching kicks a 33-yard field goal at 6:33.

Dec. 18, 1977—Chicago 12, New York Giants 9, at East Rutherford, N.J.; Giants win toss. The ball changes hands eight times before Thomas kicks a 28-yard field goal at 14:51.

Sept. 10, 1978—Cleveland 13, Cincinnati 10, at Cleveland; Browns win toss. Collins returns kickoff 41 yards to Browns' 47. Cockroft kicks 27-yard field goal at 4:30.

*Sept. 11, 1978—Minnesota 12, Denver 9, at Minnesota; Vikings win toss. Danmeier kicks 44-yard field goal at 2:56.

Sept. 24, 1978—Pittsburgh 15, Cleveland 9, at Pittsburgh; Steelers win toss. Cunningham scores on a 37-yard "gadget" pass from Bradshaw at 3:43. Steelers start winning drive on their 21.

Sept. 24, 1978—Denver 23, Kansas City 17, at Kansas City; Broncos win toss. Dilts punts to Broncos' 40 where Reed fails to make first down on fourth-and-one situation. Broncos march downfield. Preston scores two-yard touchdown at 10:28.

Oct. 1, 1978—Oakland 25, Chicago 19, at Chicago; Bears win toss. Both teams punt on first possession. On Chicago's second offensive series, Colzie intercepts Avellini's pass and returns it to Bears' 3. Three plays later, Whittington runs two yards for a touchdown at 5:19.

Oct. 15, 1978—Dallas 24, St. Louis 21, at St. Louis; Cowboys win toss. Dallas drives from its 23 into field goal range. Septien kicks 27-yard field goal at 3:28.

Oct. 29, 1978—Denver 20, Seattle 17, at Seattle; Broncos win toss. Ball changes hands four times before Turner kicks 18-yard field goal at 12:59.

Nov. 12, 1978—San Diego 29, Kansas City 23, at San Diego; Chiefs win toss. Fouts hits Jefferson for decisive 14-yard touchdown pass on the last play (15:00) of overtime period.

Nov. 12, 1978—Washington 16, New York Giants 13, at Washington; Redskins win toss. Moseley kicks winning 45-yard field goal at 8:32 after missing first down field goal attempt of 35 yards at 4:50.

Nov. 26, 1978—Green Bay 10, Minnesota 10, at Green Bay; Packers win toss. Both teams have possession of the ball four times.

Dec. 9, 1978—Cleveland 37, New York Jets 34, at Cleveland; Browns win toss. Cockroft kicks 22-yard field goal at 3:07.

Sept. 2, 1979—Atlanta 40, New Orleans 34, at New Orleans; Falcons win toss. Bartkowski's pass intercepted by Myers and returned to Falcons' 46. Erxleben punts to Falcons' 4. James punts to Chandler on Saints' 43. Erxleben punts and Ryckman returns to Falcons' 28. James punts and Chandler returns to Saints' 36. Erxleben retrieves poor snap on Saints' 1 and attempts pass. Mayberry intercepts and returns six yards for touchdown at 8:22.

Sept. 2, 1979—Cleveland 25, New York Jets 22, at New York; Jets win toss. Leahy's 43-yard field goal attempt goes wide right at 4:41. Evans's punt blocked by Dykes is recovered by Newton. Ramsey punts into end zone for touchdown. Evans punts and Harper returns to Jets' 24. Robinson's pass intercepted by Davis and returned 33 yards to Jets' 31. Cockroft kicks 27-yard field goal at 14:45.

*Sept. 3, 1979—Pittsburgh 16, New England 13, at Foxboro; Patriots win toss. Hare punts to Swann at Steelers' 31. Bahr kicks 41-yard field goal at 5:10.

Sept. 9, 1979—Tampa Bay 29, Baltimore 26, at Baltimore; Colts win toss. Landry fumbles, recovered by Kollar at Colts' 14. O'Donoghue kicks 31-yard, first-down field goal at 1:41.

Sept. 16, 1979—Denver 20, Atlanta 17, at Atlanta; Broncos win toss. Broncos march 65 yards to Falcons' 7. Turner kicks 24-yard field goal at 6:15.

Sept. 23, 1979—Houston 30, Cincinnati 27, at Cincinnati; Oilers win toss. Parsley punts and Lusby returns to Bengals' 33. Bahr's 32-yard field goal attempt is wide right at 8:05. Parsley's punt downed on Bengals' 5. McInally punts and Ellender returns to Bengals' 42. Fritsch's third down, 29-yard field goal attempt hits left upright and bounces through at 14:28.

Sept. 23, 1979—Minnesota 27, Green Bay 21, at Minnesota; Vikings win toss. Kramer throws 50-yard touchdown pass to Rashad at 3:18.

Oct. 28, 1979—Houston 27, New York Jets 24, at Houston; Oilers win toss. Oilers march 58 yards to Jets' 18. Fritsch kicks 35-yard field goal at 5:10.

Nov. 18, 1979—Cleveland 30, Miami 24, at Cleveland; Browns win toss. Sipe passes 39 yards to Rucker for touchdown at 1:59.

Nov. 25, 1979—Pittsburgh 33, Cleveland 30, at Pittsburgh; Browns win toss. Sipe's pass intercepted by Blount on Steelers' 4. Bradshaw pass intercepted by Bolton on Browns' 12. Evans punts and Bell returns to Steelers' 17. Bahr kicks 37-yard field goal at 14:51.

Nov. 25, 1979—Buffalo 16, New England 13, at Foxboro; Patriots win toss. Hare's punt downed on Bills' 38. Jackson punts and Morgan returns to Patriots' 20. Grogan's pass intercepted by Haslett and returned to Bills' 42. Ferguson's 51-yard pass to Butler sets up N. Mike-Mayer's 29-yard field goal at 9:15.

Dec. 2, 1979—Los Angeles 27, Minnesota 21, at Los Angeles; Rams win toss. Clark punts and Miller returns to Vikings' 25. Kramer's pass intercepted by Brown and returned to Rams' 40. Cromwell, holding for 22-yard field goal attempt, runs around left end untouched for winning score at 6:53.

Sept. 7, 1980—Green Bay 12, Chicago 6, at Green Bay; Bears win toss. Parsons punts and Nixon returns 16 yards. Five plays later, Marcol returns own blocked field goal attempt 24 yards for touchdown at 6:00.

*indicates Monday night game
#indicates Thursday night game

Sept. 14, 1980—San Diego 30, Oakland 24, at San Diego; Raiders win toss. Pastorini's first-down pass intercepted by Edwards. Millen intercepts Fouts' first-down pass and returns to San Diego 46. Bahr's 50-yard field goal attempt partially blocked by Williams and recovered on Chargers' 32. Eight plays later, Fouts throws 24-yard touchdown pass to Jefferson at 8:09.

Sept. 14, 1980—San Francisco 24, St. Louis 21, at San Francisco; Cardinals win toss. Swider punts and Robinson returns to 49ers' 32. San Francisco drives 52 yards to St. Louis 16, where Wersching kicks 33-yard field goal at 4:12.

Oct. 12, 1980—Green Bay 14, Tampa Bay 14, at Tampa Bay; Packers win toss. Teams trade punts twice. Lee returns second Tampa Bay punt to Green Bay 42. Dickey completes three passes to Buccaneers' 18, where Birney's 36-yard field goal attempt is wide right as time expires.

Nov. 9, 1980—Atlanta 33, St. Louis 27, at St. Louis; Falcons win toss. Strong runs 21 yards for touchdown at 4:20.

#**Nov. 20, 1980—San Diego 27, Miami 24,** at Miami; Chargers win toss. Partridge punts into end zone, Dolphins take over on their own 20. Woodley's pass for Nathan intercepted by Lowe and returned 28 yards to Dolphins' 12. Benirschke kicks 28-yard field goal at 7:14.

Nov. 23, 1980—New York Jets 31, Houston 28, at New York; Jets win toss. Leahy kicks 38-yard field goal at 3:58.

Nov. 27, 1980—Chicago 23, Detroit 17, at Detroit; Bears win toss. Williams returns kickoff 95 yards for touchdown at 0:21.

Dec. 7, 1980—Buffalo 10, Los Angeles 7, at Buffalo; Rams win toss. Corral punts and Hooks returns to Bills' 34. Ferguson's 30-yard pass to Lewis sets up N. Mike-Mayer's 30-yard field goal at 5:14.

Dec. 7, 1980—San Francisco 38, New Orleans 35, at San Francisco; Saints win toss. Erxleben's punt downed by Hardy on 49ers' 27. Wersching kicks 36-yard field goal at 7:40.

***Dec. 8, 1980—Miami 16, New England 13,** at Miami; Dolphins win toss. Von Schamann kicks 23-yard field goal at 3:20.

Dec. 14, 1980—Cincinnati 17, Chicago 14, at Chicago; Bengals win toss. Breech kicks 28-yard field goal at 4:23.

Dec. 21, 1980—Los Angeles 20, Atlanta 17, at Los Angeles; Rams win toss. Corral's punt downed at Rams' 37. James punts into end zone for touchback. Corral's punt downed on Falcons' 17. Bartkowski fumbles when hit by Harris, recovered by Delaney. Corral kicks 23-yard field goal on first play of possession at 7:00.

Sept. 27, 1981—Cincinnati 27, Buffalo 24, at Cincinnati; Bills win toss. Cater punts into end zone for touchback. Bengals drive to the Bills' 10 where Breech kicks 28-yard field goal at 9:33.

Sept. 27, 1981—Pittsburgh 27, New England 21, at Pittsburgh; Patriots win toss. Hubach punts and Smith returns five yards to midfield. Four plays later Bradshaw throws 24-yard touchdown pass to Swann at 3:19.

Oct. 4, 1981—Miami 28, New York Jets 28, at Miami; Jets win toss. Teams trade punts twice. Leahy's 48-yard field goal attempt is wide right as time expires.

Oct. 25, 1981—New York Giants 27, Atlanta 24, at Atlanta; Giants win toss. Jennings' punt goes out of bounds at New York 47. Bright returns Atlanta punt to Giants' 14. Woerner fair catches punt at own 28. Andrews fumbles on first play, recovered by Van Pelt. Danelo kicks 40-yard field goal four plays later at 9:20.

Oct. 25, 1981—Chicago 20, San Diego 17, at Chicago; Bears win toss. Teams trade punts. Bears' second punt returned by Brooks to Chargers' 33. Fouts pass intercepted by Fencik and returned 32 yards to San Diego 27. Roveto kicks 27-yard field goal seven plays later at 9:30.

Nov. 8, 1981—Chicago 16, Kansas City 13, at Kansas City; Bears win toss. Teams trade punts. Kansas City takes over on downs on its own 38. Fuller's fumble recovered by Harris on Chicago 36. Roveto's 37-yard field goal wide, but Chiefs penalized for leverage. Roveto's 22-yard field goal attempt three plays later is good at 13:07.

Nov. 8, 1981—Denver 23, Cleveland 20, at Denver; Browns win toss. D. Smith recovers Hill's fumble at Denver 48. Morton's 33-yard pass to Upchurch and six-yard run by Preston set up Steinfort's 30-yard field goal at 4:10.

Nov. 8, 1981—Miami 30, New England 27, at New England; Dolphins win toss. Orosz punts and Morgan returns six yards to New England 26. Grogan's pass intercepted by Brudzinski who returns 19 yards to Patriots' 26. Von Schamann kicks 30-yard field goal on first down at 7:09.

Nov. 15, 1981—Washington 30, New York Giants 27, at New York; Giants win toss. Nelms returns Giants' punt 26 yards to New York 47. Five plays later Moseley kicks 48-yard field goal at 3:44.

Dec. 20, 1981—New York Giants 13, Dallas 10, at New York; Cowboys win toss and kick off. Jennings punts to Dallas 40. Taylor recovers Dorsett's fumble on second down. Danelo's 33-yard field goal attempt hits right upright and bounces back. White's pass for Pearson intercepted by Hunt and returned seven yards to Dallas 24. Four plays later Danelo kicks 35-yard field goal at 6:19.

Sept. 12, 1982—Washington 37, Philadelphia 34, at Philadelphia; Redskins win toss. Theismann completes five passes for 63 yards to set up Moseley's 26-yard field goal at 4:47.

Sept. 19, 1982—Pittsburgh 26, Cincinnati 20, at Pittsburgh; Bengals win toss. Anderson's pass intended for Kreider intercepted by Woodruff and returned 30 yards to Cincinnati 2. Bradshaw completes two-yard touchdown pass to Stallworth on first down at 1:08.

Dec. 19, 1982—Baltimore 20, Green Bay 20, at Baltimore; Packers win toss. K. Anderson intercepts Dickey's first-down pass and returns to Packers' 42. Miller's 44-yard field goal attempt blocked by G. Lewis. Teams trade punts before Stenerud's 47-yard field goal attempt is wide right. Teams trade punts again before time expires in Colts possession.

Jan. 2, 1983—Tampa Bay 26, Chicago 23, at Tampa Bay; Bears win toss. Parsons punts to T. Bell at Buccaneers' 40. Capece kicks 33-yard field goal at 3:14.

Sept. 4, 1983—Baltimore 29, New England 23, at New England; Patriots win toss. Cooks runs 52 yards with fumble recovery three plays into overtime at 0:30.

Sept. 4, 1983—Green Bay 41, Houston 38, at Houston; Packers win toss. Stenerud kicks 42-yard field goal at 5:55.

Sept. 11, 1983—New York Giants 16, Atlanta 13, at Atlanta; Giants win toss. Dennis returns kickoff 54 yards to Atlanta 41. Haji-Sheikh kicks 30-yard field goal at 3:38.

Sept. 18, 1983—New Orleans 34, Chicago 31, at New Orleans; Bears win toss. Parsons punts and Groth returns five yards to New Orleans 34. Stabler pass intercepted by Schmidt at Chicago 47. Parsons punt downed by Gentry at New Orleans 2. Stabler gains 36 yards in four passes; Wilson 38 in six carries. Andersen kicks 41-yard field goal at 10:57.

Sept. 18, 1983—Minnesota 19, Tampa Bay 16, at Tampa; Vikings win toss. Coleman punts and Bell returns eight yards to Tampa Bay 47. Capece's 33-yard field goal attempt sails wide at 7:26. Dils and Young combine for 48-yard gain to Tampa Bay 27. Ricardo kicks 42-yard field goal at 9:27.

Sept. 25, 1983—Baltimore 22, Chicago 19, at Baltimore; Colts win toss. Allegre kicks 33-yard field goal nine plays later at 4:51.

Sept. 25, 1983—Cleveland 30, San Diego 24, at San Diego; Browns win toss. Walker returns kickoff 33 yards to Cleveland 37. Sipe completes 48-yard touchdown pass to Holt four plays later at 1:53.

Sept. 25, 1983—New York Jets 27, Los Angeles Rams 24, at New York; Jets win toss. Ramsey punts to Irvin who returns to 25 but penalty puts Rams on own 13. Holmes 30-yard interception return sets up Leahy's 26-yard field goal at 3:22.

Oct. 9, 1983—Buffalo 38, Miami 35, at Miami; Dolphins win toss. Von Schamann's 52-yard field goal attempt goes wide at 12:36. Cater punts to Clayton who loses 11 to own 13. Von Schamann's 43-yard field goal attempt sails wide at 5:15. Danelo kicks 36-yard field goal nine plays later at 13:58.

Oct. 9, 1983—Dallas 27, Tampa Bay 24, at Dallas; Cowboys win toss. Septien's 51-yard field goal attempt goes wide but Buccaneers penalized for roughing kicker. Septien kicks 42-yard field goal at 4:38.

Oct. 23, 1983—Kansas City 13, Houston 10, at Houston; Chiefs win toss. Lowery kicks 41-yard field goal 13 plays later at 7:41.

Oct. 23, 1983—Minnesota 20, Green Bay 17, at Green Bay; Packers win toss. Scribner's punt downed on Vikings' 42. Ricardo kicks 32-yard field goal eight plays later at 5:05.

***Oct. 24, 1983—New York Giants 20, St. Louis 20,** at St. Louis; Cardinals win toss. Teams trade punts before O'Donoghue's 44-yard field goal attempt is wide left. Jennings' punt returned by Bird to St. Louis 21. Lomax pass intercepted by Haynes who loses six yards to New York 33. Jennings' punt downed on St. Louis 17. O'Donoghue's 19-yard field goal attempt is wide right. Rutledge's pass intercepted by L. Washington who returns 25 yards to New York 25. O'Donoghue's 42-yard field goal attempt is wide right. Rutledge's pass intercepted by W. Smith at St. Louis 33 to end game.

Oct. 30, 1983—Cleveland 25, Houston 19, at Cleveland; Oilers win toss. Teams trade punts. Nielsen's pass intercepted by Whitwell who returns to Houston 20. Green runs 20 yards for touchdown on first down at 6:34.

Nov. 20, 1983—Detroit 23, Green Bay 20, at Milwaukee; Packers win toss. Scribner punts and Jenkins returns 14 yards to Green Bay 45. Murray's 33-yard field goal attempt is wide left at 9:32. Whitehurst's pass intercepted by Watkins and returned to Green Bay 27. Murray kicks 37-yard field goal four plays later at 8:30.

Nov. 27, 1983—Atlanta 47, Green Bay 41, at Atlanta; Packers win toss. K. Johnson returns interception 31 yards for touchdown at 2:13.

Nov. 27, 1983—Seattle 51, Kansas City 48, at Seattle; Seahawks win toss. Dixon's 47-yard kickoff return sets up N. Johnson's 42-yard field goal at 1:36.

Dec. 11, 1983—New Orleans 20, Philadelphia 17, at Philadelphia; Eagles win toss. Runager punts to Groth who fair catches on New Orleans 32. Stabler completes two passes for 36 yards to Goodlow to set up Andersen's 50-yard field goal at 5:30.

***Dec. 12, 1983—Green Bay 12, Tampa Bay 9,** at Tampa; Packers win toss. Stenerud kicks 23-yard field goal 11 plays later at 4:07.

Sept. 9, 1984—Detroit 27, Atlanta 24, at Atlanta; Lions win toss. Murray kicks 48-yard field goal nine plays later at 5:06.

Sept. 30, 1984—Tampa Bay 30, Green Bay 27, at Tampa; Packers win toss. Scribner punts 44 yards to Tampa Bay 2. Epps returns Garcia's punt three yards to Green Bay 27. Scribner's punt downed on Buccaneers' 33. Ariri kicks 46-yard field goal 11 plays later at 10:32.

Oct. 14, 1984—Detroit 13, Tampa Bay 7, at Detroit; Buccaneers win toss. Tampa Bay drives to Lions' 39 before Wilder fumbles. Five plays later Danielson hits Thompson with 37-yard touchdown pass at 4:34.

Oct. 21, 1984—Dallas 30, New Orleans 27, at Dallas; Cowboys win toss. Septien kicks 41-yard field goal eight plays later at 3:42.

Oct. 28, 1984—Denver 22, Los Angeles Raiders 19, at Los Angeles; Raiders win toss. Hawkins fumble recovered by Foley at Denver 7. Teams trade punts. Karlis' 42-yard field goal attempt is wide left. Teams trade punts. Wilson pass intercepted by R. Jackson at Los Angeles 45, returned 23 yards to Los Angeles 22. Karlis kicks 35-yard field goal two plays later at 15:00.

Nov. 4, 1984—Philadelphia 23, Detroit 23, at Detroit; Lions win toss. Lions drive to Eagles' 3 in eight plays. Murray's 21-yard field goal attempt hits right upright and bounces back. Jaworski's pass intercepted by Watkins at Detroit 5. Teams trade punts. Cooper returns Black's punt five yards to Eagles' 14. Time expires four plays later with Eagles on own 21.

Nov. 18, 1984—San Diego 34, Miami 28, at San Diego; Chargers win toss. McGee scores eight plays later on a 25-yard run at 3:17.

Dec. 2, 1984—Cincinnati 20, Cleveland 17, at Cleveland; Browns win toss. Simmons returns Cox's punt 30 yards to Cleveland 35. Breech kicks 35-yard field goal seven plays later at 4:34.

Dec. 2, 1984—Houston 23, Pittsburgh 20, at Houston; Oilers win toss. Cooper kicks 30-yard field goal 16 plays later at 5:53.

*indicates Monday night game
#indicates Thursday night game

Postseason

Dec. 28, 1958—Baltimore 23, New York Giants 17, at New York; Giants win toss. Maynard returns kickoff to Giants' 20. Chandler punts and Taseff returns one yard to Colts' 20. Colts win at 8:15 on a one-yard run by Ameche.

Dec. 23, 1962—Dallas Texans 20, Houston Oilers 17, at Houston; Texans win toss and kick off. Jancik returns kickoff to Oilers' 33. Norton punts and Jackson makes fair catch on Texans' 22. Wilson punts and Jancik makes fair catch on Oilers' 45. Robinson intercepts Blanda's pass and returns 13 yards to Oilers' 47. Wilson's punt rolls dead at Oilers' 12. Hull intercepts Blanda's pass and returns 23 yards to midfield. Texans win at 17:54 on a 25-yard field goal by Brooker.

Dec. 26, 1965—Green Bay 13, Baltimore 10, at Green Bay; Packers win toss. Moore returns kickoff to Packers' 22. Chandler punts and Haymond returns nine yards to Colts' 41. Gilburg punts and Wood makes fair catch at Packers' 21. Chandler punts and Haymond returns one yard to Colts' 41. Michaels misses 47-yard field goal. Packers win at 13:39 on 25-yard field goal by Chandler.

Dec. 25, 1971—Miami 27, Kansas City 24, at Kansas City; Chiefs win toss. Podolak, after a lateral from Buchanan, returns kickoff to Chiefs' 46. Stenerud's 42-yard field goal is blocked. Seiple punts and Podolak makes fair catch at Chiefs' 17. Wilson punts and Scott returns 18 yards to Dolphins' 39. Yepremian misses 62-yard field goal. Scott intercepts Dawson's pass and returns 13 yards to Dolphins' 46. Seiple punts and Podolak loses one yard to Chiefs' 15. Wilson punts and Scott makes fair catch on Dolphins' 30. Dolphins win at 22:40 on a 37-yard field goal by Yepremian.

Dec. 24, 1977—Oakland 37, Baltimore 31, at Baltimore; Colts win toss. Raiders start on own 42 following a punt late in the first overtime. Oakland works way into a threatening position on Stabler's 19-yard pass to Branch at Colts' 26. Four plays later, on the second play of the second overtime, Stabler hits Casper with a 10-yard touchdown pass at 15:43.

Jan. 2, 1982—San Diego 41, Miami 38, at Miami; Chargers win toss. San Diego drives from its 13 to Miami 8. On second-and-goal, Benirschke misses 27-yard field goal attempt wide left at 9:15. Miami has the ball twice and San Diego twice more before the Dolphins get their third possession. Miami drives from the San Diego 46 to Chargers' 17 and on fourth-and-two, von Schamann's 34-yard field goal attempt is blocked by San Diego's Winslow after 11:27. Fouts then completes four of five passes, including a 29-yarder to Joiner that puts the ball on Dolphins' 10. On first down, Benirschke kicks a 20-yard field goal at 13:52. San Diego's winning drive covered 74 yards in six plays.

Overtime Won-Lost Records, 1974—1984 (Regular Season)

	W	L	T
Atlanta	3	6	0
Buffalo	3	1	0
Chicago	4	7	0
Cincinnati	4	3	0
Cleveland	7	4	0
Dallas	5	2	0
Denver	6	1	1
Detroit	3	2	1
Green Bay	3	5	3
Houston	3	5	0
Indianapolis	3	1	1
Kansas City	3	4	0
Los Angeles Raiders	3	2	0
Los Angeles Rams	3	2	1
Miami	2	6	1
Minnesota	5	2	2
New England	0	7	0
New Orleans	2	4	0
New York Giants	3	4	1
New York Jets	3	3	1
Philadelphia	0	3	1
Pittsburgh	5	1	1
St. Louis	2	4	1
San Diego	5	4	0
San Francisco	3	2	0
Seattle	1	1	0
Tampa Bay	3	4	1
Washington	5	2	0

Overtime Games By Year (Regular Season)

1984- 9	1978-11
1983-19	1977- 6
1982- 4	1976- 5
1981-10	1975- 9
1980-13	1974- 2
1979-12	

Overtime Game Summary—1974-1984

There have been 100 overtime games in regular-season play since the rule was adopted in 1974. The breakdown follows:

68 times both teams had at least one possession (68%)

32 times the team which won the toss drove for winning score (24 FG, 8 TD) (32%)

48 times the team which won the toss won the game (48%)

44 times the team which lost the toss won the game (44%)

67 games were decided by a field goal (67%)

25 games were decided by a touchdown (25%)

8 games ended tied (8%). Last time: Philadelphia 23 at Detroit 23; 11/4/84

Shortest Overtime Games

0:21 (Chicago 23, Detroit 17; 11/27/80) Initial overtime kickoff return for a touchdown.

0:30 (Baltimore 29, New England 23; 9/4/83)

1:08 (Pittsburgh 26, Cincinnati 20; 9/19/82)

There have been six postseason overtime games dating back to 1958. In all cases, both teams had at least one possession. Last postseason overtime: San Diego 41, Miami 38; 1//2/82.

NUMBER-ONE DRAFT CHOICES

Season	Team	Player	Position	College
1985	Buffalo	Bruce Smith	DE	Virginia Tech
1984	New England	Irving Fryar	WR	Nebraska
1983	Baltimore	John Elway	QB	Stanford
1982	New England	Kenneth Sims	DT	Texas
1981	New Orleans	George Rogers	RB	South Carolina
1980	Detroit	Billy Sims	RB	Oklahoma
1979	Buffalo	Tom Cousineau	LB	Ohio State
1978	Houston	Earl Campbell	RB	Texas
1977	Tampa Bay	Ricky Bell	RB	Southern California
1976	Tampa Bay	Lee Roy Selmon	DE	Oklahoma
1975	Atlanta	Steve Bartkowski	QB	California
1974	Dallas	Ed Jones	DE	Tennessee State
1973	Houston	John Matuszak	DE	Tampa
1972	Buffalo	Walt Patulski	DE	Notre Dame
1971	New England	Jim Plunkett	QB	Stanford
1970	Pittsburgh	Terry Bradshaw	QB	Louisiana Tech
1969	Buffalo (AFL)	O. J. Simpson	RB	Southern California
1968	Minnesota	Ron Yary	T	Southern California
1967	Baltimore	Bubba Smith	DT	Michigan State
1966	Atlanta	Tommy Nobis	LB	Texas
	Miami (AFL)	Jim Grabowski	RB	Illinois
1965	New York Giants	Tucker Frederickson	RB	Auburn
	Houston (AFL)	Lawrence Elkins	E	Baylor
1964	San Francisco	Dave Parks	E	Texas Tech
	Boston (AFL)	Jack Concannon	QB	Boston College
1963	Los Angeles	Terry Baker	QB	Oregon State
	Kansas City (AFL)	Buck Buchanan	DT	Grambling
1962	Washington	Ernie Davis	RB	Syracuse
	Oakland (AFL)	Roman Gabriel	QB	North Carolina State
1961	Minnesota	Tommy Mason	RB	Tulane
	Buffalo (AFL)	Ken Rice	G	Auburn
1960	Los Angeles	Billy Cannon	RB	Louisiana State
	(AFL had no formal first pick)			
1959	Green Bay	Randy Duncan	QB	Iowa
1958	Chicago Cardinals	King Hill	QB	Rice
1957	Green Bay	Paul Hornung	HB	Notre Dame
1956	Pittsburgh	Gary Glick	DB	Colorado A&M
1955	Baltimore	George Shaw	QB	Oregon
1954	Cleveland	Bobby Garrett	QB	Stanford
1953	San Francisco	Harry Babcock	E	Georgia
1952	Los Angeles	Bill Wade	QB	Vanderbilt
1951	New York Giants	Kyle Rote	HB	Southern Methodist
1950	Detroit	Leon Hart	E	Notre Dame
1949	Philadelphia	Chuck Bednarik	C	Pennsylvania
1948	Washington	Harry Gilmer	QB	Alabama
1947	Chicago Bears	Bob Fenimore	HB	Oklahoma A&M
1946	Boston	Frank Dancewicz	QB	Notre Dame
1945	Chicago Cardinals	Charley Trippi	HB	Georgia
1944	Boston	Angelo Bertelli	QB	Notre Dame
1943	Detroit	Frank Sinkwich	HB	Georgia
1942	Pittsburgh	Bill Dudley	HB	Virginia
1941	Chicago Bears	Tom Harmon	HB	Michigan
1940	Chicago Cardinals	George Cafego	HB	Tennessee
1939	Chicago Cardinals	Ki Aldrich	C	Texas Christian
1938	Cleveland	Corbett Davis	FB	Indiana
1937	Philadelphia	Sam Francis	FB	Nebraska
1936	Philadelphia	Jay Berwanger	HB	Chicago

RECORDS

All-Time Records
Outstanding Performers
Yearly Statistical Leaders
Super Bowl Records
Postseason Game Records
AFC-NFC Pro Bowl Records

Compiled by Elias Sports Bureau
The following records reflect all available official information on the National Football League from its formation in 1920 to date. Also included are all applicable records from the American Football League, 1960-69. Rookie records are limited to those players who had never played in a professional game in the United States in any previous season.

INDIVIDUAL RECORDS

SERVICE

Most Seasons
- 26 George Blanda, Chi. Bears, 1949, 1950-58; Baltimore, 1950; Houston, 1960-66; Oakland, 1967-75
- 21 Earl Morrall, San Francisco, 1956; Pittsburgh, 1957-58; Detroit, 1958-64; N.Y. Giants, 1965-67; Baltimore, 1968-71; Miami, 1972-76
- 20 Jim Marshall, Cleveland, 1960; Minnesota, 1961-79

Most Seasons, One Club
- 19 Jim Marshall, Minnesota, 1961-79
- 18 Jim Hart, St. Louis, 1966-83
- 17 Lou Groza, Cleveland, 1950-59, 1961-67
  Johnny Unitas, Baltimore, 1956-72
  John Brodie, San Francisco, 1957-73
  Jim Bakken, St. Louis, 1962-78
  Mick Tingelhoff, Minnesota, 1962-78

Most Games Played, Career
- 340 George Blanda, Chi. Bears, 1949, 1950-58; Baltimore, 1950; Houston, 1960-66; Oakland, 1967-75
- 282 Jim Marshall, Cleveland, 1960; Minnesota, 1961-79
- 255 Earl Morrall, San Francisco, 1956; Pittsburgh, 1957-58; Detroit, 1958-64; N.Y. Giants, 1965-67; Baltimore, 1968-71; Miami, 1972-76

Most Consecutive Games Played, Career
- 282 Jim Marshall, Cleveland, 1960; Minnesota, 1961-79
- 240 Mick Tingelhoff, Minnesota, 1962-78
- 234 Jim Bakken, St. Louis, 1962-78

Most Seasons, Coach
- 40 George Halas, Chi. Bears, 1920-29, 1933-42, 1946-55, 1958-67
- 33 Earl (Curly) Lambeau, Green Bay, 1921-49; Chi. Cardinals, 1950-51; Washington, 1952-53
- 25 Tom Landry, Dallas, 1960-84

SCORING

Most Seasons Leading League
- 5 Don Hutson, Green Bay, 1940-44
  Gino Cappelletti, Boston, 1961, 1963-66
- 3 Earl (Dutch) Clark Portsmouth, 1932; Detroit, 1935-36
  Pat Harder, Chi. Cardinals, 1947-49
  Paul Hornung, Green Bay, 1959-61
- 2 Jack Manders, Chi. Bears, 1934, 1937
  Gordy Soltau, San Francisco, 1952-53
  Doak Walker, Detroit, 1950, 1955
  Gene Mingo, Denver, 1960, 1962
  Jim Turner, N.Y. Jets, 1968-69
  Fred Cox, Minnesota, 1969-70
  Chester Marcol, Green Bay, 1972, 1974
  John Smith, New England, 1979-80

Most Consecutive Seasons Leading League
- 5 Don Hutson, Green Bay, 1940-44
- 4 Gino Cappelletti, Boston, 1963-66
- 3 Pat Harder, Chi. Cardinals, 1947-49
  Paul Hornung, Green Bay, 1959-61

POINTS

Most Points, Career
- 2,002 George Blanda, Chi. Bears, 1949, 1950-58; Baltimore, 1950; Houston, 1960-66; Oakland, 1967-75 (9-td, 943-pat, 335-fg)
- 1,613 Jan Stenerud, Kansas City, 1967-79; Green Bay, 1980-83; Minnesota, 1984 (539-pat, 358-fg)
- 1,439 Jim Turner, N.Y. Jets, 1964-70; Denver, 1971-79 (1-td, 521-pat, 304-fg)

Most Points, Season
- 176 Paul Hornung, Green Bay, 1960 (15-td, 41-pat, 15-fg)
- 161 Mark Moseley, Washington, 1983 (62-pat, 33-fg)
- 155 Gino Cappelletti, Boston, 1964 (7-td, 38-pat, 25-fg)

Most Points, No Touchdowns, Season
- 161 Mark Moseley, Washington, 1983 (62-pat, 33-fg)
- 145 Jim Turner, N.Y. Jets, 1968 (43-pat, 34-fg)
- 131 Ray Wersching, San Francisco, 1984 (56-pat, 25-fg)

Most Seasons, 100 or More Points
- 7 Jan Stenerud, Kansas City, 1967-71; Green Bay, 1981, 1983
- 6 Gino Cappelletti, Boston, 1961-66
  George Blanda, Houston, 1960-61; Oakland, 1967-69, 1973
  Bruce Gossett, Los Angeles, 1966-67, 1969; San Francisco, 1970-71, 1973
- 5 Lou Michaels, Pittsburgh, 1962; Baltimore, 1964-65, 1967-68

Most Points, Rookie, Season
- 132 Gale Sayers, Chicago, 1965 (22-td)
- 128 Doak Walker, Detroit, 1950 (11-td, 38-pat, 8-fg)
  Cookie Gilchrist, Buffalo, 1962 (15-td, 14-pat, 8-fg)
  Chester Marcol, Green Bay, 1972 (29-pat, 33-fg)
- 127 Ali Haji-Sheikh, N.Y. Giants, 1983 (22-pat, 35-fg)

Most Points, Game
- 40 Ernie Nevers, Chi. Cardinals vs. Chi. Bears, Nov. 28, 1929 (6-td, 4-pat)
- 36 Dub Jones, Cleveland vs. Chi. Bears, Nov. 25, 1951 (6-td)
  Gale Sayers, Chicago vs. San Francisco, Dec. 12, 1965 (6-td)
- 33 Paul Hornung, Green Bay vs. Baltimore, Oct. 8, 1961 (4-td, 6-pat, 1-fg)

Most Consecutive Games Scoring
- 151 Fred Cox, Minnesota, 1963-73
- 133 Garo Yepremian, Miami, 1970-78; New Orleans, 1979-
- 118 Jim Turner, N.Y. Jets, 1966-70; Denver, 1971-74
  Rafael Septien, Los Angeles, 1977; Dallas, 1978-84 (current)

TOUCHDOWNS

Most Seasons Leading League
- 8 Don Hutson, Green Bay, 1935-38, 1941-44
- 3 Jim Brown, Cleveland, 1958-59, 1963
  Lance Alworth, San Diego, 1964-66
- 2 By many players

Most Consecutive Seasons Leading League
- 4 Don Hutson, Green Bay, 1935-38, 1941-44
- 3 Lance Alworth, San Diego, 1964-66
- 2 By many players

Most Touchdowns, Career
- 126 Jim Brown, Cleveland, 1957-65 (106-r, 20-p)
- 113 Lenny Moore, Baltimore, 1956-67 (63-r, 48-p, 2-ret)
- 108 John Riggins, N.Y. Jets, 1971-75; Washington, 1976-79, 1981-84 (96-r, 12-p)

Most Touchdowns, Season
- 24 John Riggins, Washington, 1983 (24-r)
- 23 O.J. Simpson, Buffalo, 1975 (16-r, 7-p)
- 22 Gale Sayers, Chicago, 1965 (14-r, 6-p, 2-ret)
  Chuck Foreman, Minnesota, 1975 (13-r, 9-p)

Most Touchdowns, Rookie, Season
- 22 Gale Sayers, Chicago, 1965 (14-r, 6-p, 2-ret)
- 20 Eric Dickerson, L.A. Rams, 1983 (18-r, 2-p)
- 16 Billy Sims, Detroit, 1980 (13-r, 3-p)

Most Touchdowns, Game
- 6 Ernie Nevers, Chi. Cardinals vs. Chi. Bears, Nov. 28, 1929 (6-r)
  Dub Jones, Cleveland vs. Chi. Bears, Nov. 25, 1951 (4-r, 2-p)
  Gale Sayers, Chicago vs. San Francisco, Dec. 12, 1965 (4-r, 1-p, 1-ret)
- 5 Bob Shaw, Chi. Cardinals vs. Baltimore, Oct. 2, 1950 (5-p)
  Jim Brown, Cleveland vs. Baltimore, Nov. 1, 1959 (5-r)
  Abner Haynes, Dall. Texans vs. Oakland, Nov. 26, 1961 (4-r, 1-p)
  Billy Cannon, Houston vs. N.Y. Titans, Dec. 10, 1961 (3-r, 2-p)
  Cookie Gilchrist, Buffalo vs. N.Y. Jets, Dec. 8, 1963 (5-r)
  Paul Hornung, Green Bay vs. Baltimore, Dec. 12, 1965 (3-r, 2-p)
  Kellen Winslow, San Diego vs. Oakland, Nov. 22, 1981 (5-p)
- 4 By many players

Most Consecutive Games Scoring Touchdowns
- 18 Lenny Moore, Baltimore, 1963-65
- 14 O.J. Simpson, Buffalo, 1975
- 13 John Riggins, Washington, 1982-83

POINTS AFTER TOUCHDOWN

Most Seasons Leading League
- 8 George Blanda, Chi. Bears, 1956; Houston, 1961-62; Oakland, 1967-69, 1972, 1974
- 4 Bob Waterfield, Cleveland, 1945; Los Angeles, 1946, 1950, 1952
- 3 Earl (Dutch) Clark Portsmouth, 1932; Detroit, 1935-36
  Jack Manders, Chi. Bears, 1933-35
  Don Hutson, Green Bay, 1941-42, 1945

Most Points After Touchdown Attempted, Career
- 959 George Blanda, Chi. Bears, 1949, 1950-58; Baltimore, 1950; Houston, 1960-66; Oakland, 1967-75
- 657 Lou Groza, Cleveland, 1950-59, 1961-67
- 558 Jan Stenerud, Kansas City, 1967-79; Green Bay, 1980-83; Minnesota, 1984

Most Points After Touchdown Attempted, Season
- 70 Uwe von Schamann, Miami, 1984
- 65 George Blanda, Houston, 1961
- 63 Mark Moseley, Washington, 1983

Most Points After Touchdown Attempted, Game
- 10 Charlie Gogolak, Washington vs. N.Y. Giants, Nov. 27, 1966
- 9 Pat Harder, Chi. Cardinals vs. N.Y. Giants, Oct. 17, 1948; vs. N.Y. Bulldogs, Nov. 13, 1949
  Bob Waterfield, Los Angeles vs. Baltimore, Oct. 22, 1950
  Bob Thomas, Chicago vs. Green Bay, Dec. 7, 1980
- 8 By many players

Most Points After Touchdown, Career
- 943 George Blanda, Chi. Bears, 1949, 1950-58; Baltimore, 1950; Houston, 1960-66; Oakland, 1967-75
- 641 Lou Groza, Cleveland, 1950-59, 1961-67
- 539 Jan Stenerud, Kansas City, 1967-79; Green Bay, 1980-83; Minnesota, 1984

Most Points After Touchdown, Season
- 66 Uwe von Schamann, Miami, 1984
- 64 George Blanda, Houston, 1961
- 62 Mark Moseley, Washington, 1983

Mos: Points After Touchdown, Game
- 9 Pat Harder, Chi. Cardinals vs. N.Y. Giants, Oct. 17, 1948
  Bob Waterfield, Los Angeles vs. Baltimore, Oct. 22, 1950
  Charlie Gogolak, Washington vs. N.Y. Giants, Nov. 27, 1966
- 8 By many players

Most Consecutive Points After Touchdown
- 234 Tommy Davis, San Francisco, 1959-65
- 221 Jim Turner, N.Y. Jets, 1967-70; Denver, 1971-74
- 201 George Blanda, Oakland, 1967-71

Highest Points After Touchdown Percentage, Career (200 points after touchdown)
- 99.43 Tommy Davis, San Francisco, 1959-69 (350-348)
- 98.33 George Blanda, Chi. Bears, 1949, 1950-58; Baltimore, 1950; Houston, 1960-66; Oakland, 1967-75 (959-943)
- 97.93 Danny Villanueva, L.A. Rams, 1960-64; Dallas, 1965-67 (241-236)

Most Points After Touchdown, No Misses, Season
- 56 Danny Villanueva, Dallas, 1966
  Ray Wersching, San Francisco, 1984
- 54 Mike Clark, Dallas, 1968
  George Blanda, Oakland, 1968
- 53 Pat Harder, Chi. Cardinals, 1948

Most Points After Touchdown, No Misses, Game
- 9 Pat Harder, Chi. Cardinals vs. N.Y. Giants, Oct. 17, 1948
  Bob Waterfield, Los Angeles vs. Baltimore, Oct. 22, 1950
- 8 By many players

FIELD GOALS

Most Seasons Leading League
5 Lou Groza, Cleveland, 1950, 1952-54, 1957
4 Jack Manders, Chi. Bears, 1933-34, 1936-37
  Ward Cuff, N.Y. Giants, 1938-39, 1943; Green Bay, 1947
  Mark Moseley, Washington, 1976-77, 1979, 1982
3 Bob Waterfield, Los Angeles, 1947, 1949, 1951
  Gino Cappelletti, Boston, 1961, 1963-64
  Fred Cox, Minnesota, 1965, 1969-70
  Jan Stenerud, Kansas City, 1967, 1970, 1975

Most Consecutive Seasons Leading League
3 Lou Groza, Cleveland, 1952-54
2 By many players

Most Field Goals Attempted, Career
638 George Blanda, Chi. Bears, 1949, 1950-58; Baltimore, 1950; Houston, 1960-66; Oakland, 1967-75
532 Jan Stenerud, Kansas City, 1967-79; Green Bay, 1980-83; Minnesota, 1984
488 Jim Turner, N.Y. Jets, 1964-70; Denver, 1971-79

Most Field Goals Attempted, Season
49 Bruce Gossett, Los Angeles, 1966
  Curt Knight, Washington, 1971
48 Chester Marcol, Green Bay, 1972
47 Jim Turner, N.Y. Jets, 1969
  David Ray, Los Angeles, 1973
  Mark Moseley, Washington, 1983

Most Field Goals Attempted, Game
9 Jim Bakken, St. Louis vs. Pittsburgh, Sept. 24, 1967
8 Lou Michaels, Pittsburgh vs. St. Louis, Dec. 2, 1962
  Garo Yepremian, Detroit vs. Minnesota, Nov. 13, 1966
  Jim Turner, N.Y. Jets vs. Buffalo, Nov. 3, 1968
7 By many players

Most Field Goals, Career
358 Jan Stenerud, Kansas City, 1967-79; Green Bay, 1980-83; Minnesota, 1984
335 George Blanda, Chi. Bears, 1949, 1950-58; Baltimore, 1950; Houston, 1960-66; Oakland, 1967-75
304 Jim Turner, N.Y. Jets, 1964-70; Denver, 1971-79

Most Field Goals, Season
35 Ali Haji-Sheikh, N.Y. Giants, 1983
34 Jim Turner, N.Y. Jets, 1968
33 Chester Marcol, Green Bay, 1972
  Mark Moseley, Washington, 1983

Most Field Goals, Rookie, Season
35 Ali Haji-Sheikh, N.Y. Giants, 1983
33 Chester Marcol, Green Bay, 1972
30 Raul Allegre, Baltimore, 1983
  Paul McFadden, Philadelphia, 1984

Most Field Goals, Game
7 Jim Bakken, St. Louis vs. Pittsburgh, Sept. 24, 1967
6 Gino Cappelletti, Boston vs. Denver, Oct. 4, 1964
  Garo Yepremian, Detroit vs. Minnesota, Nov. 13, 1966
  Jim Turner, N.Y. Jets vs. Buffalo, Nov. 3, 1968
  Tom Dempsey, Philadelphia vs. Houston, Nov. 12, 1972
  Bobby Howfield, N.Y. Jets vs. New Orleans, Dec. 3, 1972
  Jim Bakken, St. Louis vs. Atlanta, Dec. 9, 1973
  Joe Danelo, N.Y. Giants vs. Seattle, Oct. 18, 1981
  Ray Wersching, San Francisco vs. New Orleans, Oct. 16, 1983
5 By many players

Most Field Goals, One Quarter
4 Garo Yepremian, Detroit vs. Minnesota, Nov. 13, 1966 (second quarter)
  Curt Knight, Washington vs. N.Y. Giants, Nov. 15, 1970 (second quarter)
3 By many players

Most Consecutive Games Scoring Field Goals
31 Fred Cox, Minnesota, 1968-70
28 Jim Turner, N.Y. Jets, 1970; Denver, 1971-72
21 Bruce Gossett, San Francisco, 1970-72

Most Consecutive Field Goals
23 Mark Moseley, Washington, 1981-82
20 Garo Yepremian, Miami, 1978; New Orleans, 1979
16 Jan Stenerud, Kansas City, 1969
  Don Cockroft, Cleveland, 1974-75
  Rolf Benirschke, San Diego, 1978-80
  Benny Ricardo, New Orleans, 1981; Minnesota, 1983

Longest Field Goal
63 Tom Dempsey, New Orleans vs. Detroit, Nov. 8, 1970
60 Steve Cox, Cleveland vs. Cincinnati, Oct. 21, 1984
59 Tony Franklin, Philadelphia vs. Dallas, Nov. 12, 1979

Highest Field Goal Percentage, Career (100 field goals)
74.67 Nick Lowery, New England, 1978; Kansas City, 1980-84 (150-112)
72.97 Ed Murray, Detroit 1980-84 (148-108)
71.04 Rolf Benirschke, San Diego, 1977-84 (183-130)

Highest Field Goal Percentage, Season (Qualifiers)
95.24 Mark Moseley, Washington, 1982 (21-20)
91.67 Jan Stenerud, Green Bay, 1981 (24-22)
88.46 Lou Groza, Cleveland, 1953 (26-23)

Most Field Goals, No Misses, Game
6 Gino Cappelletti, Boston vs. Denver, Oct. 4, 1964
  Joe Danelo, N.Y. Giants vs. Seattle, Oct. 18, 1981
  Ray Wersching, San Francisco vs. New Orleans, Oct. 16, 1983
5 Roger LeClerc, Chicago vs. Detroit, Dec. 3, 1961
  Lou Michaels, Baltimore vs. San Francisco, Sept. 25, 1966
  Mac Percival, Chicago vs. Philadelphia, Oct. 20, 1968
  Roy Gerela, Houston vs. Miami, Sept. 28, 1969
  Jan Stenerud, Kansas City vs. Buffalo, Nov. 2, 1969; vs. Buffalo, Dec. 7, 1969; Minnesota vs. Detroit, Sept. 23, 1984
  Horst Muhlmann, Cincinnati vs. Buffalo, Nov. 8, 1970; vs. Pittsburgh, Sept. 24, 1972
  Bruce Gossett, San Francisco vs. Denver, Sept. 23, 1973
  Nick Mike-Mayer, Atlanta vs. Los Angeles, Nov. 4, 1973
  Curt Knight, Washington vs. Baltimore, Nov. 18, 1973
  Tim Mazzetti, Atlanta vs. Los Angeles, Oct. 30, 1978
  Ed Murray, Detroit vs. Green Bay, Sept. 14, 1980
  Rich Karlis, Denver vs. Seattle, Nov. 20, 1983
  Pat Leahy, N.Y. Jets vs. Cincinnati, Sept. 16, 1984

Most Field Goals, 50 or More Yards, Career
17 Jan Stenerud, Kansas City, 1967-79; Green Bay, 1980-83; Minnesota, 1984
12 Tom Dempsey, New Orleans, 1969-70; Philadelphia, 1971-74; Los Angeles, 1975-76; Houston, 1977; Buffalo, 1978-79
  Mark Moseley, Philadelphia, 1970; Houston, 1971-72; Washington, 1974-84
10 Joe Danelo, Green Bay, 1975; N.Y. Giants, 1976-82; Buffalo, 1983-84

Most Field Goals, 50 or More Yards, Season
5 Fred Steinfort, Denver, 1980
4 Horst Muhlmann, Cincinnati, 1970
  Mark Moseley, Washington, 1977
  Nick Lowery, Kansas City, 1980
  Raul Allegre, Baltimore, 1983
3 By many players

Most Field Goals, 50 or More Yards, Game
2 Jim Martin, Detroit vs. Baltimore, Oct. 23, 1960
  Tom Dempsey, New Orleans vs. Los Angeles, Dec. 6, 1970
  Chris Bahr, Cincinnati vs. Houston, Sept. 23, 1979
  Nick Lowery, Kansas City vs. Seattle, Sept. 14, 1980
  Mark Moseley, Washington vs. New Orleans, Oct. 26, 1980
  Fred Steinfort, Denver vs. Seattle, Dec. 21, 1980
  Mick Luckhurst, Atlanta vs. Denver, Dec. 5, 1982; vs. L.A. Rams, Oct. 7, 1984
  Morten Andersen, New Orleans vs. Philadelphia, Dec. 11, 1983
  Paul McFadden, Philadelphia vs. Detroit, Nov. 4, 1984

SAFETIES

Most Safeties, Career
4 Ted Hendricks, Baltimore, 1969-73; Green Bay, 1974; Oakland, 1975-81; L.A. Raiders, 1982-83
  Doug English, Detroit, 1975-79, 1981-84
3 Bill McPeak, Pittsburgh, 1949-57
  Charlie Krueger, San Francisco, 1959-73
  Ernie Stautner, Pittsburgh, 1950-63
  Jim Katcavage, N.Y. Giants, 1956-68
  Roger Brown, Detroit, 1960-66; Los Angeles, 1967-69
  Bruce Maher, Detroit, 1960-67; N.Y. Giants, 1968-69
  Ron McDole, St. Louis, 1961; Houston, 1962; Buffalo, 1963-70; Washington, 1971-78
  Alan Page, Minnesota, 1967-78; Chicago, 1979-81
2 By many players

Most Safeties, Season
2 Tom Nash, Green Bay, 1932
  Roger Brown, Detroit, 1962
  Ron McDole, Buffalo, 1964
  Alan Page, Minnesota, 1971
  Fred Dryer, Los Angeles, 1973
  Benny Barnes, Dallas, 1973
  James Young, Houston, 1977
  Tom Hannon, Minnesota, 1981
  Doug English, Detroit, 1983

Most Safeties, Game
2 Fred Dryer, Los Angeles vs. Green Bay, Oct. 21, 1973

RUSHING

Most Seasons Leading League
8 Jim Brown, Cleveland, 1957-61, 1963-65
4 Steve Van Buren, Philadelphia, 1945, 1947-49
  O.J. Simpson, Buffalo, 1972-73, 1975-76
3 Earl Campbell, Houston, 1978-80

Most Consecutive Seasons Leading League
5 Jim Brown, Cleveland, 1957-61
3 Steve Van Buren, Philadelphia, 1947-49
  Jim Brown, Cleveland, 1963-65
  Earl Campbell, Houston, 1978-80
2 Bill Paschal, N.Y. Giants, 1943-44
  Joe Perry, San Francisco, 1953-54
  Jim Nance, Boston, 1966-67
  Leroy Kelly, Cleveland, 1967-68
  O.J. Simpson, Buffalo, 1972-73; 1975-76
  Eric Dickerson, L.A. Rams, 1983-84

ATTEMPTS

Most Seasons Leading League
6 Jim Brown, Cleveland, 1958-59, 1961, 1963-65
4 Steve Van Buren, Philadelphia, 1947-50
  Walter Payton, Chicago, 1976-79
3 Cookie Gilchrist, Buffalo, 1963-64; Denver, 1965
  Jim Nance, Boston, 1966-67, 1969
  O.J. Simpson, Buffalo, 1973-75

Most Consecutive Seasons Leading League
4 Steve Van Buren, Philadelphia, 1947-50
  Walter Payton, Chicago, 1976-79
3 Jim Brown, Cleveland, 1963-65
  Cookie Gilchrist, Buffalo, 1963-64; Denver, 1965
  O.J. Simpson, Buffalo, 1973-75
2 By many players

Most Attempts, Career
3,047 Walter Payton, Chicago, 1975-84
2,949 Franco Harris, Pittsburgh, 1972-83; Seattle, 1984
2,740 John Riggins, N.Y. Jets, 1971-75; Washington, 1976-79, 1981-84

Most Attempts, Season
407 James Wilder, Tampa Bay 1984
390 Eric Dickerson, L.A. Rams, 1983
381 Walter Payton, Chicago, 1984

Most Attempts, Rookie, Season
390 Eric Dickerson, L.A. Rams, 1983
378 George Rogers, New Orleans, 1981
335 Curt Warner, Seattle, 1983

Most Attempts, Game
43 Butch Woolfolk, N.Y. Giants vs. Philadelphia, Nov. 20, 1983
  James Wilder, Tampa Bay vs. Green Bay, Sept. 30, 1984 (OT)
42 James Wilder, Tampa Bay vs. Pittsburgh, Oct. 30, 1983
41 Franco Harris, Pittsburgh vs. Cincinnati, Oct. 17, 1976

YARDS GAINED
Most Yards Gained, Career
13,309 Walter Payton, Chicago, 1975-84
12,312 Jim Brown, Cleveland, 1957-65
12,120 Franco Harris, Pittsburgh, 1972-83; Seattle, 1984
Most Seasons, 1,000 or More Yards Rushing
8 Franco Harris, Pittsburgh, 1972, 1974-79, 1983
   Walter Payton, Chicago, 1976-81, 1983-84
7 Jim Brown, Cleveland, 1958-61, 1963-65
   Tony Dorsett, Dallas, 1977-81, 1983-84
5 Jim Taylor, Green Bay, 1960-64
   O.J. Simpson, Buffalo, 1972-76
   Earl Campbell, Houston, 1978-81, 1983
   Ottis Anderson, St. Louis, 1979-81, 1983-84
   John Riggins, N.Y. Jets, 1975; Washington, 1978-79, 1983-84
Most Yards Gained, Season
2,105 Eric Dickerson, L.A. Rams, 1984
2,003 O.J. Simpson, Buffalo, 1973
1,934 Earl Campbell, Houston, 1980
Most Yards Gained, Rookie, Season
1,808 Eric Dickerson, L.A. Rams, 1983
1,674 George Rogers, New Orleans, 1981
1,605 Ottis Anderson, St. Louis, 1979
Most Yards Gained, Game
275 Walter Payton, Chicago vs. Minnesota, Nov. 20, 1977
273 O.J. Simpson, Buffalo vs. Detroit, Nov. 25, 1976
250 O.J. Simpson, Buffalo vs. New England, Sept. 16, 1973
Most Games, 200 or More Yards Rushing, Career
6 O.J. Simpson, Buffalo, 1969-77; San Francisco, 1978-79
4 Jim Brown, Cleveland, 1957-65
   Earl Campbell, Houston, 1978-84; New Orleans, 1984
2 Walter Payton, Chicago, 1975-84
   Eric Dickerson, L.A. Rams, 1983-84
Most Games, 200 or More Yards Rushing, Season
4 Earl Campbell, Houston, 1980
3 O.J. Simpson, Buffalo, 1973
2 Jim Brown, Cleveland, 1963
   O.J. Simpson, Buffalo, 1976
   Walter Payton, Chicago, 1977
   Eric Dickerson, L.A. Rams, 1984
Most Consecutive Games, 200 or More Yards Rushing
2 O.J. Simpson, Buffalo, 1973, 1976
   Earl Campbell, Houston, 1980
Most Games, 100 or More Yards Rushing, Career
63 Walter Payton, Chicago, 1975-84
58 Jim Brown, Cleveland, 1957-65
47 Franco Harris, Pittsburgh, 1972-83; Seattle, 1984
Most Games, 100 or More Yards Rushing, Season
12 Eric Dickerson, L.A. Rams, 1984
11 O.J. Simpson, Buffalo, 1973
   Earl Campbell, Houston, 1979
10 Walter Payton, Chicago, 1977
   Earl Campbell, Houston, 1980
Most Consecutive Games, 100 or More Yards Rushing
7 O.J. Simpson, Buffalo, 1972-73
   Earl Campbell, Houston, 1979
6 Jim Brown, Cleveland, 1958
   Franco Harris, Pittsburgh, 1972
   Earl Campbell, Houston, 1980
   Walter Payton, Chicago, 1984
   Eric Dickerson, L.A. Rams, 1984
5 Rob Goode, Washington, 1951
   Jim Brown, Cleveland, 1961
   Jim Nance, Boston, 1966
   O.J. Simpson, Buffalo, 1973, 1975
   Walter Payton, Chicago, 1977
Longest Run From Scrimmage
99 Tony Dorsett, Dallas vs. Minnesota, Jan. 3, 1983 (TD)
97 Andy Uram, Green Bay vs. Chi. Cardinals, Oct. 8, 1939 (TD)
   Bob Gage, Pittsburgh vs. Chi. Bears, Dec. 4, 1949 (TD)
96 Jim Spavital, Baltimore vs. Green Bay, Nov. 5, 1950 (TD)
   Bob Hoernschemeyer, Detroit vs. N.Y. Yanks, Nov. 23, 1950 (TD)

AVERAGE GAIN
Highest Average Gain, Career (700 attempts)
5.22 Jim Brown, Cleveland, 1957-65 (2,359-12,312)
5.14 Eugene (Mercury) Morris, Miami, 1969-75; San Diego, 1976 (804-4,133)
5.09 Eric Dickerson, L.A. Rams, 1983-84 (769-3,913)
Highest Average Gain, Season (Qualifiers)
9.94 Beattie Feathers, Chi. Bears, 1934 (101-1,004)
6.87 Bobby Douglass, Chicago, 1972 (141-968)
6.78 Dan Towler, Los Angeles, 1951 (126-854)
Highest Average Gain, Game (10 attempts)
17.09 Marion Motley, Cleveland vs. Pittsburgh, Oct. 29, 1950 (11-188)
16.70 Bill Grimes, Green Bay vs. N.Y. Yanks, Oct. 8, 1950 (10-167)
16.57 Bobby Mitchell, Cleveland vs. Washington, Nov. 15, 1959 (14-232)

TOUCHDOWNS
Most Seasons Leading League
5 Jim Brown, Cleveland, 1957-59, 1963, 1965
4 Steve Van Buren, Philadelphia, 1945, 1947-49
3 Abner Haynes, Dall. Texans, 1960-62
   Cookie Gilchrist, Buffalo, 1962-64
   Paul Lowe, L.A. Chargers, 1960; San Diego, 1961, 1965
   Leroy Kelly, Cleveland, 1966-68
Most Consecutive Seasons Leading League
3 Steve Van Buren, Philadelphia, 1947-49
   Jim Brown, Cleveland, 1957-59
   Abner Haynes, Dall. Texans, 1960-62
   Cookie Gilchrist, Buffalo, 1962-64
   Leroy Kelly, Cleveland, 1966-68
Most Touchdowns, Career
106 Jim Brown, Cleveland, 1957-65

96 John Riggins, N.Y. Jets, 1971-75; Washington, 1976-79, 1981-84
91 Franco Harris, Pittsburgh, 1972-83; Seattle, 1984
Most Touchdowns, Season
24 John Riggins, Washington, 1983
19 Jim Taylor, Green Bay, 1962
   Earl Campbell, Houston, 1979
   Chuck Muncie, San Diego, 1981
18 Eric Dickerson, L.A. Rams, 1983
Most Touchdowns, Rookie, Season
18 Eric Dickerson, L.A. Rams, 1983
14 Gale Sayers, Chicago, 1965
13 Cookie Gilchrist, Buffalo, 1962
   Earl Campbell, Houston, 1978
   Billy Sims, Detroit, 1980
   George Rogers, New Orleans, 1981
   Curt Warner, Seattle, 1983
Most Touchdowns, Game
6 Ernie Nevers, Chi. Cardinals vs. Chi. Bears, Nov. 28, 1929
5 Jim Brown, Cleveland vs. Baltimore, Nov. 1, 1959
   Cookie Gilchrist, Buffalo vs. N.Y. Jets, Dec. 8, 1963
4 By many players
Most Consecutive Games Rushing for Touchdowns
13 John Riggins, Washington, 1982-83
11 Lenny Moore, Baltimore, 1963-64
9 Leroy Kelly, Cleveland, 1968

PASSING
Most Seasons Leading League
6 Sammy Baugh, Washington, 1937, 1940, 1943, 1945, 1947, 1949
4 Len Dawson, Dall. Texans; 1962; Kansas City, 1964, 1966, 1968
   Roger Staubach, Dallas, 1971, 1973, 1978-79
   Ken Anderson, Cincinnati, 1974-75, 1981-82
3 Arnie Herber, Green Bay, 1932, 1934, 1936
   Norm Van Brocklin, Los Angeles, 1950, 1952, 1954
   Bart Starr, Green Bay, 1962, 1964, 1966
Most Consecutive Seasons Leading League
2 Cecil Isbell, Green Bay, 1941-42
   Milt Plum, Cleveland, 1960-61
   Ken Anderson, Cincinnati, 1974-75; 1981-82
   Roger Staubach, Dallas, 1978-79

ATTEMPTS
Most Seasons Leading League
4 Sammy Baugh, Washington, 1937, 1943, 1947-48
   Johnny Unitas, Baltimore, 1957, 1959-61
   George Blanda, Chi. Bears, 1953; Houston, 1963-65
3 Arnie Herber, Green Bay, 1932, 1934, 1936
   Sonny Jurgensen, Washington, 1966-67, 1969
2 By many players
Most Consecutive Seasons Leading League
3 Johnny Unitas, Baltimore, 1959-61
   George Blanda, Houston, 1963-65
2 By many players
Most Passes Attempted, Career
6,467 Fran Tarkenton, Minnesota, 1961-66, 1972-78; N.Y. Giants, 1967-71
5,186 Johnny Unitas, Baltimore, 1956-72; San Diego, 1973
5,076 Jim Hart, St. Louis, 1966-83; Washington, 1984
Most Passes Attempted, Season
609 Dan Fouts, San Diego, 1981
603 Bill Kenney, Kansas City, 1983
593 Tommy Kramer, Minnesota, 1981
Most Passes Attempted, Rookie, Season
450 Warren Moon, Houston, 1984
439 Jim Zorn, Seattle, 1976
392 Butch Songin, Boston, 1960
Most Passes Attempted, Game
68 George Blanda, Houston vs. Buffalo, Nov. 1, 1964
62 Joe Namath, N.Y. Jets vs. Baltimore, Oct. 18, 1970
   Steve Dils, Minnesota vs. Tampa Bay, Sept. 5, 1981
61 Tommy Kramer, Minnesota vs. Buffalo, Dec. 16, 1979

COMPLETIONS
Most Seasons Leading League
5 Sammy Baugh, Washington, 1937, 1943, 1945, 1947-48
4 George Blanda, Chi. Bears, 1953; Houston, 1963-65
   Sonny Jurgensen, Philadelphia, 1961; Washington, 1966-67, 1969
3 Arnie Herber, Green Bay, 1932, 1934, 1936
   Johnny Unitas, Baltimore, 1959-60, 1963
   John Brodie, San Francisco, 1965, 1968, 1970
   Fran Tarkenton, Minnesota, 1975-76, 1978
Most Consecutive Seasons Leading League
3 George Blanda, Houston, 1963-65
2 By many players
Most Passes Completed, Career
3,686 Fran Tarkenton, Minnesota, 1961-66, 1972-78; N.Y. Giants, 1967-71
2,830 Johnny Unitas, Baltimore, 1956-72; San Diego, 1973
2,627 Ken Anderson, Cincinnati, 1971-84
Most Passes Completed, Season
362 Dan Marino, Miami, 1984
360 Dan Fouts, San Diego, 1981
348 Dan Fouts, San Diego, 1980
Most Passes Completed, Rookie, Season
259 Warren Moon, Houston, 1984
208 Jim Zorn, Seattle, 1976
187 Butch Songin, Boston, 1960
Most Passes Completed, Game
42 Richard Todd, N.Y. Jets vs. San Francisco, Sept. 21, 1980
40 Ken Anderson, Cincinnati vs. San Diego, Dec. 20, 1982
38 Tommy Kramer, Minnesota vs. Cleveland, Dec. 14, 1980
   Tommy Kramer, Minnesota vs. Green Bay, Nov. 29, 1981
   Joe Ferguson, Buffalo vs. Miami, Oct. 9, 1983 (OT)
Most Consecutive Passes Completed
20 Ken Anderson, Cincinnati vs. Houston, Jan. 2, 1983

18 Steve DeBerg, Denver vs. L.A. Rams (17), Dec. 12, 1982; vs. Kansas City (1), Dec. 19, 1982
17 Bert Jones, Baltimore vs. N.Y. Jets, Dec. 15, 1974

COMPLETION PERCENTAGE
Most Seasons Leading League
8 Len Dawson, Dall. Texans, 1962; Kansas City, 1964-69, 1975
7 Sammy Baugh, Washington, 1940, 1942-43, 1945, 1947-49
4 Bart Starr, Green Bay, 1962, 1966, 1968-69
Most Consecutive Seasons Leading League
6 Len Dawson, Kansas City, 1964-69
3 Sammy Baugh, Washington, 1947-49
   Otto Graham, Cleveland, 1953-55
   Milt Plum, Cleveland, 1959-61
2 By many players
Highest Completion Percentage, Career (1,500 attempts)
63.75 Joe Montana, San Francisco, 1979-84 (2,077-1,324)
59.85 Ken Stabler, Oakland, 1970-79; Houston, 1980-81; New Orleans, 1982-84 (3,793-2,270)
59.44 Danny White, Dallas, 1976-84 (1,943-1,155)
Highest Completion Percentage, Season (Qualifiers)
70.55 Ken Anderson, Cincinnati, 1982 (309-218)
70.33 Sammy Baugh, Washington, 1945 (182-128)
67.29 Steve Bartkowski, Atlanta, 1984 (269-181)
Highest Completion Percentage, Rookie, Season (Qualifiers)
58.45 Dan Marino, Miami, 1983 (296-173)
57.56 Warren Moon, Houston, 1984 (450-259)
57.14 Jim McMahon, Chicago, 1982 (210-120)
Highest Completion Percentage, Game (20 attempts)
90.91 Ken Anderson, Cincinnati vs. Pittsburgh, Nov. 10, 1974 (22-20)
90.48 Lynn Dickey, Green Bay vs. New Orleans, Dec. 13, 1981 (21-19)
87.50 Danny White, Dallas vs. Philadelphia, Nov. 6, 1983 (24-21)

YARDS GAINED
Most Seasons Leading League
5 Sonny Jurgensen, Philadelphia, 1961-62; Washington, 1966-67, 1969
4 Sammy Baugh, Washington, 1937, 1940, 1947-48
   Johnny Unitas, Baltimore, 1957, 1959-60, 1963
   Dan Fouts, San Diego, 1979-82
3 Arnie Herber, Green Bay, 1932, 1934, 1936
   Sid Luckman, Chi. Bears, 1943, 1945-46
   John Brodie, San Francisco, 1965, 1968, 1970
   John Hadl, San Diego, 1965, 1968, 1971
   Joe Namath, N.Y. Jets, 1966-67, 1972
Most Consecutive Seasons Leading League
4 Dan Fouts, San Diego, 1979-82
2 By many players
Most Yards Gained, Career
47,003 Fran Tarkenton, Minnesota, 1961-66, 1972-78; N.Y. Giants, 1967-71
40,239 Johnny Unitas, Baltimore, 1956-72; San Diego, 1973
34,665 Jim Hart, St. Louis, 1966-83; Washington, 1984
Most Seasons, 3,000 or More Yards Passing
5 Sonny Jurgensen, Philadelphia, 1961-62; Washington, 1966-67, 1969
4 Brian Sipe, Cleveland, 1979-81, 1983
   Dan Fouts, San Diego, 1979-81, 1984
3 By many players
Most Yards Gained, Season
5,084 Dan Marino, Miami, 1984
4,802 Dan Fouts, San Diego, 1981
4,715 Dan Fouts, San Diego, 1980
Most Yards Gained, Rookie, Season
3,338 Warren Moon, Houston, 1984
2,571 Jim Zorn, Seattle, 1976
2,507 Dennis Shaw, Buffalo, 1970
Most Yards Gained, Game
554 Norm Van Brocklin, Los Angeles vs. N.Y. Yanks, Sept. 28, 1951
509 Vince Ferragamo, L.A. Rams vs. Chicago, Dec. 26, 1982
505 Y.A. Tittle, N.Y. Giants vs. Washington, Oct. 28, 1962
Most Games, 400 or More Yards Passing, Career
5 Sonny Jurgensen, Philadelphia, 1957-63; Washington, 1964-74
4 Dan Fouts, San Diego, 1973-84
   Dan Marino, Miami, 1983-84
3 Joe Namath, N.Y. Jets, 1965-76; Los Angeles, 1977
Most Games, 400 or More Yards Passing, Season
4 Dan Marino, Miami, 1984
2 George Blanda, Houston, 1961
   Sonny Jurgensen, Philadelphia, 1961
   Joe Namath, N.Y. Jets, 1972
   Dan Fouts, San Diego, 1982
Most Consecutive Games, 400 or More Yards Passing
2 Dan Fouts, San Diego, 1982
   Dan Marino, Miami, 1984
Most Games, 300 or More Yards Passing, Career
40 Dan Fouts, San Diego, 1973-84
26 Johnny Unitas, Baltimore, 1956-72; San Diego, 1973
25 Sonny Jurgensen, Philadelphia, 1957-63; Washington, 1964-74
Most Games, 300 or More Yards Passing, Season
9 Dan Marino, Miami, 1984
8 Dan Fouts, San Diego, 1980
7 Dan Fouts, San Diego, 1981
   Bill Kenney, Kansas City, 1983
   Neil Lomax, St. Louis, 1984
Most Consecutive Games, 300 or More Yards, Passing, Season
5 Joe Montana, San Francisco, 1982
4 Dan Fouts, San Diego, 1979
   Bill Kenney, Kansas City, 1983
3 By many players
Longest Pass Completion (All TDs except as noted)
99 Frank Filchock (to Farkas), Washington vs. Pittsburgh, Oct. 15, 1939
   George Izo (to Mitchell), Washington vs. Cleveland, Sept. 15, 1963
   Karl Sweetan (to Studstill), Detroit vs. Baltimore, Oct. 16, 1966
   Sonny Jurgensen (to Allen), Washington vs. Chicago, Sept. 15, 1968
   Jim Plunkett (to Branch), L.A. Raiders vs. Washington, Oct. 2, 1983

98 Doug Russell (to Tinsley), Chi. Cardinals vs. Cleveland, Nov. 27, 1938
   Ogden Compton (to Lane), Chi. Cardinals vs. Green Bay, Nov. 13, 1955
   Bill Wade (to Farrington), Chicago Bears vs. Detroit, Oct. 8, 1961
   Jacky Lee (to Dewveall), Houston vs. San Diego, Nov. 25, 1962
   Earl Morrall (to Jones), N.Y. Giants vs. Pittsburgh, Sept. 11, 1966
   Jim Hart (to Moore), St. Louis vs. Los Angeles, Dec. 10, 1972 (no TD)
97 Pat Coffee (to Tinsley), Chi. Cardinals vs. Chi. Bears, Dec. 5, 1937
   Bobby Layne (to Box), Detroit vs. Green Bay, Nov. 26, 1953
   George Shaw (to Tarr), Denver vs. Boston, Sept. 21, 1962

AVERAGE GAIN
Most Seasons Leading League
7 Sid Luckman, Chi. Bears, 1939-43, 1946-47
3 Arnie Herber, Green Bay, 1932, 1934, 1936
   Norm Van Brocklin, Los Angeles, 1950, 1952, 1954
   Len Dawson, Dall. Texans, 1962; Kansas City, 1966, 1968
   Bart Starr, Green Bay, 1966-68
Most Consecutive Seasons Leading League
5 Sid Luckman, Chi. Bears, 1939-43
3 Bart Starr, Green Bay, 1966-68
2 Bernie Masterson, Chi. Bears, 1937-38
   Sid Luckman, Chi. Bears, 1946-47
   Johnny Unitas, Baltimore, 1964-65
   Terry Bradshaw, Pittsburgh, 1977-78
   Steve Grogan, New England, 1980-81
Highest Average Gain, Career (1,500 attempts)
8.63 Otto Graham, Cleveland, 1950-55 (1,565-13,499)
8.42 Sid Luckman, Chi. Bears, 1939-50 (1,744-14,686)
8.16 Norm Van Brocklin, Los Angeles, 1949-57; Philadelphia, 1958-60 (2,895-23,611)
Highest Average Gain, Season (Qualifiers)
11.17 Tommy O'Connell, Cleveland, 1957 (110-1,229)
10.86 Sid Luckman, Chi. Bears, 1943 (202-2,194)
10.55 Otto Graham, Cleveland, 1953 (258-2,722)
Highest Average Gain, Rookie, Season (Qualifiers)
9.411 Greg Cook, Cincinnati, 1969 (197-1,854)
9.409 Bob Waterfield, Cleveland, 1945 (171-1,609)
8.36 Zeke Bratkowski, Chi. Bears, 1954 (130-1,087)
Highest Average Gain, Game (20 attempts)
18.58 Sammy Baugh, Washington vs. Boston, Oct. 31, 1948 (24-446)
18.50 Johnny Unitas, Baltimore vs. Atlanta, Nov. 12, 1967 (20-370)
17.71 Joe Namath, N.Y. Jets vs. Baltimore, Sept. 24, 1972 (28-496)

TOUCHDOWNS
Most Seasons Leading League
4 Johnny Unitas, Baltimore, 1957-60
   Len Dawson, Dall. Texans, 1962; Kansas City, 1963, 1965-66
3 Arnie Herber, Green Bay, 1932, 1934, 1936
   Sid Luckman, Chi. Bears, 1943, 1945-46
   Y.A. Tittle, San Francisco, 1955; N.Y. Giants, 1962-63
2 By many players
Most Consecutive Seasons Leading League
4 Johnny Unitas, Baltimore, 1957-60
2 By many players
Most Touchdown Passes, Career
342 Fran Tarkenton, Minnesota, 1961-66, 1972-78; N.Y. Giants, 1967-71
290 Johnny Unitas, Baltimore, 1956-72: San Diego, 1973
255 Sonny Jurgensen, Philadelphia, 1957-63; Washington, 1964-74
Most Touchdown Passes, Season
48 Dan Marino, Miami, 1984
36 George Blanda, Houston, 1961
   Y.A. Tittle, N.Y. Giants, 1963
34 Daryle Lamonica, Oakland, 1969
Most Touchdown Passes, Rookie, Season
22 Charlie Conerly, N.Y. Giants, 1948
   Butch Songin, Boston, 1960
20 Dan Marino, Miami, 1983
19 Jim Plunkett, New England, 1971
Most Touchdown Passes, Game
7 Sid Luckman, Chi. Bears vs. N.Y. Giants, Nov. 14, 1943
   Adrian Burk, Philadelphia vs. Washington, Oct. 17, 1954
   George Blanda, Houston vs. N.Y. Titans, Nov. 19, 1961
   Y.A. Tittle, N.Y. Giants vs. Washington, Oct. 28, 1962
   Joe Kapp, Minnesota vs. Baltimore, Sept. 28, 1969
6 By many players. Last time: Dan Fouts, San Diego vs. Oakland, Nov. 22, 1981
Most Games, Four or More Touchdown Passes, Career
17 Johnny Unitas, Baltimore, 1956-72; San Diego, 1973
13 George Blanda, Chi. Bears, 1949, 1950-58; Baltimore, 1950; Houston, 1960-66; Oakland, 1967-75
12 Sonny Jurgensen, Philadelphia, 1957-63; Washington, 1964-74
   Fran Tarkenton, Minnesota, 1961-66, 1972-78; N.Y. Giants, 1967-71
Most Games, Four or More Touchdown Passes, Season
6 Dan Marino, Miami, 1984
4 George Blanda, Houston, 1961
   Vince Ferragamo, Los Angeles, 1980
3 By many players
Most Consecutive Games, Four or More Touchdown Passes
4 Dan Marino, Miami, 1984 (current)
2 By many players
Most Consecutive Games, Touchdown Passes
47 Johnny Unitas, Baltimore, 1956-60
25 Daryle Lamonica, Oakland, 1968-70
23 Frank Ryan, Cleveland, 1965-67
   Sonny Jurgensen, Washington, 1966-68

HAD INTERCEPTED
Most Consecutive Passes Attempted, None Intercepted
294 Bart Starr, Green Bay, 1964-65
208 Milt Plum, Cleveland, 1959-60
206 Roman Gabriel, Los Angeles, 1968-69
Most Passes Had Intercepted, Career
277 George Blanda, Chi. Bears, 1949, 1950-58; Baltimore, 1950; Houston, 1960-66; Oakland, 1967-75

268 John Hadl, San Diego, 1962-72; Los Angeles, 1973-74; Green Bay, 1974-75; Houston, 1976-77
266 Fran Tarkenton, Minnesota, 1961-66, 1972-78; N.Y. Giants, 1967-71

Most Passes Had Intercepted, Season
42 George Blanda, Houston, 1962
34 Frank Tripucka, Denver, 1960
32 John Hadl, San Diego, 1968
Fran Tarkenton, Minnesota, 1978

Most Passes Had Intercepted, Game
8 Jim Hardy, Chi. Cardinals vs. Philadelphia, Sept. 24, 1950
7 Parker Hall, Cleveland vs. Green Bay, Nov. 8, 1942
Frank Sinkwich, Detroit vs. Green Bay, Oct. 24, 1943
Bob Waterfield, Los Angeles vs. Green Bay, Oct. 17, 1948
Zeke Bratkowski, Chicago vs. Baltimore, Oct. 2, 1960
Tommy Wade, Pittsburgh vs. Philadelphia, Dec. 12, 1965
Ken Stabler, Oakland vs. Denver, Oct. 16, 1977
6 By many players

Most Attempts, No Interceptions, Game
51 Scott Brunner, N.Y. Giants vs. St. Louis, Dec. 26, 1982
50 Dan Fouts, San Diego vs. Green Bay, Oct. 7, 1984
49 Greg Landry, Baltimore vs. N.Y. Jets, Dec. 2, 1979
Tommy Kramer, Minnesota vs. Cleveland, Dec. 14, 1980

LOWEST PERCENTAGE, PASSES HAD INTERCEPTED
Most Seasons Leading League, Lowest Percentage, Passes Had Intercepted
5 Sammy Baugh, Washington, 1940, 1942, 1944-45, 1947
3 Charlie Conerly, N.Y. Giants, 1950, 1956, 1959
Bart Starr, Green Bay, 1962, 1964, 1966
Roger Staubach, Dallas, 1971, 1977, 1979
Ken Anderson, Cincinnati, 1972, 1981-82
2 By many players

Lowest Percentage, Passes Had Intercepted, Career (1,500 attempts)
2.60 Joe Montana, San Francisco, 1979-84 (2,077-54)
3.31 Roman Gabriel, Los Angeles, 1962-72; Philadelphia, 1973-77 (4,498-149)
3.57 Ken Anderson, Cincinnati, 1971-84 (4,420-158)

Lowest Percentage, Passes Had Intercepted, Season (Qualifiers)
0.66 Joe Ferguson, Buffalo, 1976 (151-1)
1.16 Steve Bartkowski, Atlanta, 1983 (432-5)
1.20 Bart Starr, Green Bay, 1966 (251-3)

Lowest Percentage, Passes Had Intercepted, Rookie, Season (Qualifiers)
2.03 Dan Marino, Miami, 1983 (296-6)
2.10 Gary Wood, N.Y. Giants, 1964 (143-3)
3.11 Warren Moon, Houston, 1984 (450-14)

PASS RECEIVING

Most Seasons Leading League
8 Don Hutson, Green Bay, 1936-37, 1939, 1941-45
5 Lionel Taylor, Denver, 1960-63, 1965
3 Tom Fears, Los Angeles, 1948-50
Pete Pihos, Philadelphia, 1953-55
Billy Wilson, San Francisco, 1954, 1956-57
Raymond Berry, Baltimore, 1958-60
Lance Alworth, San Diego, 1966, 1968-69

Most Consecutive Seasons Leading League
5 Don Hutson, Green Bay, 1941-45
4 Lionel Taylor, Denver, 1960-63
3 Tom Fears, Los Angeles, 1948-50
Pete Pihos, Philadelphia, 1953-55
Raymond Berry, Baltimore, 1958-60

Most Pass Receptions, Career
657 Charlie Joiner, Houston, 1969-72; Cincinnati, 1972-75; San Diego, 1976-84
649 Charley Taylor, Washington, 1964-75, 1977
633 Don Maynard, N.Y. Giants, 1958; N.Y. Jets, 1960-72; St. Louis, 1973

Most Seasons, 50 or More Pass Receptions
7 Raymond Berry, Baltimore, 1958-62, 1965-66
Art Powell, N.Y. Titans, 1960-62; Oakland, 1963-66
Lance Alworth, San Diego, 1963-69
Charley Taylor, Washington, 1964, 1966-67, 1969, 1973-75
Steve Largent, Seattle, 1976, 1978-81, 1983-84
6 Lionel Taylor, Denver, 1960-65
Bobby Mitchell, Washington, 1962-67
Ahmad Rashad, Minnesota, 1976-81
Charlie Joiner, San Diego, 1976, 1979-81, 1983-84
5 By many players

Most Pass Receptions, Season
106 Art Monk, Washington, 1984
101 Charley Hennigan, Houston, 1964
100 Lionel Taylor, Denver, 1961

Most Pass Receptions, Rookie, Season
83 Earl Cooper, San Francisco, 1980
72 Bill Groman, Houston, 1960
67 Jack Clancy, Miami, 1967
Cris Collinsworth, Cincinnati, 1981

Most Pass Receptions, Game
18 Tom Fears, Los Angeles vs. Green Bay, Dec. 3, 1950
17 Clark Gaines, N.Y. Jets vs. San Francisco, Sept. 21, 1980
16 Sonny Randle, St. Louis vs. N.Y. Giants, Nov. 4, 1962

Most Consecutive Games, Pass Receptions
127 Harold Carmichael, Philadelphia, 1972-80
121 Mel Gray, St. Louis, 1973-82
107 Steve Largent, Seattle, 1977-84 (current)

YARDS GAINED
Most Seasons Leading League
7 Don Hutson, Green Bay, 1936, 1938-39, 1941-44
3 Raymond Berry, Baltimore, 1957, 1959-60
Lance Alworth, San Diego, 1965-66, 1968
2 By many players

Most Consecutive Seasons Leading League
4 Don Hutson, Green Bay, 1941-44
2 By many players

Most Yards Gained, Career
11,834 Don Maynard, N.Y. Giants, 1958; N.Y. Jets, 1960-72; St. Louis, 1973
10,774 Charlie Joiner, Houston, 1969-72; Cincinnati, 1972-75; San Diego, 1976-84
10,372 Harold Jackson, Los Angeles, 1968, 1973-77; Philadelphia, 1969-72; New England, 1978-81; Minnesota, 1982; Seattle, 1983

Most Seasons, 1,000 or More Yards, Pass Receiving
7 Lance Alworth, San Diego, 1963-69
6 Steve Largent, Seattle, 1978-81, 1983-84
5 Art Powell, N.Y. Titans, 1960, 1962; Oakland, 1963-64, 1966
Don Maynard, N.Y. Jets, 1960, 1962, 1965, 1967-68

Most Yards Gained, Season
1,746 Charley Hennigan, Houston, 1961
1,602 Lance Alworth, San Diego, 1965
1,555 Roy Green, St. Louis, 1984

Most Yards Gained, Rookie, Season
1,473 Bill Groman, Houston, 1960
1,231 Bill Howton, Green Bay, 1952
1,124 Harlon Hill, Chi. Bears, 1954

Most Yards Gained, Game
303 Jim Benton, Cleveland vs. Detroit, Nov. 22, 1945
302 Cloyce Box, Detroit vs. Baltimore, Dec. 3, 1950
272 Charley Hennigan, Houston vs. Boston, Oct. 13, 1961

Most Games, 200 or More Yards Pass Receiving, Career
5 Lance Alworth, San Diego, 1962-70; Dallas, 1971-72
4 Don Hutson, Green Bay, 1935-45
Charley Hennigan, Houston, 1960-66
3 Don Maynard, N.Y. Giants, 1958; N.Y. Jets, 1960-72; St. Louis, 1973

Most Games, 200 or More Yards Pass Receiving, Season
3 Charley Hennigan, Houston, 1961
2 Don Hutson, Green Bay, 1942
Gene Roberts, N.Y. Giants, 1949
Lance Alworth, San Diego, 1963
Don Maynard, N.Y. Jets, 1968

Most Games, 100 or More Yards Pass Receiving, Career
50 Don Maynard, N.Y. Giants, 1958; N.Y. Jets, 1960-72; St. Louis, 1973
41 Lance Alworth, San Diego, 1962-70; Dallas, 1971-72
32 Steve Largent, Seattle, 1976-84

Most Games, 100 or More Yards Pass Receiving, Season
10 Charley Hennigan, Houston, 1961
9 Elroy (Crazylegs) Hirsch, Los Angeles, 1951
Bill Groman, Houston, 1960
Lance Alworth, San Diego, 1965
Don Maynard, N.Y. Jets, 1967
8 Charley Hennigan, Houston, 1964
Lance Alworth, San Diego, 1967

Most Consecutive Games, 100 or More Yards Pass Receiving
7 Charley Hennigan, Houston, 1961
Bill Groman, Houston, 1961
6 Raymond Berry, Baltimore, 1960
Pat Studstill, Detroit, 1966
5 Elroy (Crazylegs) Hirsch, Los Angeles, 1951
Bob Boyd, Los Angeles, 1954
Terry Barr, Detroit, 1963
Lance Alworth, San Diego, 1966

Longest Pass Reception (All TDs except as noted)
99 Andy Farkas (from Filchock), Washington vs. Pittsburgh, Oct. 15, 1939
Bobby Mitchell (from Izo), Washington vs. Cleveland, Sept. 15, 1963
Pat Studstill (from Sweetan), Detroit vs. Baltimore, Oct. 16, 1966
Gerry Allen (from Jurgensen), Washington vs. Chicago, Sept. 15, 1968
Cliff Branch (from Plunkett), L.A. Raiders vs. Washington, Oct. 2, 1983
98 Gaynell Tinsley (from Russell), Chi. Cardinals vs. Cleveland, Nov. 17, 1938
Dick (Night Train) Lane (from Compton), Chi. Cardinals vs. Green Bay, Nov. 13, 1955
John Farrington (from Wade), Chicago vs. Detroit, Oct. 8, 1961
Willard Dewveall (from Lee), Houston vs. San Diego, Nov. 25, 1962
Homer Jones (from Morrall), N.Y. Giants vs. Pittsburgh, Sept. 11, 1966
Bobby Moore (from Hart), St. Louis vs. Los Angeles, Dec. 10, 1972 (no TD)
97 Gaynell Tinsley (from Coffee), Chi. Cardinals vs. Chi. Bears, Dec. 5, 1937
Cloyce Box (from Layne), Detroit vs. Green Bay, Nov. 26, 1953
Jerry Tarr (from Shaw), Denver vs. Boston, Sept. 21, 1962

TOUCHDOWNS
Most Seasons Leading League
9 Don Hutson, Green Bay, 1935-38, 1940-44
3 Lance Alworth, San Diego, 1964-66
2 By many players

Most Consecutive Seasons Leading League
5 Don Hutson, Green Bay, 1940-44
4 Don Hutson, Green Bay, 1935-38
3 Lance Alworth, San Diego, 1964-66

Most Touchdowns, Career
99 Don Hutson, Green Bay, 1935-45
88 Don Maynard, N.Y. Giants, 1958; N.Y. Jets, 1960-72; St. Louis, 1973
85 Lance Alworth, San Diego, 1962-70; Dallas, 1971-72
Paul Warfield, Cleveland, 1964-69, 1976-77; Miami, 1970-74

Most Touchdowns, Season
18 Mark Clayton, Miami, 1984
17 Don Hutson, Green Bay, 1942
Elroy (Crazylegs) Hirsch, Los Angeles, 1951
Bill Groman, Houston, 1961
16 Art Powell, Oakland, 1963

Most Touchdowns, Rookie, Season
13 Bill Howton, Green Bay, 1952
John Jefferson, San Diego, 1979
12 Harlon Hill, Chi. Bears, 1954
Bill Groman, Houston, 1960
Mike Ditka, Chicago, 1961
Bob Hayes, Dallas, 1965
10 Bill Swiacki, N.Y. Giants, 1948
Bucky Pope, Los Angeles, 1964
Sammy White, Minnesota, 1976
Daryl Turner, Seattle, 1984

Most Touchdowns, Game
- 5 Bob Shaw, Chi. Cardinals vs. Baltimore, Oct. 2, 1950
  - Kellen Winslow, San Diego vs. Oakland, Nov. 22, 1981
- 4 By many players

Most Consecutive Games, Touchdowns
- 11 Elroy (Crazylegs) Hirsch, Los Angeles, 1950-51
  - Buddy Dial, Pittsburgh, 1959-60
- 9 Lance Alworth, San Diego, 1963
- 8 Bill Groman, Houston, 1961
  - Dave Parks, San Francisco, 1965

INTERCEPTIONS BY

Most Seasons Leading League
- 2 Dick (Night Train) Lane, Los Angeles, 1952; Chi. Cardinals, 1954
  - Jack Christiansen, Detroit, 1953, 1957
  - Milt Davis, Baltimore, 1957, 1959
  - Dick Lynch, N.Y. Giants, 1961, 1963
  - Johnny Robinson, Kansas City, 1966, 1970
  - Bill Bradley, Philadelphia, 1971-72
  - Emmitt Thomas, Kansas City, 1969, 1974
  - Everson Walls, Dallas, 1981-82

Most Interceptions By, Career
- 81 Paul Krause, Washington, 1964-67; Minnesota, 1968-79
- 79 Emlen Tunnell, N.Y. Giants, 1948-58; Green Bay, 1959-61
- 68 Dick (Night Train) Lane, Los Angeles, 1952-53; Chi. Cardinals, 1954-59; Detroit, 1960-65

Most Interceptions By, Season
- 14 Dick (Night Train) Lane, Los Angeles, 1952
- 13 Dan Sandifer, Washington, 1948
  - Orban (Spec) Sanders, N.Y. Yanks, 1950
  - Lester Hayes, Oakland, 1980
- 12 By nine players

Most Interceptions By, Rookie, Season
- 14 Dick (Night Train) Lane, Los Angeles, 1952
- 13 Dan Sandifer, Washington, 1948
- 12 Woodley Lewis, Los Angeles, 1950
  - Paul Krause, Washington, 1964

Most Interceptions By, Game
- 4 Sammy Baugh, Washington vs. Detroit, Nov. 14, 1943
  - Dan Sandifer, Washington vs. Boston, Oct. 31, 1948
  - Don Doll, Detroit vs. Chi. Cardinals, Oct. 23, 1949
  - Bob Nussbaumer, Chi. Cardinals vs. N.Y. Bulldogs, Nov. 13, 1949
  - Russ Craft, Philadelphia vs. Chi. Cardinals, Sept. 24, 1950
  - Bobby Dillon, Green Bay vs. Detroit, Nov. 26, 1953
  - Jack Butler, Pittsburgh vs. Washington, Dec. 13, 1953
  - Austin (Goose) Gonsoulin, Denver vs. Buffalo, Sept. 18, 1960
  - Jerry Norton, St. Louis vs. Washington, Nov. 20, 1960; vs. Pittsburgh, Nov. 26, 1961
  - Dave Baker, San Francisco vs. L.A. Rams, Dec. 4, 1960
  - Bobby Ply, Dall. Texans vs. San Diego, Dec. 16, 1962
  - Bobby Hunt, Kansas City vs. Houston, Oct. 4, 1964
  - Willie Brown, Denver vs. N.Y. Jets, Nov. 15, 1964
  - Dick Anderson, Miami vs. Pittsburgh, Dec. 3, 1973
  - Willie Buchanon, Green Bay vs. San Diego, Sept. 24, 1978

Most Consecutive Games, Passes Intercepted By
- 8 Tom Morrow, Oakland, 1962-63
- 7 Paul Krause, Washington, 1964
  - Larry Wilson, St. Louis, 1966
  - Ben Davis, Cleveland, 1968
- 6 Dick (Night Train) Lane, Chi. Cardinals, 1954-55
  - Will Sherman, Los Angeles, 1954-55
  - Jim Shofner, Cleveland, 1960
  - Paul Krause, Minnesota, 1968
  - Willie Williams, N.Y. Giants, 1968
  - Kermit Alexander, San Francisco, 1968-69
  - Mel Blount, Pittsburgh, 1975
  - Eric Harris, Kansas City, 1980
  - Lester Hayes, Oakland, 1980

YARDS GAINED

Most Seasons Leading League
- 2 Dick (Night Train) Lane, Los Angeles, 1952; Chi. Cardinals, 1954
  - Herb Adderley, Green Bay, 1965, 1969
  - Dick Anderson, Miami, 1968, 1970

Most Yards Gained, Career
- 1,282 Emlen Tunnell, N.Y. Giants, 1948-58; Green Bay, 1959-61
- 1,207 Dick (Night Train) Lane, Los Angeles, 1952-53; Chi. Cardinals, 1954-59; Detroit, 1960-65
- 1,185 Paul Krause, Washington, 1964-67; Minnesota, 1968-79

Most Yards Gained, Season
- 349 Charley McNeil, San Diego, 1961
- 301 Don Doll, Detroit, 1949
- 298 Dick (Night Train) Lane, Los Angeles, 1952

Most Yards Gained, Rookie, Season
- 301 Don Doll, Detroit, 1949
- 298 Dick (Night Train) Lane, Los Angeles, 1952
- 275 Woodley Lewis, Los Angeles, 1950

Most Yards Gained, Game
- 177 Charley McNeil, San Diego vs. Houston, Sept. 24, 1961
- 167 Dick Jauron, Detroit vs. Chicago, Nov. 18, 1973
- 151 Tom Myers, New Orleans vs. Minnesota, Sept. 3, 1978
  - Mike Haynes, L.A. Raiders vs. Miami, Dec. 2, 1984

Longest Return (All TDs)
- 102 Bob Smith, Detroit vs. Chi. Bears, Nov. 24, 1949
  - Erich Barnes, N.Y. Giants vs. Dall. Cowboys, Oct. 22, 1961
  - Gary Barbaro, Kansas City vs. Seattle, Dec. 11, 1977
  - Louis Breeden, Cincinnati vs. San Diego, Nov. 8, 1981
- 101 Richie Petitbon, Chicago vs. Los Angeles, Dec. 9, 1962
  - Henry Carr, N.Y. Giants vs. Los Angeles, Nov. 13, 1966
  - Tony Greene, Buffalo vs. Kansas City, Oct. 3, 1976
  - Tom Pridemore, Atlanta vs. San Francisco, Sept. 20, 1981
- 100 Vern Huffman, Detroit vs. Brooklyn, Oct. 17, 1937
  - Mike Gaechter, Dall. Cowboys vs. Philadelphia, Oct. 14, 1962

Les (Speedy) Duncan, San Diego vs. Kansas City, Oct. 15, 1967
Tom Janik, Buffalo vs. N.Y. Jets, Sept. 29, 1968
Tim Collier, Kansas City vs. Oakland, Dec. 18, 1977

TOUCHDOWNS

Most Touchdowns, Career
- 9 Ken Houston, Houston, 1967-72; Washington, 1973-80
- 7 Herb Adderley, Green Bay, 1961-69; Dallas, 1970-72
  - Erich Barnes, Chi. Bears, 1958-60; N.Y. Giants, 1961-64; Cleveland, 1965-70
  - Lem Barney, Detroit, 1967-77
- 6 Tom Janik, Denver, 1963-64; Buffalo, 1965-68; Boston, 1969-70; New England, 1971
  - Miller Farr, Denver, 1965; San Diego, 1965-66; Houston, 1967-69; St. Louis, 1970-72; Detroit, 1973
  - Bobby Bell, Kansas City, 1963-74

Most Touchdowns, Season
- 4 Ken Houston, Houston, 1971
  - Jim Kearney, Kansas City, 1972
- 3 Dick Harris, San Diego, 1961
  - Dick Lynch, N.Y. Giants, 1963
  - Herb Adderley, Green Bay, 1965
  - Lem Barney, Detroit, 1967
  - Miller Farr, Houston, 1967
  - Monte Jackson, Los Angeles, 1976
  - Rod Perry, Los Angeles, 1978
  - Ronnie Lott, San Francisco, 1981
- 2 By many players

Most Touchdowns, Rookie, Season
- 3 Lem Barney, Detroit, 1967
  - Ronnie Lott, San Francisco, 1981
- 2 By many players

Most Touchdowns, Game
- 2 Bill Blackburn, Chi. Cardinals vs. Boston, Oct. 24, 1948
  - Dan Sandifer, Washington vs. Boston, Oct. 31, 1948
  - Bob Franklin, Cleveland vs. Chicago, Dec. 11, 1960
  - Bill Stacy, St. Louis vs. Dall. Cowboys, Nov. 5, 1961
  - Jerry Norton, St. Louis vs. Pittsburgh, Nov. 26, 1961
  - Miller Farr, Houston vs. Buffalo, Dec. 7, 1968
  - Ken Houston, Houston vs. San Diego, Dec. 19, 1971
  - Jim Kearney, Kansas City vs. Denver, Oct. 1, 1972
  - Lemar Parrish, Cincinnati vs. Houston, Dec. 17, 1972
  - Dick Anderson, Miami vs. Pittsburgh, Dec. 3, 1973
  - Prentice McCray, New England vs. N.Y. Jets, Nov. 21, 1976
  - Kenny Johnson, Atlanta vs. Green Bay, Nov. 27, 1983 (OT)
  - Mike Kozlowski, Miami vs. N.Y. Jets, Dec. 16, 1983
  - Dave Brown, Seattle vs. Kansas City, Nov. 4, 1984

PUNTING

Most Seasons Leading League
- 4 Sammy Baugh, Washington, 1940-43
  - Jerrel Wilson, Kansas City, 1965, 1968, 1972-73
- 3 Yale Lary, Detroit, 1959, 1961, 1963
  - Jim Fraser, Denver, 1962-64
  - Ray Guy, Oakland, 1974-75, 1977
- 2 By many players

Most Consecutive Seasons Leading League
- 4 Sammy Baugh, Washington, 1940-43
- 3 Jim Fraser, Denver, 1962-64
- 2 By many players

PUNTS

Most Punts, Career
- 1,083 John James, Atlanta, 1972-81; Detroit, 1982, Houston, 1982-84
- 1,072 Jerrel Wilson, Kansas City, 1963-77; New England, 1978
- 978 Mike Bragg, Washington, 1968-79; Baltimore, 1980

Most Punts, Season
- 114 Bob Parsons, Chicago, 1981
- 109 John James, Atlanta, 1978
- 106 David Beverly, Green Bay, 1978

Most Punts, Rookie, Season
- 96 Mike Connell, San Francisco, 1978
  - Chris Norman, Denver, 1984
- 93 Wilbur Summers, Detroit, 1977
  - Ken Clark, Los Angeles, 1979
  - Jim Arnold, Kansas City, 1983
- 92 Mike Horan, Philadelphia, 1984

Most Punts, Game
- 14 Dick Nesbitt, Chi. Cardinals vs. Chi. Bears, Nov. 30, 1933
  - Keith Molesworth, Chi. Bears vs. Green Bay, Dec. 10, 1933
  - Sammy Baugh, Washington vs. Philadelphia, Nov. 5, 1939
  - Carl Kinscherf, N.Y. Giants vs. Detroit, Nov. 7, 1943
  - George Taliaferro, N.Y. Yanks vs. Los Angeles, Sept. 28, 1951
- 12 Parker Hall, Cleveland vs. Green Bay, Nov. 26, 1939
  - Beryl Clark, Chi. Cardinals vs. Detroit, Sept. 15, 1940
  - Len Barnum, Philadelphia vs. Washington, Oct. 4, 1942
  - Horace Gillom, Cleveland vs. Philadelphia, Dec. 3, 1950
  - Adrian Burk, Philadelphia vs. Green Bay, Nov. 2, 1952; vs. N.Y. Giants, Dec. 12, 1954
  - Bob Scarpitto, Denver vs. Oakland, Sept. 10, 1967
  - Bill Van Heusen, Denver vs. Cincinnati, Oct. 6, 1968
  - Tom Blanchard, New Orleans vs. Minnesota, Nov. 16, 1975
  - Rusty Jackson, Los Angeles vs. San Francisco, Nov. 21, 1976
  - Wilbur Summers, Detroit vs. San Francisco, Oct. 23, 1977
  - John James, Atlanta vs. Washington, Dec. 10, 1978
  - Luke Prestridge, Denver vs. Buffalo, Oct. 25, 1981
  - Greg Coleman, Minnesota vs. Green Bay, Nov. 21, 1982
- 11 By many players

Longest Punt
- 98 Steve O'Neal, N.Y. Jets vs. Denver, Sept. 21, 1969
- 94 Joe Lintzenich, Chi. Bears vs. N.Y. Giants, Nov. 16, 1931
- 90 Don Chandler, Green Bay vs. San Francisco, Oct. 10, 1965

AVERAGE YARDAGE

Highest Average, Punting, Career (300 punts)
- 45.10 Sammy Baugh, Washington, 1937-52 (338-15,245)
- 44.68 Tommy Davis, San Francisco, 1959-69 (511-22,833)
- 44.29 Yale Lary, Detroit, 1952-53, 1956-64 (503-22,279)

Highest Average, Punting, Season (Qualifiers)
- 51.40 Sammy Baugh, Washington, 1940 (35-1,799)
- 48.94 Yale Lary, Detroit, 1963 (35-1,713)
- 48.73 Sammy Baugh, Washington, 1941 (30-1,462)

Highest Average, Punting, Rookie, Season (Qualifiers)
- 46.40 Bobby Walden, Minnesota, 1964 (72-3,341)
- 46.22 Dave Lewis, Cincinnati, 1970 (79-3,651)
- 45.92 Frank Sinkwich, Detroit, 1943 (12-551)

Highest Average, Punting, Game (4 punts)
- 61.75 Bob Cifers, Detroit vs. Chi. Bears, Nov. 24, 1946 (4-247)
- 61.60 Roy McKay, Green Bay vs. Chi. Cardinals, Oct. 28, 1945 (5-308)
- 59.40 Sammy Baugh, Washington vs. Detroit, Oct. 27, 1940 (5-297)

PUNT RETURNS

Most Seasons Leading League
- 3 Les (Speedy) Duncan, San Diego, 1965-66; Washington, 1971
  - Rick Upchurch, Denver, 1976, 1978, 1982
- 2 Dick Christy, N.Y. Titans, 1961-62
  - Claude Gibson, Oakland, 1963-64
  - Billy Johnson, Houston, 1975, 1977

PUNT RETURNS

Most Punt Returns, Career
- 258 Emlen Tunnell, N.Y. Giants, 1948-58; Green Bay, 1959-61
- 253 Alvin Haymond, Baltimore, 1964-67; Philadelphia, 1968; Los Angeles, 1969-71; Washington, 1972; Houston, 1973
- 252 Mike Fuller, San Diego, 1975-80; Cincinnati, 1981-82

Most Punt Returns, Season
- 70 Danny Reece, Tampa Bay, 1979
- 58 J. T. Smith, Kansas City, 1979
  - Greg Pruitt, L.A. Raiders, 1983
- 57 Eddie Brown, Washington, 1977
  - Danny Reece, Tampa Bay, 1980
  - Jeff Fisher, Chicago, 1984

Most Punt Returns, Rookie, Season
- 54 James Jones, Dallas, 1980
- 53 Louis Lipps, Pittsburgh, 1984
- 52 Leon Bright, N.Y. Giants, 1981
  - Robbie Martin, Detroit, 1981

Most Punt Returns, Game
- 11 Eddie Brown, Washington vs. Tampa Bay, Oct. 9, 1977
- 10 Theo Bell, Pittsburgh vs. Buffalo, Dec. 16, 1979
  - Mike Nelms, Washington vs. New Orleans, Dec. 26, 1982
- 9 Rodger Bird, Oakland vs. Denver, Sept. 10, 1967
  - Ralph McGill, San Francisco vs. Atlanta, Oct. 29, 1972
  - Ed Podolak, Kansas City vs. San Diego, Nov. 10, 1974
  - Anthony Leonard, San Francisco vs. New Orleans, Oct. 17, 1976
  - Butch Johnson, Dallas vs. Buffalo, Nov. 15, 1976
  - Larry Marshall, Philadelphia vs. Tampa Bay, Sept. 18, 1977
  - Nesby Glasgow, Baltimore vs. Kansas City, Sept. 2, 1979
  - Mike Nelms, Washington vs. St. Louis, Dec. 21, 1980
  - Leon Bright, N.Y. Giants vs. Philadelphia, Dec. 11, 1982
  - Pete Shaw, N.Y. Giants vs. Philadelphia, Nov. 20, 1983
  - Cleotha Montgomery, L.A. Raiders vs. Detroit, Dec. 10, 1984

FAIR CATCHES

Most Fair Catches, Season
- 24 Ken Graham, San Diego, 1969
- 22 Lem Barney, Detroit, 1976
- 21 Ed Podolak, Kansas City, 1970
  - Steve Schubert, Chicago, 1978
  - Stanley Morgan, New England, 1979

Most Fair Catches, Game
- 7 Lem Barney, Detroit vs. Chicago, Nov. 21, 1976
- 6 Jake Scott, Miami vs. Buffalo, Dec. 20, 1970
  - Greg Pruitt, L.A. Raiders vs. Seattle, Oct. 7, 1984
- 5 By many players

YARDS GAINED

Most Seasons Leading League
- 3 Alvin Haymond, Baltimore, 1965-66; Los Angeles, 1969
- 2 Bill Dudley, Pittsburgh, 1942, 1946
  - Emlen Tunnell, N.Y. Giants, 1951-52
  - Dick Christy, N.Y. Titans, 1961-62
  - Claude Gibson, Oakland, 1963-64
  - Rodger Bird, Oakland, 1966-67
  - J. T. Smith, Kansas City, 1979-80

Most Yards Gained, Career
- 3,008 Rick Upchurch, Denver, 1975-83
- 2,954 Billy Johnson, Houston, 1974-80; Atlanta, 1982-84
- 2,660 Mike Fuller, San Diego, 1975-80; Cincinnati, 1981-82

Most Yards Gained, Season
- 666 Greg Pruitt, L.A. Raiders, 1983
- 656 Louis Lipps, Pittsburgh, 1984
- 655 Neal Colzie, Oakland, 1975

Most Yards Gained, Rookie, Season
- 656 Louis Lipps, Pittsburgh, 1984
- 655 Neal Colzie, Oakland, 1975
- 608 Mike Haynes, New England, 1976

Most Yards Gained, Game
- 207 LeRoy Irvin, Los Angeles vs. Atlanta, Oct. 11, 1981
- 205 George Atkinson, Oakland vs. Buffalo, Sept. 15, 1968
- 184 Tom Watkins, Detroit vs. San Francisco, Oct. 6, 1963

Longest Punt Return (All TDs)
- 98 Gil LeFebvre, Cincinnati vs. Brooklyn, Dec. 3, 1933
  - Charlie West, Minnesota vs. Washington, Nov. 3, 1968
  - Dennis Morgan, Dallas vs. St. Louis, Oct. 13, 1974
- 97 Greg Pruitt, L.A. Raiders vs. Washington, Oct. 2, 1983

AVERAGE YARDAGE

Highest Average, Career (75 returns)
- 12.78 George McAfee, Chi. Bears, 1940-41, 1945-50 (112-1,431)
- 12.75 Jack Christiansen, Detroit, 1951-58 (85-1,084)
- 12.55 Claude Gibson, San Diego, 1961-62; Oakland, 1963-65 (110-1,381)

Highest Average, Season (Qualifiers)
- 23.00 Herb Rich, Baltimore, 1950 (12-276)
- 21.47 Jack Christiansen, Detroit, 1952 (15-322)
- 21.28 Dick Christy, N.Y. Titans, 1961 (18-383)

Highest Average, Rookie, Season (Qualifiers)
- 23.00 Herb Rich, Baltimore, 1950 (12-276)
- 20.88 Jerry Davis, Chi. Cardinals, 1948 (16-334)
- 20.73 Frank Sinkwich, Detroit, 1943 (11-228)

Highest Average, Game (3 returns)
- 47.67 Chuck Latourette, St. Louis vs. New Orleans, Sept. 29, 1968 (3-143)
- 47.33 Johnny Roland, St. Louis vs. Philadelphia, Oct. 2, 1966 (3-142)
- 45.67 Dick Christy, N.Y. Titans vs. Denver, Sept. 24, 1961 (3-137)

TOUCHDOWNS

Most Touchdowns, Career
- 8 Jack Christiansen, Detroit, 1951-58
  - Rick Upchurch, Denver, 1975-83
- 6 Billy Johnson, Houston, 1974-80; Atlanta, 1982-84
- 5 Emlen Tunnell, N.Y. Giants, 1948-58; Green Bay, 1959-61

Most Touchdowns, Season
- 4 Jack Christiansen, Detroit, 1951
  - Rick Upchurch, Denver, 1976
- 3 Emlen Tunnell, N.Y. Giants, 1951
  - Billy Johnson, Houston, 1975
  - LeRoy Irvin, Los Angeles, 1981
- 2 By many players

Most Touchdowns, Rookie, Season
- 4 Jack Christiansen, Detroit, 1951
- 2 By five players

Most Touchdowns, Game
- 2 Jack Christiansen, Detroit vs. Los Angeles, Oct. 14, 1951; vs. Green Bay, Nov. 22, 1951
  - Dick Christy, N.Y. Titans vs. Denver, Sept. 24, 1961
  - Rick Upchurch, Denver vs. Cleveland, Sept. 26, 1976
  - LeRoy Irvin, Los Angeles vs. Atlanta, Oct. 11, 1981

KICKOFF RETURNS

Most Seasons Leading League
- 3 Abe Woodson, San Francisco, 1959, 1962-63
- 2 Lynn Chandnois, Pittsburgh, 1951-52
  - Bobby Jancik, Houston, 1962-63
  - Travis Williams, Green Bay, 1967; Los Angeles, 1971

KICKOFF RETURNS

Most Kickoff Returns, Career
- 275 Ron Smith, Chicago, 1965, 1970-72; Atlanta, 1966-67; Los Angeles, 1968-69; San Diego, 1973; Oakland, 1974
- 243 Bruce Harper, N.Y. Jets, 1977-84
- 193 Abe Woodson, San Francisco, 1958-64; St. Louis, 1965-66

Most Kickoff Returns, Season
- 60 Drew Hill, Los Angeles, 1981
- 55 Bruce Harper, N.Y. Jets, 1978, 1979
  - David Turner, Cincinnati, 1979
  - Stump Mitchell, St. Louis, 1981
- 53 Eddie Payton, Minnesota, 1980

Most Kickoff Returns, Rookie, Season
- 55 Stump Mitchell, St. Louis, 1981
- 50 Nesby Glasgow, Baltimore, 1979
  - Dino Hall, Cleveland, 1979
- 47 Odell Barry, Denver, 1964

Most Kickoff Returns, Game
- 9 Noland Smith, Kansas City vs. Oakland, Nov. 23, 1967
  - Dino Hall, Cleveland vs. Pittsburgh, Oct. 7, 1979
- 8 George Taliaferro, N.Y. Yanks vs. N.Y. Giants, Dec. 3, 1950
  - Bobby Jancik, Houston vs. Boston, Dec. 8, 1963; vs. Oakland, Dec. 22, 1963
  - Mel Renfro, Dallas vs. Green Bay, Nov. 29, 1964
  - Willie Porter, Boston vs. N.Y. Jets, Sept. 22, 1968
  - Keith Moody, Buffalo vs. Seattle, Oct. 30, 1977
  - Brian Baschnagel, Chicago vs. Houston, Nov. 6, 1977
  - Bruce Harper, N.Y. Jets vs. New England, Oct. 29, 1978; vs. New England, Sept. 9, 1979
  - Dino Hall, Cleveland vs. Pittsburgh, Nov. 25, 1979
  - Terry Metcalf, Washington vs. St. Louis, Sept. 20, 1981
  - Harlan Huckleby, Green Bay vs. Washington, Oct. 17, 1983
- 7 By many players

YARDS GAINED

Most Seasons Leading League
- 3 Bruce Harper, N.Y. Jets, 1977-79
- 2 Marshall Goldberg, Chi. Cardinals, 1941-42
  - Woodley Lewis, Los Angeles, 1953-54
  - Al Carmichael, Green Bay, 1956-57
  - Timmy Brown, Philadelphia, 1961, 1963
  - Bobby Jancik, Houston, 1963, 1966
  - Ron Smith, Atlanta, 1966-67

Most Yards Gained, Career
- 6,922 Ron Smith, Chicago, 1965, 1970-72; Atlanta, 1966-67; Los Angeles, 1968-69; San Diego, 1973; Oakland, 1974
- 5,538 Abe Woodson, San Francisco, 1958-64; St. Louis, 1965-66
- 5,407 Bruce Harper, N.Y. Jets, 1977-84

Most Yards Gained, Season
- 1,317 Bobby Jancik, Houston, 1963
- 1,314 Dave Hampton, Green Bay, 1971
- 1,292 Stump Mitchell, St. Louis, 1981

Most Yards Gained, Rookie, Season
- 1,292 Stump Mitchell, St. Louis, 1981

1,245 Odell Barry, Denver, 1964
1,148 Noland Smith, Kansas City, 1967
Most Yards Gained, Game
294 Wally Triplett, Detroit vs. Los Angeles, Oct. 29, 1950
247 Timmy Brown, Philadelphia vs. Dallas, Nov. 6, 1966
244 Noland Smith, Kansas City vs. San Diego, Oct. 15, 1967
Longest Kickoff Return (All TDs)
106 Al Carmichael, Green Bay vs. Chi. Bears, Oct. 7, 1956
Noland Smith, Kansas City vs. Denver, Dec. 17, 1967
Roy Green, St. Louis vs. Dallas, Oct. 21, 1979
105 Frank Seno, Chi. Cardinals vs. N.Y. Giants, Oct. 20, 1946
Ollie Matson, Chi. Cardinals vs. Washington, Oct. 14, 1956
Abe Woodson, San Francisco vs. Los Angeles, Nov. 8, 1959
Timmy Brown, Philadelphia vs. Cleveland, Sept. 17, 1961
Jon Arnett, Los Angeles vs. Detroit, Oct. 29, 1961
Eugene (Mercury) Morris, Miami vs. Cincinnati, Sept. 14, 1969
Travis Williams, Los Angeles vs. New Orleans, Dec. 5, 1971
104 By many players

AVERAGE YARDAGE
Highest Average, Career (75 returns)
30.56 Gale Sayers, Chicago, 1965-71 (91-2,781)
29.57 Lynn Chandnois, Pittsburgh, 1950-56 (92-2,720)
28.69 Abe Woodson, San Francisco, 1958-64; St. Louis, 1965-66 (193-5,538)
Highest Average, Season (Qualifiers)
41.06 Travis Williams, Green Bay, 1967 (18-739)
37.69 Gale Sayers, Chicago, 1967 (16-603)
35.50 Ollie Matson, Chi. Cardinals, 1958 (14-497)
Highest Average, Rookie, Season (Qualifiers)
41.06 Travis Williams, Green Bay, 1967 (18-739)
33.08 Tom Moore, Green Bay, 1960 (12-397)
32.88 Duriel Harris, Miami, 1976 (17-559)
Highest Average, Game (3 returns)
73.50 Wally Triplett, Detroit vs. Los Angeles, Oct. 29, 1950 (4-294)
67.33 Lenny Lyles, San Francisco vs. Baltimore, Dec. 18, 1960 (3-202)
65.33 Ken Hall, Houston vs. N.Y. Titans, Oct. 23, 1960 (3-196)

TOUCHDOWNS
Most Touchdowns, Career
6 Ollie Matson, Chi. Cardinals, 1952, 1954-58; L.A. Rams, 1959-62; Detroit, 1963; Philadelphia, 1964
Gale Sayers, Chicago, 1965-71
Travis Williams, Green Bay, 1967-70; Los Angeles, 1971
5 Bobby Mitchell, Cleveland, 1958-61; Washington, 1962-68
Abe Woodson, San Francisco, 1958-64; St. Louis, 1965-66
Timmy Brown, Green Bay, 1959; Philadelphia, 1960-67; Baltimore, 1968
4 Cecil Turner, Chicago, 1968-73
Most Touchdowns, Season
4 Travis Williams, Green Bay, 1967
Cecil Turner, Chicago, 1970
3 Verda (Vitamin T) Smith, Los Angeles, 1950
Abe Woodson, San Francisco, 1963
Gale Sayers, Chicago, 1967
Raymond Clayborn, New England, 1977
2 By many players
Most Touchdowns, Rookie, Season
4 Travis Williams, Green Bay, 1967
3 Raymond Clayborn, New England, 1977
2 By six players
Most Touchdowns, Game
2 Timmy Brown, Philadelphia vs. Dallas, Nov. 6, 1966
Travis Williams, Green Bay vs. Cleveland, Nov. 12, 1967

COMBINED KICK RETURNS
Most Combined Kick Returns, Career
510 Ron Smith, Chicago, 1965, 1970-72; Atlanta, 1966-67; Los Angeles, 1968-69; San Diego, 1973; Oakland, 1974 (p-235, k-275)
426 Bruce Harper, N.Y. Jets, 1977-84 (p-183, k-243)
423 Alvin Haymond, Baltimore, 1964-67; Philadelphia, 1968; Los Angeles, 1969-71; Washington, 1972; Houston, 1973 (p-253, k-170)
Most Combined Kick Returns, Season
100 Larry Jones, Washington, 1975 (p-53, k-47)
97 Stump Mitchell, St. Louis, 1981 (p-42, k-55)
94 Nesby Glasgow, Baltimore, 1979 (p-44, k-50)
Most Combined Kick Returns, Game
13 Stump Mitchell, St. Louis vs. Atlanta, Oct. 18, 1981 (p-6, k-7)
12 Mel Renfro, Dallas vs. Green Bay, Nov. 29, 1964 (p-4, k-8)
Larry Jones, Washington vs. Dallas, Dec. 13, 1975 (p-6, k-6)
Eddie Brown, Washington vs. Tampa Bay, Oct. 9, 1977 (p-11, k-1)
Nesby Glasgow, Baltimore vs. Denver, Sept. 2, 1979 (p-9, k-3)
11 By many players

YARDS GAINED
Most Yards Returned, Career
8,710 Ron Smith, Chicago, 1965, 1970-72; Atlanta, 1966-67; Los Angeles, 1968-69; San Diego, 1973; Oakland, 1974 (p-1,788, k-6,922)
7,191 Bruce Harper, N.Y. Jets, 1977-84 (p-1,784, k-5,407)
6,740 Les (Speedy) Duncan, San Diego, 1964-70; Washington, 1971-74 (p-2,201, k-4,539)
Most Yards Returned, Season
1,737 Stump Mitchell, St. Louis, 1981 (p-445, k-1,292)
1,658 Bruce Harper, N.Y. Jets, 1978 (p-378, k-1,280)
1,591 Mike Nelms, Washington, 1981 (p-492, k-1,099)
Most Yards Returned, Game
294 Wally Triplett, Detroit vs. Los Angeles, Oct. 29, 1950 (k-294)
Woodley Lewis, Los Angeles vs. Detroit, Oct. 18, 1953 (p-120, k-174)
289 Eddie Payton, Detroit vs. Minnesota, Dec. 17, 1977 (p-105, k-184)
282 Les (Speedy) Duncan, San Diego vs. N.Y. Jets, Nov. 24, 1968 (p-102, k-180)

TOUCHDOWNS
Most Touchdowns, Career
9 Ollie Matson, Chi. Cardinals, 1952, 1954-58; Los Angeles, 1959-62; Detroit, 1963; Philadelphia, 1964-66 (p-3, k-6)

---

8 Jack Christiansen, Detroit, 1951-58 (p-8)
Bobby Mitchell, Cleveland, 1958-61; Washington, 1962-68 (p-3, k-5)
Gale Sayers, Chicago, 1965-71 (p-2, k-6)
Rick Upchurch, Denver, 1975-83 (p-8)
Billy Johnson, Houston, 1974-80; Atlanta, 1982-84 (p-6, k-2)
7 Abe Woodson, San Francisco, 1958-64; St. Louis, 1965-66 (p-2, k-5)
Most Touchdowns, Season
4 Jack Christiansen, Detroit, 1951 (p-4)
Emlen Tunnell, N.Y. Giants, 1951 (p-3, k-1)
Gale Sayers, Chicago, 1967 (p-1, k-3)
Travis Williams, Green Bay, 1967 (k-4)
Cecil Turner, Chicago, 1970 (k-4)
Billy Johnson, Houston, 1975 (p-3, k-1)
Rick Upchurch, Denver, 1976 (p-4)
3 Verda (Vitamin T) Smith, Los Angeles, 1950 (k-3)
Abe Woodson, San Francisco, 1963 (k-3)
Raymond Clayborn, New England, 1977 (k-3)
Billy Johnson, Houston, 1977 (p-2, k-1)
LeRoy Irvin, Los Angeles, 1981 (p-3)
2 By many players
Most Touchdowns, Game
2 Jack Christiansen, Detroit vs. Los Angeles, Oct. 14, 1951 (p-2); vs. Green Bay, Nov. 22, 1951 (p-2)
Jim Patton, N.Y. Giants vs. Washington, Oct. 30, 1955 (p-1, k-1)
Bobby Mitchell, Cleveland vs. Philadelphia, Nov. 23, 1958 (p-1, k-1)
Dick Christy, N.Y. Titans vs. Denver, Sept. 24, 1961 (p-2)
Al Frazier, Denver vs. Boston, Dec. 3, 1961 (p-1, k-1)
Timmy Brown, Philadelphia vs. Dallas, Nov. 6, 1966 (k-2)
Travis Williams, Green Bay vs. Cleveland, Nov. 12, 1967 (k-2); vs. Pittsburgh, Nov. 2, 1969 (p-1, k-1)
Gale Sayers, Chicago vs. San Francisco, Dec. 3, 1967 (p-1, k-1)
Rick Upchurch, Denver vs. Cleveland, Sept. 26, 1976 (p-2)
Eddie Payton, Detroit vs. Minnesota, Dec. 17, 1977 (p-1, k-1)
LeRoy Irvin, Los Angeles vs. Atlanta, Oct. 11, 1981 (p-2)

FUMBLES
Most Fumbles, Career
105 Roman Gabriel, Los Angeles, 1962-72; Philadelphia, 1973-77
95 Johnny Unitas, Baltimore, 1956-72; San Diego, 1973
90 Franco Harris, Pittsburgh, 1972-83; Seattle, 1984
Most Fumbles, Season
17 Dan Pastorini, Houston, 1973
Warren Moon, Houston, 1984
16 Don Meredith, Dallas, 1964
Joe Cribbs, Buffalo, 1980
Steve Fuller, Kansas City, 1980
Paul McDonald, Cleveland, 1984
15 Paul Christman, Chi. Cardinals, 1946
Sammy Baugh, Washington, 1947
Sam Etcheverry, St. Louis, 1961
Len Dawson, Kansas City, 1964
Terry Metcalf, St. Louis, 1976
Steve DeBerg, Tampa Bay, 1984
Most Fumbles, Game
7 Len Dawson, Kansas City vs. San Diego, Nov. 15, 1964
6 Sam Etcheverry, St. Louis vs. N.Y. Giants, Sept. 17, 1961
5 Paul Christman, Chi. Cardinals vs. Green Bay, Nov. 10, 1946
Charlie Conerly, N.Y. Giants vs San Francisco, Dec. 1, 1957
Jack Kemp, Buffalo vs. Houston, Oct. 29, 1967
Roman Gabriel, Philadelphia vs. Oakland, Nov. 21, 1976

FUMBLES RECOVERED
Most Fumbles Recovered, Career, Own and Opponents'
43 Fran Tarkenton, Minnesota, 1961-66, 1972-78; N.Y. Giants, 1967-71 (43 own)
38 Jack Kemp, Pittsburgh, 1957; L.A. Chargers, 1960; San Diego, 1961-62; Buffalo, 1962-67, 1969 (38 own)
37 Roman Gabriel, Los Angeles, 1962-72; Philadelphia, 1973-77 (37 own)
Most Fumbles Recovered, Season, Own and Opponents'
9 Don Hultz, Minnesota, 1963 (9 opp)
8 Paul Christman, Chi. Cardinals, 1945 (8 own)
Joe Schmidt, Detroit, 1955 (8 opp)
Bill Butler, Minnesota, 1963 (8 own)
Kermit Alexander, San Francisco, 1965 (4 own, 4 opp)
Jack Lambert, Pittsburgh, 1976 (1 own, 7 opp)
Danny White, Dallas, 1981 (8 own)
7 By many players
Most Fumbles Recovered, Game, Own and Opponents'
4 Otto Graham, Cleveland vs. N.Y. Giants, Oct. 25, 1953 (4 own)
Sam Etcheverry, St. Louis vs. N.Y. Giants, Sept. 17, 1961 (4 own)
Roman Gabriel, Los Angeles vs. San Francisco, Oct. 12, 1969 (4 own)
Joe Ferguson, Buffalo vs. Miami, Sept. 18, 1977 (4 own)
3 By many players

OWN FUMBLES RECOVERED
Most Own Fumbles Recovered, Career
43 Fran Tarkenton, Minnesota, 1961-66, 1972-78; N.Y. Giants, 1967-71
38 Jack Kemp, Pittsburgh, 1957; L.A. Chargers, 1960; San Diego, 1961-62; Buffalo, 1962-67, 1969
37 Roman Gabriel, Los Angeles, 1962-72; Philadelphia, 1973-77
Most Own Fumbles Recovered, Season
8 Paul Christman, Chi. Cardinals, 1945
Bill Butler, Minnesota, 1963
Danny White, Dallas, 1981
7 Sammy Baugh, Washington, 1947
Tommy Thompson, Philadelphia, 1947
John Roach, St. Louis, 1960
Jack Larscheid, Oakland, 1960
Gary Huff, Chicago, 1974
Terry Metcalf, St. Louis, 1974
Joe Ferguson, Buffalo, 1977
Fran Tarkenton, Minnesota, 1978
Greg Pruitt, L.A. Raiders, 1983
Warren Moon, Houston, 1984

6 By many players

Most Own Fumbles Recovered, Game
  4 Otto Graham, Cleveland vs. N.Y. Giants, Oct. 25, 1953
    Sam Etcheverry, St. Louis vs. N.Y. Giants, Sept. 17, 1961
    Roman Gabriel, Los Angeles vs. San Francisco, Oct. 12, 1969
    Joe Ferguson, Buffalo vs. Miami, Sept. 18, 1977
  3 By many players

OPPONENTS' FUMBLES RECOVERED
Most Opponents' Fumbles Recovered, Career
  29 Jim Marshall, Cleveland, 1960; Minnesota, 1961-79
  25 Dick Butkus, Chicago, 1965-73
  23 Carl Eller, Minnesota, 1964-78; Seattle, 1979
Most Opponents' Fumbles Recovered, Season
  9 Don Hultz, Minnesota, 1963
  8 Joe Schmidt, Detroit, 1955
  7 Alan Page, Minnesota, 1970
    Jack Lambert, Pittsburgh, 1976
Most Opponents' Fumbles Recovered, Game
  3 Corwin Clatt, Chi. Cardinals vs. Detroit, Nov. 6, 1949
    Vic Sears, Philadelphia vs. Green Bay, Nov. 2, 1952
    Ed Beatty, San Francisco vs. Los Angeles, Oct. 7, 1956
    Ron Carroll, Houston vs. Cincinnati, Oct. 27, 1974
    Maurice Spencer, New Orleans vs. Atlanta, Oct. 10, 1976
    Steve Nelson, New England vs. Philadelphia, Oct. 8, 1978
    Charles Jackson, Kansas City vs. Pittsburgh, Sept. 6, 1981
    Willie Buchanon, San Diego vs. Denver, Sept. 27, 1981
  2 By many players

YARDS RETURNING FUMBLES
Longest Fumble Run (All TDs)
  104 Jack Tatum, Oakland vs. Green Bay, Sept. 24, 1972 (opp)
  98 George Halas, Chi. Bears vs. Oorang Indians, Marion, Ohio, Nov. 4, 1923 (opp)
  97 Chuck Howley, Dallas vs. Atlanta, Oct. 2, 1966 (opp)

TOUCHDOWNS
Most Touchdowns, Career (Total)
  4 Bill Thompson, Denver, 1969-81
  3 Ralph Heywood, Detroit, 1947-48; Boston, 1948; N.Y. Bulldogs, 1949
    Leo Sugar, Chi. Cardinals, 1954-59; St. Louis, 1960; Philadelphia, 1961; Detroit, 1962
    Bud McFadin, Los Angeles, 1952-56; Denver, 1960-63; Houston, 1964-65
    Doug Cline, Houston, 1960-66; San Diego, 1966
    Bob Lilly, Dall. Cowboys, 1961-74
    Chris Hanburger, Washington, 1965-78
    Lemar Parrish, Cincinnati, 1970-77; Washington, 1978-81; Buffalo, 1982
    Paul Krause, Washington, 1964-67; Minnesota, 1968-79
    Brad Dusek, Washington, 1974-81
    David Logan, Tampa Bay, 1979-84
    Tom Howard, Kansas City, 1977-83; St. Louis, 1984
  2 By many players
Most Touchdowns, Season (Total)
  2 Harold McPhail, Boston, 1934
    Harry Ebding, Detroit, 1937
    John Morelli, Boston, 1944
    Frank Maznicki, Boston, 1947
    Fred (Dippy) Evans, Chi. Bears, 1948
    Ralph Heywood, Boston, 1948
    Art Tait, N.Y. Yanks, 1951
    John Dwyer, Los Angeles, 1952
    Leo Sugar, Chi. Cardinals, 1957
    Doug Cline, Houston, 1961
    Jim Bradshaw, Pittsburgh, 1964
    Royce Berry, Cincinnati, 1970
    Ahmad Rashad, Buffalo, 1974
    Tim Gray, Kansas City, 1977
    Charles Phillips, Oakland, 1978
    Kenny Johnson, Atlanta, 1981
    George Martin, N.Y. Giants, 1981
    Del Rodgers, Green Bay, 1982
    Mike Douglass, Green Bay, 1983
    Shelton Robinson, Seattle, 1983
Most Touchdowns, Career (Own recovered)
  2 Ken Kavanaugh, Chi. Bears, 1940-41, 1945-50
    Mike Ditka, Chicago, 1961-66; Philadelphia, 1967-68; Dallas, 1969-72
    Gail Cogdill, Detroit, 1960-68; Baltimore, 1968; Atlanta, 1969-70
    Ahrnad Rashad, St. Louis, 1972-73; Buffalo, 1974; Minnesota, 1976-82
    Jim Mitchell, Atlanta, 1969-79
    Drew Pearson, Dallas, 1973-83
    Del Rodgers, Green Bay, 1982, 1984
Most Touchdowns, Season (Own recovered)
  2 Ahmad Rashad, Buffalo, 1974
    Del Rodgers, Green Bay, 1982
  1 By many players
Most Touchdowns, Career (Opponents' recovered)
  3 Leo Sugar, Chi. Cardinals, 1954-59; St. Louis, 1960; Philadelphia, 1961; Detroit, 1962
    Doug Cline, Houston, 1960-66; San Diego, 1966
    Bud McFadin, Los Angeles, 1952-56; Denver, 1960-63; Houston, 1964-65
    Bob Lilly, Dall. Cowboys, 1961-74
    Chris Hanburger, Washington, 1965-78
    Paul Krause, Washington, 1964-67; Minnesota, 1968-79
    Lemar Parrish, Cincinnati, 1970-77; Washington, 1978-81; Buffalo, 1982
    Bill Thompson, Denver, 1969-81
    Brad Dusek, Washington, 1974-81
    David Logan, Tampa Bay, 1979-84
    Tom Howard, Kansas City, 1977-83; St. Louis, 1984
  2 By many players
Most Touchdowns, Season (Opponents' recovered)
  2 Harold McPhail, Boston, 1934
    Harry Ebding, Detroit, 1937
    John Morelli, Boston, 1944

Frank Maznicki, Boston, 1947
Fred (Dippy) Evans, Chi. Bears, 1948
Ralph Heywood, Boston, 1948
Art Tait, N.Y. Yanks, 1951
John Dwyer, Los Angeles, 1952
Leo Sugar, Chi. Cardinals, 1957
Doug Cline, Houston, 1961
Jim Bradshaw, Pittsburgh, 1964
Royce Berry, Cincinnati, 1970
Tim Gray, Kansas City, 1977
Charles Phillips, Oakland, 1978
Kenny Johnson, Atlanta, 1981
George Martin, N.Y. Giants, 1981
Mike Douglass, Green Bay, 1983
Shelton Robinson, Seattle, 1983
Most Touchdowns, Game (Opponents' recovered)
  2 Fred (Dippy) Evans, Chi. Bears vs. Washington, Nov. 28, 1948

COMBINED NET YARDS GAINED
Rushing, receiving, interception returns, punt returns, kickoff returns, and fumble returns
Most Seasons Leading League
  5 Jim Brown, Cleveland, 1958-61, 1964
  3 Cliff Battles, Boston, 1932-33; Washington, 1937
    Gale Sayers, Chicago, 1965-67
  2 By many players
Most Consecutive Seasons Leading League
  4 Jim Brown, Cleveland, 1958-61
  3 Gale Sayers, Chicago, 1965-67
  2 Cliff Battles, Boston, 1932-33
    Charley Trippi, Chi. Cardinals, 1948-49
    Timmy Brown, Philadelphia, 1962-63
    Floyd Little, Denver, 1967-68
    James Brooks, San Diego, 1981-82
    Eric Dickerson, L.A. Rams, 1983-84

ATTEMPTS
Most Attempts, Career
  3,457 Walter Payton, Chicago, 1975-84
  3,281 Franco Harris, Pittsburgh, 1972-83; Seattle, 1984
  2,992 John Riggins, N.Y. Jets, 1971-75; Washington, 1976-79, 1981-84
Most Attempts, Season
  496 James Wilder, Tampa Bay, 1984
  442 Eric Dickerson, L.A. Rams, 1983
  427 Walter Payton, Chicago, 1984
Most Attempts, Rookie, Season
  442 Eric Dickerson, L.A. Rams, 1983
  395 George Rogers, New Orleans, 1981
  390 Joe Cribbs, Buffalo, 1980
Most Attempts, Game
  48 James Wilder, Tampa Bay vs. Pittsburgh, Oct. 30, 1983
  47 James Wilder, Tampa Bay vs. Green Bay, Sept. 30, 1984 (OT)
  43 Lydell Mitchell, Baltimore vs. N.Y. Jets, Oct. 20, 1974
    Butch Woolfolk, N.Y. Giants vs. Philadelphia, Nov. 20, 1983

YARDS GAINED
Most Yards Gained, Career
  17,304 Walter Payton, Chicago, 1975-84
  15,459 Jim Brown, Cleveland, 1957-65
  14,622 Franco Harris, Pittsburgh, 1972-83; Seattle, 1984
Most Yards Gained, Season
  2,462 Terry Metcalf, St. Louis, 1975
  2,444 Mack Herron, New England, 1974
  2,440 Gale Sayers, Chicago, 1966
Most Yards Gained, Rookie, Season
  2,272 Gale Sayers, Chicago, 1965
  2,212 Eric Dickerson, L.A. Rams, 1983
  2,100 Abner Haynes, Dall. Texans, 1960
Most Yards Gained, Game
  373 Billy Cannon, Houston vs. N.Y. Titans, Dec. 10, 1961
  341 Timmy Brown, Philadelphia vs. St. Louis, Dec. 16, 1962
  339 Gale Sayers, Chicago vs. Minnesota, Dec. 18, 1966

SACKS
Sacks have been compiled since 1982.
Most Sacks, Career
  47 Mark Gastineau, N.Y. Jets, 1982-84
  37.5 Curtis Greer, St. Louis, 1982-84
  34 Doug Betters, Miami, 1982-84
    Dennis Harrison, Philadelphia, 1982-84
Most Sacks, Season
  22 Mark Gastineau, N.Y. Jets, 1984
  19 Mark Gastineau, N.Y. Jets, 1983
  18.5 Andre Tippett, New England, 1984
Most Sacks, Game
  6 Fred Dean, San Francisco vs. New Orleans, Nov. 13, 1983
  5.5 William Gay, Detroit vs. Tampa Bay, Sept. 4, 1983
  5 Howie Long, L.A. Raiders vs. Washington, Oct. 2, 1983

MISCELLANEOUS
Longest Return of Missed Field Goal (All TDs)
  101 Al Nelson, Philadelphia vs. Dallas, Sept. 26, 1971
  100 Al Nelson, Philadelphia vs. Cleveland, Dec. 11, 1966
    Ken Ellis, Green Bay vs. N.Y. Giants, Sept. 19, 1971
  99 Jerry Williams, Los Angeles vs. Green Bay, Dec. 16, 1951
    Carl Taseff, Baltimore vs. Los Angeles, Dec. 12, 1959
    Timmy Brown, Philadelphia vs. St. Louis, Sept. 16, 1962

TEAM RECORDS

CHAMPIONSHIPS
Most Seasons League Champion
  11 Green Bay, 1929-31, 1936, 1939, 1944, 1961-62, 1965-67

8 Chi. Bears, 1921, 1932-33, 1940-41, 1943, 1946, 1963
4 N.Y. Giants, 1927, 1934, 1938, 1956
    Detroit, 1935, 1952-53, 1957
    Clev. Browns, 1950, 1954-55, 1964
    Baltimore, 1958-59, 1968, 1970
    Pittsburgh, 1974-75, 1978-79
    Oakland/L.A. Raiders, 1967, 1976, 1980, 1983

Most Consecutive Seasons League Champion

3 Green Bay, 1929-31, 1965-67
2 Canton, 1922-23
    Chi. Bears, 1932-33, 1940-41
    Philadelphia, 1948-49
    Detroit, 1952-53
    Cleveland, 1954-55
    Baltimore, 1958-59
    Houston, 1960-61
    Green Bay, 1961-62
    Buffalo, 1964-65
    Miami, 1972-73
    Pittsburgh, 1974-75, 1978-79

Most Times Finishing First, Regular Season (Since 1933)

14 N.Y. Giants, 1933-35, 1938-39, 1941, 1944, 1946, 1956, 1958-59, 1961-63
    Clev./L.A. Rams, 1945, 1949-51, 1955, 1967, 1969, 1973-79
    Clev. Browns, 1950-55, 1957, 1964-65, 1967-69, 1971, 1980
12 Dallas, 1966-71, 1973, 1976-79, 1981
11 Green Bay, 1936, 1938-39, 1944, 1960-62, 1965-67, 1972
    Minnesota 1968-71, 1973-78, 1980
    Chi. Bears, 1933-34, 1937, 1940-43, 1946, 1956, 1963, 1984

Most Consecutive Times Finishing First, Regular Season (Since 1933)

7 Los Angeles, 1973-79
6 Cleveland, 1950-55
    Dallas, 1966-71
    Minnesota, 1973-78
    Pittsburgh, 1974-79
5 Oakland, 1972-76

GAMES WON

Most Consecutive Games Won (Incl. postseason games)

18 Chi. Bears, 1933-34, 1941-42
    Miami, 1972-73
17 Oakland, 1976-77
14 Washington, 1942-43

Most Consecutive Games Won (Regular season)

17 Chi. Bears, 1933-34
16 Chi. Bears, 1941-42
    Miami, 1971-73; 1983-84
15 L.A. Chargers/San Diego, 1960-61

Most Consecutive Games Without Defeat (Incl. postseason games)

24 Canton, 1922-23 (won 21, tied 3)
23 Green Bay, 1928-30 (won 21, tied 2)
18 Chi. Bears, 1933-34 (won 18); 1941-42 (won 18)
    Miami, 1972-73 (won 18)

Most Consecutive Games Without Defeat (Regular season)

24 Canton, 1922-23 (won 21, tied 3)
    Chi. Bears, 1941-43 (won 23, tied 1)
23 Green Bay, 1928-30 (won 21, tied 2)
17 Chi. Bears, 1933-34 (won 17)

Most Games Won, One Season (Incl. postseason games)

18 San Francisco, 1984
17 Miami, 1972
    Pittsburgh, 1978
16 Oakland, 1976
    San Francisco, 1981
    Washington, 1983
    Miami, 1984

Most Games Won, Season (Since 1932)

15 San Francisco, 1984
14 Miami, 1972, 1984
    Pittsburgh, 1978
    Washington, 1983
13 Chi. Bears, 1934
    Green Bay, 1962
    Oakland, 1967, 1976
    Baltimore, 1968
    San Francisco, 1981
    Denver, 1984

Most Consecutive Games Won, One Season (Incl. postseason games)

17 Miami, 1972
13 Chi. Bears, 1934
    Oakland, 1976
12 Minnesota, 1969
    San Francisco, 1984

Most Consecutive Games Won, One Season

14 Miami, 1972
13 Chi. Bears, 1934
12 Minnesota, 1969

Most Consecutive Games Won, Start of Season

14 Miami, 1972, entire season
13 Chi. Bears, 1934, entire season
11 Chi. Bears, 1942, entire season
    Cleveland, 1953
    San Diego, 1961
    Los Angeles, 1969
    Miami, 1984

Most Consecutive Games Won, End of Season

14 Miami, 1972, entire season
13 Chi. Bears, 1934, entire season
11 Chi. Bears, 1942, entire season
    Cleveland, 1951

Most Consecutive Games Without Defeat, One Season (Incl. postseason games)

17 Miami, 1972
13 Chi. Bears, 1926, 1934
    Green Bay, 1929

    Baltimore, 1967
    Oakland, 1976
12 Canton, 1922, 1923
    Minnesota, 1969
    San Francisco, 1984

Most Consecutive Games Without Defeat, One Season

14 Miami, 1972
13 Chi. Bears, 1926, 1934
    Green Bay, 1929
    Baltimore, 1967
12 Canton, 1922, 1923
    Minnesota, 1969

Most Consecutive Games Without Defeat, Start of Season

14 Miami, 1972, entire season
13 Chi. Bears, 1926, 1934, entire seasons
    Green Bay, 1929, entire season
    Baltimore, 1967
12 Canton, 1922, 1923, entire seasons

Most Consecutive Games Without Defeat, End of Season

14 Miami, 1972, entire season
13 Green Bay, 1929, entire season
    Chi. Bears, 1934, entire season
12 Canton, 1922, 1923, entire seasons

Most Consecutive Home Games Won

27 Miami, 1971-74
20 Green Bay, 1929-32
18 Oakland, 1968-70
    Dallas, 1979-81

Most Consecutive Home Games Without Defeat

30 Green Bay, 1928-33 (won 27, tied 3)
27 Miami, 1971-74 (won 27)
18 Chi. Bears, 1932-35 (won 17, tied 1); 1941-44 (won 17, tied 1)
    Oakland, 1968-70 (won 18)
    Dallas, 1979-81 (won 18)

Most Consecutive Road Games Won

11 L.A. Chargers/San Diego, 1960-61
10 Chi. Bears, 1941-42
    Dallas, 1968-69
9 Chi. Bears, 1933-34
    Kansas City, 1966-67
    Oakland, 1967-68, 1974-75, 1976-77
    Pittsburgh, 1974-75
    Washington, 1981-83
    San Francisco, 1983-84 (current)

Most Consecutive Road Games Without Defeat

13 Chi. Bears, 1941-43 (won 12, tied 1)
12 Green Bay, 1928-30 (won 10, tied 2)
11 L.A. Chargers/San Diego, 1960-61 (won 11)
    Los Angeles, 1966-68 (won 10, tied 1)

Most Shutout Games Won or Tied, Season (Since 1932)

7 Chi. Bears, 1932 (won 4, tied 3)
    Green Bay, 1932 (won 6, tied 1)
    Detroit, 1934 (won 7)
5 Chi. Cardinals, 1934 (won 5)
    N.Y. Giants, 1944 (won 5)
    Pittsburgh, 1976 (won 5)
4 By many teams

Most Consecutive Shutout Games Won or Tied (Since 1932)

7 Detroit, 1934 (won 7)
3 Chi. Bears, 1932 (tied 3)
    Green Bay, 1932 (won 3)
    New York, 1935 (won 3)
    St. Louis, 1970 (won 3)
    Pittsburgh, 1976 (won 3)
2 By many teams

GAMES LOST

Most Consecutive Games Lost

26 Tampa Bay, 1976-77
19 Chi. Cardinals, 1942-43, 1945
    Oakland, 1961-62
18 Houston, 1972-73

Most Consecutive Games Without Victory

26 Tampa Bay, 1976-77 (lost 26)
23 Washington, 1960-61 (lost 20, tied 3)

Most Games Lost, Season (Since 1932)

15 New Orleans, 1980
14 Tampa Bay, 1976, 1983
    San Francisco, 1978, 1979
    Detroit, 1979
    Baltimore, 1981
    New England, 1981
    Houston, 1983
    Buffalo, 1984
13 Oakland, 1962
    Chicago, 1969
    Pittsburgh, 1969
    Buffalo, 1971
    Houston, 1972, 1973, 1984
    Minnesota, 1984

Most Consecutive Games Lost, One Season

14 Tampa Bay, 1976
    New Orleans, 1980
    Baltimore, 1981
13 Oakland, 1962
12 Tampa Bay, 1977

Most Consecutive Games Lost, Start of Season

14 Tampa Bay, 1976, entire season
    New Orleans, 1980
13 Oakland, 1962
12 Tampa Bay, 1977

Most Consecutive Games Lost, End of Season
    14 Tampa Bay, 1976, entire season
    13 Pittsburgh, 1969
    11 Philadelphia, 1936
        Detroit, 1942, entire season
        Houston, 1972

Most Consecutive Games Without Victory, One Season
    14 Tampa Bay, 1976, entire season
        New Orleans, 1980
        Baltimore, 1981
    13 Washington, 1961
        Oakland, 1962
    12 Dall. Cowboys, 1960, entire season
        Tampa Bay, 1977

Most Consecutive Games Without Victory, Start of Season
    14 Tampa Bay, 1976, entire season
        New Orleans, 1980
    13 Washington, 1961
        Oakland, 1962
    12 Dall. Cowboys, 1960, entire season
        Tampa Bay, 1977

Most Consecutive Games Without Victory, End of Season
    14 Tampa Bay, 1976, entire season
    13 Pittsburgh, 1969
    12 Dall. Cowboys, 1960, entire season

Most Consecutive Home Games Lost
    13 Houston, 1972-73
        Tampa Bay, 1976-77
    11 Oakland, 1961-62
        Los Angeles, 1961-63
    10 Pittsburgh, 1937-39, 1943-45
        Washington, 1960-61
        N.Y. Giants, 1973-75
        New Orleans, 1979-80

Most Consecutive Home Games Without Victory
    13 Houston, 1972-73 (lost 13)
        Tampa Bay, 1976-77 (lost 13)
    12 Philadelphia, 1936-38 (lost 11, tied 1)
    11 Washington, 1960-61 (lost 10, tied 1)
        Oakland, 1961-62 (lost 11)
        Los Angeles, 1961-63 (lost 11)

Most Consecutive Road Games Lost
    23 Houston, 1981-84
    18 San Francisco, 1977-79
    16 Chicago, 1973-75

Most Consecutive Road Games Without Victory
    23 Houston, 1981-84 (lost 23)
    18 Washington, 1959-62 (lost 15, tied 3)
        New Orleans, 1971-74 (lost 17, tied 1)
        San Francisco, 1977-79 (lost 18)
    17 Denver, 1962-65 (lost 16, tied 1)

Most Shutout Games Lost or Tied, Season (Since 1932)
    6 Cincinnati, 1934 (lost 6)
       Pittsburgh, 1934 (lost 6)
       Philadelphia, 1936 (lost 6)
       Tampa Bay, 1977 (lost 6)
    5 Boston, 1932 (lost 4, tied 1), 1933 (lost 4, tied 1)
       N.Y. Giants, 1932 (lost 4, tied 1)
       Cincinnati, 1933 (lost 4, tied 1)
       Brooklyn, 1934 (lost 5), 1942 (lost 5)
       Detroit, 1942 (lost 5)
       Tampa Bay, 1976 (lost 5)
    4 By many teams

Most Consecutive Shutout Games Lost or Tied (Since 1932)
    6 Brooklyn, 1942-43 (lost 6)
    4 Chi. Bears, 1932 (lost 1, tied 3)
       Philadelphia, 1936 (lost 4)
    3 Chi. Cardinals, 1934 (lost 3), 1938 (lost 3)
       Brooklyn, 1935 (lost 3), 1937 (lost 3)
       Oakland, 1981 (lost 3)

TIE GAMES

Most Tie Games, Season
    6 Chi. Bears, 1932
    5 Frankford, 1929
    4 Chi. Bears, 1924
       Orange, 1929
       Portsmouth, 1929

Most Consecutive Tie Games
    3 Chi. Bears, 1932
    2 By many teams

SCORING

Most Seasons Leading League
    9 Chi. Bears, 1934-35, 1939, 1941-43, 1946-47, 1956
    6 Green Bay, 1932, 1936-38, 1961-62
       L.A. Rams, 1950-52, 1957, 1967, 1973
    5 Oakland, 1967-69, 1974, 1977
       Dall. Cowboys, 1966, 1968, 1971, 1978, 1980

Most Consecutive Seasons Leading League
    3 Green Bay, 1936-38
       Chi. Bears, 1941-43
       Los Angeles, 1950-52
       Oakland, 1967-69

POINTS
Most Points, Season
    541 Washington, 1983
    513 Houston, 1961
         Miami, 1984
    479 Dallas, 1983

Fewest Points, Season (Since 1932)
    37 Cincinnati/St. Louis, 1934
    38 Cincinnati, 1933
        Detroit, 1942
    51 Pittsburgh, 1934
        Philadelphia, 1936

Most Points, Game
    72 Washington vs. N.Y. Giants, Nov. 27, 1966
    70 Los Angeles vs. Baltimore, Oct. 22, 1950
    65 Chi. Cardinals vs. N.Y. Bulldogs, Nov. 13, 1949
        Los Angeles vs. Detroit, Oct. 29, 1950

Most Points, Both Teams, Game
    113 Washington (72) vs. N.Y. Giants (41), Nov. 27, 1966
    101 Oakland (52) vs. Houston (49), Dec. 22, 1963
    99   Seattle (51) vs. Kansas City (48), Nov. 27, 1983 (OT)

Fewest Points, Both Teams, Game
    0 In many games. Last time: N.Y. Giants vs. Detroit, Nov. 7, 1943

Most Points, Shutout Victory, Game
    64 Philadelphia vs. Cincinnati, Nov. 6, 1934
    59 Los Angeles vs. Atlanta, Dec. 4, 1976
    57 Chicago vs. Baltimore, Nov. 25, 1962

Fewest Points, Shutout Victory, Game
    2 Green Bay vs. Chi. Bears, Oct. 16, 1932
       Chi. Bears vs. Green Bay, Sept. 18, 1938

Most Points Overcome to Win Game
    28 San Francisco vs. New Orleans, Dec. 7, 1980 (OT) (trailed 7-35, won 38-35)
    24 Philadelphia vs. Washington, Oct. 27, 1946 (trailed 0-24, won 28-24)
        Denver vs. Boston, Oct. 23, 1960 (trailed 0-24, won 31-24)
        Miami vs. New England, Dec. 15, 1974 (trailed 0-24, won 34-27)
        Minnesota vs. San Francisco, Dec. 4, 1977 (trailed 0-24, won 28-27)
        Denver vs. Seattle, Sept. 23, 1979 (trailed 10-34, won 37-34)
        L.A. Raiders vs. San Diego, Nov. 22, 1982 (trailed 0-24, won 28-24)

Most Points Overcome to Tie Game
    31 Denver vs. Buffalo, Nov. 27, 1960 (trailed 7-38, tied 38-38)
    28 Los Angeles vs. Philadelphia, Oct. 3, 1948 (trailed 0-28, tied 28-28)

Most Points, Each Half
1st: 49 Green Bay vs. Tampa Bay, Oct. 2, 1983
      45 Green Bay vs. Cleveland, Nov. 12, 1967
2nd: 49 Chi. Bears vs. Philadelphia, Nov. 30, 1941
      48 Chi. Cardinals vs. Baltimore, Oct. 2, 1950
          N.Y. Giants vs. Baltimore, Nov. 19, 1950

Most Points, Both Teams, Each Half
1st: 70 Houston (35) vs. Oakland (35), Dec. 22, 1963
2nd: 65 Washington (38) vs. N.Y. Giants (27), Nov. 27, 1966

Most Points, One Quarter
    41 Green Bay vs. Detroit, Oct. 7, 1945 (second quarter)
        Los Angeles vs. Detroit, Oct. 29, 1950 (third quarter)
    37 Los Angeles vs. Green Bay, Sept. 21, 1980 (second quarter)
    35 Chi. Cardinals vs. Boston, Oct. 24, 1948 (third quarter)
        Green Bay vs. Cleveland, Nov. 12, 1967 (first quarter); vs. Tampa Bay, Oct. 2, 1983 (second quarter)

Most Points, Both Teams, One Quarter
    49 Oakland (28) vs. Houston (21), Dec. 22, 1963 (second quarter)
    48 Green Bay (41) vs. Detroit (7), Oct. 7, 1945 (second quarter)
        Los Angeles (41) vs. Detroit (7), Oct. 29, 1950 (third quarter)
    47 St. Louis (27) vs. Philadelphia (20), Dec. 13, 1964 (second quarter)

Most Points, Each Quarter
1st: 35 Green Bay vs. Cleveland, Nov. 12, 1967
2nd: 41 Green Bay vs. Detroit, Oct. 7, 1945
3rd: 41 Los Angeles vs. Detroit, Oct. 29, 1950
4th: 31 Oakland vs. Denver, Dec. 17, 1960; vs. San Diego, Dec. 8, 1963
          Atlanta vs. Green Bay, Sept. 13, 1981

Most Points, Both Teams, Each Quarter
1st: 42 Green Bay (35) vs. Cleveland (7), Nov. 12, 1967
2nd: 49 Oakland (28) vs. Houston (21), Dec. 22, 1963
3rd: 48 Los Angeles (41) vs. Detroit (7), Oct. 29, 1950
4th: 42 Chi. Cardinals (28) vs. Philadelphia (14), Dec. 7, 1947
          Green Bay (28) vs. Chi. Bears (14), Nov. 6, 1955
          N.Y. Jets (28) vs. Boston (14), Oct. 27, 1968
          Pittsburgh (21) vs. Cleveland (21), Oct. 18, 1969

GAMES
Most Consecutive Games Scoring
    274 Cleveland, 1950-71
    217 Oakland, 1966-81
    208 Dallas, 1970-84 (current)

TOUCHDOWNS
Most Seasons Leading League, Touchdowns
    13 Chi. Bears, 1932, 1934-35, 1939, 1941-44, 1946-48, 1956, 1965
    7   Dall. Cowboys, 1966, 1968, 1971, 1973, 1977-78, 1980
    6   Oakland, 1967-69, 1972, 1974, 1977

Most Consecutive Seasons Leading League, Touchdowns
    4 Chi. Bears, 1941-44
       Los Angeles, 1949-52
    3 Chi. Bears, 1946-48
       Baltimore, 1957-59
       Oakland, 1967-69
    2 By many teams

Most Touchdowns, Season
    70 Miami, 1984
    66 Houston, 1961
    64 Los Angeles, 1950

Fewest Touchdowns, Season (Since 1932)
    3 Cincinnati, 1933
    4 Cincinnati/St. Louis, 1934
    5 Detroit, 1942

Most Touchdowns, Game
    10 Philadelphia vs. Cincinnati, Nov. 6, 1934
        Los Angeles vs. Baltimore, Oct. 22, 1950
        Washington vs. N.Y. Giants, Nov. 27, 1966
    9   Chi. Cardinals vs. Rochester, Oct. 7, 1923; vs. N.Y. Giants, Oct. 17, 1948; vs. N.Y. Bulldogs, Nov. 13, 1949

Los Angeles vs. Detroit, Oct. 29, 1950
Pittsburgh vs. N.Y. Giants, Nov. 30, 1952
Chicago vs. San Francisco, Dec. 12, 1965; vs. Green Bay, Dec. 7, 1980
  8 By many teams.

Most Touchdowns, Both Teams, Game
 16 Washington (10) vs. N.Y. Giants (6), Nov. 27, 1966
 14 Chi. Cardinals (9) vs. N.Y. Giants (5), Oct. 17, 1948
     Los Angeles (10) vs. Baltimore (4), Oct. 22, 1950
     Houston (7) vs. Oakland (7), Dec. 22, 1963
 13 New Orleans (7) vs. St. Louis (6), Nov. 2, 1969
     Kansas City (7) vs. Seattle (6), Nov. 27, 1983 (OT)

Most Consecutive Games Scoring Touchdowns
166 Cleveland, 1957-69
 97 Oakland, 1966-73
 96 Kansas City, 1963-70

POINTS AFTER TOUCHDOWN
Most Points After Touchdown, Season
 66 Miami, 1984
 65 Houston, 1961
 62 Washington, 1983

Fewest Points After Touchdown, Season
  2 Chi. Cardinals, 1933
  3 Cincinnati, 1933
     Pittsburgh, 1934
  4 Cincinnati/St. Louis, 1934

Most Points After Touchdown, Game
 10 Los Angeles vs. Baltimore, Oct. 22, 1950
  9 Chi. Cardinals vs. N.Y. Giants, Oct. 17, 1948
     Pittsburgh vs. N.Y. Giants, Nov. 30, 1952
     Washington vs. N.Y. Giants, Nov. 27, 1966
  8 By many teams

Most Points After Touchdown, Both Teams, Game
 14 Chi. Cardinals (9) vs. N.Y. Giants (5), Oct. 17, 1948
     Houston (7) vs. Oakland (7), Dec. 22, 1963
     Washington (9) vs. N.Y. Giants (5), Nov. 27, 1966
 13 Los Angeles (10) vs. Baltimore (3), Oct. 22, 1950
 12 In many games

FIELD GOALS
Most Seasons Leading League, Field Goals
 11 Green Bay, 1935-36, 1940-43, 1946-47, 1955, 1972, 1974
  7 Washington, 1945, 1956, 1971, 1976-77, 1979, 1982
     N.Y. Giants, 1933, 1937, 1939, 1941, 1944, 1959, 1983
  5 Portsmouth/Detroit, 1932-33, 1937-38, 1980

Most Consecutive Seasons Leading League, Field Goals
  4 Green Bay, 1940-43
  3 Cleveland, 1952-54
  2 By many teams

Most Field Goals Attempted, Season
 49 Los Angeles, 1966
     Washington, 1971
 48 Green Bay, 1972
 47 N.Y. Jets, 1969
     Los Angeles, 1973
     Washington, 1983

Fewest Field Goals Attempted, Season (Since 1938)
  0 Chi. Bears, 1944
  2 Cleveland, 1939
     Card-Pitt, 1944
     Boston, 1946
     Chi. Bears, 1947
  3 Chi. Bears, 1945
     Cleveland, 1945

Most Field Goals Attempted, Game
  9 St. Louis vs. Pittsburgh, Sept. 24, 1967
  8 Pittsburgh vs. St. Louis, Dec. 2, 1962
     Detroit vs. Minnesota, Nov. 13, 1966
     N.Y. Jets vs. Buffalo, Nov. 3, 1968
  7 By many teams

Most Field Goals Attempted, Both Teams, Game
 11 St. Louis (6) vs. Pittsburgh (5), Nov. 13, 1966
     Washington (6) vs. Chicago (5), Nov. 14, 1971
     Green Bay (6) vs. Detroit (5), Sept. 29, 1974
     Washington (6) vs. N.Y. Giants (5), Nov. 14, 1976
 10 Denver (5) vs. Boston (5), Nov. 11, 1962
     Boston (7) vs. San Diego (3), Sept. 20, 1964
     Buffalo (7) vs. Houston (3), Dec. 5, 1965
     St. Louis (7) vs. Atlanta (3), Dec. 11, 1966
     Boston (7) vs. Buffalo (3), Sept. 24, 1967
     Detroit (7) vs. Minnesota (3), Sept. 20, 1971
     Washington (7) vs. Houston (3), Oct. 10, 1971
     Green Bay (5) vs. St. Louis (5), Dec. 5, 1971
     Kansas City (7) vs. Buffalo (3), Dec. 19, 1971
     Kansas City (5) vs. San Diego (5), Oct. 29, 1972
     Minnesota (6) vs. Chicago (4), Sept. 23, 1973
     Cleveland (7) vs. Denver (3), Oct. 19, 1975
     Cleveland (5) vs. Denver (5), Oct. 5, 1980
  9 In many games

Most Field Goals, Season
 35 N.Y. Giants, 1983
 34 N.Y. Jets, 1968
 33 Green Bay, 1972
     Washington, 1983

Fewest Field Goals, Season (Since 1932)
  0 Boston, 1932, 1935
     Chi. Cardinals, 1932, 1945
     Green Bay, 1932, 1944
     New York, 1932
     Brooklyn, 1944
     Card-Pitt, 1944
     Chi. Bears, 1944, 1947
     Boston, 1946

Baltimore, 1950
Dallas, 1952

Most Field Goals, Game
  7 St. Louis vs. Pittsburgh, Sept. 24, 1967
  6 Boston vs. Denver, Oct. 4, 1964
     Detroit vs. Minnesota, Nov. 13, 1966
     N.Y. Jets vs. Buffalo, Nov. 3, 1968; vs. New Orleans, Dec. 3, 1972
     Philadelphia vs. Houston, Nov. 12, 1972
     St. Louis vs. Atlanta, Dec. 9, 1973
     N.Y. Giants vs. Seattle, Oct. 18, 1981
     San Francisco vs. New Orleans, Oct. 16, 1983
  5 By many teams

Most Field Goals, Both Teams, Game
  8 Cleveland (4) vs. St. Louis (4), Sept. 20, 1964
     Chicago (5) vs. Philadelphia (3), Oct. 20, 1968
     Washington (5) vs. Chicago (3), Nov. 14, 1971
     Kansas City (5) vs. Buffalo (3), Dec. 19, 1971
     Detroit (4) vs. Green Bay (4), Sept. 29, 1974
     Cleveland (5) vs. Denver (3), Oct. 19, 1975
     New England (4) vs. San Diego (4), Nov. 9, 1975
     San Francisco (6) vs. New Orleans (2), Oct. 16, 1983
  7 In many games

Most Consecutive Games Scoring Field Goals
 31 Minnesota, 1968-70
 21 San Francisco, 1970-72
 20 Los Angeles, 1970-71
     Miami, 1970-72

SAFETIES
Most Safeties, Season
  4 Detroit, 1962
  3 Green Bay, 1932, 1975
     Pittsburgh, 1947
     N.Y. Yanks, 1950
     Detroit, 1960
     St. Louis, 1960
     Buffalo, 1964
     Minnesota, 1965, 1981
     Cleveland, 1970
     L.A. Rams, 1973, 1984
     Houston, 1977
     Dallas, 1981
     Oakland, 1981
  2 By many teams

Most Safeties, Game
  3 L.A. Rams vs. N.Y. Giants, Sept. 30, 1984
  2 Cincinnati vs. Chi. Cardinals, Nov. 19, 1933
     Detroit vs. Brooklyn, Dec. 1, 1935
     N.Y. Giants vs. Pittsburgh, Sept. 17, 1950; vs. Washington, Nov. 5, 1961
     Chicago vs. Pittsburgh, Nov. 9, 1969
     Dallas vs. Philadelphia, Nov. 19, 1972
     Los Angeles vs. Green Bay, Oct. 21, 1973
     Oakland vs. San Diego, Oct. 26, 1975
     Denver vs. Seattle, Jan. 2, 1983

Most Safeties, Both Teams, Game
  3 L.A. Rams (3) vs. N.Y. Giants (0), Sept. 30, 1984
  2 Chi. Bears (1) vs. San Francisco (1), Oct. 19, 1952
     Cincinnati (1) vs. Los Angeles (1), Oct. 22, 1972
     Atlanta (1) vs. Detroit (1), Oct. 5, 1980
     (Also see previous record)

FIRST DOWNS
Most Seasons Leading League
  9 Chi. Bears, 1935, 1939, 1941, 1943, 1945, 1947-49, 1955
  6 L.A. Rams, 1946, 1950-51, 1954, 1957, 1973
     San Diego, 1965, 1969, 1980-83
  5 Green Bay, 1940, 1942, 1944, 1960, 1962

Most Consecutive Seasons Leading League
  4 San Diego, 1980-83
  3 Chi. Bears, 1947-49
  2 By many teams

Most First Downs, Season
387 Miami, 1984
379 San Diego, 1981
374 San Diego, 1984

Fewest First Downs, Season
 51 Cincinnati, 1933
 64 Pittsburgh, 1935
 67 Philadelphia, 1937

Most First Downs, Game
 38 Los Angeles vs. N.Y. Giants, Nov. 13, 1966
 37 Green Bay vs. Philadelphia, Nov. 11, 1962
 36 Pittsburgh vs. Cleveland, Nov. 25, 1979 (OT)

Fewest First Downs, Game
  0 N.Y. Giants vs. Green Bay, Oct. 1, 1933; vs. Washington, Sept. 27, 1942
     Pittsburgh vs. Boston, Oct. 29, 1933
     Philadelphia vs. Detroit, Sept. 20, 1935
     Denver vs. Houston, Sept. 3, 1966

Most First Downs, Both Teams, Game
 59 Miami (31) vs. Buffalo (28), Oct. 9, 1983 (OT)
     Seattle (33) vs. Kansas City (26), Nov. 27, 1983 (OT)
 58 Los Angeles (30) vs. Chi. Bears (28), Oct. 24, 1954
     Denver (34) vs. Kansas City (24), Nov. 18, 1974
     Atlanta (35) vs. New Orleans (23), Sept. 2, 1979 (OT)
     Pittsburgh (36) vs. Cleveland (22), Nov. 25, 1979 (OT)
     San Diego (34) vs. Miami (24), Nov. 18, 1984 (OT)
 57 Los Angeles (32) vs. N.Y. Yanks (25), Nov. 19, 1950
     Baltimore (33) vs. N.Y. Jets (24), Dec. 15, 1974
     San Francisco (29) vs. San Diego (28), Dec. 11, 1982
     Green Bay (32) vs. Atlanta (25), Nov. 27, 1983 (OT)

Fewest First Downs, Both Teams, Game
  5 N.Y. Giants (0) vs. Green Bay (5), Oct. 1, 1933

Most First Downs, Rushing, Season
181 New England, 1978
177 Los Angeles, 1973
170 Miami, 1972
Fewest First Downs, Rushing, Season
36 Cleveland, 1942
Boston, 1944
39 Brooklyn, 1943
40 Philadelphia, 1940
Detroit, 1945
Most First Downs, Rushing, Game
25 Philadelphia vs. Washington, Dec. 2, 1951
21 Cleveland vs. Philadelphia, Dec. 13, 1959
Los Angeles vs. New Orleans, Nov. 25, 1973
Pittsburgh vs. Kansas City, Nov. 7, 1976
New England vs. Denver, Nov. 28, 1976
Oakland vs. Green Bay, Sept. 17, 1978
20 By eight teams
Fewest First Downs, Rushing, Game
0 By many teams
Most First Downs, Passing, Season
244 San Diego, 1980
243 Miami, 1984
240 San Diego, 1984
Fewest First Downs, Passing, Season
18 Pittsburgh, 1941
23 Brooklyn, 1942
N.Y. Giants, 1944
24 N.Y. Giants, 1943
Most First Downs, Passing, Game
25 Denver vs. Kansas City, Nov. 18, 1974
N.Y. Jets vs. San Francisco, Sept. 21, 1980
24 Houston vs. Buffalo, Nov. 1, 1964
Minnesota vs. Baltimore, Sept. 28, 1969
23 Dallas vs. San Francisco, Nov. 10, 1963
Denver vs. Houston, Dec. 20, 1964
San Diego vs. N.Y. Giants, Oct. 19, 1980; vs. Cincinnati, Dec. 20, 1982
Miami vs. Indianapolis, Dec. 9, 1984
Fewest First Downs, Passing, Game
0 By many teams
Most First Downs, Penalty, Season
39 Seattle, 1978
38 Buffalo, 1983
Denver, 1983
37 Cleveland, 1981
Fewest First Downs, Penalty, Season
2 Brooklyn, 1940
4 Chi. Cardinals, 1940
N.Y. Giants, 1942, 1944
Washington, 1944
Cleveland, 1952
Kansas City, 1969
5 Brooklyn, 1939
Chi. Bears, 1939
Detroit, 1953
Los Angeles, 1953
Houston, 1982
Most First Downs, Penalty, Game
9 Chi. Bears vs. Cleveland, Nov. 25, 1951
Baltimore vs. Pittsburgh, Oct. 30, 1977
8 Philadelphia vs. Detroit, Dec. 2, 1979
7 Boston vs. Houston, Sept. 19, 1965
Baltimore vs. Detroit, Nov. 19, 1967; vs. Buffalo, Dec. 17, 1978; vs. Pittsburgh, Sept. 14, 1980
Oakland vs. Boston, Oct. 6, 1968
Cleveland vs. Buffalo, Oct. 23, 1977; vs. Pittsburgh, Sept. 24, 1978; vs. Atlanta, Sept. 27, 1981
Buffalo vs. Cleveland, Oct. 29, 1978
Cincinnati vs. Oakland, Nov. 9, 1980
Miami vs. Buffalo, Oct. 9, 1983 (OT)
Fewest First Downs, Penalty, Game
0 By many teams

NET YARDS GAINED RUSHING AND PASSING
Most Seasons Leading League
12 Chi. Bears, 1932, 1934-35, 1939, 1941-44, 1947, 1949, 1955-56
6 L.A. Rams, 1946, 1950-51, 1954, 1957, 1973
Baltimore, 1958-60, 1964, 1967, 1976
Dall. Cowboys, 1966, 1968-69, 1971, 1974, 1977
San Diego, 1963, 1965, 1980-83
3 Green Bay, 1937-38, 1940
Houston, 1960-62
N.Y. Giants, 1933, 1962-63
Oakland, 1968-70
Most Consecutive Seasons Leading League
4 Chi. Bears, 1941-44
San Diego, 1980-83
3 Baltimore, 1958-60
Houston, 1960-62
Oakland, 1968-70
2 By many teams
Most Yards Gained, Season
6,936 Miami, 1984
6,744 San Diego, 1981
6,410 San Diego, 1980
Fewest Yards Gained, Season
1,150 Cincinnati, 1933
1,443 Chi. Cardinals, 1934
1,486 Chi. Cardinals, 1933
Most Yards Gained, Game
735 Los Angeles vs. N.Y. Yanks, Sept. 28, 1951
683 Pittsburgh vs. Chi. Cardinals, Dec. 13, 1958
682 Chi. Bears vs. N.Y. Giants, Nov. 14, 1943

Fewest Yards Gained, Game
−7 Seattle vs. Los Angeles, Nov. 4, 1979
−5 Denver vs. Oakland, Sept. 10, 1967
14 Chi. Cardinals vs. Detroit, Sept. 15, 1940
Most Yards Gained, Both Teams, Game
1,133 Los Angeles (636) vs. N.Y. Yanks (497), Nov. 19, 1950
1,102 San Diego (661) vs. Cincinnati (441), Dec. 20, 1982
1,087 St. Louis (589) vs. Philadelphia (498), Dec. 16, 1962
Fewest Yards Gained, Both Teams, Game
30 Chi. Cardinals (14) vs. Detroit (16), Sept. 15, 1940
Most Consecutive Games, 400 or More Yards Gained
11 San Diego, 1982-83
6 Houston, 1961-62
San Diego, 1981
5 Chi. Bears, 1947, 1955
Los Angeles, 1950
Philadelphia, 1953
Oakland, 1968
New England, 1981
Most Consecutive Games, 300 or More Yards Gained
29 Los Angeles, 1949-51
21 Miami, 1983-84 (current)
20 Chi. Bears, 1948-50

RUSHING
Most Seasons Leading League
14 Chi. Bears, 1932, 1934-35, 1939-42, 1951, 1955-56, 1968, 1977, 1983-84
6 Cleveland, 1958-59, 1963, 1965-67
5 Buffalo, 1962, 1964, 1973, 1975, 1982
Most Consecutive Seasons Leading League
4 Chi. Bears, 1939-42
3 Detroit, 1936-38
San Francisco, 1952-54
Cleveland, 1965-67
2 By many teams
Most Rushing Attempts, Season
681 Oakland, 1977
674 Chicago, 1984
671 New England, 1978
Fewest Rushing Attempts, Season
211 Philadelphia, 1982
219 San Francisco, 1982
225 Houston, 1982
Most Rushing Attempts, Game
72 Chi. Bears vs. Brooklyn, Oct. 20, 1935
70 Chi. Cardinals vs. Green Bay, Nov. 25, 1951
69 Chi. Cardinals vs. Green Bay, Dec. 6, 1936
Kansas City vs. Cincinnati, Sept. 3, 1978
Fewest Rushing Attempts, Game
6 Chi. Cardinals vs. Boston, Oct. 29, 1933
7 Oakland vs. Buffalo, Oct. 15, 1963
8 Denver vs. Oakland, Dec. 17, 1960
Buffalo vs. St. Louis, Sept. 9, 1984
Most Rushing Attempts, Both Teams, Game
108 Chi. Cardinals (70) vs. Green Bay (38), Dec. 5, 1948
105 Oakland (62) vs. Atlanta (43), Nov. 30, 1975 (OT)
103 Kansas City (53) vs. San Diego (50), Nov. 12, 1978 (OT)
Fewest Rushing Attempts, Both Teams, Game
36 Cincinnati (16) vs. Chi. Bears (20), Sept. 30, 1934
38 N.Y. Jets (13) vs. Buffalo (25), Nov. 8, 1964
39 Denver (16) vs. N.Y. Titans (23), Sept. 24, 1961
Denver (14) vs. Boston (25), Sept. 21, 1962
Denver (14) vs. Houston (25), Dec. 2, 1962

YARDS GAINED
Most Yards Gained Rushing, Season
3,165 New England, 1978
3,088 Buffalo, 1973
2,986 Kansas City, 1978
Fewest Yards Gained Rushing, Season
298 Philadelphia, 1940
467 Detroit, 1946
471 Boston, 1944
Most Yards Gained Rushing, Game
426 Detroit vs. Pittsburgh, Nov. 4, 1934
423 N.Y. Giants vs. Baltimore, Nov. 19, 1950
420 Boston vs. N.Y. Giants, Oct. 8, 1933
Fewest Yards Gained Rushing, Game
−53 Detroit vs. Chi. Cardinals, Oct. 17, 1943
−36 Philadelphia vs. Chi. Bears, Nov. 19, 1939
−33 Phil-Pitt vs. Brooklyn, Oct. 2, 1943
Most Yards Gained Rushing, Both Teams, Game
595 Los Angeles (371) vs. N.Y. Yanks (224), Nov. 18, 1951
574 Chi. Bears (396) vs. Pittsburgh (178), Oct. 10, 1934
557 Chi. Bears (406) vs. Green Bay (151), Nov. 6, 1955
Fewest Yards Gained Rushing, Both Teams, Game
−15 Detroit (−53) vs. Chi. Cardinals (38), Oct. 17, 1943
4 Detroit (−10) vs. Chi. Cardinals (14), Sept. 15, 1940
63 Chi. Cardinals (−1) vs. N.Y. Giants (64), Oct. 18, 1953

AVERAGE GAIN
Highest Average Gain, Rushing, Season
5.74 Cleveland, 1963
5.65 San Francisco, 1954
5.56 San Diego, 1963
Lowest Average Gain, Rushing, Season
0.94 Philadelphia, 1940
1.45 Boston, 1944
1.55 Pittsburgh, 1935

TOUCHDOWNS

Most Touchdowns, Rushing, Season
- 36 Green Bay, 1962
- 33 Pittsburgh, 1976
- 30 Chi. Bears, 1941
       New England, 1978
       Washington, 1983

Fewest Touchdowns, Rushing, Season
- 1 Brooklyn, 1934
- 2 Chi. Cardinals, 1933
      Cincinnati, 1933
      Pittsburgh, 1934, 1940
      Philadelphia, 1935, 1936, 1937, 1938, 1972
- 3 By many teams

Most Touchdowns, Rushing, Game
- 7 Los Angeles vs. Atlanta, Dec. 4, 1976
- 6 By many teams

Most Touchdowns, Rushing, Both Teams, Game
- 8 Los Angeles (6) vs. N.Y. Yanks (2), Nov. 18, 1951
     Cleveland (6) vs. Los Angeles (2), Nov. 24, 1957
- 7 In many games

PASSING

ATTEMPTS

Most Passes Attempted, Season
- 709 Minnesota, 1981
- 662 San Diego, 1984
- 641 Kansas City, 1983

Fewest Passes Attempted, Season
- 102 Cincinnati, 1933
- 106 Boston, 1933
- 120 Detroit, 1937

Most Passes Attempted, Game
- 68 Houston vs. Buffalo, Nov 1, 1964
- 63 Minnesota vs. Tampa Bay, Sept. 5, 1981
- 62 N.Y. Jets vs. Denver, Dec. 3, 1967; vs Baltimore, Oct. 18, 1970

Fewest Passes Attempted, Game
- 0 Green Bay vs. Portsmouth, Oct. 8, 1933; vs. Chi. Bears, Sept. 25, 1949
     Detroit vs. Cleveland, Sept. 10, 1937
     Pittsburgh vs. Brooklyn, Nov. 16, 1941; vs. Los Angeles, Nov. 13, 1949
     Cleveland vs. Philadelphia, Dec. 3, 1950

Most Passes Attempted, Both Teams, Game
- 100 Tampa Bay (54) vs. Kansas City (46), Oct. 28, 1984
- 98 Minnesota (56) vs. Baltimore (42), Sept. 28, 1969
- 97 Denver (53) vs. Houston (44), Dec. 2, 1962
      Cincinnati (56) vs. San Diego (41), Dec. 20, 1982
      San Diego (56) vs. Miami (41), Nov. 18, 1984 (OT)

Fewest Passes Attempted, Both Teams, Game
- 4 Chi. Cardinals (1) vs. Detroit (3), Nov. 3, 1935
     Detroit (0) vs. Cleveland (4), Sept. 10, 1937
- 6 Chi. Cardinals (2) vs. Detroit (4), Sept 15, 1940
- 8 Brooklyn (2) vs. Philadelphia (6), Oct. 1, 1939

COMPLETIONS

Most Passes Completed, Season
- 401 San Diego, 1984
- 382 Minnesota, 1981
- 369 Kansas City, 1983
       San Diego, 1983

Fewest Passes Completed, Season
- 25 Cincinnati, 1933
- 33 Boston, 1933
- 34 Chi. Cardinals, 1934
      Detroit, 1934

Most Passes Completed, Game
- 42 N.Y. Jets vs. San Francisco, Sept. 21, 1980
- 40 Cincinnati vs. San Diego, Dec. 20, 1982
- 38 Minnesota vs. Cleveland, Dec. 14, 1980; vs. Green Bay, Nov. 29, 1981
      Buffalo vs. Miami, Oct. 9, 1983 (OT)

Most Passes Completed, Both Teams, Game
- 66 Cincinnati (40) vs. San Diego (26), Dec. 20, 1982
- 65 San Diego (33) vs. San Francisco (32), Dec. 11, 1982
      San Diego (37) vs. Miami (28), Nov. 18, 1984 (OT)
- 63 N.Y. Jets (42) vs. San Francisco (21), Sept. 21, 1980

Fewest Passes Completed, Both Teams, Game
- 1 Chi. Cardinals (0) vs. Philadelphia (1), Nov. 8, 1936
     Detroit (0) vs. Cleveland (1), Sept. 10, 1937
     Chi. Cardinals (0) vs. Detroit (1), Sept. 15, 1940
     Brooklyn (0) vs. Pittsburgh (1), Nov. 29, 1942
- 2 Chi. Cardinals (0) vs. Detroit (2), Nov. 3, 1935
     Buffalo (0) vs. N.Y. Jets (2), Sept. 29, 1974
- 3 Brooklyn (1) vs. Philadelphia (2), Oct. 1, 1939

YARDS GAINED

Most Seasons Leading League, Passing Yardage
- 9 San Diego, 1965, 1968, 1971, 1978-83
- 8 Chi. Bears, 1932, 1939, 1941, 1943, 1945, 1949, 1954, 1964
- 7 Washington, 1938, 1940, 1944, 1947-48, 1967, 1974

Most Consecutive Seasons Leading League, Passing Yardage
- 6 San Diego, 1978-83
- 4 Green Bay, 1934-37
- 2 By many teams

Most Yards Gained, Passing, Season
- 5,018 Miami, 1984
- 4,739 San Diego, 1981
- 4,661 San Diego, 1983

Fewest Yards Gained, Passing, Season
- 302 Chi. Cardinals, 1934
- 357 Cincinnati, 1933
- 459 Boston, 1934

Most Yards Gained, Passing, Game
- 554 Los Angeles vs. N.Y. Yanks, Sept. 28, 1951
- 530 Minnesota vs. Baltimore, Sept. 28, 1969

- 506 L.A. Rams vs. Chicago, Dec. 26, 1982

Fewest Yards Gained, Passing, Game
- −53 Denver vs. Oakland, Sept. 10, 1967
- −52 Cincinnati vs. Houston, Oct. 31, 1971
- −39 Atlanta vs. San Francisco, Oct. 23, 1976

Most Yards Gained, Passing, Both Teams, Game
- 883 San Diego (486) vs. Cincinnati (397), Dec. 20, 1982
- 834 Philadelphia (419) vs. St. Louis (415), Dec. 16, 1962
- 822 N.Y. Jets (490) vs. Baltimore (332), Sept. 24, 1972

Fewest Yards Gained, Passing, Both Teams, Game
- −11 Green Bay (−10) vs. Dallas (−1), Oct. 24, 1965
- 1 Chi. Cardinals (0) vs. Philadelphia (1), Nov. 8, 1936
- 7 Brooklyn (0) vs. Pittsburgh (7), Nov. 29, 1942

TIMES SACKED

Most Seasons Leading League, Fewest Times Sacked
- 4 San Diego, 1963-64, 1967-68
     San Francisco, 1964-65, 1970-71
     Miami, 1973, 1982-84
- 3 N.Y. Jets, 1965-66, 1968
     Houston, 1961-62, 1978
     St. Louis, 1974-76
- 2 Washington, 1966-67
     L.A. Rams, 1969, 1983
     Buffalo, 1980-81
     Tampa Bay, 1979, 1982

Most Consecutive Seasons Leading League, Fewest Times Sacked
- 3 St. Louis, 1974-76
     Miami, 1982-84
- 2 By many teams

Most Times Sacked, Season
- 70 Atlanta, 1968
- 68 Dallas, 1964
- 67 Detroit, 1976
     Atlanta, 1984

Fewest Times Sacked, Season
- 8 San Francisco, 1970
     St. Louis, 1975
- 9 N.Y. Jets, 1966
- 10 N.Y. Giants, 1972

Most Times Sacked, Game
- 12 Pittsburgh vs. Dallas, Nov. 20, 1966
      Baltimore vs. St. Louis, Oct. 26, 1980
      Detroit vs. Chicago, Dec. 16, 1984
- 11 St. Louis vs. N.Y. Giants, Nov. 1, 1964
      Los Angeles vs. Baltimore, Nov. 22, 1964
      Denver vs. Buffalo, Dec. 13, 1964; vs. Oakland, Nov. 5, 1967
      Green Bay vs. Detroit, Nov. 7, 1965
      Buffalo vs. Oakland, Oct. 15, 1967
      Atlanta vs. St. Louis, Nov. 24, 1968; vs. Cleveland, Nov. 18, 1984
      Detroit vs. Dallas, Oct. 6, 1975
      Philadelphia vs. St. Louis, Dec. 18, 1983
      Cleveland vs. Kansas City, Sept. 30, 1984
      Minnesota vs. Chicago, Oct. 28, 1984
- 10 By many teams

Most Times Sacked, Both Teams, Game
- 18 Green Bay (10) vs. San Diego (8), Sept. 24, 1978
- 17 Buffalo (10) vs. N.Y. Titans (7), Nov. 23, 1961
      Pittsburgh (12) vs. Dallas (5), Nov. 20, 1966
      Atlanta (9) vs. Philadelphia (8), Dec. 16, 1984
- 16 Los Angeles (11) vs. Baltimore (5), Nov. 22, 1964
      Buffalo (11) vs. Oakland (5), Oct. 15, 1967

COMPLETION PERCENTAGE

Most Seasons Leading League, Completion Percentage
- 11 Washington, 1937, 1939-40, 1942-45, 1947-48, 1969-70
- 7 Green Bay, 1936, 1941, 1961-62, 1964, 1966, 1968
- 6 Cleveland, 1951, 1953-55, 1959-60
     Dall. Texans/Kansas City, 1962, 1964, 1966-69
     San Francisco, 1952, 1957-58, 1965, 1981, 1983

Most Consecutive Seasons Leading League, Completion Percentage
- 4 Washington, 1942-45
     Kansas City, 1966-69
- 3 Cleveland, 1953-55
- 2 By many teams

Highest Completion Percentage, Season
- 70.6 Cincinnati, 1982 (310-219)
- 64.3 Oakland, 1976 (361-232)
- 64.2 San Francisco, 1983 (528-339)

Lowest Completion Percentage, Season
- 22.9 Philadelphia, 1936 (170-39)
- 24.5 Cincinnati, 1933 (102-25)
- 25.0 Pittsburgh, 1941 (168-42)

TOUCHDOWNS

Most Touchdowns, Passing, Season
- 49 Miami, 1984
- 48 Houston, 1961
- 39 N.Y. Giants, 1963

Fewest Touchdowns, Passing, Season
- 0 Cincinnati, 1933
     Pittsburgh, 1945
- 1 Boston, 1932, 1933
     Chi. Cardinals, 1934
     Cincinnati/St. Louis, 1934
     Detroit, 1942
- 2 Chi. Cardinals, 1932, 1935
     Stapleton, 1932
     Brooklyn, 1936
     Pittsburgh, 1942

Most Touchdowns, Passing, Game
- 7 Chi. Bears vs. N.Y. Giants, Nov. 14, 1943
     Philadelphia vs. Washington, Oct. 17, 1954

Houston vs. N.Y. Titans, Nov. 19, 1961; vs. N.Y. Titans, Oct. 14, 1962
N.Y. Giants vs. Washington, Oct. 28, 1962
Minnesota vs. Baltimore, Sept. 28, 1969
San Diego vs. Oakland, Nov. 22, 1981
6   By many teams.

Most Touchdowns, Passing, Both Teams, Game
12 New Orleans (6) vs. St. Louis (6), Nov. 2, 1969
11 N.Y. Giants (7) vs. Washington (4), Oct. 28, 1962
    Oakland (6) vs. Houston (5), Dec. 22, 1963
9   In many games

PASSES HAD INTERCEPTED
Most Passes Had Intercepted, Season
48 Houston, 1962
45 Denver, 1961
41 Card-Pitt, 1944
Fewest Passes Had Intercepted, Season
5   Cleveland, 1960
    Green Bay, 1966
6   Green Bay, 1964
    St. Louis, 1982
7   Los Angeles, 1969
Most Passes Had Intercepted, Game
9   Detroit vs. Green Bay, Oct. 24, 1943
    Pittsburgh vs. Philadelphia, Dec. 12, 1965
8   Green Bay vs. N.Y. Giants, Nov. 21, 1948
    Chi. Cardinals vs. Philadelphia, Sept. 24, 1950
    N.Y. Yanks vs. N.Y. Giants, Dec. 16, 1951
    Denver vs. Houston, Dec. 2, 1962
    Chi. Bears vs. Detroit, Sept. 22, 1968
    Baltimore vs. N.Y. Jets, Sept. 23, 1973
7   By many teams. Last time: Detroit vs. Denver, Oct. 7, 1984
Most Passes Had Intercepted, Both Teams, Game
13 Denver (8) vs. Houston (5), Dec. 2, 1962
11 Philadelphia (7) vs. Boston (4), Nov. 3, 1935
    Boston (6) vs. Pittsburgh (5), Dec. 1, 1935
    Cleveland (7) vs. Green Bay (4), Oct. 30, 1938
    Green Bay (7) vs. Detroit (4), Oct. 20, 1940
    Detroit (7) vs. Chi. Bears (4), Nov. 22, 1942
    Detroit (7) vs. Cleveland (4), Nov. 26, 1944
    Chi. Cardinals (8) vs. Philadelphia (3), Sept. 24, 1950
    Washington (7) vs. N.Y. Giants (4), Dec. 8, 1963
    Pittsburgh (9) vs. Philadelphia (2), Dec 12, 1965
10 In many games

PUNTING
Most Seasons Leading League (Average Distance)
6   Washington, 1940-43, 1945, 1958
    Denver, 1962-64, 1966-67, 1982
    Kansas City, 1968, 1971-73, 1979, 1984
4   L.A. Rams, 1946, 1949, 1955-56
3   Cleveland, 1950-52
    San Francisco, 1957, 1962, 1965
    Oakland, 1974, 1975, 1977
    Cincinnati, 1970, 1978, 1981
    Baltimore, 1966, 1969, 1983
Most Consecutive Seasons Leading League (Average Distance)
4   Washington, 1940-43
3   Cleveland, 1950-52
    Denver, 1962-64
    Kansas City, 1971-73
Most Punts, Season
114 Chicago, 1981
113 Boston, 1934
    Brooklyn, 1934
112 Boston, 1935
Fewest Punts, Season
23 San Diego, 1982
31 Cincinnati, 1982
32 Chi. Bears, 1941
Most Punts, Game
17 Chi. Bears vs. Green Bay, Oct. 22, 1933
    Cincinnati vs. Pittsburgh, Oct. 22, 1933
16 Cincinnati vs. Portsmouth, Sept. 17, 1933
    Chi. Cardinals vs. Chi. Bears, Nov. 30, 1933; vs. Detroit, Sept. 15, 1940
Fewest Punts, Game
0   By many teams. Last time: New Orleans vs. Atlanta, Jan. 2, 1983
Most Punts, Both Teams, Game
31 Chi. Bears (17) vs. Green Bay (14), Oct. 22, 1933
    Cincinnati (17), vs. Pittsburgh (14), Oct. 22, 1933
29 Chi. Cardinals (15) vs. Cincinnati (14), Nov. 12, 1933
    Chi. Cardinals (16) vs. Chi. Bears (13), Nov. 30, 1933
    Chi. Cardinals (16) vs. Detroit (13), Sept. 15, 1940
Fewest Punts, Both Teams, Game
1   Dall. Cowboys (0) vs. Cleveland (1), Dec. 3, 1961
    Chicago (0) vs. Detroit (1), Oct. 1, 1972
    San Francisco (0) vs. N.Y. Giants (1), Oct. 15, 1972
    Green Bay (0) vs. Buffalo (1), Dec. 5, 1982
2   In many games

AVERAGE YARDAGE
Highest Average Distance, Punting, Season
47.6 Detroit, 1961 (56-2,664)
47.0 Pittsburgh, 1961 (73-3,431)
46.9 Pittsburgh, 1953 (80-3,752)
Lowest Average Distance, Punting, Season
32.7 Card-Pitt, 1944 (60-1,964)
33.9 Detroit, 1969 (74-2,510)
34.4 Phil-Pitt, 1943 (62-2,132)

PUNT RETURNS
Most Seasons Leading League (Average Return)
8   Detroit, 1943-45, 1951-52, 1962, 1966, 1969
5   Chi. Cardinals, 1948-49, 1955-56, 1959
    Cleveland, 1958, 1960, 1964-65, 1967
    Green Bay, 1950, 1953-54, 1961, 1972
    Dall. Texans/Kansas City, 1960, 1968, 1970, 1979-80
4   Denver, 1963, 1967, 1969, 1982
Most Consecutive Seasons Leading League (Average Return)
3   Detroit, 1943-45
2   By many teams
Most Punt Returns, Season
71 Pittsburgh, 1976
    Tampa Bay, 1979
67 Pittsburgh, 1974
    Los Angeles, 1978
    L.A. Raiders, 1984
65 San Francisco, 1976
Fewest Punt Returns, Season
12 Baltimore, 1981
    San Diego, 1982
14 Los Angeles, 1961
    Philadelphia, 1962
    Baltimore, 1982
15 Houston, 1960
    Washington, 1960
    Oakland, 1961
    N.Y. Giants, 1969
    Philadelphia, 1973
    Kansas City, 1982
Most Punt Returns, Game
12 Philadelphia vs. Cleveland, Dec. 3, 1950
11 Chi. Bears vs. Chi. Cardinals, Oct. 8, 1950
    Washington vs. Tampa Bay, Oct. 9, 1977
10 Philadelphia vs. N.Y. Giants, Nov. 26, 1950
    Philadelphia vs. Tampa Bay, Sept. 18, 1977
    Pittsburgh vs. Buffalo, Dec. 16, 1979
    Washington vs. New Orleans, Dec. 26, 1982
Most Punt Returns, Both Teams, Game
17 Philadelphia (12) vs. Cleveland (5), Dec. 3, 1950
16 N.Y. Giants (9) vs. Philadelphia (7), Dec. 12, 1954
    Washington (11) vs. Tampa Bay (5), Oct. 9, 1977
15 Detroit (8) vs. Cleveland (7), Sept. 27, 1942
    Los Angeles (8) vs. Baltimore (7), Nov. 27, 1966
    Pittsburgh (8) vs. Houston (7), Dec. 1, 1974
    Philadelphia (10) vs. Tampa Bay (5), Sept. 18, 1977
    Baltimore (9) vs. Kansas City (6), Sept. 2, 1979
    Washington (10) vs. New Orleans (5), Dec. 26, 1982

FAIR CATCHES
Most Fair Catches, Season
34 Baltimore, 1971
32 San Diego, 1969
30 St. Louis, 1967
    Minnesota, 1971
Fewest Fair Catches, Season
0   San Diego, 1975
    New England, 1976
    Tampa Bay, 1976
    Pittsburgh, 1977
    Dallas, 1982
1   Cleveland, 1974
    San Francisco, 1975
    Kansas City, 1976
    St. Louis, 1976, 1982
    San Diego, 1976
    L.A. Rams, 1982
    Tampa Bay, 1982
2   By many teams
Most Fair Catches, Game
7   Minnesota vs. Dallas, Sept. 25, 1966
    Detroit vs. Chicago, Nov. 21, 1976
6   By many teams

YARDS GAINED
Most Yards, Punt Returns, Season
781 Chi. Bears, 1948
774 Pittsburgh, 1974
729 Green Bay, 1950
Fewest Yards, Punt Returns, Season
27 St. Louis, 1965
35 N.Y. Giants, 1965
37 New England, 1972
Most Yards, Punt Returns, Game
231 Detroit vs. San Francisco, Oct. 6, 1963
225 Oakland vs. Buffalo, Sept. 15, 1968
219 Los Angeles vs. Atlanta, Oct. 11, 1981
Most Yards, Punt Returns, Both Teams, Game
282 Los Angeles (219) vs. Atlanta (63), Oct. 11, 1981
245 Detroit (231) vs. San Francisco (14), Oct. 6, 1963
244 Oakland (225) vs. Buffalo (19), Sept. 15, 1968

AVERAGE YARDS RETURNING PUNTS
Highest Average, Punt Returns, Season
20.2 Chi. Bears, 1941 (27-546)
19.1 Chi. Cardinals, 1948 (35-669)
18.2 Chi. Cardinals, 1949 (30-546)
Lowest Average, Punt Returns, Season
1.2   St. Louis, 1965 (23-27)
1.5   N.Y. Giants, 1965 (24-35)
1.7   Washington, 1970 (27-45)

TOUCHDOWNS RETURNING PUNTS
Most Touchdowns, Punt Returns, Season
  5 Chi. Cardinals, 1959
  4 Chi. Cardinals, 1948
      Detroit, 1951
      N.Y. Giants, 1951
      Denver, 1976
  3 Washington, 1941
      Detroit, 1952
      Pittsburgh, 1952
      Houston, 1975
      Los Angeles, 1981

Most Touchdowns, Punt Returns, Game
  2 Detroit vs. Los Angeles, Oct. 14, 1951; vs. Green Bay, Nov. 22, 1951
      Chi. Cardinals vs. Pittsburgh, Nov. 1, 1959; vs. N.Y. Giants, Nov. 22, 1959
      N.Y. Titans vs. Denver, Sept. 24, 1961
      Denver vs. Cleveland, Sept. 26, 1976
      Los Angeles vs. Atlanta, Oct. 11, 1981

Most Touchdowns, Punt Returns, Both Teams, Game
  2 Philadelphia (1) vs. Washington (1), Nov. 9, 1952
      Kansas City (1) vs. Buffalo (1), Sept. 11, 1966
      Baltimore (1) vs. New England (1), Nov. 18, 1979
      (Also see previous record)

KICKOFF RETURNS
Most Seasons Leading League (Average Return)
  7 Washington, 1942, 1947, 1962-63, 1973-74, 1981
  5 N.Y. Giants, 1944, 1946, 1949, 1951, 1953
      Chi. Bears, 1943, 1948, 1958, 1966, 1972
  4 Houston, 1960, 1962-63, 1968

Most Consecutive Seasons Leading League (Average Return)
  3 Denver, 1965-67
  2 By many teams

Most Kickoff Returns, Season
  88 New Orleans, 1980
  86 Minnesota, 1984
  84 Baltimore, 1981

Fewest Kickoff Returns, Season
  17 N.Y. Giants, 1944
  20 N.Y. Giants, 1941, 1943
      Chi. Bears, 1942
  23 Washington, 1942

Most Kickoff Returns, Game
  12 N.Y. Giants vs. Washington, Nov. 27, 1966
  10 By many teams

Most Kickoff Returns, Both Teams, Game
  19 N.Y. Giants (12) vs. Washington (7), Nov. 27, 1966
  18 Houston (10) vs. Oakland (8), Dec. 22, 1963
  17 Washington (9) vs. Green Bay (8), Oct. 17, 1983

YARDS GAINED
Most Yards, Kickoff Returns, Season
  1,973 New Orleans, 1980
  1,824 Houston, 1963
  1,801 Denver, 1963

Fewest Yards, Kickoff Returns, Season
  282 N.Y. Giants, 1940
  381 Green Bay, 1940
  424 Chicago, 1963

Most Yards, Kickoff Returns, Game
  362 Detroit vs. Los Angeles, Oct. 29, 1950
  304 Chi. Bears vs. Green Bay, Nov. 9, 1952
  295 Denver vs. Boston, Oct. 4, 1964

Most Yards, Kickoff Returns, Both Teams, Game
  560 Detroit (362) vs. Los Angeles (198), Oct. 29, 1950
  453 Washington (236) vs. Philadelphia (217), Sept. 28, 1947
  447 N.Y. Giants (236) vs. Cleveland (211), Dec. 4, 1966

AVERAGE YARDAGE
Highest Average, Kickoff Returns, Season
  29.4 Chicago, 1972 (52-1,528)
  28.9 Pittsburgh, 1952 (39-1,128)
  28.2 Washington, 1962 (61-1,720)

Lowest Average, Kickoff Returns, Season
  16.3 Chicago, 1963 (26-424)
  16.4 Chicago, 1983 (58-953)
  16.5 San Diego, 1961 (51-642)

TOUCHDOWNS
Most Touchdowns, Kickoff Returns, Season
  4 Green Bay, 1967
      Chicago, 1970
  3 Los Angeles, 1950
      Chi. Cardinals, 1954
      San Francisco, 1963
      Denver, 1966
      Chicago, 1967
      New England, 1977
  2 By many teams

Most Touchdowns, Kickoff Returns, Game
  2 Chi. Bears vs. Green Bay, Sept. 22, 1940; vs. Green Bay, Nov. 9, 1952
      Philadelphia vs. Dallas, Nov. 6, 1966
      Green Bay vs. Cleveland, Nov. 12, 1967

Most Touchdowns, Kickoff Returns, Both Teams, Game
  2 Washington (1) vs. Philadelphia (1), Nov. 1, 1942
      Washington (1) vs. Philadelphia (1), Sept. 28, 1947
      Los Angeles (1) vs. Detroit (1), Oct. 29, 1950
      N.Y. Yanks (1) vs. N.Y. Giants (1), Nov. 4, 1951 (consecutive)
      Baltimore (1) vs. Chi. Bears (1), Oct. 4, 1958
      Buffalo (1) vs. Boston (1), Nov. 3, 1962
      Pittsburgh (1) vs. Dallas (1), Oct. 30, 1966
      St. Louis (1) vs. Washington (1), Sept. 23, 1973 (consecutive)
      (Also see previous record)

FUMBLES
Most Fumbles, Season
  56 Chi. Bears, 1938
      San Francisco, 1978
  54 Philadelphia, 1946
  51 New England, 1973

Fewest Fumbles, Season
  8 Cleveland, 1959
  11 Green Bay, 1944
  12 Brooklyn, 1934
      Detroit, 1943
      Cincinnati, 1982
      Minnesota, 1982

Most Fumbles, Game
  10 Phil-Pitt vs. New York, Oct. 9, 1943
      Detroit vs. Minnesota, Nov. 12, 1967
      Kansas City vs. Houston, Oct. 12, 1969
      San Francisco vs. Detroit, Dec. 17, 1978
  9 Philadelphia vs. Green Bay, Oct. 13, 1946
      Kansas City vs. San Diego, Nov. 15, 1964
      N.Y. Giants vs. Buffalo, Oct. 20, 1975
      St. Louis vs. Washington, Oct. 25, 1976
      San Diego vs. Green Bay, Sept. 24, 1978
      Pittsburgh vs. Cincinnati, Oct. 14, 1979
      Cleveland vs. Seattle, Dec. 20, 1981
  8 By many teams. Last time: Tampa Bay vs. New York Jets, Dec. 12, 1982

Most Fumbles, Both Teams, Game
  14 Chi. Bears (7) vs. Cleveland (7), Nov. 24, 1940
      St. Louis (8) vs. N.Y. Giants (6), Sept. 17, 1961
      Kansas City (10) vs. Houston (4), Oct. 12, 1969
  13 Washington (8) vs. Pittsburgh (5), Nov. 14, 1937
      Philadelphia (7) vs. Boston (6), Dec. 8, 1946
      N.Y. Giants (7) vs. Washington (6), Nov. 5, 1950
      Kansas City (9) vs. San Diego (4), Nov. 15, 1964
      Buffalo (7) vs. Denver (6), Dec. 13, 1964
      N.Y. Jets (7) vs. Houston (6), Sept. 12, 1965
      Houston (8) vs. Pittsburgh (5), Dec. 9, 1973
      St. Louis (9) vs. Washington (4), Oct. 25, 1976
      Cleveland (9) vs. Seattle (4), Dec. 20, 1981
  12 In many games

FUMBLES LOST
Most Fumbles Lost, Season
  36 Chi. Cardinals, 1959
  31 Green Bay, 1952
  29 Chi. Cardinals, 1946
      Pittsburgh, 1950

Fewest Fumbles Lost, Season
  3 Philadelphia, 1938
      Minnesota, 1980
  4 San Francisco, 1960
      Kansas City, 1982
  5 Chi. Cardinals, 1943
      Detroit, 1943
      N.Y. Giants, 1943
      Cleveland, 1959
      Minnesota, 1982

Most Fumbles Lost, Game
  8 St. Louis vs. Washington, Oct. 25, 1976
  7 Cincinnati vs. Buffalo, Nov. 30, 1969
      Cleveland vs. Seattle, Dec. 20, 1981
  6 By many teams. Last time: L.A. Rams vs. New England, Dec. 11, 1983

FUMBLES RECOVERED
Most Fumbles Recovered, Season, Own and Opponents'
  58 Minnesota, 1963 (27 own, 31 opp)
  51 Chi. Bears, 1938 (37 own, 14 opp)
      San Francisco, 1978 (24 own, 27 opp)
  47 Atlanta, 1978 (22 own, 25 opp)

Fewest Fumbles Recovered, Season, Own and Opponents'
  9 San Francisco, 1982 (5 own, 4 opp)
  11 Cincinnati, 1982 (5 own, 6 opp)
  13 Baltimore, 1967 (5 own, 8 opp)
      N.Y. Jets, 1967 (7 own, 6 opp)
      Philadelphia, 1968 (6 own, 7 opp)
      Miami, 1973 (5 own, 8 opp)
      Chicago, 1982 (6 own, 7 opp)
      Denver, 1982 (6 own, 7 opp)
      Miami, 1982 (5 own, 8 opp)
      New York Giants, 1982 (7 own, 6 opp)

Most Fumbles Recovered, Game, Own and Opponents'
  10 Denver vs. Buffalo, Dec. 13, 1964 (5 own, 5 opp)
      Pittsburgh vs. Houston, Dec. 9, 1973 (5 own, 5 opp)
      Washington vs. St. Louis, Oct. 25, 1976 (2 own, 8 opp)
  9 St. Louis vs. N.Y. Giants, Sept. 17, 1961 (6 own, 3 opp)
      Houston vs. Cincinnati, Oct. 27, 1974 (4 own, 5 opp)
      Kansas City vs. Dallas, Nov. 10, 1975 (4 own, 5 opp)
  8 By many teams

Most Own Fumbles Recovered, Season
  37 Chi. Bears, 1938
  27 Philadelphia, 1946
      Minnesota, 1963
  26 Washington, 1940
      Pittsburgh, 1948

Fewest Own Fumbles Recovered, Season
  2 Washington, 1958
  3 Detroit, 1956
      Cleveland, 1959
      Houston, 1982
  4 By many teams

Most Opponents' Fumbles Recovered, Season
  31 Minnesota, 1963

29 Cleveland, 1951
28 Green Bay, 1946
Houston, 1977
Seattle, 1983
Fewest Opponents' Fumbles Recovered, Season
3 Los Angeles, 1974
4 Philadelphia, 1944
San Francisco, 1982
5 Baltimore, 1982
Most Opponents' Fumbles Recovered, Game
8 Washington vs. St. Louis, Oct. 25, 1976
7 Buffalo vs. Cincinnati, Nov. 30, 1969
Seattle vs. Cleveland, Dec. 20, 1981
6 By many teams. Last time: New England vs. L.A. Rams, Dec. 11, 1983

TOUCHDOWNS
Most Touchdowns, Fumbles Recovered, Season, Own and Opponents'
5 Chi. Bears, 1942 (1 own, 4 opp)
Los Angeles, 1952 (1 own, 4 opp)
San Francisco, 1965 (1 own, 4 opp)
Oakland, 1978 (2 own, 3 opp)
4 Chi. Bears, 1948 (1 own, 3 opp)
Boston, 1948 (4 opp)
Denver, 1979 (1 own, 3 opp), 1984 (4 opp)
Atlanta, 1981 (1 own, 3 opp)
3 By many teams
Most Touchdowns, Own Fumbles Recovered, Season
2 Chi. Bears, 1953
New England, 1973
Buffalo, 1974
Denver, 1975
Oakland, 1978
Green Bay, 1982
New Orleans, 1983
Most Touchdowns, Opponents' Fumbles Recovered, Season
4 Detroit, 1937
Chi. Bears, 1942
Boston, 1948
Los Angeles, 1952
San Francisco, 1965
Denver, 1984
3 By many teams
Most Touchdowns, Fumbles Recovered, Game, Own and Opponents'
2 Detroit vs. Cleveland, Nov. 7, 1937 (2 opp); vs. Los Angeles, Sept. 17, 1950
(1 own, 1 opp); vs. Chi. Cardinals, Dec. 6, 1959 (1 own, 1 opp);
vs. Minnesota, Dec. 9, 1962 (1 own, 1 opp)
Philadelphia vs. New York, Sept. 25, 1938 (2 opp) vs. St. Louis, Nov. 21, 1971
(1 own, 1 opp)
Chi. Bears vs. Washington, Nov. 28, 1948 (2 opp)
N.Y. Giants vs. Pittsburgh, Sept. 17, 1950 (2 opp); vs. Green Bay, Sept. 19,
1971 (2 opp)
Cleveland vs. Dall. Cowboys, Dec. 3, 1961 (2 opp); vs. N.Y. Giants, Oct. 25,
1964 (2 opp)
Green Bay vs. Dallas, Nov. 26, 1964 (2 opp)
San Francisco vs. Detroit, Nov. 14, 1965 (2 opp)
Oakland vs. Buffalo, Dec. 24, 1967 (2 opp)
Washington vs. San Diego, Sept. 16, 1973 (2 opp); vs. Minnesota, Nov. 29,
1984 (1 own, 1 opp)
New Orleans vs. San Francisco, Oct 19, 1975 (2 opp)
Cincinnati vs. Pittsburgh, Oct. 14, 1979 (2 opp)
Atlanta vs. Detroit, Oct. 5, 1980 (2 opp)
Kansas City vs. Oakland, Oct. 5, 1980 (2 opp)
New England vs. Baltimore, Nov. 23, 1980 (2 opp)
Denver vs. Green Bay, Oct. 15, 1984 (2 opp)
Most Touchdowns, Own Fumbles Recovered, Game
1 By many teams
Most Touchdowns, Opponents' Fumbles Recovered, Game
2 Detroit vs. Cleveland, Nov. 7, 1937
Philadelphia vs. N.Y. Giants, Sept. 25, 1938
Chi. Bears vs. Washington, Nov. 28, 1948
N.Y. Giants vs. Pittsburgh, Sept. 17, 1950; vs. Green Bay, Sept. 19, 1971
Cleveland vs. Dall. Cowboys, Dec. 3, 1961; vs. N.Y. Giants, Oct. 25, 1964
Green Bay vs. Dallas, Nov. 26, 1964
San Francisco vs. Detroit, Nov. 14, 1965
Oakland vs. Buffalo, Dec. 24, 1967
Washington vs. San Diego, Sept. 16, 1973
New Orleans vs. San Francisco, Oct. 19, 1975
Cincinnati vs. Pittsburgh, Oct. 14, 1979
Atlanta vs. Detroit, Oct. 5, 1980
Kansas City vs. Oakland, Oct. 5, 1980
New England vs. Baltimore, Nov. 23, 1980
Denver vs. Green Bay, Oct. 15, 1984

TURNOVERS
(Number of times losing the ball on interceptions and fumbles.)
Most Turnovers, Season
63 San Francisco, 1978
58 Chi. Bears, 1947
Pittsburgh, 1950
N.Y. Giants, 1983
57 Green Bay, 1950
Houston, 1962, 1963
Pittsburgh, 1965
Fewest Turnovers, Season
12 Kansas City, 1982
14 N.Y. Giants, 1943
Cleveland, 1959
16 San Francisco, 1960
Cincinnati, 1982
St. Louis, 1982
Washington, 1982
Most Turnovers, Game
12 Detroit vs. Chi. Bears, Nov. 22, 1942

Chi. Cardinals vs. Philadelphia, Sept. 24, 1950
Pittsburgh vs. Philadelphia, Dec. 12, 1965
11 San Diego vs. Green Bay, Sept. 24, 1978
10 Washington vs. N.Y. Giants, Dec. 4, 1938; vs. N.Y. Giants, Dec. 8, 1963
Pittsburgh vs. Green Bay, Nov. 23, 1941
Detroit vs. Green Bay, Oct. 24, 1943; vs. Denver, Oct. 7, 1984
Chi. Cardinals vs. Green Bay, Nov. 10, 1946; vs. N.Y. Giants, Nov. 2, 1952
Minnesota vs. Detroit, Dec. 9, 1962
Houston vs. Oakland, Sept. 7, 1963
Chicago vs. Detroit, Sept. 22, 1968
St. Louis vs. Washington, Oct. 25, 1976
N.Y. Jets vs. New England, Nov. 21, 1976
San Francisco vs. Dallas, Oct. 12, 1980
Cleveland vs. Seattle, Dec. 20, 1981
Most Turnovers, Both Teams, Game
17 Detroit (12) vs. Chi. Bears (5), Nov. 22, 1942
Boston (9) vs. Philadelphia (8), Dec. 8, 1946
16 Chi. Cardinals (12) vs. Philadelphia (4), Sept. 24, 1950
Chi. Cardinals (8) vs. Chi. Bears (8), Dec. 7, 1958
Minnesota (10) vs. Detroit (6), Dec. 9, 1962
Houston (9) vs. Kansas City (7), Oct. 12, 1969
15 Philadelphia (8) vs. Chi. Cardinals (7), Oct. 3, 1954
Denver (9) vs. Houston (6), Dec. 2, 1962
Washington (10) vs. N.Y. Giants (5), Dec. 8, 1963
St. Louis (9) vs. Kansas City (6), Oct. 2, 1983

PENALTIES
Most Seasons Leading League, Fewest Penalties
10 Miami, 1968, 1976-84
9 Pittsburgh, 1946-47, 1950-52, 1954, 1963, 1965, 1968
5 Green Bay, 1955-56, 1966-67, 1974
Most Consecutive Seasons Leading League, Fewest Penalties
9 Miami, 1976-84
3 Pittsburgh, 1950-52
2 By many teams
Most Seasons Leading League, Most Penalties
16 Chi. Bears, 1941-44, 1946-49, 1951, 1959-61, 1963, 1965, 1968, 1976
7 Oakland/L.A. Raiders, 1963, 1966, 1968-69, 1975, 1982, 1984
6 L.A. Rams, 1950, 1952, 1962, 1969, 1978, 1980
Most Consecutive Seasons Leading League, Most Penalties
4 Chi. Bears, 1941-44, 1946-49
3 Chi. Cardinals, 1954-56
Chi. Bears, 1959-61
Fewest Penalties, Season
19 Detroit, 1937
21 Boston, 1935
24 Philadelphia, 1936
Most Penalties, Season
144 Buffalo, 1983
143 L.A. Raiders, 1984
138 Detroit, 1984
Fewest Penalties, Game
0 By many teams. Last time: Tampa Bay vs. Detroit, Dec. 18, 1983
Most Penalties, Game
22 Brooklyn vs. Green Bay, Sept. 17, 1944
Chi. Bears vs. Philadelphia, Nov. 26, 1944
21 Cleveland vs. Chi. Bears, Nov. 25, 1951
20 Tampa Bay vs. Seattle, Oct. 17, 1976
Fewest Penalties, Both Teams, Game
0 Brooklyn vs. Pittsburgh, Oct. 28, 1934
Brooklyn vs. Boston, Sept. 28, 1936
Cleveland vs. Chi. Bears, Oct. 9, 1938
Pittsburgh vs. Philadelphia, Nov. 10, 1940
Most Penalties, Both Teams, Game
37 Cleveland (21) vs. Chi. Bears (16), Nov. 25, 1951
35 Tampa Bay (20) vs. Seattle (15), Oct. 17, 1976
33 Brooklyn (22) vs. Green Bay (11), Sept. 17, 1944

YARDS PENALIZED
Most Seasons Leading League, Fewest Yards Penalized
11 Miami, 1967-68, 1973, 1977-84
7 Pittsburgh, 1946-47, 1950, 1952, 1962, 1965, 1968
Boston/Washington, 1935, 1953-54, 1956-58, 1970
4 Philadelphia, 1936, 1940, 1951, 1964
Boston, 1962, 1964-66
Most Consecutive Seasons Leading League, Fewest Yards Penalized
8 Miami, 1977-84
3 Washington, 1956-58
Boston, 1964-66
2 By many teams
Most Seasons Leading League, Most Yards Penalized
15 Chi. Bears, 1935, 1937, 1939-44, 1946-47, 1949, 1951, 1961-62, 1968
7 Oakland/L.A. Raiders, 1963-64, 1968-69, 1975, 1982, 1984
6 Buffalo, 1962, 1967, 1970, 1972, 1981, 1983
Most Consecutive Seasons Leading League, Most Yards Penalized
6 Chi. Bears, 1939-44
3 Cleveland, 1976-78
2 By many teams
Fewest Yards Penalized, Season
139 Detroit, 1937
146 Philadelphia, 1937
159 Philadelphia, 1936
Most Yards Penalized, Season
1,274 Oakland, 1969
1,239 Baltimore, 1979
1,209 L.A. Raiders, 1984
Fewest Yards Penalized, Game
0 By many teams. Last time: Tampa Bay vs. Detroit, Dec. 18, 1983
Most Yards Penalized, Game
209 Cleveland vs. Chi. Bears, Nov. 25, 1951
190 Tampa Bay vs. Seattle, Oct. 17, 1976
189 Houston vs. Buffalo, Oct. 31, 1965

Fewest Yards Penalized, Both Teams, Game
- 0 Brooklyn vs. Pittsburgh, Oct. 28, 1934
  - Brooklyn vs. Boston, Sept. 28, 1936
  - Cleveland vs. Chi. Bears, Oct. 9, 1938
  - Pittsburgh vs. Philadelphia, Nov. 10, 1940

Most Yards Penalized, Both Teams, Game
- 374 Cleveland (209) vs. Chi. Bears (165), Nov. 25, 1951
- 310 Tampa Bay (190) vs. Seattle (120), Oct. 17, 1976
- 309 Green Bay (184) vs. Boston (125), Oct. 21, 1945

DEFENSE

SCORING

Most Seasons Leading League, Fewest Points Allowed
- 8 N.Y. Giants, 1935, 1938-39, 1941, 1944, 1958-59, 1961
- 6 Chi. Bears, 1932, 1936-37, 1942, 1948, 1963
  - Cleveland, 1951, 1953-57
- 5 Green Bay, 1935, 1947, 1962, 1965-66

Most Consecutive Seasons Leading League, Fewest Points Allowed
- 5 Cleveland, 1953-57
- 3 Buffalo, 1964-66
  - Minnesota, 1969-71
- 2 By many teams

Fewest Points Allowed, Season (Since 1932)
- 44 Chi. Bears, 1932
- 54 Brooklyn, 1933
- 59 Detroit, 1934

Most Points Allowed, Season
- 533 Baltimore, 1981
- 501 N.Y. Giants, 1966
- 487 New Orleans, 1980

Fewest Touchdowns Allowed, Season (Since 1932)
- 6 Chi. Bears, 1932
  - Brooklyn, 1933
- 7 Detroit, 1934
- 8 Green Bay, 1932

Most Touchdowns Allowed, Season
- 68 Baltimore, 1981
- 66 N.Y. Giants, 1966
- 63 Baltimore, 1950

FIRST DOWNS

Fewest First Downs Allowed Season
- 77 Detroit, 1935
- 79 Boston, 1935
- 82 Washington, 1937

Most First Downs Allowed, Season
- 406 Baltimore, 1981
- 371 Seattle, 1981
- 366 Green Bay, 1983

Fewest First Downs Allowed, Rushing, Season
- 35 Chi. Bears, 1942
- 40 Green Bay, 1939
- 41 Brooklyn, 1944

Most First Downs Allowed, Rushing, Season
- 178 New Orleans, 1980
- 175 Seattle, 1981
- 171 Buffalo, 1978
  - Green Bay, 1983

Fewest First Downs Allowed, Passing, Season
- 33 Chi. Bears, 1943
- 34 Pittsburgh, 1941
  - Washington, 1943
- 35 Detroit, 1940
  - Philadelphia, 1940, 1944

Most First Downs Allowed, Passing, Season
- 216 San Diego, 1981
- 214 Baltimore, 1981
- 206 Denver, 1984

Fewest First Downs Allowed, Penalty, Season
- 1 Boston, 1944
- 3 Philadelphia, 1940
  - Pittsburgh, 1945
  - Washington, 1957
- 4 Cleveland, 1940
  - Green Bay, 1943
  - N.Y. Giants, 1943

Most First Downs Allowed, Penalty, Season
- 43 L.A. Raiders, 1984
- 41 Detroit, 1979
- 40 Pittsburgh, 1978

NET YARDS ALLOWED RUSHING AND PASSING

Most Seasons Leading League, Fewest Yards Allowed
- 6 N.Y. Giants, 1938, 1940-41, 1951, 1956, 1959
  - Chi. Bears, 1942-43, 1948, 1958, 1963, 1984
- 5 Boston/Washington, 1935-37, 1939, 1946
  - Philadelphia, 1944-45, 1949, 1953, 1981
- 4 Cleveland, 1950, 1952, 1954-55

Most Consecutive Seasons Leading League, Fewest Yards Allowed
- 3 Boston/Washington, 1935-37
- 2 By many teams

Fewest Yards Allowed, Season
- 1,539 Chi. Cardinals, 1934
- 1,703 Chi. Bears, 1942
- 1,789 Brooklyn, 1933

Most Yards Allowed, Season
- 6,793 Baltimore, 1981
- 6,403 Green Bay, 1983
- 6,352 Minnesota, 1984

RUSHING

Most Seasons Leading League, Fewest Yards Allowed
- 7 Detroit, 1938, 1950, 1952, 1962, 1970, 1980-81
  - Chi. Bears, 1937, 1939, 1942, 1946, 1949, 1963, 1984
- 6 Dallas, 1966-69, 1972, 1978
- 5 Philadelphia, 1944-45, 1947-48, 1953

Most Consecutive Seasons Leading League, Fewest Yards Allowed
- 4 Dallas, 1966-69
- 2 By many teams

Fewest Yards Allowed, Rushing, Season
- 519 Chi. Bears, 1942
- 558 Philadelphia, 1944
- 762 Pittsburgh, 1982

Most Yards Allowed, Rushing, Season
- 3,228 Buffalo, 1978
- 3,106 New Orleans, 1980
- 3,010 Baltimore, 1978

Fewest Touchdowns Allowed, Rushing, Season
- 2 Detroit, 1934
  - Dallas, 1968
  - Minnesota, 1971
- 3 By many teams

Most Touchdowns Allowed, Rushing, Season
- 36 Oakland, 1961
- 31 N.Y. Giants, 1980
- 30 Baltimore, 1981

PASSING

Most Seasons Leading League, Fewest Yards Allowed
- 8 Green Bay, 1947-48, 1962, 1964-68
- 6 Chi. Bears, 1938, 1943-44, 1958, 1960, 1963
  - Washington, 1939, 1942, 1945, 1952-53, 1980
- 5 Pittsburgh, 1941, 1946, 1951, 1955, 1974
  - Minnesota, 1969-70, 1972, 1975-76
  - Philadelphia, 1934, 1936, 1940, 1949, 1981

Most Consecutive Seasons Leading League, Fewest Yards Allowed
- 5 Green Bay, 1964-68
- 2 By many teams

Fewest Yards Allowed, Passing, Season
- 545 Philadelphia, 1934
- 558 Portsmouth, 1933
- 585 Chi. Cardinals, 1934

Most Yards Allowed, Passing, Season
- 4,311 San Diego, 1981
- 4,128 Baltimore, 1981
- 4,115 N.Y. Jets, 1979

Fewest Touchdowns Allowed, Passing, Season
- 1 Portsmouth, 1932
  - Philadelphia, 1934
- 2 Brooklyn, 1933
  - Chi. Bears, 1934
- 3 Chi. Bears, 1932, 1936
  - Green Bay, 1932, 1934
  - N.Y. Giants, 1939, 1944

Most Touchdowns Allowed, Passing, Season
- 40 Denver, 1963
- 38 St. Louis, 1969
- 37 Washington, 1961
  - Baltimore, 1981

SACKS

Most Seasons Leading League
- 4 Boston/New England, 1961, 1963, 1977, 1979
  - Dallas, 1966, 1968-69, 1978
  - Oakland/L.A. Raiders, 1966-68, 1982
- 3 Dallas/Kansas City, 1960, 1965, 1969
  - San Francisco, 1967, 1972, 1976
- 2 Baltimore, 1964, 1975
  - San Diego, 1962, 1980

Most Consecutive Seasons Leading League
- 3 Oakland, 1966-68
- 2 Dallas, 1968-69

Most Sacks, Season
- 72 Chicago, 1984
- 67 Oakland, 1967
- 66 N.Y. Jets, 1981
  - Washington, 1984

Fewest Sacks, Season
- 11 Baltimore, 1982
- 12 Buffalo, 1982
- 13 Baltimore, 1981

Most Sacks, Game
- 12 Dallas vs. Pittsburgh, Nov. 20, 1966
  - St. Louis vs. Baltimore, Oct. 26, 1980
  - Chicago vs. Detroit, Dec. 16, 1984
- 11 N.Y. Giants vs. St. Louis, Nov. 1, 1964
  - Baltimore vs. Los Angeles, Nov. 22, 1964
  - Buffalo vs. Denver, Dec. 13, 1964
  - Detroit vs. Green Bay, Nov. 7, 1965
  - Oakland vs. Buffalo, Oct. 15, 1967; vs. Denver, Nov. 5, 1967
  - St. Louis vs. Atlanta, Nov. 24, 1968; vs. Philadelphia, Dec. 18, 1983
  - Dallas vs. Detroit, Oct. 6, 1975
  - Kansas City vs. Cleveland, Sept. 30, 1984
  - Chicago vs. Minnesota, Oct. 28, 1984
  - Cleveland vs. Atlanta, Nov. 18, 1984
- 10 By many teams

Most Opponents Yards Lost Attempting to Pass, Season
- 666 Oakland, 1967
- 583 Chicago, 1984
- 573 San Francisco, 1976

Fewest Opponents Yards Lost Attempting to Pass, Season
- 75 Green Bay, 1956
- 77 N.Y. Bulldogs, 1949
- 78 Green Bay, 1958

INTERCEPTIONS BY

Most Seasons Leading League
- 9 N.Y. Giants, 1933, 1937-39, 1944, 1948, 1951, 1954, 1961
- 8 Green Bay, 1940, 1942-43, 1947, 1955, 1957, 1962, 1965
- 6 Chi. Bears, 1935-36, 1941-42, 1946, 1963
     Kansas City, 1966-70, 1974

Most Consecutive Seasons Leading League
- 5 Kansas City, 1966-70
- 3 N.Y. Giants, 1937-39
- 2 By many teams

Most Passes Intercepted By, Season
- 49 San Diego, 1961
- 42 Green Bay, 1943
- 41 N.Y. Giants, 1951

Fewest Passes Intercepted By, Season
- 3 Houston, 1982
- 5 Baltimore, 1982
- 6 Houston, 1972
     St. Louis, 1982

Most Passes Intercepted By, Game
- 9 Green Bay vs. Detroit, Oct. 24, 1943
     Philadelphia vs. Pittsburgh, Dec. 12, 1965
- 8 N.Y. Giants vs. Green Bay, Nov. 21, 1948; vs. N.Y. Yanks, Dec. 16, 1951
     Philadelphia vs. Chi. Cardinals, Sept. 24, 1950
     Houston vs. Denver, Dec. 2, 1962
     Detroit vs. Chicago, Sept. 22, 1968
     N.Y. Jets vs. Baltimore, Sept. 23, 1973
- 7 By many teams. Last time: Denver vs. Detroit, Oct. 7, 1984

Most Consecutive Games, One or More Interceptions By
- 46 L.A. Chargers/San Diego, 1960-63
- 37 Detroit, 1960-63
- 36 Boston, 1944-47
     Washington, 1962-65

Most Yards Returning Interceptions, Season
- 929 San Diego, 1961
- 712 Los Angeles, 1952
- 697 Seattle, 1984

Fewest Yards Returning Interceptions, Season
- 5 Los Angeles, 1959
- 42 Philadelphia, 1982
- 47 Houston, 1982

Most Yards Returning Interceptions, Game
- 325 Seattle vs. Kansas City, Nov. 4, 1984
- 314 Los Angeles vs. San Francisco, Oct. 18, 1964
- 245 Houston vs. N.Y. Jets, Oct. 15, 1967

Most Touchdowns, Returning Interceptions, Season
- 9 San Diego, 1961
- 7 Seattle, 1984
- 6 Cleveland, 1960
     Green Bay, 1966
     Detroit, 1967
     Houston, 1967

Most Touchdowns Returning Interceptions, Game
- 4 Seattle vs. Kansas City, Nov. 4, 1984
- 3 Baltimore vs. Green Bay, Nov. 5, 1950
     Cleveland vs. Chicago, Dec. 11, 1960
     Philadelphia vs. Pittsburgh, Dec, 12, 1965
     Baltimore vs. Pittsburgh, Sept. 29, 1968
     Buffalo vs. N.Y. Jets, Sept. 29, 1968
     Houston vs. San Diego, Dec. 19, 1971
     Cincinnati vs. Houston, Dec. 17, 1972
     Tampa Bay vs. New Orleans, Dec. 11, 1977
- 2 By many teams

Most Touchdowns Returning Interceptions, Both Teams, Game
- 4 Philadelphia (3) vs. Pittsburgh (1), Dec. 12, 1965
     Seattle (4) vs. Kansas City (0), Nov. 4, 1984
- 3 Los Angeles (2) vs. Detroit (1), Nov. 1, 1953
     Cleveland (2) vs. N.Y. Giants (1), Dec. 18, 1960
     Pittsburgh (2) vs. Cincinnati (1), Oct. 10, 1983
     (Also see previous record)

PUNT RETURNS

Fewest Opponents Punt Returns, Season
- 7 Washington, 1962
     San Diego, 1982
- 10 Buffalo, 1982
- 11 Boston, 1962

Most Opponents Punt Returns, Season
- 71 Tampa Bay, 1976, 1977
- 69 N.Y. Giants, 1953
- 68 Cleveland, 1974

Fewest Yards Allowed, Punt Returns, Season
- 22 Green Bay, 1967
- 34 Washington, 1962
- 39 Cleveland, 1959
     Washington, 1972

Most Yards Allowed, Punt Returns, Season
- 932 Green Bay, 1949
- 913 Boston, 1947
- 906 New Orleans, 1974

Lowest Average Allowed, Punt Returns, Season
- 1.20 Chi. Cardinals, 1954 (46-55)
- 1.22 Cleveland, 1959 (32-39)
- 1.55 Chi. Cardinals, 1953 (44-68)

Highest Average Allowed, Punt Returns, Season
- 18.6 Green Bay, 1949 (50-932)
- 18.0 Cleveland, 1977 (31-558)
- 17.9 Boston, 1960 (20-357)

Most Touchdowns Allowed, Punt Returns, Season
- 4 New York, 1959
- 3 Green Bay, 1949
     Chi. Cardinals, 1951

     Los Angeles, 1951
     Washington, 1952
     Dallas, 1952
     Pittsburgh, 1959
     N.Y. Jets, 1968
     Cleveland, 1977
- 2 By many teams

KICKOFF RETURNS

Fewest Opponents Kickoff Returns, Season
- 10 Brooklyn, 1943
- 15 Detroit, 1942
     Brooklyn, 1944
- 18 Cleveland, 1941
     Boston, 1944

Most Opponents Kickoff Returns, Season
- 91 Washington, 1983
- 89 New England, 1980
- 88 San Diego, 1981

Fewest Yards Allowed, Kickoff Returns, Season
- 225 Brooklyn, 1943
- 293 Brooklyn, 1944
- 361 Seattle, 1982

Most Yards Allowed, Kickoff Returns, Season
- 2,045 Kansas City, 1966
- 1,816 N.Y. Giants, 1963
- 1,806 Dallas, 1983

Lowest Average Allowed, Kickoff Returns, Season
- 14.3 Cleveland, 1980 (71-1,018)
- 15.0 Seattle, 1982 (24-361)
- 15.8 Oakland, 1977 (63-997)

Highest Average Allowed, Kickoff Returns, Season
- 29.5 N.Y. Jets, 1972 (47-1,386)
- 29.4 Los Angeles, 1950 (48-1,411)
- 29.1 New England, 1971 (49-1,427)

Most Touchdowns Allowed, Kickoff Returns, Season
- 3 Minnesota, 1963, 1970
     Dallas, 1966
     Detroit, 1980
- 2 By many teams

FUMBLES

Fewest Opponents Fumbles, Season
- 11 Cleveland, 1956
     Baltimore, 1982
- 13 Los Angeles, 1956
     Chicago, 1960
     Cleveland, 1963, 1965
     Detroit, 1967
     San Diego, 1969
- 14 Baltimore, 1970
     Oakland, 1975
     Buffalo, 1982
     St. Louis, 1982
     San Francisco, 1982

Most Opponents Fumbles, Season
- 50 Minnesota, 1963
     San Francisco, 1978
- 48 N.Y. Giants, 1980
- 47 N.Y. Giants, 1977
     Seattle, 1984

TURNOVERS

(Number of times losing the ball on interceptions and fumbles.)

Fewest Opponents Turnovers, Season
- 11 Baltimore, 1982
- 13 San Francisco, 1982
- 15 St. Louis, 1982

Most Opponents Turnovers, Season
- 66 San Diego, 1961
- 63 Seattle, 1984
- 61 Washington, 1983

Most Opponents Turnovers, Game
- 12 Chi. Bears vs. Detroit, Nov. 22, 1942
     Philadelphia vs. Chi. Cardinals, Sept. 24, 1950; vs. Pittsburgh, Dec. 12, 1965
- 11 Green Bay vs. San Diego, Sept. 24, 1978
- 10 N.Y. Giants vs. Washington, Dec. 4, 1938; vs. Chi. Cardinals, Nov. 2, 1952; vs. Washington, Dec. 8, 1963
     Green Bay vs. Pittsburgh, Nov. 23, 1941; vs. Detroit, Oct. 24, 1943; vs. Chi. Cardinals, Nov. 10, 1946
     Detroit vs. Minnesota, Dec. 9, 1962; vs. Chicago, Sept. 22, 1968
     Oakland vs. Houston, Sept. 7, 1963
     Washington vs. St. Louis, Oct. 25, 1976
     New England vs. N.Y. Jets, Nov. 21, 1976
     Dallas vs. San Francisco, Oct. 12, 1980
     Seattle vs. Cleveland, Dec. 20, 1981
     Denver vs. Detroit, Oct. 7, 1984

OUTSTANDING PERFORMERS

1,000 YARDS RUSHING IN A SEASON

Year	Player, Team	Att.	Yards	Avg.	Long	TD
1984	Eric Dickerson, L.A. Rams[2]	379	2,105	5.6	66	14
	Walter Payton, Chicago[8]	381	1,684	4.4	72	11
	James Wilder, Tampa Bay	407	1,544	3.8	37	13
	Gerald Riggs, Atlanta	353	1,486	4.2	57	13
	Wendell Tyler, San Francisco[3]	246	1,262	5.1	40	7
	John Riggins, Washington[5]	327	1,239	3.8	24	14
	Tony Dorsett, Dallas[7]	302	1,189	3.9	31	6
	Earnest Jackson, San Diego	296	1,179	4.0	32	8
	Ottis Anderson, St. Louis[5]	289	1,174	4.1	24	6
	Marcus Allen, L.A. Raiders[2]	275	1,168	4.2	52	13
	Sammy Winder, Denver	296	1,153	3.9	24	4
	*Greg Bell, Buffalo	262	1,100	4.2	85	7
	Freeman McNeil, N.Y. Jets	229	1,070	4.7	53	5
1983	*Eric Dickerson, L.A. Rams	390	1,808	4.6	85	18
	William Andrews, Atlanta[4]	331	1,567	4.7	27	7
	*Curt Warner, Seattle	335	1,449	4.3	60	13
	Walter Payton, Chicago[7]	314	1,421	4.5	49	6
	John Riggins, Washington[4]	375	1,347	3.6	44	24
	Tony Dorsett, Dallas[6]	289	1,321	4.6	77	8
	Earl Campbell, Houston[5]	322	1,301	4.0	42	12
	Ottis Anderson, St. Louis[4]	296	1,270	4.3	43	5
	Mike Pruitt, Cleveland[4]	293	1,184	4.0	27	10
	George Rogers, New Orleans[2]	256	1,144	4.5	76	5
	Joe Cribbs, Buffalo[3]	263	1,131	4.3	45	3
	Curtis Dickey, Baltimore	254	1,122	4.4	56	4
	Tony Collins, New England	219	1,049	4.8	50	10
	Billy Sims, Detroit[3]	220	1,040	4.7	41	7
	Marcus Allen, L.A. Raiders	266	1,014	3.8	19	9
	Franco Harris, Pittsburgh[8]	279	1,007	3.6	19	5
1981	*George Rogers, New Orleans	378	1,674	4.4	79	13
	Tony Dorsett, Dallas[5]	342	1,646	4.8	75	4
	Billy Sims, Detroit[2]	296	1,437	4.9	51	13
	Wilbert Montgomery, Philadelphia[3]	286	1,402	4.9	41	8
	Ottis Anderson, St. Louis[3]	328	1,376	4.2	28	9
	Earl Campbell, Houston[4]	361	1,376	3.8	43	10
	William Andrews, Atlanta[3]	289	1,301	4.5	29	10
	Walter Payton, Chicago[6]	339	1,222	3.6	39	6
	Chuck Muncie, San Diego[2]	251	1,144	4.6	73	19
	*Joe Delaney, Kansas City	234	1,121	4.8	82	3
	Mike Pruitt, Cleveland[3]	247	1,103	4.5	21	7
	Joe Cribbs, Buffalo[2]	257	1,097	4.3	35	3
	Pete Johnson, Cincinnati	274	1,077	3.9	39	12
	Wendell Tyler, Los Angeles[2]	260	1,074	4.1	69	12
	Ted Brown, Minnesota	274	1,063	3.9	34	6
1980	Earl Campbell, Houston[3]	373	1,934	5.2	55	13
	Walter Payton, Chicago[5]	317	1,460	4.6	69	6
	Ottis Anderson, St. Louis[2]	301	1,352	4.5	52	9
	William Andrews, Atlanta[2]	265	1,308	4.9	33	4
	*Billy Sims, Detroit	313	1,303	4.2	52	13
	Tony Dorsett, Dallas[4]	278	1,185	4.3	56	11
	*Joe Cribbs, Buffalo	306	1,185	3.9	48	11
	Mike Pruitt, Cleveland[2]	249	1,034	4.2	56	6
1979	Earl Campbell, Houston[2]	368	1,697	4.6	61	19
	Walter Payton, Chicago[4]	369	1,610	4.4	43	14
	*Ottis Anderson, St. Louis	331	1,605	4.8	76	8
	Wilbert Montgomery, Philadelphia[2]	338	1,512	4.5	62	9
	Mike Pruitt, Cleveland	264	1,294	4.9	77	9
	Ricky Bell, Tampa Bay	283	1,263	4.5	49	7
	Chuck Muncie, New Orleans	238	1,198	5.0	69	11
	Franco Harris, Pittsburgh[7]	267	1,186	4.4	71	11
	John Riggins, Washington[3]	260	1,153	4.4	66	9
	Wendell Tyler, Los Angeles	218	1,109	5.1	63	9
	Tony Dorsett, Dallas[3]	250	1,107	4.4	41	6
	*William Andrews, Atlanta	239	1,023	4.3	23	3
1978	*Earl Campbell, Houston	302	1,450	4.8	81	13
	Walter Payton, Chicago[3]	333	1,395	4.2	76	11
	Tony Dorsett, Dallas[2]	290	1,325	4.6	63	7
	Delvin Williams, Miami[2]	272	1,258	4.6	58	8
	Wilbert Montgomery, Philadelphia	259	1,220	4.7	47	9
	Terdell Middleton, Green Bay	284	1,116	3.9	76	11
	Franco Harris, Pittsburgh[6]	310	1,082	3.5	37	8
	Mark van Eeghen, Oakland[3]	270	1,080	4.0	34	9
	*Terry Miller, Buffalo	238	1,060	4.5	60	7
	Tony Reed, Kansas City	206	1,053	5.1	62	5
	John Riggins, Washington[2]	248	1,014	4.1	31	5
1977	Walter Payton, Chicago[2]	339	1,852	5.5	73	14
	Mark van Eeghen, Oakland[2]	324	1,273	3.9	27	7
	Lawrence McCutcheon, Los Angeles[4]	294	1,238	4.2	48	7
	Franco Harris, Pittsburgh[5]	300	1,162	3.9	61	11
	Lydell Mitchell, Baltimore[3]	301	1,159	3.9	64	3
	Chuck Foreman, Minnesota[3]	270	1,112	4.1	51	6
	Greg Pruitt, Cleveland[3]	236	1,086	4.6	78	3
	Sam Cunningham, New England	270	1,015	3.8	31	4
	*Tony Dorsett, Dallas	208	1,007	4.8	84	12
1976	O.J. Simpson, Buffalo[5]	290	1,503	5.2	75	8
	Walter Payton, Chicago	311	1,390	4.5	60	13
	Delvin Williams, San Francisco	248	1,203	4.9	80	7
	Lydell Mitchell, Baltimore[2]	289	1,200	4.2	43	5
	Lawrence McCutcheon, Los Angeles[3]	291	1,168	4.0	40	9
	Chuck Foreman, Minnesota[2]	278	1,155	4.2	46	13
	Franco Harris, Pittsburgh[4]	289	1,128	3.9	30	14
	Mike Thomas, Washington	254	1,101	4.3	28	5
	Rocky Bleier, Pittsburgh	220	1,036	4.7	28	5
	Mark van Eeghen, Oakland	233	1,012	4.3	21	3
	Otis Armstrong, Denver[2]	247	1,008	4.1	31	5
	Greg Pruitt, Cleveland[2]	209	1,000	4.8	64	4
1975	O.J. Simpson, Buffalo[4]	329	1,817	5.5	88	16
	Franco Harris, Pittsburgh[3]	262	1,246	4.8	36	10
	Lydell Mitchell, Baltimore	289	1,193	4.1	70	11
	Jim Otis, St. Louis	269	1,076	4.0	30	5
	Chuck Foreman, Minnesota	280	1,070	3.8	31	13
	Greg Pruitt, Cleveland	217	1,067	4.9	50	8
	John Riggins, N.Y. Jets	238	1,005	4.2	42	8
	Dave Hampton, Atlanta	250	1,002	4.0	22	5
1974	Otis Armstrong, Denver	263	1,407	5.3	43	9
	*Don Woods, San Diego	227	1,162	5.1	56	7
	O.J. Simpson, Buffalo[3]	270	1,125	4.2	41	3
	Lawrence McCutcheon, Los Angeles[2]	236	1,109	4.7	23	3
	Franco Harris, Pittsburgh[2]	208	1,006	4.8	54	5
1973	O.J. Simpson, Buffalo[2]	332	2,003	6.0	80	12
	John Brockington, Green Bay[3]	265	1,144	4.3	53	3
	Calvin Hill, Dallas[2]	273	1,142	4.2	21	6
	Lawrence McCutcheon, Los Angeles	210	1,097	5.2	37	2
	Larry Csonka, Miami[3]	219	1,003	4.6	25	5
1972	O.J. Simpson, Buffalo	292	1,251	4.3	94	6
	Larry Brown, Washington[2]	285	1,216	4.3	38	8
	Ron Johnson, N.Y. Giants[2]	298	1,182	4.0	35	9
	Larry Csonka, Miami[2]	213	1,117	5.2	45	6
	Marv Hubbard, Oakland	219	1,100	5.0	39	4
	*Franco Harris, Pittsburgh	188	1,055	5.6	75	10
	Calvin Hill, Dallas	245	1,036	4.2	26	6
	Mike Garrett, San Diego[2]	272	1,031	3.8	41	6
	John Brockington, Green Bay[2]	274	1,027	3.7	30	8
	Eugene (Mercury) Morris, Miami	190	1,000	5.3	33	12
1971	Floyd Little, Denver	284	1,133	4.0	40	6
	*John Brockington, Green Bay	216	1,105	5.1	52	4
	Larry Csonka, Miami	195	1,051	5.4	28	7
	Steve Owens, Detroit	246	1,035	4.2	23	8
	Willie Ellison, Los Angeles	211	1,000	4.7	80	4
1970	Larry Brown, Washington	237	1,125	4.7	75	5
	Ron Johnson, N.Y. Giants	263	1,027	3.9	68	8
1969	Gale Sayers, Chicago[2]	236	1,032	4.4	28	8
1968	Leroy Kelly, Cleveland[3]	248	1,239	5.0	65	16
	*Paul Robinson, Cincinnati	238	1,023	4.3	87	8
1967	Jim Nance, Boston[2]	269	1,216	4.5	53	7
	Leroy Kelly, Cleveland[2]	235	1,205	5.1	42	11
	Hoyle Granger, Houston	236	1,194	5.1	67	6
	Mike Garrett, Kansas City	236	1,087	4.6	58	9
1966	Jim Nance, Boston	299	1,458	4.9	65	11
	Gale Sayers, Chicago	229	1,231	5.4	58	8
	Leroy Kelly, Cleveland	209	1,141	5.5	70	15
	Dick Bass, Los Angeles[2]	248	1,090	4.4	50	8
1965	Jim Brown, Cleveland[7]	289	1,544	5.3	67	17
	Paul Lowe, San Diego[2]	222	1,121	5.0	59	7
1964	Jim Brown, Cleveland[6]	280	1,446	5.2	71	7
	Jim Taylor, Green Bay[5]	235	1,169	5.0	84	12
	John Henry Johnson, Pittsburgh[2]	235	1,048	4.5	45	7
1963	Jim Brown, Cleveland[5]	291	1,863	6.4	80	12
	Clem Daniels, Oakland	215	1,099	5.1	74	3
	Jim Taylor, Green Bay[4]	248	1,018	4.1	40	9
	Paul Lowe, San Diego	177	1,010	5.7	66	8
1962	Jim Taylor, Green Bay[3]	272	1,474	5.4	51	19
	John Henry Johnson, Pittsburgh	251	1,141	4.5	40	7
	*Cookie Gilchrist, Buffalo	214	1,096	5.1	44	13
	Abner Haynes, Dall. Texans	221	1,049	4.7	71	13
	Dick Bass, Los Angeles	196	1,033	5.3	57	6
	Charlie Tolar, Houston	244	1,012	4.1	25	7
1961	Jim Brown, Cleveland[4]	305	1,408	4.6	38	8
	Jim Taylor, Green Bay[2]	243	1,307	5.4	53	15
1960	Jim Brown, Cleveland[3]	215	1,257	5.8	71	9
	Jim Taylor, Green Bay	230	1,101	4.8	32	11
	John David Crow, St. Louis	183	1,071	5.9	57	6
1959	Jim Brown, Cleveland[2]	290	1,329	4.6	70	14
	J. D. Smith, San Francisco	207	1,036	5.0	73	10
1958	Jim Brown, Cleveland	257	1,527	5.9	65	17
1956	Rick Casares, Chi. Bears	234	1,126	4.8	68	12
1954	Joe Perry, San Francisco[2]	173	1,049	6.1	58	8
1953	Joe Perry, San Francisco	192	1,018	5.3	51	10
1949	Steve Van Buren, Philadelphia[2]	263	1,146	4.4	41	11
	Tony Canadeo, Green Bay	208	1,052	5.1	54	4
1947	Steve Van Buren, Philadelphia	217	1,008	4.6	45	13
1934	*Beattie Feathers, Chi. Bears	101	1,004	9.9	82	8

*First year in the league.

200 YARDS RUSHING IN A GAME

Date	Player, Team, Opponent	Att.	Yards	TD
Dec. 9, 1984	Eric Dickerson, L.A. Rams vs. Houston	27	215	2
Nov. 18, 1984	*Greg Bell, Buffalo vs. Dallas	27	206	1
Nov. 4, 1984	Eric Dickerson, L.A. Rams vs. St. Louis	21	208	0
Sept. 2, 1984	Gerald Riggs, Atlanta vs. New Orleans	35	202	2
Nov. 27, 1983	*Curt Warner, Seattle vs. Kansas City (OT)	32	207	3
Nov. 6, 1983	James Wilder, Tampa Bay vs. Minnesota	31	219	1
Sept. 18, 1983	Tony Collins, New England vs. N.Y. Jets	23	212	3
Sept. 4, 1983	George Rogers, New Orleans vs. St. Louis	24	206	2
Dec. 21, 1980	Earl Campbell, Houston vs. Minnesota	29	203	1
Nov. 16, 1980	Earl Campbell, Houston vs. Chicago	31	206	0
Oct. 26, 1980	Earl Campbell, Houston vs. Cincinnati	27	202	2
Oct. 19, 1980	Earl Campbell, Houston vs. Tampa Bay	33	203	0
Nov. 26, 1978	*Terry Miller, Buffalo vs. N.Y. Giants	21	208	2
Dec. 4, 1977	*Tony Dorsett, Dallas vs. Philadelphia	23	206	2
Nov. 20, 1977	Walter Payton, Chicago vs. Minnesota	40	275	1
Oct. 30, 1977	Walter Payton, Chicago vs. Green Bay	23	205	2
Dec. 5, 1976	O.J. Simpson, Buffalo vs. Miami	24	203	1
Nov. 25, 1976	O.J. Simpson, Buffalo vs. Detroit	29	273	2

Oct. 24, 1976	Chuck Foreman, Minnesota vs. Philadelphia	28	200	2
Dec. 14, 1975	Greg Pruitt, Cleveland vs. Kansas City	26	214	3
Sept. 28, 1975	O.J. Simpson, Buffalo vs. Pittsburgh	28	227	1
Dec. 16, 1973	O.J. Simpson, Buffalo vs. N.Y. Jets	34	200	1
Dec. 9, 1973	O.J. Simpson, Buffalo vs. New England	22	219	1
Sept. 16, 1973	O.J. Simpson, Buffalo vs. New England	29	250	2
Dec. 5, 1971	Willie Ellison, Los Angeles vs. New Orleans	26	247	1
Dec. 20, 1970	John (Frenchy) Fuqua, Pittsburgh vs. Philadelphia	20	218	2
Nov. 3, 1968	Gale Sayers, Chicago vs. Green Bay	24	205	0
Oct. 30, 1966	Jim Nance, Boston vs. Oakland	38	208	2
Oct. 10, 1964	John Henry Johnson, Pittsburgh vs. Cleveland	30	200	3
Dec. 8, 1963	Cookie Gilchrist, Buffalo vs. N.Y. Jets	36	243	5
Nov. 3, 1963	Jim Brown, Cleveland vs. Philadelphia	28	223	1
Oct. 20, 1963	Clem Daniels, Oakland vs. N.Y. Jets	27	200	2
Sept. 22, 1963	Jim Brown, Cleveland vs. Dallas	20	232	2
Dec. 10, 1961	Billy Cannon, Houston vs. N.Y. Titans	25	216	3
Nov. 19, 1961	Jim Brown, Cleveland vs. Philadelphia	34	237	4
Dec. 18, 1960	John David Crow, St. Louis vs. Pittsburgh	24	203	0
Nov. 15, 1959	Bobby Mitchell, Cleveland vs. Washington	14	232	3
Nov. 24, 1957	*Jim Brown, Cleveland vs. Los Angeles	31	237	4
Dec. 16, 1956	*Tom Wilson, Los Angeles vs. Green Bay	23	223	0
Nov. 22, 1953	Dan Towler, Los Angeles vs. Baltimore	14	205	1
Nov. 12, 1950	Gene Roberts, N.Y. Giants vs. Chi. Cardinals	26	218	2
Nov. 27, 1949	Steve Van Buren, Philadelphia vs. Pittsburgh	27	205	0
Oct. 8, 1933	Cliff Battles, Boston vs. N.Y. Giants	16	215	1

First year in the league.

Times 200 or More
43 times by 30 players . . . Simpson 6; Brown, Campbell 4; Dickerson, Payton 2.

400 YARDS PASSING IN A GAME

Date	Player, Team, Opponent	Att.	Comp.	Yards	TD
Dec. 16, 1984	Neil Lomax, St. Louis vs. Washington	46	37	468	2
Dec. 9, 1984	Dan Marino, Miami vs. Indianapolis	41	29	404	4
Dec. 2, 1984	Dan Marino, Miami vs. L.A. Raiders	57	35	470	4
Nov. 25, 1984	Dave Krieg, Seattle vs. Denver	44	30	406	3
Nov. 4, 1984	Dan Marino, Miami vs. N.Y. Jets	42	23	422	2
Oct. 21, 1984	Dan Fouts, San Diego vs. L.A. Raiders	45	24	410	3
Sept. 30, 1984	Dan Marino, Miami vs. St. Louis	36	24	429	3
Sept. 2, 1984	Phil Simms, N.Y. Giants vs. Philadelphia	30	23	409	4
Dec. 11, 1983	Bill Kenney, Kansas City vs. San Diego	41	31	411	4
Nov. 20, 1983	Dave Krieg, Seattle vs. Denver	42	31	418	3
Oct. 9, 1983	Joe Ferguson, Buffalo vs. Miami (OT)	55	38	419	5
Oct. 2, 1983	Joe Theismann, Washington vs. L.A. Raiders	39	23	417	3
Sept. 25, 1983	Richard Todd, N.Y. Jets vs. L.A. Rams (OT)	50	37	446	2
Dec. 26, 1982	Vince Ferragamo, L.A. Rams vs. Chicago	46	30	509	3
Dec. 20, 1982	Dan Fouts, San Diego vs. Cincinnati	40	25	435	1
Dec. 20, 1982	Ken Anderson, Cincinnati vs. San Diego	56	40	416	2
Dec. 11, 1982	Dan Fouts, San Diego vs. San Francisco	48	33	444	5
Nov. 21, 1982	Joe Montana, San Francisco vs. St. Louis	39	26	408	3
Nov. 15, 1981	Steve Bartkowski, Atlanta vs. Pittsburgh	50	33	416	2
Oct. 25, 1981	Brian Sipe, Cleveland vs. Baltimore	41	30	444	4
Oct. 25, 1981	David Woodley, Miami vs. Dallas	37	21	408	3
Oct. 11, 1981	Tommy Kramer, Minnesota vs. San Diego	43	27	444	4
Dec. 14, 1980	Tommy Kramer, Minnesota vs. Cleveland	49	38	456	4
Nov. 16, 1980	Doug Williams, Tampa Bay vs. Minnesota	55	30	486	4
Oct. 19, 1980	Dan Fouts, San Diego vs. N.Y. Giants	41	26	444	3
Oct. 12, 1980	Lynn Dickey, Green Bay vs. Tampa Bay (OT)	51	35	418	1
Sept. 21, 1980	Richard Todd, N.Y. Jets vs. San Francisco	60	42	447	3
Oct. 3, 1976	James Harris, Los Angeles vs. Miami	29	17	436	2
Nov. 17, 1975	Ken Anderson, Cincinnati vs. Buffalo	46	30	447	2
Nov. 18, 1974	Charley Johnson, Denver vs. Kansas City	42	28	445	2
Dec. 11, 1972	Joe Namath, N.Y. Jets vs. Oakland	46	25	403	1
Sept. 24, 1972	Joe Namath, N.Y. Jets vs. Baltimore	28	15	496	6
Dec. 21, 1969	Don Horn, Green Bay vs. St. Louis	31	22	410	5
Sept. 28, 1969	Joe Kapp, Minnesota vs. Baltimore	43	28	449	7
Sept. 9, 1968	Pete Beathard, Houston vs. Kansas City	48	23	413	2
Nov. 26, 1967	Sonny Jurgensen, Washington vs. Cleveland	50	32	418	3
Oct. 1, 1967	Joe Namath, N.Y. Jets vs. Miami	39	23	415	3
Sept. 17, 1967	Johnny Unitas, Baltimore vs. Atlanta	32	22	401	2
Nov. 13, 1966	Don Meredith, Dallas vs. Washington	29	21	406	2
Nov. 28, 1965	Sonny Jurgensen, Washington vs. Dallas	43	26	411	3
Oct. 24, 1965	Fran Tarkenton, Minnesota vs. San Francisco	35	21	407	3
Nov. 1, 1964	Len Dawson, Kansas City vs. Denver	38	23	435	6
Oct. 25, 1964	Cotton Davidson, Oakland vs. Denver	36	23	427	5
Oct. 16, 1964	Babe Parilli, Boston vs. Oakland	47	25	422	4
Dec. 22, 1963	Tom Flores, Oakland vs. Houston	29	17	407	6
Nov. 17, 1963	Norm Snead, Washington vs. Pittsburgh	40	23	424	2
Nov. 10, 1963	Don Meredith, Dallas vs. San Francisco	48	30	460	3
Oct. 13, 1963	Charley Johnson, St. Louis vs. Pittsburgh	41	20	428	2
Dec. 16, 1962	Sonny Jurgensen, Philadelphia vs. St. Louis	34	15	419	5
Nov. 18, 1962	Bill Wade, Chicago vs. Dall. Cowboys	46	28	466	2
Oct. 28, 1962	Y.A. Tittle, N.Y. Giants vs. Washington	39	27	505	7
Sept. 15, 1962	Frank Tripucka, Denver vs. Buffalo	56	29	447	2
Dec. 17, 1961	Sonny Jurgensen, Philadelphia vs. Detroit	42	27	403	3
Nov. 19, 1961	George Blanda, Houston vs. N.Y. Titans	32	20	418	7
Oct. 29, 1961	Sonny Jurgensen, Philadelphia vs. Washington	41	27	436	3
Oct. 29, 1961	George Blanda, Houston vs. Buffalo	32	18	464	4
Oct. 13, 1961	Jacky Lee, Houston vs. Boston	41	27	457	2
Dec. 13, 1958	Bobby Layne, Pittsburgh vs. Chi. Cardinals	49	23	409	2
Nov. 8, 1953	Bobby Thomason, Philadelphia vs. N.Y. Giants	44	22	437	4
Oct. 4, 1952	Otto Graham, Cleveland vs. Pittsburgh	49	21	401	3
Sept. 28, 1951	Norm Van Brocklin, Los Angeles vs. N.Y. Yanks	41	27	554	5
Dec. 11, 1949	Johnny Lujack, Chi. Bears vs. Chi. Cardinals	39	24	468	6
Oct. 31, 1948	Jim Hardy, Los Angeles vs. Chi. Cardinals	53	28	406	3
Oct. 31, 1948	Sammy Baugh, Washington vs. Boston	24	17	446	4
Nov. 14, 1943	Sid Luckman, Chi. Bears vs. N.Y. Giants	32	21	433	7

Times 400 or More
65 times by 46 players . . . Jurgensen 5; Fouts, Marino 4; Namath 3; Anderson, Blanda, Johnson, Kramer, Krieg, Meredith, Todd 2.

1,000 YARDS PASS RECEIVING IN A SEASON

Year	Player, Team	No.	Yards	Avg.	Long	TD
1984	Roy Green, St. Louis[2]	78	1,555	19.9	83	12
	John Stallworth, Pittsburgh[3]	80	1,395	17.4	51	11
	Mark Clayton, Miami	73	1,389	19.0	65	18
	Art Monk, Washington	106	1,372	12.9	72	7
	James Lofton, Green Bay[4]	62	1,361	22.0	79	7
	Mark Duper, Miami[2]	71	1,306	18.4	80	8
	Steve Watson, Denver[3]	69	1,170	17.0	73	7
	Steve Largent, Seattle[6]	74	1,164	15.7	65	12
	Tim Smith, Houston[2]	69	1,141	16.5	75	4
	Stacey Bailey, Atlanta	67	1,138	17.0	61	6
	Carlos Carson, Kansas City[2]	57	1,078	18.9	57	4
	Mike Quick, Philadelphia[2]	61	1,052	17.2	90	9
	Todd Christensen, L.A. Raiders[2]	80	1,007	12.6	38	7
	Kevin House, Tampa Bay[2]	76	1,005	13.2	55	5
	Ozzie Newsome, Cleveland[2]	89	1,001	11.2	52	5
1983	Mike Quick, Philadelphia	69	1,409	20.4	83	13
	Carlos Carson, Kansas City	80	1,351	16.9	50	7
	James Lofton, Green Bay[3]	58	1,300	22.4	74	8
	Todd Christensen, L.A. Raiders	92	1,247	13.6	45	12
	Roy Green, St. Louis	78	1,227	15.7	71	14
	Charlie Brown, Washington	78	1,225	15.7	75	8
	Tim Smith, Houston	83	1,176	14.2	47	6
	Kellen Winslow, San Diego[3]	88	1,172	13.3	46	8
	Earnest Gray, N.Y. Giants	78	1,139	14.6	62	5
	Steve Watson, Denver[2]	59	1,133	19.2	78	5
	Cris Collinsworth, Cincinnati[2]	66	1,130	17.1	63	5
	Steve Largent, Seattle[5]	72	1,074	14.9	46	11
	Mark Duper, Miami	51	1,003	19.7	85	10
1982	Wes Chandler, San Diego[3]	49	1,032	21.1	66	9
1981	Alfred Jenkins, Atlanta[2]	70	1,358	19.4	67	13
	James Lofton, Green Bay[2]	71	1,294	18.2	75	8
	Frank Lewis, Buffalo[2]	70	1,244	17.8	33	4
	Steve Watson, Denver	60	1,244	20.7	95	13
	Steve Largent, Seattle[4]	75	1,224	16.3	57	9
	Charlie Joiner, San Diego[4]	70	1,188	17.0	57	7
	Kevin House, Tampa Bay	56	1,176	21.0	84	9
	Wes Chandler, N.O.-San Diego[2]	69	1,142	16.6	51	6
	Dwight Clark, San Francisco	85	1,105	13.0	78	4
	John Stallworth, Pittsburgh[2]	63	1,098	17.4	55	5
	Kellen Winslow, San Diego[2]	88	1,075	12.2	67	10
	Pat Tilley, St. Louis	66	1,040	15.8	75	3
	Stanley Morgan, New England[2]	44	1,029	23.4	76	6
	Harold Carmichael, Philadelphia[3]	61	1,028	16.9	85	6
	Freddie Scott, Detroit	53	1,022	19.3	48	5
	*Cris Collinsworth, Cincinnati	67	1,009	15.1	74	8
	Joe Senser, Minnesota	79	1,004	12.7	53	8
	Ozzie Newsome, Cleveland	69	1,002	14.5	62	6
	Sammy White, Minnesota	66	1,001	15.2	53	3
1980	John Jefferson, San Diego[2]	82	1,340	16.3	58	13
	Kellen Winslow, San Diego	89	1,290	14.5	65	9
	James Lofton, Green Bay	71	1,226	17.3	47	4
	Charlie Joiner, San Diego[3]	71	1,132	15.9	51	4
	Ahmad Rashad, Minnesota[2]	69	1,095	15.9	76	5
	Steve Largent, Seattle[3]	66	1,064	16.1	67	6
	Tony Hill, Dallas[2]	60	1,055	17.6	58	8
	Alfred Jenkins, Atlanta	57	1,026	18.0	57	6
1979	Steve Largent, Seattle[2]	66	1,237	18.7	55	9
	John Stallworth, Pittsburgh	70	1,183	16.9	65	8
	Ahmad Rashad, Minnesota	80	1,156	14.5	52	9
	John Jefferson, San Diego[2]	61	1,090	17.9	65	10
	Frank Lewis, Buffalo	54	1,082	20.0	55	2
	Wes Chandler, New Orleans	65	1,069	16.4	85	6
	Tony Hill, Dallas	60	1,062	17.7	75	10
	Drew Pearson, Dallas[2]	55	1,026	18.7	56	8
	Wallace Francis, Atlanta	74	1,013	13.7	42	8
	Harold Jackson, New England[3]	45	1,013	22.5	59	7
	Charlie Joiner, San Diego[2]	72	1,008	14.0	39	4
	Stanley Morgan, New England	44	1,002	22.8	63	12
1978	Wesley Walker, N.Y. Jets	48	1,169	24.4	77	8
	Steve Largent, Seattle	71	1,168	16.5	57	8
	Harold Carmichael, Philadelphia[2]	55	1,072	19.5	56	8
	*John Jefferson, San Diego	56	1,001	17.9	46	13
1976	Roger Carr, Baltimore	43	1,112	25.9	79	11
	Cliff Branch, Oakland[2]	46	1,111	24.2	88	12
	Charlie Joiner, San Diego	50	1,056	21.1	81	7
1975	Ken Burrough, Houston	53	1,063	20.1	77	8
1974	Cliff Branch, Oakland	60	1,092	18.2	67	13
	Drew Pearson, Dallas	62	1,087	17.5	50	2
1973	Harold Carmichael, Philadelphia	67	1,116	16.7	73	9
1972	Harold Jackson, Philadelphia[2]	62	1,048	16.9	77	4
	John Gilliam, Minnesota	47	1,035	22.0	66	7
1971	Otis Taylor, Kansas City[2]	57	1,110	19.5	82	7
1970	Gene Washington, San Francisco	53	1,100	20.8	79	12
	Marlin Briscoe, Buffalo	57	1,036	18.2	48	8
	Dick Gordon, Chicago	71	1,026	14.5	69	13
	Gary Garrison, San Diego[2]	44	1,006	22.9	67	12
1969	Warren Wells, Oakland[2]	47	1,260	26.8	80	14
	Harold Jackson, Philadelphia	65	1,116	17.2	65	9
	Roy Jefferson, Pittsburgh[2]	67	1,079	16.1	63	9
	Dan Abramowicz, New Orleans	73	1,015	13.9	49	7
	Lance Alworth, San Diego[7]	64	1,003	15.7	76	4
1968	Lance Alworth, San Diego[6]	68	1,312	19.3	80	10
	Don Maynard, N.Y. Jets[5]	57	1,297	22.8	87	10

	Player, Team	No.	Yards	Avg	Long	TD
	George Sauer, N.Y. Jets[3]	66	1,141	17.3	43	3
	Warren Wells, Oakland	53	1,137	21.5	94	11
	Gary Garrison, San Diego	52	1,103	21.2	84	10
	Roy Jefferson, Pittsburgh	58	1,074	18.5	62	11
	Paul Warfield, Cleveland	50	1,067	21.3	65	12
	Homer Jones, N.Y. Giants[3]	45	1,057	23.5	84	7
	Fred Biletnikoff, Oakland	61	1,037	17.0	82	6
	Lance Rentzel, Dallas	54	1,009	18.7	65	6
1967	Don Maynard, N.Y. Jets[4]	71	1,434	20.2	75	10
	Ben Hawkins, Philadelphia	59	1,265	21.4	87	10
	Homer Jones, N.Y. Giants[2]	49	1,209	24.7	70	13
	Jackie Smith, St. Louis	56	1,205	21.5	76	9
	George Sauer, N.Y. Jets[2]	75	1,189	15.9	61	6
	Lance Alworth, San Diego[5]	52	1,010	19.4	71	9
1966	Lance Alworth, San Diego[4]	73	1,383	18.9	78	13
	Otis Taylor, Kansas City	58	1,297	22.4	89	8
	Pat Studstill, Detroit	67	1,266	18.9	99	5
	Bob Hayes, Dallas[2]	64	1,232	19.3	95	13
	Charlie Frazier, Houston	57	1,129	19.8	79	12
	Charley Taylor, Washington	72	1,119	15.5	86	12
	George Sauer, N.Y. Jets	63	1,081	17.2	77	5
	Homer Jones, N.Y. Giants	48	1,044	21.8	98	8
	Art Powell, Oakland[5]	53	1,026	19.4	46	11
1965	Lance Alworth, San Diego[3]	69	1,602	23.2	85	14
	Dave Parks, San Francisco	80	1,344	16.8	53	12
	Don Maynard, N.Y. Jets[3]	68	1,218	17.9	56	14
	Pete Retzlaff, Philadelphia	66	1,190	18.0	78	10
	Lionel Taylor, Denver[4]	85	1,131	13.3	63	6
	Tommy McDonald, Los Angeles[3]	67	1,036	15.5	51	9
	*Bob Hayes, Dallas	46	1,003	21.8	82	12
1964	Charley Hennigan, Houston[3]	101	1,546	15.3	53	8
	Art Powell, Oakland[4]	76	1,361	17.9	77	11
	Lance Alworth, San Diego[2]	61	1,235	20.2	82	13
	Johnny Morris, Chicago	93	1,200	12.9	63	10
	Elbert Dubenion, Buffalo	42	1,139	27.1	72	10
	Terry Barr, Detroit[2]	57	1,030	18.1	58	9
1963	Bobby Mitchell, Washington[2]	69	1,436	20.8	99	7
	Art Powell, Oakland[3]	73	1,304	17.9	85	16
	Buddy Dial, Pittsburgh[2]	60	1,295	21.6	83	9
	Lance Alworth, San Diego	61	1,205	19.8	85	11
	Del Shofner, N.Y. Giants[4]	64	1,181	18.5	70	9
	Lionel Taylor, Denver[3]	78	1,101	14.1	72	10
	Terry Barr, Detroit	66	1,086	16.5	75	13
	Charley Hennigan, Houston[2]	61	1,051	17.2	83	10
	Sonny Randle, St. Louis[2]	51	1,014	19.9	68	12
	Bake Turner, N.Y. Jets	71	1,009	14.2	53	6
1962	Bobby Mitchell, Washington	72	1,384	19.2	81	11
	Sonny Randle, St. Louis	63	1,158	18.4	86	7
	Tommy McDonald, Philadelphia[2]	58	1,146	19.8	60	10
	Del Shofner, N.Y. Giants[3]	53	1,133	21.4	69	12
	Art Powell, N.Y. Titans[2]	64	1,130	17.7	80	8
	Frank Clarke, Dall. Cowboys	47	1,043	22.2	66	14
	Don Maynard, N.Y. Titans[2]	56	1,041	18.6	86	8
1961	Charley Hennigan, Houston	82	1,746	21.3	80	12
	Lionel Taylor, Denver[2]	100	1,176	11.8	52	4
	Bill Groman, Houston[2]	50	1,175	23.5	80	17
	Tommy McDonald, Philadelphia	64	1,144	17.9	66	13
	Del Shofner, N.Y. Giants[2]	68	1,125	16.5	46	11
	Jim Phillips, Los Angeles	78	1,092	14.0	69	5
	*Mike Ditka, Chicago	56	1,076	19.2	76	12
	Dave Kocourek, San Diego	55	1,055	19.2	76	4
	Buddy Dial, Pittsburgh	53	1,047	19.8	88	12
	R.C. Owens, San Francisco	55	1,032	18.8	54	5
1960	*Bill Groman, Houston	72	1,473	20.5	92	12
	Raymond Berry, Baltimore	74	1,298	17.5	70	10
	Don Maynard, N.Y. Titans	72	1,265	17.6	65	6
	Lionel Taylor, Denver	92	1,235	13.4	80	12
	Art Powell, N.Y. Titans	69	1,167	16.9	76	14
1958	Del Shofner, Los Angeles	51	1,097	21.5	92	8
1956	Bill Howton, Green Bay[2]	55	1,188	21.6	66	12
	Harlon Hill, Chi. Bears[2]	47	1,128	24.0	79	11
1954	Bob Boyd, Los Angeles	53	1,212	22.9	80	6
	*Harlon Hill, Chi. Bears	45	1,124	25.0	76	12
1953	Pete Pihos, Philadelphia	63	1,049	16.7	59	10
1952	*Bill Howton, Green Bay	53	1,231	23.2	90	13
1951	Elroy (Crazylegs) Hirsch, Los Angeles	66	1,495	22.7	91	17
1950	Tom Fears, Los Angeles[2]	84	1,116	13.3	53	7
	Cloyce Box, Detroit	50	1,009	20.2	82	11
1949	Bob Mann, Detroit	66	1,014	15.4	64	4
	Tom Fears, Los Angeles	77	1,013	13.2	51	9
1945	Jim Benton, Cleveland	45	1,067	23.7	84	8
1942	Don Hutson, Green Bay	74	1,211	16.4	73	17

*First year in the league.

250 YARDS PASS RECEIVING IN A GAME

Date	Player, Team, Opponent	No.	Yards	TD
Dec. 20, 1982	Wes Chandler, San Diego vs. Cincinnati	10	260	2
Sept. 23, 1979	*Jerry Butler, Buffalo vs. N.Y. Jets	10	255	4
Nov. 4, 1962	Sonny Randle, St. Louis vs. N.Y. Giants	16	256	1
Oct. 28, 1962	Del Shofner, N.Y. Giants vs. Washington	11	269	1
Oct. 13, 1961	Charley Hennigan, Houston vs. Boston	13	272	1
Oct. 21, 1956	Billy Howton, Green Bay vs. Los Angeles	7	257	2
Dec. 3, 1950	Cloyce Box, Detroit vs. Baltimore	12	302	4
Nov. 22, 1945	Jim Benton, Cleveland vs. Detroit	10	303	1

*First year in the league.

2,000 COMBINED NET YARDS GAINED IN A SEASON

Year	Player, Team	Rushing Att.-Yds.	Pass Rec.	Punt Ret.	Kickoff Ret.	Fum. Runs	Total Yds.
1984	Eric Dickerson, L.A. Rams	379-2,105	21-139	0-0	0-0	4-15	404-2,259
	James Wilder, Tampa Bay	407-1,544	85-685	0-0	0-0	4-0	496-2,229
	Walter Payton, Chicago	381-1,684	45-368	0-0	0-0	1-0	427-2,052
1983	*Eric Dickerson, L.A. Rams	390-1,808	51-404	0-0	0-0	1-0	442-2,212
	William Andrews, Atlanta	331-1,567	59-609	0-0	0-0	2-0	392-2,176
	Walter Payton, Chicago	314-1,421	53-607	0-0	0-0	2-0	369-2,028
1981	*James Brooks, San Diego	109-525	46-329	22-290	40-949	2-0	219-2,093
	William Andrews, Atlanta	289-1,301	81-735	0-0	1-6	2-0	370-2,036
1980	Bruce Harper, N.Y. Jets	45-126	50-634	28-242	49-1,070	3-0	175-2,072
1979	Wilbert Montgomery, Phil.	338-1,512	41-494	0-0	1-6	2-0	382-2,012
1978	Bruce Harper, N.Y. Jets	58-303	13-196	30-378	55-1,280	1-0	157-2,157
1977	Walter Payton, Chicago	339-1,852	27-269	0-0	2-95	5-0	373-2,216
	Terry Metcalf, St. Louis	149-739	34-403	14-108	32-772	1-0	230-2,022
1975	Terry Metcalf, St. Louis	165-816	43-378	23-285	35-960	2-23	268-2,462
	O.J. Simpson, Buffalo	329-1,817	28-426	0-0	0-0	1-0	358-2,243
1974	Mack Herron, New England	231-824	38-474	35-517	28-629	3-0	335-2,444
	Otis Armstrong, Denver	263-1,407	38-405	0-0	16-386	1-0	318-2,198
	Terry Metcalf, St. Louis	152-718	50-377	26-340	20-623	7-0	255-2,058
1973	O.J. Simpson, Buffalo	332-2,003	6-70	0-0	0-0	0-0	338-2,073
1966	Gale Sayers, Chicago	229-1,231	34-447	6-44	23-718	0-0	295-2,440
	Leroy Kelly, Cleveland	209-1,141	32-366	13-104	19-403	0-0	273-2,014
1965	Gale Sayers, Chicago	166-867	29-507	16-238	21-660	4-0	236-2,272
1963	Timmy Brown, Philadelphia	192-841	36-487	16-152	33-945	2-3	279-2,428
	Jim Brown, Cleveland	291-1,863	24-268	0-0	0-0	0-0	315-2,131
1962	Timmy Brown, Philadelphia	137-545	52-849	6-81	28-629	4-0	229-2,306
	Dick Christy, N.Y. Titans	114-535	62-538	15-250	38-824	2-0	231-2,147
1961	Billy Cannon, Houston	200-948	43-586	9-70	18-439	2-0	272-2,043
1960	*Abner Haynes, Dall. Texans	156-875	55-576	14-215	19-434	4-0	248-2,100

*First year in the league.

300 COMBINED NET YARDS GAINED IN A GAME

Date	Player, Team, Opponent	No.	Yards	TD
Dec. 21, 1975	Walter Payton, Chicago vs. New Orleans	32	300	1
Nov. 23, 1975	Greg Pruitt, Cleveland vs. Cincinnati	28	304	2
Nov. 1, 1970	Eugene (Mercury) Morris, Miami vs. Baltimore	17	302	0
Oct. 4, 1970	O. J. Simpson, Buffalo vs. N.Y. Jets	26	303	2
Dec. 6, 1969	Jerry LeVias, Houston vs. N.Y. Jets	18	329	1
Nov. 2, 1969	Travis Williams, Green Bay vs. Pittsburgh	11	314	3
Dec. 3, 1966	Gale Sayers, Chicago vs. Minnesota	20	339	2
Dec. 12, 1965	Gale Sayers, Chicago vs. San Francisco	17	336	6
Nov. 17, 1963	Gary Ballman, Pittsburgh vs. Washington	12	320	2
Dec. 16, 1962	Timmy Brown, Philadelphia vs. St. Louis	19	341	2
Dec. 10, 1961	Billy Cannon, Houston vs. N.Y. Titans	32	373	5
Nov 19, 1961	Jim Brown, Cleveland vs. Philadelphia	38	313	4
Dec. 3, 1950	Cloyce Box, Detroit vs. Baltimore	13	302	4
Oct. 29, 1950	Wally Triplett, Detroit vs. Los Angeles	11	331	1
Nov. 22, 1945	Jim Benton, Cleveland vs. Detroit	10	303	1

TOP 10 SCORERS

Player	Years	TD	FG	PAT	TP
George Blanda	26	9	335	943	2,002
Jan Stenerud	18	0	358	539	1,613
Jim Turner	16	1	304	521	1,439
Jim Bakken	17	0	282	534	1,380
Fred Cox	15	0	282	519	1,365
Lou Groza	17	1	234	641	1,349
Mark Moseley	14	0	266	426	1,224
Gino Cappelletti	11	42	176	350	1,130
Don Cockroft	13	0	216	432	1,080
Garo Yepremian	14	0	210	444	1,074

Cappelletti's total includes four two-point conversions.

TOP 10 TOUCHDOWN SCORERS

Player	Years	Rush	Pass Rec.	Returns	Total TD
Jim Brown	9	106	20	0	126
Lenny Moore	12	63	48	2	113
John Riggins	13	96	12	0	108
Don Hutson	11	3	99	3	105
Franco Harris	13	91	9	0	100
Walter Payton	10	89	9	0	98
Jim Taylor	10	83	10	0	93
Bobby Mitchell	11	18	65	8	91
Leroy Kelly	10	74	13	3	90
Charley Taylor	13	11	79	0	90

TOP 10 RUSHERS

Player	Years	Att.	Yards	Avg.	Long	TD
Walter Payton	10	3,047	13,309	4.4	76	89
Jim Brown	9	2,359	12,312	5.2	80	106
Franco Harris	13	2,949	12,120	4.1	75	91
O. J. Simpson	11	2,404	11,236	4.7	94	61
John Riggins	13	2,740	10,675	3.9	66	96
Tony Dorsett	8	2,136	9,525	4.5	99	59
Earl Campbell	7	2,029	8,764	4.3	81	73
Jim Taylor	10	1,941	8,597	4.4	84	83
Joe Perry	14	1,737	8,378	4.8	78	53
Larry Csonka	11	1,891	8,081	4.3	54	64

TOP 10 PASSERS

Player	Years	Att.	Comp.	Pct. Comp.	Yards	TD	Pct. TD	Int.	Pct. Int.	Avg. Gain	Rating
Joe Montana	6	2,077	1,324	63.7	15,609	106	5.1	54	2.6	7.52	92.7
Roger Staubach	11	2,958	1,685	57.0	22,700	153	5.2	109	3.7	7.67	83.4
Danny White	9	1,943	1,155	59.4	14,754	109	5.6	90	4.6	7.59	82.7
Sonny Jurgensen	18	4,262	2,433	57.1	32,224	255	6.0	189	4.4	7.56	82.6
Len Dawson	19	3,741	2,136	57.1	28,711	239	6.4	183	4.9	7.67	82.6
Ken Anderson	14	4,420	2,627	59.4	32,497	194	4.4	158	3.6	7.35	82.0
Dan Fouts	12	4,380	2,585	59.0	33,854	201	4.6	185	4.2	7.73	81.2
Bart Starr	16	3,149	1,808	57.4	24,718	152	4.8	138	4.4	7.85	80.5
Fran Tarkenton	18	6,467	3,686	57.0	47,003	342	5.3	266	4.1	7.27	80.4
Joe Theismann	11	3,301	1,877	56.9	23,432	152	4.6	122	3.7	7.10	79.0

1,500 or more attempts. The passing ratings are based on performance standards established for completion percentage, interception percentage, touchdown percentage, and average gain. Passers are allocated points according to how their marks compare with those standards.

TOP 10 PASS RECEIVERS

Player	Years	No.	Yards	Avg.	Long	TD
Charlie Joiner	16	657	10,774	16.4	87	56
Charley Taylor	13	649	9,110	14.0	88	79
Don Maynard	15	633	11,834	18.7	87	88
Raymond Berry	13	631	9,275	14.7	70	68
Harold Carmichael	14	590	8,985	15.2	85	79
Fred Biletnikoff	14	589	8,974	15.2	82	76
Harold Jackson	16	579	10,372	17.9	79	76
Lionel Taylor	10	567	7,195	12.7	80	45
Steve Largent	9	545	8,772	16.1	74	60
Lance Alworth	11	542	10,266	18.9	85	85

TOP 10 INTERCEPTORS

Player	Years	No.	Yards	Avg.	Long	TD
Paul Krause	16	81	1,185	14.6	81	3
Emlen Tunnell	14	79	1,282	16.2	55	4
Dick (Night Train) Lane	14	68	1,207	17.8	80	5
Ken Riley	15	65	596	9.2	66	5
Dick LeBeau	13	62	762	12.3	70	3
Emmitt Thomas	13	58	937	16.2	73	5
Bobby Boyd	9	57	994	17.4	74	4
Johnny Robinson	12	57	741	13.0	57	1
Mel Blount	14	57	736	12.9	52	2
Lem Barney	11	56	1,077	19.2	71	7
Pat Fischer	17	56	941	16.8	69	4

TOP 10 PUNTERS

Player	Years	No.	Yards	Avg.	Long	Blk.
Sammy Baugh	16	338	15,245	45.1	85	9
Tommy Davis	11	511	22,833	44.7	82	2
Yale Lary	11	503	22,279	44.3	74	4
Horace Gillom	7	385	16,872	43.8	80	5
Jerry Norton	11	358	15,671	43.8	78	2
Don Chandler	12	660	28,678	43.5	90	4
Jerrel Wilson	16	1,072	46,139	43.0	72	12
Norm Van Brocklin	12	523	22,413	42.9	72	3
Ray Guy	12	870	37,246	42.8	74	3
Danny Villanueva	8	488	20,862	42.8	68	2

300 or more punts.

TOP 10 PUNT RETURNERS

Player	Years	No.	Yards	Avg.	Long	TD
George McAfee	8	112	1,431	12.8	74	2
Jack Christiansen	8	85	1,084	12.8	89	8
Claude Gibson	5	110	1,381	12.6	85	3
Billy Johnson	10	240	2,954	12.3	87	6
Bill Dudley	9	124	1,515	12.2	96	3
Dana McLemore	3	83	1,008	12.1	93	3
Rick Upchurch	9	248	3,008	12.1	92	8
Mack Herron	3	84	982	11.7	66	0
Bill Thompson	13	157	1,814	11.6	60	0
Rodger Bird	3	94	1,063	11.3	78	0

75 or more returns.

TOP 10 KICKOFF RETURNERS

Player	Years	No.	Yards	Avg.	Long	TD
Gale Sayers	7	91	2,781	30.6	103	6
Lynn Chandnois	7	92	2,720	29.6	93	3
Abe Woodson	9	193	5,538	28.7	105	5
Claude (Buddy) Young	6	90	2,514	27.9	104	2
Travis Williams	5	102	2,801	27.5	105	6
Joe Arenas	7	139	3,798	27.3	96	1
Clarence Davis	8	79	2,140	27.1	76	0
Steve Van Buren	8	76	2,030	26.7	98	3
Lenny Lyles	12	81	2,161	26.7	103	3
Eugene (Mercury) Morris	8	111	2,947	26.5	105	3

75 or more returns.

YEARLY STATISTICAL LEADERS

ANNUAL SCORING LEADERS

Year	Player, Team	TD	FG	PAT	TP
1984	Ray Wersching, San Francisco, NFC	0	25	56	131
	Gary Anderson, Pittsburgh, AFC	0	24	45	117
1983	Mark Moseley, Washington, NFC	0	33	62	161
	Gary Anderson, Pittsburgh, AFC	0	27	38	119
1982	*Marcus Allen, L.A. Raiders, AFC	14	0	0	84
	Wendell Tyler, L.A. Rams, NFC	13	0	0	78
1981	Ed Murray, Detroit, NFC	0	25	46	121
	Rafael Septien, Dallas, NFC	0	27	40	121
	Jim Breech, Cincinnati, AFC	0	22	49	115
	Nick Lowery, Kansas City, AFC	0	26	37	115
1980	John Smith, New England, AFC	0	26	51	129
	*Ed Murray, Detroit, NFC	0	27	35	116
1979	John Smith, New England, AFC	0	23	46	115
	Mark Moseley, Washington, NFC	0	25	39	114
1978	*Frank Corral, Los Angeles, NFC	0	29	31	118
	Pat Leahy, N.Y. Jets, AFC	0	22	41	107
1977	Errol Mann, Oakland, AFC	0	20	39	99
	Walter Payton, Chicago, NFC	16	0	0	96
1976	Toni Linhart, Baltimore, AFC	0	20	49	109
	Mark Moseley, Washington, NFC	0	22	31	97
1975	O.J. Simpson, Buffalo, AFC	23	0	0	138
	Chuck Foreman, Minnesota, NFC	22	0	0	132
1974	Chester Marcol, Green Bay, NFC	0	25	19	94
	Roy Gerela, Pittsburgh, AFC	0	20	33	93
1973	David Ray, Los Angeles, NFC	0	30	40	130
	Roy Gerela, Pittsburgh, AFC	0	29	36	123
1972	*Chester Marcol, Green Bay, NFC	0	33	29	128
	Bobby Howfield, N.Y. Jets, AFC	0	27	40	121
1971	Garo Yepremian, Miami, AFC	0	28	33	117
	Curt Knight, Washington, NFC	0	29	27	114
1970	Fred Cox, Minnesota, NFC	0	30	35	125
	Jan Stenerud, Kansas City, AFC	0	30	26	116
1969	Jim Turner, N.Y. Jets, AFL	0	32	33	129
	Fred Cox, Minnesota, NFL	0	26	43	121
1968	Jim Turner, N.Y. Jets, AFL	0	34	43	145
	Leroy Kelly, Cleveland, NFL	20	0	0	120
1967	Jim Bakken, St. Louis, NFL	0	27	36	117
	George Blanda, Oakland, AFL	0	20	56	116
1966	Gino Cappelletti, Boston, AFL	6	16	35	119
	Bruce Gossett, Los Angeles, NFL	0	28	29	113
1965	*Gale Sayers, Chicago, NFL	22	0	0	132
	Gino Cappelletti, Boston, AFL	9	17	27	132
1964	Gino Cappelletti, Boston, AFL	7	25	36	155
	Lenny Moore, Baltimore, NFL	20	0	0	120
1963	Gino Cappelletti, Boston, AFL	2	22	35	113
	Don Chandler, N.Y. Giants, NFL	0	18	52	106
1962	Gene Mingo, Denver, AFL	4	27	32	137
	Jim Taylor, Green Bay, NFL	19	0	0	114
1961	Gino Cappelletti, Boston, AFL	8	17	48	147
	Paul Hornung, Green Bay, NFL	10	15	41	146
1960	Paul Hornung, Green Bay, NFL	15	15	41	176
	*Gene Mingo, Denver, AFL	6	18	33	123
1959	Paul Hornung, Green Bay	7	7	31	94
1958	Jim Brown, Cleveland	18	0	0	108
1957	Sam Baker, Washington	1	14	29	77
	Lou Groza, Cleveland	0	15	32	77
1956	Bobby Layne, Detroit	5	12	33	99
1955	Doak Walker, Detroit	7	9	27	96
1954	Bobby Walston, Philadelphia	11	4	36	114
1953	Gordy Soltau, San Francisco	6	10	48	114
1952	Gordy Soltau, San Francisco	7	6	34	94
1951	Elroy (Crazylegs) Hirsch, Los Angeles	17	0	0	102
1950	*Doak Walker, Detroit	11	8	38	128
1949	Pat Harder, Chi. Cardinals	8	3	45	102
	Gene Roberts, N.Y. Giants	17	0	0	102
1948	Pat Harder, Chi. Cardinals	6	7	53	110
1947	Pat Harder, Chi. Cardinals	7	7	39	102
1946	Ted Fritsch, Green Bay	10	9	13	100
1945	Steve Van Buren, Philadelphia	18	0	2	110
1944	Don Hutson, Green Bay	9	0	31	85
1943	Don Hutson, Green Bay	12	3	36	117
1942	Don Hutson, Green Bay	17	1	33	138
1941	Don Hutson, Green Bay	12	1	20	95
1940	Don Hutson, Green Bay	7	0	15	57
1939	Andy Farkas, Washington	11	0	2	68
1938	Clarke Hinkle, Green Bay	7	3	7	58
1937	Jack Manders, Chi. Bears	5	8	15	69
1936	Earl (Dutch) Clark, Detroit	7	4	19	73
1935	Earl (Dutch) Clark, Detroit	6	1	16	55
1934	Jack Manders, Chi. Bears	3	10	28	76
1933	Ken Strong, N.Y. Giants	6	5	13	64
	Glenn Presnell, Portsmouth	6	6	10	64
1932	Earl (Dutch) Clark, Portsmouth	6	3	10	55

*First year in the league.

ANNUAL LEADERS—MOST FIELD GOALS MADE

Year	Player, Team	Att.	Made	Pct.
1984	*Paul McFadden, Philadelphia, NFC	37	30	81.1
	Gary Anderson, Pittsburgh, AFC	32	24	75.0
	Matt Bahr, Cleveland, AFC	32	24	75.0
1983	*Ali Haji-Sheikh, N.Y. Giants, NFC	42	35	83.3
	*Raul Allegre, Baltimore, AFC	35	30	85.7
1982	Mark Moseley, Washington, NFC	21	20	95.2
	Nick Lowery, Kansas City, AFC	24	19	79.2
1981	Rafael Septien, Dallas, NFC	35	27	77.1
	Nick Lowery, Kansas City, AFC	36	26	72.2
1980	*Ed Murray, Detroit, NFC	42	27	64.3
	John Smith, New England, AFC	34	26	76.5
	Fred Steinfort, Denver, AFC	34	26	76.5
1979	Mark Moseley, Washington, NFC	33	25	75.8
	John Smith, New England, AFC	33	23	69.7
1978	*Frank Corral, Los Angeles, NFC	43	29	67.4
	Pat Leahy, N.Y. Jets, AFC	30	22	73.3
1977	Mark Moseley, Washington, NFC	37	21	56.8
	Errol Mann, Oakland, AFC	28	20	71.4
1976	Mark Moseley, Washington, NFC	34	22	64.7
	Jan Stenerud, Kansas City, AFC	38	21	55.3
1975	Jan Stenerud, Kansas City, AFC	32	22	68.8
	Toni Fritsch, Dallas, NFC	35	22	62.9
1974	Chester Marcol, Green Bay, NFC	39	25	64.1
	Roy Gerela, Pittsburgh, AFC	29	20	69.0
1973	David Ray, Los Angeles, NFC	47	30	63.8
	Roy Gerela, Pittsburgh, AFC	43	29	67.4
1972	*Chester Marcol, Green Bay, NFC	48	33	68.8
	Roy Gerela, Pittsburgh, AFC	41	28	68.3
1971	Curt Knight, Washington, NFC	49	29	59.2
	Garo Yepremian, Miami, AFC	40	28	70.0
1970	Fred Cox, Minnesota, NFC	46	30	65.2
	Jan Stenerud, Kansas City, AFC	42	30	71.4
1969	Jim Turner, N.Y. Jets, AFL	47	32	68.1
	Fred Cox, Minnesota, NFL	37	26	70.3
1968	Jim Turner, N.Y. Jets, AFL	46	34	73.9
	Mac Percival, Chicago, NFL	36	25	69.4
1967	Jim Bakken, St. Louis, NFL	39	27	69.2
	Jan Stenerud, Kansas City, AFL	36	21	58.3
1966	Bruce Gossett, Los Angeles, NFL	49	28	57.1
	Mike Mercer, Oakland-Kansas City, AFL	30	21	70.0
1965	Pete Gogolak, Buffalo, AFL	46	28	60.9
	Fred Cox, Minnesota, NFL	35	23	65.7
1964	Jim Bakken, St. Louis, NFL	38	25	65.8
	Gino Cappelletti, Boston, AFL	39	25	64.1
1963	Jim Martin, Baltimore, NFL	39	24	61.5
	Gino Cappelletti, Boston, AFL	38	22	57.9
1962	Gene Mingo, Denver, AFL	39	27	69.2
	Lou Michaels, Pittsburgh, NFL	42	26	61.9
1961	Steve Myhra, Baltimore, NFL	39	21	53.8
	Gino Cappelletti, Boston, AFL	32	17	53.1
1960	Tommy Davis, San Francisco, NFL	32	19	59.4
	*Gene Mingo, Denver, AFL	28	18	64.3
1959	Pat Summerall, New York Giants	29	20	69.0
1958	Paige Cothren, Los Angeles	25	14	56.0
	*Tom Miner, Pittsburgh	28	14	50.0
1957	Lou Groza, Cleveland	22	15	68.2
1956	Sam Baker, Washington	25	17	68.0
1955	Fred Cone, Green Bay	24	16	66.7
1954	Lou Groza, Cleveland	24	16	66.7
1953	Lou Groza, Cleveland	26	23	88.5
1952	Lou Groza, Cleveland	33	19	57.6
1951	Bob Waterfield, Los Angeles	23	13	56.5
1950	*Lou Groza, Cleveland	19	13	68.4
1949	Cliff Patton, Philadelphia	18	9	50.0
	Bob Waterfield, Los Angeles	16	9	56.3
1948	Cliff Patton, Philadelphia	12	8	66.7
1947	Ward Cuff, Green Bay	16	7	43.8
	Pat Harder, Chi. Cardinals	10	7	70.0
	Bob Waterfield, Los Angeles	16	7	43.8
1946	Ted Fritsch, Green Bay	17	9	52.9
1945	Joe Aguirre, Washington	13	7	53.8
1944	Ken Strong, N.Y. Giants	12	6	50.0
1943	Ward Cuff, N.Y. Giants	9	3	33.3
	Don Hutson, Green Bay	5	3	60.0
1942	Bill Daddio, Chi. Cardinals	10	5	50.0
1941	Clarke Hinkle, Green Bay	14	6	42.9
1940	Clarke Hinkle, Green Bay	14	9	64.3
1939	Ward Cuff, N.Y. Giants	16	7	43.8
1938	Ward Cuff, N.Y. Giants	9	5	55.6
	Ralph Kercheval, Brooklyn	13	5	38.5
1937	Jack Manders, Chi. Bears		8	
1936	Jack Manders, Chi. Bears		7	
	Armand Niccolai, Pittsburgh		7	
1935	Armand Niccolai, Pittsburgh		6	
	Bill Smith, Chi. Cardinals		6	
1934	Jack Manders, Chi. Bears		10	
1933	*Jack Manders, Chi. Bears		6	
	Glenn Presnell, Portsmouth		6	
1932	Earl (Dutch) Clark, Portsmouth		3	

*First year in the league.

ANNUAL RUSHING LEADERS

Year	Player, Team	Att.	Yards	Avg.	TD
1984	Eric Dickerson, L.A. Rams, NFC	379	2,105	5.6	14
	Earnest Jackson, San Diego, AFC	296	1,179	4.0	8
1983	*Eric Dickerson, L.A. Rams, NFC	390	1,808	4.6	18
	*Curt Warner, Seattle, AFC	335	1,449	4.3	13
1982	Freeman McNeil, N.Y. Jets, AFC	151	786	5.2	6
	Tony Dorsett, Dallas, NFC	177	745	4.2	5
1981	*George Rogers, New Orleans, NFC	378	1,674	4.4	13
	Earl Campbell, Houston, AFC	361	1,376	3.8	10
1980	Earl Campbell, Houston, AFC	373	1,934	5.2	13
	Walter Payton, Chicago, NFC	317	1,460	4.6	6
1979	Earl Campbell, Houston, AFC	368	1,697	4.6	19
	Walter Payton, Chicago, NFC	369	1,610	4.4	14
1978	*Earl Campbell, Houston, AFC	302	1,450	4.8	13
	Walter Payton, Chicago, NFC	333	1,395	4.2	11

1977	Walter Payton, Chicago, NFC	339	1,852	5.5	14
	Mark van Eeghen, Oakland, AFC	324	1,273	3.9	7
1976	O.J. Simpson, Buffalo, AFC	290	1,503	5.2	8
	Walter Payton, Chicago, NFC	311	1,390	4.5	13
1975	O.J. Simpson, Buffalo, AFC	329	1,817	5.5	16
	Jim Otis, St. Louis, NFC	269	1,076	4.0	5
1974	Otis Armstrong, Denver, AFC	263	1,407	5.3	9
	Lawrence McCutcheon, Los Angeles, NFC	236	1,109	4.7	3
1973	O.J. Simpson, Buffalo, AFC	332	2,003	6.0	12
	John Brockington, Green Bay, NFC	265	1,144	4.3	3
1972	O.J. Simpson, Buffalo, AFC	292	1,251	4.3	6
	Larry Brown, Washington, NFC	285	1,216	4.3	8
1971	Floyd Little, Denver, AFC	284	1,133	4.0	6
	*John Brockington, Green Bay, NFC	216	1,105	5.1	4
1970	Larry Brown, Washington, NFC	237	1,125	4.7	5
	Floyd Little, Denver, AFC	209	901	4.3	3
1969	Gale Sayers, Chicago, NFL	236	1,032	4.4	8
	Dickie Post, San Diego, AFL	182	873	4.8	6
1968	Leroy Kelly, Cleveland, NFL	248	1,239	5.0	16
	*Paul Robinson, Cincinnati, AFL	238	1,023	4.3	8
1967	Jim Nance, Boston, AFL	269	1,216	4.5	7
	Leroy Kelly, Cleveland, NFL	235	1,205	5.1	11
1966	Jim Nance, Boston, AFL	299	1,458	4.9	11
	Gale Sayers, Chicago, NFL	229	1,231	5.4	8
1965	Jim Brown, Cleveland, NFL	289	1,544	5.3	17
	Paul Lowe, San Diego, AFL	222	1,121	5.0	7
1964	Jim Brown, Cleveland, NFL	280	1,446	5.2	7
	Cookie Gilchrist, Buffalo, AFL	230	981	4.3	6
1963	Jim Brown, Cleveland, NFL	291	1,863	6.4	12
	Clem Daniels, Oakland, AFL	215	1,099	5.1	3
1962	Jim Taylor, Green Bay, NFL	272	1,474	5.4	19
	*Cookie Gilchrist, Buffalo, AFL	214	1,096	5.1	13
1961	Jim Brown, Cleveland, NFL	305	1,408	4.6	8
	Billy Cannon, Houston, AFL	200	948	4.7	6
1960	Jim Brown, Cleveland, NFL	215	1,257	5.8	9
	*Abner Haynes, Dall. Texans, AFL	156	875	5.6	9
1959	Jim Brown, Cleveland	290	1,329	4.6	14
1958	Jim Brown, Cleveland	257	1,527	5.9	17
1957	*Jim Brown, Cleveland	202	942	4.7	9
1956	Rick Casares, Chi. Bears	234	1,126	4.8	12
1955	*Alan Ameche, Baltimore	213	961	4.5	9
1954	Joe Perry, San Francisco	173	1,049	6.1	8
1953	Joe Perry, San Francisco	192	1,018	5.3	10
1952	Dan Towler, Los Angeles	156	894	5.7	10
1951	Eddie Price, N.Y. Giants	271	971	3.6	7
1950	*Marion Motley, Cleveland	140	810	5.8	3
1949	Steve Van Buren, Philadelphia	263	1,146	4.4	11
1948	Steve Van Buren, Philadelphia	201	945	4.7	10
1947	Steve Van Buren, Philadelphia	217	1,008	4.6	13
1946	Bill Dudley, Pittsburgh	146	604	4.1	3
1945	Steve Van Buren, Philadelphia	143	832	5.8	15
1944	Bill Paschal, N.Y. Giants	196	737	3.8	9
1943	*Bill Paschal, N.Y. Giants	147	572	3.9	10
1942	*Bill Dudley, Pittsburgh	162	696	4.3	5
1941	Clarence (Pug) Manders, Brooklyn	111	486	4.4	5
1940	Byron (Whizzer) White, Detroit	146	514	3.5	5
1939	*Bill Osmanski, Chicago	121	699	5.8	7
1938	*Byron (Whizzer) White, Pittsburgh	152	567	3.7	4
1937	Cliff Battles, Washington	216	874	4.0	5
1936	*Alphonse (Tuffy) Leemans, N.Y. Giants	206	830	4.0	2
1935	Doug Russell, Chi. Cardinals	140	499	3.6	0
1934	*Beattie Feathers, Chi. Bears	101	1,004	9.9	8
1933	Jim Musick, Boston	173	809	4.7	5
1932	*Cliff Battles, Boston	148	576	3.9	3

**First year in the league.*

ANNUAL PASSING LEADERS

Year	Player, Team	Att.	Comp.	Yards	TD	Int.
1984	Dan Marino, Miami, AFC	564	362	5,084	48	17
	Joe Montana, San Francisco, NFC	432	279	3,630	28	10
1983	Steve Bartkowski, Atlanta, NFC	432	274	3,167	22	5
	*Dan Marino, Miami, AFC	296	173	2,210	20	6
1982	Ken Anderson, Cincinnati, AFC	309	218	2,495	12	9
	Joe Theismann, Washington, NFC	252	161	2,033	13	9
1981	Ken Anderson, Cincinnati, AFC	479	300	3,754	29	10
	Joe Montana, San Francisco, NFC	488	311	3,565	19	12
1980	Brian Sipe, Cleveland, AFC	554	337	4,132	30	14
	Ron Jaworski, Philadelphia, NFC	451	257	3,529	27	12
1979	Roger Staubach, Dallas, NFC	461	267	3,586	27	11
	Dan Fouts, San Diego, AFC	530	332	4,082	24	24
1978	Roger Staubach, Dallas, NFC	413	231	3,190	25	16
	Terry Bradshaw, Pittsburgh, AFC	368	207	2,915	28	20
1977	Bob Griese, Miami, AFC	307	180	2,252	22	13
	Roger Staubach, Dallas, NFC	361	210	2,620	18	9
1976	Ken Stabler, Oakland, AFC	291	194	2,737	27	17
	James Harris, Los Angeles, NFC	158	91	1,460	8	6
1975	Ken Anderson, Cincinnati, AFC	377	228	3,169	21	11
	Fran Tarkenton, Minnesota, NFC	425	273	2,994	25	13
1974	Ken Anderson, Cincinnati, AFC	328	213	2,667	18	10
	Sonny Jurgensen, Washington, NFC	167	107	1,185	11	5
1973	Roger Staubach, Dallas, NFC	286	179	2,428	23	15
	Ken Stabler, Oakland, AFC	260	163	1,997	14	10
1972	Norm Snead, N.Y. Giants, NFC	325	196	2,307	17	12
	Earl Morrall, Miami, AFC	150	83	1,360	11	7
1971	Roger Staubach, Dallas, NFC	211	126	1,882	15	4
	Bob Griese, Miami, AFC	263	145	2,089	19	9
1970	John Brodie, San Francisco, NFC	378	223	2,941	24	10
	Daryle Lamonica, Oakland, AFC	356	179	2,516	22	15
1969	Sonny Jurgensen, Washington, NFL	442	274	3,102	22	15
	*Greg Cook, Cincinnati, AFL	197	106	1,854	15	11
1968	Len Dawson, Kansas City, AFL	224	131	2,109	17	9
	Earl Morrall, Baltimore, NFL	317	182	2,909	26	17
1967	Sonny Jurgensen, Washington, NFL	508	288	3,747	31	16
	Daryle Lamonica, Oakland, AFL	425	220	3,228	30	20
1966	Bart Starr, Green Bay, NFL	251	156	2,257	14	3
	Len Dawson, Kansas City, AFL	284	159	2,527	26	10
1965	Rudy Bukich, Chicago, NFL	312	176	2,641	20	9
	John Hadl, San Diego, AFL	348	174	2,798	20	21
1964	Len Dawson, Kansas City, AFL	354	199	2,879	30	18
	Bart Starr, Green Bay, NFL	272	163	2,144	15	4
1963	Y.A. Tittle, N.Y. Giants, NFL	367	221	3,145	36	14
	Tobin Rote, San Diego, AFL	286	170	2,510	20	17
1962	Len Dawson, Dall. Texans, AFL	310	189	2,759	29	17
	Bart Starr, Green Bay, NFL	285	178	2,438	12	9
1961	George Blanda, Houston, AFL	362	187	3,330	36	22
	Milt Plum, Cleveland, NFL	302	177	2,416	18	10
1960	Milt Plum, Cleveland, NFL	250	151	2,297	21	5
	Jack Kemp, L.A. Chargers, AFL	406	211	3,018	20	25
1959	Charlie Conerly, N.Y. Giants	194	113	1,706	14	4
1958	Eddie LeBaron, Washington	145	79	1,365	11	10
1957	Tommy O'Connell, Cleveland	110	63	1,229	9	8
1956	Ed Brown, Chi. Bears	168	96	1,667	11	12
1955	Otto Graham, Cleveland	185	98	1,721	15	8
1954	Norm Van Brocklin, Los Angeles	260	139	2,637	13	21
1953	Otto Graham, Cleveland	258	167	2,722	11	9
1952	Norm Van Brocklin, Los Angeles	205	113	1,736	14	17
1951	Bob Waterfield, Los Angeles	176	88	1,566	13	10
1950	Norm Van Brocklin, Los Angeles	233	127	2,061	18	14
1949	Sammy Baugh, Washington	255	145	1,903	18	14
1948	Tommy Thompson, Philadelphia	246	141	1,965	25	11
1947	Sammy Baugh, Washington	354	210	2,938	25	15
1946	Bob Waterfield, Los Angeles	251	127	1,747	18	17
1945	Sammy Baugh, Washington	182	128	1,669	11	4
	Sid Luckman, Chi. Bears	217	117	1,725	14	10
1944	Frank Filchock, Washington	147	84	1,139	13	9
1943	Sammy Baugh, Washington	239	133	1,754	23	19
1942	Cecil Isbell, Green Bay	268	146	2,021	24	14
1941	Cecil Isbell, Green Bay	206	117	1,479	15	11
1940	Sammy Baugh, Washington	177	111	1,367	12	10
1939	*Parker Hall, Cleveland	208	106	1,227	9	13
1938	Ed Danowski, N.Y. Giants	129	70	848	7	8
1937	*Sammy Baugh, Washington	171	81	1,127	8	14
1936	Arnie Herber, Green Bay	173	77	1,239	11	13
1935	Ed Danowski, N.Y. Giants	113	57	794	10	9
1934	Arnie Herber, Green Bay	115	42	799	8	12
1933	*Harry Newman, N.Y. Giants	136	53	973	11	17
1932	Arnie Herber, Green Bay	101	37	639	9	9

**First year in the league.*

ANNUAL PASS RECEIVING LEADERS

Year	Player, Team	No.	Yards	Avg.	TD
1984	Art Monk, Washington, NFC	106	1,372	12.9	7
	Ozzie Newsome, Cleveland, AFC	89	1,001	11.2	5
1983	Todd Christensen, L.A. Raiders, AFC	92	1,247	13.6	12
	Roy Green, St. Louis, NFC	78	1,227	15.7	14
	Charlie Brown, Washington, NFC	78	1,225	15.7	8
	Earnest Gray, N.Y. Giants, NFC	78	1,139	14.6	5
1982	Dwight Clark, San Francisco, NFC	60	913	15.2	5
	Kellen Winslow, San Diego, AFC	54	721	13.4	6
1981	Kellen Winslow, San Diego, AFC	88	1,075	12.2	10
	Dwight Clark, San Francisco, NFC	85	1,105	13.0	4
1980	Kellen Winslow, San Diego, AFC	89	1,290	14.5	9
	*Earl Cooper, San Francisco, NFC	83	567	6.8	4
1979	Joe Washington, Baltimore, AFC	82	750	9.1	3
	Ahmad Rashad, Minnesota, NFC	80	1,156	14.5	9
1978	Rickey Young, Minnesota, NFC	88	704	8.0	5
	Steve Largent, Seattle, AFC	71	1,168	16.5	8
1977	Lydell Mitchell, Baltimore, AFC	71	620	8.7	4
	Ahmad Rashad, Minnesota, NFC	51	681	13.4	2
1976	MacArthur Lane, Kansas City, AFC	66	686	10.4	1
	Drew Pearson, Dallas, NFC	58	806	13.9	6
1975	Chuck Foreman, Minnesota, NFC	73	691	9.5	9
	Reggie Rucker, Cleveland, AFC	60	770	12.8	3
	Lydell Mitchell, Baltimore, AFC	60	544	9.1	4
1974	Lydell Mitchell, Baltimore, AFC	72	544	7.6	2
	Charles Young, Philadelphia, NFC	63	696	11.0	3
1973	Harold Carmichael, Philadelphia, NFC	67	1,116	16.7	9
	Fred Willis, Houston, AFC	57	371	6.5	1
1972	Harold Jackson, Philadelphia, NFC	62	1,048	16.9	4
	Fred Biletnikoff, Oakland, AFC	58	802	13.8	7
1971	Fred Biletnikoff, Oakland, AFC	61	929	15.2	9
	Bob Tucker, N.Y. Giants, NFC	59	791	13.4	4
1970	Dick Gordon, Chicago, NFC	71	1,026	14.5	13
	Marlin Briscoe, Buffalo, AFC	57	1,036	18.2	8
1969	Dan Abramowicz, New Orleans, NFL	73	1,015	13.9	7
	Lance Alworth, San Diego, AFL	64	1,003	15.7	4
1968	Clifton McNeil, San Francisco, NFL	71	994	14.0	7
	Lance Alworth, San Diego, AFL	68	1,312	19.3	10
1967	George Sauer, N.Y. Jets, AFL	75	1,189	15.9	6
	Charley Taylor, Washington, NFL	70	990	14.1	9
1966	Lance Alworth, San Diego, AFL	73	1,383	18.9	13
	Charley Taylor, Washington, NFL	72	1,119	15.5	12
1965	Lionel Taylor, Denver, AFL	85	1,131	13.3	6
	Dave Parks, San Francisco, NFL	80	1,344	16.8	12
1964	Charley Hennigan, Houston, AFL	101	1,546	15.3	8
	Johnny Morris, Chicago, NFL	93	1,200	12.9	10
1963	Lionel Taylor, Denver, AFL	78	1,101	14.1	10
	Bobby Joe Conrad, St. Louis, NFL	73	967	13.2	10
1962	Lionel Taylor, Denver, AFL	77	908	11.8	4
	Bobby Mitchell, Washington, NFL	72	1,384	19.2	11
1961	Lionel Taylor, Denver, AFL	100	1,176	11.8	4
	Jim (Red) Phillips, Los Angeles, NFL	78	1,092	14.0	5
1960	Lionel Taylor, Denver, AFL	92	1,235	13.4	12
	Raymond Berry, Baltimore, NFL	74	1,298	17.5	10
1959	Raymond Berry, Baltimore	66	959	14.5	14
1958	Raymond Berry, Baltimore	56	794	14.2	9

Year	Player, Team			
	Pete Retzlaff, Philadelphia	56	766	13.7	2
1957	Billy Wilson, San Francisco	52	757	14.6	6
1956	Billy Wilson, San Francisco	60	889	14.8	5
1955	Pete Pihos, Philadelphia	62	864	13.9	7
1954	Pete Pihos, Philadelphia	60	872	14.5	10
	Billy Wilson, San Francisco	60	830	13.8	5
1953	Pete Pihos, Philadelphia	63	1,049	16.7	10
1952	Mac Speedie, Cleveland	62	911	14.7	5
1951	Elroy (Crazylegs) Hirsch, Los Angeles	66	1,495	22.7	17
1950	Tom Fears, Los Angeles	84	1,116	13.3	7
1949	Tom Fears, Los Angeles	77	1,013	13.2	9
1948	*Tom Fears, Los Angeles	51	698	13.7	4
1947	Jim Keane, Chi. Bears	64	910	14.2	10
1946	Jim Benton, Los Angeles	63	981	15.6	6
1945	Don Hutson, Green Bay	47	834	17.7	9
1944	Don Hutson, Green Bay	58	866	14.9	9
1943	Don Hutson, Green Bay	47	776	16.5	11
1942	Don Hutson, Green Bay	74	1,211	16.4	17
1941	Don Hutson, Green Bay	58	738	12.7	10
1940	*Don Looney, Philadelphia	58	707	12.2	4
1939	Don Hutson, Green Bay	34	846	24.9	6
1938	Gaynell Tinsley, Chi. Cardinals	41	516	12.6	1
1937	Don Hutson, Green Bay	41	552	13.5	7
1936	Don Hutson, Green Bay	34	536	15.8	8
1935	*Tod Goodwin, N.Y. Giants	26	432	16.6	4
1934	Joe Carter, Philadelphia	16	238	14.9	4
	Morris (Red) Badgro, N.Y. Giants	16	206	12.9	1
1933	John (Shipwreck) Kelly, Brooklyn	22	246	11.2	3
1932	Ray Flaherty, N.Y. Giants	21	350	16.7	3

*First year in the league.

ANNUAL INTERCEPTION LEADERS

Year	Player, Team	No.	Yards	TD
1984	Ken Easley, Seattle, AFC	10	126	2
	*Tom Flynn, Green Bay, NFC	9	106	0
1983	Mark Murphy, Washington, NFC	9	127	0
	Ken Riley, Cincinnati, AFC	8	89	2
	Vann McElroy, L.A. Raiders, AFC	8	68	0
1982	Everson Walls, Dallas, NFC	7	61	0
	Ken Riley, Cincinnati, AFC	5	88	1
	Bobby Jackson, N.Y. Jets, AFC	5	84	1
	Dwayne Woodruff, Pittsburgh, AFC	5	53	0
	Donnie Shell, Pittsburgh, AFC	5	27	0
1981	*Everson Walls, Dallas, NFC	11	133	0
	John Harris, Seattle, AFC	10	155	2
1980	Lester Hayes, Oakland, AFC	13	273	1
	Nolan Cromwell, Los Angeles, NFC	8	140	1
1979	Mike Reinfeldt, Houston, AFC	12	205	0
	Lemar Parrish, Washington, NFC	9	65	0
1978	Thom Darden, Cleveland, AFC	10	200	0
	Ken Stone, St. Louis, NFC	9	139	0
	Willie Buchanon, Green Bay, NFC	9	93	1
1977	Lyle Blackwood, Baltimore, AFC	10	163	0
	Rolland Lawrence, Atlanta, NFC	7	138	0
1976	Monte Jackson, Los Angeles, NFC	10	173	3
	Ken Riley, Cincinnati, AFC	9	141	1
1975	Mel Blount, Pittsburgh, AFC	11	121	0
	Paul Krause, Minnesota, NFC	10	201	0
1974	Emmitt Thomas, Kansas City, AFC	12	214	2
	Ray Brown, Atlanta, NFC	8	164	1
1973	Dick Anderson, Miami, AFC	8	163	2
	Mike Wagner, Pittsburgh, AFC	8	134	0
	Bobby Bryant, Minnesota, NFC	7	105	1
1972	Bill Bradley, Philadelphia, NFC	9	73	0
	Mike Sensibaugh, Kansas City, AFC	8	65	0
1971	Bill Bradley, Philadelphia, NFC	11	248	0
	Ken Houston, Houston, AFC	9	220	4
1970	Johnny Robinson, Kansas City, AFC	10	155	0
	Dick LeBeau, Detroit, NFC	9	96	0
1969	Mel Renfro, Dallas, NFL	10	118	0
	Emmitt Thomas, Kansas City, AFL	9	146	1
1968	Dave Grayson, Oakland, AFL	10	195	1
	Willie Williams, N.Y. Giants, NFL	10	103	0
1967	Miller Farr, Houston, AFL	10	264	3
	*Lem Barney, Detroit, NFL	10	232	3
	Tom Janik, Buffalo, AFL	10	222	2
	Dave Whitsell, New Orleans, NFL	10	178	2
	Dick Westmoreland, Miami, AFL	10	127	1
1966	Larry Wilson, St. Louis, NFL	10	180	2
	Johnny Robinson, Kansas City, AFL	10	136	1
	Bobby Hunt, Kansas City, AFL	10	113	0
1965	W.K. Hicks, Houston, AFL	9	156	0
	Bobby Boyd, Baltimore, NFL	9	78	1
1964	Dainard Paulson, N.Y. Jets, AFL	12	157	1
	*Paul Krause, Washington, NFL	12	140	1
1963	Fred Glick, Houston, AFL	12	180	1
	Dick Lynch, N.Y. Giants, NFL	9	251	3
	Roosevelt Taylor, Chicago, NFL	9	172	1
1962	Lee Riley, N.Y. Titans, AFL	11	122	0
	Willie Wood, Green Bay, NFL	9	132	0
1961	Billy Atkins, Buffalo, AFL	10	158	0
	Dick Lynch, N.Y. Giants, NFL	9	60	1
1960	*Austin (Goose) Gonsoulin, Denver, AFL	11	98	0
	Dave Baker, San Francisco, NFL	10	96	0
	Jerry Norton, St. Louis, NFL	10	96	0
1959	Dean Derby, Pittsburgh	7	127	0
	Milt Davis, Baltimore	7	119	1
	Don Shinnick, Baltimore	7	70	0
1958	Jim Patton, N.Y. Giants	11	183	0
1957	*Milt Davis, Baltimore	10	219	2
	Jack Christiansen, Detroit	10	137	1
	Jack Butler, Pittsburgh	10	85	0
1956	Lindon Crow, Chi. Cardinals	11	170	0
1955	Will Sherman, Los Angeles	11	101	0
1954	Dick (Night Train) Lane, Chi. Cardinals	10	181	0
1953	Jack Christiansen, Detroit	12	238	1
1952	*Dick (Night Train) Lane, Los Angeles	14	298	2
1951	Otto Schnellbacher, N.Y. Giants	11	194	2
1950	*Orban (Spec) Sanders, N.Y. Yanks	13	199	0
1949	Bob Nussbaumer, Chi. Cardinals	12	157	0
1948	*Dan Sandifer, Washington	13	258	2
1947	Frank Reagan, N.Y. Giants	10	203	0
	Frank Seno, Boston	10	100	0
1946	Bill Dudley, Pittsburgh	10	242	1
1945	Roy Zimmerman, Philadelphia	7	90	0
1944	*Howard Livingston, N.Y. Giants	9	172	1
1943	Sammy Baugh, Washington	11	112	0
1942	*Clyde (Bulldog) Turner, Chi. Bears	8	96	1
1941	Marshall Goldberg, Chi. Cardinals	7	54	0
	*Art Jones, Pittsburgh	7	35	0
1940	Clarence (Ace) Parker, Brooklyn	6	146	1
	Kent Ryan, Detroit	6	65	0
	Don Hutson, Green Bay	6	24	0

*First year in the league.

ANNUAL PUNTING LEADERS

Year	Player, Team	No.	Avg.	Long
1984	Jim Arnold, Kansas City, AFC	98	44.9	63
	*Brian Hansen, New Orleans, NFC	69	43.8	66
1983	Rohn Stark, Baltimore, AFC	91	45.3	68
	*Frank Garcia, Tampa Bay, NFC	95	42.2	64
1982	Luke Prestridge, Denver, AFC	45	45.0	65
	Carl Birdsong, St. Louis, NFC	54	43.8	65
1981	Pat McInally, Cincinnati, AFC	72	45.4	62
	Tom Skladany, Detroit, NFC	64	43.5	74
1980	Dave Jennings, N.Y. Giants, NFC	94	44.8	63
	Luke Prestridge, Denver, AFC	70	43.9	57
1979	*Bob Grupp, Kansas City, AFC	89	43.6	74
	Dave Jennings, N.Y. Giants, NFC	104	42.7	72
1978	Pat McInally, Cincinnati, AFC	91	43.1	65
	*Tom Skladany, Detroit, NFC	86	42.5	63
1977	Ray Guy, Oakland, AFC	59	43.3	74
	Tom Blanchard, New Orleans, NFC	82	42.4	66
1976	Marv Bateman, Buffalo, AFC	86	42.8	78
	John James, Atlanta, NFC	101	42.1	67
1975	Ray Guy, Oakland, AFC	68	43.8	64
	Herman Weaver, Detroit, NFC	80	42.0	61
1974	Ray Guy, Oakland, AFC	74	42.2	66
	Tom Blanchard, New Orleans, NFC	88	42.1	71
1973	Jerrel Wilson, Kansas City, AFC	80	45.5	68
	*Tom Wittum, San Francisco, NFC	79	43.7	62
1972	Jerrel Wilson, Kansas City, AFC	66	44.8	69
	Dave Chapple, Los Angeles, NFC	53	44.2	70
1971	Dave Lewis, Cincinnati, AFC	72	44.8	56
	Tom McNeill, Philadelphia, NFC	73	42.0	64
1970	*Dave Lewis, Cincinnati, AFC	79	46.2	63
	*Julian Fagan, New Orleans, NFC	77	42.5	64
1969	David Lee, Baltimore, NFL	57	45.3	66
	Dennis Partee, San Diego, AFL	71	44.6	62
1968	Jerrel Wilson, Kansas City, AFL	63	45.1	70
	Billy Lothridge, Atlanta, NFL	75	44.3	70
1967	Bob Scarpitto, Denver, AFL	105	44.9	73
	Billy Lothridge, Atlanta, NFL	87	43.7	62
1966	Bob Scarpitto, Denver, AFL	76	45.8	70
	*David Lee, Baltimore, NFL	49	45.6	64
1965	Gary Collins, Cleveland, NFL	65	46.7	71
	Jerrel Wilson, Kansas City, AFL	69	45.4	64
1964	*Bobby Walden, Minnesota, NFL	72	46.4	73
	Jim Fraser, Denver, AFL	73	44.2	67
1963	Yale Lary, Detroit, NFL	35	48.9	73
	Jim Fraser, Denver, AFL	81	44.4	66
1962	Tommy Davis, San Francisco, NFL	48	45.6	82
	Jim Fraser, Denver, AFL	55	43.6	75
1961	Yale Lary, Detroit, NFL	52	48.4	71
	Billy Atkins, Buffalo, AFL	85	44.5	70
1960	Jerry Norton, St. Louis, NFL	39	45.6	62
	*Paul Maguire, L.A. Chargers, AFL	43	40.5	61
1959	Yale Lary, Detroit	45	47.1	67
1958	Sam Baker, Washington	48	45.4	64
1957	Don Chandler, N.Y. Giants	60	44.6	61
1956	Norm Van Brocklin, Los Angeles	48	43.1	72
1955	Norm Van Brocklin, Los Angeles	60	44.6	61
1954	Pat Brady, Pittsburgh	66	43.2	72
1953	Pat Brady, Pittsburgh	80	46.9	64
1952	Horace Gillom, Cleveland	61	45.7	73
1951	Horace Gillom, Cleveland	73	45.5	66
1950	*Fred (Curly) Morrison, Chi. Bears	57	43.3	65
1949	*Mike Boyda, N.Y. Bulldogs	56	44.2	61
1948	Joe Muha, Philadelphia	57	47.3	82
1947	Jack Jacobs, Green Bay	57	43.5	74
1946	Roy McKay, Green Bay	64	42.7	64
1945	Roy McKay, Green Bay	44	41.2	73
1944	Frank Sinkwich, Detroit	45	41.0	73
1943	Sammy Baugh, Washington	50	45.9	81
1942	Sammy Baugh, Washington	37	48.2	74
1941	Sammy Baugh, Washington	30	48.7	75
1940	Sammy Baugh, Washington	35	51.4	85
1939	*Parker Hall, Cleveland	58	40.8	80

*First year in the league.

ANNUAL PUNT RETURN LEADERS

Year	Player, Team	No.	Yards	Avg.	Long	TD
1984	Mike Martin, Cincinnati, AFC	24	376	15.7	55	0
	Henry Ellard, L.A. Rams, NFC	30	403	13.4	83	2
1983	*Henry Ellard, L.A. Rams, NFC	16	217	13.6	72	1
	Kirk Springs, N.Y. Jets, AFC	23	287	12.5	76	1

Year	Player, Team	No.	Yards	Avg.	Long	TD
1982	Rick Upchurch, Denver, AFC	15	242	16.1	78	2
	Billy Johnson, Atlanta, NFC	24	273	11.4	71	0
1981	LeRoy Irvin, Los Angeles, NFC	46	615	13.4	84	3
	*James Brooks, San Diego, AFC	22	290	13.2	42	0
1980	J. T. Smith, Kansas City, AFC	40	581	14.5	75	2
	*Kenny Johnson, Atlanta, NFC	23	281	12.2	56	0
1979	John Sciarra, Philadelphia, NFC	16	182	11.4	38	0
	*Tony Nathan, Miami, AFC	28	306	10.9	86	1
1978	Rick Upchurch, Denver, AFC	36	493	13.7	75	1
	Jackie Wallace, Los Angeles, NFC	52	618	11.9	58	0
1977	Billy Johnson, Houston, AFC	35	539	15.4	87	2
	Larry Marshall, Philadelphia, NFC	46	489	10.6	48	0
1976	Rick Upchurch, Denver, AFC	39	536	13.7	92	4
	Eddie Brown, Washington, NFC	48	646	13.5	71	1
1975	Billy Johnson, Houston, AFC	40	612	15.3	83	3
	Terry Metcalf, St. Louis, NFC	23	285	12.4	69	1
1974	Lemar Parrish, Cincinnati, AFC	18	338	18.8	90	2
	Dick Jauron, Detroit, NFC	17	286	16.8	58	0
1973	Bruce Taylor, San Francisco, NFC	15	207	13.8	61	0
	Ron Smith, San Diego, AFC	27	352	13.0	84	2
1972	*Ken Ellis, Green Bay, NFC	14	215	15.4	80	1
	Chris Farasopoulos, N.Y. Jets, AFC	17	179	10.5	65	1
1971	Les (Speedy) Duncan, Washington, NFC	22	233	10.6	33	0
	Leroy Kelly, Cleveland, AFC	30	292	9.7	74	0
1970	Ed Podolak, Kansas City, AFC	23	311	13.5	60	0
	*Bruce Taylor, San Francisco, NFC	43	516	12.0	76	0
1969	Alvin Haymond, Los Angeles, NFL	33	435	13.2	52	0
	*Bill Thompson, Denver, AFL	25	288	11.5	40	0
1968	Bob Hayes, Dallas, NFL	15	312	20.8	90	2
	Noland Smith, Kansas City, AFL	18	270	15.0	80	1
1967	Floyd Little, Denver, AFL	16	270	16.9	72	1
	Ben Davis, Cleveland, NFL	18	229	12.7	52	1
1966	Les (Speedy) Duncan, San Diego, AFL	18	238	13.2	81	1
	Johnny Roland, St. Louis, NFL	20	221	11.1	86	1
1965	Leroy Kelly, Cleveland, NFL	17	265	15.6	67	2
	Les (Speedy) Duncan, San Diego, AFL	30	464	15.5	66	2
1964	Bobby Jancik, Houston, AFL	12	220	18.3	82	1
	Tommy Watkins, Detroit, NFL	16	238	14.9	68	2
1963	Dick James, Washington, NFL	16	214	13.4	39	0
	Claude (Hoot) Gibson, Oakland, AFL	26	307	11.8	85	2
1962	Dick Christy, N.Y. Titans, AFL	15	250	16.7	73	2
	Pat Studstill, Detroit, NFL	29	457	15.8	44	0
1961	Dick Christy, N.Y. Titans, AFL	18	383	21.3	70	2
	Willie Wood, Green Bay, NFL	14	225	16.1	72	2
1960	*Abner Haynes, Dall. Texans, AFL	14	215	15.4	46	0
	Abe Woodson, San Francisco, NFL	13	174	13.4	48	0
1959	Johnny Morris, Chi. Bears	14	171	12.2	78	1
1958	Jon Arnett, Los Angeles	18	223	12.4	58	0
1957	Bert Zagers, Washington	14	217	15.5	76	2
1956	Ken Konz, Cleveland	13	187	14.4	65	1
1955	Ollie Matson, Chi. Cardinals	13	245	18.8	78	2
1954	*Veryl Switzer, Green Bay	24	306	12.8	93	1
1953	Charley Trippi, Chi. Cardinals	21	239	11.4	38	0
1952	Jack Christiansen, Detroit	15	322	21.5	79	2
1951	Claude (Buddy) Young, N.Y. Yanks	12	231	19.3	79	1
1950	*Herb Rich, Baltimore	12	276	23.0	86	1
1949	Verda (Vitamin T) Smith, Los Angeles	27	427	15.8	85	1
1948	George McAfee, Chi. Bears	30	417	13.9	60	1
1947	*Walt Slater, Pittsburgh	28	435	15.5	33	0
1946	Bill Dudley, Pittsburgh	27	385	14.3	52	0
1945	*Dave Ryan, Detroit	15	220	14.7	56	0
1944	*Steve Van Buren, Philadelphia	15	230	15.3	55	1
1943	Andy Farkas, Washington	15	168	11.2	33	0
1942	Merlyn Condit, Brooklyn	21	210	10.0	23	0
1941	Byron (Whizzer) White, Detroit	19	262	13.8	64	0

First year in the league.

ANNUAL KICKOFF RETURN LEADERS

Year	Player, Team	No.	Yards	Avg.	Long	TD
1984	*Bobby Humphery, N.Y. Jets, AFC	22	675	30.7	97	1
	Barry Redden, L.A. Rams, NFC	23	530	23.0	40	0
1983	Fulton Walker, Miami, AFC	36	962	26.7	78	0
	Darrin Nelson, Minnesota, NFC	18	445	24.7	50	0
1982	*Mike Mosley, Buffalo, AFC	18	487	27.1	66	0
	Alvin Hall, Detroit, NFC	16	426	26.6	96	1
1981	Mike Nelms, Washington, NFC	37	1,099	29.7	84	0
	Carl Roaches, Houston, AFC	28	769	27.5	96	1
1980	Horace Ivory, New England, AFC	36	992	27.6	98	1
	Rich Mauti, New Orleans, NFC	31	798	25.7	52	0
1979	Larry Brunson, Oakland, AFC	17	441	25.9	89	0
	*Jimmy Edwards, Minnesota, NFC	44	1,103	25.1	83	0
1978	Steve Odom, Green Bay, NFC	25	677	27.1	95	1
	*Keith Wright, Cleveland, AFC	30	789	26.3	86	0
1977	*Raymond Clayborn, New England, AFC	28	869	31.0	101	3
	*Wilbert Montgomery, Philadelphia, NFC	23	619	26.9	99	1
1976	*Duriel Harris, Miami, AFC	17	559	32.9	69	0
	Cullen Bryant, Los Angeles, NFC	16	459	28.7	90	1
1975	*Walter Payton, Chicago, NFC	14	444	31.7	70	0
	Harold Hart, Oakland, AFC	17	518	30.5	102	1
1974	Terry Metcalf, St. Louis, NFC	20	623	31.2	94	1
	Greg Pruitt, Cleveland, AFC	22	606	27.5	88	1
1973	Carl Garrett, Chicago, NFC	16	486	30.4	67	0
	*Wallace Francis, Buffalo, AFC	23	687	29.9	101	2
1972	Ron Smith, Chicago, NFC	30	924	30.8	94	1
	*Bruce Laird, Baltimore, AFC	29	843	29.1	73	0
1971	Travis Williams, Los Angeles, NFC	25	743	29.7	105	1
	Eugene (Mercury) Morris, Miami, AFC	15	423	28.2	94	1
1970	Jim Duncan, Baltimore, AFC	20	707	35.4	99	1
	Cecil Turner, Chicago, NFC	23	752	32.7	96	4
1969	Bobby Williams, Detroit, NFL	17	563	33.1	96	1
	*Bill Thompson, Denver, AFL	18	513	28.5	63	0
1968	Preston Pearson, Baltimore, NFL	15	527	35.1	102	2
	*George Atkinson, Oakland, AFL	32	802	25.1	60	0
1967	*Travis Williams, Green Bay, NFL	18	739	41.1	104	4
	*Zeke Moore, Houston, AFL	14	405	28.9	92	1
1966	Gale Sayers, Chicago, NFL	23	718	31.2	93	2
	*Goldie Sellers, Denver, AFL	19	541	28.5	100	2
1965	Tommy Watkins, Detroit, NFL	17	584	34.4	94	0
	Abner Haynes, Denver, AFL	34	901	26.5	60	0
1964	*Clarence Childs, N.Y. Giants, NFL	34	987	29.0	100	1
	Bo Roberson, Oakland, AFL	36	975	27.1	59	0
1963	Abe Woodson, San Francisco, NFL	29	935	32.2	103	3
	Bobby Jancik, Houston, AFL	45	1,317	29.3	53	0
1962	Abe Woodson, San Francisco, NFL	37	1,157	31.3	79	0
	*Bobby Jancik, Houston, AFL	24	826	30.3	61	0
1961	Dick Bass, Los Angeles, NFL	23	698	30.3	64	0
	*Dave Grayson, Dall. Texans, AFL	16	453	28.3	73	0
1960	*Tom Moore, Green Bay, NFL	12	397	33.1	84	0
	Ken Hall, Houston, AFL	19	594	31.3	104	1
1959	Abe Woodson, San Francisco	13	382	29.4	105	1
1958	Ollie Matson, Chi. Cardinals	14	497	35.5	101	2
1957	*Jon Arnett, Los Angeles	18	504	28.0	98	1
1956	*Tom Wilson, Los Angeles	15	477	31.8	103	1
1955	Al Carmichael, Green Bay	14	418	29.9	100	1
1954	Billy Reynolds, Cleveland	14	413	29.5	51	0
1953	Joe Arenas, San Francisco	16	551	34.4	82	0
1952	Lynn Chandnois, Pittsburgh	17	599	35.2	93	2
1951	Lynn Chandnois, Pittsburgh	12	390	32.5	55	0
1950	Verda (Vitamin T) Smith, Los Angeles	22	742	33.7	97	3
1949	*Don Doll, Detroit	21	536	25.5	56	0
1948	*Joe Scott, N.Y. Giants	20	569	28.5	99	1
1947	Eddie Saenz, Washington	29	797	27.5	94	2
1946	Abe Karnofsky, Boston	21	599	28.5	97	1
1945	Steve Van Buren, Philadelphia	13	373	28.7	98	1
1944	Bob Thurbon, Card.-Pitt	12	291	24.3	55	0
1943	Ken Heineman, Brooklyn	16	444	27.8	69	0
1942	Marshall Goldberg, Chi. Cardinals	15	393	26.2	95	1
1941	Marshall Goldberg, Chi. Cardinals	12	290	24.2	41	0

First year in the league.

POINTS SCORED

Year	Team	Points
1984	Miami, AFC	513
	San Francisco, NFC	475
1983	Washington, NFC	541
	L.A. Raiders, AFC	442
1982	San Diego, AFC	288
	Dallas, NFC	226
	Green Bay, NFC	226
1981	San Diego, AFC	478
	Atlanta, NFC	426
1980	Dallas, NFC	454
	New England, AFC	441
1979	Pittsburgh, AFC	416
	Dallas, NFC	371
1978	Dallas, NFC	384
	Miami, AFC	372
1977	Oakland, AFC	351
	Dallas, NFC	345
1976	Baltimore, AFC	417
	Los Angeles, NFC	351
1975	Buffalo, AFC	420
	Minnesota, NFC	377
1974	Oakland, AFC	355
	Washington, NFC	320
1973	Los Angeles, NFC	388
	Denver, AFC	354
1972	Miami, AFC	385
	San Francisco, NFC	353
1971	Dallas, NFC	406
	Oakland, AFC	344
1970	San Francisco, NFC	352
	Baltimore, AFC	321
1969	Minnesota, NFL	379
	Oakland, AFL	377
1968	Oakland, AFL	453
	Dallas, NFL	431
1967	Oakland, AFL	468
	Los Angeles, NFL	398
1966	Kansas City, AFL	448
	Dallas, NFL	445
1965	San Francisco, NFL	421
	San Diego, AFL	340
1964	Baltimore, NFL	428
	Buffalo, AFL	400
1963	N.Y. Giants, NFL	448
	San Diego, AFL	399
1962	Green Bay, NFL	415
	Dall. Texans, AFL	389
1961	Houston, AFL	513
	Green Bay, NFL	391
1960	N.Y. Titans, AFL	382
	Cleveland, NFL	362
1959	Baltimore	374
1958	Baltimore	381
1957	Los Angeles	307
1956	Chi. Bears	363
1955	Cleveland	349
1954	Detroit	337
1953	San Francisco	372
1952	Los Angeles	349
1951	Los Angeles	392
1950	Los Angeles	466
1949	Philadelphia	364
1948	Chi. Cardinals	395
1947	Chi. Bears	363
1946	Chi. Bears	289
1945	Philadelphia	272
1944	Philadelphia	267
1943	Chi. Bears	303
1942	Chi. Bears	376
1941	Chi. Bears	396
1940	Washington	245
1939	Chi. Bears	298
1938	Green Bay	223
1937	Green Bay	220
1936	Green Bay	248
1935	Chi. Bears	192
1934	Chi. Bears	286
1933	N.Y. Giants	244
1932	Green Bay	152

TOTAL YARDS GAINED

Year	Team	Yards
1984	Miami, AFC	6,936
	San Francisco, NFC	6,366
1983	San Diego, AFC	6,197
	Green Bay, NFC	6,172
1982	San Diego, AFC	4,048
	San Francisco, NFC	3,242
1981	San Diego, AFC	6,744
	Detroit, NFC	5,933
1980	San Diego, AFC	6,410
	Los Angeles, NFC	6,006
1979	Pittsburgh, AFC	6,258
	Dallas, NFC	5,968
1978	New England, AFC	5,965
	Dallas, NFC	5,959
1977	Dallas, NFC	4,812
	Oakland, AFC	4,736
1976	Baltimore, AFC	5,236
	St. Louis, NFC	5,136
1975	Buffalo, AFC	5,467
	Dallas, NFC	5,025
1974	Dallas, NFC	4,983
	Oakland, AFC	4,718
1973	Los Angeles, NFC	4,906
	Oakland, AFC	4,773
1972	Miami, AFC	5,036
	N.Y. Giants, NFC	4,483
1971	Dallas, NFC	5,035
	San Diego, AFC	4,738
1970	Oakland, AFC	4,829
	San Francisco, NFC	4,503
1969	Dallas, NFL	5,122
	Oakland, AFL	5,036
1968	Oakland, AFL	5,696
	Dallas, NFL	5,117
1967	N.Y. Jets, AFL	5,152
	Baltimore, NFL	5,008
1966	Dallas, NFL	5,145
	Kansas City, AFL	5,114
1965	San Francisco, NFL	5,270
	San Diego, AFL	5,188
1964	Buffalo, AFL	5,206
	Baltimore, NFL	4,779
1963	San Diego, AFL	5,153
	N.Y. Giants, NFL	5,024
1962	N.Y. Giants, NFL	5,005
	Houston, AFL	4,971
1961	Houston, AFL	6,288
	Philadelphia, NFL	5,112

1960	Houston, AFL	4,936
	Baltimore, NFL	4,245
1959	Baltimore	4,458
1958	Baltimore	4,539
1957	Los Angeles	4,143
1956	Chi. Bears	4,537
1955	Chi. Bears	4,316
1954	Los Angeles	5,187
1953	Philadelphia	4,811
1952	Cleveland	4,352
1951	Los Angeles	5,506
1950	Los Angeles	5,420
1949	Chi. Bears	4,873
1948	Chi. Cardinals	4,705
1947	Chi. Bears	5,053
1946	Los Angeles	3,793
1945	Washington	3,549
1944	Chi. Bears	3,239
1943	Chi. Bears	4,045
1942	Chi. Bears	3,900
1941	Chi. Bears	4,265
1940	Green Bay	3,400
1939	Chi. Bears	3,988
1938	Green Bay	3,037
1937	Green Bay	3,201
1936	Detroit	3,703
1935	Chi. Bears	3,454
1934	Chi. Bears	3,900
1933	N.Y. Giants	2,973
1932	Chi. Bears	2,755

YARDS RUSHING

Year	Team	Yards
1984	Chicago, NFC	2,974
	N.Y. Jets, AFC	2,189
1983	Chicago, NFC	2,727
	Baltimore, AFC	2,695
1982	Buffalo, AFC	1,371
	Dallas, NFC	1,313
1981	Detroit, NFC	2,795
	Kansas City, AFC	2,633
1980	Los Angeles, NFC	2,799
	Houston, AFC	2,635
1979	N.Y. Jets, AFC	2,646
	St. Louis, NFC	2,582
1978	New England, AFC	3,165
	Dallas, NFC	2,783
1977	Chicago, NFC	2,811
	Oakland, AFC	2,627
1976	Pittsburgh, AFC	2,971
	Los Angeles, NFC	2,528
1975	Buffalo, AFC	2,974
	Dallas, NFC	2,432
1974	Dallas, NFC	2,454
	Pittsburgh, AFC	2,417
1973	Buffalo, AFC	3,088
	Los Angeles, NFC	2,925
1972	Miami, AFC	2,960
	Chicago, NFC	2,360
1971	Miami, AFC	2,429
	Detroit, NFC	2,376
1970	Dallas, NFC	2,300
	Miami, AFC	2,082
1969	Dallas, NFL	2,276
	Kansas City, AFL	2,220
1968	Chicago, NFL	2,377
	Kansas City, AFL	2,227
1967	Cleveland, NFL	2,139
	Houston, AFL	2,122
1966	Kansas City, AFL	2,274
	Cleveland, NFL	2,166
1965	Cleveland, NFL	2,331
	San Diego, AFL	2,085
1964	Green Bay, NFL	2,276
	Buffalo, AFL	2,040
1963	Cleveland, NFL	2,639
	San Diego, AFL	2,203
1962	Buffalo, AFL	2,480
	Green Bay, NFL	2,460
1961	Green Bay, NFL	2,350
	Dall. Texans, AFL	2,189
1960	St. Louis, NFL	2,356
	Oakland, AFL	2,056
1959	Cleveland	2,149
1958	Cleveland	2,526
1957	Los Angeles	2,142
1956	Chi. Bears	2,468
1955	Chi. Bears	2,388
1954	San Francisco	2,498
1953	San Francisco	2,230
1952	San Francisco	1,905
1951	Chi. Bears	2,408
1950	N.Y. Giants	2,336
1949	Philadelphia	2,607
1948	Chi. Cardinals	2,560
1947	Los Angeles	2,171
1946	Green Bay	1,765
1945	Cleveland	1,714
1944	Philadelphia	1,661
1943	Phil-Pitt	1,730
1942	Chi. Bears	1,881
1941	Chi. Bears	2,263
1940	Chi. Bears	1,818
1939	Chi. Bears	2,043
1938	Detroit	1,893
1937	Detroit	2,074
1936	Detroit	2,885
1935	Chi. Bears	2,096
1934	Chi. Bears	2,847
1933	Boston	2,260
1932	Chi. Bears	1,770

YARDS PASSING

Leadership in this category has been based on net yards since 1952.

Year	Team	Yards
1984	Miami, AFC	5,018
	St. Louis, NFC	4,257
1983	San Diego, AFC	4,661
	Green Bay, NFC	4,365
1982	San Diego, AFC	2,927
	San Francisco, NFC	2,502
1981	San Diego, AFC	4,739
	Minnesota, NFC	4,333
1980	San Diego, AFC	4,531
	Minnesota, NFC	3,688
1979	San Diego, AFC	3,915
	San Francisco, NFC	3,641
1978	San Diego, AFC	3,375
	Minnesota, NFC	3,243
1977	Buffalo, AFC	2,530
	St. Louis, NFC	2,499
1976	Baltimore, AFC	2,933
	Minnesota, NFC	2,855
1975	Cincinnati, AFC	3,241
	Washington, NFC	2,917
1974	Washington, NFC	2,978
	Cincinnati, AFC	2,804
1973	Philadelphia, NFC	2,998
	Denver, AFC	2,519
1972	N.Y. Jets, AFC	2,777
	San Francisco, NFC	2,735
1971	San Diego, AFC	3,134
	Dallas, NFC	2,786
1970	San Francisco, NFC	2,923
	Oakland, AFC	2,865
1969	Oakland, AFL	3,271
	San Francisco, NFL	3,158
1968	San Diego, AFL	3,623
	Dallas, NFL	3,026
1967	N.Y. Jets, AFL	3,845
	Washington, NFL	3,730
1966	N.Y. Jets, AFL	3,464
	Dallas, NFL	3,023
1965	San Francisco, NFL	3,487
	San Diego, AFL	3,103
1964	Houston, AFL	3,527
	Chicago, NFL	2,841
1963	Baltimore, NFL	3,296
	Houston, AFL	3,222
1962	Denver, AFL	3,404
	Philadelphia, NFL	3,385
1961	Houston, AFL	4,392
	Philadelphia, NFL	3,605
1960	Houston, AFL	3,203
	Baltimore, NFL	2,956
1959	Baltimore	2,753
1958	Pittsburgh	2,752
1957	Baltimore	2,388
1956	Los Angeles	2,419
1955	Philadelphia	2,472
1954	Chi. Bears	3,104
1953	Philadelphia	3,089
1952	Cleveland	2,566
1951	Los Angeles	3,296
1950	Los Angeles	3,709
1949	Chi. Bears	3,055
1948	Washington	2,861
1947	Washington	3,336
1946	Los Angeles	2,080
1945	Chi. Bears	1,857
1944	Washington	2,021
1943	Chi. Bears	2,310
1942	Green Bay	2,407
1941	Chi. Bears	2,002
1940	Washington	1,887
1939	Chi. Bears	1,965
1938	Washington	1,536
1937	Green Bay	1,398
1936	Green Bay	1,629
1935	Green Bay	1,449
1934	Green Bay	1,165
1933	N.Y. Giants	1,348
1932	Chi. Bears	1,013

FEWEST POINTS ALLOWED

Year	Team	Points
1984	San Francisco, NFC	227
	Denver, AFC	241
1983	Miami, AFC	250
	Detroit, NFC	286
1982	Washington, AFC	128
	Miami, AFC	131
1981	Philadelphia, NFC	221
	Miami, AFC	275
1980	Philadelphia, NFC	222
	Houston, AFC	251
1979	Tampa Bay, NFC	237
	San Diego, AFC	246
1978	Pittsburgh, AFC	195
	Dallas, NFC	208
1977	Atlanta, NFC	129
	Denver, AFC	148
1976	Pittsburgh, AFC	138
	Minnesota, NFC	176
1975	Los Angeles, NFC	135
	Pittsburgh, AFC	162
1974	Los Angeles, NFC	181
	Pittsburgh, AFC	189
1973	Miami, AFC	150
	Minnesota, NFC	168
1972	Miami, AFC	171
	Washington, NFC	218
1971	Minnesota, NFC	139
	Baltimore, AFC	140
1970	Minnesota, NFC	143
	Miami, AFC	228
1969	Minnesota, NFL	133
	Kansas City, AFL	177
1968	Baltimore, NFL	144
	Kansas City, AFL	170
1967	Los Angeles, NFL	196
	Houston, AFL	199
1966	Green Bay, NFL	163
	Buffalo, AFL	255
1965	Green Bay, NFL	224
	Buffalo, AFL	226
1964	Baltimore, NFL	225
	Buffalo, AFL	242
1963	Chicago, NFL	144
	San Diego, AFL	255
1962	Green Bay, NFL	148
	Dall. Texans, AFL	233
1961	San Diego, AFL	219
	N.Y. Giants, NFL	220
1960	San Francisco, NFL	205
	Dall. Texans, AFL	253
1959	N.Y. Giants	170
1958	N.Y. Giants	183
1957	Cleveland	172
1956	Cleveland	177
1955	Cleveland	218
1954	Cleveland	162
1953	Cleveland	162
1952	Detroit	192
1951	Cleveland	152
1950	Philadelphia	141
1949	Philadelphia	134
1948	Chi. Bears	151
1947	Green Bay	210
1946	Pittsburgh	117
1945	Washington	121
1944	N.Y. Giants	75
1943	Washington	137
1942	Chi. Bears	84
1941	N.Y. Giants	114
1940	Brooklyn	120
1939	N.Y. Giants	85
1938	N.Y. Giants	79
1937	Chi. Bears	100
1936	Chi. Bears	94
1935	Green Bay	96
	N.Y. Giants	96
1934	Detroit	59
1933	Brooklyn	54
1932	Chi. Bears	44

FEWEST TOTAL YARDS ALLOWED

Year	Team	Yards
1984	Chicago, NFC	3,863
	Cleveland, AFC	4,641
1983	Cincinnati, AFC	4,327
	New Orleans, NFC	4,691
1982	Miami, AFC	2,312
	Tampa Bay, NFC	2,442
1981	Philadelphia, NFC	4,447
	N.Y. Jets, AFC	4,871
1980	Buffalo, AFC	4,101
	Philadelphia, NFC	4,443
1979	Tampa Bay, NFC	3,949
	Pittsburgh, AFC	4,270
1978	Los Angeles, NFC	3,893
	Pittsburgh, AFC	4,168
1977	Dallas, NFC	3,213
	New England, AFC	3,638
1976	Pittsburgh, AFC	3,323
	San Francisco, NFC	3,562
1975	Minnesota, NFC	3,153
	Oakland, AFC	3,629
1974	Pittsburgh, AFC	3,074
	Washington, NFC	3,285
1973	Los Angeles, NFC	2,951
	Oakland, AFC	3,160
1972	Miami, AFC	3,297
	Green Bay, NFC	3,474
1971	Baltimore, AFC	2,852
	Minnesota, NFC	3,406
1970	Minnesota, NFC	2,803
	N.Y. Jets, AFC	3,655
1969	Minnesota, NFL	2,720
	Kansas City, AFL	3,163
1968	Los Angeles, NFL	3,118
	N.Y. Jets, AFL	3,363
1967	Oakland, AFL	3,294
	Green Bay, NFL	3,300
1966	St. Louis, NFL	3,492
	Oakland, AFL	3,910
1965	San Diego, AFL	3,262
	Detroit, NFL	3,557
1964	Green Bay, NFL	3,179
	Buffalo, AFL	3,878
1963	Chicago, NFL	3,176
	Boston, AFL	3,834
1962	Detroit, NFL	3,217
	Dall. Texans, AFL	3,951
1961	San Diego, AFL	3,726
	Baltimore, NFL	3,782
1960	St. Louis, NFL	3,029
	Buffalo, AFL	3,866
1959	N.Y. Giants	2,843
1958	Chi. Bears	3,066
1957	Pittsburgh	2,791
1956	N.Y. Giants	3,081
1955	Cleveland	2,841
1954	Cleveland	2,658
1953	Philadelphia	2,998
1952	Cleveland	3,075
1951	N.Y. Giants	3,250
1950	Cleveland	3,154
1949	Philadelphia	2,831
1948	Chi. Bears	2,931
1947	Green Bay	3,396
1946	Washington	2,451
1945	Philadelphia	2,073
1944	Philadelphia	1,943
1943	Chi. Bears	2,262
1942	Chi. Bears	1,703
1941	N.Y. Giants	2,368
1940	N.Y. Giants	2,219
1939	Washington	2,116
1938	N.Y. Giants	2,029
1937	Washington	2,123
1936	Boston	2,181
1935	Boston	1,996
1934	Chi. Cardinals	1,539
1933	Brooklyn	1,789

FEWEST YARDS RUSHING ALLOWED

Year	Team	Yards
1984	Chicago, NFC	1,377
	Pittsburgh, AFC	1,617
1983	Washington, NFC	1,289
	Cincinnati, AFC	1,499
1982	Pittsburgh, AFC	762
	Detroit, NFC	854
1981	Detroit, NFC	1,623
	Kansas City, AFC	1,747
1980	Detroit, NFC	1,599
	Cincinnati, AFC	1,680
1979	Denver, AFC	1,693
	Tampa Bay, NFC	1,873
1978	Dallas, NFC	1,721
	Pittsburgh, AFC	1,774
1977	Denver, AFC	1,531
	Dallas, NFC	1,651
1976	Pittsburgh, AFC	1,457
	Los Angeles, NFC	1,564
1975	Minnesota, NFC	1,532
	Houston, AFC	1,680
1974	Los Angeles, NFC	1,302
	New England, AFC	1,587
1973	Los Angeles, NFC	1,270
	Oakland, AFC	1,470
1972	Dallas, NFC	1,515
	Miami, AFC	1,548
1971	Baltimore, AFC	1,113
	Dallas, NFC	1,144
1970	Detroit, NFC	1,152
	N.Y. Jets, AFC	1,283
1969	Dallas, NFL	1,050
	Kansas City, AFL	1,091
1968	Dallas, NFL	1,195
	N.Y. Jets, AFL	1,195
1967	Dallas, NFL	1,081
	Oakland, AFL	1,129
1966	Buffalo, AFL	1,051
	Dallas, NFL	1,176
1965	San Diego, AFL	1,094
	Los Angeles, NFL	1,409
1964	Buffalo, AFL	913
	Los Angeles, NFL	1,501
1963	Boston, AFL	1,107
	Chicago, NFL	1,442
1962	Detroit, NFL	1,231
	Dall. Texans, AFL	1,250
1961	Boston, AFL	1,041
	Pittsburgh, NFL	1,463
1960	St. Louis, NFL	1,212
	Dall. Texans, AFL	1,338

Year	Team	Yards
1959	N.Y. Giants	1,261
1958	Baltimore	1,291
1957	Baltimore	1,174
1956	N.Y. Giants	1,443
1955	Cleveland	1,189
1954	Cleveland	1,050
1953	Philadelphia	1,117
1952	Detroit	1,145
1951	N.Y. Giants	913
1950	Detroit	1,367
1949	Chi. Bears	1,196
1948	Philadelphia	1,209
1947	Philadelphia	1,329
1946	Chi. Bears	1,060
1945	Philadelphia	817
1944	Philadelphia	558
1943	Phil-Pitt	793
1942	Chi. Bears	519
1941	Washington	1,042
1940	N.Y. Giants	977
1939	Chi. Bears	812
1938	Detroit	1,081
1937	Chi. Bears	933
1936	Boston	1,148
1935	Boston	998
1934	Chi. Cardinals	954
1933	Brooklyn	964
1939	Washington	1,116
1938	Chi. Bears	897
1937	Detroit	804
1936	Philadelphia	853
1935	Chi. Cardinals	793
1934	Philadelphia	545
1933	Portsmouth	558

FEWEST YARDS PASSING ALLOWED

Leadership in this category has been based on net yards since 1952.

Year	Team	Yards
1984	New Orleans, NFC	2,453
	Cleveland, AFC	2,696
1983	New Orleans, NFC	2,691
	Cincinnati, AFC	2,828
1982	Miami, AFC	1,027
	Tampa Bay, NFC	1,384
1981	Philadelphia, NFC	2,696
	Buffalo, AFC	2,870
1980	Washington, NFC	2,171
	Buffalo, AFC	2,282
1979	Tampa Bay, NFC	2,076
	Buffalo, AFC	2,530
1978	Buffalo, AFC	1,960
	Los Angeles, NFC	2,048
1977	Atlanta, NFC	1,384
	San Diego, AFC	1,725
1976	Minnesota, NFC	1,575
	Cincinnati, AFC	1,758
1975	Minnesota, NFC	1,621
	Cincinnati, AFC	1,729
1974	Pittsburgh, AFC	1,466
	Atlanta, NFC	1,572
1973	Miami, AFC	1,290
	Atlanta, NFC	1,430
1972	Minnesota, NFC	1,699
	Cleveland, AFC	1,736
1971	Atlanta, NFC	1,638
	Baltimore, AFC	1,739
1970	Minnesota, NFC	1,438
	Kansas City, AFC	2,010
1969	Minnesota, NFL	1,631
	Kansas City, AFL	2,072
1968	Houston, AFL	1,671
	Green Bay, NFL	1,796
1967	Green Bay, NFL	1,377
	Buffalo, AFL	1,825
1966	Green Bay, NFL	1,959
	Oakland, AFL	2,118
1965	Green Bay, NFL	1,981
	San Diego, AFL	2,168
1964	Green Bay, NFL	1,647
	San Diego, AFL	2,518
1963	Chicago, NFL	1,734
	Oakland, AFL	2,589
1962	Green Bay, NFL	1,746
	Oakland, AFL	2,306
1961	Baltimore, NFL	1,913
	San Diego, AFL	2,363
1960	Chicago, NFL	1,388
	Buffalo, AFL	2,124
1959	N.Y. Giants	1,582
1958	Chi. Bears	1,769
1957	Cleveland	1,300
1956	Cleveland	1,103
1955	Pittsburgh	1,295
1954	Cleveland	1,608
1953	Washington	1,751
1952	Washington	1,580
1951	Pittsburgh	1,687
1950	Cleveland	1,581
1949	Philadelphia	1,607
1948	Green Bay	1,626
1947	Green Bay	1,790
1946	Pittsburgh	939
1945	Washington	1,121
1944	Chi. Bears	1,052
1943	Chi. Bears	980
1942	Washington	1,093
1941	Pittsburgh	1,168
1940	Philadelphia	1,012

SUPER BOWL RECORDS

Compiled by Elias Sports Bureau

1967: Super Bowl I	1974: Super Bowl VIII	1980: Super Bowl XIV
1968: Super Bowl II	1975: Super Bowl IX	1981: Super Bowl XV
1969: Super Bowl III	1976: Super Bowl X	1982: Super Bowl XVI
1970: Super Bowl IV	1977: Super Bowl XI	1983: Super Bowl XVII
1971: Super Bowl V	1978: Super Bowl XII	1984: Super Bowl XVIII
1972: Super Bowl VI	1979: Super Bowl XIII	1985: Super Bowl XIX
1973: Super Bowl VII		

INDIVIDUAL RECORDS

SERVICE

Most Games
- 5 Marv Fleming, Green Bay, 1967-68; Miami, 1972-74
  - Larry Cole, Dallas, 1971-72, 1976, 1978-79
  - Cliff Harris, Dallas, 1971-72, 1976, 1978-79
  - D.D. Lewis, Dallas, 1971-72, 1976, 1978-79
  - Preston Pearson, Baltimore, 1969; Pittsburgh, 1975; Dallas, 1976, 1978-79
  - Charlie Waters, Dallas, 1971-72, 1976, 1978-79
  - Rayfield Wright, Dallas, 1971-72, 1976, 1978-79
- 4 By many players

Most Games, Winning Team
- 4 By many players

Most Games, Coach
- 6 Don Shula, Baltimore, 1969; Miami, 1972-74, 1983, 1985
- 5 Tom Landry, Dallas, 1971-72, 1976, 1978-79
- 4 Bud Grant, Minnesota, 1970, 1974-75, 1977
  - Chuck Noll, Pittsburgh, 1975-76, 1979-80

Most Games, Winning Team, Coach
- 4 Chuck Noll, Pittsburgh, 1975-76, 1979-80
- 2 Vince Lombardi, Green Bay, 1967-68
  - Tom Landry, Dallas, 1972, 1978
  - Don Shula, Miami, 1973-74
  - Tom Flores, Oakland, 1981; L.A. Raiders, 1984
  - Bill Walsh, San Francisco, 1982, 1985

Most Games, Losing Team, Coach
- 4 Bud Grant, Minnesota, 1970, 1974-75, 1977
  - Don Shula, Baltimore, 1969; Miami, 1972, 1983, 1985
- 3 Tom Landry, Dallas, 1971, 1976, 1979
- 1 By eight coaches

SCORING

POINTS

Most Points, Career
- 24 Franco Harris, Pittsburgh, 4 games (4-td)
- 22 Ray Wersching, San Francisco, 2 games (7-pat, 5-fg)
- 20 Don Chandler, Green Bay, 2 games (8-pat, 4-fg)

Most Points, Game
- 18 Roger Craig, San Francisco vs. Miami, 1985 (3-td)
- 15 Don Chandler, Green Bay vs. Oakland, 1968 (3-pat, 4-fg)
- 14 Ray Wersching, San Francisco vs. Cincinnati, 1982 (2-pat, 4-fg)

TOUCHDOWNS

Most Touchdowns, Career
- 4 Franco Harris, Pittsburgh, 4 games (4-r)
- 3 John Stallworth, Pittsburgh, 4 games (3-p)
  - Lynn Swann, Pittsburgh, 4 games (3-p)
  - Cliff Branch, Oakland-L.A. Raiders, 3 games (3-p)
  - Roger Craig, San Francisco, 1 game (1-r, 2-p)
- 2 By many players

Most Touchdowns, Game
- 3 Roger Craig, San Francisco vs. Miami, 1985 (1-r, 2-p)
- 2 Max McGee, Green Bay vs. Kansas City, 1967 (2-p)
  - Elijah Pitts, Green Bay vs. Kansas City, 1967 (2-r)
  - Bill Miller, Oakland vs. Green Bay, 1968 (2-p)
  - Larry Csonka, Miami vs. Minnesota, 1974 (2-r)
  - Pete Banaszak, Oakland vs. Minnesota, 1977 (2-r)
  - John Stallworth, Pittsburgh vs. Dallas, 1979 (2-p)
  - Franco Harris, Pittsburgh vs. Los Angeles, 1980 (2-r)
  - Cliff Branch, Oakland vs. Philadelphia, 1981 (2-p)
  - Dan Ross, Cincinnati vs. San Francisco, 1982 (2-p)
  - Marcus Allen, L.A. Raiders vs. Washington, 1984 (2-r)

POINTS AFTER TOUCHDOWN

Most Points After Touchdown, Career
- 8 Don Chandler, Green Bay, 2 games (8 att)
  - Roy Gerela, Pittsburgh, 3 games (9 att)
  - Chris Bahr, Oakland-L.A. Raiders, 2 games (8 att)
- 7 Ray Wersching, San Francisco, 2 games (7 att)
- 5 Garo Yepremian, Miami, 3 games (5 att)

Most Points After Touchdown, Game
- 5 Don Chandler, Green Bay vs. Kansas City, 1967 (5 att)
  - Roy Gerela, Pittsburgh vs. Dallas, 1979 (5 att)
  - Chris Bahr, L.A. Raiders vs. Washington, 1984 (5 att)
  - Ray Wersching, San Francisco vs. Miami, 1985 (5 att)
- 4 Rafael Septien, Dallas vs. Pittsburgh, 1979 (4 att)
  - Matt Bahr, Pittsburgh vs. Los Angeles, 1980 (4 att)

FIELD GOALS

Field Goals Attempted, Career
- 7 Roy Gerela, Pittsburgh, 3 games
- 6 Jim Turner, N.Y. Jets-Denver, 2 games
- 5 Efren Herrera, Dallas, 1 game
  - Ray Wersching, San Francisco, 2 games

Most Field Goals Attempted, Game
- 5 Jim Turner, N.Y. Jets vs. Baltimore, 1969
  - Efren Herrera, Dallas vs. Denver, 1978
- 4 Don Chandler, Green Bay vs. Oakland, 1968
  - Roy Gerela, Pittsburgh vs. Dallas, 1976

Ray Wersching, San Francisco vs. Cincinnati, 1982

Most Field Goals, Career
- 5 Ray Wersching, San Francisco, 2 games (5 att)
- 4 Don Chandler, Green Bay, 2 games (4 att)
  - Jim Turner, N.Y. Jets-Denver, 2 games (6 att)
  - Uwe von Schamann, Miami, 2 games (4 att)
- 3 Mike Clark, Dallas, 2 games (3 att)
  - Jan Stenerud, Kansas City, 1 game (3 att)
  - Chris Bahr, Oakland-L.A. Raiders, 2 games (4 att)
  - Mark Moseley, Washington, 2 games (4 att)

Most Field Goals, Game
- 4 Don Chandler, Green Bay vs. Oakland, 1968
  - Ray Wersching, San Francisco vs. Cincinnati, 1982
- 3 Jim Turner, N.Y. Jets vs. Baltimore, 1969
  - Jan Stenerud, Kansas City vs. Minnesota, 1970
  - Uwe von Schamann, Miami vs. San Francisco, 1985

Longest Field Goal
- 48 Jan Stenerud, Kansas City vs. Minnesota, 1970
- 47 Jim Turner, Denver vs. Dallas, 1978
- 46 Chris Bahr, Oakland vs. Philadelphia, 1981

SAFETIES

Most Safeties, Game
- 1 Dwight White, Pittsburgh vs. Minnesota, 1975
  - Reggie Harrison, Pittsburgh vs. Dallas, 1976

RUSHING

ATTEMPTS

Most Attempts, Career
- 101 Franco Harris, Pittsburgh, 4 games
- 64 John Riggins, Washington, 2 games
- 57 Larry Csonka, Miami, 3 games

Most Attempts, Game
- 38 John Riggins, Washington vs. Miami, 1983
- 34 Franco Harris, Pittsburgh vs. Minnesota, 1975
- 33 Larry Csonka, Miami vs. Minnesota, 1974

YARDS GAINED

Most Yards Gained, Career
- 354 Franco Harris, Pittsburgh, 4 games
- 297 Larry Csonka, Miami, 3 games
- 230 John Riggins, Washington, 2 games

Most Yards Gained, Game
- 191 Marcus Allen, L.A. Raiders vs. Washington, 1984
- 166 John Riggins, Washington vs. Miami, 1983
- 158 Franco Harris, Pittsburgh vs. Minnesota, 1975

Longest Run From Scrimmage
- 74 Marcus Allen, L.A. Raiders vs. Washington, 1984 (TD)
- 58 Tom Matte, Baltimore vs. N.Y. Jets, 1969
- 49 Larry Csonka, Miami vs. Washington, 1973

AVERAGE GAIN

Highest Average Gain, Career (20 attempts)
- 9.6 Marcus Allen, L.A. Raiders, 1 game (20-191)
- 5.3 Walt Garrison, Dallas, 2 games (26-139)
- 5.2 Tony Dorsett, Dallas, 2 games (31-162)

Highest Average Gain, Game (10 attempts)
- 10.5 Tom Matte, Baltimore vs. N.Y. Jets, 1969 (11-116)
- 9.6 Marcus Allen, L.A. Raiders vs. Washington, 1984 (20-191)
- 8.6 Clarence Davis, Oakland vs. Minnesota, 1977 (16-137)

TOUCHDOWNS

Most Touchdowns, Career
- 4 Franco Harris, Pittsburgh, 4 games
- 2 Elijah Pitts, Green Bay, 1 game
  - Jim Kiick, Miami, 3 games
  - Larry Csonka, Miami, 3 games
  - Pete Banaszak, Oakland, 2 games
  - Marcus Allen, L.A. Raiders, 1 game
  - John Riggins, Washington, 2 games

Most Touchdowns, Game
- 2 Elijah Pitts, Green Bay vs. Kansas City, 1967
  - Larry Csonka, Miami vs. Minnesota, 1974
  - Pete Banaszak, Oakland vs. Minnesota, 1977
  - Franco Harris, Pittsburgh vs. Los Angeles, 1980
  - Marcus Allen, L.A. Raiders vs. Washington, 1984

PASSING

ATTEMPTS

Most Passes Attempted, Career
- 98 Roger Staubach, Dallas, 4 games
- 89 Fran Tarkenton, Minnesota, 3 games
- 84 Terry Bradshaw, Pittsburgh, 4 games

Most Passes Attempted, Game
- 50 Dan Marino, Miami vs. San Francisco, 1985
- 38 Ron Jaworski, Philadelphia vs. Oakland, 1981
- 35 Fran Tarkenton, Minnesota vs. Oakland, 1977
  - Joe Theismann, Washington vs. L.A. Raiders, 1984
  - Joe Montana, San Francisco vs. Miami, 1985

COMPLETIONS

Most Passes Completed, Career
- 61 Roger Staubach, Dallas, 4 games
- 49 Terry Bradshaw, Pittsburgh, 4 games
- 46 Fran Tarkenton, Minnesota, 3 games

Most Passes Completed, Game
- 29 Dan Marino, Miami vs. San Francisco, 1985
- 25 Ken Anderson, Cincinnati vs. San Francisco, 1982
- 24 Joe Montana, San Francisco vs. Miami, 1985

Most Consecutive Completions, Game
 8 Len Dawson, Kansas City vs. Green Bay, 1967
    Joe Theismann, Washington vs. Miami, 1983

COMPLETION PERCENTAGE
Highest Completion Percentage, Career (40 attempts)
 66.7 Joe Montana, San Francisco, 2 games (57-38)
 63.6 Len Dawson, Kansas City, 2 games (44-28)
 63.4 Bob Griese, Miami, 3 games (41-26)
Highest Completion Percentage, Game (20 attempts)
 73.5 Ken Anderson, Cincinnati vs. San Francisco, 1982 (34-25)
 69.6 Bart Starr, Green Bay vs. Kansas City, 1967 (23-16)
 68.6 Joe Montana, San Francisco vs. Miami, 1985 (35-24)

YARDS GAINED
Most Yards Gained, Career
 932 Terry Bradshaw, Pittsburgh, 4 games
 734 Roger Staubach, Dallas, 4 games
 489 Fran Tarkenton, Minnesota, 3 games
Most Yards Gained, Game
 331 Joe Montana, San Francisco vs. Miami, 1985
 318 Terry Bradshaw, Pittsburgh vs. Dallas, 1979
      Dan Marino, Miami vs. San Francisco, 1985
 309 Terry Bradshaw, Pittsburgh vs. Los Angeles, 1980
Longest Pass Completion
 80 Jim Plunkett (to King), Oakland vs. Philadelphia, 1981 (TD)
 76 David Woodley (to Cefalo), Miami vs. Washington, 1983 (TD)
 75 Johnny Unitas (to Mackey), Baltimore vs. Dallas, 1971 (TD)
     Terry Bradshaw (to Stallworth), Pittsburgh vs. Dallas, 1979 (TD)

AVERAGE GAIN
Highest Average Gain, Career (40 attempts)
 11.10 Terry Bradshaw, Pittsburgh, 4 games (84-932)
 9.62   Bart Starr, Green Bay, 2 games (47-452)
 9.41   Jim Plunkett, Oakland-L.A. Raiders, 2 games (46-433)
Highest Average Gain, Game (20 attempts)
 14.71 Terry Bradshaw, Pittsburgh vs. Los Angeles, 1980 (21-309)
 12.43 Jim Plunkett, Oakland vs. Philadelphia, 1981 (21-261)
 10.87 Bart Starr, Green Bay vs. Kansas City, 1967 (23-250)

TOUCHDOWNS
Most Touchdown Passes, Career
 9 Terry Bradshaw, Pittsburgh, 4 games
 8 Roger Staubach, Dallas, 4 games
 4 Jim Plunkett, Oakland-L.A. Raiders, 2 games
    Joe Montana, San Francisco, 2 games
Most Touchdown Passes, Game
 4 Terry Bradshaw, Pittsburgh vs. Dallas, 1979
 3 Roger Staubach, Dallas vs. Pittsburgh, 1979
    Jim Plunkett, Oakland vs. Philadelphia, 1981
    Joe Montana, San Francisco vs. Miami, 1985
 2 By many players

HAD INTERCEPTED
Lowest Percentage, Passes Had Intercepted, Career (40 attempts)
 0.00 Jim Plunkett, Oakland-L.A. Raiders, 2 games (46-0)
       Joe Montana, San Francisco, 2 games (57-0)
 2.13 Bart Starr, Green Bay, 2 games (47-1)
 4.08 Roger Staubach, Dallas, 4 games (98-4)
Most Attempts, Without Interception, Game
 35 Joe Montana, San Francisco vs. Miami, 1985
 28 Joe Namath, N.Y. Jets vs. Baltimore, 1969
 25 Roger Staubach, Dallas vs. Denver, 1978
     Jim Plunkett, L.A. Raiders vs. Washington, 1984
Most Passes Had Intercepted, Career
 7 Craig Morton, Dallas-Denver, 2 games
 6 Fran Tarkenton, Minnesota, 3 games
 4 Earl Morrall, Baltimore-Miami, 4 games
    Roger Staubach, Dallas, 4 games
    Terry Bradshaw, Pittsburgh, 4 games
    Joe Theismann, Washington, 2 games
Most Passes Had Intercepted, Game
 4 Craig Morton, Denver vs. Dallas, 1978
 3 By seven players

PASS RECEIVING

RECEPTIONS
Most Receptions, Career
 16 Lynn Swann, Pittsburgh, 4 games
 15 Chuck Foreman, Minnesota, 3 games
 14 Cliff Branch, Oakland-L.A. Raiders, 3 games
Most Receptions, Game
 11 Dan Ross, Cincinnati vs. San Francisco, 1982
 10 Tony Nathan, Miami vs. San Francisco, 1985
 8 George Sauer, N.Y. Jets vs. Baltimore, 1969

YARDS GAINED
Most Yards Gained, Career
 364 Lynn Swann, Pittsburgh, 4 games
 268 John Stallworth, Pittsburgh, 4 games
 181 Cliff Branch, Oakland-L.A. Raiders, 3 games
Most Yards Gained, Game
 161 Lynn Swann, Pittsburgh vs. Dallas, 1976
 138 Max McGee, Green Bay vs. Kansas City, 1967
 133 George Sauer, N.Y. Jets vs. Baltimore, 1969
Longest Reception
 80 Kenny King (from Plunkett), Oakland vs. Philadelphia, 1981 (TD)
 76 Jimmy Cefalo (from Woodley), Miami vs. Washington, 1983 (TD)
 75 John Mackey (from Unitas), Baltimore vs. Dallas, 1971 (TD)
     John Stallworth (from Bradshaw), Pittsburgh vs. Dallas, 1979 (TD)

AVERAGE GAIN
Highest Average Gain, Career (8 receptions)
 24.4 John Stallworth, Pittsburgh, 4 games (11-268)
 22.8 Lynn Swann, Pittsburgh, 4 games (16-364)
 17.0 Charlie Brown, Washington, 2 games (9-153)
Highest Average Gain, Game (3 receptions)
 40.33 John Stallworth, Pittsburgh vs. Los Angeles, 1980 (3-121)
 40.25 Lynn Swann, Pittsburgh vs. Dallas, 1979 (4-161)
 38.33 John Stallworth, Pittsburgh vs. Dallas, 1979 (3-115)

TOUCHDOWNS
Most Touchdowns, Career
 3 John Stallworth, Pittsburgh, 4 games
    Lynn Swann, Pittsburgh, 4 games
    Cliff Branch, Oakland-L.A. Raiders, 3 games
 2 Max McGee, Green Bay, 2 games
    Bill Miller, Oakland, 1 game
    Butch Johnson, Dallas, 2 games
    Dan Ross, Cincinnati, 1 game
    Roger Craig, San Francisco, 1 game
Most Touchdowns, Game
 2 Max McGee, Green Bay vs. Kansas City, 1967
    Bill Miller, Oakland vs. Green Bay, 1968
    John Stallworth, Pittsburgh vs. Dallas, 1979
    Cliff Branch, Oakland vs. Philadelphia, 1981
    Dan Ross, Cincinnati vs. San Francisco, 1982
    Roger Craig, San Francisco vs. Miami, 1985

INTERCEPTIONS BY
Most Interceptions By, Career
 3 Chuck Howley, Dallas, 2 games
    Rod Martin, Oakland-L.A. Raiders, 2 games
 2 Randy Beverly, N.Y. Jets, 1 game
    Jake Scott, Miami, 3 games
    Mike Wagner, Pittsburgh, 3 games
    Mel Blount, Pittsburgh, 4 games
    Eric Wright, San Francisco, 2 games
Most Interceptions By, Game
 3 Rod Martin, Oakland vs. Philadelphia, 1981
 2 Randy Beverly, N.Y. Jets vs. Baltimore, 1969
    Chuck Howley, Dallas vs. Baltimore, 1971
    Jake Scott, Miami vs. Washington, 1973

YARDS GAINED
Most Yards Gained, Career
 75 Willie Brown, Oakland, 2 games
 63 Chuck Howley, Dallas, 2 games
     Jake Scott, Miami, 3 games
 60 Herb Adderley, Green Bay-Dallas, 4 games
Most Yards Gained, Game
 75 Willie Brown, Oakland vs. Minnesota, 1977
 63 Jake Scott, Miami vs. Washington, 1973
 60 Herb Adderley, Green Bay vs. Oakland, 1968
Longest Return
 75 Willie Brown, Oakland vs. Minnesota, 1977 (TD)
 60 Herb Adderley, Green Bay vs. Oakland, 1968 (TD)
 55 Jake Scott, Miami vs. Washington, 1973

TOUCHDOWNS
Most Touchdowns, Game
 1 Herb Adderley, Green Bay vs. Oakland, 1968
    Willie Brown, Oakland vs. Minnesota, 1977
    Jack Squirek, L.A. Raiders vs. Washington, 1984

PUNTING
Most Punts, Career
 17 Mike Eischeid, Oakland-Minnesota, 3 games
 15 Larry Seiple, Miami, 3 games
 14 Ron Widby, Dallas, 2 games
     Ray Guy, Oakland-L.A. Raiders, 3 games
Most Punts, Game
 9 Ron Widby, Dallas vs. Baltimore, 1971
 7 By seven players
Longest Punt
 61 Jerrel Wilson, Kansas City vs. Green Bay, 1967
 59 Jerrel Wilson, Kansas City vs. Minnesota, 1970
     Bobby Walden, Pittsburgh vs. Dallas, 1976
     Ken Clark, Los Angeles vs. Pittsburgh, 1980
 57 Larry Seiple, Miami vs. Minnesota, 1974

AVERAGE YARDAGE
Highest Average, Punting, Career (10 punts)
 46.5 Jerrel Wilson, Kansas City, 2 games (11-151)
 41.9 Ray Guy, Oakland-L.A. Raiders, 3 games (14-587)
 41.3 Larry Seiple, Miami, 3 games (15-620)
Highest Average, Punting, Game (4 punts)
 48.5 Jerrel Wilson, Kansas City vs. Minnesota, 1970 (4-194)
 46.3 Jim Miller, San Francisco vs. Cincinnati, 1982 (4-185)
 45.3 Jerrel Wilson, Kansas City vs. Green Bay, 1967 (7-317)

PUNT RETURNS
Most Punt Returns, Career
 6 Willie Wood, Green Bay, 2 games
    Jake Scott, Miami, 3 games
    Theo Bell, Pittsburgh, 2 games
    Mike Nelms, Washington, 1 game
 5 Dana McLemore, San Francisco, 1 game
 4 By seven players
Most Punt Returns, Game
 6 Mike Nelms, Washington vs. Miami, 1983
 5 Willie Wood, Green Bay vs. Oakland, 1968
    Dana McLemore, San Francisco vs. Miami, 1985
 4 By six players

Most Fair Catches, Game
   3 Ron Gardin, Baltimore vs. Dallas, 1971
      Golden Richards, Dallas vs. Pittsburgh, 1976
      Greg Pruitt, L.A. Raiders vs. Washington, 1984

YARDS GAINED
Most Yards Gained, Career
  52 Mike Nelms, Washington, 1 game
  51 Dana McLemore, San Francisco, 1 game
  45 Jake Scott, Miami, 3 games
Most Yards Gained, Game
  52 Mike Nelms, Washington vs. Miami, 1983
  51 Dana McLemore, San Francisco vs. Miami, 1985
  43 Neal Colzie, Oakland vs. Minnesota, 1977
Longest Return
  34 Darrell Green, Washington vs. L.A. Raiders, 1984
  31 Willie Wood, Green Bay vs. Oakland, 1968
  28 Dana McLemore, San Francisco vs. Miami, 1985

AVERAGE YARDAGE
Highest Average, Career (4 returns)
  10.8 Neal Colzie, Oakland, 1 game (4-43)
  10.2 Dana McLemore, San Francisco, 1 game (5-51)
   8.8 Mike Fuller, Cincinnati, 1 game (4-35)
Highest Average, Game (3 returns)
  11.3 Lynn Swann, Pittsburgh vs. Minnesota, 1975 (3-34)
  10.8 Neal Colzie, Oakland vs. Minnesota, 1977 (4-43)
  10.2 Dana McLemore, San Francisco vs. Miami, 1985 (5-51)

TOUCHDOWNS
Most Touchdowns, Game
     None

KICKOFF RETURNS
Most Kickoff Returns, Career
   8 Larry Anderson, Pittsburgh, 2 games
      Fulton Walker, Miami, 2 games
   7 Preston Pearson, Baltimore-Pittsburgh-Dallas, 5 games
   6 Eugene (Mercury) Morris, Miami, 3 games
Most Kickoff Returns, Game
   5 Larry Anderson, Pittsburgh vs. Los Angeles, 1980
      Billy Campfield, Philadelphia vs. Oakland, 1981
      David Verser, Cincinnati vs. San Francisco, 1982
      Alvin Garrett, Washington vs. L.A. Raiders, 1984
   4 By seven players

YARDS GAINED
Most Yards Gained, Career
  283 Fulton Walker, Miami, 2 games
  207 Larry Anderson, Pittsburgh, 2 games
  123 Eugene (Mercury) Morris, Miami, 3 games
Most Yards Gained, Game
  190 Fulton Walker, Miami vs. Washington, 1983
  162 Larry Anderson, Pittsburgh vs. Los Angeles, 1980
  100 Alvin Garrett, Washington vs. L.A. Raiders, 1984
Longest Return
  98 Fulton Walker, Miami vs. Washington, 1983 (TD)
  67 Rick Upchurch, Denver vs. Dallas, 1978
  48 Thomas Henderson, Dallas vs. Pittsburgh, 1976 (lateral)

AVERAGE YARDAGE
Highest Average, Career (4 returns)
  35.4 Fulton Walker, Miami, 2 games (8-283)
  25.9 Larry Anderson, Pittsburgh, 2 games (8-207)
  22.5 Jim Duncan, Baltimore, 1 game (4-90)
Highest Average, Game (3 returns)
  47.5 Fulton Walker, Miami vs. Washington, 1983 (4-190)
  32.4 Larry Anderson, Pittsburgh vs. Los Angeles, 1980 (5-162)
  31.3 Rick Upchurch, Denver vs. Dallas, 1978 (3-94)

TOUCHDOWNS
Most Touchdowns, Game
   1 Fulton Walker, Miami vs. Washington, 1983

FUMBLES
Most Fumbles, Career
   5 Roger Staubach, Dallas, 4 games
   3 Franco Harris, Pittsburgh, 4 games
      Terry Bradshaw, Pittsburgh, 4 games
   2 By five players
Most Fumbles, Game
   3 Roger Staubach, Dallas vs. Pittsburgh, 1976
   2 Franco Harris, Pittsburgh vs. Minnesota, 1975
      Butch Johnson, Dallas vs. Denver, 1978
      Terry Bradshaw, Pittsburgh vs. Dallas, 1979

RECOVERIES
Most Fumbles Recovered, Career
   2 Jake Scott, Miami, 3 games (1 own, 1 opp)
      Fran Tarkenton, Minnesota, 3 games (2 own)
      Franco Harris, Pittsburgh, 4 games (2 own)
      Roger Staubach, Dallas, 4 games (2 own)
      Bobby Walden, Pittsburgh, 2 games (2 own)
      John Fitzgerald, Dallas, 4 games (2 own)
      Randy Hughes, Dallas, 3 games (2 opp)
      Butch Johnson, Dallas, 2 games (2 own)
Most Fumbles Recovered, Game
   2 Jake Scott, Miami vs. Minnesota, 1974 (1 own, 1 opp)
      Roger Staubach, Dallas vs. Pittsburgh, 1976 (2 own)
      Randy Hughes, Dallas vs. Denver, 1978 (2 opp)
      Butch Johnson, Dallas vs. Denver, 1978 (2 own)

YARDS GAINED
Most Yards Gained, Game
  49 Mike Bass, Washington vs. Miami, 1973 (opp)
  37 Mike Hegman, Dallas vs. Pittsburgh, 1979 (opp)
  21 Randy Hughes, Dallas vs. Denver, 1978 (opp)
Longest Return
  49 Mike Bass, Washington vs. Miami, 1973 (TD)
  37 Mike Hegman, Dallas vs. Pittsburgh, 1979 (TD)
  19 Randy Hughes, Dallas vs. Denver, 1978

TOUCHDOWNS
Most Touchdowns, Game
   1 Mike Bass, Washington vs. Miami, 1973 (opp 49 yds)
      Mike Hegman, Dallas vs. Pittsburgh, 1979 (opp 37 yds)

COMBINED NET YARDS GAINED
ATTEMPTS
Most Attempts, Career
  108 Franco Harris, Pittsburgh, 4 games
  66 John Riggins, Washington, 2 games
  60 Larry Csonka, Miami, 3 games
Most Attempts, Game
  39 John Riggins, Washington vs. Miami, 1983
  35 Franco Harris, Pittsburgh vs. Minnesota, 1975
  34 Matt Snell, N.Y. Jets vs. Baltimore, 1969

YARDS GAINED
Most Yards Gained, Career
  468 Franco Harris, Pittsburgh, 4 games
  391 Lynn Swann, Pittsburgh, 4 games
  314 Larry Csonka, Miami, 3 games
Most Yards Gained, Game
  209 Marcus Allen, L.A. Raiders vs. Washington, 1984
  190 Fulton Walker, Miami vs. Washington, 1983
  181 John Riggins, Washington vs. Miami, 1983

TEAM RECORDS

GAMES, VICTORIES, DEFEATS
Most Games
   5 Dallas, 1971-72, 1976, 1978-79
      Miami, 1972-74, 1983, 1985
   4 Minnesota, 1970, 1974-75, 1977
      Pittsburgh, 1975-76, 1979-80
      Oakland/L.A. Raiders, 1968, 1977, 1981, 1984
   3 Washington, 1973, 1983-84
Most Consecutive Games
   3 Miami, 1972-74
   2 Green Bay, 1967-68
      Dallas, 1971-72
      Minnesota, 1974-75
      Pittsburgh, 1975-76, 1979-80
      Washington, 1983-84
Most Games Won
   4 Pittsburgh, 1975-76, 1979-80
   3 Oakland/L.A. Raiders, 1977, 1981, 1984
   2 Green Bay, 1967-68
      Miami, 1973-74
      Dallas, 1972, 1978
      San Francisco, 1982, 1985
Most Consecutive Games Won
   2 Green Bay, 1967-68
      Miami, 1973-74
      Pittsburgh, 1975-76, 1979-80
Most Games Lost
   4 Minnesota, 1970, 1974-75, 1977
   3 Dallas, 1971, 1976, 1979
      Miami, 1972, 1983, 1985
   2 Washington, 1973, 1984
Most Consecutive Games Lost
   2 Minnesota, 1974-75

SCORING
Most Points, Game
  38 L.A. Raiders vs. Washington, 1984
      San Francisco vs. Miami, 1985
  35 Green Bay vs. Kansas City, 1967
      Pittsburgh vs. Dallas, 1979
  33 Green Bay vs. Kansas City, 1967
Fewest Points, Game
   3 Miami vs. Dallas, 1972
   6 Minnesota vs. Pittsburgh, 1975
   7 By four teams
Most Points, Both Teams, Game
  66 Pittsburgh (35) vs. Dallas (31), 1979
  54 San Francisco (38) vs. Miami (16), 1985
  50 Pittsburgh (31) vs. Los Angeles (19), 1980
Fewest Points, Both Teams, Game
  21 Washington (7) vs. Miami (14), 1973
  22 Minnesota (6) vs. Pittsburgh (16), 1975
  23 Baltimore (7) vs. N.Y. Jets (16), 1969
Largest Margin of Victory, Game
  29 L.A. Raiders vs. Washington, 1984 (38-9)
  25 Green Bay vs. Kansas City, 1967 (35-10)
  22 San Francisco vs. Miami, 1985 (38-16)
Most Points, Each Half
1st: 28 San Francisco vs. Miami, 1985
2nd: 21 Green Bay vs. Kansas City, 1967
         Pittsburgh vs. Los Angeles, 1980
         Cincinnati vs. San Francisco, 1982
Most Points, Each Quarter
1st: 14 Miami vs. Minnesota, 1974

Oakland vs. Philadelphia, 1981
2nd: 21 San Francisco vs. Miami, 1985
3rd: 14 Green Bay vs. Kansas City, 1967
L.A. Raiders vs. Washington, 1984
4th: 14 Pittsburgh vs. Dallas, 1976; vs. Dallas, 1979; vs. Los Angeles, 1980
Dallas vs. Pittsburgh, 1979
Cincinnati vs. San Francisco, 1982
Washington vs. Miami, 1983

Most Points, Both Teams, Each Half
1st: 44 San Francisco (28) vs. Miami (16), 1985
2nd: 31 Dallas (17) vs. Pittsburgh (14), 1979

Fewest Points, Both Teams, Each Half
1st: 2 Minnesota (0) vs. Pittsburgh (2), 1975
2nd: 7 Miami (0) vs. Washington (7), 1973

Most Points, Both Teams, Each Quarter
1st: 17 Miami (10) vs. San Francisco (7), 1985
2nd: 27 San Francisco (21) vs. Miami (6), 1985
3rd: 20 L.A. Raiders (14) vs. Washington (6), 1984
4th: 28 Dallas (14) vs. Pittsburgh (14), 1979

TOUCHDOWNS
Most Touchdowns, Game
5 Green Bay vs. Kansas City, 1967
Pittsburgh vs. Dallas, 1979
L.A. Raiders vs. Washington, 1984
San Francisco vs. Miami, 1985
4 Oakland vs. Minnesota, 1977
Dallas vs. Pittsburgh, 1979
Pittsburgh vs. Los Angeles, 1980
3 By many teams

Fewest Touchdowns, Game
0 Miami vs. Dallas, 1972
1 By 12 teams

Most Touchdowns, Both Teams, Game
9 Pittsburgh (5) vs. Dallas (4), 1979
6 Green Bay (5) vs. Kansas City (1), 1967
Oakland (4) vs. Minnesota (2), 1977
Pittsburgh (4) vs. Los Angeles (2), 1980
L.A. Raiders (5) vs. Washington (1), 1984
San Francisco (5) vs. Miami (1), 1985

Fewest Touchdowns, Both Teams, Game
2 Baltimore (1) vs. N.Y. Jets (1), 1969
3 In five games

POINTS AFTER TOUCHDOWN
Most Points After Touchdown, Game
5 Green Bay vs. Kansas City, 1967
Pittsburgh vs. Dallas, 1979
L.A. Raiders vs. Washington, 1984
San Francisco vs. Miami, 1985
4 Dallas vs. Pittsburgh, 1979
Pittsburgh vs. Los Angeles, 1980

Most Points After Touchdown, Both Teams, Game
9 Pittsburgh (5) vs. Dallas (4), 1979
6 Green Bay (5) vs. Kansas City (1), 1967
San Francisco (5) vs. Miami (1), 1985

Fewest Points After Touchdown, Both Teams, Game
2 Baltimore (1) vs. N.Y. Jets (1), 1969
Baltimore (1) vs. Dallas (1), 1971
Minnesota (0) vs. Pittsburgh (2), 1975

FIELD GOALS
Most Field Goals Attempted, Game
5 N.Y. Jets vs. Baltimore, 1969
Dallas vs. Denver, 1978
4 Green Bay vs. Oakland, 1968
Pittsburgh vs. Dallas, 1976
San Francisco vs. Cincinnati, 1982

Most Field Goals Attempted, Both Teams, Game
7 N.Y. Jets (5) vs. Baltimore (2), 1969
6 Dallas (5) vs. Denver (1), 1978
5 Green Bay (4) vs. Oakland (1), 1968
Pittsburgh (4) vs. Dallas (1), 1976
Oakland (3) vs. Philadelphia (2), 1981

Fewest Field Goals Attempted, Both Teams, Game
1 Minnesota (0) vs. Miami (1), 1974
2 Green Bay (0) vs. Kansas City (2), 1967
Miami (1) vs. Washington (1), 1973
Dallas (1) vs. Pittsburgh (1), 1979

Most Field Goals, Game
4 Green Bay vs. Oakland, 1968
San Francisco vs. Cincinnati, 1982
3 N.Y. Jets vs. Baltimore, 1969
Kansas City vs. Minnesota, 1970
Miami vs. San Francisco, 1985

Most Field Goals, Both Teams, Game
4 Green Bay (4) vs. Oakland (0), 1968
San Francisco (4) vs. Cincinnati (0), 1982
Miami (3) vs. San Francisco (1), 1985
3 In seven games

Fewest Field Goals, Both Teams, Game
0 Miami vs. Washington, 1973
Pittsburgh vs. Minnesota, 1975
1 Green Bay (0) vs. Kansas City (1), 1967
Minnesota (0) vs. Miami (1), 1974
Pittsburgh (0) vs. Dallas (1), 1979

SAFETIES
Most safeties, Game
1 Pittsburgh vs. Minnesota, 1975 vs. Dallas, 1976

FIRST DOWNS
Most First Downs, Game
31 San Francisco vs. Miami, 1985
24 Cincinnati vs. San Francisco, 1982
Washington vs. Miami, 1983
23 Dallas vs. Miami, 1972

Fewest First Downs, Game
9 Minnesota vs. Pittsburgh, 1975
Miami vs. Washington, 1983
10 Dallas vs. Baltimore, 1971
Miami vs. Dallas, 1972
11 Denver vs. Dallas, 1978

Most First Downs, Both Teams, Game
50 San Francisco (31) vs. Miami (19), 1985
44 Cincinnati (24) vs. San Francisco (20), 1982
41 Oakland (21) vs. Minnesota (20), 1977

Fewest First Downs, Both Teams, Game
24 Dallas (10) vs. Baltimore (14), 1971
26 Minnesota (9) vs. Pittsburgh (17), 1975
27 Pittsburgh (13) vs. Dallas (14), 1976

RUSHING
Most First Downs, Rushing, Game
16 San Francisco vs. Miami, 1985
15 Dallas vs. Miami, 1972
14 Washington vs. Miami, 1983

Fewest First Downs, Rushing, Game
2 Minnesota vs. Kansas City, 1970; vs. Pittsburgh, 1975; vs. Oakland, 1977
Pittsburgh vs. Dallas, 1979
Miami vs. San Francisco, 1985
3 Miami vs. Dallas, 1972
Philadelphia vs. Oakland, 1981
4 Kansas City vs. Green Bay, 1967
Baltimore vs. Dallas, 1971
Dallas vs. Baltimore, 1971

Most First Downs, Rushing, Both Teams, Game
21 Washington (14) vs. Miami (7), 1983
18 Dallas (15) vs. Miami (3), 1972
Miami (13) vs. Minnesota (5), 1974
San Francisco (16) vs. Miami (2), 1985
17 N.Y. Jets (10) vs. Baltimore (7), 1969

Fewest First Downs, Rushing, Both Teams, Game
8 Baltimore (4) vs. Dallas (4), 1971
Pittsburgh (2) vs. Dallas (6), 1979
9 Philadelphia (3) vs. Oakland (6), 1981
10 Minnesota (2) vs. Kansas City (8), 1970

PASSING
Most First Downs, Passing, Game
17 Miami vs. San Francisco, 1985
15 Minnesota vs. Oakland, 1977
Pittsburgh vs. Dallas, 1979
San Francisco vs. Miami, 1985
14 Philadelphia vs. Oakland, 1981

Fewest First Downs, Passing, Game
1 Denver vs. Dallas, 1978
2 Miami vs. Washington, 1983
4 Miami vs. Minnesota, 1974

Most First Downs, Passing, Both Teams, Game
32 Miami (17) vs. San Francisco (15), 1985
28 Pittsburgh (15) vs. Dallas (13), 1979
24 Philadelphia (14) vs. Oakland (10), 1981

Fewest First Downs, Passing, Both Teams, Game
9 Denver (1) vs. Dallas (8), 1978
10 Minnesota (5) vs. Pittsburgh (5), 1975
11 Dallas (5) vs. Baltimore (6), 1971
Miami (2) vs. Washington (9), 1983

PENALTY
Most First Downs, Penalty, Game
4 Baltimore vs. Dallas, 1971
Miami vs. Minnesota, 1974
Cincinnati vs. San Francisco, 1982
3 Kansas City vs. Minnesota, 1970
Minnesota vs. Oakland, 1977

Most First Downs, Penalty, Both Teams, Game
6 Cincinnati (4) vs. San Francisco (2), 1982
5 Baltimore (4) vs. Dallas (1), 1971
Miami (4) vs. Minnesota (1), 1974
4 Kansas City (3) vs. Minnesota (1), 1970

Fewest First Downs, Penalty, Both Teams, Game
0 Dallas vs. Miami, 1972
Miami vs. Washington, 1973
Dallas vs. Pittsburgh, 1976
Miami vs. San Francisco, 1985
1 Green Bay (0) vs. Kansas City (1), 1967
Miami (0) vs. Washington (1), 1983

NET YARDS GAINED RUSHING AND PASSING
Most Yards Gained, Game
537 San Francisco vs. Miami, 1985
429 Oakland vs. Minnesota, 1977
400 Washington vs. Miami, 1983

Fewest Yards Gained, Game
119 Minnesota vs. Pittsburgh, 1975
156 Denver vs. Dallas, 1978
176 Miami vs. Washington, 1983

Most Yards Gained, Both Teams, Game
851 San Francisco (537) vs. Miami (314), 1985
782 Oakland (429) vs. Minnesota (353), 1977
737 Oakland (377) vs. Philadelphia (360), 1981

Fewest Yards Gained, Both Teams, Game
- 452   Minnesota (119) vs. Pittsburgh (333), 1975
- 481   Washington (228) vs. Miami (253), 1973
-         Denver (156) vs. Dallas (325), 1978
- 497   Minnesota (238) vs. Miami (259), 1974

RUSHING

ATTEMPTS
Most Attempts, Game
- 57   Pittsburgh vs. Minnesota, 1975
- 53   Miami vs. Minnesota, 1974
- 52   Oakland vs. Minnesota, 1977
-      Washington vs. Miami, 1983

Fewest Attempts, Game
- 9   Miami vs. San Francisco, 1985
- 19   Kansas City vs. Green Bay, 1967
-      Minnesota vs. Kansas City, 1970
- 20   Oakland vs. Green Bay, 1968
-      Miami vs. Dallas, 1972

Most Attempts, Both Teams, Game
- 81   Washington (52) vs. Miami (29), 1983
- 78   Pittsburgh (57) vs. Minnesota (21), 1975
-      Oakland (52) vs. Minnesota (26), 1977
- 77   Miami (53) vs. Minnesota (24), 1974
-      Pittsburgh (46) vs. Dallas (31), 1976

Fewest Attempts, Both Teams, Game
- 49   Miami (9) vs. San Francisco (40), 1985
- 52   Kansas City (19) vs. Green Bay (33), 1967
- 56   Pittsburgh (24) vs. Dallas (32), 1979

YARDS GAINED
Most Yards Gained, Game
- 276   Washington vs. Miami, 1983
- 266   Oakland vs. Minnesota, 1977
- 252   Dallas vs. Miami, 1972

Fewest Yards Gained, Game
- 17   Minnesota vs. Pittsburgh, 1975
- 25   Miami vs. San Francisco, 1985
- 66   Pittsburgh vs. Dallas, 1979

Most Yards Gained, Both Teams, Game
- 372   Washington (276) vs. Miami (96), 1983
- 337   Oakland (266) vs. Minnesota (71), 1977
- 332   Dallas (252) vs. Miami (80), 1972

Fewest Yards Gained, Both Teams, Game
- 171   Baltimore (69) vs. Dallas (102), 1971
- 186   Philadelphia (69) vs. Oakland (117), 1981
- 191   Pittsburgh (84) vs. Los Angeles (107), 1980

AVERAGE GAIN
Highest Average Gain, Game
- 7.00   L.A. Raiders vs. Washington, 1984 (33-231)
- 6.22   Baltimore vs. N.Y. Jets, 1969 (23-143)
- 5.35   Oakland vs. Green Bay, 1968 (20-107)

Lowest Average Gain, Game
- 0.81   Minnesota vs. Pittsburgh, 1975 (21-17)
- 2.23   Baltimore vs. Dallas, 1971 (31-69)
- 2.27   Pittsburgh vs. Los Angeles, 1980 (37-84)

TOUCHDOWNS
Most Touchdowns, Game
- 3   Green Bay vs. Kansas City, 1967
-     Miami vs. Minnesota, 1974
- 2   Oakland vs. Minnesota, 1977
-     Pittsburgh vs. Los Angeles, 1980
-     L.A. Raiders vs. Washington, 1984
-     San Francisco vs. Miami, 1985

Fewest Touchdowns, Game
- 0   By 13 teams

Most Touchdowns, Both Teams, Game
- 4   Miami (3) vs. Minnesota (1), 1974
- 3   Green Bay (3) vs. Kansas City (0), 1967
-     Pittsburgh (2) vs. Los Angeles (1), 1980
-     L.A. Raiders (2) vs. Washington (1), 1984

Fewest Touchdowns, Both Teams, Game
- 0   Pittsburgh vs. Dallas, 1976
-     Oakland vs. Philadelphia, 1981
- 1   In seven games

PASSING

ATTEMPTS
Most Passes Attempted, Game
- 50   Miami vs. San Francisco, 1985
- 44   Minnesota vs. Oakland, 1977
- 41   Baltimore vs. N.Y. Jets, 1969

Fewest Passes Attempted, Game
- 7   Miami vs. Minnesota, 1974
- 11   Miami vs. Washington, 1973
- 14   Pittsburgh vs. Minnesota, 1975

Most Passes Attempted, Both Teams, Game
- 85   Miami (50) vs. San Francisco (35), 1985
- 70   Baltimore (41) vs. N.Y. Jets (29), 1969
- 63   Minnesota (44) vs. Oakland (19), 1977

Fewest Passes Attempted, Both Teams, Game
- 35   Miami (7) vs. Minnesota (28), 1974
- 39   Miami (11) vs. Washington (28), 1973
- 40   Pittsburgh (14) vs. Minnesota (26), 1975
-      Miami (17) vs. Washington (23), 1983

COMPLETIONS
Most Passes Completed, Game
- 29   Miami vs. San Francisco, 1985
- 25   Cincinnati vs. San Francisco, 1982

- 24   Minnesota vs. Oakland, 1977
-      San Francisco vs. Miami, 1985

Fewest Passes Completed, Game
- 4   Miami vs. Washington, 1983
- 6   Miami vs. Minnesota, 1974
- 8   Miami vs. Washington, 1973
-    Denver vs. Dallas, 1978

Most Passes Completed, Both Teams, Game
- 53   Miami (29) vs. San Francisco (24), 1985
- 39   Cincinnati (25) vs. San Francisco (14), 1982
- 36   Minnesota (24) vs. Oakland (12), 1977

Fewest Passes Completed, Both Teams, Game
- 19   Miami (4) vs. Washington (15), 1983
- 20   Pittsburgh (9) vs. Minnesota (11), 1975
- 22   Miami (8) vs. Washington (14), 1973

COMPLETION PERCENTAGE
Highest Completion Percentage, Game (20 attempts)
- 73.5   Cincinnati vs. San Francisco, 1982 (34-25)
- 68.6   San Francisco vs. Miami, 1985 (35-24)
- 67.9   Dallas vs. Denver, 1978 (28-19)

Lowest Completion Percentage, Game (20 attempts)
- 32.0   Denver vs. Dallas, 1978 (25-8)
- 41.5   Baltimore vs. N.Y. Jets, 1969 (41-17)
- 42.3   Minnesota vs. Pittsburgh, 1975 (26-11)

YARDS GAINED
Most Yards Gained, Game
- 326   San Francisco vs. Miami, 1985
- 309   Pittsburgh vs. Los Angeles, 1980
- 291   Pittsburgh vs. Dallas, 1979
-      Philadelphia vs. Oakland, 1981

Fewest Yards Gained, Game
- 35   Denver vs. Dallas, 1978
- 63   Miami vs. Minnesota, 1974
- 69   Miami vs. Washington, 1973

Most Yards Gained, Both Teams, Game
- 615   San Francisco (326) vs. Miami (289), 1985
- 551   Philadelphia (291) vs. Oakland (260), 1981
- 503   Pittsburgh (309) vs. Los Angeles (194), 1980

Fewest Yards Gained, Both Teams, Game
- 156   Miami (69) vs. Washington (87), 1973
- 186   Pittsburgh (84) vs. Minnesota (102), 1975
- 205   Dallas (100) vs. Miami (105), 1972

TIMES SACKED
Most Times Sacked, Game
- 7   Dallas vs. Pittsburgh, 1976
- 6   Kansas City vs. Green Bay, 1967
-    Washington vs. L.A. Raiders, 1984
- 5   Dallas vs. Denver, 1978; vs. Pittsburgh, 1979
-    Cincinnati vs. San Francisco, 1982

Fewest Times Sacked, Game
- 0   Baltimore vs. N.Y. Jets, 1969; vs. Dallas, 1971
-    Minnesota vs. Pittsburgh, 1975
-    Pittsburgh vs. Los Angeles, 1980
-    Philadelphia vs. Oakland, 1981
- 1   By seven teams

Most Times Sacked, Both Teams, Game
- 9   Kansas City (6) vs. Green Bay (3), 1967
-    Dallas (7) vs. Pittsburgh (2), 1976
-    Dallas (5) vs. Denver (4), 1978
-    Dallas (5) vs. Pittsburgh (4), 1979
- 8   Washington (6) vs. L.A. Raiders (2), 1984
- 7   Green Bay (4) vs. Oakland (3), 1968

Fewest Times Sacked, Both Teams, Game
- 1   Philadelphia (0) vs. Oakland (1), 1981
- 2   Baltimore (0) vs. N.Y. Jets (2), 1969
-    Baltimore (0) vs. Dallas (2), 1971
-    Minnesota (0) vs. Pittsburgh (2), 1975
- 3   In three games

TOUCHDOWNS
Most Touchdowns, Game
- 4   Pittsburgh vs. Dallas, 1979
- 3   Dallas vs. Pittsburgh, 1979
-    Oakland vs. Philadelphia, 1981
-    San Francisco vs. Miami, 1985
- 2   By 10 teams

Fewest Touchdowns, Game
- 0   By 10 teams

Most Touchdowns, Both Teams, Game
- 7   Pittsburgh (4) vs. Dallas (3), 1979
- 4   Dallas (2) vs. Pittsburgh (2), 1976
-    Oakland (3) vs. Philadelphia (1), 1981
-    San Francisco (3) vs. Miami (1), 1985
- 3   In six games

Fewest Touchdowns, Both Teams, Game
- 0   N.Y. Jets vs. Baltimore, 1969
-    Miami vs. Minnesota, 1974
- 1   In four games

INTERCEPTIONS BY
Most Interceptions By, Game
- 4   N.Y. Jets vs. Baltimore, 1969
-    Dallas vs. Denver, 1978
- 3   By eight teams

Most Interceptions By, Both Teams, Game
- 6   Baltimore (3) vs. Dallas (3), 1971
- 4   In five games

YARDS GAINED
Most Yards Gained, Game
  95 Miami vs. Washington, 1973
  91 Oakland vs. Minnesota, 1977
  89 Pittsburgh vs. Dallas, 1976
Most Yards Gained, Both Teams, Game
  95 Miami (95) vs. Washington (0), 1973
  91 Oakland (91) vs. Minnesota (0), 1977
  89 Pittsburgh (89) vs. Dallas (0), 1976

TOUCHDOWNS
Most Touchdowns, Game
  1 Green Bay vs. Oakland, 1968
     Oakland vs. Minnesota, 1977
     L.A. Raiders vs. Washington, 1984

PUNTING

Most Punts, Game
  9 Dallas vs. Baltimore, 1971
  8 Washington vs. L.A. Raiders, 1984
  7 By six teams
Fewest Punts, Game
  2 Pittsburgh vs. Los Angeles, 1980
  3 By eight teams
Most Punts, Both Teams, Game
  15 Washington (8) vs. L.A. Raiders (7), 1984
  13 Dallas (9) vs. Baltimore (4), 1971
      Pittsburgh (7) vs. Minnesota (6), 1975
  12 In three games
Fewest Punts, Both Teams, Game
  6 Oakland (3) vs. Philadelphia (3), 1981
  7 In four games

AVERAGE YARDAGE
Highest Average, Game (4 punts)
  48.50 Kansas City vs. Minnesota, 1970 (4-194)
  46.25 San Francisco vs. Cincinnati, 1982 (4-185)
  45.29 Kansas City vs. Green Bay, 1967 (7-317)
Lowest Average, Game (4 punts)
  31.20 Washington vs. Miami, 1973 (5-156)
  32.38 Washington vs. L.A. Raiders, 1984 (8-259)
  32.40 Oakland vs. Minnesota, 1977 (5-162)

PUNT RETURNS

Most Punt Returns, Game
  6 Washington vs. Miami, 1983
  5 By five teams
Fewest Punt Returns, Game
  0 Minnesota vs. Miami, 1974
  1 By eight teams
Most Punt Returns, Both Teams, Game
  9 Pittsburgh (5) vs. Minnesota (4), 1975
  8 Green Bay (5) vs. Oakland (3), 1968
     Baltimore (5) vs. Dallas (3), 1971
     Washington (6) vs. Miami (2), 1983
  7 Green Bay (4) vs. Kansas City (3), 1967
     Oakland (4) vs. Minnesota (3), 1977
     San Francisco (5) vs. Miami (2), 1985
Fewest Punt Returns, Both Teams, Game
  2 Dallas (1) vs. Miami (1), 1972
  3 Kansas City (1) vs. Minnesota (2), 1970
     Minnesota (0) vs. Miami (3), 1974
  4 L.A. Raiders (2) vs. Washington (2), 1984

YARDS GAINED
Most Yards Gained, Game
  52 Washington vs. Miami, 1983
  51 San Francisco vs. Miami, 1985
  43 Oakland vs. Minnesota, 1977
Fewest Yards Gained, Game
  −1 Dallas vs. Miami, 1972
   0 By four teams
Most Yards Gained, Both Teams, Game
  74 Washington (52) vs. Miami (22), 1983
  66 San Francisco (51) vs. Miami (15), 1985
  60 Dallas (33) vs. Pittsburgh (27), 1979
Fewest Yards Gained, Both Teams, Game
  13 Miami (4) vs. Washington (9), 1973
  18 Kansas City (0) vs. Minnesota (18), 1970
  20 Dallas (−1) vs. Miami (21), 1972
     Minnesota (0) vs. Miami (20), 1974

AVERAGE RETURN
Highest Average, Game (3 returns)
  10.8 Oakland vs. Minnesota, 1977 (4-43)
  10.2 San Francisco vs. Miami, 1985 (5-51)
   8.8 Cincinnati vs. San Francisco, 1982 (4-35)

TOUCHDOWNS
Most Touchdowns, Game
     None

KICKOFF RETURNS

Most Kickoff Returns, Game
  7 Oakland vs. Green Bay, 1968
     Minnesota vs. Oakland, 1977
     Cincinnati vs. San Francisco, 1982
     Washington vs. L.A. Raiders, 1984
     Miami vs. San Francisco, 1985
  6 By six teams
Fewest Kickoff Returns, Game
  1 N.Y. Jets vs. Baltimore, 1969

     L.A. Raiders vs. Washington, 1984
  2 By six teams
Most Kickoff Returns, Both Teams, Game
  11 Los Angeles (6) vs. Pittsburgh (5), 1980
      Miami (7) vs. San Francisco (4), 1985
  10 Oakland (7) vs. Green Bay (3), 1968
   9 In seven games
Fewest Kickoff Returns, Both Teams, Game
  5 N.Y. Jets (1) vs. Baltimore (4), 1969
     Miami (2) vs. Washington (3), 1973
  6 In three games

YARDS GAINED
Most Yards Gained, Game
  222 Miami vs. Washington, 1983
  173 Denver vs. Dallas, 1978
  162 Pittsburgh vs. Los Angeles, 1980
Fewest Yards Gained, Game
  17 L.A. Raiders vs. Washington, 1984
  25 N.Y. Jets vs. Baltimore, 1969
  32 Pittsburgh vs. Minnesota, 1975
Most Yards Gained, Both Teams, Game
  279 Miami (222) vs. Washington (57), 1983
  231 Pittsburgh (162) vs. Los Angeles (79), 1980
  224 Denver (173) vs. Dallas (51), 1978
Fewest Yards Gained, Both Teams, Game
  78 Miami (33) vs. Washington (45), 1973
  82 Pittsburgh (32) vs. Minnesota (50), 1975
  92 San Francisco (40) vs. Cincinnati (52), 1982

AVERAGE GAIN
Highest Average, Game (3 returns)
  37.0 Miami vs. Washington, 1983 (6-222)
  32.4 Pittsburgh vs. Los Angeles, 1980 (5-162)
  28.8 Denver vs. Dallas, 1978 (6-173)

TOUCHDOWNS
Most Touchdowns, Game
  1 Miami vs. Washington, 1983

PENALTIES

Most Penalties, Game
  12 Dallas vs. Denver, 1978
  10 Dallas vs. Baltimore, 1971
   9 Dallas vs. Pittsburgh, 1979
Fewest Penalties, Game
  0 Miami vs. Dallas, 1972
     Pittsburgh vs. Dallas, 1976
  1 Green Bay vs. Oakland, 1968
     Miami vs. Minnesota, 1974; vs. San Francisco, 1985
  2 By four teams
Most Penalties, Both Teams, Game
  20 Dallas (12) vs. Denver (8), 1978
  16 Cincinnati (8) vs. San Francisco (8), 1982
  14 Dallas (10) vs. Baltimore (4), 1971
      Dallas (9) vs. Pittsburgh (5), 1979
Fewest Penalties, Both Teams, Game
  2 Pittsburgh (0) vs. Dallas (2), 1976
  3 Miami (0) vs. Dallas (3), 1972
     Miami (1) vs. San Francisco (2), 1985
  5 Green Bay (1) vs. Oakland (4), 1968

YARDS PENALIZED
Most Yards Penalized, Game
  133 Dallas vs. Baltimore, 1971
  122 Pittsburgh vs. Minnesota, 1975
   94 Dallas vs. Denver, 1978
Fewest Yards Penalized, Game
  0 Miami vs. Dallas, 1972
     Pittsburgh vs. Dallas, 1976
  4 Miami vs. Minnesota, 1974
  10 Miami vs. San Francisco, 1985
      San Francisco vs. Miami, 1985
Most Yards Penalized, Both Teams, Game
  164 Dallas (133) vs. Baltimore (31), 1971
  154 Dallas (94) vs. Denver (60), 1978
  140 Pittsburgh (122) vs. Minnesota (18), 1975
Fewest Yards Penalized, Both Teams, Game
  15 Miami (0) vs. Dallas (15), 1972
  20 Pittsburgh (0) vs. Dallas (20), 1976
     Miami (10) vs. San Francisco (10), 1985
  43 Green Bay (12) vs. Oakland (31), 1968

FUMBLES

Most Fumbles, Game
  6 Dallas vs. Denver, 1978
  5 Baltimore vs. Dallas, 1971
  4 In four games
Fewest Fumbles, Game
  0 In six games
Most Fumbles, Both Teams, Game
  10 Dallas (6) vs. Denver (4), 1978
   8 Dallas (4) vs. Pittsburgh (4), 1976
   7 Pittsburgh (4) vs. Minnesota (3), 1975
Fewest Fumbles, Both Teams, Game
  0 Los Angeles vs. Pittsburgh, 1980
  1 Oakland (0) vs. Minnesota (1), 1977
     Oakland (0) vs. Philadelphia (1), 1981
  2 In three games
Most Fumbles Lost, Game
  4 Baltimore vs. Dallas, 1971
     Denver vs. Dallas, 1978
  2 In many games

Most Fumbles Recovered, Game
- 8 Dallas vs. Denver, 1978 (4 own, 4 opp)
- 4 Pittsburgh vs. Minnesota, 1975 (2 own, 2 opp)
- Dallas vs. Pittsburgh, 1976 (4 own)

TURNOVERS
(Number of times losing the ball on interceptions and fumbles.)

Most Turnovers, Game
- 8 Denver vs. Dallas, 1978
- 7 Baltimore vs. Dallas, 1971
- 5 In three games

Fewest Turnovers, Game
- 0 Green Bay vs. Oakland, 1968
- Miami vs. Minnesota, 1974
- Pittsburgh vs. Dallas, 1976
- Oakland vs. Minnesota, 1977; vs. Philadelphia, 1981
- 1 By many teams

Most Turnovers, Both Teams, Game
- 11 Baltimore (7) vs. Dallas (4), 1971
- 10 Denver (8) vs. Dallas (2), 1978
- 7 Minnesota (5) vs. Pittsburgh (2), 1975

Fewest Turnovers, Both Teams, Game
- 2 Green Bay (1) vs. Kansas City (1), 1967
- Miami (0) vs. Minnesota (2), 1974
- 3 Green Bay (0) vs. Oakland (3), 1968
- Pittsburgh (0) vs. Dallas (3), 1976
- Oakland (0) vs. Minnesota (3), 1977
- 4 In five games

Compiled by Elias Sports Bureau

Throughout this all-time postseason record section, the following abbreviations are used to indicate various levels of postseason games:

SB   Super Bowl (1966 to date)
AFC   AFC Championship Game (1970 to date) or AFL Championship Game (1960-69)
NFC   NFC Championship Game (1970 to date) or NFL Championship Game (1933-69)
AFC-D   AFC Divisional Playoff Game (1970 to date), AFC Second-Round Playoff Game (1982), AFL Inter-Divisional Playoff Game (1969), or special playoff game to break tie for AFL Division Championship (1963, 1968)
NFC-D   NFC Divisional Playoff Game (1970 to date), NFC Second-Round Playoff Game (1982), NFL Conference Championship Game (1967-69), or special playoff game to break tie for NFL Division or Conference Championship (1941, 1943, 1947, 1950, 1952, 1957, 1958, 1965)
AFC-FR   AFC First-Round Playoff Game (1978 to date)
NFC-FR   NFC First-Round Playoff Game (1978 to date)

Year references are to the season following which the postseason game occurred, even if the game was played in the next calendar year.

POSTSEASON GAME COMPOSITE STANDINGS

	W	L	Pct.	Pts.	OP
Green Bay Packers	13	5	.722	416	259
Pittsburgh Steelers	15	8	.652	533	447
San Francisco 49ers	9	5	.643	328	271
Los Angeles Raiders*	19	11	.633	741	508
Kansas City Chiefs**	5	3	.625	144	147
Detroit Lions	6	4	.600	221	208
Seattle Seahawks	3	2	.600	95	95
Miami Dolphins	13	9	.591	497	416
Philadelphia Eagles	7	5	.583	219	173
Dallas Cowboys	20	15	.571	805	620
New York Jets	4	3	.571	137	119
Baltimore Colts	8	7	.533	264	262
Chicago Bears	8	8	.500	353	338
Houston Oilers	6	6	.500	168	267
Washington Redskins***	11	11	.500	443	449
Minnesota Vikings	10	12	.455	378	427
Los Angeles Rams****	10	16	.385	414	576
Buffalo Bills	3	5	.375	138	171
Cleveland Browns	7	13	.350	354	433
San Diego Chargers†	4	8	.333	230	279
Cincinnati Bengals	2	5	.286	137	180
Denver Broncos	2	5	.286	105	166
New York Giants	6	15	.286	308	438
Atlanta Falcons	1	3	.250	85	100
Tampa Bay Buccaneers	1	3	.250	41	94
New England Patriots††	1	4	.200	84	142
St. Louis Cardinals†††	1	4	.200	81	134

*24 games played when franchise was in Oakland. (Won 15, lost 9, 587 points scored, 435 points allowed)
**One game played when franchise was in Dallas (Texans). (Won 20-17)
***One game played when franchise was in Boston. (Lost 21-6)
****One game played when franchise was in Cleveland. (Won 15-14)
†One game played when franchise was in Los Angeles. (Lost 24-16)
††Two games played when franchise was in Boston. (Won 26-8, lost 51-10)
†††Two games played when franchise was in Chicago. (Won 28-21, lost 7-0)

INDIVIDUAL RECORDS

SERVICE

Most Games, Career
27   D. D. Lewis, Dallas (SB-5, NFC-9, NFC-D 12, NFC-FR 1)
26   Larry Cole, Dallas (SB-5, NFC-8, NFC-D-12, NFC-FR 1)
25   Charlie Waters, Dallas (SB-5, NFC-9, NFC-D 10, NFC-FR 1)

SCORING

POINTS
Most Points, Career
115   George Blanda, Chi. Bears-Houston-Oakland, 19 games (49-pat, 22-fg)
102   Franco Harris, Pittsburgh, 19 games (17-td)
95   Rafael Septien, L.A. Rams-Dallas, 14 games (41-pat, 18-fg)
Most Points, Game
19   Pat Harder, NFC-D: Detroit vs. Los Angeles, 1952 (2-td, 4-pat, 1-fg)
   Paul Hornung, NFC: Green Bay vs. N.Y. Giants, 1961 (1-td, 4-pat, 3-fg)
18   By 15 players

TOUCHDOWNS
Most Touchdowns, Career
17   Franco Harris, Pittsburgh, 19 games (16-r, 1-p)
12   John Riggins, Washington, 9 games (12-r)
   John Stallworth, Pittsburgh, 18 games (12-p)
10   Fred Biletnikoff, Oakland, 19 games (10-p)
   Larry Csonka, Miami, 12 games (9-r, 1-p)
   Tony Dorsett, Dallas, 16 games (9-r, 1-p)
Most Touchdowns, Game
3   Andy Farkas, NFC-D: Washington vs. N.Y. Giants, 1943 (3-r)
   Tom Fears, NFC-D: Los Angeles vs. Chi. Bears, 1950 (3-p)
   Otto Graham, NFC: Cleveland vs. Detroit, 1954 (3-r)
   Gary Collins, NFC: Cleveland vs. Baltimore, 1964 (3-p)
   Craig Baynham, NFC-D: Dallas vs. Cleveland, 1967 (2-r, 1-p)

   Fred Biletnikoff, AFC-D: Oakland vs. Kansas City, 1968 (3-p)
   Tom Matte, NFC: Baltimore vs. Cleveland, 1968 (3-r)
   Larry Schreiber, NFC-D: San Francisco vs. Dallas, 1972 (3-r)
   Larry Csonka, AFC: Miami vs. Oakland, 1973 (3-r)
   Franco Harris, AFC-D: Pittsburgh vs. Buffalo, 1974 (3-r)
   Preston Pearson, NFC: Dallas vs. Los Angeles, 1975 (3-p)
   Dave Casper, AFC-D: Oakland vs. Baltimore, 1977 (OT) (3-p)
   Alvin Garrett, NFC-FR: Washington vs. Detroit, 1982 (3-p)
   John Riggins, NFC-D: Washington vs. L.A. Rams, 1983 (3-r)
   Roger Craig, SB: San Francisco vs. Miami, 1984 (1-r, 2-p)

Most Consecutive Games Scoring Touchdowns
8   John Stallworth, Pittsburgh, 1978-83
7   John Riggins, Washington, 1982-84 (current)
6   Marcus Allen, L.A. Raiders, 1982-84 (current)

POINTS AFTER TOUCHDOWN
Most Points After Touchdown, Career
49   George Blanda, Chi. Bears-Houston-Oakland, 19 games (49 att)
41   Rafael Septien, L.A. Rams-Dallas, 14 games (41 att)
38   Fred Cox, Minnesota, 18 games (40 att)
Most Points After Touchdown, Game
8   Lou Groza, NFC: Cleveland vs. Detroit, 1954 (8 att)
   Jim Martin, NFC: Detroit vs. Cleveland, 1957 (8 att)
   George Blanda, AFC-D: Oakland vs. Houston, 1969 (8 att)
7   Danny Villanueva, NFC-D: Dallas vs. Cleveland, 1967 (7 att)
6   George Blair, AFC: San Diego vs. Boston, 1963 (6 att)
   Mark Moseley, NFC-D: Washington vs. L.A. Rams, 1983 (6 att)
   Uwe von Schamann, AFC: Miami vs. Pittsburgh, 1984 (6 att)
Most Points After Touchdown, No Misses, Career
49   George Blanda, Chi. Bears-Houston-Oakland, 19 games
41   Rafael Septien, L.A. Rams-Dallas, 14 games
32   Uwe von Schamann, Miami, 10 games

FIELD GOALS
Most Field Goals Attempted, Career
39   George Blanda, Chi. Bears-Houston-Oakland, 19 games
27   Roy Gerela, Houston-Pittsburgh, 15 games
25   Toni Fritsch, Dallas-Houston, 14 games
Most Field Goals Attempted, Game
6   George Blanda, AFC: Oakland vs. Houston, 1967
   David Ray, NFC-D: Los Angeles vs. Dallas, 1973
5   Jerry Kramer, NFC: Green Bay vs. N.Y. Giants, 1962
   Gino Cappelletti, AFC-D: Boston vs. Buffalo, 1963
   Pete Gogolak, AFC: Buffalo vs. San Diego, 1965
   Jan Stenerud, AFC-D: Kansas City vs. N.Y. Jets, 1969
   George Blanda, AFC-D: Oakland vs. Pittsburgh, 1973
   Ed Murray, NFC-D: Detroit vs. San Francisco, 1983
   Mark Moseley, NFC: Washington vs. San Francisco, 1983
4   By many players
Most Field Goals, Career
22   George Blanda, Chi. Bears-Houston-Oakland, 19 games
20   Toni Fritsch, Dallas-Houston, 14 games
18   Rafael Septien, L.A. Rams-Dallas, 14 games
Most Field Goals, Game
4   Gino Cappelletti, AFC-D: Boston vs. Buffalo, 1963
   George Blanda, AFC: Oakland vs. Houston, 1967
   Don Chandler, SB: Green Bay vs. Oakland, 1967
   Curt Knight, NFC: Washington vs. Dallas, 1972
   George Blanda, AFC-D: Oakland vs. Pittsburgh, 1973
   Ray Wersching, SB: San Francisco vs. Cincinnati, 1981
3   By many players
Most Consecutive Field Goals
15   Rafael Septien, Dallas, 1978-82
Longest Field Goal
54   Ed Murray, NFC-D: Detroit vs. San Francisco, 1983
52   Lou Groza, NFC: Cleveland vs. Los Angeles, 1951
   Curt Knight, NFC-D: Washington vs. Minnesota, 1973
   Matt Bahr, AFC-FR: Cleveland vs. L.A. Raiders, 1982
50   Garo Yepremian, AFC-D: Miami vs. Cincinnati, 1973
   Rafael Septien, NFC-D: Dallas vs. Green Bay, 1982
Highest Field Goal Percentage, Career (10 field goals)
85.7   Rafael Septien, L.A. Rams-Dallas, 14 games (21-18)
81.3   Chris Bahr, Oakland-L.A. Raiders, 10 games (16-13)
80.0   Toni Fritsch, Dallas-Houston, 14 games (25-20)

SAFETIES
Most Safeties, Game
1   Bill Willis, NFC-D: Cleveland vs. N.Y. Giants, 1950
   Carl Eller, NFC-D: Minnesota vs. Los Angeles, 1969
   George Andrie, NFC-D: Dallas vs. Detroit, 1970
   Alan Page, NFC-D: Minnesota vs. Dallas, 1971
   Dwight White, SB: Pittsburgh vs. Minnesota, 1974
   Reggie Harrison, SB: Pittsburgh vs. Dallas, 1975
   Jim Jensen, NFC-D: Dallas vs. Los Angeles, 1976
   Ted Washington, AFC: Houston vs. Pittsburgh, 1978
   Randy White, NFC-D: Dallas vs. Los Angeles, 1979

RUSHING

ATTEMPTS
Most Attempts, Career
400   Franco Harris, Pittsburgh, 19 games
285   Tony Dorsett, Dallas, 16 games
251   John Riggins, Washington, 9 games
Most Attempts, Game
38   Ricky Bell, NFC-D: Tampa Bay vs. Philadelphia, 1979
   John Riggins, SB: Washington vs. Miami, 1982
37   Lawrence McCutcheon, NFC-D: Los Angeles vs. St. Louis, 1975
   John Riggins, NFC-D: Washington vs. Minnesota, 1982

36 John Riggins, NFC: Washington vs. Dallas, 1982
John Riggins, NFC: Washington vs. San Francisco, 1983

YARDS GAINED
Most Yards Gained, Career
1,556 Franco Harris, Pittsburgh, 19 games
1,325 Tony Dorsett, Dallas, 16 games
996 John Riggins, Washington, 9 games
Most Yards Gained, Game
206 Keith Lincoln, AFC: San Diego vs. Boston, 1963
202 Lawrence McCutcheon, NFC-D: Los Angeles vs. St. Louis, 1975
Freeman McNeil, AFC-FR: N.Y. Jets vs. Cincinnati, 1982
196 Steve Van Buren, NFC: Philadelphia vs. Los Angeles, 1949
Most Games, 100 or More Yards Rushing, Career
6 John Riggins, Washington, 9 games
5 Franco Harris, Pittsburgh, 19 games
4 Larry Csonka, Miami, 12 games
Chuck Foreman, Minnesota, 13 games
Most Consecutive Games, 100 or More Yards Rushing
6 John Riggins, Washington, 1982-83
3 Larry Csonka, Miami, 1973-74
Franco Harris, Pittsburgh, 1974-75
Marcus Allen, L.A. Raiders, 1983
Longest Run From Scrimmage
74 Marcus Allen, SB: L.A. Raiders vs. Washington, 1983 (TD)
71 Hugh McElhenny, NFC-D: San Francisco vs. Detroit, 1957
James Lofton, NFC-D: Green Bay vs. Dallas, 1982 (TD)
70 Elmer Angsman, NFC: Chi. Cardinals vs. Philadelphia, 1947 (twice, 2 TDs)

AVERAGE GAIN
Highest Average Gain, Career (50 attempts)
6.67 Paul Lowe, L.A. Chargers-San Diego, 5 games (57-380)
5.93 Marcus Allen, L.A. Raiders, 6 games (107-635)
5.68 Roger Staubach, Dallas, 20 games (76-432)
Highest Average Gain, Game (10 attempts)
15.90 Elmer Angsman, NFC: Chi. Cardinals vs. Philadelphia, 1947 (10-159)
15.85 Keith Lincoln, AFC: San Diego vs. Boston, 1963 (13-206)
10.90 Bill Osmanski, NFC: Chi. Bears vs. Washington, 1940 (10-109)

TOUCHDOWNS
Most Touchdowns, Career
16 Franco Harris, Pittsburgh, 19 games
12 John Riggins, Washington, 9 games
9 Larry Csonka, Miami, 12 games
Tony Dorsett, Dallas, 16 games
Most Touchdowns, Game
3 Andy Farkas, NFC-D: Washington vs. N.Y. Giants, 1943
Otto Graham, NFC: Cleveland vs. Detroit, 1954
Tom Matte, NFC: Baltimore vs. Cleveland, 1968
Larry Schreiber, NFC-D: San Francisco vs. Dallas, 1972
Larry Csonka, AFC: Miami vs. Oakland, 1973
Franco Harris, AFC-D: Pittsburgh vs. Buffalo, 1974
John Riggins, NFC-D: Washington vs. L.A. Rams, 1983
Most Consecutive Games Rushing for Touchdowns
7 John Riggins, Washington, 1982-84 (current)
5 Franco Harris, Pittsburgh, 1974-75
Franco Harris, Pittsburgh, 1977-79
3 By many players

PASSING

ATTEMPTS
Most Passes Attempted, Career
456 Terry Bradshaw, Pittsburgh, 19 games
410 Roger Staubach, Dallas, 20 games
351 Ken Stabler, Oakland-Houston, 13 games
Most Passes Attempted, Game
53 Dan Fouts, AFC-D: San Diego vs. Miami, 1981 (OT)
Danny White, NFC-FR: Dallas vs. L.A. Rams, 1983
51 Richard Todd, AFC-FR: N.Y. Jets vs. Buffalo, 1981
Neil Lomax, NFC-FR: St. Louis vs. Green Bay, 1982
50 Dan Marino, SB: Miami vs. San Francisco, 1984

COMPLETIONS
Most Passes Completed, Career
261 Terry Bradshaw, Pittsburgh, 19 games
223 Roger Staubach, Dallas, 20 games
203 Ken Stabler, Oakland-Houston, 13 games
Most Passes Completed, Game
33 Dan Fouts, AFC-D: San Diego vs. Miami, 1981 (OT)
32 Neil Lomax, NFC-FR: St. Louis vs. Green Bay, 1982
Danny White, NFC-FR: Dallas vs. L.A. Rams, 1983
29 Don Strock, AFC-D: Miami vs. San Diego, 1981 (OT)
Dan Marino, SB: Miami vs. San Francisco, 1984

COMPLETION PERCENTAGE
Highest Completion Percentage, Career (100 attempts)
66.3 Ken Anderson, Cincinnati, 6 games (166-110)
61.2 Dan Pastorini, Houston, 5 games (116-71)
61.1 Joe Montana, San Francisco, 8 games (275-168)
Highest Completion Percentage, Game (15 completions)
84.2 David Woodley, AFC-FR: Miami vs. New England, 1982 (19-16)
78.9 Norm Van Brocklin, NFC-D: Los Angeles vs. Detroit, 1952 (19-15)
78.3 Joe Theismann, NFC-D: Washington vs. L.A. Rams, 1983 (23-18)

YARDS GAINED
Most Yards Gained, Career
3,833 Terry Bradshaw, Pittsburgh, 19 games
2,791 Roger Staubach, Dallas, 20 games
2,641 Ken Stabler, Oakland-Houston, 13 games
Most Yards Gained, Game
433 Dan Fouts, AFC-D: San Diego vs. Miami, 1981 (OT)
421 Dan Marino, AFC: Miami vs. Pittsburgh, 1984
403 Don Strock, AFC-D: Miami vs. San Diego, 1981 (OT)

Most Games, 300 or More Yards Passing, Career
5 Dan Fouts, San Diego, 7 games
4 Joe Montana, San Francisco, 8 games
3 Terry Bradshaw, Pittsburgh, 19 games
Danny White, Dallas, 17 games
Dan Marino, Miami, 4 games
Most Consecutive Games, 300 or More Yards Passing
4 Dan Fouts, San Diego, 1979-81
2 Daryle Lamonica, Oakland, 1968
Ken Anderson, Cincinnati, 1981-82 (current)
Terry Bradshaw, Pittsburgh, 1979-82
Joe Montana, San Francisco, 1983-84
Dan Marino, Miami, 1984 (current)
Longest Pass Completion
93 Daryle Lamonica (to Dubenion), AFC-D: Buffalo vs. Boston, 1963 (TD)
88 George Blanda (to Cannon), AFC: Houston vs. L.A. Chargers, 1960 (TD)
86 Don Meredith (to Hayes), NFC-D: Dallas vs. Cleveland, 1967 (TD)

AVERAGE GAIN
Highest Average Gain, Career (100 attempts)
8.47 Dan Marino, Miami, 4 games (141-1,194)
8.45 Joe Theismann, Washington, 10 games (211-1,782)
8.43 Jim Plunkett, Oakland-L.A. Raiders, 10 games (272-2,293)
Highest Average Gain, Game (20 attempts)
14.71 Terry Bradshaw, SB: Pittsburgh vs. Los Angeles, 1979 (21-309)
13.33 Bob Waterfield, NFC-D: Los Angeles vs. Chi. Bears, 1950 (21-280)
13.16 Dan Marino, AFC: Miami vs. Pittsburgh, 1984 (32-421)

TOUCHDOWNS
Most Touchdown Passes, Career
30 Terry Bradshaw, Pittsburgh, 19 games
24 Roger Staubach, Dallas, 20 games
19 Daryle Lamonica, Buffalo-Oakland, 13 games
Ken Stabler, Oakland-Houston, 13 games
Most Touchdown Passes, Game
6 Daryle Lamonica, AFC-D: Oakland vs. Houston, 1969
5 Sid Luckman, NFC: Chi. Bears vs. Washington, 1943
Daryle Lamonica, AFC-D: Oakland vs. Kansas City, 1968
4 Otto Graham, NFC: Cleveland vs. Los Angeles, 1950
Tobin Rote, NFC: Detroit vs. Cleveland, 1957
Bart Starr, NFC: Green Bay vs. Dallas, 1966
Ken Stabler, AFC-D: Oakland vs. Miami, 1974
Roger Staubach, NFC: Dallas vs. Los Angeles, 1975
Terry Bradshaw, SB: Pittsburgh vs. Dallas, 1978
Don Strock, AFC-D: Miami vs. San Diego, 1981 (OT)
Lynn Dickey, NFC-FR: Green Bay vs. St. Louis, 1982
Dan Marino, AFC: Miami vs. Pittsburgh, 1984
Most Consecutive Games, Touchdown Passes
10 Ken Stabler, Oakland, 1973-77
8 Terry Bradshaw, Pittsburgh, 1977-82
Joe Montana, San Francisco, 1981-84 (current)
6 Bart Starr, Green Bay, 1965-67
Terry Bradshaw, Pittsburgh, 1972-74
Dan Fouts, San Diego, 1980-82 (current)
Joe Theismann, Washington, 1982-83

HAD INTERCEPTED
Lowest Percentage, Passes Had Intercepted, Career (100 attempts)
1.41 Bart Starr, Green Bay, 10 games (213-3)
3.32 Joe Theismann, Washington, 10 games (211-7)
3.42 Joe Namath, N.Y. Jets, 3 games (117-4)
Most Attempts Without Interception, Game
47 Daryle Lamonica, AFC: Oakland vs. N.Y. Jets, 1968
42 Dan Fouts, AFC-FR: San Diego vs. Pittsburgh, 1982
39 Daryle Lamonica, AFC-D: Oakland vs. Kansas City, 1968
Ron Jaworski, NFC-D: Philadelphia vs. Tampa Bay, 1979
Tommy Kramer, NFC-D: Minnesota vs. Washington, 1982
Most Passes Had Intercepted, Career
26 Terry Bradshaw, Pittsburgh, 19 games
19 Roger Staubach, Dallas, 20 games
17 George Blanda, Chi. Bears-Houston-Oakland, 19 games
Fran Tarkenton, Minnesota, 11 games
Most Passes Had Intercepted, Game
6 Frank Filchock, NFC: N.Y. Giants vs. Chi. Bears, 1946
Bobby Layne, NFC: Detroit vs. Cleveland, 1954
Norm Van Brocklin, NFC: Los Angeles vs. Cleveland, 1955
5 Frank Filchock, NFC: Washington vs. Chi. Bears, 1940
George Blanda, AFC: Houston vs. San Diego, 1961
George Blanda, AFC: Houston vs. Dall. Texans, 1962 (OT)
Y. A. Tittle, NFC: N.Y. Giants vs. Chicago, 1963
Mike Phipps, AFC-D: Cleveland vs. Miami, 1972
Dan Pastorini, AFC: Houston vs. Pittsburgh, 1978
Dan Fouts, AFC-D: San Diego vs. Houston, 1979
Tommy Kramer, NFC-D: Minnesota vs. Philadelphia, 1980
Dan Fouts, AFC-D: San Diego vs. Miami, 1982
Richard Todd, AFC: N.Y. Jets vs Miami, 1982
Gary Danielson, NFC-D: Detroit vs. San Francisco, 1983
4 By many players

PASS RECEIVING

RECEPTIONS
Most Receptions, Career
73 Cliff Branch, Oakland-L.A. Raiders, 22 games
70 Fred Biletnikoff, Oakland, 19 games
67 Drew Pearson, Dallas, 22 games
Most Receptions, Game
13 Kellen Winslow, AFC-D: San Diego vs. Miami, 1981 (OT)
12 Raymond Berry, NFC: Baltimore vs. N.Y. Giants, 1958
11 Dante Lavelli, NFC: Cleveland vs. Los Angeles, 1950
Dan Ross, SB: Cincinnati vs. San Francisco, 1981
Franco Harris, AFC-FR: Pittsburgh vs. San Diego, 1982
Steve Watson, AFC-D: Denver vs. Pittsburgh, 1984

Most Consecutive Games, Pass Receptions
22   Drew Pearson, Dallas, 1973-83
18   Paul Warfield, Cleveland-Miami, 1964-74
     Cliff Branch, Oakland-L.A. Raiders, 1974-83
17   John Stallworth, Pittsburgh, 1974-84 (current)

YARDS GAINED
Most Yards Gained, Career
1,289   Cliff Branch, Oakland-L.A. Raiders, 22 games
1,167   Fred Biletnikoff, Oakland, 19 games
1,121   Paul Warfield, Cleveland-Miami, 18 games
Most Yards Gained, Game
198   Tom Fears, NFC-D: Los Angeles vs. Chi. Bears, 1950
190   Fred Biletnikoff, AFC: Oakland vs. N.Y. Jets, 1968
186   Cliff Branch, AFC: Oakland vs. Pittsburgh, 1974
Most Games, 100 or More Yards Receiving, Career
5   John Stallworth, Pittsburgh, 18 games
4   Fred Biletnikoff, Oakland, 19 games
3   Tom Fears, L.A. Rams, 6 games
   Cliff Branch, Oakland-L.A. Raiders, 22 games
   Dwight Clark, San Francisco, 6 games
Most Consecutive Games, 100 or More Yards Receiving, Career
3   Tom Fears, Los Angeles, 1950-51
2   Lenny Moore, Baltimore, 1958-59
   Fred Biletnikoff, Oakland, 1968
   Paul Warfield, Miami, 1971
   Charlie Joiner, San Diego, 1981
   Dwight Clark, San Francisco, 1981
   Cris Collinsworth, Cincinnati, 1981-82
   John Stallworth, Pittsburgh, 1979-82
   Wesley Walker, N.Y. Jets, 1982
   Charlie Brown, Washington, 1983
Longest Reception
93   Elbert Dubenion (from Lamonica), AFC-D: Buffalo vs. Boston, 1963 (TD)
88   Billy Cannon (from Blanda), AFC: Houston vs. L.A. Chargers, 1960 (TD)
86   Bob Hayes (from Meredith), NFC: Dallas vs. Cleveland, 1967 (TD)

AVERAGE GAIN
Highest Average Gain, Career (20 receptions)
22.8   Harold Jackson, L.A. Rams-New England-Minnesota-Seattle, 14 games (24-548)
20.7   Charlie Brown, Washington, 8 games (31-643)
20.5   Frank Lewis, Pittsburgh-Buffalo, 12 games (27-553)
Highest Average Gain, Game (3 receptions)
46.3   Harold Jackson, NFC: Los Angeles vs. Minnesota, 1974 (3-139)
42.7   Billy Cannon, AFC: Houston vs. L.A. Chargers, 1960 (3-128)
42.0   Lenny Moore, NFC: Baltimore vs. N.Y. Giants, 1959 (3-126)

TOUCHDOWNS
Most Touchdowns, Career
12   John Stallworth, Pittsburgh, 18 games
10   Fred Biletnikoff, Oakland, 19 games
9   Lynn Swann, Pittsburgh, 16 games
Most Touchdowns, Game
3   Tom Fears, NFC-D: Los Angeles vs. Chi. Bears, 1950
   Gary Collins, NFC: Cleveland vs. Baltimore, 1964
   Fred Biletnikoff, AFC-D: Oakland vs. Kansas City, 1968
   Preston Pearson, NFC: Dallas vs. Los Angeles, 1975
   Dave Casper, AFC-D: Oakland vs. Baltimore, 1977 (OT)
   Alvin Garrett, NFC-FR: Washington vs. Detroit, 1982
Most Consecutive Games, Touchdown Passes Caught
8   John Stallworth, Pittsburgh, 1978-83
4   Lynn Swann, Pittsburgh, 1978-79
   Harold Carmichael, Philadelphia, 1978-80
   Fred Solomon, San Francisco, 1983-84
3   By many players

INTERCEPTIONS BY
Most Interceptions, Career
9   Charlie Waters, Dallas, 25 games
   Bill Simpson, Los Angeles-Buffalo, 11 games
8   Lester Hayes, Oakland-L.A. Raiders, 12 games
7   Willie Brown, Oakland, 17 games
   Dennis Thurman, Dallas, 13 games
Most Interceptions, Game
4   Vernon Perry, AFC-D: Houston vs. San Diego, 1979
3   Joe Laws, NFC: Green Bay vs. N.Y. Giants, 1944
   Charlie Waters, NFC-D: Dallas vs. Chicago, 1977
   Rod Martin, SB: Oakland vs. Philadelphia, 1980
   Dennis Thurman, NFC-D: Dallas vs. Green Bay, 1982
   A.J. Duhe, AFC: Miami vs. N.Y. Jets, 1982
2   By many players

YARDS GAINED
Most Yards Gained, Career
196   Willie Brown, Oakland, 17 games
151   Glen Edwards, Pittsburgh-San Diego, 17 games
149   Bill Simpson, Los Angeles-Buffalo, 11 games
Most Yards Gained, Game
98   Darrol Ray, AFC-FR: N.Y. Jets vs. Cincinnati, 1982
94   LeRoy Irvin, NFC-FR: L.A. Rams vs. Dallas, 1983
88   Walt Sumner, NFC-D: Cleveland vs. Dallas, 1969
Longest Return
98   Darrol Ray, AFC-FR: N.Y. Jets vs. Cincinnati, 1982 (TD)
94   LeRoy Irvin, NFC-FR: L.A. Rams vs. Dallas, 1983
88   Walt Sumner, NFC-D: Cleveland vs. Dallas, 1969 (TD)

TOUCHDOWNS
Most Touchdowns, Career
3   Willie Brown, Oakland, 17 games
2   Lester Hayes, Oakland-L.A. Raiders, 12 games

Most Touchdowns, Game
1   By 37 players

PUNTING
Most Punts, Career
109   Ray Guy, Oakland-L.A. Raiders, 21 games
84   Danny White, Dallas, 17 games
73   Mike Eischeid, Oakland-Minnesota, 14 games
Most Punts, Game
12   David Lee, AFC-D: Baltimore vs. Oakland, 1977 (OT)
11   Ken Strong, NFC: N.Y. Giants vs. Chi. Bears, 1933
   Jim Norton, AFC: Houston vs. Oakland, 1967
10   Keith Molesworth, NFC: Chi. Bears vs. N.Y. Giants, 1933
   Riley Smith, NFC: Boston vs. Green Bay, 1936
   Len Younce, NFC: N.Y. Giants vs. Green Bay, 1944
   Curley Johnson, AFC: N.Y. Jets vs. Oakland, 1968
   Tom Orosz, AFC: Miami vs. N.Y. Jets, 1982
Longest Punt
76   Ed Danowski, NFC: N.Y. Giants vs. Detroit, 1935
72   Charlie Conerly, NFC-D: N.Y. Giants vs. Cleveland, 1950
71   Ray Guy, AFC: Oakland vs. San Diego, 1980

AVERAGE YARDAGE
Highest Average, Career (20 punts)
43.4   Jerrel Wilson, Kansas City-New England, 8 games (43-1,866)
43.1   Don Chandler, N.Y. Giants-Green Bay, 14 games (53-2,282)
42.5   Ray Guy, Oakland-L.A. Raiders, 21 games (109-4,637)
Highest Average, Game (4 punts)
56.0   Ray Guy, AFC: Oakland vs. San Diego, 1980 (4-224)
52.5   Sammy Baugh, NFC: Washington vs. Chi. Bears, 1942 (6-315)
51.4   John Hadl, AFC: San Diego vs. Buffalo, 1965 (5-257)

PUNT RETURNS
Most Punt Returns, Career
25   Theo Bell, Pittsburgh-Tampa Bay, 10 games
19   Willie Wood, Green Bay, 10 games
   Butch Johnson, Dallas-Denver, 18 games
18   Neal Colzie, Oakland-Miami-Tampa Bay, 10 games
Most Punt Returns, Game
7   Ron Gardin, AFC-D: Baltimore vs. Cincinnati, 1970
   Carl Roaches, AFC-FR: Houston vs. Oakland, 1980
6   George McAfee, NFC-D: Chi. Bears vs. Los Angeles, 1950
   Eddie Brown, NFC-D: Washington vs. Minnesota, 1976
   Theo Bell, AFC: Pittsburgh vs. Houston, 1978
   Eddie Brown, NFC: Los Angeles vs. Tampa Bay, 1979
   John Sciarra, NFC: Philadelphia vs. Dallas, 1980
   Kurt Sohn, AFC: N.Y. Jets vs. Miami, 1982
   Mike Nelms, SB: Washington vs. Miami, 1982
5   By many players

YARDS GAINED
Most Yards Gained, Career
221   Neal Colzie, Oakland-Miami-Tampa Bay, 10 games
208   Butch Johnson, Dallas-Denver, 18 games
204   Theo Bell, Pittsburgh-Tampa Bay, 10 games
Most Yards Gained, Game
141   Bob Hayes, NFC-D: Dallas vs. Cleveland, 1967
102   Charley Trippi, NFC: Chi. Cardinals vs. Philadelphia, 1947
101   Bosh Pritchard, NFC-D: Philadelphia vs. Pittsburgh, 1947
Longest Return
81   Hugh Gallarneau, NFC-D: Chi. Bears vs. Green Bay, 1941 (TD)
79   Bosh Pritchard, NFC-D: Philadelphia vs. Pittsburgh, 1947 (TD)
75   Charley Trippi, NFC: Chi. Cardinals vs. Philadelphia, 1947 (TD)

AVERAGE YARDAGE
Highest Average, Career (10 returns)
12.6   Bob Hayes, Dallas, 15 games (12-151)
12.4   Mike Fuller, San Diego-Cincinnati, 7 games (13-161)
12.3   Neal Colzie, Oakland-Miami-Tampa Bay, 10 games (18-221)
Highest Average Gain, Game (3 returns)
47.0   Bob Hayes, NFC-D: Dallas vs. Cleveland, 1967 (3-141)
29.0   George (Butch) Byrd, AFC: Buffalo vs. San Diego, 1965 (3-87)
25.3   Bosh Pritchard, NFC-D: Philadelphia vs. Pittsburgh, 1947 (4-101)

TOUCHDOWNS
Most Touchdowns
1   Hugh Gallarneau, NFC-D: Chicago Bears vs. Green Bay, 1941
   Bosh Pritchard, NFC-D: Philadelphia vs. Pittsburgh, 1947
   Charley Trippi, NFC: Chicago Cardinals vs. Philadelphia, 1947
   Verda (Vitamin T) Smith, NFC-D: Los Angeles vs. Detroit, 1952
   George (Butch) Byrd, AFC: Buffalo vs. San Diego, 1965
   Golden Richards, NFC: Dallas vs. Minnesota, 1973
   Wes Chandler, AFC-D: San Diego vs. Miami, 1981 (OT)

KICKOFF RETURNS
Most Kickoff Returns, Career
26   Fulton Walker, Miami, 9 games
19   Preston Pearson, Baltimore-Pittsburgh-Dallas, 22 games
18   Charlie West, Minnesota, 9 games
Most Kickoff Returns, Game
7   Don Bingham, NFC: Chi. Bears vs. N.Y. Giants, 1956
   Reggie Brown, NFC-FR: Atlanta vs. Minnesota, 1982
   David Verser, AFC-FR: Cincinnati vs. N.Y. Jets, 1982
   Del Rodgers, NFC-D: Green Bay vs. Dallas, 1982
   Henry Ellard, NFC-D: L.A. Rams vs. Washington, 1983
6   Wallace Francis, AFC-D: Buffalo vs. Pittsburgh, 1974
   Eddie Brown, NFC-D: Washington vs. Minnesota, 1976
   Eddie Payton, NFC-D: Minnesota vs. Philadelphia, 1980
   Alvin Hall, NFC-FR: Detroit vs. Washington, 1982
   Fulton Walker, AFC-D: Miami vs. Seattle, 1983
5   By many players

YARDS GAINED
Most Yards Gained, Career
- 618 Fulton Walker, Miami, 9 games
- 481 Carl Garrett, Oakland, 5 games
- 458 Cullen Bryant, L.A. Rams-Seattle, 19 games

Most Yards Gained, Game
- 190 Fulton Walker, SB: Miami vs. Washington, 1982
- 170 Les (Speedy) Duncan, NFC-D: Washington vs. San Francisco, 1971
- 169 Carl Garrett, AFC-D: Oakland vs. Baltimore, 1977 (OT)

Longest Return
- 98 Fulton Walker, SB: Miami vs. Washington, 1982 (TD)
- 97 Vic Washington, NFC-D: San Francisco vs. Dallas, 1972 (TD)
- 89 Nat Moore, AFC-D: Miami vs. Oakland, 1974 (TD)
  - Rod Hill, NFC-D: Dallas vs. Green Bay, 1982

AVERAGE YARDAGE
Highest Average, Career (10 returns)
- 30.1 Carl Garrett, Oakland, 5 games (16-481)
- 27.9 George Atkinson, Oakland, 16 games (12-335)
- 24.2 Larry Anderson, Pittsburgh, 6 games (16-387)

Highest Average, Game (3 returns)
- 56.7 Les (Speedy) Duncan, NFC-D: Washington vs. San Francisco, 1971 (3-170)
- 51.3 Ed Podolak, AFC-D: Kansas City vs. Miami, 1971 (OT) (3-154)
- 49.0 Les (Speedy) Duncan, AFC: San Diego vs. Buffalo, 1964 (3-147)

TOUCHDOWNS
Most Touchdowns
- 1 Vic Washington, NFC-D: San Francisco vs. Dallas, 1972
  - Nat Moore, AFC-D: Miami vs. Oakland, 1974
  - Marshall Johnson, AFC-D: Baltimore vs. Oakland, 1977 (OT)
  - Fulton Walker, SB: Miami vs. Washington, 1982

FUMBLES

Most Fumbles, Career
- 13 Tony Dorsett, Dallas, 16 games
- 10 Franco Harris, Pittsburgh, 19 games
  - Terry Bradshaw, Pittsburgh, 19 games
  - Roger Staubach, Dallas, 20 games
- 9 Chuck Foreman, Minnesota, 13 games

Most Fumbles, Game
- 4 Brian Sipe, AFC-D: Cleveland vs. Oakland, 1980
- 3 Y.A. Tittle, NFC-D: San Francisco vs. Detroit, 1957
  - Bill Nelsen, AFC-D: Cleveland vs. Baltimore, 1972
  - Chuck Foreman, NFC: Minnesota vs. Los Angeles, 1974
  - Lawrence McCutcheon, NFC-D: Los Angeles vs. St. Louis, 1975
  - Roger Staubach, SB: Dallas vs. Pittsburgh, 1975
  - Terry Bradshaw, AFC: Pittsburgh vs. Houston, 1978
  - Earl Campbell, AFC: Houston vs. Pittsburgh, 1978
  - Franco Harris, AFC: Pittsburgh vs. Houston, 1978
  - Chuck Muncie, AFC: San Diego vs. Cincinnati, 1981
  - Andra Franklin, AFC-FR: Miami vs. New England, 1982
- 2 By many players

RECOVERIES
Most Own Fumbles Recovered, Career
- 5 Roger Staubach, Dallas, 20 games
- 4 Fran Tarkenton, Minnesota, 11 games
- 3 Alex Webster, N.Y. Giants, 7 games
  - Don Meredith, Dallas, 4 games
  - Franco Harris, Pittsburgh, 19 games
  - Gerry Mullins, Pittsburgh, 18 games
  - Ron Jaworski, Los Angeles-Philadelphia, 10 games
  - Lyle Blackwood, Cincinnati-Baltimore-Miami, 12 games

Most Opponents' Fumbles Recovered, Career
- 4 Cliff Harris, Dallas, 21 games
  - Harvey Martin, Dallas, 22 games
  - Ted Hendricks, Baltimore-Oakland-L.A. Raiders, 21 games
- 3 Paul Krause, Minnesota, 19 games
  - Jack Lambert, Pittsburgh, 18 games
  - Fred Dryer, Los Angeles, 14 games
  - Charlie Waters, Dallas, 25 games
  - Jack Ham, Pittsburgh, 16 games
  - Mike Hegman, Dallas, 15 games
  - Tom Jackson, Denver, 7 games

Most Fumbles Recovered, Game, Own and Opponents'
- 3 Jack Lambert, AFC: Pittsburgh vs. Oakland, 1975 (3 opp)
  - Ron Jaworski, NFC-FR: Philadelphia vs. N.Y. Giants, 1981 (3 own)

YARDS GAINED
Longest Return
- 93 Andy Russell, AFC-D: Pittsburgh vs. Baltimore, 1975 (opp, TD)
- 60 Mike Curtis, NFC-D: Baltimore vs. Minnesota, 1968 (opp, TD)
  - Hugh Green, NFC-FR: Tampa Bay vs. Dallas, 1982 (opp, TD)
- 50 Lee Artoe, NFC: Chi. Bears vs. Washington, 1942 (opp, TD)

TOUCHDOWNS
Most Touchdowns
- 1 By 19 players

TEAM RECORDS

GAMES, VICTORIES, DEFEATS
Most Consecutive Seasons Participating in Postseason Games
- 9 Dallas, 1975-83
- 8 Dallas, 1966-73
  - Pittsburgh, 1972-79
  - Los Angeles, 1973-80
- 6 Cleveland, 1950-55
  - Oakland, 1972-77
  - Minnesota, 1973-78

Most Games
- 35 Dallas, 1966-73, 1975-83
- 30 Oakland/L. A. Raiders, 1967-70, 1973-77, 1980, 1982-84
- 26 Cleveland, L. A. Rams, 1945, 1949-52, 1955, 1967, 1969, 1973-80, 1983-84

Most Games Won
- 20 Dallas, 1967, 1970-73, 1975, 1977-78, 1980-82
- 19 Oakland/L. A. Raiders, 1967-70, 1973-77, 1980, 1982-83
- 15 Pittsburgh, 1972, 1974-76, 1978-79, 1984

Most Consecutive Games Won
- 9 Green Bay, 1961-62, 1965-67
- 7 Pittsburgh, 1974-76
- 6 Miami, 1972-73
  - Pittsburgh, 1978-79
  - Washington, 1982-83

Most Games Lost
- 16 L.A. Rams, 1949-50, 1952, 1955, 1967, 1969, 1973-80, 1983-84
- 15 Dallas, 1966-70, 1972-73, 1975-76, 1978-83
  - N. Y. Giants, 1933, 1935, 1939, 1941, 1943-44, 1946, 1950, 1958-59, 1961-63, 1981, 1984
- 13 Cleveland, 1951-53, 1957-58, 1965, 1967-69, 1971-72, 1980, 1982

Most Consecutive Games Lost
- 6 N. Y. Giants, 1939, 1941, 1943-44, 1946, 1950
- 5 N. Y. Giants, 1958-59, 1961-63
  - Los Angeles, 1952, 1955, 1967, 1969, 1973
  - Cleveland, 1969, 1971-72, 1980, 1982 (current)
  - Denver, 1977-79, 1983-84 (current)
- 4 Washington, 1972-74, 1976
  - Baltimore, 1971, 1975-77 (current)
  - Miami, 1974, 1978-79, 1981
  - Chi. Cards/St. Louis, 1948, 1974-75, 1982 (current)
  - Boston/New England, 1963, 1976, 1978, 1982 (current)

SCORING

Most Points, Game
- 73 NFC: Chi. Bears vs. Washington, 1940
- 59 NFC: Detroit vs. Cleveland, 1957
- 56 NFC: Cleveland vs. Detroit, 1954
  - AFC-D: Oakland vs. Houston, 1969

Most Points, Both Teams, Game
- 79 AFC-D: San Diego (41) vs. Miami (38), 1981 (OT)
- 73 NFC: Chi. Bears (73) vs. Washington (0), 1940
  - NFC: Detroit (59) vs. Cleveland (14), 1957
  - AFC: Miami (45) vs. Pittsburgh (28), 1984
- 68 AFC-D: Oakland (37) vs. Baltimore (31), 1977 (OT)

Fewest Points, Both Teams, Game
- 5 NFC-D: Detroit (0) vs. Dallas (5), 1970
- 7 NFC: Chi. Cardinals (0) vs. Philadelphia (7), 1948
- 9 NFC: Tampa Bay (0) vs. Los Angeles (9), 1979

Largest Margin of Victory, Game
- 73 NFC: Chi. Bears vs. Washington, 1940 (73-0)
- 49 AFC-D: Oakland vs. Houston, 1969 (56-7)
- 46 NFC: Cleveland vs. Detroit, 1954 (56-10)

Most Points, Shutout Victory, Game
- 73 NFC: Chi. Bears vs. Washington, 1940
- 38 NFC-D: Dallas vs. Tampa Bay, 1981
- 37 NFC: Green Bay vs. N.Y. Giants, 1961

Most Points Overcome to Win Game
- 20 NFC-D: Detroit vs. San Francisco, 1957 (trailed 7-27, won 31-27)
- 18 NFC-D: Dallas vs. San Francisco, 1972 (trailed 3-21, won 30-28)
- 14 NFC-D: Philadelphia vs. Minnesota, 1980 (trailed 0-14, won 31-16)
  - NFC-D: Dallas vs. Atlanta, 1980 (trailed 10-24, won 30-27)

Most Points, Each Half
1st:	38	NFC-D: Washington vs. L.A. Rams, 1983
	35	NFC: Cleveland vs. Detroit, 1954
		AFC-D: Oakland vs. Houston, 1969
	34	NFC: N. Y. Giants vs. Chi. Bears, 1956
2nd:	45	NFC: Chi. Bears vs. Washington, 1940
	28	NFC: Chi. Bears vs. N.Y. Giants, 1941
		NFC: Detroit vs. Cleveland, 1957
		NFC-D: Dallas vs. Cleveland, 1967
		NFC-D: Dallas vs. Tampa Bay, 1981
	27	NFC: N. Y. Giants vs. Chi. Bears, 1934
		NFC: Dallas vs. Washington, 1943
		NFC: Cleveland vs. Baltimore, 1964

Most Points, Each Quarter
1st:	28	AFC-D: Oakland vs. Houston, 1969
	24	AFC-D: San Diego vs. Miami, 1981 (OT)
	21	NFC: Chi. Bears vs. Washington, 1940
		AFC: San Diego vs. Boston, 1963
		AFC-D: Oakland vs. Kansas City, 1968
		AFC: Oakland vs. San Diego, 1980
2nd:	26	AFC-D: Pittsburgh vs. Buffalo, 1974
	24	NFC-D: Chi. Bears vs. Green Bay, 1941
		NFC: Green Bay vs. N. Y. Giants, 1961
	21	NFC: Cleveland vs. Detroit, 1954
		NFC: N. Y. Giants vs. Chi. Bears, 1956
		AFC-D: Houston vs. New England, 1978
		NFC-FR: Green Bay vs. St. Louis, 1982
		NFC-D: Washington vs. L.A. Rams, 1983
		SB: San Francisco vs. Miami, 1984
3rd:	26	NFC: Chi. Bears vs. Washington, 1940
	21	NFC-D: Dallas vs. Cleveland, 1967
		NFC-D: Dallas vs. Tampa Bay, 1981
		AFC-D: L.A. Raiders vs. Pittsburgh, 1983
	17	NFC: Cleveland vs. Baltimore, 1964
		NFC-D: Dallas vs. Chicago, 1977
4th	27	NFC: N. Y. Giants vs. Chi. Bears, 1934
	24	NFC: Baltimore vs. N. Y. Giants, 1959
	21	AFC: Pittsburgh vs. Oakland, 1974
		NFC: Dallas vs. Los Angeles, 1978
		AFC-FR: N. Y. Jets vs. Cincinnati, 1982
		NFC: San Francisco vs. Washington, 1983

OT: 6 NFC: Baltimore vs. N.Y. Giants, 1958
AFC-D: Oakland vs. Baltimore, 1977

TOUCHDOWNS
Most Touchdowns, Game
11 NFC: Chi. Bears vs. Washington, 1940
8 NFC: Cleveland vs. Detroit, 1954
NFC: Detroit vs. Cleveland, 1957
AFC-D: Oakland vs. Houston, 1969
7 AFC: San Diego vs. Boston, 1963
NFC-D: Dallas vs. Cleveland, 1967

Most Touchdowns, Both Teams, Game
11 NFC: Chi. Bears (11) vs. Washington (0), 1940
10 NFC: Detroit (8) vs. Cleveland (2), 1957
AFC-D: Miami (5) vs. San Diego (5), 1981 (OT)
AFC: Miami (6) vs. Pittsburgh (4), 1984
9 NFC: Chi. Bears (6) vs. Washington (3), 1943
NFC: Cleveland (8) vs. Detroit (1), 1954
NFC-D: Dallas (7) vs. Cleveland (2), 1967
AFC-D: Oakland (8) vs. Houston (1), 1969
AFC-D: Oakland (5) vs. Baltimore (4), 1977 (OT)
SB: Pittsburgh (5) vs. Dallas (4), 1978

Fewest Touchdowns, Both Teams, Game
0 NFC-D: N.Y. Giants vs. Cleveland, 1950
NFC-D: Dallas vs. Detroit, 1970
NFC: Los Angeles vs. Tampa Bay, 1979
1 NFC: Chi. Cardinals (0) vs. Philadelphia (1), 1948
AFC: San Diego (0) vs. Houston (1), 1961
AFC-D: N.Y. Jets (0) vs. Kansas City (1), 1969
NFC-D: Green Bay (0) vs. Washington (1), 1972
2 In many games

POINTS AFTER TOUCHDOWN
Most Points After Touchdown, Game
8 NFC: Cleveland vs. Detroit, 1954
NFC: Detroit vs. Cleveland, 1957
AFC-D: Oakland vs. Houston, 1969
7 NFC: Chi. Bears vs. Washington, 1940
NFC-D: Dallas vs. Cleveland, 1967
6 AFC: San Diego vs. Boston, 1963
NFC-D: Washington vs. L.A. Rams, 1983
AFC: Miami vs. Pittsburgh, 1984

Most Points After Touchdown, Both Teams, Game
10 NFC: Detroit (8) vs. Cleveland (2), 1957
AFC-D: Miami (5) vs. San Diego (5), 1981 (OT)
AFC: Miami (6) vs. Pittsburgh (4), 1984
9 NFC: Cleveland (8) vs. Detroit (1), 1954
NFC-D: Dallas (7) vs. Cleveland (2), 1967
AFC-D: Oakland (8) vs. Houston (1), 1969
8 In many games

Fewest Points After Touchdown, Both Teams, Game
0 NFC-D: N.Y. Giants vs. Cleveland, 1950
NFC-D: Dallas vs. Detroit, 1970
NFC: Los Angeles vs. Tampa Bay, 1979

FIELD GOALS
Most Field Goals, Game
4 AFC-D: Boston vs. Buffalo, 1963
AFC: Oakland vs. Houston, 1967
SB: Green Bay vs. Oakland, 1967
NFC: Washington vs. Dallas, 1972
AFC-D: Oakland vs. Pittsburgh, 1973
SB: San Francisco vs. Cincinnati, 1981
3 By many teams

Most Field Goals, Both Teams, Game
5 NFC: Green Bay (3) vs. Cleveland (2), 1965
AFC: Oakland (3) vs. N.Y. Jets (2), 1968
NFC: Washington (4) vs. Dallas (1), 1972
AFC-D: Cincinnati (3) vs. Miami (2), 1973
NFC-D: Los Angeles (3) vs. Dallas (2), 1973
NFC-D: Dallas (3) vs. Green Bay (2), 1982
NFC-FR: N.Y. Giants (3) vs. L.A. Rams (2), 1984
4 In many games

Most Field Goals Attempted, Game
6 AFC: Oakland vs. Houston, 1967
NFC-D: Los Angeles vs. Dallas, 1973
5 By many teams

Most Field Goals Attempted, Both Teams, Game
8 NFC-D: Los Angeles (6) vs. Dallas (2), 1973
NFC-D: Detroit (5) vs. San Francisco (3), 1983
7 In many games

SAFETIES
Most Safeties, Game
1 By 12 teams

FIRST DOWNS
Most First Downs, Game
34 AFC-D: San Diego vs. Miami, 1981 (OT)
31 SB: San Francisco vs. Miami, 1984
29 AFC-D: Pittsburgh vs. Buffalo, 1974
AFC-D: Pittsburgh vs. Baltimore, 1976
NFC-FR: Dallas vs. Los Angeles, 1980
NFC-FR: Dallas vs. Tampa Bay, 1982
AFC-FR: San Diego vs. Pittsburgh, 1982
AFC-D: Miami vs. San Diego, 1982

Fewest First Downs, Game
6 NFC: N.Y. Giants vs. Green Bay, 1961
7 NFC: Green Bay vs. Boston, 1936
NFC-D: Pittsburgh vs. Philadelphia, 1947
NFC: Chi. Cardinals vs. Philadelphia, 1948
NFC: Los Angeles vs. Philadelphia, 1949
NFC-D: Cleveland vs. N.Y. Giants, 1958

AFC-D: Cincinnati vs. Baltimore, 1970
NFC-D: Detroit vs. Dallas, 1970
8 By many teams

Most First Downs, Both Teams, Game
59 AFC-D: San Diego (34) vs. Miami (25), 1981 (OT)
55 AFC-FR: San Diego (29) vs. Pittsburgh (26), 1982
50 AFC: Oakland (28) vs. Baltimore (22), 1977 (OT)
NFC-FR: St. Louis (28) vs. Green Bay (22), 1982
AFC-FR: N.Y. Jets (27) vs. Cincinnati (23), 1982
AFC: Miami (28) vs. Pittsburgh (22), 1984
SB: San Francisco (31) vs. Miami (19), 1984

Fewest First Downs, Both Teams, Game
15 NFC: Green Bay (7) vs. Boston (8), 1936
19 NFC: N.Y. Giants (9) vs. Green Bay (10), 1939
NFC: Washington (9) vs. Chi. Bears (10), 1942
20 NFC-D: Cleveland (9) vs. N.Y. Giants (11), 1950

RUSHING
Most First Downs, Rushing, Game
19 NFC-FR: Dallas vs. Los Angeles, 1980
18 AFC-D: Miami vs. Cincinnati, 1973
AFC-D: Pittsburgh vs. Buffalo, 1974
16 NFC: Philadelphia vs. Chi. Cardinals, 1948
NFC: Dallas vs. San Francisco, 1970

Fewest First Downs, Rushing, Game
0 NFC: Los Angeles vs. Philadelphia, 1949
AFC-D: Buffalo vs. Boston, 1963
AFC: Oakland vs. Pittsburgh, 1974
1 NFC: N.Y. Giants vs. Green Bay, 1961
AFC-D: Houston vs. Oakland, 1969
NFC: Los Angeles vs. Dallas, 1975
AFC-FR: Cleveland vs. L.A. Raiders, 1982
2 By many teams

Most First Downs, Rushing, Both Teams, Game
25 NFC-FR: Dallas (19) vs. Los Angeles (6), 1980
23 NFC: Cleveland (15) vs. Detroit (8), 1952
AFC-D: Miami (18) vs. Cincinnati (5), 1973
AFC-D: Pittsburgh (18) vs. Buffalo (5), 1974
22 AFC: Miami (18) vs. Oakland (4), 1973
AFC-D: Buffalo (11) vs. Cincinnati (11), 1981
AFC-D: L.A. Raiders (13) vs. Pittsburgh (9), 1983

Fewest First Downs, Rushing, Both Teams, Game
5 AFC-D: Buffalo (0) vs. Boston (5), 1963
6 NFC: Green Bay (2) vs. Boston (4), 1936
NFC-D: Baltimore (2) vs. Minnesota (4), 1968
AFC-D: Houston (1) vs. Oakland (5), 1969
7 NFC-D: Washington (2) vs. N.Y. Giants (5), 1943
NFC: Baltimore (3) vs. N.Y. Giants (4), 1959
NFC: Washington (3) vs. Dallas (4), 1972
AFC-FR: N.Y. Jets (3) vs. Buffalo (4), 1981

PASSING
Most First Downs, Passing, Game
21 AFC-D: Miami vs. San Diego, 1981 (OT)
AFC-D: San Diego vs. Miami, 1981 (OT)
20 NFC-FR: Dallas vs. L.A. Rams, 1983
19 NFC-FR: St. Louis vs. Green Bay, 1982
NFC-FR: Dallas vs. Tampa Bay, 1982
AFC-FR: Pittsburgh vs. San Diego, 1982
AFC-FR: San Diego vs. Pittsburgh, 1982
NFC: Dallas vs. Washington, 1982

Fewest First Downs, Passing, Game
0 NFC: Philadelphia vs. Chi. Cardinals, 1948
1 NFC-D: N.Y. Giants vs. Washington, 1943
NFC: Cleveland vs. Detroit, 1953
SB: Denver vs. Dallas, 1977
2 By many teams

Most First Downs, Passing, Both Teams, Game
42 AFC-D: Miami (21) vs. San Diego (21), 1981 (OT)
38 AFC-FR: Pittsburgh (19) vs. San Diego (19), 1982
32 NFC-FR: St. Louis (19) vs. Green Bay (13), 1982
AFC: Miami (18) vs. Pittsburgh (14), 1984
SB: Miami (17) vs. San Francisco (15), 1984

Fewest First Downs, Passing, Both Teams, Game
2 NFC: Philadelphia (0) vs. Chi. Cardinals (2), 1948
4 NFC-D: Cleveland (2) vs. N.Y. Giants (2), 1950
5 NFC: Detroit (2) vs. N.Y. Giants (3), 1935
NFC: Green Bay (2) vs. N.Y. Giants (3), 1939

PENALTY
Most First Downs, Penalty, Game
7 AFC-D: New England vs. Oakland, 1976
5 AFC-FR: Cleveland vs. L.A. Raiders, 1982
4 By many teams

Most First Downs, Penalty, Both Teams, Game
9 AFC-D: New England (7) vs. Oakland (2), 1976
8 NFC-FR: Atlanta (4) vs. Minnesota (4), 1982
7 AFC-D: Baltimore (4) vs. Oakland (3), 1977 (OT)

NET YARDS GAINED RUSHING AND PASSING
Most Yards Gained, Game
610 AFC: San Diego vs. Boston, 1963
569 AFC: Miami vs. Pittsburgh, 1984
564 AFC-D: San Diego vs. Miami, 1981 (OT)

Fewest Yards Gained, Game
86 NFC-D: Cleveland vs. N.Y. Giants, 1958
99 NFC: Chi. Cardinals vs. Philadelphia, 1948
114 NFC-D: N.Y. Giants vs. Washington, 1943

Most Yards Gained, Both Teams, Game
1,036 AFC-D: San Diego (564) vs. Miami (472), 1981 (OT)
1,024 AFC: Miami (569) vs. Pittsburgh (455), 1984
912 AFC-FR: N.Y. Jets (517) vs. Cincinnati (395), 1982

Fewest Yards Gained, Both Teams, Game
- 331 NFC: Chi. Cardinals (99) vs. Philadelphia (232), 1948
- 332 NFC-D: N.Y. Giants (150) vs. Cleveland (182), 1950
- 336 NFC: Boston (116) vs. Green Bay (220), 1936

RUSHING

ATTEMPTS
Most Attempts, Game
- 65 NFC: Detroit vs. N.Y. Giants, 1935
- 61 NFC: Philadelphia vs. Los Angeles, 1949
- 57 NFC: Chi. Bears vs. Washington, 1940
  - NFC: Philadelphia vs. Chi. Cardinals, 1948
  - SB: Pittsburgh vs. Minnesota, 1974

Fewest Attempts, Game
- 9 SB: Miami vs. San Francisco, 1984
- 12 AFC-D: Buffalo vs. Boston, 1963
- 13 NFC-D: Cleveland vs. N.Y. Giants, 1958
  - AFC: Buffalo vs. Kansas City, 1966
  - NFC-D: Minnesota vs. Philadelphia, 1980

Most Attempts, Both Teams, Game
- 109 NFC: Detroit (65) vs. N.Y. Giants (44), 1935
- 97 AFC-D: Baltimore (50) vs. Oakland (47), 1977 (OT)
- 91 NFC: Philadelphia (57) vs. Chi. Cardinals (34), 1948

Fewest Attempts, Both Teams, Game
- 45 AFC-FR: N.Y. Jets (22) vs. Buffalo (23), 1981
- 46 AFC: Buffalo (13) vs. Kansas City (33), 1966
- 48 AFC-D: Buffalo (12) vs. Boston (36), 1963
  - AFC: Boston (16) vs. San Diego (32), 1963

YARDS GAINED
Most Yards Gained, Game
- 382 NFC: Chi. Bears vs. Washington, 1940
- 338 NFC-FR: Dallas vs. Los Angeles, 1980
- 318 AFC: San Diego vs. Boston, 1963

Fewest Yards Gained, Game
- 7 AFC-D: Buffalo vs. Boston, 1963
- 17 SB: Minnesota vs. Pittsburgh, 1974
- 21 NFC: Los Angeles vs. Philadelphia, 1949

Most Yards Gained, Both Teams, Game
- 430 NFC-FR: Dallas (338) vs. Los Angeles (92), 1980
- 426 NFC: Cleveland (227) vs. Detroit (199), 1952
- 404 NFC: Chi. Bears (382) vs. Washington (22), 1940

Fewest Yards Gained, Both Teams, Game
- 90 AFC-D: Buffalo (7) vs. Boston (83), 1963
- 106 NFC: Boston (39) vs. Green Bay (67), 1936
- 128 NFC-FR: Philadelphia (53) vs. Atlanta (75), 1978

AVERAGE GAIN
Highest Average Gain, Game
- 9.94 AFC: San Diego vs. Boston, 1963 (32-318)
- 9.29 NFC-D: Green Bay vs. Dallas, 1982 (17-158)
- 7.35 NFC-FR: Dallas vs. Los Angeles, 1980 (46-338)

Lowest Average Gain, Game
- 0.58 AFC-D: Buffalo vs. Boston, 1963 (12-7)
- 0.81 SB: Minnesota vs. Pittsburgh, 1974 (21-17)
- 0.88 NFC: Los Angeles vs. Philadelphia, 1949 (24-21)

TOUCHDOWNS
Most Touchdowns, Game
- 7 NFC: Chi. Bears vs. Washington, 1940
- 5 NFC: Cleveland vs. Detroit, 1954
- 4 NFC: Detroit vs. N.Y. Giants, 1935
  - AFC: San Diego vs. Boston, 1963
  - NFC-D: Dallas vs. Cleveland, 1967
  - NFC: Baltimore vs. Cleveland, 1968
  - NFC-FR: Dallas vs. Los Angeles, 1980
  - AFC-D: L.A. Raiders vs. Pittsburgh, 1983

Most Touchdowns, Both Teams, Game
- 7 NFC: Chi. Bears (7) vs. Washington (0), 1940
- 6 NFC: Cleveland (5) vs. Detroit (1), 1954
- 5 NFC: Chi. Cardinals (3) vs. Philadelphia (2), 1947
  - AFC: San Diego (4) vs. Boston (1), 1963
  - AFC-D: Cincinnati (3) vs. Buffalo (2), 1981

PASSING

ATTEMPTS
Most Attempts, Game
- 54 AFC-D: San Diego vs. Miami, 1981 (OT)
- 53 NFC-FR: Dallas vs. L.A. Rams, 1983
- 51 NFC: Washington vs. Chi. Bears, 1940
  - AFC-FR: N.Y. Jets vs. Buffalo, 1981
  - NFC-FR: St. Louis vs. Green Bay, 1982

Fewest Attempts, Game
- 5 NFC: Detroit vs. N.Y. Giants, 1935
- 6 AFC: Miami vs. Oakland, 1973
- 7 SB: Miami vs. Minnesota, 1973

Most Attempts, Both Teams, Game
- 102 AFC-D: San Diego (54) vs. Miami (48), 1981 (OT)
- 96 AFC: N.Y. Jets (49) vs. Oakland (47), 1968
- 85 AFC-FR: N.Y. Jets (51) vs. Buffalo (34), 1981
  - SB: Miami (50) vs. San Francisco (35), 1984

Fewest Attempts, Both Teams, Game
- 18 NFC: Detroit (5) vs. N.Y. Giants (13), 1935
- 21 NFC: Chi. Bears (7) vs. N.Y. Giants (14), 1933
- 23 NFC: Chi. Cardinals (11) vs. Philadelphia (12), 1948

COMPLETIONS
Most Completions, Game
- 33 AFC-D: San Diego vs. Miami, 1981 (OT)
- 32 NFC-FR: St. Louis vs. Green Bay, 1982
  - NFC-FR: Dallas vs. L.A. Rams, 1983
- 31 AFC-D: Miami vs. San Diego, 1981 (OT)

Fewest Completions, Game
- 2 NFC: Detroit vs. N.Y. Giants, 1935
  - NFC: Philadelphia vs. Chi. Cardinals, 1948
- 3 NFC: N.Y. Giants vs. Chi. Bears, 1941
  - NFC: Green Bay vs. N.Y. Giants, 1944
  - NFC: Chi. Cardinals vs. Philadelphia, 1947
  - NFC: Chi. Cardinals vs. Philadelphia, 1948
  - NFC-D: Cleveland vs. N.Y. Giants, 1950
  - NFC-D: N.Y. Giants vs. Cleveland, 1950
  - NFC: Cleveland vs. Detroit, 1953
  - AFC: Miami vs. Oakland, 1973
- 4 NFC-D: Dallas vs. Detroit, 1970
  - AFC: Miami vs. Baltimore, 1971
  - SB: Miami vs. Washington, 1982
  - AFC-FR: Seattle vs. L.A. Raiders, 1984

Most Completions, Both Teams, Game
- 64 AFC-D: San Diego (33) vs. Miami (31), 1981 (OT)
- 55 AFC-FR: Pittsburgh (28) vs. San Diego (27), 1982
- 53 SB: Miami (29) vs. San Francisco (24), 1984

Fewest Completions, Both Teams, Game
- 5 NFC: Philadelphia (2) vs. Chi. Cardinals (3), 1948
- 6 NFC: Detroit (2) vs. N.Y. Giants (4), 1935
  - NFC-D: Cleveland (3) vs. N.Y. Giants (3), 1950
- 11 NFC: Green Bay (3) vs. N.Y. Giants (8), 1944
  - NFC-D: Dallas (4) vs. Detroit (7), 1970

COMPLETION PERCENTAGE
Highest Completion Percentage, Game (20 attempts)
- 80.0 NFC-D: Washington vs. L.A. Rams, 1983 (25-20)
- 79.2 AFC-D: Pittsburgh vs. Baltimore, 1976 (24-19)
- 78.3 AFC: Miami vs. San Diego, 1982 (23-18)

Lowest Completion Percentage, Game (20 attempts)
- 18.5 NFC: Tampa Bay vs. Los Angeles, 1979 (27-5)
- 20.0 NFC-D: N.Y. Giants vs. Washington, 1943 (20-4)
- 25.8 NFC: Chi. Bears vs. Washington, 1937 (31-8)

YARDS GAINED
Most Yards Gained, Game
- 435 AFC: Miami vs. Pittsburgh, 1984
- 415 AFC-D: San Diego vs. Miami, 1981 (OT)
- 394 AFC-D: Miami vs. San Diego, 1981 (OT)

Fewest Yards Gained, Game
- 3 NFC: Chi. Cardinals vs. Philadelphia, 1948
- 7 NFC: Philadelphia vs. Chi. Cardinals, 1948
- 9 NFC-D: N.Y. Giants vs. Cleveland, 1950
  - NFC: Cleveland vs. Detroit, 1953

Most Yards Gained, Both Teams, Game
- 809 AFC-D: San Diego (415) vs. Miami (394), 1981 (OT)
- 747 AFC: Miami (435) vs. Pittsburgh (312), 1984
- 658 AFC-FR: San Diego (333) vs. Pittsburgh (325), 1982

Fewest Yards Gained, Both Teams, Game
- 10 NFC: Chi. Cardinals (3) vs. Philadelphia (7), 1948
- 38 NFC-D: N.Y. Giants (9) vs. Cleveland (29), 1950
- 102 NFC-D: Dallas (22) vs. Detroit (80), 1970

TIMES SACKED
Most Times Sacked, Game
- 9 AFC: Kansas City vs. Buffalo, 1966
  - NFC: Chicago vs. San Francisco, 1984
- 8 NFC: Green Bay vs. Dallas, 1967
- 7 NFC-D: Dallas vs. Los Angeles, 1973
  - SB: Dallas vs. Pittsburgh, 1975
  - AFC-FR: Houston vs. Oakland, 1980
  - NFC-D: Washington vs. Chicago, 1984

Most Times Sacked, Both Teams, Game
- 13 AFC: Kansas City (9) vs. Buffalo (4), 1966
- 12 NFC-D: Dallas (7) vs. Los Angeles (5), 1973
  - NFC-D: Washington (7) vs. Chicago (5), 1984
  - NFC: Chicago (9) vs. San Francisco (3), 1984
- 10 AFC-FR: Houston (7) vs. Oakland (3), 1980
  - NFC-D: N.Y. Giants (6) vs. San Francisco (4), 1984

Fewest Times Sacked, Both Teams, Game
- 0 AFC-D: Buffalo vs. Pittsburgh, 1974
  - AFC-FR: Pittsburgh vs. San Diego, 1982
- 1 In many games

TOUCHDOWNS
Most Touchdowns, Game
- 6 AFC-D: Oakland vs. Houston, 1969
- 5 NFC: Chi. Bears vs. Washington, 1943
  - NFC: Detroit vs. Cleveland, 1957
  - AFC-D: Oakland vs. Kansas City, 1968
- 4 NFC: Cleveland vs. Los Angeles, 1950
  - NFC: Green Bay vs. Dallas, 1966
  - AFC-D: Oakland vs. Miami, 1974
  - NFC: Dallas vs. Los Angeles, 1975
  - SB: Pittsburgh vs. Dallas, 1978
  - AFC-D: Miami vs. San Diego, 1981 (OT)
  - NFC-FR: Green Bay vs. St. Louis, 1982
  - AFC: Miami vs. Pittsburgh, 1984

Most Touchdowns, Both Teams, Game
- 7 NFC: Chi. Bears (5) vs. Washington (2), 1943
  - AFC-D: Oakland (6) vs. Houston (1), 1969
  - SB: Pittsburgh (4) vs. Dallas (3), 1978
  - AFC-D: Miami (4) vs. San Diego (3), 1981 (OT)
  - AFC: Miami (4) vs. Pittsburgh (3), 1984
- 6 NFC-FR: Green Bay (4) vs. St. Louis (2), 1982
- 5 In many games

INTERCEPTIONS BY
Most Interceptions By, Game
- 8 NFC: Chi. Bears vs. Washington, 1940
- 7 NFC: Cleveland vs. Los Angeles, 1955

6 NFC: Green Bay vs. N.Y. Giants, 1939
NFC: Chi. Bears vs. N.Y. Giants, 1946
NFC: Cleveland vs. Detroit, 1954
AFC: San Diego vs. Houston, 1961

Most Interceptions By, Both Teams, Game
10 NFC: Cleveland (7) vs. Los Angeles (3), 1955
AFC: San Diego (6) vs. Houston (4), 1961
9 NFC: Green Bay (6) vs. N.Y. Giants (3), 1939
8 NFC: Chi. Bears (8) vs. Washington (0), 1940
NFC: Chi. Bears (6) vs. N.Y. Giants (2), 1946
NFC: Cleveland (6) vs. Detroit (2), 1954
AFC-FR: Buffalo (4) vs. N.Y. Jets (4), 1981
AFC: Miami (5) vs. N.Y. Jets (3), 1982

YARDS GAINED
Most Yards Gained, Game
138 AFC-FR: N.Y. Jets vs. Cincinnati, 1982
136 AFC: Dall. Texans vs. Houston, 1962 (OT)
130 NFC-D: Los Angeles vs. St. Louis, 1975
Most Yards Gained, Both Teams, Game
156 NFC: Green Bay (123) vs. N.Y. Giants (33), 1939
149 NFC: Cleveland (103) vs. Los Angeles (46), 1955
141 AFC-FR: Buffalo (79) vs. N.Y. Jets (62), 1981

TOUCHDOWNS
Most Touchdowns, Game
3 NFC: Chi. Bears vs. Washington, 1940
2 NFC-D: Los Angeles vs. St. Louis, 1975
1 In many games

PUNTING
Most Punts, Game
13 NFC: N.Y. Giants vs. Chi. Bears, 1933
AFC-D: Baltimore vs. Oakland, 1977 (OT)
11 AFC: Houston vs. Oakland, 1967
AFC-D: Houston vs. Oakland, 1969
10 In many games
Fewest Punts, Game
0 NFC-FR: St. Louis vs. Green Bay, 1982
AFC-FR: N.Y. Jets vs. Cincinnati, 1982
1 NFC-D: Cleveland vs. Dallas, 1969
AFC: Miami vs. Oakland, 1973
AFC-D: Oakland vs. Cincinnati, 1975
AFC-D: Pittsburgh vs. Baltimore, 1976
AFC: Pittsburgh vs. Houston, 1978
NFC-FR: Green Bay vs. St. Louis, 1982
AFC-FR: Miami vs. New England, 1982
AFC-FR: San Diego vs. Pittsburgh, 1982
2 In many games
Most Punts, Both Teams, Game
23 NFC: N.Y. Giants (13) vs. Chi. Bears (10), 1933
21 AFC-D: Baltimore (13) vs. Oakland (8), 1977 (OT)
20 NFC: Green Bay (10) vs. N.Y. Giants (10), 1944
AFC: Miami (10) vs. N.Y. Jets (10), 1982
Fewest Punts, Both Teams, Game
1 NFC-FR: St. Louis (0) vs. Green Bay (1), 1982
2 AFC-FR: N.Y. Jets (0) vs. Cincinnati (2), 1982
3 AFC: Miami (1) vs. Oakland (2), 1973
AFC-FR: San Diego (1) vs. Pittsburgh (2), 1982

AVERAGE YARDAGE
Highest Average, Punting, Game (4 punts)
56.0 AFC: Oakland vs. San Diego, 1980
52.5 NFC: Washington vs. Chi. Bears, 1942
51.3 AFC: Pittsburgh vs. Miami, 1972
Lowest Average, Punting, Game (4 punts)
24.9 NFC: Washington vs. Chi. Bears, 1937
25.5 NFC: Green Bay vs. N.Y. Giants, 1962
27.8 AFC-D: San Diego vs. Buffalo, 1980

PUNT RETURNS
Most Punt Returns, Game
8 NFC: Green Bay vs. N.Y. Giants, 1944
7 NFC-D: Washington vs. N.Y. Giants, 1943
NFC-D: Chi. Bears vs. Los Angeles, 1950
AFC-D: Baltimore vs. Cincinnati, 1970
NFC: Los Angeles vs. Minnesota, 1976
AFC-FR: Houston vs. Oakland, 1980
AFC-D: Cleveland vs. Oakland, 1980
6 By many teams
Most Punt Returns, Both Teams, Game
13 AFC-FR: Houston (7) vs. Oakland (6), 1980
11 NFC: Green Bay (8) vs. N.Y. Giants (3), 1944
NFC-D: Green Bay (6) vs. Baltimore (5), 1965
10 In many games
Fewest Punt Returns, Both Teams, Game
0 NFC: Chi. Bears vs. N.Y. Giants, 1941
AFC: Boston vs. San Diego, 1963
NFC-FR: Green Bay vs. St. Louis, 1982
1 AFC: Miami (0) vs. Pittsburgh (1), 1972
AFC: Cincinnati (0) vs. San Diego (1), 1981
AFC-FR: Cincinnati (0) vs. N.Y. Jets (1), 1982
AFC-FR: San Diego (0) vs. Pittsburgh (1), 1982
NFC-D: Minnesota (0) vs. Washington (1), 1982
AFC: Seattle (0) vs. L.A. Raiders (1), 1983
2 In many games

YARDS GAINED
Most Yards Gained, Game
155 NFC-D: Dallas vs. Cleveland, 1967
150 NFC: Chi. Cardinals vs. Philadelphia, 1947
112 NFC-D: Philadelphia vs. Pittsburgh, 1947

Fewest Yards Gained, Game
−10 NFC: Green Bay vs. Cleveland, 1965
−9 NFC: Dallas vs. Green Bay, 1966
AFC-D: Kansas City vs. Oakland, 1968
−5 AFC-D: Miami vs. Oakland, 1970
NFC-D: San Francisco vs. Dallas, 1972
NFC: Dallas vs. Washington, 1972
Most Yards Gained, Both Teams, Game
166 NFC-D: Dallas (155) vs. Cleveland (11), 1967
160 NFC: Chi. Cardinals (150) vs. Philadelphia (10), 1947
146 NFC-D: Philadelphia (112) vs. Pittsburgh (34), 1947
Fewest Yards Gained, Both Teams, Game
−9 NFC: Dallas (−9) vs. Green Bay (0), 1966
−6 AFC-D: Miami (−5) vs. Oakland (−1), 1970
−3 NFC-D: San Francisco (−5) vs. Dallas (2), 1972

TOUCHDOWNS
Most Touchdowns, Game
1 By seven teams

KICKOFF RETURNS
Most Kickoff Returns, Game
10 NFC-D: L.A. Rams vs. Washington, 1983
9 NFC: Chi. Bears vs. N.Y. Giants, 1956
AFC: Boston vs. San Diego, 1963
AFC: Houston vs. Oakland, 1967
8 By many teams
Most Kickoff Returns, Both Teams, Game
13 NFC-D: Green Bay (7) vs. Dallas (6), 1982
12 AFC: Boston (9) vs. San Diego (3), 1963
NFC: Dallas (6) vs. Green Bay (6), 1966
AFC-D: Baltimore (6) vs. Oakland (6), 1977 (OT)
AFC: Oakland (6) vs. San Diego (6), 1980
AFC-D: Miami (6) vs. San Diego (6), 1981 (OT)
NFC-D: N.Y. Giants (7) vs. San Francisco (5), 1981
AFC-FR: Cincinnati (8) vs. N.Y. Jets (4), 1982
NFC-D: L.A. Rams (10) vs. Washington (2), 1983
11 In many games
Fewest Kickoff Returns, Both Teams, Game
1 NFC: Green Bay (0) vs. Boston (1), 1936
2 NFC-D: Los Angeles (0) vs. Chi. Bears (2), 1950
AFC: Houston (0) vs. San Diego (2), 1961
AFC-D: Oakland (1) vs. Pittsburgh (1), 1972
AFC-D: N.Y. Jets (0) vs. L.A. Raiders (2), 1982
AFC: Miami (1) vs. N.Y. Jets (1), 1982
3 In many games

YARDS GAINED
Most Yards Gained, Game
225 NFC: Washington vs. Chi. Bears, 1940
222 SB: Miami vs. Washington, 1982
215 AFC: Houston vs. Oakland, 1967
Most Yards Gained, Both Teams, Game
379 AFC-D: Baltimore (193) vs. Oakland (186), 1977 (OT)
321 NFC-D: Dallas (173) vs. Green Bay (148), 1982
318 AFC-D: Miami (183) vs. Oakland (135), 1974
Fewest Yards Gained, Both Teams, Game
31 NFC-D: Los Angeles (0) vs. Chi. Bears (31), 1950
32 NFC: Green Bay (0) vs. Boston (32), 1936
46 NFC-D: Philadelphia (15) vs. Pittsburgh (31), 1947
AFC-D: Baltimore (0) vs. Cincinnati (46), 1970

TOUCHDOWNS
Most Touchdowns, Game
1 NFC-D: San Francisco vs. Dallas, 1972
AFC-D: Miami vs. Oakland, 1974
AFC-D: Baltimore vs. Oakland, 1977 (OT)
SB: Miami vs. Washington, 1982

PENALTIES
Most Penalties, Game
14 AFC-FR: Oakland vs. Houston, 1980
NFC-D: San Francisco vs. N.Y. Giants, 1981
12 NFC-D: Chi. Bears vs. Green Bay, 1941
AFC-D: Pittsburgh vs. Baltimore, 1976
SB: Dallas vs. Denver, 1977
AFC-FR: N.Y. Jets vs. Cincinnati, 1982
11 NFC: N.Y. Giants vs. Green Bay, 1944
AFC-D: Oakland vs. New England, 1976
AFC-D: Pittsburgh vs. Denver, 1978
NFC-FR: Dallas vs. Los Angeles, 1980
Fewest Penalties, Game
0 NFC: Philadelphia vs. Green Bay, 1960
NFC-D: Detroit vs. Dallas, 1970
AFC-D: Miami vs. Oakland, 1970
SB: Miami vs. Dallas, 1971
NFC-D: Washington vs. Minnesota, 1973
SB: Pittsburgh vs. Dallas, 1975
1 By many teams
Most Penalties, Both Teams, Game
22 AFC-FR: Oakland (14) vs. Houston (8), 1980
NFC-D: San Francisco (14) vs. N.Y. Giants (8), 1981
21 AFC-D: Oakland (11) vs. New England (10), 1976
20 SB: Dallas (12) vs. Denver (8), 1977
Fewest Penalties, Both Teams, Game
2 NFC: Washington (1) vs. Chi. Bears (1), 1937
NFC-D: Washington (0) vs. Minnesota (2), 1973
SB: Pittsburgh (0) vs. Dallas (2), 1975
3 AFC: Miami (1) vs. Baltimore (2), 1971
NFC: San Francisco (1) vs. Dallas (2), 1971
SB: Miami (0) vs. Dallas (3), 1971
AFC-D: Pittsburgh (1) vs. Oakland (2), 1972

AFC-D: Miami (1) vs. Cincinnati (2), 1973
SB: Miami (1) vs. San Francisco (2), 1984
4   NFC-D: Cleveland (2) vs. Dallas (2), 1967
NFC-D: Minnesota (1) vs. San Francisco (3), 1970
AFC-D: Miami (0) vs. Oakland (4), 1970
NFC-D: Dallas (2) vs. Minnesota (2), 1971

YARDS PENALIZED
Most Yards Penalized, Game
145 NFC-D: San Francisco vs. N.Y. Giants, 1981
133 SB: Dallas vs. Baltimore, 1970
128 NFC-D: Chi. Bears vs. Green Bay, 1941
Fewest Yards Penalized, Game
0   By six teams
Most Yards Penalized, Both Teams, Game
206 NFC-D: San Francisco (145) vs. N.Y. Giants (61), 1981
192 AFC-D: Denver (104) vs. Pittsburgh (88), 1978
182 NFC-FR: Atlanta (98) vs. Minnesota (84), 1982
Fewest Yards Penalized, Both Teams, Game
9   NFC-D: Washington (0) vs. Minnesota (9), 1973
15 SB: Miami (0) vs. Dallas (15), 1971
20 NFC: Washington (5) vs. Chi. Bears (15), 1937
AFC-D: Pittsburgh (5) vs. Oakland (15), 1972
SB: Pittsburgh (0) vs. Dallas (20), 1975
Miami (10) vs. San Francisco (10), 1984

FUMBLES

Most Fumbles, Game
6   By nine teams
Most Fumbles, Both Teams, Game
12 AFC: Houston (6) vs. Pittsburgh (6), 1978
10 NFC: Chi. Bears (5) vs. N.Y. Giants (5), 1934
SB: Dallas (6) vs. Denver (4), 1977
9   NFC-D: San Francisco (6) vs. Detroit (3), 1957
NFC-D: San Francisco (5) vs. Dallas (4), 1972
NFC: Dallas (5) vs. Philadelphia (4), 1980
Most Fumbles Lost, Game
4   NFC: N.Y. Giants vs. Baltimore, 1958 (OT)
AFC: Kansas City vs. Oakland, 1969
SB: Baltimore vs. Dallas, 1970
AFC: Pittsburgh vs. Oakland, 1975
SB: Denver vs. Dallas, 1977
AFC: Houston vs. Pittsburgh, 1978
3   By many teams
Fewest Fumbles, Both Teams, Game
0   NFC: Green Bay vs. Cleveland, 1965
AFC: Buffalo vs. San Diego, 1965
AFC-D: Oakland vs. Miami, 1974
AFC-D: Houston vs. San Diego, 1979
NFC-D: Dallas vs. Los Angeles, 1979
SB: Los Angeles vs. Pittsburgh, 1979
AFC-D: Buffalo vs. Cincinnati, 1981
1   In many games

RECOVERIES
Most Total Fumbles Recovered, Game
8   SB: Dallas vs. Denver, 1977 (4 own, 4 opp)
7   NFC: Chi. Bears vs. N.Y. Giants, 1934 (5 own, 2 opp)
NFC-D: San Francisco vs. Detroit, 1957 (4 own, 3 opp)
NFC-D: San Francisco vs. Dallas, 1972 (4 own, 3 opp)
AFC: Pittsburgh vs. Houston, 1978 (3 own, 4 opp)
6   AFC: Houston vs. San Diego, 1961 (4 own, 2 opp)
AFC-D: Cleveland vs. Baltimore, 1971 (4 own, 2 opp)
AFC-D: Cleveland vs. Oakland, 1980 (5 own, 1 opp)
NFC: Philadelphia vs. Dallas, 1980 (3 own, 3 opp)
Most Own Fumbles Recovered, Game
5   NFC: Chi. Bears vs. N.Y. Giants, 1934
AFC-D: Cleveland vs. Oakland, 1980
4   By many teams

TURNOVERS
(Numbers of times losing the ball on interceptions and fumbles.)
Most Turnovers, Game
9   NFC: Washington vs. Chi. Bears, 1940
NFC: Detroit vs. Cleveland, 1954
AFC: Houston vs. Pittsburgh, 1978
8   NFC: N.Y. Giants vs. Chi. Bears, 1946
NFC: Los Angeles vs. Cleveland, 1955
NFC: Cleveland vs. Detroit, 1957
SB: Denver vs. Dallas, 1977
NFC-D: Minnesota vs. Philadelphia, 1980
7   AFC: Houston vs. San Diego, 1961
SB: Baltimore vs. Dallas, 1970
AFC: Pittsburgh vs. Oakland, 1975
NFC-D: Chicago vs. Dallas, 1977
NFC: Los Angeles vs. Dallas, 1978
AFC-D: San Diego vs. Miami, 1982
Fewest Turnovers, Game
0   By many teams
Most Turnovers, Both Teams, Game
14 AFC: Houston (9) vs. Pittsburgh (5), 1978
13 NFC: Detroit (9) vs. Cleveland (4), 1954
AFC: Houston (7) vs. San Diego (6), 1961
12 AFC: Pittsburgh (7) vs. Oakland (5), 1975
Fewest Turnovers, Both Teams, Game
1   AFC-D: Baltimore (0) vs. Cincinnati (1), 1970
AFC-D: Pittsburgh (0) vs. Buffalo (1), 1974
AFC: Oakland (0) vs. Pittsburgh (1), 1976
NFC-D: Minnesota (0) vs. Washington (1), 1982
2   In many games

Compiled by Elias Sports Bureau

INDIVIDUAL RECORDS

SERVICE

Most Games
- 9 *Ken Houston, Houston, 1971-73; Washington, 1974-79
  Joe Greene, Pittsburgh, 1971-77, 1979-80
  Jack Lambert, Pittsburgh, 1976-84
- 8 Tom Mack, Los Angeles, 1971-76, 1978-79
  *Franco Harris, Pittsburgh, 1973-76, 1978-81
  Lemar Parrish, Cincinnati, 1971-72, 1975-77; Washington, 1978, 1980-81
  Art Shell, Oakland, 1973-79, 1981
  Ted Hendricks, Baltimore, 1972-74; Green Bay, 1975; Oakland, 1981-82; L.A. Raiders, 1983-84
- 7 Ron Yary, Minnesota, 1972-78
  Elvin Bethea, Houston, 1972-76, 1979-80
  Roger Wehrli, St. Louis, 1971-72, 1975-78, 1980
  Jack Youngblood, Los Angeles, 1974-80
  Ray Guy, Oakland, 1974-79, 1981
  Robert Brazile, Houston, 1977-83
  Randy Gradishar, Denver, 1976, 1978-80, 1982-84
  *John Hannah, New England, 1977, 1979-83, 1985
  Walter Payton, Chicago, 1977-81, 1984-85
  *Randy White, Dallas, 1978, 1980-85
  Mike Webster, Pittsburgh, 1979-85
  *Also selected, but did not play, in one additional game

SCORING

POINTS

Most Points, Career
- 30 Jan Stenerud, Kansas City, 1971-72, 1976; Green Bay, 1985 (6-pat, 8-fg)
- 18 John Brockington, Green Bay, 1972-74 (3-td)
  Earl Campbell, Houston, 1979-82, 1984 (3-td)
  Chuck Muncie, New Orleans, 1980; San Diego, 1982-83 (3-td)
  William Andrews, Atlanta, 1981-84 (3-td)
- 16 Garo Yepremian, Miami, 1974, 1979 (1-pat, 5-fg)

Most Points, Game
- 18 John Brockington, Green Bay, 1973 (3-td)
- 15 Garo Yepremian, Miami, 1974 (5-fg)
- 14 Jan Stenerud, Kansas City, 1972 (2-pat, 4-fg)

TOUCHDOWNS

Most Touchdowns, Career
- 3 John Brockington, Green Bay, 1972-74 (2-r, 1-p)
  Earl Campbell, Houston, 1979-82, 1984 (3-r)
  Chuck Muncie, New Orleans, 1980; San Diego, 1982-83 (3-r)
  William Andrews, Atlanta, 1981-84 (1-r, 2-p)
- 2 By 10 players

Most Touchdowns, Game
- 3 John Brockington, Green Bay, 1973 (2-r, 1-p)
- 2 Mel Renfro, Dallas, 1971 (2-ret)
  Earl Campbell, Houston, 1980 (2-r)
  Chuck Muncie, New Orleans, 1980 (2-r)
  William Andrews, Atlanta, 1984 (2-p)

POINTS AFTER TOUCHDOWN

Most Points After Touchdown, Career
- 6 Chester Marcol, Green Bay, 1973, 1975 (6 att)
  Mark Moseley, Washington, 1980, 1983 (7 att)
  Ali Haji-Sheikh, N.Y. Giants, 1984 (6 att)
  Jan Stenerud, Kansas City, 1971-72, 1976; Green Bay, 1985 (6 att)

Most Points After Touchdown, Game
- 6 Ali Haji-Sheikh, N.Y. Giants, 1984 (6 att)
- 4 Chester Marcol, Green Bay, 1973 (4 att)
  Mark Moseley, Washington, 1980 (5 att)

FIELD GOALS

Most Field Goals Attempted, Career
- 15 Jan Stenerud, Kansas City, 1971-72, 1976; Green Bay, 1985
- 7 Garo Yepremian, Miami, 1974, 1979
  Mark Moseley, Washington, 1980, 1983
- 6 Ed Murray, Detroit, 1981

Most Field Goals Attempted, Game
- 6 Jan Stenerud, Kansas City, 1972
  Ed Murray, Detroit, 1981
  Mark Moseley, Washington, 1983
- 5 Garo Yepremian, Miami, 1974
- 4 Jan Stenerud, Kansas City, 1976

Most Field Goals, Career
- 8 Jan Stenerud, Kansas City, 1971-72, 1976; Green Bay, 1985
- 5 Garo Yepremian, Miami, 1974, 1979
- 4 Ed Murray, Detroit, 1981

Most Field Goals, Game
- 5 Garo Yepremian, Miami, 1974 (5 att)
- 4 Jan Stenerud, Kansas City, 1972 (6 att)
  Ed Murray, Detroit, 1981 (6 att)
- 2 By many players

Longest Field Goal
- 48 Jan Stenerud, Kansas City, 1972
- 43 Gary Anderson, Pittsburgh, 1984
- 42 Jim Bakken, St. Louis, 1976

SAFETIES

Most Safeties, Game
- 1 Art Still, Kansas City, 1983
  Mark Gastineau, N.Y. Jets, 1985

RUSHING

ATTEMPTS

Most Attempts, Career
- 73 Walter Payton, Chicago, 1977-81, 1984-85
- 68 O.J. Simpson, Buffalo, 1973-77
- 46 Franco Harris, Pittsburgh, 1973-76, 1978-81
  Earl Campbell, Houston, 1979-82, 1984

Most Attempts, Game
- 19 O.J. Simpson, Buffalo, 1974
- 17 Marv Hubbard, Oakland, 1974
- 16 O.J. Simpson, Buffalo, 1973

YARDS GAINED

Most Yards Gained, Career
- 356 O.J. Simpson, Buffalo, 1973-77
- 330 Walter Payton, Chicago, 1977-81, 1984-85
- 220 Earl Campbell, Houston, 1979-82, 1984

Most Yards Gained, Game
- 112 O. J. Simpson, Buffalo, 1973
- 104 Marv Hubbard, Oakland, 1974
- 77 Walter Payton, Chicago, 1978

Longest Run From Scrimmage
- 41 Lawrence McCutcheon, Los Angeles, 1976
- 30 O.J. Simpson, Buffalo, 1975
- 29 Franco Harris, Pittsburgh, 1973

AVERAGE GAIN

Highest Average Gain, Career (20 attempts)
- 5.81 Marv Hubbard, Oakland, 1972-74 (36-209)
- 5.71 Wilbert Montgomery, Philadelphia, 1979-80 (21-120)
- 5.36 Larry Csonka, Miami, 1971-72, 1975 (22-118)

Highest Average Gain, Game (10 attempts)
- 7.00 O.J. Simpson, Buffalo, 1973 (16-112)
  Ottis Anderson, St. Louis, 1981 (10-70)
- 6.91 Walter Payton, Chicago, 1985 (11-76)
- 6.90 Earl Campbell, Houston, 1980 (10-69)

TOUCHDOWNS

Most Touchdowns, Career
- 3 Earl Campbell, Houston, 1979-82, 1984
  Chuck Muncie, New Orleans, 1980; San Diego, 1982-83
- 2 John Brockington, Green Bay, 1972-74
  O.J. Simpson, Buffalo, 1973-77
  Walter Payton, Chicago, 1977-81, 1984-85

Most Touchdowns, Game
- 2 John Brockington, Green Bay, 1973
  Earl Campbell, Houston, 1980
  Chuck Muncie, New Orleans, 1980

PASSING

ATTEMPTS

Most Attempts, Career
- 93 Dan Fouts, San Diego, 1980-84
- 88 Bob Griese, Miami, 1971-72, 1974-75, 1977, 1979
- 56 Ken Anderson, Cincinnati, 1976-77, 1982-83

Most Attempts, Game
- 32 Bill Kenney, Kansas City, 1984
- 30 Dan Fouts, San Diego, 1983
- 28 Jim Hart, St. Louis, 1976

COMPLETIONS

Most Completions, Career
- 47 Dan Fouts, San Diego, 1980-84
- 44 Bob Griese, Miami, 1971-72, 1974-75, 1977, 1979
- 33 Ken Anderson, Cincinnati, 1976-77, 1982-83

Most Completions, Game
- 21 Joe Theismann, Washington, 1984
- 17 Dan Fouts, San Diego, 1983
- 14 Norm Snead, N.Y. Giants, 1973
  Ken Anderson, Cincinnati, 1983
  Danny White, Dallas, 1983

COMPLETION PERCENTAGE

Highest Completion Percentage, Career (40 attempts)
- 68.9 Joe Theismann, Washington, 1983-84 (45-31)
- 58.9 Ken Anderson, Cincinnati, 1976-77, 1982-83 (56-33)
- 50.5 Dan Fouts, San Diego, 1980-84 (93-47)

Highest Completion Percentage, Game (10 attempts)
- 90.0 Archie Manning, New Orleans, 1980 (10-9)
- 77.8 Joe Theismann, Washington, 1984 (27-21)
- 71.4 Joe Montana, San Francisco, 1985 (14-10)

YARDS GAINED

Most Yards Gained, Career
- 717 Dan Fouts, San Diego, 1980-84
- 554 Bob Griese, Miami, 1971-72, 1974-75, 1977, 1979
- 398 Ken Anderson, Cincinnati, 1976-77, 1982-83

Most Yards Gained, Game
- 274 Dan Fouts, San Diego, 1983
- 242 Joe Theismann, Washington, 1984
- 192 Neil Lomax, St. Louis, 1985

Longest Completion
- 64 Dan Pastorini, Houston (to Burrough, Houston), 1976 (TD)
- 57 James Harris, Los Angeles (to Gray, St. Louis), 1976
  Ken Anderson, Cincinnati (to G. Pruitt, Cleveland), 1977
- 56 Dan Marino, Miami (to Allen, L.A. Raiders), 1985

AVERAGE GAIN
Highest Average Gain, Career (40 attempts)
- 7.71 Dan Fouts, San Diego, 1980-84 (93-717)
- 7.64 Joe Theismann, Washington, 1983-84 (45-344)
- 7.11 Ken Anderson, Cincinnati, 1976-77, 1982-83 (56-398)

Highest Average Gain, Game (10 attempts)
- 11.40 Ken Anderson, Cincinnati, 1977 (10-114)
- 11.20 Archie Manning, New Orleans, 1980 (10-112)
- 11.09 Greg Landry, Detroit, 1972 (11-122)

TOUCHDOWNS
Most Touchdowns, Career
- 3 Joe Theismann, Washington, 1983-84
-    Joe Montana, San Francisco, 1982, 1984-85
- 2 James Harris, Los Angeles, 1975
-    Mike Boryla, Philadelphia, 1976
-    Ken Anderson, Cincinnati, 1976-77, 1982-83

Most Touchdowns, Game
- 3 Joe Theismann, Washington, 1984
- 2 James Harris, Los Angeles, 1975
-    Mike Boryla, Philadelphia, 1976
-    Ken Anderson, Cincinnati, 1977

HAD INTERCEPTED
Most Passes Had Intercepted, Career
- 6 Jim Hart, St. Louis, 1975-78
- 5 Ken Stabler, Oakland, 1974-75, 1978
-    Dan Fouts, San Diego, 1980-84
- 4 Roger Staubach, Dallas, 1972, 1977, 1979-80

Most Passes Had Intercepted, Game
- 5 Jim Hart, St. Louis, 1977
- 4 Ken Stabler, Oakland, 1974
- 2 By many players

Most Attempts, Without Interception, Game
- 27 Joe Theismann, Washington, 1984
- 26 John Brodie, San Francisco, 1971
-     Danny White, Dallas, 1983
- 21 Roman Gabriel, Los Angeles, 1974
-     Dan Marino, Miami, 1985

PERCENTAGE, PASSES HAD INTERCEPTED
Lowest Percentage, Passes Had Intercepted, Career (40 attempts)
- 0.00 Joe Theismann, Washington, 1983-84 (45-0)
- 3.41 Bob Griese, Miami, 1971-72, 1974-75, 1977, 1979 (88-3)
- 5.36 Ken Anderson, Cincinnati, 1976-77, 1982-83 (56-3)

PASS RECEIVING
RECEPTIONS
Most Receptions, Career
- 14 Walter Payton, Chicago, 1977-81, 1984-85
-     John Stallworth, Pittsburgh, 1980, 1983, 1985
- 13 William Andrews, Atlanta, 1981-84
- 12 Kellen Winslow, San Diego, 1981-84
-     James Lofton, Green Bay, 1979, 1981-85

Most Receptions, Game
- 7 John Stallworth, Pittsburgh, 1983
- 6 John Stallworth, Pittsburgh, 1980
-    Kellen Winslow, San Diego, 1982
- 5 By many players

YARDS GAINED
Most Yards Gained, Career
- 179 Kellen Winslow, San Diego, 1981-84
- 169 John Jefferson, San Diego, 1979-81; Green Bay, 1983
- 163 Cliff Branch, Oakland, 1975-78

Most Yards Gained, Game
- 96 Ken Burrough, Houston, 1976
- 91 Alfred Jenkins, Atlanta, 1981
- 89 Ahmad Rashad, Minnesota, 1979

Longest Reception
- 64 Ken Burrough, Houston (from Pastorini, Houston), 1976 (TD)
- 57 Mel Gray, St. Louis (from Harris, Los Angeles), 1975
-     Greg Pruitt, Cleveland (from Anderson, Cincinnati), 1977
- 56 Marcus Allen, L.A. Raiders (from Marino, Miami), 1985

TOUCHDOWNS
Most Touchdowns, Career
- 2 Mel Gray, St. Louis, 1975-78
-    Cliff Branch, Oakland, 1975-78
-    Terry Metcalf, St. Louis, 1975-76, 1978
-    Tony Hill, Dallas, 1979-80
-    William Andrews, Atlanta, 1981-84
-    James Lofton, Green Bay, 1979, 1981-85

Most Touchdowns, Game
- 2 William Andrews, Atlanta, 1984

INTERCEPTIONS BY
Most Interceptions, Career
- 4 Everson Walls, Dallas, 1982-84
- 3 Ken Houston, Houston, 1971-73; Washington, 1975-79
-    Jack Lambert, Pittsburgh, 1976-84
-    Ted Hendricks, Baltimore, 1972-74; Green Bay, 1975; Oakland, 1981-82; L.A. Raiders, 1983-84
- 2 By five players

Most Interceptions By, Game
- 2 Mel Blount, Pittsburgh, 1977
-    Everson Walls, Dallas, 1982, 1983

YARDS GAINED
Most Yards Gained, Career
- 77 Ted Hendricks, Baltimore, 1972-74; Green Bay, 1975; Oakland, 1981-82; L.A. Raiders, 1983-84
- 44 Nolan Cromwell, L.A. Rams, 1981-84

- 40 Tom Myers, New Orleans, 1980
-     Everson Walls, Dallas, 1982-84

Most Yards Gained, Game
- 65 Ted Hendricks, Baltimore, 1973
- 44 Nolan Cromwell, L.A. Rams, 1984
- 40 Tom Myers, New Orleans, 1980

Longest Gain
- 65 Ted Hendricks, Baltimore, 1973
- 44 Nolan Cromwell, L.A. Rams, 1984 (TD)
- 40 Tom Myers, New Orleans, 1980

TOUCHDOWNS
Most Touchdowns, Game
- 1 Bobby Bell, Kansas City, 1973
-    Nolan Cromwell, L.A. Rams, 1984

PUNTING
Most Punts, Career
- 33 Ray Guy, Oakland, 1974-79, 1981
- 19 Dave Jennings, N.Y. Giants, 1979-81, 1983
- 16 Jerrel Wilson, Kansas City, 1971-73
-     Tom Wittum, San Francisco, 1974-75

Most Punts, Game
- 10 Reggie Roby, Miami, 1985
- 9 Tom Wittum, San Francisco, 1974
- 8 Jerrel Wilson, Kansas City, 1971
-    Tom Skladany, Detroit, 1982

Longest Punt
- 64 Tom Wittum, San Francisco, 1974
- 61 Reggie Roby, Miami, 1985
- 60 Ron Widby, Dallas, 1972

AVERAGE YARDAGE
Highest Average, Career (10 punts)
- 45.25 Jerrel Wilson, Kansas City, 1971-73 (16-724)
- 44.64 Ray Guy, Oakland, 1974-79, 1981 (33-1,473)
- 44.63 Tom Wittum, San Francisco, 1974-75 (16-714)

Highest Average, Game (4 punts)
- 49.00 Ray Guy, Oakland, 1974 (4-196)
- 47.75 Bob Grupp, Kansas City, 1980 (4-191)
- 47.40 Ray Guy, Oakland, 1976 (5-237)

PUNT RETURNS
Most Punt Returns, Career
- 13 Rick Upchurch, Denver, 1977, 1979-80, 1983
- 10 Mike Nelms, Washington, 1981-83
- 9 Greg Pruitt, Cleveland, 1974-75, 1977-78; L.A. Raiders, 1984

Most Punt Returns, Game
- 6 Henry Ellard, L.A. Rams, 1985
- 5 Rick Upchurch, Denver, 1980
-    Mike Nelms, Washington, 1981
-    Carl Roaches, Houston, 1982
- 4 By six players

Most Fair Catches, Game
- 2 Jerry Logan, Baltimore, 1971
-    Dick Anderson, Miami, 1974
-    Henry Ellard, L.A. Rams, 1985

YARDS GAINED
Most Yards Gained, Career
- 183 Billy Johnson, Houston, 1976, 1978; Atlanta, 1984
- 138 Rick Upchurch, Denver, 1977, 1979-80, 1983
- 119 Mike Nelms, Washington, 1981-83

Most Yards Gained, Game
- 159 Billy Johnson, Houston, 1976
- 138 Mel Renfro, Dallas, 1971
- 117 Wally Henry, Philadelphia, 1980

Longest Punt Return
- 90 Billy Johnson, Houston, 1976 (TD)
- 86 Wally Henry, Philadelphia, 1980 (TD)
- 82 Mel Renfro, Dallas, 1971 (TD)

TOUCHDOWNS
Most Touchdowns, Game
- 2 Mel Renfro, Dallas, 1971
- 1 Billy Johnson, Houston, 1976
-    Wally Henry, Philadelphia, 1980

KICKOFF RETURNS
Most Kickoff Returns, Career
- 10 Rick Upchurch, Denver, 1977, 1979-80, 1983
-     Greg Pruitt, Cleveland, 1974-75, 1977-78; L.A. Raiders, 1984
- 8 Mike Nelms, Washington, 1981-83
- 6 Terry Metcalf, St. Louis, 1975-76, 1978

Most Kickoff Returns, Game
- 6 Greg Pruitt, L.A. Raiders, 1984
- 5 Les (Speedy) Duncan, Washington, 1972
-    Ron Smith, Chicago, 1973
-    Herb Mul-Key, Washington, 1974
- 4 By four players

YARDS GAINED
Most Yards Gained, Career
- 309 Greg Pruitt, Cleveland, 1974-75, 1977-78; L.A. Raiders, 1984
- 222 Rick Upchurch, Denver, 1977, 1979-80, 1983
- 175 Les (Speedy) Duncan, Washington, 1972

Most Yards Gained, Game
- 192 Greg Pruitt, L.A. Raiders, 1984
- 175 Les (Speedy) Duncan, Washington, 1972
- 152 Ron Smith, Chicago, 1973

Longest Kickoff Return
- 62 Greg Pruitt, L.A. Raiders, 1984
- 61 Eugene (Mercury) Morris, Miami, 1972
- 55 Ron Smith, Chicago, 1973

TOUCHDOWNS
Most Touchdowns, Game
- None

FUMBLES

Most Fumbles, Career
- 6 Dan Fouts, San Diego, 1980-84
- 4 Lawrence McCutcheon, Los Angeles, 1974-78
-    Franco Harris, Pittsburgh, 1973-76, 1978-81
- 3 O.J. Simpson, Buffalo, 1973-77
-    William Andrews, Atlanta, 1981-84
-    Joe Montana, San Francisco, 1982, 1984-85
-    Walter Payton, Chicago, 1977-81, 1984-85

Most Fumbles, Game
- 3 Dan Fouts, San Diego, 1982
- 2 By eight players

RECOVERIES
Most Fumbles Recovered, Career
- 3 Harold Jackson, Philadelphia, 1973; Los Angeles, 1974, 1976, 1978 (3-own)
-    Dan Fouts, San Diego, 1980-84 (3-own)
- 2 By many players

Most Fumbles Recovered, Game
- 2 Dick Anderson, Miami, 1974 (1-own, 1-opp)
-    Harold Jackson, Los Angeles, 1974 (2-own)
-    Dan Fouts, San Diego, 1982 (2-own)

YARDAGE
Longest Fumble Return
- 83 Art Still, Kansas City, 1985 (TD, opp)
- 51 Phil Villapiano, Oakland, 1974 (opp)
- 34 Rick Upchurch, Denver, 1980 (own)

TOUCHDOWNS
Most Touchdowns, Game
- 1 Art Still, Kansas City, 1985

TEAM RECORDS

SCORING

Most Points, Game
- 45 NFC, 1984
Fewest Points, Game
- 3 AFC, 1984
Most Points, Both Teams, Game
- 64 NFC (37) vs. AFC (27), 1980
Fewest Points, Both Teams, Game
- 20 AFC (7) vs. NFC (13), 1979

TOUCHDOWNS
Most Touchdowns, Game
- 6 NFC, 1984
Fewest Touchdowns, Game
- 0 AFC, 1971, 1974, 1984
Most Touchdowns, Both Teams, Game
- 8 AFC (4) vs. NFC (4), 1973
-    NFC (5) vs. AFC (3), 1980
Fewest Touchdowns, Both Teams, Game
- 1 AFC (0) vs. NFC (1), 1974

POINTS AFTER TOUCHDOWN
Most Points After Touchdown, Game
- 6 NFC, 1984
Most Points After Touchdown, Both Teams, Game
- 7 NFC (4) vs. AFC (3), 1973
-    NFC (4) vs. AFC (3), 1980

FIELD GOALS
Most Field Goals Attempted, Game
- 6 AFC, 1972
-    NFC, 1981, 1983
Most Field Goals Attempted, Both Teams, Game
- 9 NFC (6) vs. AFC (3), 1983
Most Field Goals, Game
- 5 AFC, 1974
Most Field Goals, Both Teams, Game
- 7 AFC (5) vs. NFC (2), 1974

NET YARDS GAINED RUSHING AND PASSING

Most Yards Gained, Game
- 466 AFC, 1983
Fewest Yards Gained, Game
- 146 AFC, 1971
Most Yards Gained, Both Teams, Game
- 811 AFC (466) vs. NFC (345), 1983
Fewest Yards Gained, Both Teams, Game
- 468 NFC (159) vs. AFC (309), 1972

RUSHING

ATTEMPTS
Most Attempts, Game
- 50 AFC, 1974
Fewest Attempts, Game
- 18 AFC, 1984
Most Attempts, Both Teams, Game
- 80 AFC (50) vs. NFC (30), 1974

Fewest Attempts, Both Teams, Game
- 54 AFC (27) vs. NFC (27), 1983
-    AFC (18) vs. NFC (36), 1984

YARDS GAINED
Most Yards Gained, Game
- 224 NFC, 1976
Fewest Yards Gained, Game
- 64 NFC, 1974
Most Yards Gained, Both Teams, Game
- 425 NFC (224) vs. AFC (201), 1976
Fewest Yards Gained, Both Teams, Game
- 178 AFC (66) vs. NFC (112), 1971

TOUCHDOWNS
Most Touchdowns, Game
- 2 AFC, 1973, 1980, 1982
-    NFC, 1973, 1977, 1980

PASSING

ATTEMPTS
Most Attempts, Game
- 50 AFC, 1983
Fewest Attempts, Game
- 17 NFC, 1972
Most Attempts, Both Teams, Game
- 94 AFC (50) vs. NFC (44), 1983
Fewest Attempts, Both Teams, Game
- 42 NFC (17) vs. AFC (25), 1972

COMPLETIONS
Most Completions, Game
- 31 AFC, 1983
Fewest Completions, Game
- 7 NFC, 1972, 1982
Most Completions, Both Teams, Game
- 55 AFC (31) vs. NFC (24), 1983
Fewest Completions, Both Teams, Game
- 18 NFC (7) vs. AFC (11), 1972

YARDS GAINED
Most Yards Gained, Game
- 387 AFC, 1983
Fewest Yards Gained, Game
- 42 NFC, 1982
Most Yards Gained, Both Teams, Game
- 608 AFC (387) vs. NFC (221), 1983
Fewest Yards Gained, Both Teams, Game
- 215 NFC (89) vs. AFC (126), 1972

TIMES SACKED
Most Times Sacked, Game
- 9 NFC, 1985
Fewest Times Sacked, Game
- 0 NFC, 1971
Most Times Sacked, Both Teams, Game
- 17 NFC (9) vs. AFC (8), 1985
Fewest Times Sacked, Both Teams, Game
- 4 AFC (2) vs. NFC (2), 1978

TOUCHDOWNS
Most Touchdowns, Game
- 4 NFC, 1984
Fewest Touchdowns, Game
- 0 AFC, 1971, 1974, 1982, 1984
-    NFC, 1977
Most Touchdowns, Both Teams, Game
- 4 NFC (3) vs. AFC (1), 1976
Fewest Touchdowns, Both Teams, Game
- 1 AFC (0) vs. NFC (1), 1971
-    AFC (0) vs. NFC (1), 1974
-    AFC (0) vs. NFC (1), 1982

INTERCEPTIONS BY

Most Interceptions By, Game
- 6 AFC, 1977
Most Interceptions By, Both Teams, Game
- 7 AFC (6) vs. NFC (1), 1977

YARDS GAINED
Most Yards Gained, Game
- 77 AFC, 1973
Most Yards Gained, Both Teams, Game
- 99 NFC (64) vs. AFC (35), 1975

TOUCHDOWNS
Most Touchdowns, Game
- 1 AFC, 1973
-    NFC, 1984

PUNTING

Most Punts, Game
- 10 AFC, 1985
Fewest Punts, Game
- 2 NFC, 1984
Most Punts, Both Teams, Game
- 16 AFC (10) vs. NFC (6), 1985
Fewest Punts, Both Teams, Game
- 6 NFC (2) vs. AFC (4), 1984

AVERAGE YARDAGE
Highest Average, Game
 49.00 AFC, 1974 (4-196)

PUNT RETURNS

Most Punt Returns, Game
 7 NFC, 1985
Fewest Punt Returns, Game
 0 AFC, 1984
Most Punt Returns, Both Teams, Game
 11 NFC (7) vs. AFC (4), 1985
Fewest Punt Returns, Both Teams, Game
 3 AFC (0) vs. NFC (3), 1984

YARDS GAINED
Most Yards Gained, Game
 177 AFC, 1976
Fewest Yards Gained, Game
 0 AFC, 1984
Most Yards Gained, Both Teams, Game
 263 AFC (177) vs. NFC (86), 1976
Fewest Yards Gained, Both Teams, Game
 16 AFC (0) vs. NFC (16), 1984

TOUCHDOWNS
Most Touchdowns, Game
 2 NFC, 1971

KICKOFF RETURNS

Most Kickoff Returns, Game
 7 AFC, 1984
Fewest Kickoff Returns, Game
 1 NFC, 1971, 1984
Most Kickoff Returns, Both Teams, Game
 10 AFC (5) vs. NFC (5), 1976
Fewest Kickoff Returns, Both Teams, Game
 5 NFC (2) vs. AFC (3), 1979

YARDS GAINED
Most Yards Gained, Game
 215 AFC, 1984
Fewest Yards Gained, Game
 6 NFC, 1971
Most Yards Gained, Both Teams, Game
 293 NFC (200) vs. AFC (93), 1972
Fewest Yards Gained, Both Teams, Game
 108 AFC (49) vs. NFC (59), 1979

TOUCHDOWNS
Most Touchdowns, Game
 None

FUMBLES

Most Fumbles, Game
 10 NFC, 1974
Most Fumbles, Both Teams, Game
 15 NFC (10) vs. AFC (5), 1974

RECOVERIES
Most Fumbles Recovered, Game
 10 NFC, 1974 (6 own, 4 opp)
Most Fumbles Lost, Game
 4 AFC, 1974

YARDS GAINED
Most Yards Gained, Game
 87 AFC, 1985

TOUCHDOWNS
Most Touchdowns, Game
 1 AFC, 1985

TURNOVERS

(Number of times losing the ball on interceptions and fumbles.)
Most Turnovers, Game
 8 AFC, 1974
Fewest Turnovers, Game
 1 AFC, 1972, 1976, 1978, 1979, 1985
   NFC, 1976, 1980, 1983
Most Turnovers, Both Teams, Game
 12 AFC (8) vs. NFC (4), 1974
Fewest Turnovers, Both Teams, Game
 2 AFC (1) vs. NFC (1), 1976

RULES

1985 NFL Roster of Officials
Official Signals
Digest of Rules

1985 NFL Roster of Officials

Art McNally, Supervisor of Officials
Jack Reader, Assistant Supervisor of Officials
Nick Skorich, Assistant Supervisor of Officials
Mark Burns, Officiating Assistant
Joe Gardi, Officiating Assistant
Tony Veteri, Officiating Assistant

No.	Name	Position	College
115	Ancich, Hendi	Umpire	Harbor College
81	Anderson, Dave	Head Linesman	Salem College
34	Austin, Gerald	Side Judge	Western Carolina
22	Baetz, Paul	Back Judge	Heidelberg
14	Barth, Gene	Referee	St. Louis
59	Beeks, Bob	Line Judge	Lincoln
17	Bergman, Jerry	Head Linesman	Duquesne
83	Blum, Ron	Line Judge	Marin College
110	Botchan, Ron	Umpire	Occidental
101	Boylston, Bob	Umpire	Alabama
43	Cashion, Red	Referee	Texas A&M
16	Cathcart, Royal	Side Judge	UC Santa Barbara
24	Clymer, Roy	Back Judge	New Mexico State
27	Conway, Al	Umpire	Army
61	Creed, Dick	Side Judge	Louisville
78	Demmas, Art	Umpire	Vanderbilt
45	DeSouza, Ron	Line Judge	Morgan State
74	Dodez, Ray	Side Judge	Wooster
31	Dolack, Dick	Field Judge	Ferris State
6	Dooley, Tom	Referee	VMI
102	Douglas, Merrill	Side Judge	Utah
12	Dreith, Ben	Referee	Colorado State
39	Fette, Jack	Line Judge	No College
57	Fiffick, Ed	Umpire	Marquette
47	Fincken, Tom	Side Judge	Emporia State
111	Frantz, Earnie	Head Linesman	No College
71	Frederic, Bob	Referee	Colorado
62	Gandy, Duwayne	Side Judge	Tulsa
50	Gereb, Neil	Umpire	California
72	Gierke, Terry	Head Linesman	Portland State
15	Glass, Bama	Line Judge	Colorado
85	Glover, Frank	Head Linesman	Morris Brown
23	Grier, Johnny	Field Judge	D.C. Teachers
75	Habel, Don	Field Judge	Western Oregon
63	Hagerty, Ligouri	Head Linesman	Syracuse
40	Haggerty, Pat	Referee	Colorado State
96	Hakes, Don	Field Judge	Bradley
104	Hamer, Dale	Head Linesman	Calif. State, Pa.
42	Hamilton, Dave	Umpire	Utah
105	Hantak, Dick	Back Judge	Southeast Missouri
66	Hawk, Dave	Side Judge	Southern Methodist
112	Haynes, Joe	Line Judge	Alcorn State
46	Heberling, Chuck	Referee	Wash. & Jefferson
19	Hensley, Tommy	Umpire	Tennessee
54	Johnson, Jack	Line Judge	Pacific Lutheran
114	Johnson, Tom	Head Linesman	Miami, Ohio
97	Jones, Nathan	Side Judge	Lewis & Clark
60	Jorgensen, Dick	Referee	Wisconsin
106	Jury, Al	Back Judge	San Bernardino Valley
107	Kearney, Jim	Back Judge	Pennsylvania
67	Keck, John	Umpire	Cornell College
25	Kelleher, Tom	Back Judge	Holy Cross
65	Kragseth, Norm	Head Linesman	Northwestern
86	Kukar, Bernie	Field Judge	St. John's

No.	Name	Position	College
120	Lane, Gary	Side Judge	Missouri
18	Lewis, Bob	Field Judge	No College
21	Liske, Pete	Back Judge	Penn State
49	Look, Dean	Side Judge	Michigan State
90	Mace, Gil	Side Judge	Westminster
82	Mallette, Pat	Field Judge	Nebraska
26	Marion, Ed	Head Linesman	Pennsylvania
9	Markbreit, Jerry	Referee	Illinois
94	Marshall, Vern	Line Judge	Linfield
116	McCallum, Chuck	Field Judge	Michigan State
48	McCarter, Gordon	Referee	Western Reserve
95	McElwee, Bob	Referee	Navy
41	McKenzie, Dick	Line Judge	Ashland
76	Merrifield, Ed	Field Judge	Missouri
35	Miles, Leo	Head Linesman	Virginia State
117	Montgomery, Ben	Umpire	Morehouse
36	Moore, Bob	Back Judge	Dayton
88	Moss, Dave	Umpire	Dartmouth
20	Nemmers, Larry	Side Judge	VPI
51	Orem, Dale	Line Judge	Louisville
77	Orr, Don	Field Judge	Vanderbilt
64	Parry, Dave	Side Judge	Wabash
44	Peters, Walt	Line Judge	Indiana State, Pa.
10	Phares, Ron	Head Linesman	Upper Iowa
92	Poole, Jim	Back Judge	San Diego State
58	Quinby, Bill	Side Judge	Iowa State
53	Reynolds, Bill	Line Judge	West Chester State
80	Rice, Bob	Side Judge	Denison
33	Roe, Howard	Line Judge	Wichita State
98	Rosser, Jimmy	Back Judge	Auburn
29	Sanders, J. W.	Back Judge	Southern Illinois
56	Shannon, Carver	Line Judge	Southern Illinois
70	Seeman, Jerry	Referee	Winona State
109	Semon, Sid	Head Linesman	So. California
7	Silva, Fred	Referee	San Jose State
73	Skelton, Bobby	Field Judge	Alabama
3	Smith, Boyce	Line Judge	Vanderbilt
119	Spitler, Ron	Field Judge	Panhandle State
91	Stanley, Bill	Field Judge	Redlands
103	Stuart, Rex	Umpire	Appalachian State
38	Swanson, Bill	Back Judge	Lake Forest
37	Toler, Burl	Head Linesman	San Francisco
52	Tompkins, Ben	Back Judge	Texas
32	Tunney, Jim	Referee	Occidental
93	Vaughan, Jack	Field Judge	Mississippi State
100	Wagner, Bob	Umpire	Penn State
28	Wedge, Don	Back Judge	Ohio Wesleyan
89	Wells, Gordon	Umpire	Occidental
30	Wilford, Dan	Line Judge	Mississippi
99	Williams, Banks	Back Judge	Houston
8	Williams, Dale	Head Linesman	Cal St.-Northridge
84	Wortman, Bob	Field Judge	Findlay
11	Wyant, Fred	Referee	West Virginia

Numerical Roster

No.	Name	
3	Boyce Smith	LJ
6	Tom Dooley	R
7	Fred Silva	R
8	Dale Williams	HL
9	Jerry Markbreit	R
10	Ron Phares	HL
11	Fred Wyant	R
12	Ben Dreith	R
14	Gene Barth	R
15	Bama Glass	LJ
16	Royal Cathcart	SJ
17	Jerry Bergman	HL
18	Bob Lewis	FJ
19	Tommy Hensley	U
20	Larry Nemmers	SJ
21	Pete Liske	BJ
22	Paul Baetz	BJ
23	Johnny Grier	FJ
24	Roy Clymer	BJ
25	Tom Kelleher	BJ
26	Ed Marion	HL
27	Al Conway	U
28	Don Wedge	BJ
29	J. W. Sanders	BJ
30	Dan Wilford	LJ
31	Dick Dolack	FJ
32	Jim Tunney	R
33	Howard Roe	LJ
34	Gerald Austin	SJ
35	Leo Miles	HL
36	Bob Moore	BJ
37	Burl Toler	HL
38	Bill Swanson	BJ
39	Jack Fette	LJ
40	Pat Haggerty	R
41	Dick McKenzie	LJ
42	Dave Hamilton	U
43	Red Cashion	R
44	Walt Peters	LJ
45	Ron DeSouza	LJ
46	Chuck Heberling	R
47	Tom Fincken	SJ
48	Gordon McCarter	R
49	Dean Look	SJ
50	Neil Gereb	U
51	Dale Orem	LJ
52	Ben Tompkins	BJ
53	Bill Reynolds	LJ
54	Jack Johnson	LJ
56	Carver Shannon	LJ
57	Ed Fiffick	U
58	Bill Quinby	SJ
59	Bob Beeks	LJ
60	Dick Jorgensen	R
61	Dick Creed	SJ
62	Duwayne Gandy	SJ
63	Ligouri Hagerty	HL
64	Dave Parry	SJ
65	Norm Kragseth	HL
66	Dave Hawk	SJ
67	John Keck	U
70	Jerry Seeman	R
71	Bob Frederic	R
72	Terry Gierke	HL
73	Bobby Skelton	FJ
74	Ray Dodez	SJ
75	Don Habel	FJ
76	Ed Merrifield	FJ
77	Don Orr	FJ
78	Art Demmas	U
80	Bob Rice	SJ
81	Dave Anderson	HL
82	Pat Mallette	FJ
83	Ron Blum	LJ
84	Bob Wortman	FJ
85	Frank Glover	HL
86	Bernie Kukar	FJ
88	Dave Moss	U
89	Gordon Wells	U
90	Gil Mace	SJ
91	Bill Stanley	FJ
92	Jim Poole	BJ
93	Jack Vaughan	FJ
94	Vern Marshall	LJ
95	Bob McElwee	R
96	Don Hakes	FJ
97	Nathan Jones	SJ
98	Jimmy Rosser	BJ
99	Banks Williams	BJ
100	Bob Wagner	U
101	Bob Boylston	U
102	Merrill Douglas	SJ
103	Rex Stuart	U
104	Dale Hamer	HL
105	Dick Hantak	BJ
106	Al Jury	BJ
107	Jim Kearney	BJ
109	Sid Semon	HL
110	Ron Botchan	U
111	Earnie Frantz	HL
112	Joe Haynes	LJ
114	Tom Johnson	HL
115	Hendi Ancich	U
116	Chuck McCallum	FJ
117	Ben Montgomery	U
119	Ron Spitler	FJ
120	Gary Lane	SJ

1985 Officials at a Glance

Referees

Gene Barth, No. **14,** St. Louis, president, oil company, 15th year.

Red Cashion, No. **43,** Texas A&M, chairman of the board, insurance company, 14th year.

Tom Dooley, No. **6,** VMI, general contractor, 8th year.

Ben Dreith, No. **12,** Colorado State, teacher-counselor, 26th year.

Bob Frederic, No. **71,** Colorado, president, printing and lithographing company, 18th year.

Pat Haggerty, No. **40,** Colorado State, teacher-coach, 21st year.

Chuck Heberling, No. **46,** Washington & Jefferson, executive administrator, state high school athletic program, 21st year.

Dick Jorgensen, No. **60,** Wisconsin, president, commercial bank, 18th year.

Jerry Markbreit, No. **9,** Illinois, trade and barter manager, 10th year.

Gordon McCarter, No. **48,** Western Reserve, industrial sales, 19th year.

Bob McElwee, No. **95,** U.S. Naval Academy, owner, construction company, 10th year.

Jerry Seeman, No. **70,** Winona State, assistant superintendent, 11th year.

Fred Silva, No. **7,** San Jose State, vice-president, director, chain store sales, 19th year.

Jim Tunney, No. **32,** Occidental, president of motivation company, professional speaker, 26th year.

Fred Wyant, No. **11,** West Virginia, executive insurance sales director, former NFL player, 20th year.

Umpires

Hendi Ancich, No. **115,** Harbor, longshoreman, 4th year.

Ron Botchan, No. **110,** Occidental, college professor, former AFL player, 6th year.

Bob Boylston, No. **101,** Alabama, manufacturers representative, 8th year.

Al Conway, No. **27,** Army, national director, industrial sales, 17th year.

Art Demmas, No. **78,** Vanderbilt, investments and financial planning, insurance company, 18th year.

Ed Fiffick, No. **57,** Marquette, podiatric physician, 7th year.

Neil Gereb, No. **50,** California, supervisor, aircraft company, 5th year.

Dave Hamilton, No. **42,** Utah, hospital administrator, 11th year.

Tommy Hensley, No. **19,** Tennessee, owner, land development and management company, 19th year.

John Keck, No. **67,** Cornell, petroleum distributor, 14th year.

Ben Montgomery, No. **117,** Morehouse, school administrator, 4th year.

Dave Moss, No. **88,** Dartmouth, insurance, 6th year.

Rex Stuart, No. **103,** Appalachian State, agency manager, life and health insurance, 2nd year.

Bob Wagner, No. **100,** Penn State, business administrator, 1st year.

Gordon Wells, No. **89,** Occidental, college professor, physical education, 14th year.

Head Linesmen

Dave Anderson, No. **81,** Salem, district sales manager, health insurance, 2nd year.

Jerry Bergman, No. **17,** Duquesne, executive director, pension fund, 20th year.

Earnie Frantz, No. **111,** vice-president and manager, land title company, 5th year.

Terry Gierke, No. **72,** Portland State, real estate broker, 5th year.

Frank Glover, No. **85,** Morris Brown, assistant area superintendent, 14th year.

Ligouri Hagerty, No. **63,** Syracuse, manager, sporting goods company, 10th year.

Dale Hamer, No. **104,** California State, Pa., senior planning specialist, 8th year.

Tom Johnson, No. **114,** Miami, Ohio, teacher and coach, 4th year.

Norm Kragseth, No. **65,** Northwestern, chairman, physical education department, 12th year.

Ed Marion, No. **26,** Pennsylvania, vice-president-pension marketing, insurance company, 26th year.

Leo Miles, No. **35,** Virginia State, university athletic director, former NFL player, 17th year.

Ron Phares, No. **10,** Upper Iowa, vice-president, general contracting firm, 1st year.

Sid Semon, No. **109,** Southern California, chairman, physical education department, 8th year.

Burl Toler, No. **37,** San Francisco, director, certificated services, 21st year.

Dale Williams, No. **8,** Cal State-Northridge, coordinator, athletic officials, 6th year.

Line Judges

Bob Beeks, No. **59,** Lincoln, law enforcement officer, 18th year.

Ron Blum, No. **83,** Marin College, manager, golf course, 1st year.

Ron DeSouza, No. **45,** Morgan State, vice-president, student affairs, 6th year.

Jack Fette, No. **39,** district sales manager, sporting goods company, 21st year.

Bama Glass, No. **15,** Colorado, owner, consumer products, 7th year.

Joe Haynes, No. **112,** Alcorn State, public schools deputy superintendent, 2nd year.

Jack Johnson, No. **54,** Pacific Lutheran, fund raising consultant, 10th year.

Vern Marshall, No. **94,** Linfield College, counseling coordinator, 10th year.

Dick McKenzie, No. **41,** Ashland, treasurer, Wellington schools, 8th year.

Dale Orem, No. **51,** Louisville, public official and owner, sporting goods company, 6th year.

Walt Peters, No. **44,** Indiana State, Pa., insurance broker, 18th year.

Bill Reynolds, No. **53,** West Chester State, teacher and athletic director, 11th year.

Howard Roe, No. **33,** Wichita State, manager and administrator, human resources, 2nd year.

Carver Shannon, No. **56,** Southern Illinois, head administrator, reprographics, former NFL player, 3rd year.

Boyce Smith, No. **3,** Vanderbilt, president and general manager, steel company, 5th year.

Dan Wilford, No. **30,** Mississippi, hospital executive, 3rd year.

Back Judges

Paul Baetz, No. **22,** Heidelberg, financial consultant, 8th year.

Roy Clymer, No. **24,** New Mexico State, area manager, gas company, 6th year.

Dick Hantak, No. **105,** Southeast Missouri, chairman, high school department, 8th year.

Al Jury, No. **106,** San Bernardino Valley, state traffic officer, 8th year.

Jim Kearney, No. **107,** Pennsylvania, marketing manager, 8th year.

Tom Kelleher, No. **25,** Holy Cross, president, marketing company, 26th year.

Pete Liske, No. **21,** Penn State, general manager, manufacturer and sales company, former NFL player, 3rd year.

Bob Moore, No. **36,** Dayton, attorney, 2nd year.

Jim Poole, No. **92,** San Diego State, college physical education professor, 11th year.

Jimmy Rosser, No. **98,** Auburn, personnel director, 9th year.

J.W. Sanders, No. **29,** Southern Illinois, physical education professor, 6th year.

Bill Swanson, No. **38,** Lake Forest, real estate appraiser, 21st year.

Ben Tompkins, No. **52,** Texas, attorney, 15th year.

Don Wedge, No. **28,** Ohio Wesleyan, regional sales manager, 14th year.

Banks Williams, No. **99,** Houston, vice-president sales, concrete company, 8th year.

Side Judges

Gerald Austin, No. **34,** Western Carolina, high school principal, 4th year.

Royal Cathcart, No. **16,** UC-Santa Barbara, real estate broker, former NFL player, 15th year.

Richard Creed, No. **61,** Louisville, real estate management, 8th year.

Ray Dodez, No. **74,** Wooster, communications consultant, 18th year.

Merrill Douglas, No. **102,** Utah, deputy sheriff, former NFL player, 5th year.

Tom Fincken, No. **47,** Emporia State, high school teacher, 2nd year.

Duwayne Gandy, No. **62,** Tulsa, sales-public relations, oil field wireline service, 5th year.

Dave Hawk, No. **66,** Southern Methodist, co-owner, warehousing company, 14th year.

Nate Jones, No. **97,** Lewis and Clark, high school principal, 9th year.

Gary Lane, No. **120,** Missouri, independent marketing consultant, former NFL player, 4th year.

Dean Look, No. **49,** Michigan State, director, marketing and sales, former AFL player, 14th year.

Gil Mace, No. **90,** Westminster, national accounts manager, 12th year.

Larry Nemmers, No. **20,** VPI, high school principal, 1st year.

Dave Parry, No. **64,** Wabash, high school athletic director, 11th year.

Bill Quinby, No. **58,** Iowa State, director, personnel services, 8th year.

Bob Rice, No. **80,** Denison, chairman, physical education department, 17th year.

Field Judges

Dick Dolack, No. **31,** Ferris State, pharmacist, 20th year.

Johnny Grier, No. **23,** D.C. Teachers, planning engineer, telephone company, 5th year.

Don Habel, No. **75,** Western Oregon, auto claim superintendent, 2nd year.

Don Hakes, No. **96,** Bradley, high school dean of students, 9th year.

Bernie Kukar, No. **86,** St. John's, health insurance representative, 2nd year.

Bob Lewis, No. **18,** supervisor, air force base, 10th year.

Pat Mallette, No. **82,** Nebraska, real estate broker, 17th year.

Chuck McCallum, No. **116,** Michigan State, director, advertising, public relations, and promotions, 4th year.

Ed Merrifield, No. **76,** Missouri, sales manager, heavy equipment, 11th year.

Don Orr, No. **77,** Vanderbilt, president, machine company, 15th year.

Bobby Skelton, No. **73,** Alabama, industrial representative, 1st year.

Ron Spitler, No. **119,** Panhandle State, transportation director, 4th year.

Bill Stanley, No. **91,** Redlands, college athletic director, 12th year.

Jack Vaughan, No. **93,** Mississippi State, insurance-field underwriter, 10th year.

Bob Wortman, No. **84,** Findlay, owner, insurance company, 20th year.

1

**TOUCHDOWN, FIELD GOAL,
or SUCCESSFUL TRY**
Both arms extended above head.

2

SAFETY
Palms together above head.

3

FIRST DOWN
Arms pointed toward defensive
team's goal.

4

**DEAD BALL or NEUTRAL
ZONE ESTABLISHED**
One arm above head
with an open hand.
With fist closed: **Fourth Down.**

5

**BALL ILLEGALLY
TOUCHED, KICKED,
OR BATTED**
Fingertips tap both shoulders.

6

TIME OUT
Hands crisscrossed above head.
Same signal followed by placing one
hand on top of cap: **Referee's Time Out.**
Same signal followed by arm swung at
side: **Touchback.**

7

**NO TIME OUT or
TIME IN WITH WHISTLE**
Full arm circled to
simulate moving clock.

8

**DELAY OF GAME,
ILLEGAL SUBSTITUTION
OR EXCESS TIME OUT**
Folded arms.

9

FALSE START, ILLEGAL SHIFT, ILLEGAL PROCEDURE, ILLEGAL FORMATION, or KICKOFF OR SAFETY KICK OUT OF BOUNDS
Forearms rotated over and over in front of body.

10

PERSONAL FOUL
One wrist striking the other above head.
Same signal followed by swinging leg: **Running Into or Roughing Kicker.**
Same signal followed by raised arm swinging forward: **Running Into or Roughing Passer.**
Same signal followed by hand striking back of calf: **Clipping.**

11

HOLDING
Grasping one wrist, the fist clenched, in front of chest.

12

ILLEGAL USE OF HANDS, ARMS, OR BODY
Grasping one wrist, the hand open and facing forward, in front of chest.

13

PENALTY REFUSED, INCOMPLETE PASS, PLAY OVER or MISSED GOAL
Hands shifted in horizontal plane.

14

PASS JUGGLED INBOUNDS AND CAUGHT OUT OF BOUNDS
Hands up and down in front of chest (following incomplete pass signal).

15

ILLEGAL FORWARD PASS
One hand waved behind back followed by loss of down signal.

16

INTENTIONAL GROUNDING OF PASS
Parallel arms waved in a diagonal plane across body. Followed by loss of down signal (23).

17

INTERFERENCE WITH FORWARD PASS or FAIR CATCH
Hands open
and extended forward from
shoulders with hands vertical.

18

INVALID FAIR CATCH SIGNAL
One hand waved above head.

19

INELIGIBLE RECEIVER or INELIGIBLE MEMBER OF KICKING TEAM DOWNFIELD
Right hand touching top of cap.

20

ILLEGAL CONTACT
One open hand extended forward.

21

OFFSIDE or ENCROACHING
Hands on hips.

22

ILLEGAL MOTION AT SNAP
Horizontal arc with one hand.

23

LOSS OF DOWN
Both hands held behind head.

24

CRAWLING, INTERLOCKING INTERFERENCE, PUSHING, or HELPING RUNNER
Pushing movement of hands
to front with arms downward.

25

**TOUCHING A FORWARD
PASS OR SCRIMMAGE KICK**
Diagonal motion of
one hand across another.

26

**UNSPORTSMANLIKE
CONDUCT (Non-contact fouls)**
Arms outstretched, palms down.
(Same signal means continuous
action fouls are disregarded.)

27

**ILLEGAL CUT or
BLOCKING BELOW
THE WAIST**
Hand striking front of thigh
preceded by personal foul
signal (10).

28

ILLEGAL CRACKBACK
Strike of an open right hand
against the right mid thigh
preceded by personal foul
signal (10).

29

PLAYER DISQUALIFIED
Ejection signal.

30

TRIPPING
Repeated action of right foot
in back of left heel.

NFL Digest of Rules

This Digest of Rules of the National Football League has been prepared to aid players, fans, and members of the press, radio, and television media in their understanding of the game.

It is not meant to be a substitute for the official rule book. In any case of conflict between these explanations and the official rules, the rules always have precedence.

In order to make it easier to coordinate the information in this digest the topics discussed generally follow the order of the rule book.

Officials' Jurisdictions, Positions, and Duties

Referee—General oversight and control of game. Gives signals for all fouls and is final authority for rule interpretations. Takes a position in backfield 10 to 12 yards behind line of scrimmage, favors right side (if quarterback is right-handed passer). Determines legality of snap, observes deep back(s) for legal motion. On running play, observes quarterback during and after handoff, remains with him until action has cleared away, then proceeds downfield, checking on runner and contact behind him. When runner is downed, Referee determines forward progress from wing official and if necessary, adjusts final position of ball.

On pass plays, drops back as quarterback begins to fade back, picks up legality of blocks by near linemen. Changes to complete concentration on quarterback as defenders approach. Primarily responsible to rule on possible roughing action on passer and if ball becomes loose, rules whether ball is free on a fumble or dead on an incomplete pass.

During kicking situations, Referee has primary responsibility to rule on kicker's actions and whether or not any subsequent contact by a defender is legal.

Umpire—Primary responsibility to rule on players' equipment, as well as their conduct and actions on scrimmage line. Lines up approximately four to five yards downfield, varying position from in front of weakside tackle to strongside guard. Looks for possible false start by offensive linemen. Observes legality of contact by both offensive linemen while blocking and by defensive players while they attempt to ward off blockers. Is prepared to call rule infractions if they occur on offense or defense. Moves forward to line of scrimmage when pass play develops in order to insure that interior linemen do not move illegally downfield. If offensive linemen indicate screen pass is to be attempted, Umpire shifts attention toward screen side, picks up potential receiver in order to insure that he will legally be permitted to run his pattern and continues to rule on action of blockers. Umpire is to assist in ruling on incomplete or trapped passes when ball is thrown overhead or short.

Head Linesman—Primarily responsible for ruling on offside, encroachment, and actions pertaining to scrimmage line prior to or at snap. Keys on closest setback on his side of the field. On pass plays, Linesman is responsible to clear this receiver approximately seven yards downfield as he moves to a point five yards beyond the line. Linesman's secondary responsibility is to rule on any illegal action taken by defenders on any delay receiver moving downfield. Has full responsibility for ruling on sideline plays on his side, e.g., pass receiver or runner in or out of bounds. Together with Referee, Linesman is responsible for keeping track of number of downs and is in charge of mechanics of his chain crew in connection with its duties.

Linesman must be prepared to assist in determining forward progress by a runner on play directed toward middle or into his side zone. He, in turn, is to signal Referee or Umpire what forward point ball has reached. Linesman is also responsible to rule on legality of action involving any receiver who approaches his side zone. He is to call pass interference when the infraction occurs and is to rule on legality of blockers and defenders on plays involving ball carriers, whether it is entirely a running play, a combination pass and run, or a play involving a kick.

Line Judge—Straddles line of scrimmage on side of field opposite Linesman. Keeps time of game as a backup for clock operator. Along with Linesman is responsible for offside, encroachment, and actions pertaining to scrimmage line prior to or at snap. Line Judge keys on closest setback on his side of field. Line Judge is to observe his receiver until he moves at least seven yards downfield. He then moves toward backfield side, being especially alert to rule on any back in motion and on flight of ball when pass is made (he must rule whether forward or backward). Line Judge has primary responsibility to rule whether or not passer is behind or beyond line of scrimmage when pass is made. He also assists in observing actions by blockers and defenders who are on his side of field. After pass is thrown, Line Judge directs attention toward activities that occur in back of Umpire. During punting situations, Line Judge remains at line of scrimmage to be sure that only the end men move downfield until kick has been made. He also rules whether or not the kick crossed line and then observes action by members of the kicking team who are moving downfield to cover the kick.

Back Judge—Operates on same side of field as Line Judge, 17 yards deep. Keys on wide receiver on his side. Concentrates on path of end or back, observing legality of his potential block(s) or of actions taken against him. Is prepared to rule from deep position on holding or illegal use of hands by end or back or on defensive infractions committed by player guarding him. Has primary responsibility to make decisions involving sideline on his side of field, e.g., pass receiver or runner in or out of bounds.

Back Judge makes decisions involving catching, recovery, or illegal touching of a loose ball beyond line of scrimmage; rules on plays involving pass receiver, including legality of catch or pass interference; assists in covering actions of runner, including blocks by teammates and that of defenders; calls clipping on punt returns; and, together with Field Judge, rules whether or not field goal attempts are successful.

Side Judge—Operates on same side of field as Linesman, 17 yards deep. Keys on wide receiver on his side. Concentrates on path of end or back, observing legality of his potential block(s) or of actions taken against him. Is prepared to rule from deep position on holding or illegal use of hands by end or back or on defensive infractions committed by player guarding him. Has primary responsibility to make decisions involving sideline on his side of field, e.g., pass receiver or runner in or out of bounds.

Side Judge makes decisions involving catching, recovery, or illegal touching of a loose ball beyond line of scrimmage; rules on plays involving pass receiver, including legality of catch or pass interference; assists in covering actions of runner, including blocks by teammates and that of defenders; and calls clipping on punt returns.

Field Judge—Takes a position 25 yards downfield. In general, favors the tight end's side of field. Keys on tight end, concentrates on his path and observes legality of tight end's potential block(s) or of actions taken against him. Is prepared to rule from deep position on holding or illegal use of hands by end or back or on defensive infractions committed by player guarding him.

Field Judge times interval between plays on 30-second clock plus intermission between two periods of each half; makes decisions involving catching, recovery, or illegal touching of a loose ball beyond line of scrimmage; is responsible to rule on plays involving end line; calls pass interference, fair catch infractions, and clipping on kick returns; and, together with Back Judge, rules whether or not field goals and conversions are successful.

Definitions

1. **Chucking:** Warding off an opponent who is in front of a defender by contacting him with a quick extension of arm or arms, followed by the return of arm(s) to a flexed position, thereby breaking the original contact.
2. **Clipping:** Throwing the body across the back of an opponent's leg or hitting him from the back below the waist while moving up from behind unless the opponent is a runner or the action is in close line play.
3. **Close Line Play:** The area between the positions normally occupied by the offensive tackles, extending three yards on each side of the line of scrimmage.
4. **Crackback:** Eligible receivers who take or move to a position more than two yards outside the tackle may not block an opponent below the waist if they then move back inside to block.
5. **Dead Ball:** Ball not in play.
6. **Double Foul:** A foul by each team during the same down.
7. **Down:** The period of action that starts when the ball is put in play and ends when it is dead.
8. **Encroachment:** When a player enters the neutral zone and makes contact with an opponent before the ball is snapped.
9. **Fair Catch:** An unhindered catch of a kick by a member of the receiving team who must raise one arm a full length above his head while the kick is in flight.
10. **Foul:** Any violation of a playing rule.
11. **Free Kick:** A kickoff, kick after a safety, or kick after a fair catch. It may be a placekick, dropkick, or punt, except a punt may not be used on a kickoff.
12. **Fumble:** The loss of possession of the ball.
13. **Impetus:** The action of a player that gives momentum to the ball.
14. **Live Ball:** A ball legally free kicked or snapped. It continues in play until the down ends.
15. **Loose Ball:** A live ball not in possession of any player.
16. **Muff:** The touching of a loose ball by a player in an unsuccessful attempt to obtain possession.
17. **Neutral Zone:** The space the length of a ball between the two scrimmage lines. The offensive team and defensive team must remain behind their end of the ball.
    Exception: The offensive player who snaps the ball.
18. **Offside:** A player is offside when any part of his body is beyond his scrimmage or free kick line when the ball is snapped.
19. **Own Goal:** The goal a team is guarding.
20. **Pocket Area (Pass):** Applies from a point two yards outside of either offensive tackle and includes the tight end if he drops off the line of scrimmage to pass protect. Pocket extends longitudinally behind the line back to offensive team's own end line.
21. **Pocket Area (Run):** Applies from a point two yards outside of either offensive tackle (five normally spaced down linemen) and extends three yards beyond the line of scrimmage when contact is made. This area remains constant and could be shifted by an unbalanced line but cannot be expanded through use of an additional lineman.
22. **Possession:** When a player controls the ball throughout the act of clearly touching both feet, or any other part of his body other than his hand(s), to the ground inbounds.
23. **Punt:** A kick made when a player drops the ball and kicks it while it is in flight.
24. **Safety:** The situation in which the ball is dead on or behind a team's own goal if the impetus comes from a player on that team. Two points are scored for the opposing team.
25. **Shift:** The movement of two or more offensive players at the same time before the snap.
26. **Striking:** The act of swinging, clubbing, or propelling the arm or forearm in contacting an opponent.
27. **Sudden Death:** The continuation of a tied game into sudden death overtime in which the team scoring first (by safety, field goal, or touchdown) wins.
28. **Touchback:** When a ball is dead on or behind a team's own goal line, provided the impetus came from an opponent and provided it is not a touchdown or a missed field goal.

29. **Touchdown:** When any part of the ball, legally in possession of a player in-bounds, is on, above, or over the opponent's goal line, provided it is not a touchback.
30. **Unsportsmanlike Conduct:** Any act contrary to the generally understood principles of sportsmanship.

Summary of Penalties
Automatic First Down
1. Awarded to offensive team on all defensive fouls with these exceptions:
   (a) Offside.
   (b) Encroachment.
   (c) Delay of game.
   (d) Illegal substitution.
   (e) Excessive time out(s).
   (f) Incidental grasp of face mask.
   (g) Prolonged, excessive or premeditated celebrations by individual players or groups of players.

Loss of Down (No yardage)
1. Second forward pass behind the line.
2. Forward pass strikes ground, goal post, or crossbar.
3. Forward pass goes out of bounds.
4. Forward pass is first touched by eligible receiver who has gone out of bounds and returned.
5. Forward pass touches or is caught by an ineligible receiver on or behind line.
6. Forward pass thrown from behind line of scrimmage after ball once crossed the line.

Five Yards
1. Crawling.
2. Defensive holding or illegal use of hands (automatic first down).
3. Delay of game.
4. Encroachment.
5. Too many time outs.
6. False start.
7. Illegal formation.
8. Illegal shift.
9. Illegal motion.
10. Illegal substitution.
11. Kickoff out of bounds between goal lines and not touched.
12. Invalid fair catch signal.
13. More than 11 players on the field at snap for either team.
14. Less than seven men on offensive line at snap.
15. Offside.
16. Failure to pause one second after shift or huddle.
17. Running into kicker (automatic first down).
18. More than one man in motion at snap.
19. Grasping face mask of opponent.
20. Player out of bounds at snap.
21. Ineligible member(s) of kicking team going beyond line of scrimmage before ball is kicked.
22. Illegal return.
23. Failure to report change of eligibility.
24. Prolonged, excessive or premeditated celebrations by individual players or groups of players.

10 Yards
1. Offensive pass interference.
2. Ineligible player downfield during passing down.
3. Holding, illegal use of hands, arms or body by offense.
4. Tripping by a member of either team.
5. Helping the runner.
6. Illegal batting or punching a loose ball.
7. Deliberately kicking a loose ball.

15 Yards
1. Clipping below the waist.
2. Fair catch interference.
3. Illegal crackback block by offense.
4. Piling on (automatic first down).
5. Roughing the kicker (automatic first down).
6. Roughing the passer (automatic first down).
7. Twisting, turning, or pulling an opponent by the face mask.
8. Unnecessary roughness.
9. Unsportsmanlike conduct.
10. Delay of game at start of either half.
11. Illegal blocking below the waist.
12. A tackler using his helmet to butt, spear, or ram an opponent.
13. Any player who uses the top of his helmet unnecessarily.
14. A punter, placekicker or holder who simulates being roughed by a defensive player.
15. A defender who takes a running start from beyond the line of scrimmage in an attempt to block a field goal or point after touchdown.

Five Yards and Loss of Down
1. Forward pass thrown from beyond line of scrimmage.

10 Yards and Loss of Down
1. Intentional grounding of forward pass (safety if passer is in own end zone). If foul occurs more than 10 yards behind line, play results in loss of down at spot of foul.

15 Yards and Loss of Coin Toss Option
1. Team's late arrival on the field prior to scheduled kickoff.

15 Yards (and disqualification if flagrant)
1. Striking opponent with fist.
2. Kicking or kneeing opponent.

3. Striking opponent on head or neck with forearm, elbow, or hands whether or not the initial contact is made below the neck area.
4. Roughing kicker.
5. Roughing passer.
6. Malicious unnecessary roughness.
7. Unsportsmanlike conduct.
8. Palpably unfair act. (Distance penalty determined by the Referee after consultation with other officials.)

15 Yards and Automatic Disqualification
1. Using a helmet that is not worn as a weapon.

Suspension From Game
1. Illegal equipment. (Player may return after one down when legally equipped.)

Touchdown
1. When Referee determines a palpably unfair act deprived a team of a touchdown. (Example: Player comes off bench and tackles runner apparently en route to touchdown.)

Field
1. Sidelines and end lines are out of bounds. The goal line is actually in the end zone. A player with the ball in his possession scores when the ball is on, above, or over the goal line.
2. The field is rimmed by a white border, a minimum six feet wide, along the sidelines. All of this is out of bounds.
3. The hashmarks (inbound lines) are 70 feet, 9 inches from each sideline.
4. Goal posts must be single-standard type, offset from the end line and painted bright gold. The goal posts must be 18 feet, 6 inches wide and the top face of the crossbar must be 10 feet above the ground. Vertical posts extend at least 30 feet above the crossbar. A ribbon 4 inches by 42 inches long is to be attached to the top of each post. The actual goal is the plane extending indefinitely above the crossbar and between the outer edges of the posts.
5. The field is 360 feet long and 160 feet wide. The end zones are 30 feet deep. The line used in try-for-point plays is two yards out from the goal line.
6. Chain crew members and ball boys must be uniformly identifiable.
7. All clubs must use standardized sideline markers. Pylons must be used for goal line and end line markings.
8. End zone markings and club identification at 50 yard line must be approved by the Commissioner to avoid any confusion as to delineation of goal lines, sidelines, and end lines.

Ball
1. The home club must have 24 balls available for testing by the Referee one hour before game time. In case of bad weather, a playable ball is to be substituted on request of the offensive team captain.

Coin Toss
1. The toss of coin will take place within three minutes of kickoff in center of field. The toss will be called by the visiting captain. The winner may choose one of two privileges and the loser gets the other:
   (a) Receive or kick
   (b) Goal his team will defend
2. Immediately prior to the start of the second half, the captains of both teams must inform the officials of their respective choices. The loser of the original coin toss gets first choice.

Timing
1. The stadium clock is official. In case it stops or is operating incorrectly, the Line Judge takes over the official timing on the field.
2. Each period is 15 minutes. The intermission between the periods is two minutes. Halftime is 15 minutes, unless otherwise specified.
3. On charged team time outs, the Field Judge starts watch and blows whistle after 1 minute 30 seconds, unless it is during the last two minutes of a half when the time is reduced to 60 seconds. However, Referee may allow two minutes for injured player and three minutes for equipment repair.
4. Each team is allowed three time outs each half.
5. Offensive team has 30 seconds to put the ball in play. The time is displayed on two 30-second clocks, which are visible to the players, officials, and fans. Field Judge is to call a delay of game penalty (five yards) when the time limit is exceeded. In case 30-second clocks are not operating, Field Judge takes over the official timing on the field.
6. Clock will start running when ball is snapped following all changes of team possession.

Sudden Death
1. The sudden death system of determining the winner shall prevail when score is tied at the end of the regulation playing time of all NFL games. The team scoring first during overtime play shall be the winner and the game automatically ends upon any score (by safety, field goal, or touchdown) or when a score is awarded by Referee for a palpably unfair act.
2. At the end of regulation time the Referee will immediately toss coin at center of field in accordance with rules pertaining to the usual pregame toss. The captain of the visiting team will call the toss.
3. Following a three-minute intermission after the end of the regulation game, play will be continued in 15-minute periods or until there is a score. There is a two-minute intermission between subsequent periods. The teams change goals at the start of each period. Each team has three time outs and general provisions for play in the last two-minutes of a half shall prevail. Disqualified players are not allowed to return.
   Exception: In preseason and regular season games there shall be a maximum of 15 minutes of sudden death with two time outs instead of three. General provisions for play in the last two minutes of a half will be in force.

Timing in Final Two Minutes of Each Half

1. On kickoff, clock does not start until the ball has been legally touched by player of either team in the field of play. (In all other cases, clock starts with kickoff.)
2. A team cannot "buy" an excess time out for a penalty. However, a fourth time out is allowed without penalty for an injured player, who must be removed immediately. A fifth time out or more is allowed for an injury and a five-yard penalty is assessed if the clock was running. Additionally, if the clock was running and the score is tied or the team in possession is losing, the ball cannot be put in play for at least 10 seconds on the fourth or more time out. The half or game can end while those 10 seconds are run off on the clock.
3. If the defensive team is behind in the score and commits a foul when it has no time outs left in the final 30 seconds of either half, the offensive team can decline the penalty for the foul and have the time on the clock expire.

Try-for-Point

1. After a touchdown, the scoring team is allowed a try-for-point during one scrimmage down. The ball may be spotted anywhere between the in-bounds lines, two or more yards from the goal line. The successful conversion counts one point, whether by run, kick, or pass.
2. The defensive team never can score on a try-for-point. As soon as defense gets possession, or kick is blocked, ball is dead.
3. Any distance penalty for fouls committed by the defense that prevent the try from being attempted can be enforced on the succeeding kickoff. Any foul committed on a successful try will result in a distance penalty being assessed on the ensuing kickoff.

Players-Substitutions

1. Each team is permitted 11 men on the field at the snap.
2. Unlimited substitution is permitted. However, players may enter the field only when the ball is dead. Players who have been substituted for are not permitted to linger on the field. Such lingering will be interpreted as unsportsmanlike conduct.
3. Players leaving the game must be out of bounds on their own side, clearing the field between the end lines, before a snap or free kick. If player crosses end line leaving field, it is delay of game (five-yard penalty).

Kickoff

1. The kickoff shall be from the kicking team's 35 yard line at the start of each half and after a field goal and try-for-point. A kickoff is one type of free kick.
2. Either a one-, two-, or three-inch tee may be used (no tee permitted for field goal or try-for-point plays). The ball is put in play by a placekick or dropkick.
3. If kickoff clears the opponent's goal posts it is not a field goal.
4. A kickoff is illegal unless it travels 10 yards OR is touched by the receiving team. Once the ball is touched by the receiving team it is a free ball. Receivers may recover and advance. Kicking team may recover but NOT advance UNLESS receiver had possession and lost the ball.
5. When a kickoff goes out of bounds between the goal lines without being touched by the receiving team, it must be kicked again. There is a five-yard penalty for a short kick or an out-of-bounds kick.
6. When a kickoff goes out of bounds between the goal lines and is touched last by receiving team, it is receiver's ball at out-of-bounds spot.

Free Kick

1. In addition to a kickoff, the other free kicks are a kick after a safety and a kick after a fair catch. In both cases, a dropkick, placekick, or punt may be used (a punt may not be used on a kickoff.)
2. On free kick after a fair catch, captain of receiving team has the option to put ball in play by punt, dropkick, or placekick without a tee, or by snap. If the placekick or dropkick goes between the uprights a field goal is scored.
3. On a free kick after a safety, the team scored upon puts ball in play by a punt, dropkick, or placekick without tee. No score can be made on a free kick following a safety, even if a series of penalties places team in position. (A field goal can be scored only on a play from scrimmage or a free kick after a fair catch.)

Field Goal

1. All field goals attempted and missed from scrimmage line beyond the 20 yard line will result in the defensive team taking possession of the ball at the scrimmage line. On any field goal attempted and missed from scrimmage line inside the 20 yard line, ball will revert to defensive team at the 20 yard line.

Safety

1. The important factor in a safety is impetus. Two points are scored for the opposing team when the ball is dead on or behind a team's own goal line if the impetus came from a player on that team.

Examples of Safety:

(a) Blocked punt goes out of kicking team's end zone. Impetus was provided by punting team. The block only changes direction of ball, not impetus.
(b) Ball carrier retreats from field of play into his own end zone and is downed. Ball carrier provides impetus.
(c) Offensive team commits a foul and spot of enforcement is behind its own goal line.
(d) Player on receiving team muffs punt and, trying to get ball, forces or illegally kicks it into end zone where he or a teammate recovers. He has given new impetus to the ball.

Examples of Non-Safety:

(a) Player intercepts a pass inside his own 5 yard line and his momentum carries him into his own end zone. Ball is put in play at spot of interception.

(b) Player intercepts a pass in his own end zone and is downed. Impetus came from passing team, not from defense. (Touchback)
(c) Player passes from behind his own goal line. Opponent bats down ball in end zone. (Incomplete pass)

Measuring

1. The forward point of the ball is used when measuring.

Position of Players at Snap

1. Offensive team must have at least seven players on line.
2. Offensive players, not on line, must be at least one yard back at snap. (**Exception:** player who takes snap.)
3. No interior lineman may move after taking or simulating a three-point stance.
4. No player of either team may invade neutral zone before snap.
5. No player of offensive team may charge or move, after assuming set position, in such manner as to lead defense to believe snap has started.
6. If a player changes his eligibility, the Referee must alert the defensive captain after player has reported to him.
7. All players of offensive team must be stationary at snap, except one back who may be in motion parallel to scrimmage line or backward (not forward).
8. After a shift or huddle all players on offensive team must come to an absolute stop for at least one second with no movement of hands, feet, head, or swaying of body.
9. Quarterbacks can be called for a false start penalty (five yards) if their actions are judged to be an obvious attempt to draw an opponent offside.

Use of Hands, Arms, and Body

1. No player on offense may assist a runner except by blocking for him. There shall be no interlocking interference.
2. A runner may ward off opponents with his hands and arms but no other player on offense may use hands or arms to obstruct an opponent by grasping with hands, pushing, or encircling any part of his body during a block.
3. Pass blocking is the obstruction of an opponent by use of that part of the body above the knees. During a legal block, hands (open or closed) must be inside the blocker's elbows and can be thrust forward to contact an opponent as long as the contact is inside the frame. Hands cannot be thrust forward above the frame to contact an opponent on the neck, face, or head. (**Note:** The frame is defined as that part of the opponent's body below the neck that is presented to the blocker.) Blocker cannot use his hands or arms to push from behind, hang onto, or encircle an opponent in a manner that restricts his movements as the play develops. By use of up and down action of arm(s), the blocker is permitted to ward off the opponent's attempt to grasp his jersey or arm(s) and prevent legal contact to the head.
4. Run blocking is an aggressive action by a blocker to obstruct an opponent from the ball carrier. During a legal block, contact can be made with the head, shoulders, hands, and/or outer surface of the forearm, or any other part of the body. Hands with extended arms can be thrust forward to contact an opponent as long as the contact is inside the frame and inside the pocket area. [See Pocket Area (Run) Definitions, page 322.] As the play develops, a blocker is permitted to work for and maintain position on an opponent as long as he does not push from behind or clip (outside legal clip zone). A blocker who makes contact with extended arms within the pocket area may maintain such contact outside of the pocket area as long as the action is continuous. A blocker cannot make initial contact with extended arms outside the pocket area. A blocker lined up more than 2 yards outside the tackle is subject, also, to the crackback rule.
5. A defensive player may not tackle or hold an opponent other than a runner. Otherwise, he may use his hands, arms, or body only:
   (a) To defend or protect himself against an obstructing opponent.
   Exception: An eligible receiver is considered to be an obstructing opponent ONLY to a point five yards beyond the line of scrimmage unless the player who receives the snap clearly demonstrates no further intention to pass the ball. Within this five-yard zone, a defensive player may make contact with an eligible receiver that may be maintained as long as it is continuous and unbroken. The defensive player cannot use his hands or arms to push from behind, hang onto, or encircle an eligible receiver in a manner that restricts movement as the play develops. Beyond this five-yard limitation, a defender may use his hands or arms ONLY to defend or protect himself against impending contact caused by a receiver. In such reaction, the defender may not contact a receiver who attempts to take a path to evade him.
   (b) To push or pull opponent out of the way on line of scrimmage.
   (c) In actual attempt to get at or tackle runner.
   (d) To push or pull opponent out of the way in a legal attempt to recover a loose ball.
   (e) During a legal block on an opponent who is not an eligible pass receiver.
   (f) When legally blocking an eligible pass receiver above the waist.
   Exception: Eligible receivers lined up within two yards of the tackle, whether on or immediately behind the line, may be blocked below the waist at or behind the line of scrimmage. NO eligible receiver may be blocked below the waist after he goes beyond the line.
   Note: Once the quarterback hands off or pitches the ball to a back, or if the quarterback leaves the pocket area, the restrictions on the defensive team relative to the offensive receivers will end, provided the ball is not in the air.
6. A defensive player must not contact an opponent above the shoulders with the palm of his hand except to ward him off on the line. This exception is permitted only if it is not a repeated act against the same opponent during

any one contact. In all other cases the palms may be used on head, neck, or face only to ward off or push an opponent in legal attempt to get at the ball.

7. Any offensive player who pretends to possess the ball or to whom a team-mate pretends to give the ball may be tackled provided he is crossing his scrimmage line between the ends of a normal tight offensive line.

8. An offensive player who lines up more than two yards outside his own tackle or a player who, at the snap, is in a backfield position and subsequently takes a position more than two yards outside a tackle may not clip an opponent anywhere nor may he contact an opponent below the waist if the blocker is moving toward the ball and if contact is made within an area five yards on either side of the line.

9. A player of either team may block at any time provided it is not pass interference, fair catch interference, or unnecessary roughness.

10. A player may not bat or punch:
    (a) A loose ball (in field of play) toward his opponent's goal line or in any direction in either end zone.
    (b) A ball in player possession or attempt to get possession.
    (c) A pass in flight forward toward opponent's goal line.
    Exception: A forward or backward pass may be batted in any direction at any time by the defense.

11. No player may deliberately kick any ball except as a punt, dropkick, or placekick.

Forward Pass

1. A forward pass may be touched or caught by any eligible receiver. All members of the defensive team are eligible. Eligible receivers on the offensive team are players on either end of line (other than center, guard, or tackle) or players at least one yard behind the line at the snap. A T-formation quarterback is not eligible to receive a forward pass during a play from scrimmage. **Exception:** T-formation quarterback becomes eligible if pass is previously touched by an eligible receiver.

2. An offensive team may make only one forward pass during each play from scrimmage (Loss of down).

3. The passer must be behind his line of scrimmage (Loss of down and five yards, enforced from the spot of pass).

4. Any eligible offensive player may catch a forward pass. If a pass is touched by one offensive player and touched or caught by a second eligible offensive player, pass completion is legal. Further, all offensive players become eligible once a pass is touched by an eligible receiver or any defensive player.

5. The rules concerning a forward pass and ineligible receivers:
    (a) If ball is touched accidentally by an ineligible receiver on or behind his line: loss of down.
    (b) If ineligible receiver is illegally downfield: loss of 10 yards.
    (c) If touched or caught (intentionally or accidentally) by ineligible receiver beyond the line: loss of 10 yards.
    (d) If ineligible receiver is illegally downfield: loss of 10 yards.

6. If a forward pass is caught simultaneously by eligible players on opposing teams, possession goes to passing team.

7. Any forward pass becomes incomplete and ball is dead if:
    (a) Pass hits the ground or goes out of bounds.
    (b) Hits the goal post or the cross bar of either team.
    (c) Is caught by offensive player after touching ineligible receiver.
    (d) An illegal pass is caught by the passer.

8. A forward pass is complete when a receiver clearly touches the ground with both feet inbounds while in possession of the ball. If a receiver is carried out of bounds by an opponent while in possession in the air, pass is complete at the out-of-bounds spot.

9. If an eligible receiver goes out of bounds accidentally or is forced out by a defender and returns to catch a pass, the play is regarded as a pass caught out of bounds. (Loss of down, no yardage.)

10. On a fourth down pass—when the offensive team is inside the opposition's 20 yard line—an incomplete pass results in a loss of down at the line of scrimmage.

11. If a personal foul is committed by the defense prior to the completion of a pass, the penalty is 15 yards from the spot where ball becomes dead.

12. If a personal foul is committed by the offense prior to the completion of a pass, the penalty is 15 yards from the previous line of scrimmage.

Intentional Grounding of Forward Pass

1. Intentional grounding of a forward pass is a foul: loss of down and 10 yards from previous spot if passer is in the field of play or loss of down at the spot of the foul if it occurs more than 10 yards behind the line or safety if passer is in his own end zone when ball is released.

2. It is considered intentional grounding of a forward pass when the ball strikes the ground after the passer throws, tosses, or lobs the ball to prevent a loss of yards by his team.

Protection of Passer

1. By interpretation, a pass begins when the passer—with possession of ball —starts to bring his hand forward. If ball strikes ground after this action has begun, play is ruled an incomplete pass. If passer loses control of ball prior to his bringing his hand forward, play is ruled a fumble.

2. No defensive player may run into a passer of a legal forward pass after the ball has left his hand (15 yards). The Referee must determine whether opponent had a reasonable chance to stop his momentum during an attempt to block the pass or tackle the passer while he still had the ball.

3. Officials are to blow the play dead as soon as the quarterback is clearly in the grasp of any tackler.

Pass Interference

1. There shall be no interference with a forward pass thrown from behind the line. The restriction for the passing team starts with the snap. The restriction on the defensive team starts when the ball leaves the passer's hand. Both restrictions end when the ball is touched by anyone.

2. The penalty for defensive pass interference is an automatic first down at the spot of the foul. If interference is in the end zone, it is first down for the offense on the defense's 1 yard line. If previous spot was inside the defense's 1 yard line, penalty is half the distance to the goal line.

3. The penalty for offensive pass interference is 10 yards from the previous spot.

4. It is pass interference by either team when any player movement beyond the offensive line significantly hinders the progress of an eligible player or such player's opportunity to catch the ball during a legal forward pass. When a player establishes a position to catch the ball in which an opponent cannot reach the ball without first contacting the player in a manner that prevents the player from catching the ball, such action by the opponent shall be considered interference. Provided an eligible player is not interfered with in such a manner, the following exceptions to pass interference will prevail:
    (a) If neither player is looking for the ball and there is incidental contact in the act of moving to the ball that does not materially affect the route of an eligible player, there is no interference. If there is any question whether the incidental contact materially affects the route, the ruling shall be no interference.
    Note: Inadvertent tripping is not a foul in this situation.
    (b) Any eligible player looking for and intent on playing the ball who initiates contact, however severe, while attempting to move to the spot of completion or interception will not be called for interference.
    (c) Any eligible player who makes contact, however severe, with one or more eligible players while looking for and making a genuine attempt to catch or bat a reachable ball, will not be called for interference.
    (d) It must be remembered that defensive players have as much right to the ball as offensive eligible receivers.
    (e) Pass interference by the defense is not to be called when the forward pass is clearly uncatchable.
    (f) Note: There is no defensive pass interference behind the line.

Backward Pass

1. Any pass not a forward pass is regarded as a backward pass or lateral. A pass parallel to the line is a backward pass. A runner may pass backward at any time. Any player on either team may catch the pass or recover the ball after it touches the ground.

2. A backward pass that strikes the ground can be recovered and advanced by offensive team.

3. A backward pass that strikes the ground can be recovered but cannot be advanced by the defensive team.

4. A backward pass caught in the air can be advanced by the defensive team.

Fumble

1. The distinction between a fumble and a muff should be kept in mind in considering rules about fumbles. A fumble is the loss of possession of the ball. A muff is the touching of a loose ball by a player in an unsuccessful attempt to obtain possession.

2. A fumble may be advanced by any player on either team regardless of whether recovered before or after ball hits the ground.

3. If an offensive player fumbles anywhere on the field during a fourth down play, or if a player fumbles on any down after the two-minute warning in a half, only the fumbling player is permitted to recover and/or advance the ball. If recovered by any other offensive player, the ball is dead at the spot of the fumble unless it is recovered behind the spot of the fumble. In that case, ball is dead at spot of recovery. Any defensive player may recover and/or advance any fumble.
    Exception: The fourth-down fumble rule does not apply if a player touches, but does not possess, a direct snap from center, i.e., a snap in flight as opposed to a hand-to-hand exchange.

Kicks From Scrimmage

1. Any punt or missed field goal that touches a goal post is dead.

2. During a kick from scrimmage, only the end men, as eligible receivers on the line of scrimmage at the time of the snap, are permitted to go beyond the line before the ball is kicked.
    Exception: An eligible receiver who, at the snap, is aligned or in motion behind the line and more than one yard outside the end man on his side of the line, clearly making him the outside receiver, REPLACES that end man as the player eligible to go downfield after the snap. All other members of the kicking team must remain at the line of scrimmage until the ball has been kicked.

3. Any punt that is blocked and does not cross the line of scrimmage can be recovered and advanced by either team. However, if offensive team recovers it must make the yardage necessary for its first down to retain possession if punt was on fourth down.

4. The kicking team may never advance its own kick even though legal recovery is made beyond the line of scrimmage. Possession only.

5. A member of the receiving team may not run into or rough a kicker who kicks from behind his line unless contact is:
    (a) Incidental to and after he had touched ball in flight.
    (b) Caused by kicker's own motions.
    (c) Occurs during a quick kick, or a kick made after a run, or after kicker recovers a loose ball. Ball is loose when kicker muffs snap or snap hits ground.

(d) Defender is blocked into kicker.

The penalty for running into the kicker is 5 yards and an automatic first down. For roughing the kicker: 15 yards and disqualification if flagrant.

6. If a member of the kicking team attempting to down the ball on or inside opponent's 5 yard line carries the ball into the end zone, it is a touchback.
7. Fouls during a punt are enforced from the previous spot (line of scrimmage). **Exception:** Illegal touching, illegal fair catch, invalid fair catch signal, and fouls by the receiving team during loose ball after ball is kicked.
8. While the ball is in the air or rolling on the ground following a punt or field goal attempt and receiving team commits a foul before gaining possession, receiving team will retain possession and will be penalized for its foul.
9. It will be illegal for a defensive player to jump or stand on any player, or be picked up by a teammate or to use a hand or hands on a teammate to gain additional height in an attempt to block a kick (Penalty 15 yards, unsportsmanlike conduct).
10. A punted ball remains a kicked ball until it is declared dead or in possession of either team.
11. Any member of the punting team may down the ball anywhere in the field of play. However, it is illegal touching (Official's time out and receiver's ball at spot of illegal touching). This foul does not offset any foul by receivers during the down.
12. Defensive team may advance all kicks from scrimmage (including unsuccessful field goal) whether or not ball crosses defensive team's goal line. Rules pertaining to kicks from scrimmage apply until defensive team gains possession.

Fair Catch

1. The member of the receiving team must raise one arm a full length above his head and wave it from side to side while kick is in flight. (Failure to give proper sign: receivers' ball five yards behind spot of signal.)
2. No opponent may interfere with the fair catcher, the ball, or his path to the ball. Penalty: 15 yards from spot of foul and fair catch is awarded.
3. A player who signals for a fair catch is not required to catch the ball. However, if a player signals for a fair catch, he may not block or initiate contact with any player on the kicking team until the ball touches a player. Penalty: snap 15 yards behind spot of foul.
4. If ball hits ground or is touched by member of kicking team in flight, fair catch signal is off and all rules for a kicked ball apply.
5. Any undue advance by a fair catch receiver is delay of game. No specific distance is specified for "undue advance" as ball is dead at spot of catch. If player comes to a reasonable stop, no penalty. For violation, five yards.
6. If time expires while ball is in play and a fair catch is awarded, receiving team may choose to extend the period with one free kick down. However, placekicker may not use tee.

Foul on Last Play of Half or Game

1. On a foul by defense on last play of half or game, the down is replayed if penalty is accepted.
2. On a foul by the offense on last play of half or game, the down is not replayed and the play in which the foul is committed is nullified.
   Exception: Fair catch interference, foul following change of possession, illegal touching. No score by offense counts.
3. On double foul on last play of half or game, down is replayed.

Spot of Enforcement of Foul

1. There are four basic spots at which a penalty for a foul is enforced:
   (a) Spot of foul: The spot where the foul is committed.
   (b) Previous spot: The spot where the ball was put in play.
   (c) Spot of snap, pass, fumble, return kick, or free kick: The spot where the act connected with the foul occurred.
   (d) Succeeding spot: The spot where the ball next would be put in play if no distance penalty were to be enforced.
      Exception: If foul occurs after a touchdown and before the whistle for a try-for-point, succeeding spot is spot of next kickoff.
2. All fouls committed by offensive team behind the line of scrimmage and in the field of play shall be penalized from the previous spot.
3. When spot of enforcement for fouls involving defensive holding or illegal use of hands by the defense is behind the line of scrimmage, any penalty yardage to be assessed on that play shall be measured from the line if the foul occurred beyond the line.

Double Foul

1. If there is a double foul during a down in which there is a change of possession, the team last gaining possession may keep the ball unless its foul was committed prior to the change of possession.
2. If double foul occurs after a change of possession, the defensive team retains the ball at the spot of its foul or dead ball spot.
3. If one of the fouls of a double foul involves disqualification, that player must be removed, but no penalty yardage is to be assessed.
4. If the kickers foul during a punt before possession changes and the receivers foul after possession changes, penalties will be offset and the down is replayed.

Penalty Enforced on Following Kickoff

1. When a team scores by touchdown, field goal, extra point, or safety and either team commits a personal foul, unsportsmanlike conduct, or obvious unfair act during the down, the penalty will be assessed on the following kickoff.

NOTES

NOTES